30s
All-American Ads

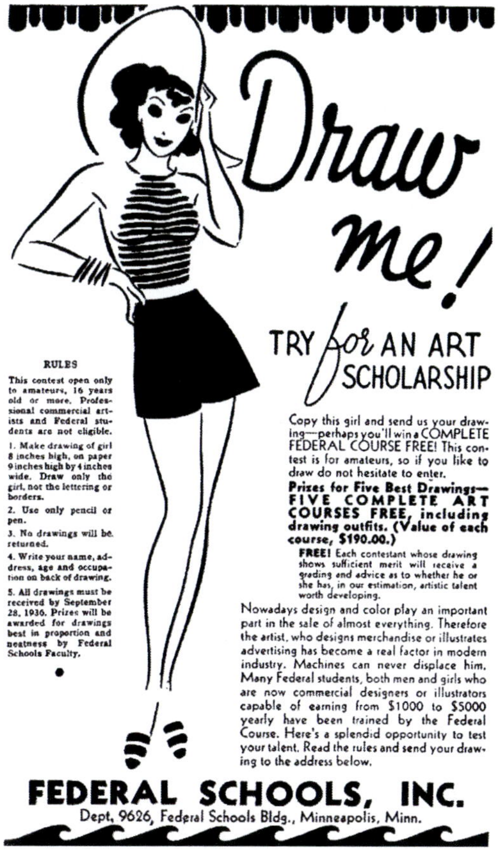

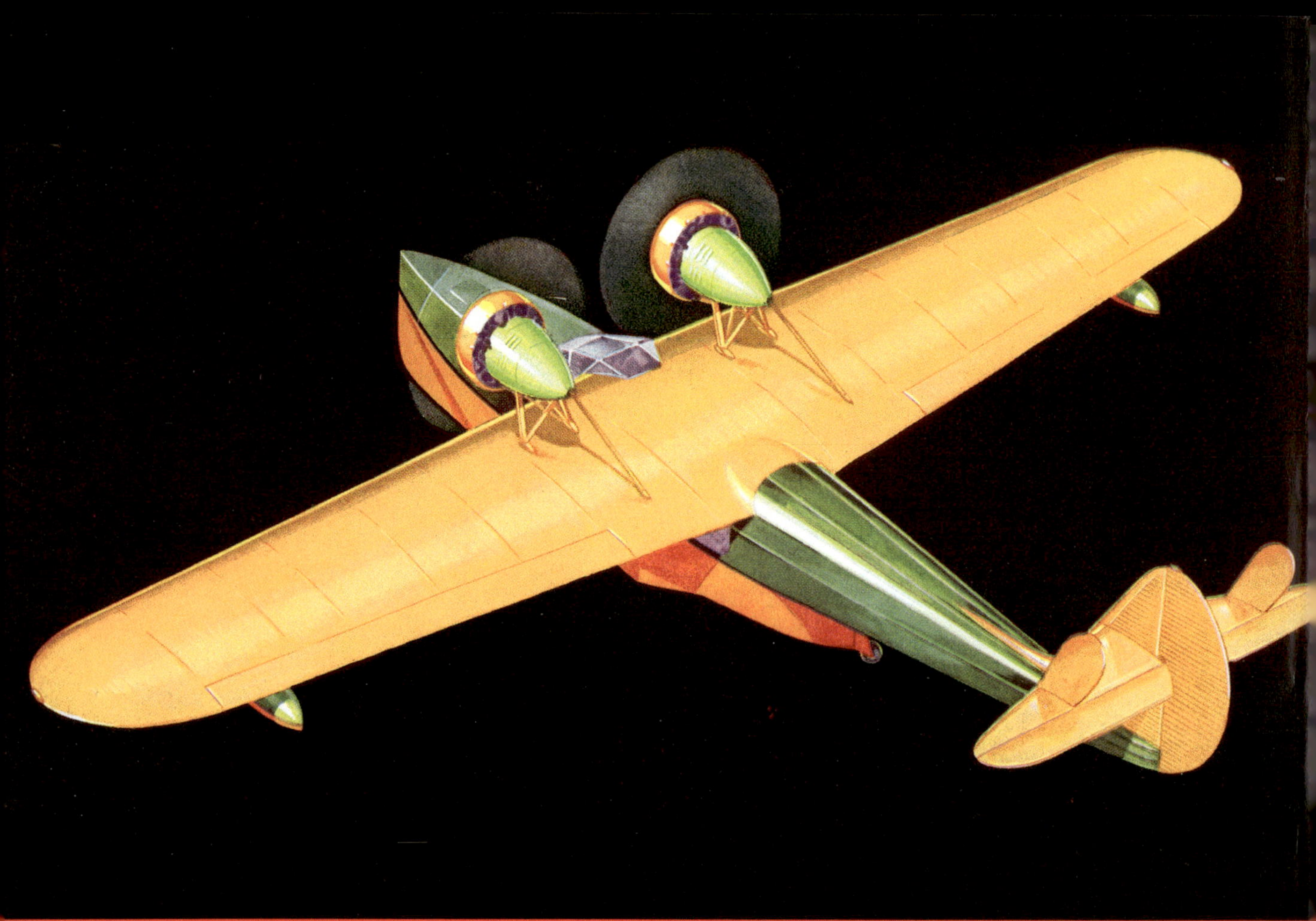

Imprint

Want to see more? Visit taschen.com to view our current publications, browse our latest magazine, and subscribe to our newsletter.

Hohenzollernring 53, D–50672 Köln
www.taschen.com

German translation:
Harald Hellmann, Cologne
French translation:
Philippe Safavi, Paris

Printed in Slovakia
ISBN 978–3–8365–8866–9

page 1: Federal Schools, Inc., 1937
above: Douglas Aircraft Co., 1931
right: Paramount, 1932
page 10–11: Thompson Products, 1935
page 16–17: RCA Victor, 1933

30s

All-American Ads

Edited by Jim Heimann
with an introduction by Steven Heller

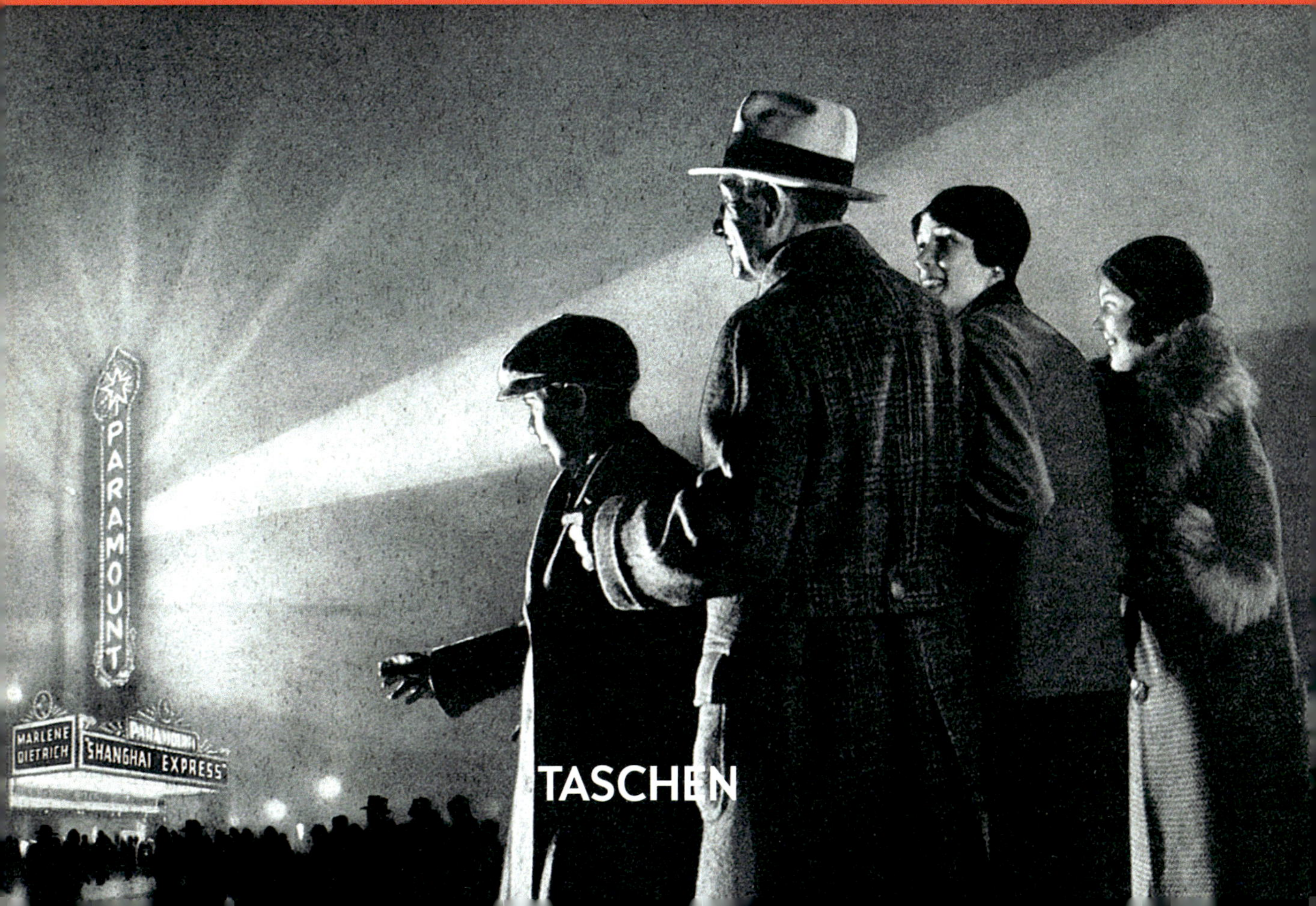

TASCHEN

Steven Heller

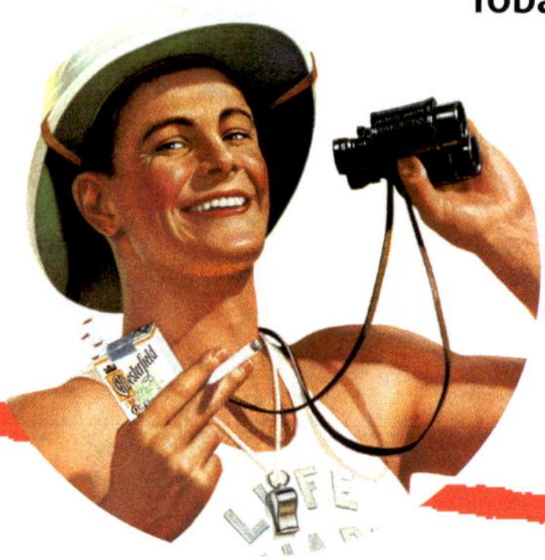

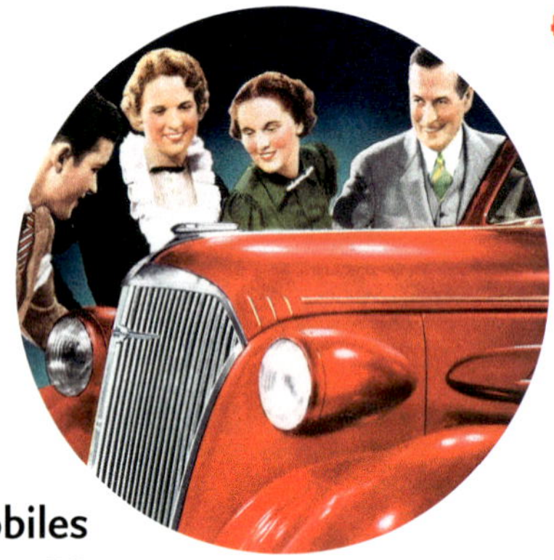

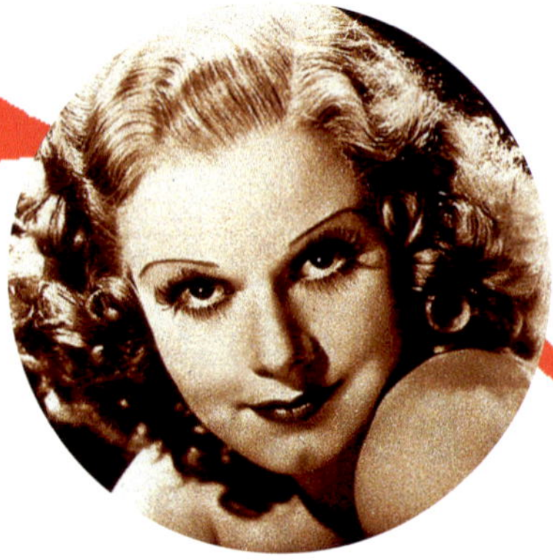

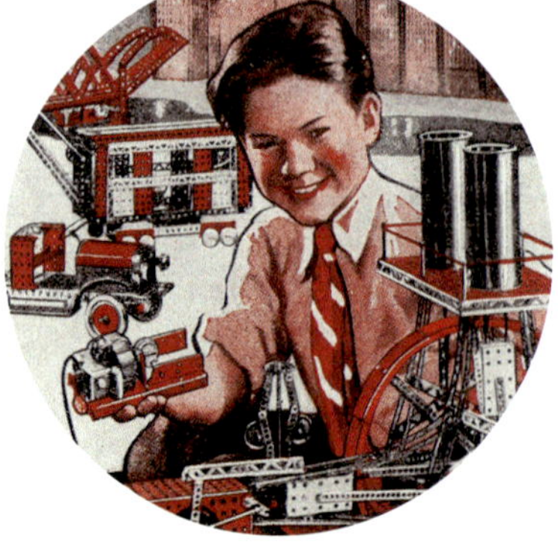

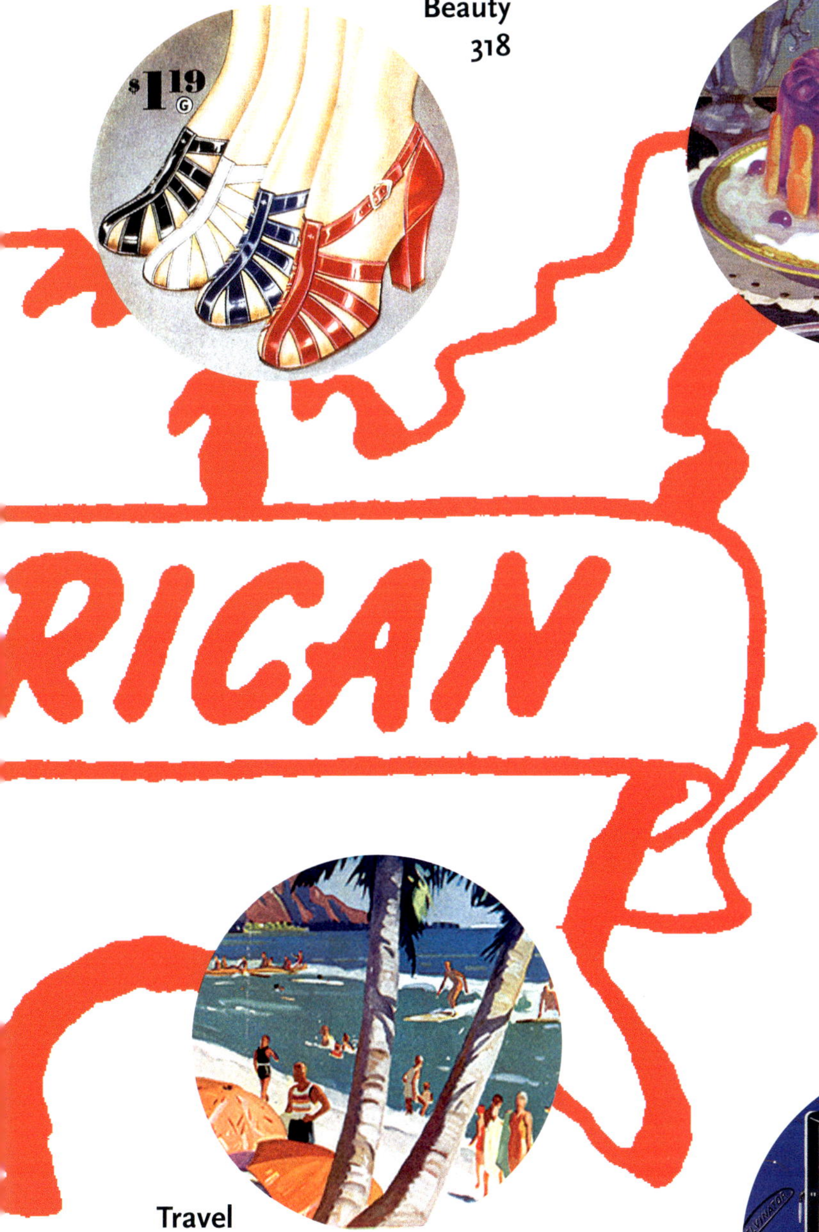
$1.19
RICAN

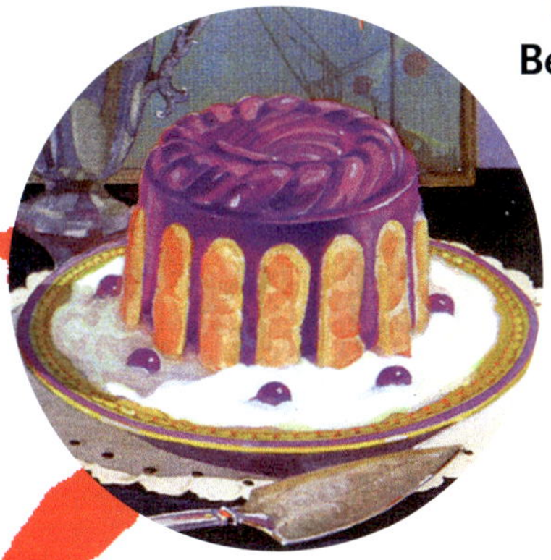

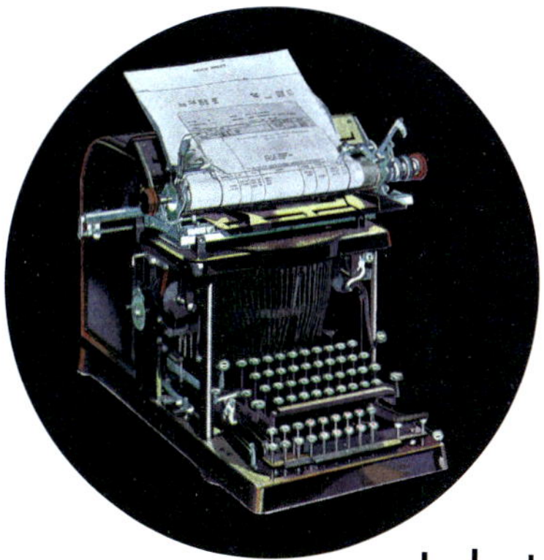

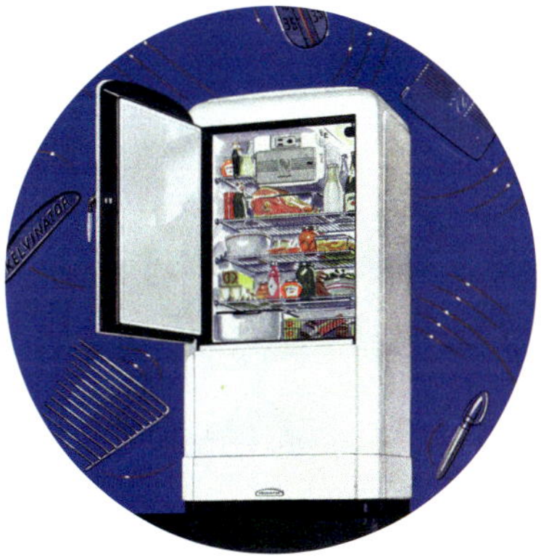

Advertisements of the Thirties

From Modernism to Shirt-Sleevism

by Steven Heller

American advertising of the thirties was born in 1925 in Paris along the banks of the Seine. The Exposition Internationale des Arts Décoratifs et Industriels Modernes, a playground of modernity, was laid out in boulevards lined with pavilions decorated with geometric ornamentation and neo-classical friezes. The world's leading clothing, furniture, and houseware manufacturers, along with many grand emporia, exhibited their latest products and designs. But one player was noticeably absent.

The United States, the world's greatest industrial nation, declined an invitation to participate. The leaders of American industry believed, as historian Terry Smith explained, "that they could not match the French designers either in making a stripped Arts and Crafts 'modernism' or by boldly countering with a national style."

And they were right. American products were either nondescript or laden with beaux-arts ornament to camouflage a mass-produced look. Although mass production was the foundation on which the modern American economy was built, many cultural critics argued that items coming off the assembly line lacked good taste. While the Bauhaus and other European modern avant-gardes had embraced the machine, American industrialists, who could easily afford to improve their products aesthetically, were apathetic. What they did not resist, however, were marketing strategies that would stimulate higher profits. So industry frantically tried to find a new means of increasing sales through the art, science, and hucksterism of advertising.

The man who helped revolutionize American advertising from the mid twenties through the thirties was Earnest Elmo Calkins, an advertising pioneer, design reformer, and founder of the New York-based Calkins and Holden Advertising Co. Inspired by the Exposition Internationale des Arts Décoratifs et Industriels Modernes, he described the array of cubistic and futuristic graphics, packages, and displays in the department-store pavilions thus in a treatise on the subject: "It is extremely 'new art' and some of it too bizarre, but it achieves a certain exciting harmony, and in detail is entertaining to a degree." Upon returning to the United States he proffered a vision of how American advertising could benefit from European modernism and modern art.

In Paris Calkins witnessed an approach to illustration—at that time the primary means of creating and disseminating images—that was not sentimentally representational but used symbols and metaphors to create a "magical" atmosphere for consumables. Boxes and bottles were not mere utilitarian vessels, but rather signifiers of the essence of a product. Calkins wrote: "Modernism offered the opportunity of expressing the inexpressible, of suggesting not so much a motor car as speed, not so much a gown as style, not so much a compact as beauty." And if this had a similar ring to one of F. T. Marinetti's futurist manifestoes, it was because Calkins borrowed his language from the European avant-garde, while at the same time he eschewed its radicalism.

No other advertising man was more responsible for the American consumerist revolution than Calkins, who looked more like a Midwestern preacher than a New York huckster. Yet he was instrumental in such progressive modern marketing concepts as "consumption engineering," "forced obsolescence," and "styling the goods". And these buzzwords were the core of an advertising strategy that insinuated modern art and graphic design into a heretofore copy-ruled, devoutly conservative profession whose primary service was purchasing ad space from magazines and newspapers.

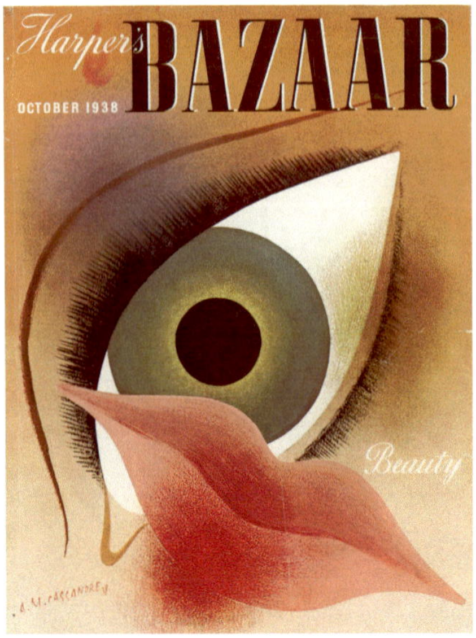

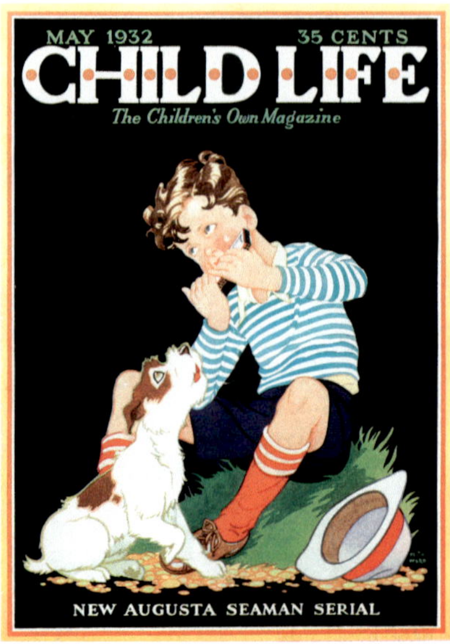

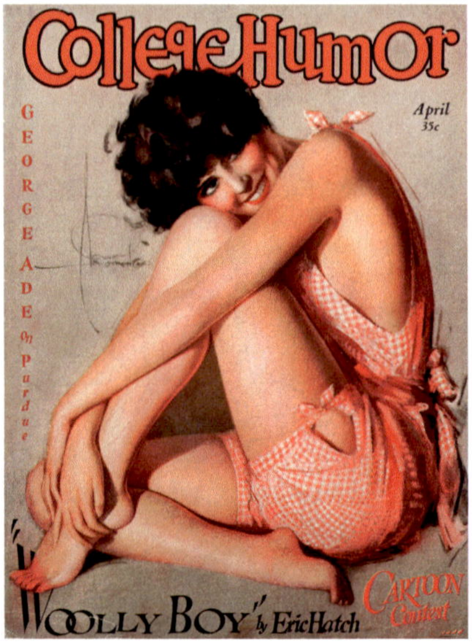

It was no longer possible "to make an advertisement striking, conspicuous and attractive by still pictures and realistic groups," asserted Calkins, who sought to take advantage of new color printing technologies, photographic effects, and aesthetic trends to make "art" that was memorable and monumental. By integrating modern art into stodgy mainstream commercial culture, Calkins revived interest in old products and also forced consumers to anticipate a bright future filled with consumables. Nonetheless, his so-called radical ideas met with opposition from those who wanted to sell in a less artsy manner. His ideas were indeed making headway, but the vast majority of advertisements were copy-laden tracts designed to avoid misperception and ambiguity of any kind.

Conservative ad men argued that fancy advertising images were elitist distractions, unresponsive to the tastes of ordinary consumers, and therefore doomed to fail. Calkins, they said, had a conflated sense of his own class values as opposed to a reflection of the whole society. To the contrary, Calkins felt that "artistic advertising" could be a democratizing force in terms of the middle classes. Indeed, he targeted solely an economic class that he called "people of taste," rather than inducing unattainable longings in the so-called have-nots.

Calkins believed that cluttered design (Wheaties, p. 402), comic strips (Camel, pp. 29–31), as well as puerile drawings and copy (Saraka, p. 267) were demeaning and confusing. Instead he proffered techniques that created mystiques through stylized, symbolic, and abstract forms. This meant that advertising could be less dependent on copy because the image was the primary mode of communication. More important, this model also elevated the art director above the copywriter in the hierarchy of advertising. Calkins felt that the so-called "art expert" was just as important as a literate copy chief. Throughout the twenties and thirties agency art directors acquired newfound prominence—indeed, art directors used illustration to create modern auras. Given Calkins' method, commonplace objects—toasters, refrigerators, pencils, shortening, and coffee tins—were presented against dynamic patterns and at skewed angles; and contemporary industrial wares were often shown in surrealistic and futuristic settings.

Modern art was a value additive and valuable camouflage. "When the uglier utilities of business cannot be beautified," wrote Calkins, "art is used to make them disappear." Suggesting a special relationship between the advertisement and goods by graphic style was something Calkins called "atmosphere," a fetishistic trait that ultimately rubbed off on the product itself.

Nonetheless, Calkins was a pragmatist. The cleverness of advertising could not exceed the public's capacity to understand what was being advertised—and be hooked in the process. He sought to raise the overall standard, yet this was accomplished in the "most advanced yet acceptable" manner and "style" was the means, not the end. Advertisements for Palmolive (p. 212), Old Gold (p. 44), and Thompson Products (pp. 10–11), to name but a few, were a true synthesis of the modern style and traditional commercial art. This was not simply a pyrrhic victory; Calkins was honestly content to create modernistic allusions because, he explained, "Improving the physiognomy of advertising had a twofold result. It directly influenced the taste of the public and indirectly conditioned the production of goods."

In some quarters the new commercial advertising style increased sales, which triggered greater production, which then

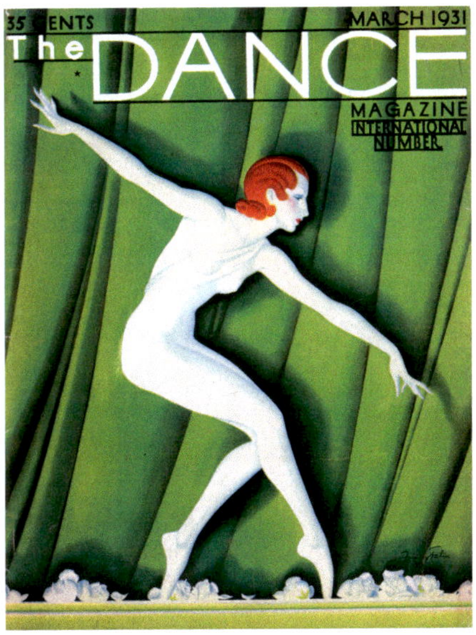

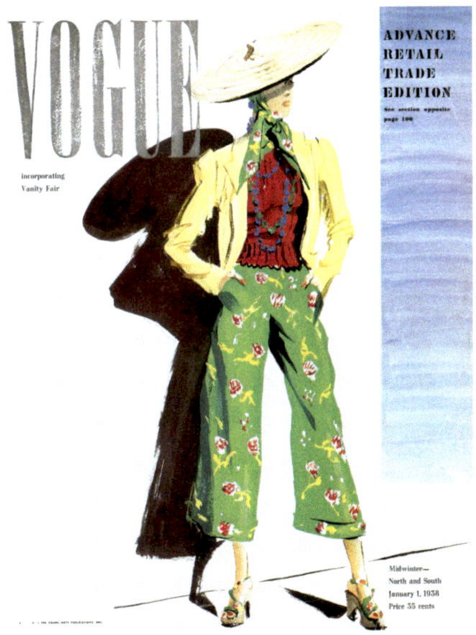

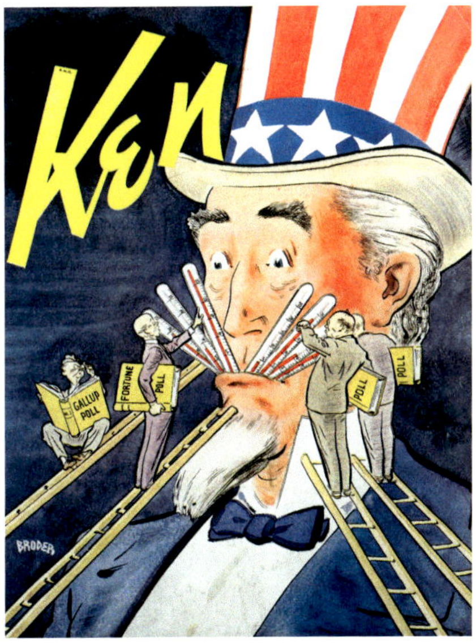

stimulated the economy. Manufacturers and retailers were happy, and designers and artists were major contributors to this bounty. A commercial artist of the day once wrote, "I've seen this styling idea coming closer and closer to the thing that really counts... a container that millions of hands stretch out to buy because it says something to them that they can't resist!"

But there was a downside to the success of Calkins' approach. In the early thirties American industry was actually producing too many goods to sustain high levels of repeat consumption. Moreover, the mammoth stock market crash of 1929 had, to say the least, put a huge crimp into mass buying power. By 1933 Calkins' style engineering reached its point of diminished return. Overzealous advertising and product manufacturing during the earlier bull market did not directly cause this catastrophic economic downslide—triggering America's Great Depression—but it was symptomatic of what N. W. Ayer's executive Harry Batten described as economic overconfidence, "a sort of gambling fever [that] spread into every level of society." By the mid thirties, still stinging from the Depression, advertisers and advertising had adopted what was called shirt-sleeve advertising, which fills much of this volume.

As the rising tide of the Depression washed away all the impressive economic gains of the postwar boom years, Calkins' agency and the scores of other big New York "shops" had to give clients what they wanted: sales. Certain "modernisms" were retained in post-Depression advertising, but the vast majority of advertisements returned to hard-sell techniques, including celebrity testimonials (for cigarettes), multi-image pictorials (for cars), sentimental landscapes (for travel), and well-stocked, glistening refrigerators (for food and drink). The most progressive art in the world was not going to sell detergent, toothpaste, deodorant, vegetable oil, or light bulbs. Subtlety was out, irony was barely a consideration, and comedy—unless in the form of easy-to-comprehend comics—was useless if the goods stayed on the shelves.

Calkins charged copywriter-artist/art director teams with the job of making creatively balanced advertisements and campaigns, but in the wake of the Depression shrill displays of screaming headlines and purple testimonials replaced any artistic nuances. Before the age of television, print advertising in newspapers, magazines, and on billboards (and radio, of course) was the most effective way of directly tempting the consumer. But advertising could not afford the luxury of the subtle tease. Ads had to make bold claims followed by stark promises, ending with memorable taglines. For example, an ad for Jantzen swimwear (p. 373), illustrated by the master of softcore allure, George Petty, promised women they'd have gorgeous men while promising men the prize of similarly endowed women if only they bought the product. The suggestive headline "Perfectly suited by Jantzen" further demonstrates that someone with a flair for clever phraseology was involved in the campaign.

The Jantzen ad was actually more artful than most in its genre. Conversely, an artless Chipso ad for a curiously named laundry detergent was a more common sort. A color photograph showing a children's tea party with a freshly coifed homemaker and three happy lassies in clean party clothes sits above the lengthy title: "Our clothes look new for more than one season's wear... thanks to Chipso," says the mother of happy little girls. It is a typically unimaginative testimonial type of ad. The grammatically challenged tag-

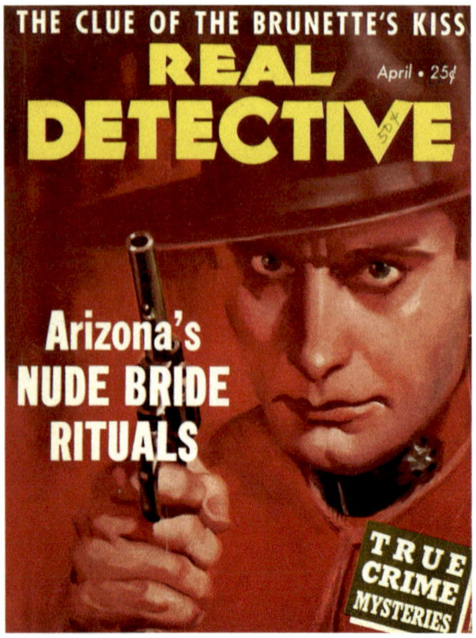

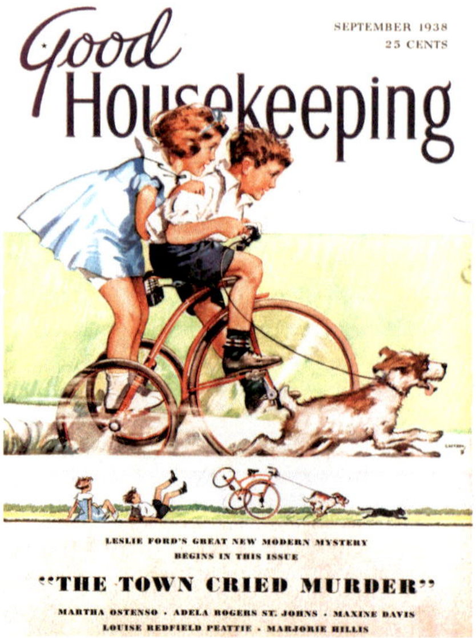

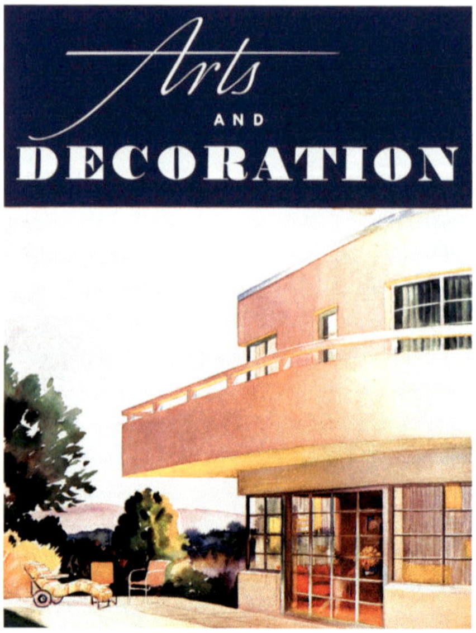

line "Chipso makes clothes wear—longer" (under a photo of mom in her apron at the slop sink with a box of the magical flakes) further reinforces the idea that happiness is cleanliness and cleanliness comes in a box.

Chipso may have been at the lower rung of the creative ladder but it was nonetheless influenced by better-known, more solidly financed national campaigns, like the one for Coca-Cola that left nothing to the imagination. "Home... to the pause that refreshes" (p. 462) is laden with layers of text and visual effluvia. A headline featuring Coca-Cola's venerable tagline sits atop a stylized painting of two happy, sugar-crazed pre-teen siblings (although the face of the girl perhaps intentionally looks much older and wiser than her body would suggest). Mom has just returned home from a shopping spree with arms full of packages (wishful thinking during the Depression) to receive the joyful greeting of her youngest child (presumably already sated by Coca-Cola and cookies). As if the painting doesn't offer enough narrative, two ancillary photographs show a "real life" mom buying and serving the dark, sweet elixir. And if all this is not enough reinforcement, think again. The text block, "When you shop you get something you don't bargain for. You get tired... and thirsty," knocks the reader over the head and brands the famous logo "Drink Coca-Cola" onto the cerebral cortex.

Advertisements like this filled the pages of *Life*, *Look*, *The Saturday Evening Post*, *Collier's*, and countless other weekly and monthly magazines. Despite the falling fortunes brought on by the Depression, commercial magazines rode crests of success—like movies they were diversions from the humdrum of the everyday. The ads not only sold the goods, they provided a sense of normalcy that helped consumers find their respective centers amid social turmoil.

Advertising of the thirties ultimately served two important functions: to stimulate want, thus generating sales; and to exhort American capitalism, thereby instilling a sense of optimism during dark times. To look at the advertisements in this volume one would never guess that Americans were suffering from severe hardships. The more artful specimens of the early thirties gave way to hard-selling (a symbolic indicator of hard times) but advertising for most commodities and a few luxuries was just as ubiquitous, and indeed exuberant, as before the crash. By the end of the decade, as war clouds formed over Europe, advertising helped artificially stimulate American consumerism. The shirt-sleeves had been rolled up, the economy was beginning to chug along, and then came World War II. Every aspect of American life would be forever altered and advertising would change its demeanor once again.

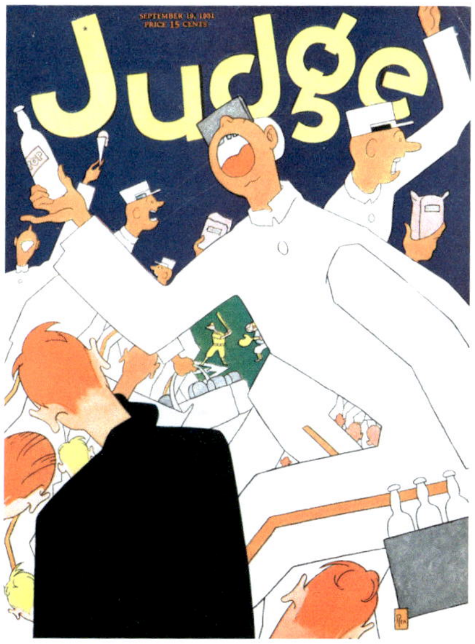

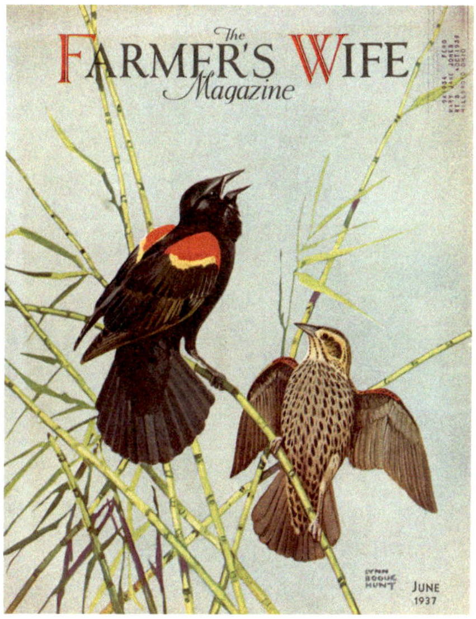

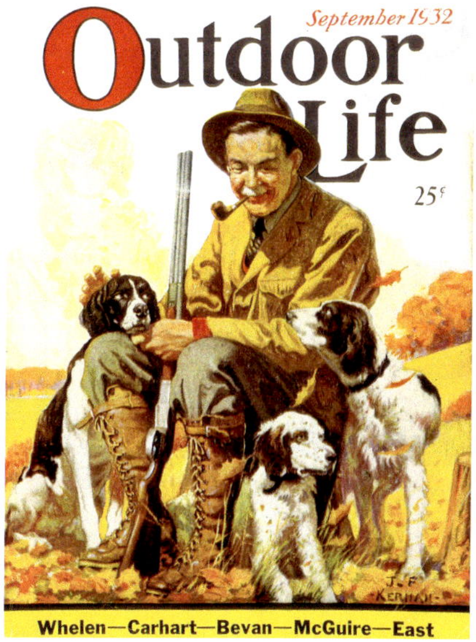

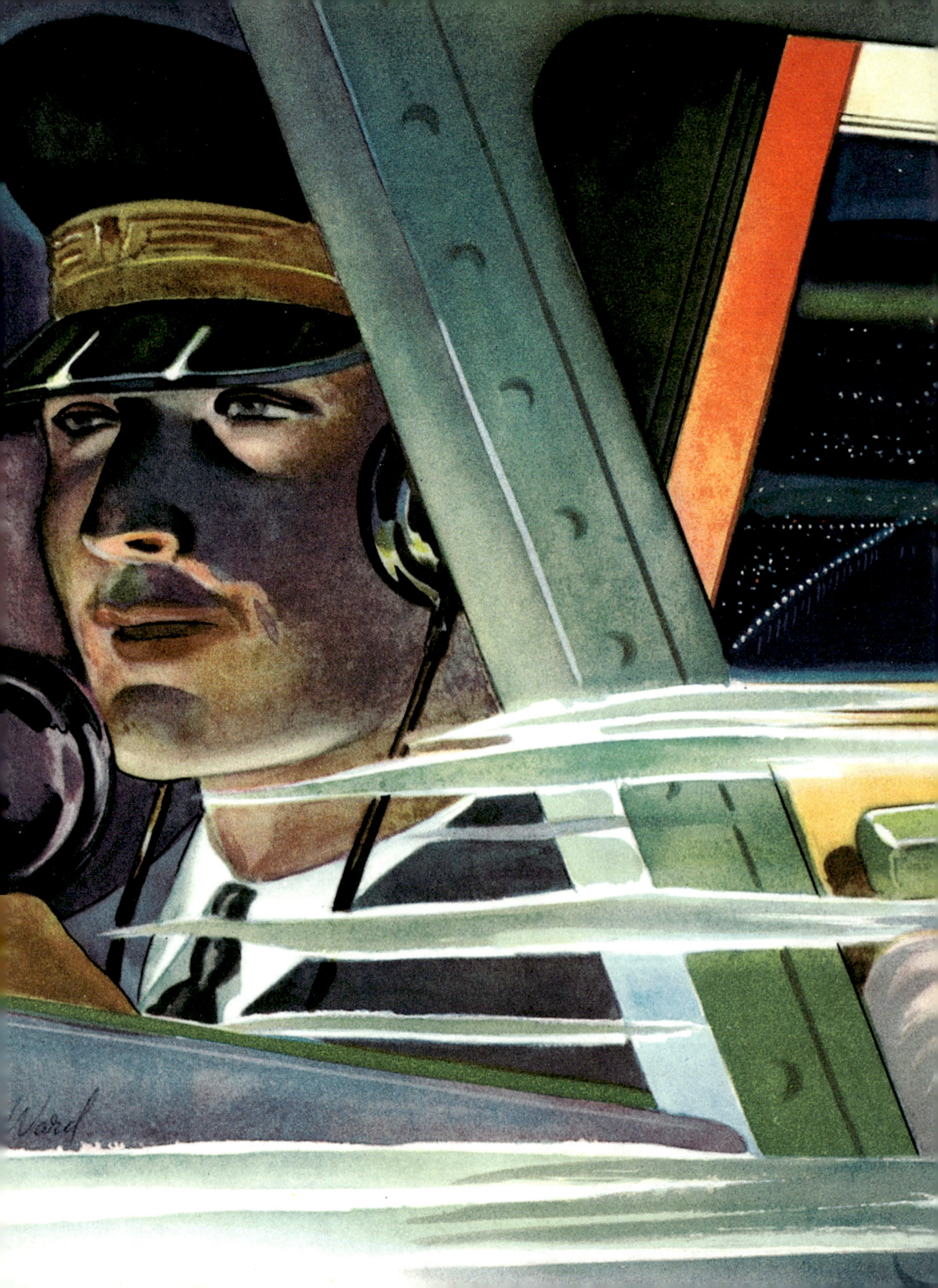

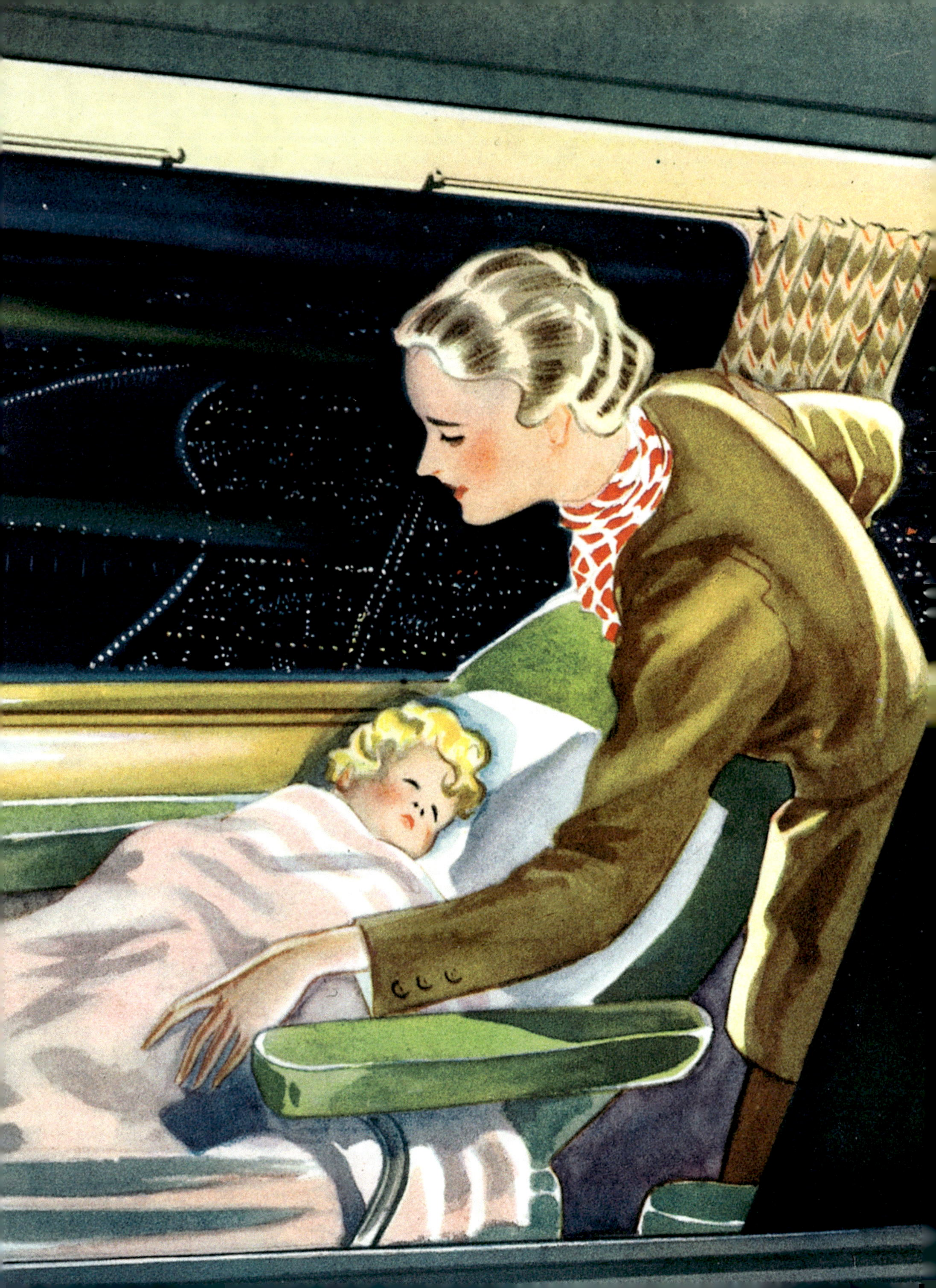

Werbung in den dreißiger Jahren

Vom Modernismus zur Machermentalität

von Steven Heller

Die amerikanische Werbung der dreißiger Jahre erblickte 1925 an den Ufern der Seine das Licht der Welt. Auf der *Exposition Internationale des Arts Décoratifs et Industriels Modernes*, einem Schaufenster der Moderne, wurden großzügige Boulevards von Pavillons gesäumt, die mit geometrischen Ornamenten und neoklassizistischen Friesen geschmückt waren. Die weltweit führenden Produzenten von Bekleidung, Möbeln und Haushaltswaren stellten hier gemeinsam mit vielen großen Warenhäusern ihre neuesten Produkte und Designs vor. Ein wichtiger Mitbewerber am Markt glänzte jedoch durch Abwesenheit.

Die Vereinigten Staaten, die bedeutendste Industrienation der Welt, hatten die Einladung zur Teilnahme ausgeschlagen. Die Marktführer der amerikanischen Wirtschaft fürchteten, so der Kunsthistoriker Terry Smith, „sie hätten den französischen Designern nichts entgegenzusetzen, weder sachliche Arts-and-Crafts-Modernität noch einen eigenständigen Stil".

Und damit hatten sie Recht. Amerikanische Produkte waren entweder gesichtslos oder viel zu verschnörkelt, um ihre schlichte Herstellung am Fließband zu verschleiern. Obgleich die Massenfertigung das Fundament der modernen amerikanischen Wirtschaft war, bemängelten viele Kritiker die Fließbandprodukte als geschmacklos. In Europa hatten das Bauhaus und andere avantgardistische Strömungen die maschinelle Fertigung als Herausforderung begriffen. Die amerikanische Industrie hingegen, die ihre Produkte ohne großen Aufwand ästhetisch hätte aufwerten können, verhielt sich hingegen passiv. Für neue Marketingstrategien, die Umsatzsteigerungen versprachen, war sie jedoch empfänglich.

Maßgeblich an der Revolutionierung der Werbung in den USA beteiligt war von Mitte der zwanziger bis Ende der dreißiger Jahre Earnest Elmo Calkins, ein Pionier auf diesem Gebiet, ein Designreformer und Gründer der in New York ansässigen Agentur Calkins and Holden Advertising Co. Beflügelt von der *Exposition Internationale des Arts Décoratifs et Industriels Moderne*, beschrieb Calkins die vielen kubistisch und futuristisch inspirierten Werbegrafiken, Verpackungen und Displays in den Pavillons der Warenhäuser: „Es ist zwar alles ausgesprochen ‚modern', einiges auch zu bizarr, erzielt jedoch immer eine gewisse spannende Harmonie und ist bisweilen sogar unterhaltsam." Calkins nahm eine Vision davon, wie die amerikanische Werbung von der europäischen Moderne profitieren könnte, mit zurück in die Staaten.

In Paris hatte Calkins eine Herangehensweise an die Illustration – damals das wichtigste Mittel der Bildproduktion und -verbreitung – kennengelernt, die sich nicht sklavisch ans reine Abbilden hielt, sondern Symbole und Metaphern benutzte, um Gebrauchsgütern eine „magische" Atmosphäre zu verleihen. Kartons und Flaschen waren mehr als nur zweckmäßige Behältnisse, sie verwiesen auf den Charakter eines Produkts. Calkins schrieb: „Die Moderne bietet die Gelegenheit, das Unausdrückbare auszudrücken, nicht auf ein Auto, sondern auf Geschwindigkeit zu verweisen, nicht auf ein Kleid, sondern auf Stil, nicht auf eine Puderdose, sondern auf Schönheit." Wenn das an eines der futuristischen Manifeste von F. T. Marinetti erinnert, liegt das daran, dass Calkins seine Terminologie der europäischen Avantgarde entlehnte, deren Radikalität er allerdings vermied.

Kein anderer Werbefachmann hat die Werbung in den USA derart revolutioniert wie Calkins, der eher einem Prediger aus dem Mittelwesten als einem ausgefuchsten Reklameprofi aus New York ähnelte. Dennoch war er maßgeblich an der Entwicklung moderner Werbekonzepte und -termini wie

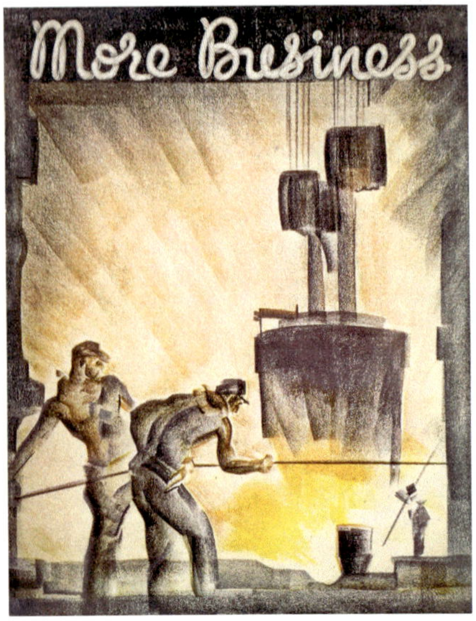

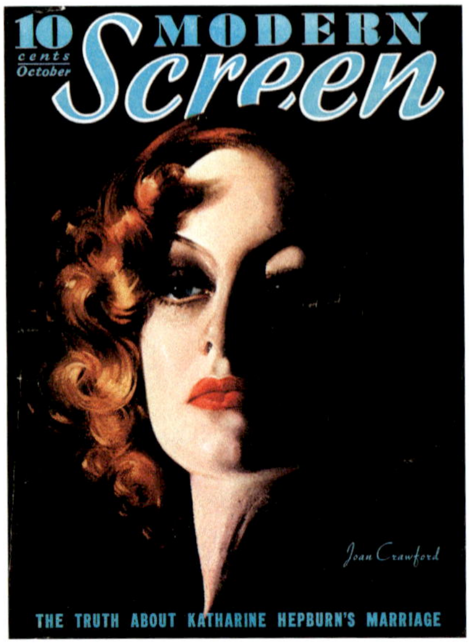

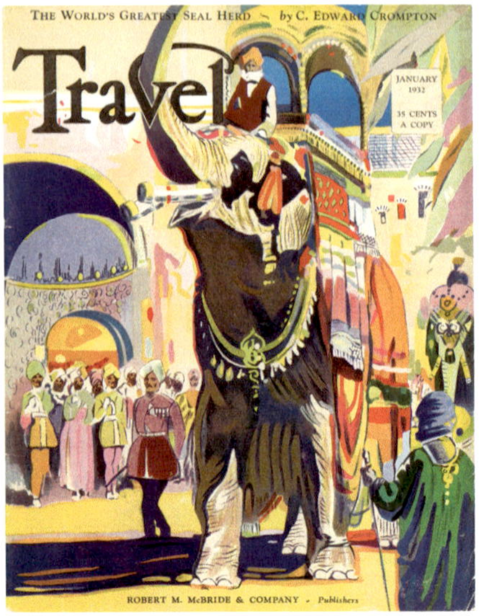

„consumption engineering", „forced obsolence" und „styling the goods" beteiligt. Diese Schlagworte standen im Mittelpunkt einer Werbestrategie, die moderne Kunst und modernes Grafikdesign geschickt in eine Profession einbrachte, die bis dahin textorientiert und durch und durch konservativ gewesen war, und deren Dienstleistung hauptsächlich darin bestand, Anzeigenplätze in Illustrierten und Zeitungen zu buchen.

Calkins setzte auf moderne Farbdruckverfahren, fotografische Effekte und ästhetische Trends, um eine einprägsame und herausragende „Kunst" zu erschaffen. Indem er modernes Artwork in die fade Standardwerbung integrierte, frischte Calkins das Interesse an bereits eingeführten Produkten auf und brachte darüber hinaus den Verbraucher dazu, freudig einer Zukunft voll schöner Konsumgüter entgegenzusehen. Seine „radikalen Ideen" stießen jedoch auf Ablehnung bei denen, die eine weniger kunstorientierte Werbung bevorzugten. Seine Ideen waren in der Tat bahnbrechend, doch die große Mehrheit der Anzeigen wies weiterhin Bleiwüsten auf, die tunlichst jedes erdenkliche Missverständnis, jede Zweideutigkeit ausschließen sollten.

Konservative Werbeleute vertraten die Ansicht, eine zu fantasievolle Werbung sei elitär und ginge am Geschmack der breiten Masse vorbei. Sie fanden, Calkins könne sich nicht von den Wertvorstellungen seiner eigenen Klasse frei machen und die Gesellschaft im Ganzen sehen. Calkins hingegen glaubte, dass „künstlerische Werbung" eine demokratisierende Kraft für den Mittelstand sein könnte. Seine eigentliche Zielgruppe waren „Menschen von Geschmack", wie er sagte; ihm lag nichts daran, in den sogenannten Habenichtsen unerfüllbare Wünsche zu wecken.

Für Calkins waren eine zu unruhige Gestaltung (Wheaties, S. 402), Bildergeschichten (Camel, S. 29–31) sowie läppische Zeichnungen und Texte (Saraka, S. 267) eine Zumutung, die den Verbraucher nur verwirrten. Er propagierte Techniken, die durch stilisierte, symbolische und abstrakte Formen eine geheimnisvolle Aura erzeugten. Da die Bildaussage nun im Vordergrund stand, verlor der Text für die Werbung zwangsläufig an Bedeutung. Während der zwanziger und dreißiger Jahre kamen die Artdirectors daher zu bislang nicht gekanntem Ansehen – ja, sie verliehen den Dingen durch die optische Gestaltung tatsächlich ein modernes Gesicht.

Nach Calkins' Rezeptur wurden alltägliche Gebrauchsgegenstände vor einem dynamisch gemusterten Hintergrund und aus ungewohnten Perspektiven präsentiert; zeitgenössische Industrieprodukte wurden oft in einem surrealistischen oder futuristischen Kontext gezeigt.

Das moderne Artwork war ein Gewinn, der sich auszahlte, und es diente der Tarnung. „Wenn man die hässlicheren Gebrauchsgegenstände nicht verschönern kann", so Calkins, „hat das Artwork die Aufgabe, sie unsichtbar zu machen." Eine durch grafische Mittel angedeutete besondere Beziehung zwischen Produkt und Anzeige war das, was Calkins „Atmosphäre" nannte, ein Fetischcharakter, der letzten Endes auf das Produkt selbst abfärbte.

Doch Calkins blieb ein Pragmatiker. Die Werbung durfte den Verbraucher nicht überfordern, sondern musste ihn fesseln. Er wollte das allgemeine Niveau heben, doch obwohl das mit den „fortschrittlichsten Methoden" geschehen sollte, war der Stil nur Mittel, nicht Endzweck. Anzeigen für Palmolive (S. 212), Old Gold (S. 44) und Thompson Products (S. 10–11), um nur einige zu nennen, stellen eine echte Synthese von modernem Stil und traditioneller Werbegrafik dar. Dies war kein Pyrrhussieg;

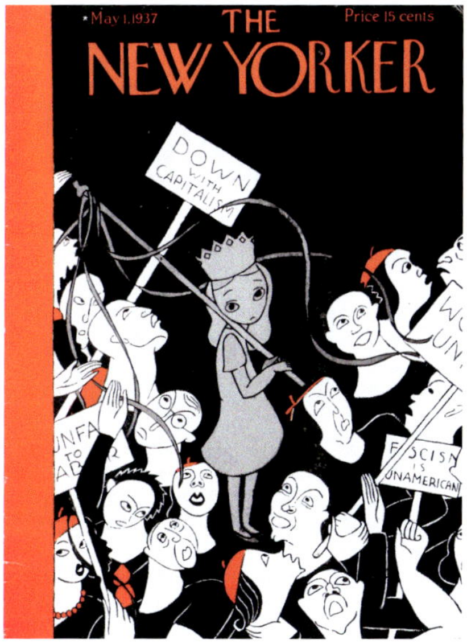

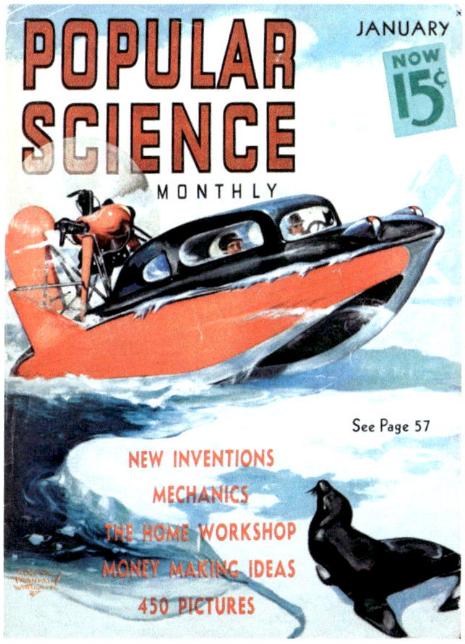

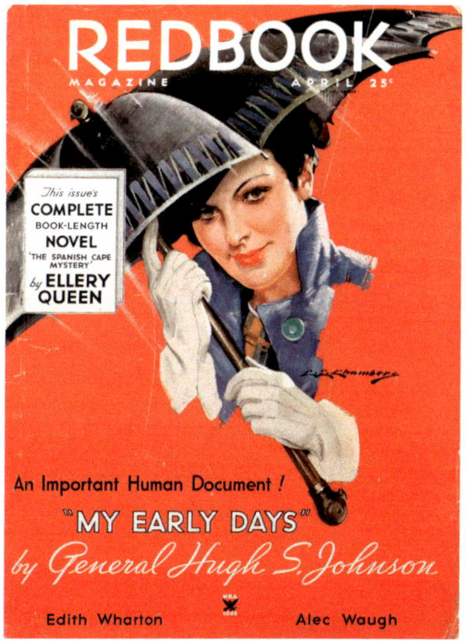

Calkins war vielmehr überzeugt: „Wenn man das Erscheinungsbild der Werbung optimiert, erreicht man zweierlei. Es beeinflusst unmittelbar den Geschmack der Öffentlichkeit und wirkt sich indirekt positiv auf die Warenproduktion aus.“

Calkins’ erfolgreiche Methode hatte jedoch auch einen Nachteil. In den frühen dreißiger Jahren produzierte die amerikanische Industrie einfach mehr, als der Markt aufnehmen konnte. Darüber hinaus wirkte sich der katastrophale Börsenkrach von 1929 nicht eben positiv auf die Kaufkraft aus. 1933 kam Calkins’ Pionierarbeit in Sachen Stil an den Punkt, an dem sie sich einfach nicht mehr rentierte. Übereifriges Werben und die Überproduktion während des Wirtschaftsbooms früherer Tage waren nicht unmittelbar für den Niedergang der amerikanischen Wirtschaft und die große Depression verantwortlich, aber sie waren symptomatisch für das, was Harry Batten von der renommierten Werbeagentur NW Ayer als einen übertriebenen wirtschaftlichen Optimismus beschreibt, eine „Art von Spielsucht“, die alle gesellschaftlichen Bereiche erfasst hatte. Mitte der dreißiger Jahre hatten sich die immer noch von der Wirtschafskrise gebeutelten Anzeigenkunden und Werbefachleute auf einen lässigen Werbestil der Machermentalität besonnen, für den sich im vorliegenden Band die meisten Beispiele finden.

Als die bedrohliche Flut der Depression alle Profite der Boomjahre vor dem Krieg fortgespült hatte, musste Calkins’ Agentur wie alle anderen großen New Yorker „Shops“ ihren Klienten nur noch eins verschaffen: reißenden Absatz. Eine gewisse Modernität wurde nach der Wirtschaftskrise beibehalten, aber der überwiegende Teil der Werbung offenbarte eine Rückkehr zu plumpen Methoden. Man warb mit Prominenten (für Zigaretten), mit zahllosen kleinen Bildern (für Automobile), mit romantischen Landschaften (für die Reisebranche) und mit gut gefüllten, glänzenden Kühlschränken (für Lebensmittel). Subtilität war out, Ironie nicht minder und witzige Einfälle – außer in Form leicht verständlicher Comics – sinnlos, wenn die Waren in den Regalen liegen blieben.

Calkins betraute Teams von Werbetextern und Illustratoren oder Artdirectors damit, kreativ ausbalancierte Anzeigen und Kampagnen zu entwerfen, aber im Gefolge der Wirtschaftskrise verdrängten marktschreierische Slogans und Lobeshymnen „zufriedener Kunden“ jedwede künsterischen Zwischentöne. Die Werbung konnte sich den Luxus der subtilen Verführung nicht mehr leisten. Anzeigen mussten markige Behauptungen aufstellen, vollmundige Versprechen folgen lassen und mit einem einprägsamen Slogan enden.

Eine Anzeige für Jantzens Bademoden (S. 373), illustriert von George Petty, dem Großmeister der erotischen Illustration, versprach den Frauen ganze Kerle und den Männern kurvige Frauen, wenn sie das Produkt kauften. Die doppelsinnige Headline „Perfectly suited by Jantzen“ zeigt, dass ein Texter mit Sprachgefühl an der Kampagne beteiligt war. Damit war die Anzeige von Jantzen anspruchsvoller als die meisten anderen in diesem Genre.

Eine anspruchslose Anzeige für Chipso, ein Waschmittel mit skurrilem Namen, entsprach da schon eher der Regel. Ein Farbfoto zeigt Kinder, die Kaffeeklatsch spielen, eine frisch frisierte Hausfrau und drei strahlende Mädchen in blitzsauberen Partykleidchen, während die zu lang geratene Unterzeile verrät: „Our clothes look new for more than one season’s wear ... thanks to Chipso.“ Das ist die klassische, einfallslose Anzeige mit der Aussage einer zufriedenen Konsumentin. Der grammatikalisch zweifelhafte Slogan „Chipso makes clothes wear – longer“ (unter dem Foto der

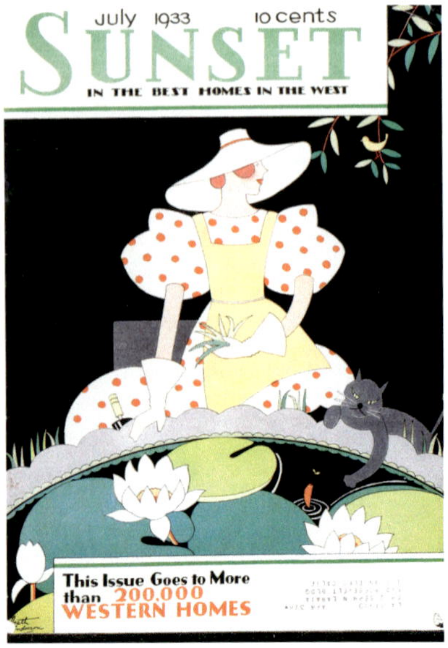

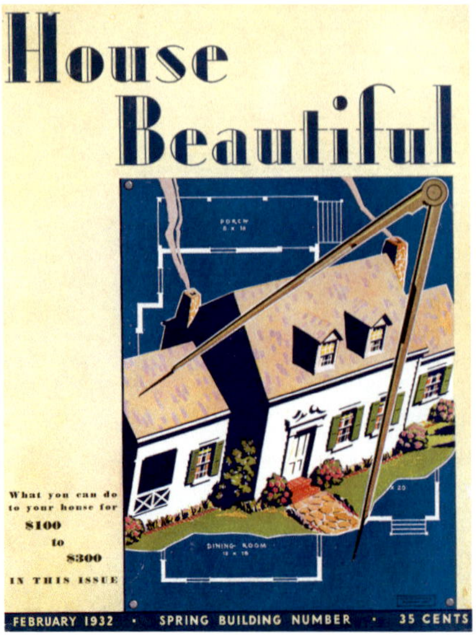

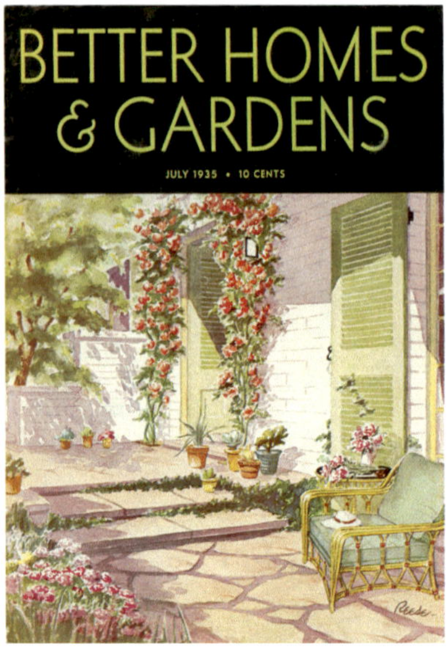

Mutter, die in ihrer Schürze am Waschbecken steht, in der Hand einen Karton des Zaubermittels) unterstreicht noch die Botschaft, dass nur Sauberkeit wahres Glück bedeutet und diese Sauberkeit in dem Karton steckt.

Chipso mag kein kreatives Highlight gewesen sein, aber die Anzeige lässt durchaus den Einfluss bekannterer und besser finanzierter Werbekampagnen erkennen, etwa der für Coca-Cola, die es auch tunlichst vermied, Fragen offen zu lassen. „Home... to the pause that refreshes" (S. 462) erschlägt einen mit Text und Bildern. Der klassische Coca-Cola-Slogan prangt als Headline über einer stilisierten Illustration, die zwei kleine, glückliche, zuckersüchtige Geschwister zeigt. Deren Mutter kehrt gerade schwer bepackt vom Einkauf zurück (reines Wunschdenken in Zeiten der Rezession) und wird von ihrem jüngsten Kind begeistert begrüßt. Als wäre dies noch nicht Narration genug, zeigen zwei begleitende Fotografien eine „echte" Mutter dabei, wie sie das dunkle, süße Elixier einkauft und kredenzt. Und wer es noch immer nicht verstehen will, bekommt als Nachschlag den Textblock „When you shop you get something you don't bargain for. You get tired ... and thirsty" an den Kopf geworfen, der ihm das berühmte Logo „Drink Coca-Cola" in die Großhirnrinde brennt.

Anzeigen dieser Machart füllten die Seiten von *Life, Look, The Saturday Evening Post, Collier's* und zahlloser anderer wöchentlich oder monatlich erscheinender Illustrierten. Trotz der wirtschaftlichen Misere ging es den Illustrierten gut – wie das Kino lenkten sie die Menschen von ihrem tristen Alltag ab. Die Anzeigen förderten nicht nur den Verkauf der Produkte, sie schufen auch eine Atmosphäre der Normalität, die den Menschen half, im allgemeinen gesellschaftlichen Chaos nicht die Orientierung zu verlieren.

Die Werbung der dreißiger Jahre erfüllte zwei wichtige Aufgaben: zum einen förderte sie natürlich die Kauflust und folglich den Absatz, zum anderen beschwor sie die Selbstheilungskraft des amerikanischen Kapitalismus und weckte so in düsteren Zeiten einen gewissen Optimismus. Wenn man die Anzeigen in diesem Band betrachtet, würde man niemals vermuten, dass Amerika damals in einer ernsthaften Krise steckte. Die stilvolleren Anzeigen der frühen dreißiger Jahre wichen aggressiveren Werbekonzepten (immer ein Indikator für düstere Zeiten), aber die Werbung für die meisten Gebrauchsgegenstände und einige wenige Luxusartikel blieb so allgegenwärtig und überschwänglich wie vor dem Börsenkrach. Und gegen Ende des Jahrzehnts, als bereits düstere Kriegswolken über Europa aufzogen, gelang es der Werbung, die Nachfrage in Amerika künstlich zu steigern. Man krempelte die Ärmel hoch, die Wirtschaft fand wieder Tritt – und dann kam der Zweite Weltkrieg. Alle Aspekte amerikanischen Lebens sollten sich für immer ändern, und auch die Werbung sollte wieder ein neues Gesicht bekommen.

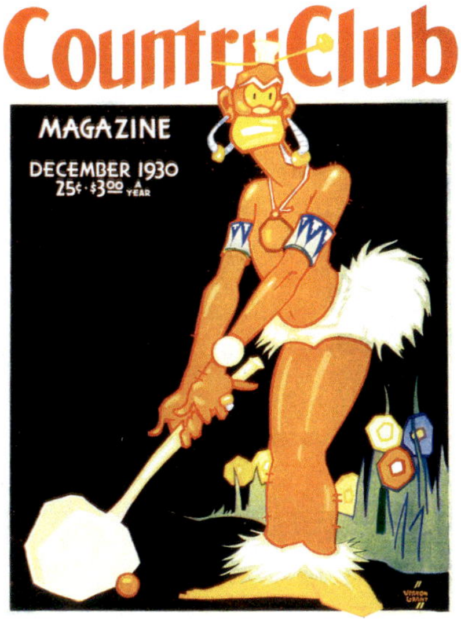

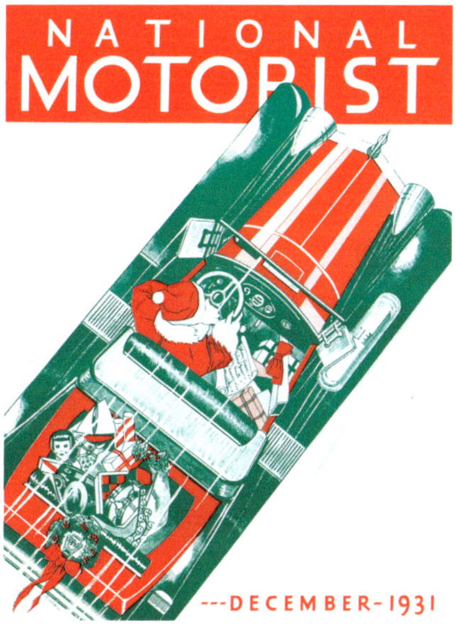

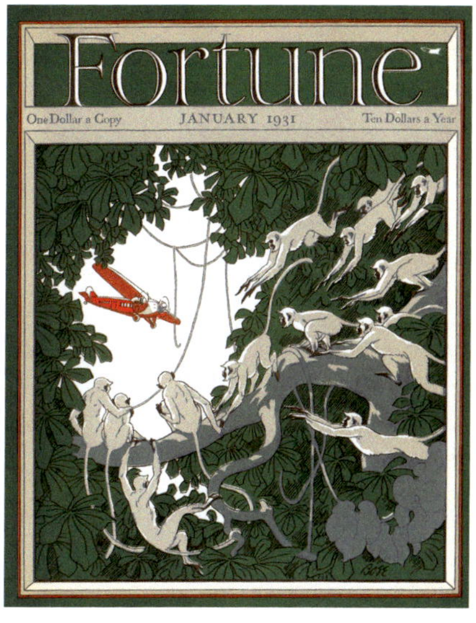

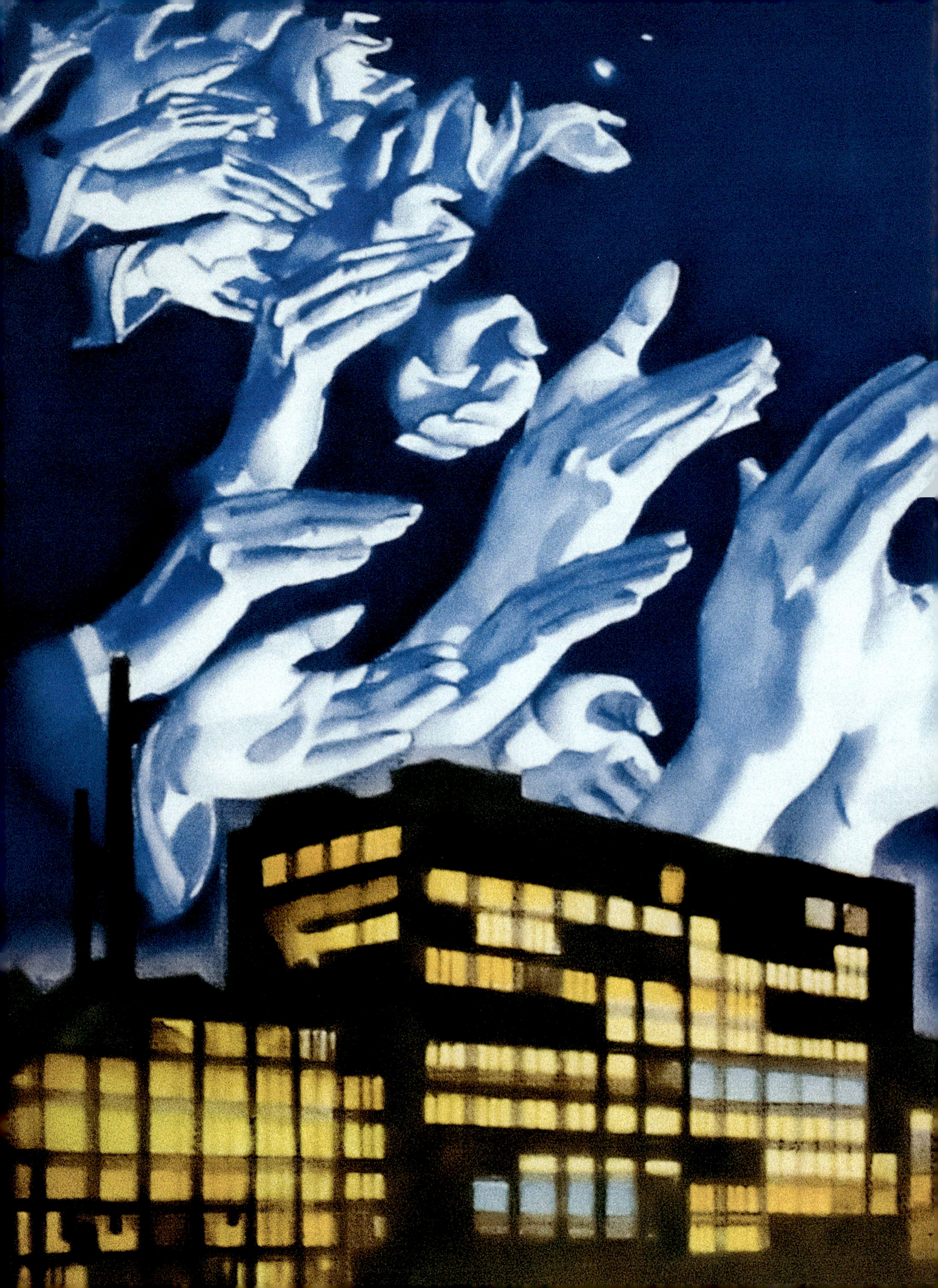

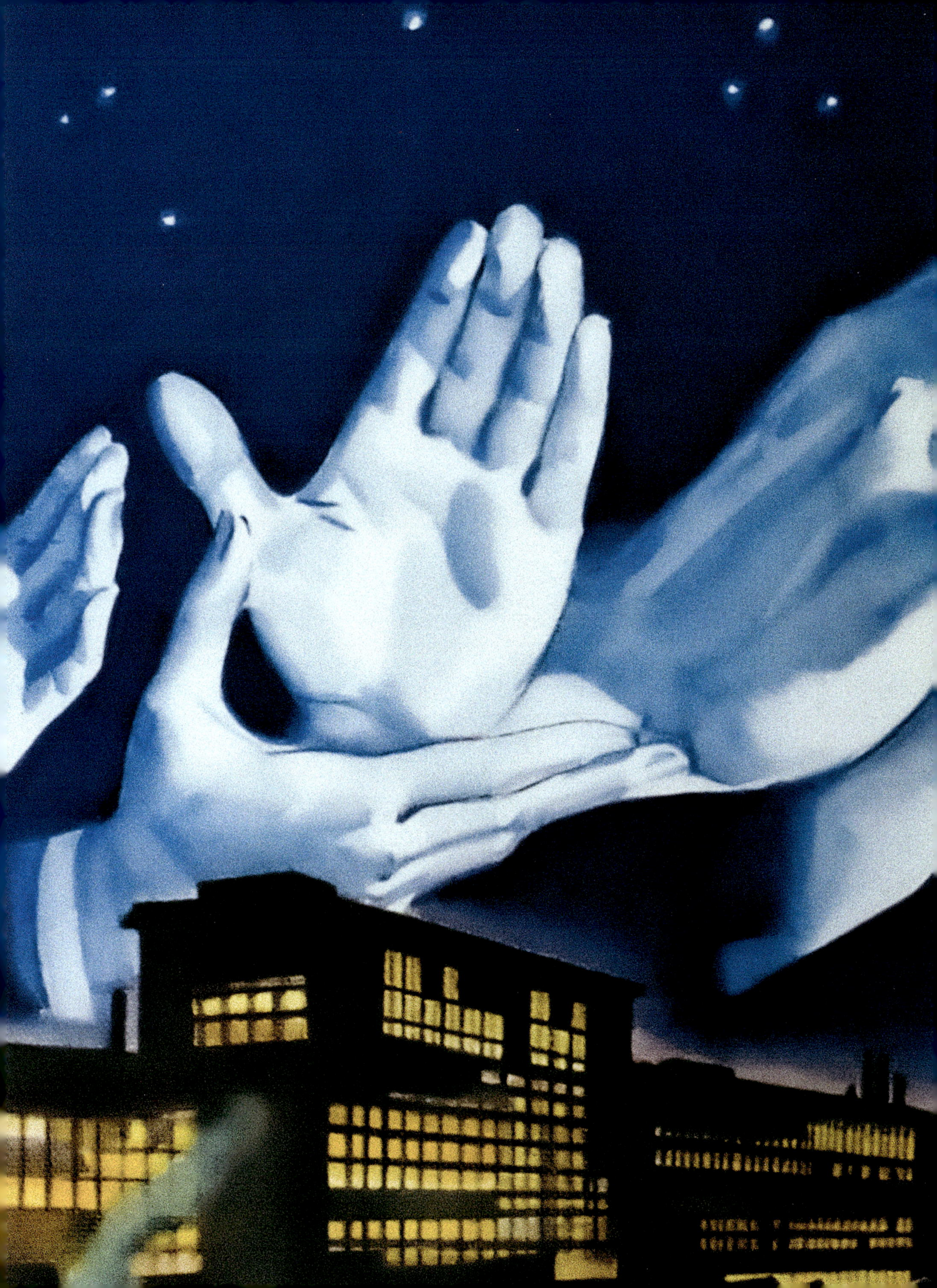

Les publicités des années 30

Du modernisme à la méthode coup de poing

par Steven Heller

La publicité américaine des années trente est née en 1925 à Paris. L'Exposition internationale des arts décoratifs et industriels modernes, creuset de la modernité, s'étirait de part et d'autre de la Seine dans des pavillons ornés de motifs géométriques et de frises néoclassiques. Venus du monde entier, les principaux créateurs de prêt-à-porter, de mobilier et d'articles ménagers, ainsi que de nombreux grands magasins, y exposaient leurs derniers produits et leurs dernières inventions. Toutefois, l'un des acteurs brillait par son absence.

Les États-Unis, la plus grande nation industrielle, avaient décliné l'invitation. Comme l'explique l'historien Terry Smith, les barons de l'industrie américaine « se sentaient incapables de rivaliser avec les créateurs français en produisant un “modernisme” dépouillé à la Arts and Crafts ou en osant créer un style propre ».

À juste titre. Quand ils n'étaient pas insipides, les produits américains étaient surchargés d'ornements censés dissimuler le fait qu'ils étaient fabriqués en série. Bien que l'économie américaine moderne reposait entièrement sur la production de masse, nombreux étaient les critiques décriant le mauvais goût des articles sortant des chaînes de montage. En Europe, le Bauhaus et d'autres mouvements d'avant-garde avaient intégré la machine, mais les industriels américains restaient apathiques alors qu'ils avaient largement les moyens d'améliorer l'esthétique de leurs produits. En revanche, ils n'étaient pas indifférents aux stratégies commerciales susceptibles d'accroître leurs profits. Tous recherchaient frénétiquement de nouveaux moyens pour stimuler leurs ventes grâce à l'art et à la science de la publicité.

L'homme qui contribua le plus à révolutionner la publicité américaine à partir du milieu des années 20 et jusque dans les années 30 fut Earnest Elmo Calkins, publicitaire de la première heure, réformateur du design et fondateur de l'agence new-yorkaise Calkins and Holden Advertising Co. Enthousiasmé par l'exposition parisienne de 1925, il rédigea un traité décrivant les graphismes, les emballages et les étalages cubistes et futuristes présentés dans les pavillons des grands magasins : « C'est un art extrêmement “nouveau”, parfois bizarre mais atteignant un degré d'harmonie fascinant, qui, dans le détail, est plutôt divertissant. » De retour aux États-Unis, il tenta de démontrer comment la publicité américaine pouvait tirer profit du modernisme et de l'art moderne européens.

À Paris, Calkins avait été frappé par une nouvelle forme d'illustration – alors principal vecteur de création et de diffusion d'images – qui n'était plus figurative, mais qui recourait à des symboles et à des métaphores pour entourer les biens de consommation d'une aura « magique ». Les boîtes et les flacons n'étaient plus de simples contenants utilitaires, mais les signifiants de l'essence d'un produit. Calkins note dans ses écrits : « Le modernisme permet d'exprimer l'inexprimable, d'évoquer non pas une automobile mais la vitesse, non pas une robe du soir mais l'élégance, non pas un poudrier mais la beauté. » Si cela n'est pas sans rappeler le futurisme de Marinetti, c'est parce que Calkins empruntait au langage de l'avant-garde européenne sans pour autant approuver son radicalisme.

Aucun publicitaire ne contribua autant que lui à la révolution consumériste des États-Unis. Calkins ressemblait davantage à un prédicateur de l'Amérique profonde qu'à un publicitaire new-yorkais. Il joua pourtant un rôle crucial dans l'avènement de concepts de marketing progressistes comme « l'ingénierie de la consommation », « l'obsolescence forcée » et « l'habillage de produits ». Ces mots clés formaient le noyau dur d'une stratégie publicitaire qui fit entrer l'art moderne et la création graphique dans un univers farouchement conservateur et dominé jusqu'alors par le texte, dont l'activité première était d'acheter de l'espace publicitaire dans les journaux et les magazines.

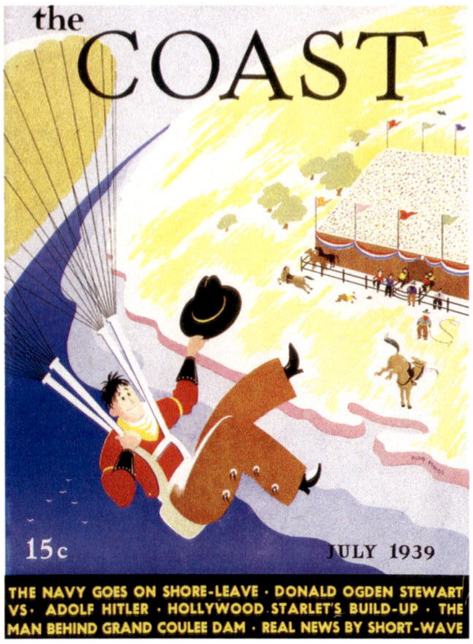

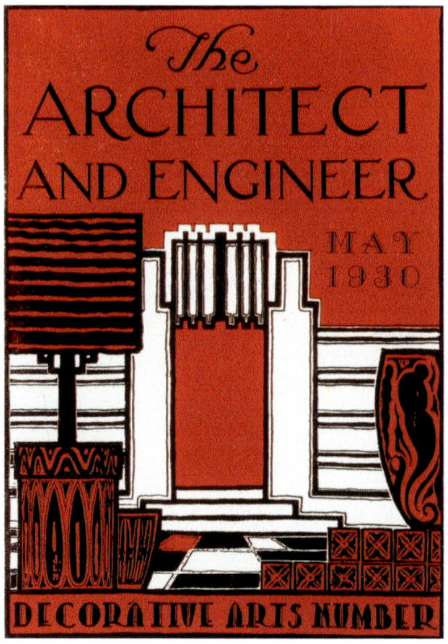

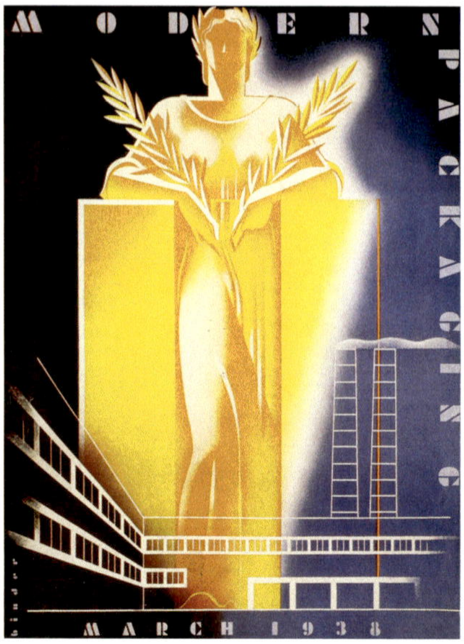

Pour Calkins, il n'était plus concevable « de produire une annonce frappante, remarquable et séduisante avec des images figées et des compositions réalistes ». Il chercha à mettre à profit les nouvelles technologies d'impression en couleur, les effets photographiques et les dernières tendances esthétiques pour créer un « art » mémorable et monumental. En intégrant l'art moderne dans l'indigeste culture commerciale grand public, Calkins ranima l'intérêt pour les produits anciens et obligea les consommateurs à imaginer un avenir radieux rempli de biens de consommation. Cependant, ses idées « radicales » se heurtèrent à l'opposition de ceux qui voulaient vendre « sans faire de chichis ». Si sa vision gagnait du terrain, la grande majorité des publicités n'étaient encore que des tracts surchargés de textes conçus pour lever toute ambiguïté quant à la nature du produit proposé.

Les publicitaires conservateurs estimaient que les images publicitaires sophistiquées étaient élitistes, qu'elles ne correspondaient pas aux goûts du consommateur moyen et qu'elles étaient donc vouées à l'échec. Pour eux, Calkins avait un sens exagéré de ses propres valeurs sociales qui ne reflétaient pas la société dans son ensemble. De son côté, Calkins pensait que la « publicité artistique » pouvait être un facteur de démocratisation pour les classes moyennes. Plutôt que de susciter des désirs nécessairement frustrés chez les plus démunis, il s'adressait exclusivement à une classe socioéconomique qu'il appelait « les gens de goût ».

Calkins considérait comme bêtifiants et déroutants les affiches surchargées (Wheaties, p. 402), les bandes dessinées (Camel, p. 29–31), les dessins et les slogans puérils (Saraka, p. 267). À leur place, il préconisait des techniques capables de créer une mystique par le biais de formes abstraites, stylisées et symboliques. La publicité pouvait donc s'affranchir du texte, l'image devenant le principal vecteur de communication. Plus important encore, ce modèle élevait le directeur artistique au-dessus du rédacteur dans la hiérarchie publicitaire. Calkins estimait que la fonction de l'« expert en art » était aussi importante que celle d'un chef de rédaction cultivé. Tout au long des années 20 et 30, les directeurs artistiques des agences de publicité – recourant à l'illustration pour créer des auras modernes – acquirent un rôle de premier plan. Suivant la méthode de Calkins, ils commencèrent à présenter des objets courants (grille-pain, réfrigérateurs, crayons, paquets de café) de guingois et sur des fonds aux motifs dynamiques. De même, les articles industriels étaient souvent mis en scène dans des décors surréalistes et futuristes.

L'art moderne constituait une valeur ajoutée et un précieux camouflage. « Lorsque les nécessités du commerce ne peuvent être embellies, écrit Calkins, l'art sert à les faire disparaître. » Il appelait « atmosphère » le style graphique suggérant un lien privilégié entre la publicité et le produit, un trait fétichiste qui finit par déteindre sur l'article lui-même.

Toutefois, Calkins était un pragmatique. Une publicité qui péchait par excès d'ingéniosité risquait de perdre son public qui, ne comprenant plus ce qu'on cherchait à lui vendre, ne se laissait plus séduire. Il cherchait à relever le niveau général de la manière « la plus moderne possible, et néanmoins acceptable » ; le « style » était un moyen, et non une fin. Les publicités pour Palmolive (p. 212), Old Gold (p. 44) et Thompson Products (p. 10–11), pour n'en citer que quelques-unes, constituent une véritable synthèse du style moderne et de la création publicitaire traditionnelle. Il ne s'agit pas là que d'une victoire à la Pyrrhus. Ces allusions modernistes satisfaisaient pleinement Calkins qui expliquera plus tard que « l'amélioration de l'aspect de la publicité a eu deux effets : elle a directement influencé le goût du public et indirectement conditionné la production des biens de consommation ».

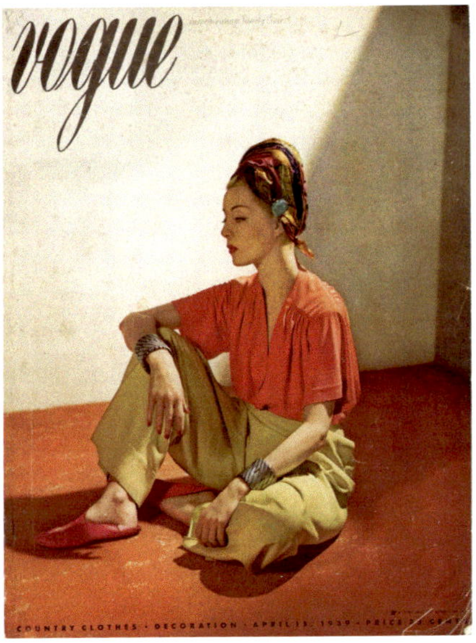

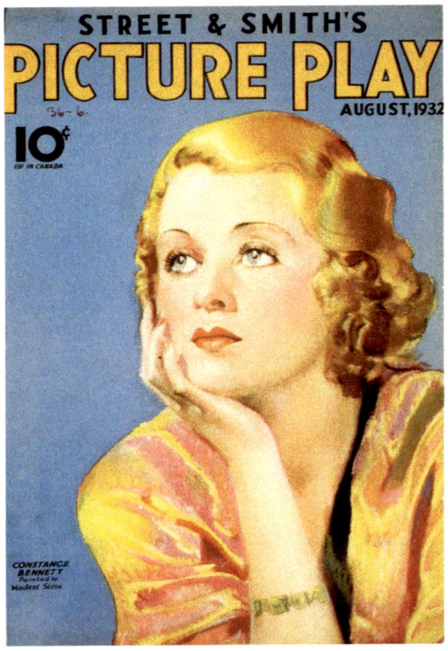

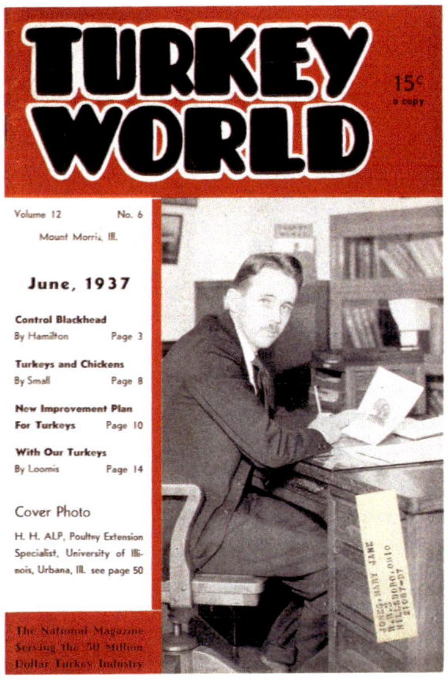

Dans certains secteurs, le nouveau style publicitaire stimula les ventes, ce qui relança la production et dopa l'économie. Fabricants et détaillants étaient ravis, tout comme les designers et les artistes en grande partie responsables de ce succès. Un illustrateur de l'époque témoigne : « J'ai vu cette nouvelle esthétique se rapprocher de plus en plus de ce qui comptait réellement… un contenant vers lequel des millions de mains d'acheteurs se tendent parce qu'il leur dit quelque chose d'irrésistible ! »

Cependant, le succès de la démarche de Calkins eut également son revers. Au début des années 30, l'industrie américaine produisait trop pour entretenir un niveau de consommation élevé et continu. En outre, le krach de 1929 avait sérieusement entravé le pouvoir d'achat des Américains… quand il ne l'avait pas totalement anéanti. En 1933, la réforme de Calkins atteignit ses limites et la tendance commença à s'inverser. Certes, le soin excessif apporté aux campagnes publicitaires et à la fabrication des produits pendant la période d'euphorie d'avant 1929 n'était pas directement responsable de la débâcle économique, mais il était symptomatique de ce que Harry Batten, de chez N. W. Ayer, a décrit comme un excès de confiance économique, « une sorte de fièvre du jeu [qui] s'était propagée dans toutes les couches de la société ». Au milieu des années 30, dans un monde encore en pleine dépression, les publicitaires se rabattirent sur ce qu'on a appelé « la publicité coup de poing », que cet ouvrage vise à illustrer.

Face au raz-de-marée de la crise de 1929, qui balaya toutes les grandes avancées économiques de l'immédiat après-guerre, l'agence de Calkins et les nombreuses autres « boutiques » newyorkaises durent donner à leurs clients ce qu'ils réclamaient : des ventes. Au lendemain de la Grande Dépression, certaines publicités conservèrent quelques aspects modernistes, mais la plupart des annonceurs renouèrent avec leurs techniques de vente agressives, faisant de nouveau appel aux témoignages de célébrités (pour les cigarettes), aux planches d'illustrations (pour les automobiles), aux paysages romantiques (pour les voyages) et aux réfrigérateurs rutilants et bien remplis (pour les produits alimentaires). L'art le plus progressiste du monde ne pouvait vendre des lessives, du dentifrice, des déodorants, de l'huile végétale ou des ampoules électriques. Si les produits restaient dans les rayons, la subtilité devenait hors sujet, l'ironie inconcevable, et l'humour (hormis dans des bandes dessinées faciles à comprendre) inutile.

Calkins confia à des équipes de rédacteurs-artistes-directeurs artistiques le soin de créer des annonces et des campagnes publicitaires créatives et équilibrées, mais, dans un contexte de dépression économique, les slogans tonitruants et les témoignages ampoulés remplacèrent toutes les nuances artistiques. Avant l'ère de la télévision, la publicité imprimée dans les journaux, dans les magazines et sur les panneaux d'affichage (sans compter les spots radiophoniques, naturellement) constituait le moyen le plus efficace pour s'adresser directement au consommateur. Toutefois, elle ne pouvait s'offrir le luxe de le séduire avec finesse. Les annonces lançaient des affirmations grandiloquentes, suivies de promesses saisissantes, et s'achevaient sur un mot de la fin mémorable. Ainsi, une publicité pour les costumes de bain Jantzen (p. 373) illustrée par George Petty, maître de l'érotisme chic, assure aux femmes qu'elles séduiront des hommes superbes tout en promettant aux hommes de tomber des créatures de rêve. Et l'accroche affirme : « Jantzen vous va comme un gant. »

À dire vrai, cette publicité pour Jantzen était plus sophistiquée que la plupart des autres du même genre. Plus représentative de l'époque, une publicité pour une lessive au nom sans ambiguïté, Chipso (de

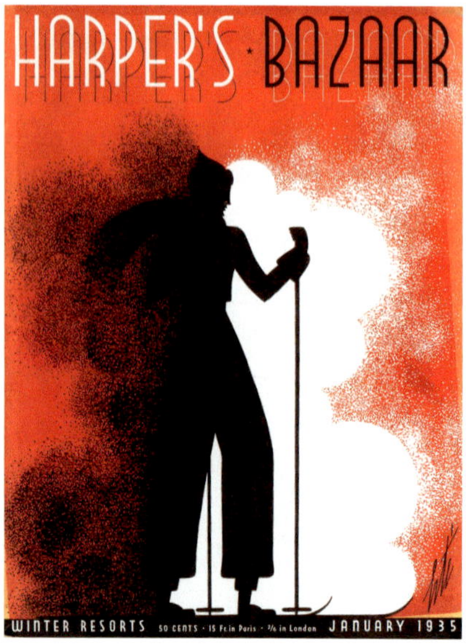

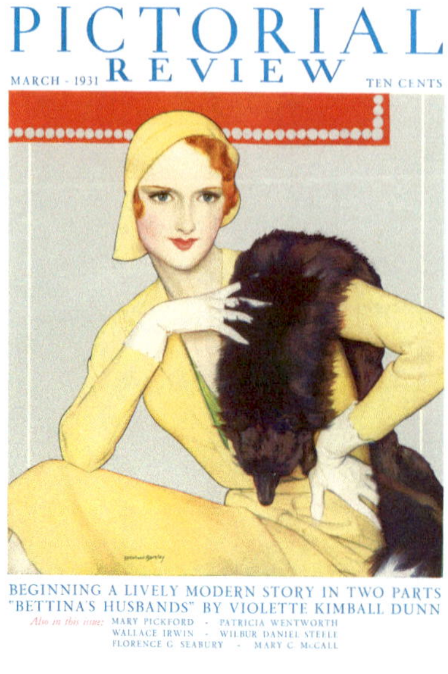

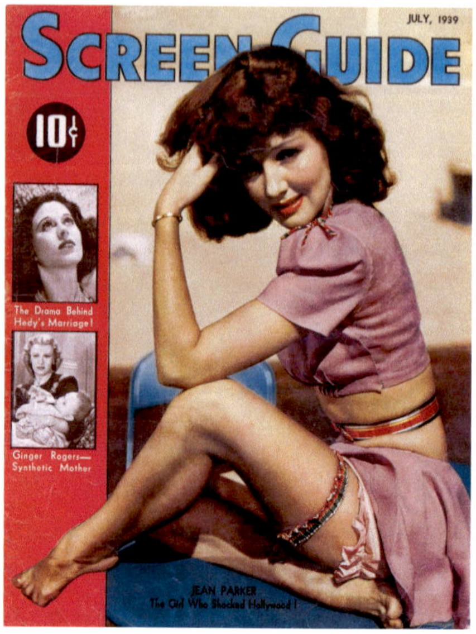

« cheap », bon marché), ne fait pas dans la dentelle. Une photographie en couleurs montre un goûter : trois fillettes radieuses et endimanchées sont accompagnées de leur maman qui semble sortir de chez le coiffeur et qui déclare : « Nos vêtements semblent neufs alors qu'ils ont plus d'une saison... grâce à Chipso. » Le manque de créativité de cette publicité-témoignage est typique. La légende finale « Chipso fait durer les vêtements plus longtemps » (sous une photo de Maman en tablier devant l'évier avec un paquet de cristaux magiques) vient renforcer l'idée que la propreté fait le bonheur et qu'elle s'achète en boîte.

Chipso se trouvait peut-être en bas de l'échelle de la créativité, mais elle n'en était pas moins influencée par des campagnes plus connues et mieux financées, comme celles de Coca-Cola, qui ne laissaient rien à l'imagination. « À la maison... pour la pause fraîcheur » (p. 462) est surchargée de textes et de visuels. La vénérable accroche de la marque couronne une illustration stylisée montrant deux enfants radieux se gavant de sucreries (le visage de la fille semble, peut-être intentionnellement, plus mûr que son corps ne le laisse penser). Maman, qui rentre des courses les bras chargés de paquets (un pur fantasme en cette période de grave récession), est accueillie par sa petite dernière (apparemment déjà repue de Coca-Cola et de gâteaux). Comme si l'image n'était pas déjà suffisamment explicite, deux photographies montrent une « vraie » maman en train d'acheter et de servir le fameux élixir sucré. Au cas où l'on n'aurait toujours pas compris, la légende assène : « Faire les courses n'est pas toujours une partie de plaisir. Cela fatigue... et donne soif. » Le célèbre logo « Buvez Coca-Cola » est ensuite marqué au fer rouge sur le cortex cérébral du lecteur.

Des publicités de ce genre remplissaient les pages de *Life*, *Look*, *The Saturday Evening Post*, *Collier's* et d'innombrables autres hebdomadaires et mensuels. Malgré des recettes fortement réduites par la Grande Dépression, les magazines florissaient. À l'instar du cinéma, ils offraient une distraction toujours bienvenue dans la grisaille ambiante. Les publicités faisaient non seulement vendre, mais elles entretenaient l'illusion que rien n'avait changé, donnant aux consommateurs une impression de normalité dans une époque de grands bouleversements sociaux.

La publicité des années 30 joua deux rôles principaux : elle stimula la demande, et donc les ventes, et elle encouragea le capitalisme américain, servant de vecteur d'optimisme pendant cette période sombre. À voir les publicités publiées dans cet ouvrage, qui aurait pensé que les Américains subissaient à l'époque de dures épreuves ? Les exemples plus artistiques du début de la décennie cédèrent le pas à des réclames plus agressives (indicateur symbolique d'une grave récession), mais la publicité pour la plupart des biens de consommation et certains produits de luxe resta aussi omniprésente, voire envahissante, qu'avant le krach boursier. À la fin des années 30, alors que le spectre de la guerre planait au-dessus de l'Europe, la publicité contribua à stimuler artificiellement la consommation américaine. Chacun avait retroussé ses manches et l'économie commençait à reprendre du poil de la bête... quand survint la Seconde Guerre mondiale. La vie américaine sous tous ses aspects allait s'en trouver à jamais altérée et, une fois de plus, la publicité allait devoir s'adapter.

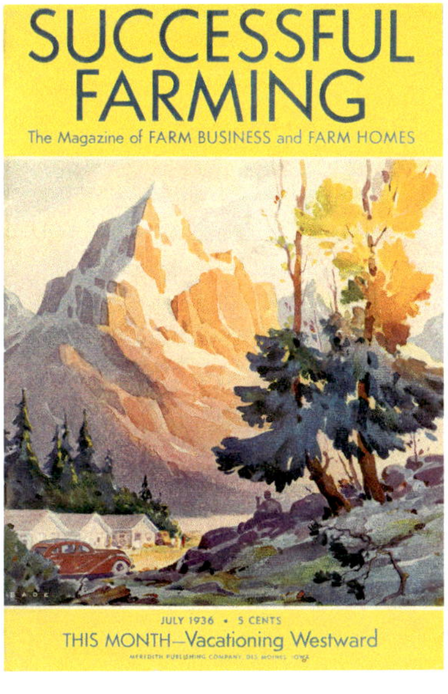

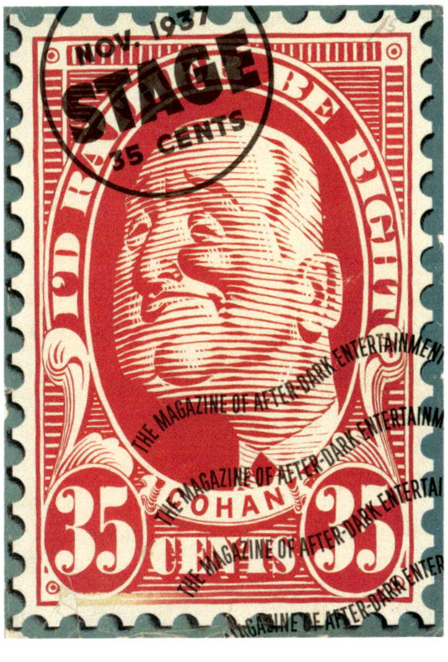

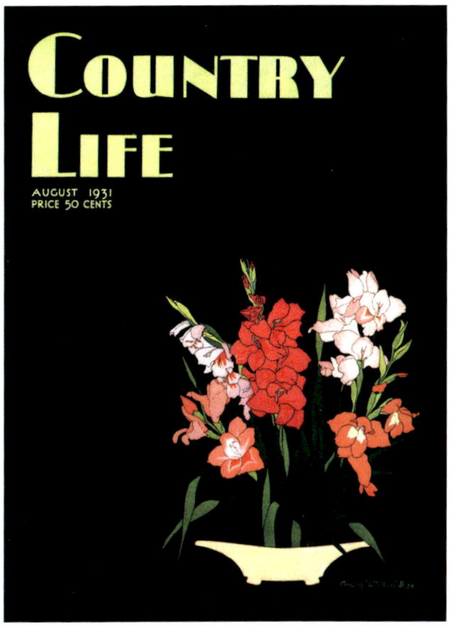

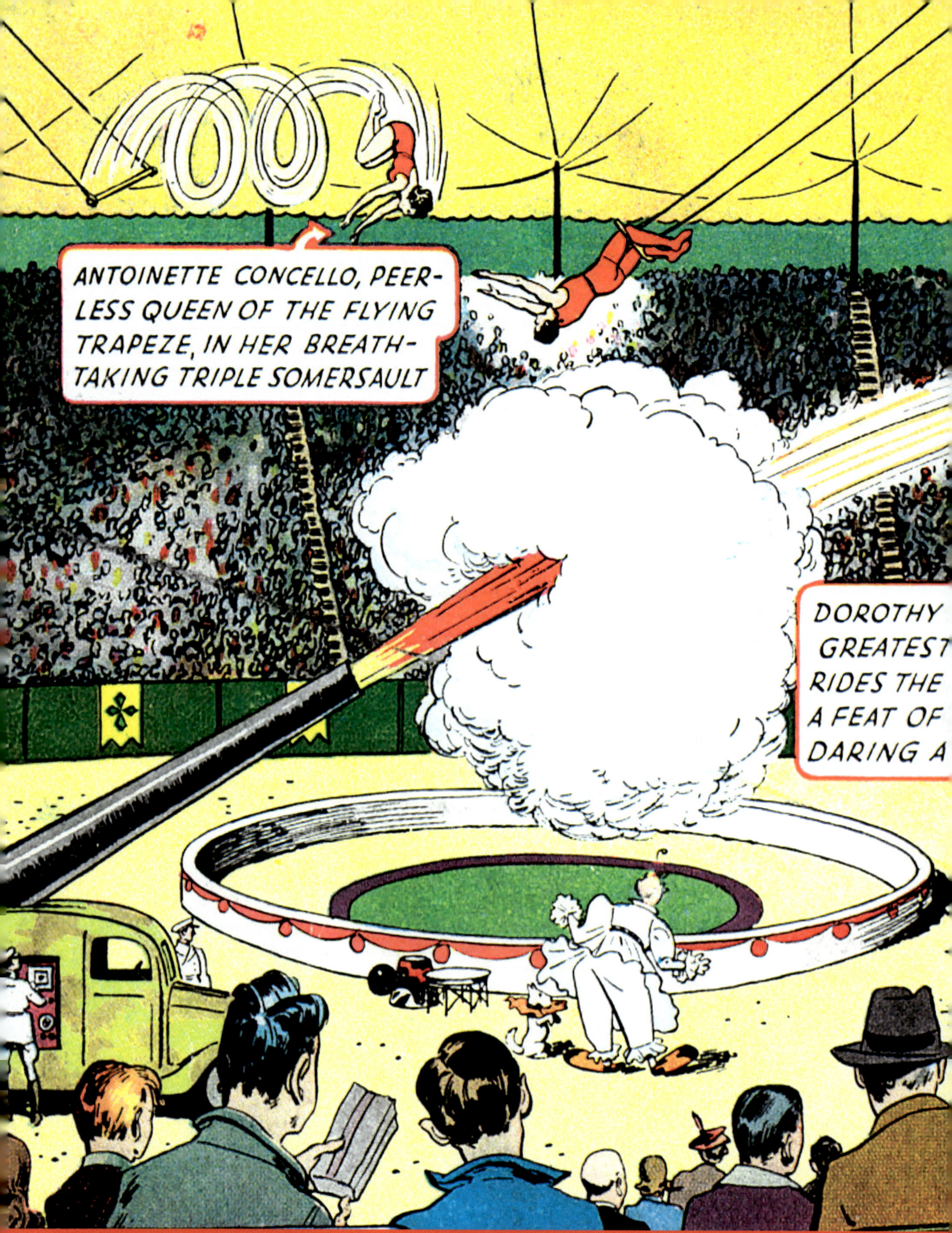
ANTOINETTE CONCELLO, PEERLESS QUEEN OF THE FLYING TRAPEZE, IN HER BREATH-TAKING TRIPLE SOMERSAULT
DOROTHY
GREATEST
RIDES THE
A FEAT OF
DARING A

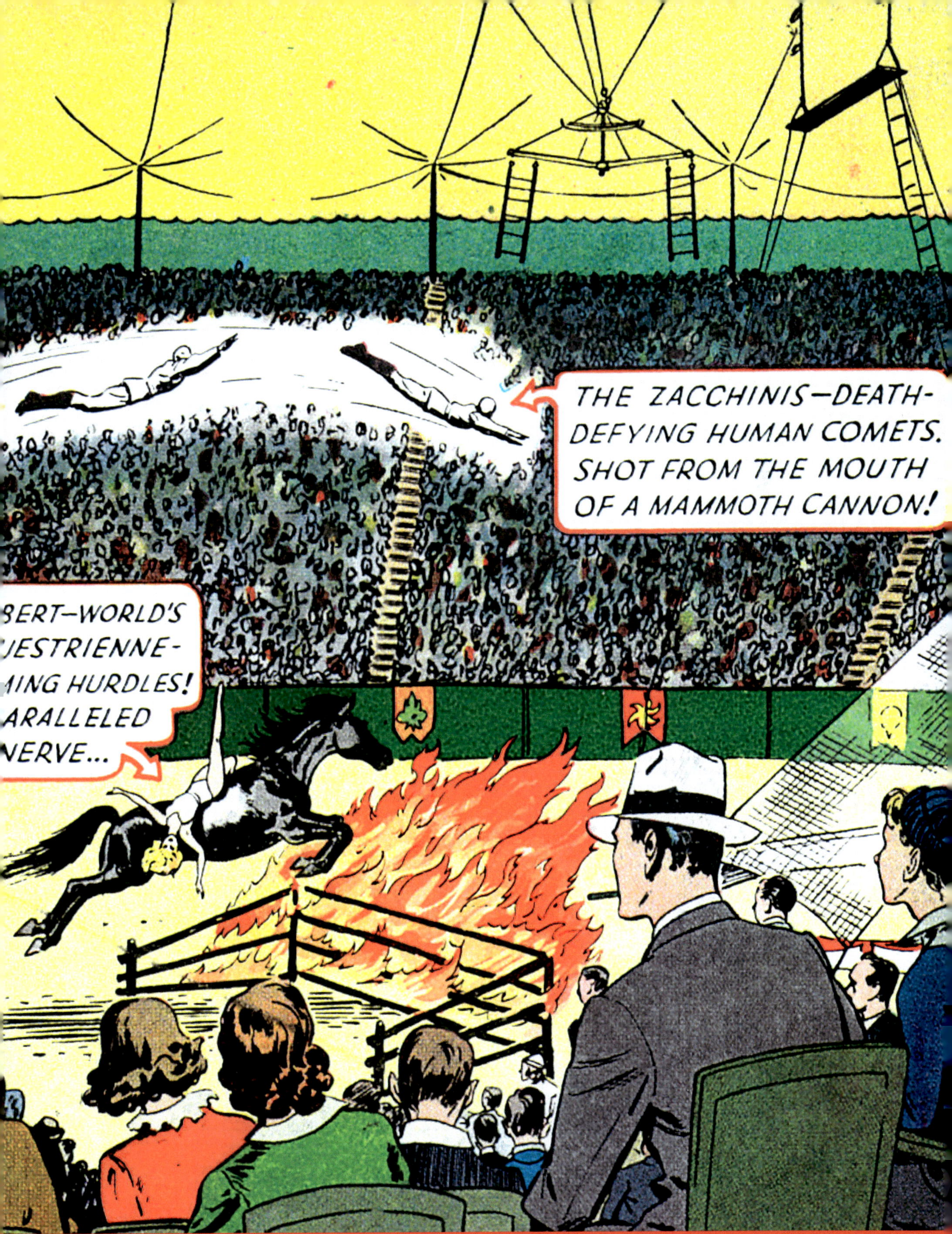
THE ZACCHINIS—DEATH-DEFYING HUMAN COMETS. SHOT FROM THE MOUTH OF A MAMMOTH CANNON!
BERT—WORLD'S JESTRIENNE-MING HURDLES! ARALLELED NERVE...

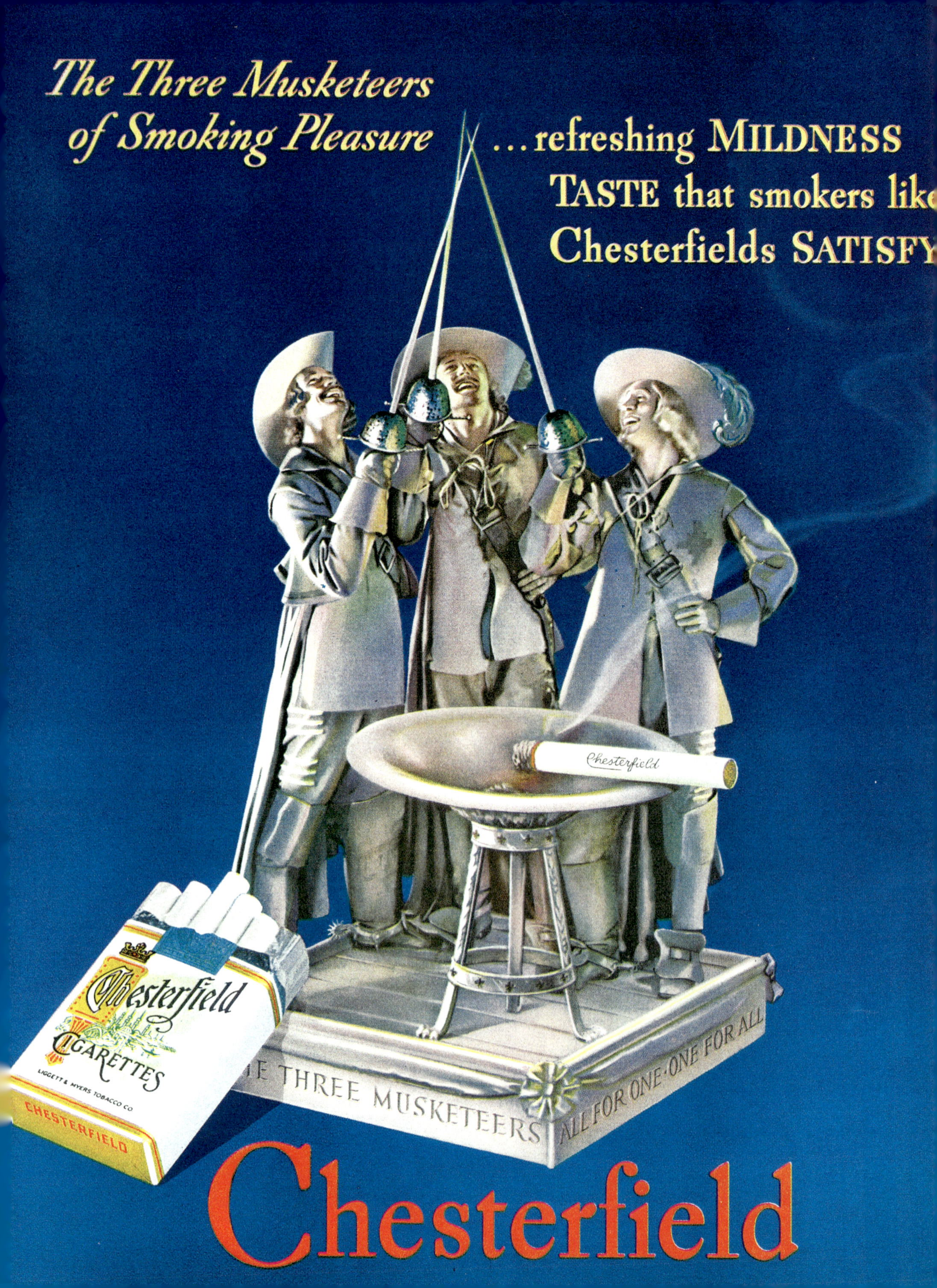
The Three Musketeers
of Smoking Pleasure
...refreshing MILDNESS
TASTE that smokers like
Chesterfields SATISFY
Chesterfield
Chesterfield
CIGARETTES
LIGGETT & MYERS TOBACCO CO
CHESTERFIELD
E THREE MUSKETEERS
ALL FOR ONE · ONE FOR ALL
Chesterfield

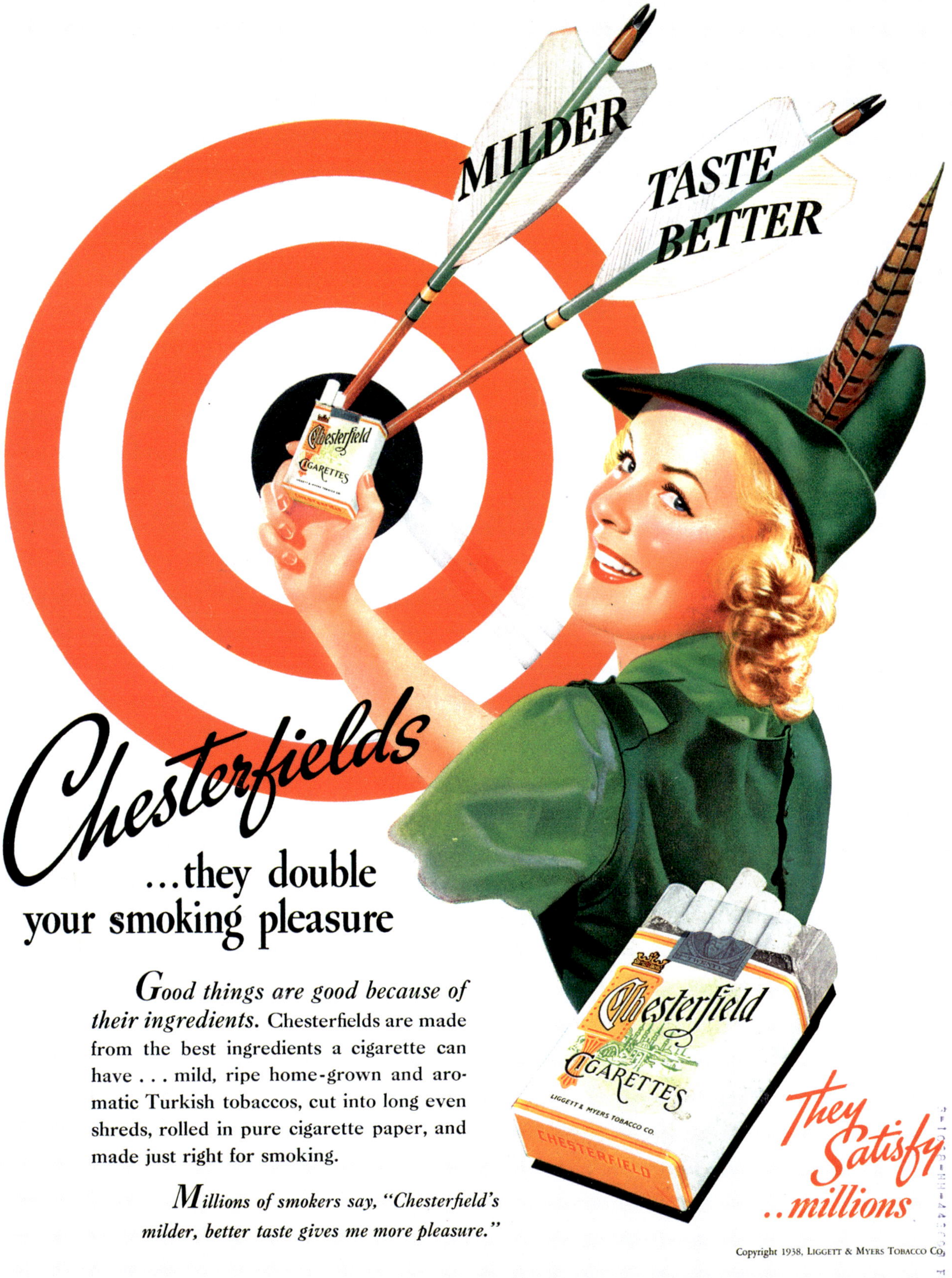

Camels, 1937 ◂◂ Chesterfield, 1937 ◂

Chesterfield, 1938

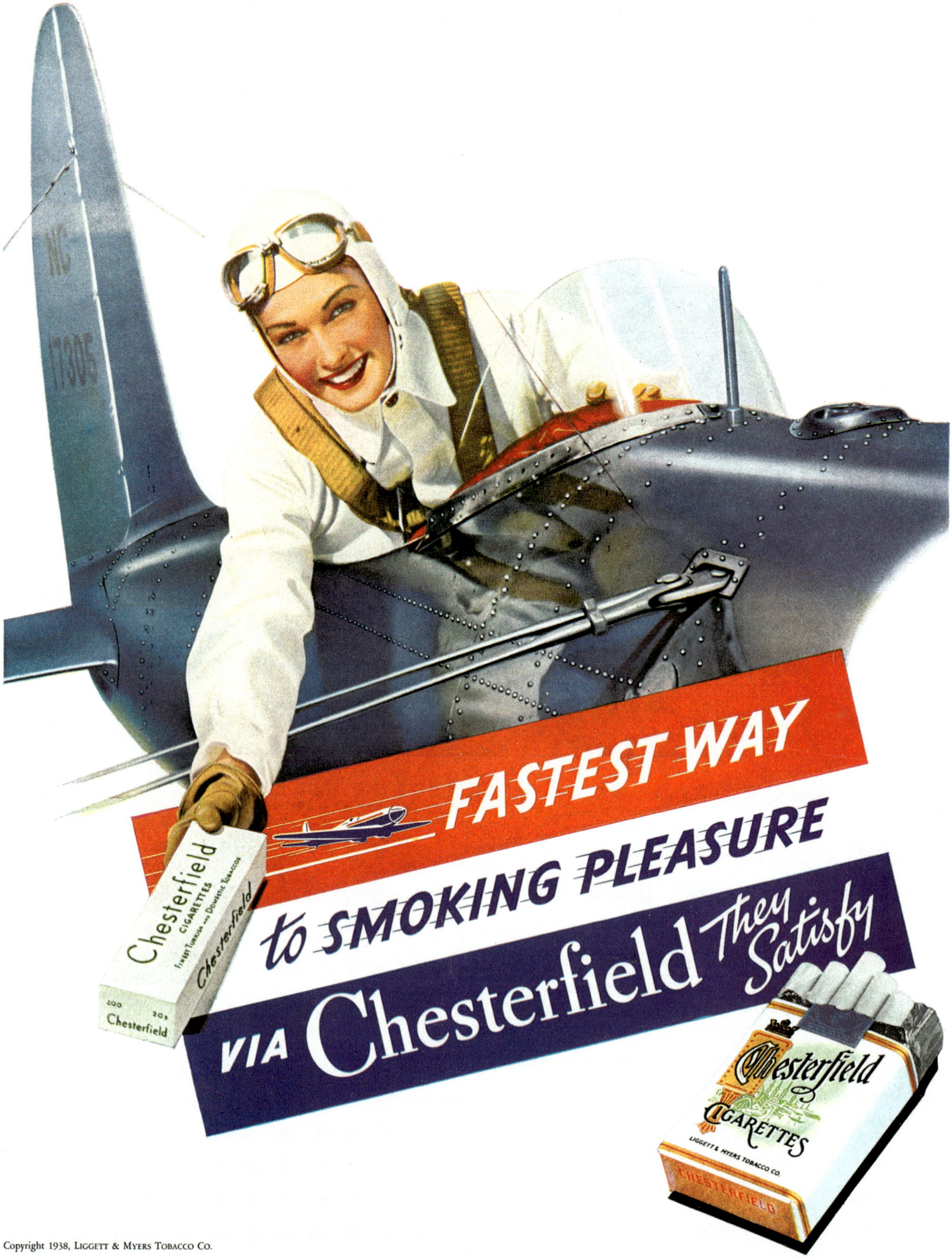

Chesterfield, 1938

▸ *Chesterfield, 1937*

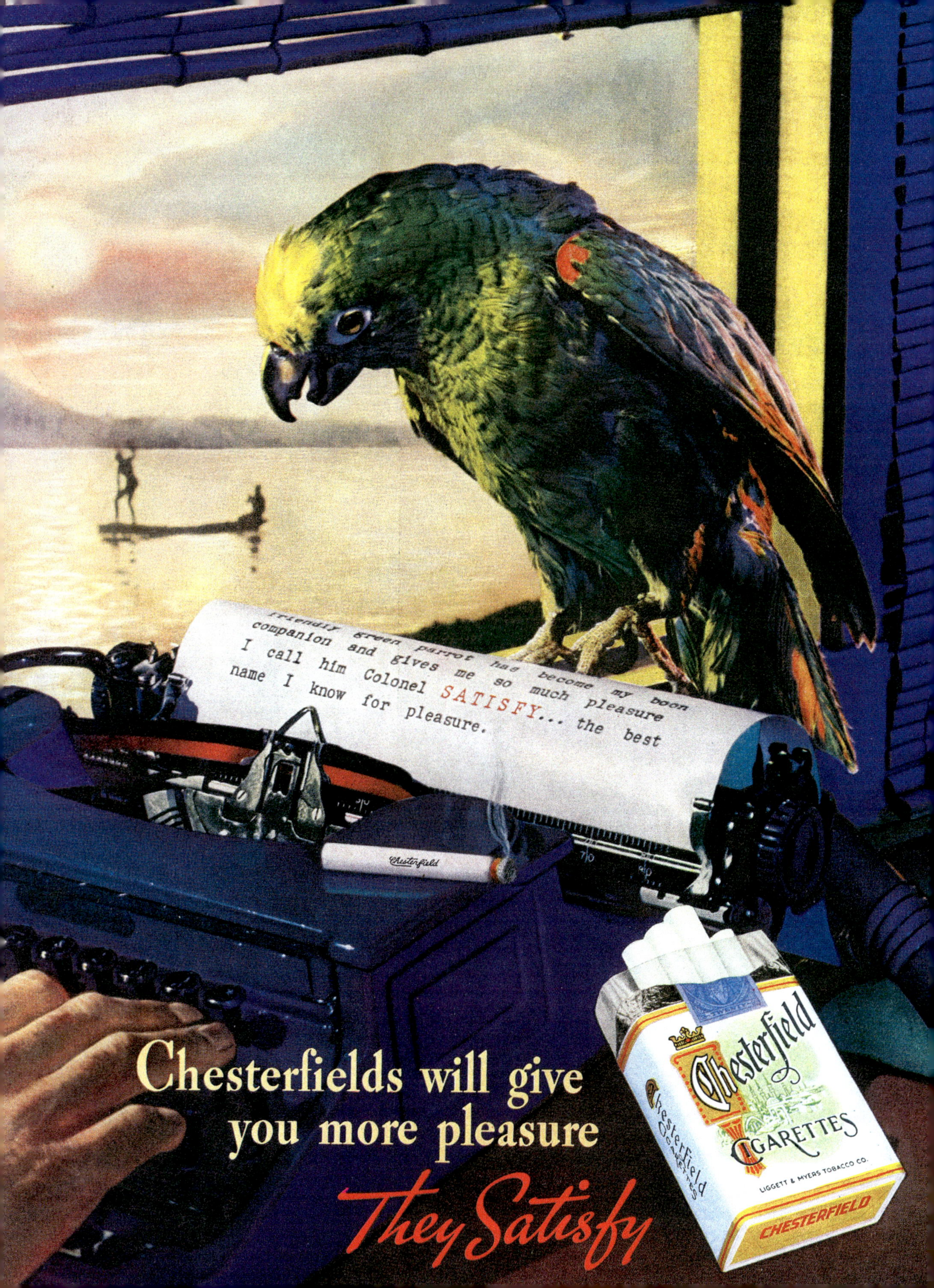

friendly green parrot has become my boon
companion and gives me so much pleasure
I call him Colonel SATISFY... the best
name I know for pleasure.
Chesterfield
Chesterfields will give
you more pleasure
They Satisfy
Chesterfield
CIGARETTES
LIGGETT & MYERS TOBACCO CO.
CHESTERFIELD

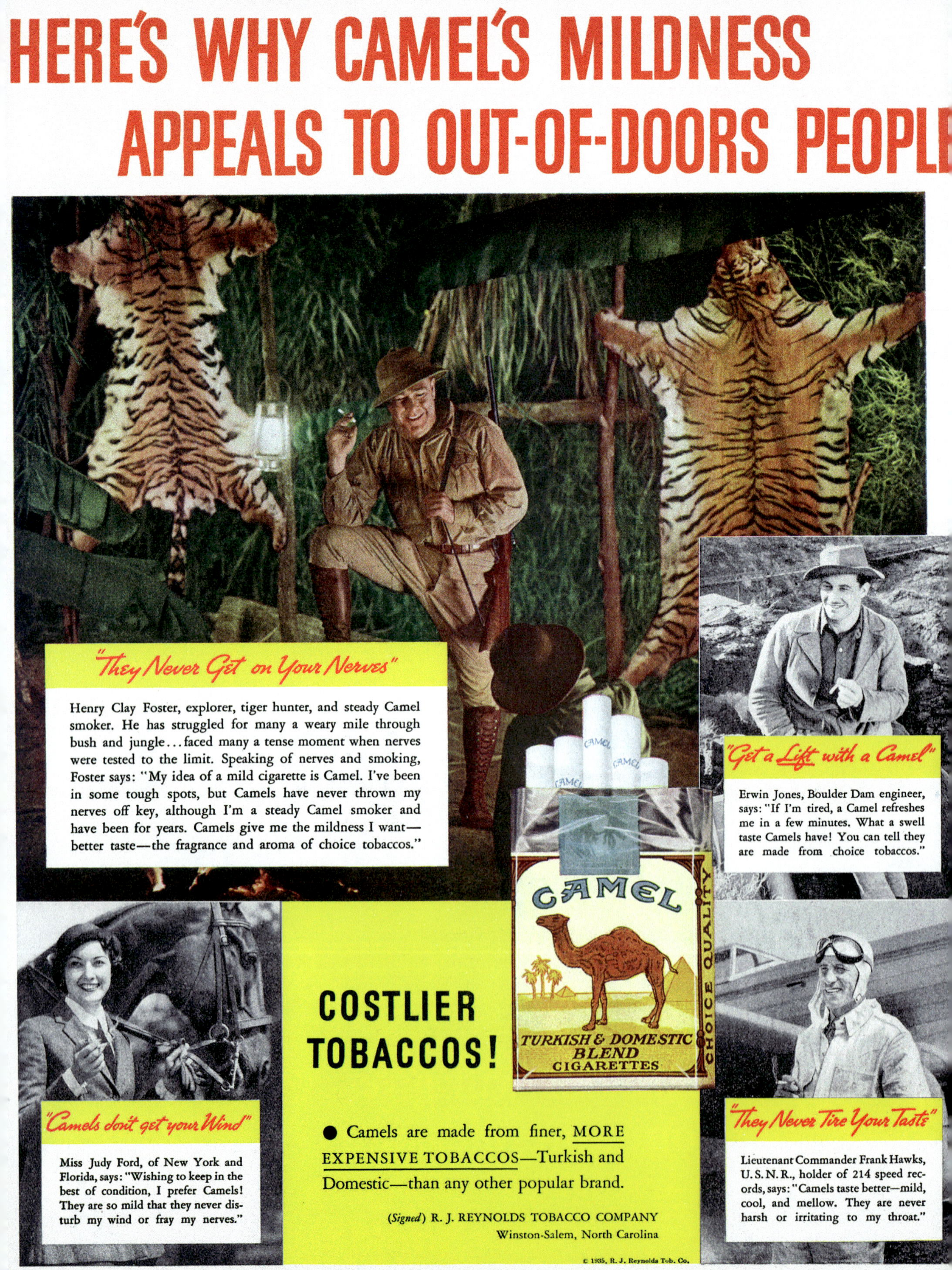
HERE'S WHY CAMEL'S MILDNESS
APPEALS TO OUT-OF-DOORS PEOPL
"They Never Get on Your Nerves"
Henry Clay Foster, explorer, tiger hunter, and steady Camel smoker. He has struggled for many a weary mile through bush and jungle...faced many a tense moment when nerves were tested to the limit. Speaking of nerves and smoking, Foster says: "My idea of a mild cigarette is Camel. I've been in some tough spots, but Camels have never thrown my nerves off key, although I'm a steady Camel smoker and have been for years. Camels give me the mildness I want—better taste—the fragrance and aroma of choice tobaccos."
"Get a Lift with a Camel"
Erwin Jones, Boulder Dam engineer, says: "If I'm tired, a Camel refreshes me in a few minutes. What a swell taste Camels have! You can tell they are made from choice tobaccos."
CAMEL
TURKISH & DOMESTIC BLEND CIGARETTES
CHOICE QUALITY
COSTLIER TOBACCOS!
"Camels don't get your Wind"
Miss Judy Ford, of New York and Florida, says: "Wishing to keep in the best of condition, I prefer Camels! They are so mild that they never disturb my wind or fray my nerves."
● Camels are made from finer, MORE EXPENSIVE TOBACCOS—Turkish and Domestic—than any other popular brand.
(Signed) R. J. REYNOLDS TOBACCO COMPANY
Winston-Salem, North Carolina
"They Never Tire Your Taste"
Lieutenant Commander Frank Hawks, U.S.N.R., holder of 214 speed records, says: "Camels taste better—mild, cool, and mellow. They are never harsh or irritating to my throat."
© 1935, R. J. Reynolds Tob. Co.

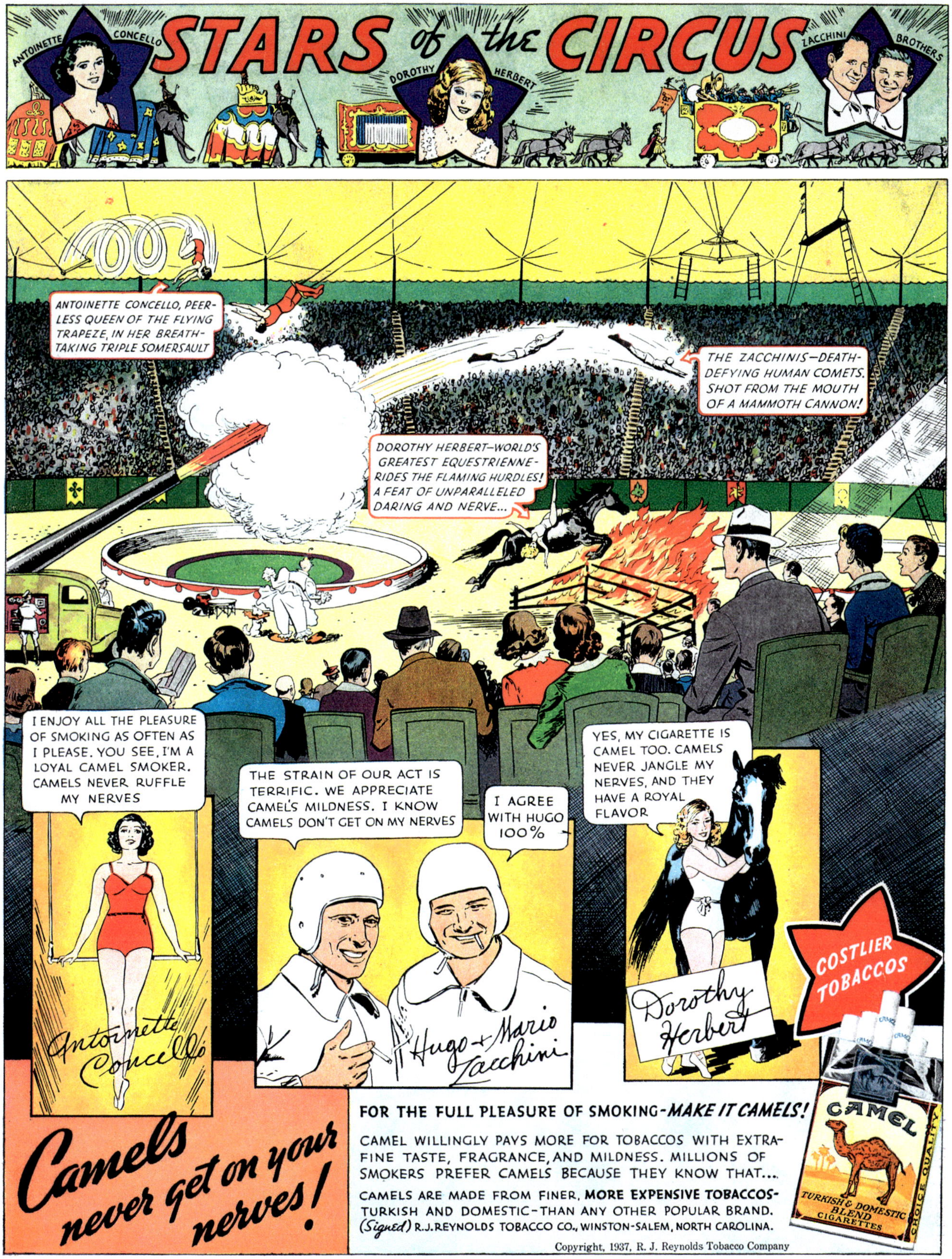

Camels, 1935 ◂

Camels, 1937

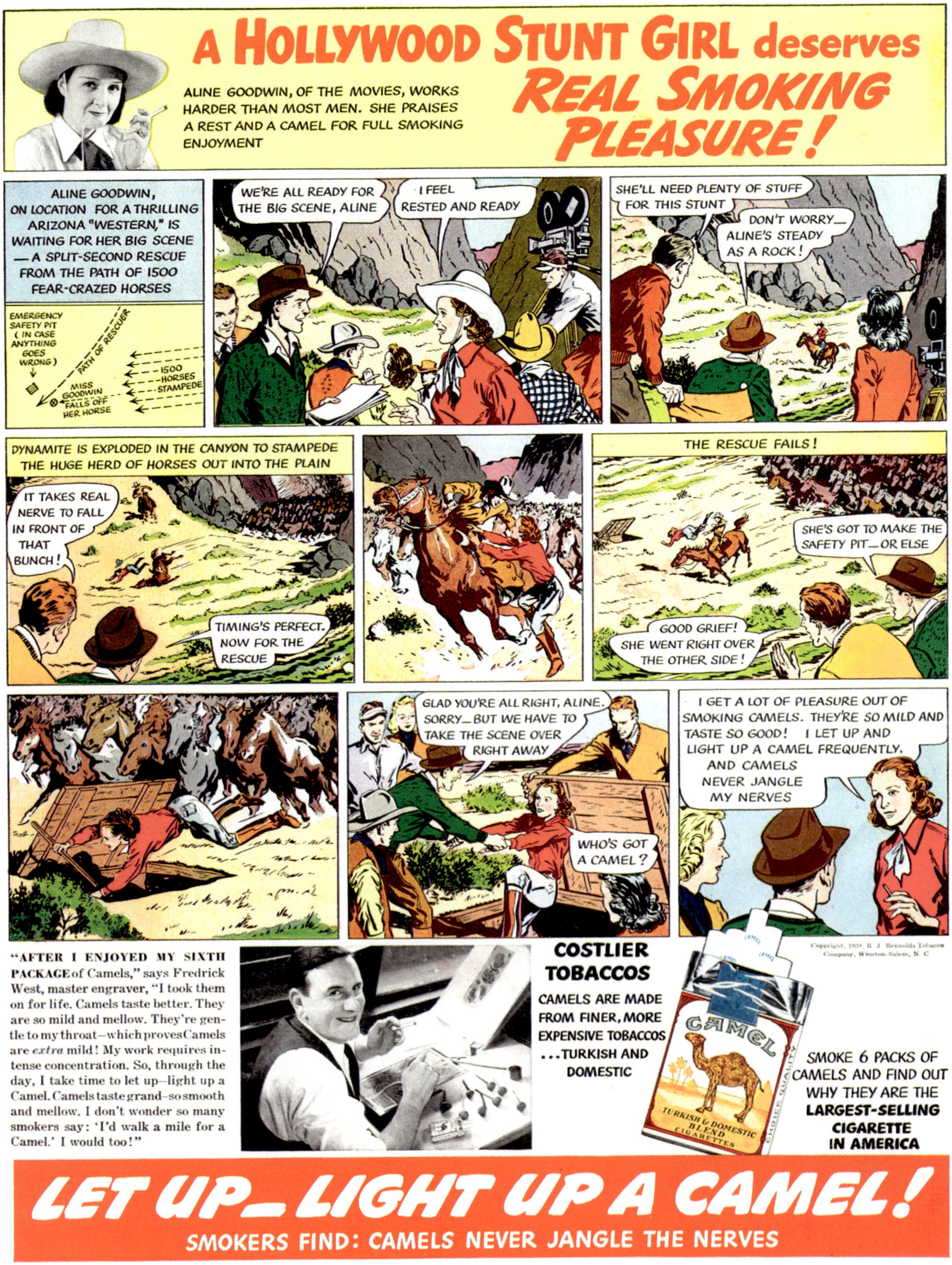

A HOLLYWOOD STUNT GIRL deserves REAL SMOKING PLEASURE!
ALINE GOODWIN, OF THE MOVIES, WORKS HARDER THAN MOST MEN. SHE PRAISES A REST AND A CAMEL FOR FULL SMOKING ENJOYMENT
ALINE GOODWIN, ON LOCATION FOR A THRILLING ARIZONA "WESTERN," IS WAITING FOR HER BIG SCENE — A SPLIT-SECOND RESCUE FROM THE PATH OF 1500 FEAR-CRAZED HORSES
EMERGENCY SAFETY PIT (IN CASE ANYTHING GOES WRONG)
PATH OF RESCUER
1500 HORSES STAMPEDE
MISS GOODWIN FALLS OFF HER HORSE
WE'RE ALL READY FOR THE BIG SCENE, ALINE
I FEEL RESTED AND READY
SHE'LL NEED PLENTY OF STUFF FOR THIS STUNT
DON'T WORRY — ALINE'S STEADY AS A ROCK!
DYNAMITE IS EXPLODED IN THE CANYON TO STAMPEDE THE HUGE HERD OF HORSES OUT INTO THE PLAIN
IT TAKES REAL NERVE TO FALL IN FRONT OF THAT BUNCH!
TIMING'S PERFECT. NOW FOR THE RESCUE
THE RESCUE FAILS!
SHE'S GOT TO MAKE THE SAFETY PIT — OR ELSE
GOOD GRIEF! SHE WENT RIGHT OVER THE OTHER SIDE!
GLAD YOU'RE ALL RIGHT, ALINE. SORRY — BUT WE HAVE TO TAKE THE SCENE OVER RIGHT AWAY
WHO'S GOT A CAMEL?
I GET A LOT OF PLEASURE OUT OF SMOKING CAMELS. THEY'RE SO MILD AND TASTE SO GOOD! I LET UP AND LIGHT UP A CAMEL FREQUENTLY. AND CAMELS NEVER JANGLE MY NERVES
Copyright, 1939, R. J. Reynolds Tobacco Company, Winston-Salem, N. C.
"AFTER I ENJOYED MY SIXTH PACKAGE of Camels," says Fredrick West, master engraver, "I took them on for life. Camels taste better. They are so mild and mellow. They're gentle to my throat—which proves Camels are *extra* mild! My work requires intense concentration. So, through the day, I take time to let up—light up a Camel. Camels taste grand—so smooth and mellow. I don't wonder so many smokers say: 'I'd walk a mile for a Camel.' I would too!"
COSTLIER TOBACCOS
CAMELS ARE MADE FROM FINER, MORE EXPENSIVE TOBACCOS ...TURKISH AND DOMESTIC
CAMEL
TURKISH & DOMESTIC BLEND CIGARETTES
CHOICE QUALITY
SMOKE 6 PACKS OF CAMELS AND FIND OUT WHY THEY ARE THE LARGEST-SELLING CIGARETTE IN AMERICA
LET UP — LIGHT UP A CAMEL!
SMOKERS FIND: CAMELS NEVER JANGLE THE NERVES

Camels, 1939

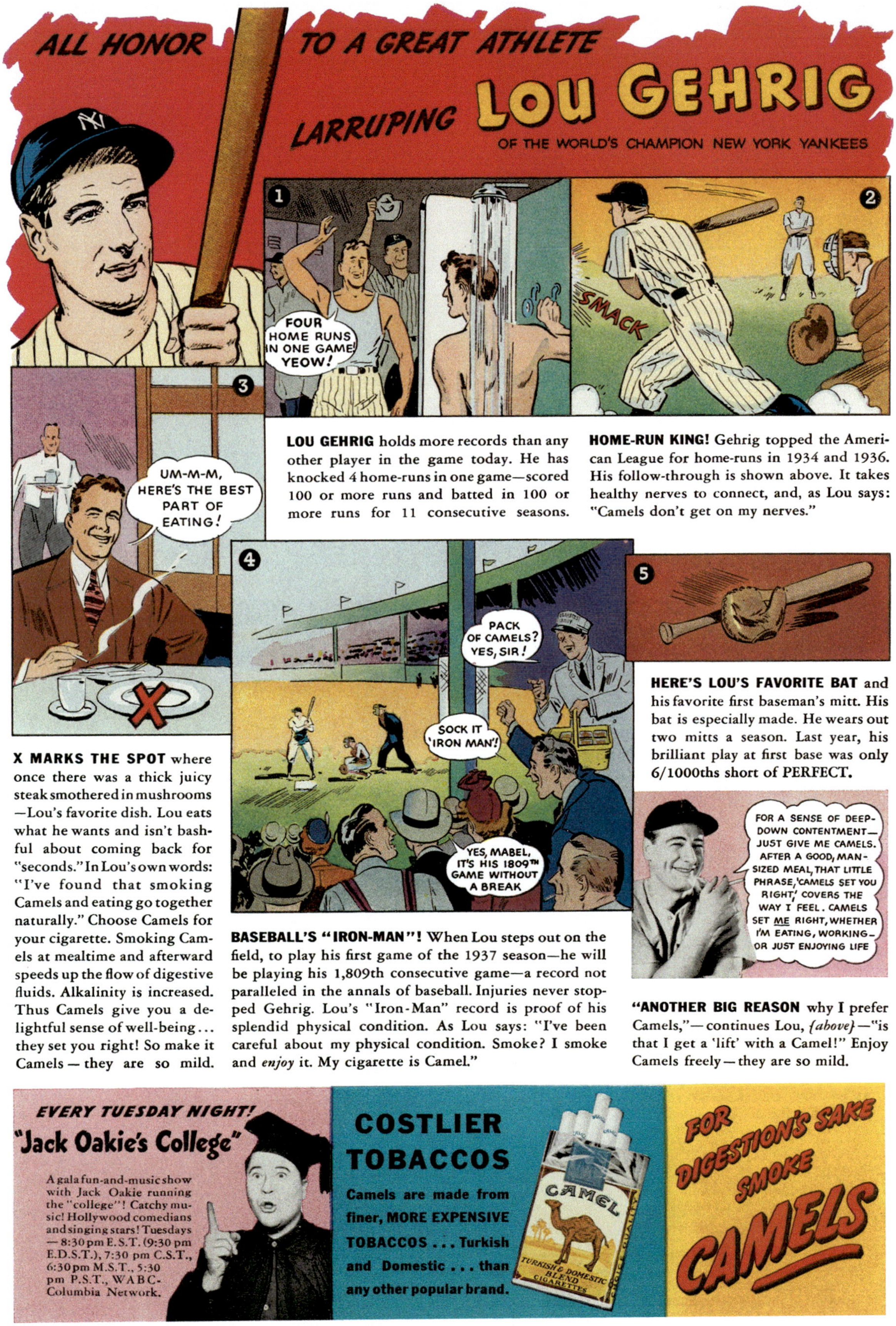
ALL HONOR TO A GREAT ATHLETE
LARRUPING LOU GEHRIG
OF THE WORLD'S CHAMPION NEW YORK YANKEES
1
FOUR HOME RUNS IN ONE GAME! YEOW!
2
SMACK
3
UM-M-M, HERE'S THE BEST PART OF EATING!
LOU GEHRIG holds more records than any other player in the game today. He has knocked 4 home-runs in one game—scored 100 or more runs and batted in 100 or more runs for 11 consecutive seasons.
HOME-RUN KING! Gehrig topped the American League for home-runs in 1934 and 1936. His follow-through is shown above. It takes healthy nerves to connect, and, as Lou says: "Camels don't get on my nerves."
4
PACK OF CAMELS? YES, SIR!
SOCK IT 'IRON MAN'!
YES, MABEL, IT'S HIS 1809TH GAME WITHOUT A BREAK
5
HERE'S LOU'S FAVORITE BAT and his favorite first baseman's mitt. His bat is especially made. He wears out two mitts a season. Last year, his brilliant play at first base was only 6/1000ths short of PERFECT.
FOR A SENSE OF DEEP-DOWN CONTENTMENT—JUST GIVE ME CAMELS. AFTER A GOOD, MAN-SIZED MEAL, THAT LITTLE PHRASE, 'CAMELS SET YOU RIGHT,' COVERS THE WAY I FEEL. CAMELS SET ME RIGHT, WHETHER I'M EATING, WORKING—OR JUST ENJOYING LIFE
X MARKS THE SPOT where once there was a thick juicy steak smothered in mushrooms—Lou's favorite dish. Lou eats what he wants and isn't bashful about coming back for "seconds." In Lou's own words: "I've found that smoking Camels and eating go together naturally." Choose Camels for your cigarette. Smoking Camels at mealtime and afterward speeds up the flow of digestive fluids. Alkalinity is increased. Thus Camels give you a delightful sense of well-being... they set you right! So make it Camels—they are so mild.
BASEBALL'S "IRON-MAN"! When Lou steps out on the field, to play his first game of the 1937 season—he will be playing his 1,809th consecutive game—a record not paralleled in the annals of baseball. Injuries never stopped Gehrig. Lou's "Iron-Man" record is proof of his splendid physical condition. As Lou says: "I've been careful about my physical condition. Smoke? I smoke and enjoy it. My cigarette is Camel."
"ANOTHER BIG REASON why I prefer Camels,"—continues Lou, (above)—"is that I get a 'lift' with a Camel!" Enjoy Camels freely—they are so mild.
EVERY TUESDAY NIGHT!
"Jack Oakie's College"
A gala fun-and-music show with Jack Oakie running the "college"! Catchy music! Hollywood comedians and singing stars! Tuesdays—8:30 pm E.S.T. (9:30 pm E.D.S.T.), 7:30 pm C.S.T., 6:30 pm M.S.T., 5:30 pm P.S.T., WABC-Columbia Network.
COSTLIER TOBACCOS
Camels are made from finer, MORE EXPENSIVE TOBACCOS... Turkish and Domestic... than any other popular brand.
CAMEL
TURKISH & DOMESTIC BLEND CIGARETTES
FOR DIGESTION'S SAKE SMOKE CAMELS

Camels, 1937

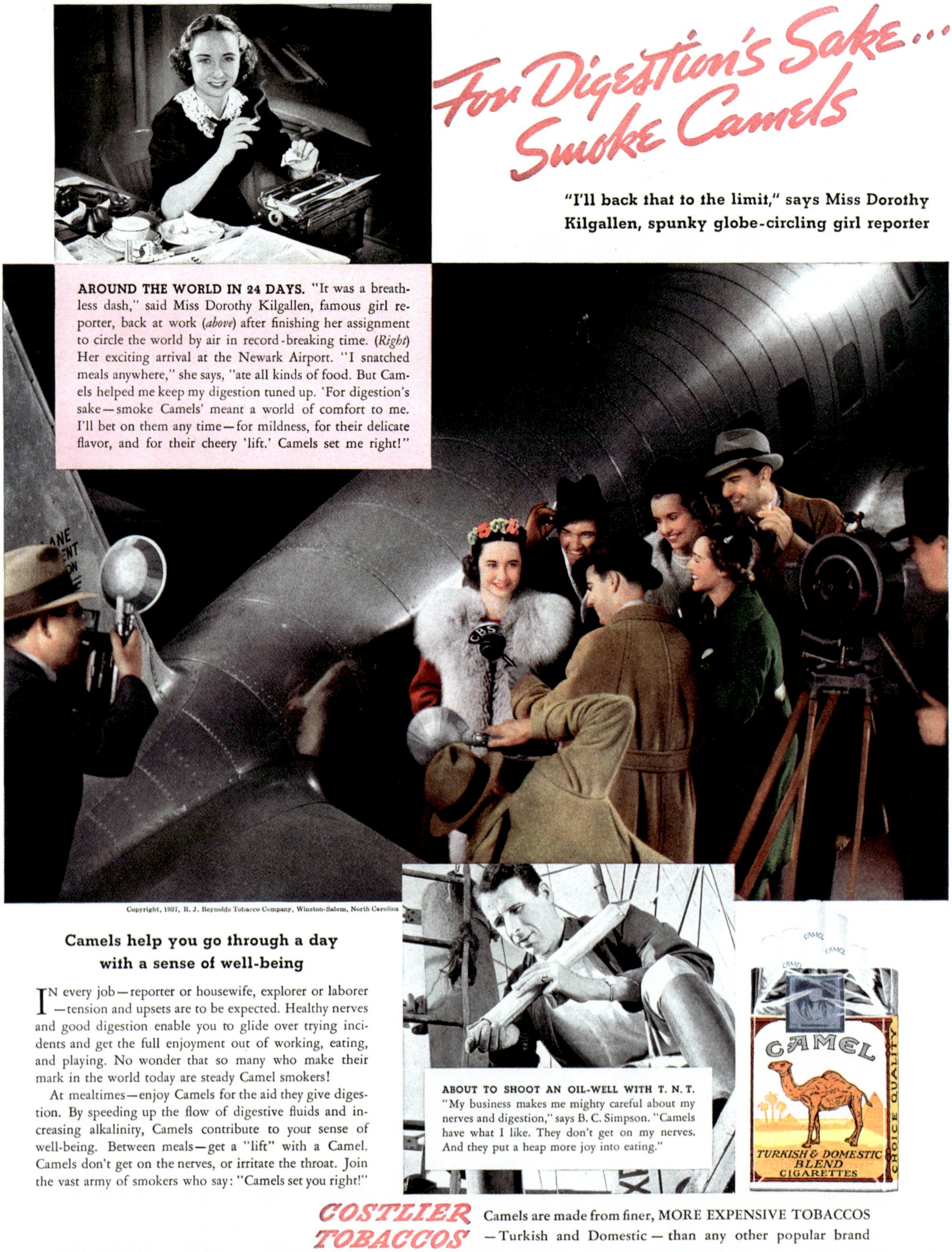

Camels, 1937

► *Camels, 1938*

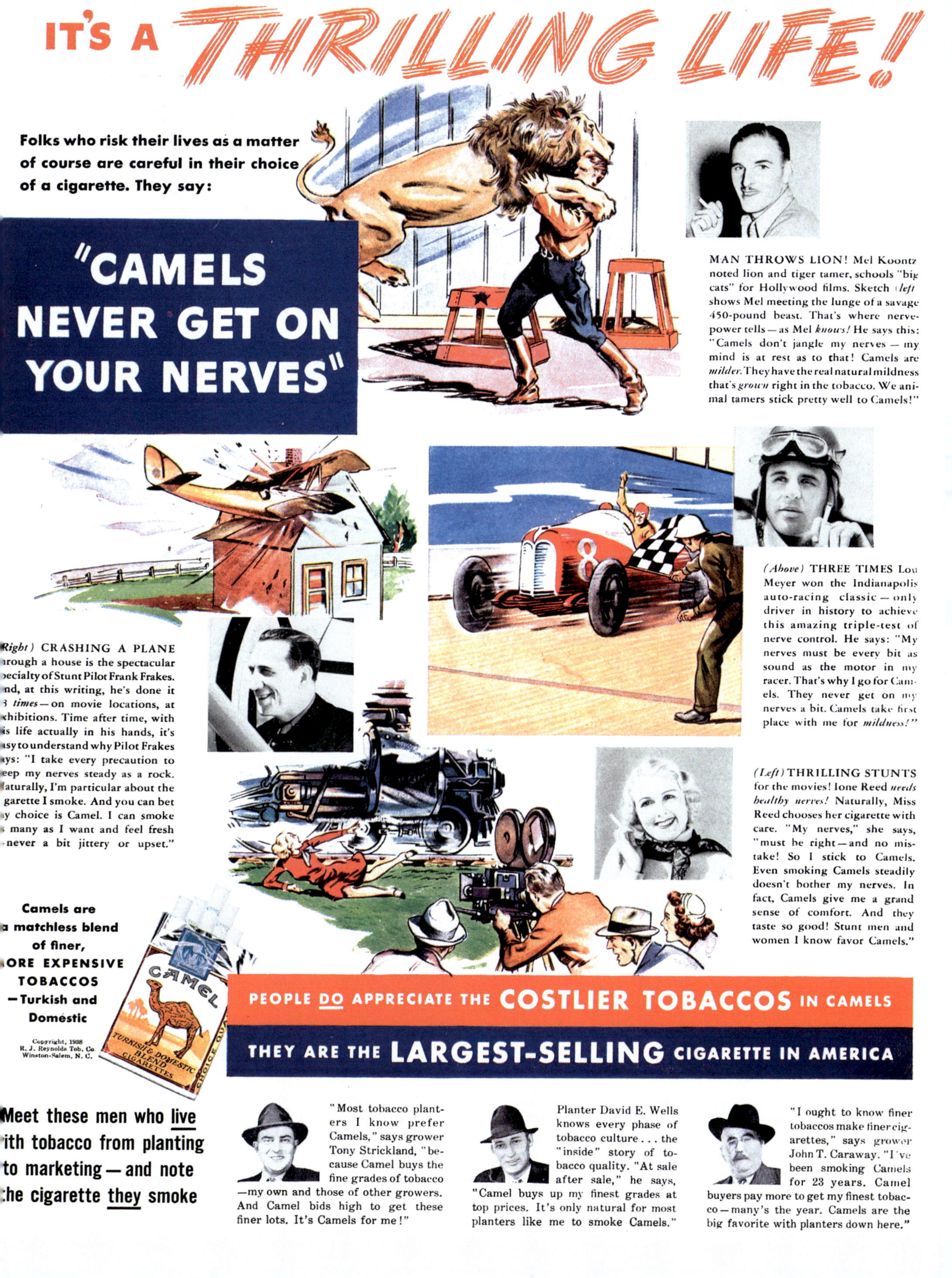

IT'S A THRILLING LIFE!
Folks who risk their lives as a matter of course are careful in their choice of a cigarette. They say:
"CAMELS NEVER GET ON YOUR NERVES"
MAN THROWS LION! Mel Koontz noted lion and tiger tamer, schools "big cats" for Hollywood films. Sketch (left) shows Mel meeting the lunge of a savage 450-pound beast. That's where nerve-power tells — as Mel knows! He says this: "Camels don't jangle my nerves — my mind is at rest as to that! Camels are milder. They have the real natural mildness that's grown right in the tobacco. We animal tamers stick pretty well to Camels!"
(Above) THREE TIMES Lou Meyer won the Indianapolis auto-racing classic — only driver in history to achieve this amazing triple-test of nerve control. He says: "My nerves must be every bit as sound as the motor in my racer. That's why I go for Camels. They never get on my nerves a bit. Camels take first place with me for mildness!"
Right) CRASHING A PLANE rough a house is the spectacular ecialty of Stunt Pilot Frank Frakes. nd, at this writing, he's done it 3 times — on movie locations, at xhibitions. Time after time, with is life actually in his hands, it's asy to understand why Pilot Frakes ays: "I take every precaution to eep my nerves steady as a rock. aturally, I'm particular about the garette I smoke. And you can bet y choice is Camel. I can smoke many as I want and feel fresh never a bit jittery or upset."
(Left) THRILLING STUNTS for the movies! Ione Reed needs healthy nerves! Naturally, Miss Reed chooses her cigarette with care. "My nerves," she says, "must be right — and no mistake! So I stick to Camels. Even smoking Camels steadily doesn't bother my nerves. In fact, Camels give me a grand sense of comfort. And they taste so good! Stunt men and women I know favor Camels."
Camels are a matchless blend of finer, ORE EXPENSIVE TOBACCOS — Turkish and Domestic
Copyright, 1938 R. J. Reynolds Tob. Co. Winston-Salem, N. C.
CAMEL
TURKISH & DOMESTIC BLEND CIGARETTES
PEOPLE DO APPRECIATE THE COSTLIER TOBACCOS IN CAMELS
THEY ARE THE LARGEST-SELLING CIGARETTE IN AMERICA
Meet these men who live ith tobacco from planting to marketing — and note he cigarette they smoke
"Most tobacco planters I know prefer Camels," says grower Tony Strickland, "because Camel buys the fine grades of tobacco — my own and those of other growers. And Camel bids high to get these finer lots. It's Camels for me!"
Planter David E. Wells knows every phase of tobacco culture . . . the "inside" story of tobacco quality. "At sale after sale," he says, "Camel buys up my finest grades at top prices. It's only natural for most planters like me to smoke Camels."
"I ought to know finer tobaccos make finer cigarettes," says grower John T. Caraway. "I've been smoking Camels for 23 years. Camel buyers pay more to get my finest tobacco — many's the year. Camels are the big favorite with planters down here."

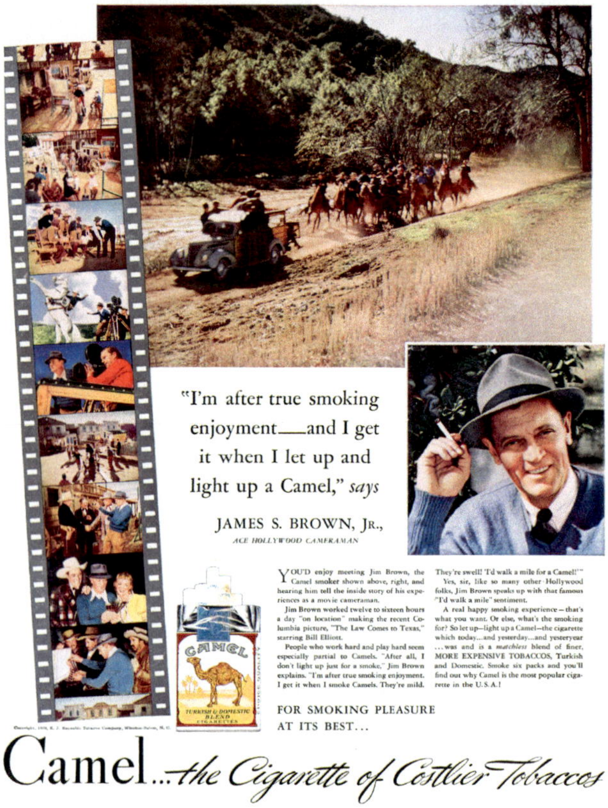

Camels, 1939

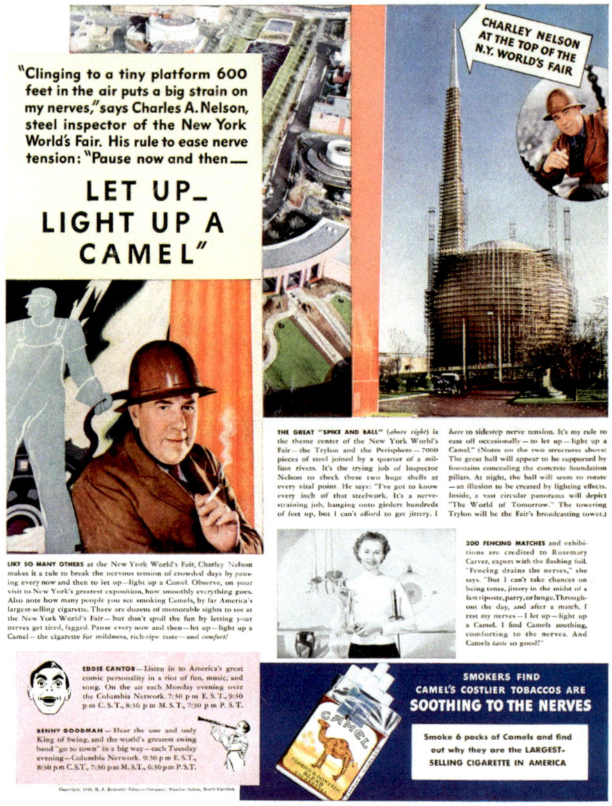

Camels, 1939

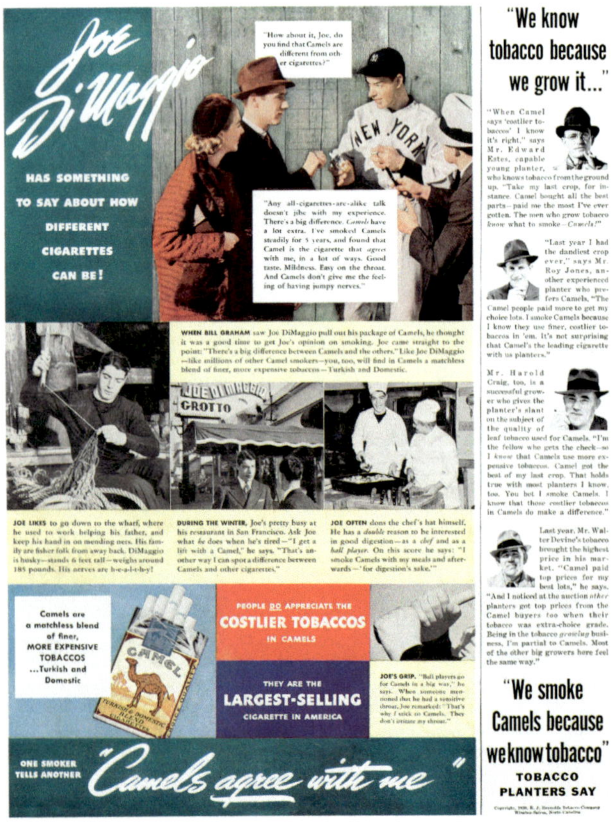

Camels, 1938

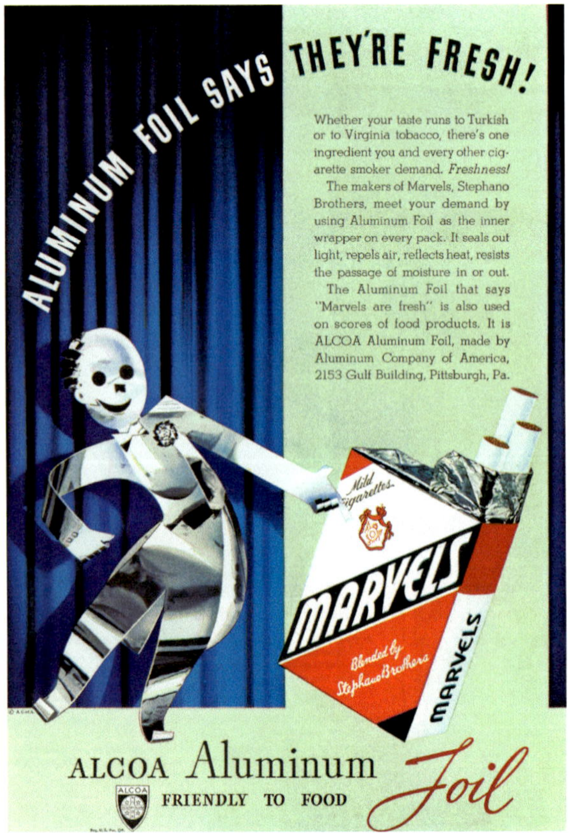

Alcoa Aluminum, 1939

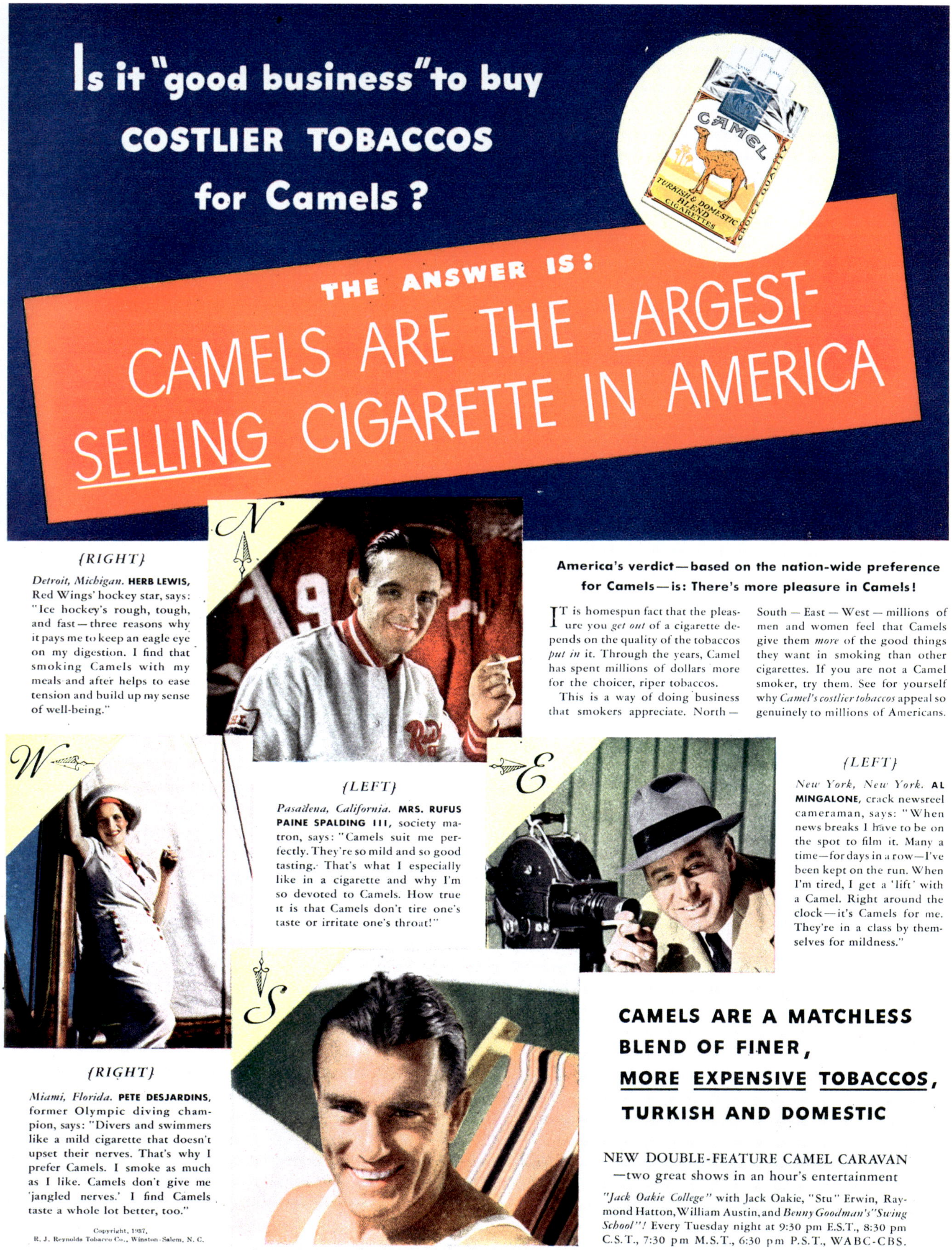
Is it "good business" to buy
COSTLIER TOBACCOS
for Camels?
CAMEL
TURKISH & DOMESTIC BLEND CIGARETTES
CHOICE QUALITY
THE ANSWER IS:
CAMELS ARE THE LARGEST-SELLING CIGARETTE IN AMERICA
N
{RIGHT}
Detroit, Michigan. HERB LEWIS, Red Wings' hockey star, says: "Ice hockey's rough, tough, and fast—three reasons why it pays me to keep an eagle eye on my digestion. I find that smoking Camels with my meals and after helps to ease tension and build up my sense of well-being."
America's verdict—based on the nation-wide preference for Camels—is: There's more pleasure in Camels!
IT is homespun fact that the pleasure you get out of a cigarette depends on the quality of the tobaccos put in it. Through the years, Camel has spent millions of dollars more for the choicer, riper tobaccos.
This is a way of doing business that smokers appreciate. North—South—East—West—millions of men and women feel that Camels give them more of the good things they want in smoking than other cigarettes. If you are not a Camel smoker, try them. See for yourself why Camel's costlier tobaccos appeal so genuinely to millions of Americans.
W
{LEFT}
Pasadena, California. MRS. RUFUS PAINE SPALDING III, society matron, says: "Camels suit me perfectly. They're so mild and so good tasting. That's what I especially like in a cigarette and why I'm so devoted to Camels. How true it is that Camels don't tire one's taste or irritate one's throat!"
E
{LEFT}
New York, New York. AL MINGALONE, crack newsreel cameraman, says: "When news breaks I have to be on the spot to film it. Many a time—for days in a row—I've been kept on the run. When I'm tired, I get a 'lift' with a Camel. Right around the clock—it's Camels for me. They're in a class by themselves for mildness."
S
{RIGHT}
Miami, Florida. PETE DESJARDINS, former Olympic diving champion, says: "Divers and swimmers like a mild cigarette that doesn't upset their nerves. That's why I prefer Camels. I smoke as much as I like. Camels don't give me 'jangled nerves.' I find Camels taste a whole lot better, too."
Copyright, 1937, R. J. Reynolds Tobacco Co., Winston-Salem, N. C.
CAMELS ARE A MATCHLESS BLEND OF FINER, MORE EXPENSIVE TOBACCOS, TURKISH AND DOMESTIC
NEW DOUBLE-FEATURE CAMEL CARAVAN —two great shows in an hour's entertainment
"Jack Oakie College" with Jack Oakie, "Stu" Erwin, Raymond Hatton, William Austin, and Benny Goodman's "Swing School"! Every Tuesday night at 9:30 pm E.S.T., 8:30 pm C.S.T., 7:30 pm M.S.T., 6:30 pm P.S.T., WABC-CBS.

Camels, 1937

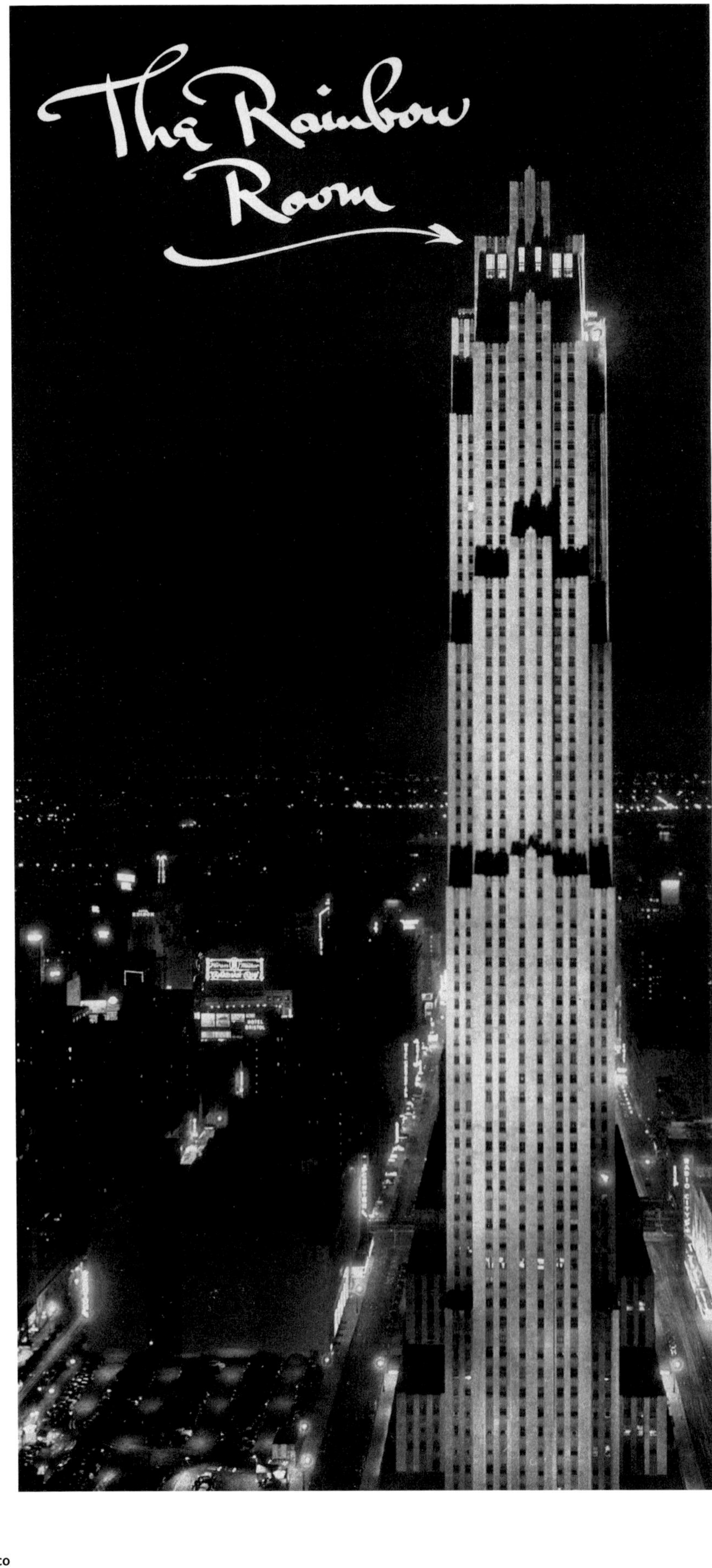

Brief introduction to the thr
of dining and dancing
65 floors above Fifth Avenu

TOWERING 800 feet above Fifth A
nue, the Rainbow Room is the worl
loftiest supper club. *Right*—dinner gue
enjoying a quiet moment in a gala e
ning. New Yorkers from the glossier
gions of the upper East Side brush elbo
amiably with, mayhap, a visiting pot
tate or a personable British Lady bou
for Hollywood. In its ever-changing ent
tainment, the Rainbow Room excels in s
ire. A puppet show debunks popular hero
Or a mimic makes her commentary on
modes and manners of her audience—a
makes them like it. As for the clientel
"They come from all parts of the worl
says the Maître d'Hôtel, adding, "and
note that most of them prefer Camel

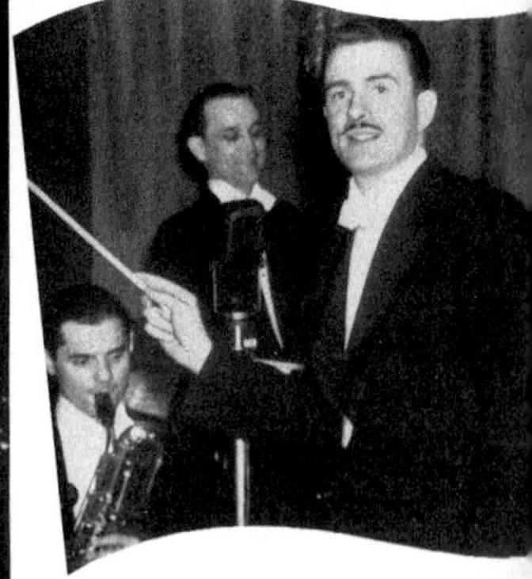

GLEN GRAY, leading his Casa Loma band. Their smooth orchestrations, spiced with vocals by Pee Wee Hunt and Kenny Sargent, are admired by all, including those astute judges of good music – the young college crowd. Equally discriminating in their choice of a cigarette, the undergraduates show a definite preference for Camels—both here and on the campus.

THE FAVORITE *(right)*. "Camels a
favorite cigarette in the Rainbow R
says the Maître d'Hôtel, "during bot
dinner *and* supper hours." This is no su
since, of course, Camels help dig
Smoking Camels speeds up the flow of
tive fluids. Increases alkalinity. Builds
sense of mealtime comfort and good c

Camels are made from finer, M
EXPENSIVE TOBACCOS – *Turkis*
Domestic—than any other popular b

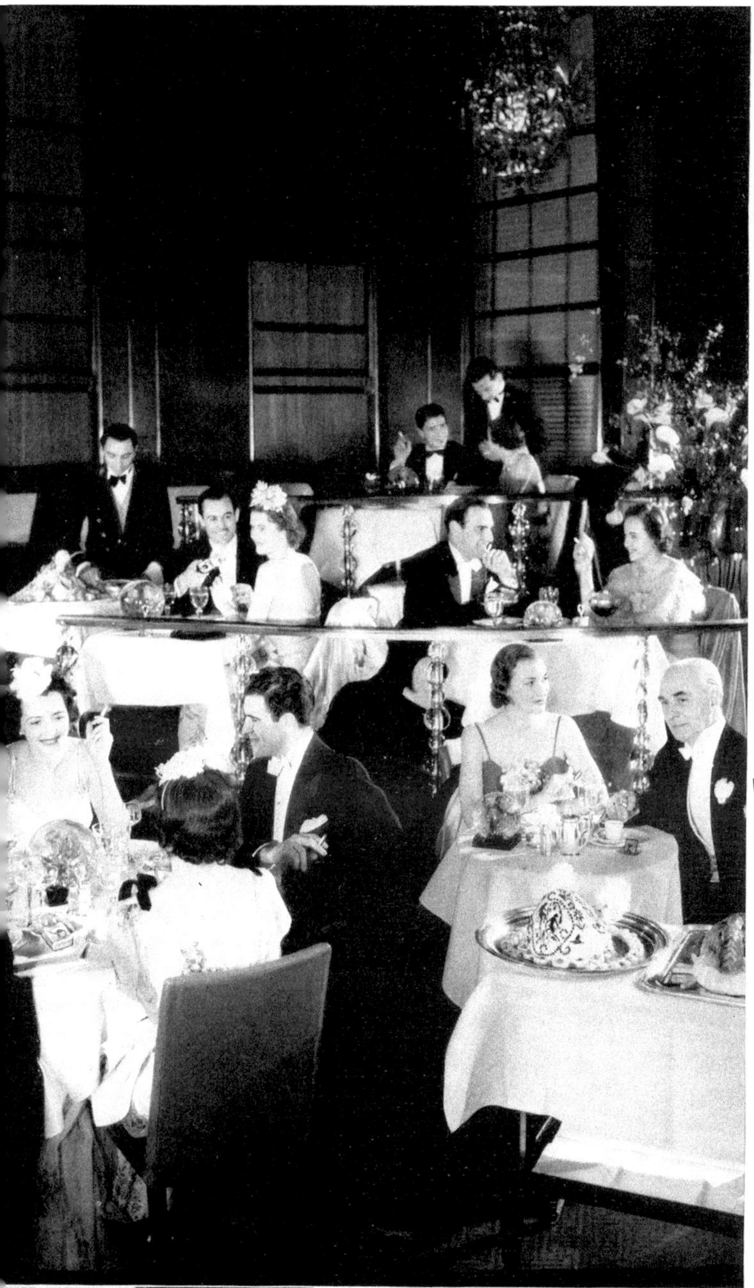

Copyright, 1937, R. J. Reynolds Tobacco Co., Winston-Salem, N. C.

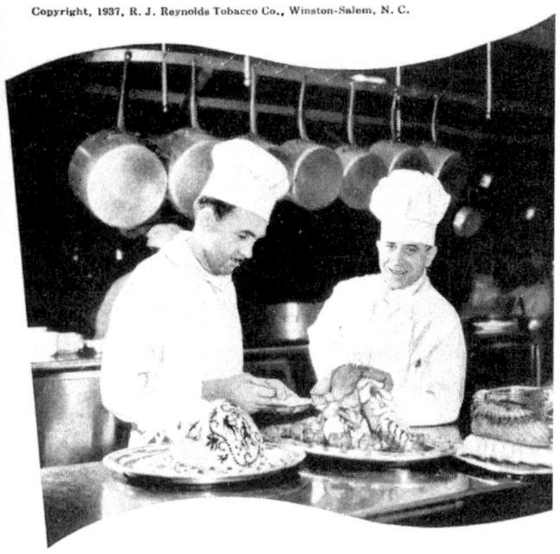

WITH GOOD DIGESTION in mind, Chef Frederic *(smiling above)* will probably serve well over 100,000 meals in 1937. Asked to name his specialty, he replied: "Just the classic dishes of *all* nations!" This includes Poularde Rose de Maie which serves 8 nicely—for $20. Here one may dine well, and—for digestion's sake, smoke Camels between courses and after.

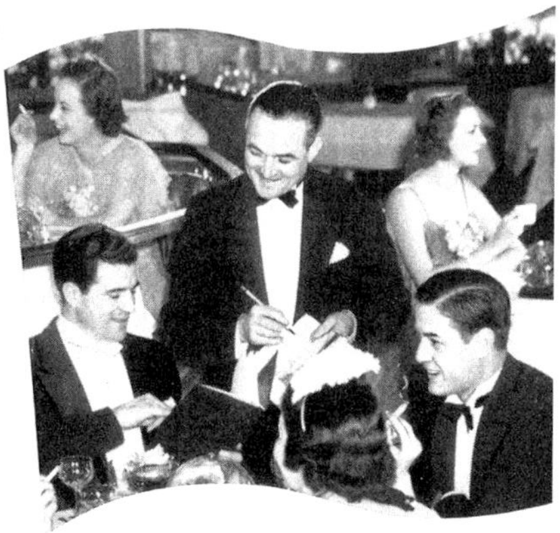

MAÎTRE D'HÔTEL *(standing)*. "There are three things," Joseph says, "that make up a perfect evening—finer food, rare entertainment, Camel's costlier tobaccos. And you'll find all three at the Rainbow Room." When 2 A. M. rolls around, and you have hours of steady smoking behind you, costlier tobaccos are more appreciated than ever. Camels never get on your nerves. And they give a cheering lift!

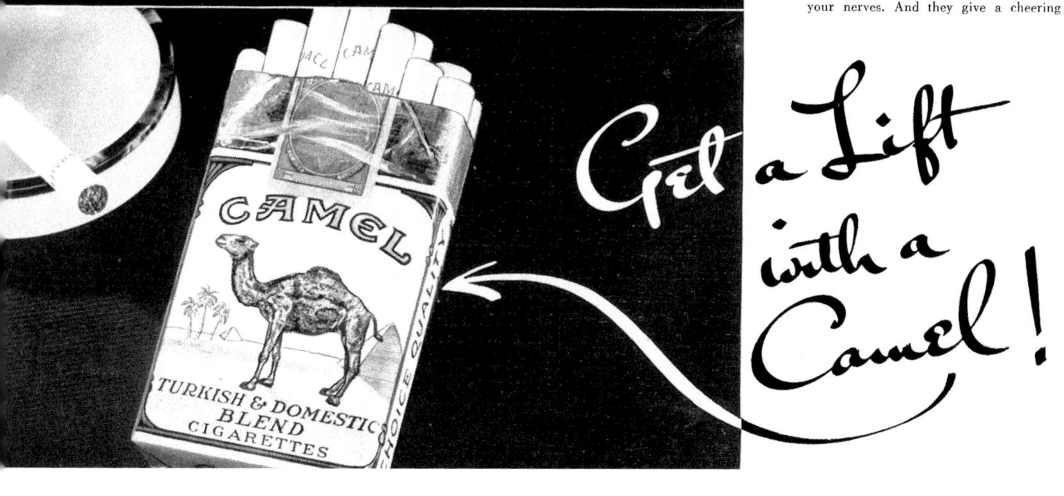

Camels, 1937

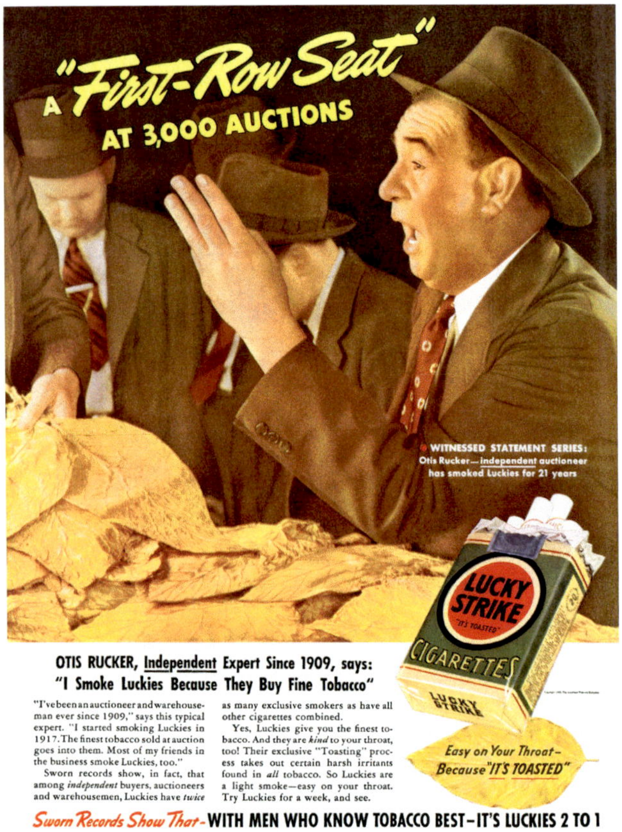

Lucky Strike, 1938

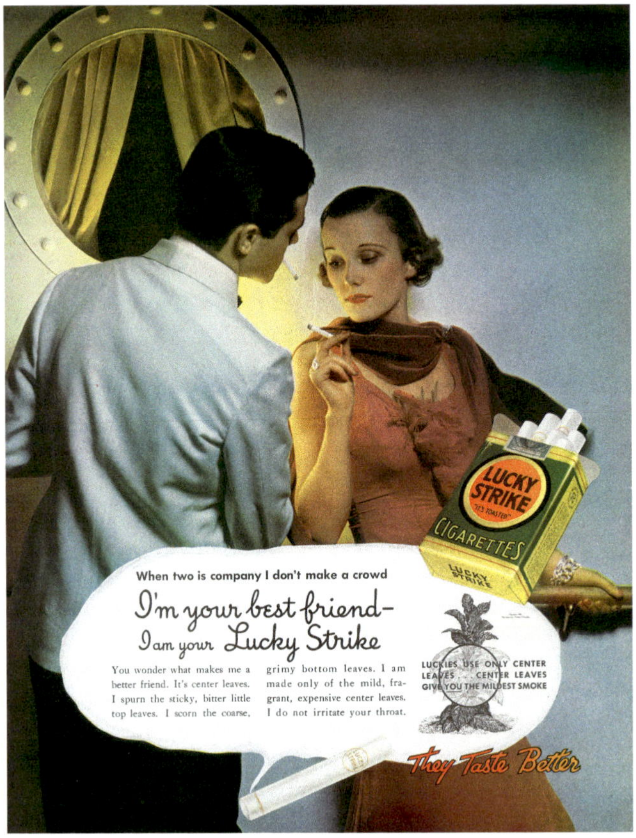

Lucky Strike, 1935

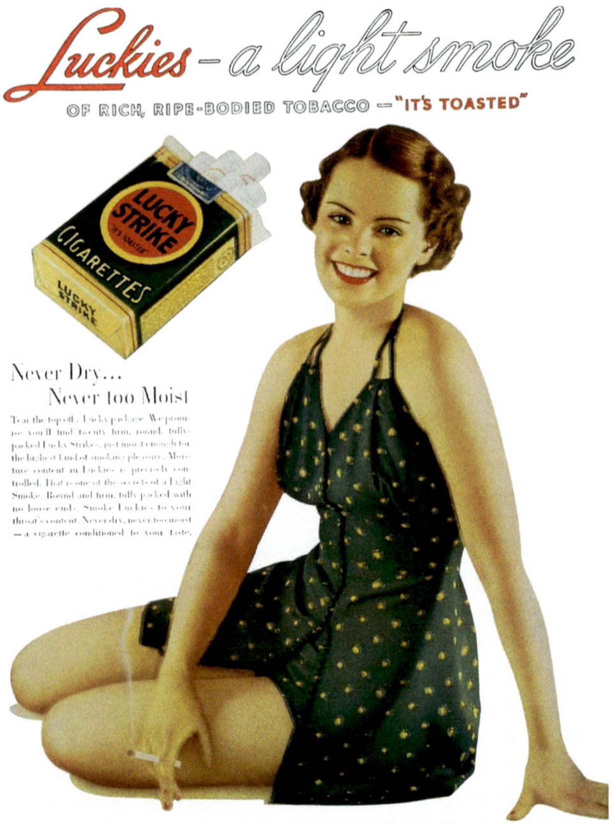

Lucky Strike, 1936

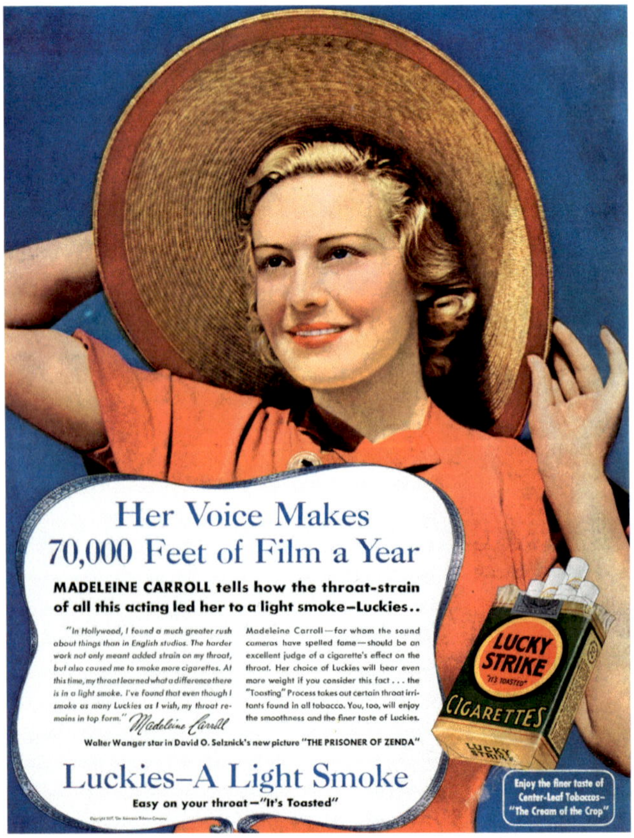

Lucky Strike, 1937

▸ Lucky Strike, 1932

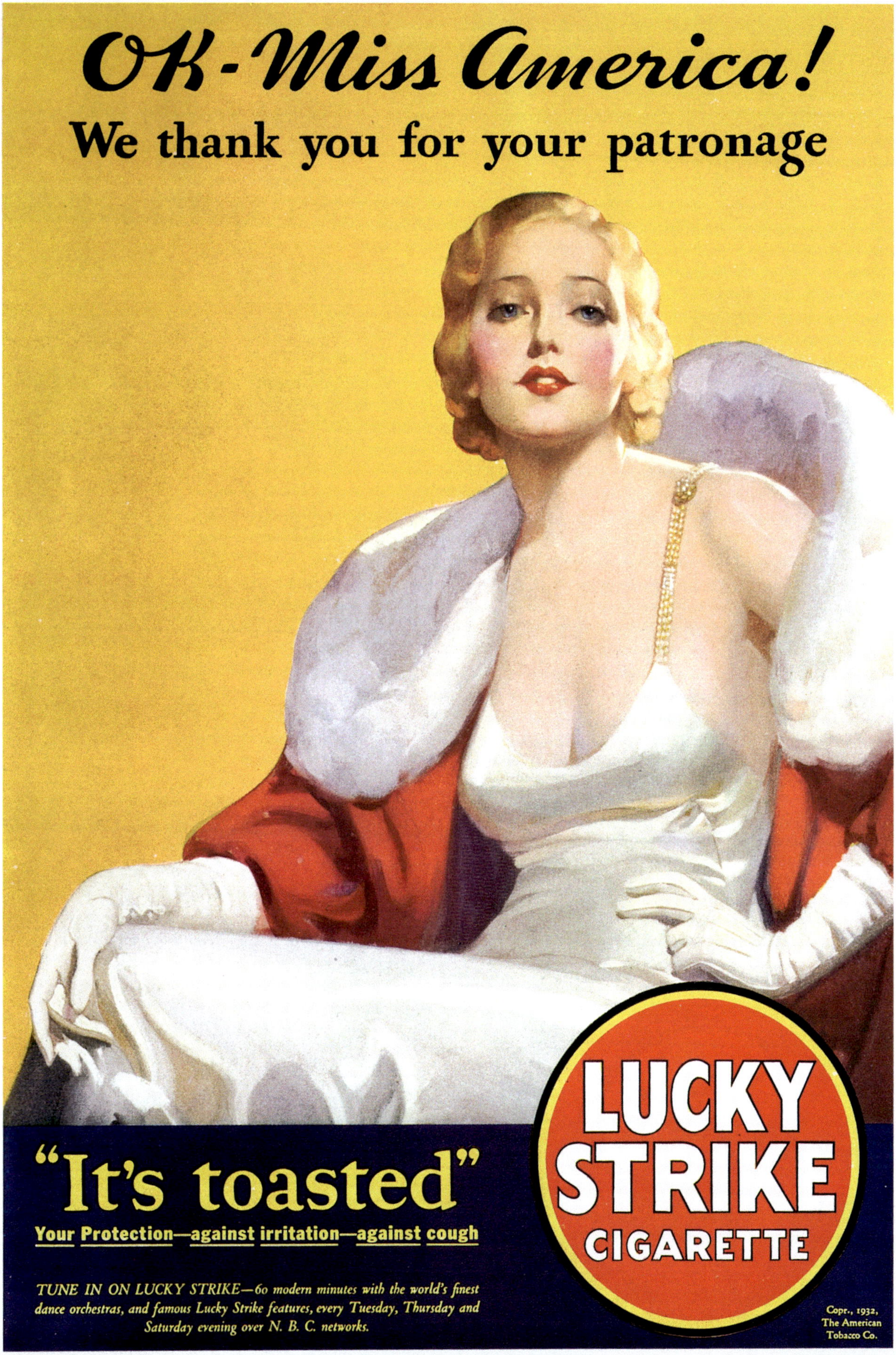
OK-Miss America!
We thank you for your patronage
"It's toasted"
Your Protection—against irritation—against cough
TUNE IN ON LUCKY STRIKE—60 modern minutes with the world's finest dance orchestras, and famous Lucky Strike features, every Tuesday, Thursday and Saturday evening over N. B. C. networks.
LUCKY STRIKE
CIGARETTE
Copr., 1932, The American Tobacco Co.

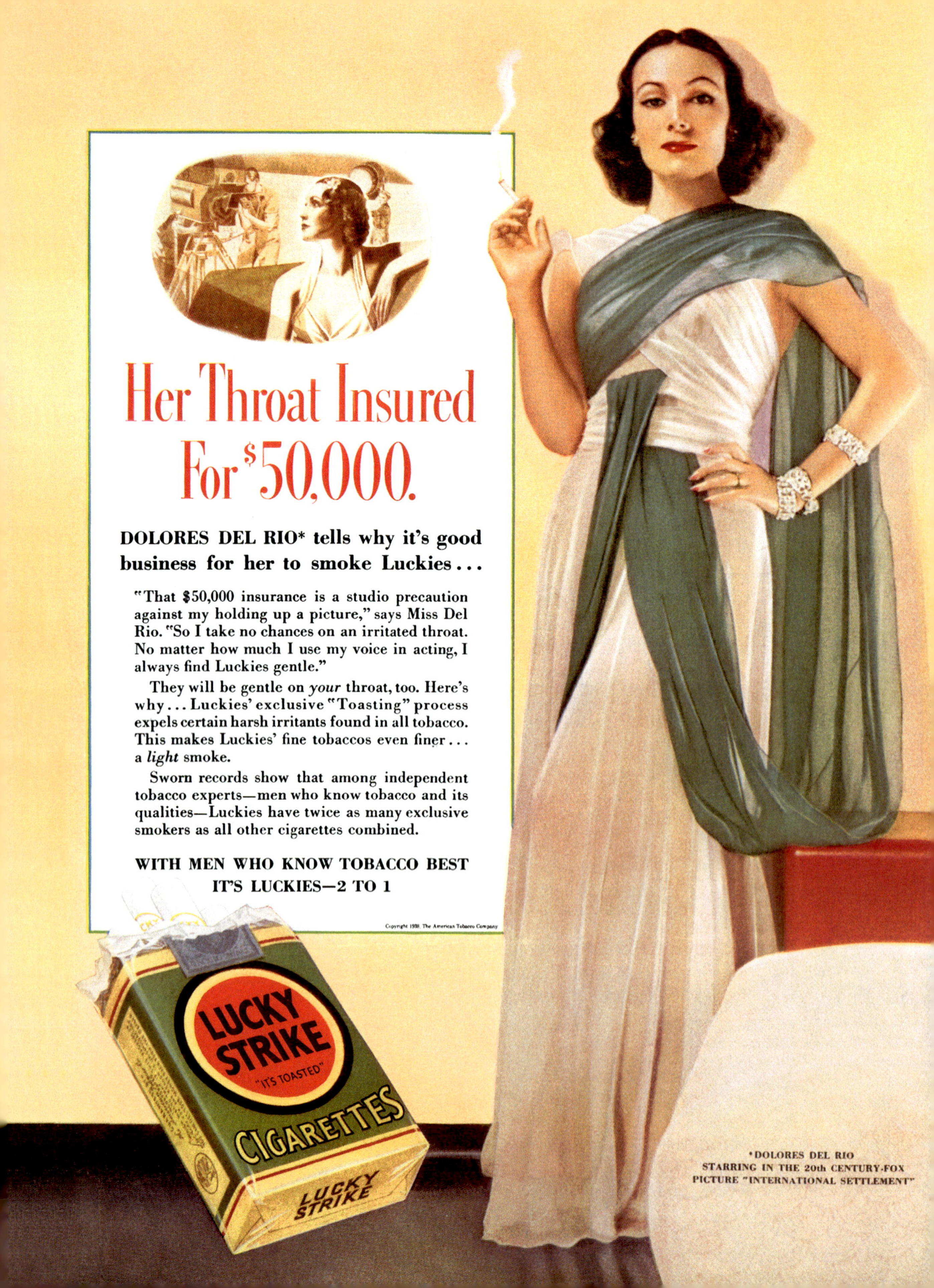
Her Throat Insured For $50,000.
DOLORES DEL RIO* tells why it's good business for her to smoke Luckies...
"That $50,000 insurance is a studio precaution against my holding up a picture," says Miss Del Rio. "So I take no chances on an irritated throat. No matter how much I use my voice in acting, I always find Luckies gentle."
They will be gentle on *your* throat, too. Here's why... Luckies' exclusive "Toasting" process expels certain harsh irritants found in all tobacco. This makes Luckies' fine tobaccos even finer... a *light* smoke.
Sworn records show that among independent tobacco experts—men who know tobacco and its qualities—Luckies have twice as many exclusive smokers as all other cigarettes combined.
WITH MEN WHO KNOW TOBACCO BEST IT'S LUCKIES—2 TO 1
Copyright 1938, The American Tobacco Company
LUCKY STRIKE
"IT'S TOASTED"
CIGARETTES
LUCKY STRIKE
*DOLORES DEL RIO STARRING IN THE 20th CENTURY-FOX PICTURE "INTERNATIONAL SETTLEMENT"

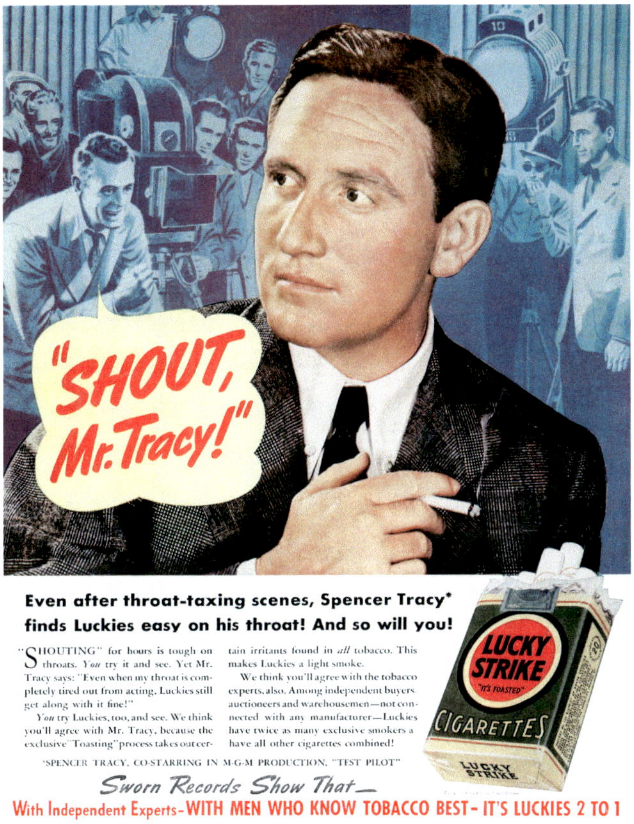

Lucky Strike, 1938

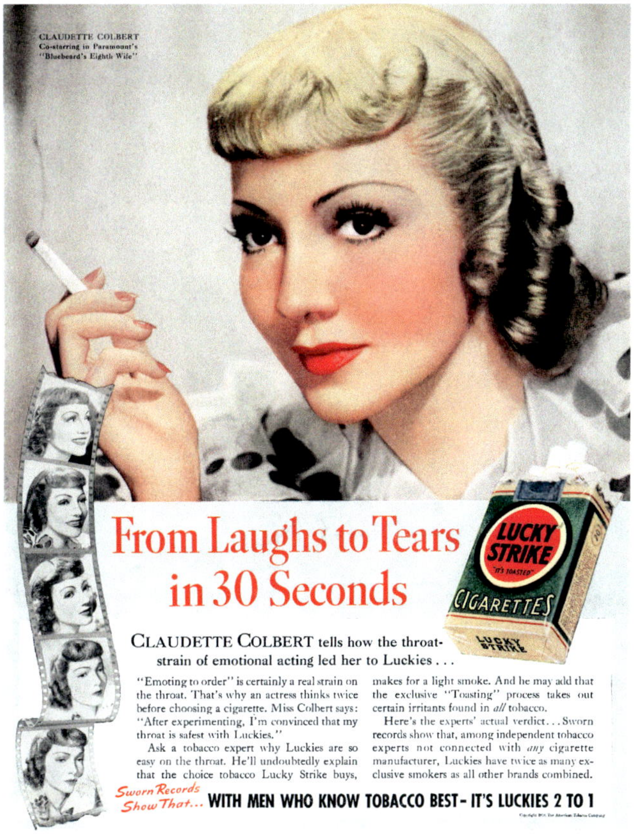

Lucky Strike, 1938

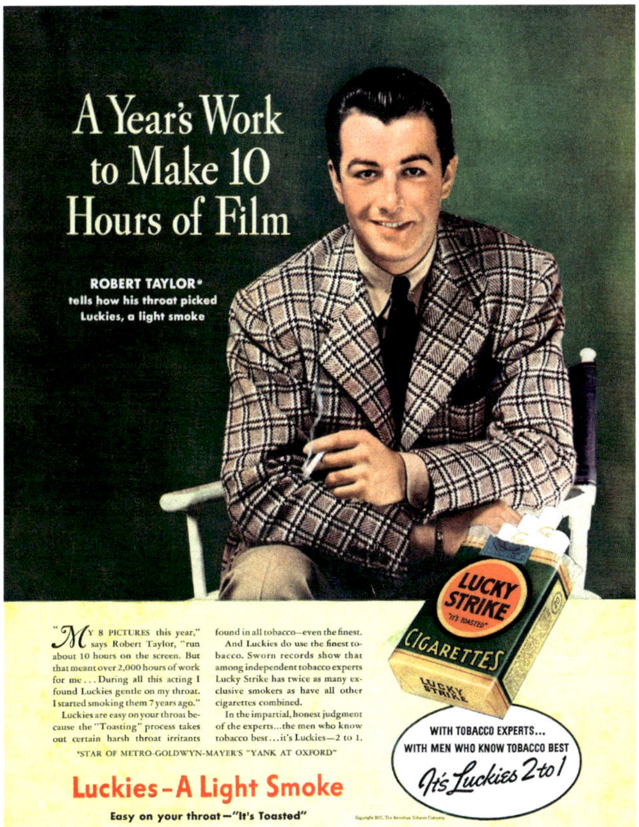

Lucky Strike, 1938 ◂ Lucky Strike, 1937

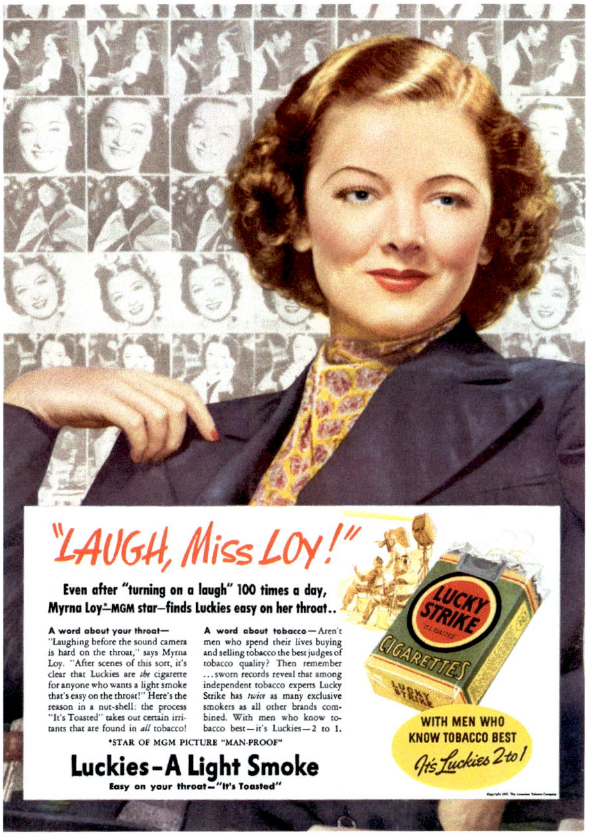

Lucky Strike, 1938

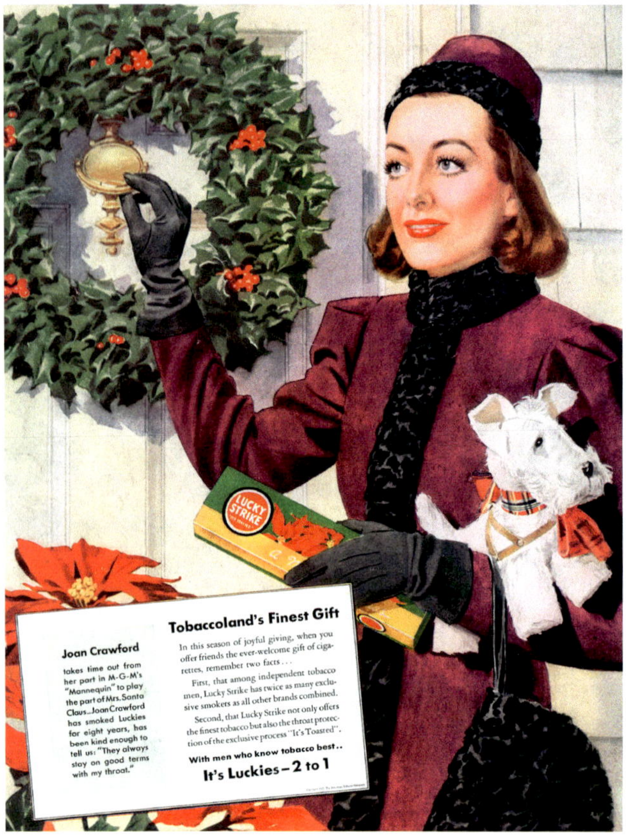

Lucky Strike, 1935

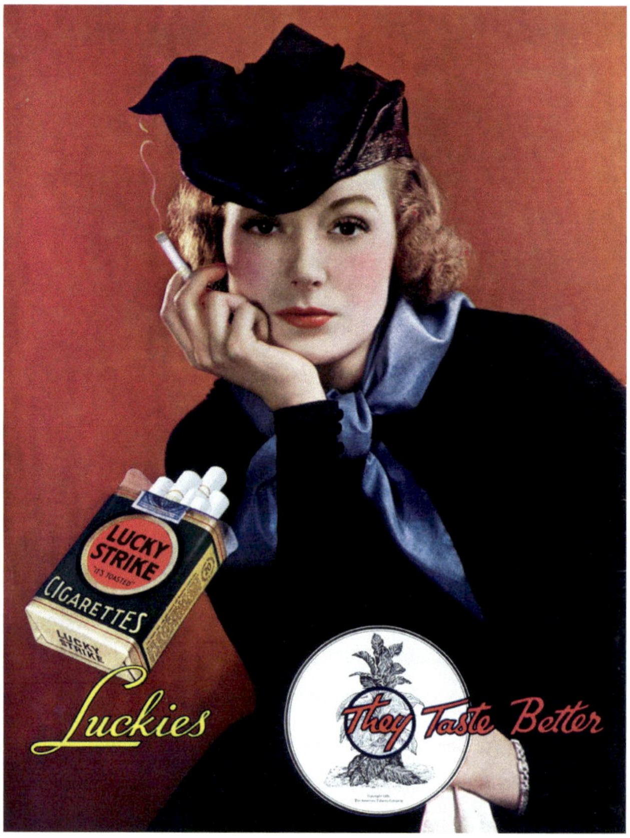

Lucky Strike, 1935

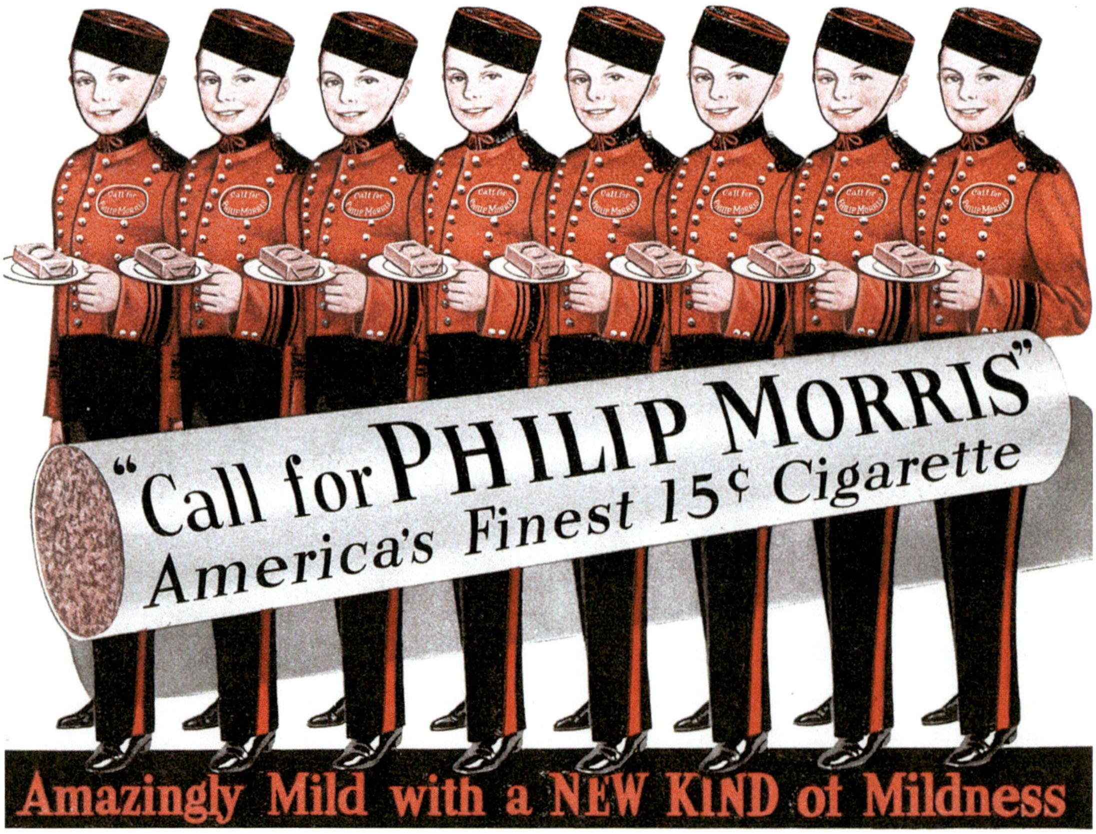

Philip Morris, 1934

▸ Philip Morris, 1938

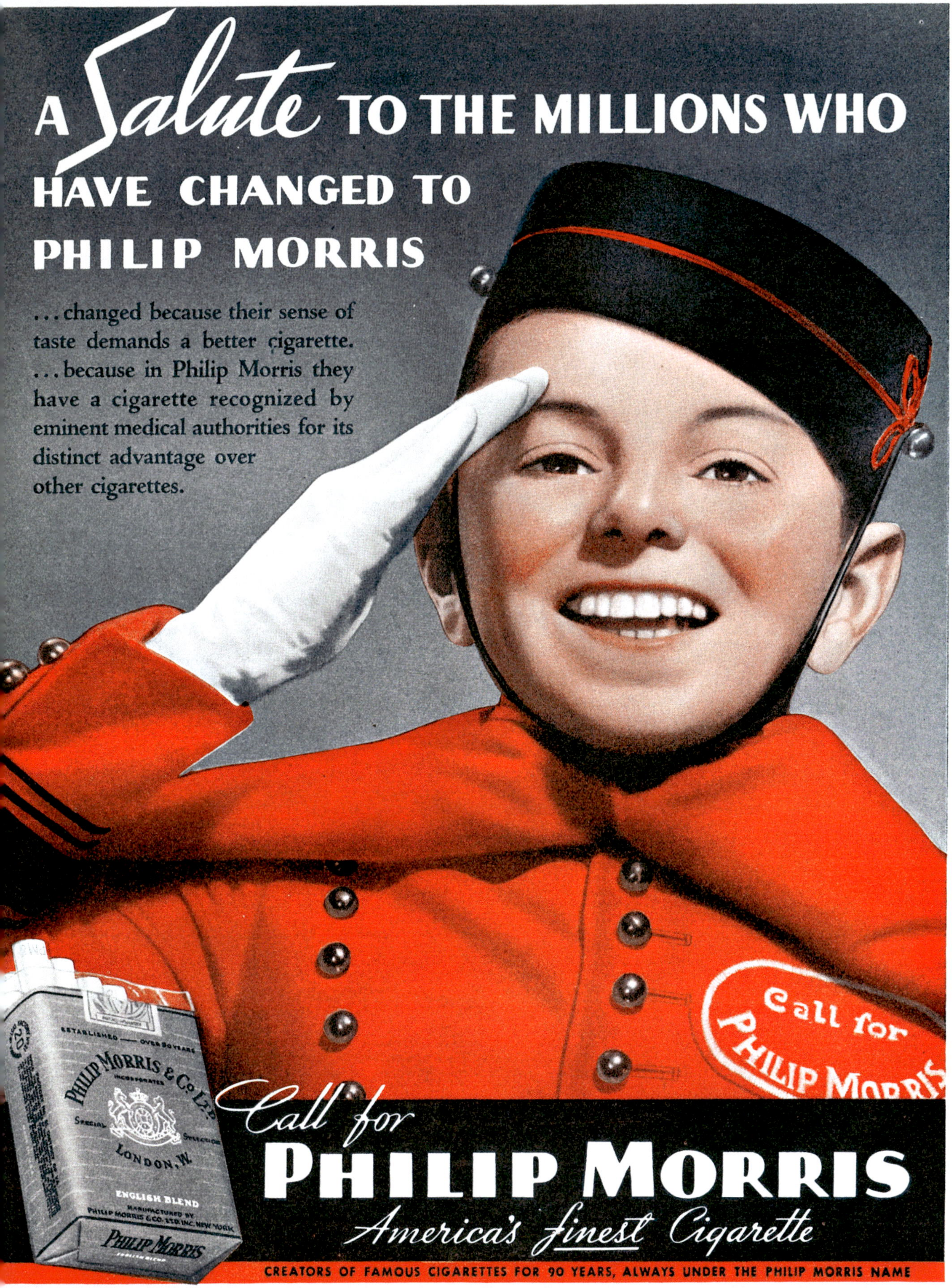
A Salute TO THE MILLIONS WHO HAVE CHANGED TO PHILIP MORRIS
...changed because their sense of taste demands a better cigarette. ...because in Philip Morris they have a cigarette recognized by eminent medical authorities for its distinct advantage over other cigarettes.
Call for PHILIP MORRIS
PHILIP MORRIS & Co. LTD.
LONDON, W.
ENGLISH BLEND
PHILIP MORRIS
Call for
PHILIP MORRIS
America's Finest Cigarette
CREATORS OF FAMOUS CIGARETTES FOR 90 YEARS, ALWAYS UNDER THE PHILIP MORRIS NAME

Tortured by a Tele-phoney?

. . . light an Old Gold

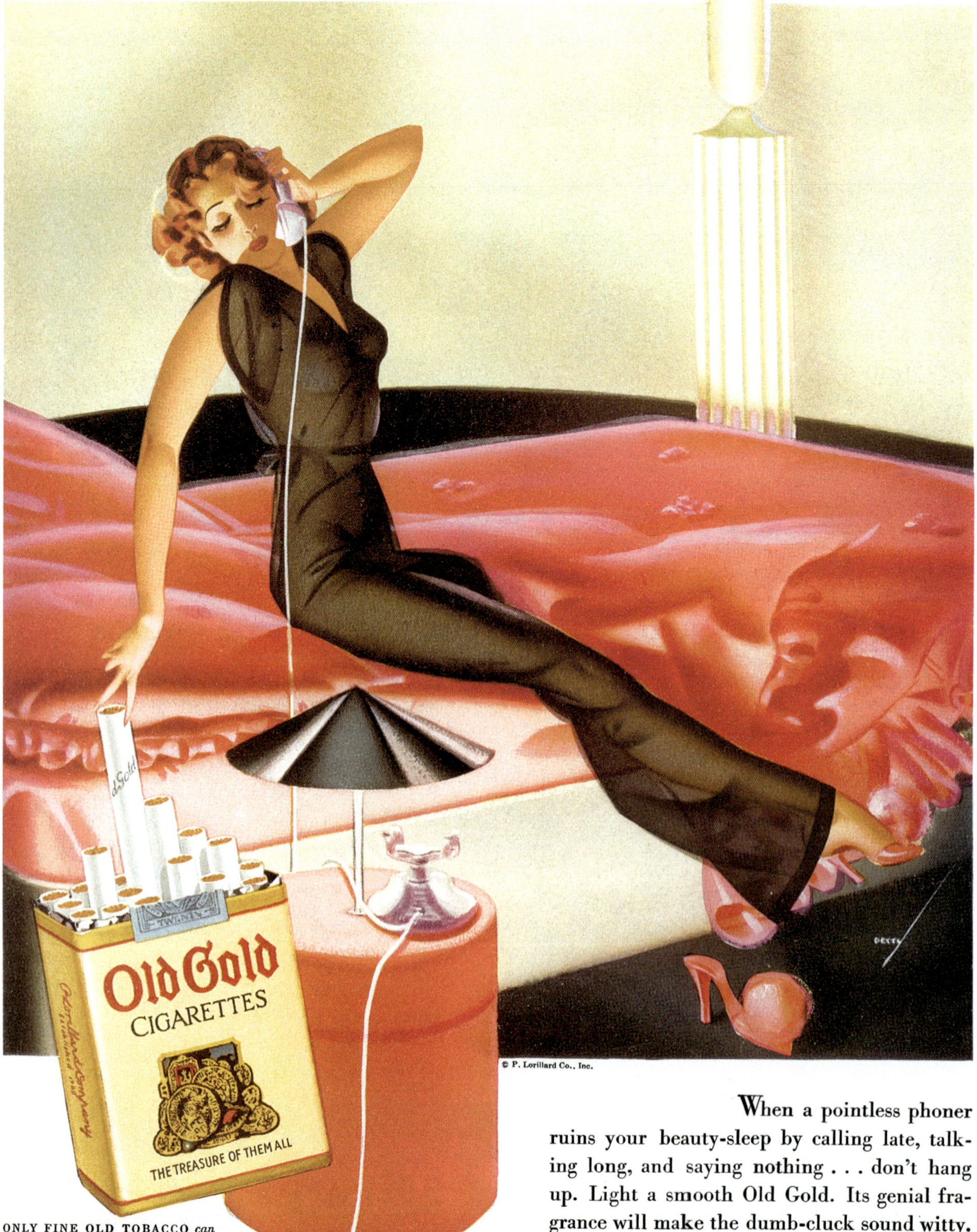

ONLY FINE OLD TOBACCO *can give that natural aroma and fragrance*

When a pointless phoner ruins your beauty-sleep by calling late, talking long, and saying nothing . . . don't hang up. Light a smooth Old Gold. Its genial fragrance will make the dumb-cluck sound witty.

AT TRYING TIMES. . . . TRY A *Smooth* OLD GOLD

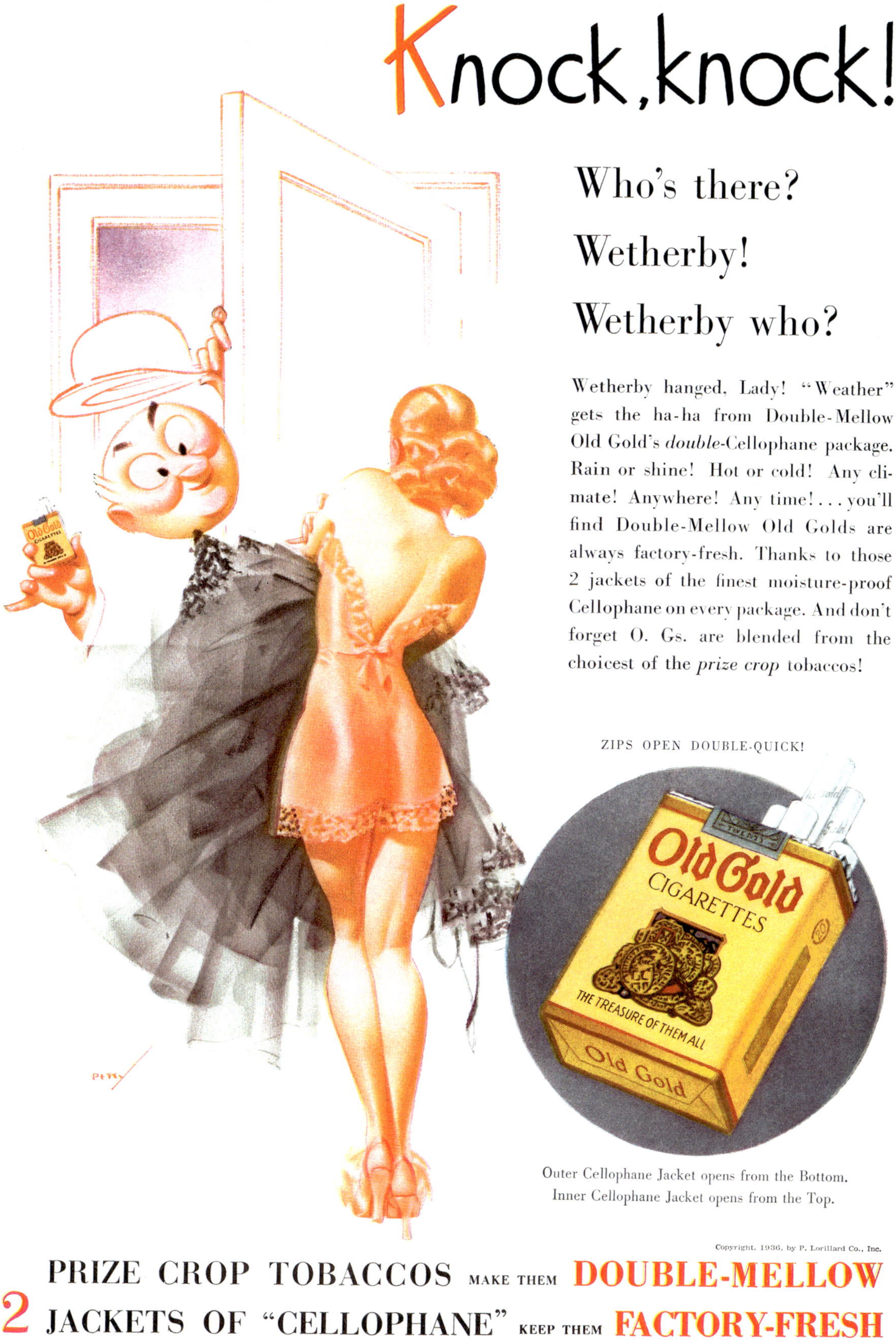

Old Gold, 1935 ◄

Old Gold, 1936

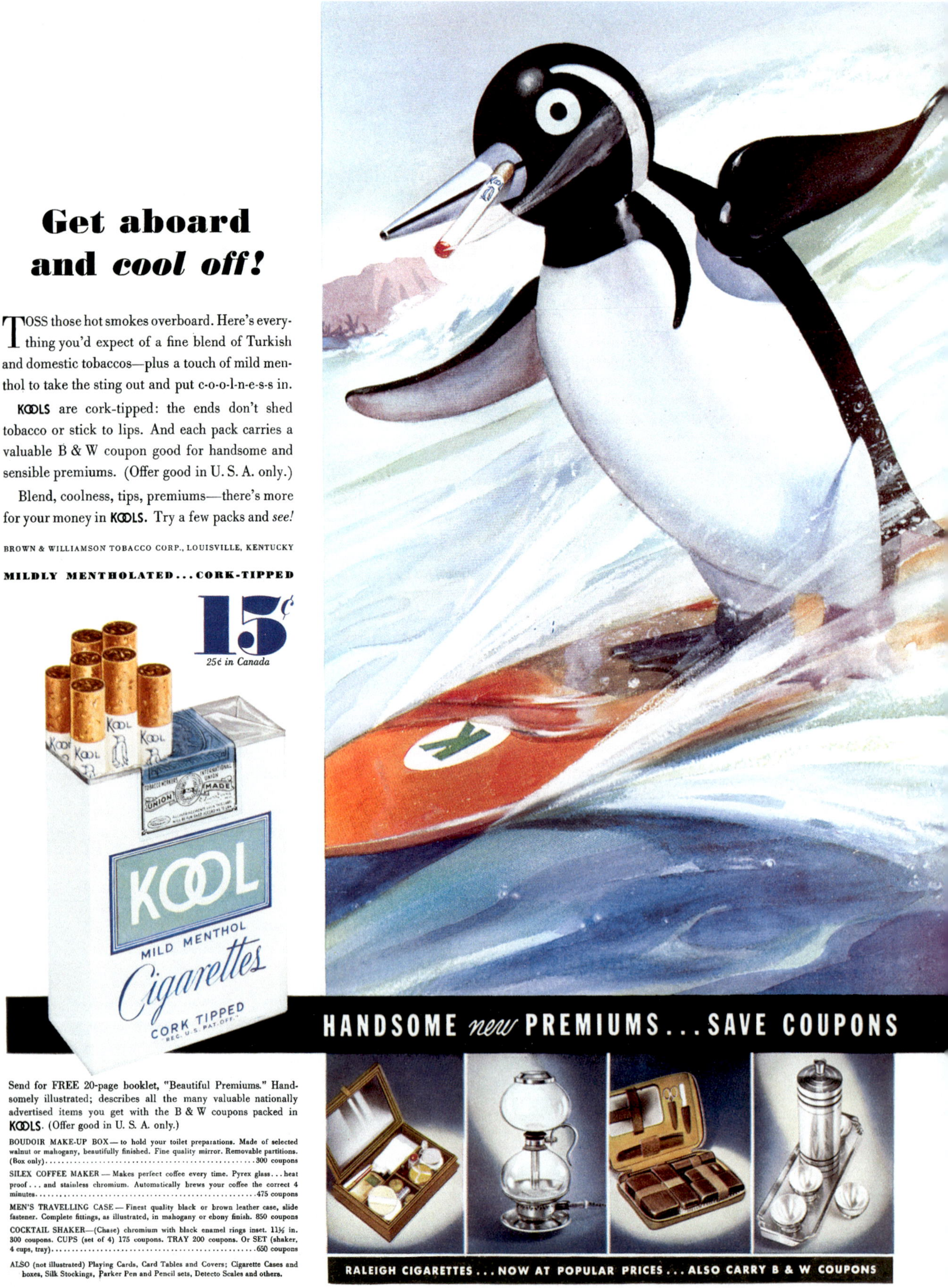
Get aboard and cool off!
TOSS those hot smokes overboard. Here's everything you'd expect of a fine blend of Turkish and domestic tobaccos—plus a touch of mild menthol to take the sting out and put c-o-o-l-n-e-s-s in.
KOOLS are cork-tipped: the ends don't shed tobacco or stick to lips. And each pack carries a valuable B & W coupon good for handsome and sensible premiums. (Offer good in U. S. A. only.)
Blend, coolness, tips, premiums—there's more for your money in KOOLS. Try a few packs and see!
BROWN & WILLIAMSON TOBACCO CORP., LOUISVILLE, KENTUCKY
MILDLY MENTHOLATED... CORK-TIPPED
15¢
25¢ in Canada
KOOL
MILD MENTHOL
Cigarettes
CORK TIPPED
REG. U. S. PAT. OFF.
HANDSOME new PREMIUMS... SAVE COUPONS
Send for FREE 20-page booklet, "Beautiful Premiums." Handsomely illustrated; describes all the many valuable nationally advertised items you get with the B & W coupons packed in KOOLS. (Offer good in U. S. A. only.)
BOUDOIR MAKE-UP BOX—to hold your toilet preparations. Made of selected walnut or mahogany, beautifully finished. Fine quality mirror. Removable partitions. (Box only)....300 coupons
SILEX COFFEE MAKER—Makes perfect coffee every time. Pyrex glass... heat proof... and stainless chromium. Automatically brews your coffee the correct 4 minutes....475 coupons
MEN'S TRAVELLING CASE—Finest quality black or brown leather case, slide fastener. Complete fittings, as illustrated, in mahogany or ebony finish. 850 coupons
COCKTAIL SHAKER—(Chase) chromium with black enamel rings inset. 11½ in. 300 coupons. CUPS (set of 4) 175 coupons. TRAY 200 coupons. Or SET (shaker, 4 cups, tray)....650 coupons
ALSO (not illustrated) Playing Cards, Card Tables and Covers; Cigarette Cases and boxes, Silk Stockings, Parker Pen and Pencil sets, Detecto Scales and others.
RALEIGH CIGARETTES... NOW AT POPULAR PRICES... ALSO CARRY B & W COUPONS

▲► *Kool*, 1935

Judge: "YOUR VERDICT, GENTLEMEN?"

Jury: "WE'RE ALL IN FAVOR OF KOOLS"

THE nation echoes the decision, KOOLS on the first ballot. They're so much cooler—a touch of mild menthol to refresh your throat. Tastier, because the fine Turkish-and-domestic tobacco flavor is fully retained. Easy on lips, don't spill tobacco crumbs—they're cork-tipped . . . And a pleasant dividend in the valuable B & W coupon in each pack. (Offer good in U.S.A. only.)

No wonder KOOL smokers tell others; the preference for KOOLS grows and grows. If you haven't made the big discovery, what better time than now? Give your throat a change.

And those premiums! Send for the illustrated booklet.

BROWN & WILLIAMSON TOBACCO CORP., LOUISVILLE, KENTUCKY

MILDLY MENTHOLATED . . . CORK TIPPED

15¢

25¢ in Canada

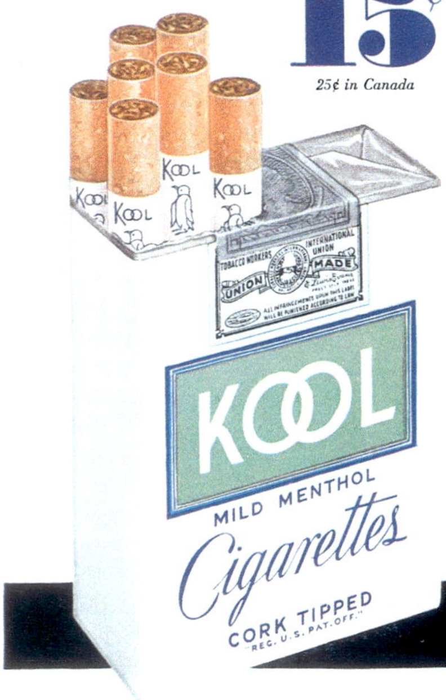

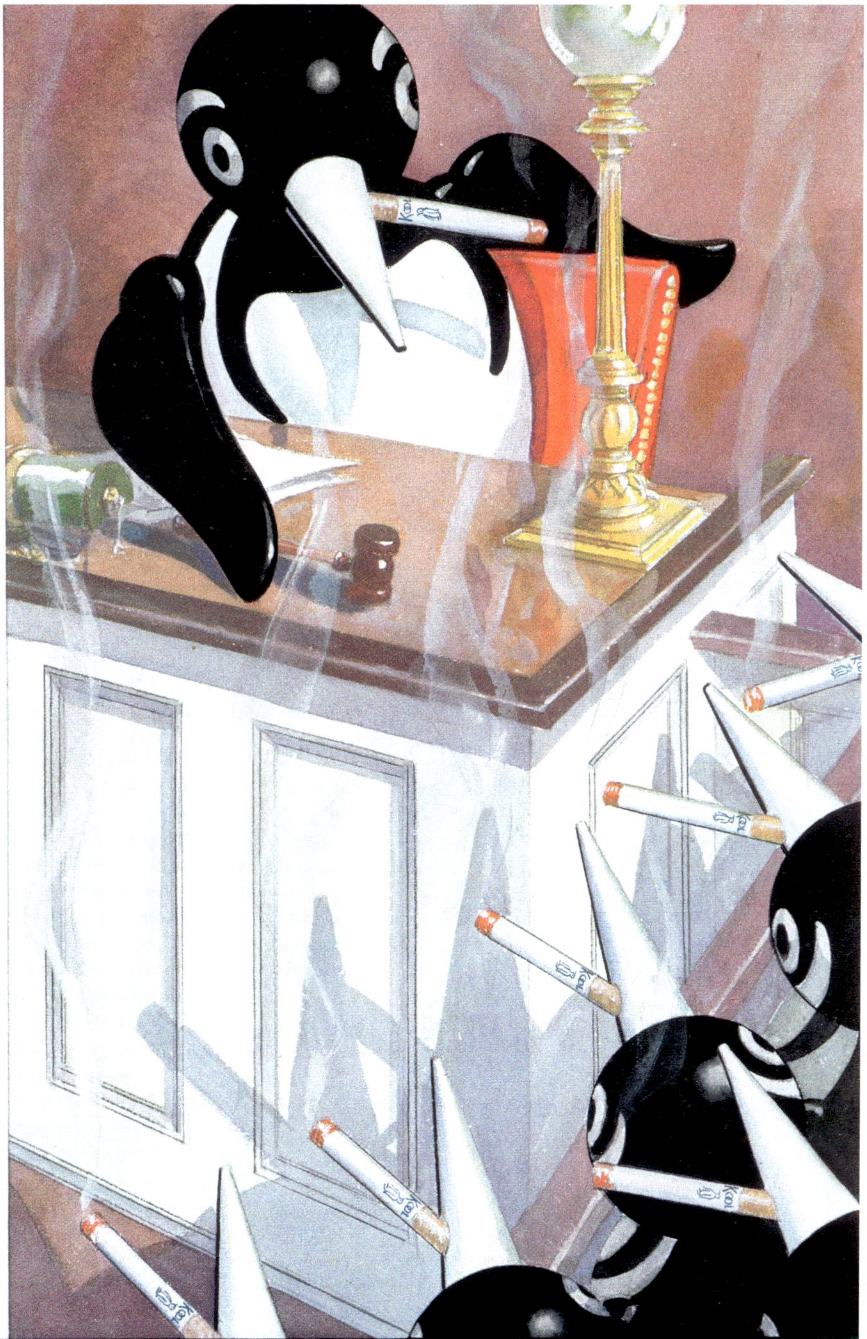

SAVE B & W COUPONS FOR HANDSOME *new* PREMIUMS

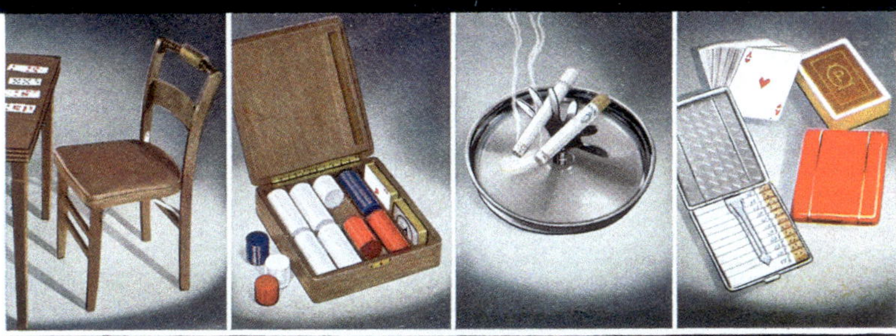

RALEIGH CIGARETTES . . . NOW AT POPULAR PRICES . . . ALSO CARRY B & W COUPONS

Send for FREE booklet, "Beautiful Premiums." Handsomely illustrated; describes all the many desirable and valuable nationally advertised items you get with the B & W coupons packed in KOOLS. (Offer good in U. S. A. only.)

BRIDGE CHAIRS—Hitchcock style folding chair. Satin walnut finish, brown leatherette seat, Sturdy, compact. 1 chair. . . . . .600 coupons; 2 chairs. . . . . . .1000 coupons.

POKER CHIP SET—Hand rubbed solid walnut case—special hardware. Holds 300 chips and 2 decks of cards. Case only, 325 coupons. 50 chips (choice of white, red, blue or yellow in units of 50), 75 coupons. *Complete* poker set (case, 300 chips. 2 decks cards) . . . . .800 coupons.

ASH TRAY—Polished chromium, beautifully modern. "Hand" at top holds five lighted cigarettes, drops them in tray when burned down .50 coupons.

PLAYING CARDS—U. S. Congress quality gilt-edge (initial or fancy back), DECK 60 coupons. BRIDGE SET (2 decks). . . . . .100 coupons.

CIGARETTE CASE—Elgin Sport Model. Florentine Enameled. Choice several strikingly beautiful colors. . . . . .100 coupons.

ALSO (not illustrated) Pen and Pencil Sets, Card Tables and Covers, Bathroom Scale, Suede-finish Table Covers, Silk Stockings, Bridge Luncheon Sets, and others.

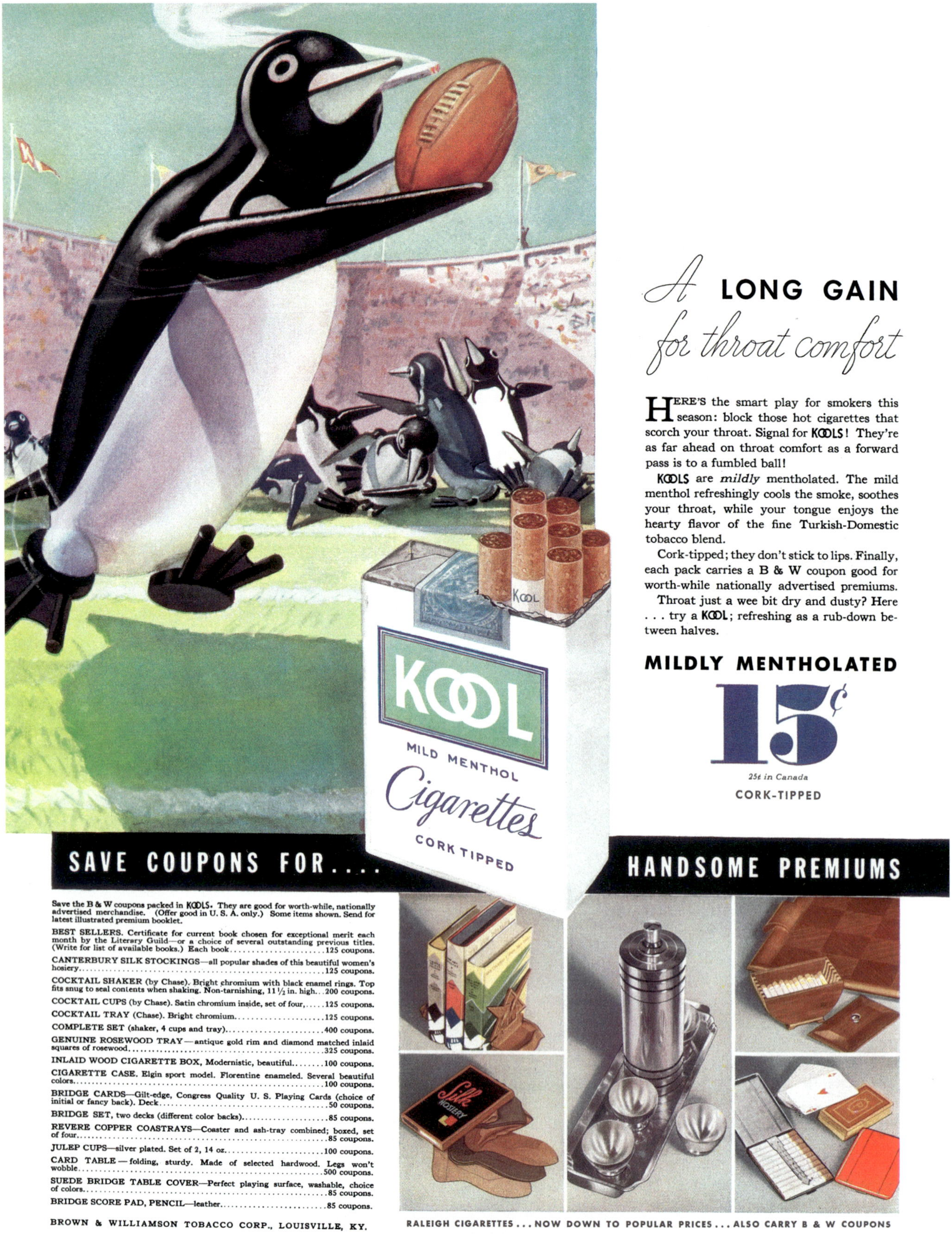
A LONG GAIN
for throat comfort
HERE'S the smart play for smokers this season: block those hot cigarettes that scorch your throat. Signal for KOOLS! They're as far ahead on throat comfort as a forward pass is to a fumbled ball!
KOOLS are mildly mentholated. The mild menthol refreshingly cools the smoke, soothes your throat, while your tongue enjoys the hearty flavor of the fine Turkish-Domestic tobacco blend.
Cork-tipped; they don't stick to lips. Finally, each pack carries a B & W coupon good for worth-while nationally advertised premiums.
Throat just a wee bit dry and dusty? Here . . . try a KOOL; refreshing as a rub-down between halves.
MILDLY MENTHOLATED
15¢
25¢ in Canada
CORK-TIPPED
KOOL
MILD MENTHOL
Cigarettes
CORK TIPPED
SAVE COUPONS FOR.... HANDSOME PREMIUMS
Save the B & W coupons packed in KOOLS. They are good for worth-while, nationally advertised merchandise. (Offer good in U. S. A. only.) Some items shown. Send for latest illustrated premium booklet.
BEST SELLERS. Certificate for current book chosen for exceptional merit each month by the Literary Guild—or a choice of several outstanding previous titles. (Write for list of available books.) Each book........125 coupons.
CANTERBURY SILK STOCKINGS—all popular shades of this beautiful women's hosiery........125 coupons.
COCKTAIL SHAKER (by Chase). Bright chromium with black enamel rings. Top fits snug to seal contents when shaking. Non-tarnishing, 11½ in. high...200 coupons.
COCKTAIL CUPS (by Chase). Satin chromium inside, set of four,.....125 coupons.
COCKTAIL TRAY (Chase). Bright chromium........125 coupons.
COMPLETE SET (shaker, 4 cups and tray)........400 coupons.
GENUINE ROSEWOOD TRAY—antique gold rim and diamond matched inlaid squares of rosewood........325 coupons.
INLAID WOOD CIGARETTE BOX, Modernistic, beautiful........100 coupons.
CIGARETTE CASE. Elgin sport model. Florentine enameled. Several beautiful colors........100 coupons.
BRIDGE CARDS—Gilt-edge, Congress Quality U. S. Playing Cards (choice of initial or fancy back). Deck........50 coupons.
BRIDGE SET, two decks (different color backs)........85 coupons.
REVERE COPPER COASTRAYS—Coaster and ash-tray combined; boxed, set of four........85 coupons.
JULEP CUPS—silver plated. Set of 2, 14 oz........100 coupons.
CARD TABLE—folding, sturdy. Made of selected hardwood. Legs won't wobble........500 coupons.
SUEDE BRIDGE TABLE COVER—Perfect playing surface, washable, choice of colors........85 coupons.
BRIDGE SCORE PAD, PENCIL—leather........85 coupons.
BROWN & WILLIAMSON TOBACCO CORP., LOUISVILLE, KY.
Silk HOSIERY
RALEIGH CIGARETTES ... NOW DOWN TO POPULAR PRICES ... ALSO CARRY B & W COUPONS

▲► *Kool*, 1935

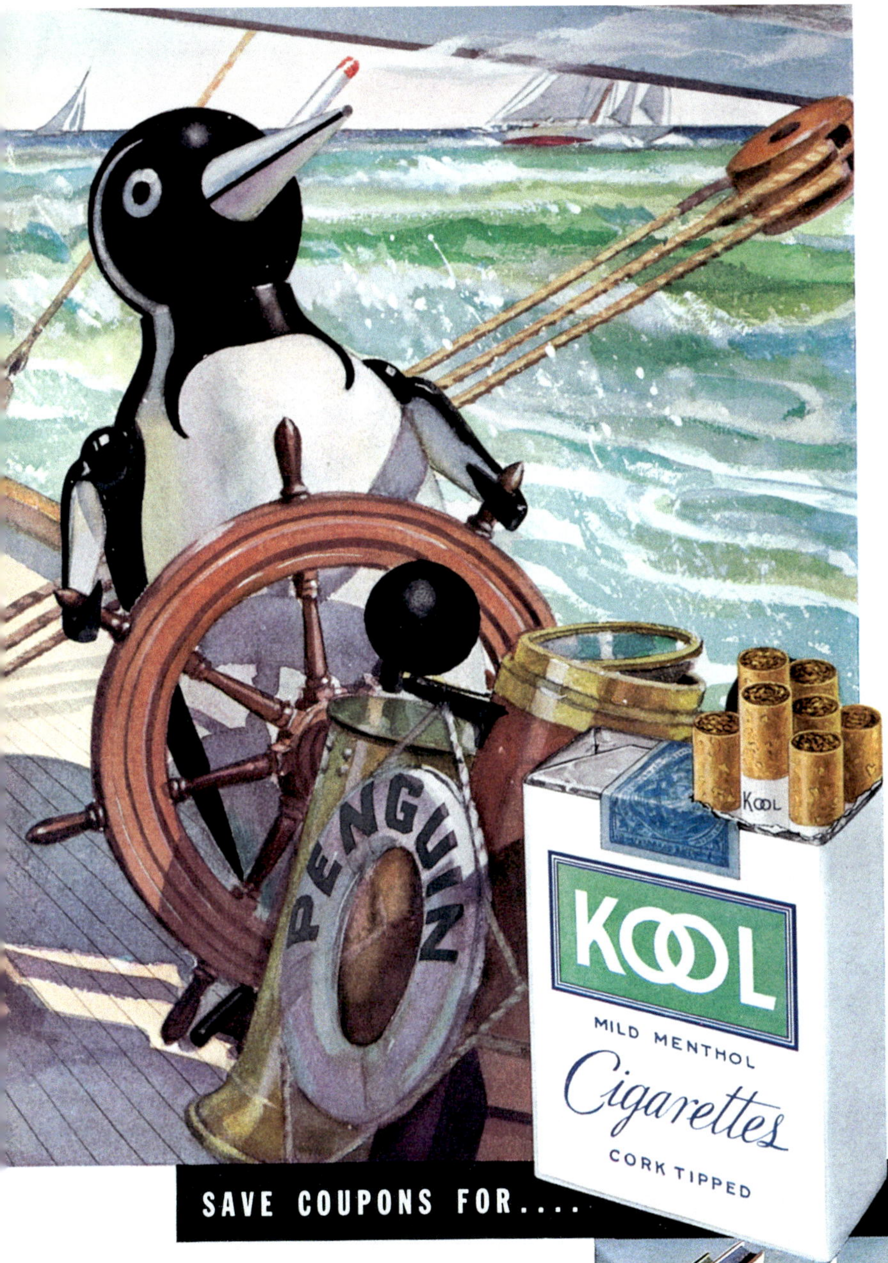

NOW

the leader in

MENTHOLATED CIGARETTES

STEER your course for true throat comfort. Light a KOOL! Refreshing as the forward deck in a spanking breeze!

Light a KOOL! Feel that smoke-weary throat relax. The mild menthol cools the smoke, eases your throat—and yet brings out the flavor of the fine tobaccos to the fullest.

Light a KOOL! Those cork tips don't stick to lips.

Light a KOOL! Each pack carries a valuable B & W coupon good for desirable, nationally advertised merchandise.

The man who wrote "all the world is sad and dreary" never heard of KOOLS. Head for KOOLS and light up.

MILDLY MENTHOLATED

15¢

25¢ in Canada

CORK-TIPPED

SAVE COUPONS FOR.... HANDSOME MERCHANDISE

Save the B & W coupons packed in KOOLS. They are good for worthwhile, nationally advertised merchandise. (Offer good in U. S. A. only.) Some items shown. Send for complete illustrated list.

BEST SELLERS. Certificate good for the current book chosen for exceptional merit each month by the Literary Guild—or a choice of several outstanding previous selections. (Write for list of available titles.) Each book..............125 coupons

GENUINE ROSEWOOD TRAY—"Adler Royal," antique gold rim and diamond matched inlaid squares of rosewood..............325 coupons

CHROMIUM COCKTAIL SHAKER (by Chase). Bright chromium with black enamel rings. Top fits snug to seal contents when shaking. Non-tarnishing, 11½ inches high..............200 coupons

COCKTAIL CUPS (by Chase). Satin chromium inside, set of 4 cups..125 coupons

COCKTAIL TRAY (by Chase). Polished chromium..............125 coupons

COMPLETE SET (shaker, four cups, and tray)..............400 coupons

CARD TABLE*—"Adler Royal" folding, extremely sturdy. Three tones of wood inlaid in a smart, modern effect. Legs won't wobble..............500 coupons

INITIALED BRIDGE CARDS—Gilt-edge, Congress Quality U. S. Playing Cards (Initial or fancy-back). Deck..............50 coupons

BRIDGE SET, two decks (different color backs)..............85 coupons

CANTERBURY SILK STOCKINGS—all popular shades of this beautiful women's hosiery..............125 coupons

ALSO (not illustrated) Revere Copper Coastrays—Coaster and ash-tray combined; set of four......85 coupons. Julep Cups—silver plated. Set of 2, full 14 oz.......100 coupons. Suede Bridge Table Cover—choice of colors....85 coupons. Leather Bridge Score Pad, Pencil—choice of colors......85 coupons. Inlaid Wood Cigarette Box, modernistic and beautiful......100 coupons. Send for complete illustrated list.

**Card tables sent express "collect" from our nearest warehouse. All other premiums sent "prepaid."*

BROWN & WILLIAMSON TOBACCO CORP., LOUISVILLE, KY.

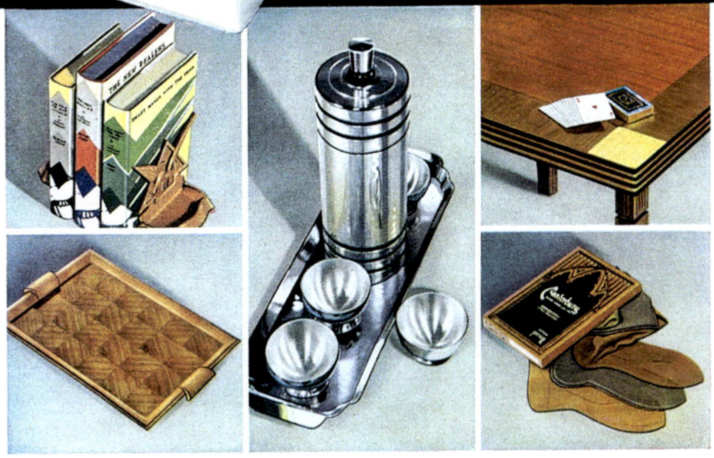

RALEIGH CIGARETTES... NOW DOWN TO POPULAR PRICES... ALSO CARRY B & W COUPONS

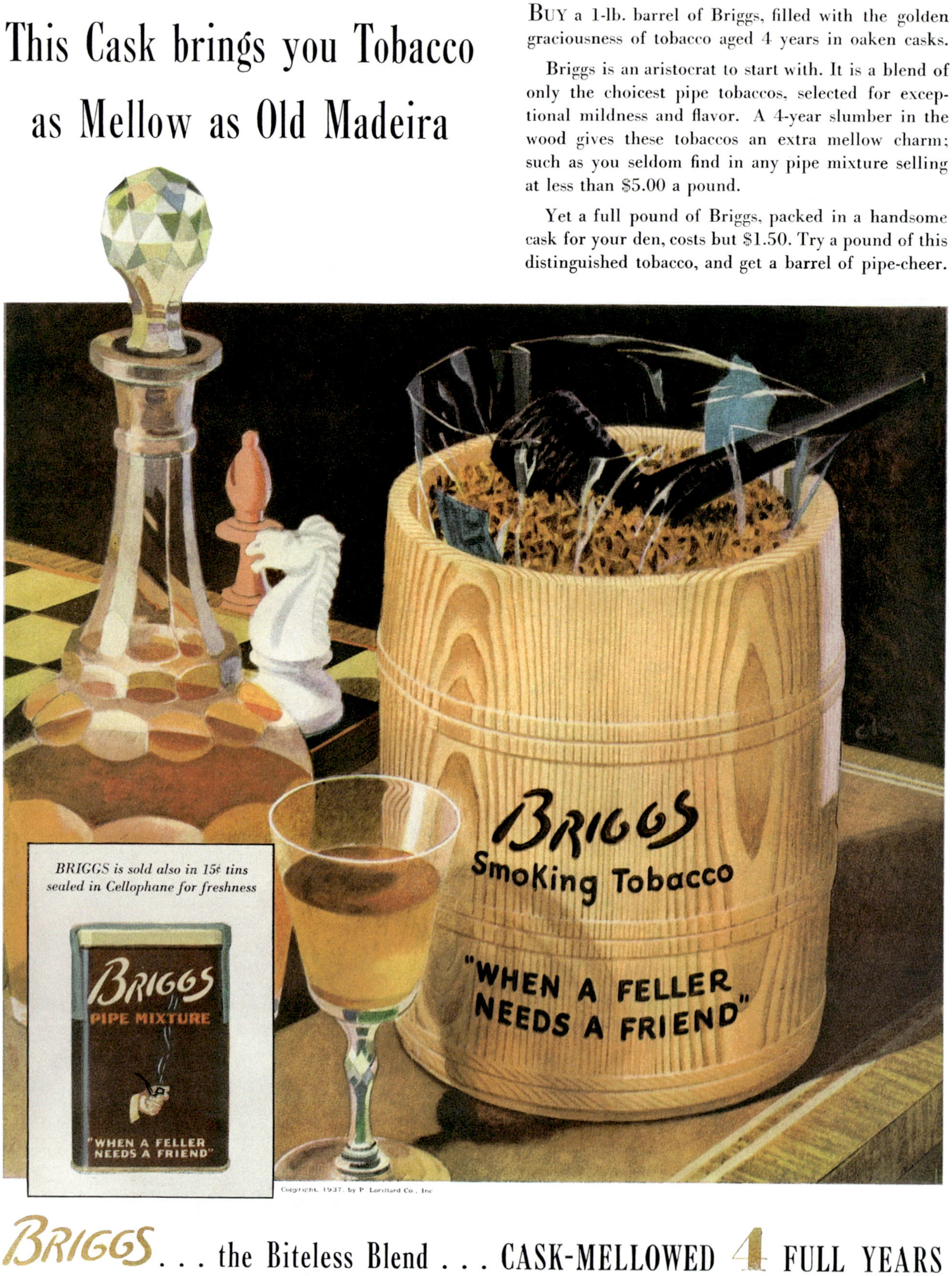

Briggs Tobacco, 1937

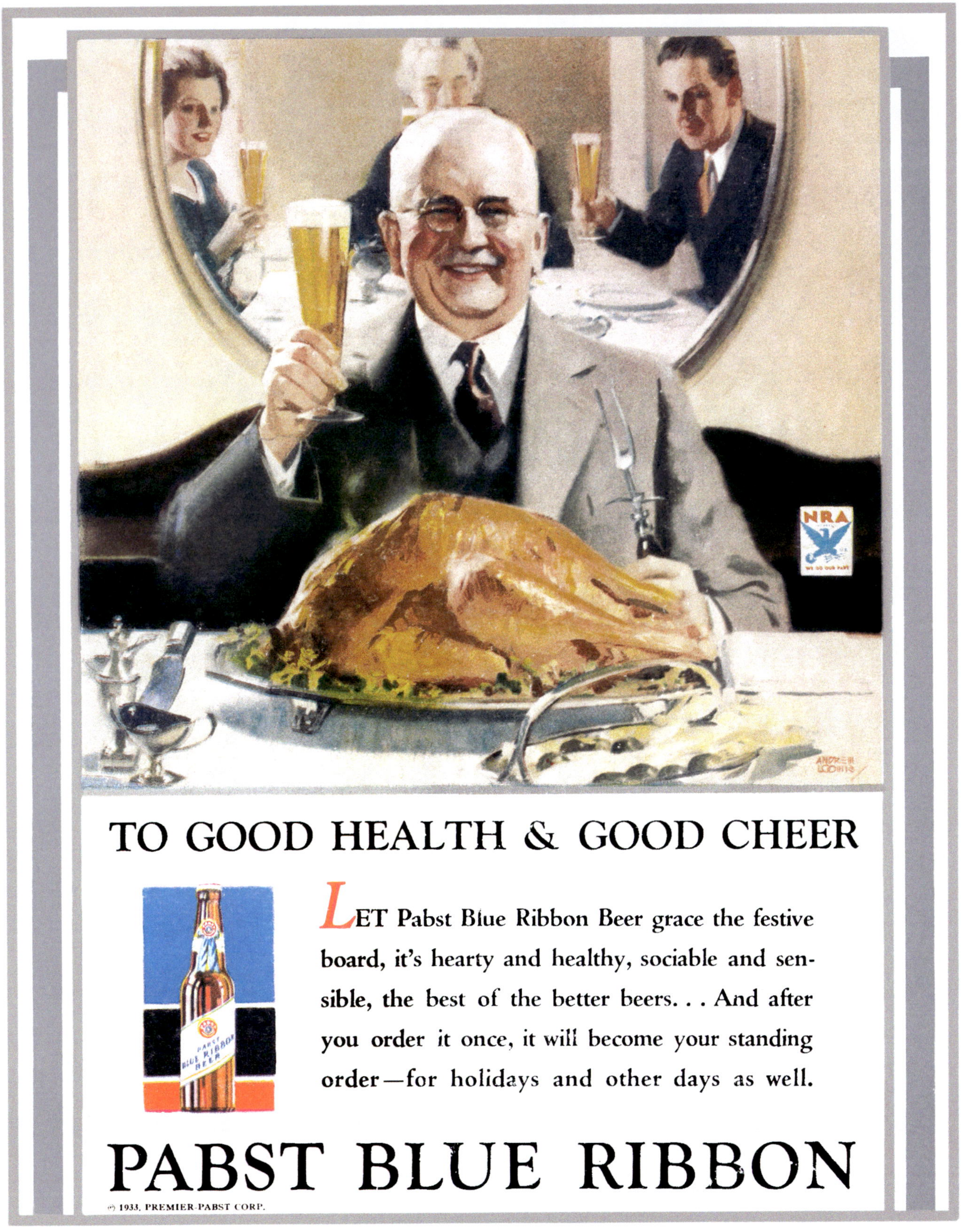

Pabst Blue Ribbon, 1933

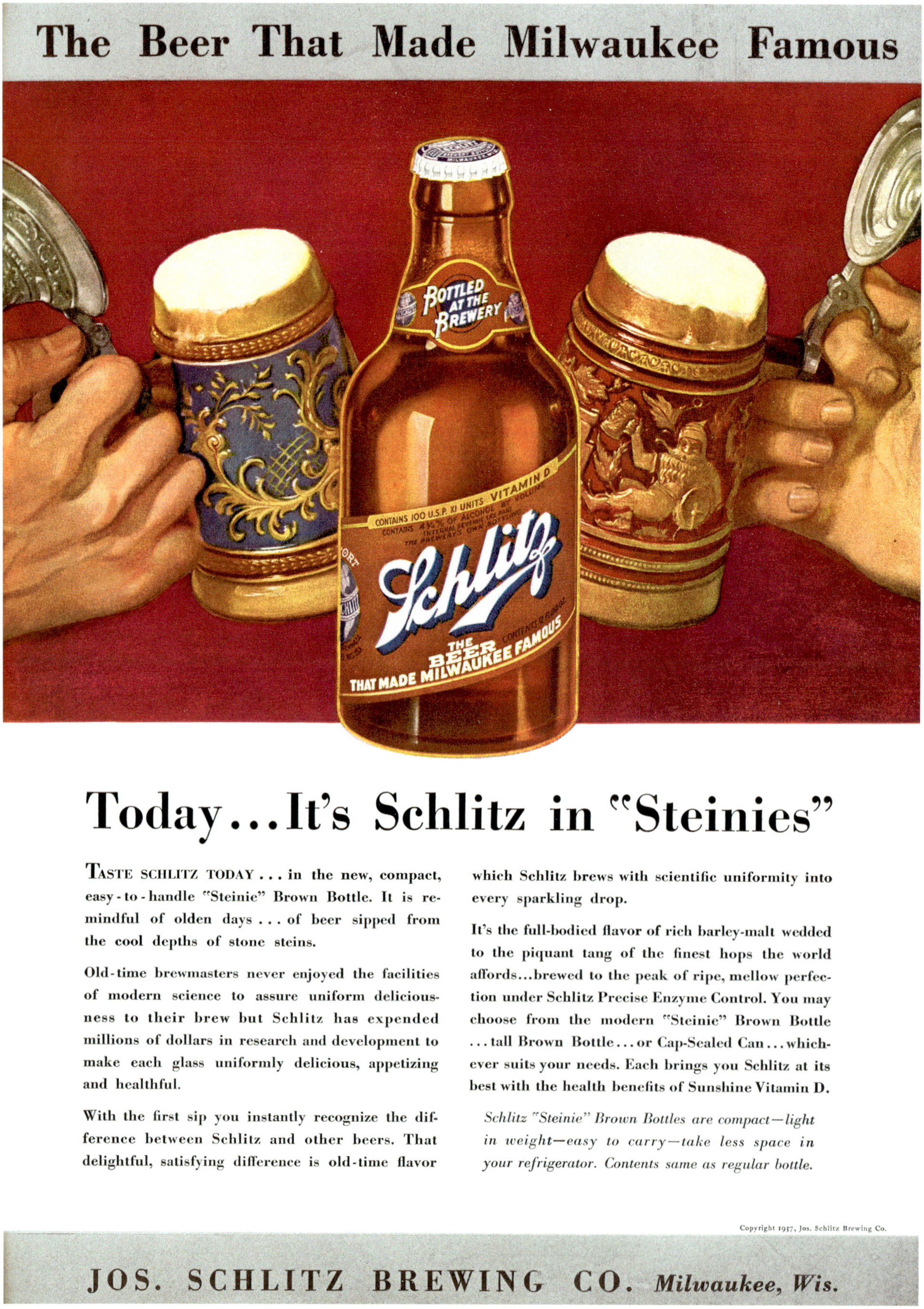

Schlitz, 1937

► *Budweiser, 1933*

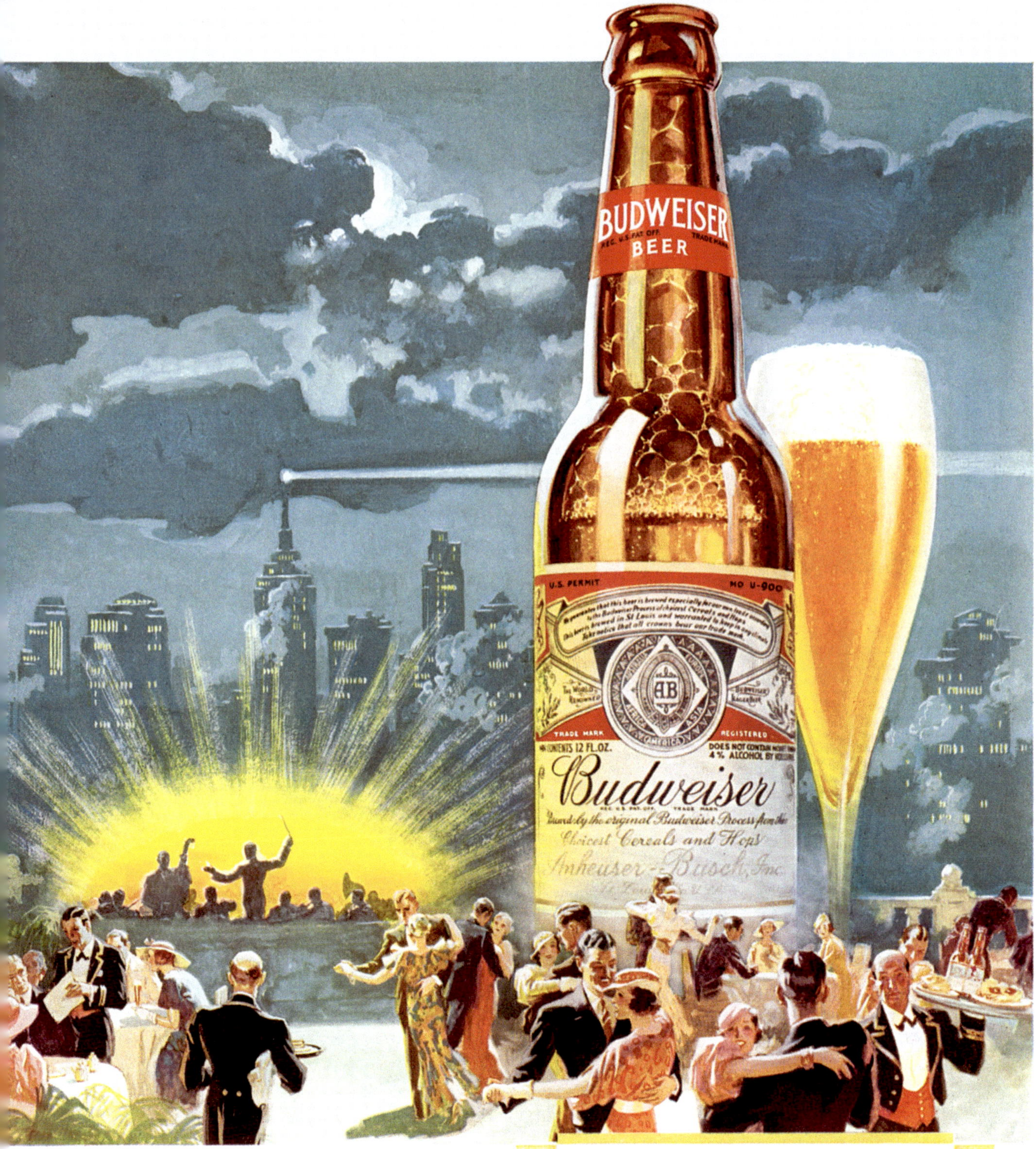

Because it fits so gracefully and so gaily into the scheme of good living, BUDWEISER is recognized as the King of Bottled Beer. Millions who welcomed beer back, are finding there is only one BUDWEISER—brewed and fully aged in the world's largest brewery.

Budweiser

KING OF BOTTLED BEER

N H E U S E R - B U S C H - S T . L O U I S

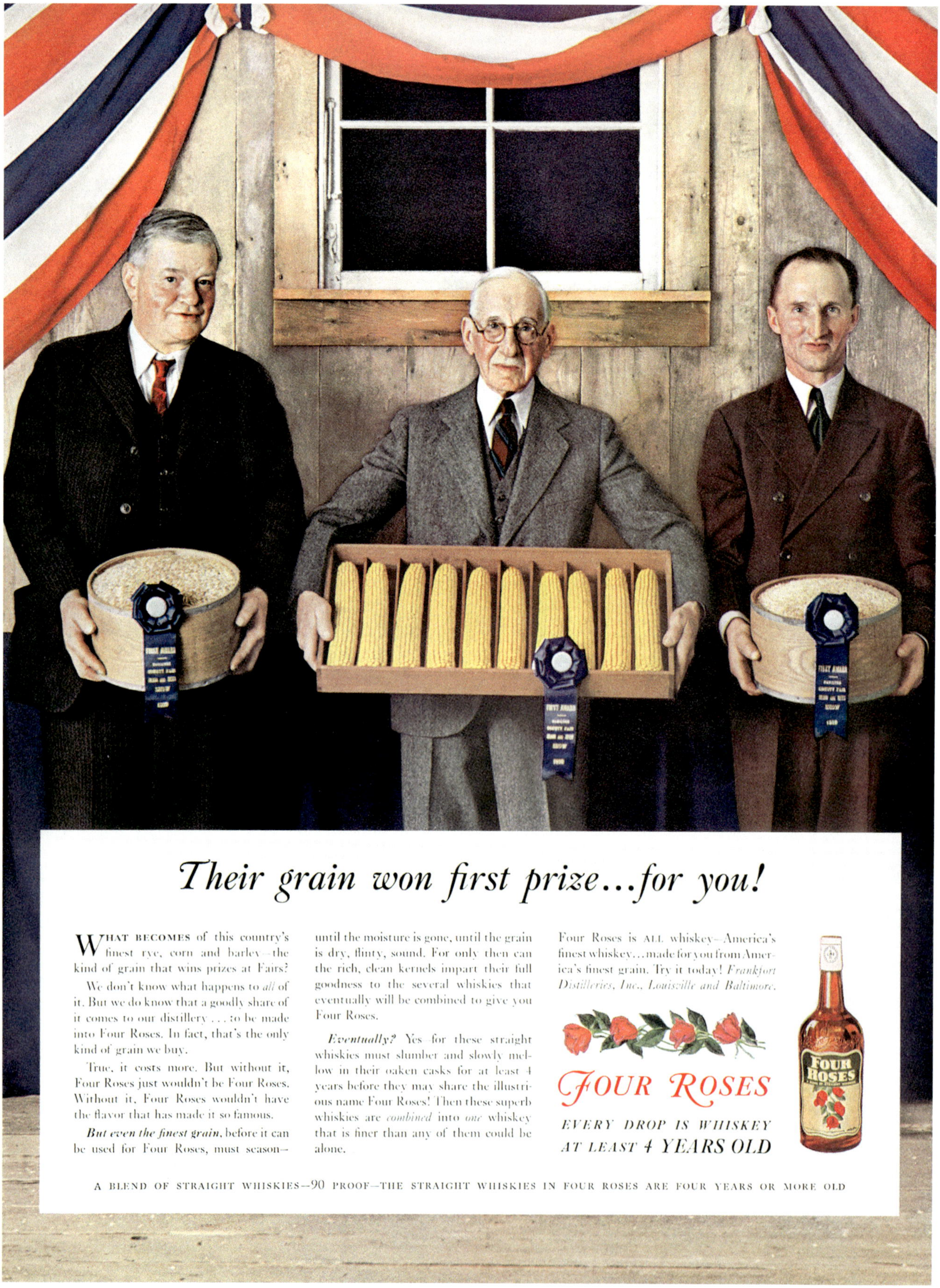

Four Roses, 1939

► *Four Roses, 1938*

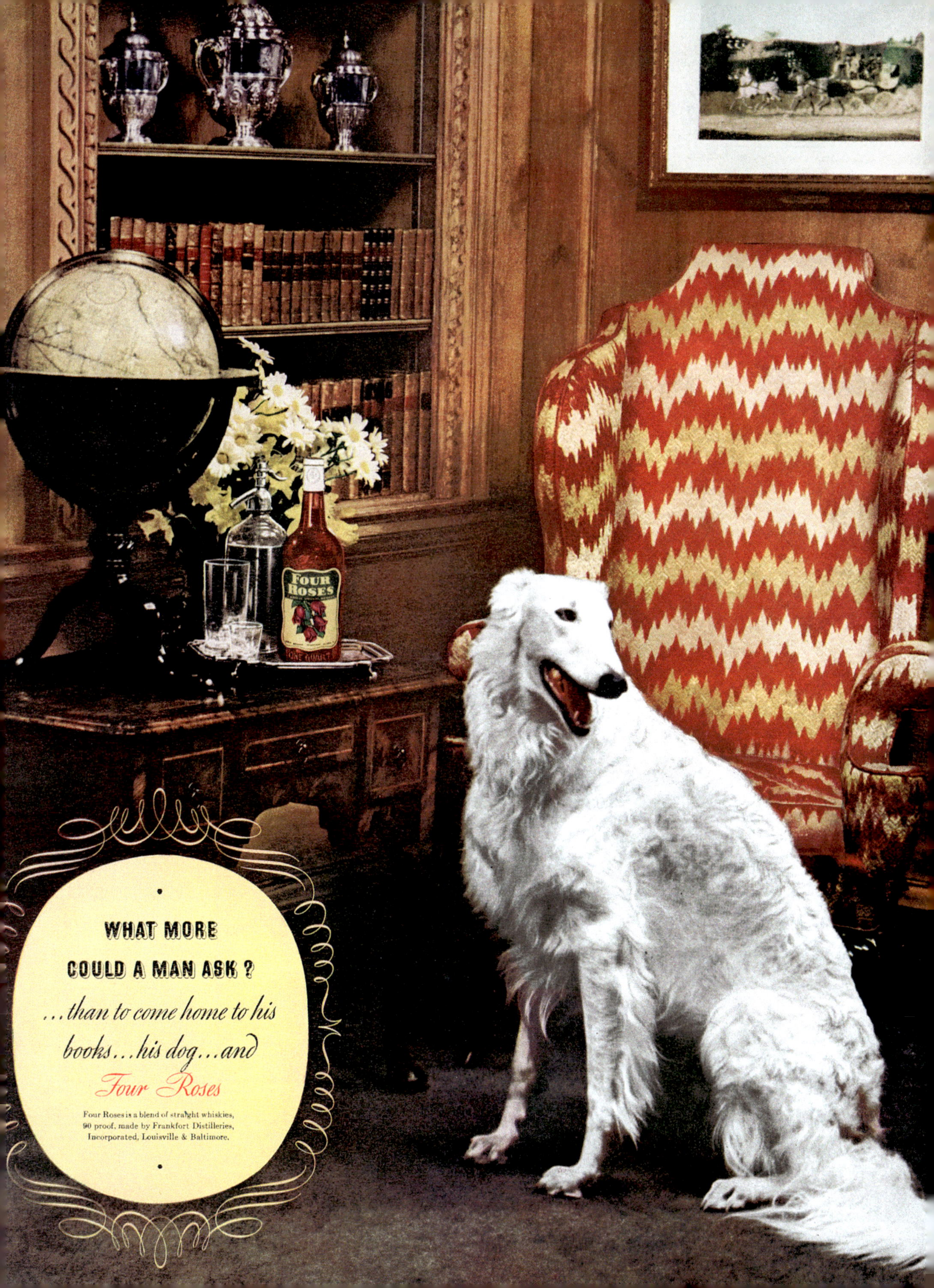
FOUR ROSES
WHAT MORE
COULD A MAN ASK ?
...than to come home to his
books...his dog...and
Four Roses
Four Roses is a blend of straight whiskies,
90 proof, made by Frankfort Distilleries,
Incorporated, Louisville & Baltimore.

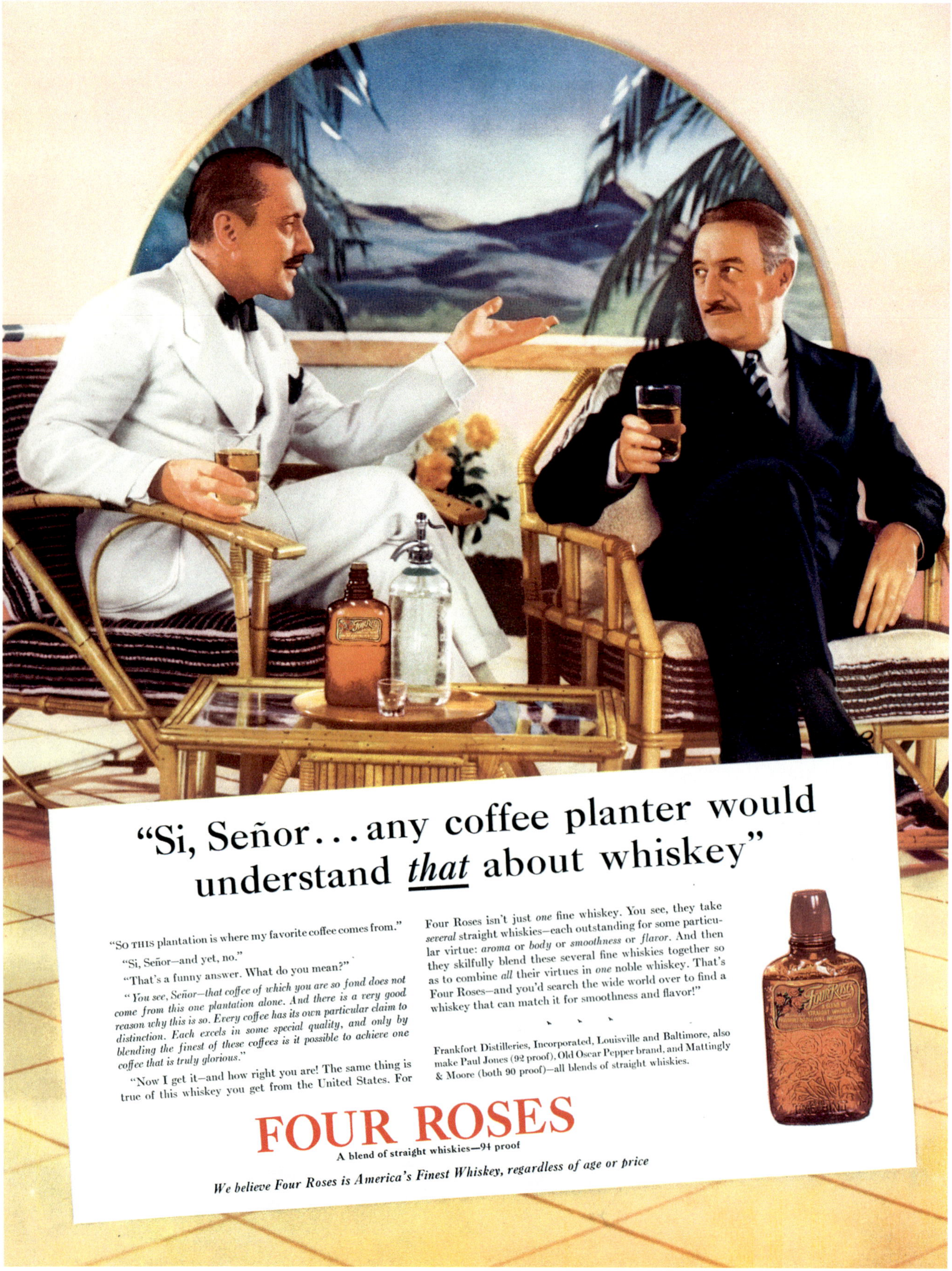

▲▶ *Four Roses, 1937*

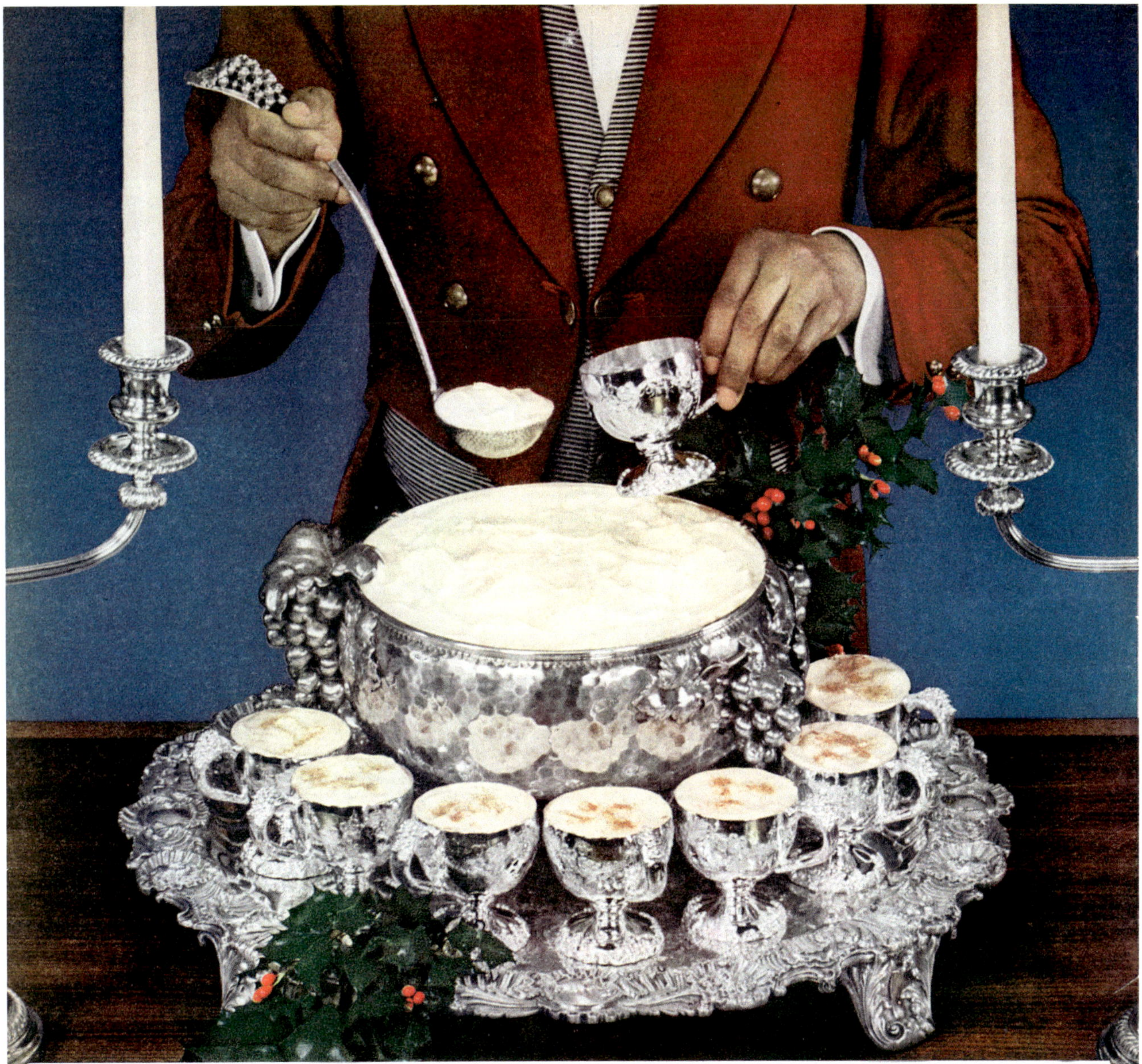

ONCE AGAIN...IT'S TIME TO MAKE A BOWL OF

Merry Christmas!

FOR A PERFECT EGG-NOG—Beat separately the yolks and whites of 6 fresh eggs. Add ½ cup of sugar to the yolks while beating, and ¼ cup of sugar to the whites after they have been beaten very stiff. Mix the egg whites with the yolks. Stir in 1 pint of rich cream and 1 pint of milk. Then add 1 pint of Four Roses Whiskey and 1 ounce of Jamaica Rum. Stir thoroughly, and serve very cold with grated nutmeg on each glass. (Makes 5 pints of Egg-nog.)

Just one thing—be mighty sure that you make your Christmas Egg-nog with Four Roses. For Four Roses is *the* whiskey that makes an Egg-nog a gloriously heart-warming Bowl of Merry Christmas. Because, while Four Roses is *ALL* whiskey, it's more than just *one* straight whiskey. It's a superb combination of *several* great whiskies, each outstanding for some particular quality. Blended together, these whiskies unite *all* their noble virtues in *one* truly magnificent whiskey —*Four Roses!*

Four Roses is a blend of straight whiskies—and that means ALL whiskey—90 proof. Frankfort Distilleries, Incorporated, Louisville and Baltimore.

FOUR ROSES

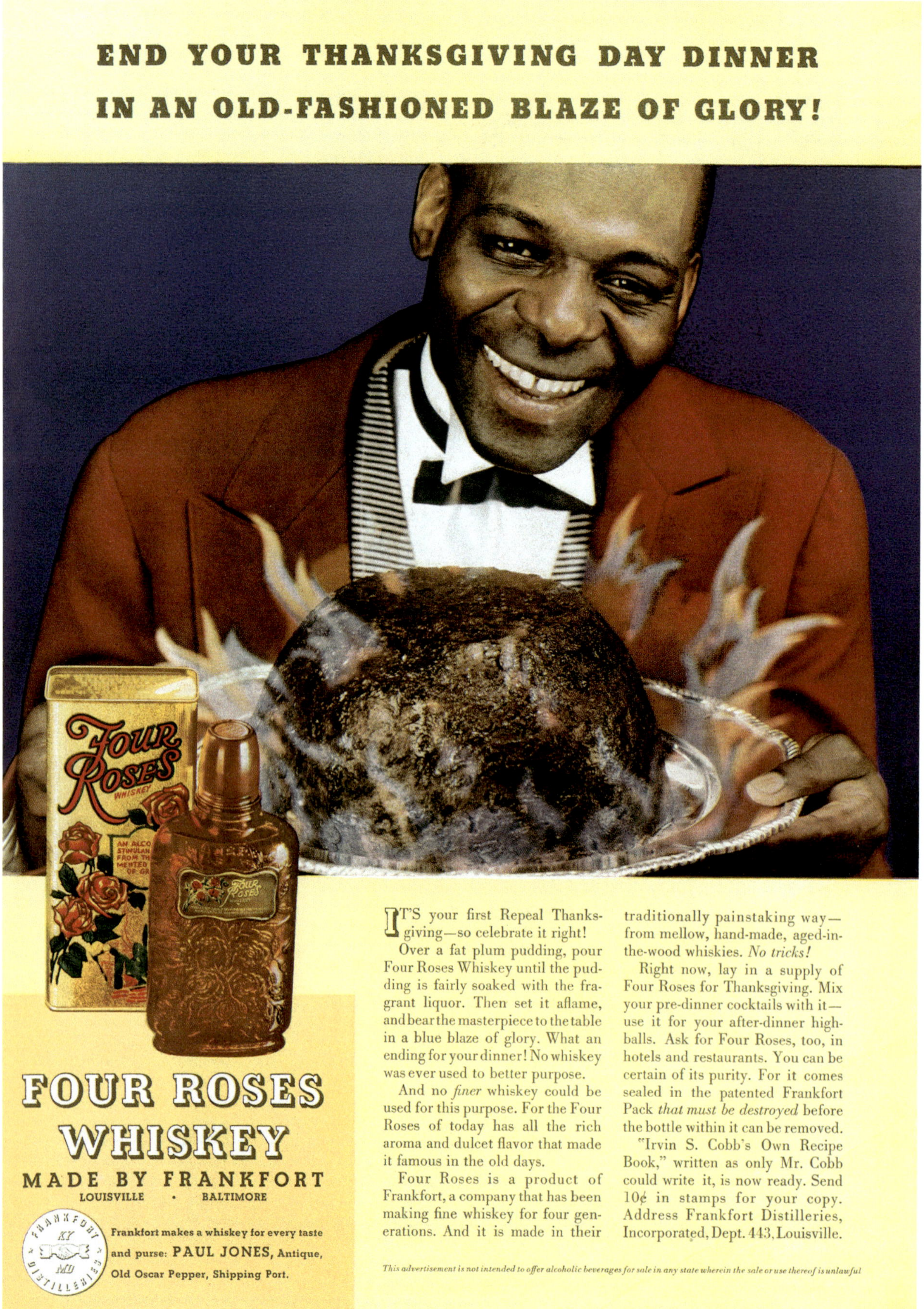

Four Roses, 1934

► Four Roses, 1937

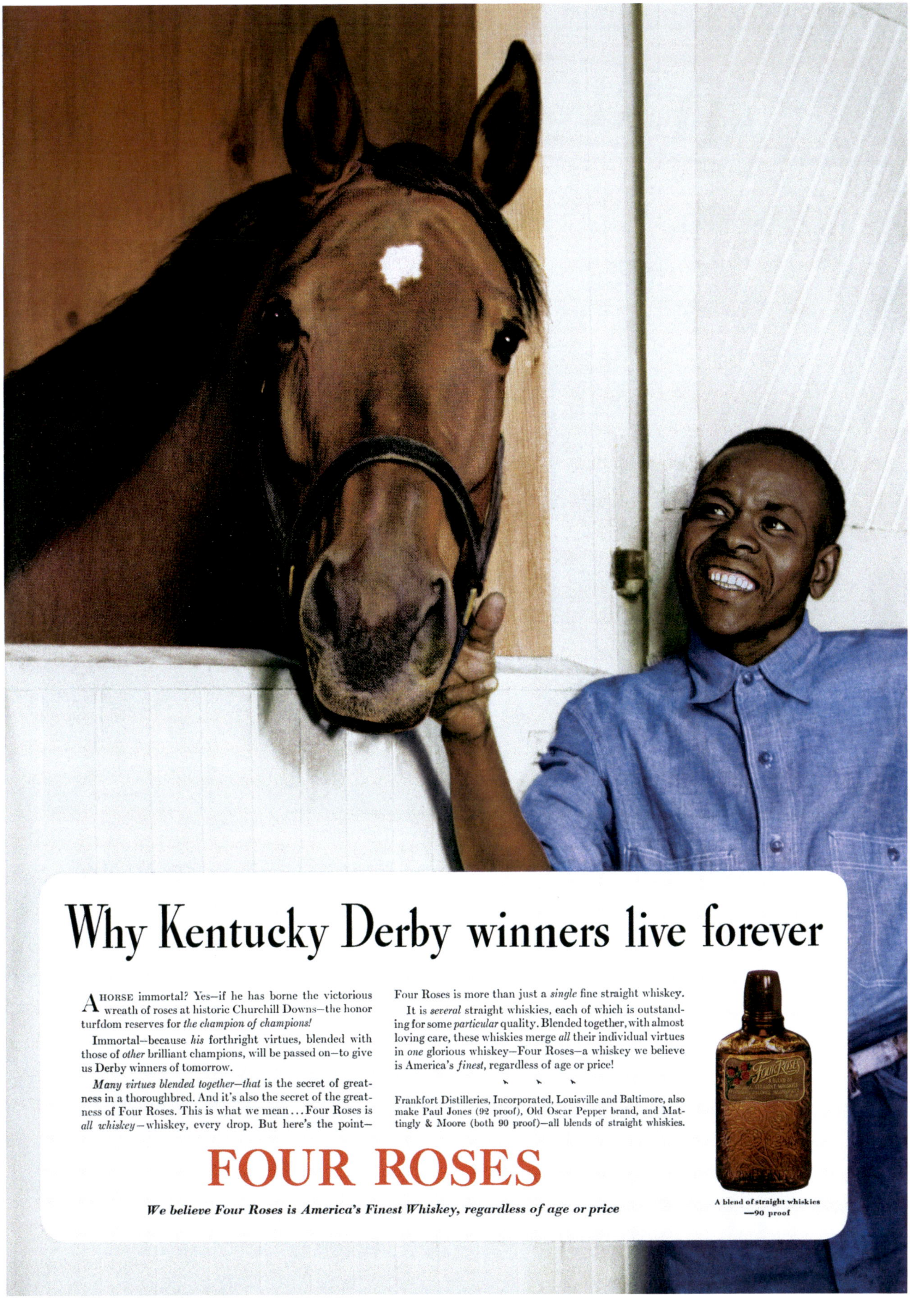
Why Kentucky Derby winners live forever
A HORSE immortal? Yes—if he has borne the victorious wreath of roses at historic Churchill Downs—the honor turfdom reserves for *the champion of champions!*
Immortal—because *his* forthright virtues, blended with those of *other* brilliant champions, will be passed on—to give us Derby winners of tomorrow.
Many virtues blended together—that is the secret of greatness in a thoroughbred. And it's also the secret of the greatness of Four Roses. This is what we mean . . . Four Roses is *all whiskey*—whiskey, every drop. But here's the point—Four Roses is more than just a *single* fine straight whiskey.
It is *several* straight whiskies, each of which is outstanding for some *particular* quality. Blended together, with almost loving care, these whiskies merge *all* their individual virtues in *one* glorious whiskey—Four Roses—a whiskey we believe is America's *finest*, regardless of age or price!
Frankfort Distilleries, Incorporated, Louisville and Baltimore, also make Paul Jones (92 proof), Old Oscar Pepper brand, and Mattingly & Moore (both 90 proof)—all blends of straight whiskies.
FOUR ROSES
We believe Four Roses is America's Finest Whiskey, regardless of age or price
A blend of straight whiskies —90 proof

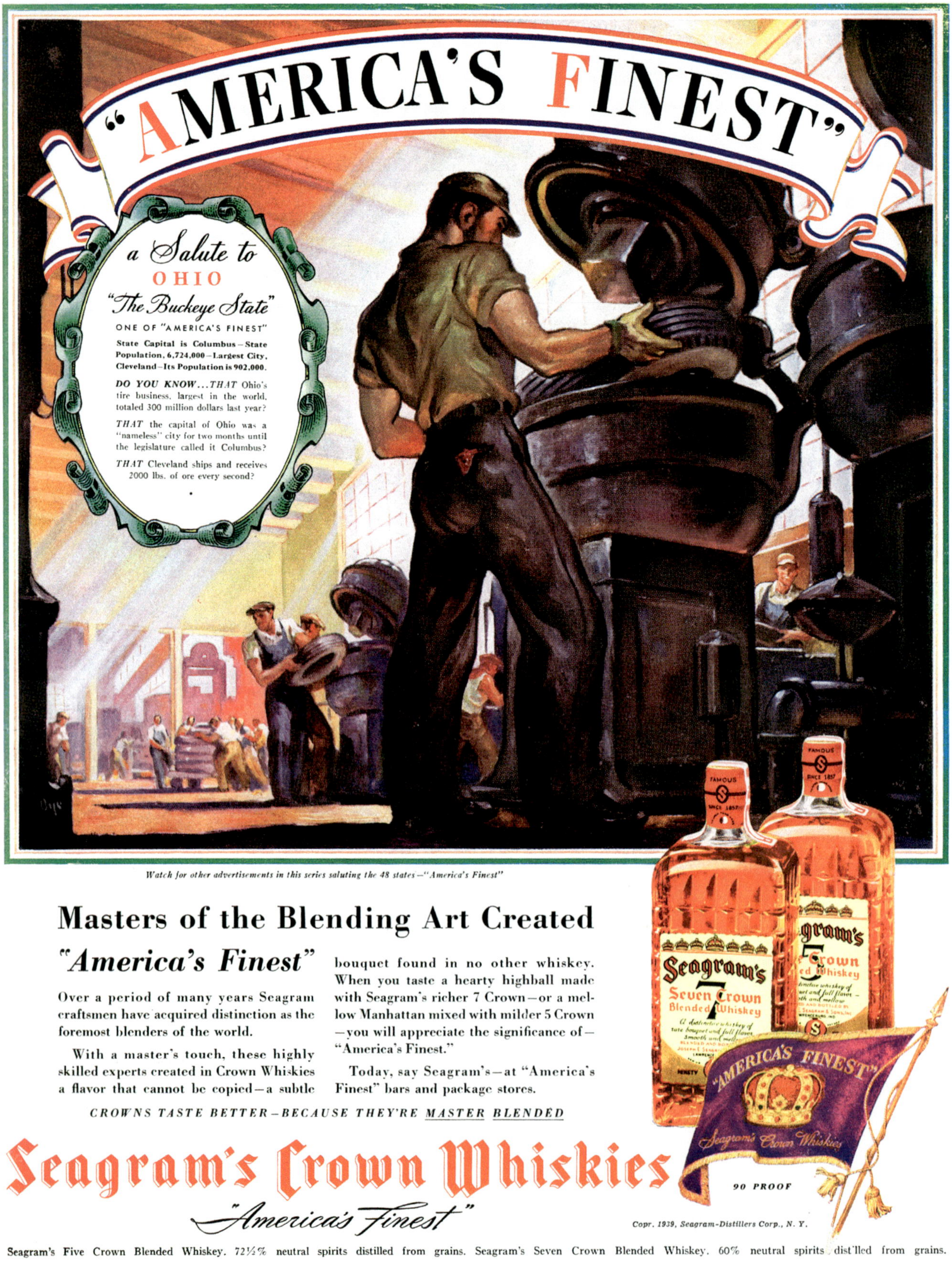

▲▶ *Seagram's, 1939*

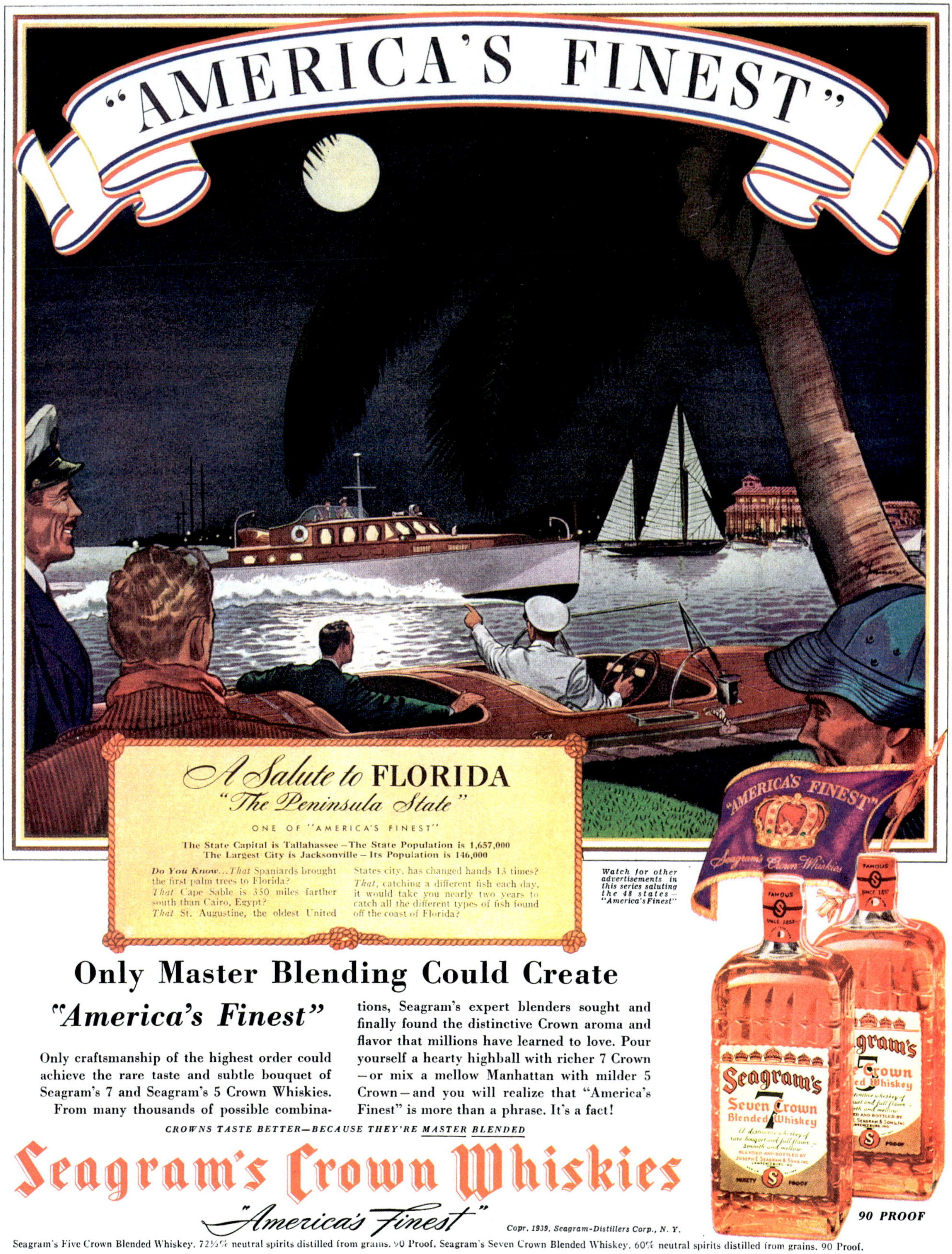

"AMERICA'S FINEST"
A Salute to FLORIDA
"The Peninsula State"
ONE OF "AMERICA'S FINEST"
The State Capital is Tallahassee – The State Population is 1,657,000
The Largest City is Jacksonville – Its Population is 146,000
Do You Know... That Spaniards brought the first palm trees to Florida?
That Cape Sable is 350 miles farther south than Cairo, Egypt?
That St. Augustine, the oldest United States city, has changed hands 13 times?
That, catching a different fish each day, it would take you nearly two years to catch all the different types of fish found off the coast of Florida?
Watch for other advertisements in this series saluting the 48 states – "America's Finest"
AMERICA'S FINEST
Seagram's Crown Whiskies
Only Master Blending Could Create
"America's Finest"
Only craftsmanship of the highest order could achieve the rare taste and subtle bouquet of Seagram's 7 and Seagram's 5 Crown Whiskies. From many thousands of possible combinations, Seagram's expert blenders sought and finally found the distinctive Crown aroma and flavor that millions have learned to love. Pour yourself a hearty highball with richer 7 Crown – or mix a mellow Manhattan with milder 5 Crown – and you will realize that "America's Finest" is more than a phrase. It's a fact!
CROWNS TASTE BETTER—BECAUSE THEY'RE MASTER BLENDED
Seagram's Crown Whiskies
"America's Finest"
Copr. 1939, Seagram-Distillers Corp., N. Y.
Seagram's Seven Crown Blended Whiskey
90 PROOF
Seagram's Five Crown Blended Whiskey. 72½% neutral spirits distilled from grains. 90 Proof. Seagram's Seven Crown Blended Whiskey. 60% neutral spirits distilled from grains. 90 Proof.

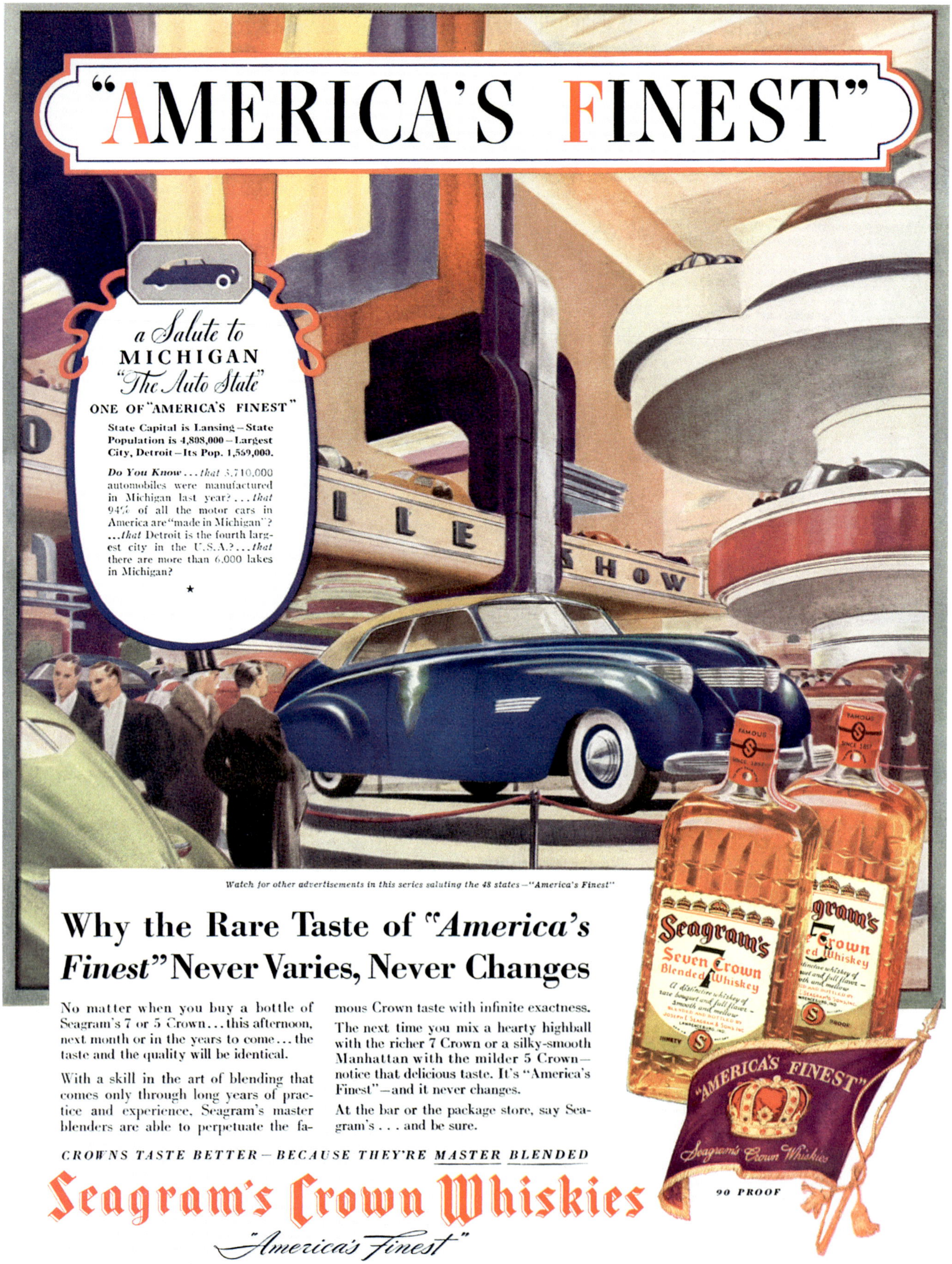

Seagram's, 1938

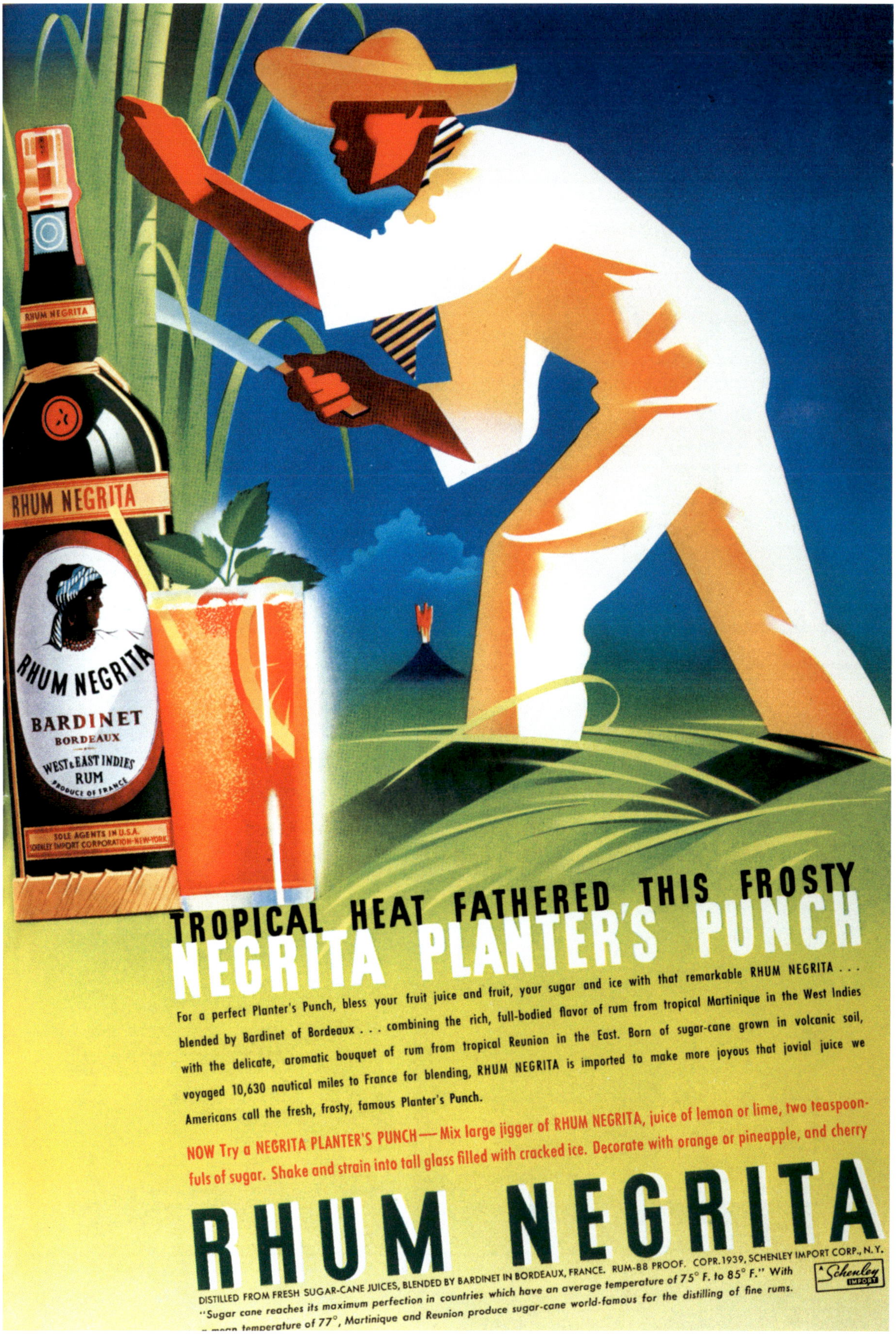

Rhum Negrita, 1939

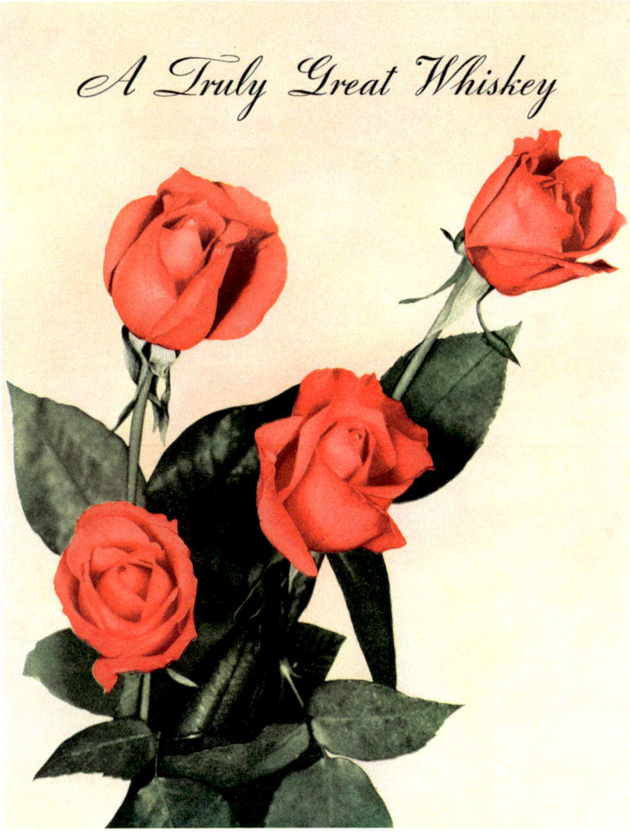

Four Roses, 1938

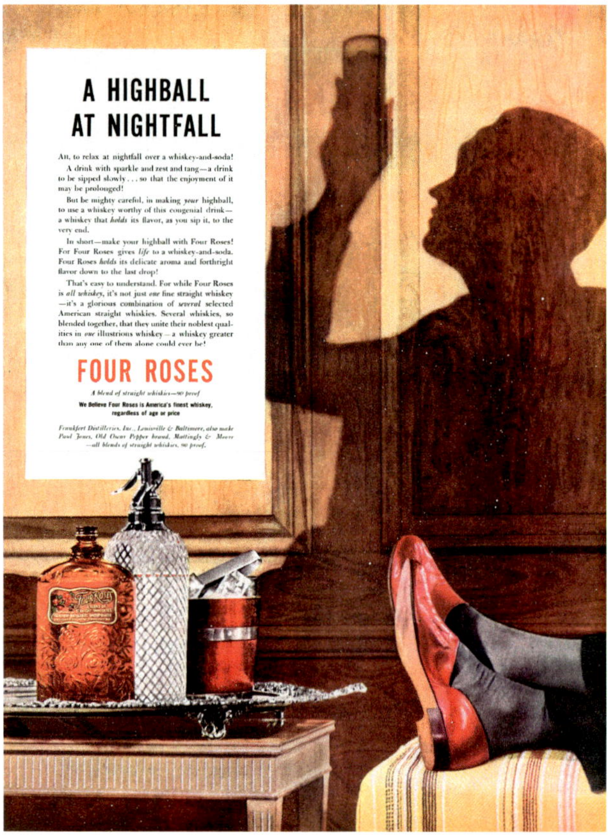

Four Roses, 1937

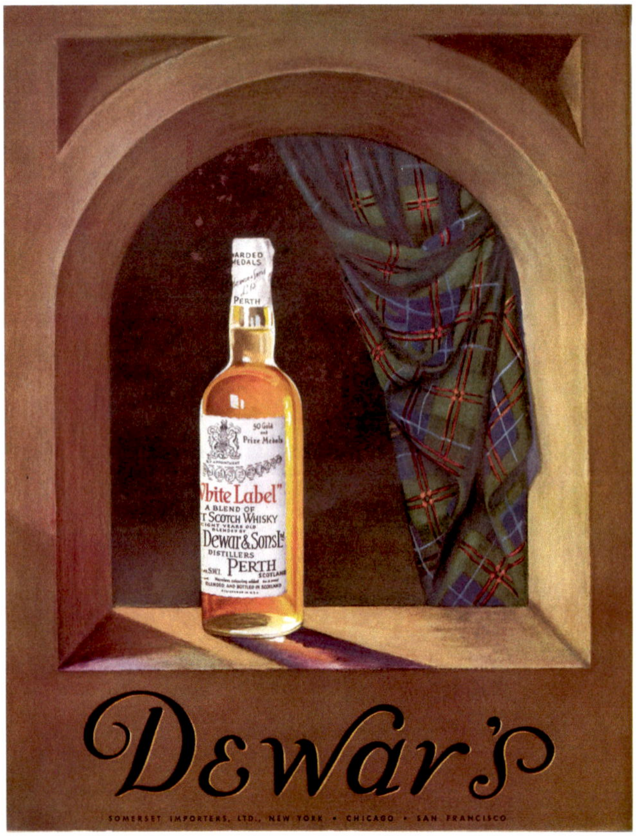

Dewar's, 1934

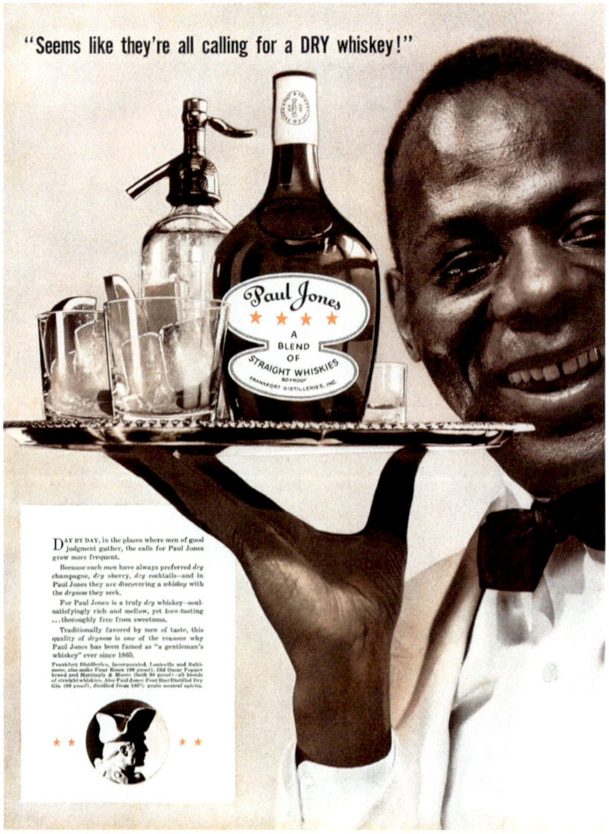

Paul Jones, 1937

▸ *Paul Jones, 1938*

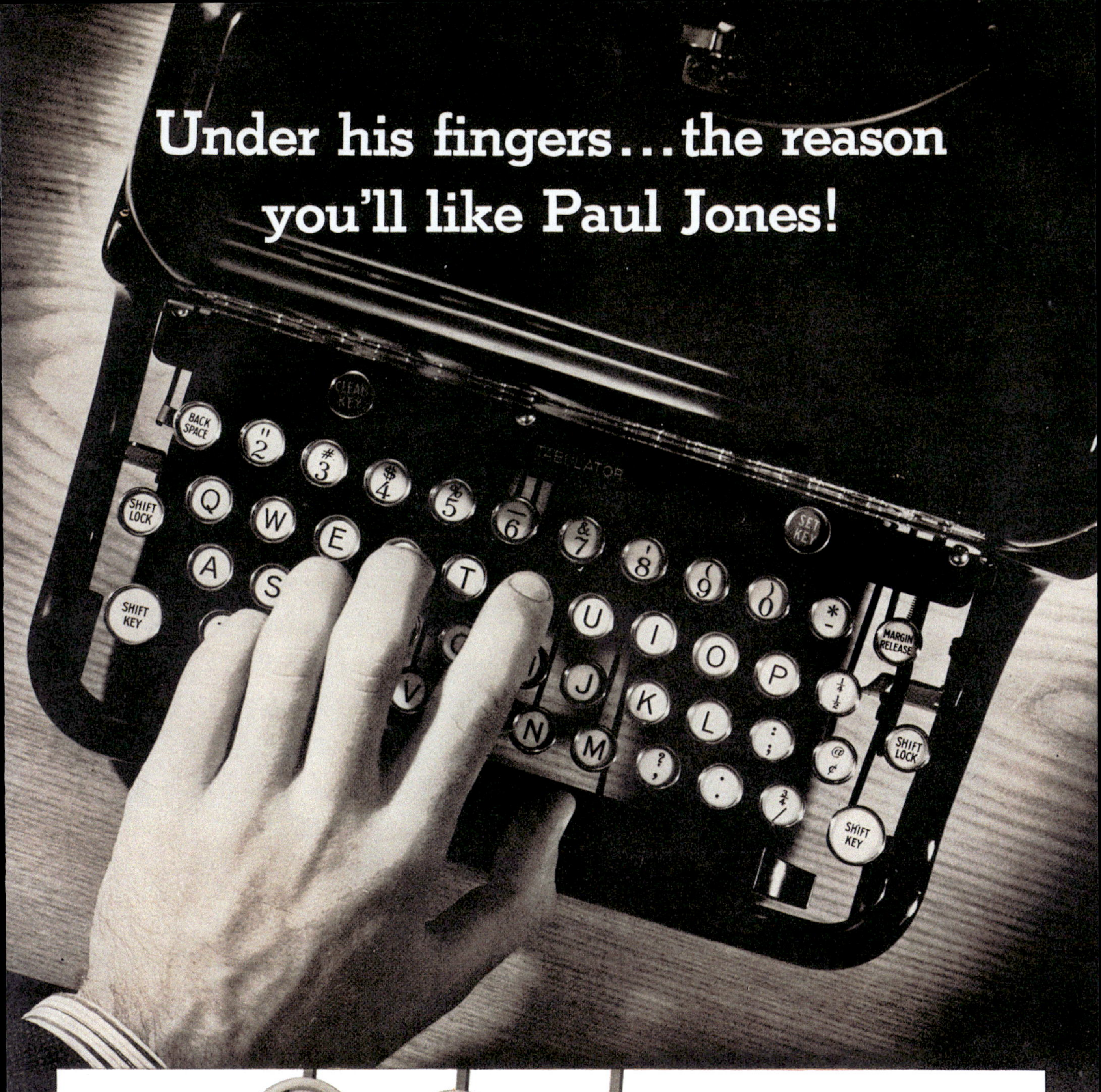

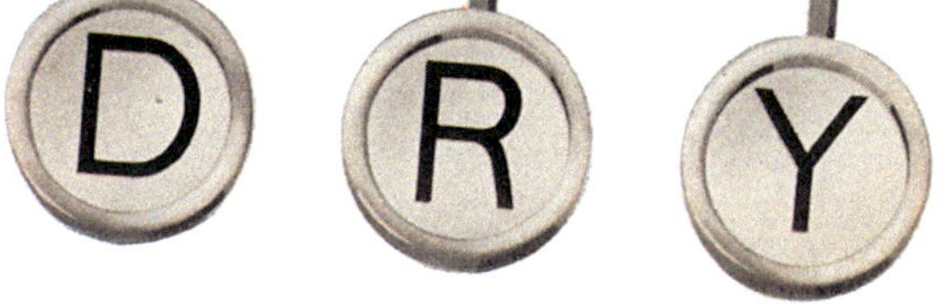

YES, those three letters . . . D-R-Y . . . spell one big reason why so many men of discerning taste find Paul Jones Whiskey very much to their liking!

For Paul Jones, you see, is a truly DRY whiskey — hearty and robust (as a man's whiskey *should* be!) . . . yet without a trace of sweetness in its make-up.

And this crisp, clean-flavored quality of DRYNESS is just one of *many* reasons why Paul Jones has been famous as "A Gentleman's Whiskey" since 1865. Try Paul Jones — discover *all* the reasons! Frankfort Distilleries, Incorporated, Louisville & Baltimore.

★ ★ ★ ★

A blend of straight whiskies.
100% straight whiskies — 90 proof

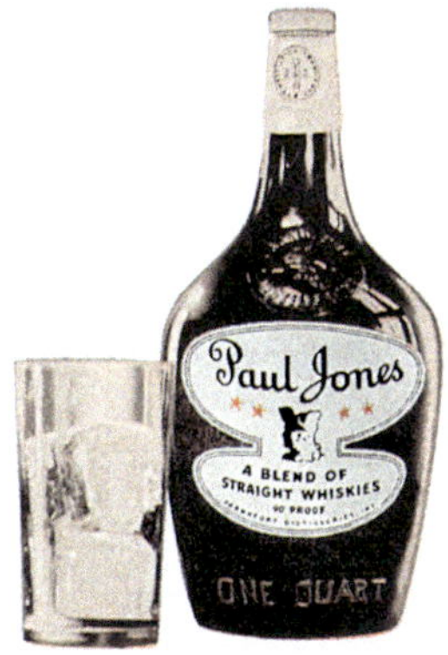

WHO SAID FIJI IS UNCIVILIZED?

"I suppose most of you Americans still think of the Fijis as populated by side-show head-hunters," a prominent British official writes.

"But what would you think if I told you that one of the fearsome-looking natives who guided us on our semi-annual inspection tour had a genuine talent for the finer things? Yes, he did—he knew at just what trading post we would be able to pick up a bottle of Canadian Club!

"I guess you're absolutely right when you say in your ads that Canadian Club's mellow flavor appeals to everyone."

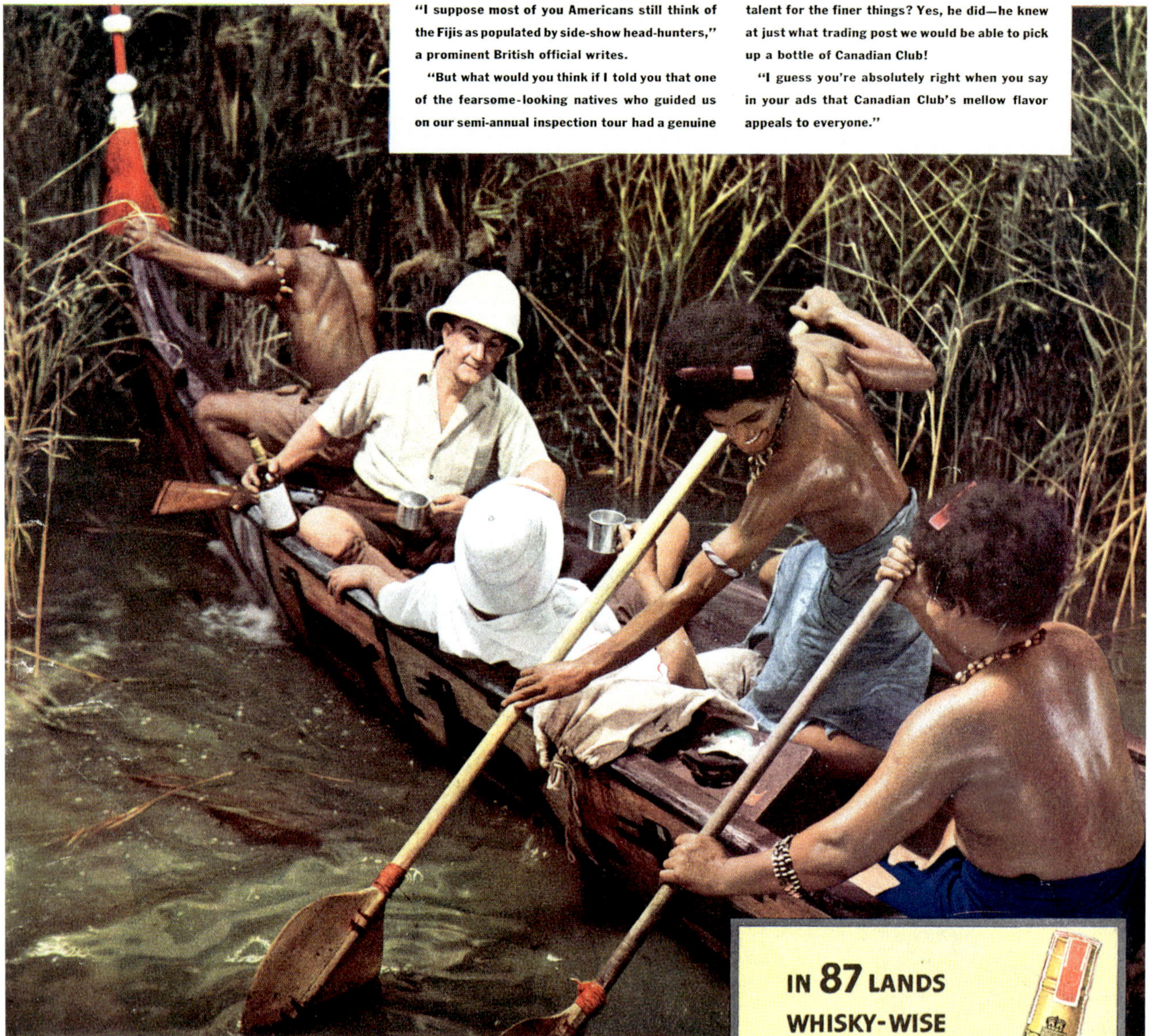

IN 87 LANDS WHISKY-WISE MEN ASK FOR

"Canadian Club"

6 YEARS OLD

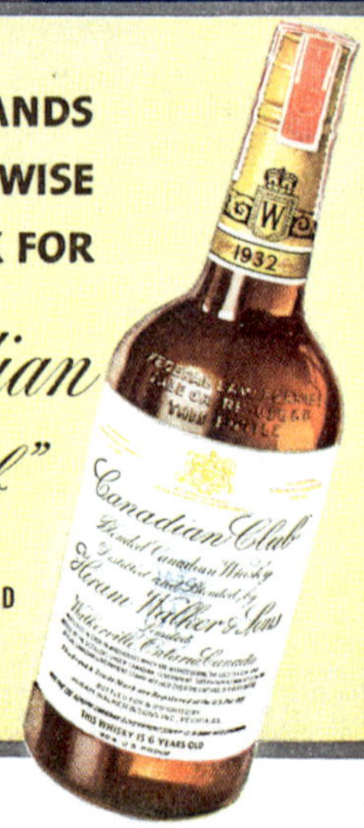

Why so many Americans have changed to this imported whisky...

Fiji, Canada, and the U.S.A. aren't alone in appreciating Canadian Club. **In 87 lands it is a favorite.** In London itself, and throughout the British Isles the biggest-selling imported whisky is Canadian Club. No other whisky has won such acclaim.

Of Interest to You

But of much more interest to *you* is the fact that many *Americans* who formerly preferred Scotch, bourbon, or rye, have changed to Canadian Club. Today, twice as many Americans regularly ask for Canadian Club as did two years ago!

Taste for yourself why Canadian Club has achieved this record of success equalled by no other whisky. Try it, as many others have, in a "show-me" mood. The instant you experience Canadian Club's distinctive mellowness, rich in flavor yet light in body, you'll see why we can say that **there is only one Canadian Club**...only *one* rare, imported whisky with this unique, appealing flavor all its own.

And—remember this—you can stick to this same whisky from start to finish. In Manhattan or Old-Fashioned before dinner, or in a highball or two after... enjoy Canadian Club today.

Canadian Club Blended Canadian Whisky. 90.4 proof. Hiram Walker & Sons Inc., Peoria, Illinois.

Canadian Club, 1939

A Tale of Two Countries

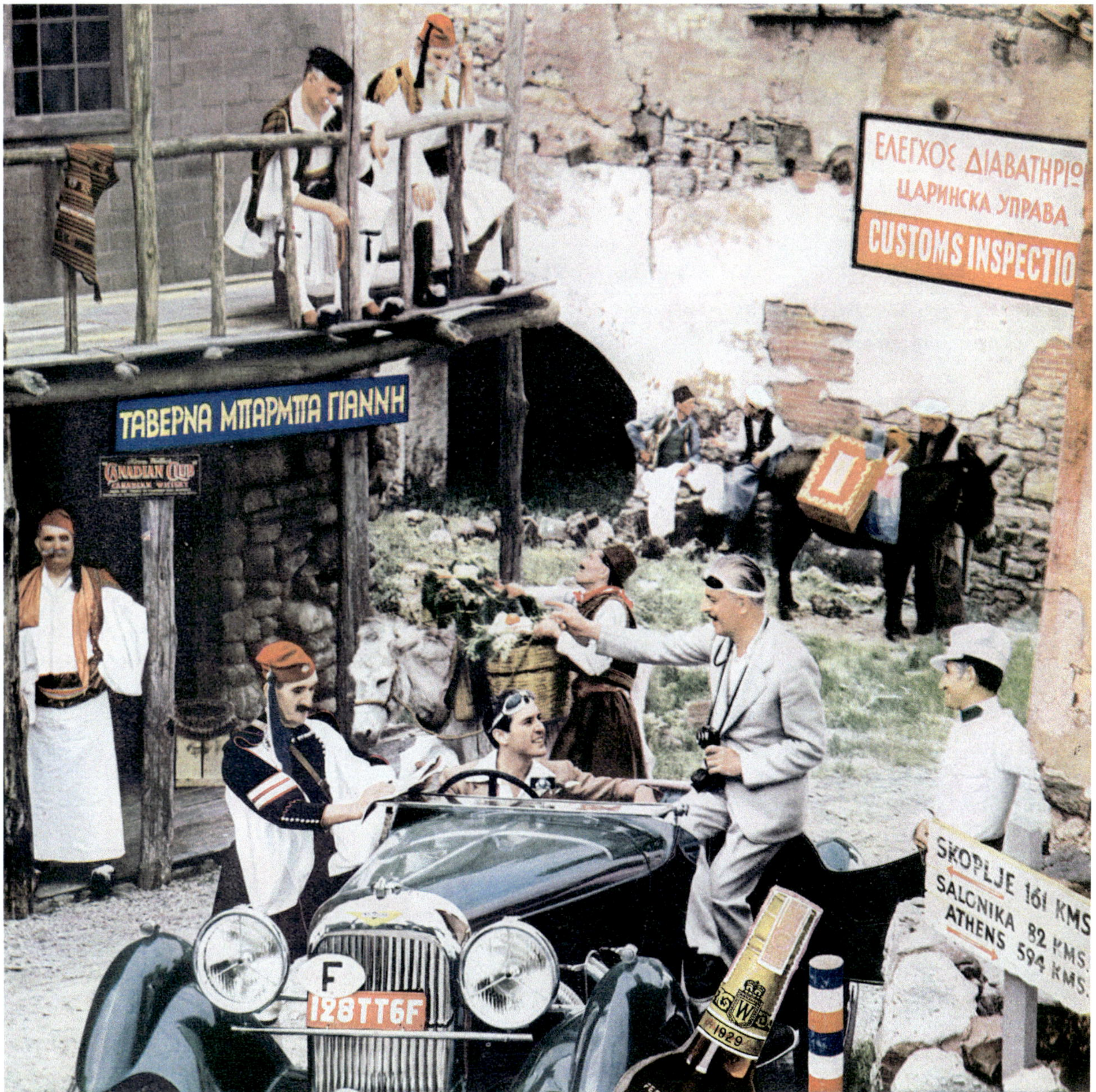

"Crossing borders was our specialty on our motor trip through the Balkans," writes H. T. Hudson of Texas. "When we arrived at the fourth one in two days, with our front wheels in Greece and our rear wheels in Yugoslavia, we were hot and thirsty. I wanted a whisky and soda—but my Greek dictionary offered the discouraging comment that the 'Greeks had no word for it'! Then I noticed that on the local inn there was a sign and it read 'Canadian Club'! It wasn't long before we were enjoying the mellow flavor of your very fine whisky. So it seems that, like us, the Greeks do have a word for it—or, rather two words . . . 'Canadian Club'! Lucky Greeks!"

"Canadian Club" is the only whisky of its kind. But Hiram Walker also makes ryes, bourbons, gins—whatever you like, at whatever you like to pay. At dealers, clubs, bars, hotels.

Hiram Walker & Sons, Peoria, Ill. Walkerville, Ont. Glasgow, Scotland

AMBASSADOR OF GOOD WILL TO 87 COUNTRIES

Hiram Walker's **"CANADIAN CLUB"**

Canadian Club, 1937

The *finale* to a perfect dinner

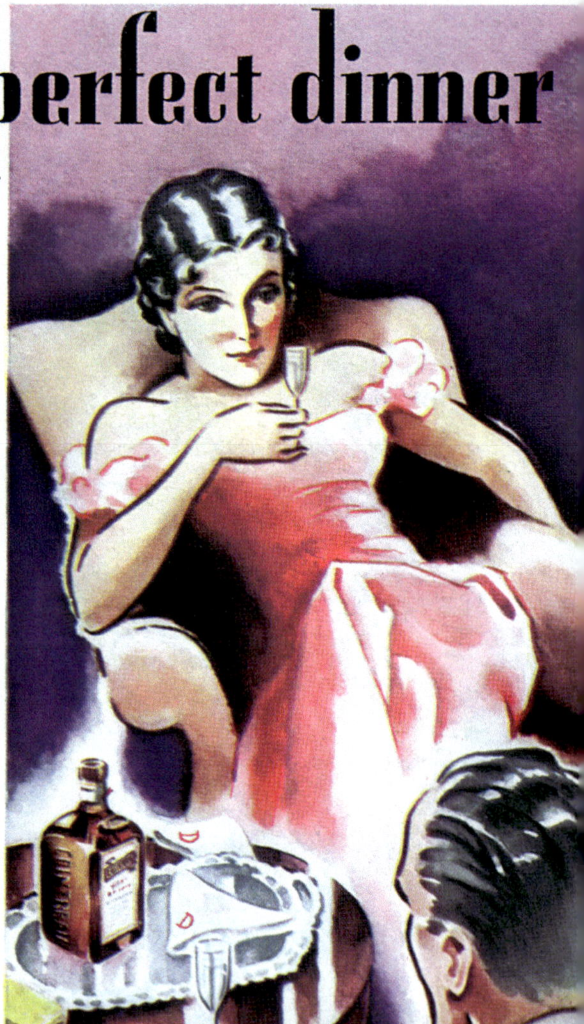

COINTREAU! . . . the after-dinner liqueur, just before stories start, to make tongues glib and wit sparkle.

COINTREAU! . . . the heart of the SIDE-CAR*, drink of the sophisticates.

COINTREAU! . . . make certain you ask for, and get, the original and genuine. Under any other name, it is never real "COINTREAU".

*RECIPE: ⅓ Cointreau, ⅓ Brandy (Rémy Martin, preferably) ⅓ Lemon Juice. Ice, shake, serve.

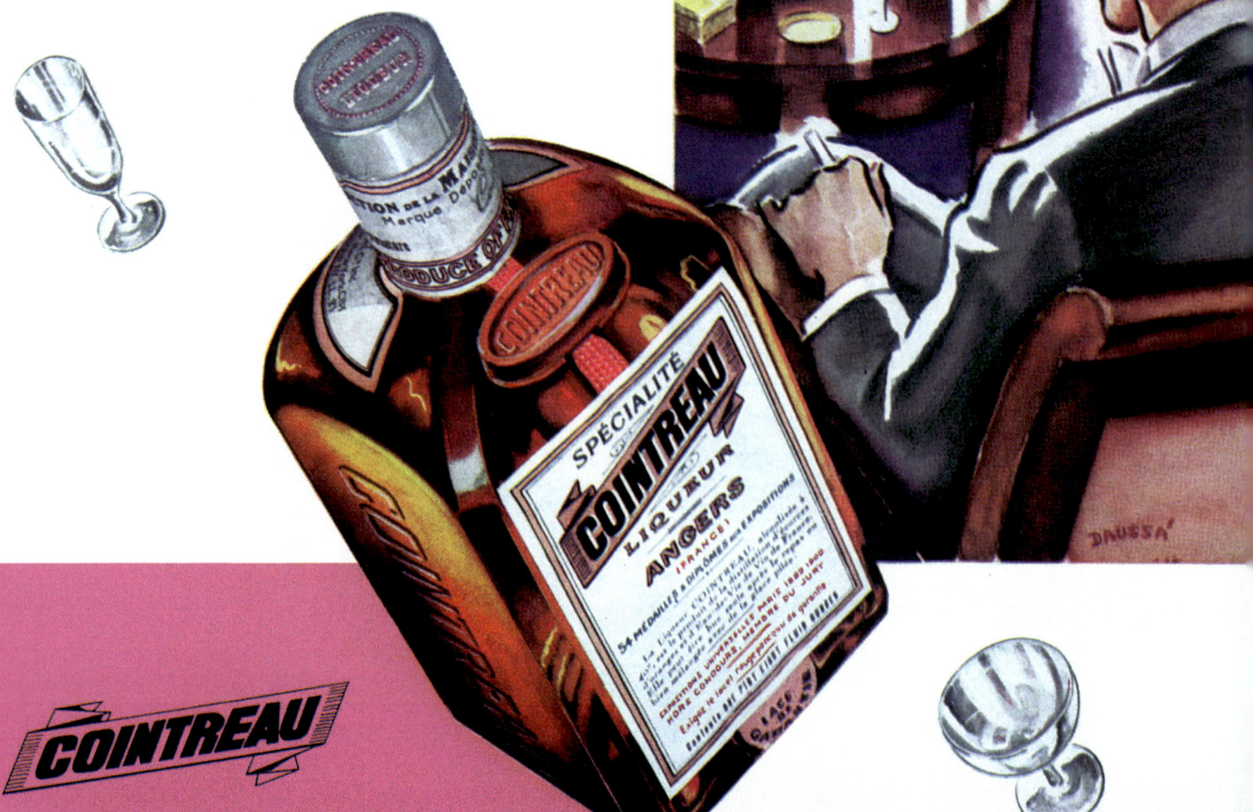

COINTREAU

Agents: BROWNE VINTNERS CO., INC. NEW YORK & SAN FRANCISCO

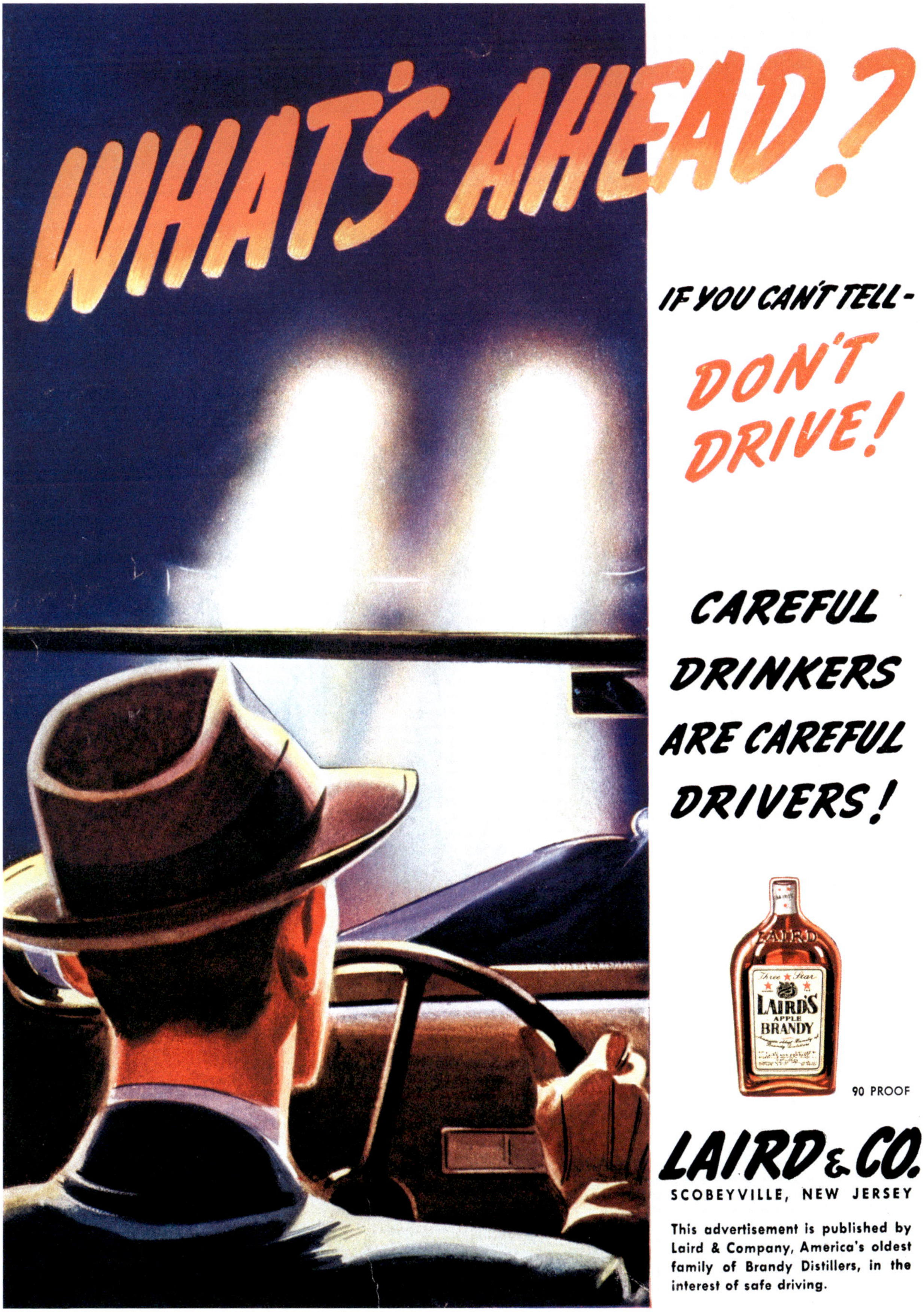

Cointreau, 1934 ◄

Laird's, 1939

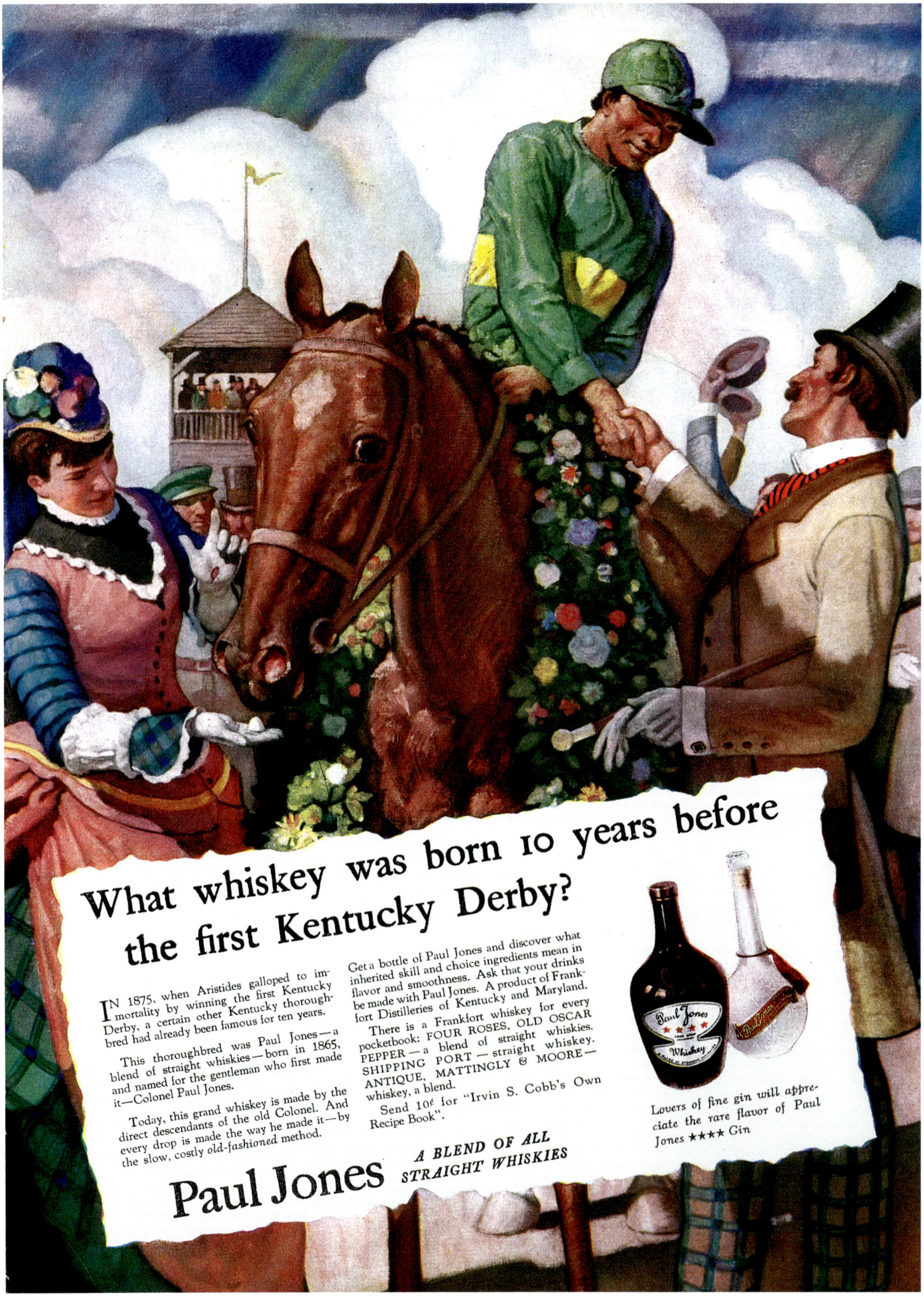
What whiskey was born 10 years before the first Kentucky Derby?
IN 1875, when Aristides galloped to immortality by winning the first Kentucky Derby, a certain other Kentucky thoroughbred had already been famous for ten years.
This thoroughbred was Paul Jones—a blend of straight whiskies—born in 1865, and named for the gentleman who first made it—Colonel Paul Jones.
Today, this grand whiskey is made by the direct descendants of the old Colonel. And every drop is made the way he made it—by the slow, costly old-fashioned method.
Get a bottle of Paul Jones and discover what inherited skill and choice ingredients mean in flavor and smoothness. Ask that your drinks be made with Paul Jones. A product of Frankfort Distilleries of Kentucky and Maryland.
There is a Frankfort whiskey for every pocketbook: FOUR ROSES, OLD OSCAR PEPPER—a blend of straight whiskies. SHIPPING PORT—straight whiskey. ANTIQUE, MATTINGLY & MOORE—whiskey, a blend.
Send 10¢ for "Irvin S. Cobb's Own Recipe Book".
Paul Jones
Whiskey
Lovers of fine gin will appreciate the rare flavor of Paul Jones ★★★★ Gin
Paul Jones
A BLEND OF ALL STRAIGHT WHISKIES

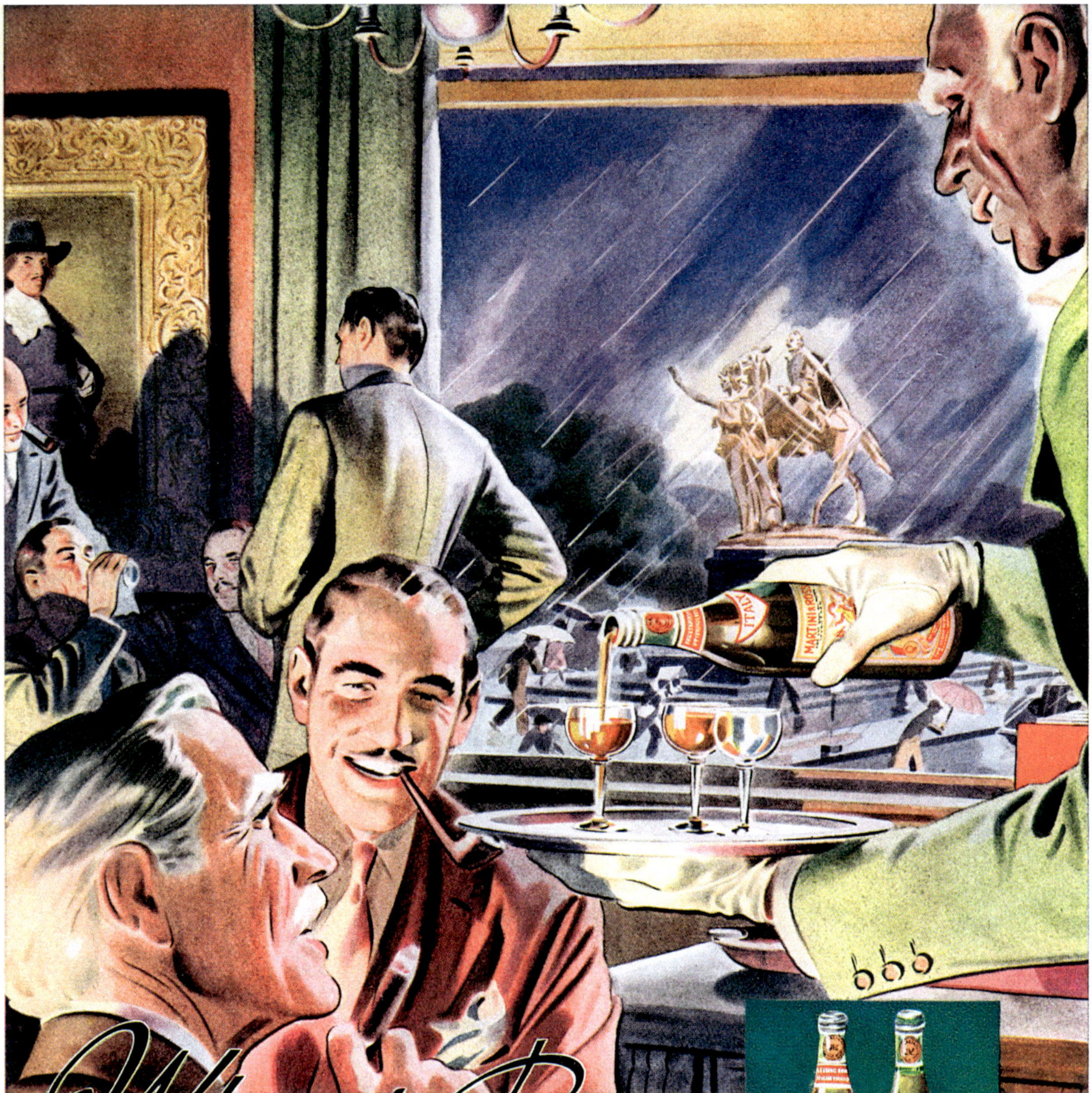

When it Pours–

CHEERFULNESS *Reigns* INSIDE

THERE'S a lot of sunshine in a bottle of vermouth—it seems as if you could taste it. Do you think that's imagination?—well, try a glass. Try it straight (chilled) so you can get the full spicy, bitter-sweet flavor—and you'll think of vineyards and herb farms under the warm Italian sun. Try it straight and you'll *find out what makes a cocktail taste good*. You'll realize why vermouth is enjoyed in every country on the globe—the great appetizer before meals, and one of the most universal of drinks.

Straight or in a cocktail it will make your lunch or dinner look more inviting. With soda, it's the conservative drink for a long evening—vermouth is versatile! But make sure you taste it straight—for vermouth, one of Europe's oldest drinks, is the newest drink of America! We mean Martini & Rossi, of course—it's the standard.

SOLE AGENTS FOR U. S. A., W. A. TAYLOR & CO., NEW YORK

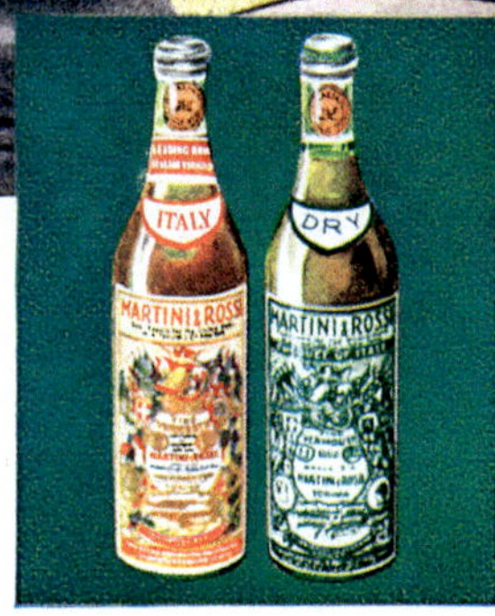

Alcohol by vol.
Italy, 15.95%
Dry, 18%

3 MOODS IN 1 BOTTLE
(Either Bottle)

1. Be gay—have a Manhattan or Martini.
2. Be moderate—have vermouth straight. Served chilled in cocktail glass.
3. Be conservative—have vermouth and soda. Mixed like a highball, using vermouth instead of whiskey.

MARTINI & ROSSI
VERMOUTH

Paul Jones, 1935 ◄

Martini & Rossi, 1939

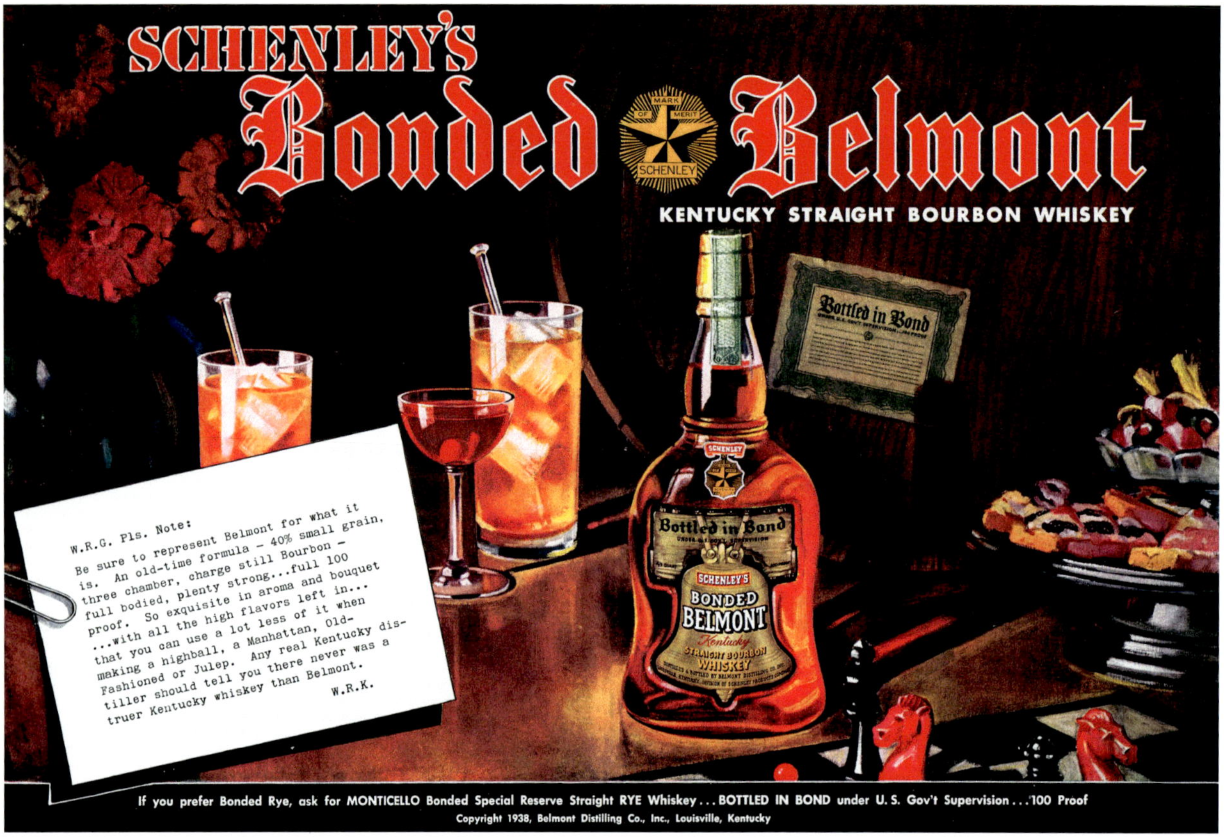

Bonded Belmont, 1938

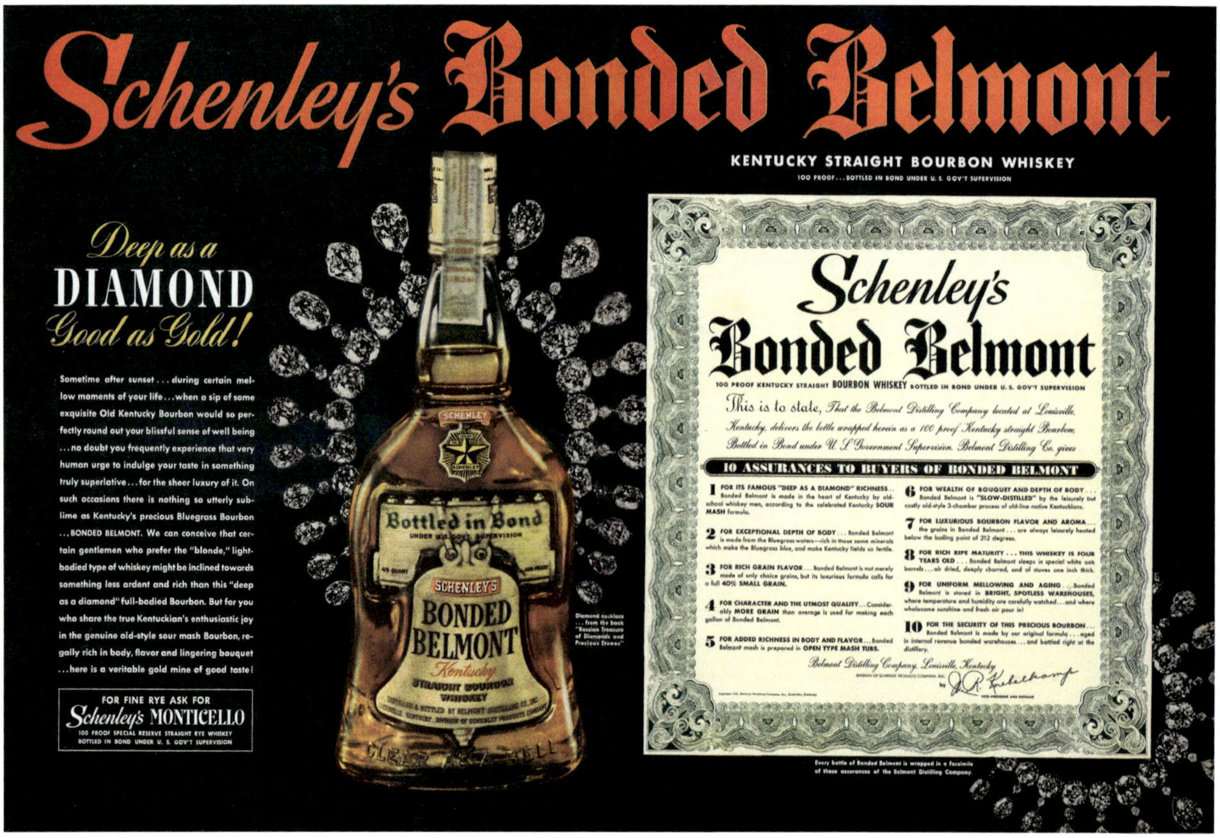

Bonded Belmont, 1938

▸ *Bonded Belmont, 1938*

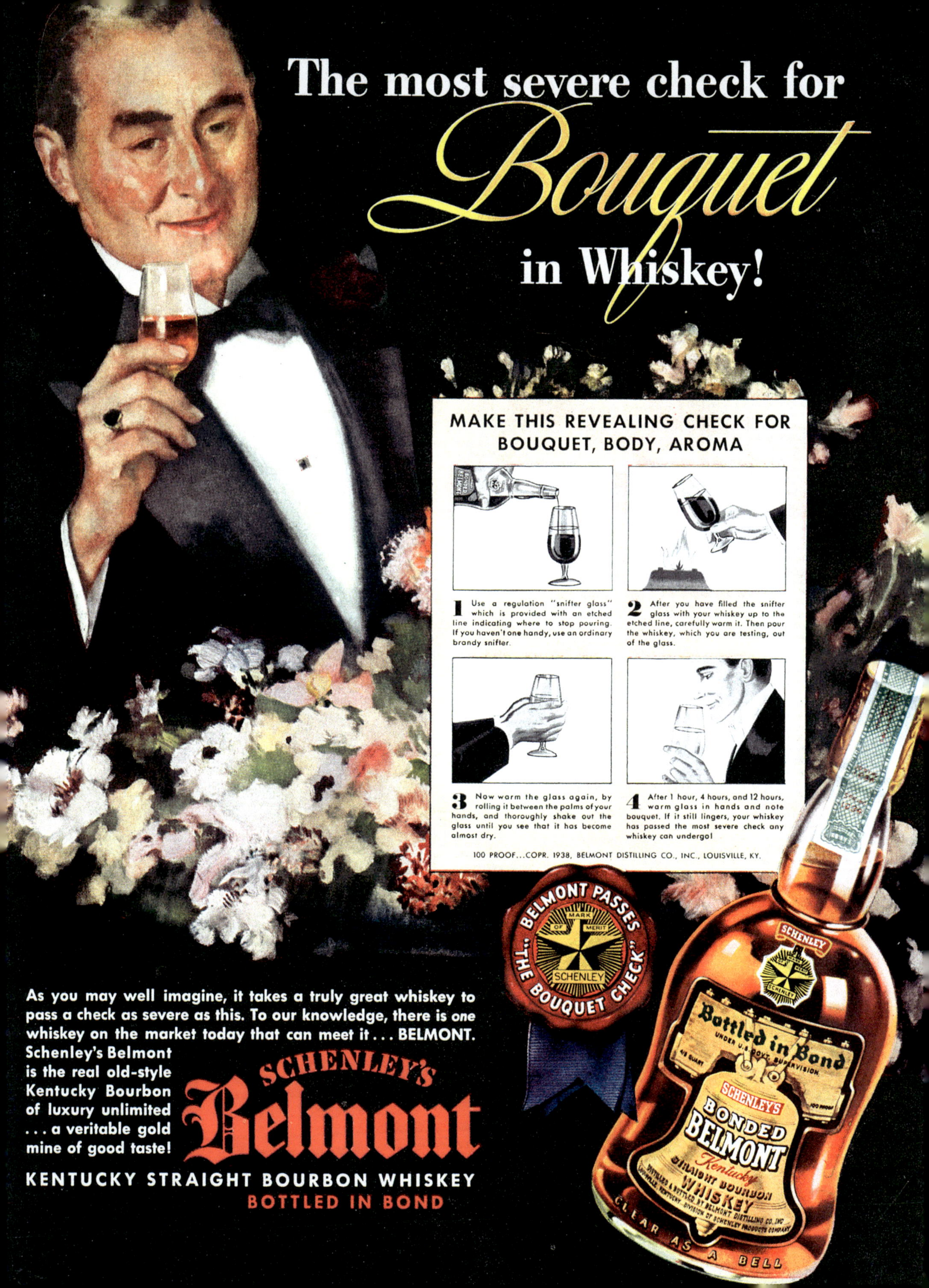

The most severe check for
Bouquet
in Whiskey!
MAKE THIS REVEALING CHECK FOR BOUQUET, BODY, AROMA
1 Use a regulation "snifter glass" which is provided with an etched line indicating where to stop pouring. If you haven't one handy, use an ordinary brandy snifter.
2 After you have filled the snifter glass with your whiskey up to the etched line, carefully warm it. Then pour the whiskey, which you are testing, out of the glass.
3 Now warm the glass again, by rolling it between the palms of your hands, and thoroughly shake out the glass until you see that it has become almost dry.
4 After 1 hour, 4 hours, and 12 hours, warm glass in hands and note bouquet. If it still lingers, your whiskey has passed the most severe check any whiskey can undergo!
100 PROOF...COPR. 1938, BELMONT DISTILLING CO., INC., LOUISVILLE, KY.
BELMONT PASSES "THE BOUQUET CHECK"
MARK OF MERIT
SCHENLEY
As you may well imagine, it takes a truly great whiskey to pass a check as severe as this. To our knowledge, there is one whiskey on the market today that can meet it . . . BELMONT.
Schenley's Belmont is the real old-style Kentucky Bourbon of luxury unlimited . . . a veritable gold mine of good taste!
SCHENLEY'S
Belmont
KENTUCKY STRAIGHT BOURBON WHISKEY
BOTTLED IN BOND
SCHENLEY
Bottled in Bond
UNDER U.S. GOVT. SUPERVISION
SCHENLEY'S
BONDED BELMONT
Kentucky
STRAIGHT BOURBON
WHISKEY
100 PROOF
CLEAR AS A BELL

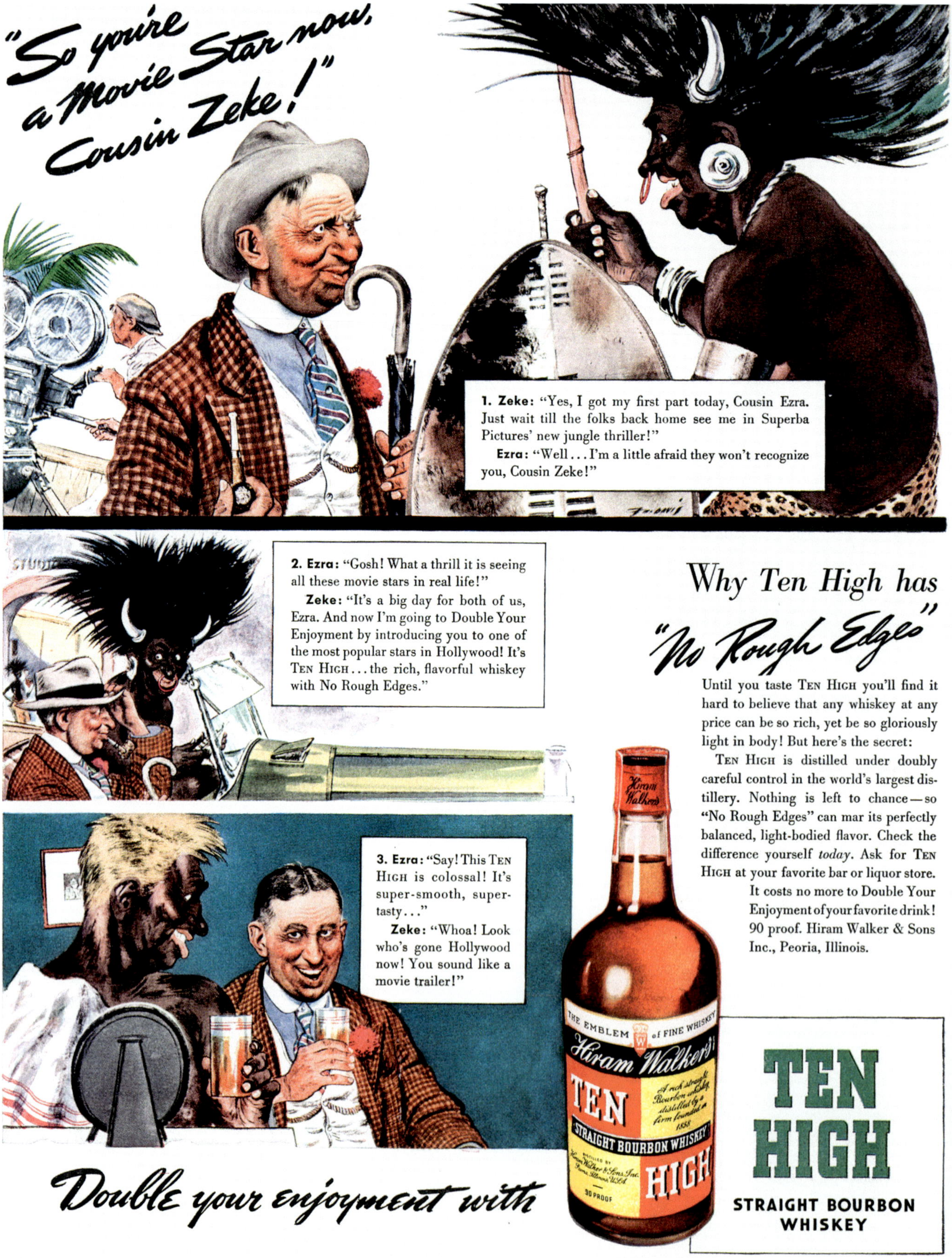

▲▶ *Ten High*, 1939

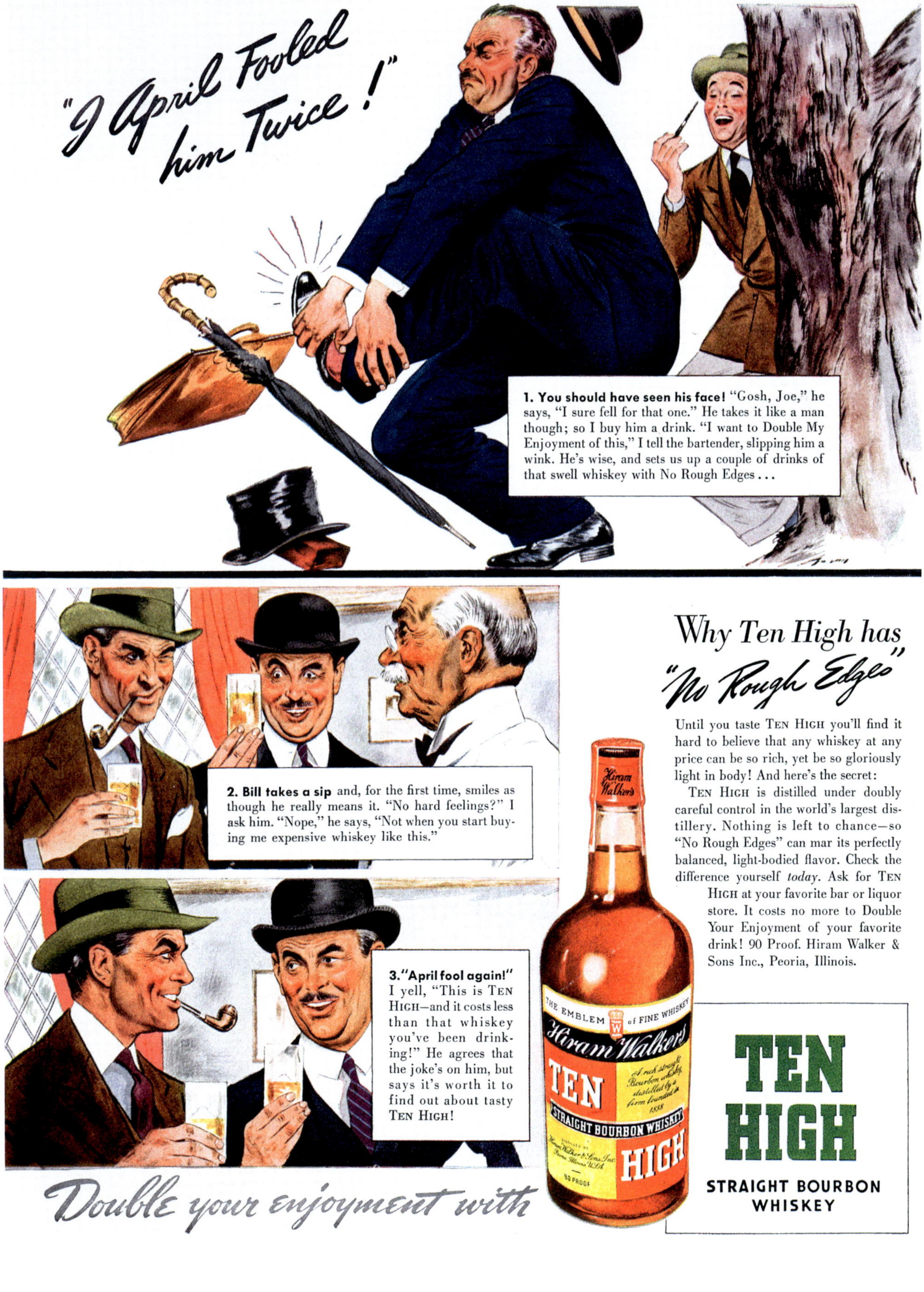
"I April Fooled him Twice!"
1. You should have seen his face! "Gosh, Joe," he says, "I sure fell for that one." He takes it like a man though; so I buy him a drink. "I want to Double My Enjoyment of this," I tell the bartender, slipping him a wink. He's wise, and sets us up a couple of drinks of that swell whiskey with No Rough Edges . . .
2. Bill takes a sip and, for the first time, smiles as though he really means it. "No hard feelings?" I ask him. "Nope," he says, "Not when you start buying me expensive whiskey like this."
3. "April fool again!" I yell, "This is TEN HIGH—and it costs less than that whiskey you've been drinking!" He agrees that the joke's on him, but says it's worth it to find out about tasty TEN HIGH!
Why Ten High has "No Rough Edges"
Until you taste TEN HIGH you'll find it hard to believe that any whiskey at any price can be so rich, yet be so gloriously light in body! And here's the secret:
TEN HIGH is distilled under doubly careful control in the world's largest distillery. Nothing is left to chance—so "No Rough Edges" can mar its perfectly balanced, light-bodied flavor. Check the difference yourself today. Ask for TEN HIGH at your favorite bar or liquor store. It costs no more to Double Your Enjoyment of your favorite drink! 90 Proof. Hiram Walker & Sons Inc., Peoria, Illinois.
Hiram Walker's
THE EMBLEM of FINE WHISKEY
Hiram Walker's
TEN
STRAIGHT BOURBON WHISKEY
HIGH
90 PROOF
Double your enjoyment with
TEN HIGH
STRAIGHT BOURBON WHISKEY

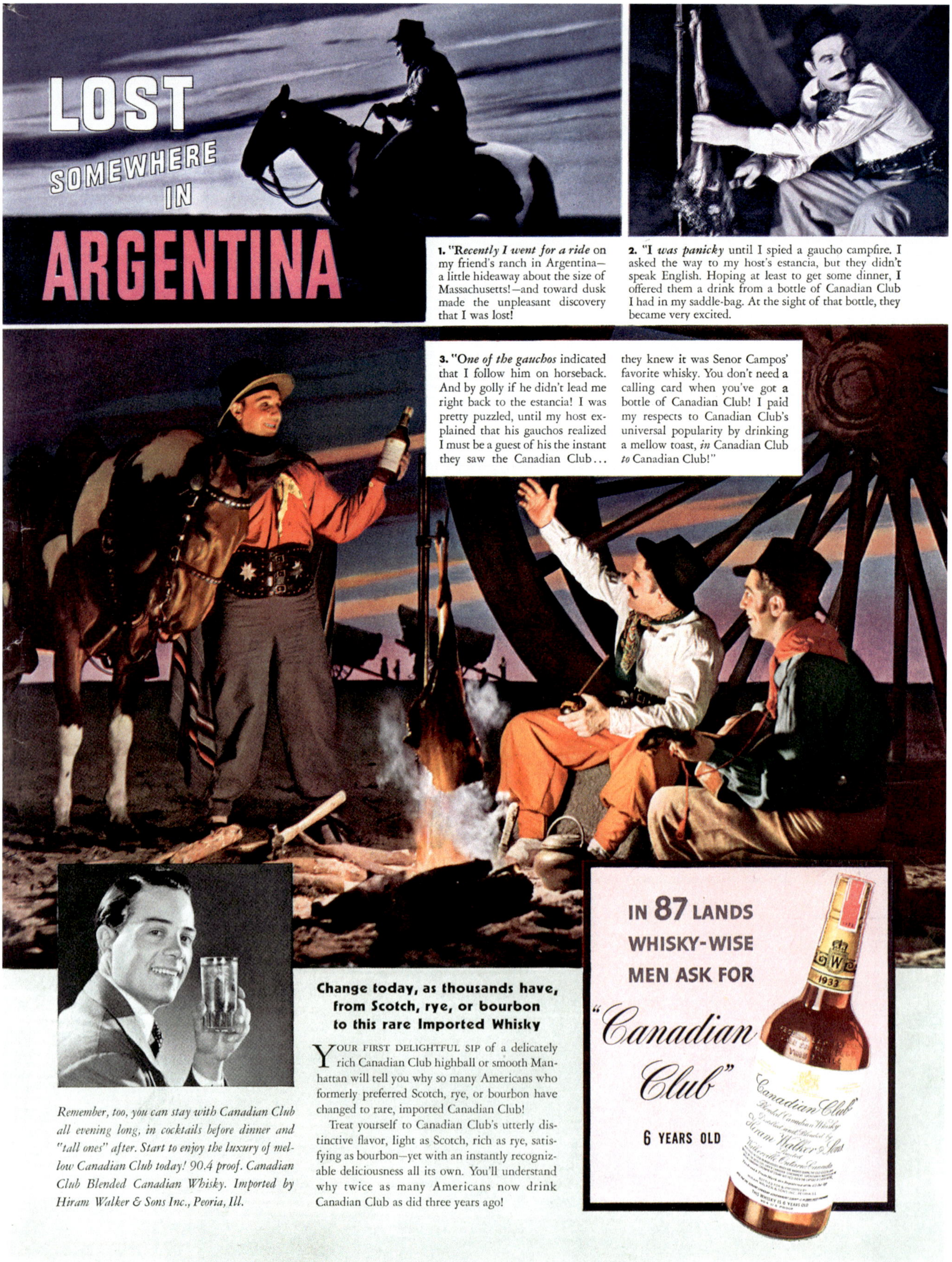

▲► *Canadian Club, 1939*

RARER THAN THE AUSTRALIAN GLORIA-MARIUS

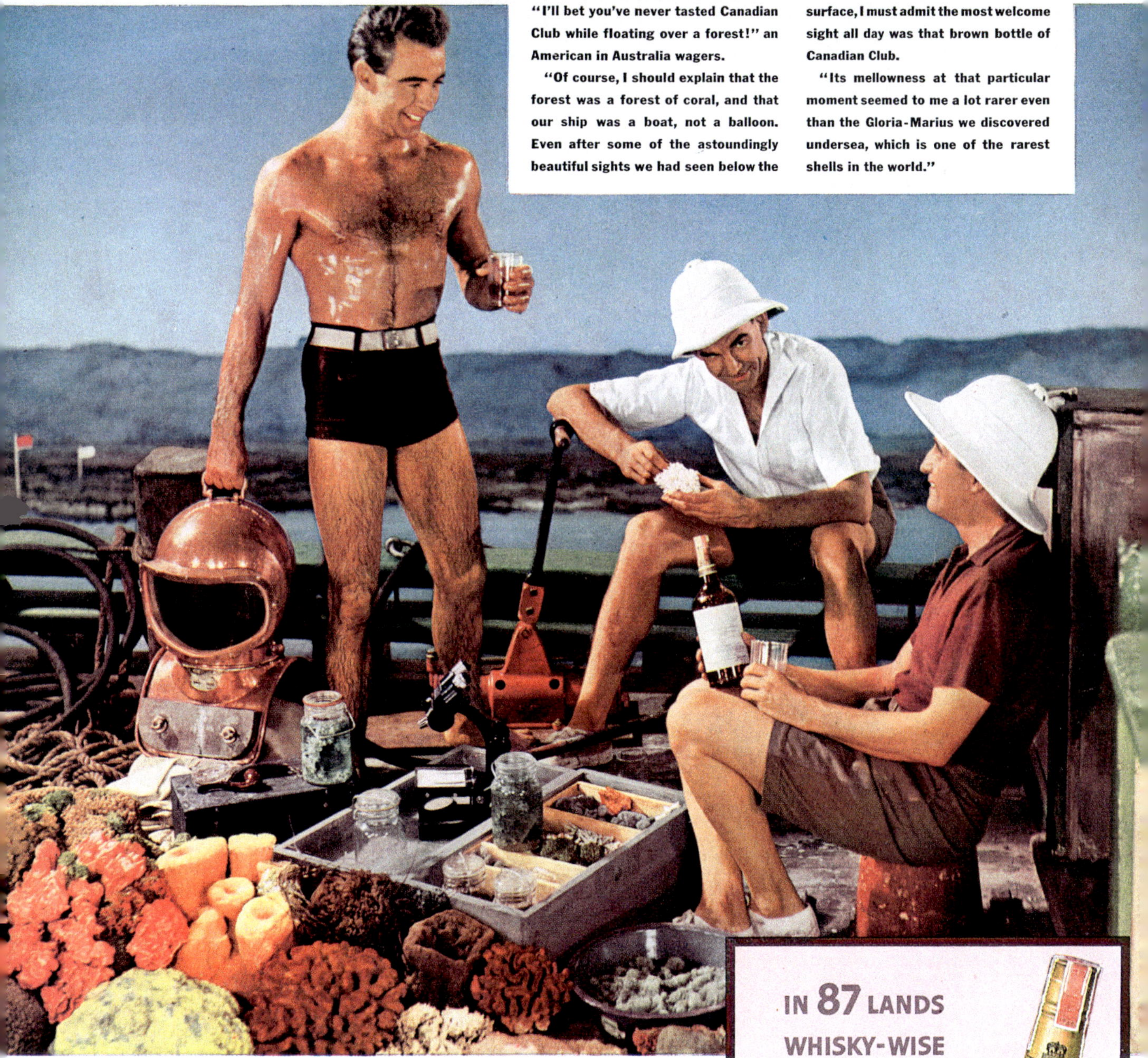

"I'll bet you've never tasted Canadian Club while floating over a forest!" an American in Australia wagers.

"Of course, I should explain that the forest was a forest of coral, and that our ship was a boat, not a balloon. Even after some of the astoundingly beautiful sights we had seen below the surface, I must admit the most welcome sight all day was that brown bottle of Canadian Club.

"Its mellowness at that particular moment seemed to me a lot rarer even than the Gloria-Marius we discovered undersea, which is one of the rarest shells in the world."

Why so many Americans have changed to this Imported Whisky...

In 87 countries Canadian Club is a favorite. In London itself and throughout the British Isles it is the **leading imported whisky.**

But of more interest to you is this fact: many *Americans* who formerly preferred Scotch, bourbon, or rye have changed to Canadian Club. Today, twice as many *Americans* now drink Canadian Club at home and at the bar as did only two years ago! **Try Canadian Club yourself**—try it in a "show-me" mood. Experience its distinctive mellowness, rich yet light. You'll see why we can say that **there is only one Canadian Club**... only one rare, imported whisky with this unique, appealing taste all its own. Start to enjoy Canadian Club today.

IN 87 LANDS
WHISKY-WISE
MEN ASK FOR
"Canadian Club"
6 YEARS OLD

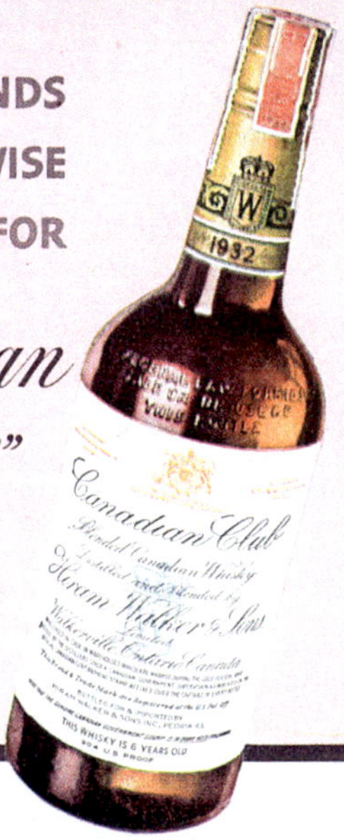

Stay with Canadian Club! In Manhattan or Old-Fashioned before dinner, or a highball or two after. Canadian Club Blended Canadian Whisky. 90.4 proof. Imported by Hiram Walker & Sons Inc., Peoria, Illinois.

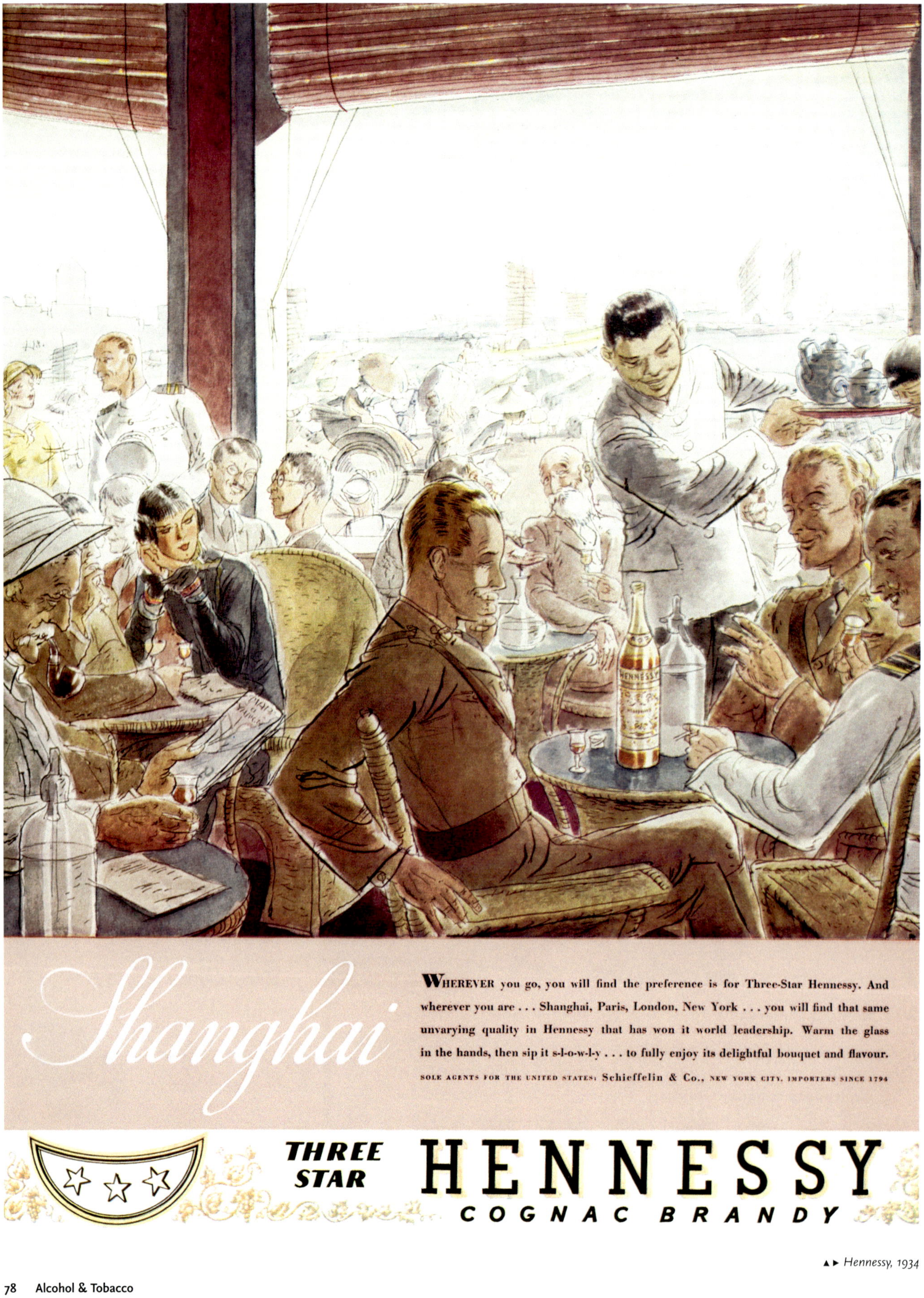

▲▶ *Hennessy, 1934*

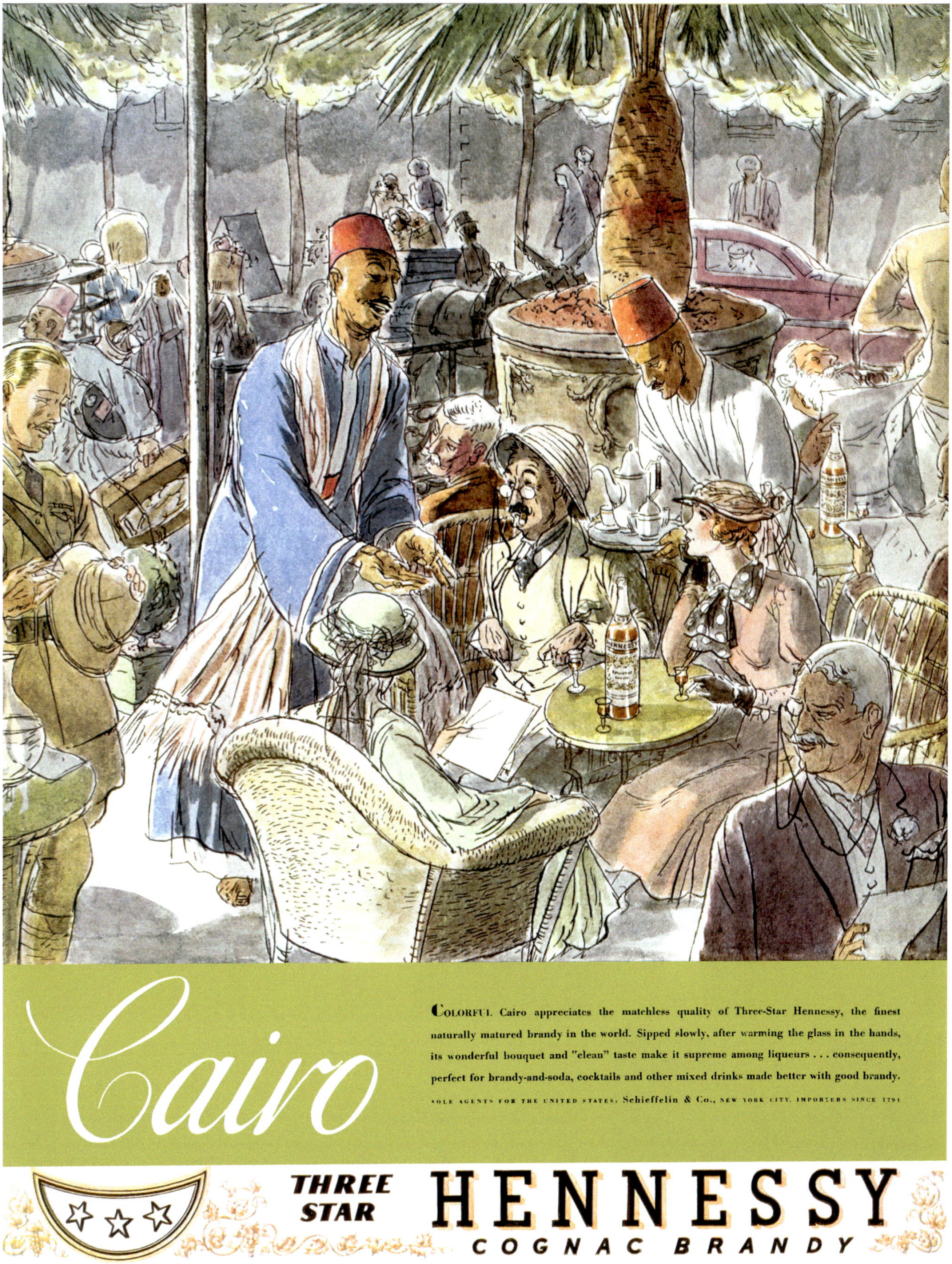
Cairo
COLORFUL Cairo appreciates the matchless quality of Three-Star Hennessy, the finest naturally matured brandy in the world. Sipped slowly, after warming the glass in the hands, its wonderful bouquet and "clean" taste make it supreme among liqueurs . . . consequently, perfect for brandy-and-soda, cocktails and other mixed drinks made better with good brandy.
SOLE AGENTS FOR THE UNITED STATES: Schieffelin & Co., NEW YORK CITY. IMPORTERS SINCE 1794
THREE STAR
HENNESSY
COGNAC BRANDY

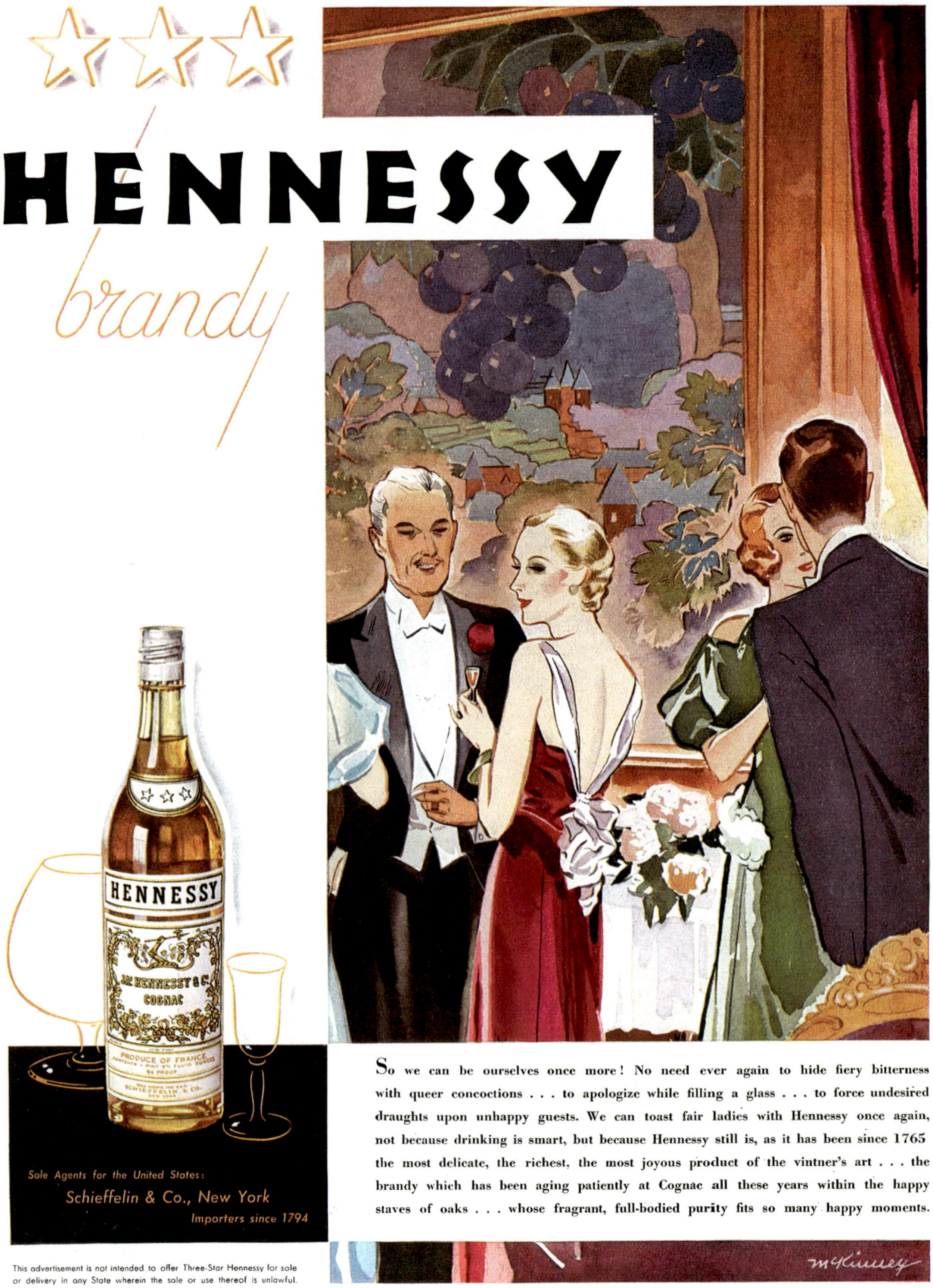

Hennessy, 1933

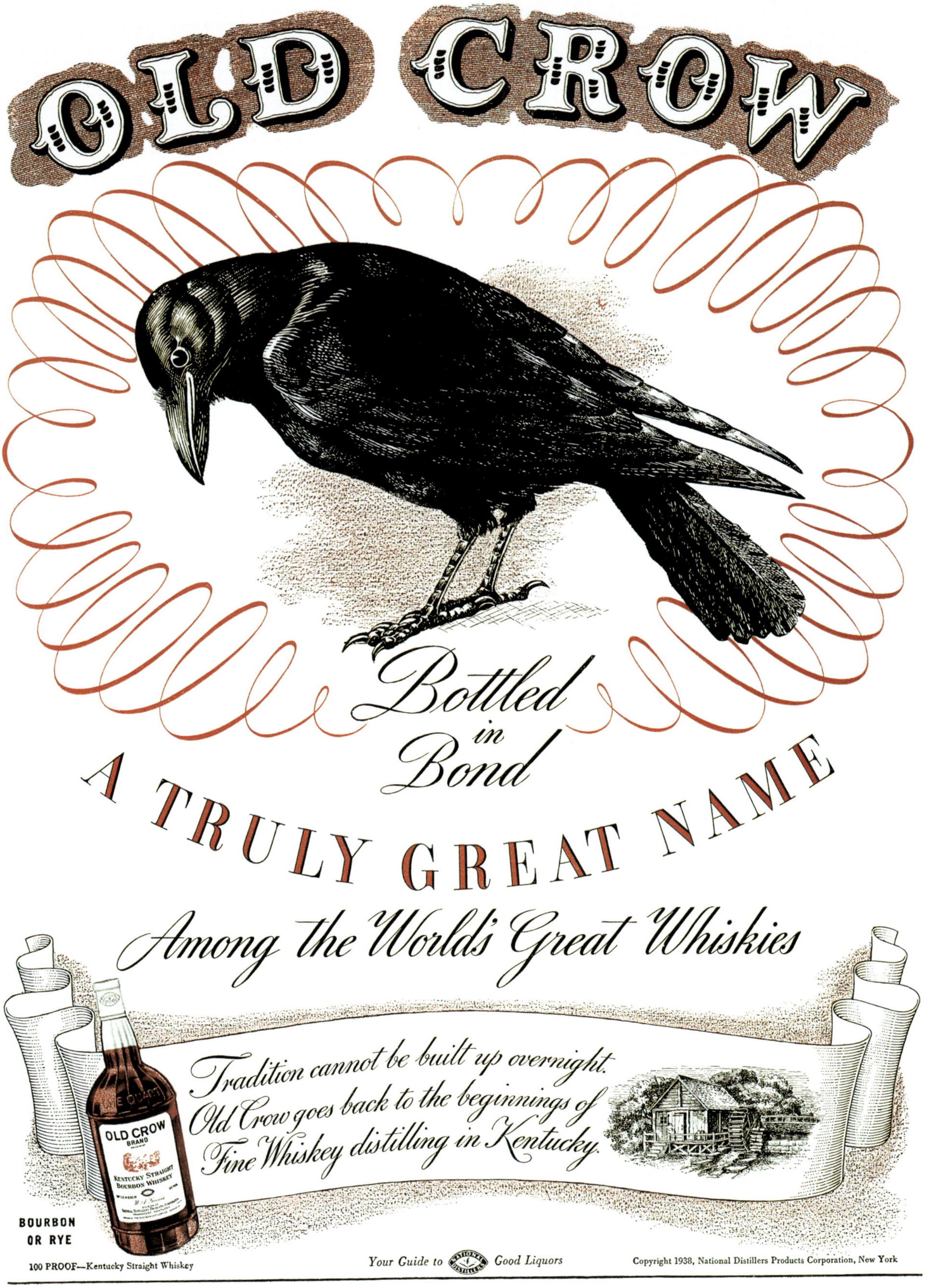

Old Crow, 1938

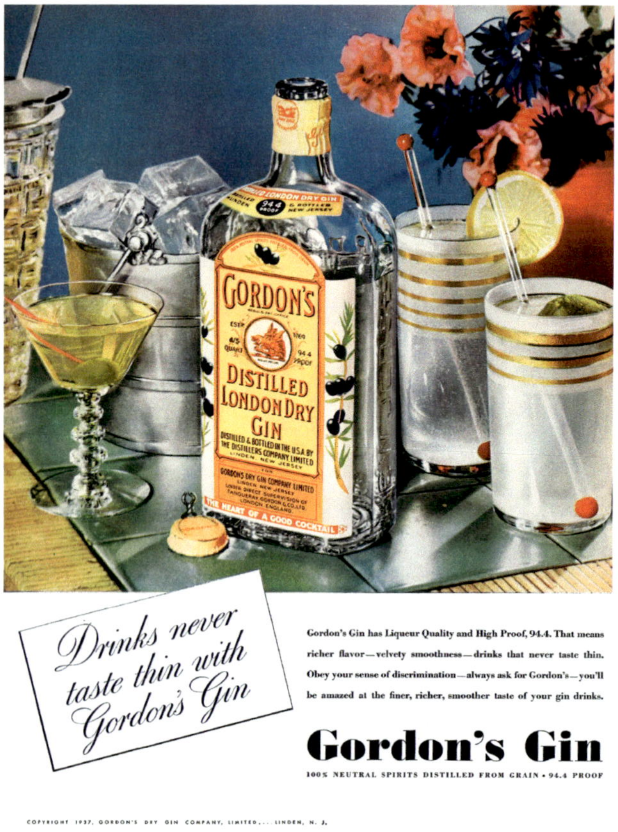

Gordon's Gin, 1937

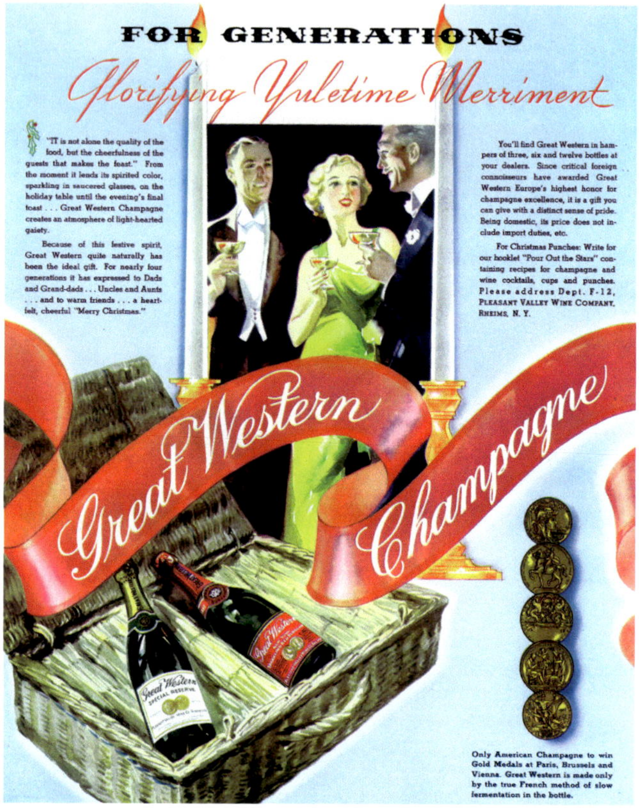

Great Western Champagne, 1935

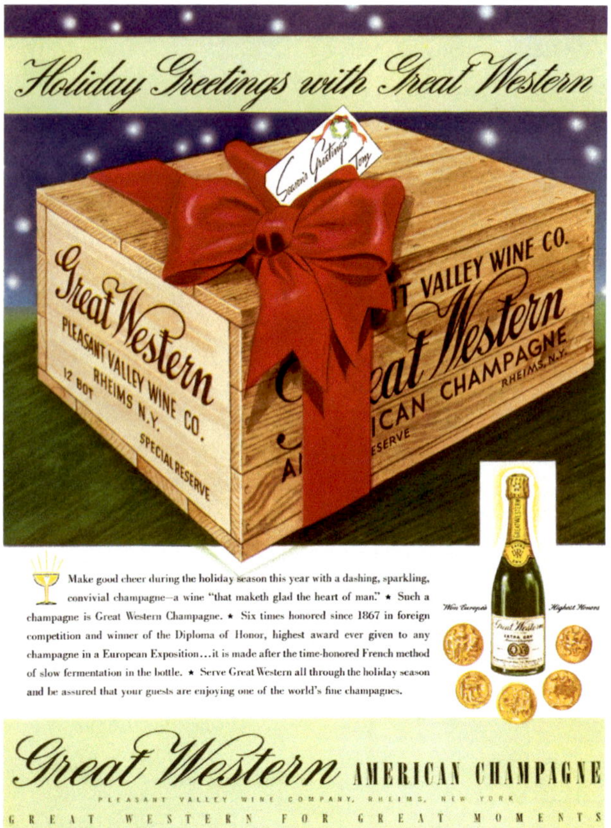

Great Western Champagne, 1937

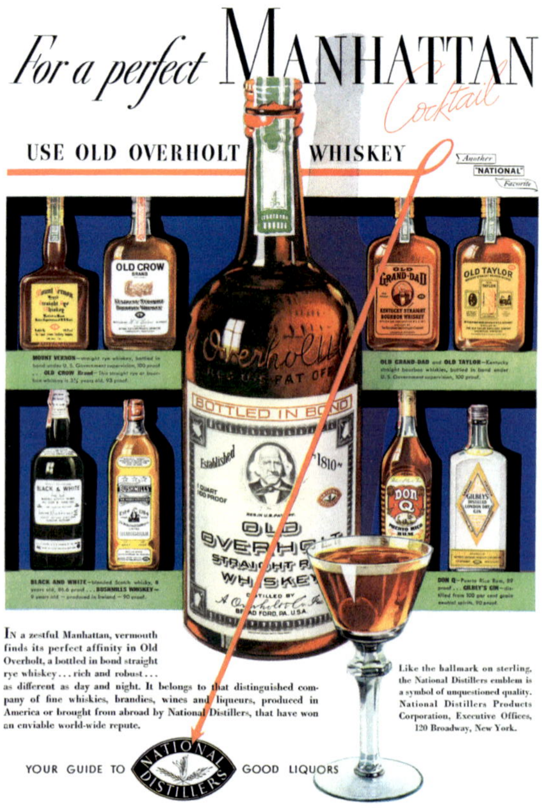

Old Overholt, 1937

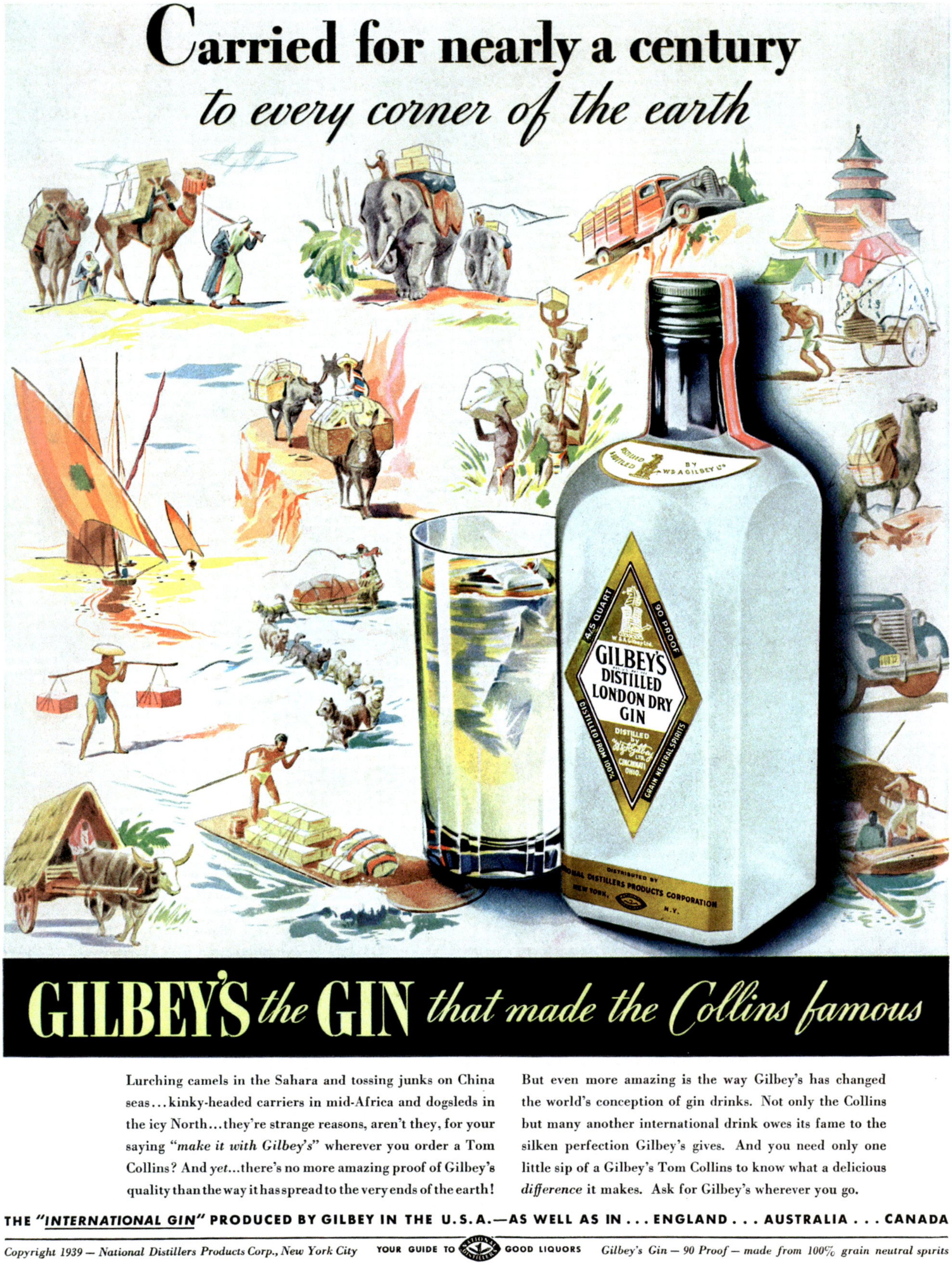

Gilbey's Gin, 1939

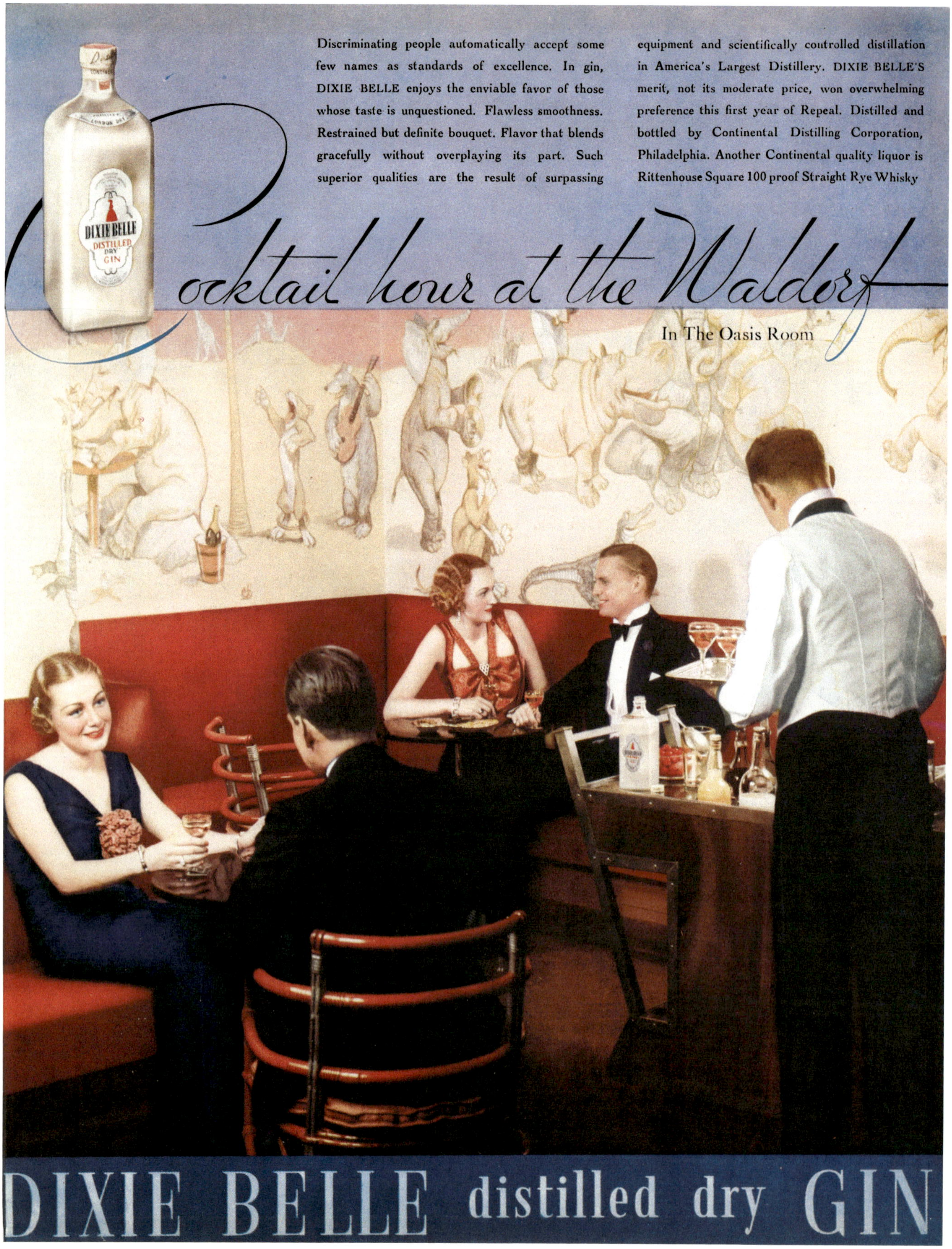

▲▶ *Dixie Belle Gin, 1934*

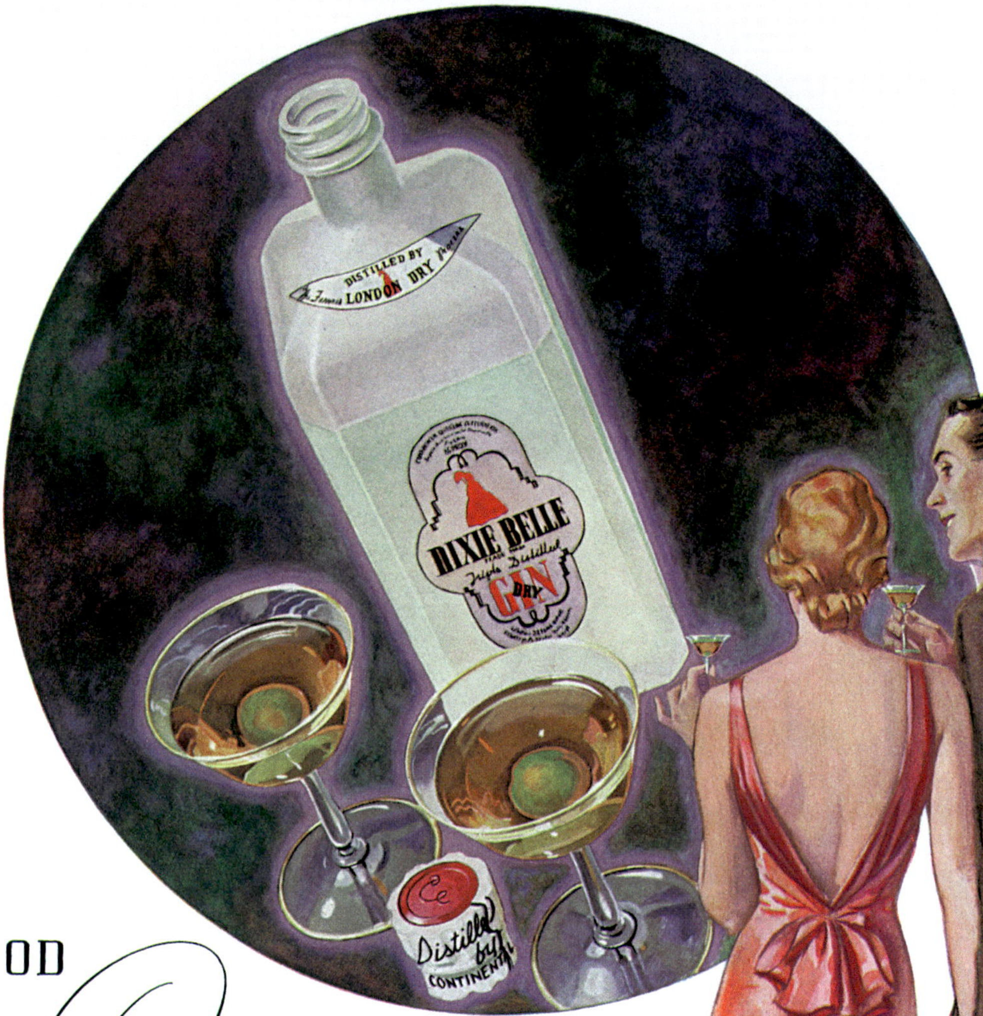

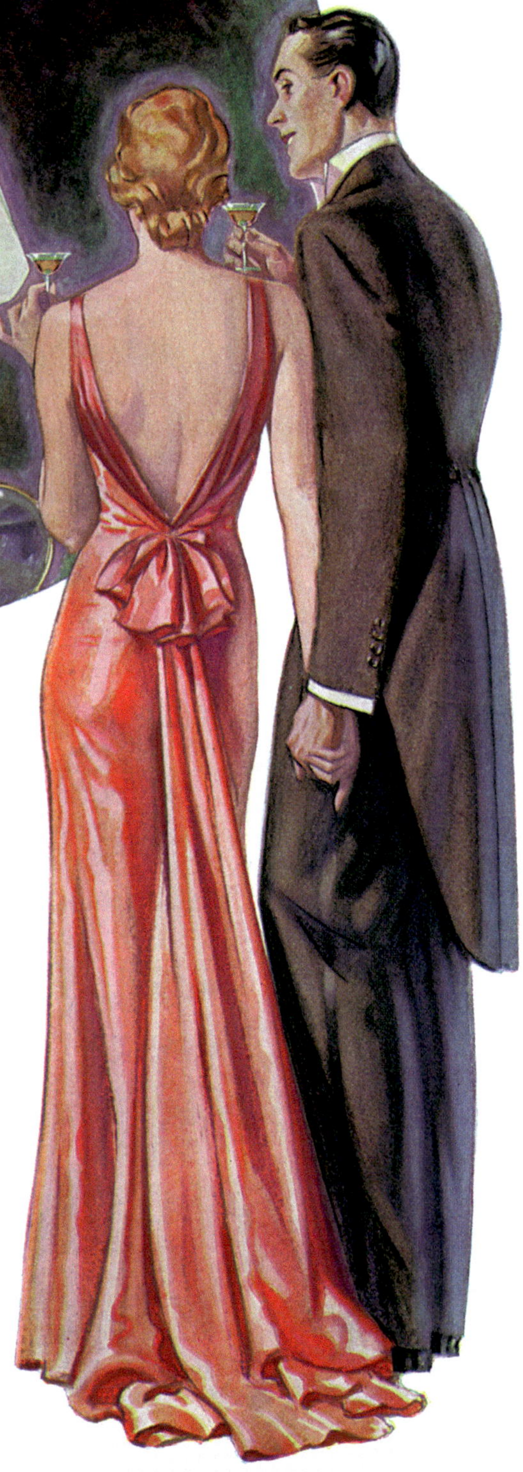

THE GOOD *Companion*

Among those whose standards demand more than superficial merit, the distinguished quality of DIXIE BELLE Dry Gin is a revelation. Such refinement of bouquet, such gracious smoothness, such readiness to merge discreetly with your chosen cocktails and highballs, are instant tokens of a gin of the highest character . . . "Distilled by Continental."

Also distillers of Sweep Stakes, Snug Harbor and Envoy Club Blended Whiskies and Cavalier Distilled Dry Gin

CONTINENTAL DISTILLING CORPORATION, Philadelphia

This advertisement is not intended to offer alcoholic beverages for sale or delivery in any state wherein the sale or use thereof is unlawful.

DIXIE BELLE

DISTILLED DRY

Gin

And the winner is...

The Celebrity Sell

In copy impossible to print by today's standards, advertisers trumpeted the perceived benefits of smoking to consumers of the 1930s. In this ad targeted at female smokers, Miss Lombard's voice teacher advises her to smoke as much as she wants without fear of damaging her throat. This claim is reinforced by "experts" who state that Luckies® "toasted" technology removes certain throat irritants found in tobacco. Surrounded by all this glamour and vague hints of a healthy pastime, who would not be seduced into smoking?

Paffen mit Prominenten

Heute undenkbar, aber dieser Werbetext preist die Vorzüge des Rauchens! Miss Lombards Lehrer für Sprech- und Atemtechnik, so möchte diese Anzeige einer weiblichen Klientel weismachen, habe garantiert, dass sie ohne Sorge um ihre Stimme so viel rauchen könne, wie sie wolle. Unterstrichen wird die Behauptung durch „Expertenstimmen", die der speziellen Verarbeitungstechnik der Luckies bescheinigen, sie entziehe dem Tabak die Kehle reizende Schadstoffe. Bei so viel Glamour und vagen Hinweisen auf einen gesundheitlich unbedenklichen Zeitvertreib, wer würde sich da keine anzünden wollen?

La célébrité fait vendre

Avec des textes qui nous paraissent aujourd'hui impensables, les annonceurs vantaient aux consommateurs des années 30 ce qu'on croyait être les bienfaits du tabac. Dans cette publicité s'adressant aux fumeuses, le professeur de chant de Miss Lombard affirme qu'elle peut fumer autant qu'elle veut sans craindre pour sa gorge. Cette déclaration est appuyée par des « experts » selon lesquels la technologie de « torréfaction » de Luckies® élimine certains irritants de la gorge présents dans le tabac. Devant tant de glamour, comment ne pas céder à une tentation si saine ?

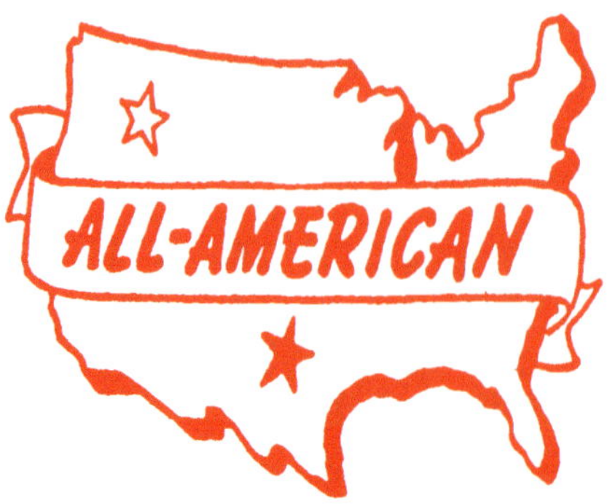

Lucky Strike, 1937

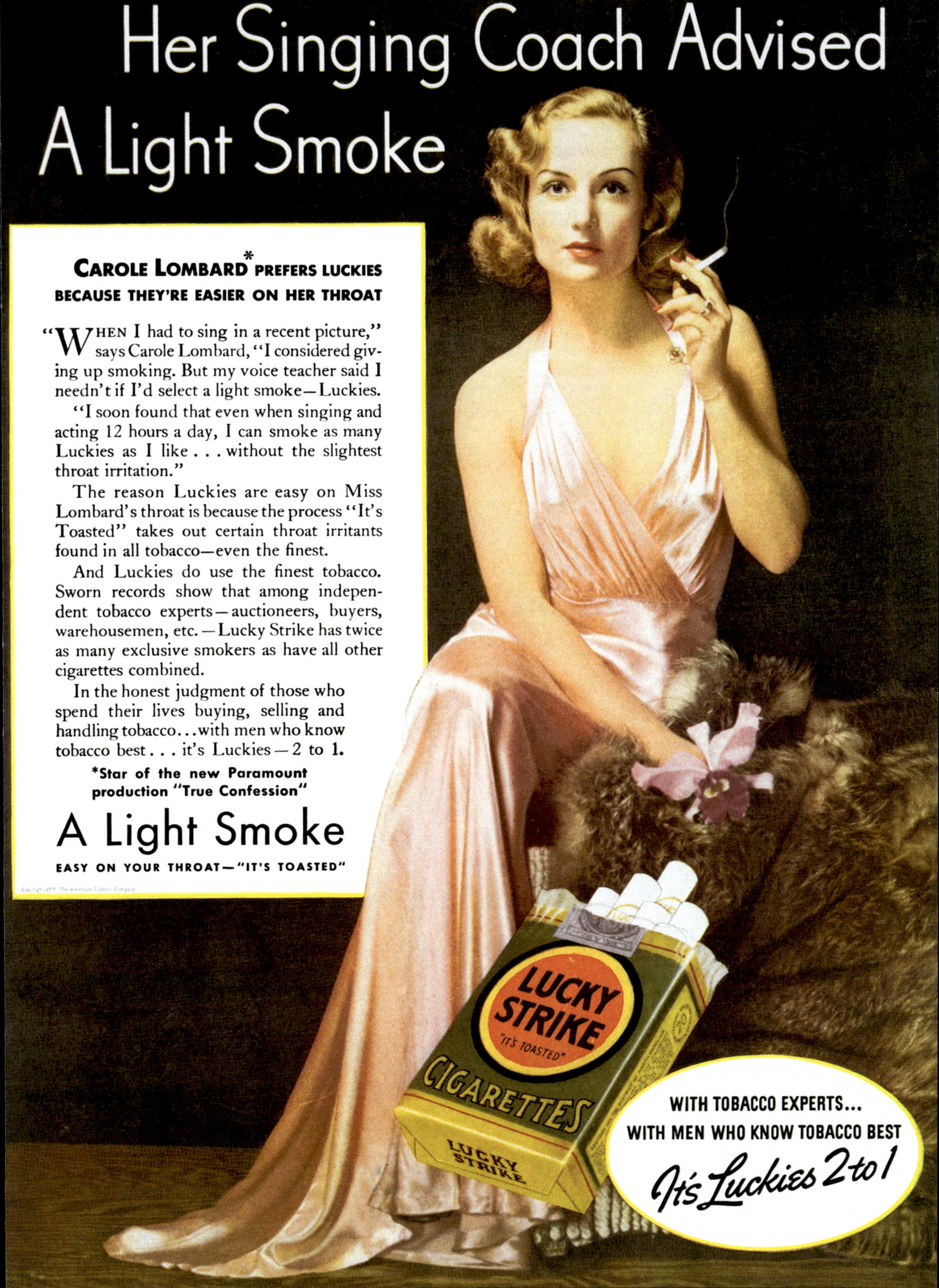
Her Singing Coach Advised
A Light Smoke
CAROLE LOMBARD* PREFERS LUCKIES
BECAUSE THEY'RE EASIER ON HER THROAT
"WHEN I had to sing in a recent picture," says Carole Lombard, "I considered giving up smoking. But my voice teacher said I needn't if I'd select a light smoke—Luckies.
"I soon found that even when singing and acting 12 hours a day, I can smoke as many Luckies as I like . . . without the slightest throat irritation."
The reason Luckies are easy on Miss Lombard's throat is because the process "It's Toasted" takes out certain throat irritants found in all tobacco—even the finest.
And Luckies do use the finest tobacco. Sworn records show that among independent tobacco experts—auctioneers, buyers, warehousemen, etc.—Lucky Strike has twice as many exclusive smokers as have all other cigarettes combined.
In the honest judgment of those who spend their lives buying, selling and handling tobacco...with men who know tobacco best . . . it's Luckies—2 to 1.
*Star of the new Paramount production "True Confession"
A Light Smoke
EASY ON YOUR THROAT—"IT'S TOASTED"
LUCKY STRIKE
"IT'S TOASTED"
CIGARETTES
LUCKY STRIKE
WITH TOBACCO EXPERTS...
WITH MEN WHO KNOW TOBACCO BEST
It's Luckies 2 to 1

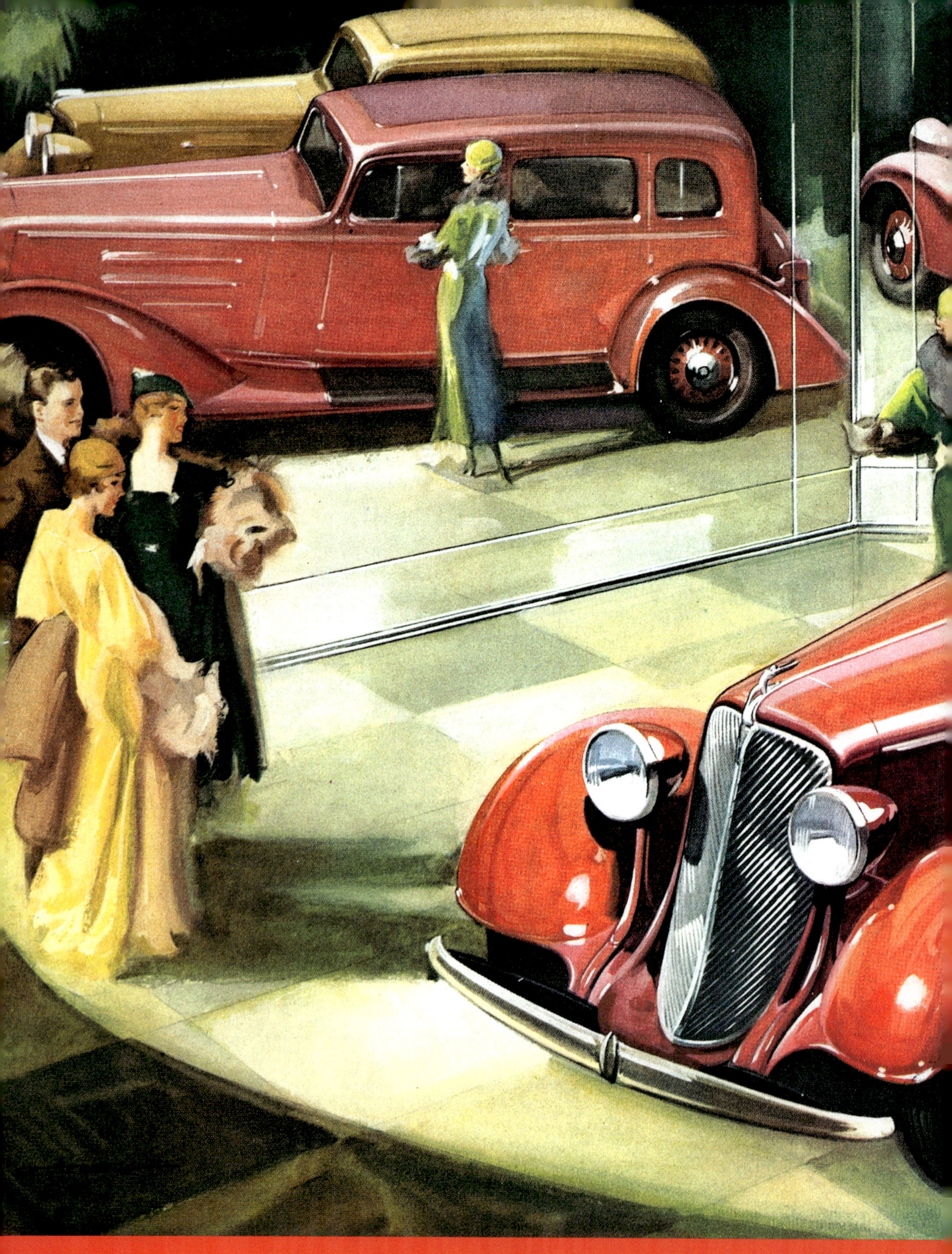

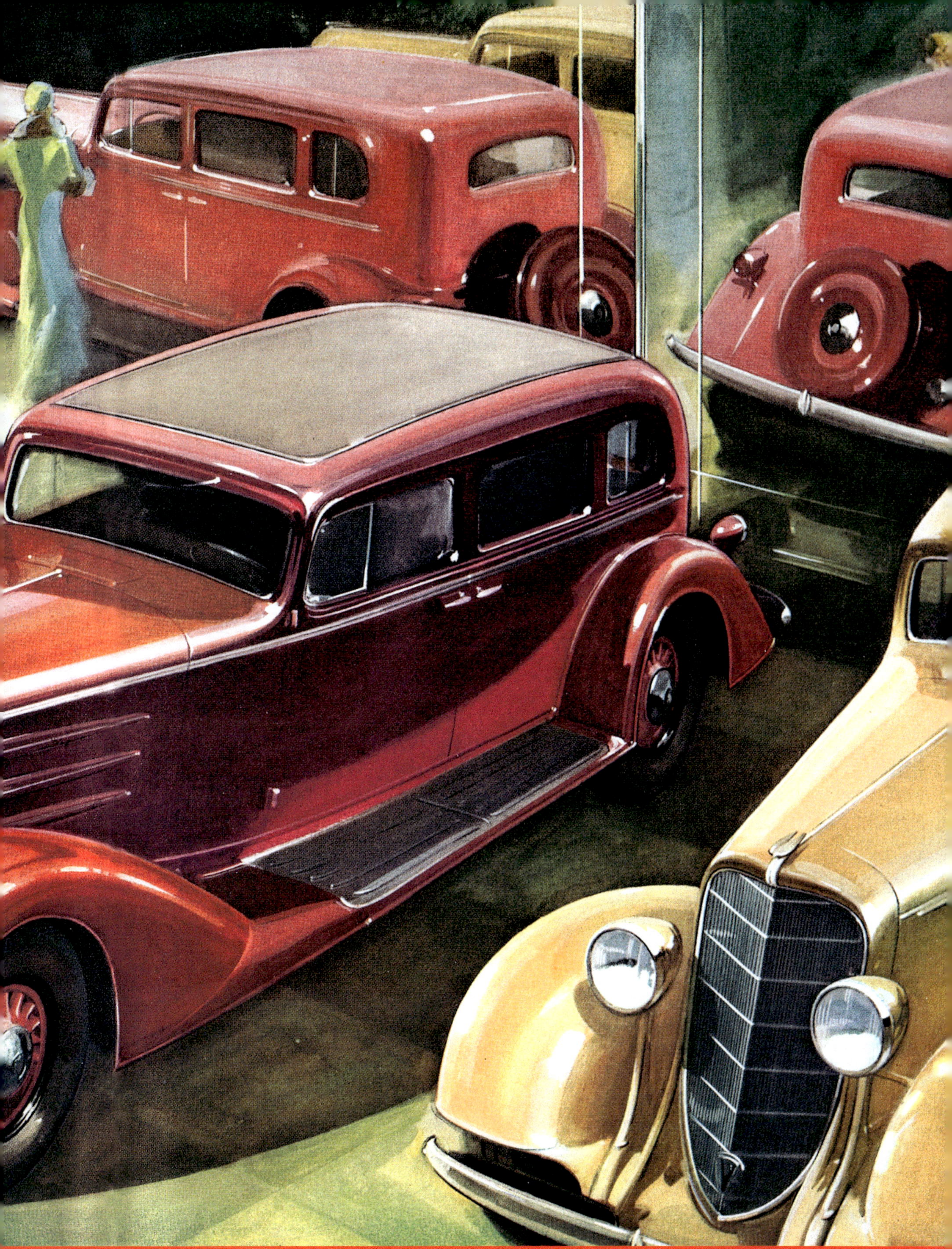

A FAMOUS NAME . . . A FINER CA

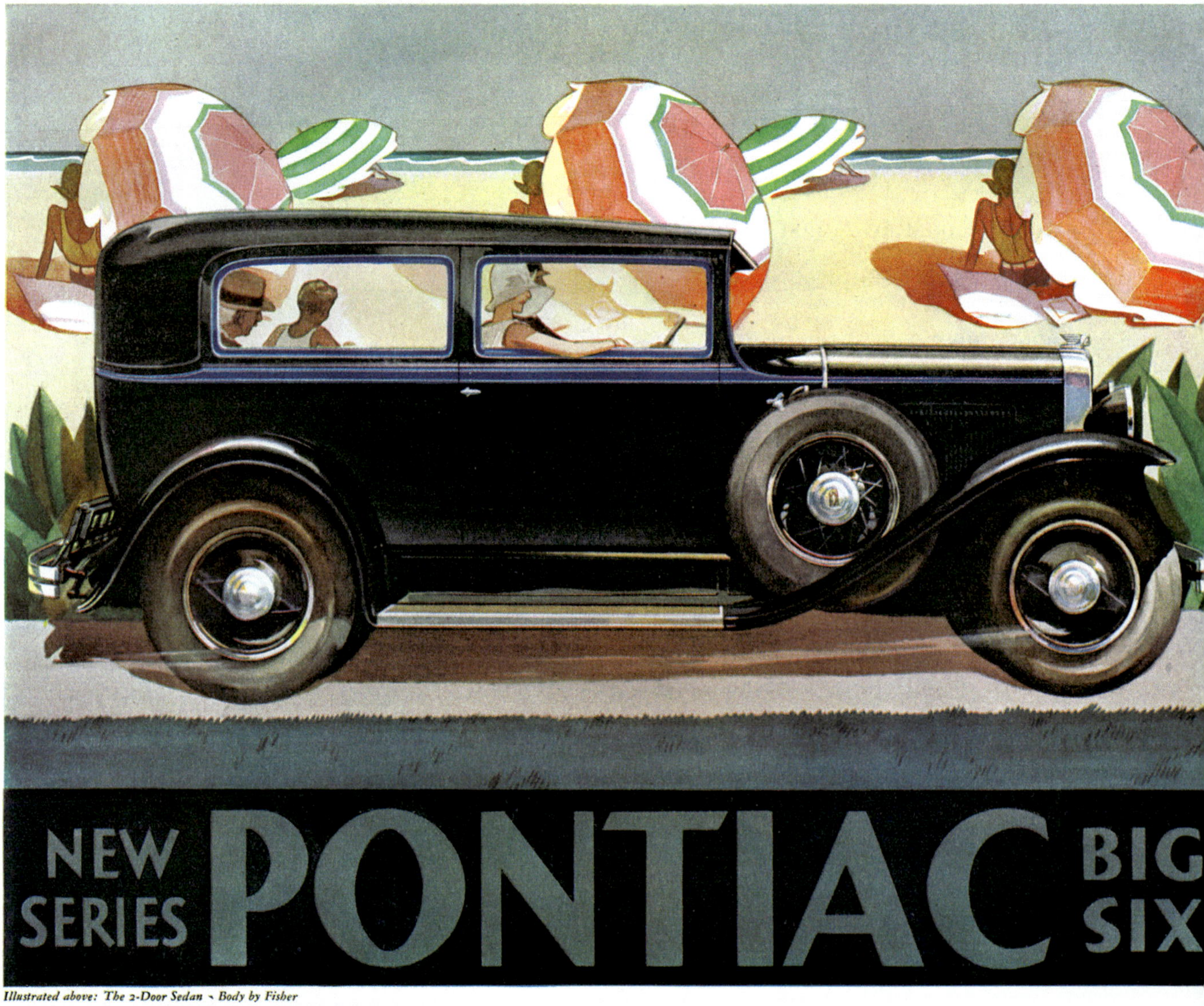

Illustrated above: The 2-Door Sedan · Body by Fisher

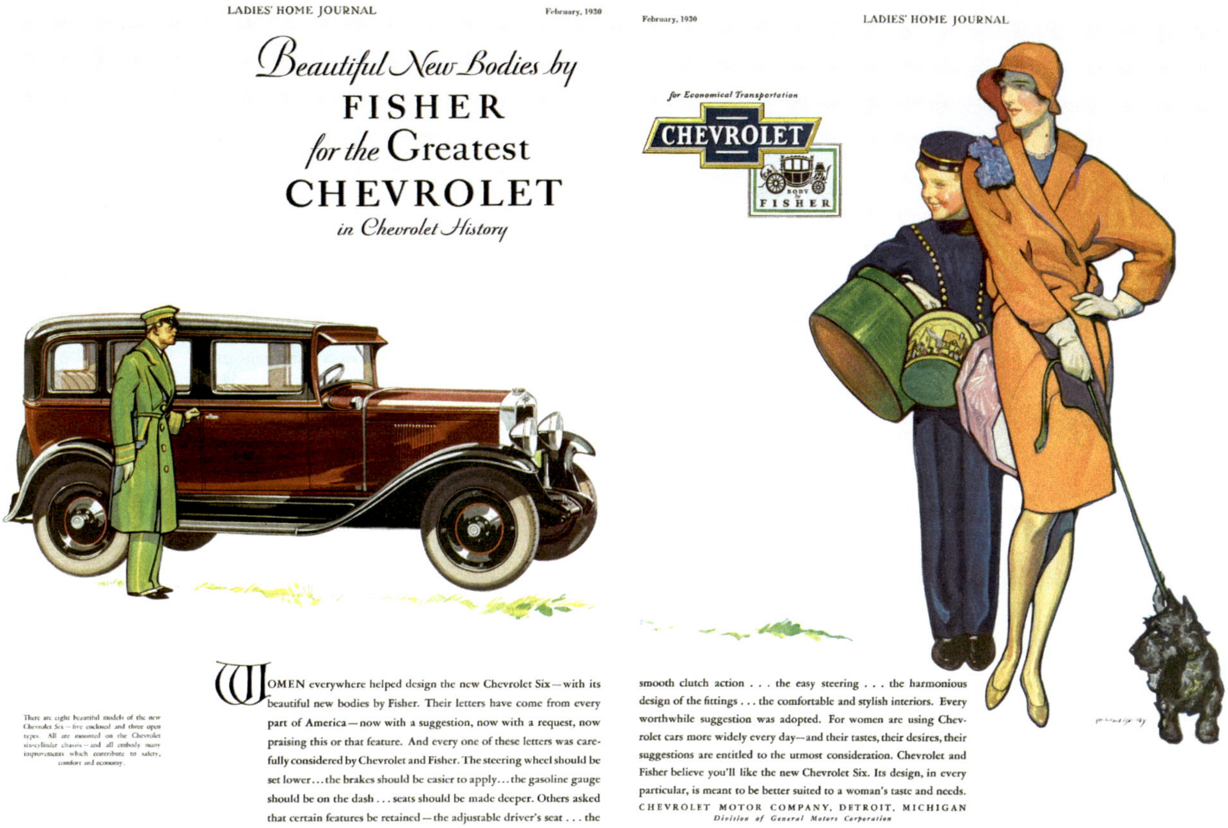

Oldsmobile, 1933 ◄◄ Pontiac, 1930 ◄ Chevrolet, 1930

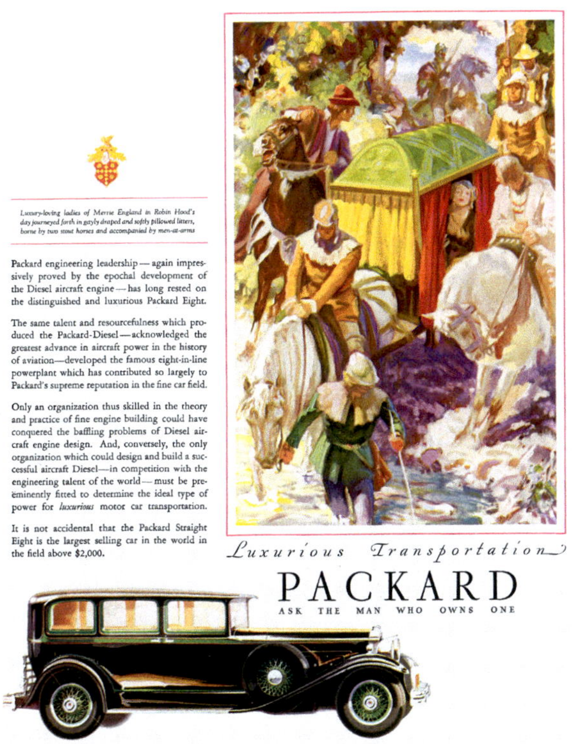

Packard, 1930

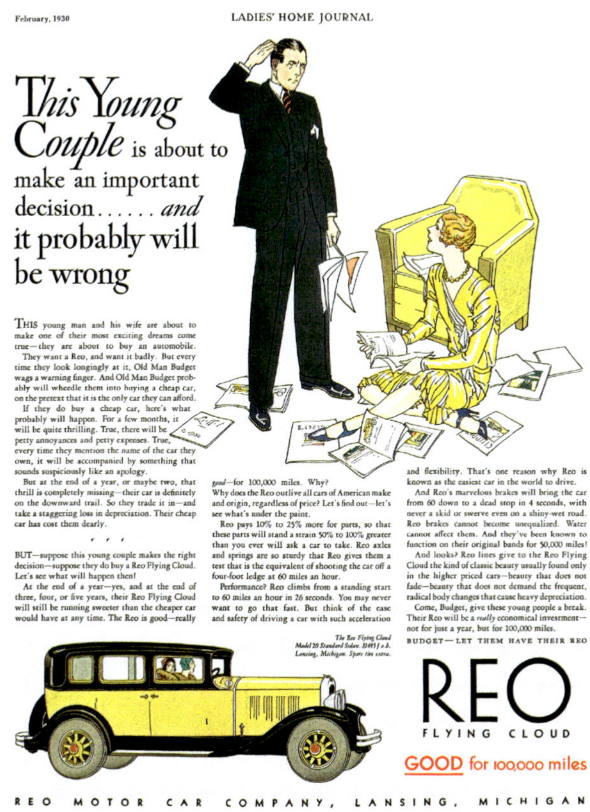

Reo Motor Car Co., 1930

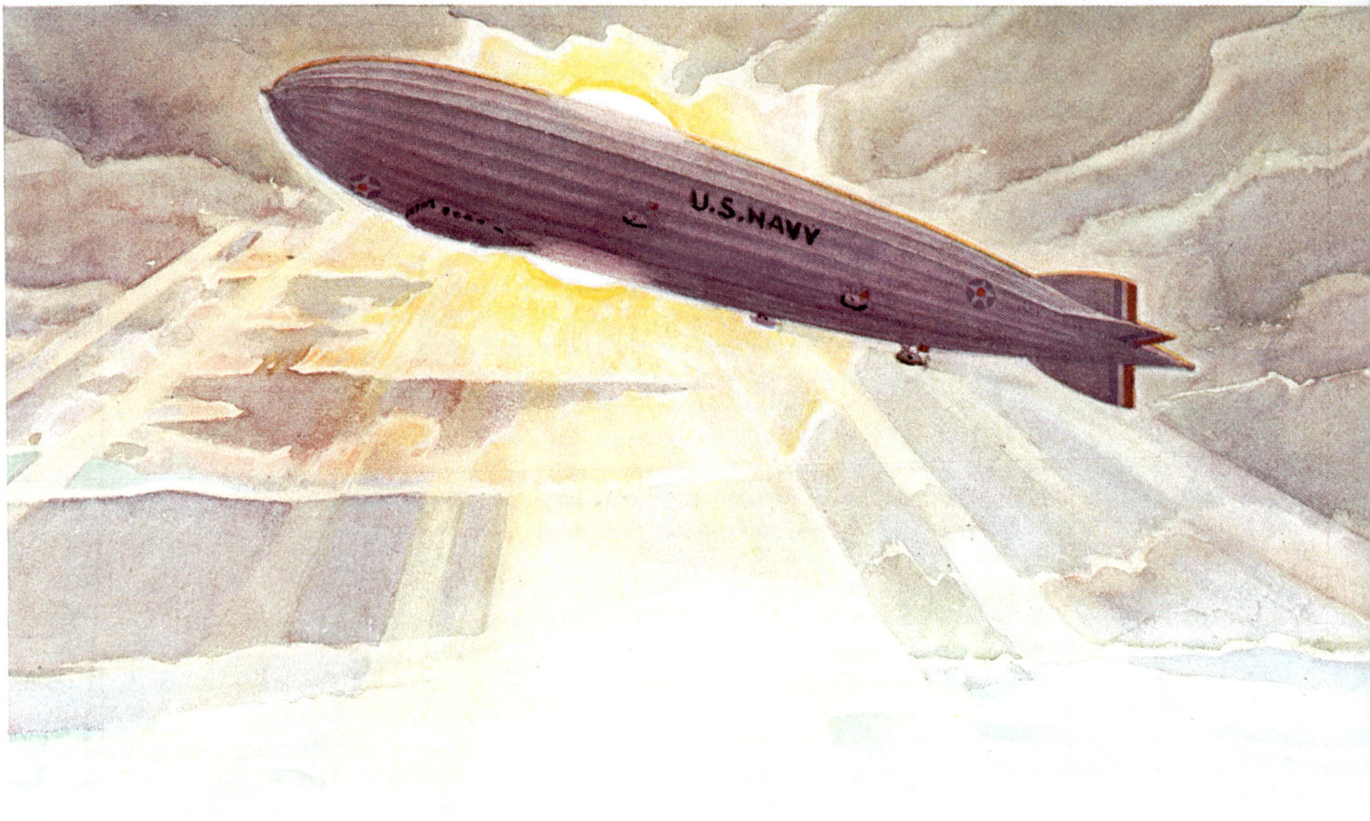

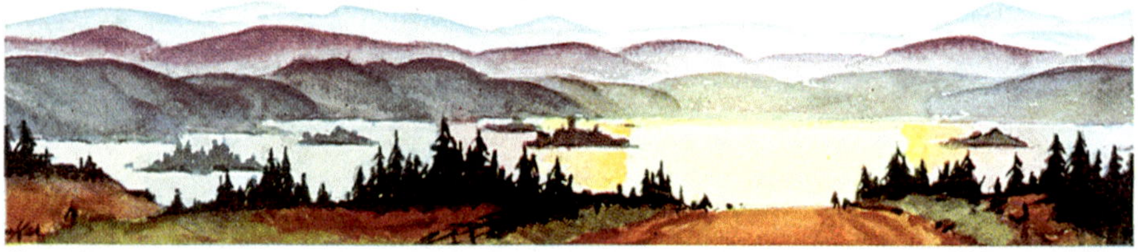

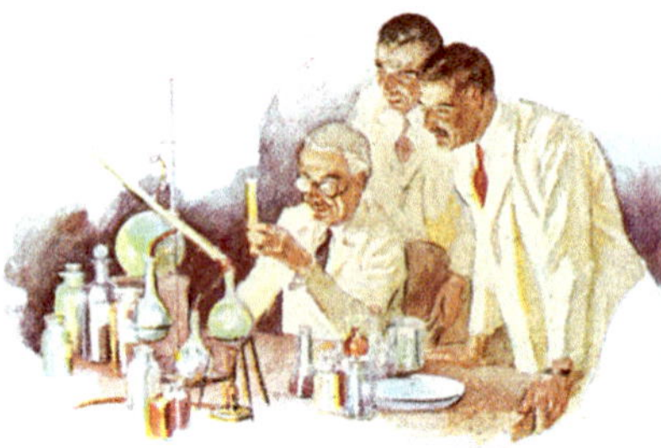

RESEARCH . . . THE GUIDE TO PROGR
Anticipating every development; insuring ever higher standa
quality . . . Texaco Laboratories are the source of Texaco pro

The "Pride of the Navy" served by Texaco . . .

Sailing high above the clouds or battling raging headwinds, the Los Angeles has demonstrated again and again its ability to meet every test.

For more than four years the motors of this leviathan of the air have been lubricated efficiently with Texaco Airplane Oil. Here again, as with Hawks on his record breaking flights from Coast to Coast—as with the Sun-God on its epoch making non-stop refueling flight, specialized Texaco Aviation Products have demonstra their dependability.

On land, at sea and in the air—in e of our 48 States, in 46 foreign count the name Texaco has become a symbo quality for petroleum products.

Motorists everywhere can assure th selves of this same uniform quality a dependable performance by stopp under the Texaco Red Star with the Gr T when they need gasoline and motor

TEXACO

The mark of quality for petroleum products

THE TEXAS COMPANY

Refiners of a complete line of Texaco Petroleum Products, including Gasoline, Motor Oil, Industrial Lubricants, Railroad and Marine Lubricants, Farm Lubricants, Road Asphalts and Asphalt Roofing.

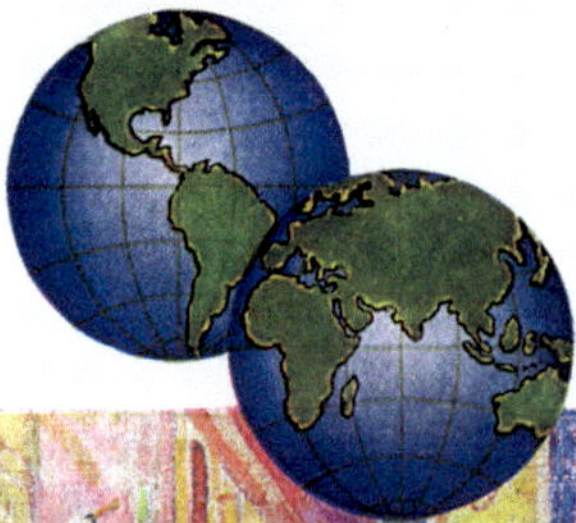

TEXACO IS SOLD IN 46 FOREIGN COUNTRIES

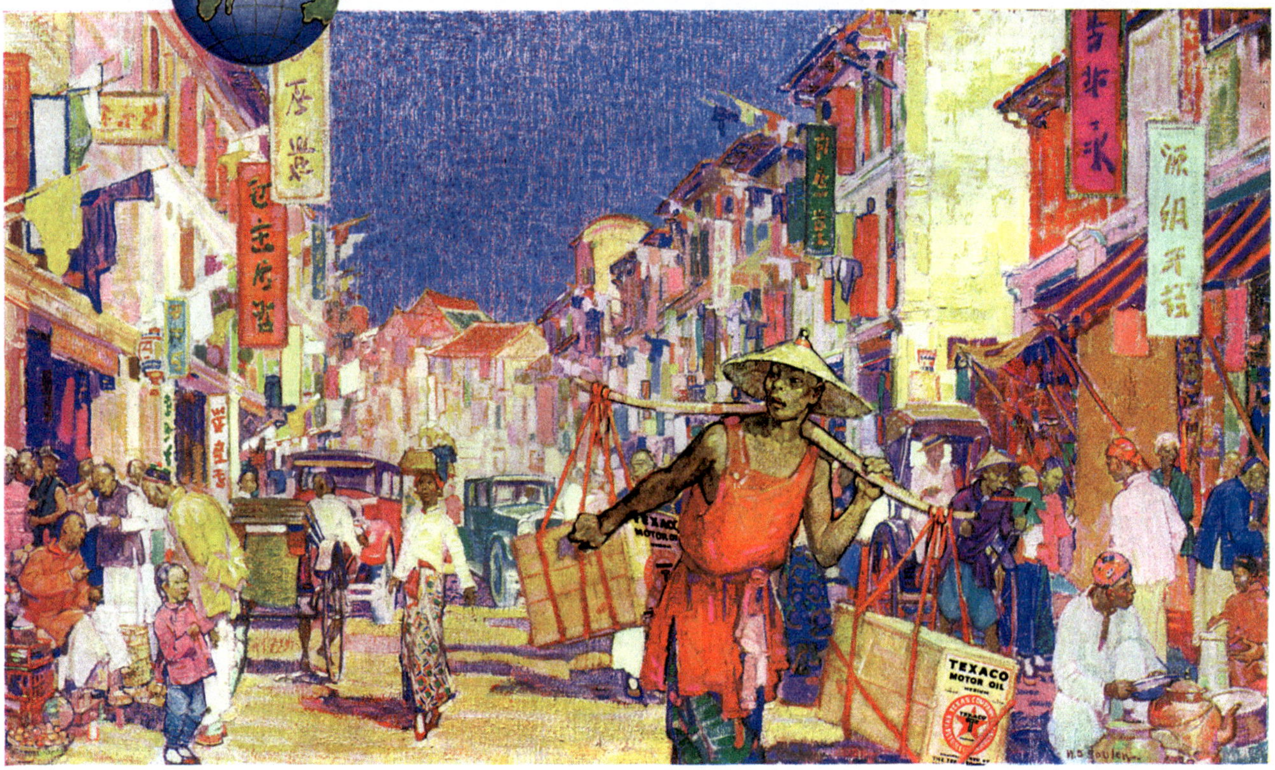

and in Singapore

you can buy the same TEXACO sold in your own home town

From the ports of the fabled Orient to the land of the midnight sun—in 'most every corner of the civilized globe—there you will find the familiar Texaco Red Star with the Green T!

And there you will find the same pure Texaco Golden Motor Oil that is sold from coast to coast—in each of our forty-eight States! For neither clime nor distance halts the progress of the Texaco Star!

In Singapore on the equator, where an engine's heat is magnified by a sun like polished brass, motorists depend implicitly on Texaco Golden Motor Oil!

And in Iceland, where the mercury hits thirty below, there, too, you will find Texaco Golden Motor Oil demonstrating its ability to meet efficiently all lubricating requirements.

The whole wide world knows Texaco quality — knows its purity, its golden color! And this international preference is added proof of Texaco superiority.

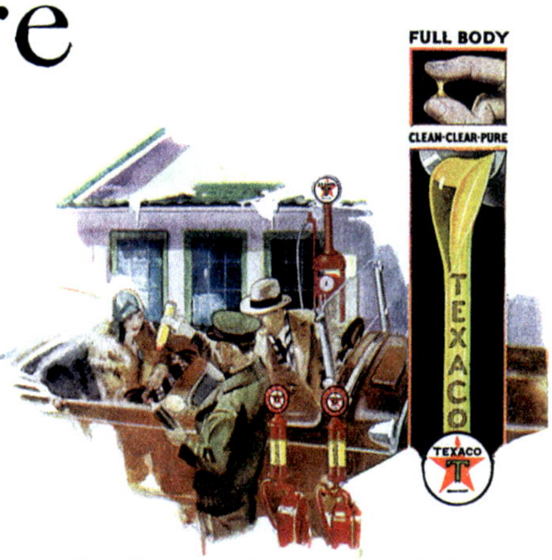

Let a Texaco man demonstrate to you the free-flowing quality of Texaco at low temperatures.

TEXACO

THE TEXAS COMPANY

Refiners of a complete line of Texaco Petroleum Products, including Gasoline, Motor Oil, Industrial Lubricants, Railroad and Marine Lubricants, Farm Lubricants, Road Asphalts and Asphalt Roofing.

Texaco, 1930 ◄▲

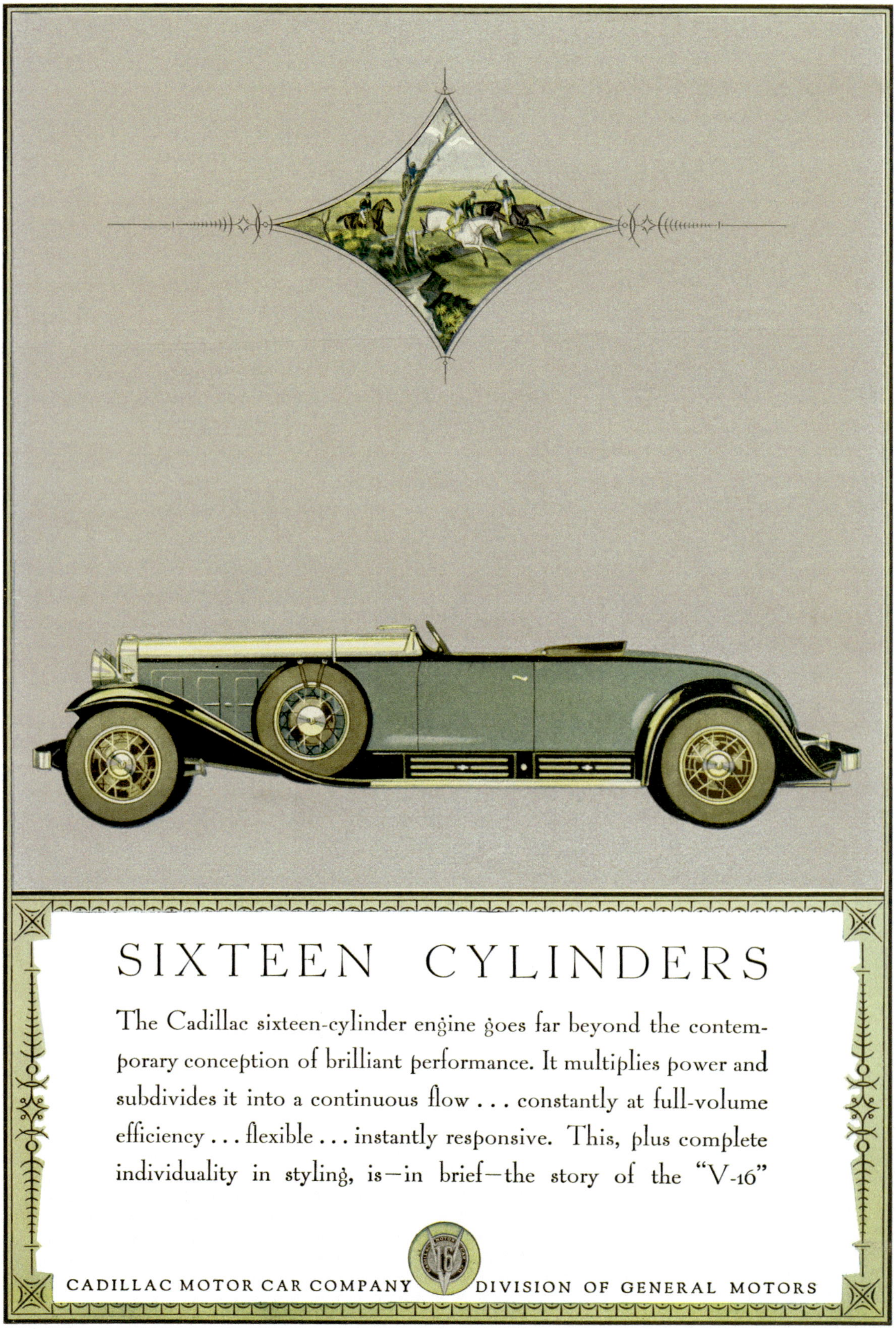

July 1930 Good Housekeeping

Cadillac, 1930

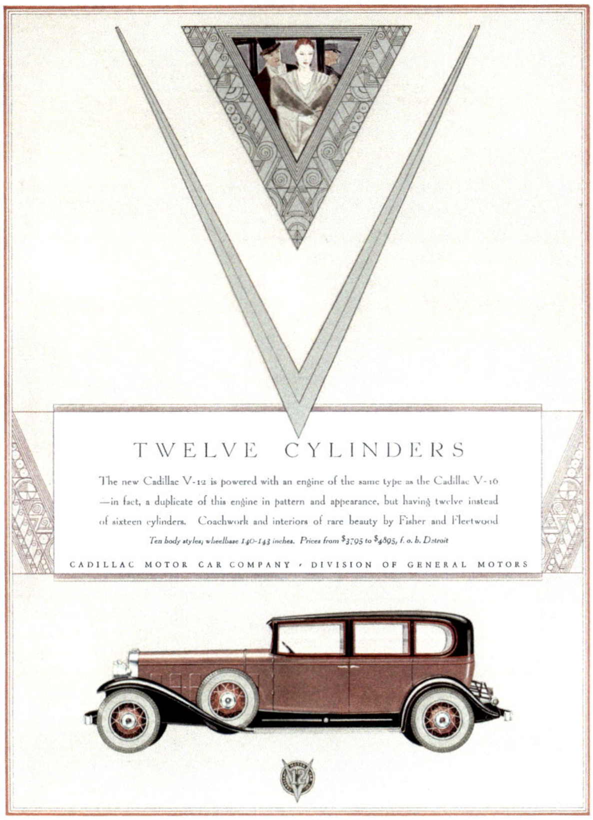

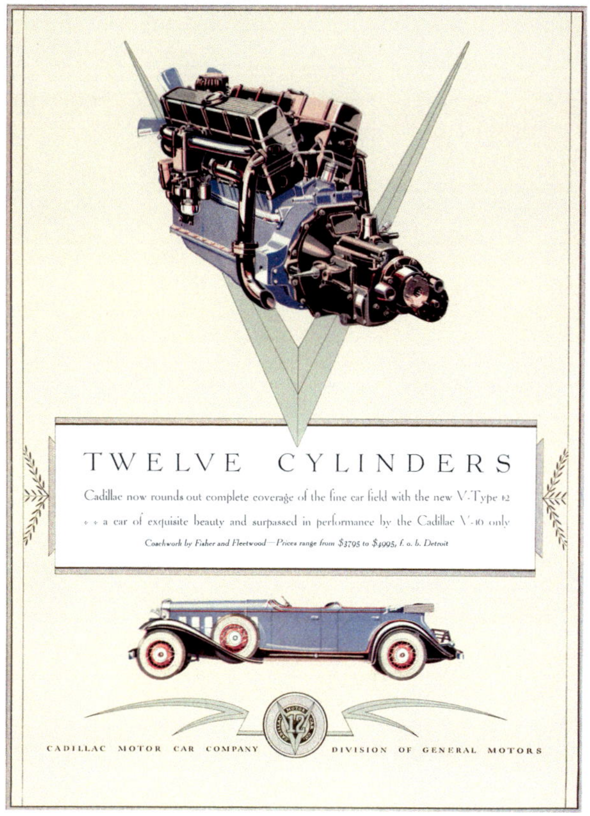

Cadillac, 1930

Cadillac, 1930

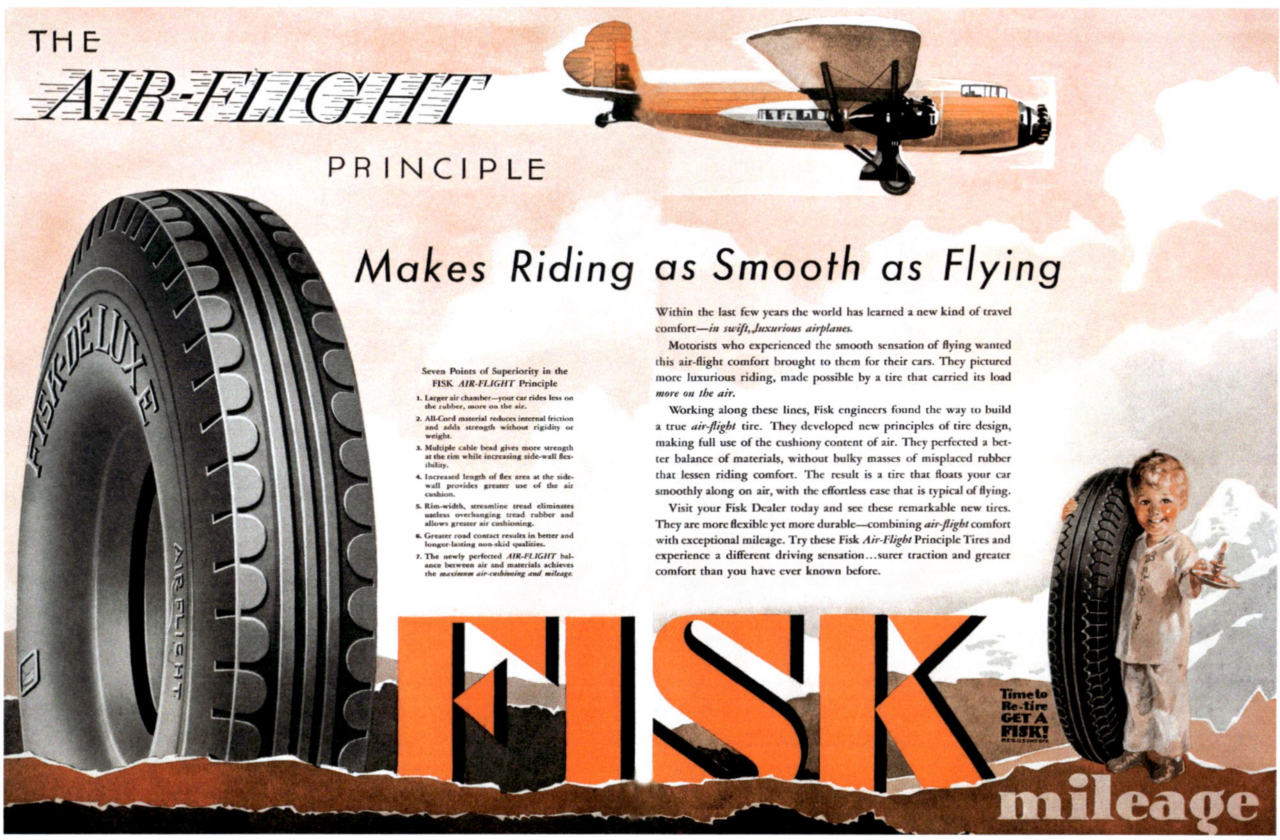

Fisk, 1930

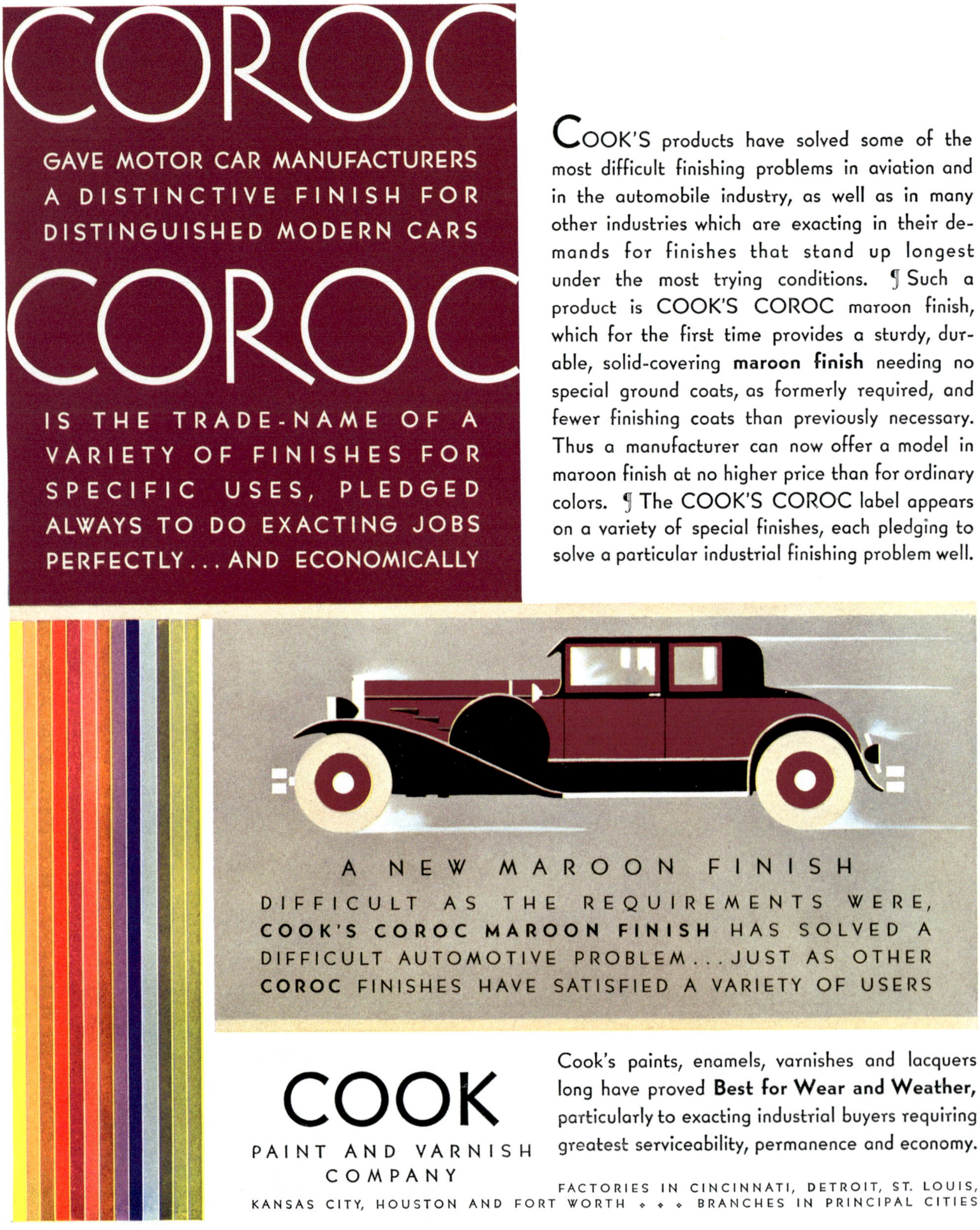

Cook Paint & Varnish Co., 1930

A joyous car for golden summer days

MANY are the delights of the Ford Roadster these golden summer days. Short the miles and pleasant because of its alert and sprightly performance, its safety and its easy-riding comfort.

And what a joy it is to travel along the way with the top down, the blue sky overhead and the fresh, cool air brushing a rosy glow upon your cheeks! Rare indeed the woman who has not hoped that some day such a car might be her very own.

That dream, long cherished, may now come true. For the new Ford Roadster, with all its beauty of line and unusual mechanical excellence, is most conveniently priced. Many months of glorious motoring await your beckoning.

Ford

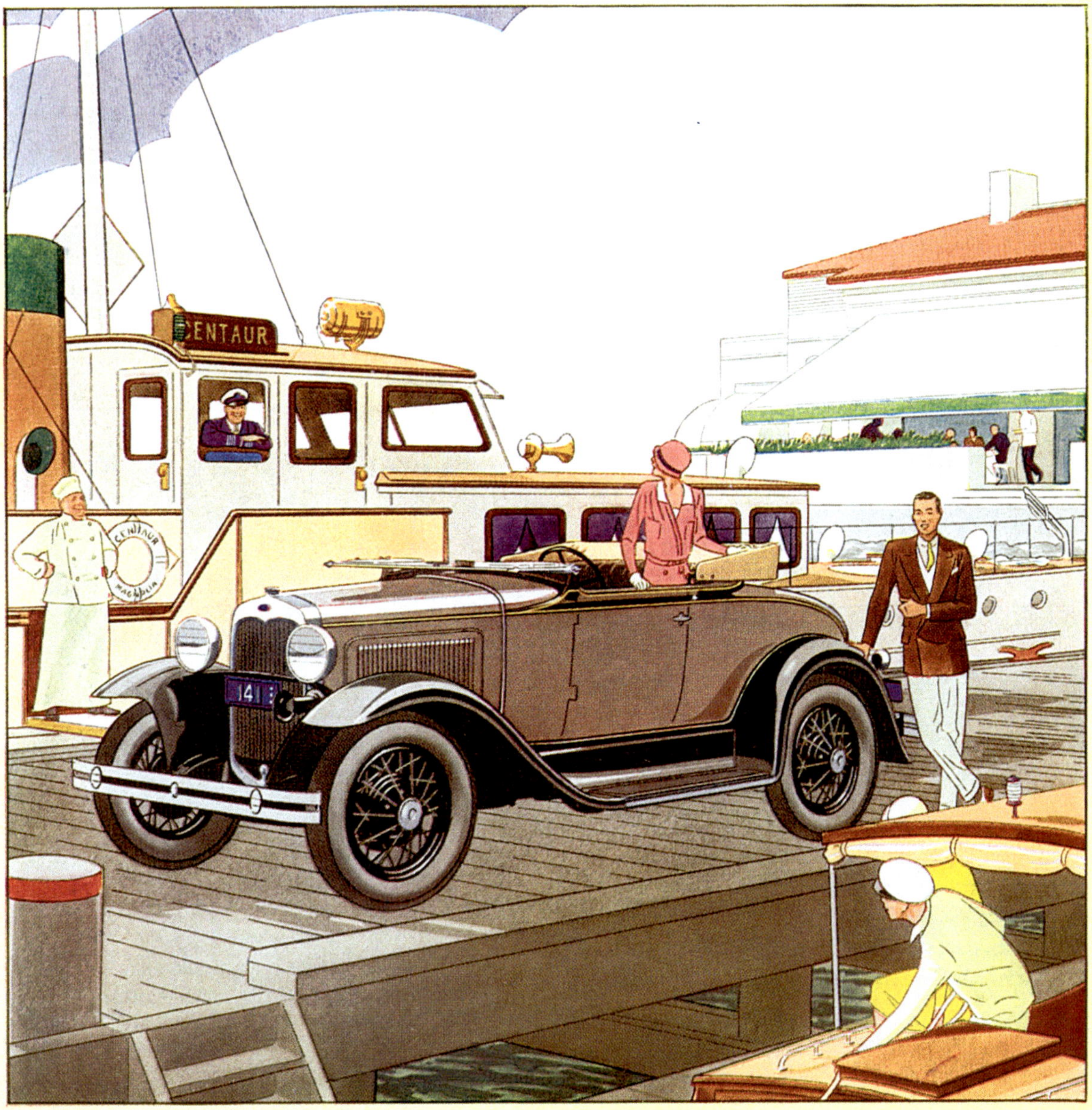

THE NEW FORD ROADSTER

Ford, 1930

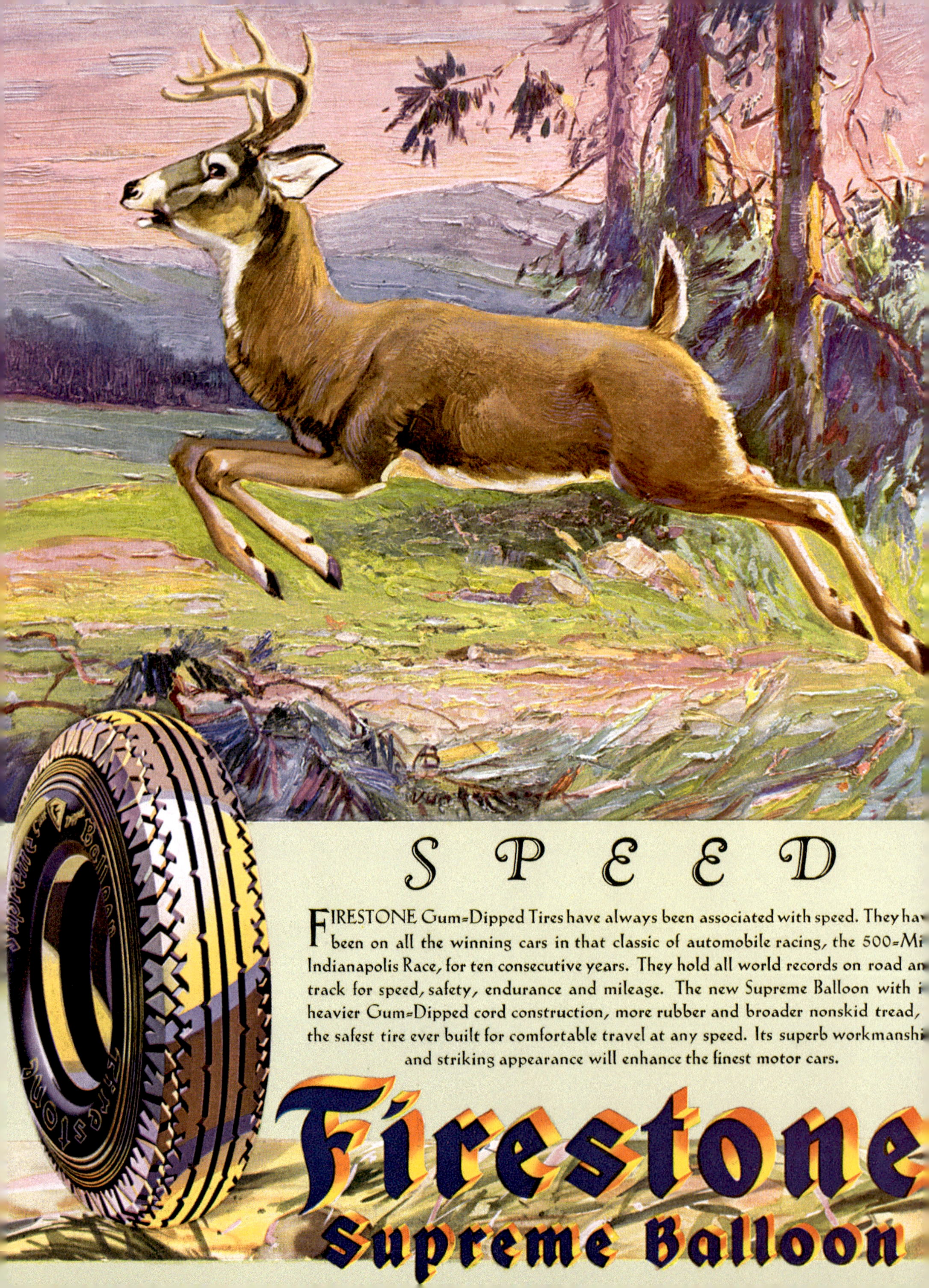

SPEED
FIRESTONE Gum-Dipped Tires have always been associated with speed. They ha been on all the winning cars in that classic of automobile racing, the 500-Mi Indianapolis Race, for ten consecutive years. They hold all world records on road an track for speed, safety, endurance and mileage. The new Supreme Balloon with i heavier Gum-Dipped cord construction, more rubber and broader nonskid tread, the safest tire ever built for comfortable travel at any speed. Its superb workmanshi and striking appearance will enhance the finest motor cars.
Firestone
Supreme Balloon

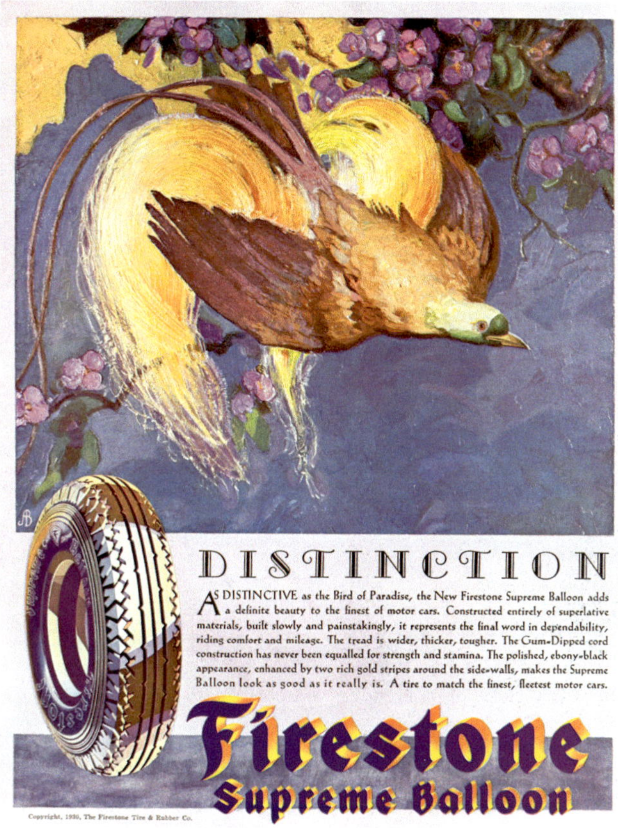

Firestone, 1930

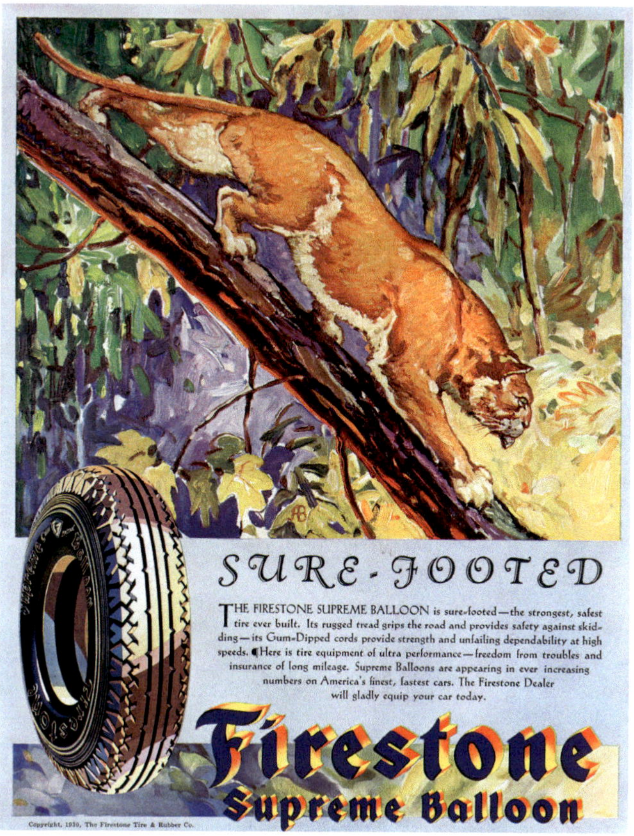

Firestone, 1930

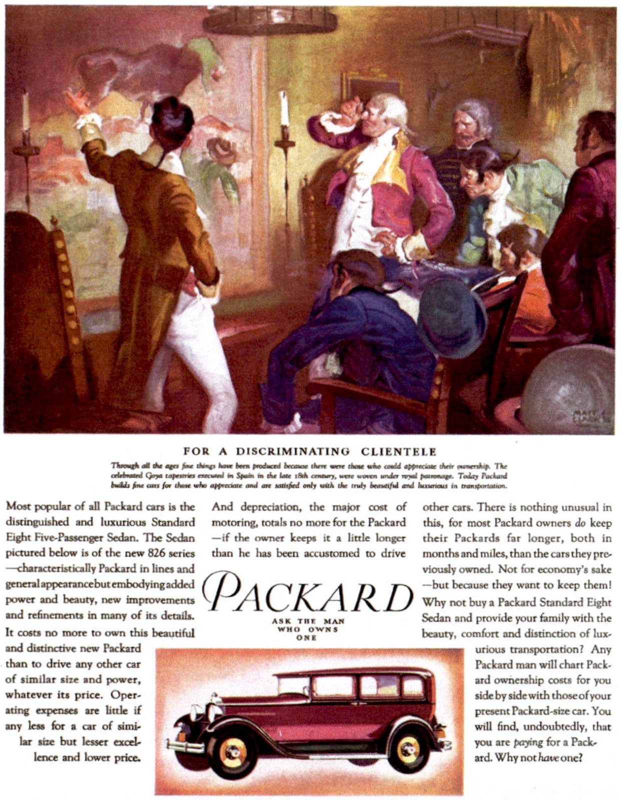

Firestone, 1930 ◂ Packard, 1930

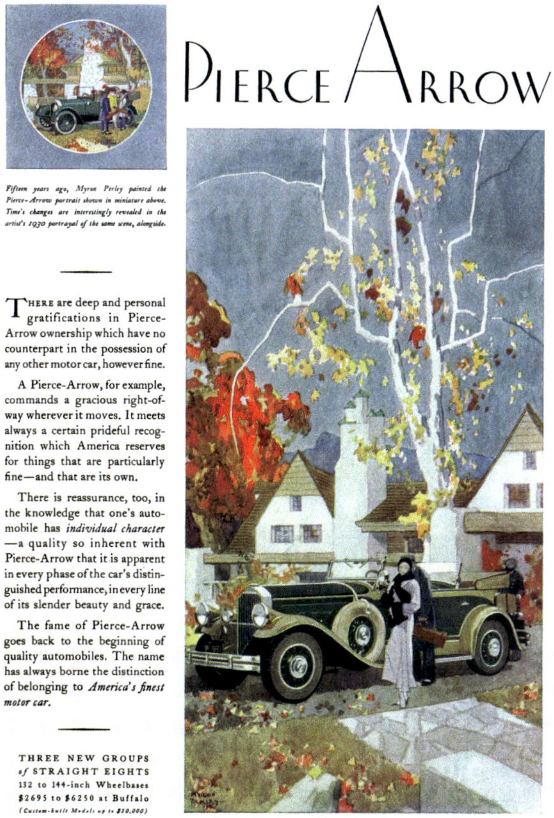

Pierce Arrow, 1930

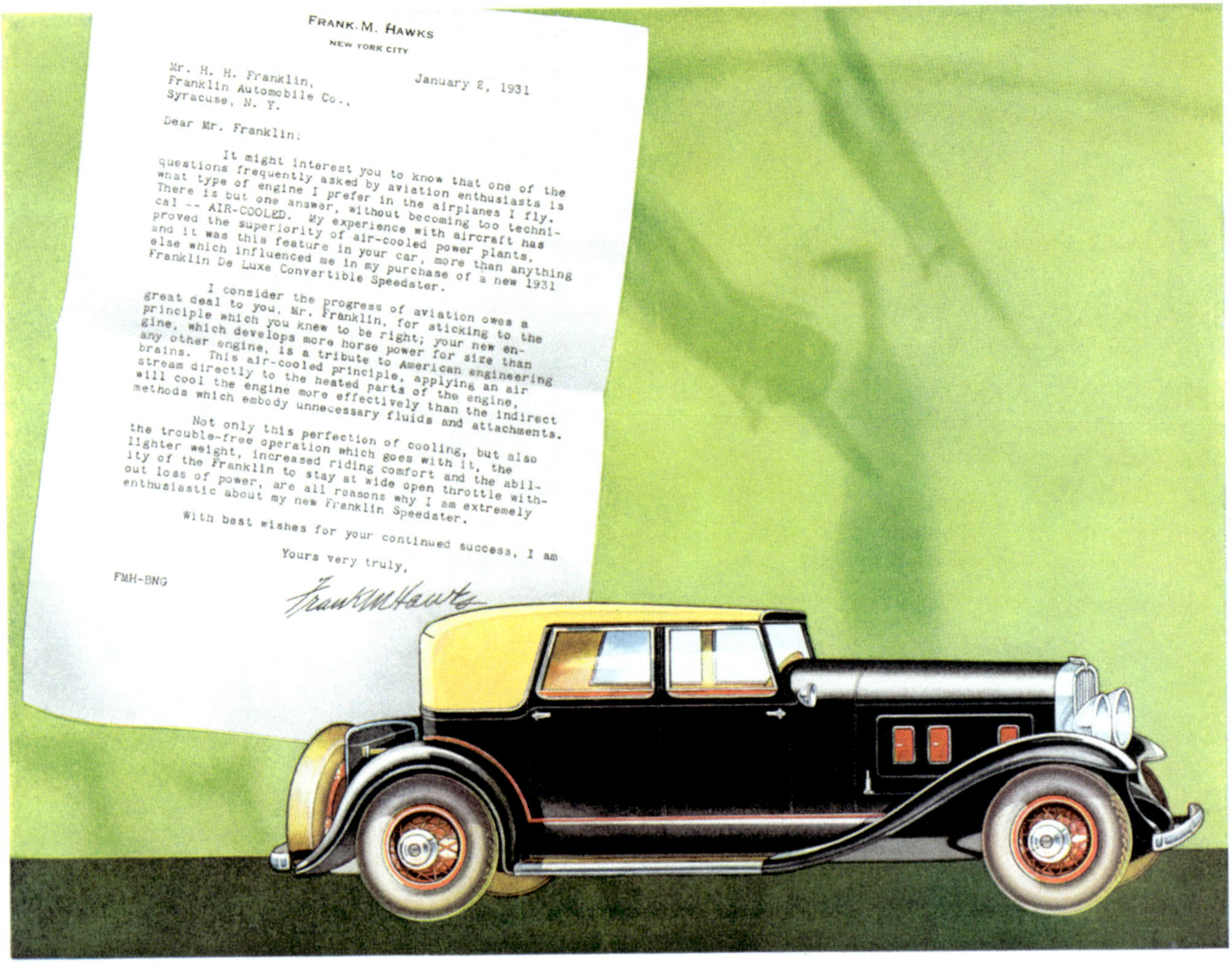

*C*APTAIN HAWKS *buys an* *air-cooled* FRANKLIN

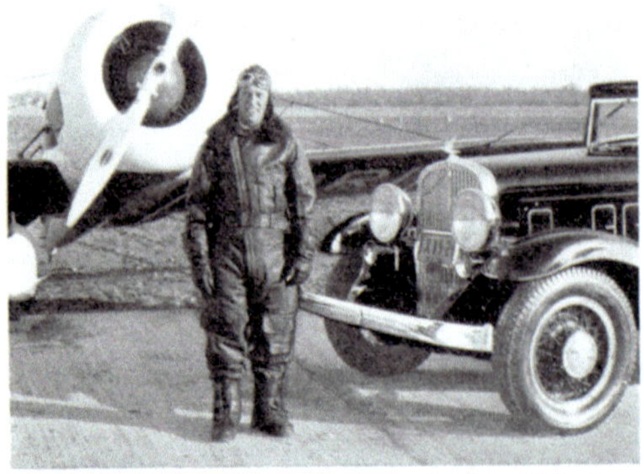
Captain Hawks, his airplane and his new Franklin Convertible Speedster

Have you ever flown an airplane? Flashed through space at 125 miles an hour—yet felt the pace to be much slower? Glided from cloud to cloud with perfect ease and comfort? It's all fascinating and thrilling.

Captain Hawks—speed monarch of the sky—knows every thrill of the air. Knows the great superiority of the air-cooled engine, which has made possible famous flights and dramatic aircraft progress. In his first Franklin ride, Captain Hawks sensed that Franklin, too, through the superiority of the air-cooled engine, has achieved brilliant performance and comfort. For the first time, he found the *airplane feel* in a motor car. He enjoyed the ease with which Franklin could be *directed.* The riding like gliding, with 80 miles an hour like 50, thrilled him.

Franklin—America's truly airplane-type car—presents a bright picture for the future of the automobile. Because of the great progress of air-cooling, many automobile authorities are saying, "Eventually all cars will be air-cooled."

Try a Franklin ride. Put the car to every test. You'll find new comfort and a new feeling of safety. The exclusive Franklin features, made possible by air-cooling, are translated into the finest motoring the world has ever known.

In outward beauty, Dietrich has styled the new De Luxe Franklin to be as modern and progressive as Franklin engineering. Through its lower price level Franklin is now available to a greatly widened group of fine car buyers. Call your local dealer for a trial ride. Franklin Automobile Company, Syracuse, N. Y.

THE AIR-COOLED AIRPLANE-TYPE CAR

Franklin, 1930

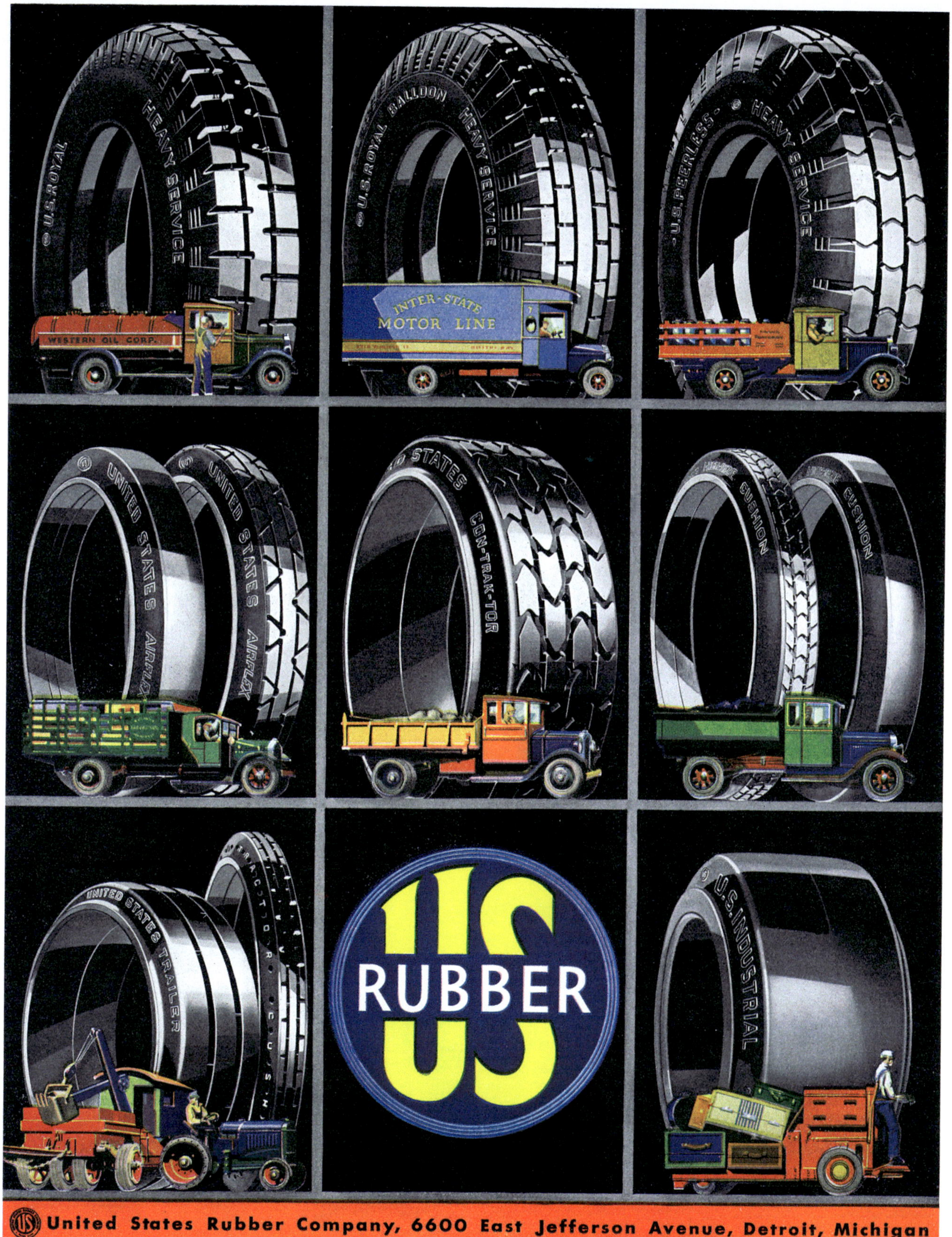

U.S. Rubber Co., 1930

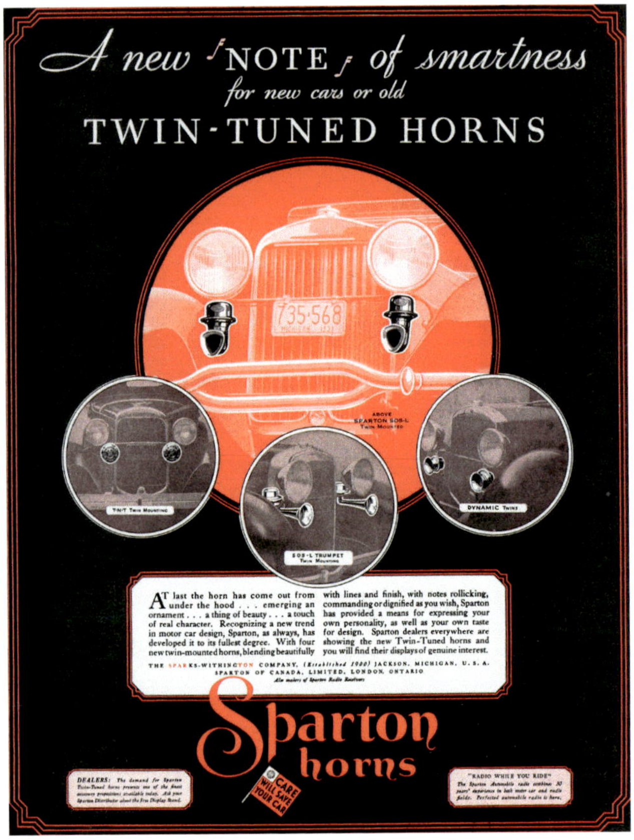

Sparton Horns, 1931

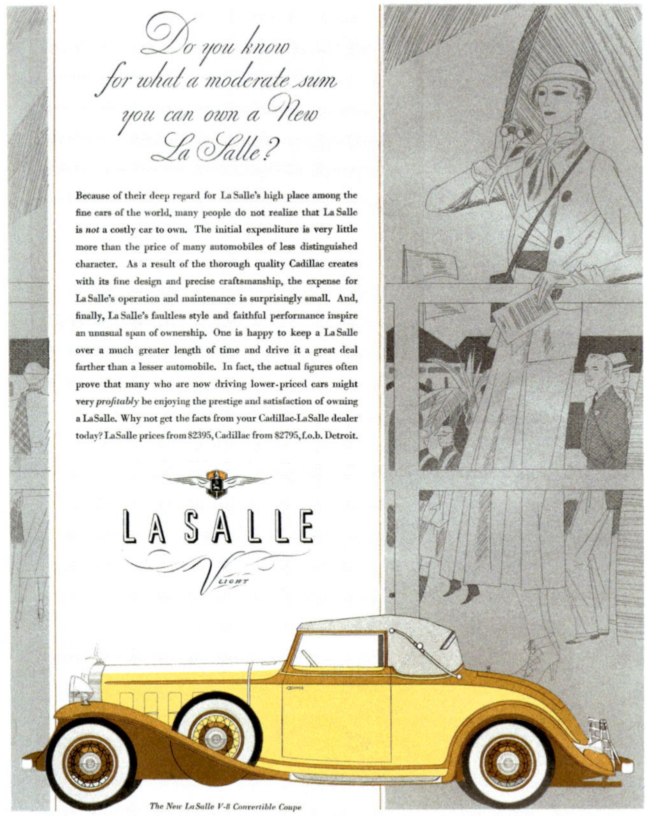

La Salle, 1931

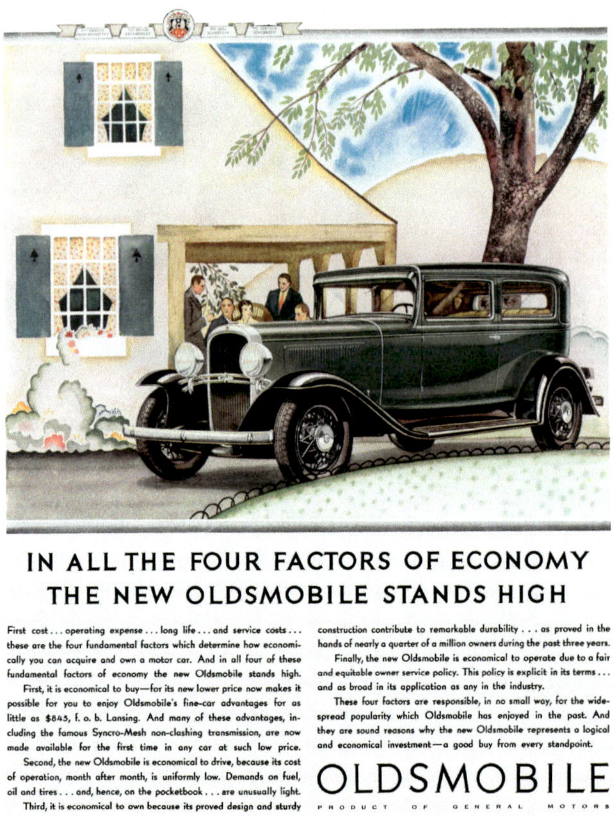

Oldsmobile, 1931

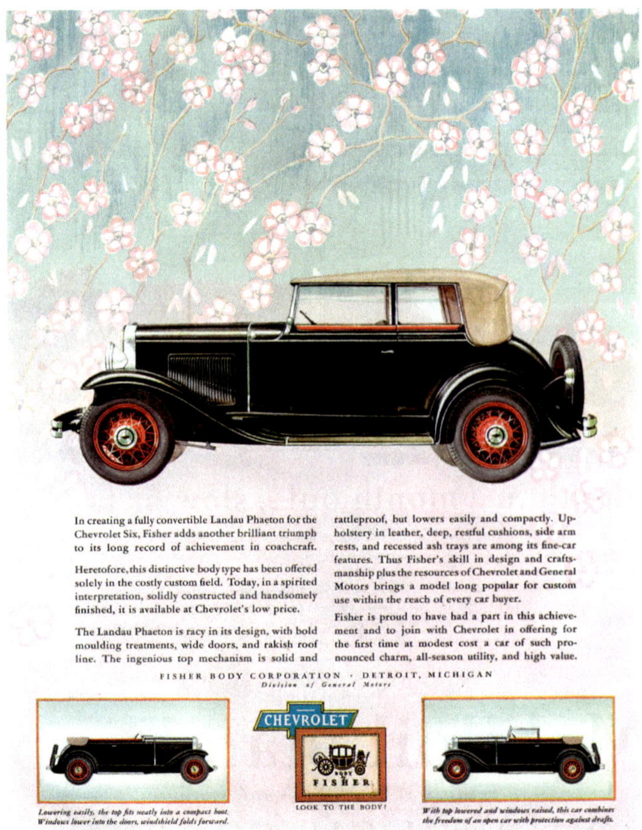

Chevrolet, 1931

► Chrysler, 1931

CHRYSLER IMPERIAL

WITH PATENTED
FLOATING POWER

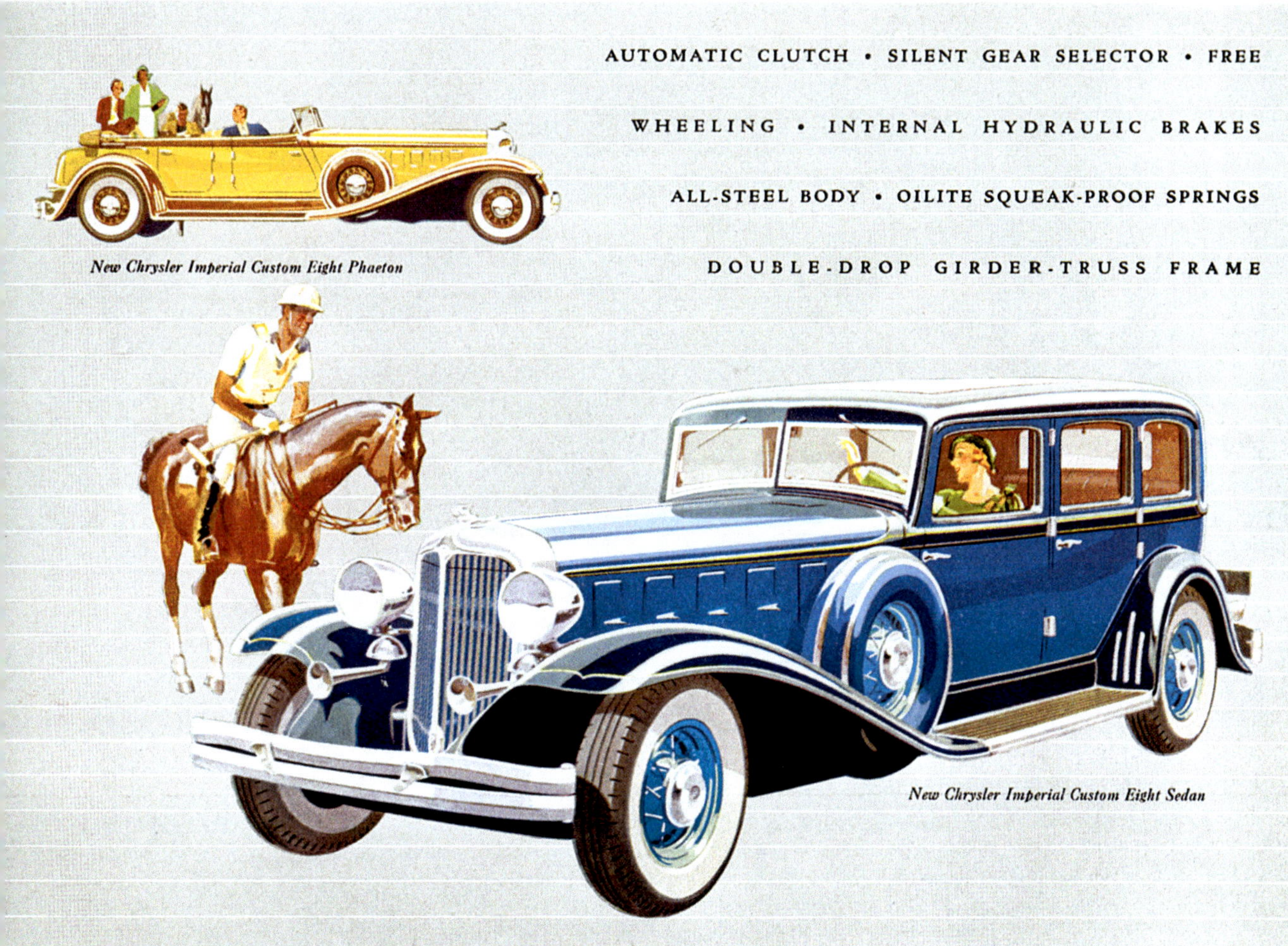

New Chrysler Imperial Custom Eight Phaeton

New Chrysler Imperial Custom Eight Sedan

CHRYSLER'S FINEST MOTOR CARS

[T]AKE THE WHEEL . . . enjoy the most [u]nforgettable ride you've ever had

[T]he new Chrysler Imperial Eights are everything [t]he word "Imperial" signifies . . . as the dictionary [s]ays, "fit for an emperor; magnificent; imposing; [su]perior in size or quality."

Styled, appointed and engineered for those who [w]ant the finest—and only the finest motor cars—these [n]ew Imperials have a "luxury" of performance [h]eretofore unknown in *any* motor car at *any* price.

In these cars you get the last word in up-to-date [e]ngineering. We promise you a new sensation. We [p]romise you the easiest, silkiest, quietest ride to be [h]ad on wheels.

Floating Power engine suspension works a seem[in]g miracle in performance. Creates an altogether new *feeling* in motoring. Wipes out power tremor completely at all car speeds. Eliminates all sense or suggestion of engine effort.

Even if you have a chauffeur, you'll want to do most of the driving. For these cars have an Automatic Clutch that is *absolutely* automatic. They have the latest and finest in Free Wheeling. They have a new Silent Gear Selector—enabling an instant, silent change to a higher or a lower gear at any car speed with no more effort than moving a lead pencil.

They have Oilite Squeak-Proof Springs—patented springs that *never* need lubrication, and *never* squeak. And Chrysler's world-famous Hydraulic Brakes for quick, positive, *cushioned* stopping—with new Centrifuse brake drums of steel with a lining of cast iron fused permanently to the steel. Resulting in cooler brakes. Safer brakes. Longer-lasting brakes.

You'll be happier with a Chrysler

The new Chrysler Imperial Eight with 125-horsepower engine may be had in two chassis sizes—a 135-inch wheelbase, carrying Chrysler's All-Steel Bodies, and a 146-inch wheelbase, carrying custom bodies by Chrysler and Le Baron.

•

A new Chrysler Imperial Custom Eight, six body models, $2895 to $3595; a new Chrysler Imperial Eight, three body models, $1925 to $2195; a new Chrysler Eight, five body models, $1435 to $1695; a new Chrysler Six, five body models, $885 to $935 (Automatic Clutch and Oilite Squeak-Proof Springs on all Sixes at slight extra cost). F. O. B. Factory. Duplate Safety Plate Glass standard on Custom Eights. Obtainable on Six and Eight Sedans, $17.50; on Imperial Sedans, $20; all 2-passenger Coupes, $9.50.

Chrysler Eight De Luxe

PATTERNED AFTER THE CHRYSLER IMPERIAL EIGHT

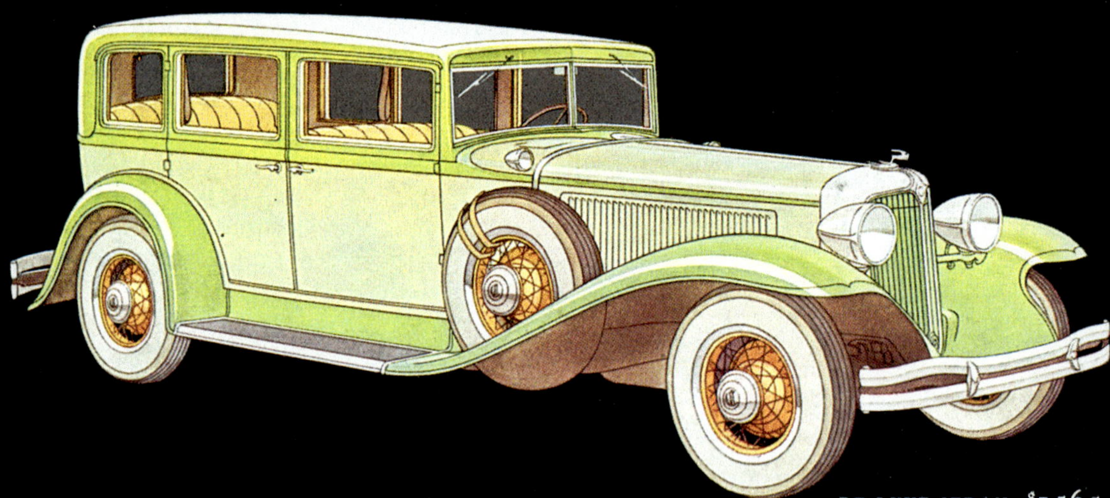

DE LUXE SEDAN, $1565

De Luxe Style—De Luxe Comfort—De Luxe Performance

CHRYSLER, so often the pioneer to better things, has now pioneered with an entirely new and better kind of luxury and performance in a car of moderate price—the new Chrysler Eight De Luxe, available in five magnificent body models.

It is a *de luxe* car through and through, from start to finish, inside and outside.

The de luxe power of a bigger engine. The de luxe comfort of bigger bodies and longer springs. The de luxe smartness of a divided windshield with *inside* adjustable sun visors. De luxe upholstery of Bedford cord. De luxe interior panels and mouldings of dark walnut finish. De luxe fitments . . . Everything about the car suggests a car of much higher price.

Its big, quiet engine is completely insulated from the frame by live rubber; has a large, perfectly balanced crankshaft, fully counterweighted—and develops with velvety ease a good 95 horsepower.

Eighty miles an hour—if you like speed—but whether you travel that fast or not, the power that makes such speed possible enables you to glide along at moderate speeds without consciousness of engine effort.

This de luxe performance owes much to Chrysler's exclusive Multi-Range four-speed transmission with Dual High gears. *Both are internal-mesh gears which make it possible to shift instantly at any time from one to the other, at any car speed, without clashing.* Two high gears *double* the range of high gear performance. There is one high gear for flashing pick-up and bursts of speed in traffic, and another higher gear for the open road.

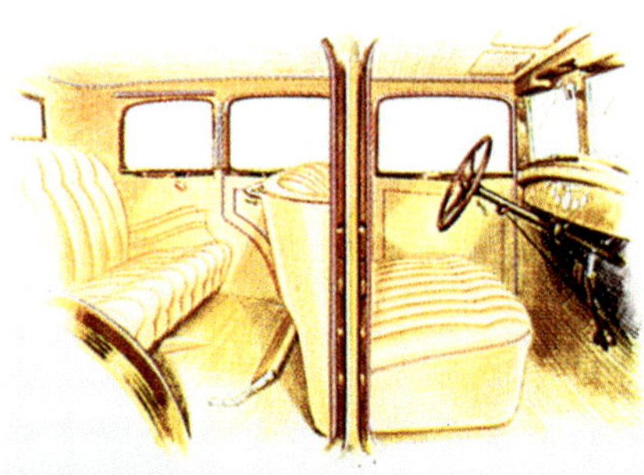

Drive this Chrysler. Learn from it th fascinating difference between Chrysler per formance and other performance. Enjoy th difference in the way it clings to the road a all speeds; the way it takes the turns; th way it soars up the hills; the ease of its piv otal steering; the positive control and safety o its internal self-equalizing hydraulic brakes

Chrysler's fine quality, Chrysler's geniu for engineering progress, Chrysler's carefu craftsmanship, all have made this Chrysle Eight De Luxe a motor car you'll drive wit unending pride and supreme satisfaction.

This is a case of fine automobile value mad almost unbelievably finer. See for yourself

•

CHRYSLER SIX	$885 to $93
CHRYSLER "70"	$1245 to $129
CHRYSLER EIGHT	$1495 to $166
CHRYSLER EIGHT DE LUXE	$1525 to $158
(Five wire wheels standard; six wire wheels $35 extra)	
CHRYSLER IMPERIAL EIGHT	$2745 to $314
(CUSTOM MODELS $3150 TO $3575)	

All prices f. o. b. factory; special equipment extra.

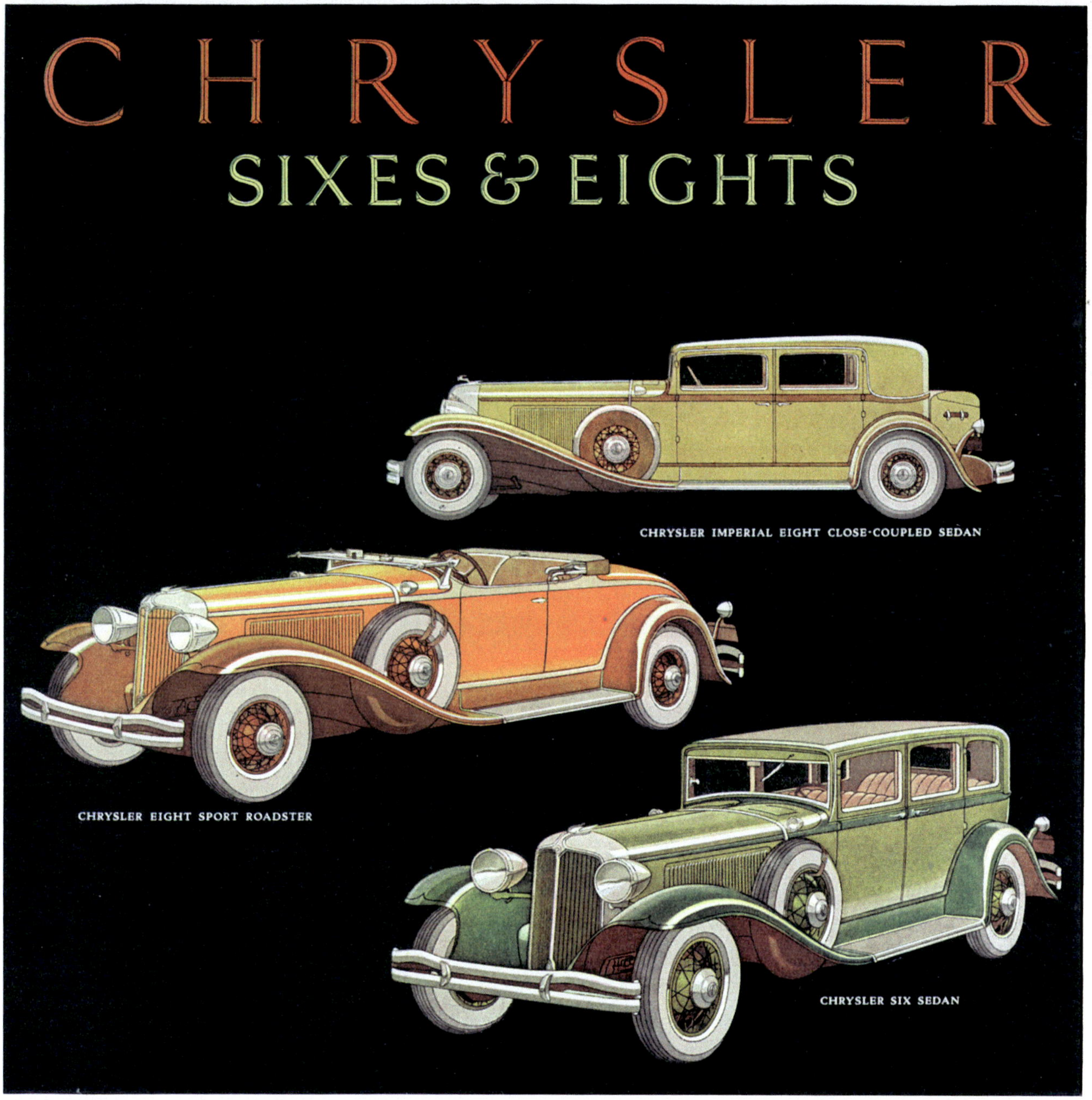

Own a Chrysler—Enjoy the Difference

OWN a Chrysler and you have a car you'll *really* enjoy—because there is a very real difference between a Chrysler and all other cars.

Sit at the wheel of a Chrysler — *any* Chrysler — and you will discover things about Chrysler performance that will stir your pulse and make your eyes sparkle. A distinctly different sensation of almost boundless power. A difference in breath-taking pick-up. A different kind of smoothness. And thrilling speed with a complete feeling of security and ease of control.

Chrysler is giving this vividly different performance in a wide range of Chryslers priced within the reach of practically every purse and income. All smart cars that inspire pride — and challenging all comparison in value.

An entirely new Chrysler Six styled like the smart Chrysler Eights—a fine, big Six with a 116-inch wheelbase; a double-drop frame; a 70-horsepower engine and safety bodies of strong steel.

And the Chrysler "70"—with its 93-horsepower engine and its Multi-Range 4-speed transmission, which together have made it world-famous for performance.

And the Chrysler Eight—with its distinguished appearance, low center of gravity, safety steel bodies, Dual High gears and quick, quiet gear shift.

And the Chrysler Imperial Eight — the embodiment of all motoring luxury — a magnificent car with a 145-inch wheelbase and a 125-horsepower engine—a car for the connoisseurs of motor cars.

Drive a Chrysler — *any* Chrysler — and learn what a difference there is in favor of Chrysler.

CHRYSLER SIX	$885 to $895
CHRYSLER "70"	$1245 to $1295
CHRYSLER EIGHT	$1495 to $1665
CHRYSLER IMPERIAL EIGHT	$2745 to $3145

(CUSTOM MODELS $3150 to $3575)

All prices f. o. b. factory; special equipment extra.

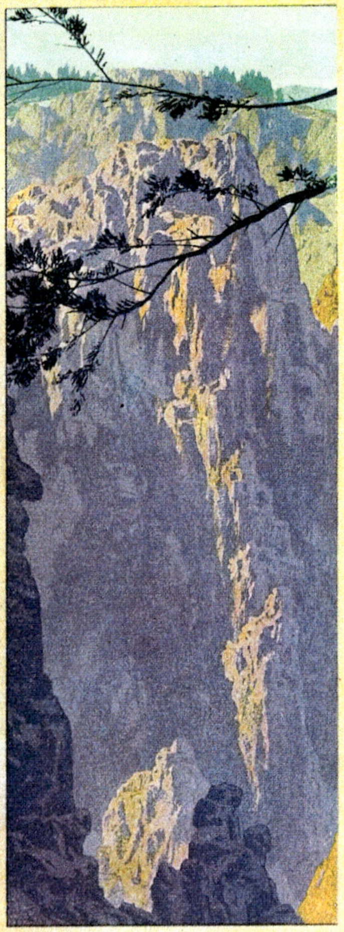

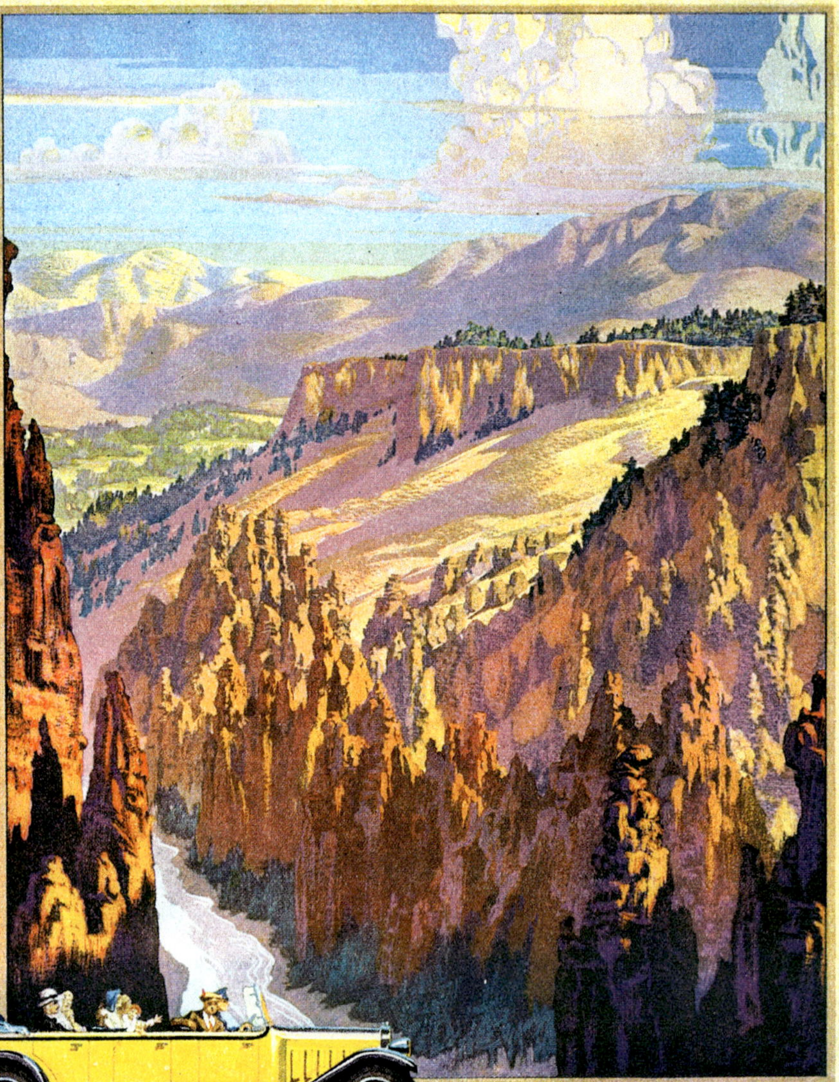

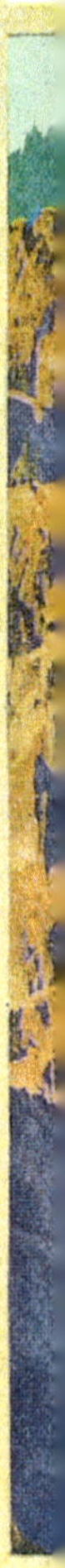

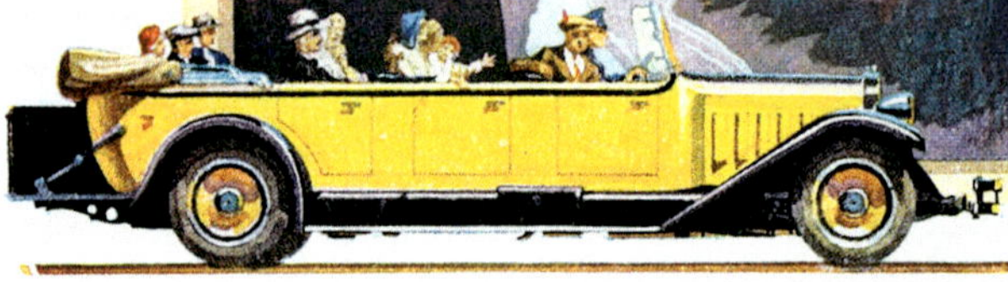

Through such gigantic chasms of rock as this, the fleet of the Yellowstone Park Transportation Company carries thousands and ten thousands each year in safety and comfort

There is no greater kaleidoscope in nature than the Grand Canyon of the Yellowstone — crimsons, ambers, ochres, cobalts—splashed with port wine and shot with lemon, vermilion, snow white and silver gray

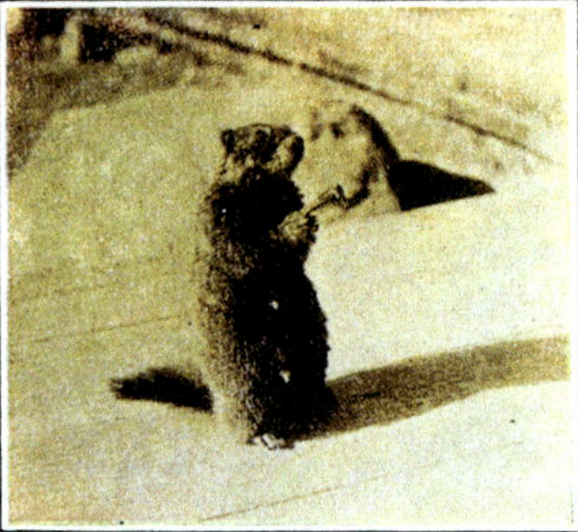

You feel particularly intimate with nature, for the wild life of Yellowstone meets you trustingly at every turn

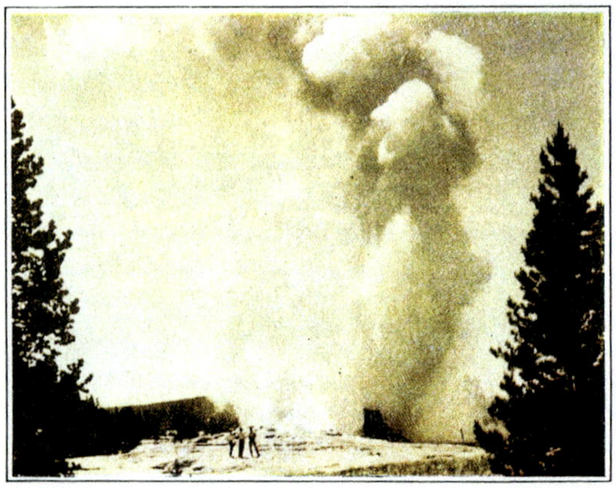

Then there is the ghostly glory of the geysers — hundreds of them. To hear them roar with eager vehemence into the sky — to watch them poise aloft with feathery florescence, is an experience never forgotten

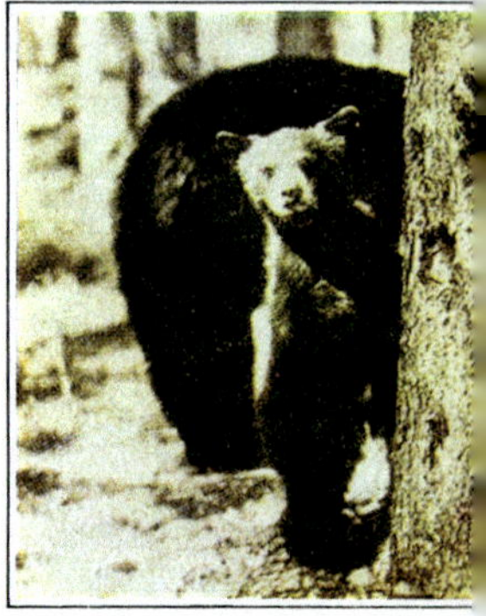

Friendly bear and bison, deer and beaver r
beside the roads you travel in Yellowstone, ad
touch of completeness to this land of m

Goodyear, 1931

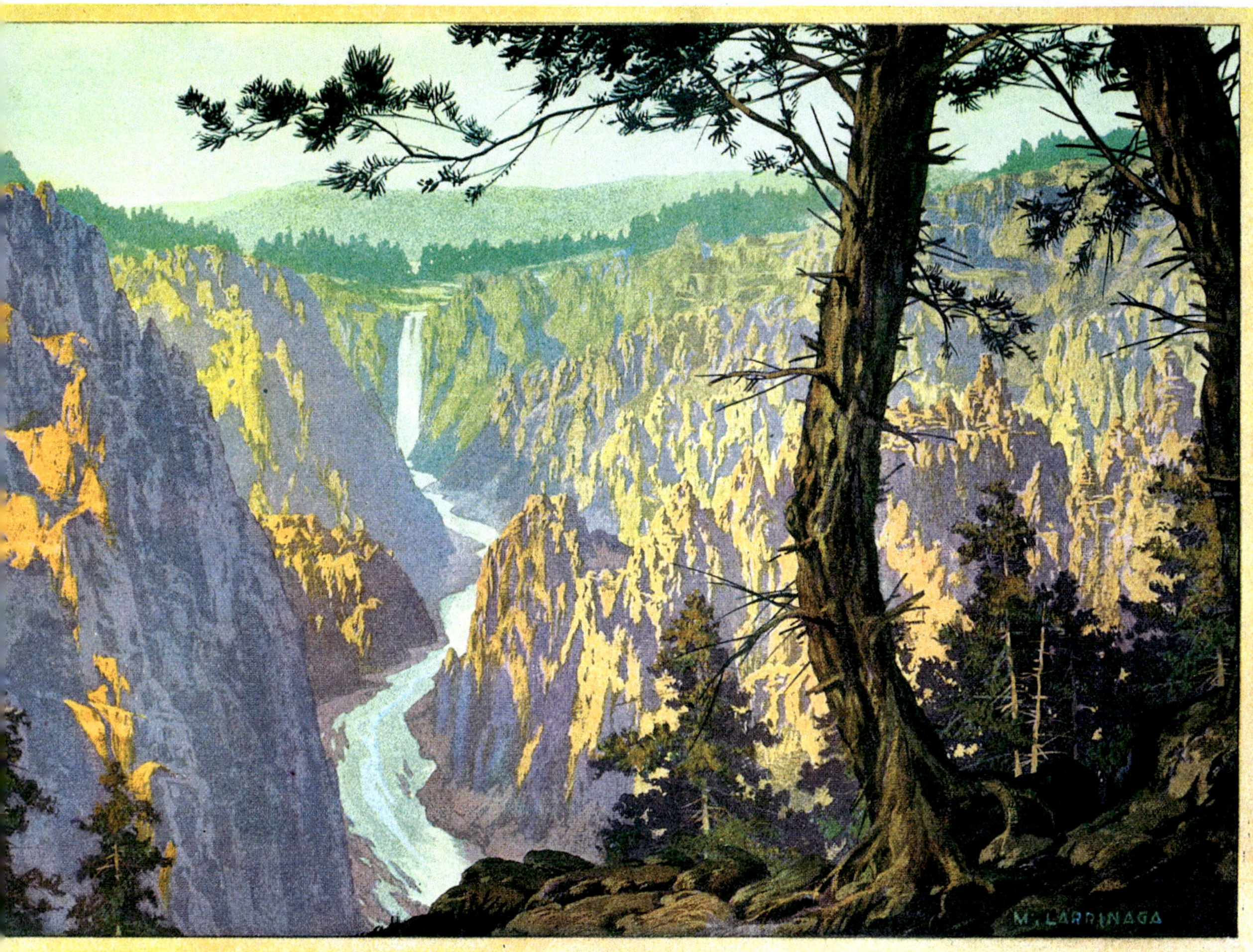

LLOWSTONE PROVES

at it pays to decide: the

"I WILL BUY ONLY ~~A~~ LEADING MAKE OF TIRE"

Soon after the jingling horse team and stage coach gave way to motor transport in Yellowstone Park, all other tires yielded place to Goodyears on the great Yellowstone fleet. ¶ Unchallenged, Goodyears have held that place for fourteen years. ¶ During almost exactly the same period of time, Goodyears have led all other tires in sales to the public. Since 1915, it has been consistently true that *"more people ride on Goodyear Tires than on any other kind."* ¶ There is, in these two facts, more than coincidence. ¶ For the responsibility of transportation through the world's most magnificent wilderness and wonderland, Yellowstone chooses only *the* leading make of tire . . . Isn't there, in this method of choosing tires, a mighty sound thought for you?

THE GREATEST NAME IN RUBBER

GOODYEAR

▸▸ *Cadillac, 1931*

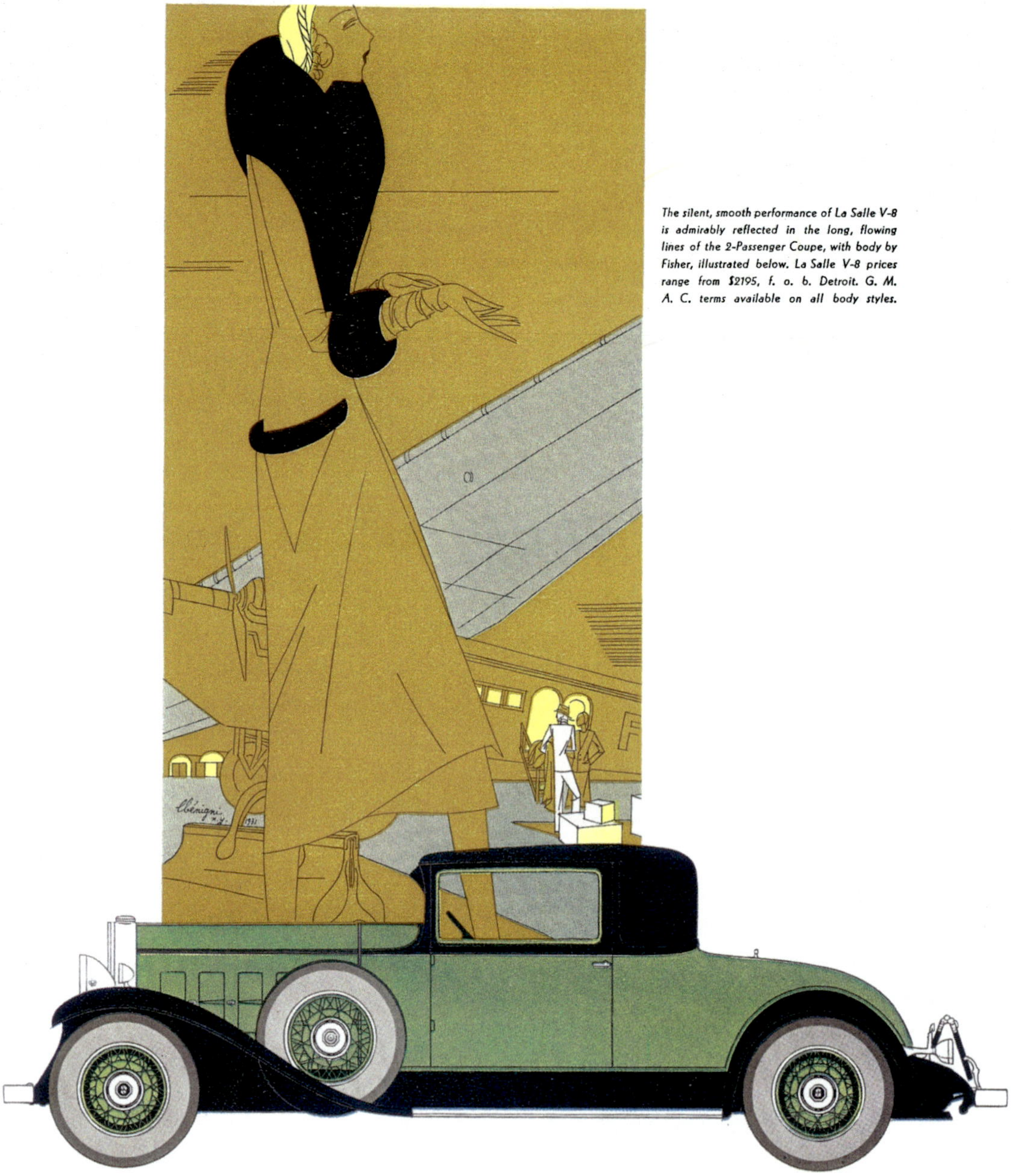

The silent, smooth performance of La Salle V-8 is admirably reflected in the long, flowing lines of the 2-Passenger Coupe, with body by Fisher, illustrated below. La Salle V-8 prices range from $2195, f. o. b. Detroit. G. M. A. C. terms available on all body styles.

So completely is the ideal of fine workmanship ingrained at the Cadillac plant that, no matter whether it be for Cadillac or for La Salle, every detail of design and manufacture is approached with the same meticulous care. There is only *one* standard of excellence, regardless of the task to be done. As a result, the La Salle V-8 provides a degree of quality and a type of performance far beyond those suggested by its moderate price—for it is built with the same exactitude as Cadillac itself.

LA SALLE V-8

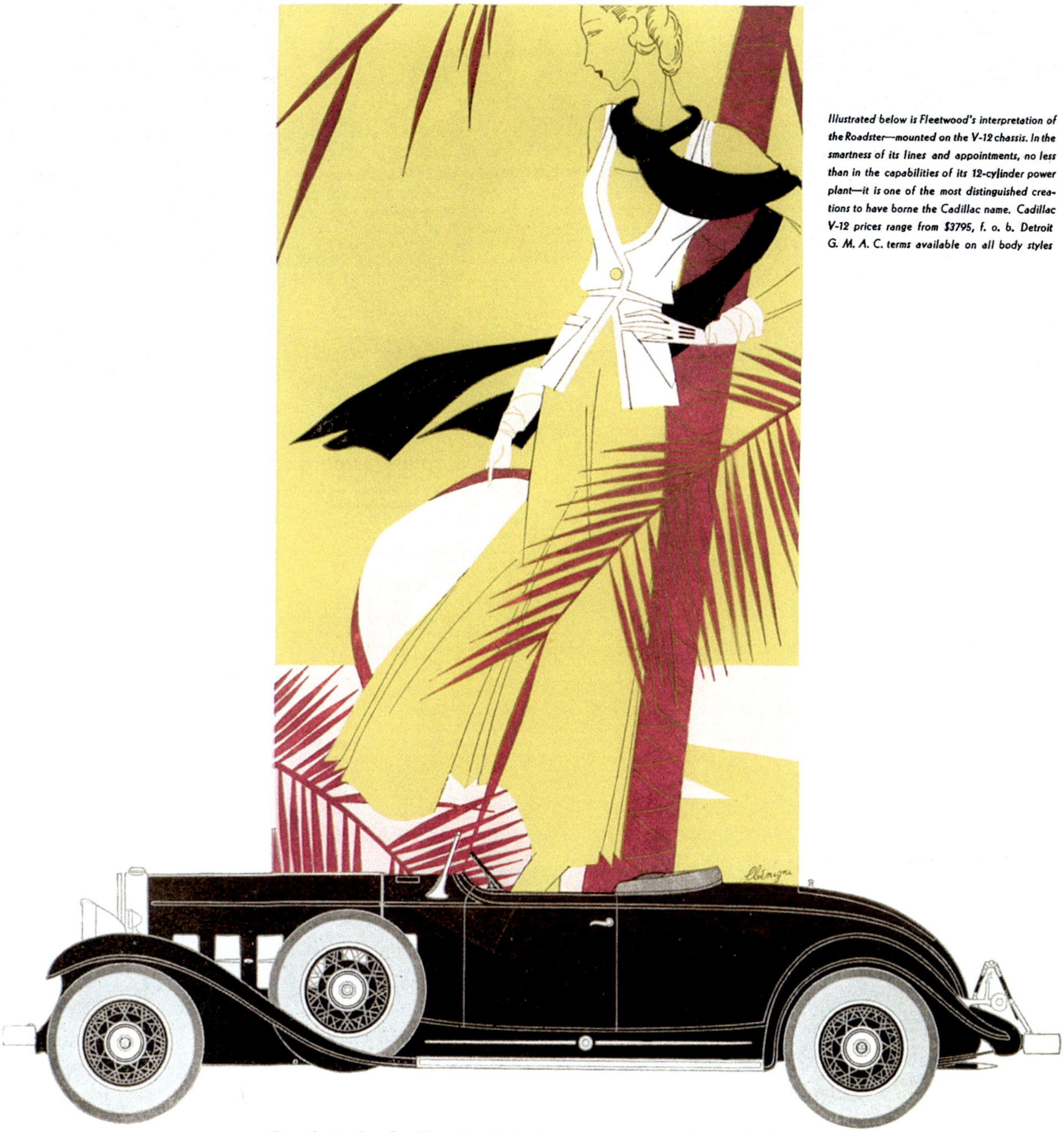

Illustrated below is Fleetwood's interpretation of the Roadster—mounted on the V-12 chassis. In the smartness of its lines and appointments, no less than in the capabilities of its 12-cylinder power plant—it is one of the most distinguished creations to have borne the Cadillac name. Cadillac V-12 prices range from $3795, f. o. b. Detroit G. M. A. C. terms available on all body styles

To ride in the Cadillac V-12 is to know at once why it is ranked so highly among the fine cars of the world—for the appeal of its 12-cylinder performance is well-nigh irresistible. Even those who are accustomed to the foremost automobiles, are finding in the V-12 a new conception of motoring luxury. In fact, a V-12 demonstration, almost without exception, makes conventional cars seem commonplace.

CADILLAC V 8 12 16

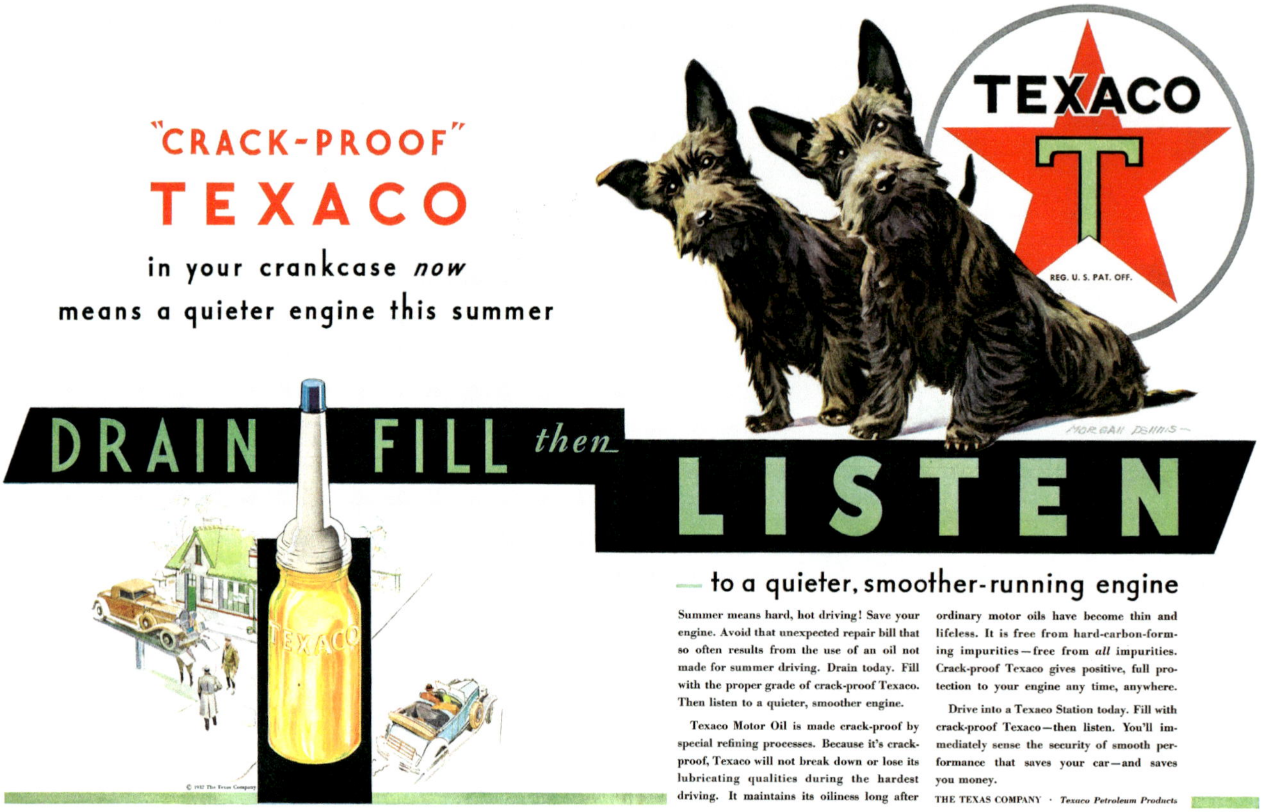

Texaco, 1931

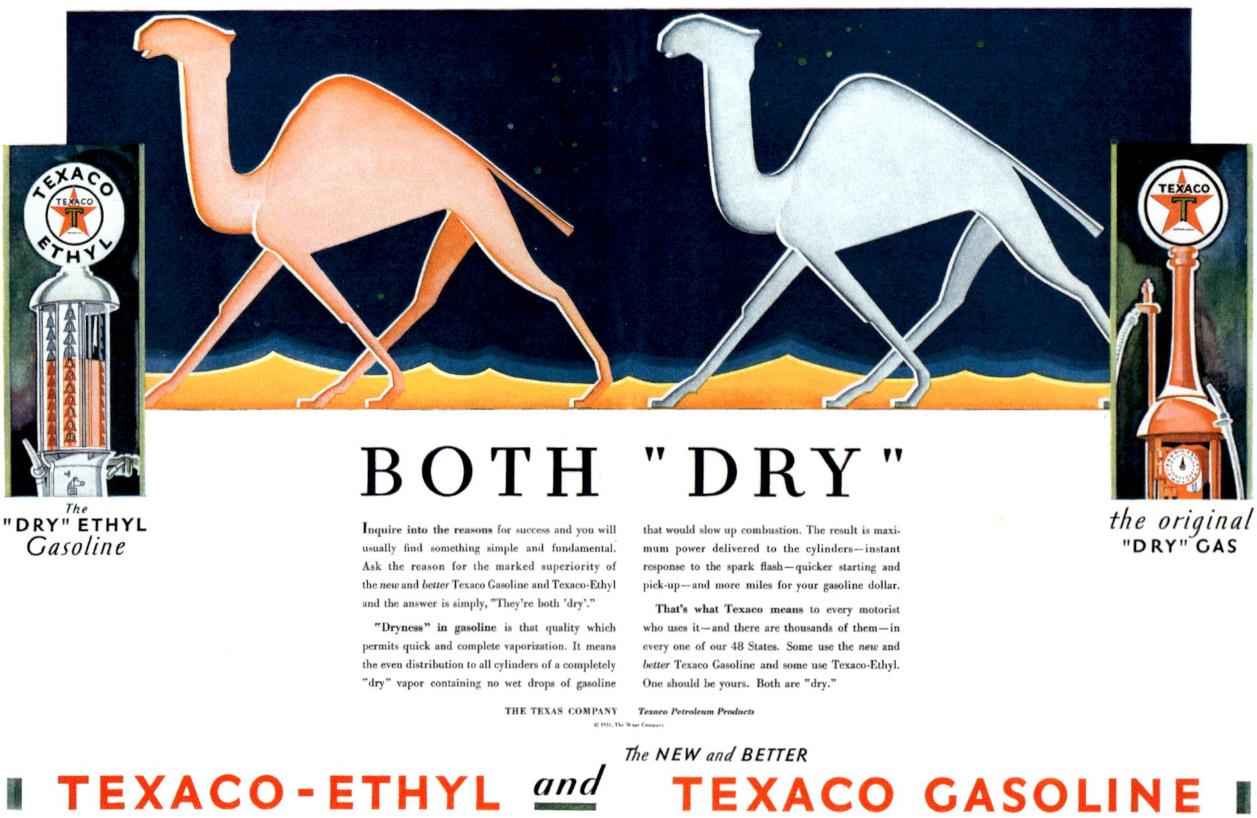

Texaco, 1931

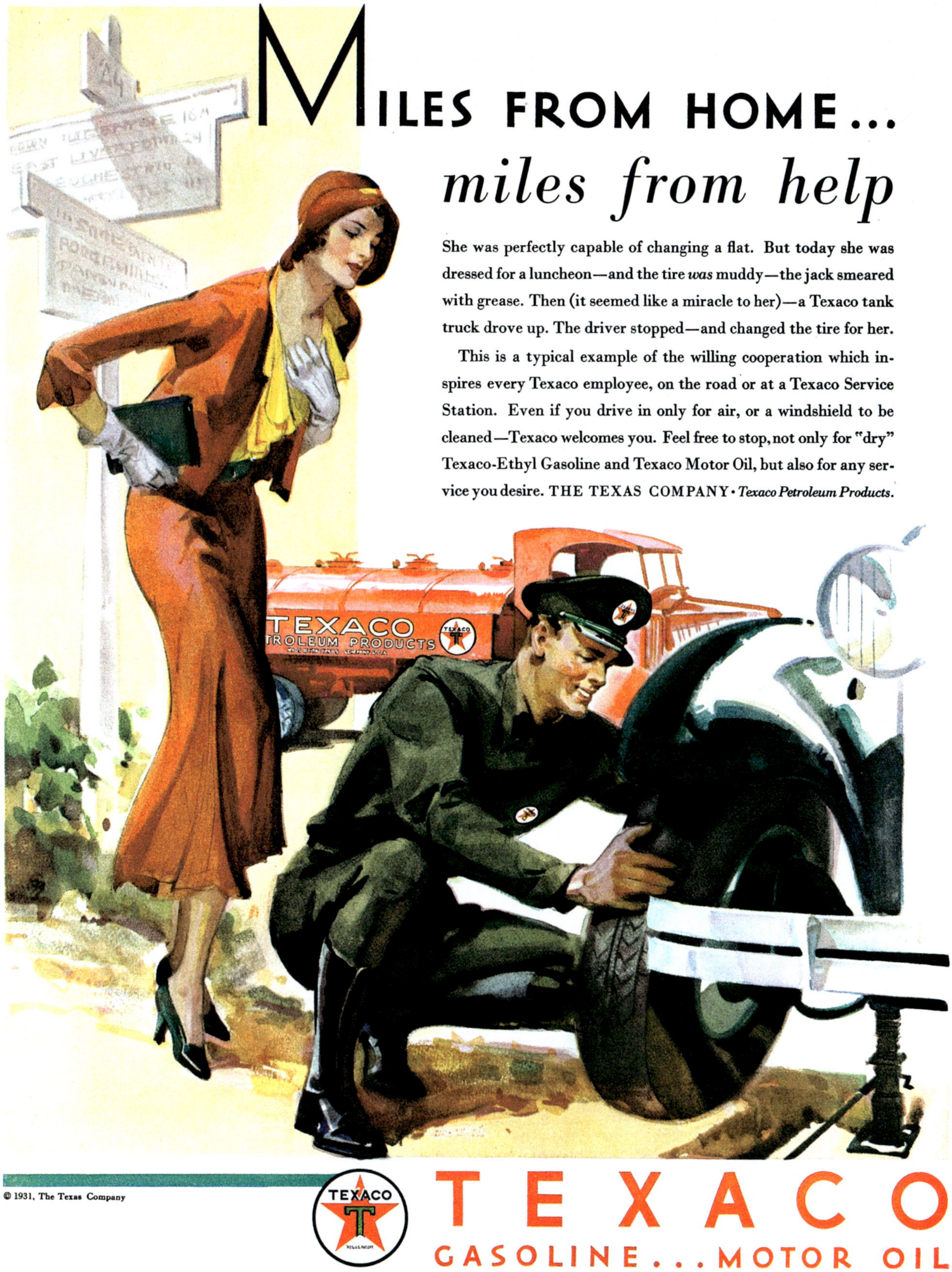
MILES FROM HOME...
miles from help
She was perfectly capable of changing a flat. But today she was dressed for a luncheon—and the tire *was* muddy—the jack smeared with grease. Then (it seemed like a miracle to her)—a Texaco tank truck drove up. The driver stopped—and changed the tire for her.
This is a typical example of the willing cooperation which inspires every Texaco employee, on the road or at a Texaco Service Station. Even if you drive in only for air, or a windshield to be cleaned—Texaco welcomes you. Feel free to stop, not only for "dry" Texaco-Ethyl Gasoline and Texaco Motor Oil, but also for any service you desire. THE TEXAS COMPANY · *Texaco Petroleum Products.*
TEXACO
TROLEUM PRODUCTS
© 1931, The Texas Company
TEXACO
TEXACO
GASOLINE . . . MOTOR OIL

Texaco, 1931

MANY A FINE CAR OWNER IS SELECTING OAKLAND FOR PERSONAL USE . . .

There are several reasons for the present trend toward Oakland V-8 as a personal car. For your personal car has a place all its own. It need not be as long or weighty perhaps as the largest cars you own, but it must meet your personal ideas of taste and style, and it must have the ability on the road to do the things that you ask.

We find that owners accustomed to fine automobiles see much in Oakland V-8 to meet their approval. They know its V-8 motor is in the certain trend of today's engine design for fine cars, boats or aircraft. They see the Syncro-mesh transmission as an evidence of thoughtfulness for their convenience.

In the Fisher-built bodies they find an understanding of their tastes and standards—a feeling of thorough care and of work well done.

It is an added virtue that a car like this may be had at a moderate price. Its expense for running and maintenance, too, comes within a sensible budget.

We want to turn one of these fine cars over to you for a two or three days' trial. Drive it anywhere you wish, and give it a real test.

THE SPORT COUPE

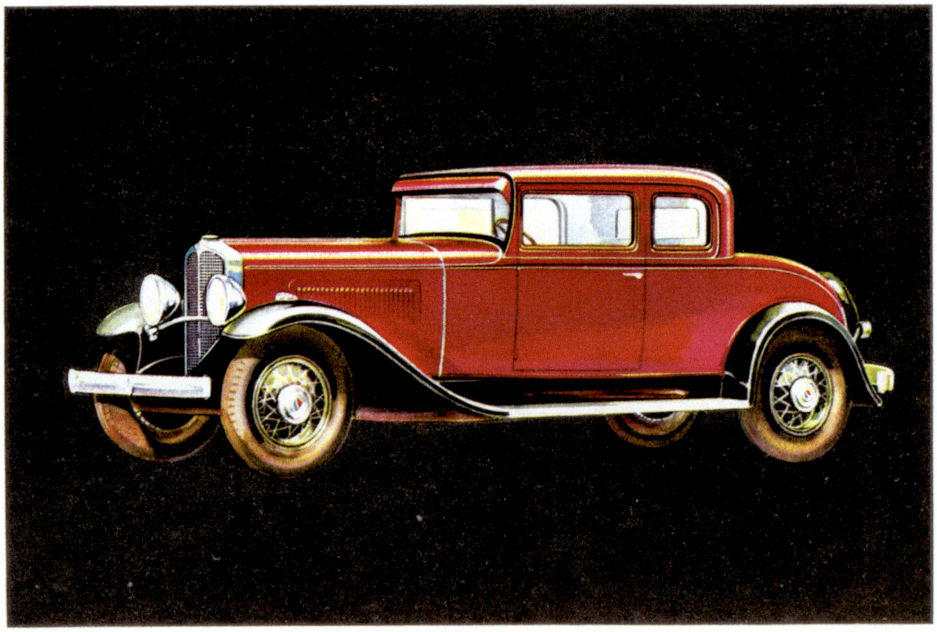

MAKING NEW FRIENDS AND KEEPING THE OLD

OAKLAND

PRODUCT OF GENERAL MOTORS · BODY BY FISHER

The Convertible Coupe

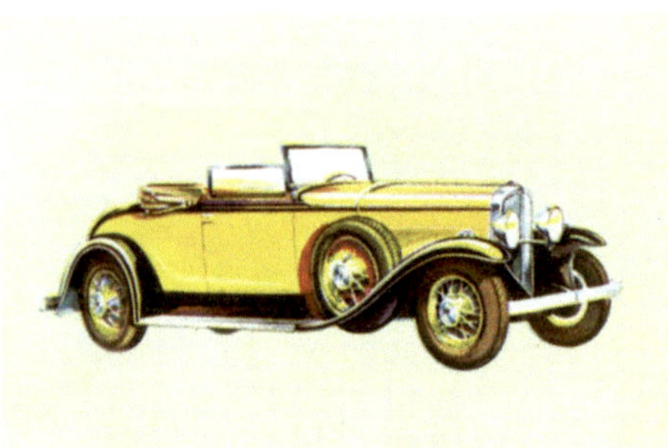

Oakland, 1931

► *Chrysler, 1931*

Y O U ' L L   B E   H A P P I E R   W I T H   A   C H R Y S L E R

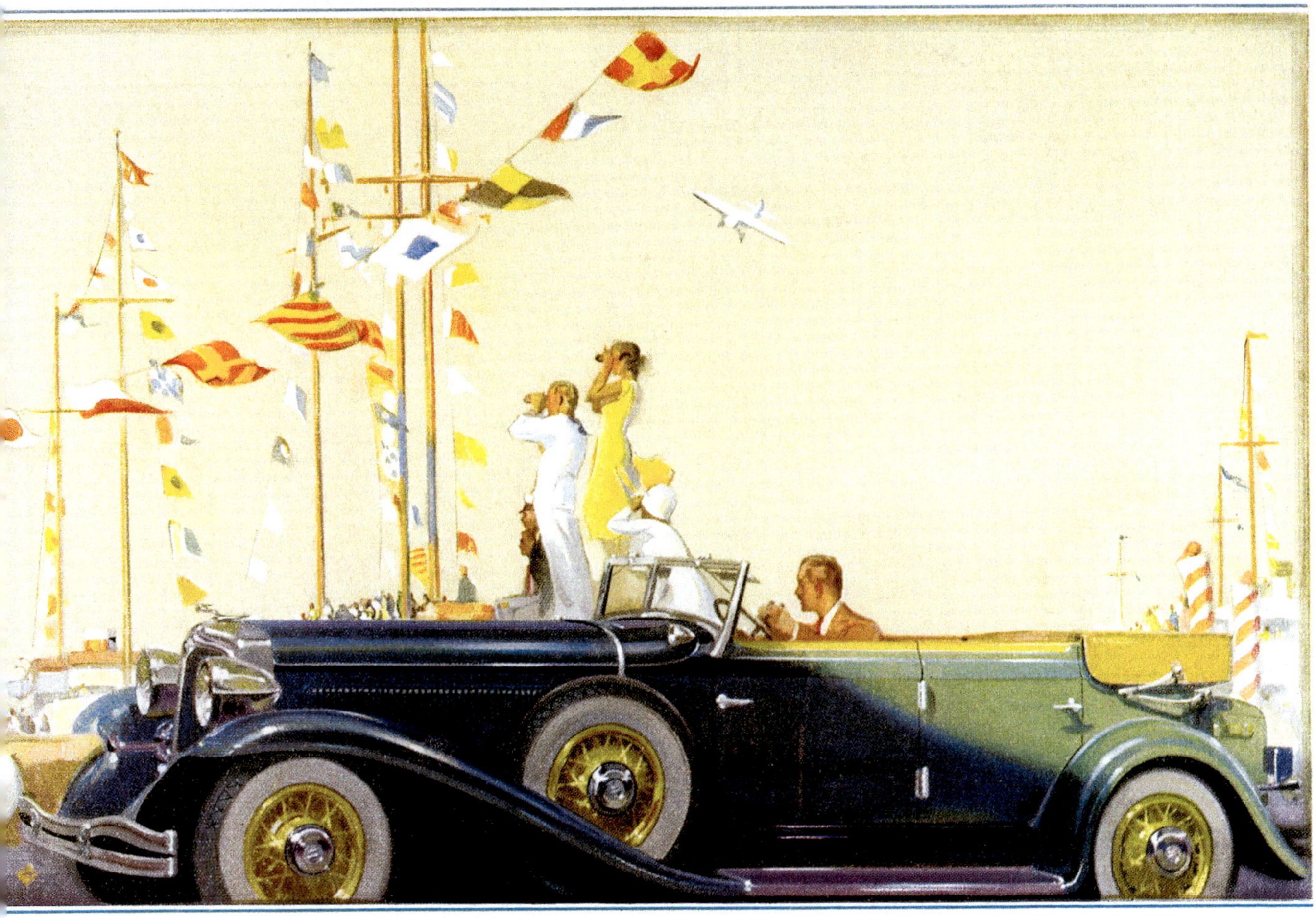

This is The Life!

AYBE it's because convertible cars have a particular swank; maybe it's because they have two-in-one utility—in either case, or ·th, it is obvious that convertible sedans and coupes are strongly in vogue. The increasing popularity of these smart and useful body types finds ırysler in the forefront, with convertibles meeting every desire. ırysler has created outstanding convertible sedans and coupes in four fferent chassis sizes—ranging all the way from $935 to $3595.

The convertible sedan pictured above is that of the Chrysler Impeal Eight, listing at $2195. Wheelbase, 135 inches; engine, 125 horse-·wer . . . a magnetic and magnificent motor car. Just to look at it akes you want to drive it.

Together with all the style and luxury of Chrysler's new convertibles, and of all other Chrysler models, there is an entirely new sensation in Chrysler performance. New results due to Floating Power engine mountings. Smoothest, quietest power you have ever experienced. Not the slightest engine tremor at any car speed. Not the slightest suggestion of engine effort.

The most refreshing of all cars to drive. Shock-proof steering. Effortless gear shifting. Squeak-proof springs. Strongest, safest bodies. Surest, safest brakes. Chrysler's unrivaled Hydraulic Brakes are always self-equalizing, and have Centrifuse drums that give *five times* the wear of ordinary brakes.

There's everything about a Chrysler to make you like it—and keep on liking it. There's just no equaling Chrysler engineering or Chrysler results.

new Chrysler Imperial Custom Eight, six body models, $2895 to $3595 · a new Chrysler Imperial Eight, three body models, $1925 to $2195 · a new Chrysler Eight, five dy models, $1435 to $1695 · a new Chrysler Six, five body models, $885 to $935 F. O. B. Factory · (On Sixes, the Automatic Clutch is optional at $8 extra and lite Squeak-Proof Springs are optional at $10 extra) · Duplate Safety Plate Glass standard on Custom Eights. Obtainable on Six and Eight Sedans, $17.50; on Imperial Sedans, $20 · all 2-passenger Coupes, $9.50. All closed models wired for PHILCO-TRANSITONE RADIO.

FLOATING POWER · AUTOMATIC CLUTCH · SILENT GEAR SELECTOR · FREE WHEELING · INTERNAL HYDRAULIC BRAKES · OILITE SQUEAK-PROOF SPRINGS · DOUBLE-DROP GIRDER-TRUSS FRAME

C H R Y S L E R

I M P E R I A L

WITH PATENTED

FLOATING POWER

ıne in on CHRYSLER MOTORS RADIO PROGRAM **"Ziegfeld Radio Show"** personally conducted by Flo Ziegfeld — Columbia Coast-to-Coast Network; every Sunday evening

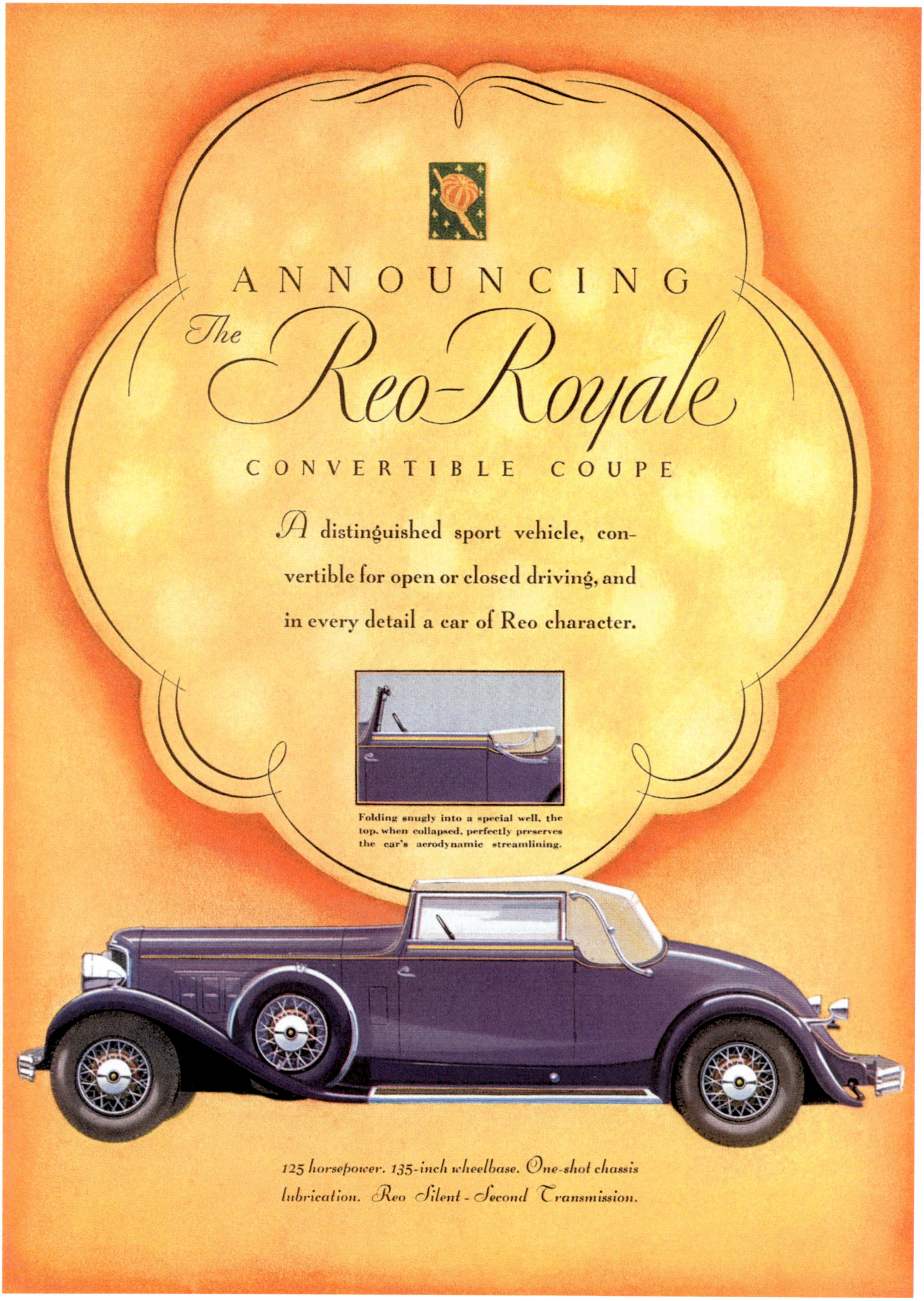

Reo-Royale, 1931

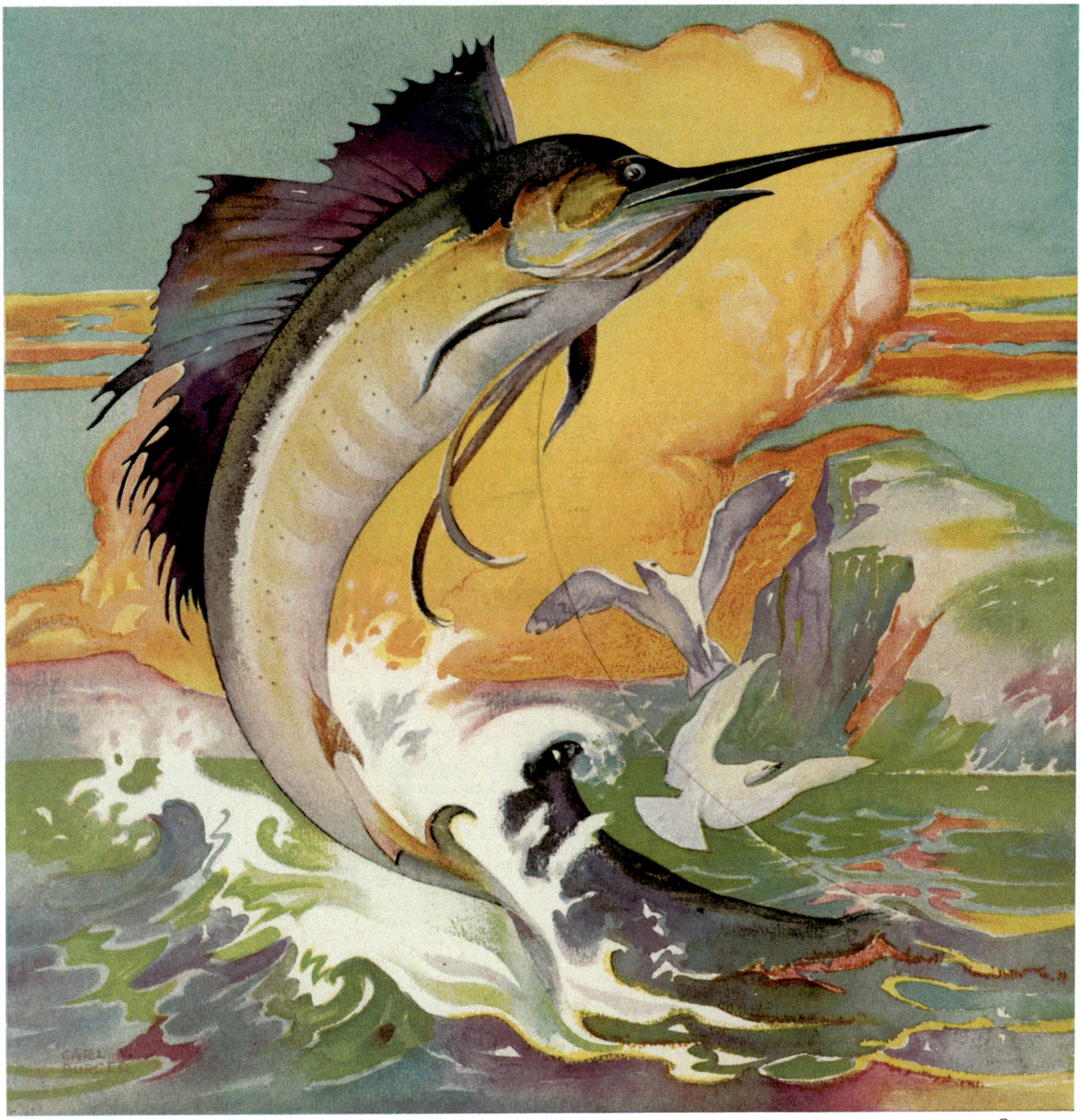

©E. G. C. 1931

AS POWERFUL AS ETHYL GASOLINE

THE leaping, racing fight of the sailfish is a breath-taking display of power under perfect control.

To put the power of gasoline under control, leading oil refiners add Ethyl fluid. This prevents the uneven explosions that cause power-waste, harmful "knock" and overheating. It *controls combustion*, delivering power to the pistons with a smoothly increasing pressure.

Controlled combustion makes such an improvement in car performance that Ethyl Gasoline is now the biggest selling motor fuel in the country. Practically all leading refiners add Ethyl fluid to good gasoline to form Ethyl Gasoline, and nearly every filling station now has one or more Ethyl pumps. Look for the Ethyl emblem. Ethyl Gasoline Corporation, New York City.

WITH ETHYL BRAND OF ANTI-KNOCK COMPOUND ETHYL GASOLINE CORPORATION NEW YORK, U.S.A. Controls Combustion

GOOD GASOLINE + ETHYL FLUID = ETHYL GASOLINE

FOR SUMMER DRIVING — *Ethyl Gasoline keeps the motor cooler because combustion is controlled. In summer, as in other seasons, Ethyl fluid is mixed with base gasoline that is best suited to the season.*

THE ACTIVE INGREDIENT USED IN ETHYL FLUID IS LEAD

examine value

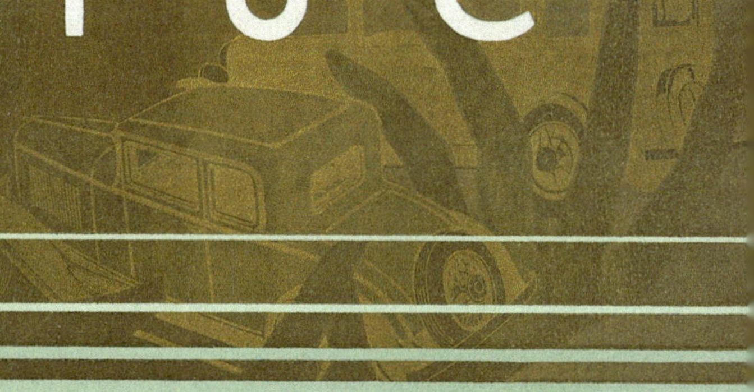

GM
GENERAL MOTORS

The General Motors Corporation maintains a creative staff known as the Art and Color Section to aid and counsel the division engineers in the style development of General Motors cars. The special province of this staff embraces style, color and appointments, and under its skillful handling, lines and proportions yield to fashion influences well in advance of the prevailing mode. Through the activities of the Art and Color Section, General Motors is kept abreast of style changes, and in co-operation with division engineers conscientious effort is made to secure the most pleasing effects. Thus the divisions of the General Motors Corporation are supported in their creative work by unusual art and style facilities which contribute deeply to the outstanding values in General Motors cars.

A Car for Every Purse and Purpose

Chevrolet Roadster	$ 475
Chevrolet Sport Roadster	495
Chevrolet Phaeton	510
Chevrolet Coupe	535
Chevrolet Coupe (5 Windows)	545
Chevrolet Coach	545
Chevrolet Sport Coupe	575
Chevrolet 5 passenger Coupe	595
Chevrolet Convertible Cabriolet	615
Chevrolet Sedan	635
Chevrolet Special Sedan	650
Chevrolet Landau Phaeton	650
Pontiac Coupe	675
Pontiac Sedan, 2-Door	675
Pontiac Sport Coupe	715
Pontiac Sedan, 4-Door	745
Pontiac Convertible Coupe	745
Pontiac Custom Sedan	785
Oldsmobile Sedan, 2-Door	$ 845
Oldsmobile Coupe	845
Oldsmobile Sport Coupe	895
Oakland Coupe	895
Oakland Sedan, 2-Door	895
Oldsmobile Sedan, 4-Door	925
Oldsmobile Convertible Roadster	935
Oldsmobile Patrician Sedan	960
Oakland Sport Coupe	975
Oakland Sedan, 4-Door	995
Oakland Convertible Coupe	995
Buick 2 Pass. Business Coupe "56"	1,025
Buick 2 Door Sedan "50"	1,035
Oakland Custom Sedan	1,055
Buick Sport Roadster "54"	1,055
Buick Phaeton "55"	1,058
Buick 4 Pass. Special Coupe "56S"	1,055
Buick 4 Door Sedan "57"	1,095
Buick 4 Pass. Conv. Coupe "8-56C"	1,095
Buick 2 Pass. Business Coupe "66"	$1,285
Buick 4 Pass. Special Coupe "66S"	1,325
Buick Sport Roadster "64"	1,335
Buick Phaeton "65"	1,335
Buick 4 Door Sedan "67"	1,355
Buick 4 Pass. Coupe "86"	1,535
Buick 4 Door Sedan "87"	1,565
Buick Sport Roadster "94"	1,610
Buick 7 Pass. Phaeton "95"	1,620
Buick 4 Pass. Country Club Coupe "96S"	1,720
Buick 5 Pass. Coupe "96"	1,765
Buick 4 Door Sedan "91"	1,785
Buick 4 Pass. Conv. Coupe "8-96C"	1,785
Buick 7 Pass. 4 Door Sedan "90"	1,935
Buick 7 Pass. Limousine "90L"	2,035
La Salle V-8 Coupe, 2 Passenger	2,195
La Salle V-8 Roadster	2,245
La Salle V-8 Convertible Coupe	2,295
La Salle V-8 Sedan, 5 Passenger	$2,295
La Salle V-8 Coupe, 5 Passenger	2,295
La Salle V-8 7 Pass. Touring	2,345
La Salle V-8 5 Pass. Town Sedan	2,345
La Salle V-8 Sedan, 7 Passenger	2,475
La Salle V-8 Imperial	2,595
Cadillac V-8 Coupe, 2 Passenger	2,695
Cadillac V-8 Coupe, 5 Passenger	2,795
Cadillac V-8 Sedan, 5 Passenger	2,795
Cadillac V-8 Roadster, 2 Passenger	2,845
Cadillac V-8 Town Sedan	2,845
Cadillac V-8 Phaeton	2,945
Cadillac V-8 Convertible Coupe	2,945
Cadillac V-8 Sedan, 7 Passenger	2,945
Cadillac V-8 Imperial	3,095
Cadillac V-8 Touring	3,195
La Salle V-8 All-Weather Phaeton	3,245
La Salle V-8 Sedanet	3,245
La Salle V-8 5 Pass. Sedanet Cab.	3,245
Cadillac V-8 All-Weather Phaeton	$
Cadillac V-12 Coupe, 2 Passenger	
Cadillac V-12 Coupe, 5 Passenger	
Cadillac V-12 Sedan, 5 Passenger	
Cadillac V-12 Roadster	
Cadillac V-12 Town Sedan	
Cadillac V-12 Phaeton	
Cadillac V-12 Convertible Coupe	
Cadillac V-12 Sedan, 7 Passenger	
Cadillac V-12 Touring	
Cadillac V-12 Imperial	
Cadillac V-12 All-Weather Phaeton	
Cadillac V-16, 31 Fleetwood Custom Models	$5,350 to $
Cadillac V-16, Special Custom Models	up to $1

All prices f. o. b. factories. G. M. A time payment plan available on all G eral Motors Products sold to the pu

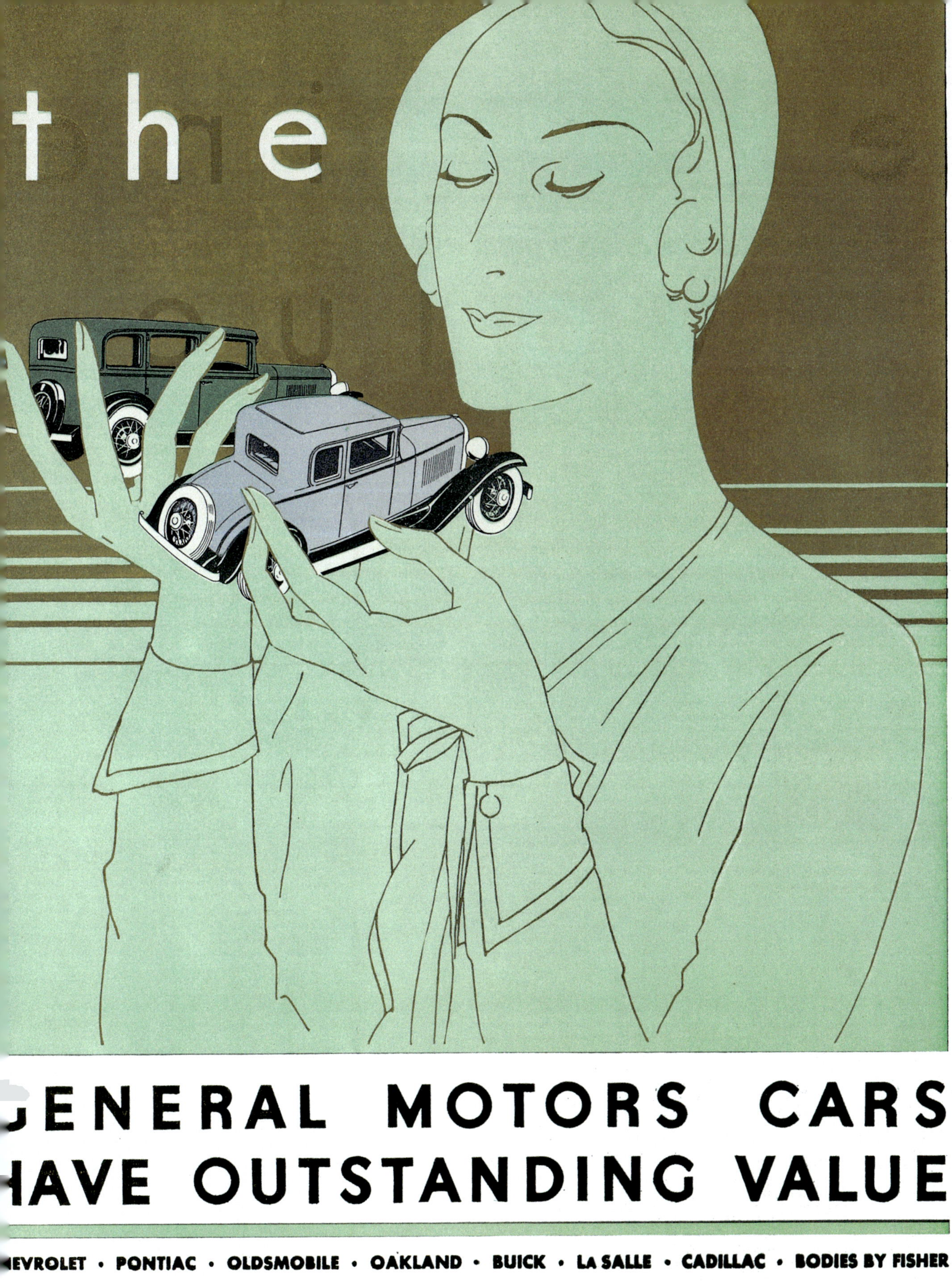
the
ENERAL MOTORS CARS
AVE OUTSTANDING VALUE
EVROLET • PONTIAC • OLDSMOBILE • OAKLAND • BUICK • LA SALLE • CADILLAC • BODIES BY FISHER

A NEW FRIEZE UPHOLSTERY by Chase

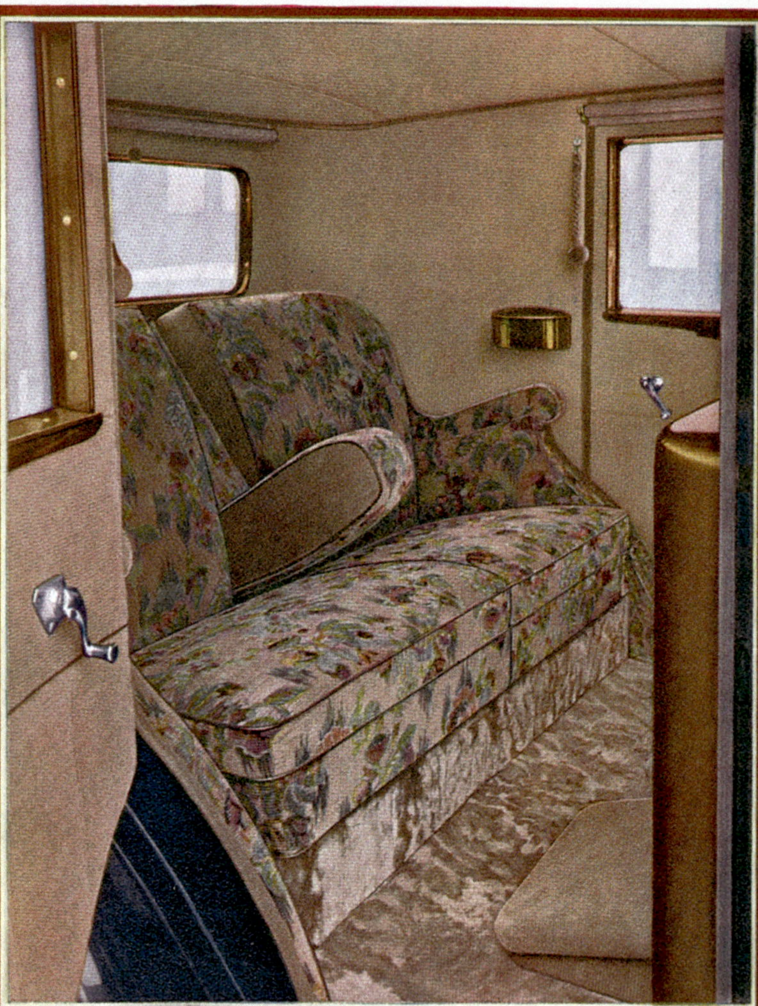

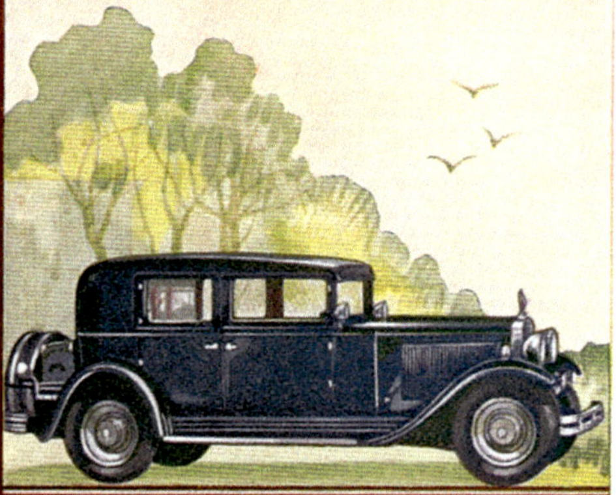

ZENOBIA - A NEW FABRIC AND DESIGN AS USED IN A SPECIAL NASH EIGHT SEDAN

THE revolt against lustreless, monotones in motor car upholstery is here evidenced in this interesting car interior.

Here, indeed, is a striking example of a modern application of an old-world art . . . hand block-printing on a beautiful Mohair Frieze. The elegance of the design . . . a rich floral motif . . . the superb pastel colorings employed and the enduring nature of the fabric, are indicative of a new upholstery trend.

The noticeable swing-back to fine, mohair fabrics for motor cars is evidence of growing dissatisfaction with delicate upholstery materials which are only adaptations for automobile use and are not pre-eminently "travel fabrics" . . . a distinction enjoyed for many years by Chase Angora mohair fabrics.

There is one of a variety of unusual Chase Velmo fabrics which will enhance the beauty of your car. Full co-operation offered to your dealer in its selection or samples for the asking.

Product of . . . . SANFORD MILLS: *Selling Agents:* L. C. Chase & Co., Boston, New York . . Detroit . . San Francisco . . Chicago

The unique Frieze Upholstery, used so effectively in the interior of this de Luxe motor car owned by Mr. J. C. Tills of the Pittsburgh Plate Glass Company is complemented by a solid color side-wall and deck-lining Chase Frieze and also Imperial Mohair floor rug . . . both of the same ground tone as the seat covering.

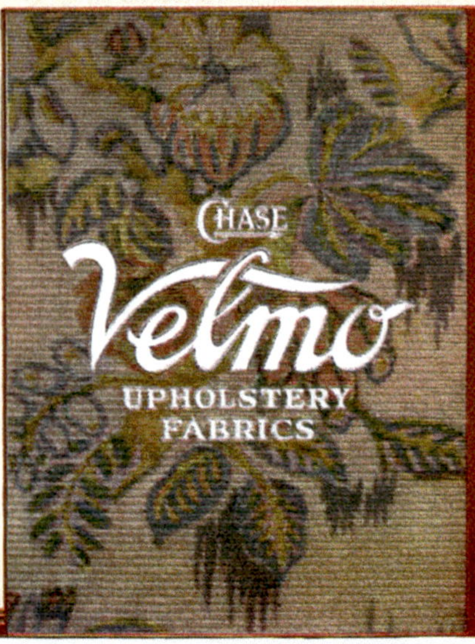

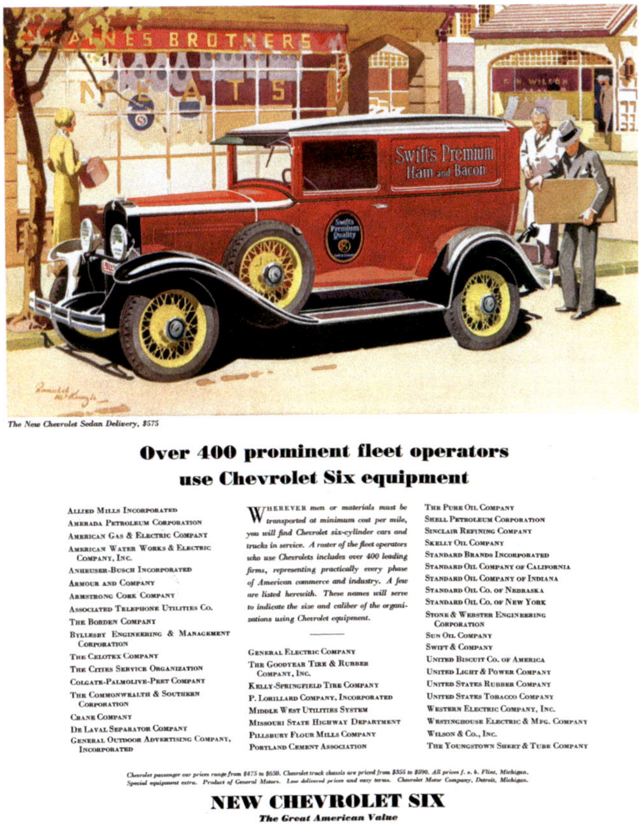

Chevrolet, 1931

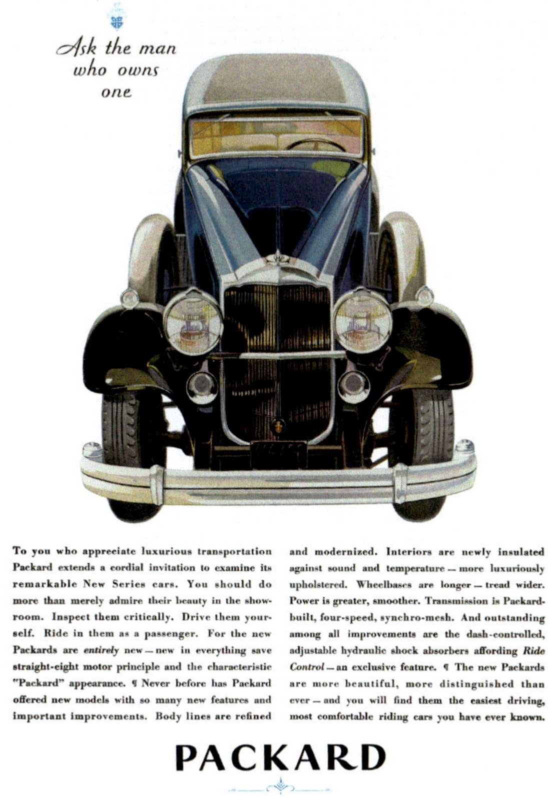

Packard, 1931

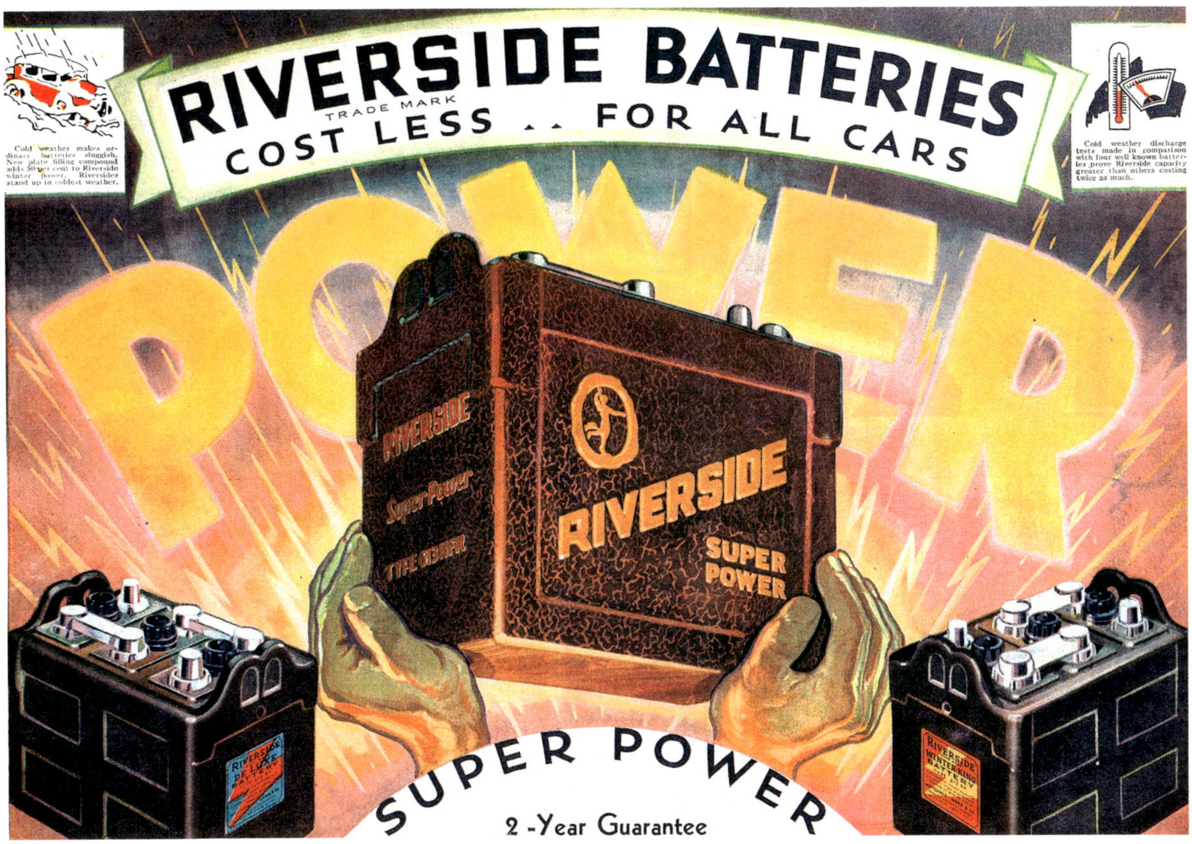

Velmo Upholstery Fabrics, 1931 ◄ Riverside Batteries, 1931

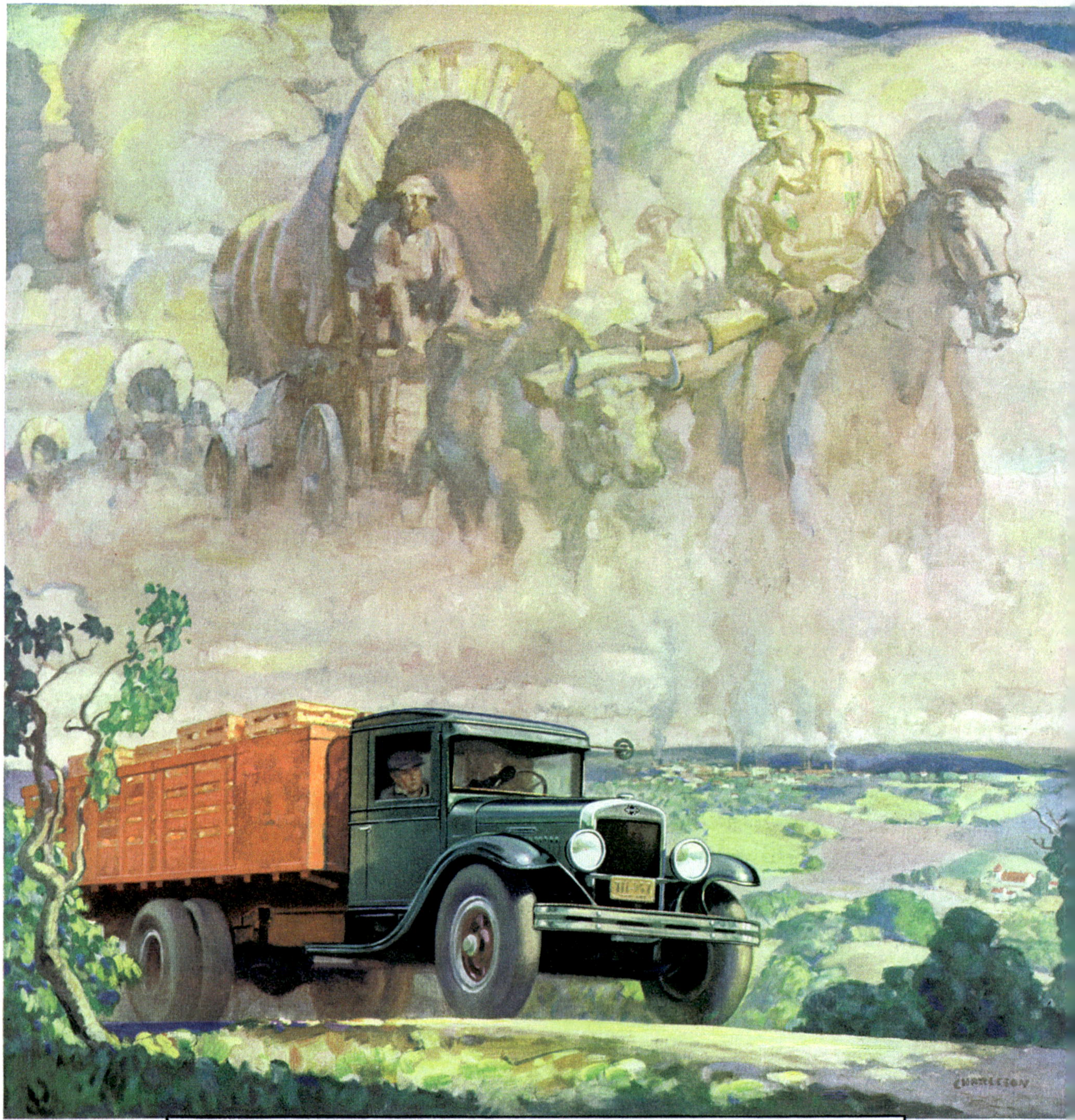

THE INTERNATIONAL MOTOR TRUCK—1931

Product of a Full Century of Manufacturing Experience

Today the service of International Harvester in the field of Transportation goes far beyond Agriculture. Three-fourths of its great annual output in trucks is absorbed by Commerce and Industry—a striking demonstration of universal acceptance, proof of the merit in manufacture that grows out of generations of accumulated experience.

1 8 3 1

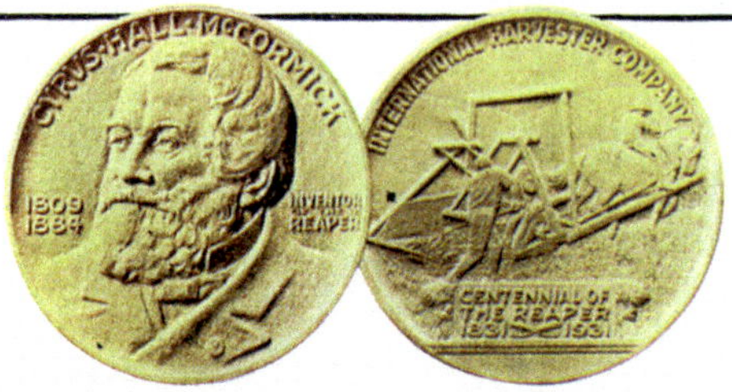

1 9 3 1

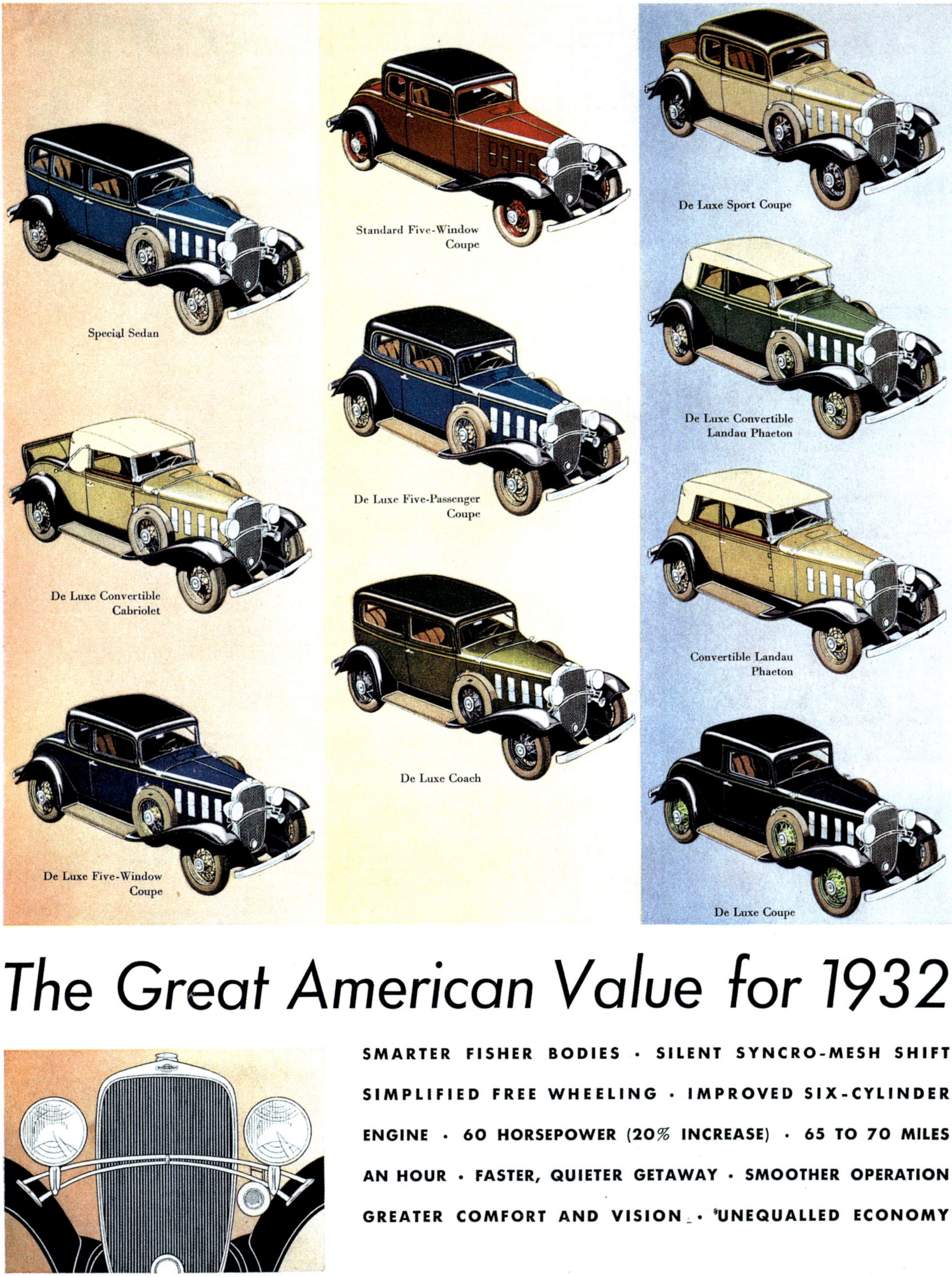

Chevrolet, 1931 ◄▲

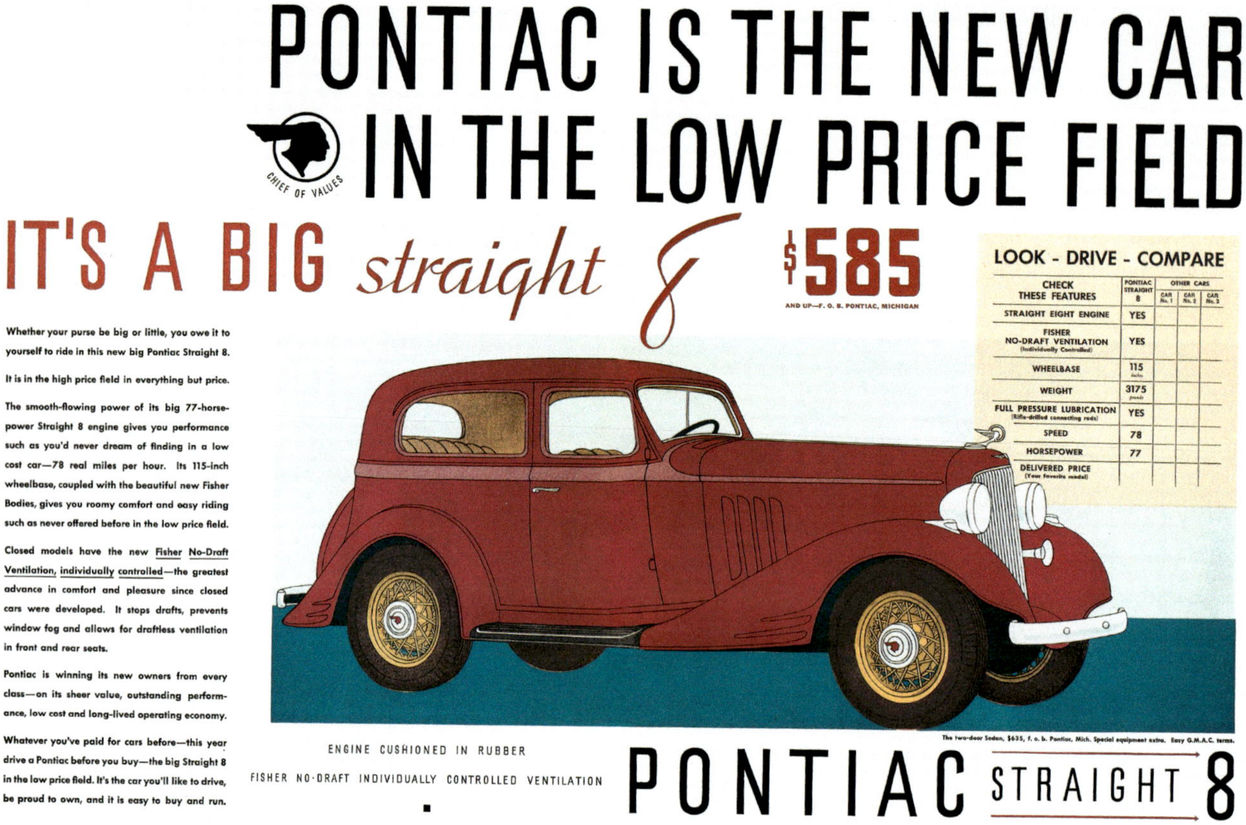

Pontiac, 1931

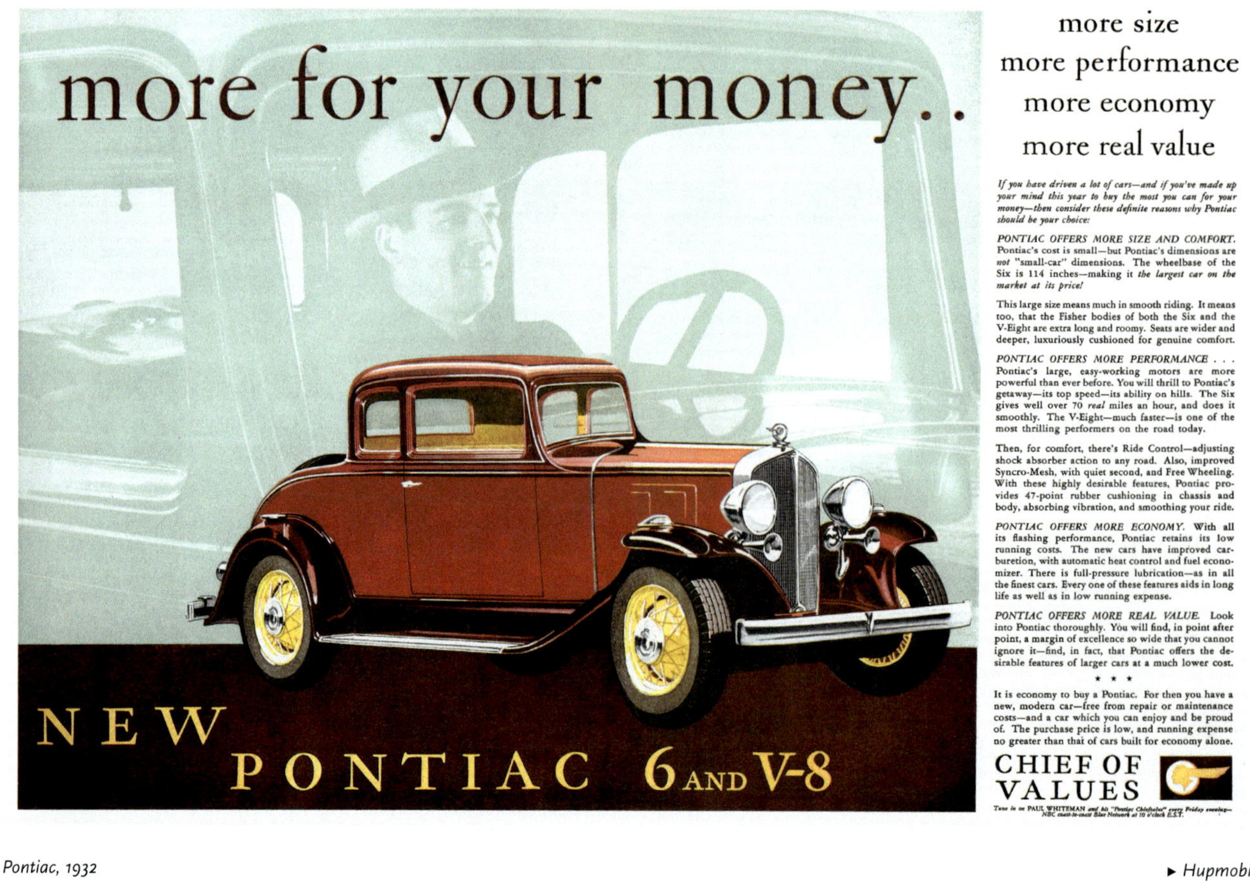

Pontiac, 1932

► *Hupmobile, 1932*

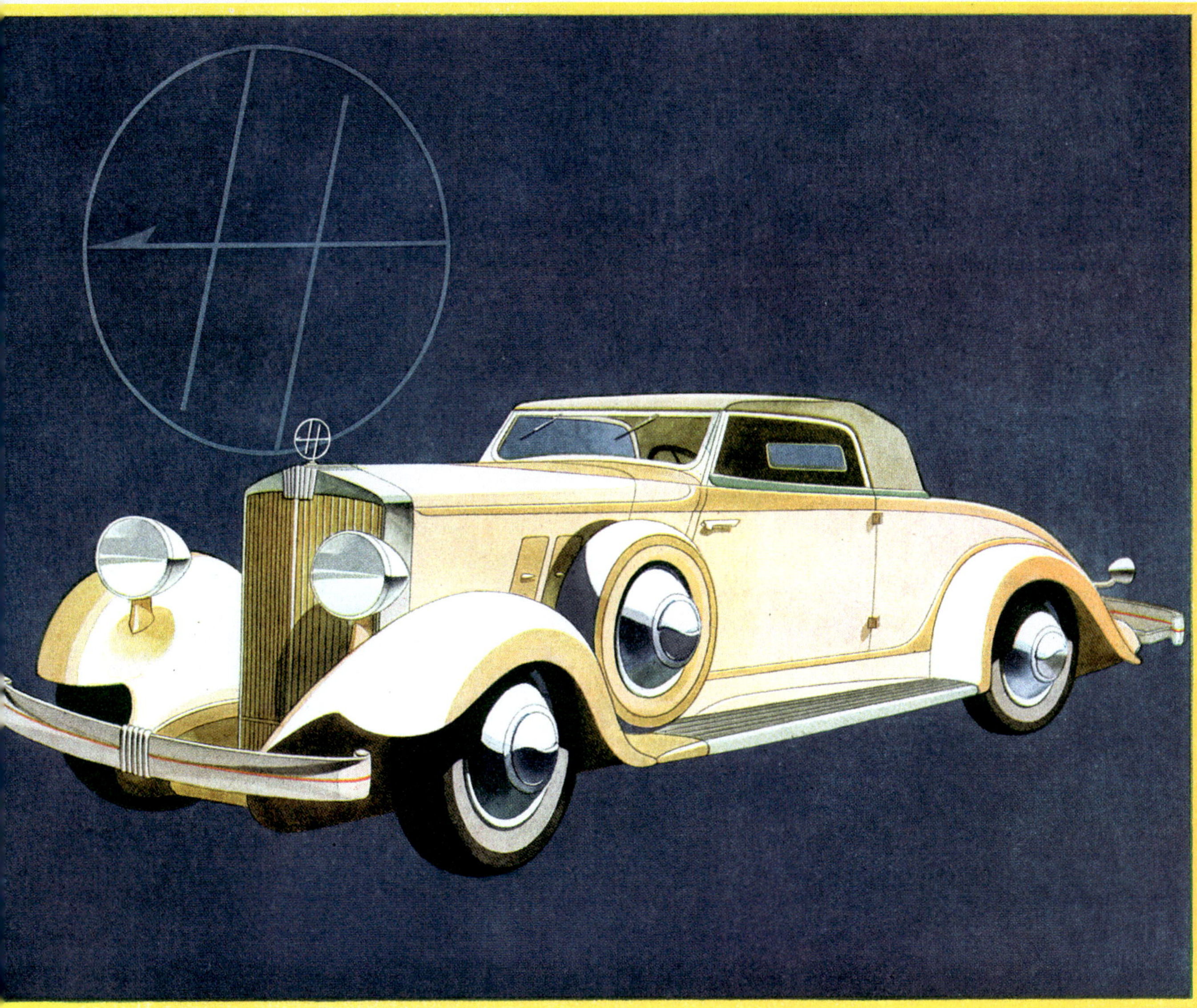

MEETING·THE·NEW·TIMES

WITH GREATER HUPMOBILE SIXES AND EIGHTS
26 MODELS . . . . $795 AND UP
AT THE FACTORY

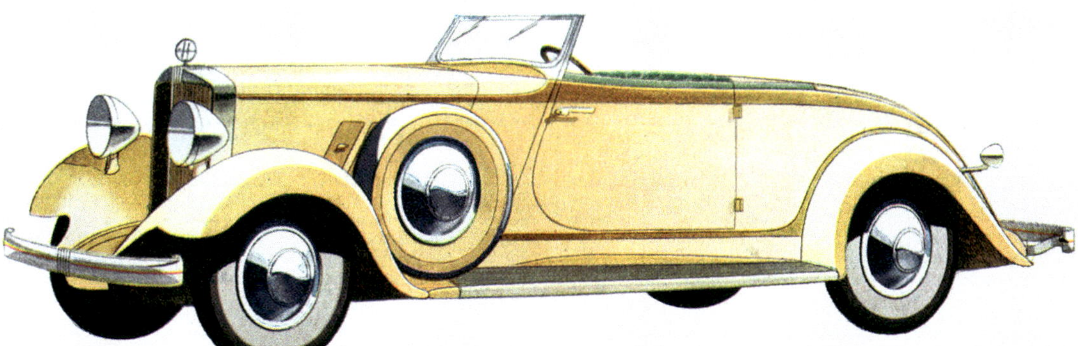

Two views of the Cabriolet-Roadster. Note how top completely disappears, leaving just a smooth expanse of gleaming metal.

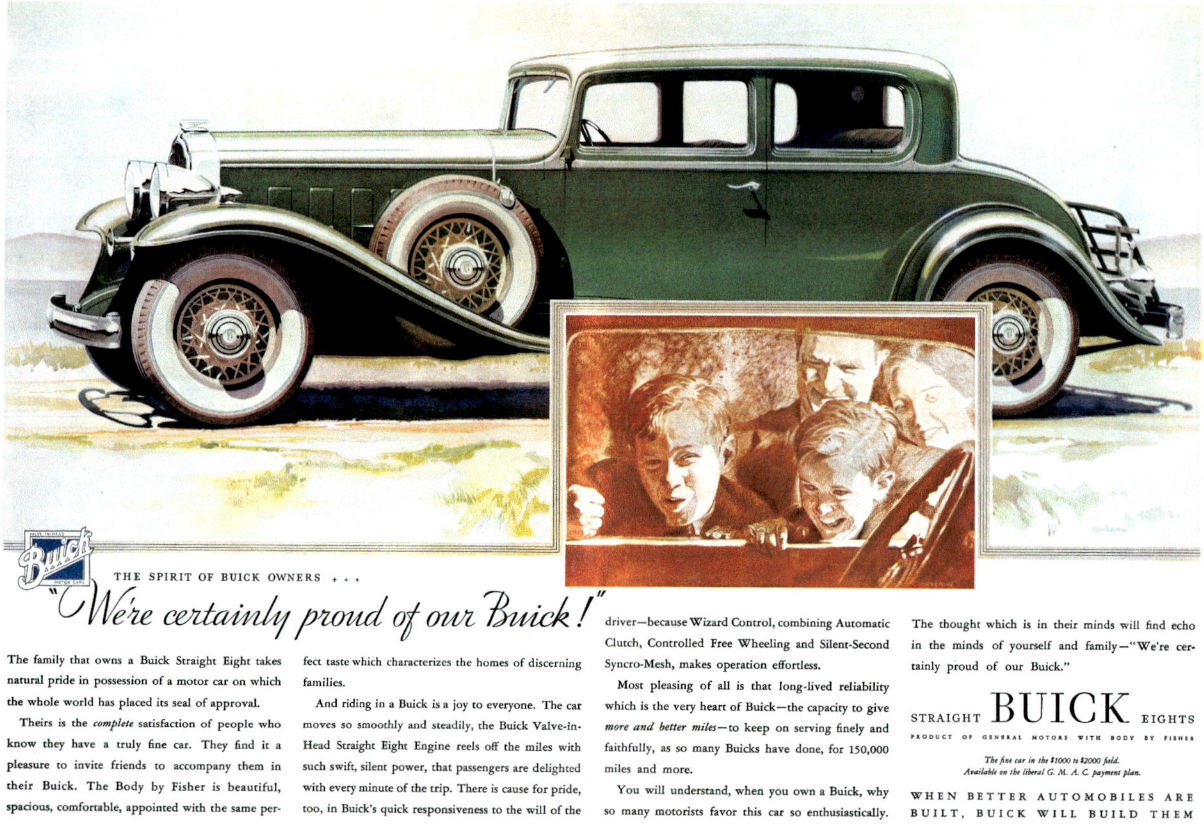

Buick, 1932

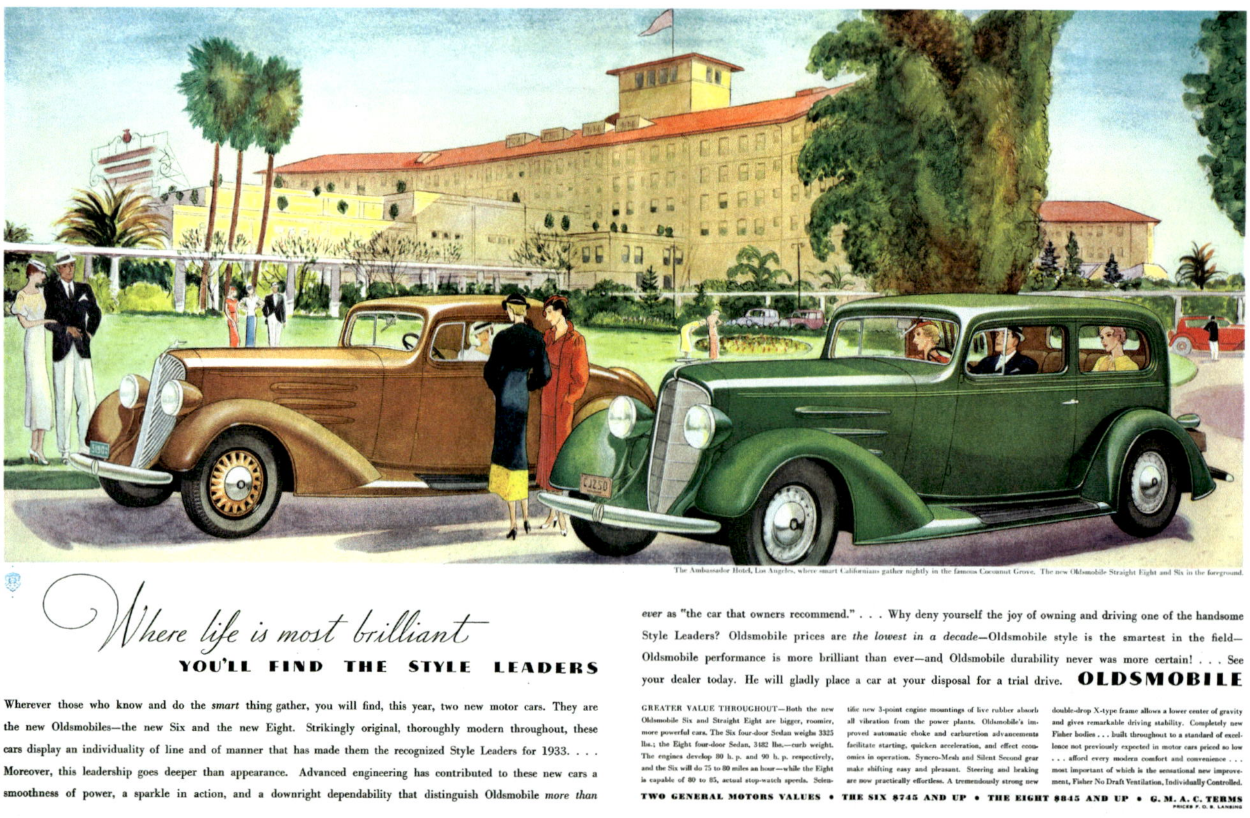

Oldsmobile, 1932

▸ *General Motors, 1932* ▸▸ *La Salle, 1932*

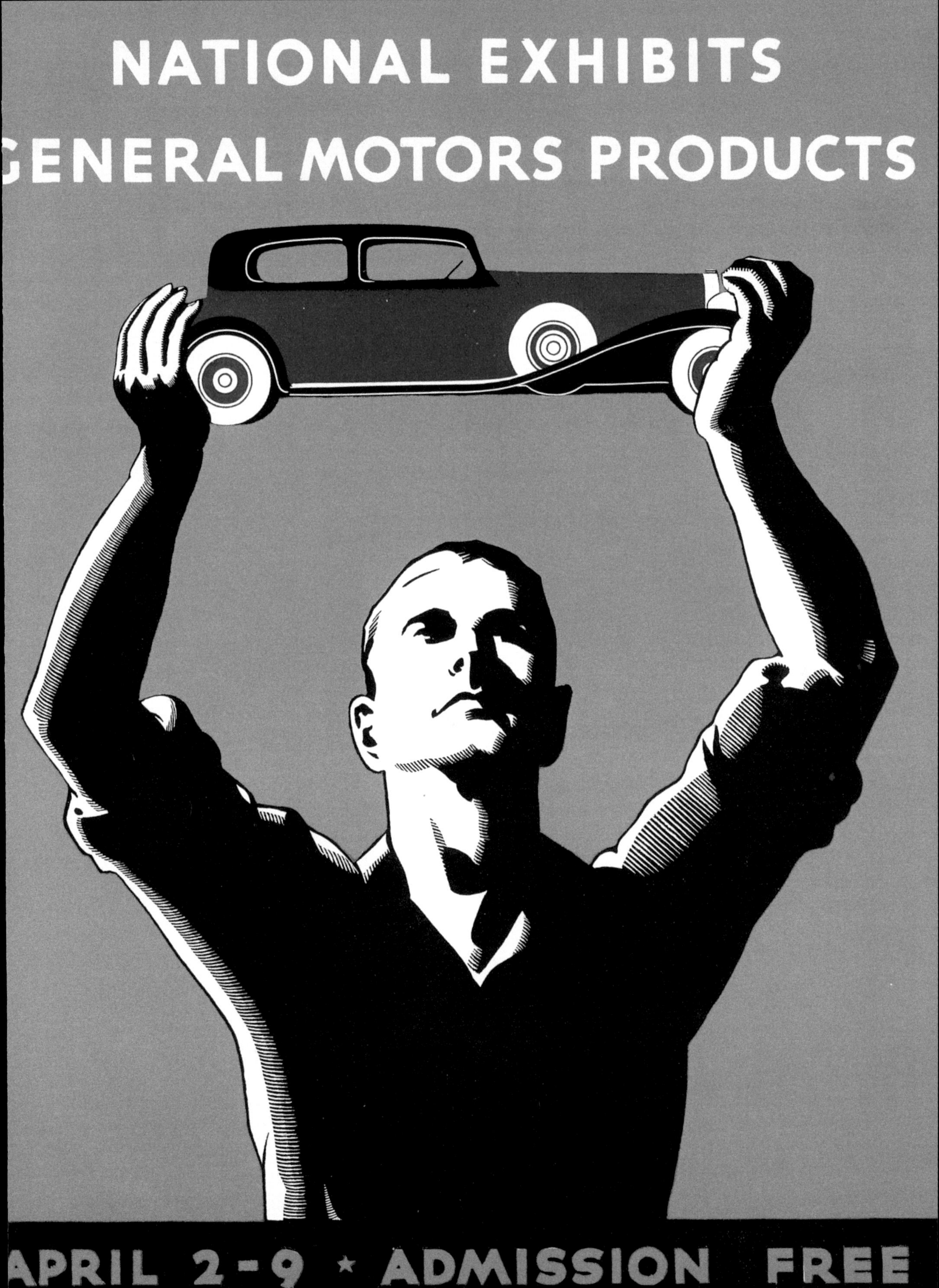
NATIONAL EXHIBITS
GENERAL MOTORS PRODUCTS
APRIL 2-9 ★ ADMISSION FREE

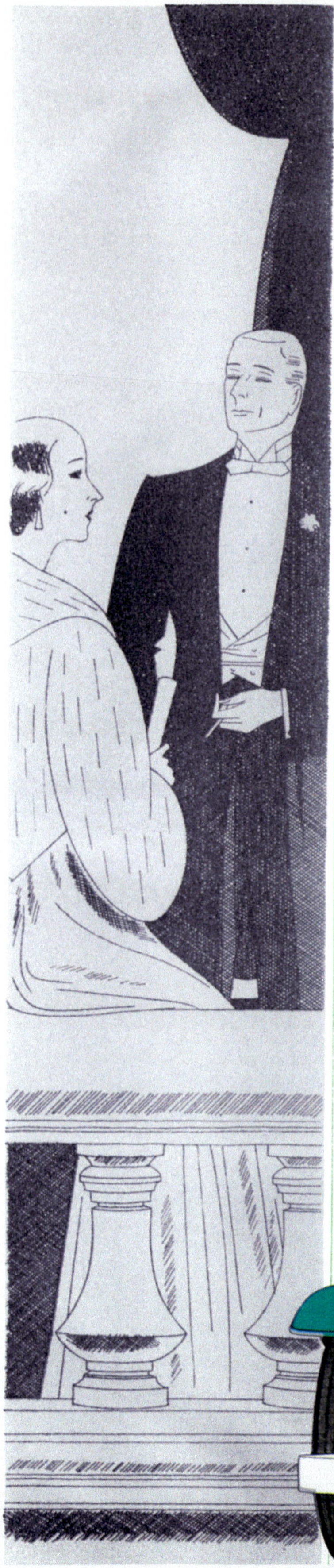

Do you know for what a moderate sum you can own a New La Salle?

Because of their deep regard for La Salle's high place among the fine cars of the world, many people do not realize that La Salle is *not* a costly car to own. The initial expenditure is very little more than the price of many automobiles of less distinguished character. As a result of the thorough quality Cadillac creates with its fine design and precise craftsmanship, the expense for La Salle's operation and maintenance is surprisingly small. And, finally, La Salle's faultless style and faithful performance inspire an unusual span of ownership. One is happy to keep a La Salle over a much greater length of time and drive it a great deal farther than a lesser automobile. In fact, the actual figures often prove that many who are now driving lower-priced cars might very *profitably* be enjoying the prestige and satisfaction of owning a La Salle. Why not get the facts from your Cadillac-La Salle dealer today? La Salle prices from \$2395, Cadillac from \$2795, f. o. b. Detroit.

LA SALLE

V EIGHT

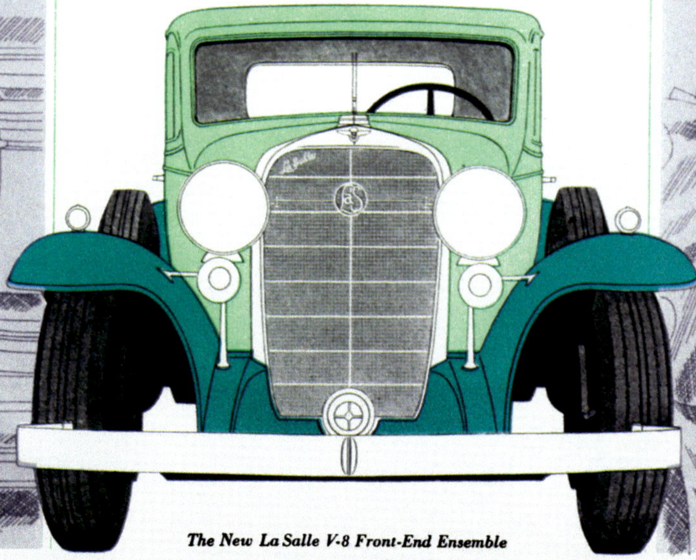

The New La Salle V-8 Front-End Ensemble

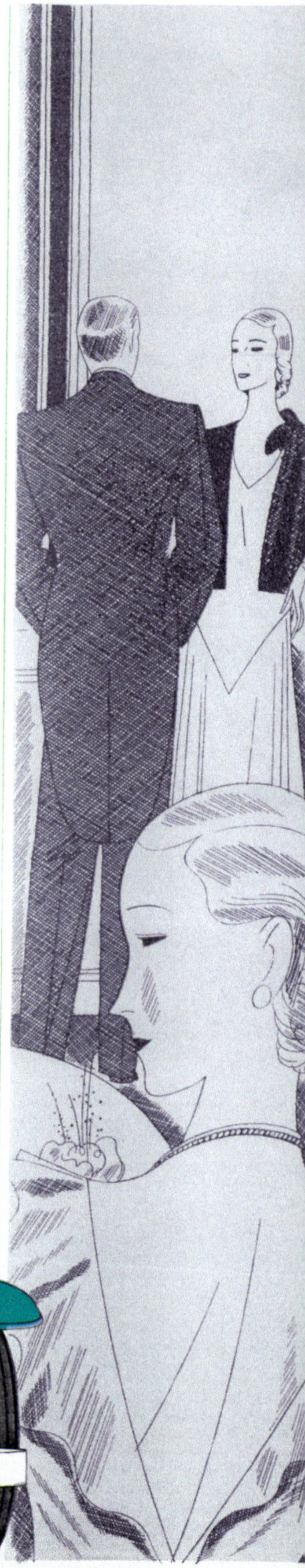

SONDERFARBE

Standard of the World

A man is known by his automobile

Of all those material possessions which bespeak a man's place among his fellow men—none is more instantly recognized than his automobile. Wherever he goes and whatever he does, his car has come to be accepted as a symbol of his tastes, his standing and his business success. Because of this, there has grown up about Cadillac and LaSalle a degree of respect which is unusual in America's business life. Men who have given the problem serious thought will have no other automobile; for here is the "Standard of the World"—the car which has stood, for thirty years, as the emblem of all that is fine. They know, when they drive a Cadillac or LaSalle, that they have the masterpiece itself—and that it is given the recognition which a masterpiece always inspires. LaSalle prices range from $2395, Cadillac from $2795, f. o. b. Detroit.

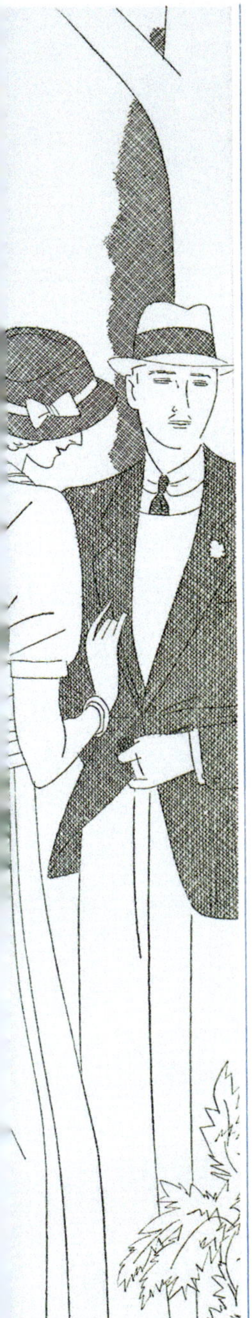

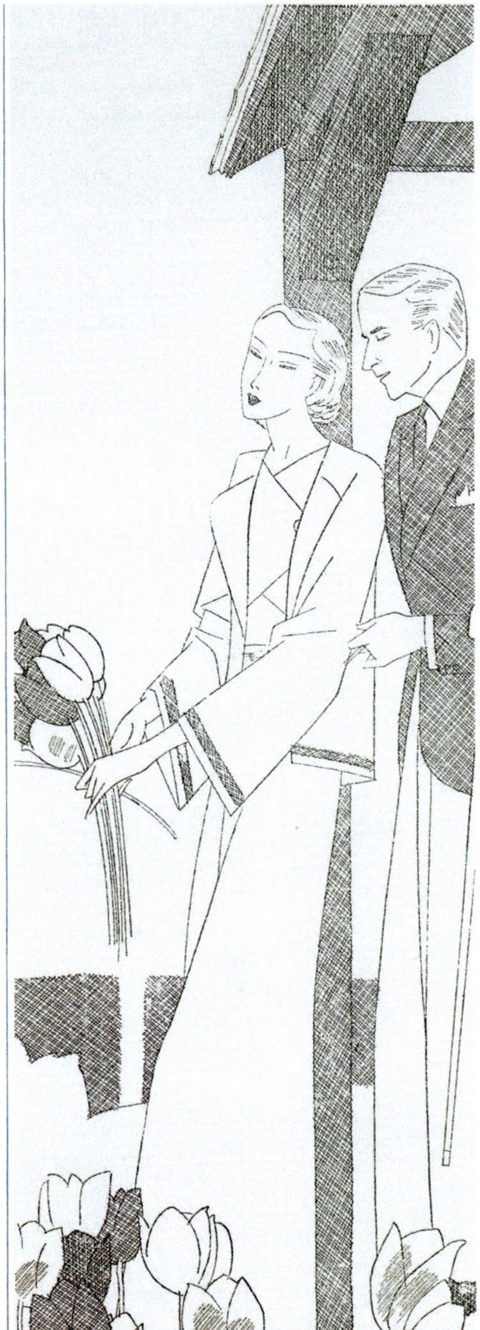

CADILLAC

V 8 12 16

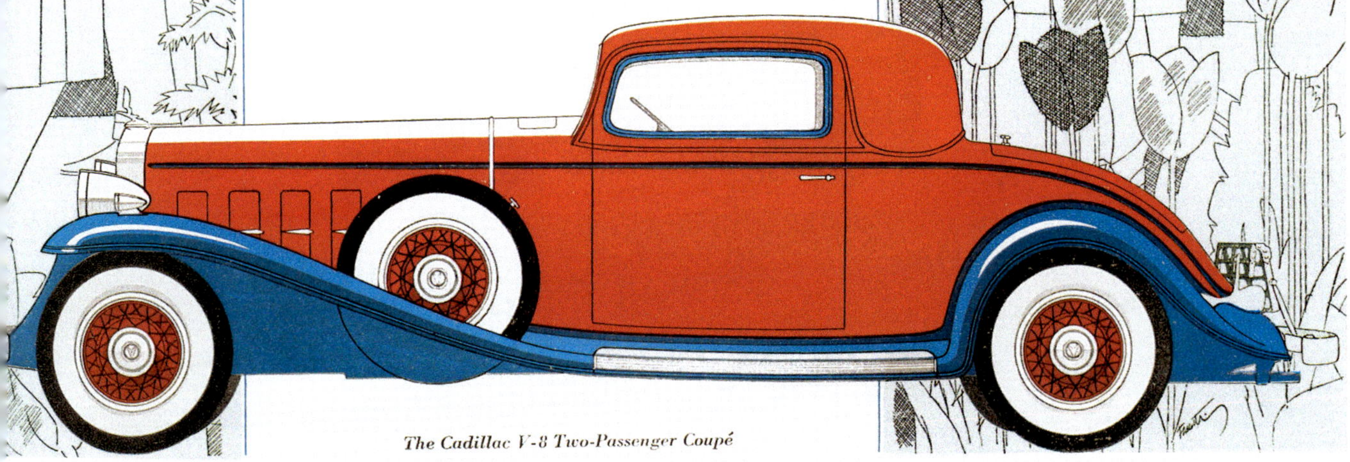

The Cadillac V-8 Two-Passenger Coupé

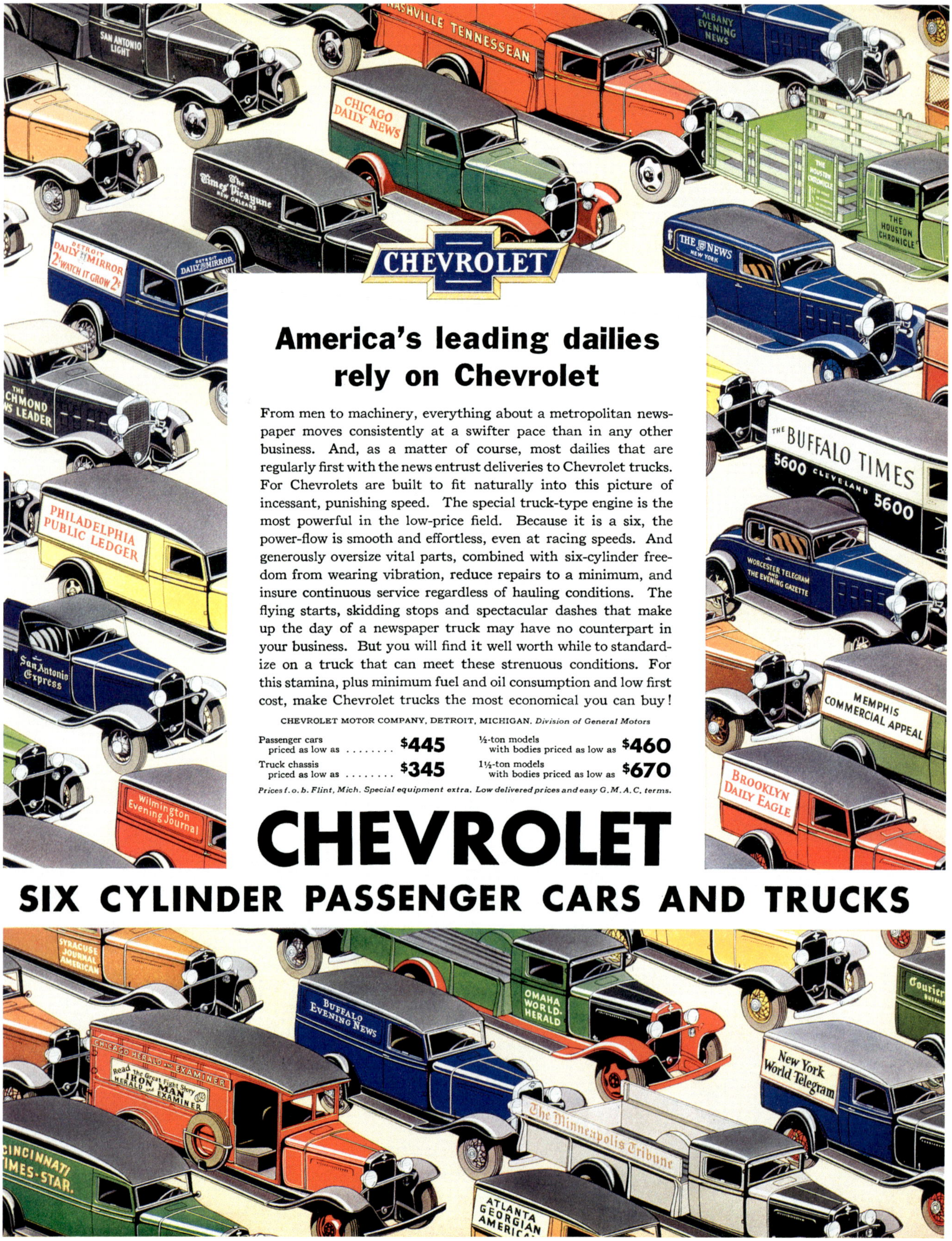

Cadillac, 1932 ◂◂ *Chevrolet*, 1932

▸ *Chevrolet*, 1931 ▸▸ *Firestone*, 1934

SIX-CYLINDER SMOOTHNESS
—at lower cost than ever

For over two years, it has been Chevrolet's distinction to build the world's lowest ced six-cylinder car. And today, by utilizing the t resources at its disposal, the Chevrolet Motor mpany is able to present: *a bigger and better six-inder automobile selling at even lower prices.* The performance of Chevrolet's 50-horsepower six-cylinder motor is made even more satisfying and enjoyable. Steady, quiet power at every speed . . . exceptional flexibility in traffic . . . positive pick-up . . . effortless high speeds . . . unusual dependability and long life . . . all these advantages of six-cylinder smoothness

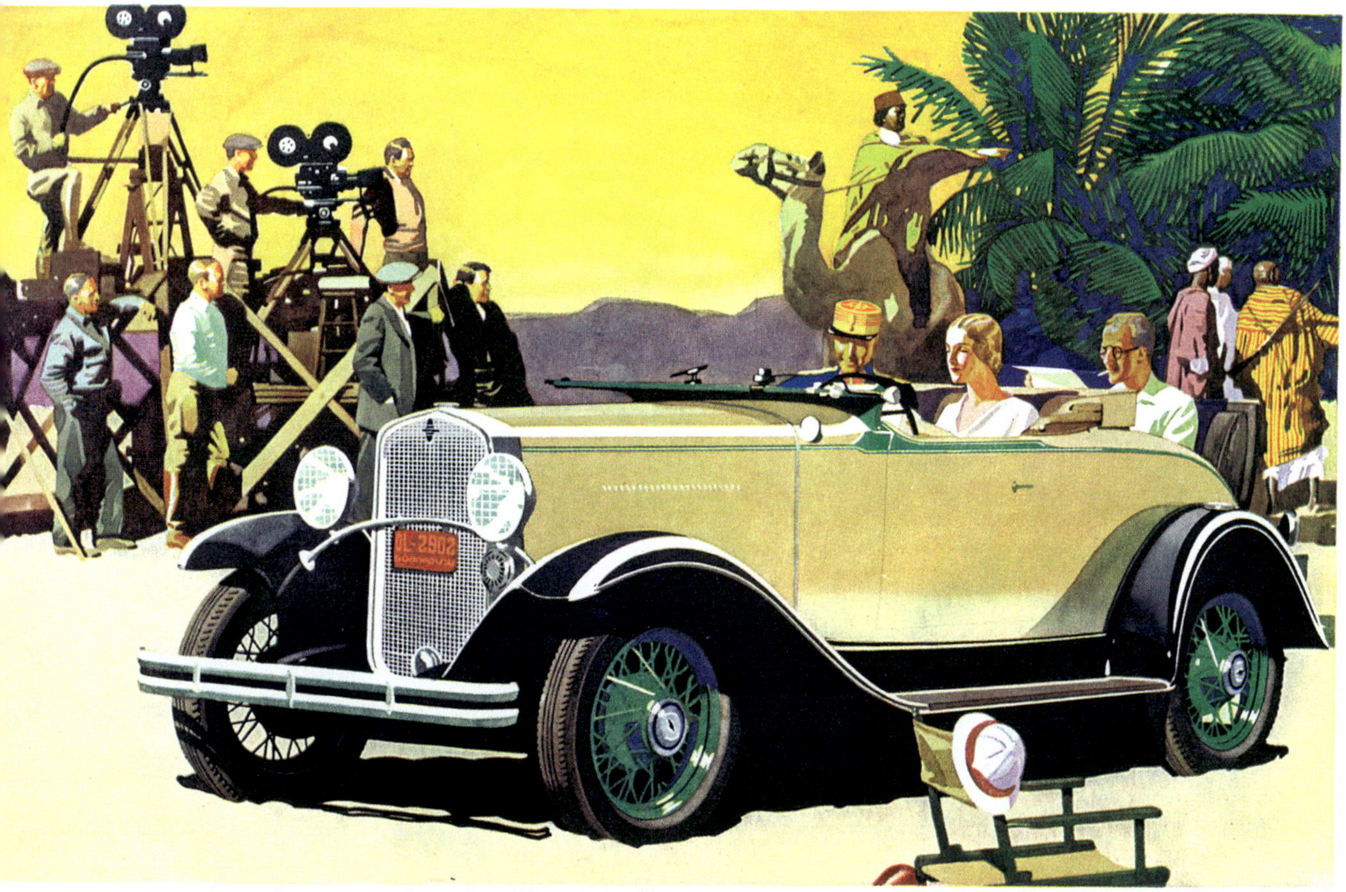

The Chevrolet Sport Roadster with rumble seat

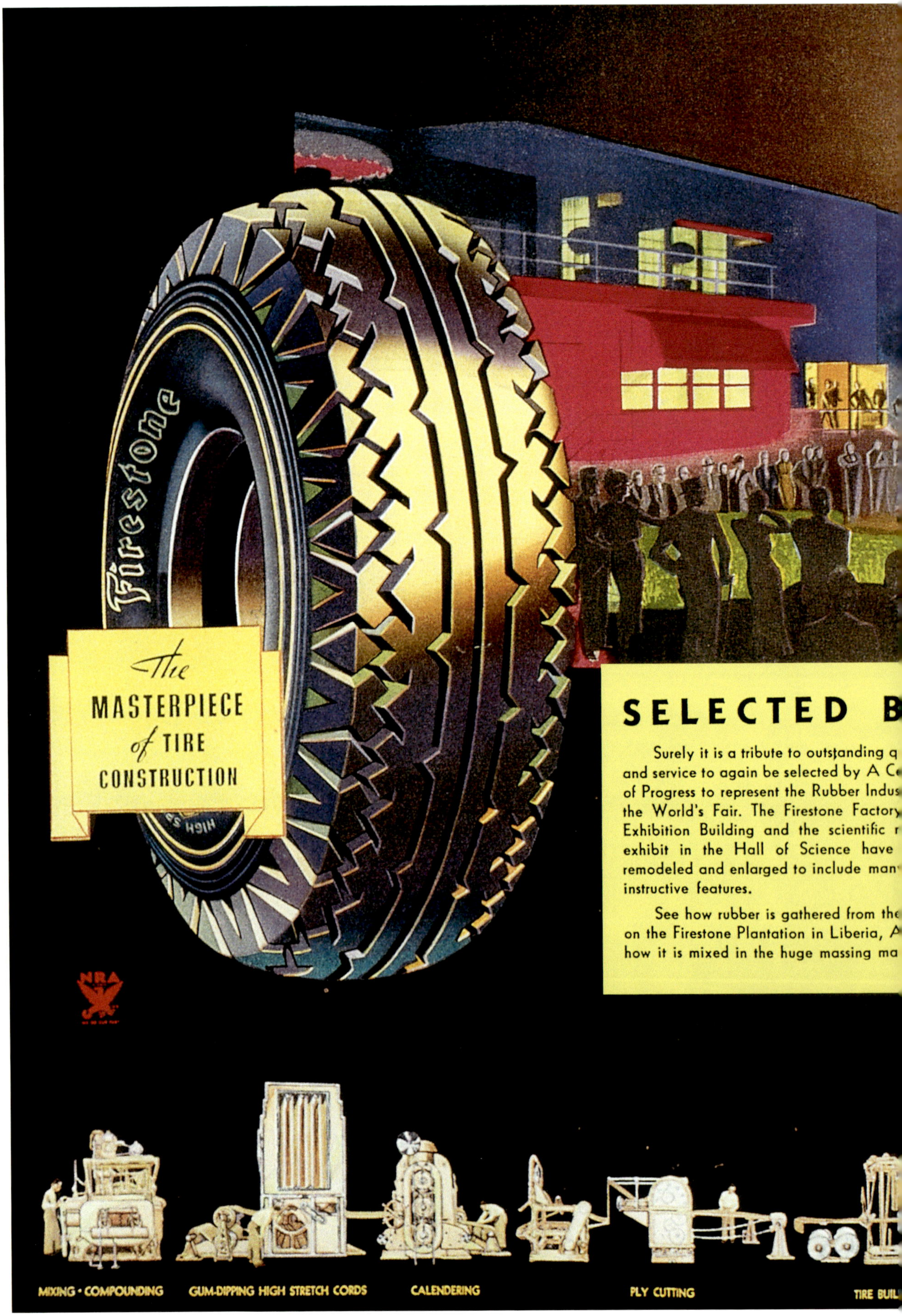
Firestone
The MASTERPIECE of TIRE CONSTRUCTION
SELECTED B
Surely it is a tribute to outstanding q
and service to again be selected by A Ce
of Progress to represent the Rubber Indus
the World's Fair. The Firestone Factory
Exhibition Building and the scientific r
exhibit in the Hall of Science have
remodeled and enlarged to include man
instructive features.
See how rubber is gathered from the
on the Firestone Plantation in Liberia, A
how it is mixed in the huge massing ma
NRA
MIXING • COMPOUNDING
GUM-DIPPING HIGH STRETCH CORDS
CALENDERING
PLY CUTTING
TIRE BUIL

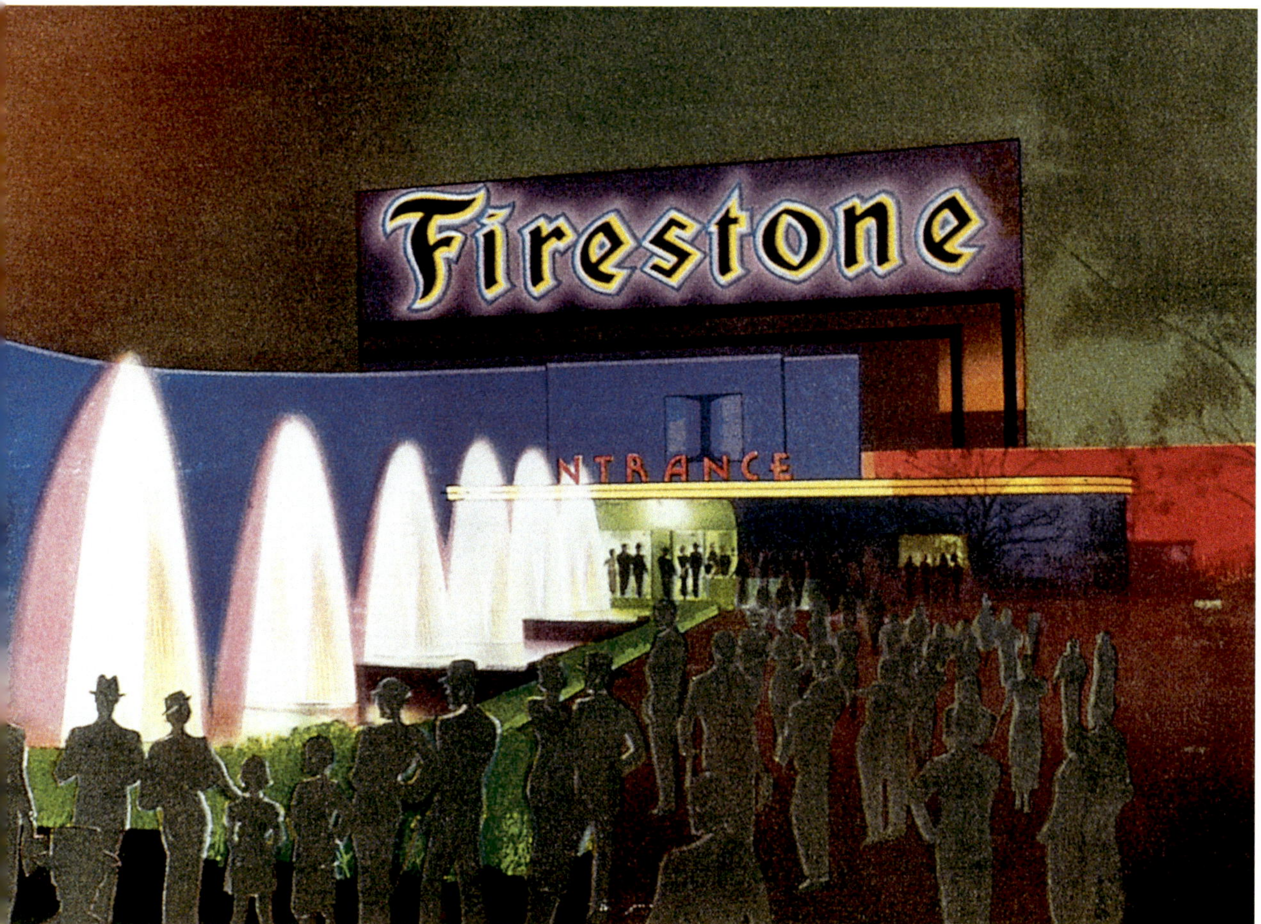

CENTURY OF PROGRESS FOR 1934

ow the millions of cotton fibers in Firestone high stretch are automatically soaked and coated with liquid rubber e Firestone patented process of Gum-Dipping, providing er strength, safety and blowout protection; how the new one Low Pressure Air Balloon tire is made, from the g of the rubber to the finished tire, as illustrated below.

See the demonstrations of extra power and long life in one Batteries and Spark Plugs, and the extra braking ency of Firestone Brake Linings, all developed by one engineers and manufactured in Firestone factories. See the dynamic exhibits of the new Firestone Low Pressure Tractor Tires, Wheels and Rims. Visit the Singing Color Fountains in the Firestone gardens—concerts every day and night—the only spectacle of its kind in the world.

Before you motor to the Fair have the Firestone Service Dealer or Service Store in your community inspect your tires, test your brakes, battery and spark plugs, that you may have an enjoyable and trouble-free trip. There is no charge for this service.

Listen to Lawrence Tibbett or Richard Crooks and Harvey Firestone, Jr., every Monday night—N. B. C. Network

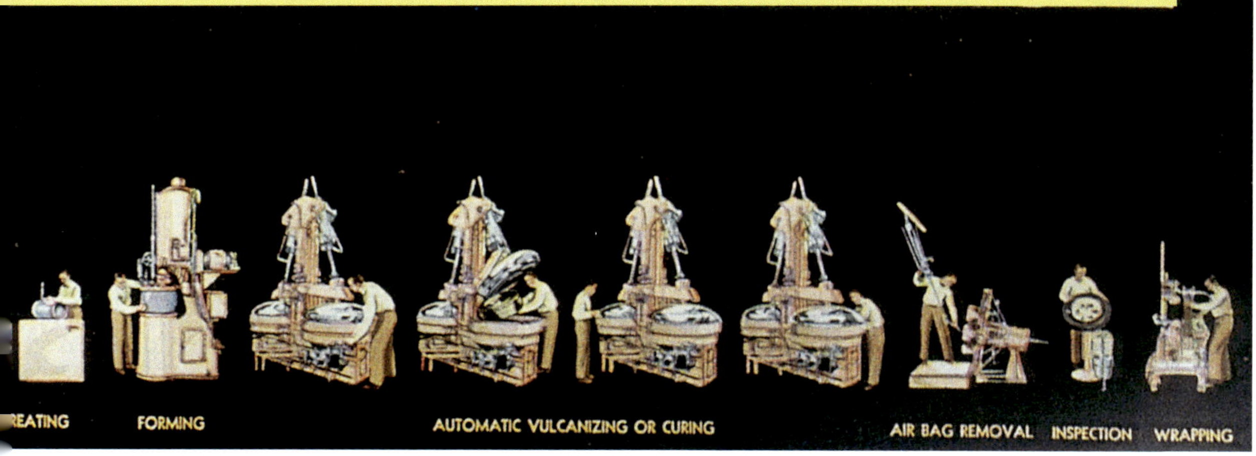

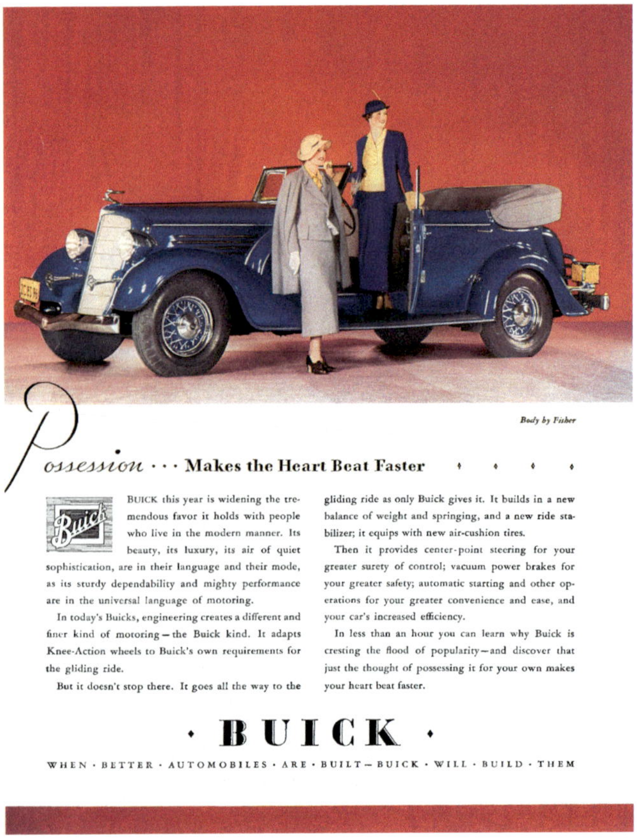

Buick, 1934

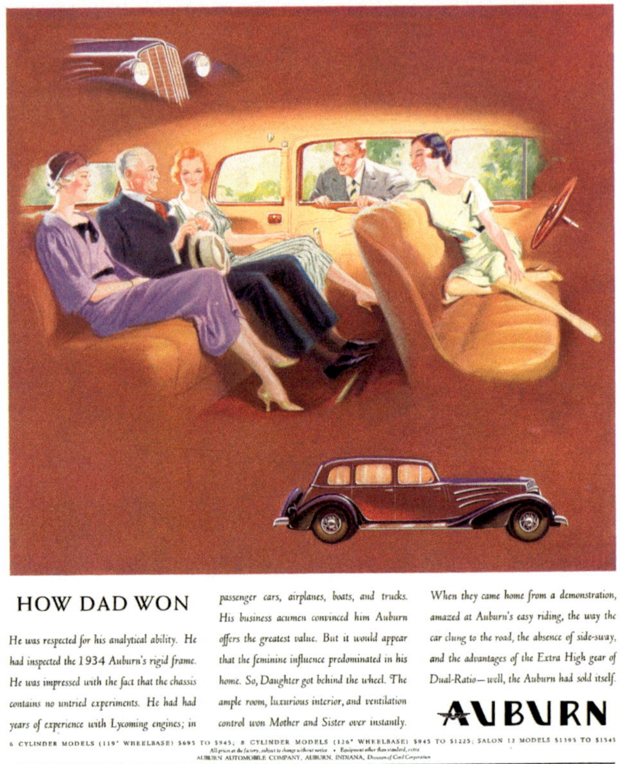

Auburn, 1934

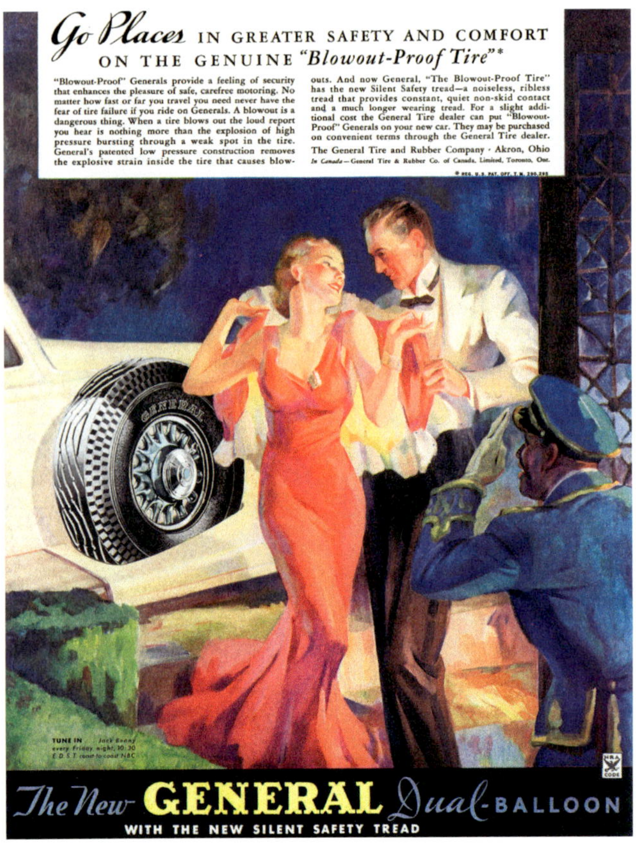

General Tires, 1934

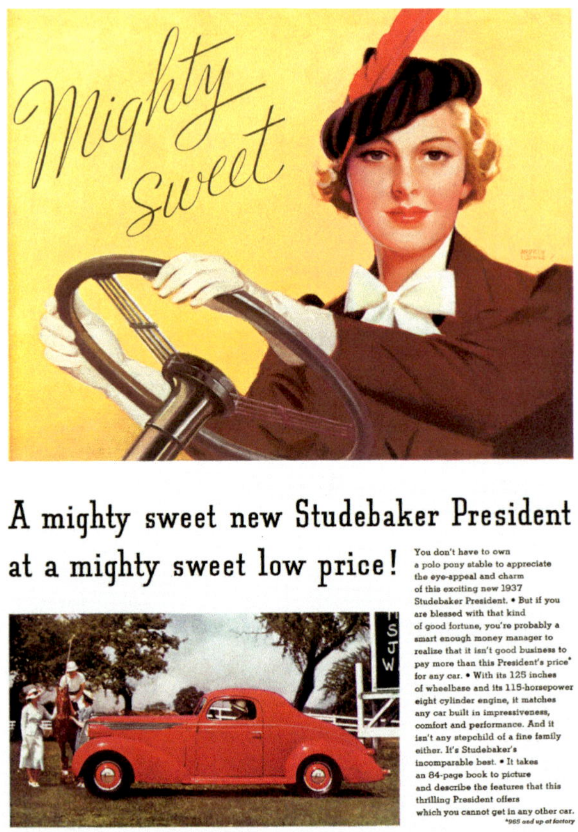

Studebaker, 1936

► La Salle, 1934

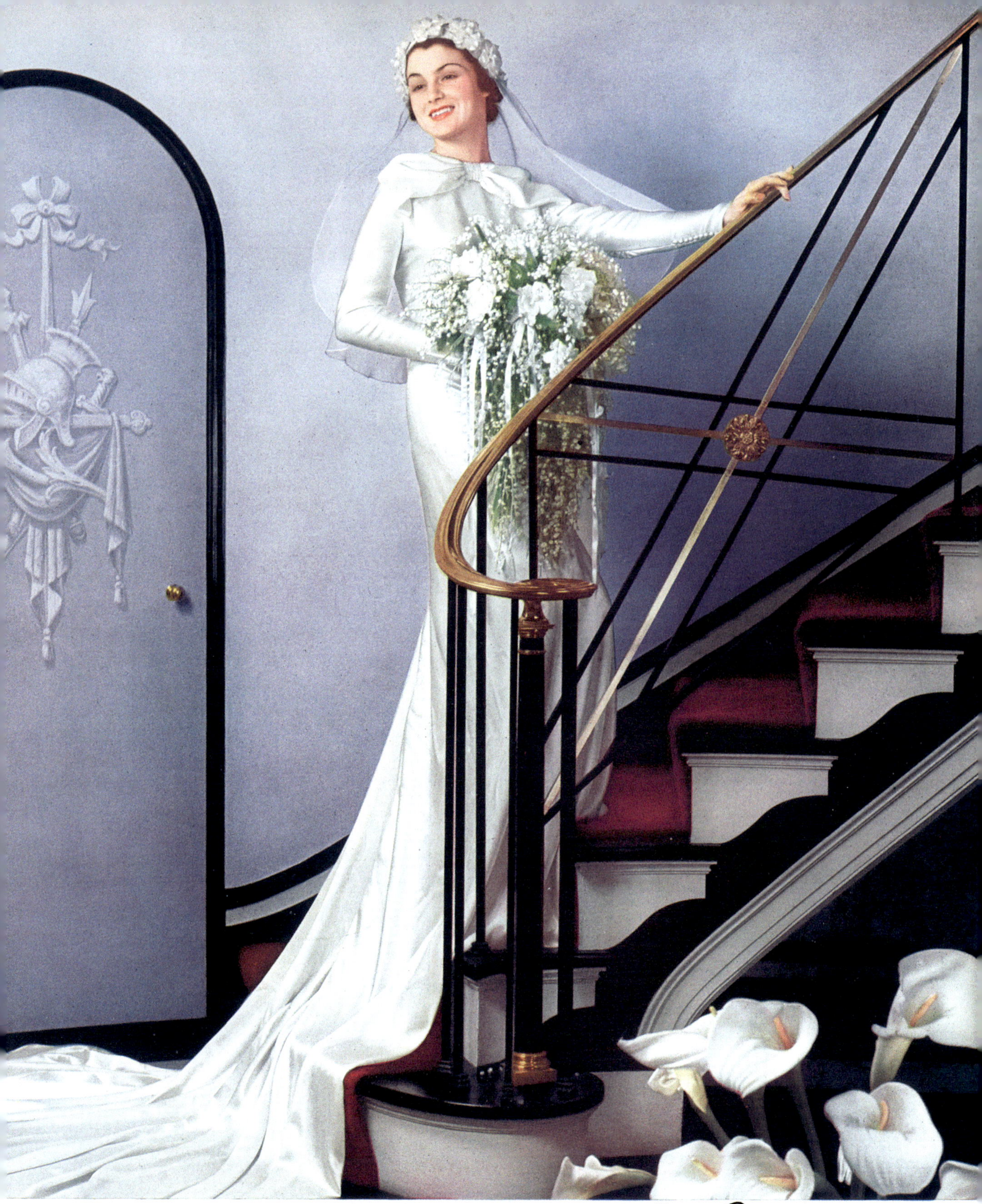

and Dad gave us a new La Salle

There is no

MISTAKING

a

PIERCE-ARROW

. . . PARTICULARLY, THE NEW TWELVES AND EIGHTS OF 1934 . . .
THE FINEST, THE EASIEST-RIDING CARS EVER BUILT BY PIERCE-ARROW

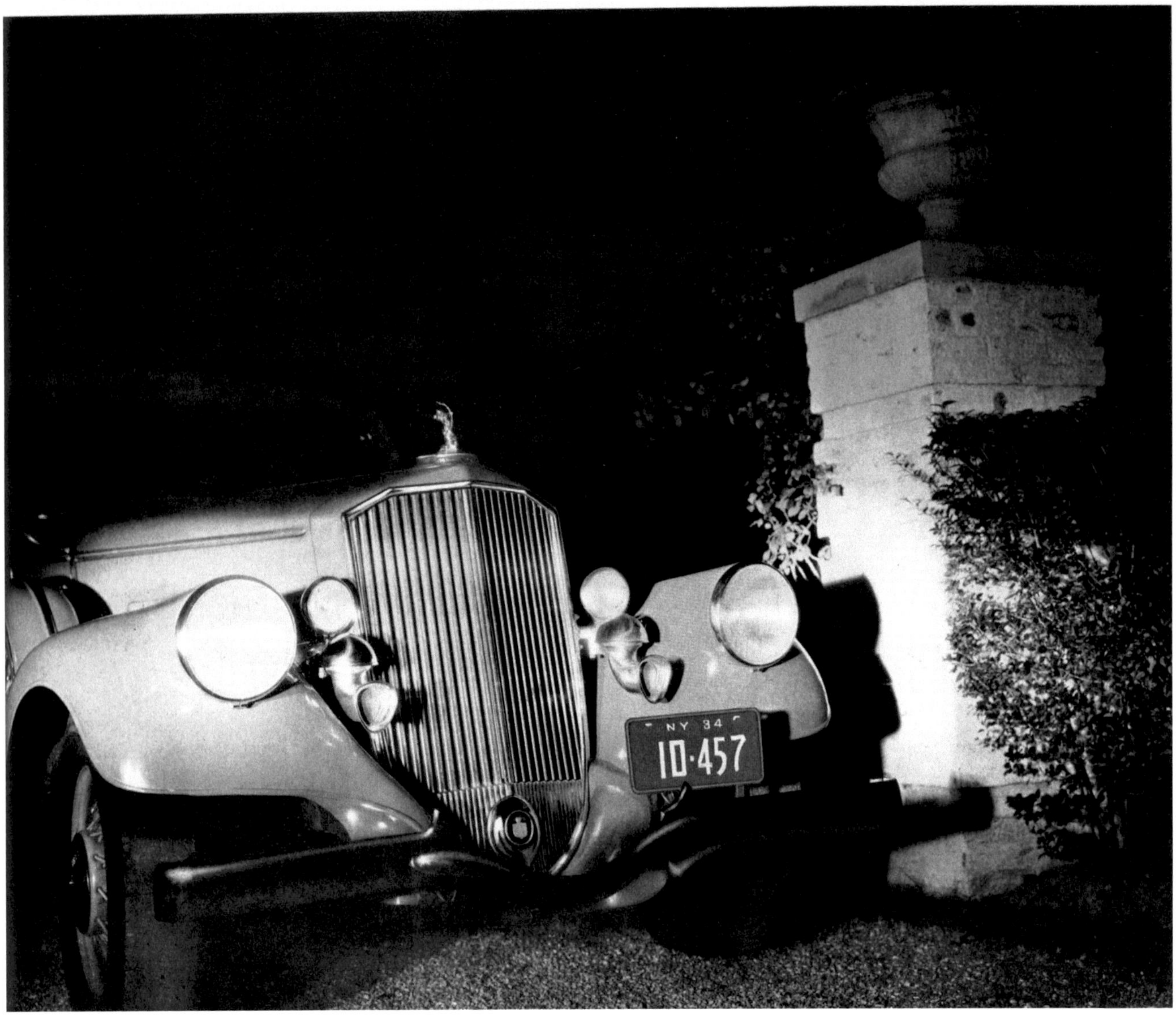

▲► *Pierce Arrow, 1934*

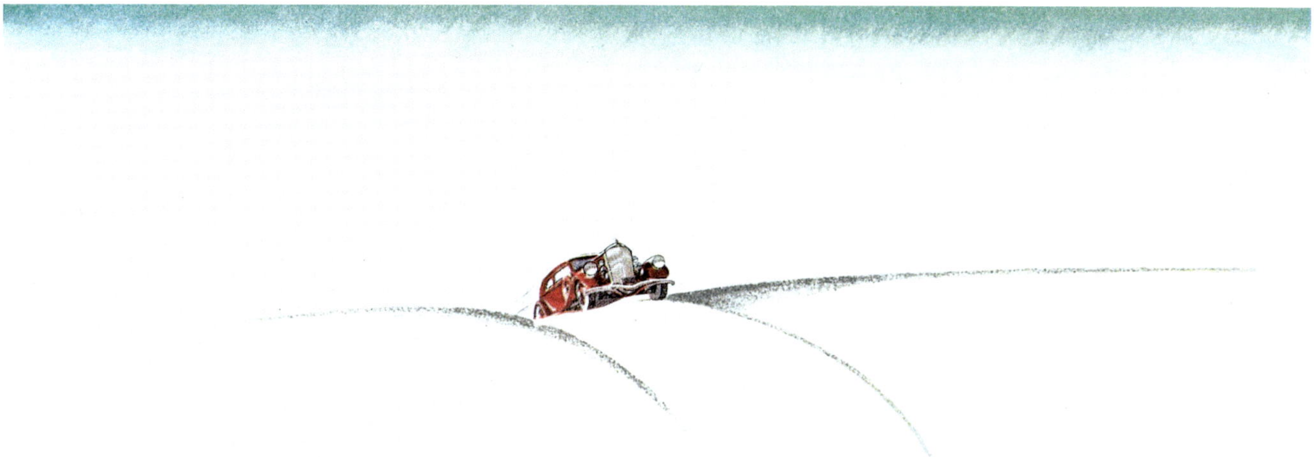

"HERE COME THE HOYTS"

THERE is something about a Pierce-Arrow that brings a friendly wave of the hand from traffic-officers . . . Even truckmen pull over a little more quickly, and doormen salute a little more smartly. This instinctive deference is not due to the distinctive appearance of the car . . . nor its extra-ordinary comfort . . . nor the unparalleled control of its full-power brakes . . . nor even the quiet smoothness of its engine, so superb that it recently broke 14 world records for speed and endurance. No one feature is responsible. The only explanation is that Pierce-Arrows are Pierce-Arrows. And the new models of 1934 will tend to deserve and to extend this deference.

PIERCE ARROW

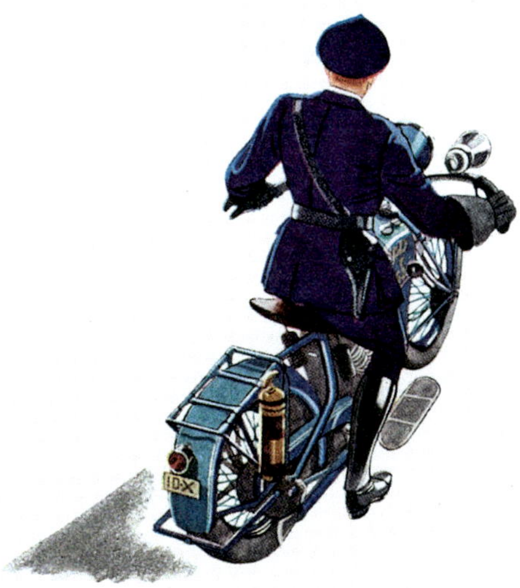

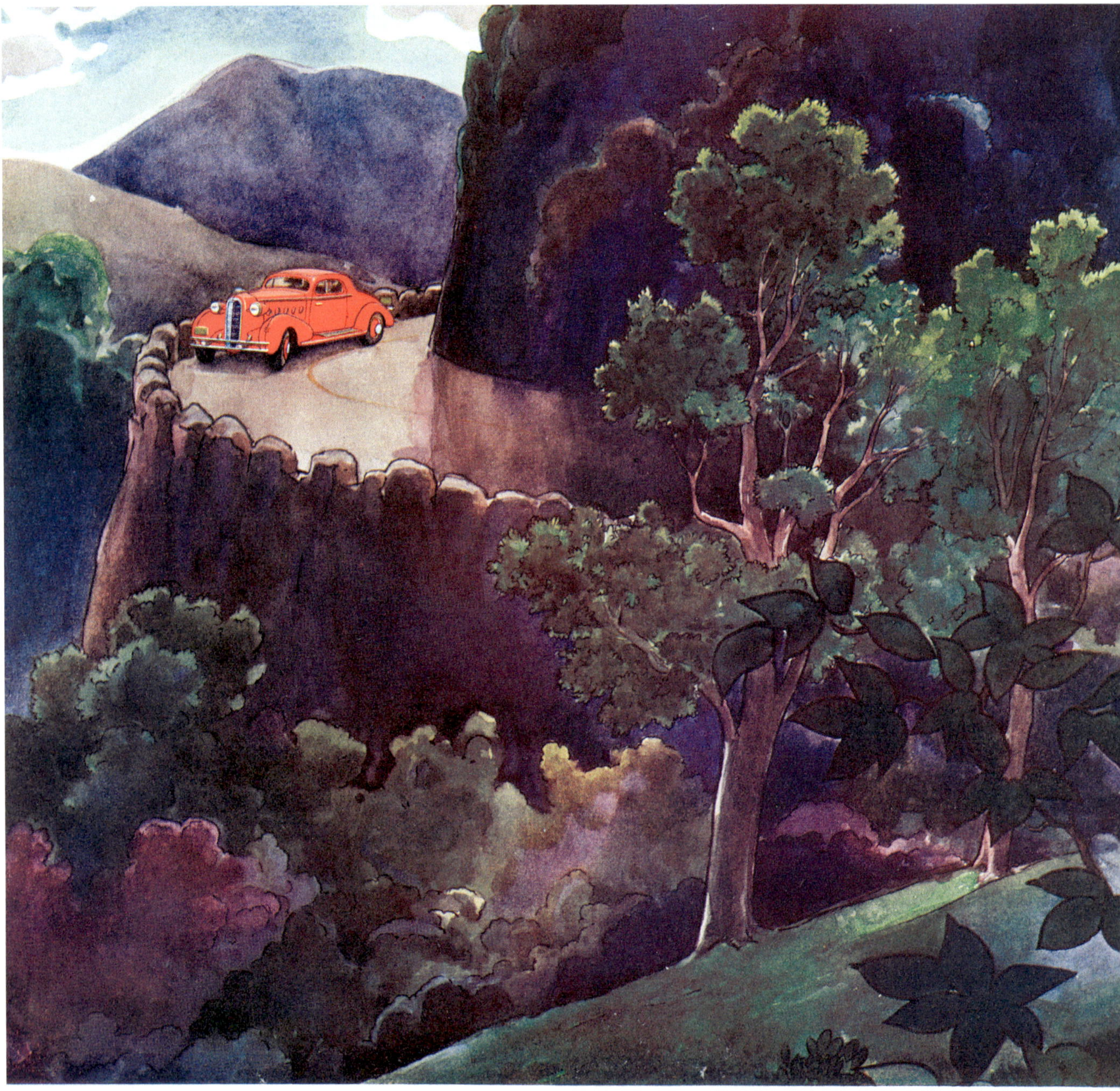

TRUST IT . . FOR IT'S *Cadillac* BUILT

You will feel much more at *ease* in the beautiful streamlined La Salle than you have *ever* felt in other automobiles. . . . You will experience greater *mental* comfort and greater *physical* comfort as well. . . . You will have the same feeling of assurance whether you happen to be parking at a fashionable club—or traveling over a rough road—or climbing a steep mountain trail far from human habitation. . . . In all of these situations, *peace of mind* is the constant companion of the man or woman who drives a new streamlined La Salle.

. . . You can trust it implicitly —for it is Cadillac-built.

La Salle

$1595 AND $1695
AT DETROIT
PRICES SUBJECT TO CHANGE WITHOUT NOTICE

La Salle, 1934

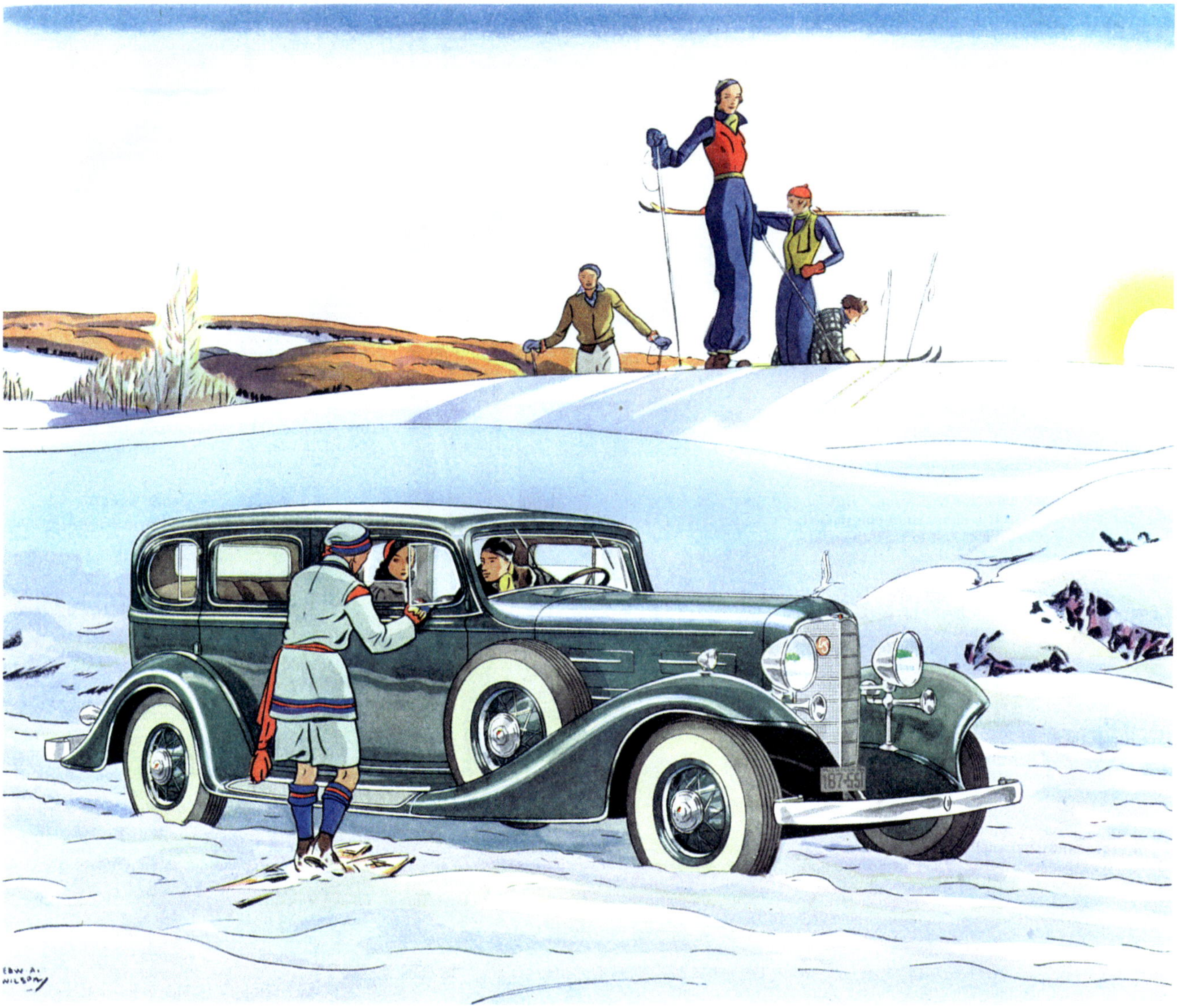

A FINER AND FAR MORE DISTINGUISHED LA SALLE

. . . at an even more moderate price

It was an occasion for great rejoicing among men and women who admire fine possessions when the new La Salle V-Eight appeared upon the American scene a few weeks ago. For here was something they had been seeking. Here was a motor car of proud lineage, enriched throughout in its quality—yet offered at prices in perfect keeping with the current economic scheme. . . . No need to question the correctness of the youthful grace which is the dominating note in its appearance—for the style of the new La Salle was created by the most accomplished designers at the command of the Fisher studios. No need to wonder about its mechanical fitness or the nature of its performance—for La Salle is the product of the same skilled craftsmen who build those magnificent motor cars, the Cadillac V-Eight, V-Twelve, and V-Sixteen. . . . The new La Salle is powered by the 115-horsepower Cadillac V-type eight-cylinder engine. Throughout chassis and body are many refinements and developments of major importance, including the new Fisher No-Draft Ventilation system, individually controlled. Yet the standard five-passenger sedan is now reduced to $2245, f.o.b. Detroit—a price most attractively reasonable for a car of Cadillac design, Cadillac construction, and genuine Cadillac quality.

La Salle V-8

A GENERAL MOTORS VALUE

La Salle, 1933

TOUR WITH TEXACO!

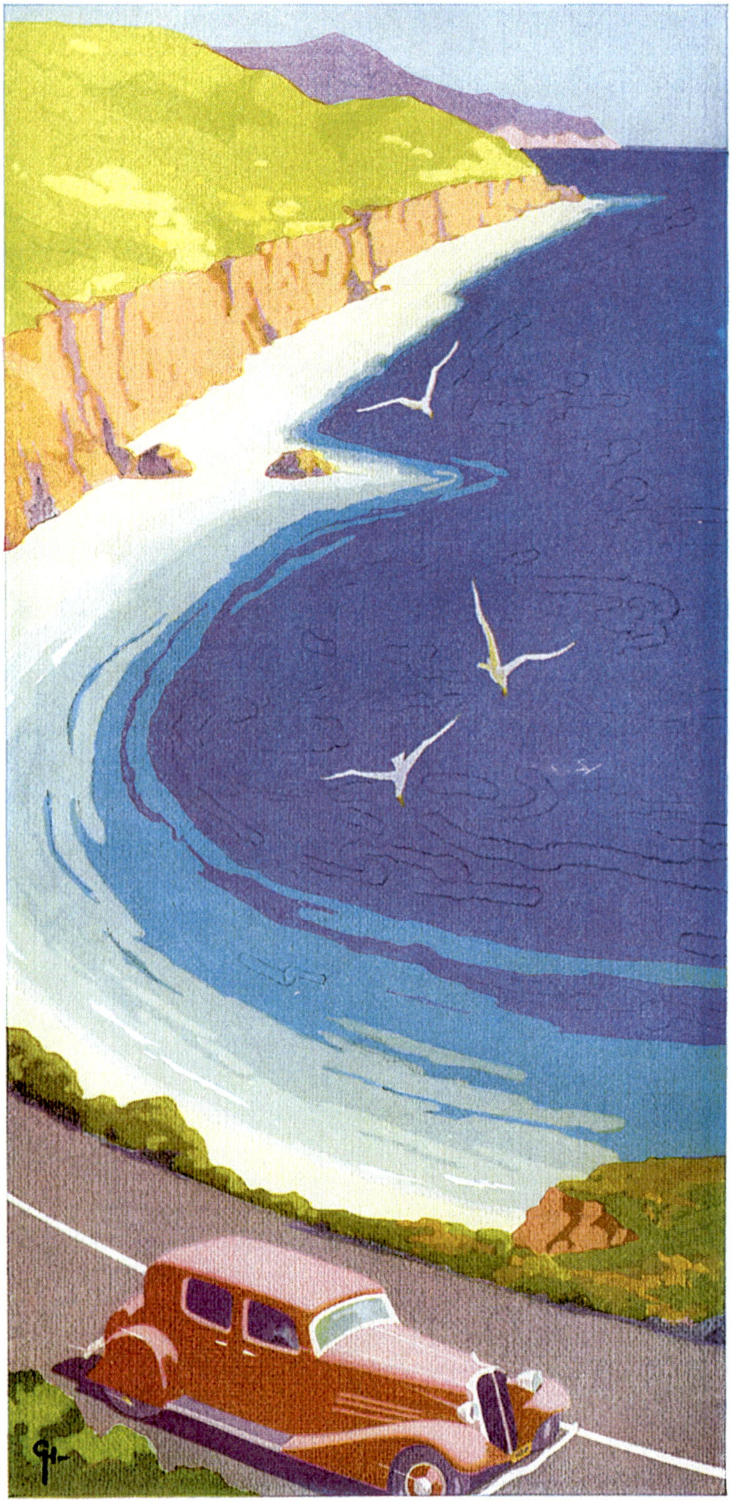

LAVISH NATURE packed this western land with beauty spots . . . forested mountains . . . rushing streams and dusky canyons . . . flowering plains, picturesque seashore and desert oases. Men laced this playground empire with roads like great, smooth ribbons. There's romance, and youth and joy around the bend of the open road.

Hundreds of users declare TEXACO *FIRE-CHIEF* Gasoline performance makes motoring definitely more enjoyable. Quick starts, abundant power, and economical mileage are built into *FIRE-CHIEF* at the refinery, by following—and *exceeding*—highest U.S. Government specifications for "emergency" motor fuel. Addition of *tetraethyl lead* rounds out this famous gasoline used by more tourists than any other kind.

FIRE-CHIEF is available wherever you go, in all our 48 states—and in 106 foreign countries. Drive into your nearest TEXACO station today, and learn why the wisest motorists *tour with Texaco!*

THE TEXAS COMPANY
A CALIFORNIA CORPORATION

HEAR ED WYNN · EVERY TUESDAY NIGHT
5:30 PACIFIC TIME · NBC · COAST-TO-COAST

TEXACO FIRE-CHIEF

Texaco, 1934

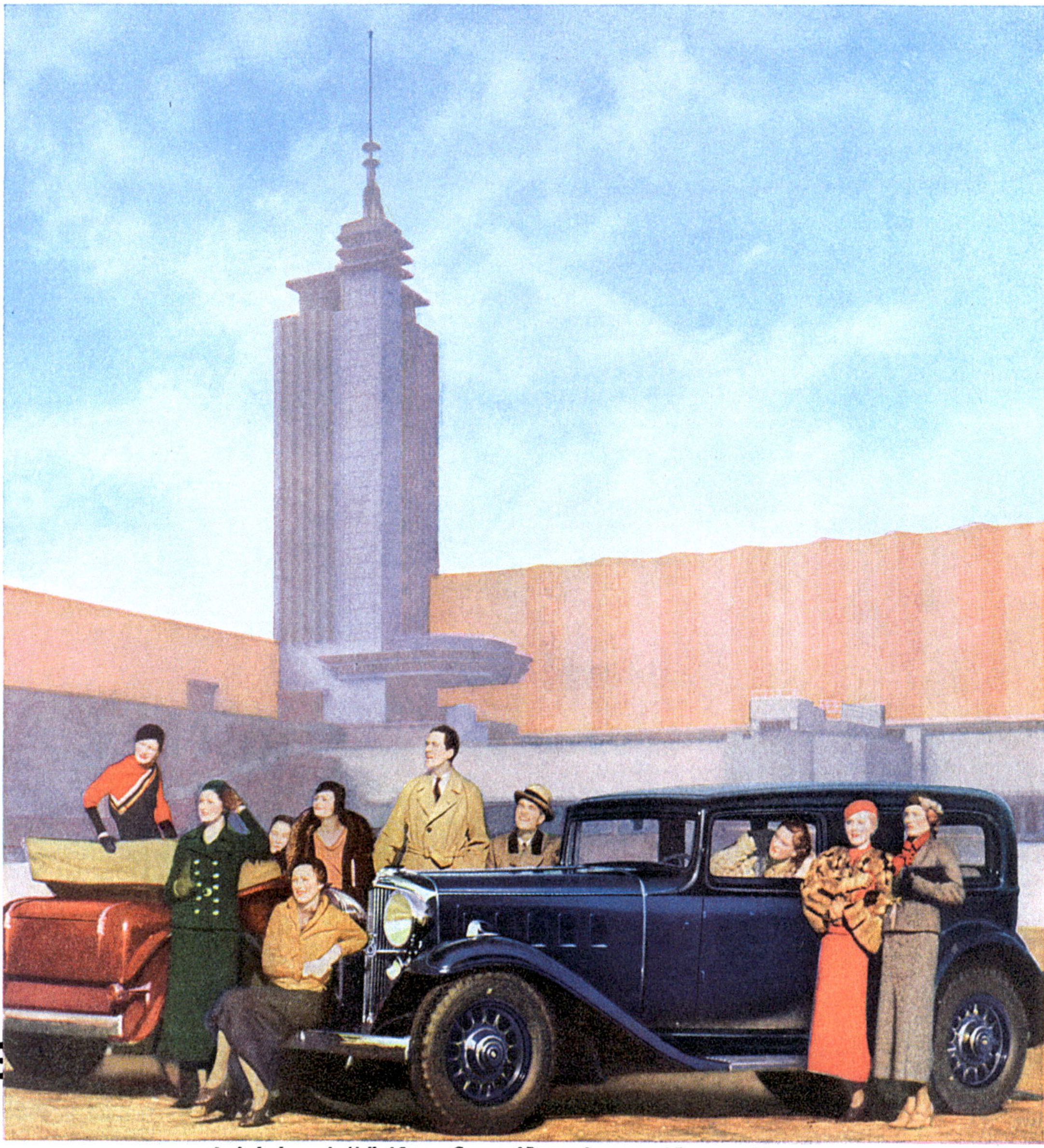

In the background—Hall of Science, Century of Progress International Exposition, Chicago, 1933

Eminent In Quality—Thrifty In Price

Nash is committed unalterably to the quality ideal. And for 1933, the five new series of Nash cars unmistakably represent the very best that Nash ever has built—in design, engineering, appearance and performance.

No one, this year, or any other year, ever will be able to say of Nash, "they don't build them as well as formerly."

The solid, substantial worth of a Nash car, the unusual brilliance of its performance, will be remembered long after price is forgotten.

And the price of a 1933 Nash car will not soon be forgotten. Nash prices for 1933 are the lowest ever placed on cars of comparable quality!

NASH

The Nash Standard Eight Sedan, one of the finest performing Eights in America today, is $145 lower than in 1932. The 116-inch wheelbase, 75 horsepower, Nash Big Six Sedan is now $695, *$130 under 1932*. The big Special Eight and the Twin-Ignition, Underslung-Worm-Drive Advanced and Ambassador Eights likewise offer the Nash owner maximum quality at minimum price.

Nash for 1933 — cars you would rather drive, at prices you would rather pay!

Nash, 1933

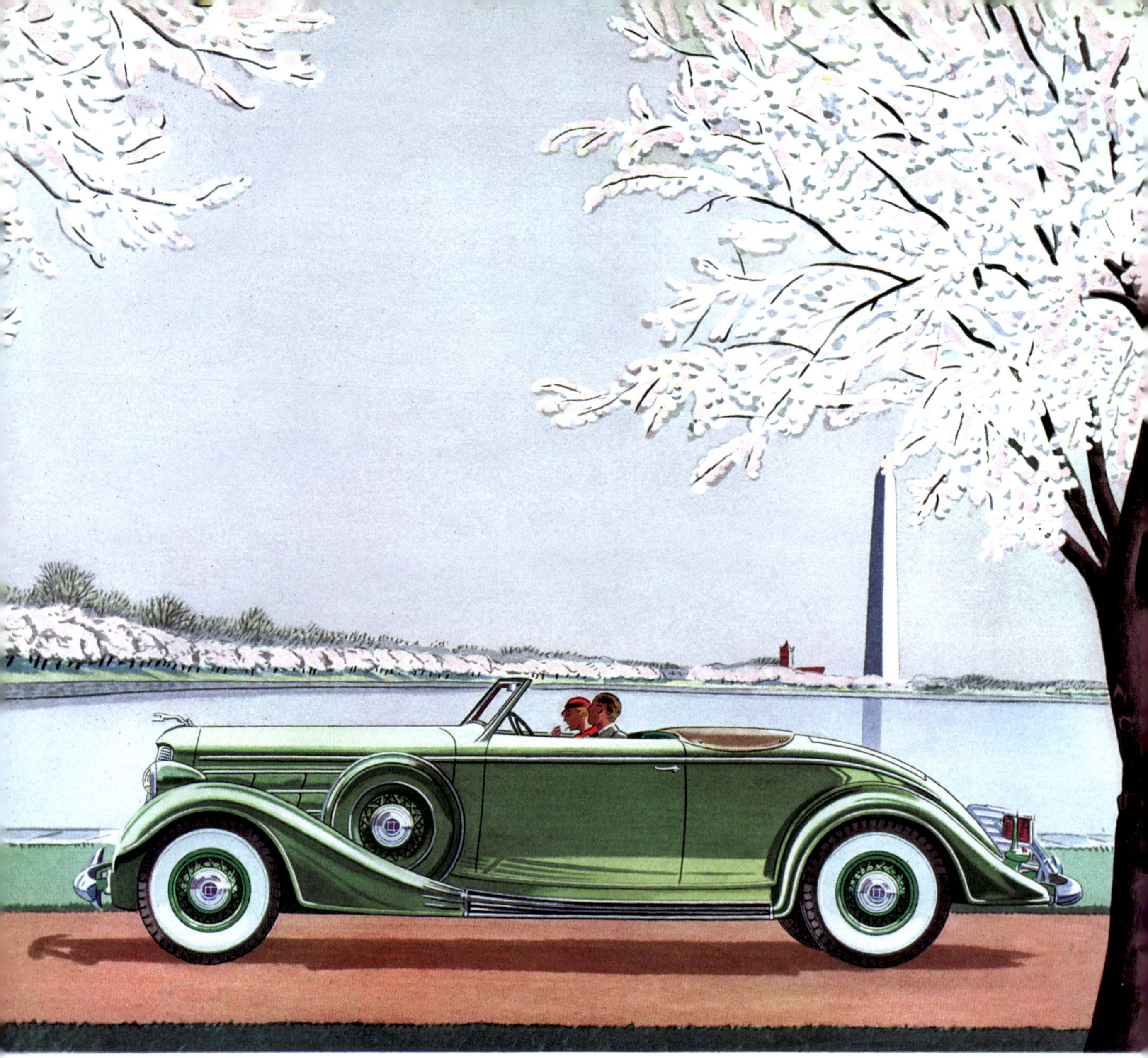

LE BARON CONVERTIBLE ROADS

THE LINCOLN

The Lincoln appeals first to the sophisticated motorist. Those who know the most about motor cars, who need not compromise with price, are its loyal adherents. They have owned four, six, or ten Lincolns.... Even more than its predecessors, the new Lincoln merits the allegiance of owners, old and new. This year, the powerful V-12 cylinder engine is placed forward several inches in the frame. As a result the luxurious body becomes roomier, and rear-seat passengers ride poised ahead of the axle, rather than directly over it. Thus the new Lincoln is a more comfortable car than ever before.... And it is an easier car to handle. It surges lightly, swiftly ahead with a touch of the accelerator. Shifting is smoother. Springs are more flexible.... Modern beauty has been achieved without the sacrifice of the dignity traditional with Lincoln. Eighteen body types designed to meet every motoring requirement, formal or informal, are available

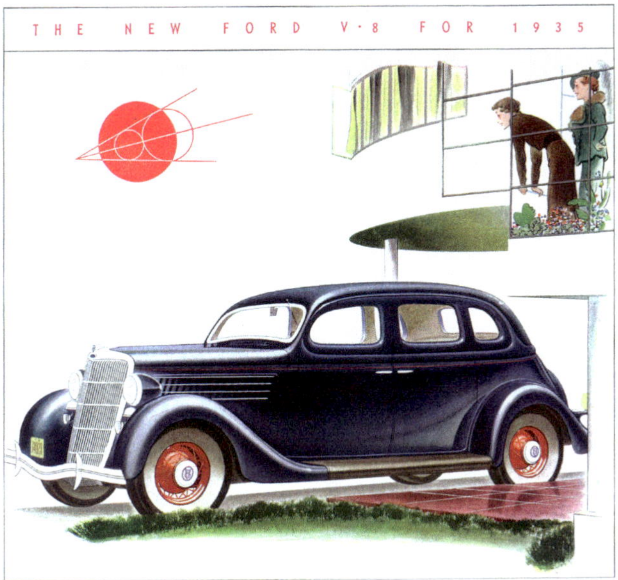

Modern Comfort and Modern Beauty

One of the most important features of the New Ford V-8 for 1935 is its remarkable riding comfort—especially in the back seat. This is achieved by fundamental changes in weight distribution, new seat position, and longer springs of unusual flexibility. You ride forward, toward the center of the car—center-poised between the springs. This gives rear-seat passengers the comfort of a "front-seat ride" and makes every road a smoother road. . . . There's increased leg room, body room and luggage room and the front seats are 4 to 5½ inches wider. . . . New and modern also are the distinctive lines and colors of the New Ford V-8 and the luxurious upholstery and appointments of the De Luxe body types. . . . The all-steel bodies are equipped with Safety Glass throughout at no additional cost. . . . Ease of steering, new easy-pressure clutch, improved quick-stopping brakes, and the dependable, economical performance of the V-8 engine are additional reasons why it is such a satisfactory choice for the woman motorist. . . . The New Ford V-8 for 1935 is modern in every detail.

Ford, 1934

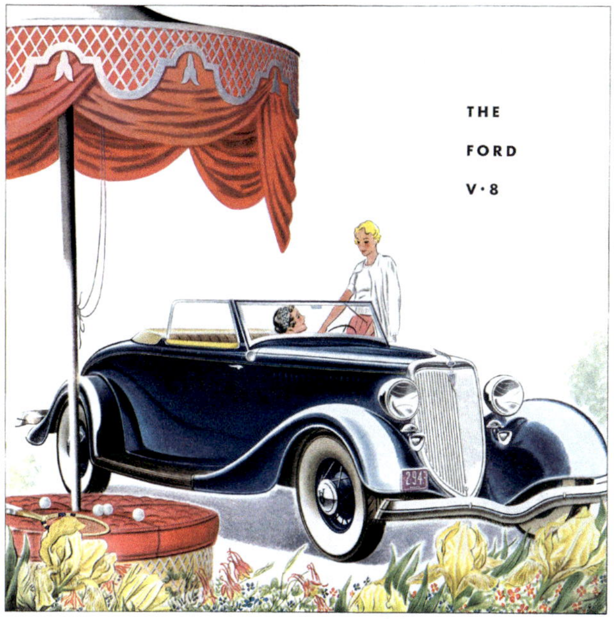

THE FORD IS PART OF THE PICTURE

The alert, capable Ford V-8 is part of the picture of every activity. . . . For the gay, glad spirit of Youth is in it—an eagerness to be doing things and going places in a thoroughly modern manner. . . . You catch a suggestion of this as you watch the Fords go by—trim, lithe and colorful. You are very sure of it as you drive the car and note how swiftly, silently and comfortably you travel along. . . . Smooth power flows through quiet gears—the quick response of the car commands your confidence—you realize that it makes quite a difference when there's a V-8 cylinder engine under the hood. . . . Truly, a new thrill in motoring awaits you in the Ford V-8.

Ford, 1934

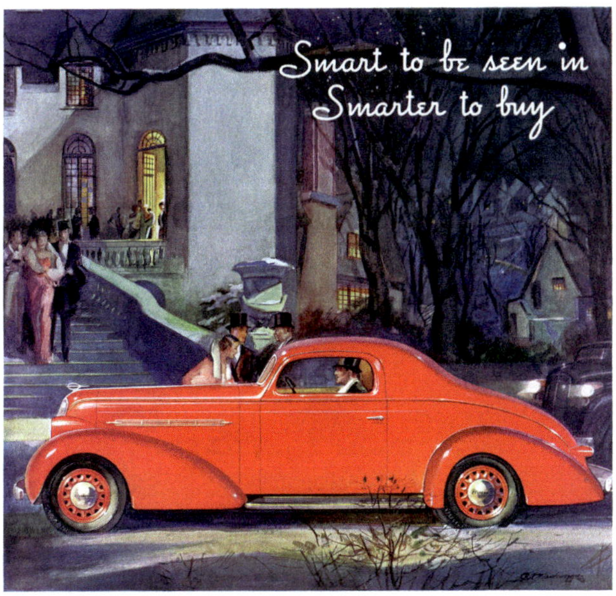

NEW 1936 STUDEBAKERS ··· PRICED AS MUCH AS $300 LOWER

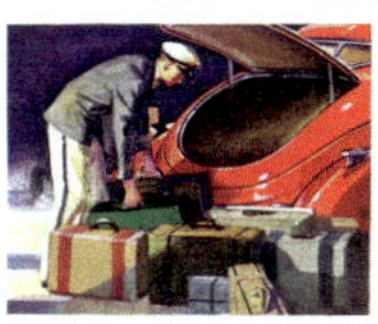

The Studebaker 3-passenger coupe has an enormous storage compartment. Sedans, with or without special trunks, have proportionately spacious accommodations for carrying luggage, spare tire and tools enclosed.

You are looking at a picture of the thrilling new automobile that is the toast of motoring America . . . the big, thrifty, incomparably beautiful, new 1936 Studebaker Champion . . . offering 97 advancements that you have not seen combined in any other car!

New prices—as much as $300 less—give these Champions a buy appeal so decisive that, once you see them, ride in them and drive them, you'll wonder how anybody could possibly make any choice but Studebaker.

$665 and up, at the factory

Beneath this new Champion's glowing harmony of suave, smooth, competent-looking exterior line, flows the lovely melody of America's smartest fittings and appointments . . . gracing interiors so roomy, you feel almost lost in their spaciousness when you drive alone . . . and so restful, on any road or at any speed, you unqualifiedly award the comfort of the 1936 Studebaker ride your first prize.

New Studebaker engines, brilliantly responsive and tremendously powerful, wring every ounce of energy out of every drop of fuel so efficiently, your oil as well as your gasoline costs stay under your budget, week after week and month after month. And with feather-touch hydraulic brakes, finger-tip straight-line steering and the world's strongest, quietest all-steel bodies, reinforced by steel, you are safer than you've ever been in a motor car before. Choose the Champion you prefer . . . a matchless new 90-horsepower Dictator Six . . . a superb new 115-horsepower President Eight.

Lincoln, 1935 ◄ Studebaker, 1935

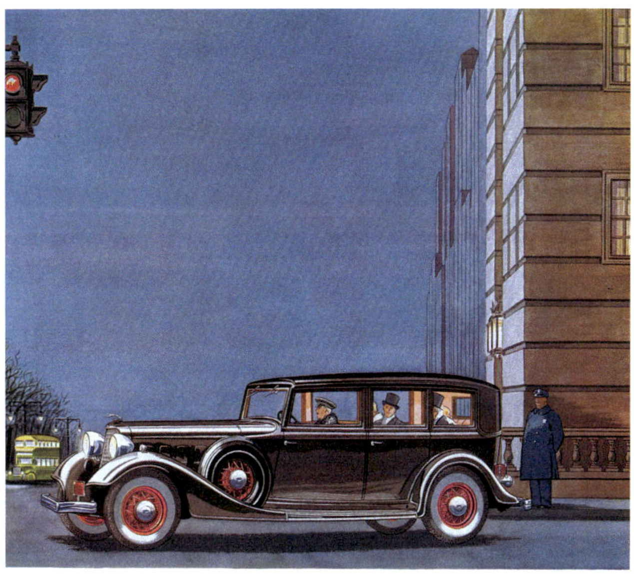

THE WILLOUGHBY LIMOUSINE

The LINCOLN

The Lincoln, a versatile car, continually astonishes loyal owners who put it to supreme tests of one kind, and then, on another occasion, find that it can meet wholly new and different tests. Thus, a rancher in Wyoming, accustomed to mountain and desert driving, learns from his wife of the car's agility in city traffic. A business man, to whom the Lincoln is a triumph of engineering, suddenly realizes, as he emerges from the opera, how beautiful a car he drives. The Lincoln is all things to all people. . . . This is a luxurious car, a safe car, with a V-12 cylinder, 150-horsepower engine powerful enough to take steep hills in high and at an almost incredible pace. Lincoln engineers affirm it the finest they have yet designed, and experience on the road confirms that judgment. And it is a car which imparts to the owner, no less than to the maker, pride in its beauty and pleasure in its high achievements. Available in twenty-three standard and custom-built body types.

Lincoln, 1934

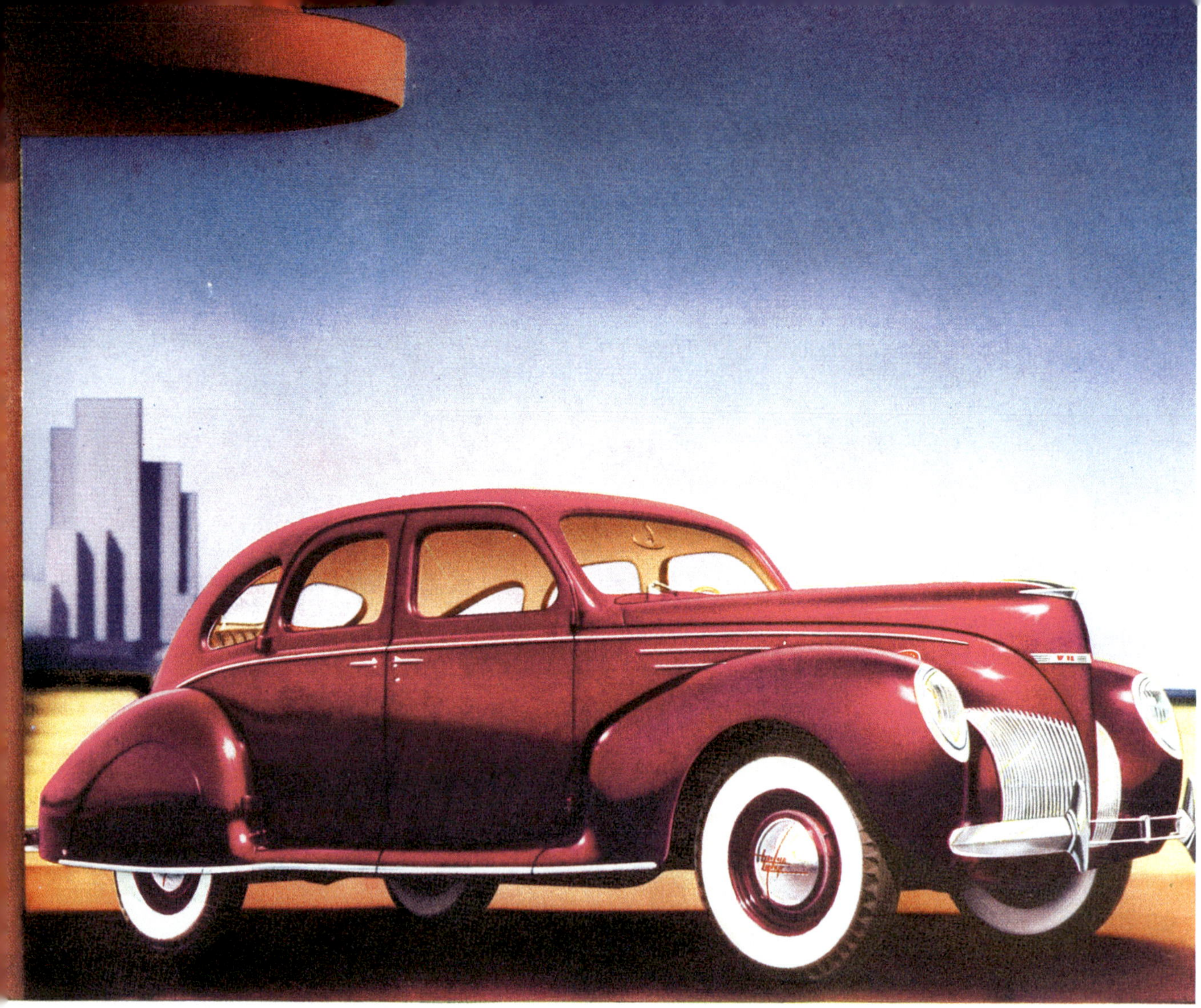

IT BRINGS VACATION JOYS TO TOWN!

Summer spent, you turn again toward the city. Places you visited and the pleasures of being away are still in your mind. If you own a Lincoln-Zephyr you can bring vacation joys back with you! This car will satisfy on city streets near home as it did on the open road!

The V-type 12-cylinder engine that responded with confident power up a mountain now idles quietly in traffic. You move smoothly when lanes are crowded. Emergency speed is there if you need it. And for all the stops and starts at lights, the Lincoln-Zephyr will go along with thrift and ease!

This is a big car. Three of you can ride comfortably from home to office or theater on the front seat. Yet the Lincoln-Zephyr handles lightly. Parking places are not so small as they seem! And the wide windshield gives you a clear view of what goes on.

The unique body-and-frame, exclusive to Lincoln-Zephyr, is built for comfort. In all closed types, steel panels are welded to a framework of steel trusses. The whole is suspended over soft transverse springs 136 inches apart. The Lincoln-Zephyr's center of gravity is low; the car holds to the ground. Passenger and car weight is balanced toward the center.

This car is justly called "style leader." Its graceful streamlines have influenced the designs of an industry. But look *beneath* the style! Here, for travel in country or town, is a combination of features at medium price not to be matched at any price! Lincoln Motor Company, Division of Ford Motor Company.

BENEATH ITS OUTWARD BEAUTY

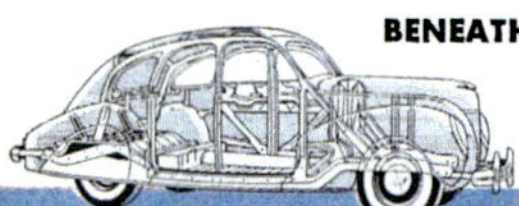

Lincoln-Zephyr V-12

A combination of features that makes the Lincoln-Zephyr the only car of its kind. 1. ***Unit-body-and-frame—steel panels welded to steel trusses.*** **2.** ***V-type 12-cylinder engine—smooth, quiet and economical power.*** **3.** ***High power-to-weight ratio—low center of gravity.*** **4.** ***Comfort for six, "amidships" in chair-high seats—gliding ride—direct entrance—high visibility.*** **5.** ***Hydraulic brakes.***

THE STYLE LEADER

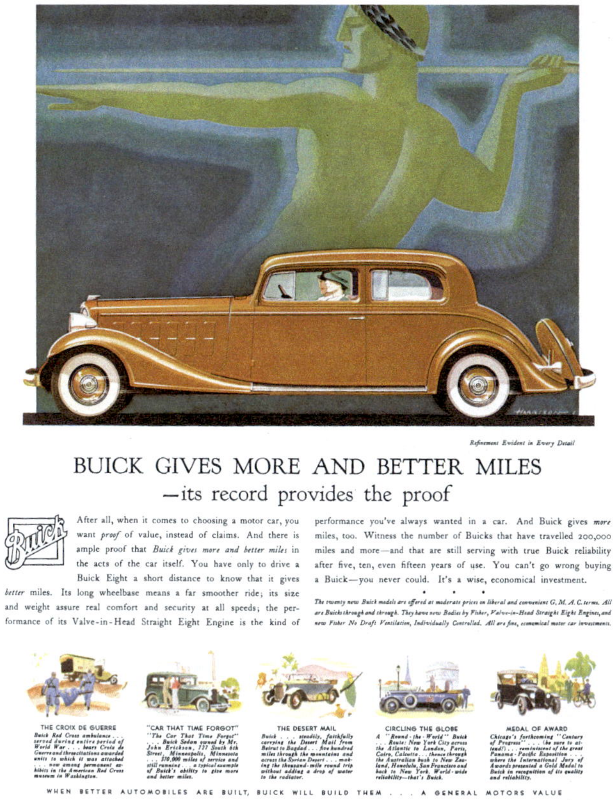

Buick, 1932

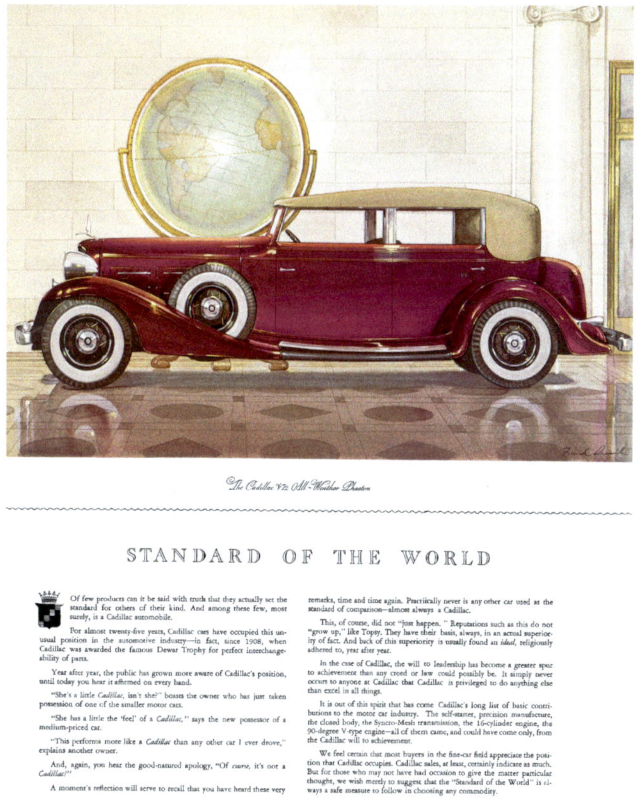

Cadillac, 1933

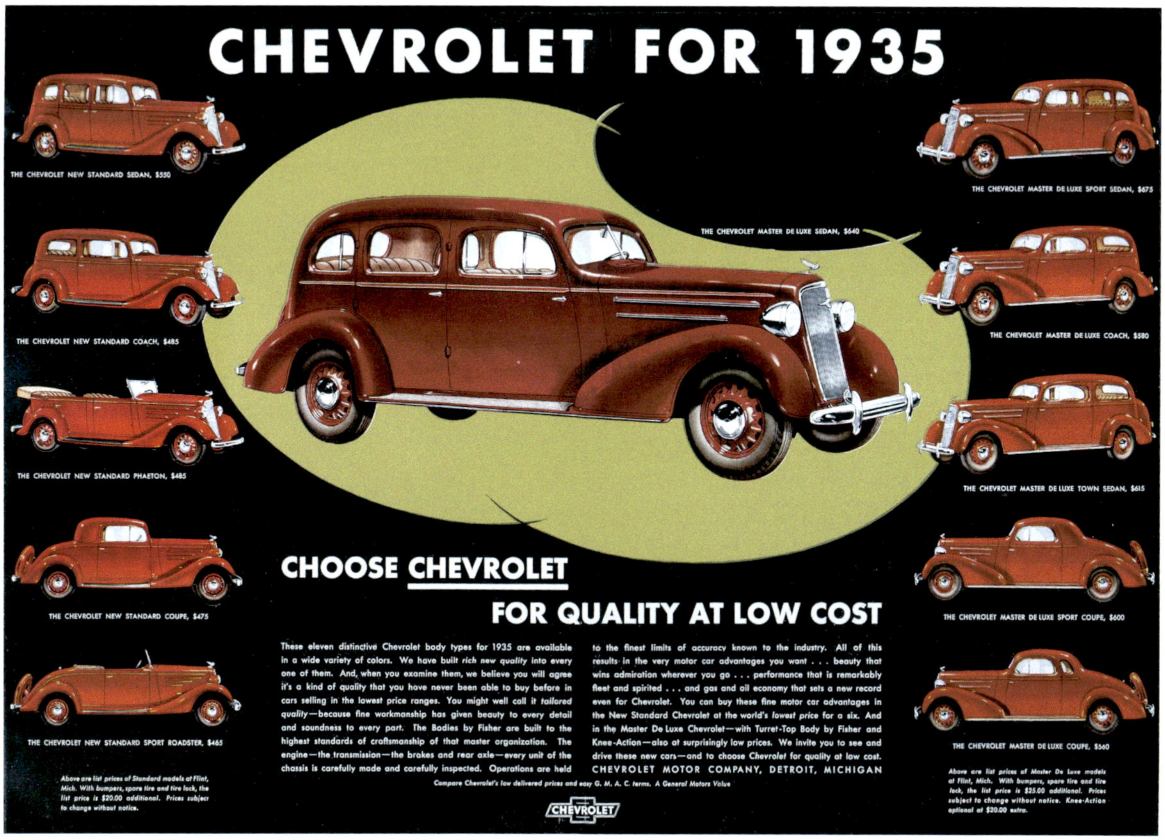

Lincoln, 1935 ◄ Chevrolet, 1935

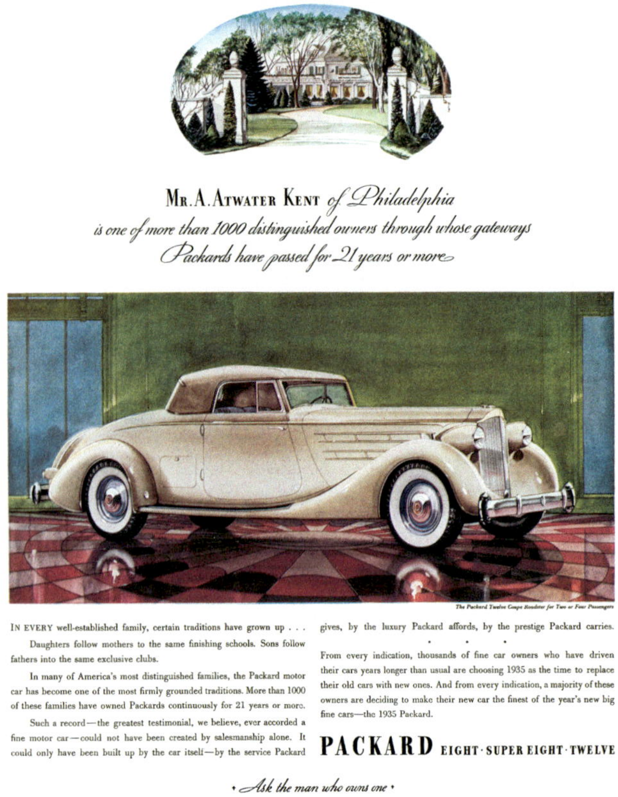

Packard, 1935

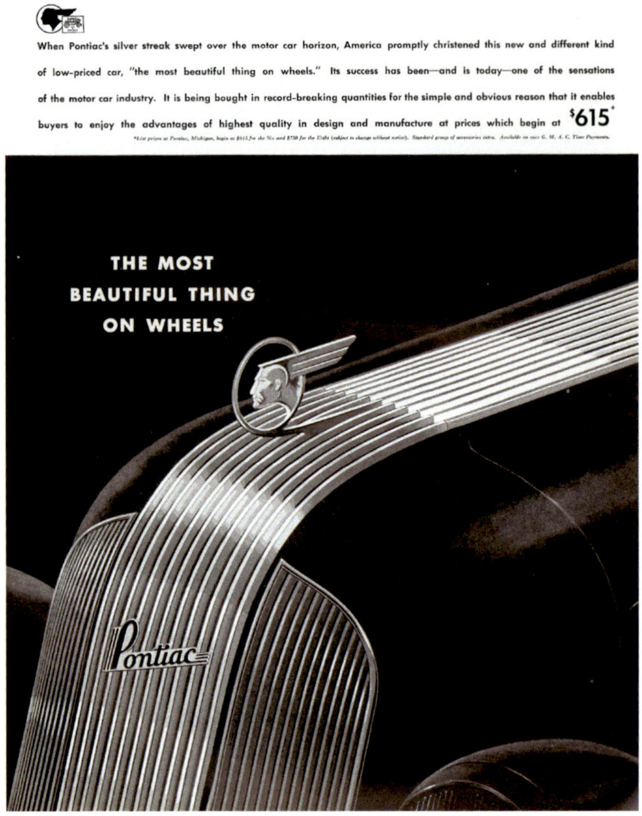

Pontiac, 1935

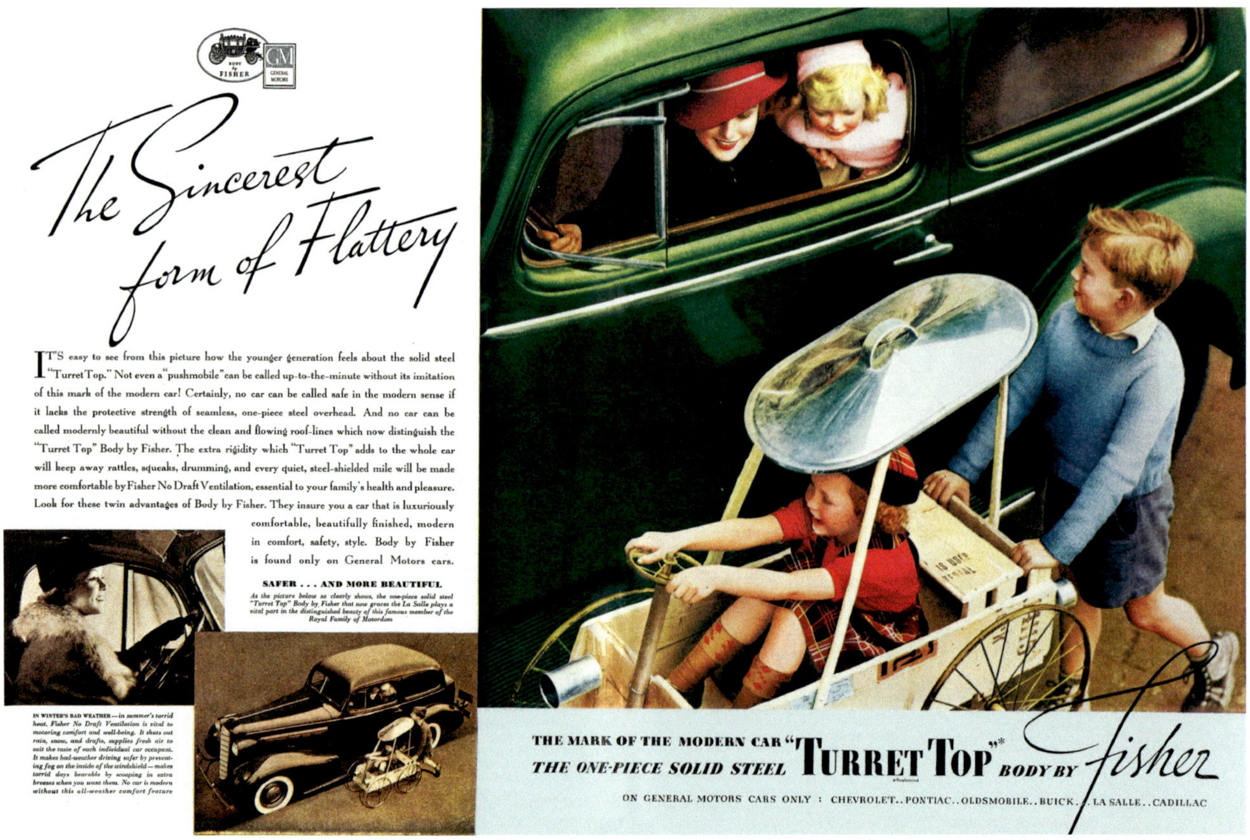

Body by Fisher, 1936

▸ La Salle, 1935 ▸▸ Chevrolet, 1935

Today a brilliant

NEW LaSALLE

with flashing new performance

ENTERS A LOWER-PRICE FIELD

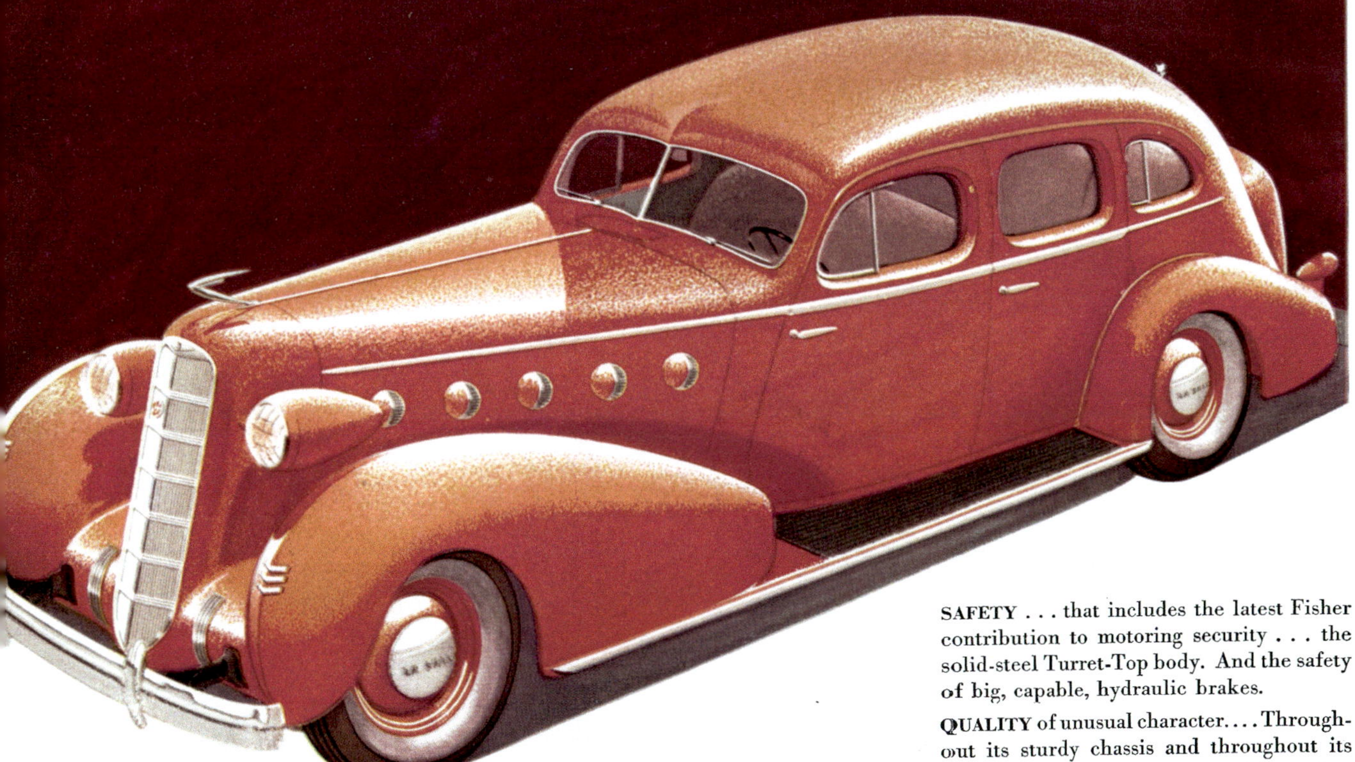

$1225

and up, list price at the Cadillac factory, Detroit, Michigan. Offered in four models. Model illustrated, the Four-Door Touring Sedan, list price, $1295. Special equipment extra. La Salle is a product of General Motors, and available on convenient G. M. A. C. terms.

CADILLAC is proud today to announce its latest achievement . . . a brilliant, flashing new La Salle, with . . .

PERFORMANCE of an inspiring new type . . . responsively eager in traffic, swift and unlabored on the hills, faster and smoother on the open road. Yet performance that carries with it new economies of operation.

STYLING . . . that is smarter than that of the style-setting La Salle of last year.

SAFETY . . . that includes the latest Fisher contribution to motoring security . . . the solid-steel Turret-Top body. And the safety of big, capable, hydraulic brakes.

QUALITY of unusual character. . . . Throughout its sturdy chassis and throughout its luxurious interior, trimly tailored in quality fabrics, the new La Salle is a tribute to fine car ideals. This is but natural . . . for it is designed and built by Cadillac.

The new La Salle is now on display at the salesrooms of your Cadillac-La Salle dealer. You are cordially invited to see it and to drive it . . . to judge its exceptional value and its brilliant performance for yourself.

CADILLAC MOTOR CAR COMPANY

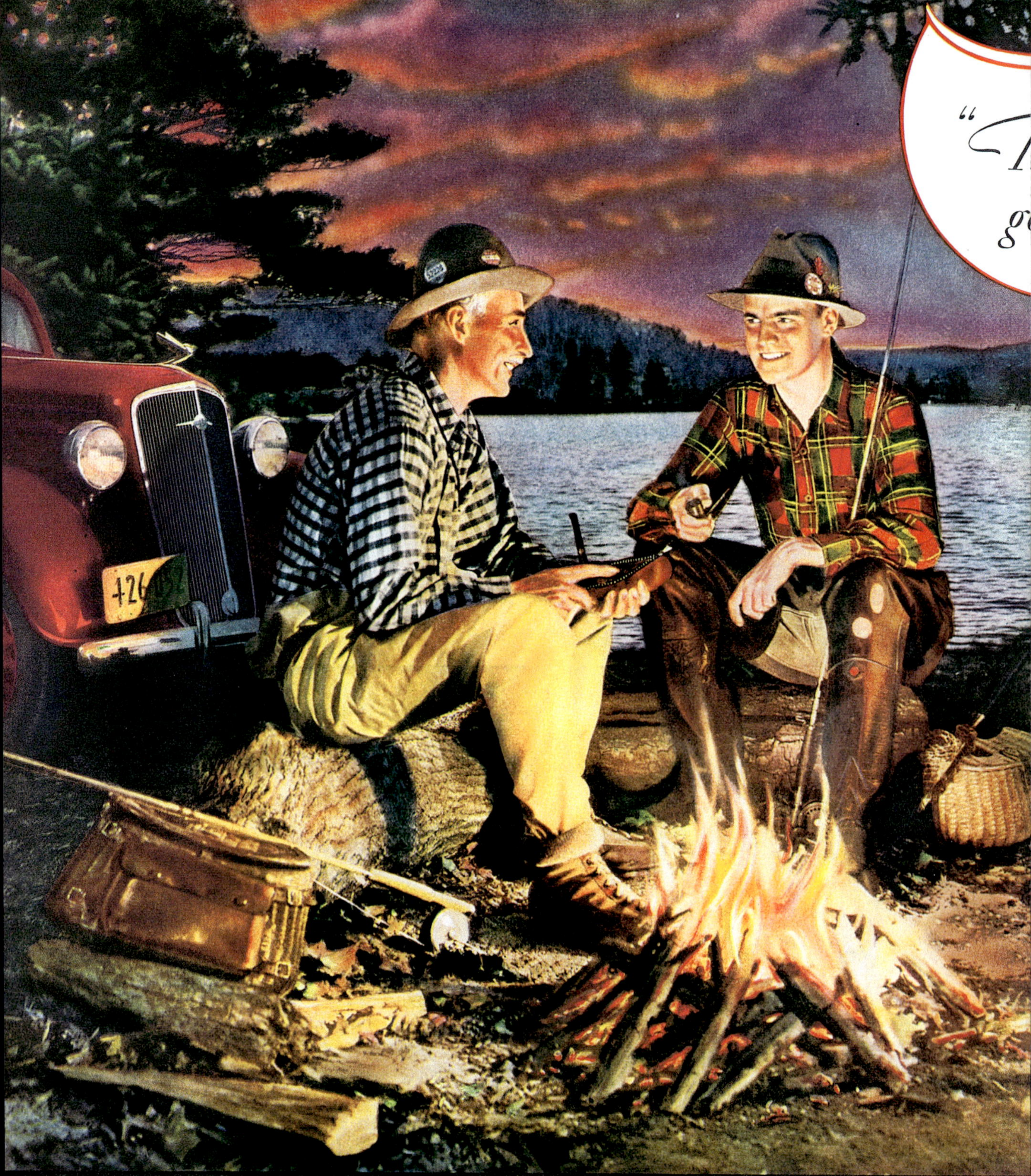

We shall be glad to send you, free of charge, a print of this illustration, suitable for framing. Mail your request to Advertising Department, Chevrolet Motor Company, General Motors Building, Detroit, Michigan.

CHEVROLET *for* 1935

CHEVROLET

"...od motor car - like the
...riend . . . is the motor car
that wears well!"

Feature after Feature
tells you to
CHOOSE CHEVROLET
FOR QUALITY AT
LOW COST

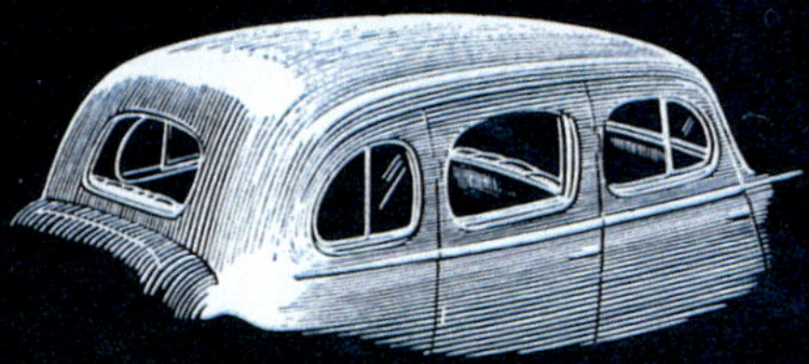

SOLID STEEL TURRET-TOP BODY BY FISHER
(with Fisher No Draft Ventilation)
for your comfort and safety

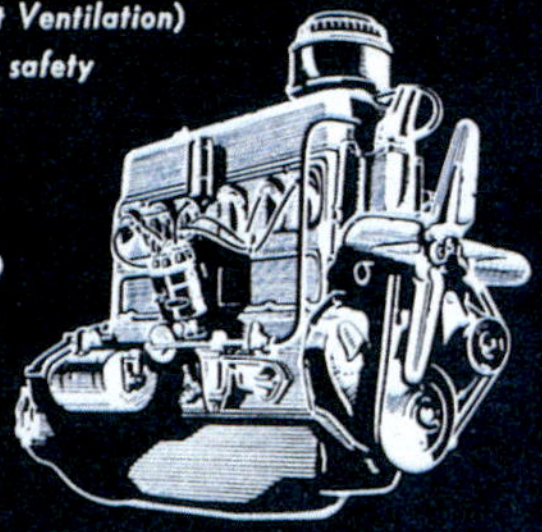

BLUE-FLAME
VALVE-IN-HEAD
ENGINE
(with Pressure Stream Oiling)
for performance with economy

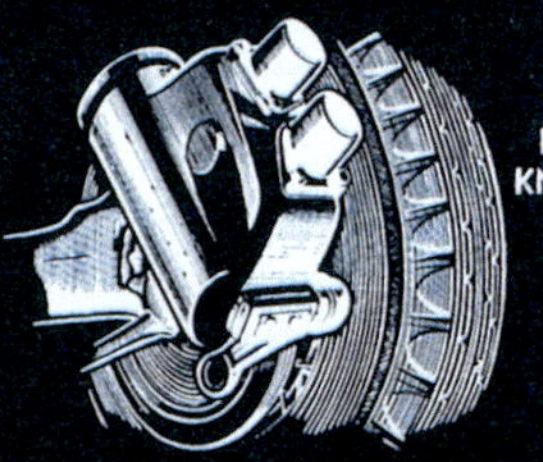

IMPROVED
KNEE-ACTION
RIDE
for your comfort and safety

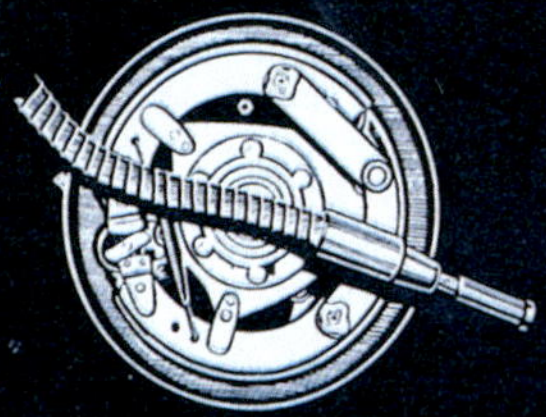

WEATHERPROOF
CABLE-
CONTROLLED
BRAKES
for quick, smooth, positive braking

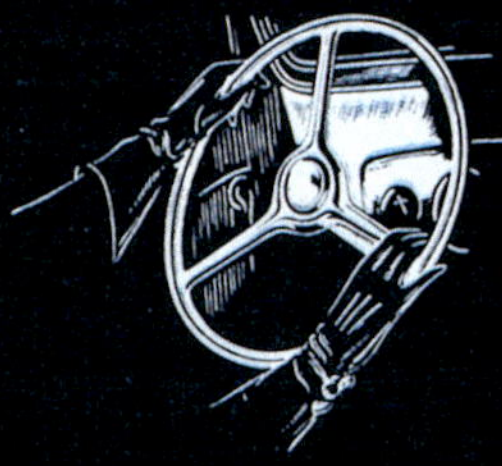

SHOCK-PROOF
STEERING
for greater driving ease

● Your Chevrolet is your friend . . . brightening your social hours . . . helping you in the work-a-day world . . . whisking you out into the countryside for healthful recreation . . . giving *much* and asking *very little* in return! And, like a good friend, your Chevrolet wears well. You *know* that, or *will* know it, when you have driven a Chevrolet for any length of time. Because this car is made right, of the very best materials, with genuine quality in every part. Chevrolet's Blue-Flame valve-in-head engine *keeps on* performing smoothly and dependably . . . its comfortable Knee-Action Ride is *always* comfortable . . . and its beautiful Body by Fisher *remains* beautiful because it is of Turret-Top construction—the strongest and most durable known. All that your Chevrolet asks of you, in return, is a *minimum* of gas and oil . . . a *minimum* of attention . . . *and your continued friendship* . . . for that is Chevrolet's finest and most valued possession.

CHEVROLET MOTOR COMPANY, DETROIT, MICHIGAN

Compare Chevrolet's low delivered prices and easy G.M.A.C. terms
A General Motors Value

Master De Luxe Coupe

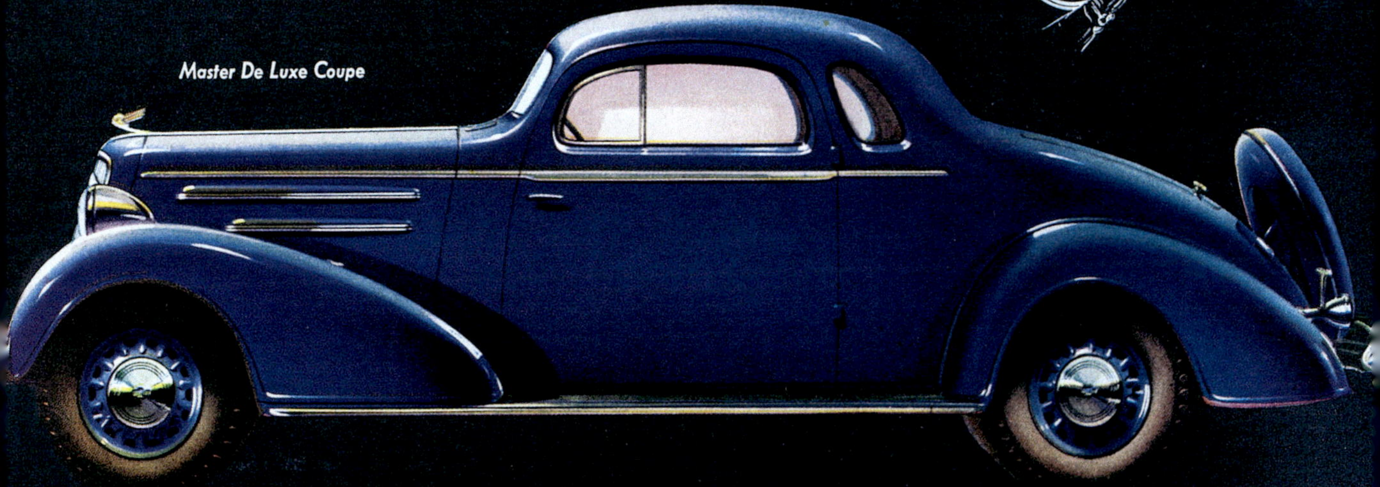

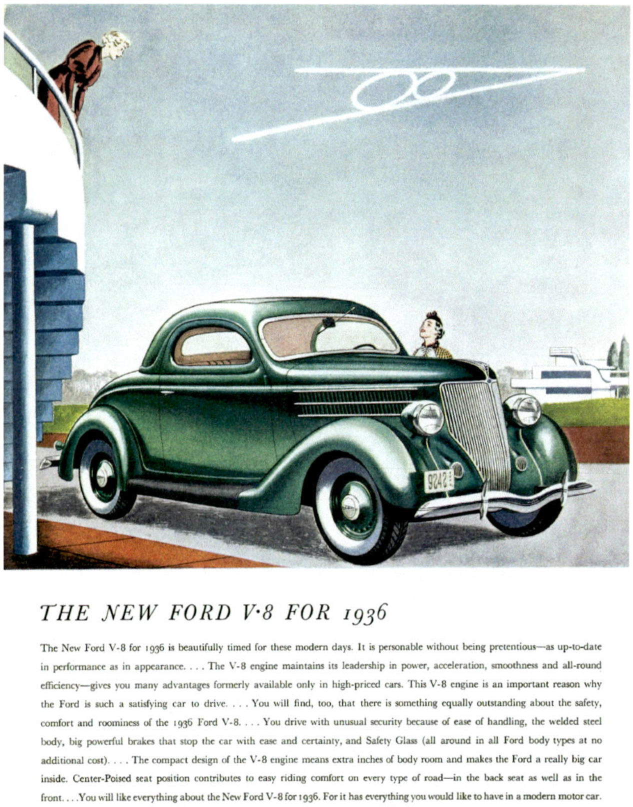

Ford, 1936

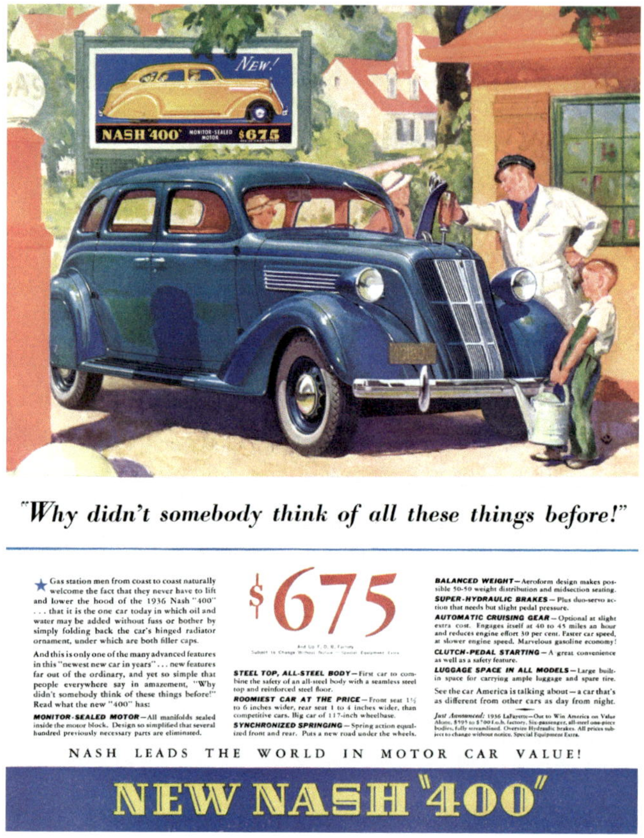

Nash, 1935

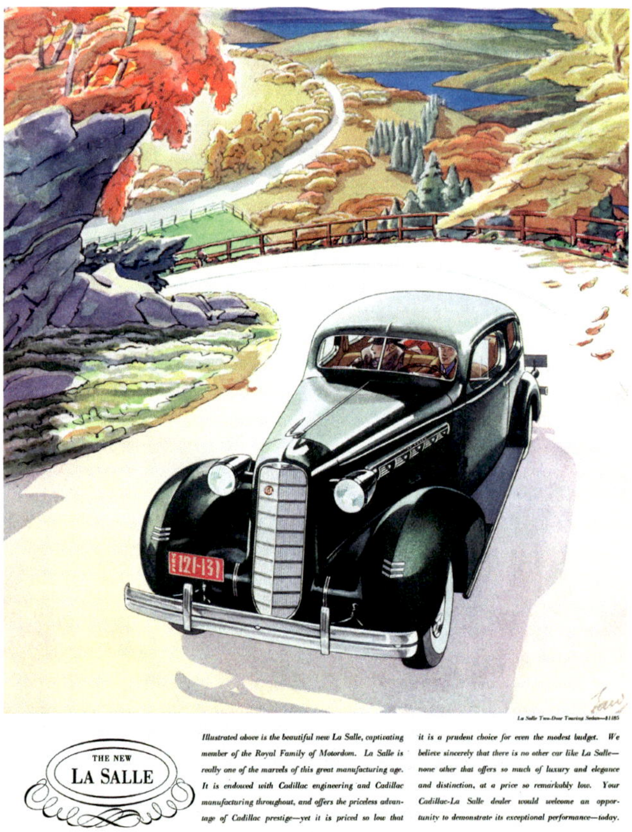

La Salle, 1935

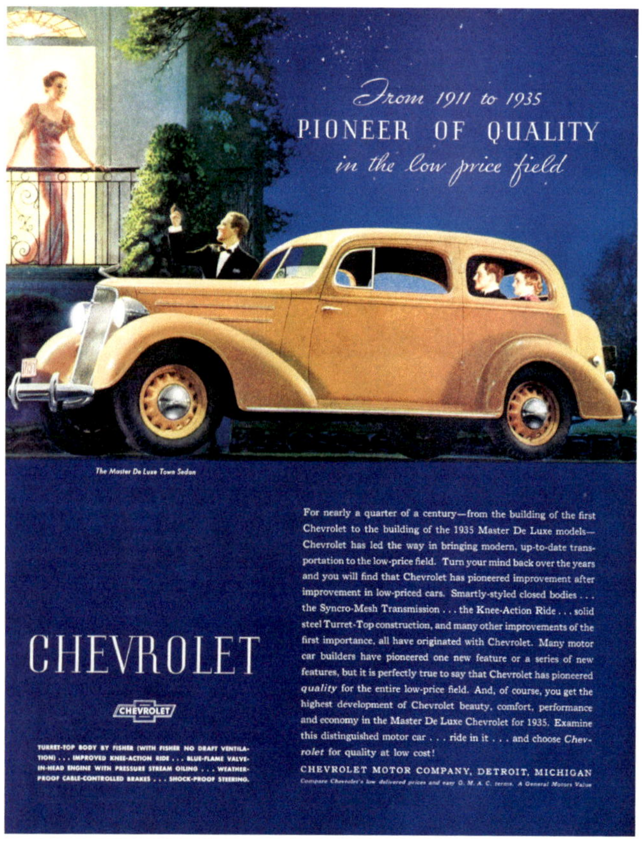

Chevrolet, 1935

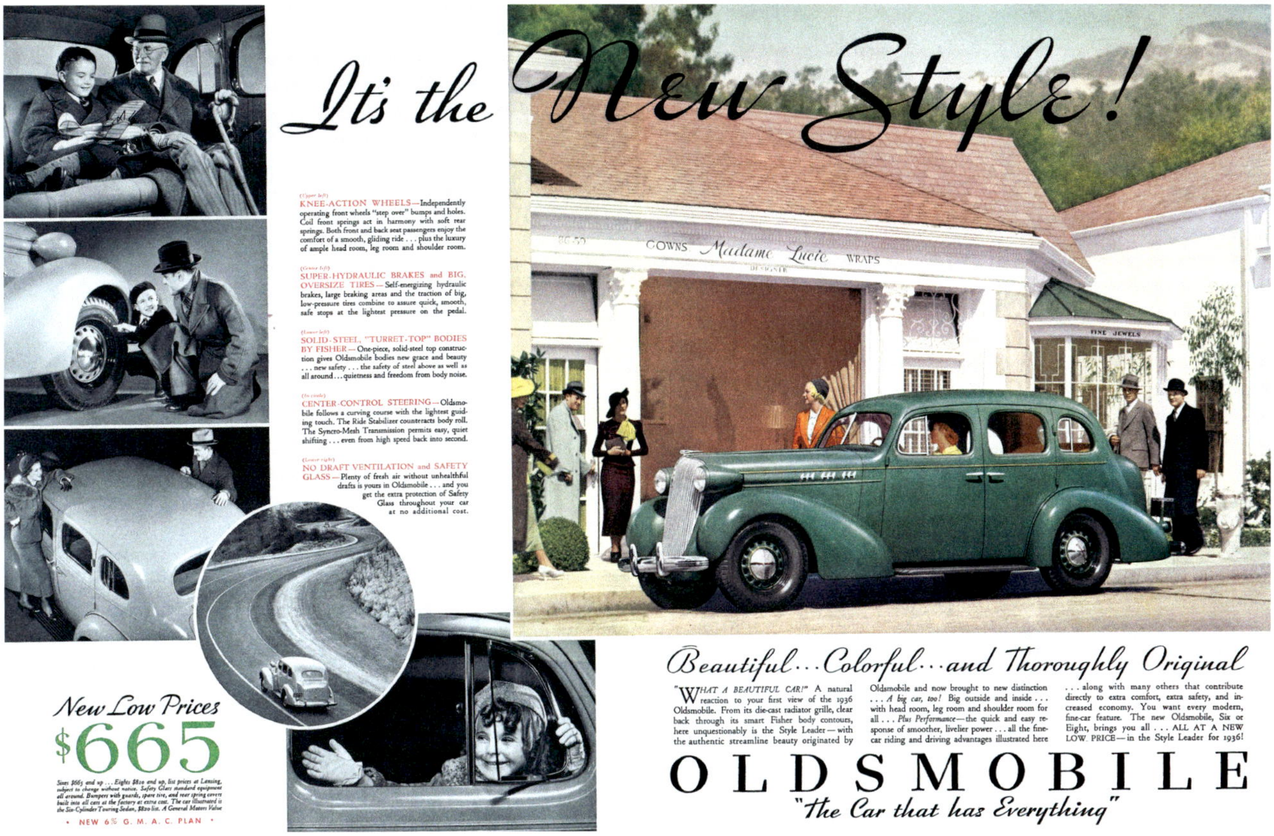

Oldsmobile, 1936

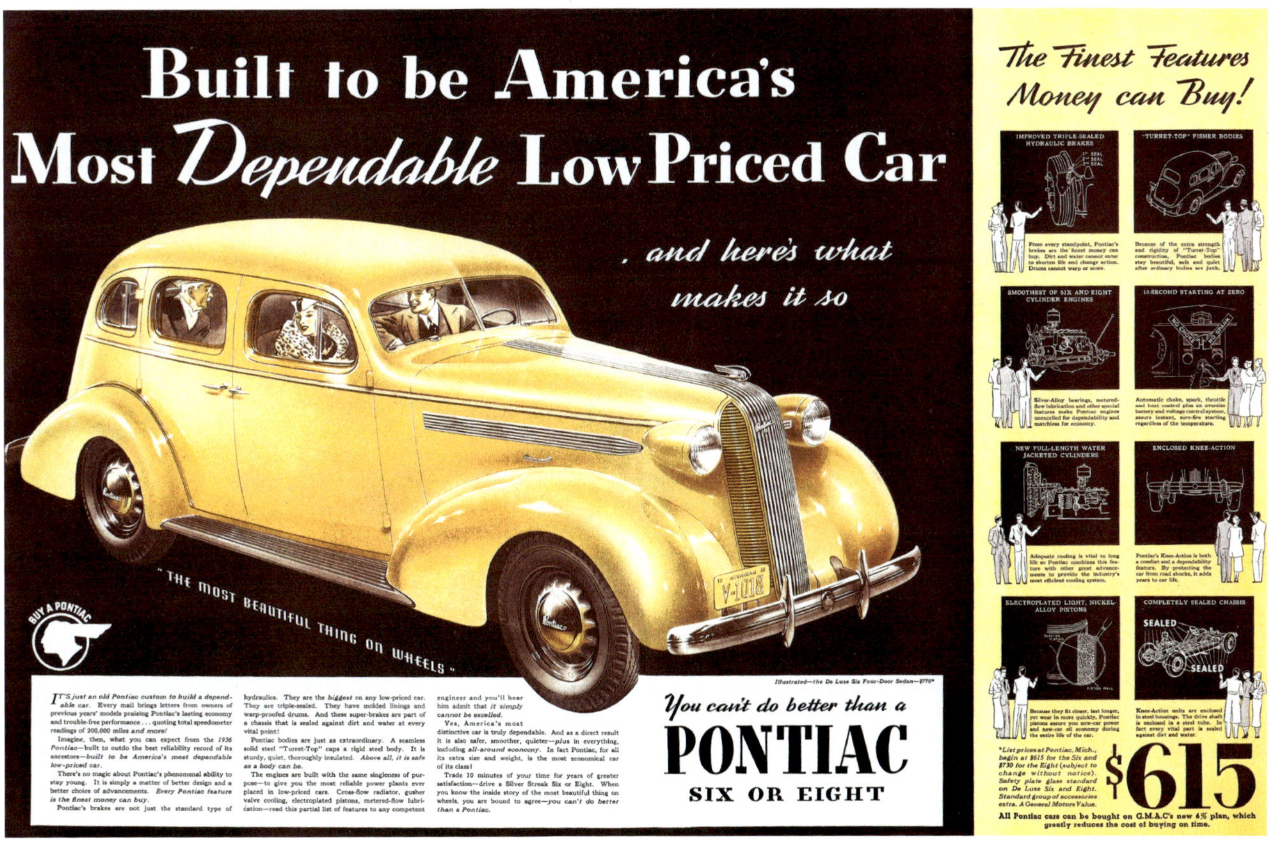

Pontiac, 1936

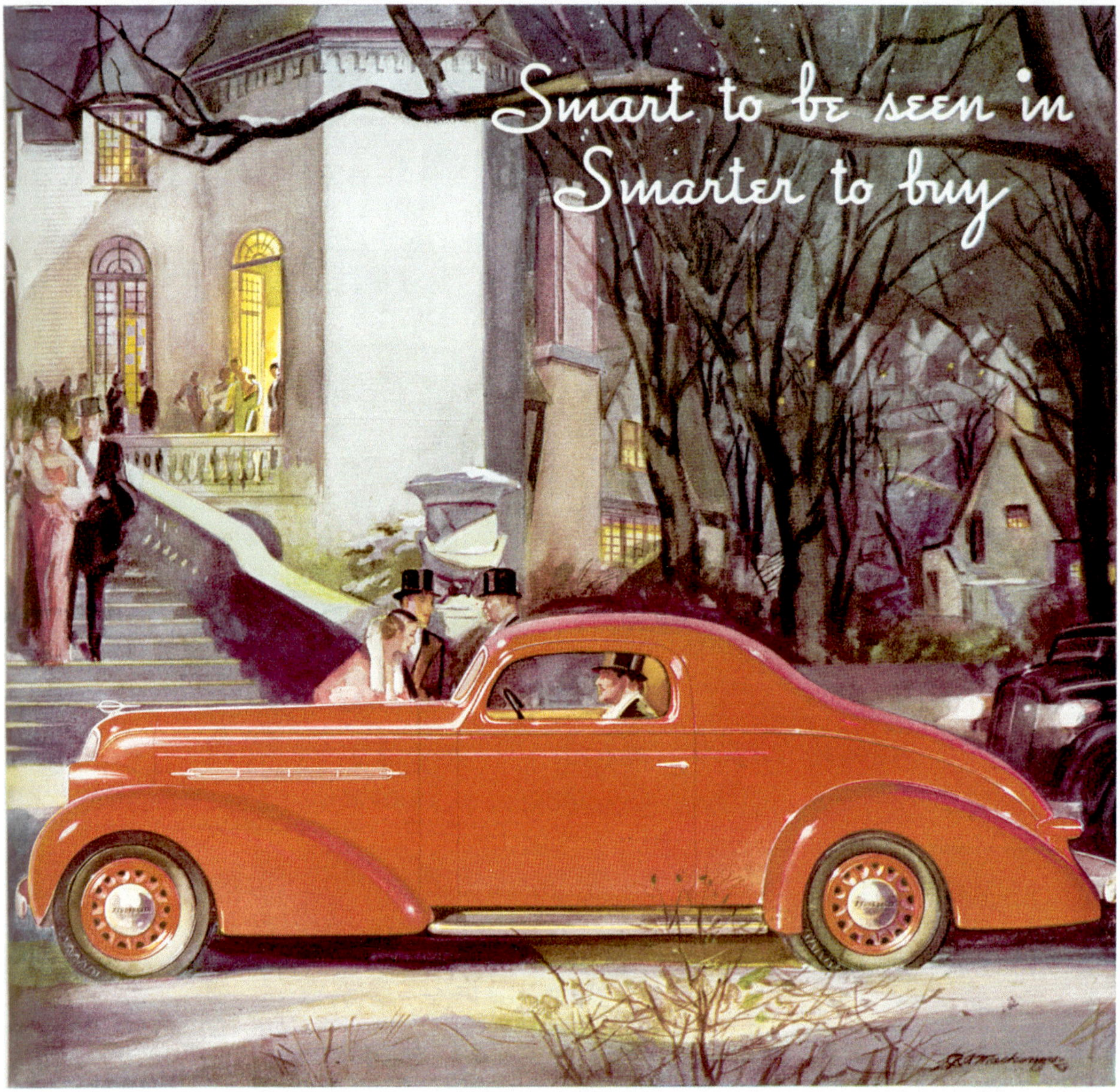

AND THIS BEAUTIFUL 1936 STUDEBAKER COSTS ALMOST AS LITTLE

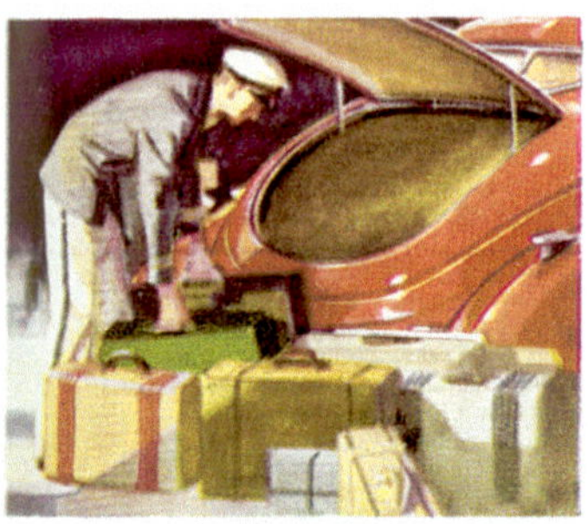

It's America's best looking coupe

here isn't another 1936 automobile that even half approaches the huing beauty of this big thrifty new 3-passenger Dictator. And you areil have to take our word for that. If you're seen all the other new reare you know! In that sweeping rear deck there's the largest carrying compartment you've ever seen in a coupe . . . more room for baggage than most people ever require . . . so much room in fact that many motorists are choosing this Dictator coupe for its carrying capacity wholly aside from its luxury and beauty.

AS LOWEST PRICE CARS

$665 and up at the factory

NOW priced as low as $665 at the factory, this big, thrifty, thoroughly new Studebaker sells itself on sight. Exquisitely appointed, styled by the gifted Helen Dryden, it won two first places in the Gilmore Yosemite 352-mile Run—the national gas economy classic . . . an average of 24.27 miles per gallon for the Dictator Six—20.34 miles per gallon for the President Eight!

Sedan rear seats are chair-height with 58⅝ inches of elbow room . . . and 3 extra inches of toe room on the flat, comfortable rear floor. The beautifully contoured steel body is the world's strongest—with the world's largest one-piece solid steel top. Feather-touch hydraulic brakes! Straight-line steering! Swift acceleration!

But for real proof, you must drive this matchless new Studebaker. Dictator prices begin at $665—President prices at $965. And the new Studebaker C. I. T. 6% plan offers a new low in time payments. The Studebaker Corporation, South Bend, Indiana.

World's only car with
AUTOMATIC HILL HOLDER
The most gratifying experience you ever had in driving . . . prevents your rolling back when you come to a stop on any upgrade . . . the most important safety advancement of 1936.

Spectacular economy with
GAS-SAVING OVERDRIVE
With this invention, a development of Studebaker free wheeling, your engine uses gas only 2 miles while your car is traveling 3 miles.

* * *

SAFER ALL-STEEL BODIES . . . ROOMIER INTERIORS . . . FLAT, COMFORTABLE FLOORS

NEW 1936 Studebaker

SMART TO BE SEEN IN . . . SMARTER TO BUY

Studebaker, 1936

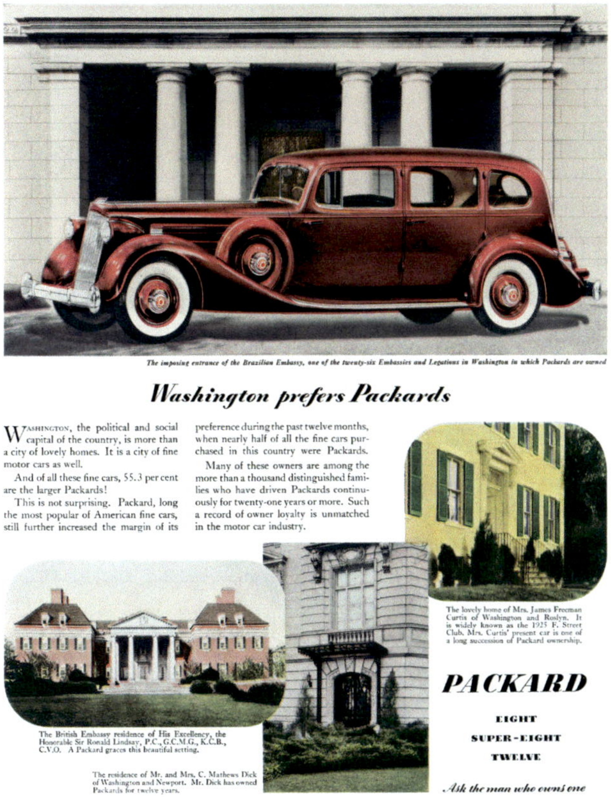

Packard, 1936

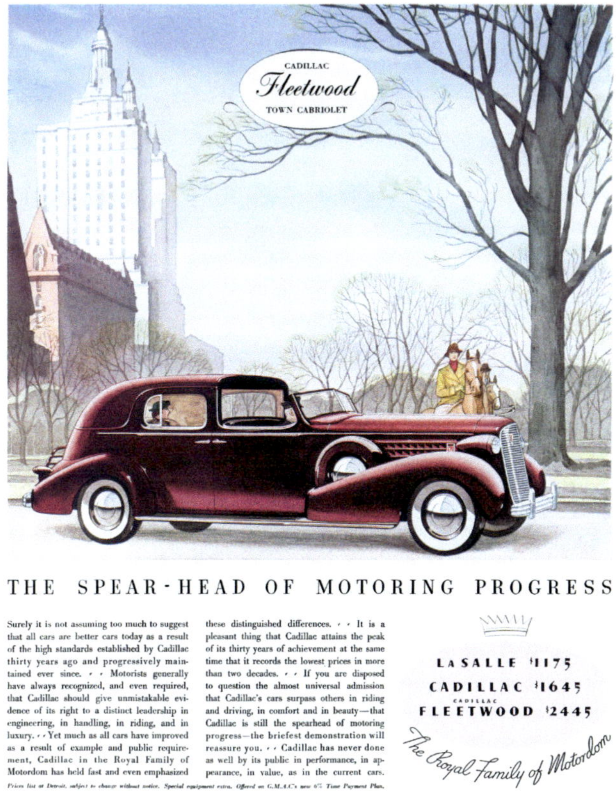

Cadillac, 1936

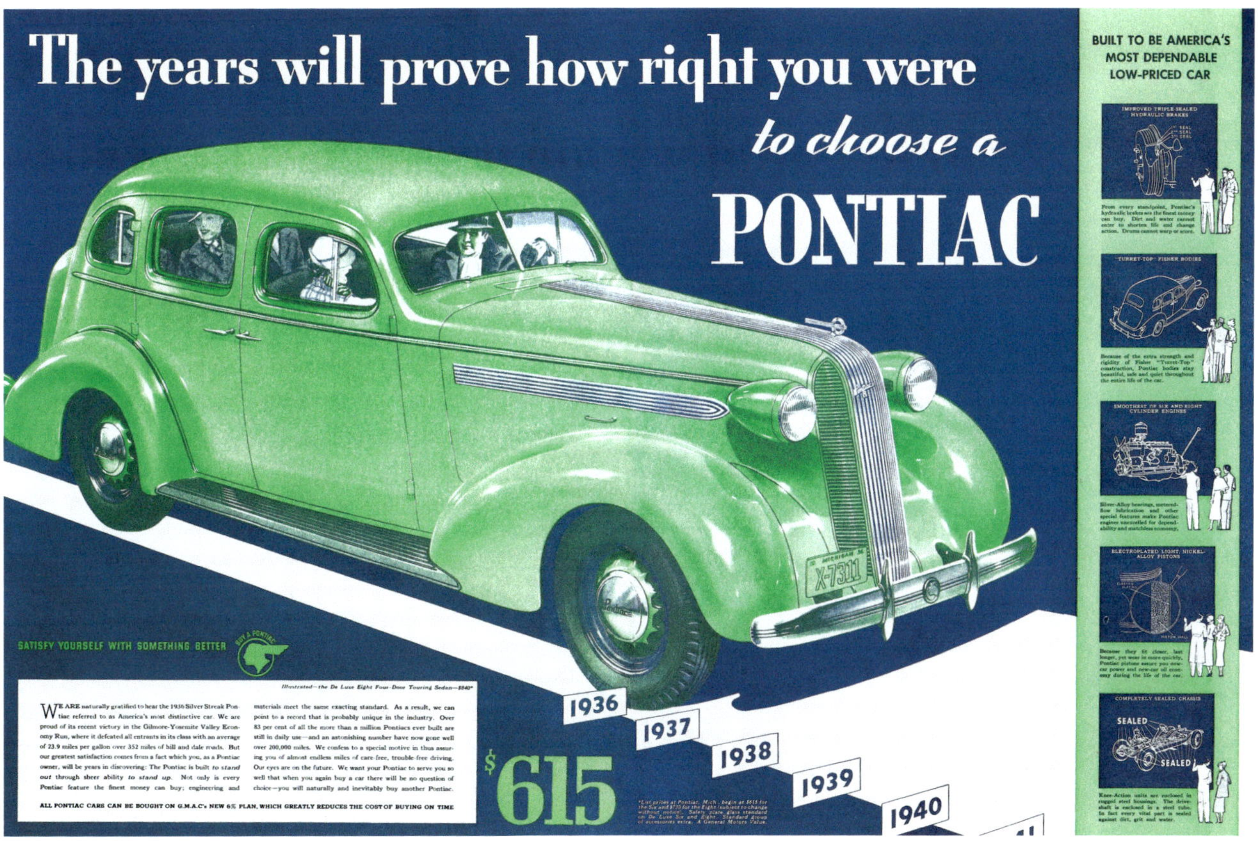

Pontiac, 1936

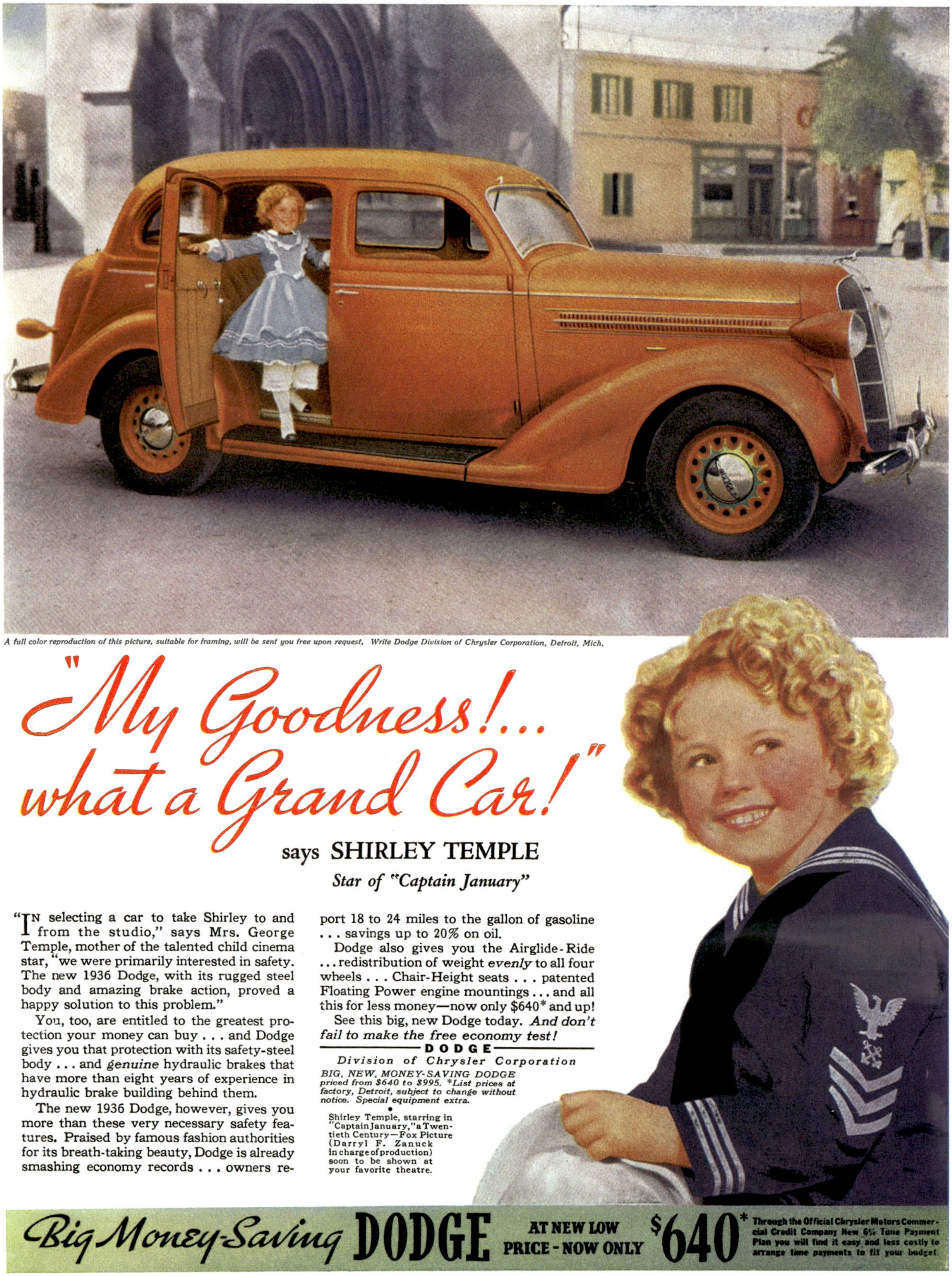
A full color reproduction of this picture, suitable for framing, will be sent you free upon request. Write Dodge Division of Chrysler Corporation, Detroit, Mich.
"My Goodness!... what a Grand Car!"
says SHIRLEY TEMPLE
Star of "Captain January"
"IN selecting a car to take Shirley to and from the studio," says Mrs. George Temple, mother of the talented child cinema star, "we were primarily interested in safety. The new 1936 Dodge, with its rugged steel body and amazing brake action, proved a happy solution to this problem."
You, too, are entitled to the greatest protection your money can buy . . . and Dodge gives you that protection with its safety-steel body . . . and genuine hydraulic brakes that have more than eight years of experience in hydraulic brake building behind them.
The new 1936 Dodge, however, gives you more than these very necessary safety features. Praised by famous fashion authorities for its breath-taking beauty, Dodge is already smashing economy records . . . owners report 18 to 24 miles to the gallon of gasoline . . . savings up to 20% on oil.
Dodge also gives you the Airglide-Ride . . . redistribution of weight evenly to all four wheels . . . Chair-Height seats . . . patented Floating Power engine mountings . . . and all this for less money—now only $640* and up!
See this big, new Dodge today. And don't fail to make the free economy test!
DODGE
Division of Chrysler Corporation
BIG, NEW, MONEY-SAVING DODGE priced from $640 to $995. *List prices at factory, Detroit, subject to change without notice. Special equipment extra.
Shirley Temple, starring in "Captain January," a Twentieth Century—Fox Picture (Darryl F. Zanuck in charge of production) soon to be shown at your favorite theatre.
Big Money-Saving DODGE
AT NEW LOW PRICE - NOW ONLY $640*
Through the Official Chrysler Motors Commercial Credit Company New 6% Time Payment Plan you will find it easy and less costly to arrange time payments to fit your budget.

▲▶ *Dodge, 1936*

"WHY SHOULD I BUY AN EXPENSIVE CAR–

When the New Dodge offers such Unusual Beauty and Economy?"

says **GINGER ROGERS**

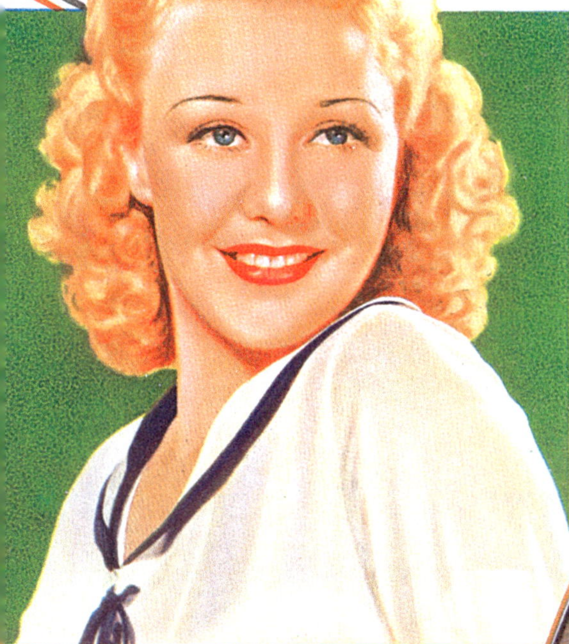

LIKE many another who could afford a more expensive car, the combination of beauty and economy won Miss Rogers to the big, new, Money-Saving Dodge. Acclaimed by fashion authorities the "Beauty Winner" of 1936, Dodge is smashing economy records . . . owners report 18 to 24 miles to the gallon of gas and oil savings up to 20%.

But with a Dodge you get more than style and economy. Dodge gives you the protection of safety-steel bodies, pioneered by Dodge, and *genuine* hydraulic brakes, plus a wealth of expensive-car features such as the Airglide-Ride . . . redistribution of weight equally to all four wheels . . . Chair-Height seats . . . patented Floating Power engine mountings . . . and many other advancements.

See the new Dodge today. Drive it. See the free economy test . . . And bear in mind that it is not unusual that dependable Dodge cars give their owners up to 200,000 and even more miles of service. And don't forget, Dodge—at new, low prices—now costs only a few dollars more than the lowest-priced cars.

DODGE

Division of Chrysler Corporation

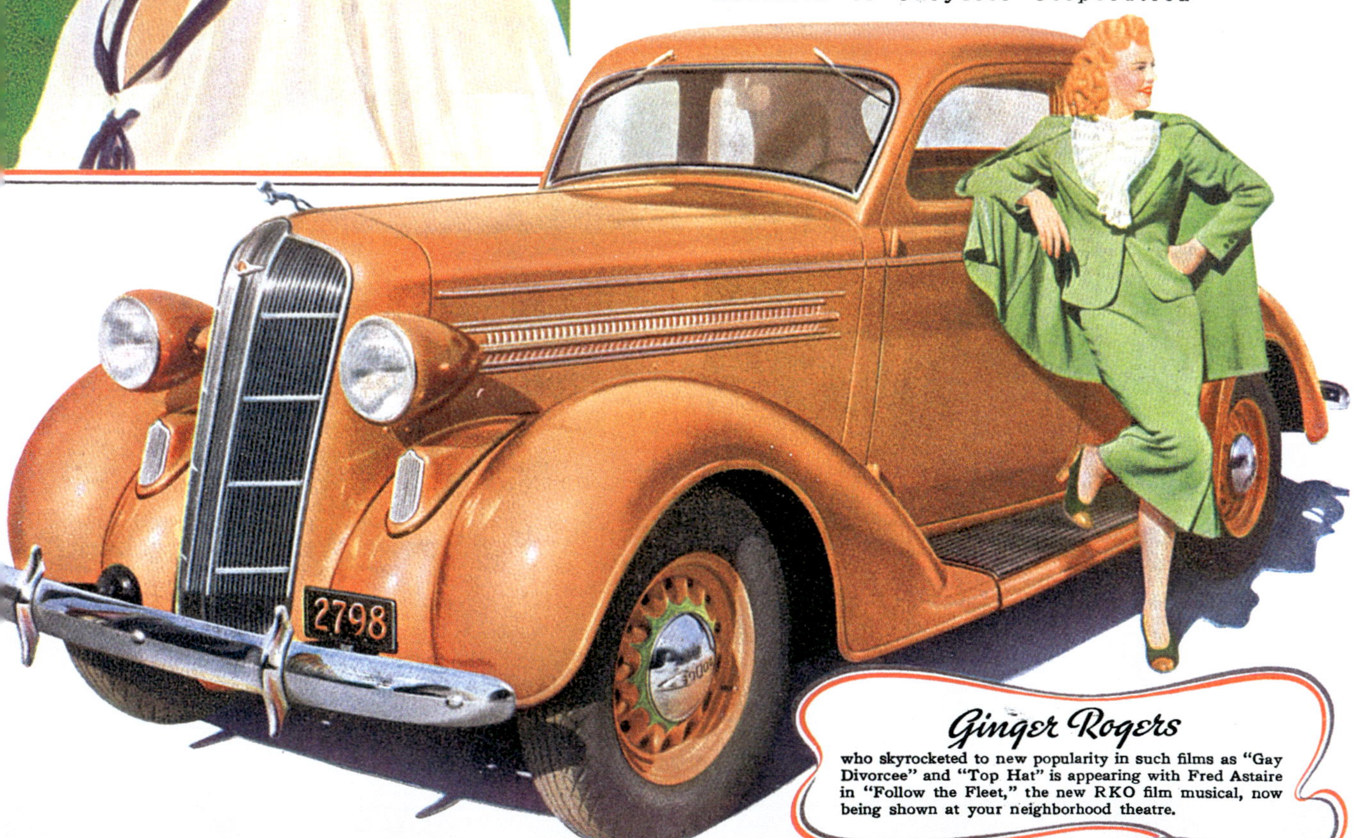

Ginger Rogers

who skyrocketed to new popularity in such films as "Gay Divorcee" and "Top Hat" is appearing with Fred Astaire in "Follow the Fleet," the new RKO film musical, now being shown at your neighborhood theatre.

...g, Money-Saving **DODGE** *new low price--only* **$640***

*Priced from $640 to $995. *List prices at factory, Detroit, subject to change without notice. Special equipment extra.*

Through the Official Chrysler Motors Commercial Credit Company New 6% Time Payment Plan you will find it easy and economical to arrange time payments to fit your budget.

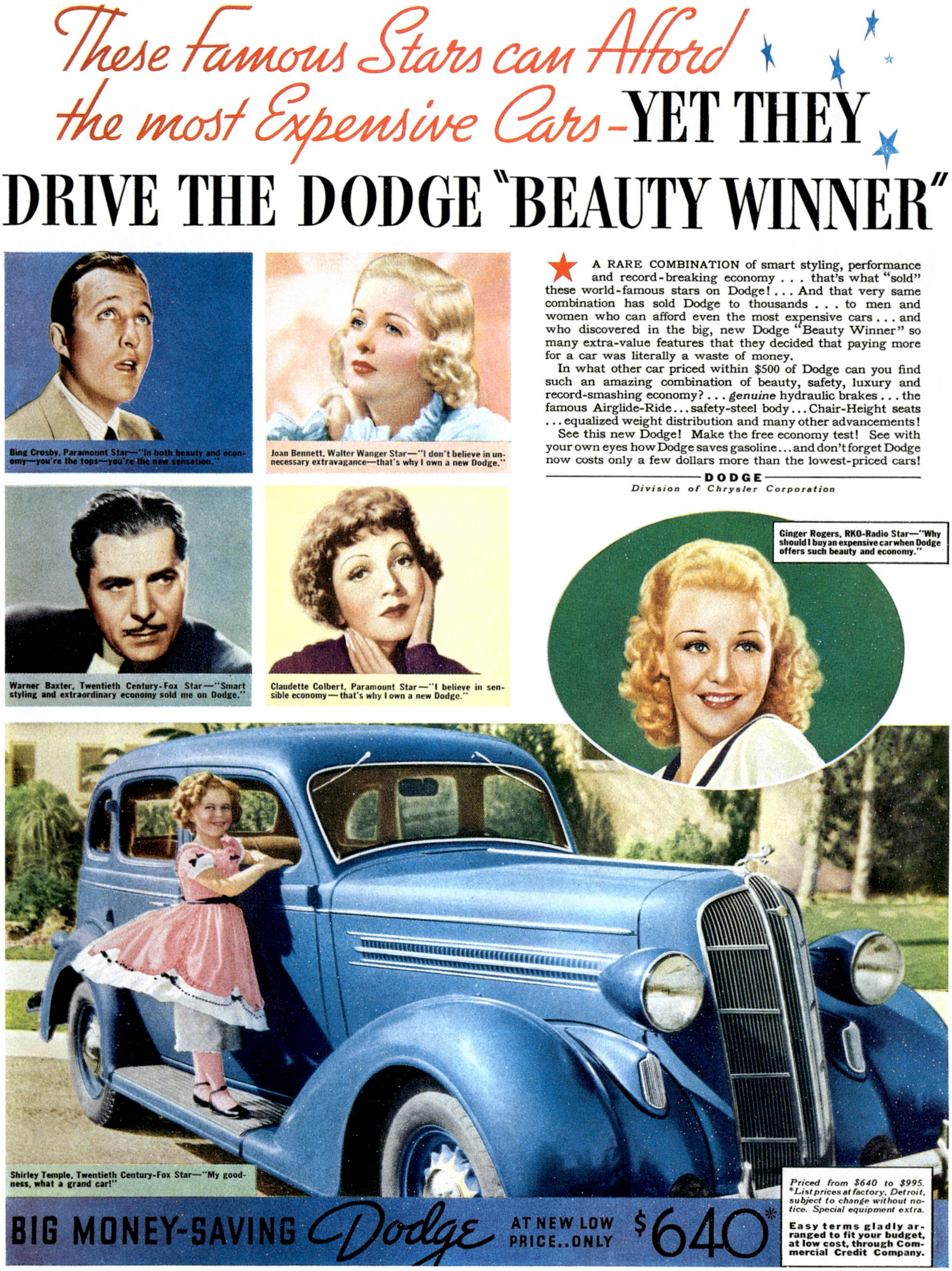
These Famous Stars can Afford the most Expensive Cars-YET THEY
DRIVE THE DODGE "BEAUTY WINNER"
A RARE COMBINATION of smart styling, performance and record-breaking economy . . . that's what "sold" these world-famous stars on Dodge! . . . And that very same combination has sold Dodge to thousands . . . to men and women who can afford even the most expensive cars . . . and who discovered in the big, new Dodge "Beauty Winner" so many extra-value features that they decided that paying more for a car was literally a waste of money.
In what other car priced within $500 of Dodge can you find such an amazing combination of beauty, safety, luxury and record-smashing economy? . . . genuine hydraulic brakes . . . the famous Airglide-Ride . . . safety-steel body . . . Chair-Height seats . . . equalized weight distribution and many other advancements!
See this new Dodge! Make the free economy test! See with your own eyes how Dodge saves gasoline . . . and don't forget Dodge now costs only a few dollars more than the lowest-priced cars!
DODGE
Division of Chrysler Corporation
Bing Crosby, Paramount Star—"In both beauty and economy—you're the tops—you're the new sensation."
Joan Bennett, Walter Wanger Star—"I don't believe in unnecessary extravagance—that's why I own a new Dodge."
Warner Baxter, Twentieth Century-Fox Star—"Smart styling and extraordinary economy sold me on Dodge."
Claudette Colbert, Paramount Star—"I believe in sensible economy—that's why I own a new Dodge."
Ginger Rogers, RKO-Radio Star—"Why should I buy an expensive car when Dodge offers such beauty and economy."
Shirley Temple, Twentieth Century-Fox Star—"My goodness, what a grand car!"
BIG MONEY-SAVING Dodge AT NEW LOW PRICE..ONLY $640*
Priced from $640 to $995. *List prices at factory, Detroit, subject to change without notice. Special equipment extra.
Easy terms gladly arranged to fit your budget, at low cost, through Commercial Credit Company.

Dodge, 1936

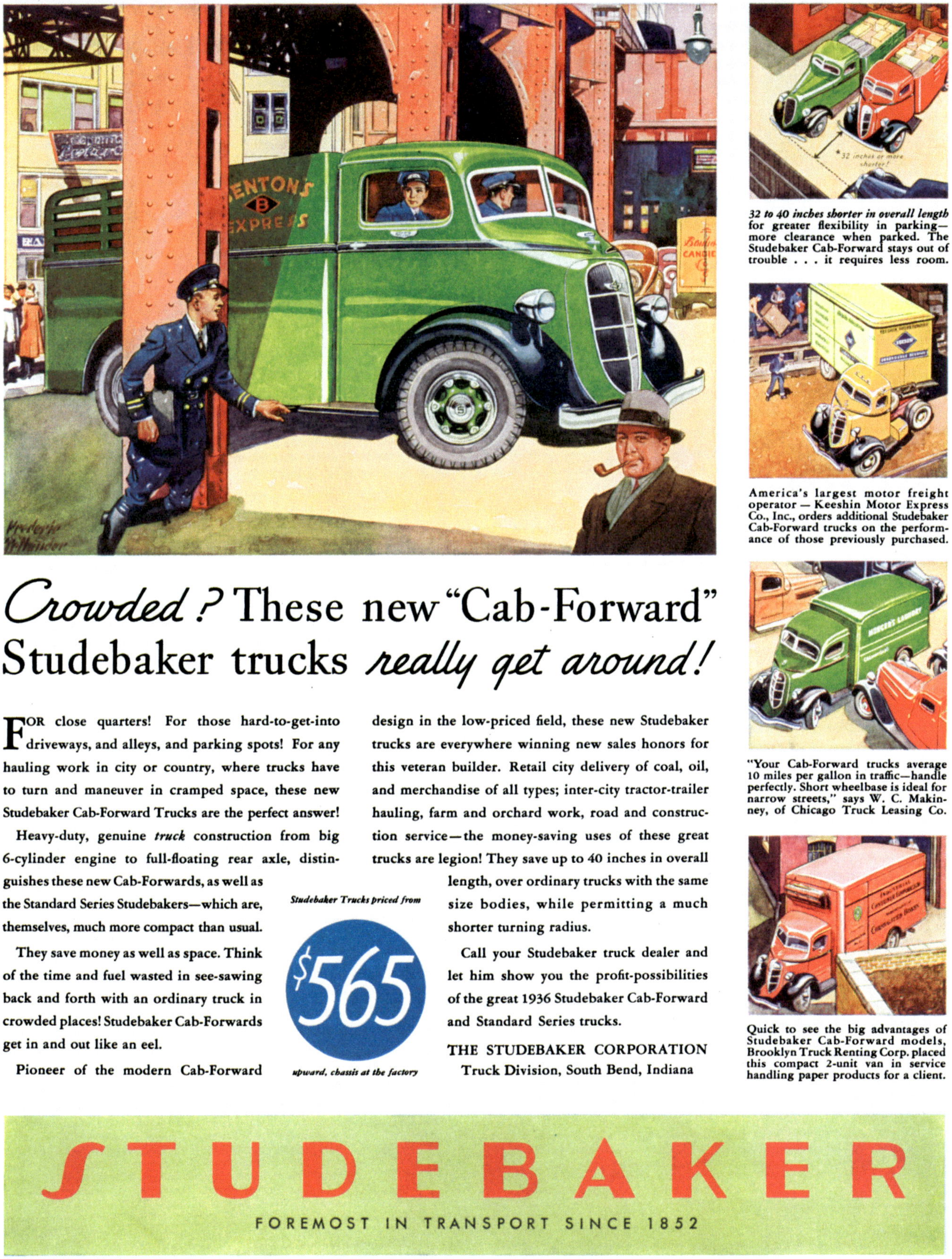

Studebaker, 1936

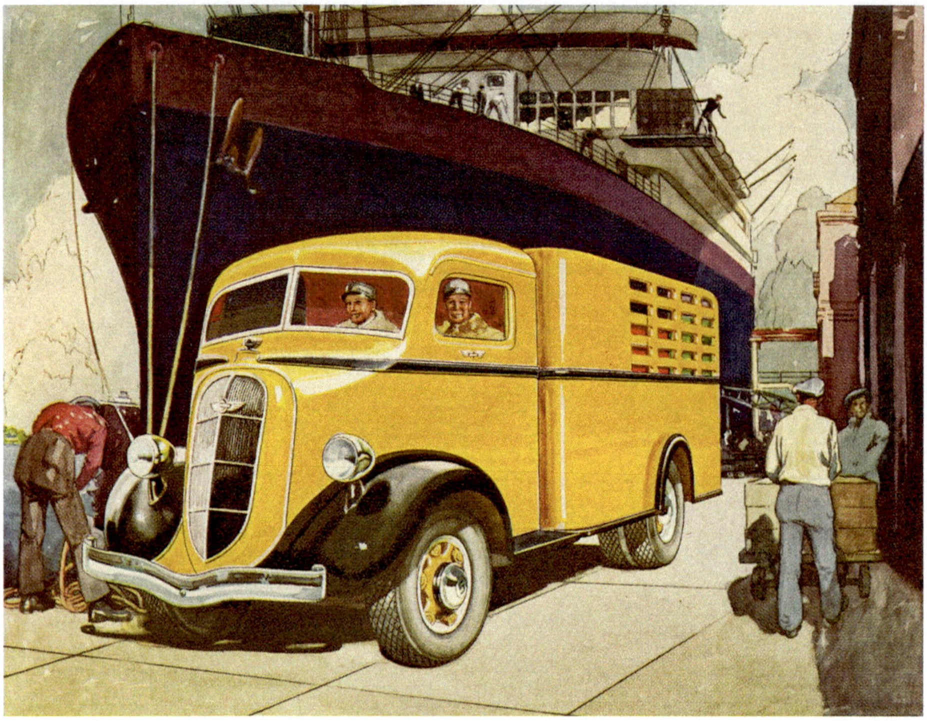

These new Studebaker "Cab-Forward" trucks *get in and out where other trucks can't!*

MINUTES saved on countless turn-arounds in crowded quarters! Fuel and oil saved! Tempers saved! Garage space saved! Crumpled fenders and property-damage saved! Get in, get out, turn, park, where ordinary trucks can't be driven! That's the Studebaker "Cab-Forward" sensational extra profit story!

Up to 40 inches in overall length is saved by this very practical modern truck chassis design, with no sacrifice of body room and a big gain in maneuverability over conventional types.

First complete trucks of their type in the low-priced field, these new Studebaker "cab-forward" trucks are heavy-duty through and through. Big, 6-cylinder *truck* engines, sturdy full-floating rear axles, big hydraulic brakes, true truck frames and springs—and furthermore—*a comfort-cab that's really been engineered for the job!*

Studebaker Trucks priced from

$565

upward, chassis at the factory

Easy for the driver to get in and out from either side—no mountainous "hump" to climb over! Elbow-room and knee-room are ample for full-sized men!

Any wonder these new Studebakers are the hit of the season? Everyone concerned with city trucking is vitally interested. Also orchard men and farmers—inter-city tractor-trailer operators—these and scores of other big, important truck-operating industries are finding these great new Studebaker "Cab-Forward" trucks the perfect answer to modern low cost hauling conditions.

New Standard Series Studebaker Trucks, too, are extra compact. Call your Studebaker dealer and let him show you how 1936 Studebaker Motor Trucks can save you money.

•

THE STUDEBAKER CORP.
Truck Division, South Bend, Ind.

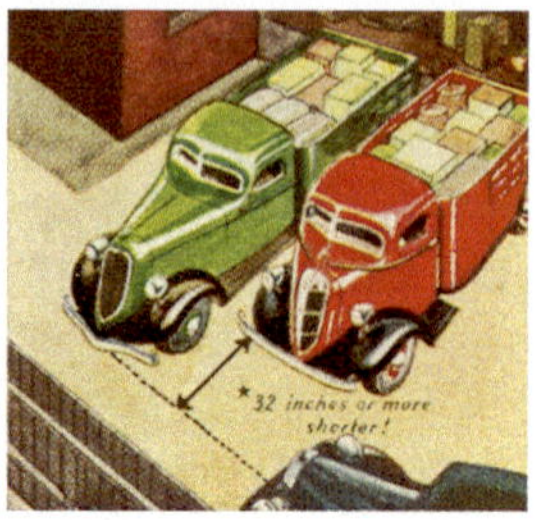

32 to 40 inches shorter in overall length for greater flexibility in parking—more clearance when parked. The Studebaker "Cab-Forward" trucks stay out of trouble...avoid many traffic difficulties... require less room.

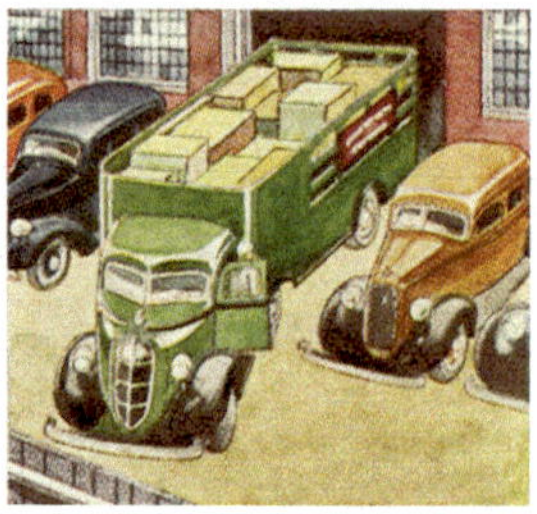

Easy to Back Up and Park! Studebaker's new extra-compact design, short turning radius and good visibility save the time and gasoline wasted in maneuvering ordinary type trucks into crowded quarters.

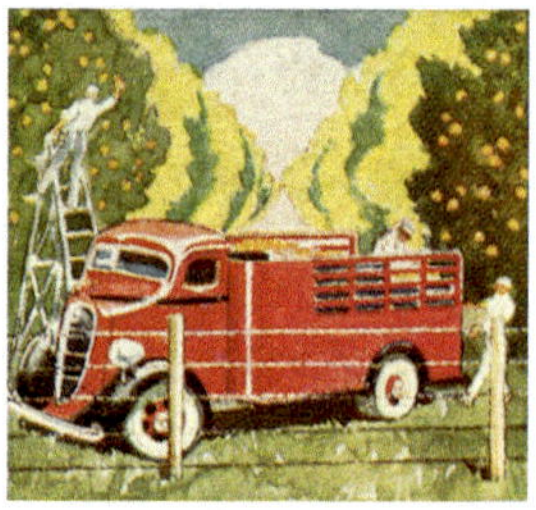

For Orchard and Farm Work! The "Cab-Forward" truck gets in between rows—makes sharp turns—avoids damage to trees or crops. Studebaker sturdiness stands up under rough-road and farm use.

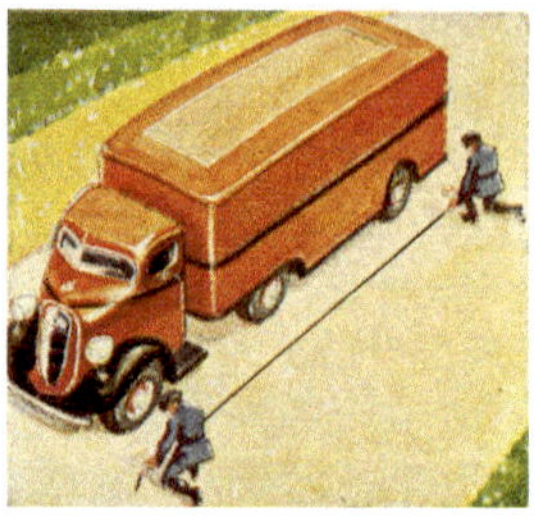

Keeps Overall Length Down! By saving as much as 40 inches without sacrificing of body room, the "Cab-Forward" design permits maximum capacity within limits of length legal in most states.

STUDEBAKER

FOREMOST IN TRANSPORT SINCE 1852

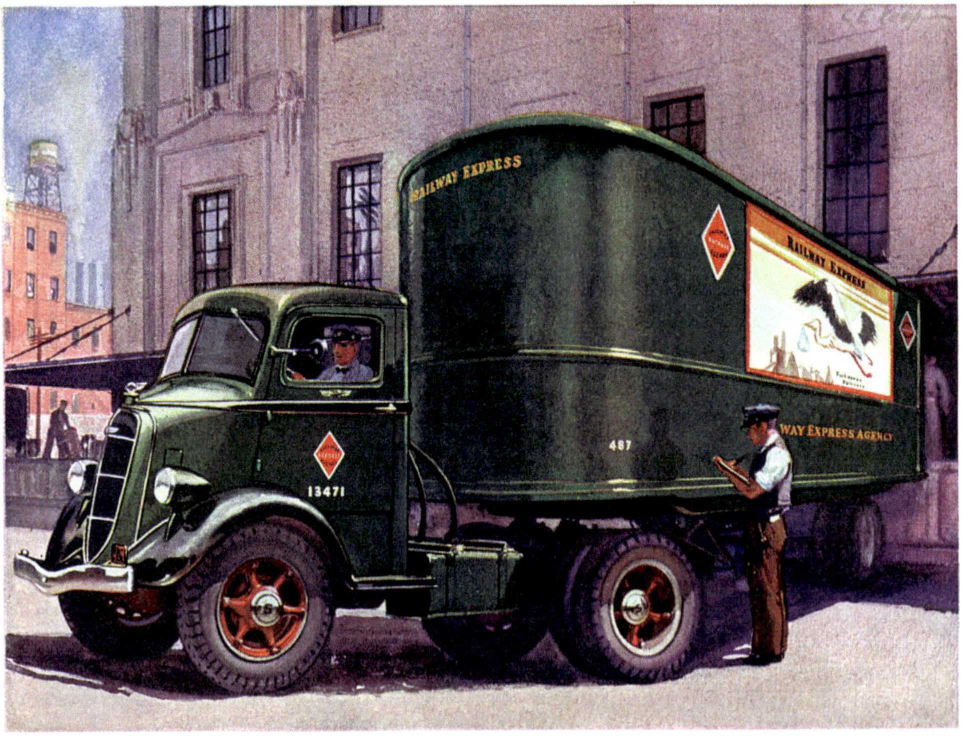

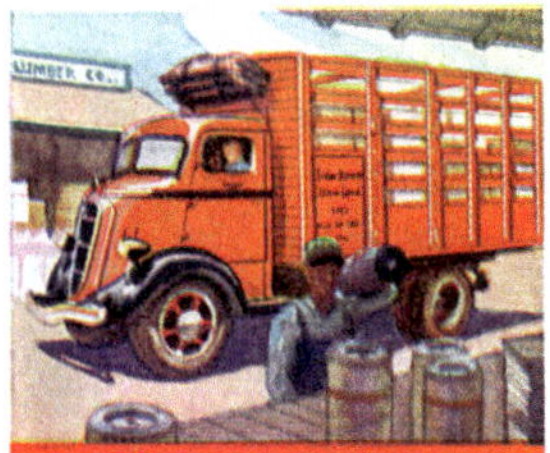

JOHNS-MANVILLE

Heavy-duty hauling in crowded factory and warehouse districts emphasizes the time- and trouble-saving advantages of close-coupled Cab-Forward design. Studebaker delivers goods for less money.

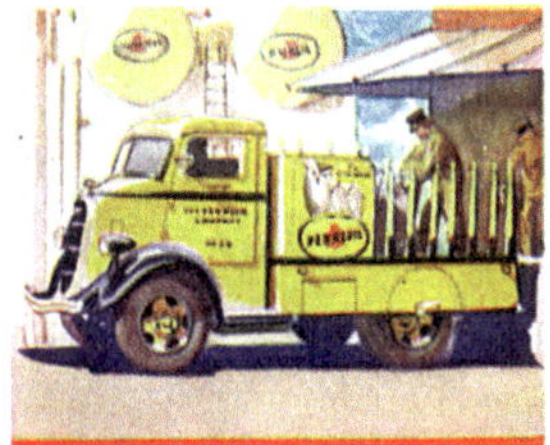

PENNZOIL

This smart Cab-Forward truck, delivering Pennzoil products on the Pacific Coast, quickly gets in and out of places where trucks of conventional design waste time and gas backing and turning.

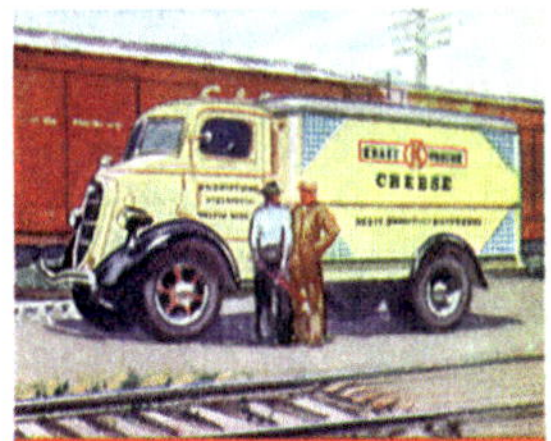

KRAFT-PHENIX

Speeding the transport of perishable dairy products, this Cab-Forward Studebaker, in the service of a Kraft-Phenix distributor, earns extra dividends in time saved, in customer good will.

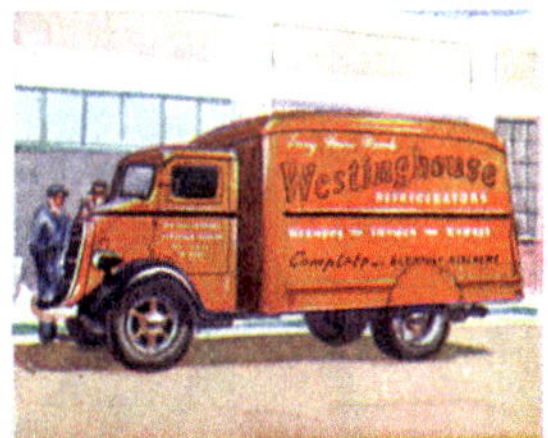

WESTINGHOUSE

Fine merchandise deserves to be handled in a way that reflects credit upon manufacturer and merchant. The smartness and efficiency of the Cab-Forward truck (illustrated) in Westinghouse distributing service do just that.

Cab-Forward sweeping the field!

Studebaker serves 25 of the 60 largest truck fleets

FROM its very introduction, Studebaker Cab-Forward design has swept swiftly into the high regard of America's foremost truck fleet operators. Of the 60 largest and best known fleets in the United States, 25 now employ Studebaker trucks!

One fleet began with an order of 10 Studebaker Cab-Forward trucks—quickly followed by an order for 75 more! Another fleet of 70 Studebakers is growing every month. A nationally known baking company's fleet now includes 102 Studebakers. Still another added 25 more Studebakers in September alone!

Cab-Forward convenience, maneuverability and service-ease *save money.* Less room, less time and less fuel are needed to turn, back up, park these great trucks. Carrying full-length bodies on much less wheelbase, they facilitate full load within legal overall length limits. Weight is more equally distributed. Sidesway is notably reduced. Traction is better.

Studebaker's exclusive safety feature—the Automatic Hill Holder, raises Studebaker extra value still higher. And a final potent advantage is Studebaker's greater *pulling power* (actual torque output) which is greatest of all trucks of anywhere near the Studebaker price range.

Your delivery budget can benefit from Cab-Forward efficiency. Call your Studebaker dealer for demonstration.

GREATEST *Pulling Power* **OF ALL TRUCKS at anywhere near the price**

THE STUDEBAKER CORPORATION
Truck Division, South Bend, Indiana

STUDEBAKER
TRUCKS AND BUSES

Studebaker, 1936 ◄▲

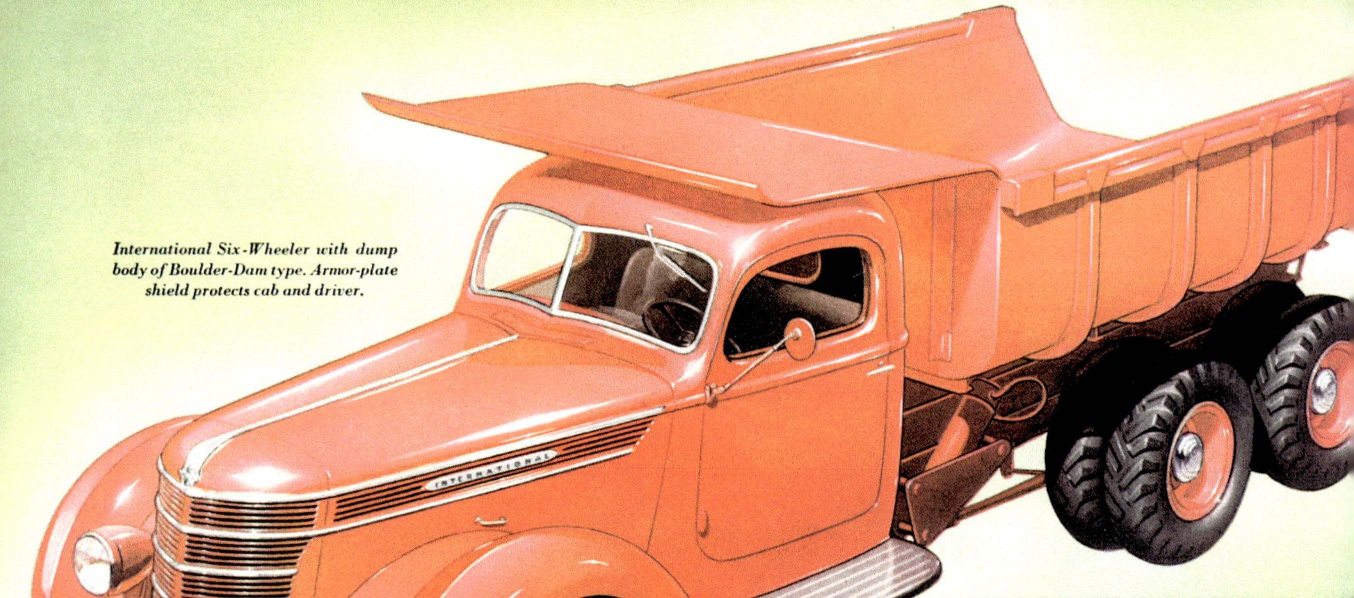

International Six-Wheeler with dump body of Boulder-Dam type. Armor-plate shield protects cab and driver.

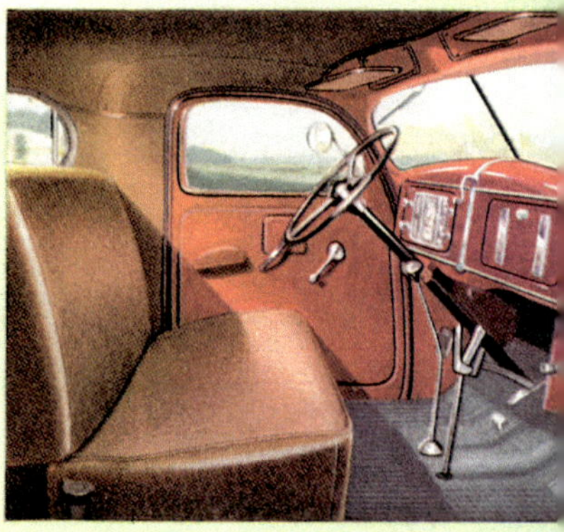

The ALL STEEL CAB—one of the many advanced features in the new International line. Illustration at the right shows the interior of the roomy, well-appointed de luxe cab. Driver comfort, clear vision, and safety are assured in every International model, Half-Ton up.

THE *New* INTERNATIONAL

Heavy-duty champion of the truck world at the top of his form—another of the new Internationals, a powerful six-wheeler shown with armored dump body.

International Harvester presents to users of trucks the latest and finest products of its automotive plants—trucks at the peak of today's efficiency with a styling of exterior that is yours to judge. *All the new Internationals are as NEW in engine and chassis, in structural refinement, in every vital detail, as they are NEW in streamlined distinction for the highway. All are ALL-TRUCK, and all are as modern as today's fine cars.*

The International line offers a trim, streamlined unit for the Half-Ton field and a wide range of sizes for every type of load and hauling requirement. Here at the far end of the *complete line* is a truck for big tonnage, brute performance, and economy on an impressive scale—a finer product for the heavy-duty field to which International sells *twice as many trucks as any other manufacturer.*

See the new Internationals. Whatever your own exact hauling needs, there is the right model and size awaiting your pleasure in the new array of trucks now on display at all International branch and dealer showrooms.

INTERNATIONAL HARVESTER COMPANY
606 S. Michigan Ave. (INCORPORATED) Chicago, Illinois

Read what this driver writes:

International Harvester Company,
Chicago, Ill.

As one of the drivers in the Payne fleet at Grand Coulee Dam, I was very much interested in your recent ad on the subject.

I am majoring in mechanical engineering at the University of Washington. I earn my expenses driving and repairing heavy trucks during vacations and other times. I have worked for practically all of the major trucking contractors in this part of the country, driving all the more popular brands of heavy dump trucks.

I am a most enthusiastic booster for the International six-wheelers. I drove the one belonging to Goodfellow Bros., Wenatchee, Wash., during its term of operation at Coulee Dam. Operating side by side with other dual-drives, the International was invariably picked for the toughest assignments. It became known without question as the toughest, most dependable, yet cheapest truck to operate per yard-mile of any truck on the project.

Yours respectfully,

Seattle, Wash.
February 13, 1937

Harold T. Smith
4014 Brooklyn St.

INTERNATIONAL TRUCK

HEAVY-DUTY STAMINA IN A HALF-TON TRUCK

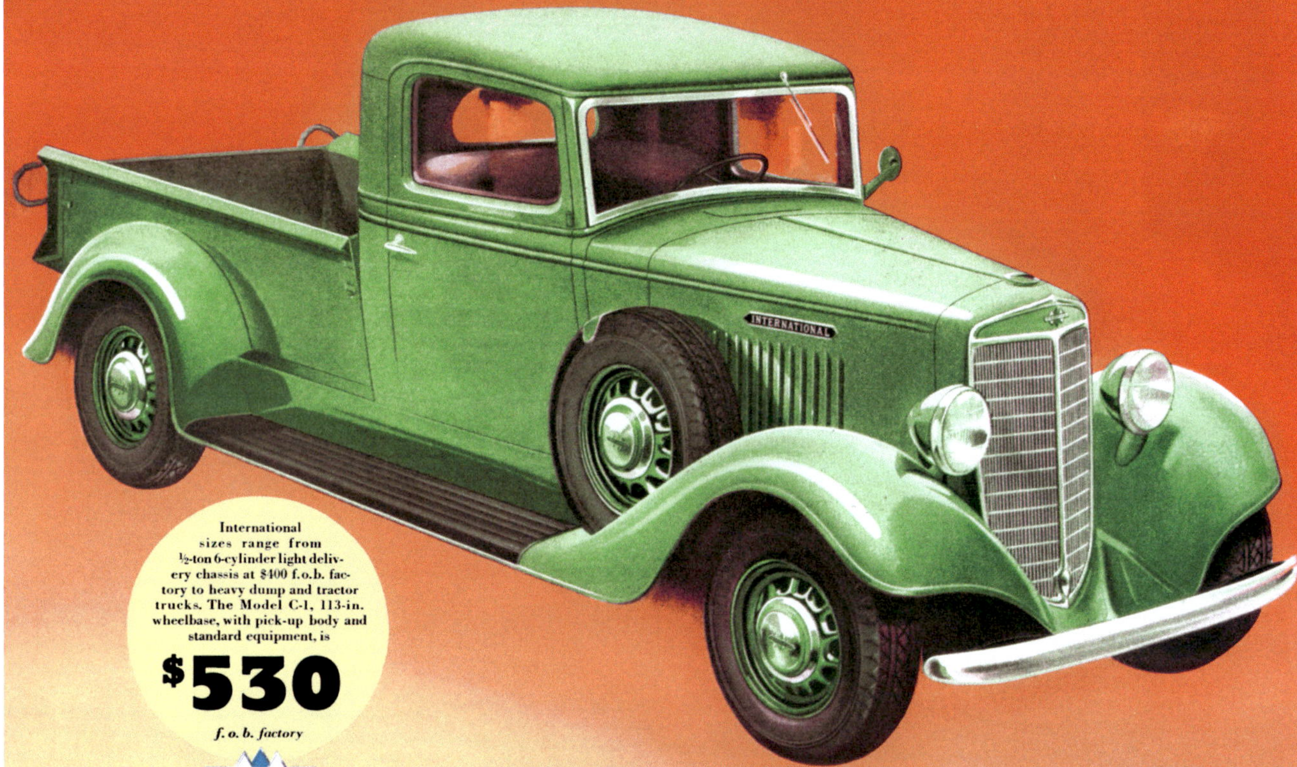

International sizes range from ½-ton 6-cylinder light delivery chassis at $400 f.o.b. factory to heavy dump and tractor trucks. The Model C-1, 113-in. wheelbase, with pick-up body and standard equipment, is

$530

f. o. b. factory

INTERNATIONAL

In the Half-Ton International Model C-1 are incorporated many of the features of truck design that provide the stamina for which the big heavy-duty Internationals have long been famous.

The all-truck construction of this dependable truck provides not only unequaled economy but handling ease and speed-with-safety that any driver will appreciate.

Your first glance at the C-1 will register beauty, but remember that under those good looks are rugged stamina in every working part, and power to spare.

Put it up to this half-ton truck and you will do your hauling job with new efficiency—and a new economy that will be a source of profit to you year after year.

The Model C-1 comes in two wheelbase lengths—113 inches and 125 inches—making a great variety of body adaptations possible. The longer size is a special International feature in a half-ton truck.

Some other features that account for the great popularity of this Half-Ton International are: handsome V-type radiator with satin-finish grill and chromium trim; valanced fenders; full-length running boards; airplane-type instrument panel.

The 6-cylinder engine develops maximum brake h. p. of 78.5—real heavy-duty power in a half-ton truck. Phone any branch or dealer for a demonstration. Other International sizes up to powerful Six-Wheelers.

INTERNATIONAL HARVESTER COMPANY
606 So. Michigan Ave. (INCORPORATED) Chicago, Illinois

INTERNATIONAL TRUCKS

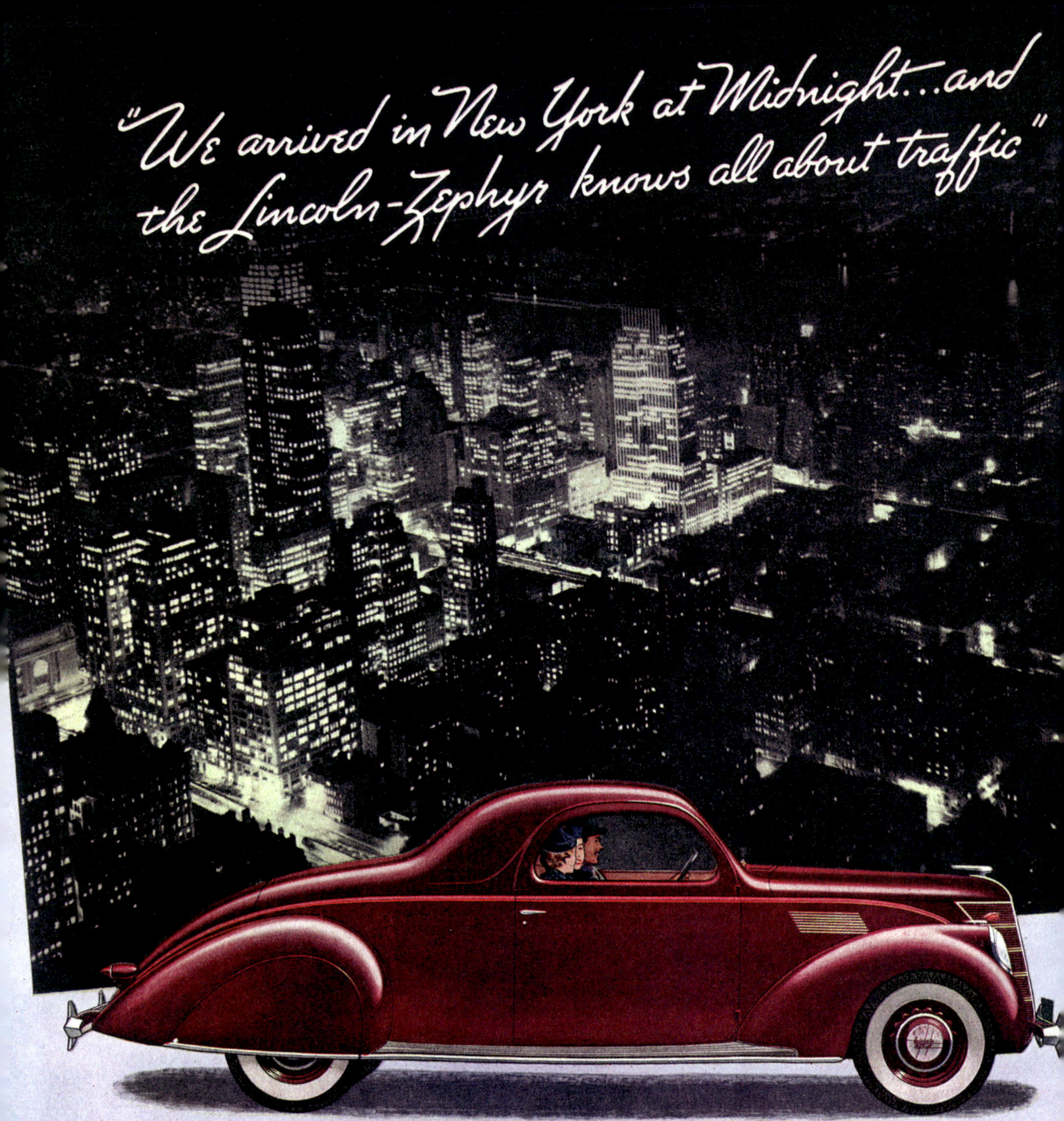

THIS new kind of car conquers all roads, all circumstances of travel. In city or country, on roads good and bad, the LINCOLN-ZEPHYR rolls up new records of performance.

Ask, as you consider this car, what it offers that other cars in its price field do not. The LINCOLN-ZEPHYR has a 12-cylinder engine—the V-type. Twelve cylinders mean greater smoothness . . . greater flexibility. And twelve cylinders, here, *mean 14 to 18 miles per gallon!*

The LINCOLN-ZEPHYR has a unique body structure. *This is the only car of its kind.* Body and frame are one, welded together. You ride surrounded by steel. And you ride amidships. This car flows along like a sloop in a favoring breeze.

The LINCOLN-ZEPHYR has extra roominess. It is a big car. The wheelbase is 122 inches. The engine is compact, and interiors thus longer. There are no conventional running boards; seats, like divans, are wider. Three may sit comfortably on the front seat or the back. THE LINCOI ZEPHYR, finally, has the Lincoln background. is built in the Lincoln plant. Lincoln precisi methods are LINCOLN-ZEPHYR precision metho Mechanical standards for the one are mechani standards for the other.

Prices now are lower. Convenient terms can arranged through Authorized Universal Cre Company Finance Plans. *Lincoln Motor Compar builders of the Lincoln and Lincoln-Zephy*

LINCOLN-ZEPHYR V·12

Lincoln Zephyr V-12

THIS IS THE CAR THAT IS PRICE BELOW ITS SPECIFICATION

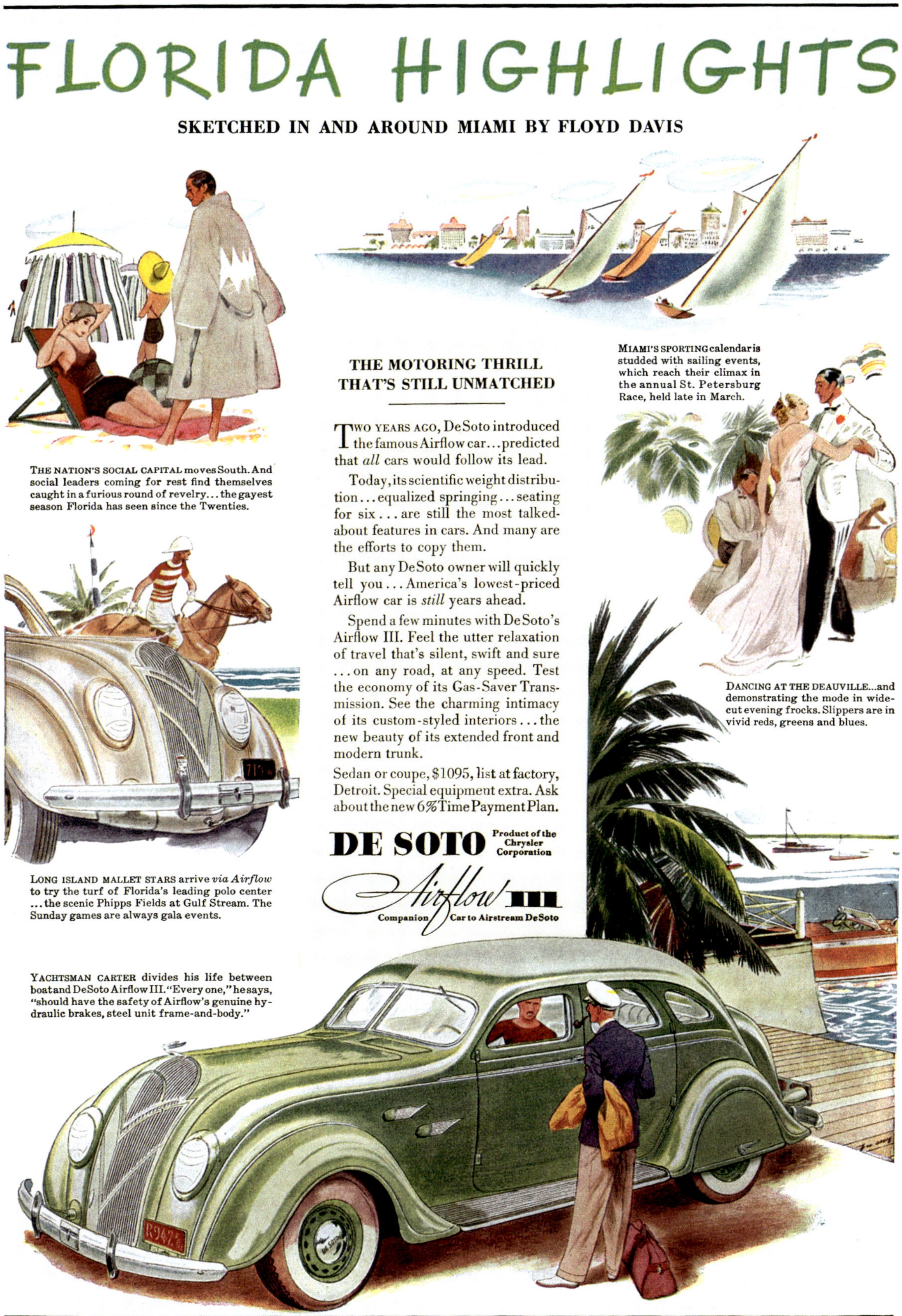
FLORIDA HIGHLIGHTS
SKETCHED IN AND AROUND MIAMI BY FLOYD DAVIS
THE NATION'S SOCIAL CAPITAL moves South. And social leaders coming for rest find themselves caught in a furious round of revelry... the gayest season Florida has seen since the Twenties.
LONG ISLAND MALLET STARS arrive via Airflow to try the turf of Florida's leading polo center ... the scenic Phipps Fields at Gulf Stream. The Sunday games are always gala events.
YACHTSMAN CARTER divides his life between boat and DeSoto Airflow III. "Every one," he says, "should have the safety of Airflow's genuine hydraulic brakes, steel unit frame-and-body."
THE MOTORING THRILL THAT'S STILL UNMATCHED
TWO YEARS AGO, DeSoto introduced the famous Airflow car... predicted that all cars would follow its lead.
Today, its scientific weight distribution... equalized springing... seating for six... are still the most talked-about features in cars. And many are the efforts to copy them.
But any DeSoto owner will quickly tell you... America's lowest-priced Airflow car is still years ahead.
Spend a few minutes with DeSoto's Airflow III. Feel the utter relaxation of travel that's silent, swift and sure ...on any road, at any speed. Test the economy of its Gas-Saver Transmission. See the charming intimacy of its custom-styled interiors... the new beauty of its extended front and modern trunk.
Sedan or coupe, $1095, list at factory, Detroit. Special equipment extra. Ask about the new 6% Time Payment Plan.
DE SOTO
Product of the Chrysler Corporation
Airflow III
Companion Car to Airstream DeSoto
MIAMI'S SPORTING calendar is studded with sailing events, which reach their climax in the annual St. Petersburg Race, held late in March.
DANCING AT THE DEAUVILLE...and demonstrating the mode in wide-cut evening frocks. Slippers are in vivid reds, greens and blues.

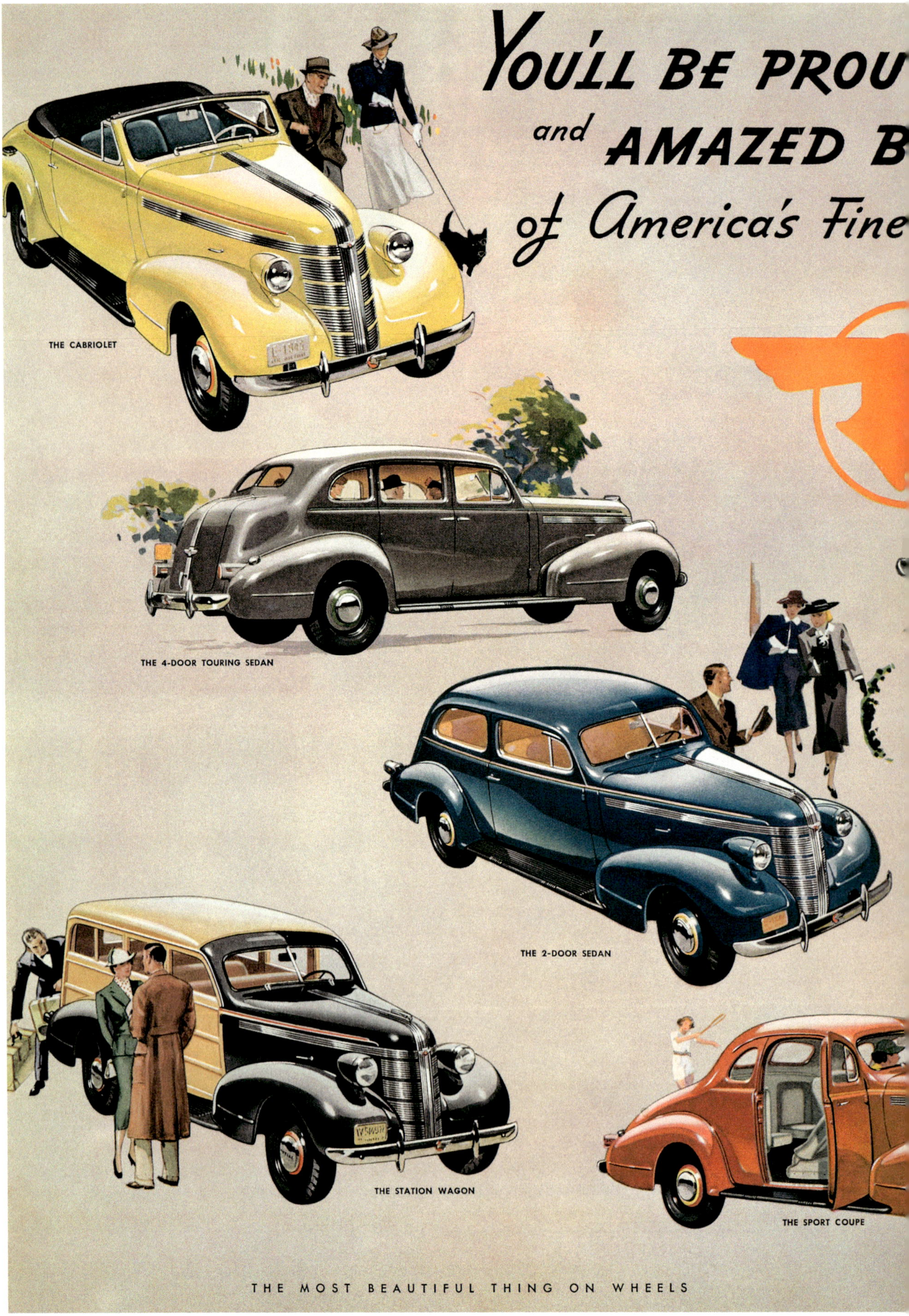

YOU'LL BE PROU
and AMAZED B
of America's Fine
THE CABRIOLET
THE 4-DOOR TOURING SEDAN
THE 2-DOOR SEDAN
THE STATION WAGON
THE SPORT COUPE
THE MOST BEAUTIFUL THING ON WHEELS

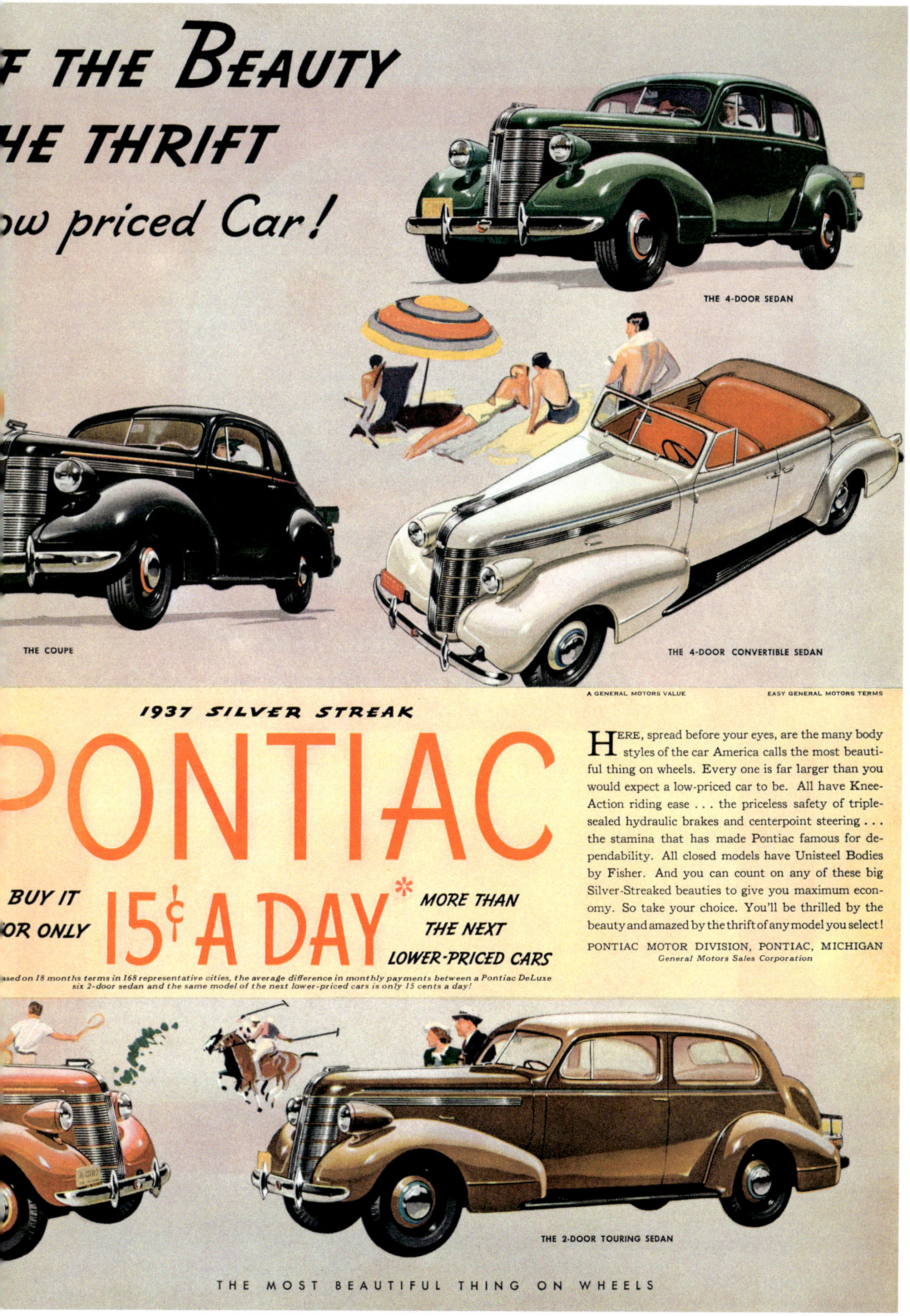
F THE BEAUTY
HE THRIFT
ow priced Car!
THE 4-DOOR SEDAN
THE COUPE
THE 4-DOOR CONVERTIBLE SEDAN
A GENERAL MOTORS VALUE
EASY GENERAL MOTORS TERMS
1937 SILVER STREAK
PONTIAC
BUY IT
OR ONLY
15¢ A DAY*
MORE THAN
THE NEXT
LOWER-PRICED CARS
ased on 18 months terms in 168 representative cities, the average difference in monthly payments between a Pontiac DeLuxe six 2-door sedan and the same model of the next lower-priced cars is only 15 cents a day!
HERE, spread before your eyes, are the many body styles of the car America calls the most beautiful thing on wheels. Every one is far larger than you would expect a low-priced car to be. All have Knee-Action riding ease . . . the priceless safety of triple-sealed hydraulic brakes and centerpoint steering . . . the stamina that has made Pontiac famous for dependability. All closed models have Unisteel Bodies by Fisher. And you can count on any of these big Silver-Streaked beauties to give you maximum economy. So take your choice. You'll be thrilled by the beauty and amazed by the thrift of any model you select!
PONTIAC MOTOR DIVISION, PONTIAC, MICHIGAN
General Motors Sales Corporation
THE 2-DOOR TOURING SEDAN
THE MOST BEAUTIFUL THING ON WHEELS

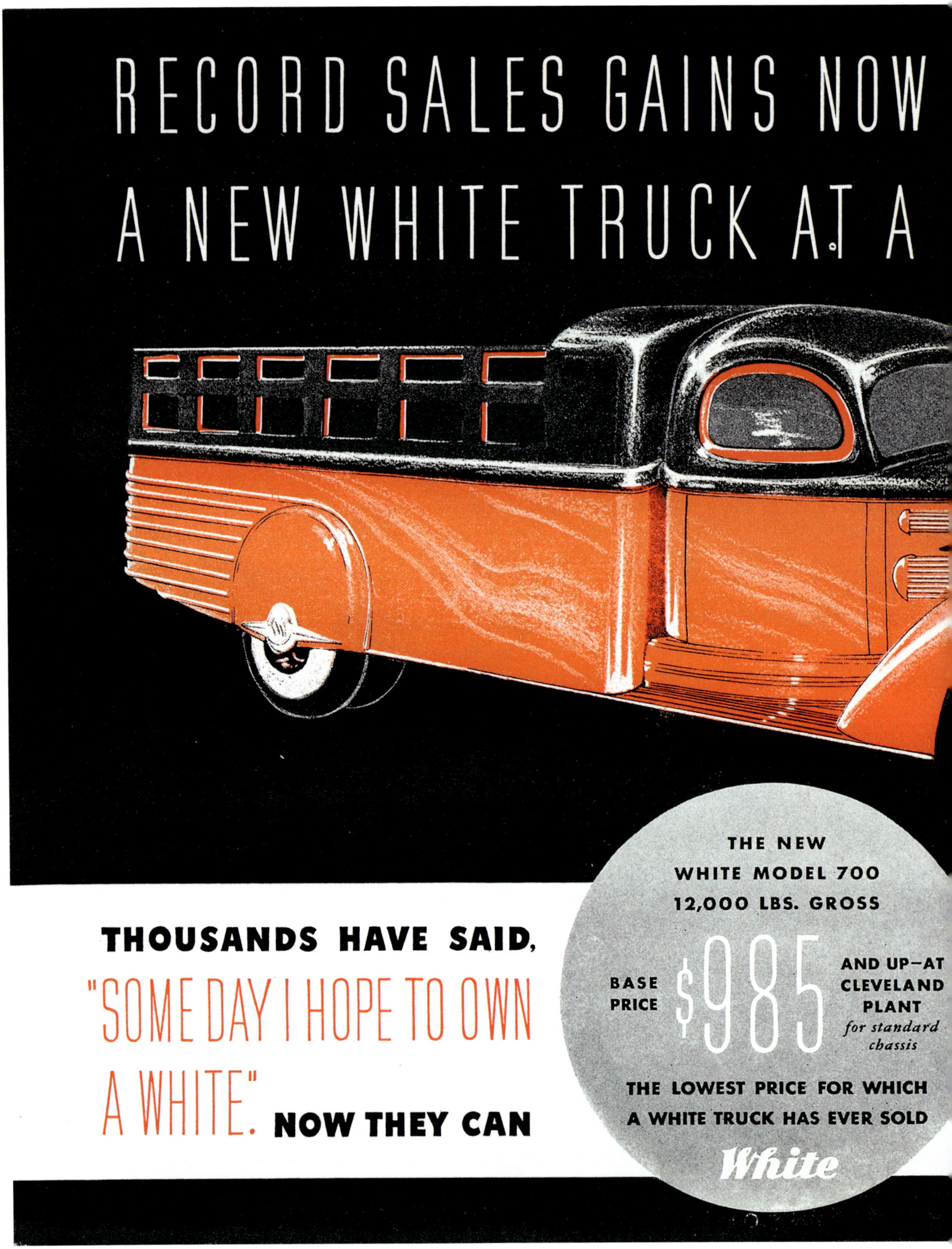

White Trucks, 1937

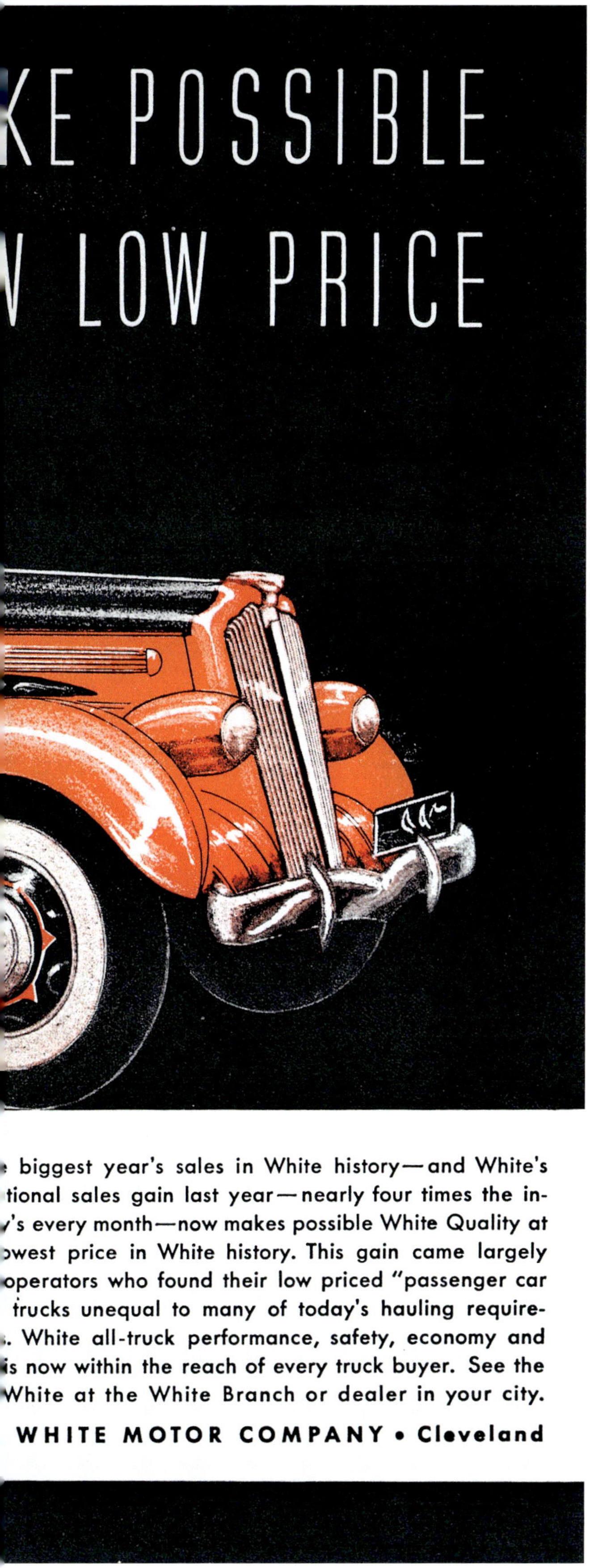

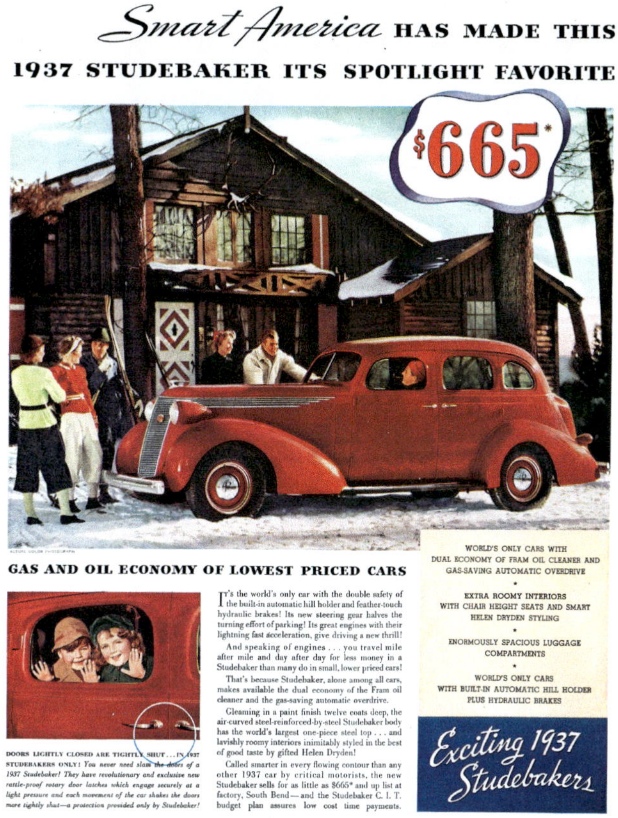

Studebaker, 1937

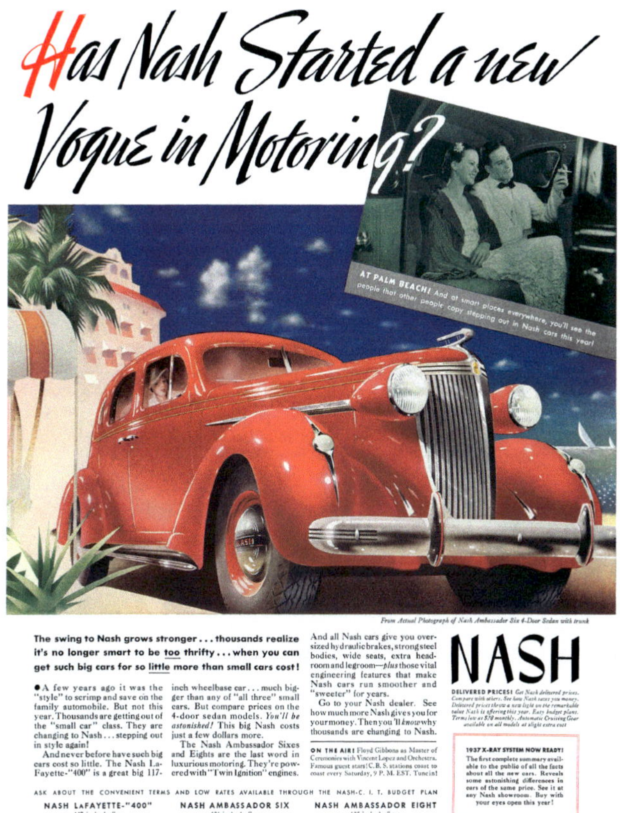

Nash, 1937

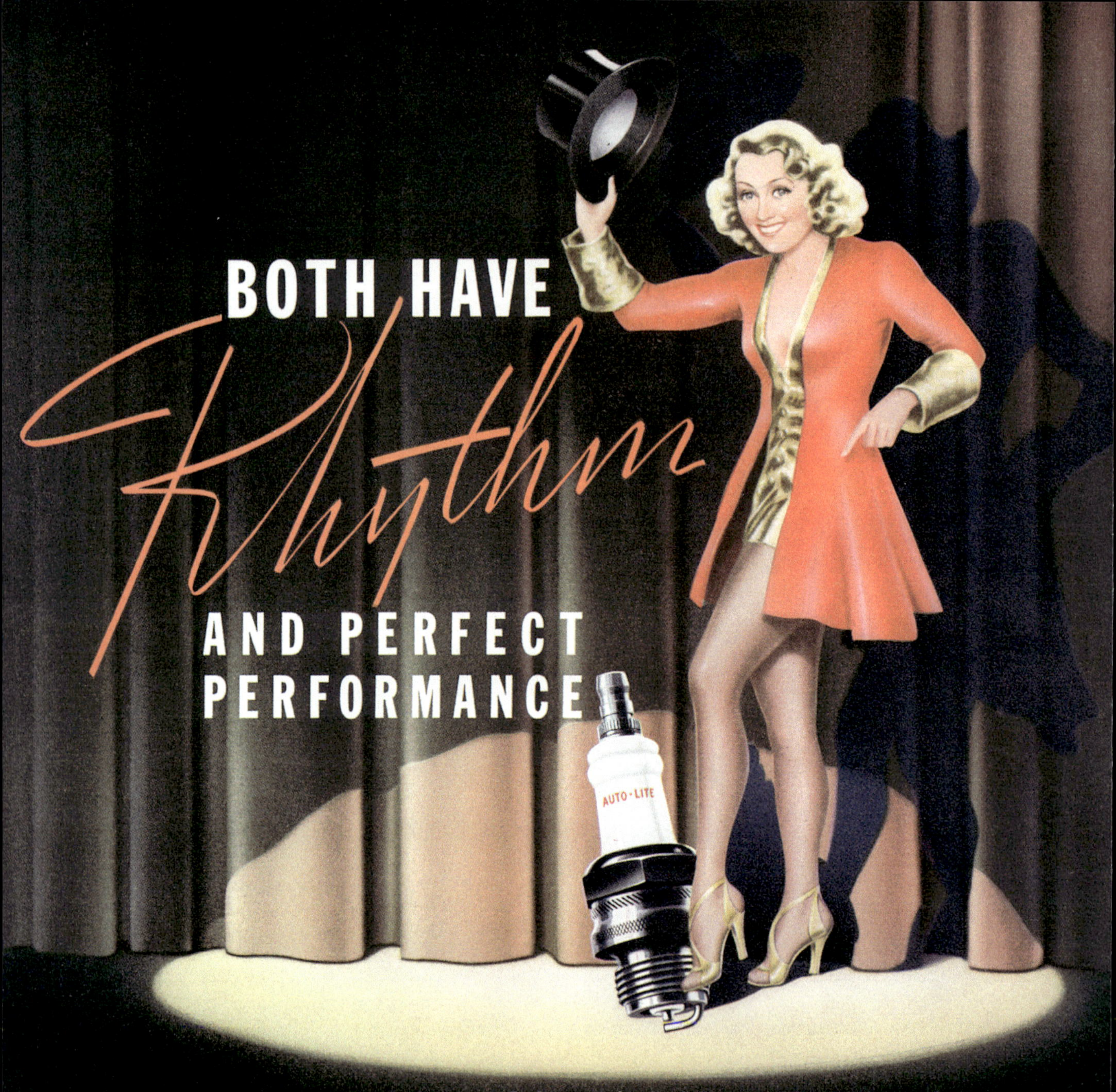

The world applauds the perfect performance. Perfect performances don't "just happen." For twenty-five years, the Electric Auto-Lite Company has been the foremost builder of Starting, Lighting and Ignition systems for the leading motor cars of America. . . . With this record of knowledge and experience, Auto-Lite engineers now introduce the perfected spark plug—the final link in perfect ignition performance—the Auto-Lite Spark Plug, Ignition Engineered by Ignition Engineers. Now you can get the most out of motoring—Greater Economy, Increased Acceleration and—Perfect Performance. Replace with Auto-Lite Spark Plugs today. Merchandising Division, The Auto-Lite Company, Toledo, Ohio.

AUTO-LITE SPARK PLUGS

Ignition Engineered by Ignition Enginee

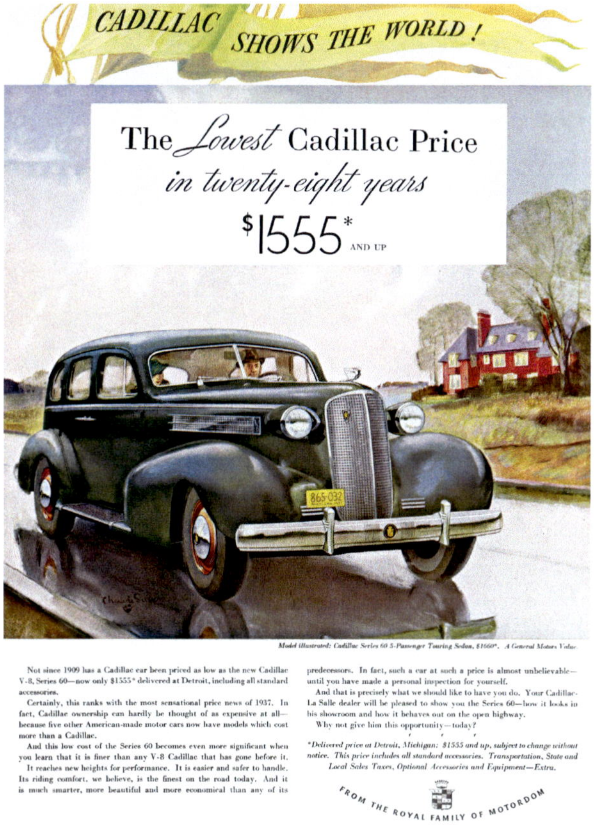

Cadillac, 1937

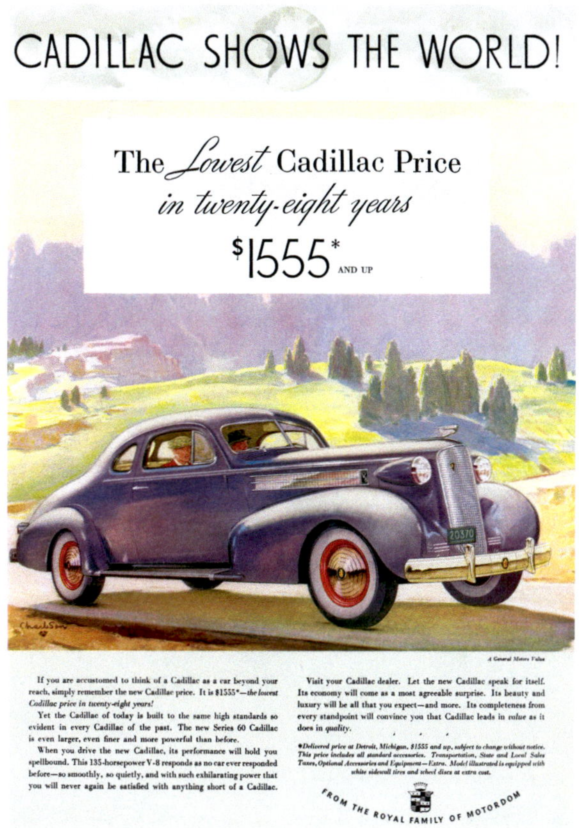

Cadillac, 1937

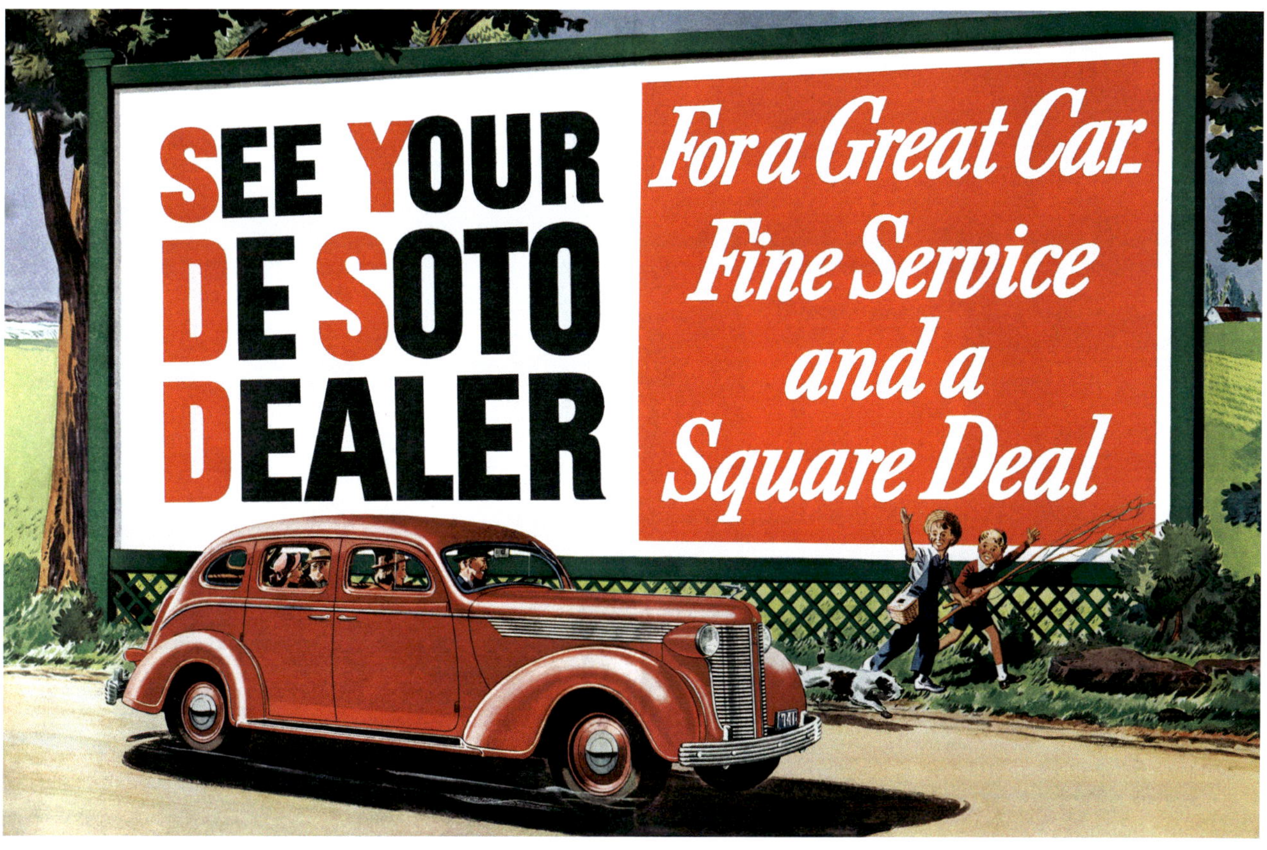

Auto-Lite Spark Plugs, 1937 ◂ De Soto, 1937

COSTS LESS TO BUY TO RU

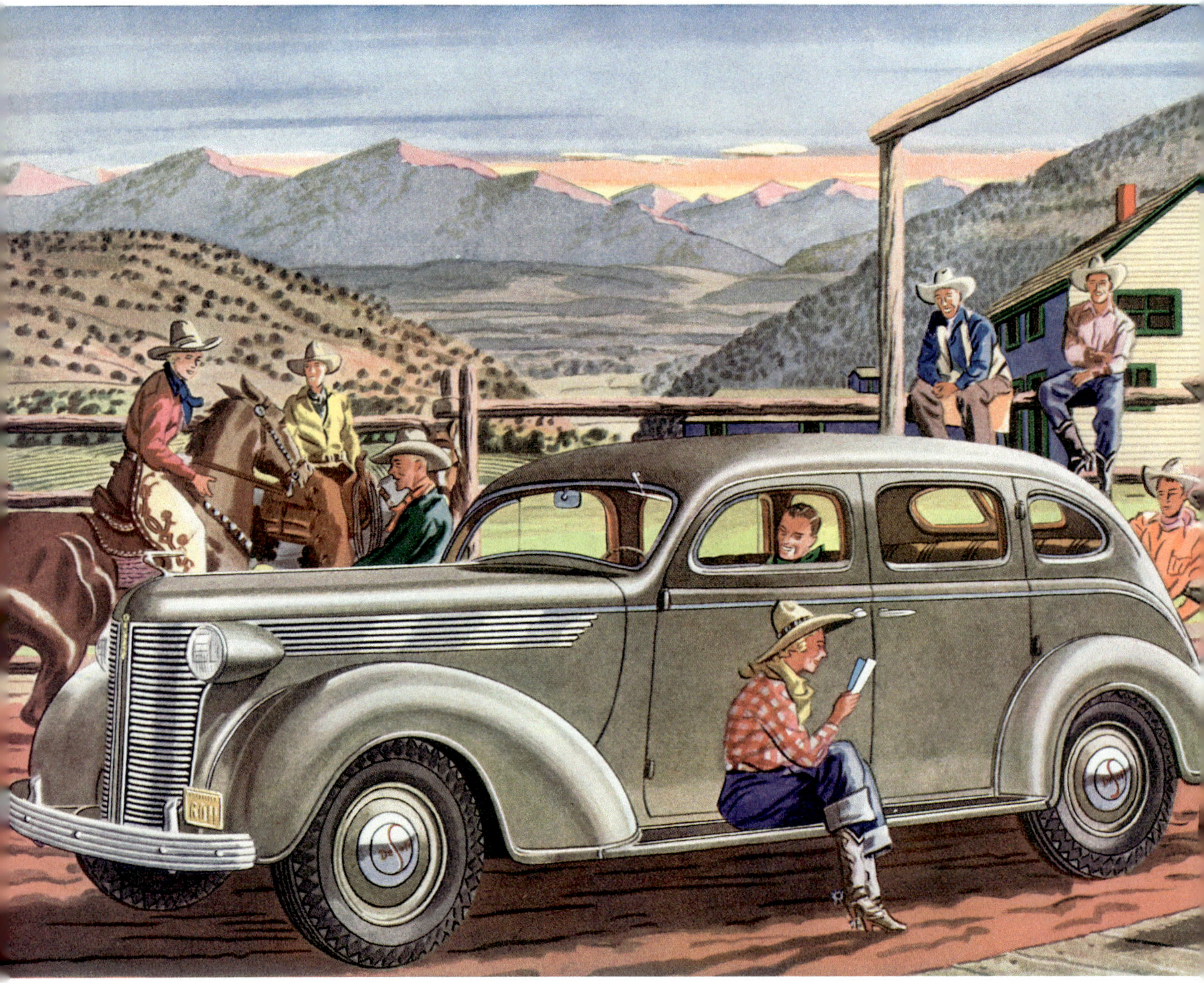

"Sure De Soto's Big and Beautiful, but What Does It Cost to Run?"

WE LIKE to have people ask about De Soto's mileage.

We carefully avoided making gas-mileage claims for De Soto's new "Economy Engine" at announcement time. We waited until tens of thousands of new De Sotos were actually on the road.

NOW reports are pouring in! "Getting 17 to 21 miles a gallon in hard city driving"..."In 8,576 miles my average is 20.3 on 'regular' gas!"..."Best gas and oil mileage I ever had on a car!"

Owners have proved it! This new car . . . big De Soto ever built . . . costs *even less* to run!

NOW ADD THIS FACT: Lower prices now De Soto within a *few dollars* of the lowest-pri cars. You save money every mile you drive. you get SMARTNESS, pride of ownership, that could not possibly enjoy in a small car.

Drive a De Soto! See your dealer. DE SOTO D SION OF CHRYSLER CORPORATION, Detroit, Mic

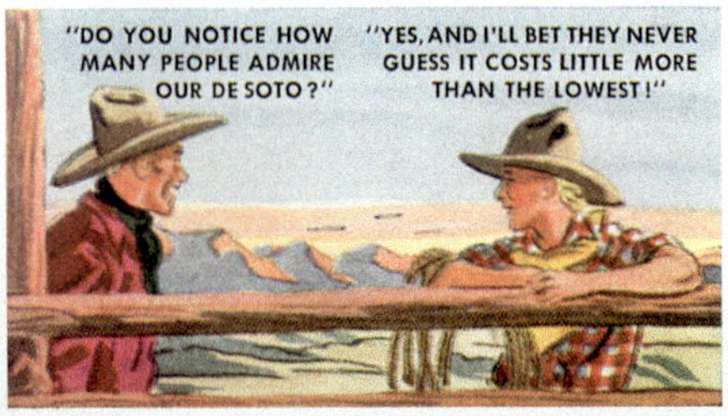

"HEARD ABOUT DE SOTO? IT'S NOW PRICED JUST ABOVE THE LOWEST!"

HIGH LIGHT FEATURES: 1. New 93-h.p. "Economy Engine." 2. New ride . . . with 14 "Float" Body Mountings and "Airplane-type" Shock-absorbers. 3. First complete Sound-Proofing. 4. Safety-Steel Body, one-piece steel top. 5. Genuine Hydraulic Brakes. Ask for Official Commercial Credit Company Finance Plan.

TUNE IN MAJOR BOWES' AMATEUR HOUR—Columbia network, Thursdays, 9 to 10 p.m., E.D.S.T.

DE SOTO

America's Smartes Low-Priced Car!

IT'S AMERICA'S SMARTEST LOW-PRICED CAR

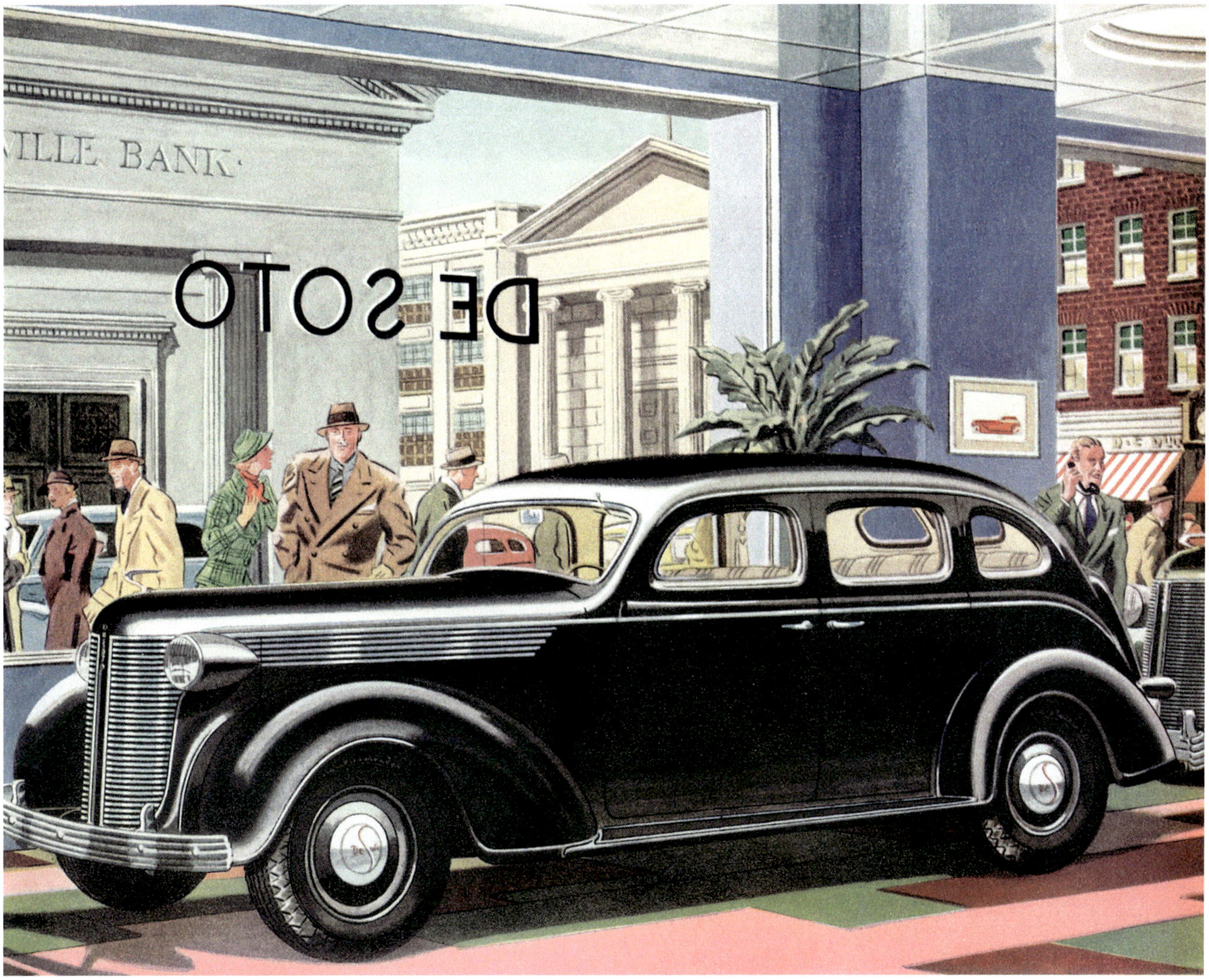

Join the Smart Set of Motoring who are Buying this Big, New, Lower-priced De Soto!

THERE'S JUST ONE THING that stands between you and a new De Soto. That's the plate-glass window of your De Soto dealer!

It's admitted . . . De Soto *does* look extravagant. Tremendously big. Sleek . . . rakish . . . exciting. And we don't deny that it's being driven by plenty of people "in the money."

But don't guess . . . step in and see the price-tag yourself. A new De Soto is practically in your garage right now!

Let's begin at the beginning. This De Soto—the one you're looking at—sells for just a few dollars more than the lowest-priced cars on the market!

Next: what, exactly, do these few dollars bring you? Well . . . it's the difference between "just style" and De Soto's smart Park Avenue air. The difference between cramped seating and De Soto's spacious room for six. The difference between simply "getting there" and De Soto . . . that carries you softly, silently, safely—over any road.

Above and beyond all that . . . your money buys a *finer-built* car. The best of Chrysler Corporation engineering. Genuine hydraulic brakes. Safety-steel body, with one-piece steel top. Four big "aero" hydraulic shock-absorbers. All-silent transmission. Sound-proofed Safety Interior. Hypoid rear axle . . . 87 fine-car features.

. . . .

TO SUM UP: it's the biggest, most beautiful De Soto ever built. Yet owners testify to amazing savings in gas and oil . . . with De Soto's new "Economy Engine."

Afford a De Soto? That's easy . . . with the new low prices. This big style leader is priced just above the lowest! So—don't stay outside looking in. Go in and get De Soto's thrill yourself!

Ask your dealer about the Official Commercial Credit Company Finance Plan. DE SOTO DIVISION OF CHRYSLER CORPORATION, DETROIT, MICHIGAN.

AMERICA'S SMARTEST LOW-PRICED CAR

DE SOTO

Now Priced just above the Lowest

De Soto, 1937 ◄▲

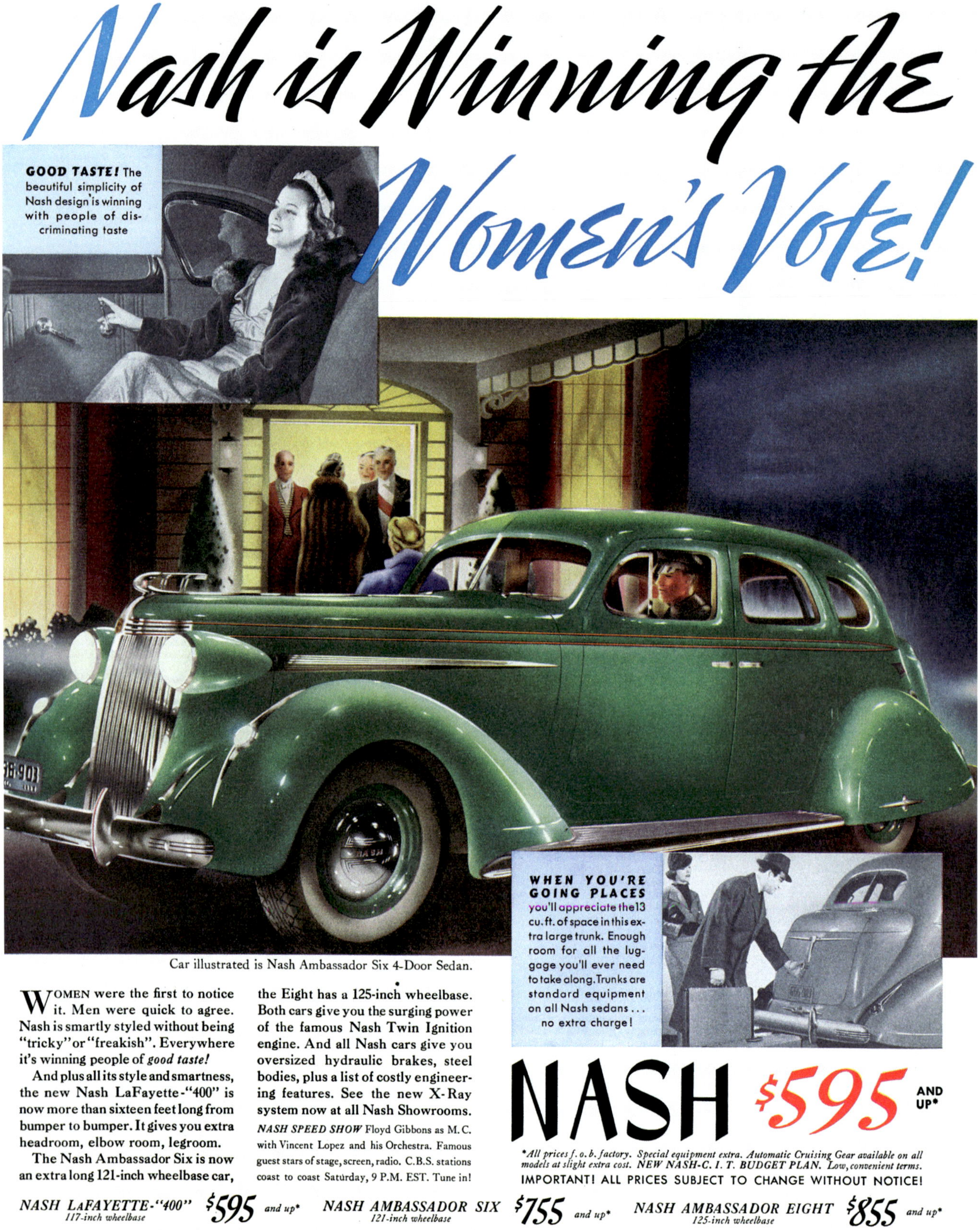

Nash, 1937

▸ Oldsmobile, 1937

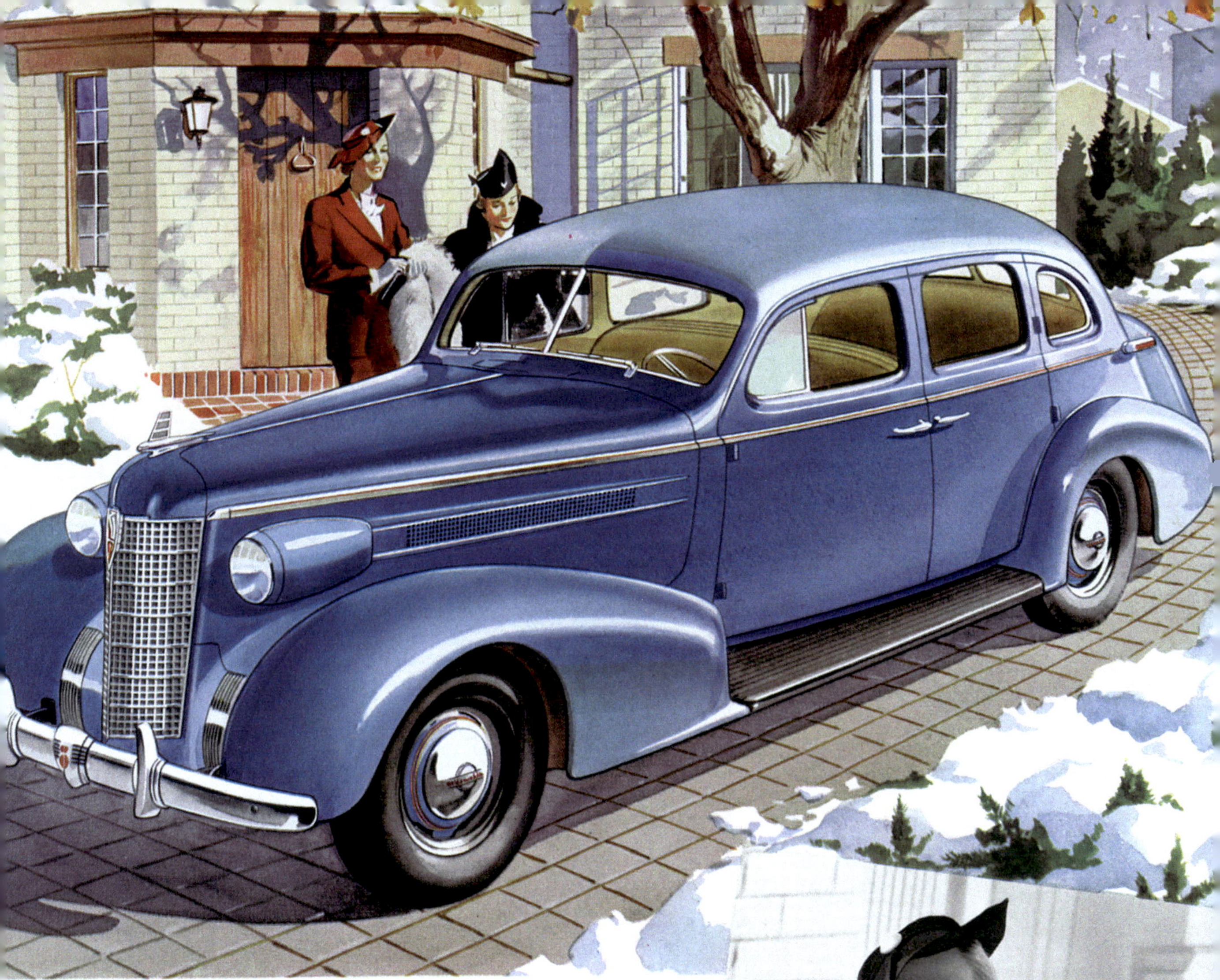

"as though it were made-to-order . . . for me"

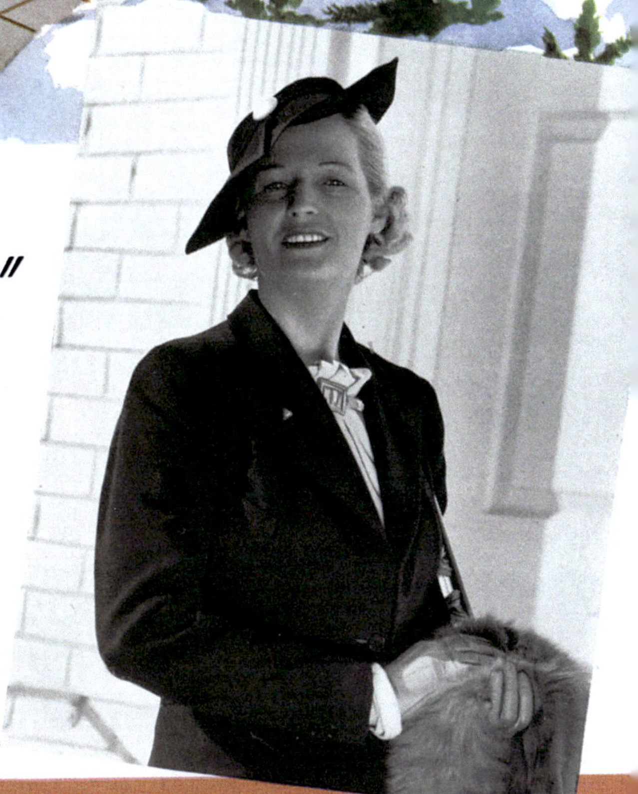

"IF I WERE to list all the things I want in my ideal motor car, I couldn't improve on our new Oldsmobile Eight. In its smartness and styling . . . and the quality of its fittings and appointments . . . it really seems made-to-order."

Even those motorists who have formerly paid twice as much for their cars state with enthusiasm that the 1937 Oldsmobile Eight gives a greater return in satisfaction than any of their previous cars. And no wonder, when you consider that Oldsmobile provides the spacious comfort of Unisteel Turret Top Bodies by Fisher, the brilliant performance of a big 110 h. p. eight-cylinder engine, and a combination of features that spells true luxury in motoring.

LIST PRICES REDUCED *on all 8-Cylinder Enclosed Models. Now as low as *$785 and up, list at Lansing. The car illustrated is the 4-door Touring Sedan, $915 list. Prices subject to change without notice. Special Accessory Groups Extra.* GENERAL MOTORS INSTALMENT PLAN

937 Oldsmobile Eight $785

AND UP

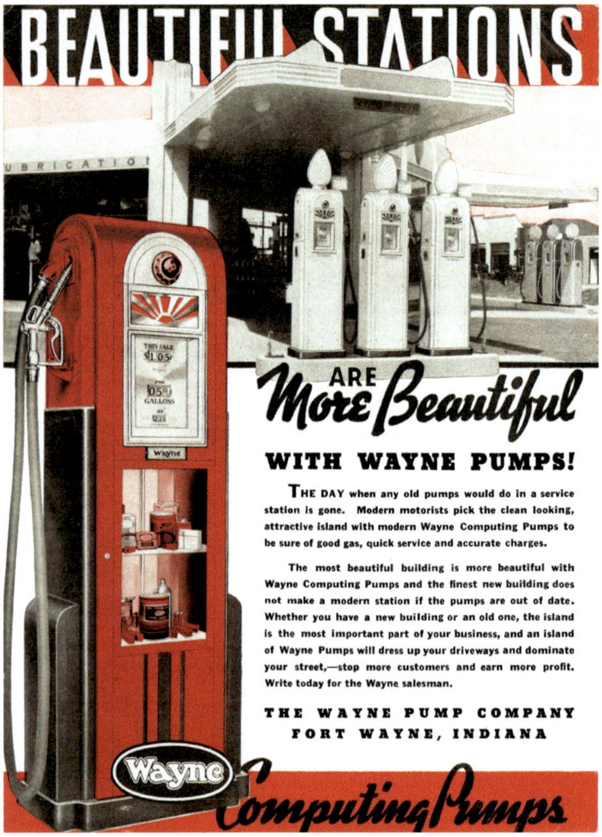

Wayne Computing Pumps, 1937

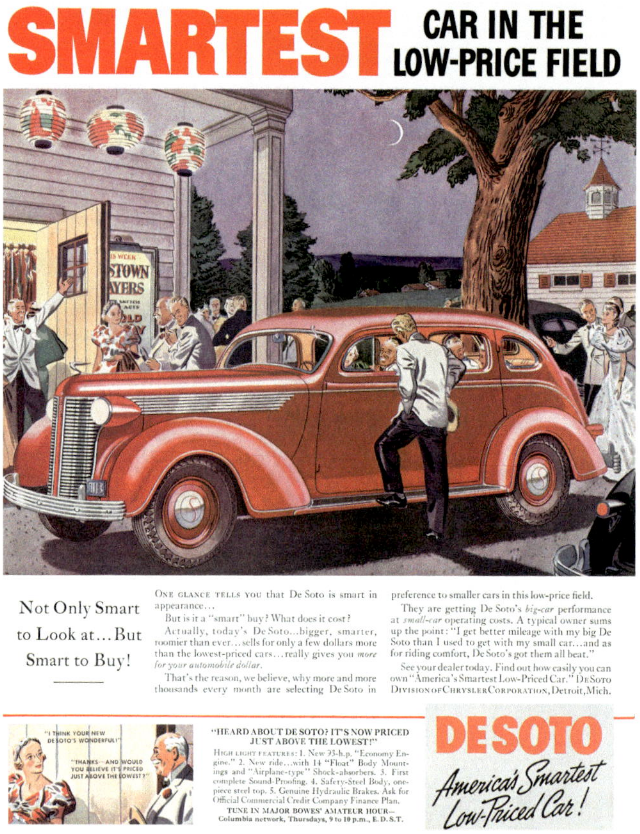

De Soto, 1937

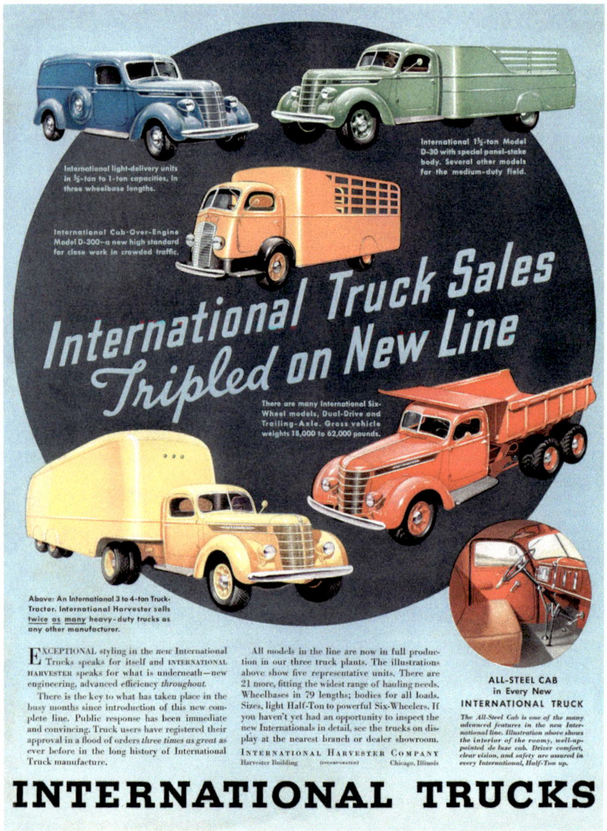

International Trucks, 1937

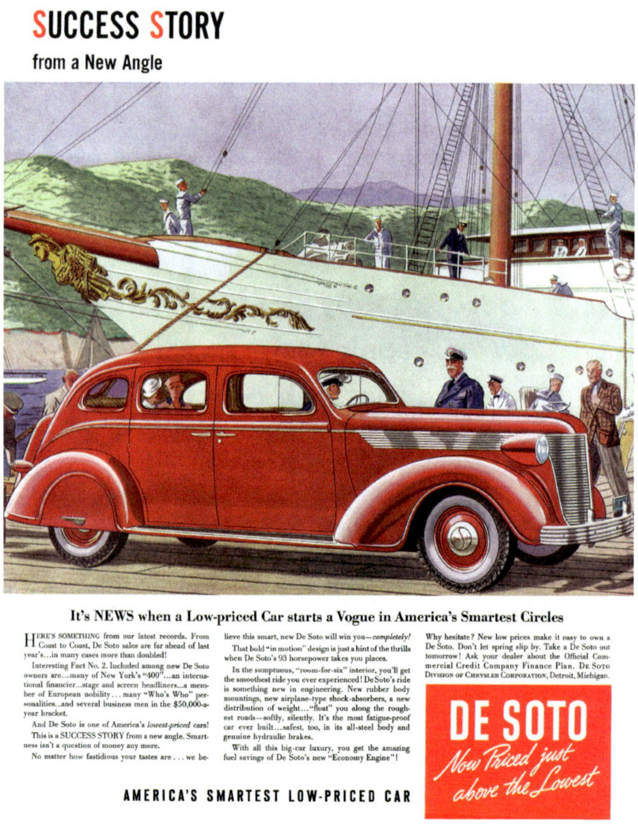

De Soto, 1937

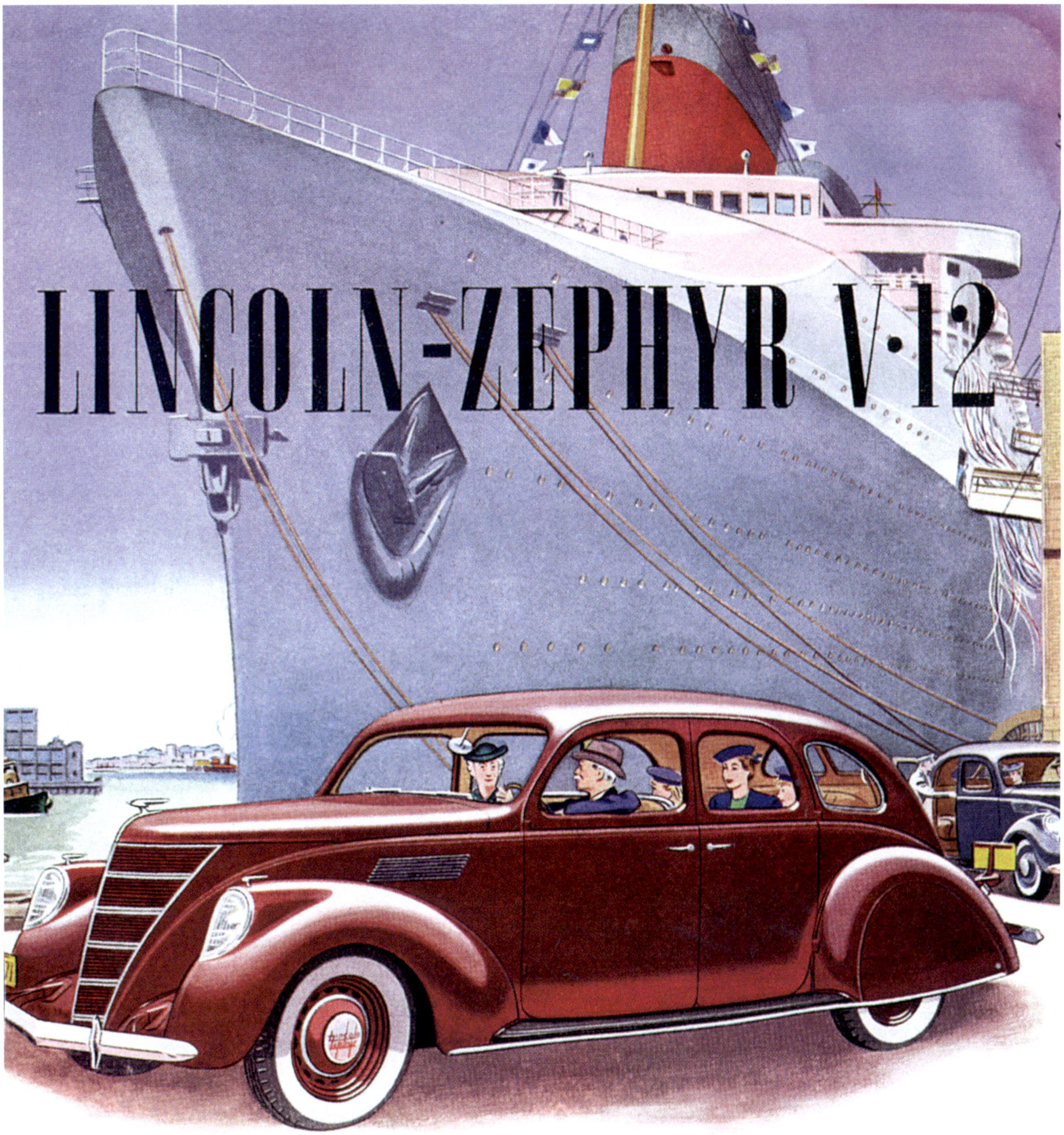

TRAVEL THE MODERN WAY!

RUNNING in luxury through blue waters, a modern ruler of the seas joins two continents in four days. . . . Cleaving white highways, a modern ship of the land, the LINCOLN-ZEPHYR, brings far places together with an ease not known before!

This car has four wheels, but there the similarity between the LINCOLN-ZEPHYR and others ends. The LINCOLN-ZEPHYR is different in design, different in the way it behaves on the roads, different in its effect upon owners. People talk about this advanced type of transportation as they talk about a fine horse, a trip abroad, a new home. Something stimulating has come into their lives!

First in their conversation is the LINCOLN-ZEPHYR engine. It has twelve cylinders in V-style, develops 110 horsepower. It gives 14 to 18 miles to the gallon, an extraordinary record. But this is an extraordinary car! From the unique all-steel body and frame combined in a single piece, to the inclusion of so many fine-car features, the car stands out in *value* as it stands out along a country-club driveway.

Have you thought, up to now, that all cars are basically alike? *Travel the modern way!* Lincoln Motor Company, builders of Lincoln and Lincoln-Zephyr V-12 motor cars.

Lincoln, 1937 ▸▸ *Oldsmobile, 1937*

"You Can't Beat Ol

"I've driven Oldsmobiles for many years, but this new Oldsmobile of mine tops them all. It not only does everything I ask of it — and does it better than any car I ever drove—but it combines surprising gas and oil economy with its brilliant, all-round performance. You simply can't beat it!"

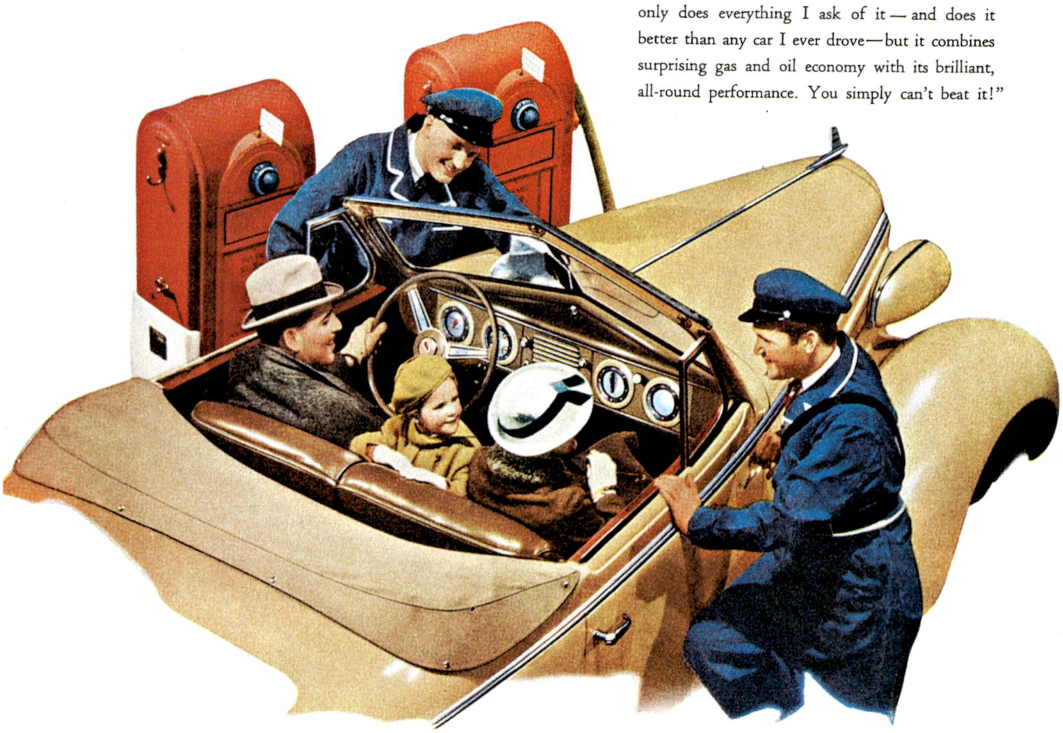

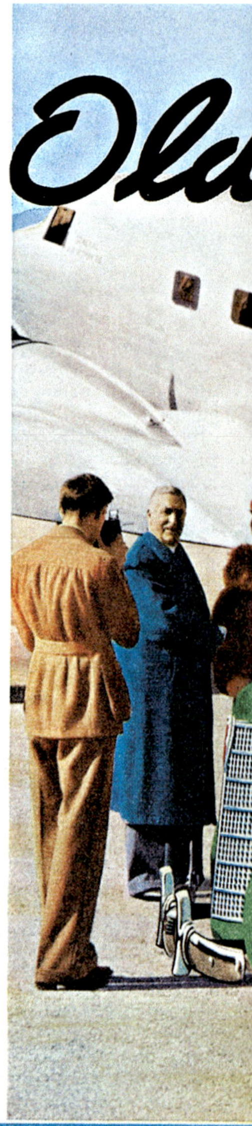

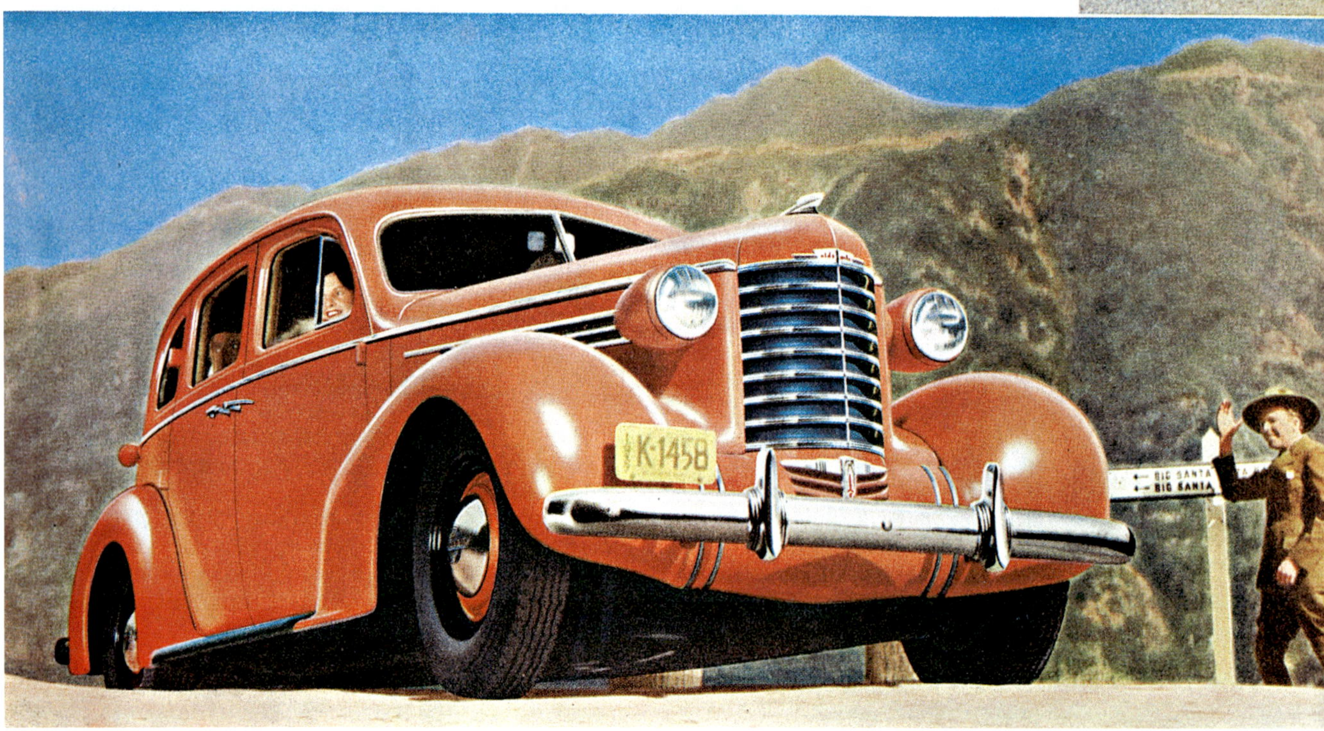

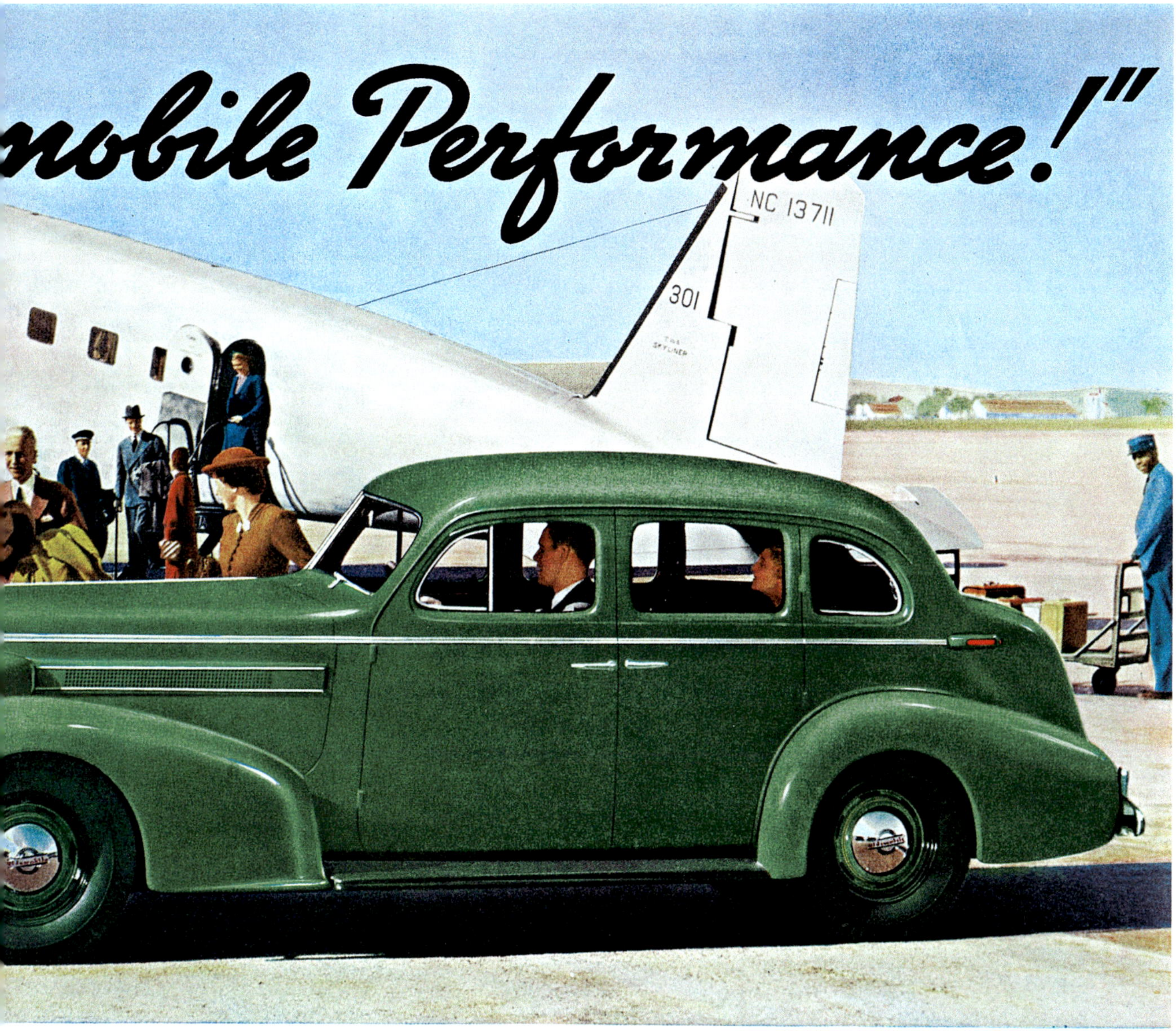

NOTHING ELSE LIKE IT FOR POWER AND SNAP AND SMOOTHNESS • • • PLUS REAL ALL-ROUND ECONOMY. A TRIAL WILL PROVE IT!

EVEN the most experienced drivers discover an altogether new kind of performance at the wheel of an Oldsmobile—an inspiring combination of engine smoothness and quietness, of luxurious comfort and peace of mind, and a most satisfying economy of operation and upkeep. These are but the natural results of Oldsmobile's finely balanced precision design, Oldsmobile's size and roominess and Oldsmobile's special provisions for safe and dependable travel. You will find the full measure of all these desirable qualities in both the modern, distinctive Oldsmobile Six and the big, distinguished Oldsmobile Eight. A trial drive over your favorite route will soon convince you, too, that you can't beat an Oldsmobile for performance, dependability or value. *Drive* it—and *prove* it!

DELIVERED PRICES at Lansing, Mich.: Sixes, $765 and up; Eights, $880 and up; subject to change without notice. Cars illustrated: at left, Six 4-Door Sedan, $885; above, Eight 4-Door Touring Sedan, $1015. These prices include safety glass, bumpers, bumper guards, spare tire and tube, rear spring covers. Transportation, state and local taxes, optional accessories and equipment, extra. Monthly payments to suit your purse. GENERAL MOTORS INSTALMENT PLAN

95-horsepower SIX with 117-inch wheelbase . . . 110-horsepower EIGHT with 124-inch wheelbase . . . Unisteel Turret Top Bodies by Fisher . . . Knee-Action Wheels . . . Triple Sealed Super-Hydraulic Brakes . . . Center-Control Steering . . . Dual Ride Stabilizers . . . Unobstructed Floors . . . Safety Glass Standard Throughout . . . Scientific Sound Proofing . . . And Many Other Fine-Car Features.

Oldsmobile 6 & 8

THE CARS THAT HAVE EVERYTHING

A NOSE FOR NEWS! THAT'S WHY LOWELL THOMAS PICKS DESOTO AS CAR OF YEAR

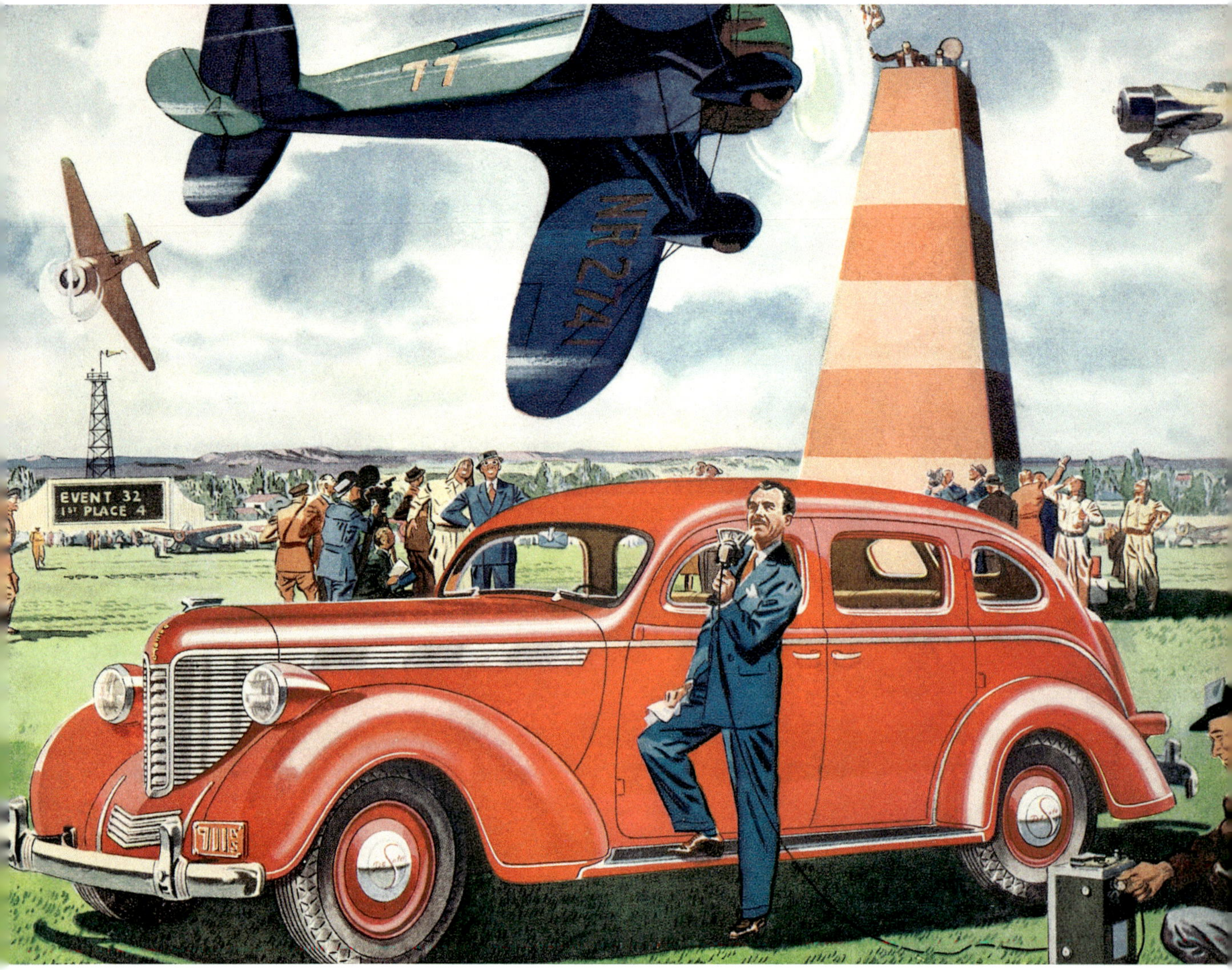

America's Ace Radio Commentator has a Big Story about his new De Soto Car

"IT'S AMERICA'S SMARTEST low-priced car!" That's the motor news of the year—flashed to you by De Soto-owner Lowell Thomas.

Here's what he says: "The great new De Soto is news because it *interests* people. It attracted thousands at the auto shows and it's being talked about all over America! I'm certainly sold on mine!"

No wonder! This great car is more luxurious than ever...both inside and out. Faster pick-up...easier handling...bigger, *genuine* hydraulic brakes...more comfortable Safety Interior...the year's smartest styling—every great new De Soto feature is a page one headline story!

And here's the best news yet: De Soto is priced just a few dollars above the lowest! This *big* car actually costs no more to run than most *small* cars!

It's easy to own! See your De Soto dealer. DE SOTO DIVISION OF CHRYSLER CORPORATION, Detroit, Mich.

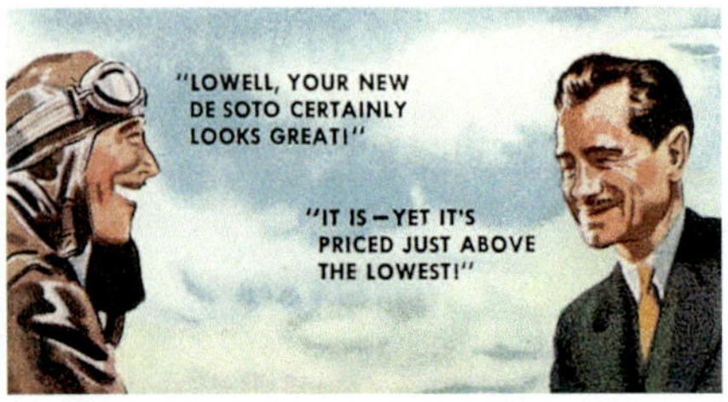

IT'S AMERICA'S SMARTEST LOW-PRICED CAR

QUICK FACTS: 1. "Lightning-fast" pick-up... Improved 93-h.p. "Economy Engine." 2. Patented Floating Power engine mountings. 3. Longer wheelbase...119 inches. 4. Bigger hydraulic brakes. 5. Easier shifting. 6. Safety-steel body rubber-mounted on a bigger, stronger frame. 7. Luxurious Safety Interior. 8. "Cushioned" ride with airplane-type shock-absorbers. 9. Easier steering...no "road-shock." Ask for Official Commercial Credit Company Finance Plan.

TUNE IN MAJOR BOWES' AMATEUR HOUR—COLUMBIA NETWORK—THURSDAYS, 9 TO 10 P. M., E. S. T.

SEE YOUR DE SOTO DEALER FOR A GREAT CAR, FINE SERVICE AND A SQUARE DEAL

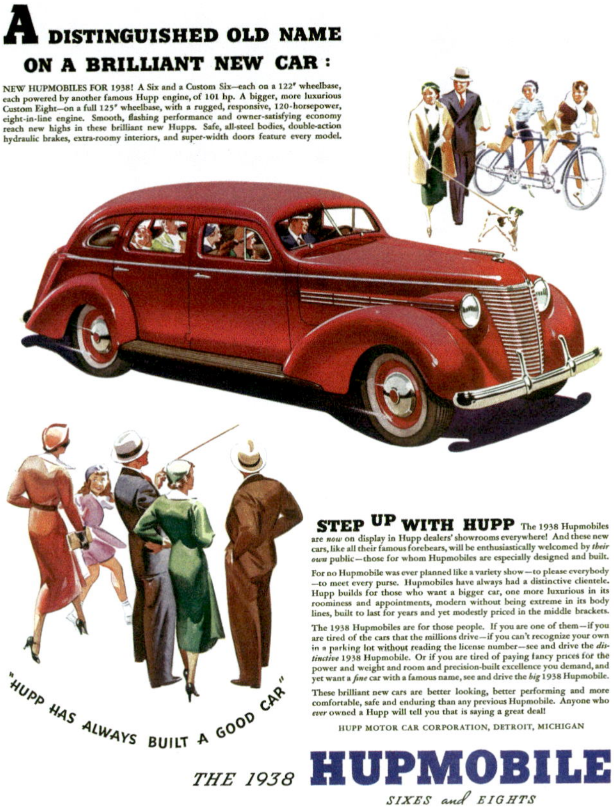

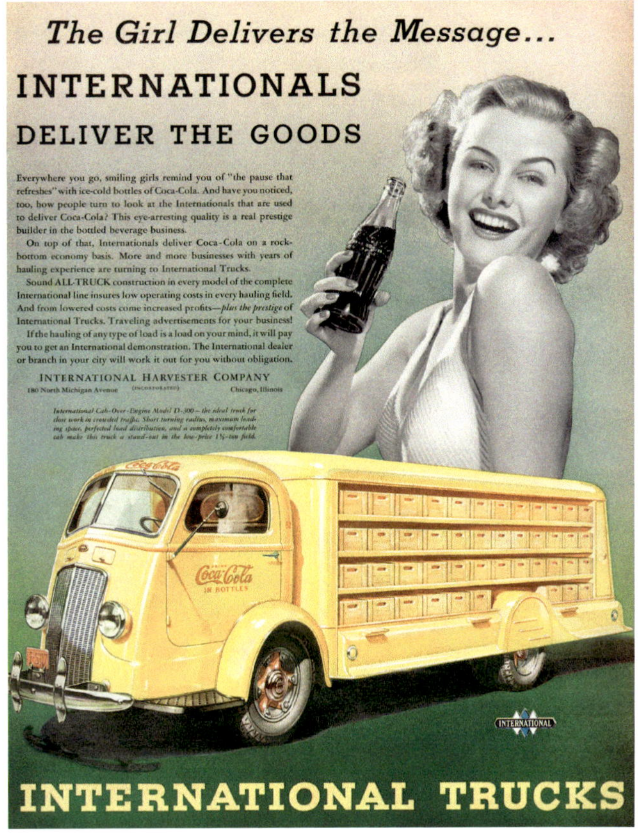

Hupmobile, 1937

International Trucks, 1938

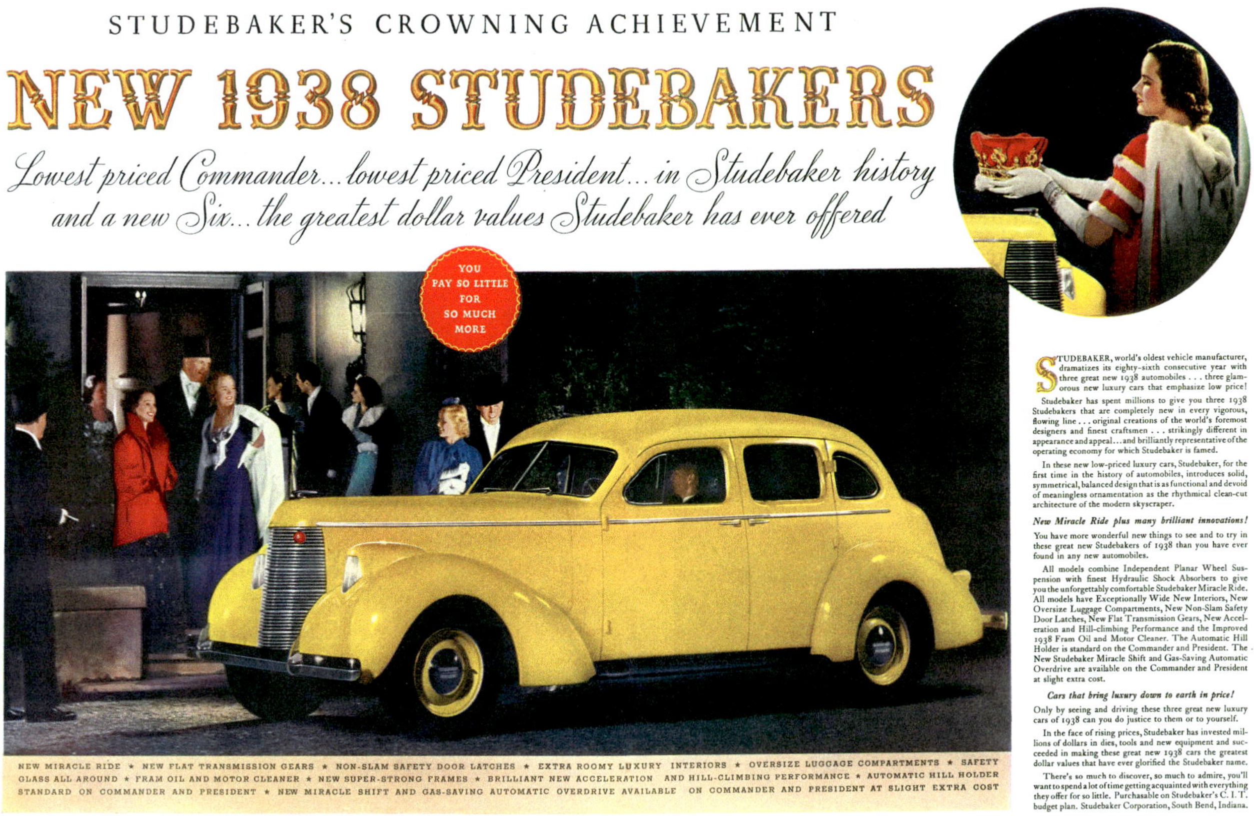

De Soto, 1937 ◂ Studebaker, 1937

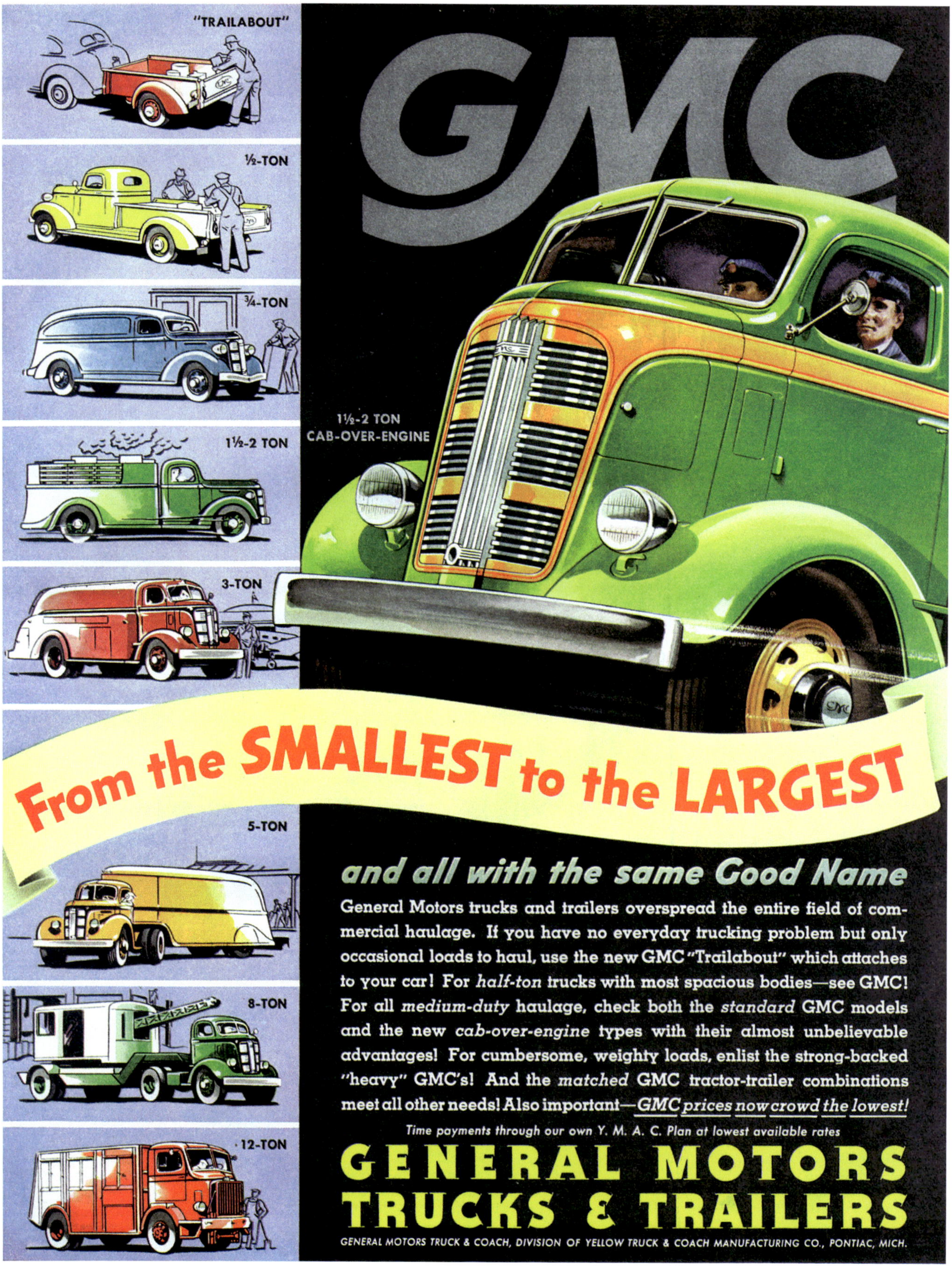

General Motors, 1937

▸ *Autocar Trucks, 1937*

A low-priced, light-duty truck is one thing . . . but a medium-priced, light-duty Autocar is a thing apart.

"FOLLOW THE LEADERS FOR THEY KNOW THE WAY"

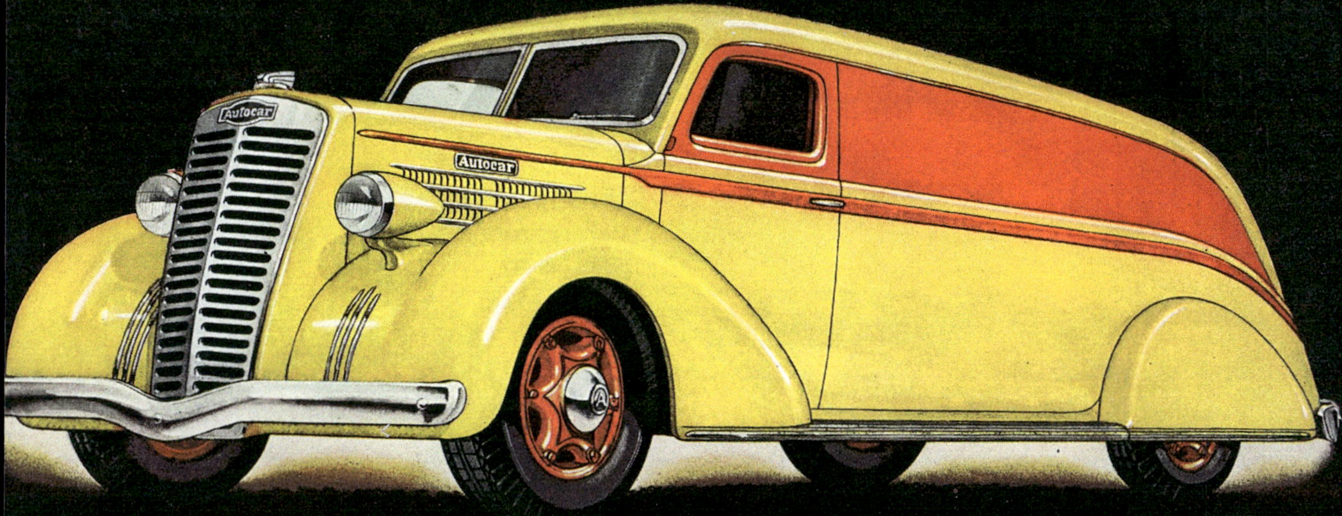

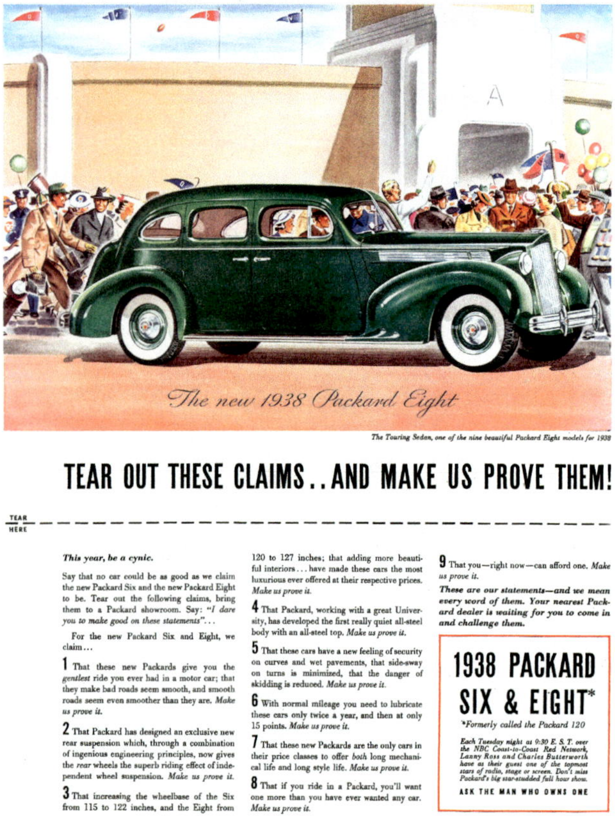

Packard, 1937

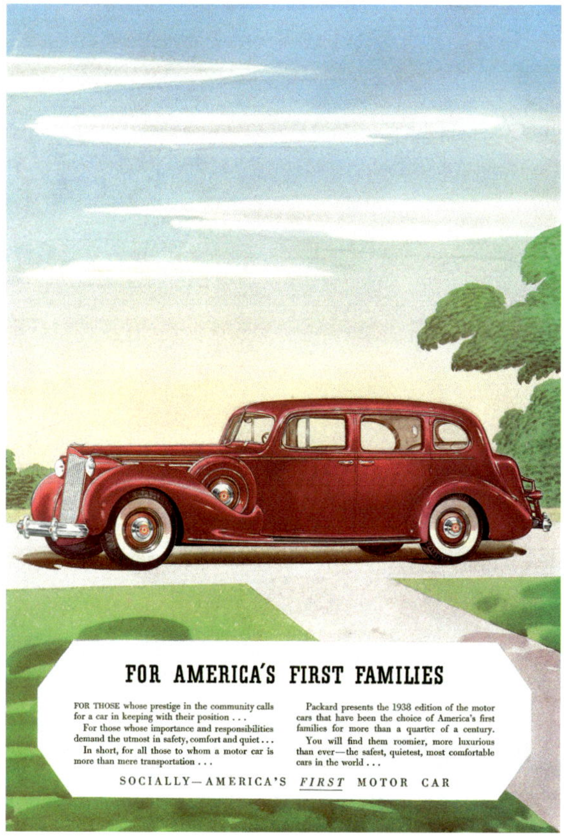

Packard, 1937

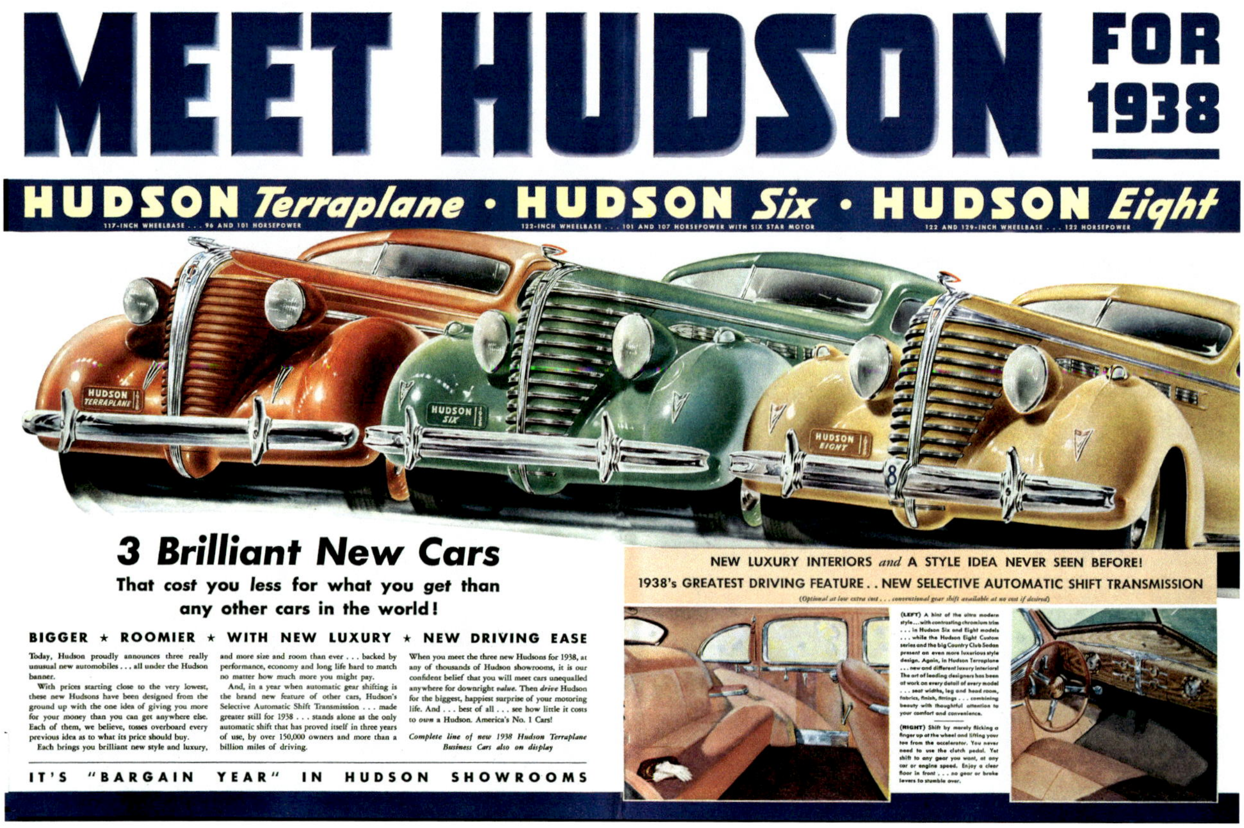

Hudson, 1937

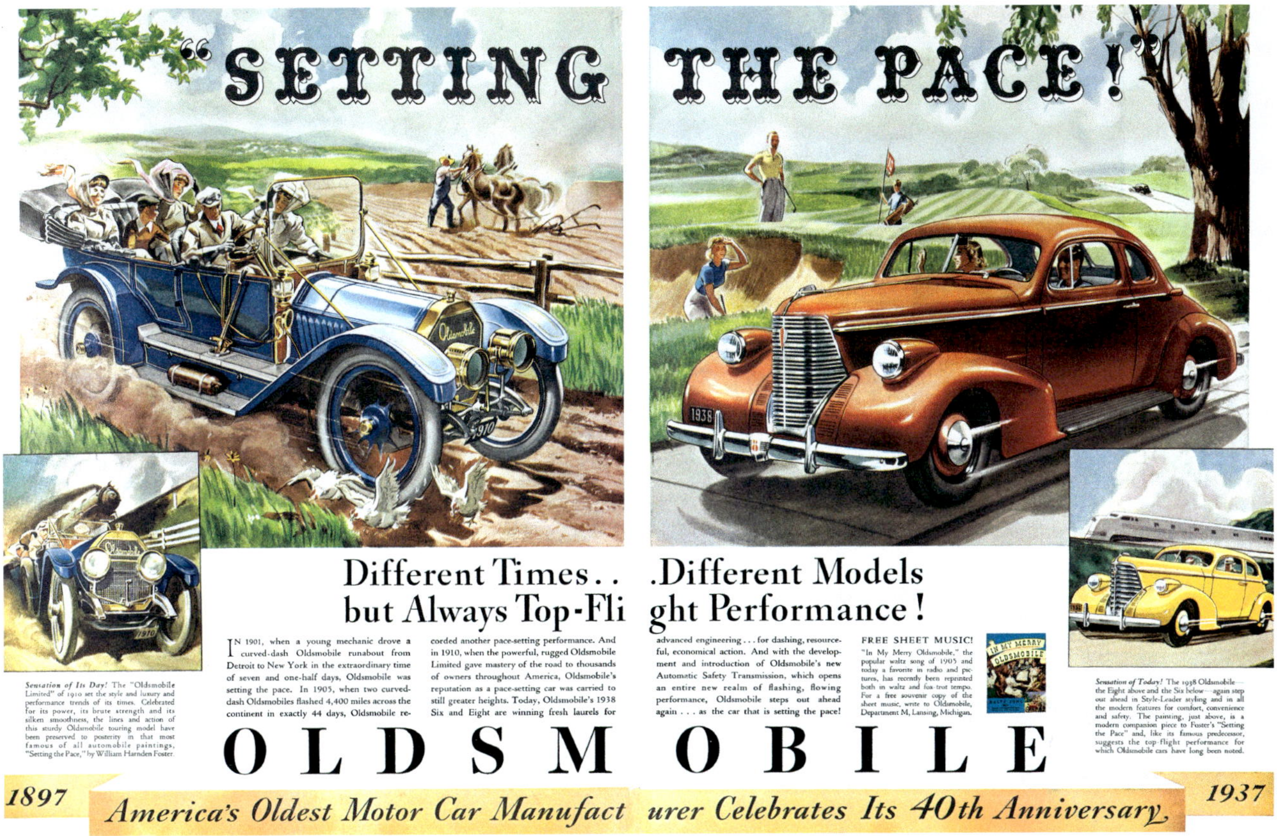

Oldsmobile, 1937

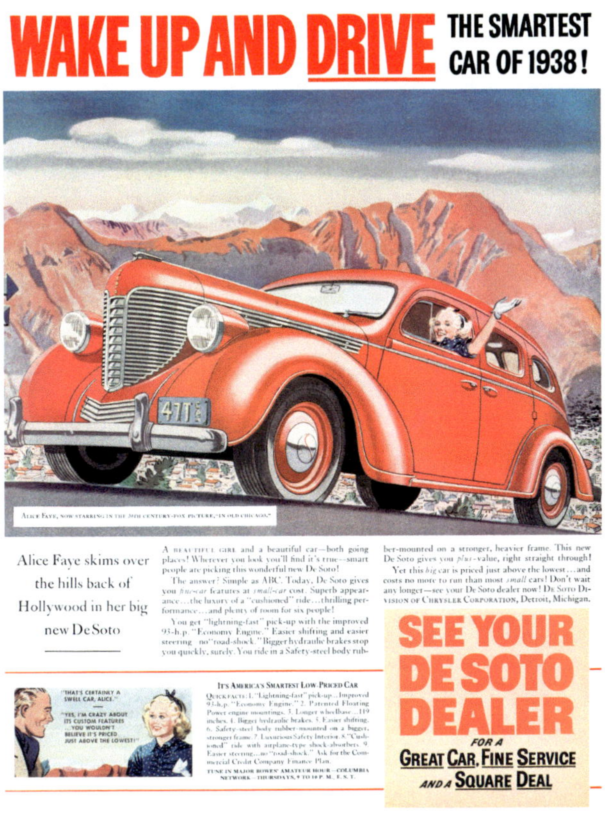

De Soto, 1937

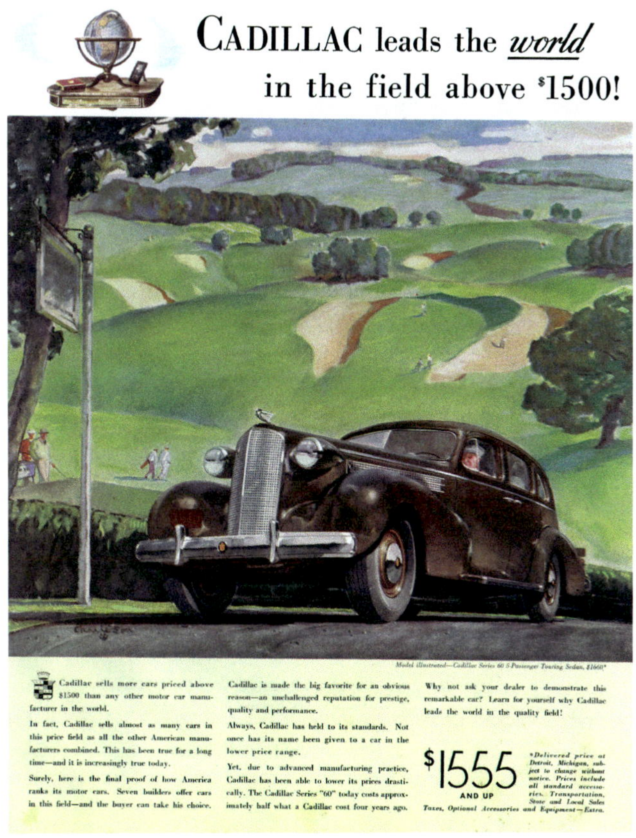

Cadillac, 1937

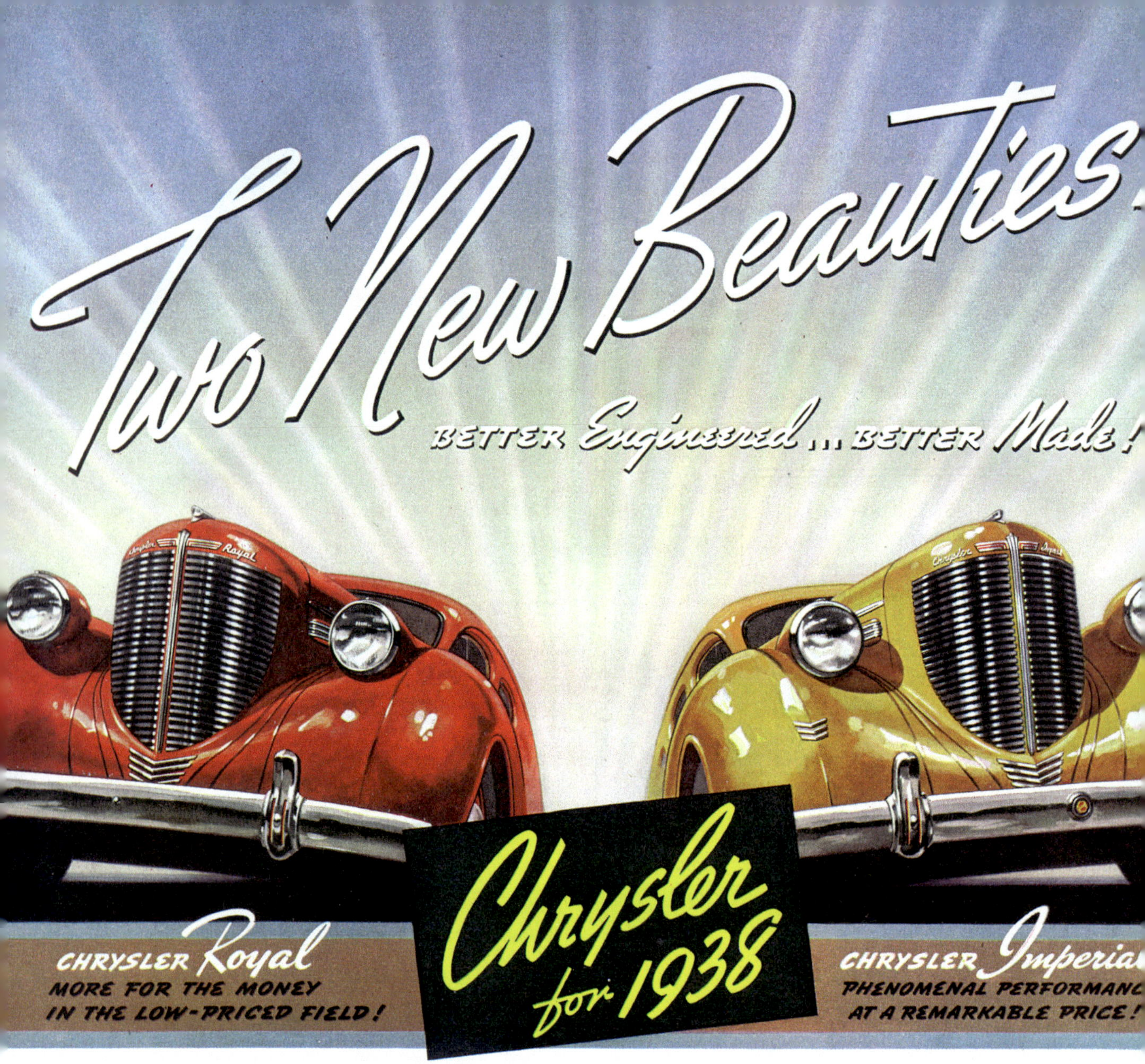

BIGGER . . . and a beauty. That's the new Chrysler Royal for 1938. Three inches more wheelbase than the 1937 Royal which invaded the low-priced field with such spectacular success.

Look at that proud, commanding radiator . . . the jewel-like modeling of the radiator grille . . . the graceful union of hood and fenders and streamlined headlamps.

Inside, beauty greets you again. The instrument panel sets the keynote . . . rich, smart, luxurious . . . blending in color harmony with the striking new steering wheel and its ring-type horn control . . . complementing the superb upholstery in new short-nap mohair or broadcloth.

A new, larger 95 horsepower Gold Seal engine . . . amazingly thrifty . . . silky smooth with Floating Power.

Glorious roominess! 119 inches of wheelbase. 96¼ inches from windshield to rear window! A 49 inch rear seat! The most spacious luggage capacity you ever saw!

High-priced riding comfort! Safety *All-Steel* Bodies . . . time-tested hydraulic brakes . . . finger-touch steering . . . toe-touch stopping . . . synchronized gear-shifting. A big, beautiful, luxurious car that tops everything in the low-priced field.

The Luxurious Imperial

The beautiful, high-powered Chrysler Imperial for 1938! More fine car for the money than America has ever seen!

Long famous as Chrysler's top-ranking car, the magnificent Imperial is now in the medium-priced field.

The proud, commanding beauty that comes from added length and size! Wheelbase increased to 125 inches . . . for low-swung smartness and grace . . . for the roominess of true fine-car luxury.

Deep, wide, chair-high seats! Beautiful appointments! Matchless riding ease . . . the buoyant, gliding smoothness of longer wheelbase . . . balanced weight distribution . . . independently sprung front wheels . . . slow-recoil springs and Aero Hydraulic Shock Absorbers.

Under that long, impressive hood, the electrifying response of 110 horsepower . . . cradled by Floating Pow

The safety and reliability of Chrysl great engineering features . . . all at t finest expression. Safety *All-Steel* Bo . . . hydraulic brakes . . . steering and g shifting perfection that makes this powerful car as effortless as the bree

See this great, new Imperial . you'll thrill to its beauty . . . marve its price.

★ ★ ★

Easy to buy on convenient terms with official Commercial Credit Company p

☆ **NEW 1938 ROYAL** . . . 95 horsepow 119-inch wheelbase. Ten body types.

☆ **NEW 1938 IMPERIAL** . . . 110 horsepow 125-inch wheelbase. Six body types.

☆ **NEW 1938 CUSTOM IMPERIAL** . . . 130 ho power, 144-inch wheelbase. Three body ty

Tune in on Major Bowes, Columbia Netw every Thursday, 9 to 10:00 P. M., E. S

★ CHRYSLER SWEEPS ON IN THE LOW-PRICED FIELD!

PRESENTING THE SENSATIONAL NEW

CADILLAC *Sixty* SPECIAL

THE NEWEST CAR IN THE WORLD

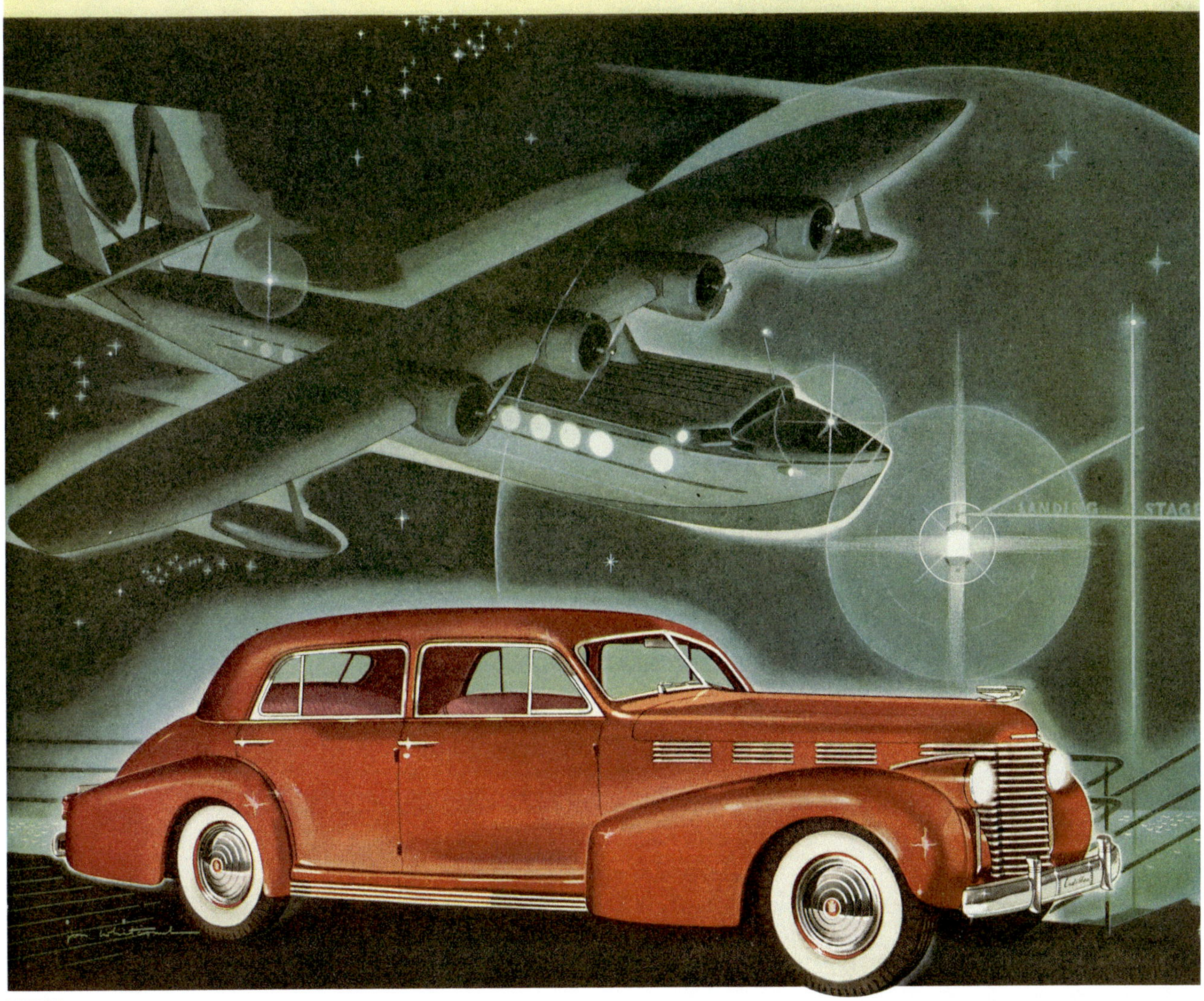

THERE HAS NEVER BEEN a car like the *new* Cadillac Sixty Special . . . a car with such definite modernity of line, yet so obviously right in taste . . . a precedent-breaking car prophetic of motor cars not yet on other drawing boards, yet a car wholly devoid of freakish trappings.

THERE HAS NEVER BEEN anything like the vivid, spirited performance of this car . . . with its inexhaustible vitality, its eager-flowing power, its quiet, obedient responsiveness! There has never been anything like its inviting, all-embracing comfort . . . davenport seats, with extra width and extra depth. There has never been anything like the vision with which you drive the Cadillac Sixty Special . . . there is more outward vision than in any closed car ever built heretofore.

THERE ARE BOLD STROKES OF INSPIRED DESIGN in the Sixty Special. There are no runningboards —you step right in, through doors of generous width. From every angle—the Cadillac Sixty Special is, beyond dispute, *the newest car in the world!*

IF YOU ARE TIRED OF THE COMMONPLACE—if you want the only really different car of the year—then by all means accept our invitation to drive this matchless Cadillac Sixty Special. Its performance . . . in your own hands . . . will make the most extravagant description seem faint praise indeed!

There is also a new Cadillac Sixty in more conventional mold, and selling at a price we believe represents the greatest value in the motor car market. It differs from the Special in appearance and appointment—it is one with the Special in quality and in performance. And as to performance . . . the Cadillac Sixty is unquestionably America's finest-performing eight cylinder car! See it!

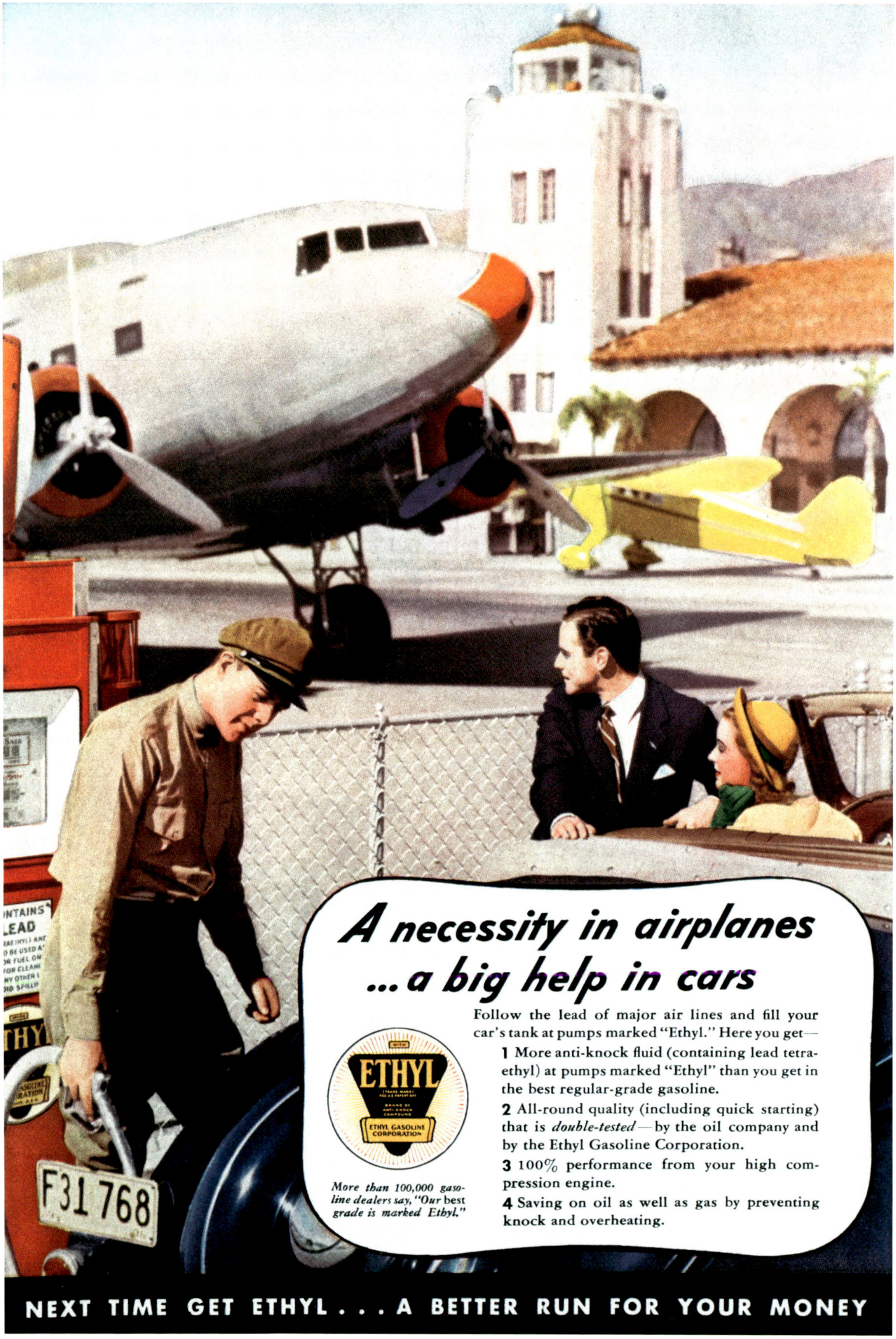

Ethyl, 1937

▸ *Packard, 1937* ▸▸ *Plymouth, 1938*

SOCIALLY—AMERICA'S FIRST MOTOR CAR

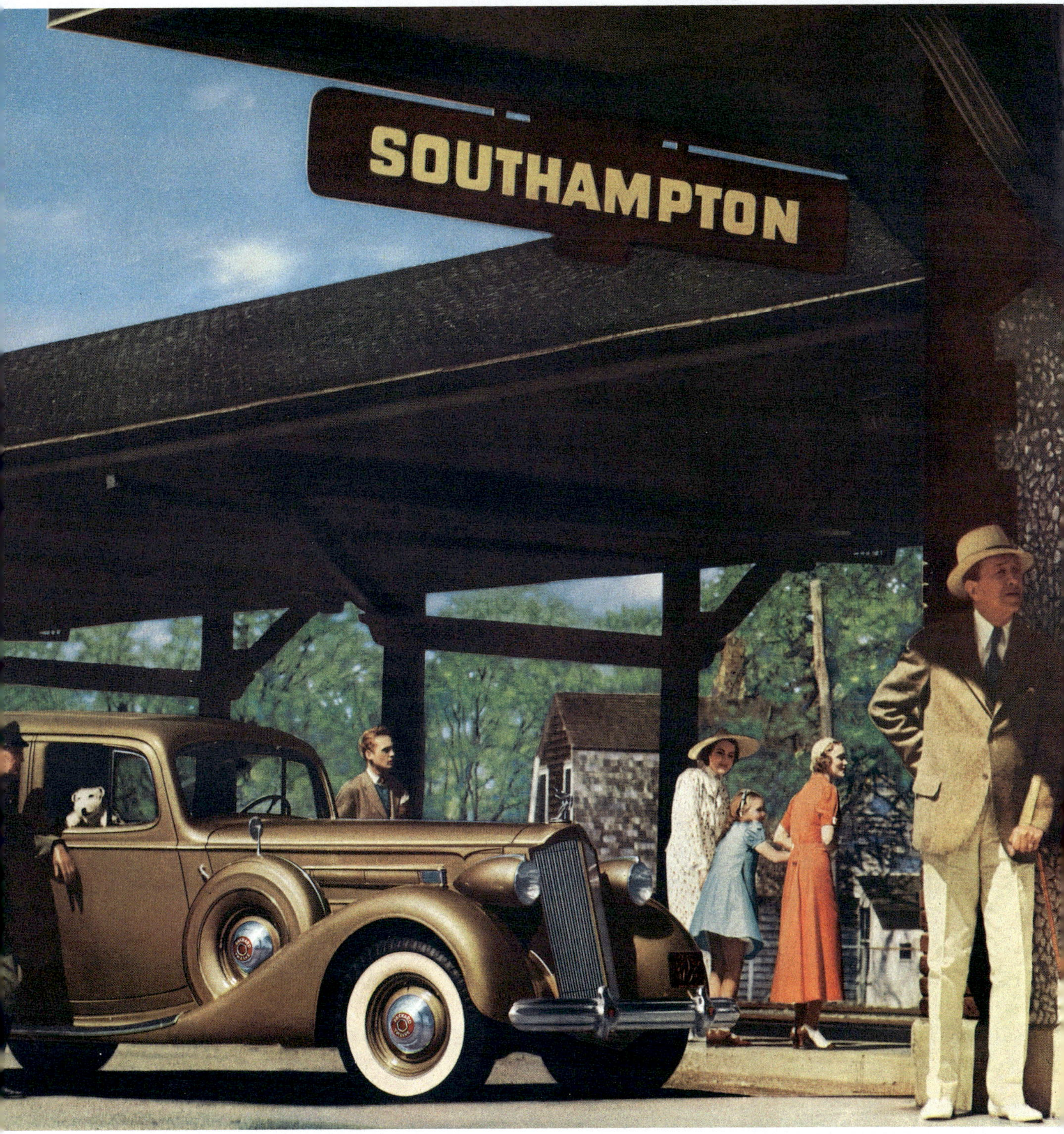

MEETING "THE CANNON BALL" AT SOUTHAMPTON, LONG ISLAND

AT THOSE vacation and week-end resorts which year after year attract America's most socially prominent families, more large Packards are habitually in evidence than any other fine car.

This is a striking fact, but a most natural one. For in such families Packard ownership has become as traditional as attendance at certain schools, membership in certain clubs.

In fact, more than a thousand of America's most distinguished families have owned Packards continuously for twenty-five years or longer.

PACKARD

THE TWELVE

THE SUPER • EIGHT

ASK THE MAN WHO OWNS ONE

Great Value at an A

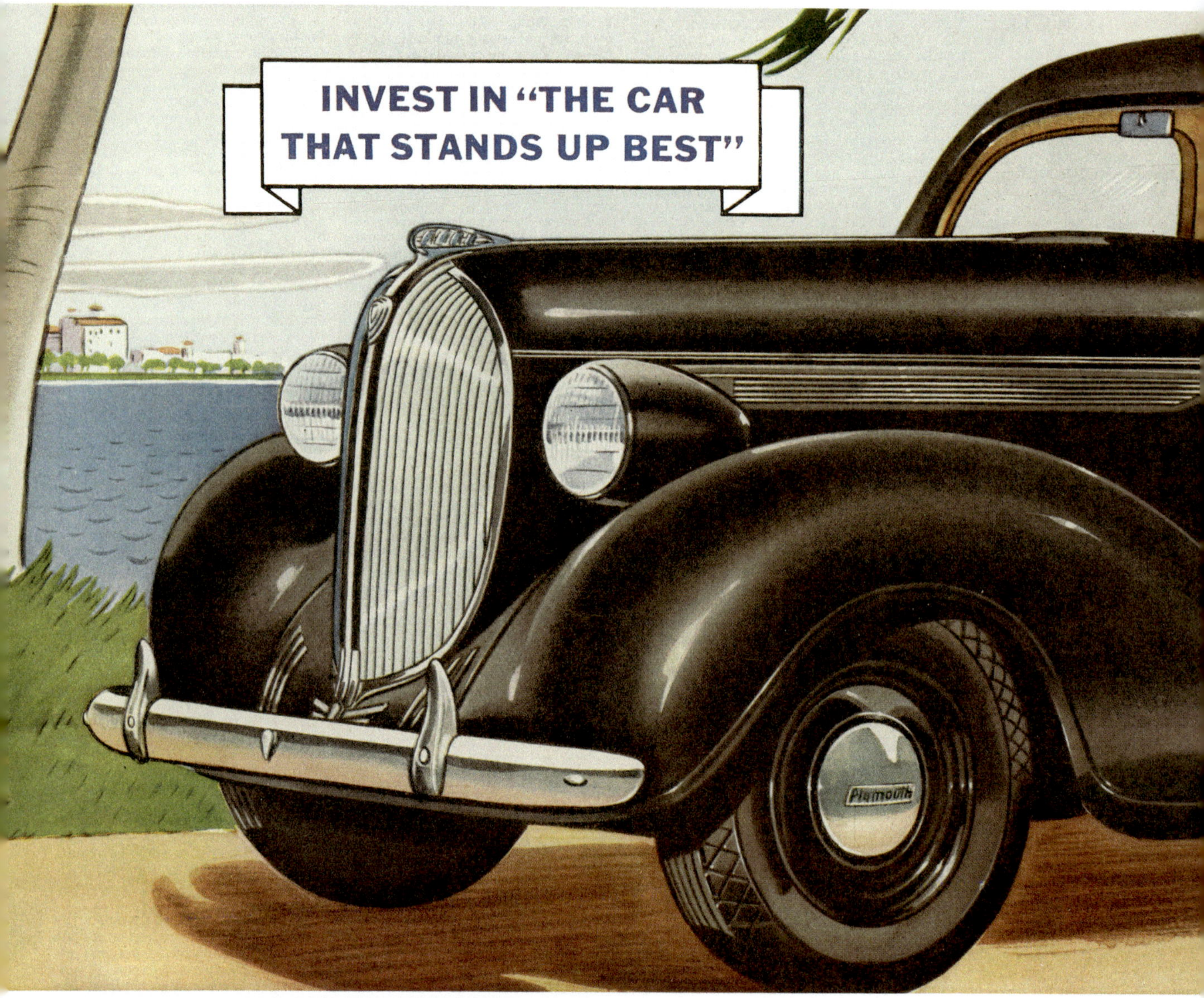

NEW 1938 PLYMOUTH OFFERS

More for the Money!

THIS BIG BEAUTIFUL CAR is the
Plymouth. It offers you more *d*
dollar value than any low-priced
offered you before!

There is news in Plymouth's low c
prices...and what you get for your

Go see Plymouth—drive it! That
the whole story. Look at its size—
features! Get the sensation of Ply
great new ride!...there's no matchin

Plymouth is the *only* low-priced

PLYMOUTH BUI

nazing Low Price!

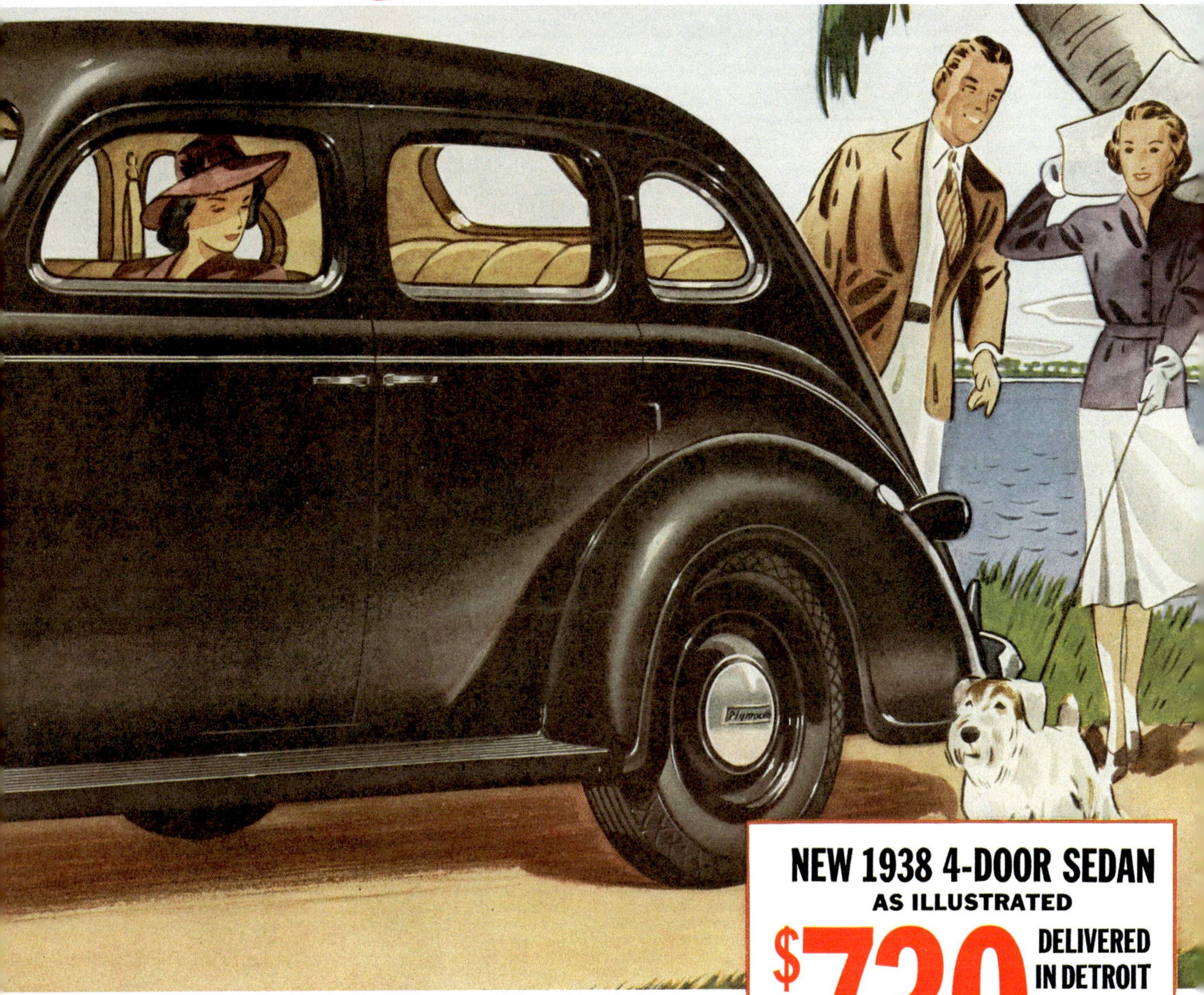

you the *extra value* of "live" rubber mountings that block out road noise vibration..."radio studio" sound-proof- .airplane-type shock-absorbers...and nted Floating Power engine mountings.

ere's *extra value* in Plymouth's safety, Plymouth's *double-action* hydraulic es stop you smoothly, safely. Around over you, under you, is the security of -steel body...welded into one rigid unit. e 1938 Plymouth steers faster, handles easier...the windshield has 12% more vision. And the whole interior is Safety-Styled.

In every way, this is the greatest Plymouth ever built. You cannot know this car until you've ridden in it—driven it. See it today—and find out about Plymouth's great value. See any Dodge, De Soto or Chrysler dealer. Plymouth Division of Chrysler Corporation, Detroit, Michigan.

TUNE IN MAJOR BOWES' AMATEUR HOUR... COLUMBIA NETWORK, THURSDAYS, 9 TO 10 P. M., E.S.T.

NEW 1938 4-DOOR SEDAN
AS ILLUSTRATED

$730 **DELIVERED IN DETROIT**

Including Federal taxes. Local, State taxes not included.

BUSINESS MODELS—Coupe, $645; 2-Door Sedan, $685; 4-Door Sedan, $730.

DE LUXE MODELS—Coupe, $730; Coupe with Rumble Seat, $770; Convertible Coupe, $850; 2-Door Sedan, $773; 2-Door Touring Sedan, $785; 4-Door Sedan, $803; 4-Door Touring Sedan, $815.

All the above are "delivered in Detroit" prices, including Federal taxes. Local, State taxes not included. For delivered prices in your locality, see your Dodge, De Soto or Chrysler dealer.

OS GREAT CARS

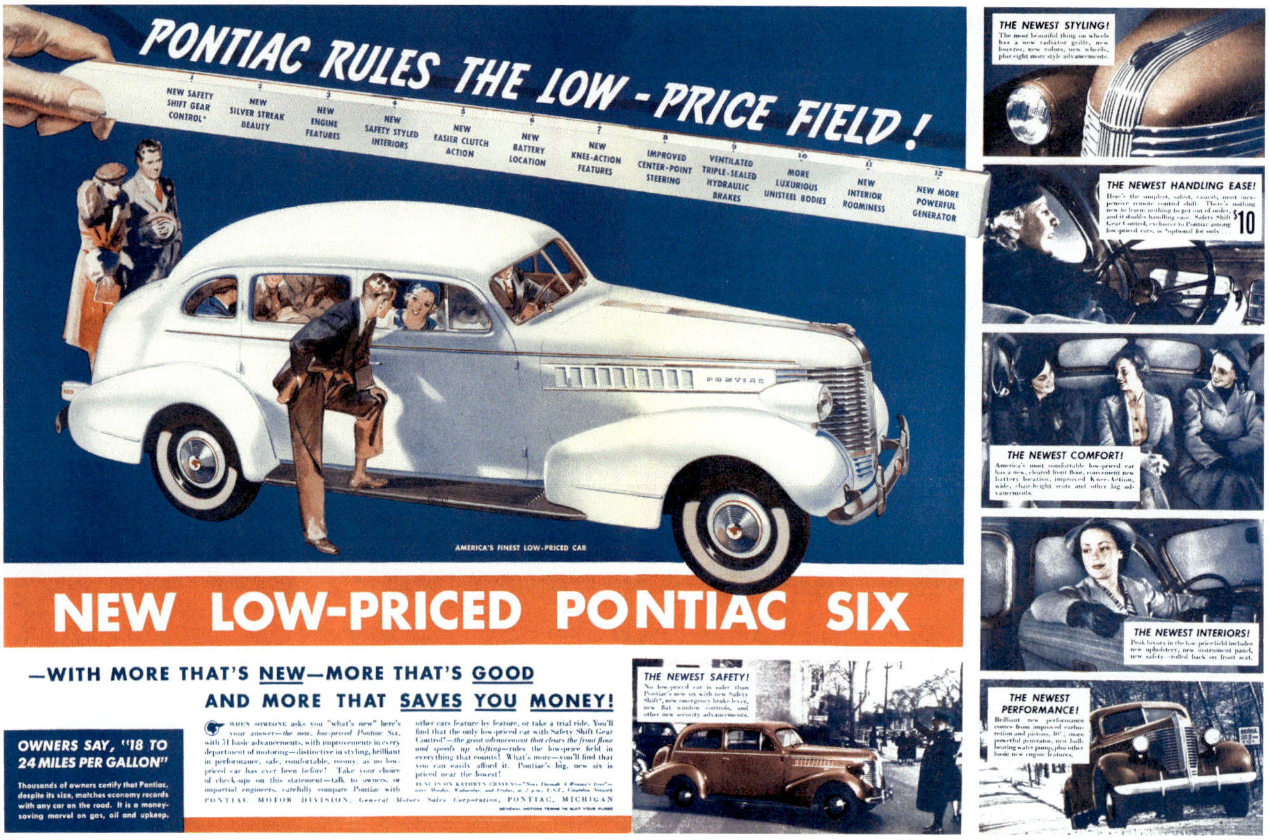

Pontiac, 1938

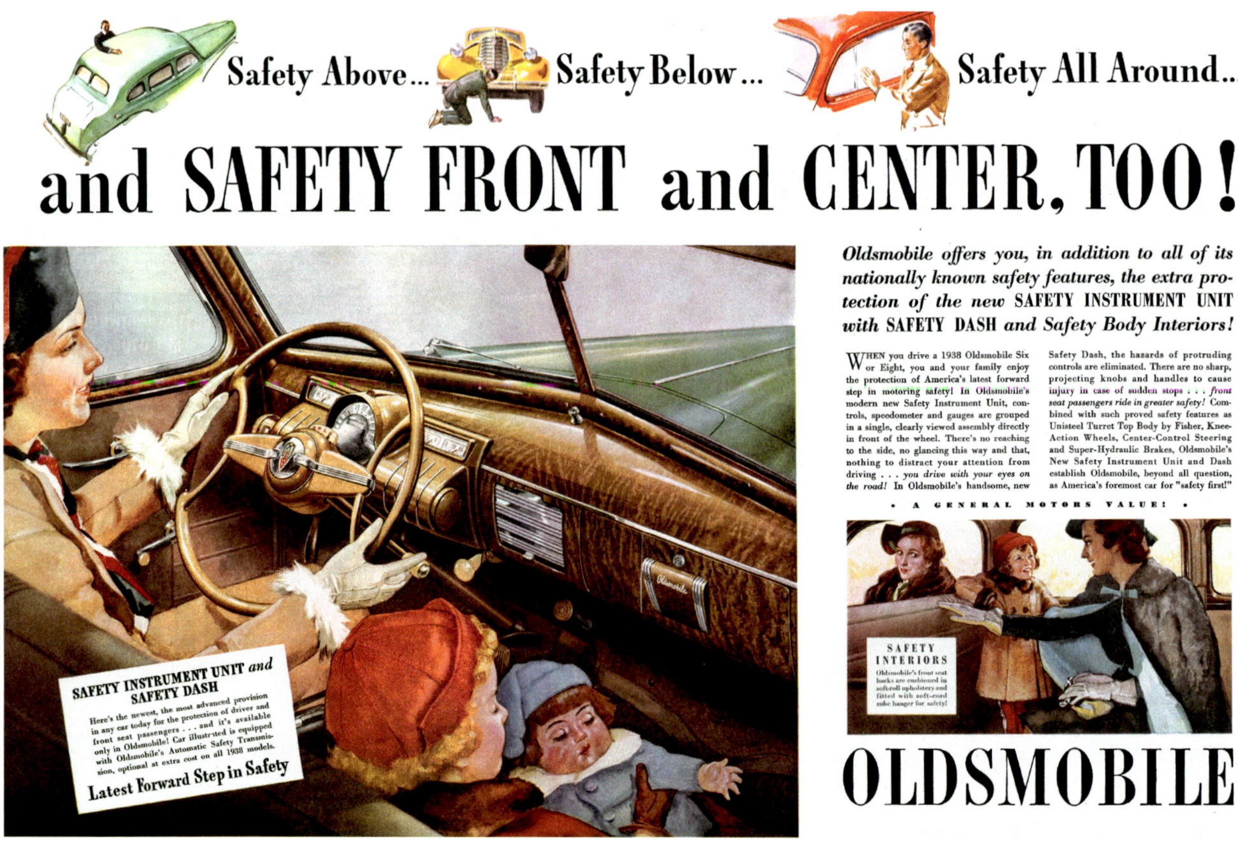

Oldsmobile, 1938

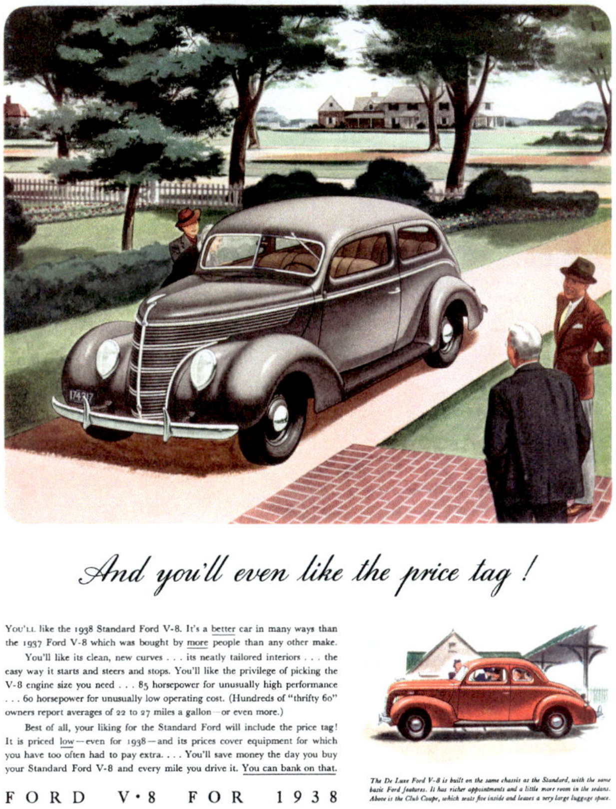

Ford, 1938

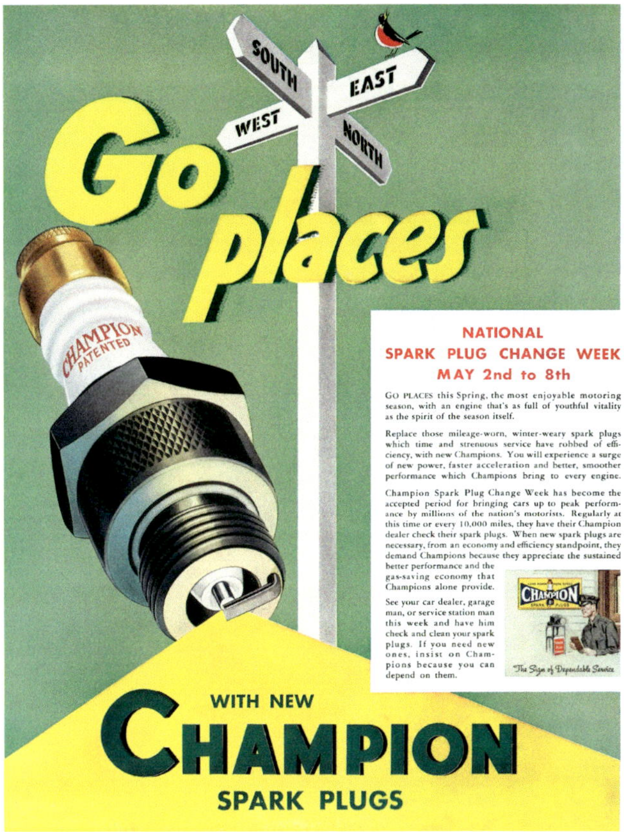

Champion Spark Plugs, 1938

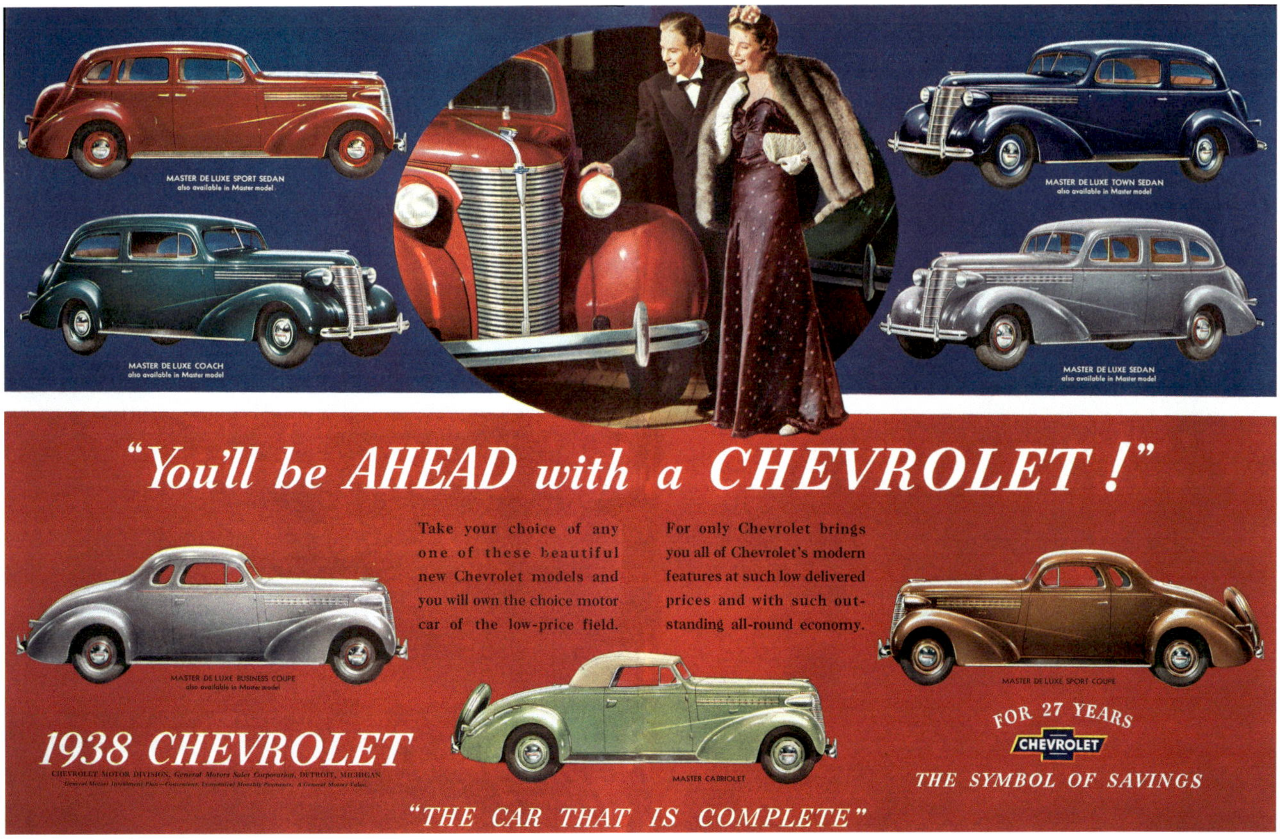

Chevrolet, 1938

Every Motoring Family will applaud

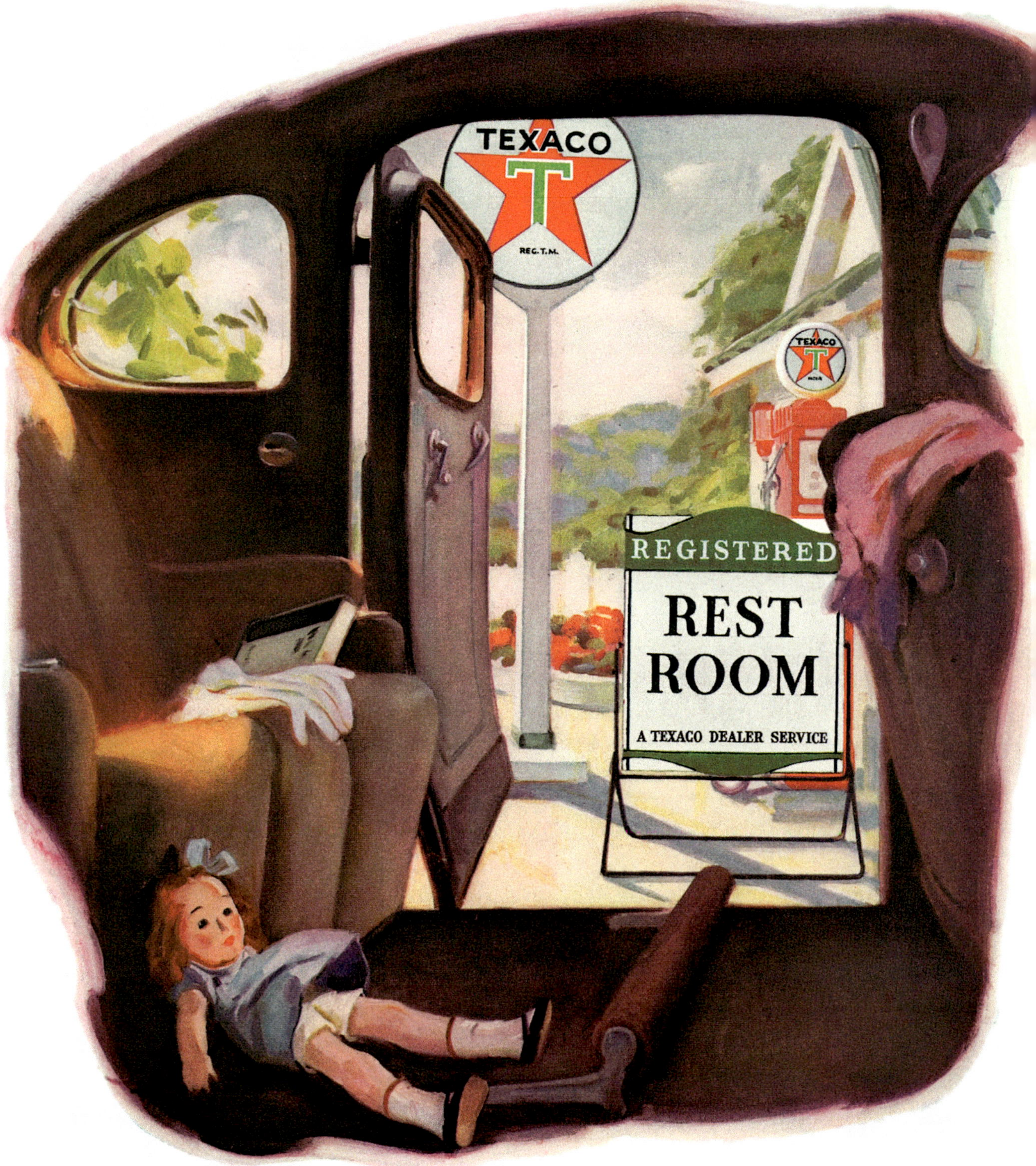

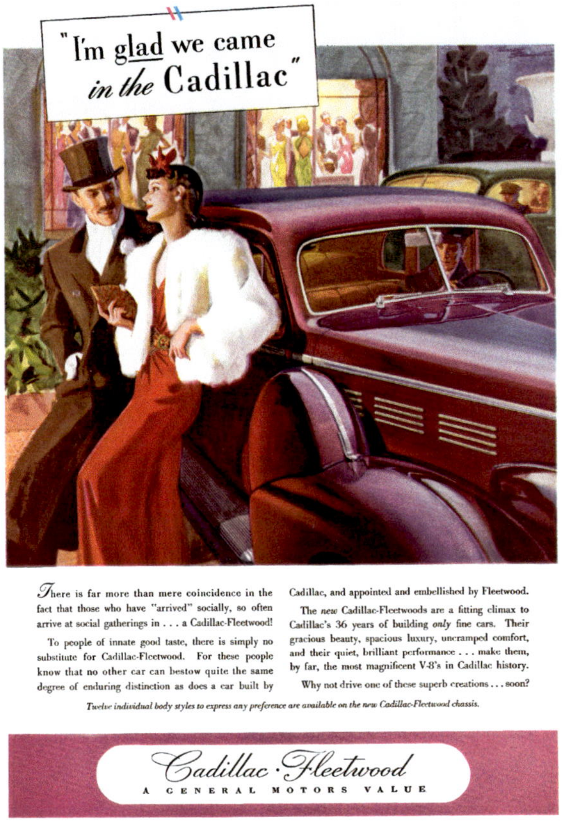

Cadillac, 1938

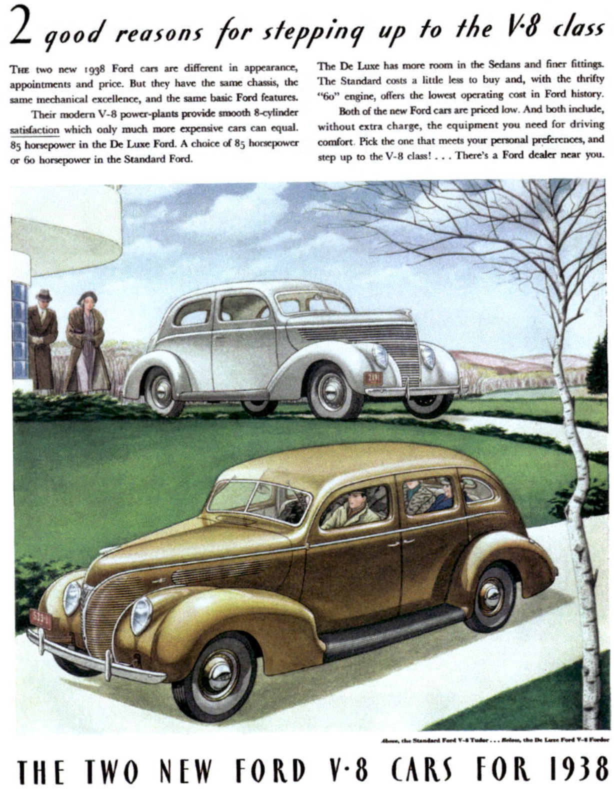

Ford, 1938

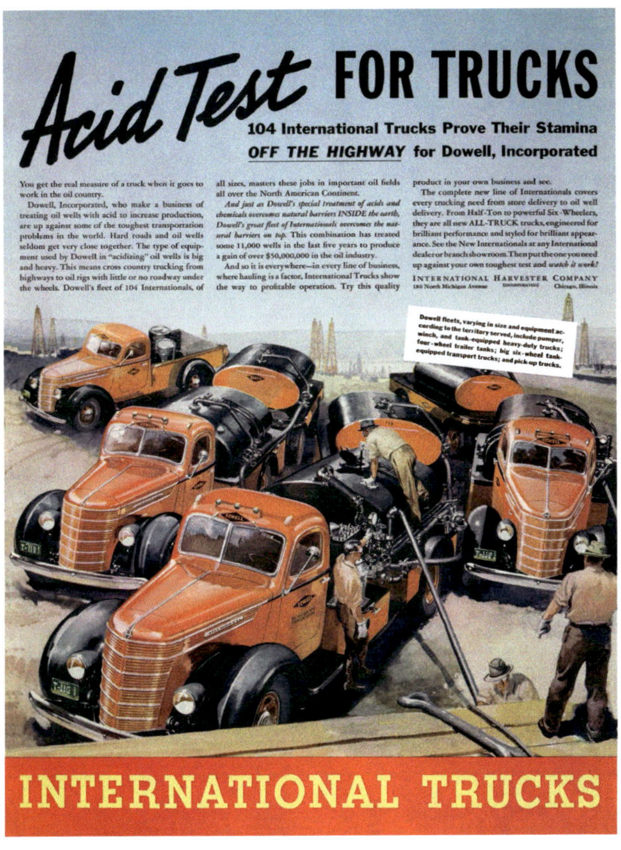

Texaco, 1938 ◄ International Trucks, 1938

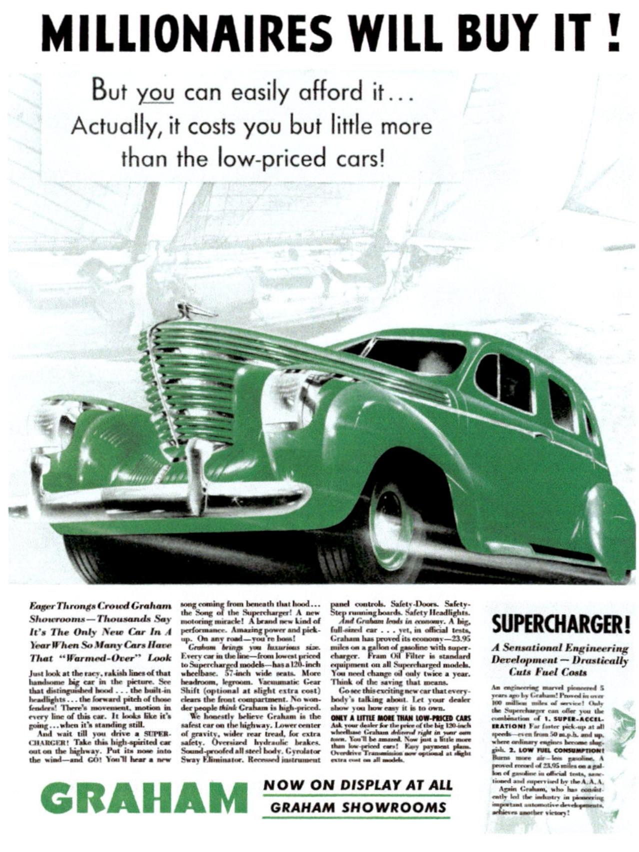

Graham, 1938

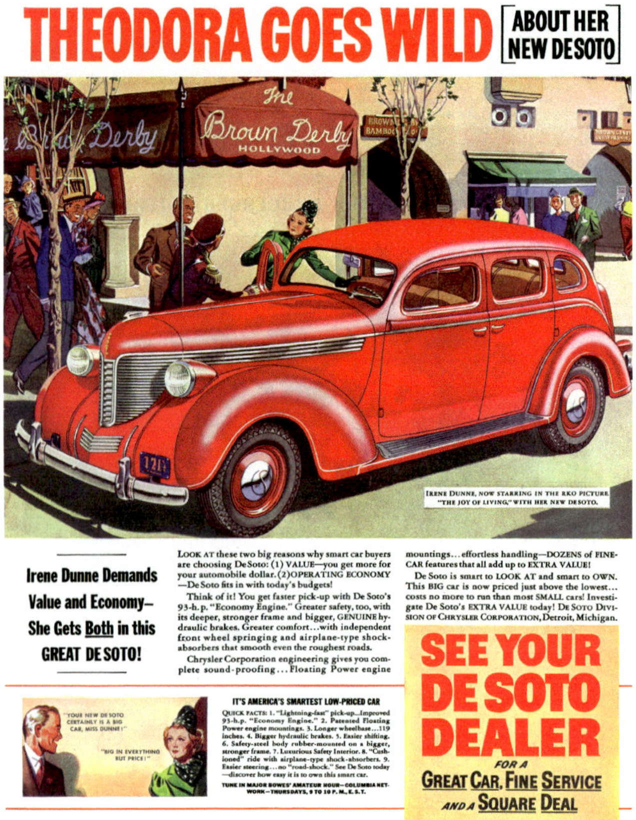

De Soto, 1938

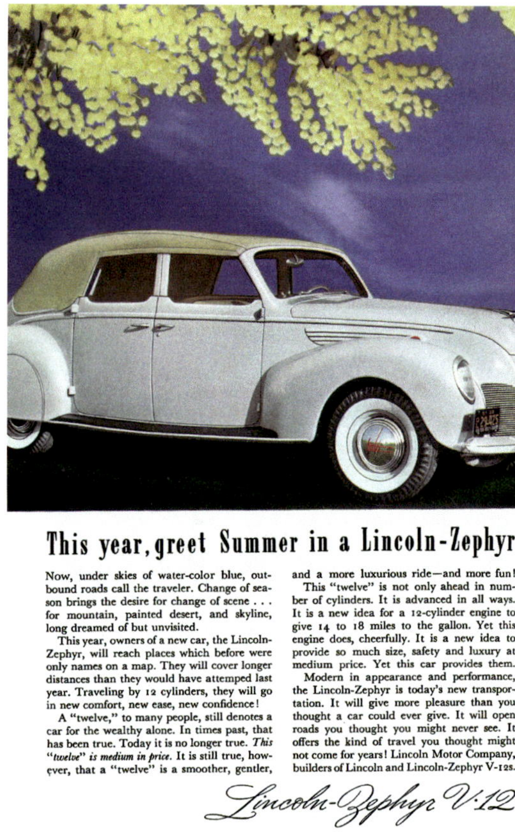

Lincoln, 1938

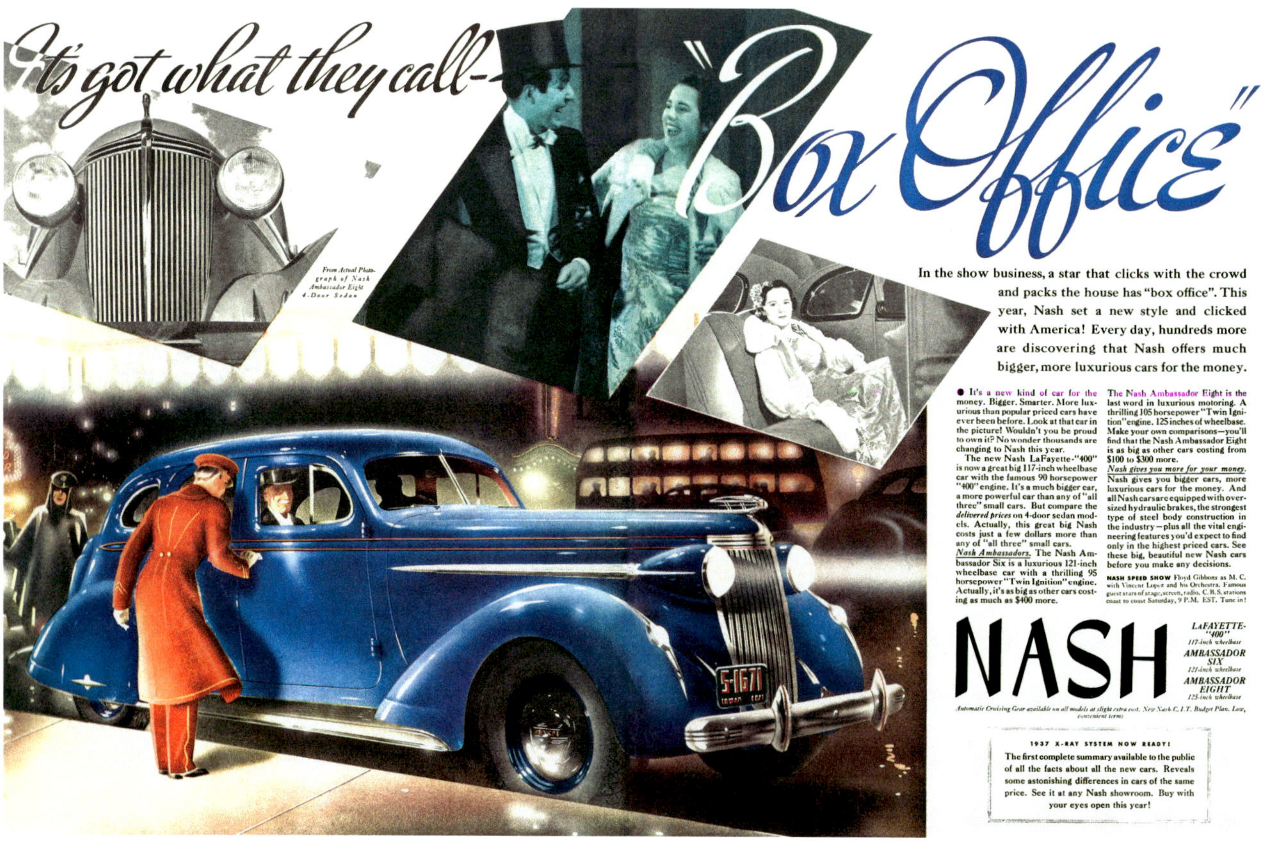

Nash, 1939

▸ AC Spark Plug, 1938

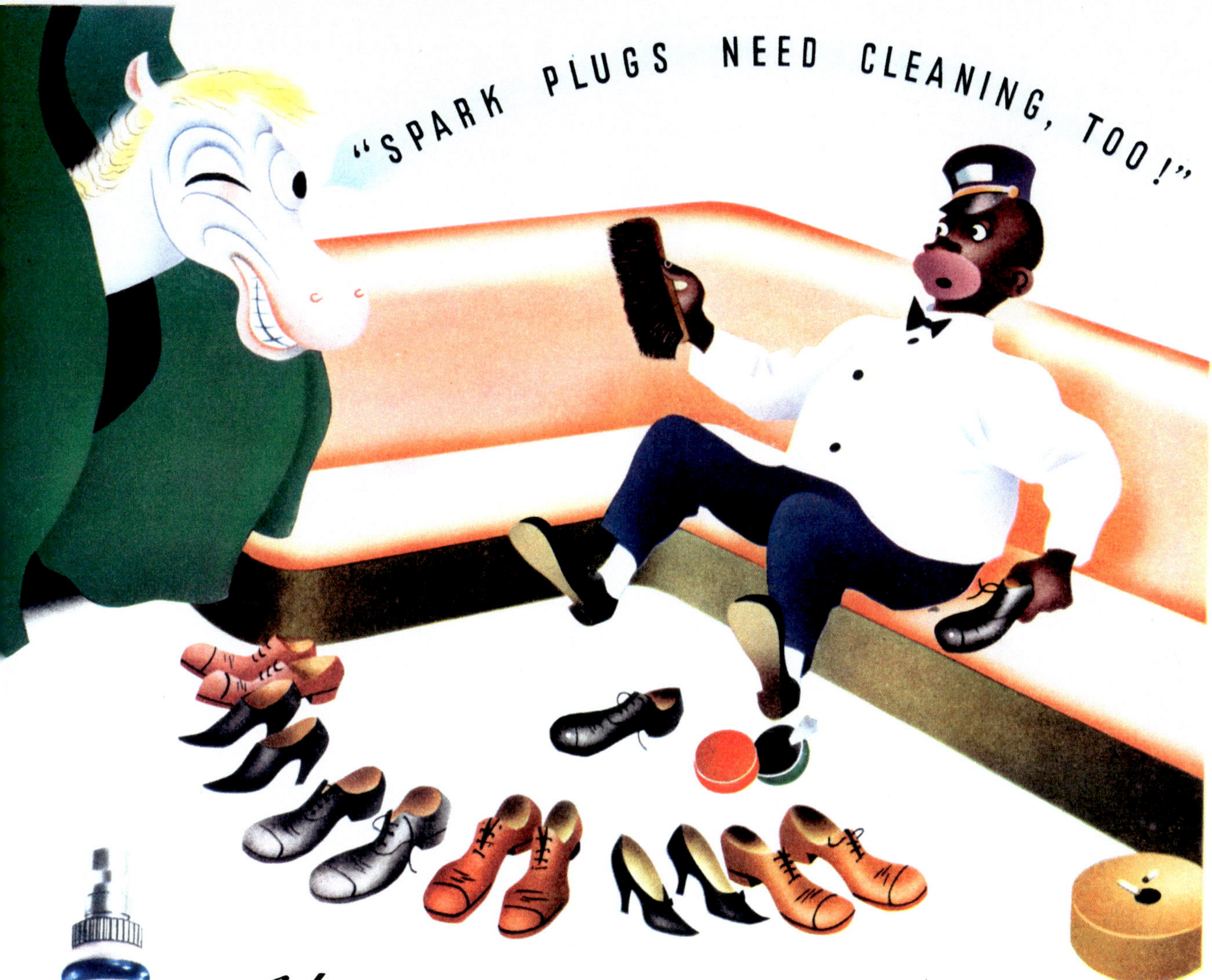

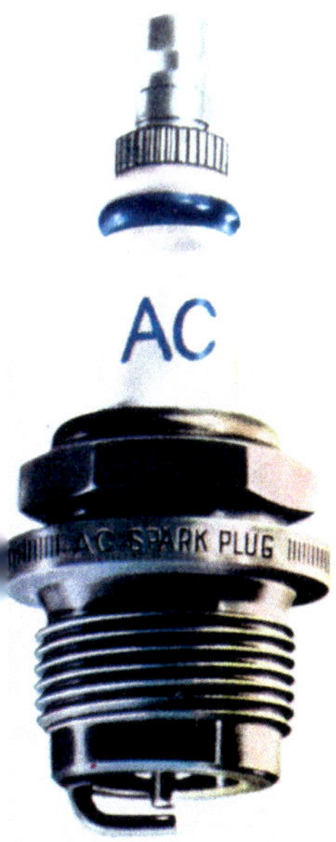

Had your plugs cleaned lately?

Plug cleaning *by the AC Method* completely and thoroughly removes the gas-wasting, power-stealing soot, carbon, and oxide coating. The cost is only 5c a plug.

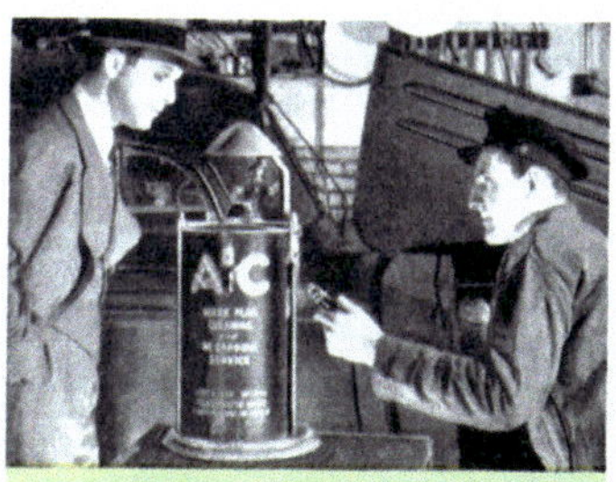

"There's enough oxide coating on your plugs to steal 10% of your gas."

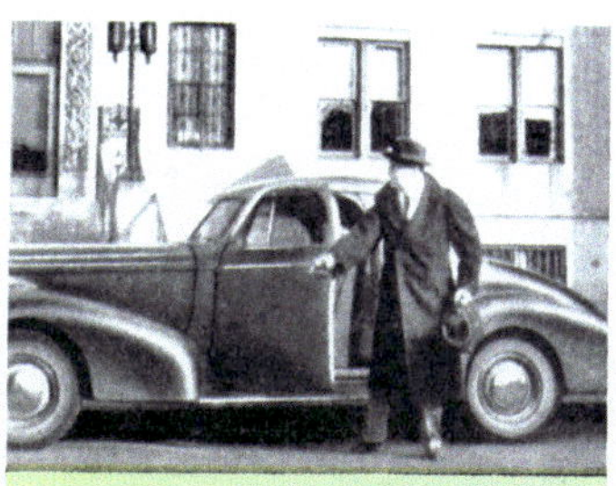

Many a doctor has arrived "in time" thanks to clean, reliable plugs.

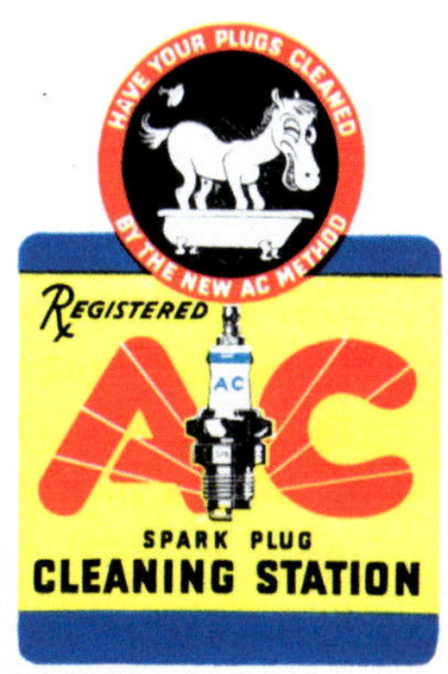

THIS SIGN identifies Registered AC Spark Plug Cleaning Stations. Look for it.

C Quality Spark Plugs
for peak performance

ty years of building quality plugs—for the car maker and ie car owner—are behind these y products. For full spark plug action, install a set of new park plugs every 10,000 miles.

SPARK PLUG DIVISION · *General Motors Corporation* · FLINT, MICHIGAN

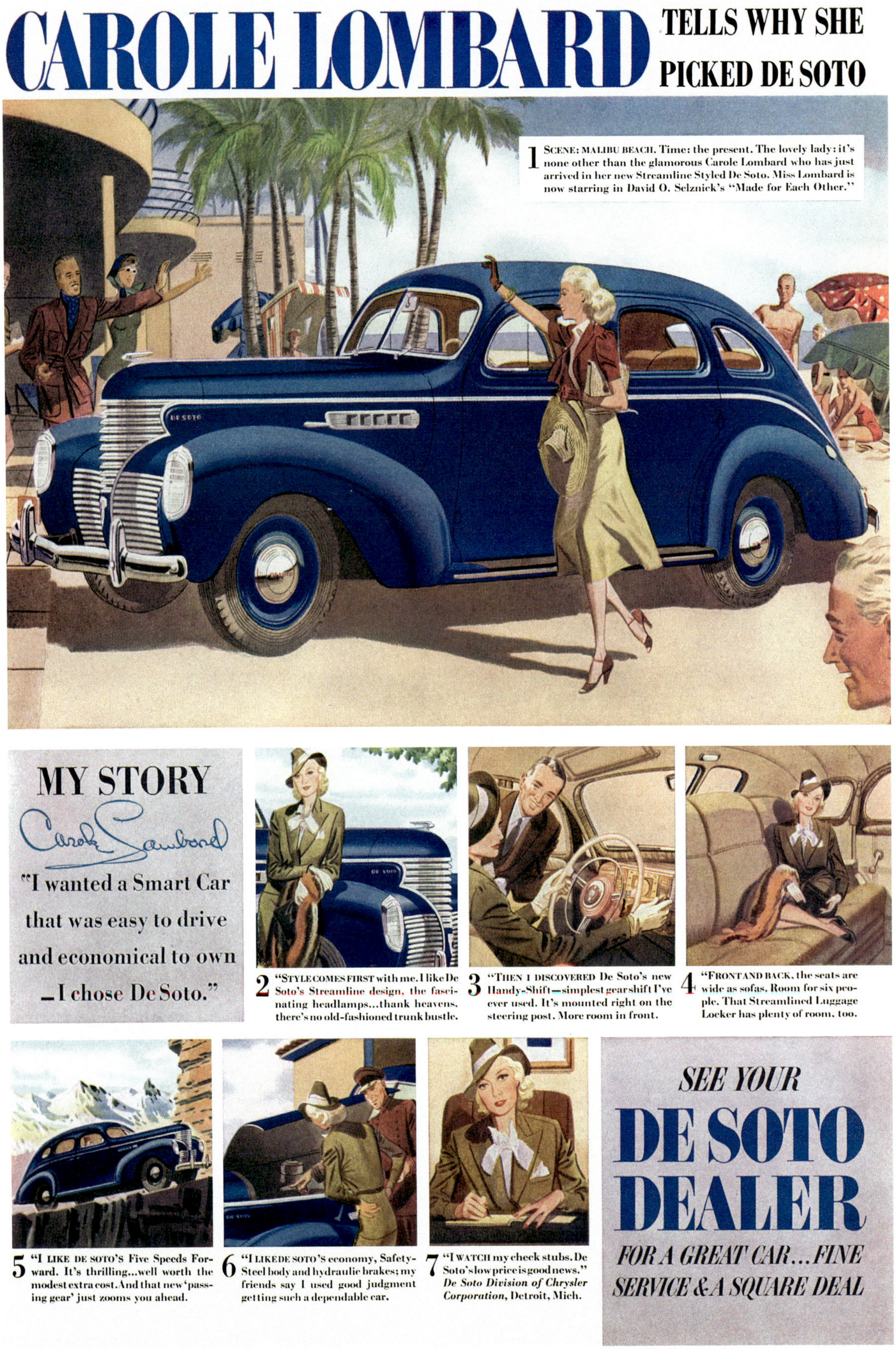

De Soto, 1938

▸ *Nash, 1938*

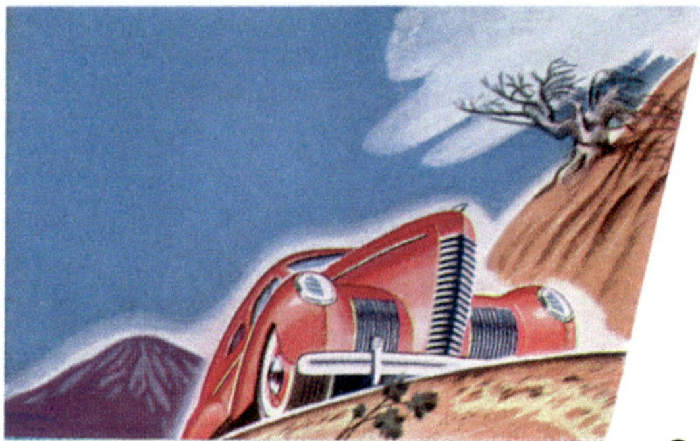

EXCITING NEW NASH "HURRICANE POWER"! Even in lowest priced models you flash from 15 to 50 M.P.H. in 13 seconds *in high!* And with this performance, economy is even better than last year.

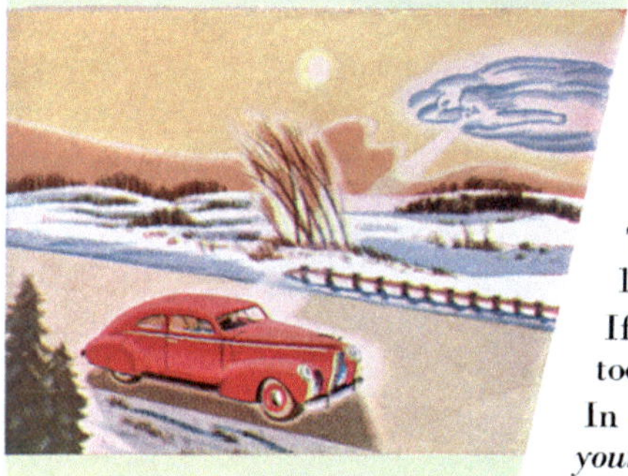

CONDITIONED AIR for Winter Driving—now made *automatic!* "Tune in" the comfort you want . . . the "Weather Eye" keeps it constant.

SOMETHING'S GOING TO HAPPEN TO YOU

On the Road Today . . . a New 1939 Nash . . . with the Ride and Drive of Your Lifetime!

YOU'LL see it pass you on the road . . . sometime this week. A sudden rush of wind . . . a silver streak, snaking ahead of traffic, silent as a shadow.

Then you'll know that the first new 1939 Nash is in town.

If you thrill to a thoroughbred, you, too, will soon drive a Nash.

In sober truth, *you have never had your hands on such a car in all your life.* It has glamour, character. It is lithe, low and *fire* on four wheels.

Simply touch that throttle . . . and in three fast shifts you can break the hearts of the best of them.

Then a *fourth speed forward* is like "wings" on your car!

Want to try the "Weather Eye"?

Just set that dial in front, and you ride all winter in fresh, balmy June air—*automatically* kept at your comfort level!

Ten old driving peeves have been abolished. You start, stop, shift, and steer with new ease, *speed!*

Spacious interiors . . . seats that quickly make up into a big double bed . . . exquisite appointments. Literally, it's a home on wheels.

It is, we believe, the world's most modern car. Certainly, it is the most exciting. And prices are something to cheer about!

See your Nash Dealer, *drive* it! NASH MOTORS DIVISION, Nash-Kelvinator Corp., Detroit, Mich.

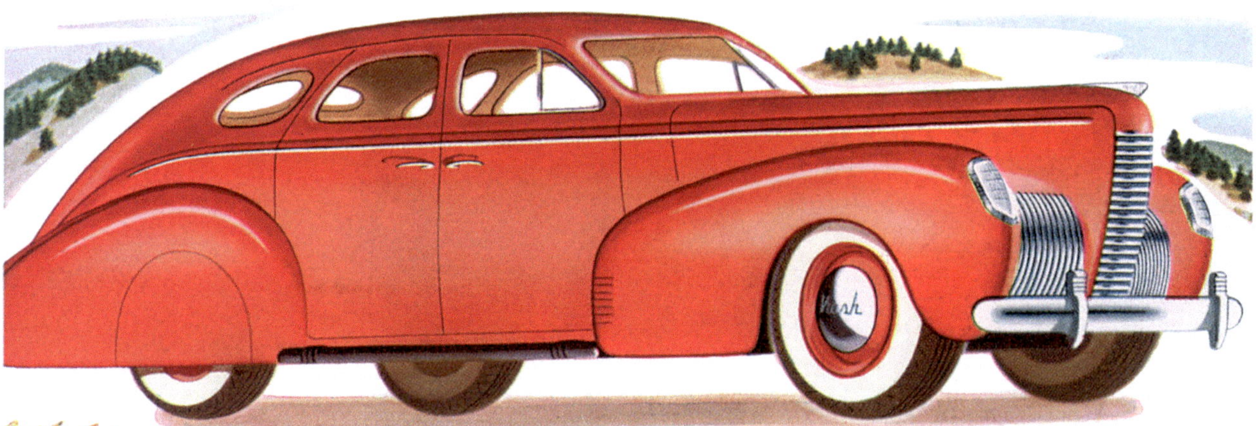

NOW ON DISPLAY . . . FOUR SERIES OF GREAT CARS . . . 21 MODELS
Nine of Them Priced Right Next to the Lowest . . . See them today

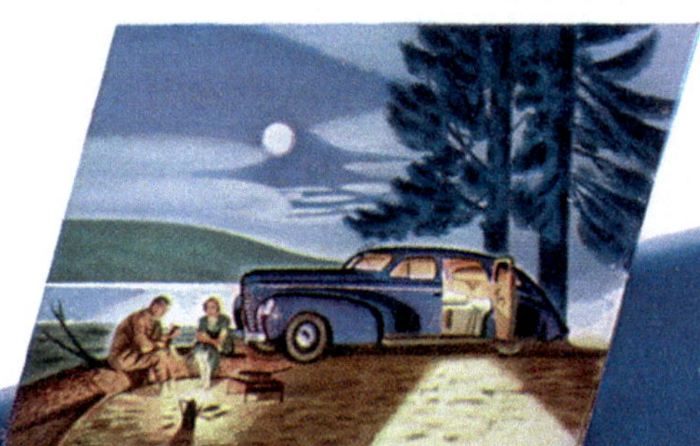

500 MILES a day is an easy, delightful trip. Then you can sleep in your Nash—in a double bed.

It's that New NASH

Put Yourself in This Picture

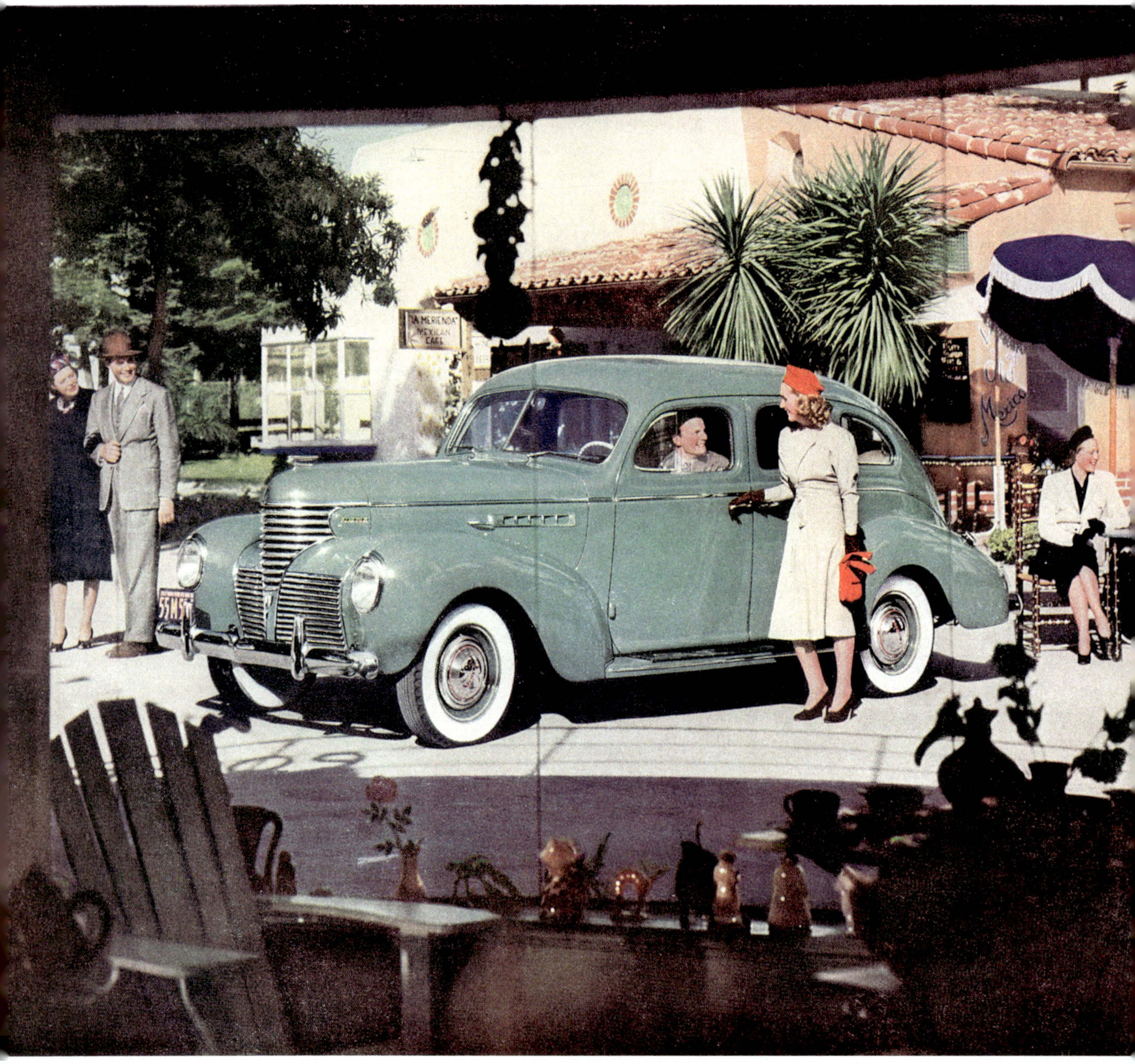

It is happening in Hollywood . . . all over America . . . and it can happen right in front of your own home. We mean that honest-to-goodness kick you get when heads turn, necks crane, and people stop . . . and stare.

That thrill is yours . . . in De Soto—America's smartest low-priced car. Notice the headlamps flush in the fenders, wisely declaring the car's full width to oncoming drivers at night. A streamlined luggage locker provides more room . . . obsoletes the old-fashioned trunk bulge.

A higher, wider windshield and bigger windows increase visibility . . . make driving safer. Giant, Constant-Speed Windshield Wipers eliminate "peephole" driving . . . take the guesswork out of rainy weather travel.

Four inches wider in front, De Soto's roomy body takes the squeeze out of three-in-front driving. Overall, there's elbow room for six big adults on luxuriously-cushioned sofa-wide seats. The shifting lever is gone from the floor... providing more leg room. You flick your way from low to high easily and quickly with the new Handy-Shift on the steering column.

But that's not half the story. Beneath De Soto's sleek streamlining is the renowned dependability of Chrysler Corporation engineering. See De Soto today! It offers you real pride of ownership at a surprisingly low cost.

Easy to own...your present car will probably represent a large part of De Soto's low delivered price; balance in low monthly instalments. De Soto Division of Chrysler Corporation, Detroit, Michigan.

Tune in Major Bowes' Amateur Hour, Colum
Network, Thursdays, 9 to 10 P. M., E. S. T

DE SOTO

America's Smartes
Low-Priced Car

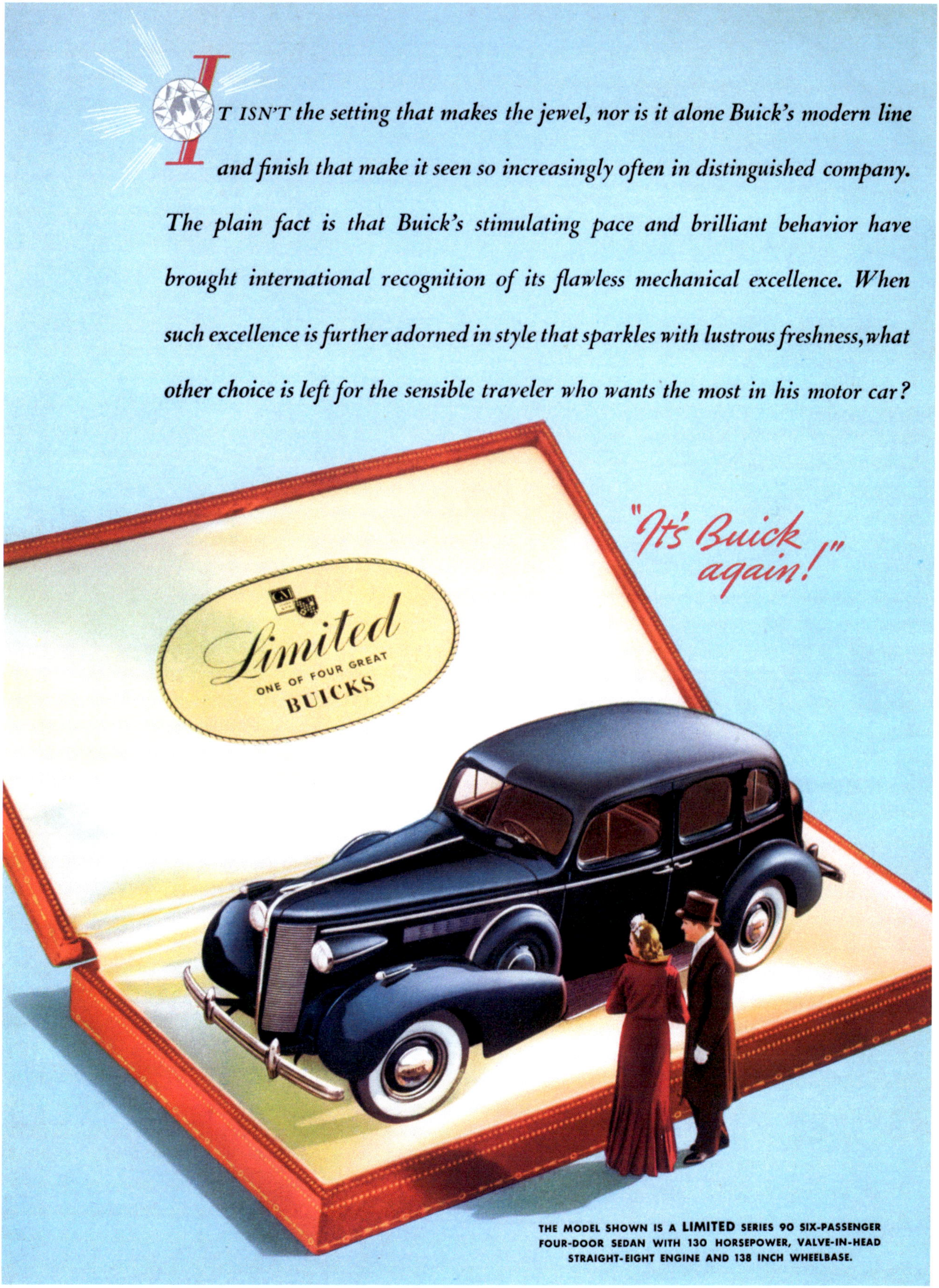

De Soto, 1939 ◄

Buick, 1937

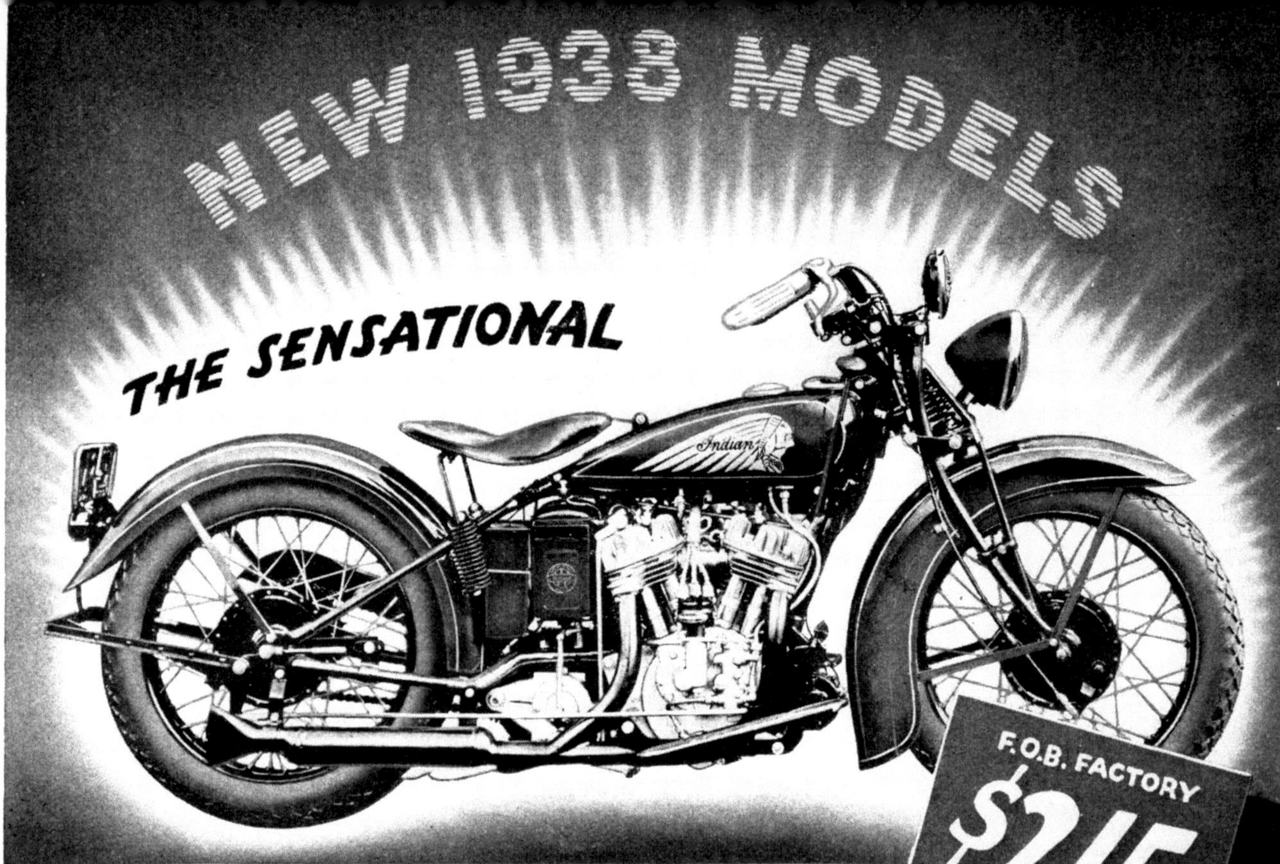

Indian JUNIOR SCOUT

THE TWIN CYLINDER MOTORCYCLE MARVEL

THE NEW 1938 INDIANS ARE READY to flash you over the open road to fun and adventure! New Indian triumphs, all of them—great motorcycles built as only Indian can build them.

Heading the parade is the new Indian Junior Scout—the greatest twin cylinder "buy" in all motorcycle-dom! It's a great machine—an engineering marvel easy to handle, easy to start, with plenty of power and pep to flash you along with the leaders. And it costs so little to run—*you'll get 70 miles to the gallon easily!*

NOW OWN AN INDIAN ON EASY PAYMENTS

The Junior Scout is still the lowest priced "twin" in America! So why wait? Visit your Indian dealer today and let him tell you how easy it is to own any Indian model on easy payments.

3 OTHER '38 MODELS

DE LUXE 4—the only four cylinder motorcycle made in America—quiet, smooth, comfortable.

CHIEF 74—for the rider who places a premium on "top speed" and performance.

SPORT SCOUT—a racing model for the man who wants to be a winner in sporting events, an easy-to-handle machine that's "out in front" always.

Get this fine RIDER'S HELMET and INDIAN PIN absolutely FREE when you place your order.

BOY—HOW THEY TRAVEL!

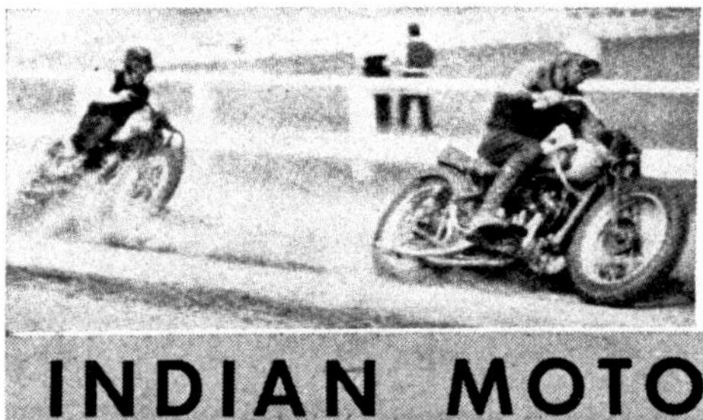

Don't forget our great FREE OFFER

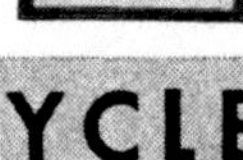

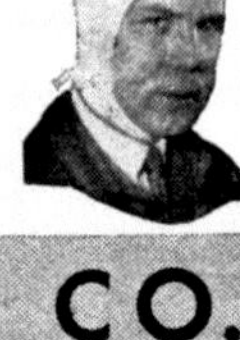

MAIL COUPON TODAY!

INDIAN MOTOCYCLE CO., Springfield, Mass.

Please send me at once, without obligation, your illustrated Folder showing the new 1938 Indian Motocycles, and CERTIFICATE of VALUE entitling me to FREE RIDER'S HELMET and INDIAN PIN, as illustrated, when I place my order.

Name..........

Address..........

Please be sure to check your age group: PSM 1

☐ 16-19 years ☐ 20-30 years ☐ 31 years and up ☐ under 16 years

INDIAN MOTOCYCLE CO., Springfield, Mass.

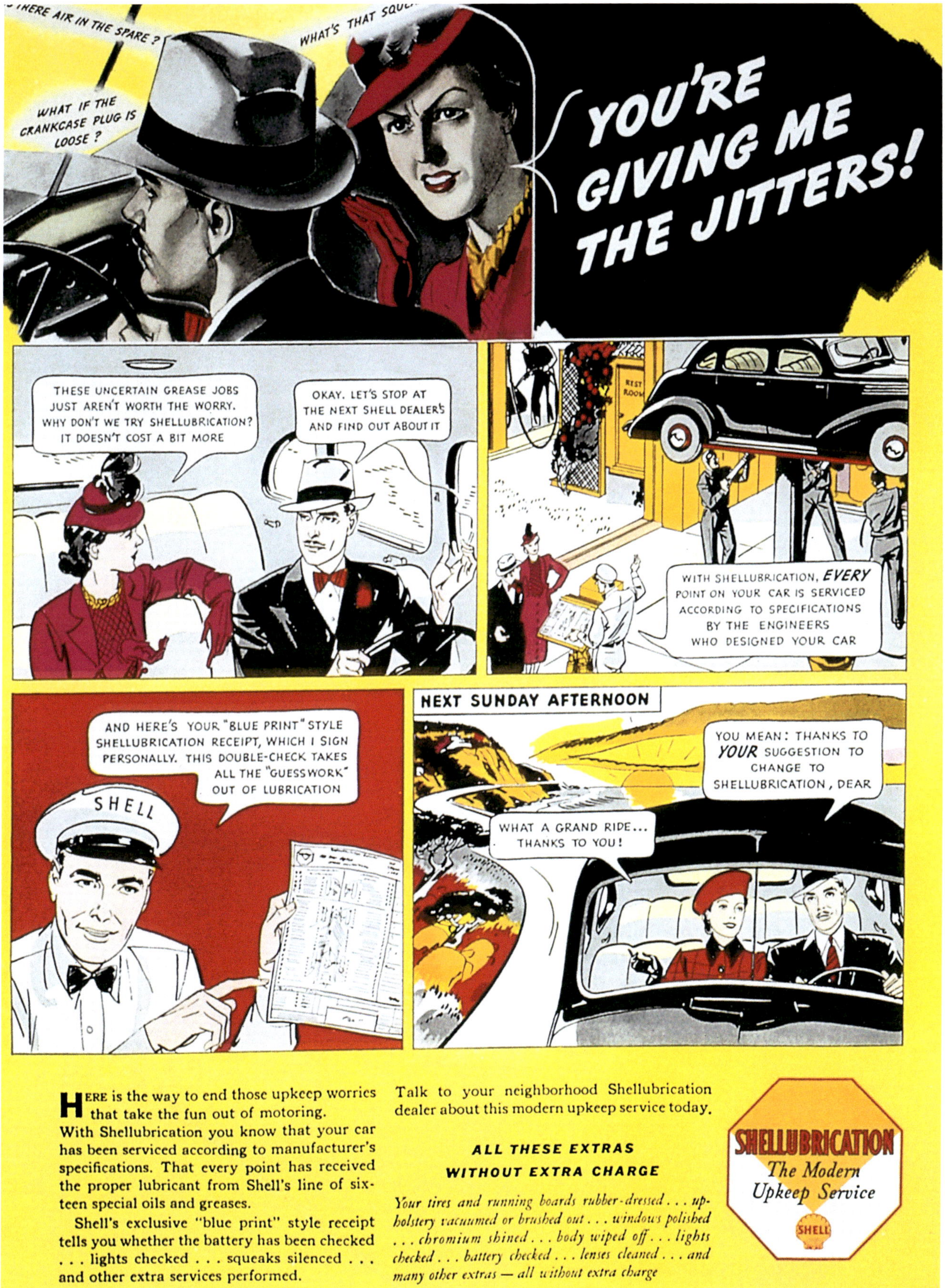

Indian Motocycle, 1938 ◂

Shell, 1938 ▸▸ Cadillac, 1939

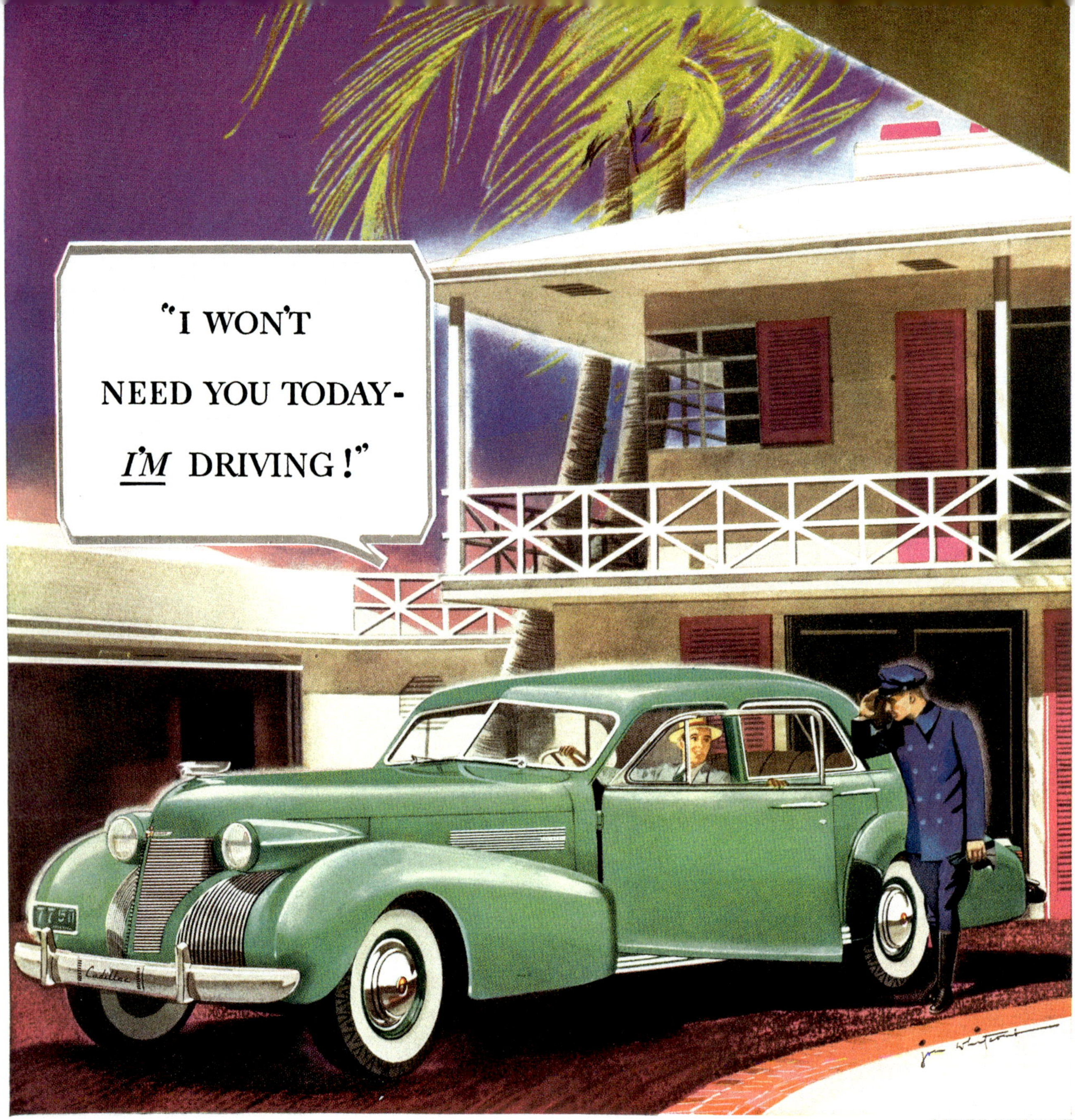

A GENERAL MOTORS VALUE

THE CADILLAC SIXTY SPECIAL is the most fascinating car to drive in all the world.

This is the verdict of owners without number—many of whom have driven every car of reputation the market affords.

Indeed, hundreds who had vowed they would never again drive a motor car have gone back to the wheel with a whoop—in charge of their Cadillac Sixty Specials.

It is hard to explain what happens in a Sixty Special that *doesn't* happen in other cars—for the difference encompasses *everything*.

First of all, there's the marvelous smoothness of the engine. The throttle feels like velvet under your foot, and the steering wheel is as kind to your hand as a chamois glove.

Then there's the way the car rides the road. You don't bobble, you don't sidesway, you don't roll. You just settle down like Man o' War on the home stretch and stick tight to the pavement. It's a tremendous sensation.

And how you snuggle down into those seats! Your favorite chair at the club was never more inviting. It's the most *relaxing* ride you can imagine.

And the *time* you make is terrific—yet you do it without once showing a heavy foot. The car is simply so quick and nimble and well-balanced that you post a high average without excessive speed.

Yes—this car is an experience. And it's an experience no man who loves a motor car should ever think of missing.

How about it for you? Your Cadillac dealer has the Sixty Special. All you need do is provide the time—and name the place.

THE NEW

CADILLAC
Sixty
SPECIAL

Also, see the Cadillac Sixty-One—the lowest-priced Cadillac for 1939. Its remarkable performance and luxurious riding comfort make it a worthy companion car to the famous Sixty Special. Your Cadillac dealer will be happy to demonstrate both cars at your convenience.

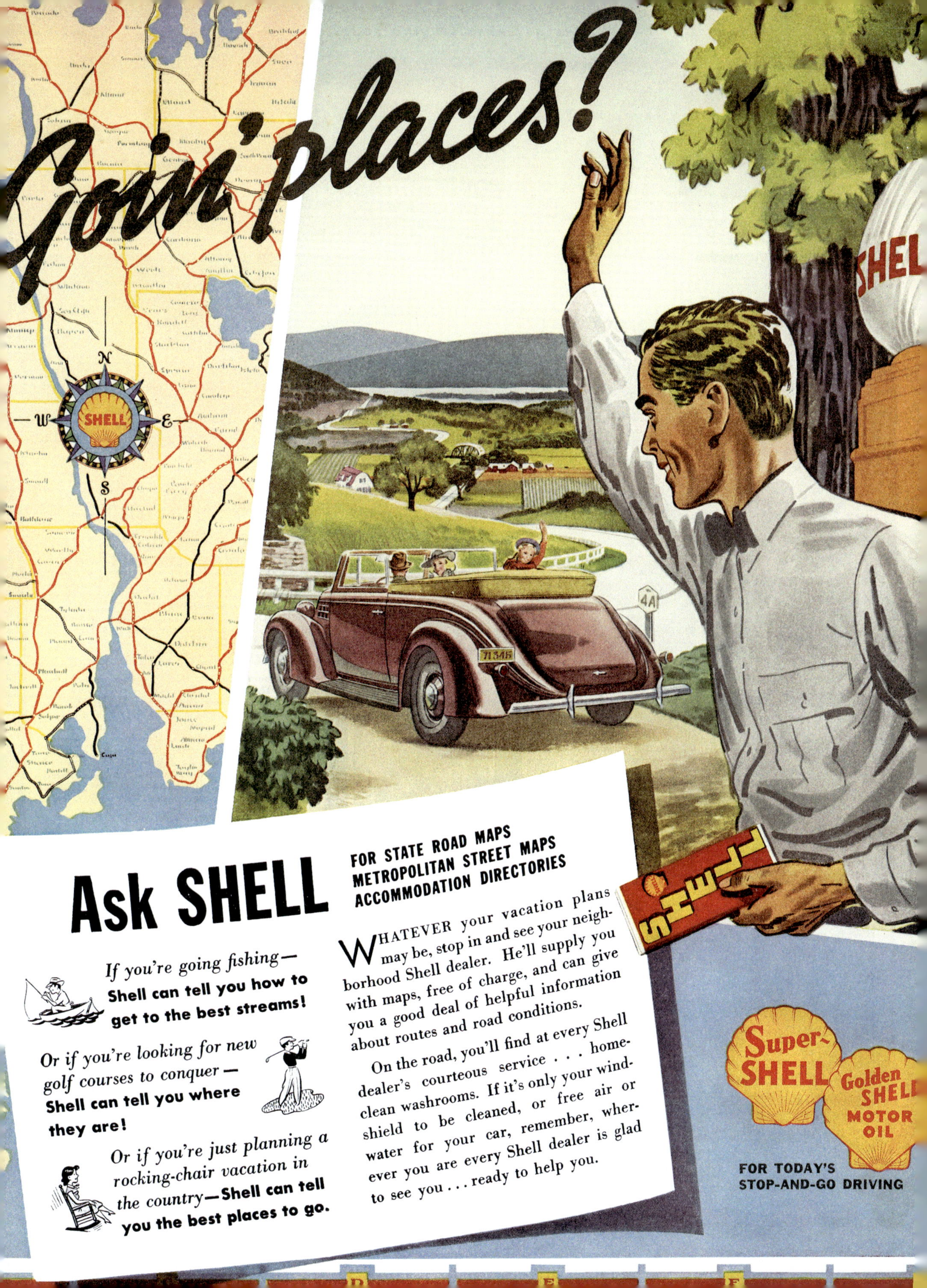

Goin' places?
SHELL
N
S
E
W
4A
71345
SHELL
Ask SHELL
FOR STATE ROAD MAPS
METROPOLITAN STREET MAPS
ACCOMMODATION DIRECTORIES
If you're going fishing—Shell can tell you how to get to the best streams!
Or if you're looking for new golf courses to conquer—Shell can tell you where they are!
Or if you're just planning a rocking-chair vacation in the country—Shell can tell you the best places to go.
WHATEVER your vacation plans may be, stop in and see your neighborhood Shell dealer. He'll supply you with maps, free of charge, and can give you a good deal of helpful information about routes and road conditions.
On the road, you'll find at every Shell dealer's courteous service . . . home-clean washrooms. If it's only your windshield to be cleaned, or free air or water for your car, remember, wherever you are every Shell dealer is glad to see you . . . ready to help you.
Super-SHELL
Golden SHELL MOTOR OIL
FOR TODAY'S STOP-AND-GO DRIVING

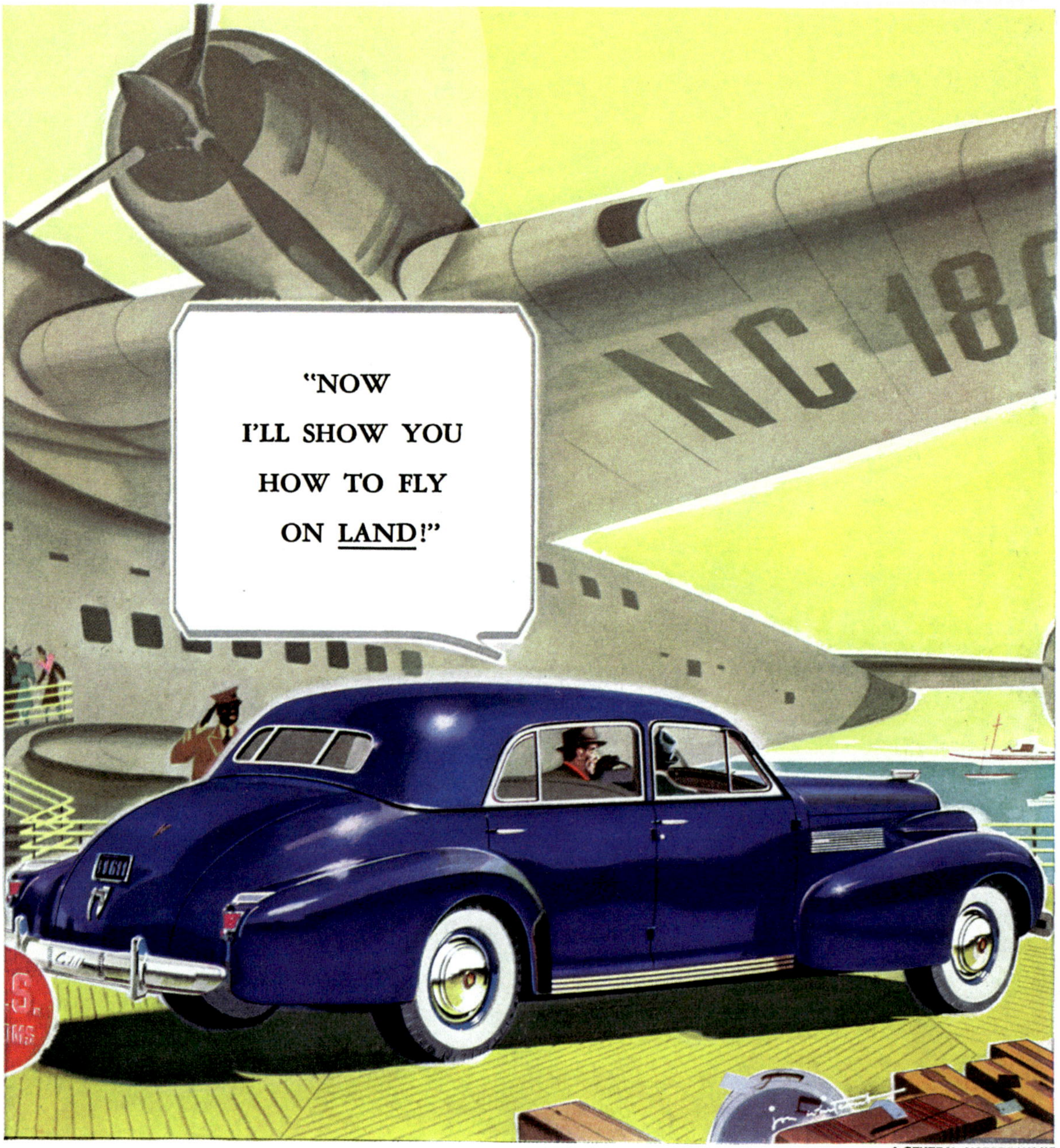

A GENERAL MOTORS VALUE

MOST PEOPLE WHO purchase the Cadillac Sixty Special are attracted, first of all, by its striking appearance. Without doubt, it is the most distinctive car in America.

But when they take the wheel, they find yet *another* reason for choosing the Sixty Special . . . and a big one, too. We refer to its unduplicated performance. It is not merely that the Sixty Special is dynamic in acceleration and unbelievably smooth in operation—the *whole conception* of its performance is different. The way it rides . . . the way it hugs the road . . . the way it handles in traffic . . . *everything* is delightfully different.

Only a ride can fully reveal what this difference means in terms of additional satisfaction. It actually makes all other performance seem commonplace by comparison.

May we prove this—by an extended road demonstration? Your Cadillac dealer has the car. Just tell him the time—and place. He will do the rest.

THE NEW

CADILLAC *Sixty* SPECIAL

Also, see the new Cadillac Sixty-One—the lowest-priced Cadillac for 1939—available in four body types. Its remarkable performance and luxurious riding comfort make it a worthy companion car to the famous Sixty Special. Your Cadillac dealer will be happy to demonstrate both cars at your convenience.

Shell, 1938 ◂◂ *Cadillac, 1938*

Young Henry Ford went to the Fair

It was summer, 1893. The Chicago World's Fair was crowded, clamorous, exciting. But a thirty-year-old mechanic named Ford forgot everything else as he studied a small gasoline engine mounted on a fire hosecart. He had been working a long time to develop just such a power-plant. Here was proof that his plans were sound! He hurried home to his little shop in Detroit, and by 1896 produced a horseless carriage that would really run.

OUT of that early Fair came a Ford *conviction*, as well as a Ford car. The conviction that expositions are *education*. The conviction that if you show men's most advanced ideas to the minds of other men, progress is inevitable and everybody benefits.

That's why the Ford Motor Company has been a big exhibitor at every important fair since its founding. And that's why Ford is one of the largest industrial exhibitors at the New York World's Fair this year.

Mr. Ford believes that all these exhibits will help eager young people to gain inspiration and knowledge for inventions that will be as important to the world of tomorrow as mass motor car production has been to the world of today.

You are cordially invited to visit the Ford Building, shown below.

Here a ride on the Road of Tomorrow will give you a grand view of the entire Fair. Here you can watch the complete cycle of Ford production on a tremendous turntable, with striking lighting and moving figures. Here, too, you'll see the world's first animated mural, and many actual production and testing operations which highlight the quality of all Ford-built cars.

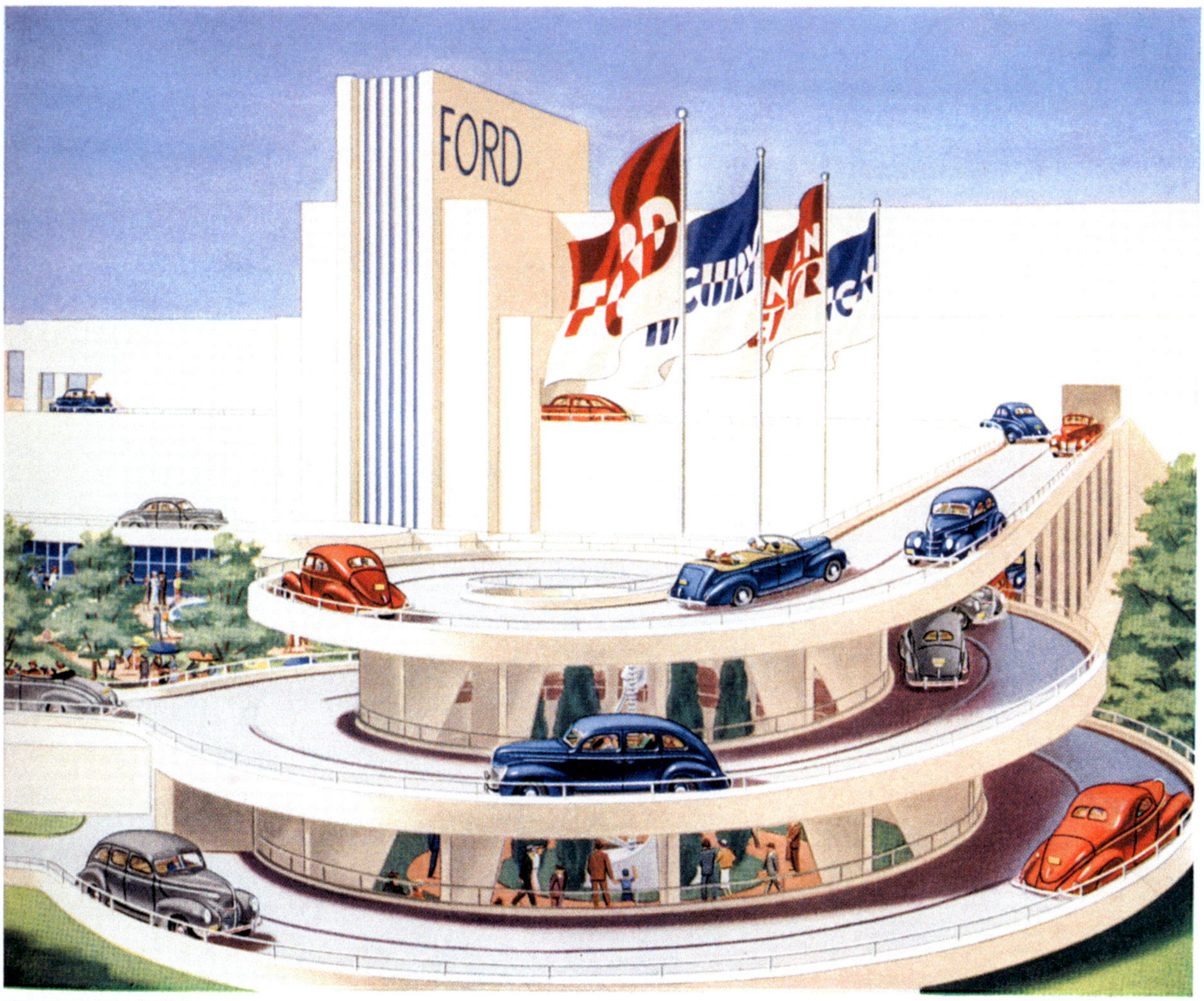

The Ford Building, above, also appears in section D6 of the World's Fair Map which occupies the next two pages. This view shows part of the Road of Tomorrow and the elm-shaded patio, where visitors may rest and relax.

New International DELIVERY TRUCKS

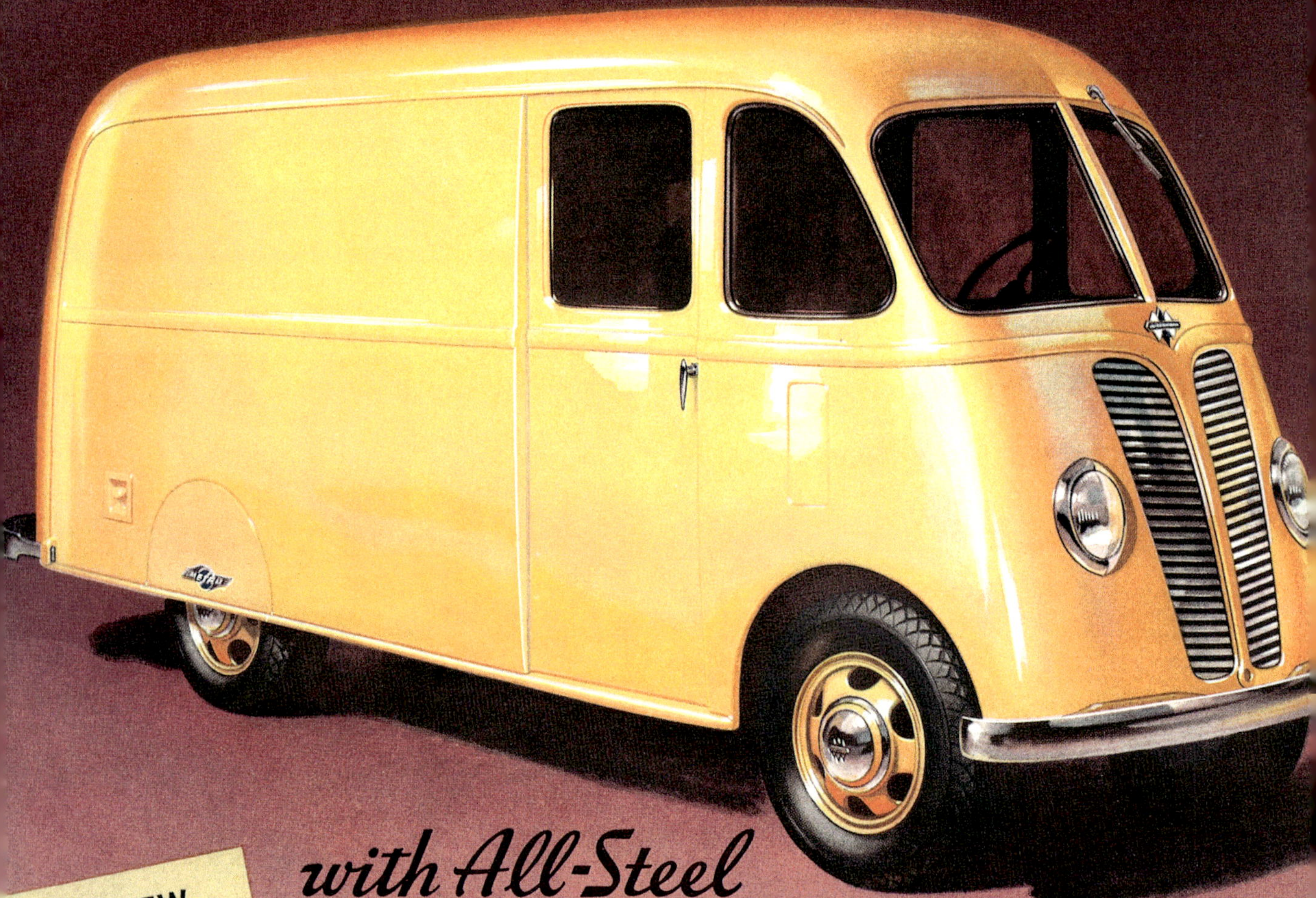

with All-Steel ... Streamlined METRO *Bodies*

TWO NEW CHASSIS

These new International Trucks with Metro Bodies are new in every respect—completely International designed and built. They are not so-called body-builders' conversions.

D-2-M

½-ton Chassis in 2 wheelbase lengths: 102-inch, for the 7½-foot body; and 113-inch, for the 9½-foot body.

D-15-M

¾- to 1-ton Chassis in 2 wheelbase lengths: 102-inch, for the 7½-foot body; and 113-inch, for the 9½-foot body.

Double the cubic capacity of the standard panel body on the same wheelbase length is now offered you in these new International Trucks with the new Metro Bodies.

And only in these two International Trucks can you get these new Metro Bodies.

There are no fenders, no running boards, no hood. There is a smooth floor, a greater area for loads, better distribution of weight. Modern insulation throughout; refrigerator insulation also available.

These new trucks handle easier, park easier and in less space. They are easier on the driver, because they are easier to drive, easier to get in and out of, easier to load and unload. There are wider doors, there is more headroom, the driver is farther front, the gear-shift control is on the steering column, and there is greater visibility.

Never before, to our knowledge, have streamlined beauty, increased utility, and absolute economy been combined to greater advantage for multi-stop service.

If this does not happen to be the type of truck you need in your business; if you need just a small half-ton pick-up or a great powerful 6-wheel dump, or any size or type in between, you will find it in the complete International line.

There's an International Dealer or Branch in your immediate vicinity—ready and eager to demonstrate the right International chassis and the correct International body for increasing your trucking efficiency and profit.

INTERNATIONAL HARVESTER COMPANY
(INCORPORATED)
180 North Michigan Avenue Chicago, Illinois

INTERNATIONAL TRUCKS

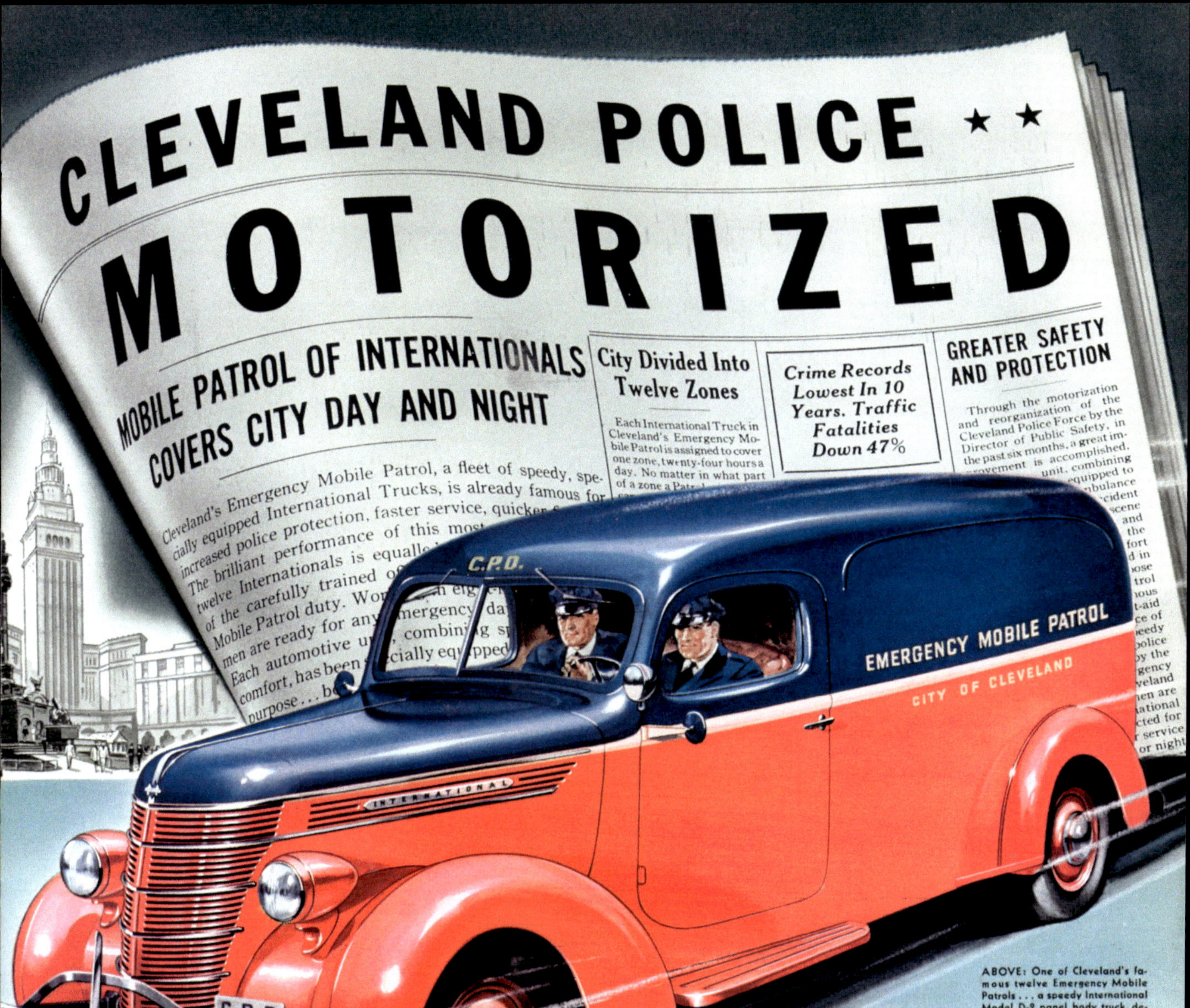

ABOVE: One of Cleveland's famous twelve Emergency Mobile Patrols . . . a speedy International Model D-2 panel body truck, designed for both ambulance and patrol service. All twelve have radio receiving sets, heaters, sirens, spotlights, and police identifying lights.

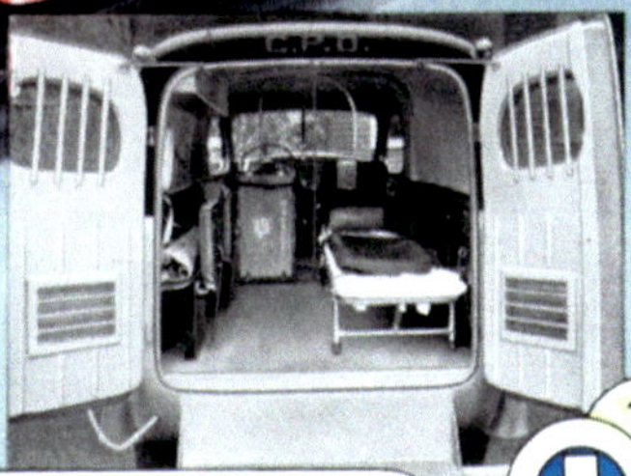

LEFT: Interior of specially built, two-seated Emergency Mobile Patrol Truck showing steel floor, special rear step, barred rear doors, heavy screen partition behind driving compartment.

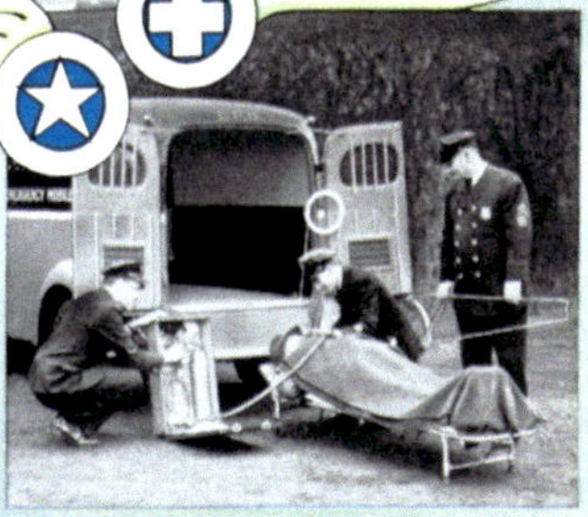

ABOVE: Each unit is a complete ambulance with finest riding comfort. Equipment includes first-aid kit, inhalator, stretcher, and all other accessories required for emergency rescue work.

CLEVELAND is prouder than ever of its Police Force hich is now entirely motorized with the exception of e traffic detail.

The city's Emergency Mobile Patrol is making history helping daily in the reduction of crime and traffic fatal-es. The entire nation is focusing its attention on this asterly stroke of police-pioneering.

Twelve motor units, fully equipped for double-duty ser-ce as ambulances and patrols, are manned by officers all of hom have hospital and first-aid training. Many of them are llege graduates. The proved results in greater safety and rvice of this innovation in patrol work are spectacular.

All twelve of these new Cleveland Police Patrols are ternational Model D-2 panel body trucks. And the per-rmance of these Internationals is thoroughly in keeping ith the reputation Internationals have established for economy, durability and dependability in every line of work.

That kind of performance and that reputation explain why International Harvester sells more heavy-duty trucks, 2-ton and up, than any other three truck manufacturers combined.

What does *your* business require in truck service or hauling? Whether you're a grocer or a farmer, a baker or a builder, there's an International designed for your special needs. The International Dealer or Branch nearest you is ready at any time to demonstrate International top performance, rock-bottom economy, and brilliant appearance.

INTERNATIONAL HARVESTER COMPANY
(INCORPORATED)
180 North Michigan Avenue Chicago, Illinois

INTERNATIONAL TRUCKS

Why Spencer Tracy Owns a De Soto!

IT'S ONE LOW-PRICED CAR THAT OFFERS:

1. BIG SIZE—Plenty of room for six big adults...more space for luggage...actually 23 cubic feet of luggage room.

2. STREAMLINE STYLING—De Soto's design will be modern for years. Smarter now...adds to resale value later.

AND REMEMBER, DESOTO IS EASY TO BUY—Your present car will probably represent a large part of De Soto's low price.

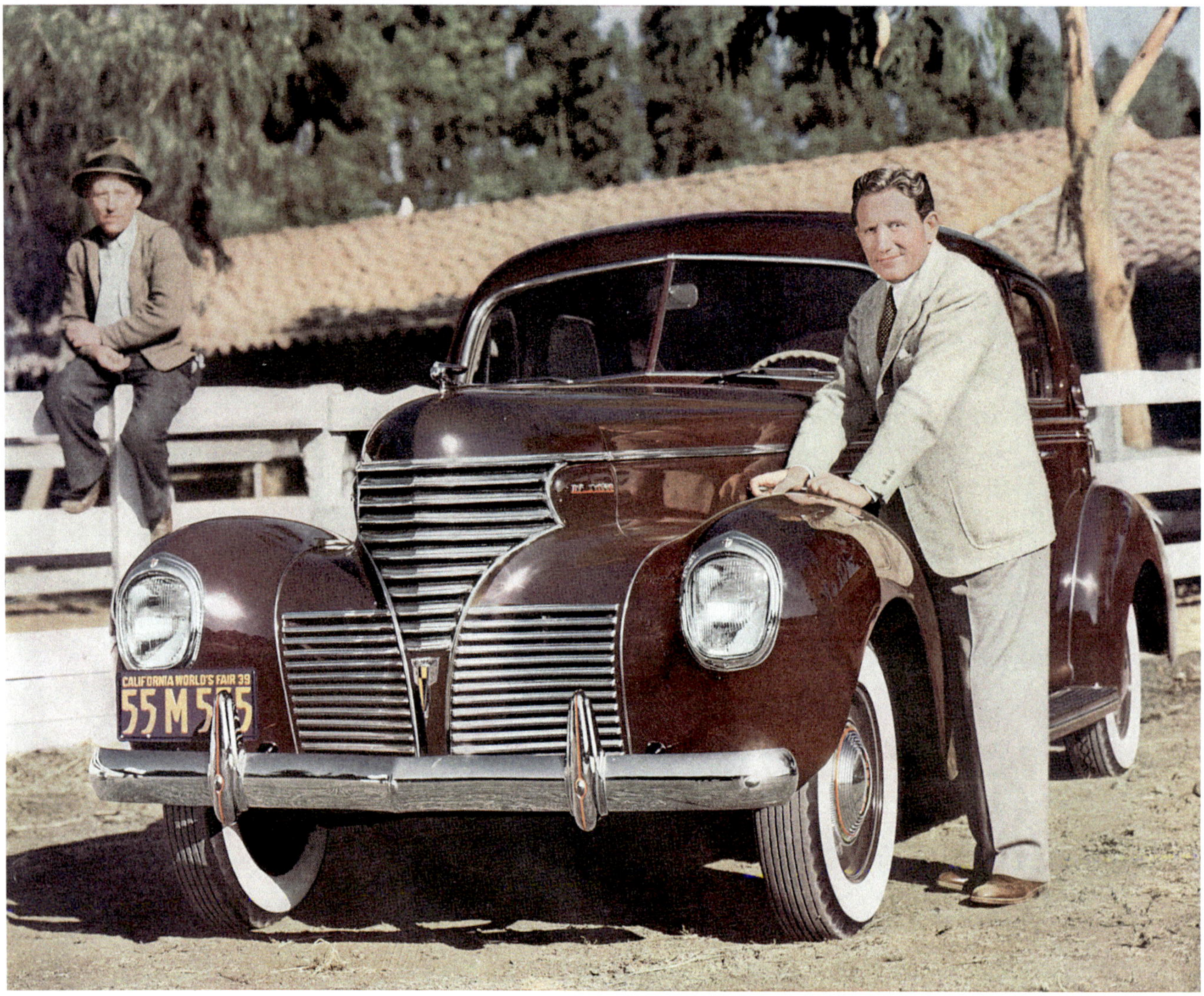

Actor, polo player, Spencer Tracy talked a lot of "horse sense" when he chose his new De Soto—"She looks great, but has she got it?"

"Try it," we urged. He did. And liked it. And today De Soto is his car!

Nimble as a colt, De Soto answers the Tracy call for action. A hint of pressure on the throttle sends it winging down the road from Mr. Tracy's home to the Riviera Country Club. With a one-two-three flick of the Handy-Shift, you're from first, second, to high.

But safety first! Right there on the dash De Soto's Safety-Signal Speedometer becomes a reminding red. It shows green from 0 to 30; amber from 30 to 50; and red on up. Ingenious? It eliminates back-seat drivers!

There's more room, too. The De Soto body is 4 inches wider at the front, with no gear-lever to take up floor space. Six big adults ride in relaxed comfort. The windshield is bigger, increasing visibility. Giant, Constant-Speed Electric Windshield Wipers give you the low-down on highways in rainy weather.

And smart! Streamlining eliminates the old-fashioned trunk bulge...gives you much more luggage space...makes De Soto a beauty, coming or going.

Find out yourself how easy it is to own the most beautiful low-priced car in America. De Soto Division of Chrysler Corporation, Detroit, Michigan.

Tune in Major Bowes' Original Amateur Hour, Columbia Network, Thursdays, 9 to 10 p.m., E.S.T.

ABSOLUTELY THE MOST BEAUTIFUL LOW-PRICED CAR IN AMERICA

De Soto

WATCH FOR SPENCER TRACY, POPULAR M-G-M STAR, IN HIS NEXT PICTURE.

De Soto, 1939

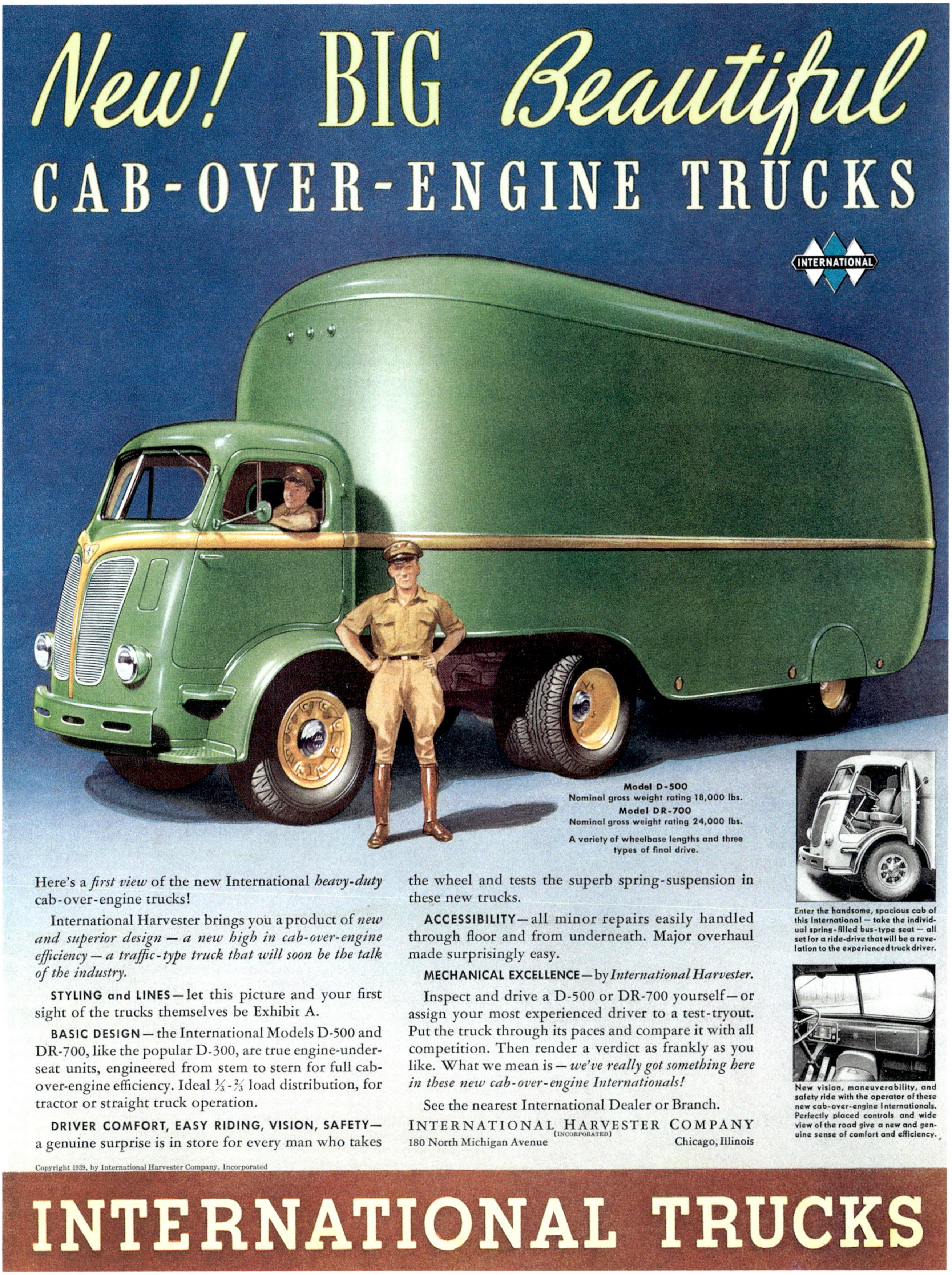

International Trucks, 1939

And the winner is...

A Dollar Saved Is a Dollar Earned

Known primarily for their motorcycles, Indian Motorcyle Co. offered a three-wheeled vehicle that both dispatched mechanics on calls and served as an advertising device and status symbol. Selling the image of a modern, efficient business was deemed as important as the dependability of a vehicle in the lean 1930s. Novelty factor withstanding, the claims of this ad serve as a reminder to the gas-guzzling twenty-first century that you don't need a Hummer® to get the job done.

Ein gesparter Dollar ist ein verdienter Dollar

In erster Linie für ihre Motorräder bekannt, bot die Indian Motorcycle Co. auch dieses dreirädrige Gefährt an. Es sollte Mechaniker zu ihren Notfällen kutschieren und gleichzeitig als Werbemittel und Statussymbol dienen. In den finanziell klammen Dreißigern war ein modernes, effizientes Image mindestens so verkaufsfördernd wie die Zuverlässigkeit eines Fahrzeugs. Vom Skurrilitätsfaktor einmal abgesehen: Die Anzeige ist für die verschwendungssüchtigen Amerikaner auch insofern nicht uninteressant, als sie daran erinnert, dass benzinschluckende Monster eine lange Tradition haben.

Un dollar épargné est un dollar gagné

Surtout connu pour ses motos, Indian Motorcycle Co. proposa dans les années 30 un véhicule à trois roues servant à la fois de moyen de transport aux mécaniciens dépanneurs, de support publicitaire et de signe extérieur de réussite. En ces années de vaches maigres, afficher une image d'entreprise moderne et efficace était aussi important que de pouvoir dépendre d'un véhicule fiable. Au-delà de l'aspect gadget, cette publicité rappelle au 21e siècle grand amateur de pétrole qu'on peut être efficace sans consommer beaucoup d'essence.

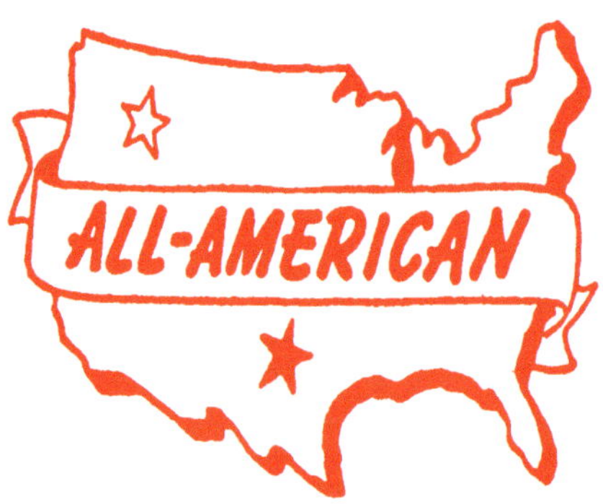

Indian Motocycle Co., 1937

GREATEST MONEY MAKER EVER OFFERED SERVICE STATIONS

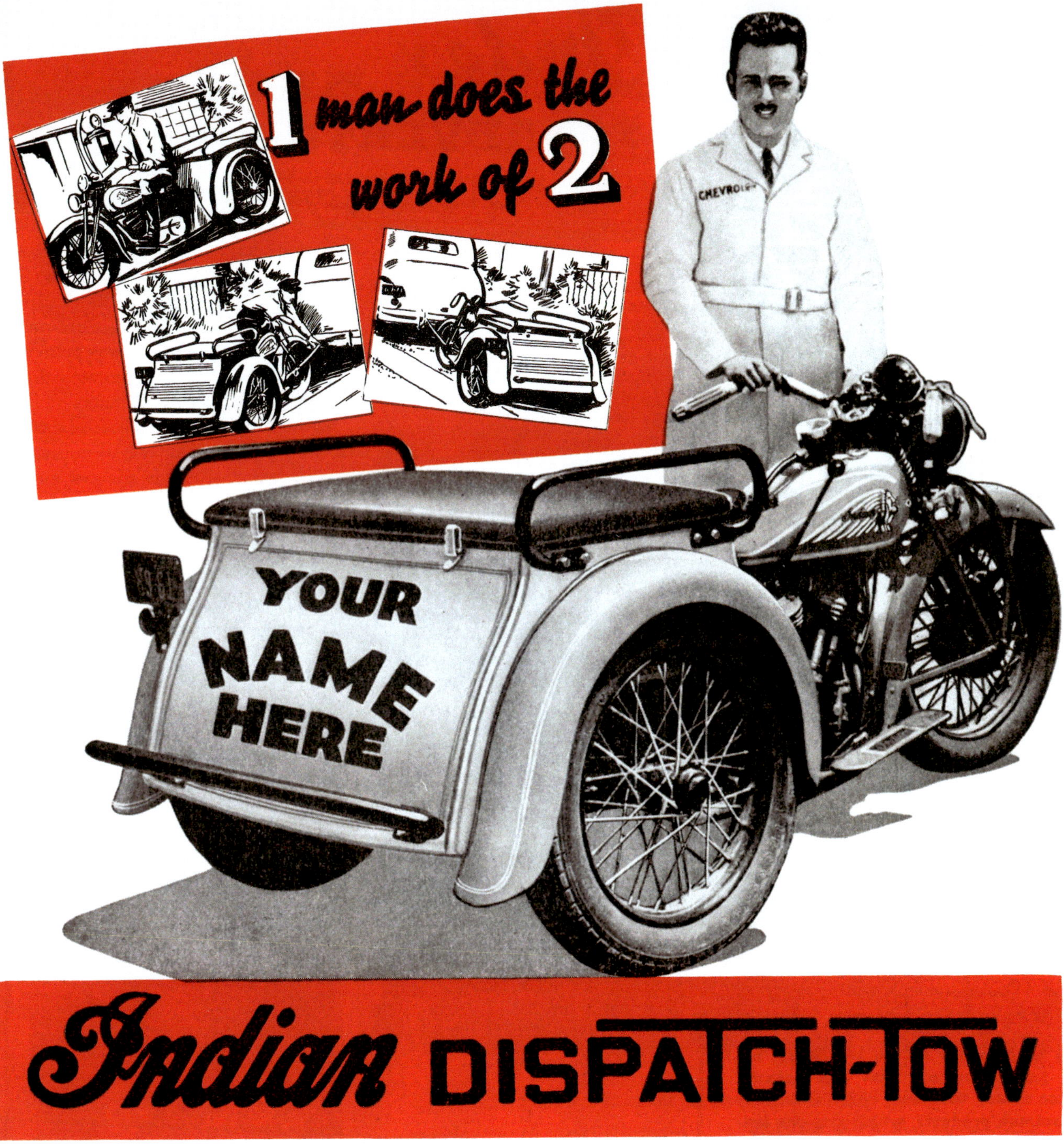

Indian DISPATCH-TOW

PROGRESSIVE SERVICE STATIONS use this modern equipment to *speed service, save time, cut costs.* Indian Dispatch-Tow makes pick up and delivery just a one-man job—releasing a man for more profitable work. Outside servicing costs are cut two-thirds through lower overhead, saved time, saved man-power. Dependable Dispatch-Tow costs only about 1c a mile to operate, turns idle hours into profitable working time.

BIG ADVERTISING VALUE—MONEY MAKER

Service stations are judged by the equipment they keep. Your name on an Indian Dispatch-Tow flashing about town is not only great advertising — it also stamps your station as efficient and modern. You can give better service at smaller cost—win new customers, make more money—with snappy Indian Dispatch-Tow service. *Write for proof based on experience,* and complete information. Address Dept. SS-7.

INDIAN MOTOCYCLE CO., *Springfield, Mass.*

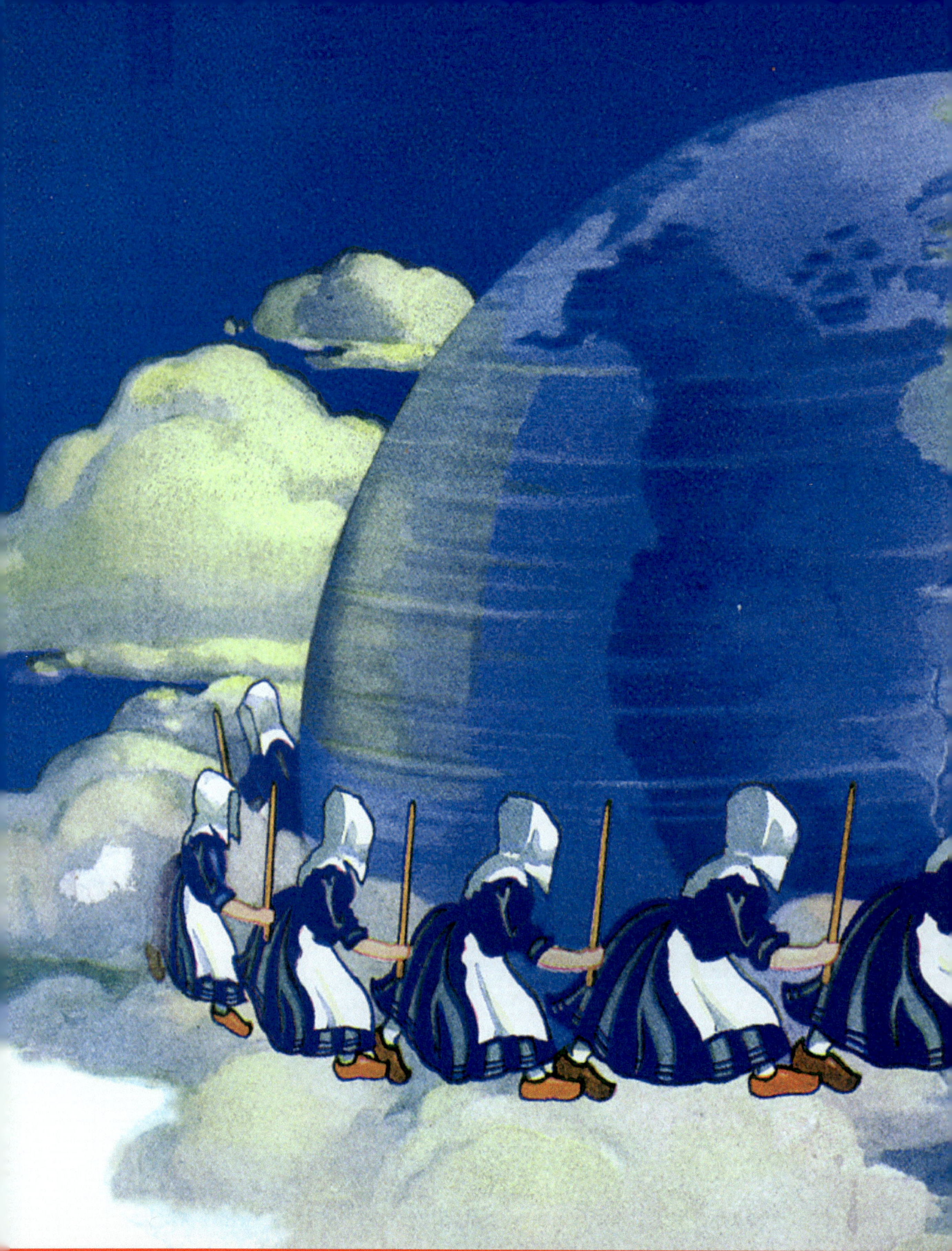

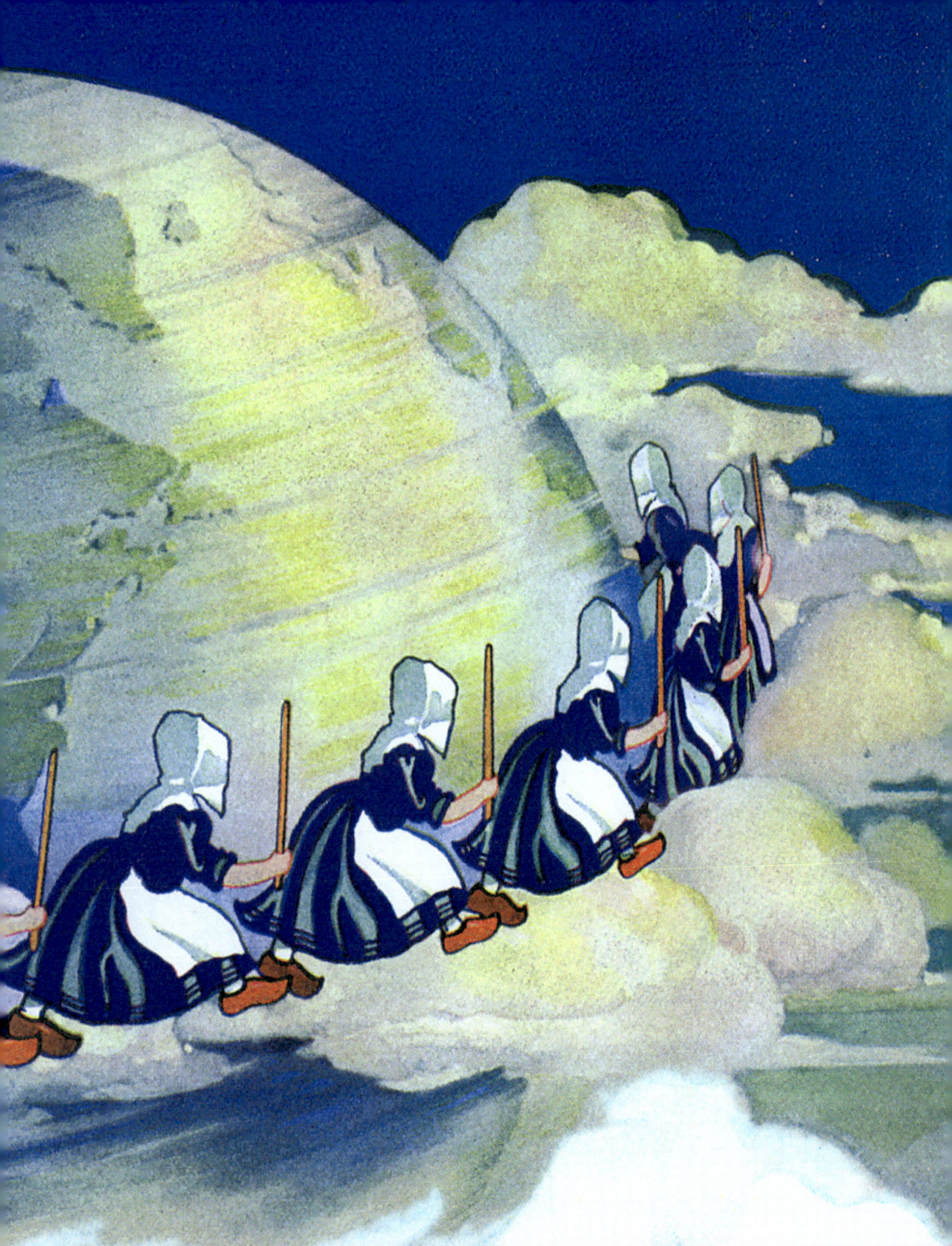

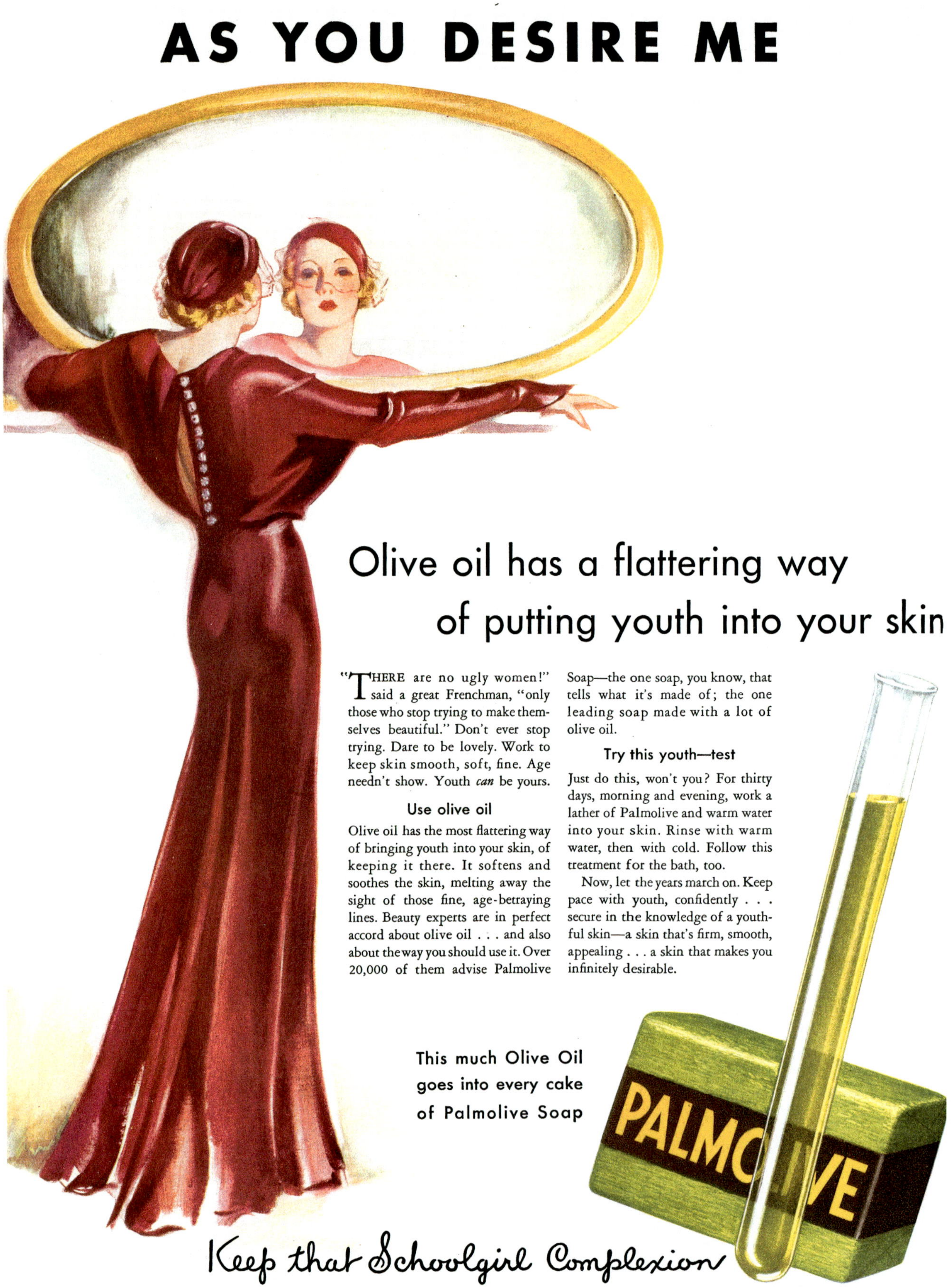

Old Dutch Girl, 1931 ◂◂ *Palmolive, 1933*

▸ *Ivory Flakes, 1937*

FREE $30,000 CASH

nd 15,000 PAIRS of $1.35 Silk Stockings

(GOTHAM GOLD STRIPE ADJUSTABLES)

6 Big Weekly Contests

ENTER EACH WEEK . . . 7530 PRIZES IN ALL!

FIVE $1000 CASH PRIZES EACH WEEK

ALSO EACH WEEK 1250 PRIZES OF 2 PAIRS OF $1.35 GOTHAM GOLD STRIPE SILK STOCKINGS

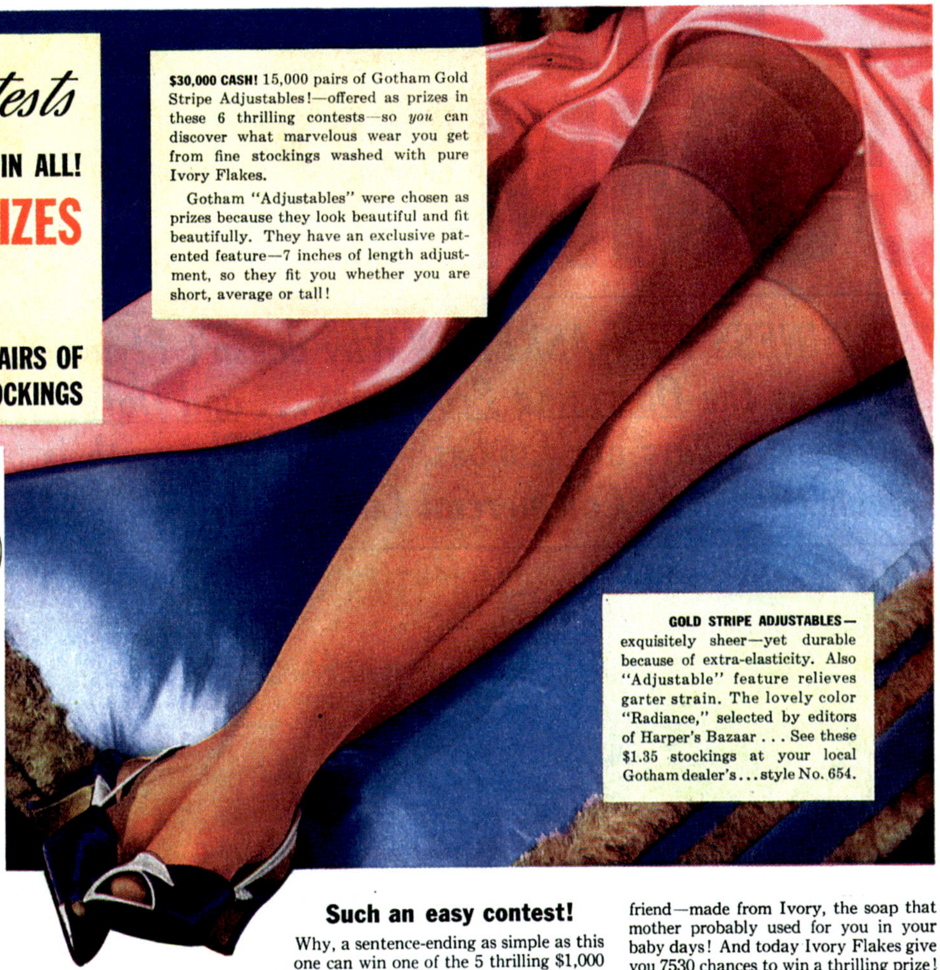

$30,000 CASH! 15,000 pairs of Gotham Gold Stripe Adjustables!—offered as prizes in these 6 thrilling contests—so *you* can discover what marvelous wear you get from fine stockings washed with pure Ivory Flakes.

Gotham "Adjustables" were chosen as prizes because they look beautiful and fit beautifully. They have an exclusive patented feature—7 inches of length adjustment, so they fit you whether you are short, average or tall!

GOLD STRIPE ADJUSTABLES— exquisitely sheer—yet durable because of extra-elasticity. Also "Adjustable" feature relieves garter strain. The lovely color "Radiance," selected by editors of Harper's Bazaar . . . See these $1.35 stockings at your local Gotham dealer's . . . style No. 654.

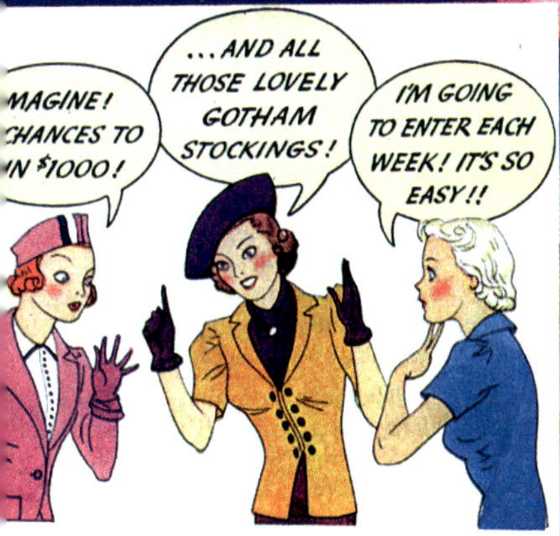

START NOW! COMPLETE THIS SENTENCE:

"I use Ivory Flakes washing my silk ckings because ______"

(IN 25 ADDITIONAL WORDS OR LESS)

G—GOING—a simply thrilling array of prizes! ances to win $1,000! 7500 chances to win 2 of luxurious Gotham Adjustables always sold 35 a pair!

ne! Here's a chance to tell what you know about tra-safety of pure Ivory Flakes! You probably know from personal experience how gentle Ivory Flakes are to colors, how safe they are for stockings because Ivory's famous purity keeps the silk springy and strong.

So don't hesitate. This is such an easy contest! Enter now—enter each week. Only 25 words or less may bring you one of the 7530 generous prizes!

Such an easy contest!

Why, a sentence-ending as simple as this one can win one of the 5 thrilling $1,000 cash prizes offered each and every week:

"I use Ivory Flakes for washing my silk stockings because my stockings keep their color and they wear longer, too, when they're protected by the purity of Ivory Flakes."

See how easy it is! Just sit down and let *yourself* talk. It's your experience we want, not fancy words. Write as to a friend. Because Ivory Flakes *are* your friend—made from Ivory, the soap that mother probably used for you in your baby days! And today Ivory Flakes give you 7530 chances to win a thrilling prize!

Listen to these RADIO PROGRAMS for more CONTEST NEWS!

"THE O'NEILLS"	"MARY MARLIN"
10:00 A.M. NBC Blue Network; 2:45 P.M. NBC Red Network	11:15 A.M. NBC Red Network; 4:00 P.M. NBC Blue Network

(All times Eastern Standard Time)

ENTRY BLANK

use Ivory Flakes for washing my lk stockings because ______________

"

FINISH THIS SENTENCE IN 25 ADDITIONAL WORDS . . . OR LESS)
RY FLAKES, Dept. S-57, Box 828, Cincinnati, Ohio
attach the top from one box of Ivory Flakes (or facsimile).

My stocking size is ________

IE ________
EET ________
Y. ________ STATE ________
dealer's name is ________

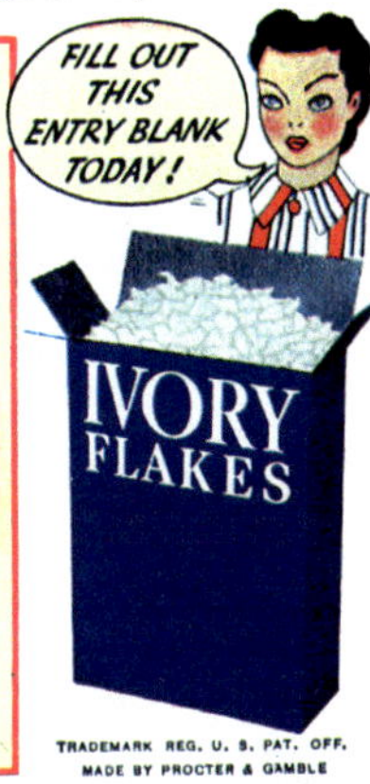

TRADEMARK REG. U. S. PAT. OFF.
MADE BY PROCTER & GAMBLE

FOLLOW THESE RULES

1. Finish the sentence shown on the entry blank in 25 additional words or less. Write your sentence on entry blank, or on one side of a sheet of paper, signing your name and address. Give the name of the dealer who sold you Ivory Flakes.

2. Attach the top from a box of Ivory Flakes (or a facsimile) to your entry. Mail to IVORY FLAKES, Dept. S-57, Box 828, Cincinnati, Ohio.

3. There will be 6 weekly contests, each with a separate list of prizes. Opening and closing dates are as follows:

	OPENING	CLOSING
1st Contest—	Now	Sat. May 29
2nd Contest—	Sun. May 30	Sat. June 5
3rd Contest—	Sun. June 6	Sat. June 12
4th Contest—	Sun. June 13	Sat. June 19
5th Contest—	Sun. June 20	Sat. June 26
6th Contest—	Sun. June 27	Sat. July 3

4. Entries for each week's contest must be postmarked before Saturday midnight. Entries will be entered in each week's contest as received.

5. Enter each week's contest as often as you choose.

6. Entries will be judged for clearness, sincerity, and individuality of thought. Your own words are most important. Fancy entries will not count extra. Contests judged by Miss Elsie Rushmore, National Contest Consultant, and her associates. Duplicate prizes awarded in case of ties. Entries, contents, and ideas therein become the property of Procter & Gamble. No entries returned.

7. Anyone may compete except employees of Procter & Gamble, their advertising agencies, and their families. Contests limited to the United States and subject to Federal, State and Local regulations.

8. Prizes in each weekly contest are: Five first prizes each of $1000 cash. Twelve hundred and fifty additional prizes of 2 pairs of Gotham Gold Stripe Adjustables "Radiance" shade, proper size.

9. Each dealer mentioned by the 30 cash prizewinners will also receive $50 in cash.

10. All $1000 prize-winners will be announced shortly after each contest closes, over "The O'Neills" radio program and "Mary Marlin."

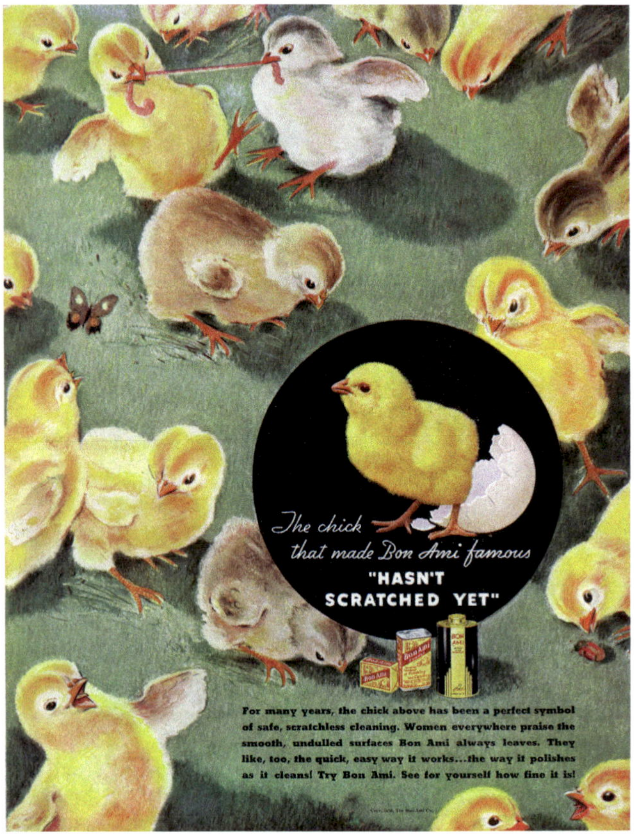

Bon Ami, 1935

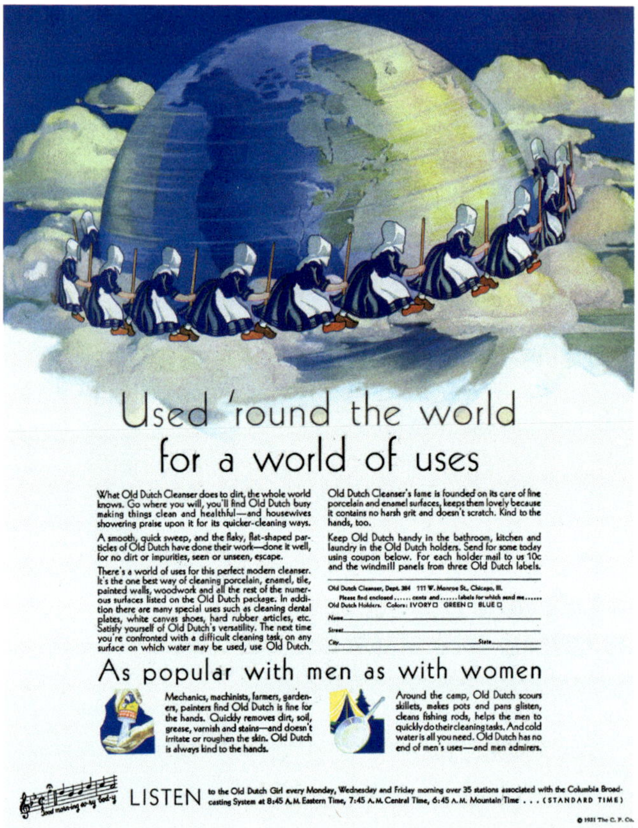

Old Dutch Girl, 1931

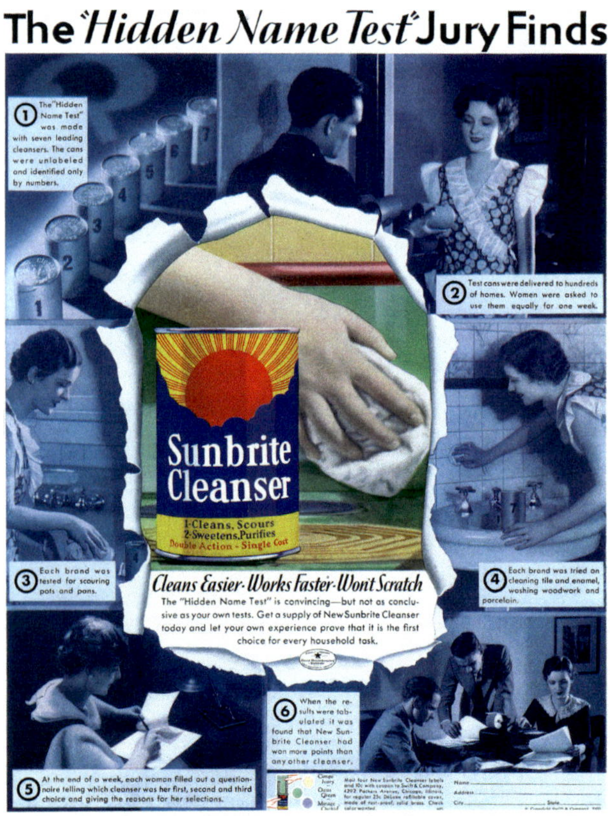

Sunbrite Cleanser, 1933

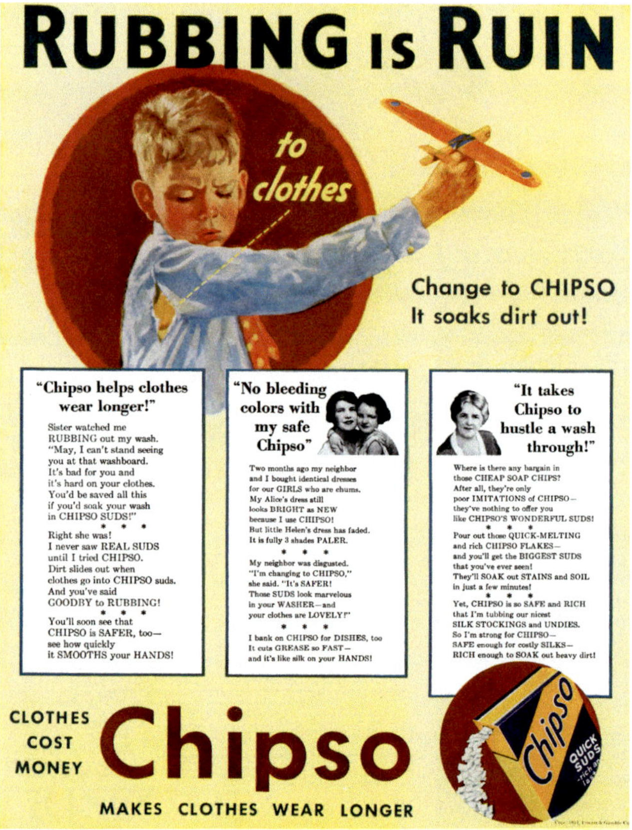

Chipso, 1932

▸ *Bon Ami, 1937*

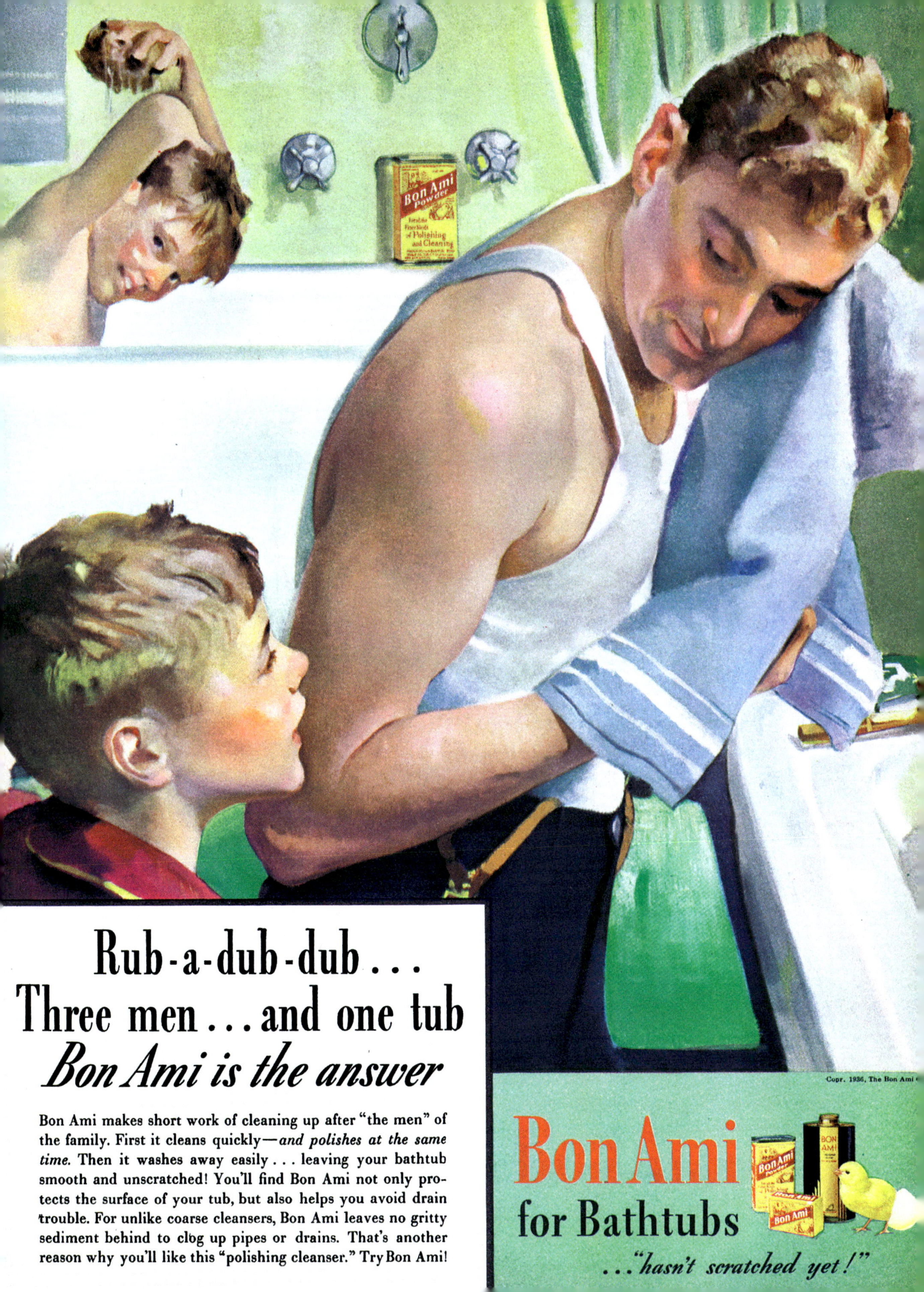
Rub-a-dub-dub . . .
Three men . . . and one tub
Bon Ami is the answer
Bon Ami makes short work of cleaning up after "the men" of the family. First it cleans quickly—*and polishes at the same time.* Then it washes away easily . . . leaving your bathtub smooth and unscratched! You'll find Bon Ami not only protects the surface of your tub, but also helps you avoid drain trouble. For unlike coarse cleansers, Bon Ami leaves no gritty sediment behind to clog up pipes or drains. That's another reason why you'll like this "polishing cleanser." Try Bon Ami!
Copr. 1936, The Bon Ami Co.
Bon Ami
for Bathtubs
. . . "hasn't scratched yet!"

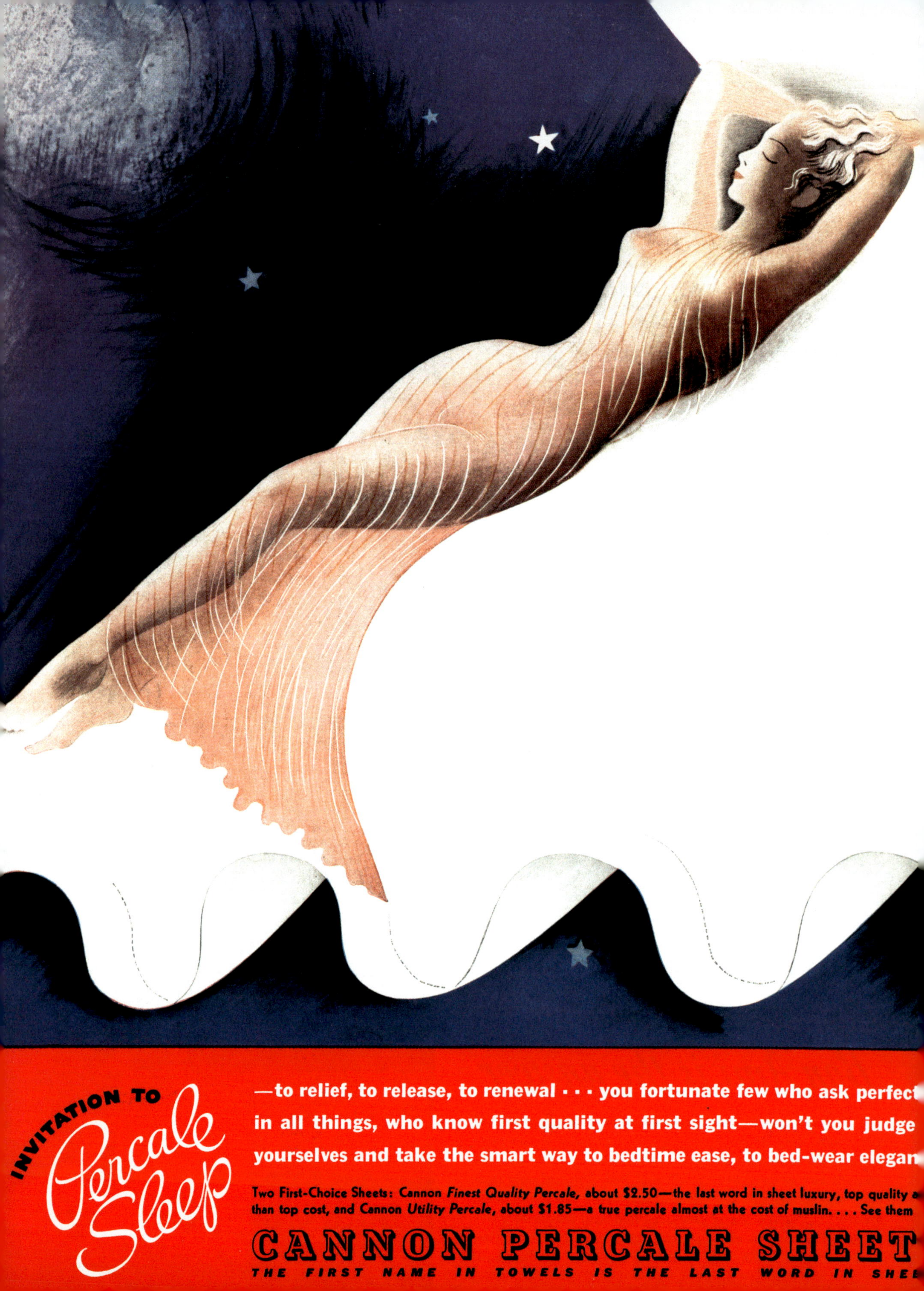

INVITATION TO
Percale Sleep
—to relief, to release, to renewal · · · you fortunate few who ask perfect
in all things, who know first quality at first sight—won't you judge
yourselves and take the smart way to bedtime ease, to bed-wear elegan
Two First-Choice Sheets: Cannon *Finest Quality Percale,* about $2.50—the last word in sheet luxury, top quality a
than top cost, and Cannon *Utility Percale*, about $1.85—a true percale almost at the cost of muslin. . . . See them
CANNON PERCALE SHEET
THE FIRST NAME IN TOWELS IS THE LAST WORD IN SHEE

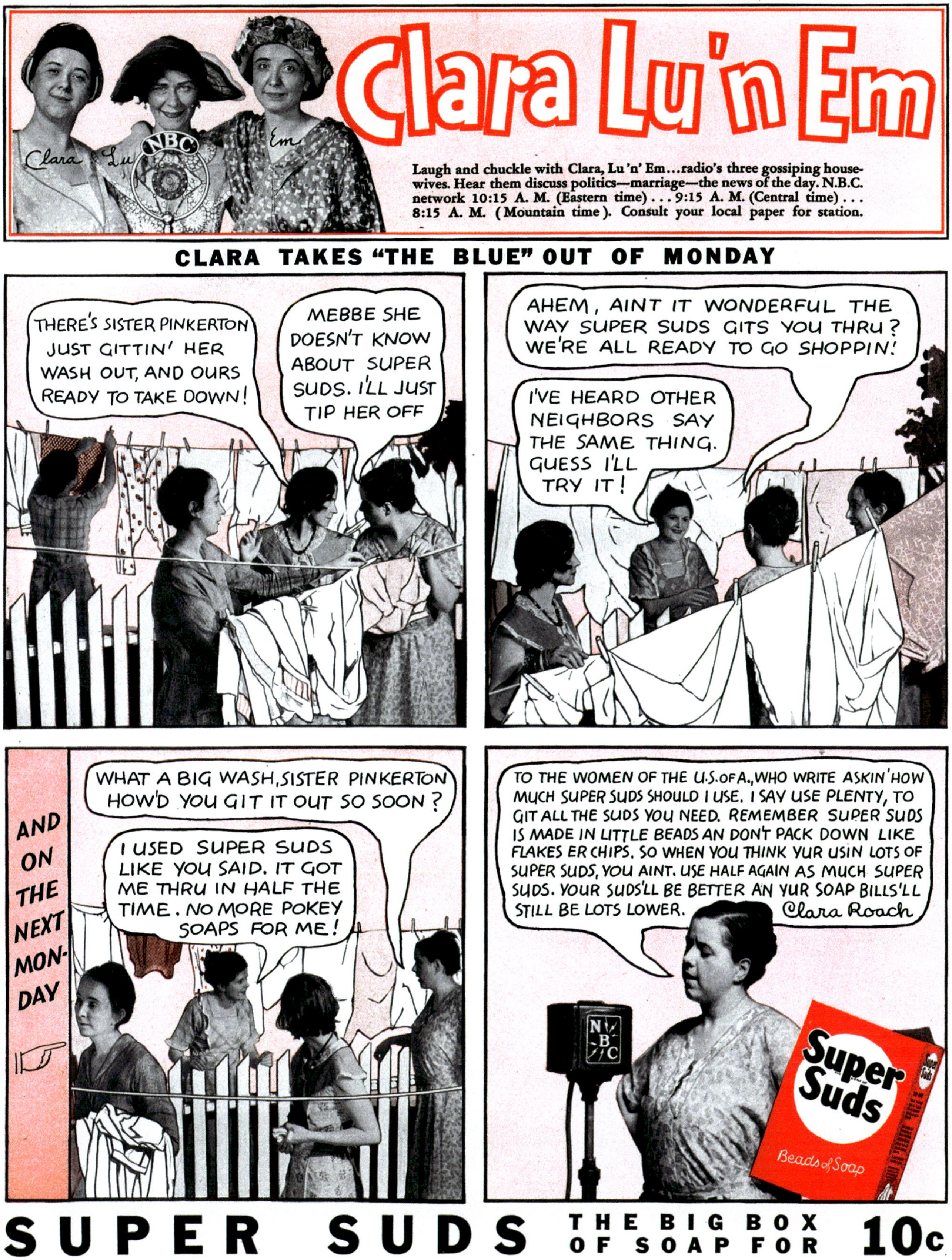

Cannon, 1937 ◄

Super Suds, 1932

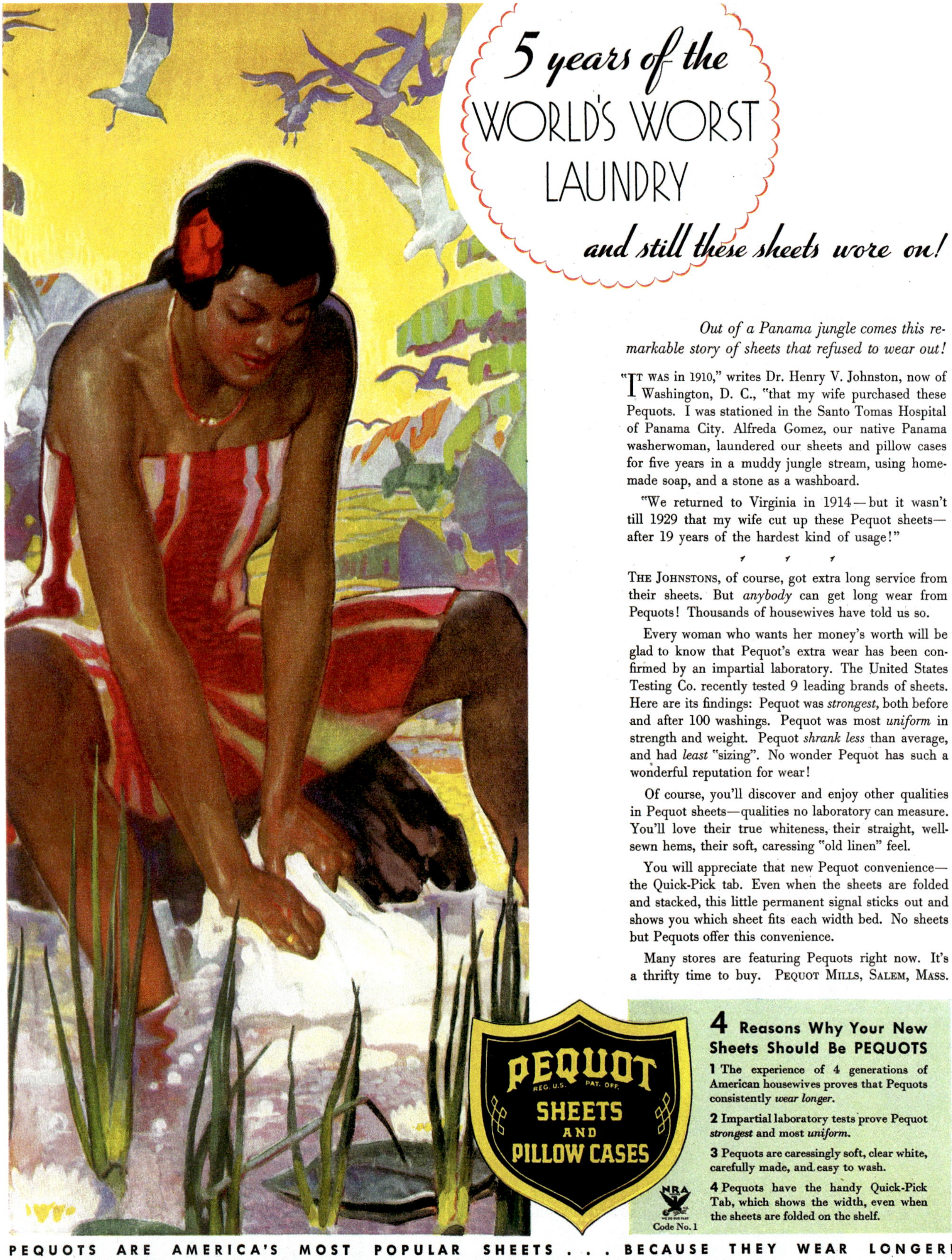
5 years of the
WORLD'S WORST LAUNDRY
and still these sheets wore on!
Out of a Panama jungle comes this remarkable story of sheets that refused to wear out!
"IT WAS in 1910," writes Dr. Henry V. Johnston, now of Washington, D. C., "that my wife purchased these Pequots. I was stationed in the Santo Tomas Hospital of Panama City. Alfreda Gomez, our native Panama washerwoman, laundered our sheets and pillow cases for five years in a muddy jungle stream, using homemade soap, and a stone as a washboard.
"We returned to Virginia in 1914—but it wasn't till 1929 that my wife cut up these Pequot sheets—after 19 years of the hardest kind of usage!"
THE JOHNSTONS, of course, got extra long service from their sheets. But anybody can get long wear from Pequots! Thousands of housewives have told us so.
Every woman who wants her money's worth will be glad to know that Pequot's extra wear has been confirmed by an impartial laboratory. The United States Testing Co. recently tested 9 leading brands of sheets. Here are its findings: Pequot was strongest, both before and after 100 washings. Pequot was most uniform in strength and weight. Pequot shrank less than average, and had least "sizing". No wonder Pequot has such a wonderful reputation for wear!
Of course, you'll discover and enjoy other qualities in Pequot sheets—qualities no laboratory can measure. You'll love their true whiteness, their straight, well-sewn hems, their soft, caressing "old linen" feel.
You will appreciate that new Pequot convenience—the Quick-Pick tab. Even when the sheets are folded and stacked, this little permanent signal sticks out and shows you which sheet fits each width bed. No sheets but Pequots offer this convenience.
Many stores are featuring Pequots right now. It's a thrifty time to buy. PEQUOT MILLS, SALEM, MASS.
PEQUOT REG. U.S. PAT. OFF.
SHEETS AND PILLOW CASES
4 Reasons Why Your New Sheets Should Be PEQUOTS
1 The experience of 4 generations of American housewives proves that Pequots consistently wear longer.
2 Impartial laboratory tests prove Pequot strongest and most uniform.
3 Pequots are caressingly soft, clear white, carefully made, and easy to wash.
4 Pequots have the handy Quick-Pick Tab, which shows the width, even when the sheets are folded on the shelf.
NRA
Code No. 1
PEQUOTS ARE AMERICA'S MOST POPULAR SHEETS . . . BECAUSE THEY WEAR LONGER!

Pequot, 1934

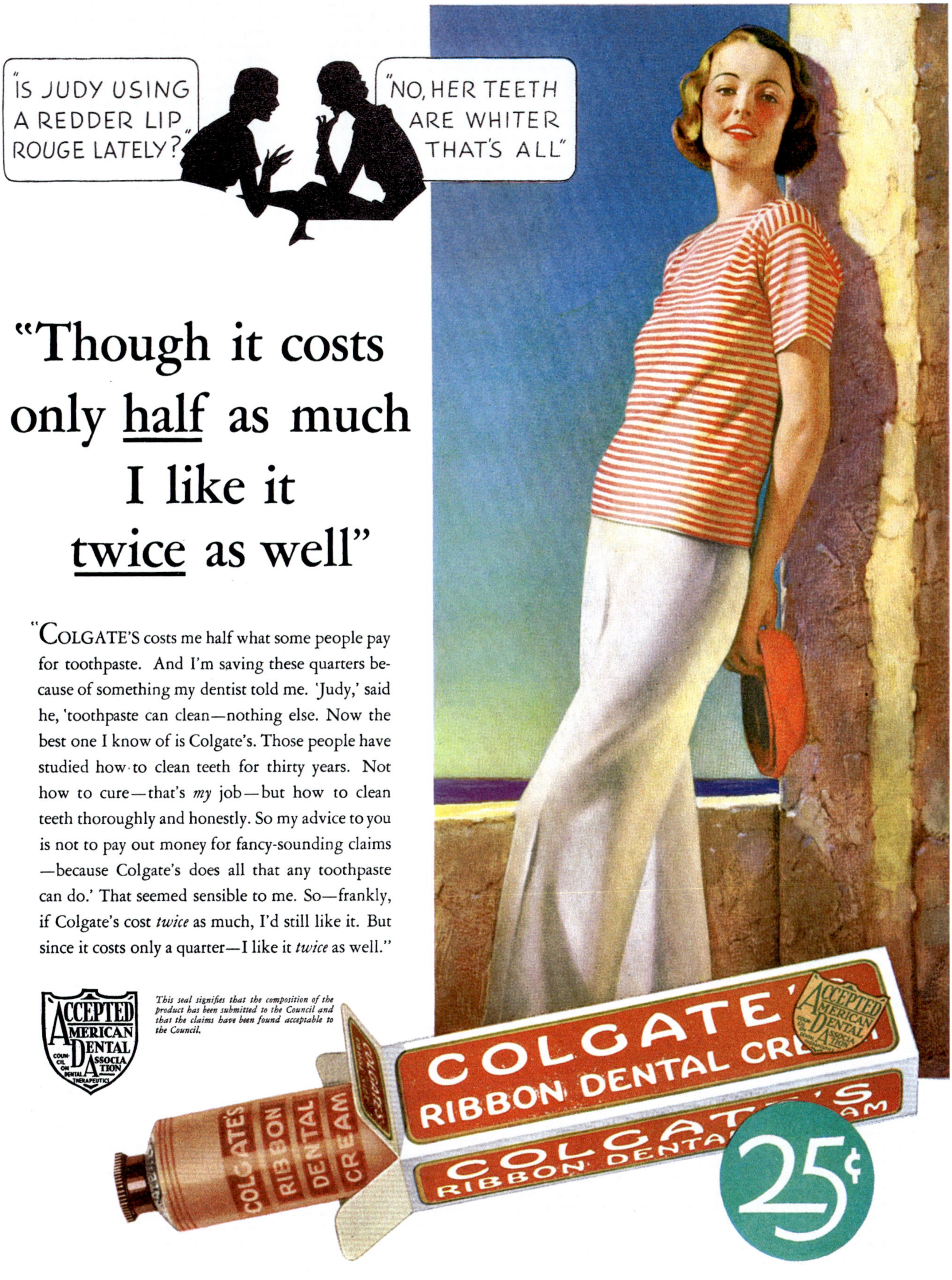

Colgate, 1937

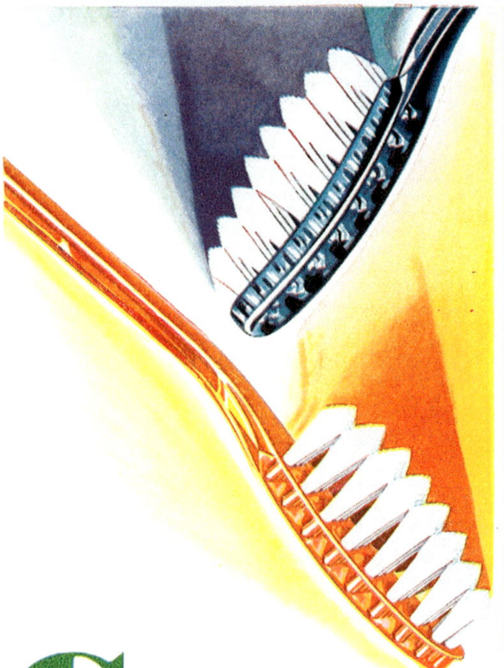

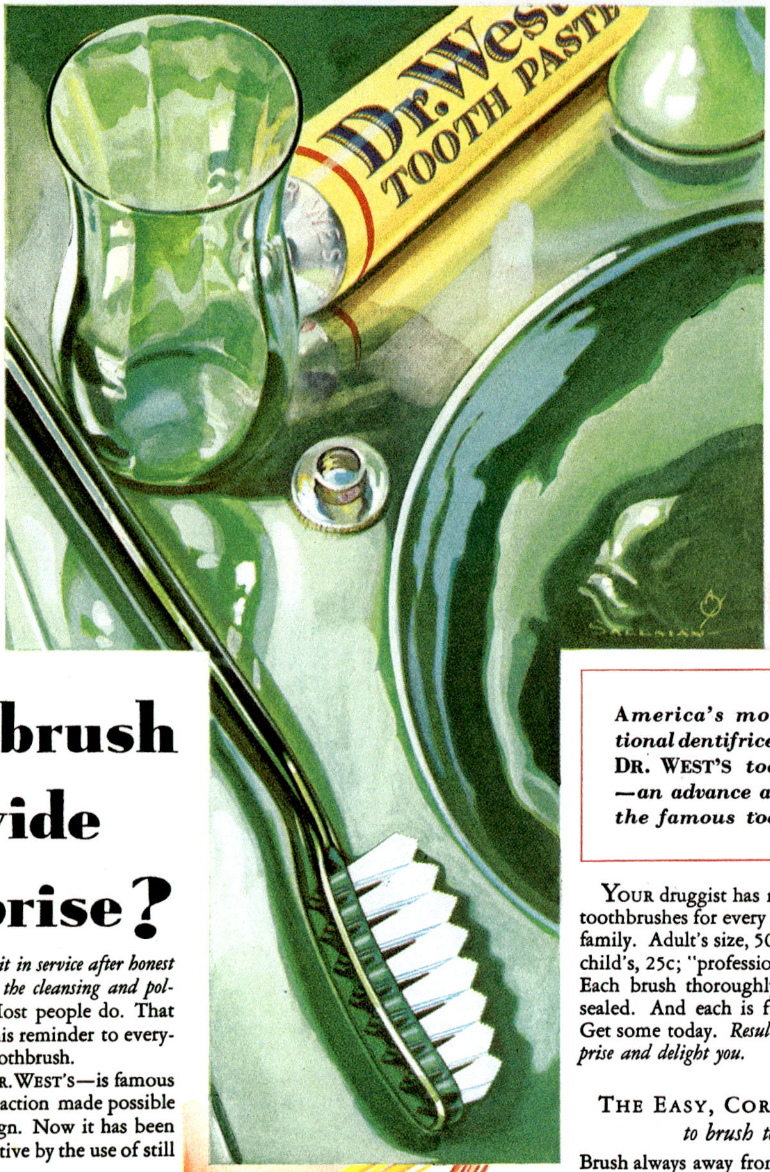

Can *any* toothbrush actually provide a pleasant surprise?

With one of these replace the brush you used this morning —then compare results

If your toothbrush gives you whiter, cleaner teeth it does you a lot of good for a very small sum of money.

And the right brush, properly used, will do exactly *that* for you. It will *not* make you a million dollars, or turn you into a movie star overnight. *But it will give you whiter teeth—*

Just get the right brush—one *small* enough and of proper shape to do the best possible job of cleaning teeth. Then—*don't keep it in service after honest wear has impaired the cleansing and polishing qualities.* Most people do. That is why we offer this reminder to everyone who uses a toothbrush.

This brush—Dr. West's—is famous for the polishing action made possible by its correct design. Now it has been made doubly effective by the use of still finer materials.

These snowy, springy bristles are the costliest the world's markets supply. Only Dr. West's new brushes have them. They are specially trimmed and spaced to enter and sweep clean all crevices—as well as to polish the surfaces.

America's most sensa- tional dentifrice success Dr. West's tooth pas —an advance as great the famous toothbrus

Your druggist has new Dr. W toothbrushes for every member o family. Adult's size, 50c; youth', child's, 25c; "professional brush, Each brush thoroughly sterilize sealed. And each is fully guara Get some today. *Results may rea prise and delight you.*

The Easy, Correct W *to brush teeth*

Brush always away from gums tc the cutting edges of the teeth; *with* the crevices, never across. what dentists advise. And they r mend Dr. West's because it is o shape and size to make correct br easy. Do this twice daily, and soon have whiter teeth.

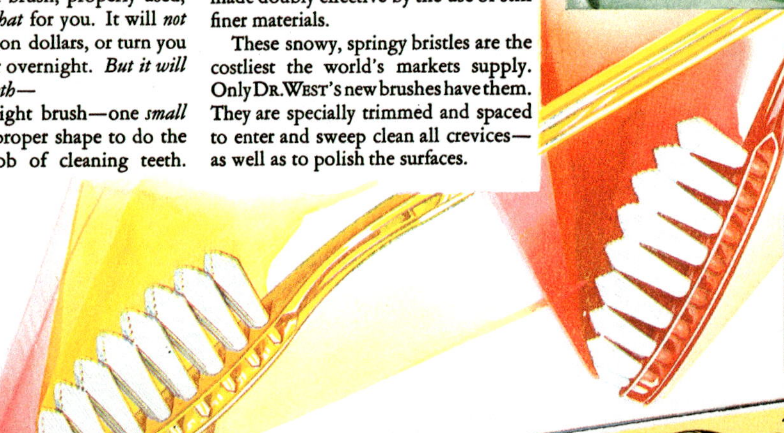

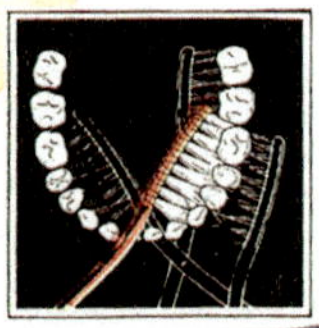

Why It Cleans *every tooth and*

This diagram shows how Dr. Wes rect design enables you to swee crevice clean—and to cleanse the ous inside curve of teeth, or te back, as thoroughly as those in fro

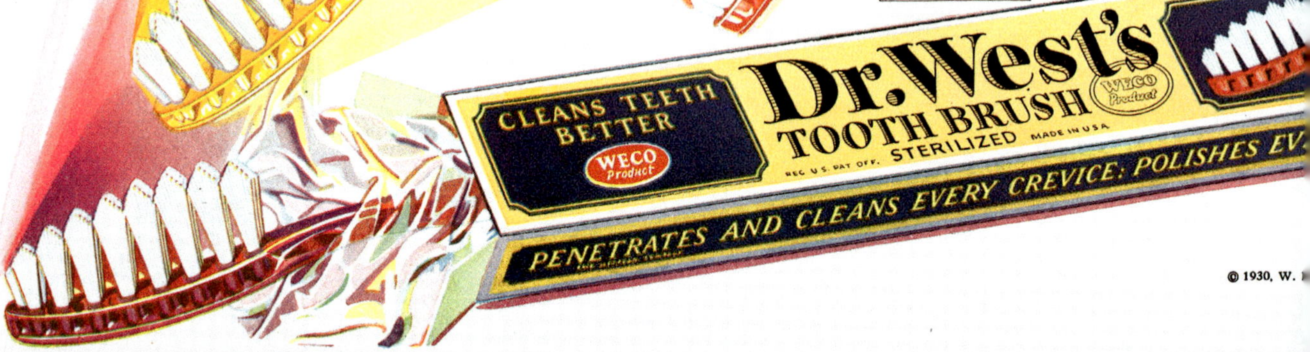

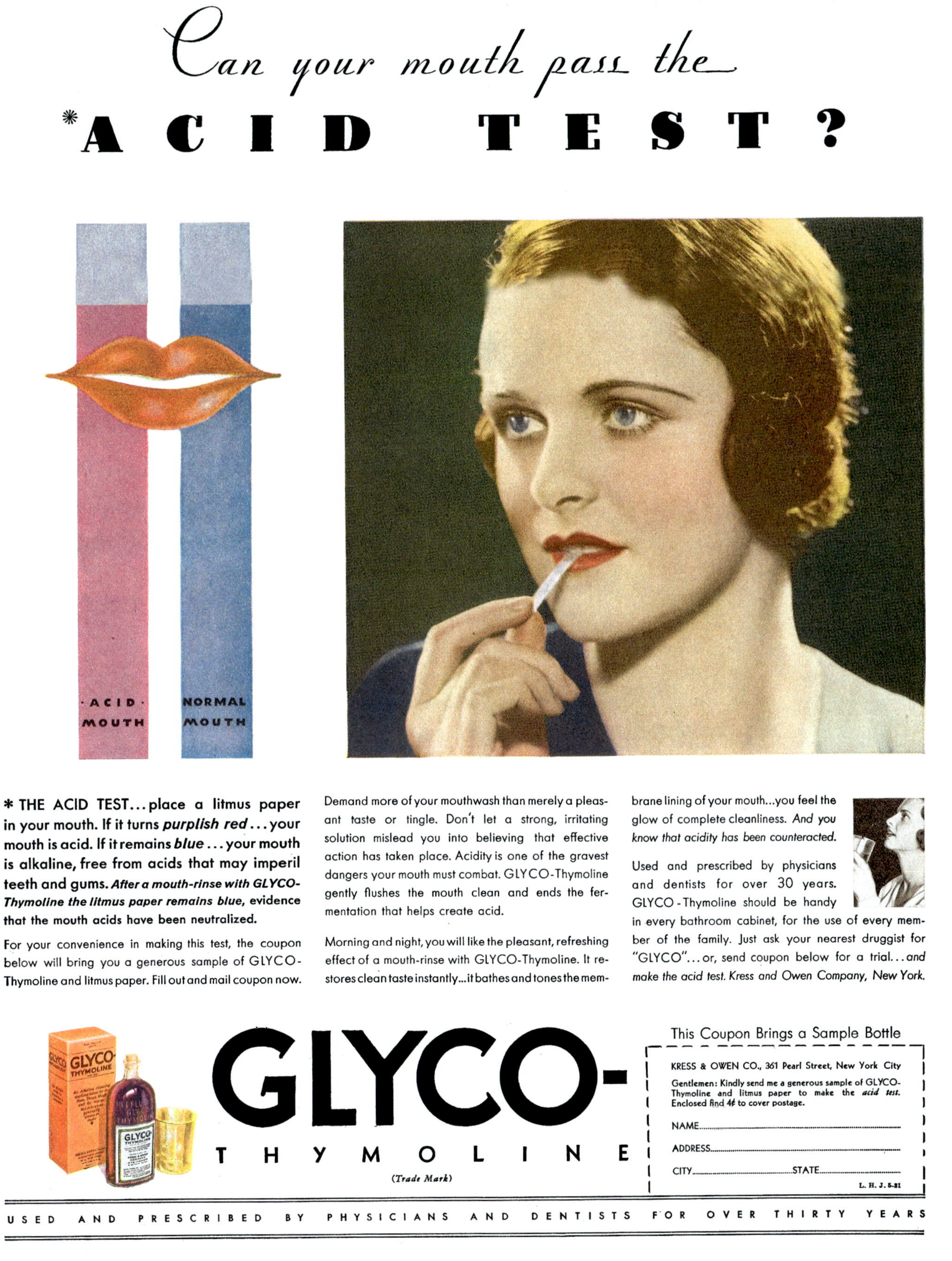

Dr. West's Toothbrush, 1930 ◄

Glyco, 1931

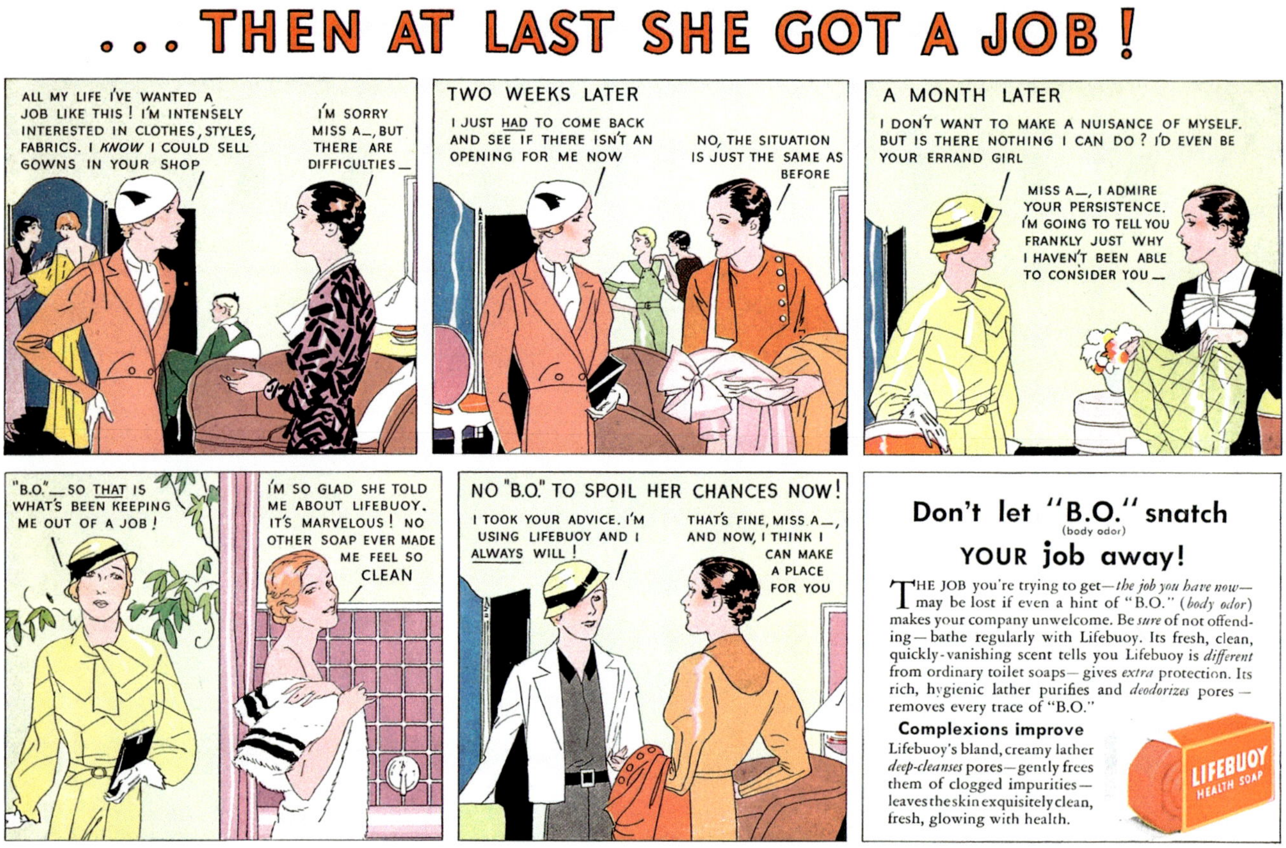

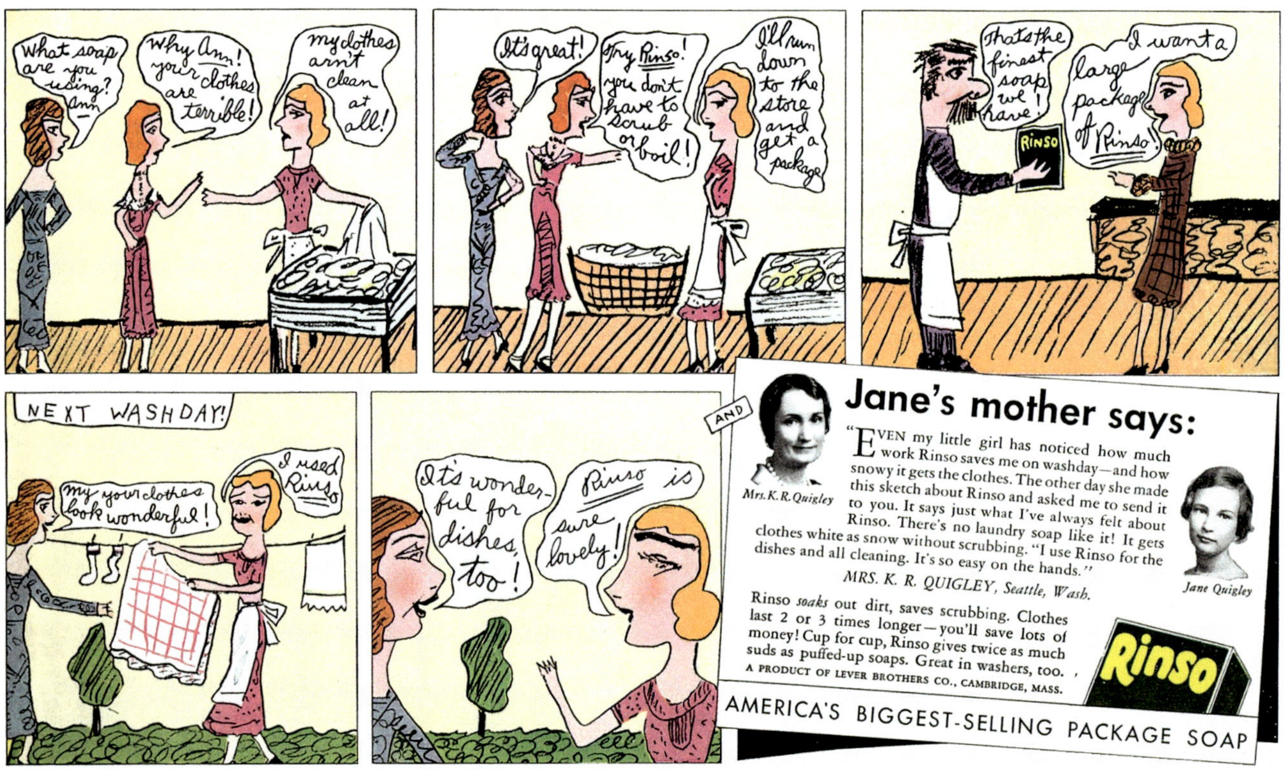

Rinso, 1933

► U.S. Savings Bonds, 1935

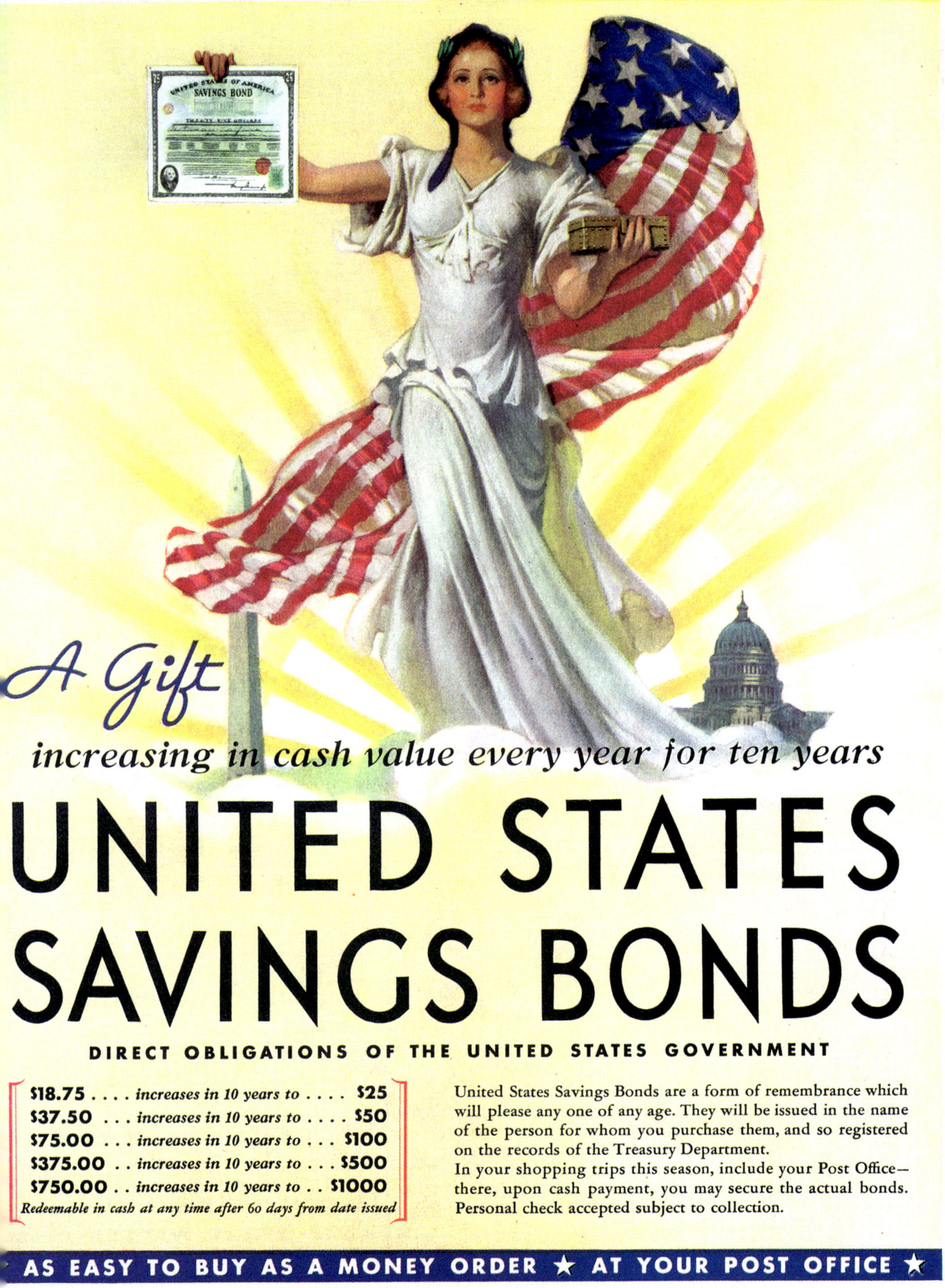
A Gift
increasing in cash value every year for ten years
UNITED STATES
SAVINGS BONDS
DIRECT OBLIGATIONS OF THE UNITED STATES GOVERNMENT
$18.75 . . . . increases in 10 years to $25
$37.50 . . . increases in 10 years to $50
$75.00 . . . increases in 10 years to . . . $100
$375.00 . . increases in 10 years to . . . $500
$750.00 . . increases in 10 years to . . $1000
Redeemable in cash at any time after 60 days from date issued
United States Savings Bonds are a form of remembrance which will please any one of any age. They will be issued in the name of the person for whom you purchase them, and so registered on the records of the Treasury Department.
In your shopping trips this season, include your Post Office—there, upon cash payment, you may secure the actual bonds. Personal check accepted subject to collection.
AS EASY TO BUY AS A MONEY ORDER ★ AT YOUR POST OFFICE ★

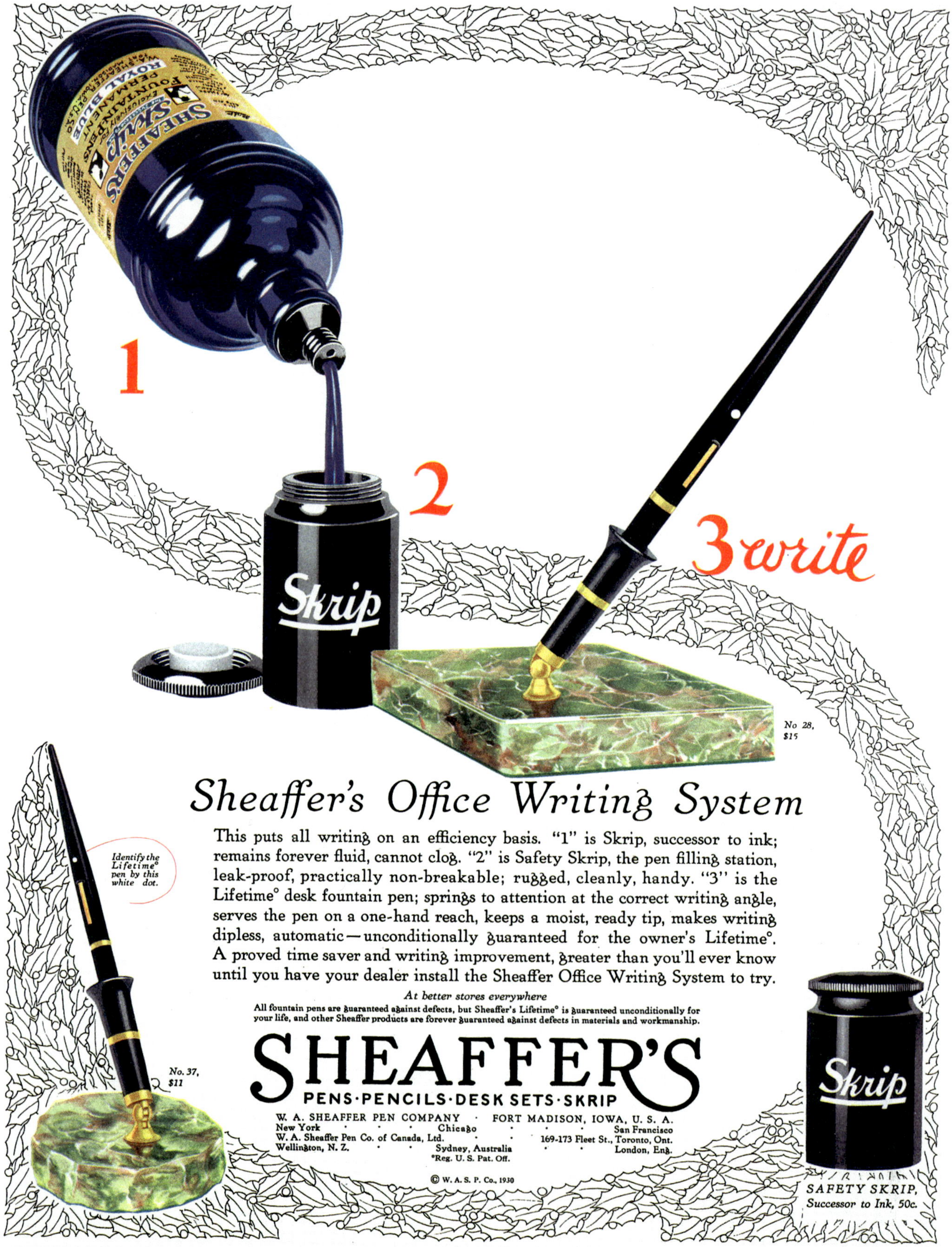

Sheaffer's, 1930

▸ *Sheaffer's, 1939*

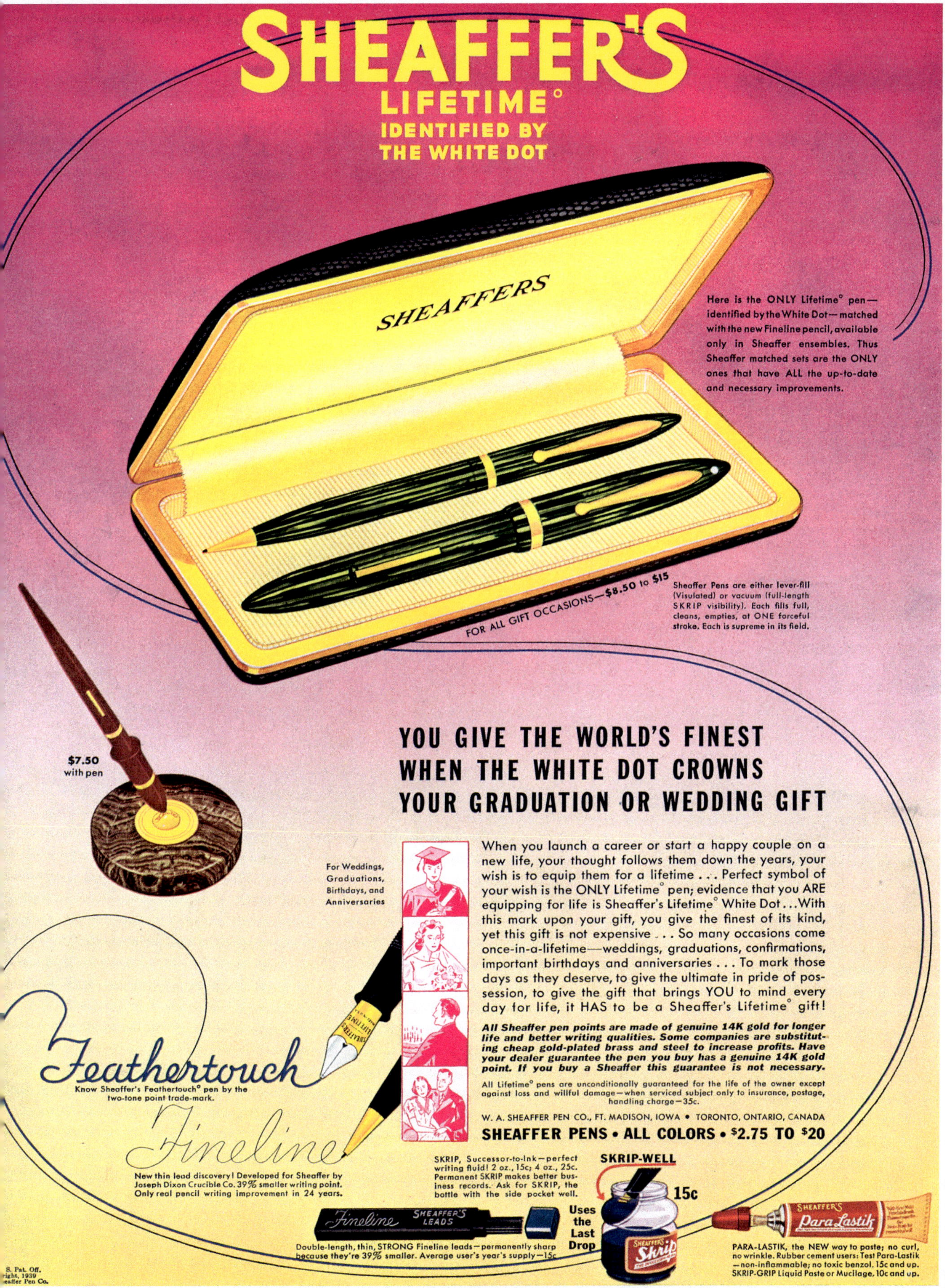

SHEAFFER'S
LIFETIME°
IDENTIFIED BY THE WHITE DOT
SHEAFFERS
Here is the ONLY Lifetime° pen—identified by the White Dot—matched with the new Fineline pencil, available only in Sheaffer ensembles. Thus Sheaffer matched sets are the ONLY ones that have ALL the up-to-date and necessary improvements.
FOR ALL GIFT OCCASIONS—$8.50 to $15
Sheaffer Pens are either lever-fill (Visulated) or vacuum (full-length SKRIP visibility). Each fills full, cleans, empties, at ONE forceful stroke. Each is supreme in its field.
$7.50 with pen
YOU GIVE THE WORLD'S FINEST WHEN THE WHITE DOT CROWNS YOUR GRADUATION OR WEDDING GIFT
For Weddings, Graduations, Birthdays, and Anniversaries
When you launch a career or start a happy couple on a new life, your thought follows them down the years, your wish is to equip them for a lifetime . . . Perfect symbol of your wish is the ONLY Lifetime° pen; evidence that you ARE equipping for life is Sheaffer's Lifetime° White Dot . . . With this mark upon your gift, you give the finest of its kind, yet this gift is not expensive . . . So many occasions come once-in-a-lifetime—weddings, graduations, confirmations, important birthdays and anniversaries . . . To mark those days as they deserve, to give the ultimate in pride of possession, to give the gift that brings YOU to mind every day for life, it HAS to be a Sheaffer's Lifetime° gift!
All Sheaffer pen points are made of genuine 14K gold for longer life and better writing qualities. Some companies are substituting cheap gold-plated brass and steel to increase profits. Have your dealer guarantee the pen you buy has a genuine 14K gold point. If you buy a Sheaffer this guarantee is not necessary.
All Lifetime° pens are unconditionally guaranteed for the life of the owner except against loss and willful damage—when serviced subject only to insurance, postage, handling charge—35c.
W. A. SHEAFFER PEN CO., FT. MADISON, IOWA • TORONTO, ONTARIO, CANADA
SHEAFFER PENS • ALL COLORS • $2.75 TO $20
Feathertouch
Know Sheaffer's Feathertouch° pen by the two-tone point trade-mark.
Fineline
New thin lead discovery! Developed for Sheaffer by Joseph Dixon Crucible Co. 39% smaller writing point. Only real pencil writing improvement in 24 years.
SKRIP, Successor-to-Ink—perfect writing fluid! 2 oz., 15c; 4 oz., 25c. Permanent SKRIP makes better business records. Ask for SKRIP, the bottle with the side pocket well.
SKRIP-WELL
15c
Uses the Last Drop
Fineline SHEAFFER'S LEADS
Double-length, thin, STRONG Fineline leads—permanently sharp because they're 39% smaller. Average user's year's supply—15c
SHEAFFER'S Skrip
SHEAFFER'S Para Lastik
PARA-LASTIK, the NEW way to paste; no curl, no wrinkle. Rubber cement users: Test Para-Lastik—non-inflammable; no toxic benzol. 15c and up. SKRIP-GRIP Liquid Paste or Mucilage, 10c and up.
S. Pat. Off.
right, 1939
eaffer Pen Co.

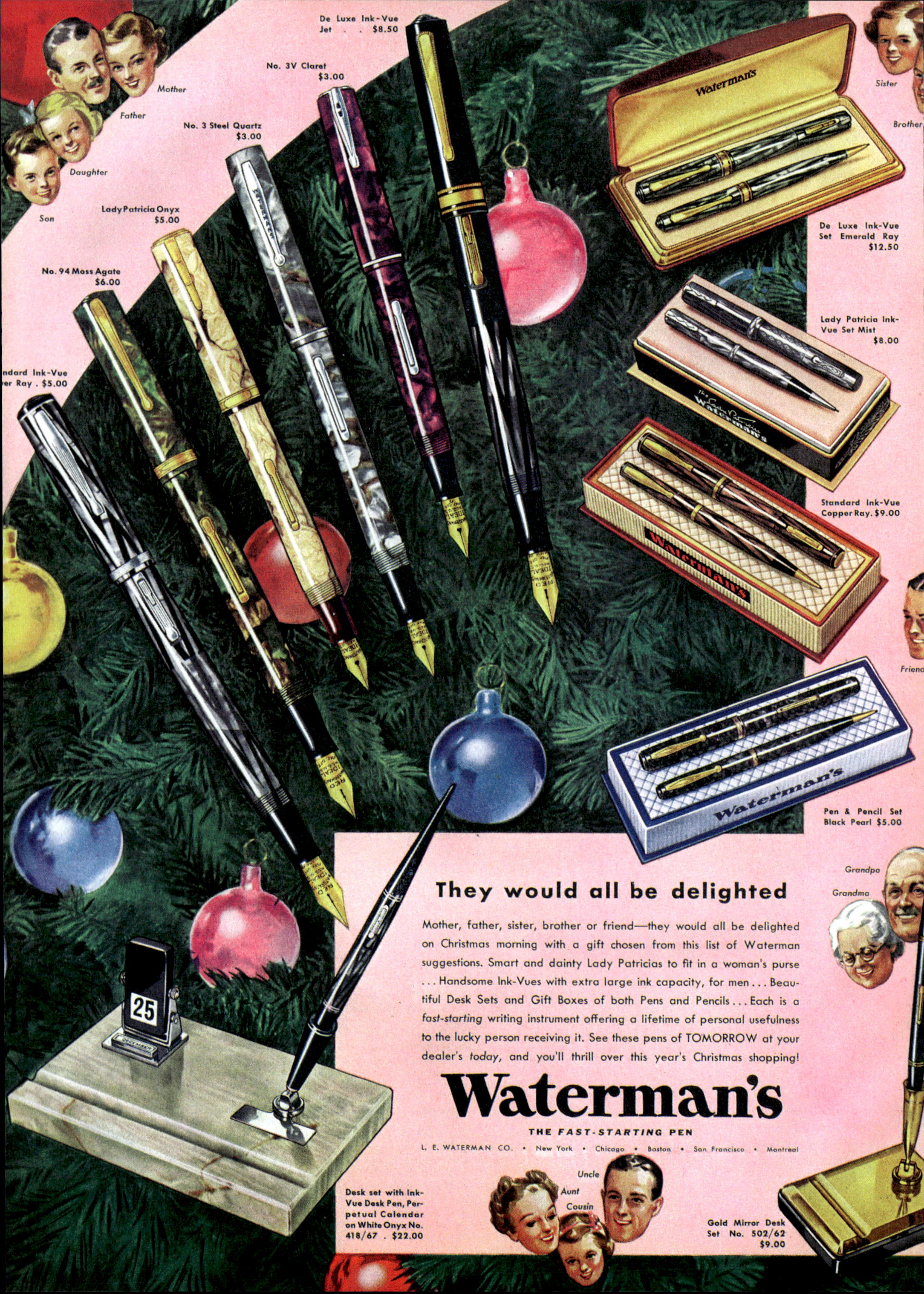

Mother
Father
Daughter
Son
Sister
Brother
De Luxe Ink-Vue Jet . . $8.50
No. 3V Claret $3.00
No. 3 Steel Quartz $3.00
Lady Patricia Onyx $5.00
No. 94 Moss Agate $6.00
ndard Ink-Vue
er Ray . $5.00
De Luxe Ink-Vue Set Emerald Ray $12.50
Lady Patricia Ink-Vue Set Mist $8.00
Standard Ink-Vue Copper Ray. $9.00
Pen & Pencil Set Black Pearl $5.00
Grandpa
Grandma
They would all be delighted
Mother, father, sister, brother or friend—they would all be delighted on Christmas morning with a gift chosen from this list of Waterman suggestions. Smart and dainty Lady Patricias to fit in a woman's purse . . . Handsome Ink-Vues with extra large ink capacity, for men . . . Beautiful Desk Sets and Gift Boxes of both Pens and Pencils . . . Each is a fast-starting writing instrument offering a lifetime of personal usefulness to the lucky person receiving it. See these pens of TOMORROW at your dealer's today, and you'll thrill over this year's Christmas shopping!
Waterman's
THE FAST-STARTING PEN
L. E. WATERMAN CO. • New York • Chicago • Boston • San Francisco • Montreal
Uncle
Aunt
Cousin
Desk set with Ink-Vue Desk Pen, Perpetual Calendar on White Onyx No. 418/67 . $22.00
Gold Mirror Desk Set No. 502/62 $9.00

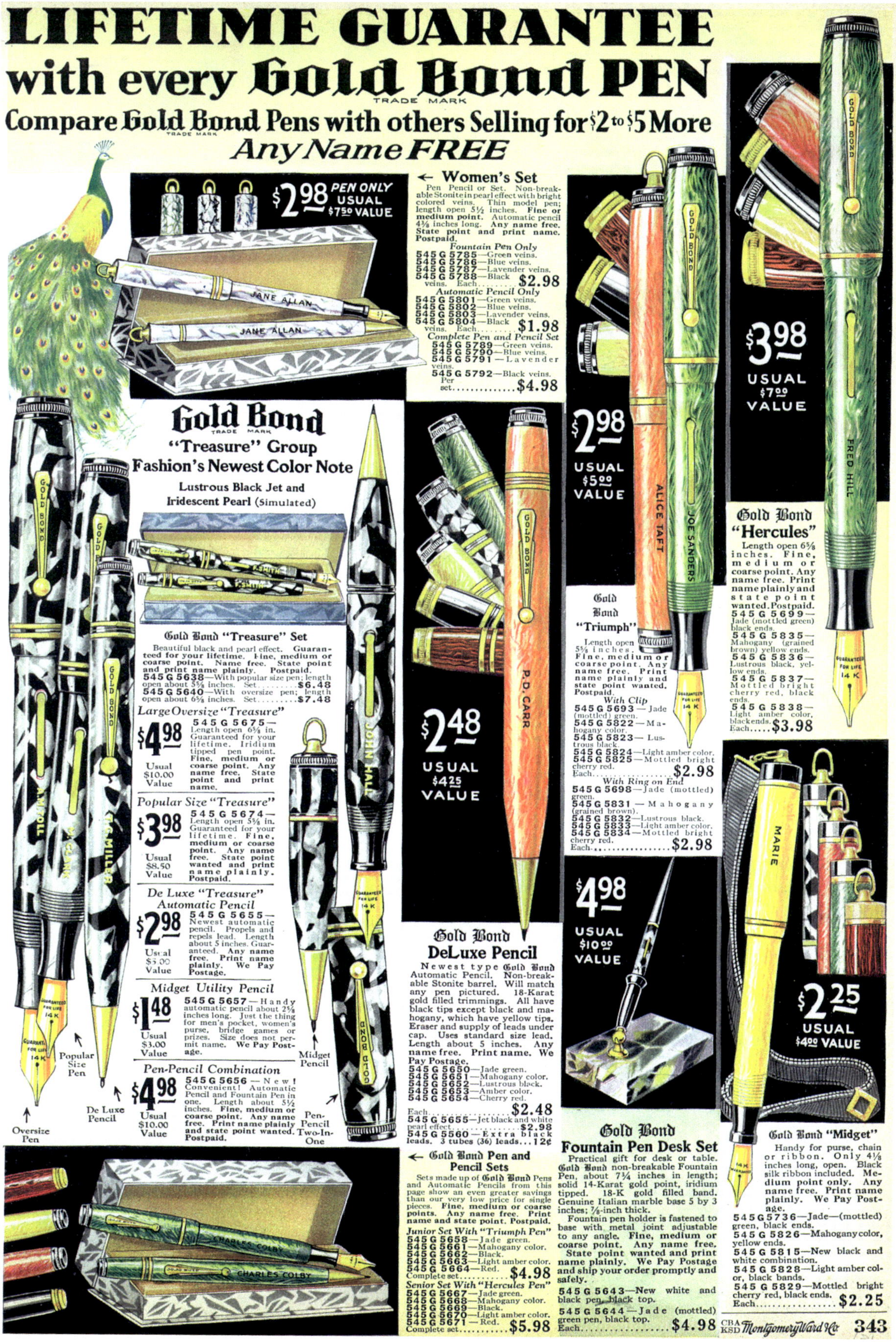

Waterman's, 1937 ◄

Gold Bond Pen, 1931

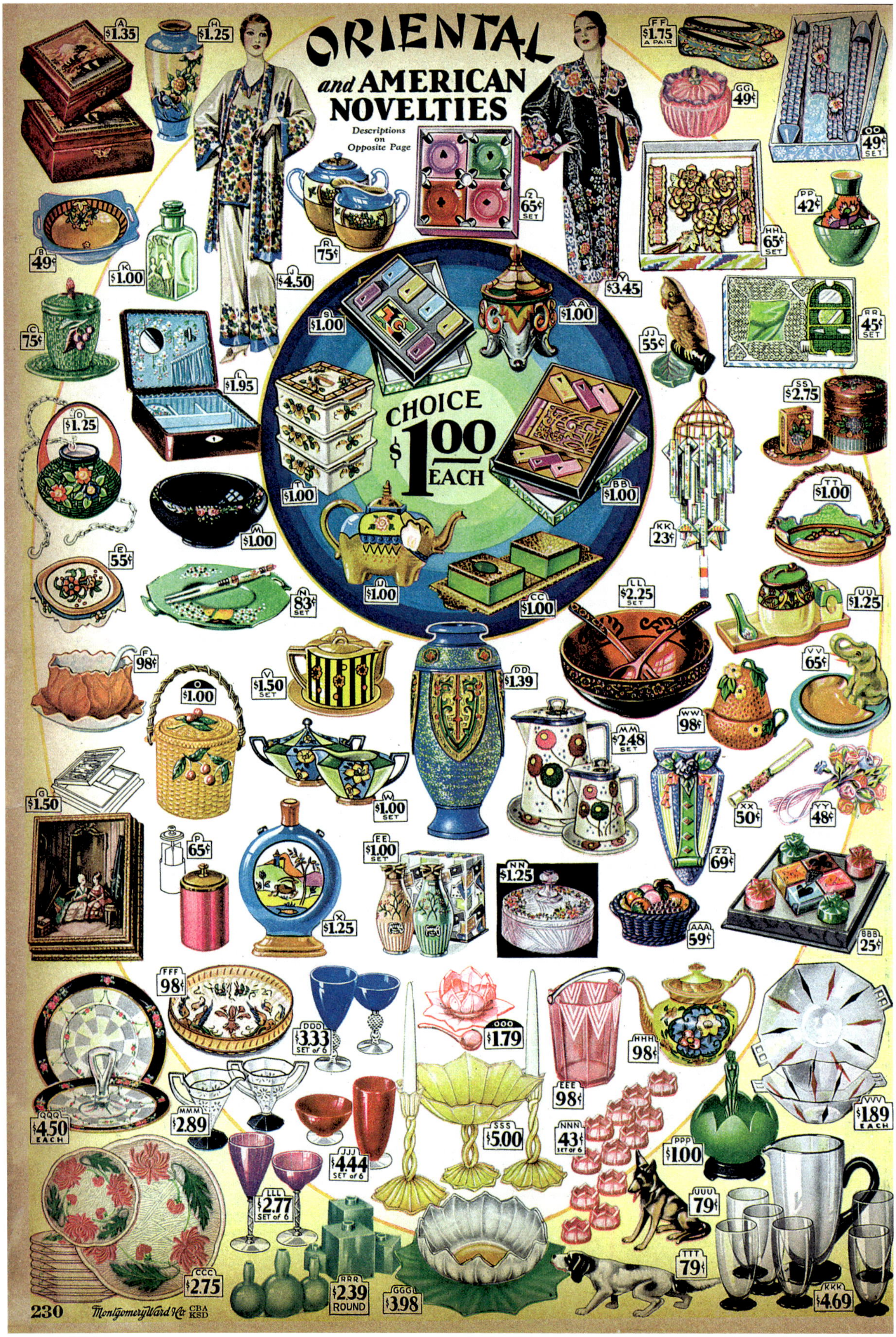

Oriental Novelties, 1931

▸ *The New Yorker Magazine, 1936* ▸▸ *Time-Fortune Magazines, 1933*

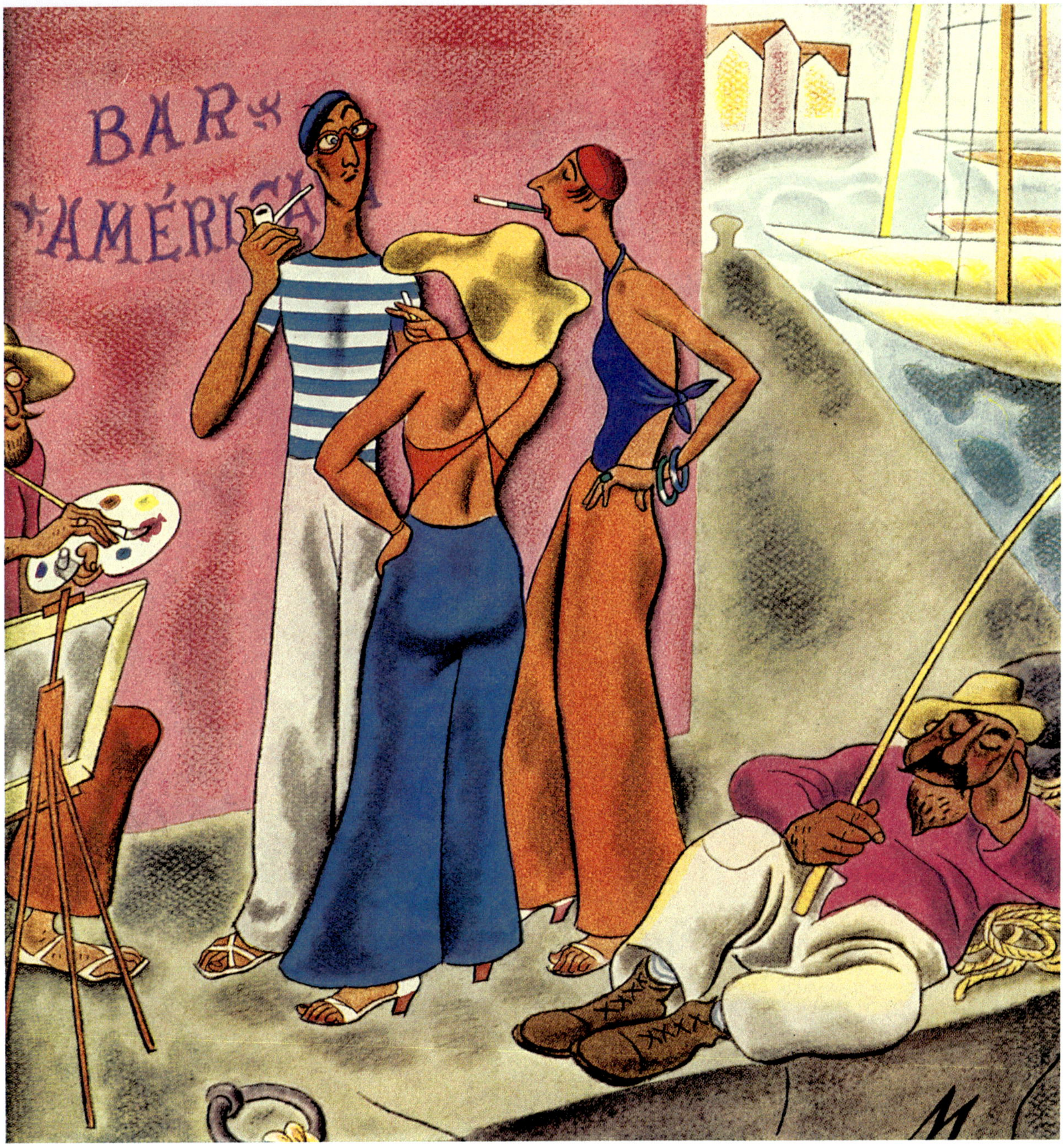

IF YOU HAD BEEN AWAY THREE YEARS—

AND returned to New York just before dinner one evening—what would you do? Where would you dine; what play or movie would you see; where would you dance and have an early breakfast? Or, if you stayed in (which you probably wouldn't), what book (if any) would you read?

THE NEW YORKER, considering you reasonably intelligent, would tell you. Reading it is the only way you could find out, unless you knew and talked with all THE NEW YORKER writers and all the people they write about. And they are a great many.

So if you turned to THE NEW YORKER you would find a conscientious guide of all current amusement offerings worthwhile—*theatres, motion pictures, musical events, art exhibitions, sports,* and *miscellaneous entertainment*—providing a ready answer to the prevalent query, "What shall we do this evening?" You would be apprised of what is going on in the public and semi-public smart gathering places—*clubs, hotels, cafés, supper clubs, cabarets,* and other resorts. You would be told where to lunch and dine and dance.

THE NEW YORKER is published avowedly for a metropolitan audience. Its character is perfectly expressed by its art which has set a new standard in American publishing.

In addition, it prints *prose* and *verse, humor, satirical paragraphs,* and *stories* about the people and events that make New York the most fascinating island in the world. These you will find in no other publication.

THE
NEW YORKER,
25 WEST 45TH STREET,
NEW YORK

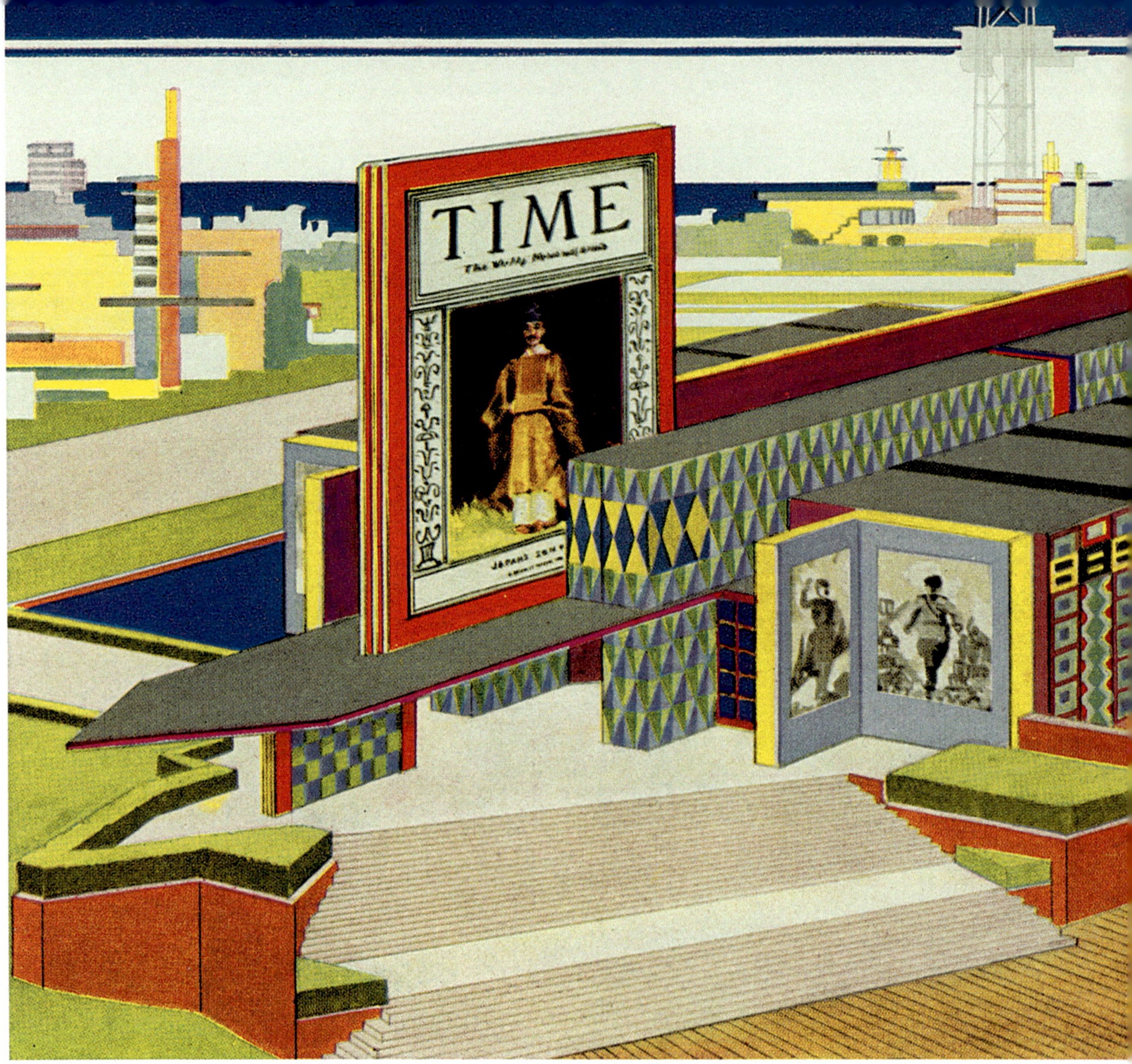

REPORTING ON YOUR BUILDING AT A CENTURY OF PROGRESS

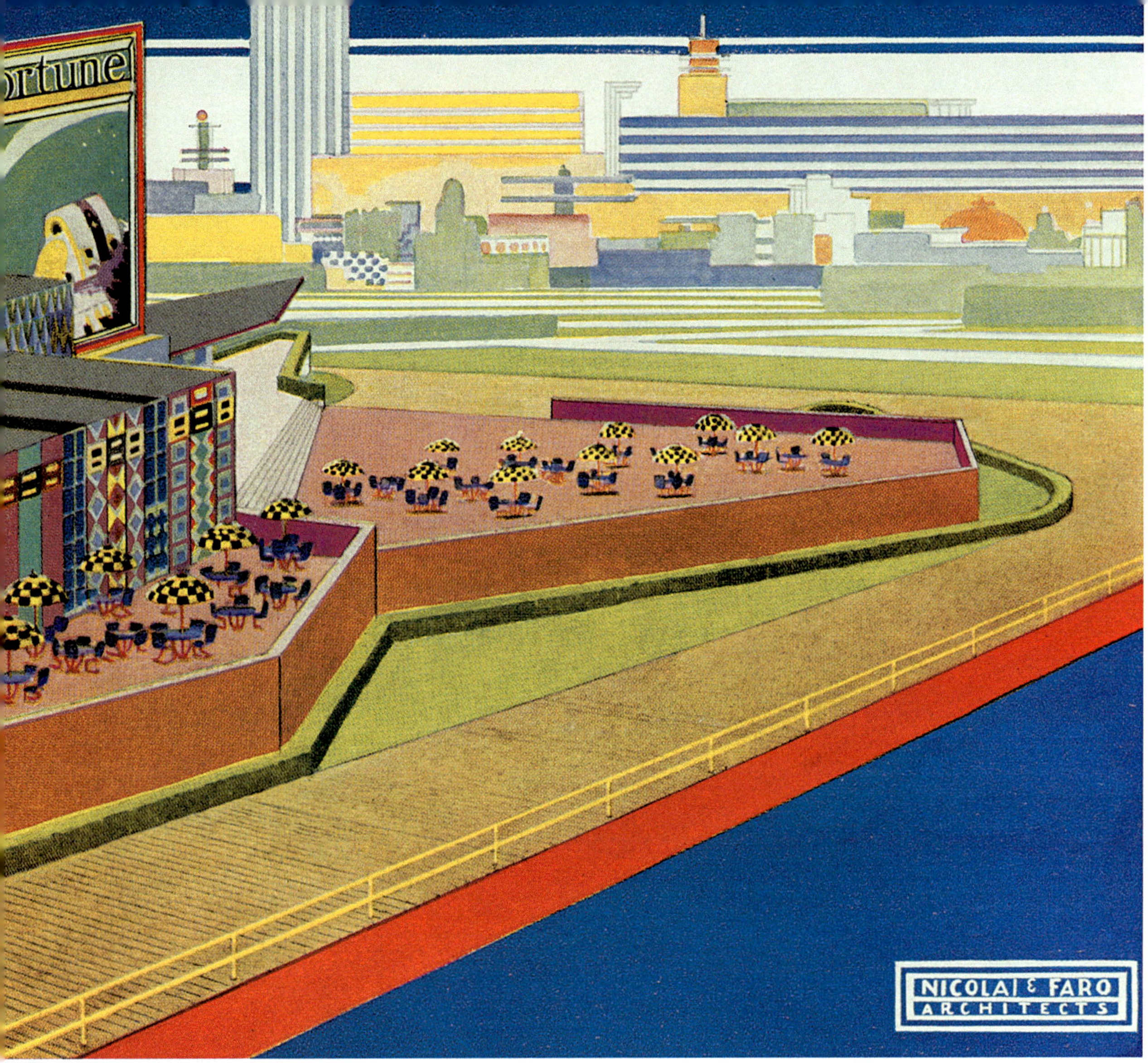

hether or not you were among the many TIME ıders to visit the TIME-FORTUNE Building at A ntury of Progress in Chicago, you may be inter- ed in its record.

It offered visitors a place for rest and reading. world's largest magazine rack with over 1500 riodicals from all over the world was in constant e. Here are outstanding facts about the building.

VISITORS TO BUILDING—91,000 a week. (A word to vertisers: thousands of these people were high grade alers in their respective towns, many of them learning out the TIME idea for the first time. That's "dealer luence," the same strong kind that has been created, d is being created by "The March of Time" on the lio.)

BOOKLETS TO VISITORS—400,000. (Further acquaint- new friends with the TIME idea.)

NEW TIME SUBSCRIBERS—4,700 trial subscriptions. 20 regular subscriptions.

- NEW FORTUNE SUBSCRIBERS—330.
- LETTERS WRITTEN AT BUILDING—246,000.
- POST CARDS—123,800.
- MAGAZINE MOST SUBSCRIBED TO (Visitors to the building could subscribe to any of the 1500 magazines displayed. No visitors were high-pressured, and TIME charged no fee, received no pay for taking subscriptions.) Not including TIME, FORTUNE and THE ARCHITECTURAL FORUM the magazines most subscribed to were *Magazine Digest, Reader's Digest, Child Life.*
- MOST FREQUENT BONER—middle aged ladies asking if this was the place where fortunes were told.
- NUMBER OF PEOPLE WHO SAW THE BUILDING: Over 20 million eyes couldn't have missed the large reproductions of TIME and FORTUNE covers on the building.
- COPIES OF ARCHITECTURAL FORUM SOLD (July issue, A Century of Progress Reference number, price $1.00): 3000.
- NET RESULT: Better than all expectations.

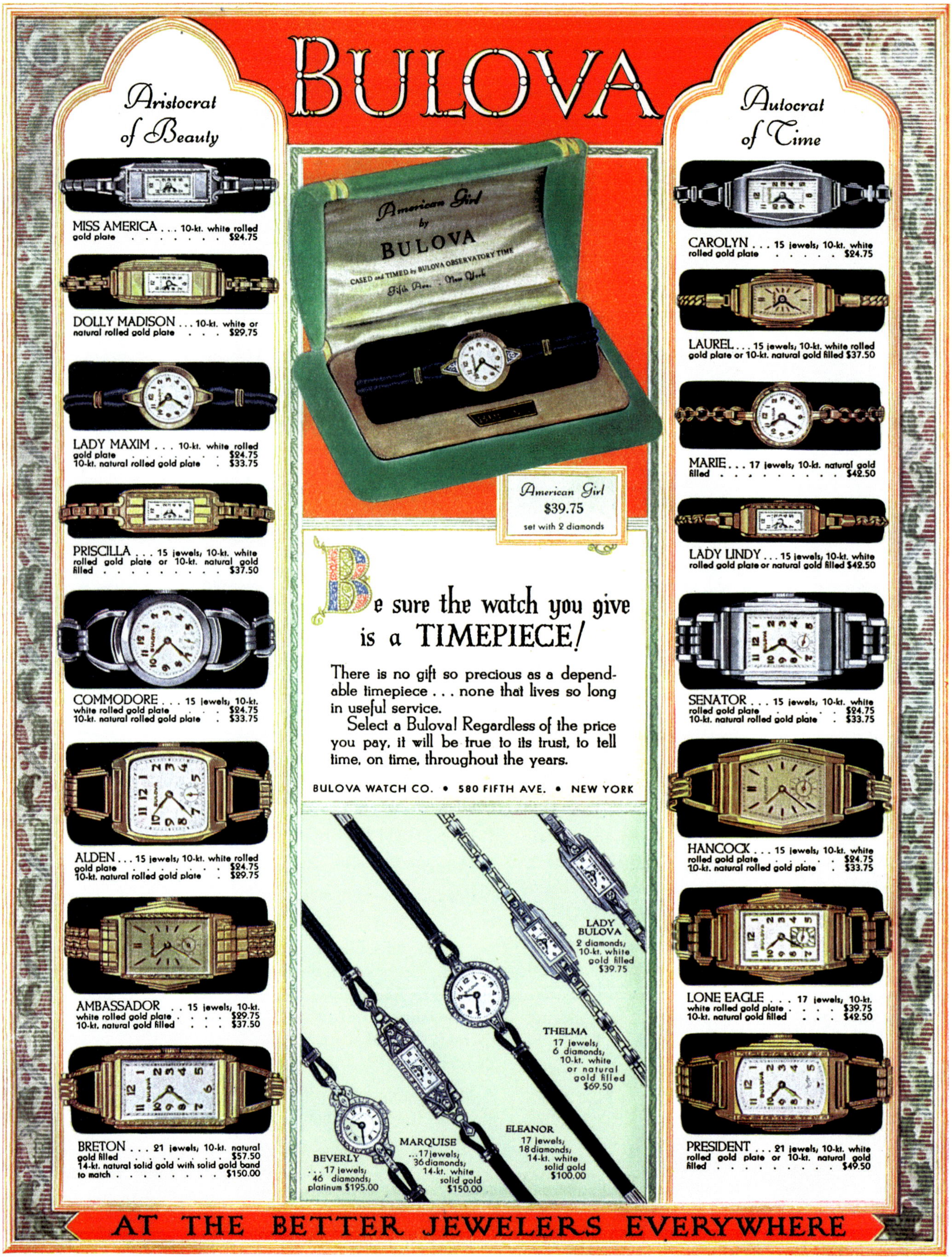
BULOVA
Aristocrat of Beauty
Autocrat of Time
MISS AMERICA . . . 10-kt. white rolled gold plate $24.75
DOLLY MADISON . . . 10-kt. white or natural rolled gold plate . . . $29.75
LADY MAXIM . . . 10-kt. white rolled gold plate . . . $24.75
10-kt. natural rolled gold plate . $33.75
PRISCILLA . . . 15 jewels, 10-kt. white rolled gold plate or 10-kt. natural gold filled $37.50
COMMODORE . . . 15 jewels, 10-kt. white rolled gold plate . . $24.75
10-kt. natural rolled gold plate . $33.75
ALDEN . . . 15 jewels, 10-kt. white rolled gold plate . . . $24.75
10-kt. natural rolled gold plate . $29.75
AMBASSADOR . . 15 jewels, 10-kt. white rolled gold plate . . . $29.75
10-kt. natural gold filled . . . $37.50
BRETON . . . 21 jewels, 10-kt. natural gold filled $57.50
14-kt. natural solid gold with solid gold band to match $150.00
American Girl by BULOVA
CASED and TIMED by BULOVA OBSERVATORY TIME
Fifth Ave. - New York
American Girl
$39.75
set with 2 diamonds
Be sure the watch you give is a TIMEPIECE!
There is no gift so precious as a dependable timepiece . . . none that lives so long in useful service.
Select a Bulova! Regardless of the price you pay, it will be true to its trust, to tell time, on time, throughout the years.
BULOVA WATCH CO. • 580 FIFTH AVE. • NEW YORK
LADY BULOVA
2 diamonds, 10-kt. white gold filled $39.75
THELMA
17 jewels, 6 diamonds, 10-kt. white or natural gold filled $69.50
ELEANOR
17 jewels, 18 diamonds, 14-kt. white solid gold $100.00
MARQUISE
. . . 17 jewels, 36 diamonds, 14-kt. white solid gold $150.00
BEVERLY
. . . 17 jewels, 46 diamonds, platinum $195.00
CAROLYN . . . 15 jewels, 10-kt. white rolled gold plate $24.75
LAUREL . . . 15 jewels, 10-kt. white rolled gold plate or 10-kt. natural gold filled $37.50
MARIE . . . 17 jewels, 10-kt. natural gold filled $42.50
LADY LINDY . . . 15 jewels, 10-kt. white rolled gold plate or natural gold filled $42.50
SENATOR . . . 15 jewels, 10-kt. white rolled gold plate . . . $24.75
10-kt. natural rolled gold plate . $33.75
HANCOCK . . . 15 jewels, 10-kt. white rolled gold plate . . . $24.75
10-kt. natural rolled gold plate . $33.75
LONE EAGLE . . . 17 jewels, 10-kt. white rolled gold plate . . . $39.75
10-kt. natural gold filled . . . $42.50
PRESIDENT . . . 21 jewels, 10-kt. white rolled gold plate or 10-kt. natural gold filled $49.50
AT THE BETTER JEWELERS EVERYWHERE

Bulova, 1935

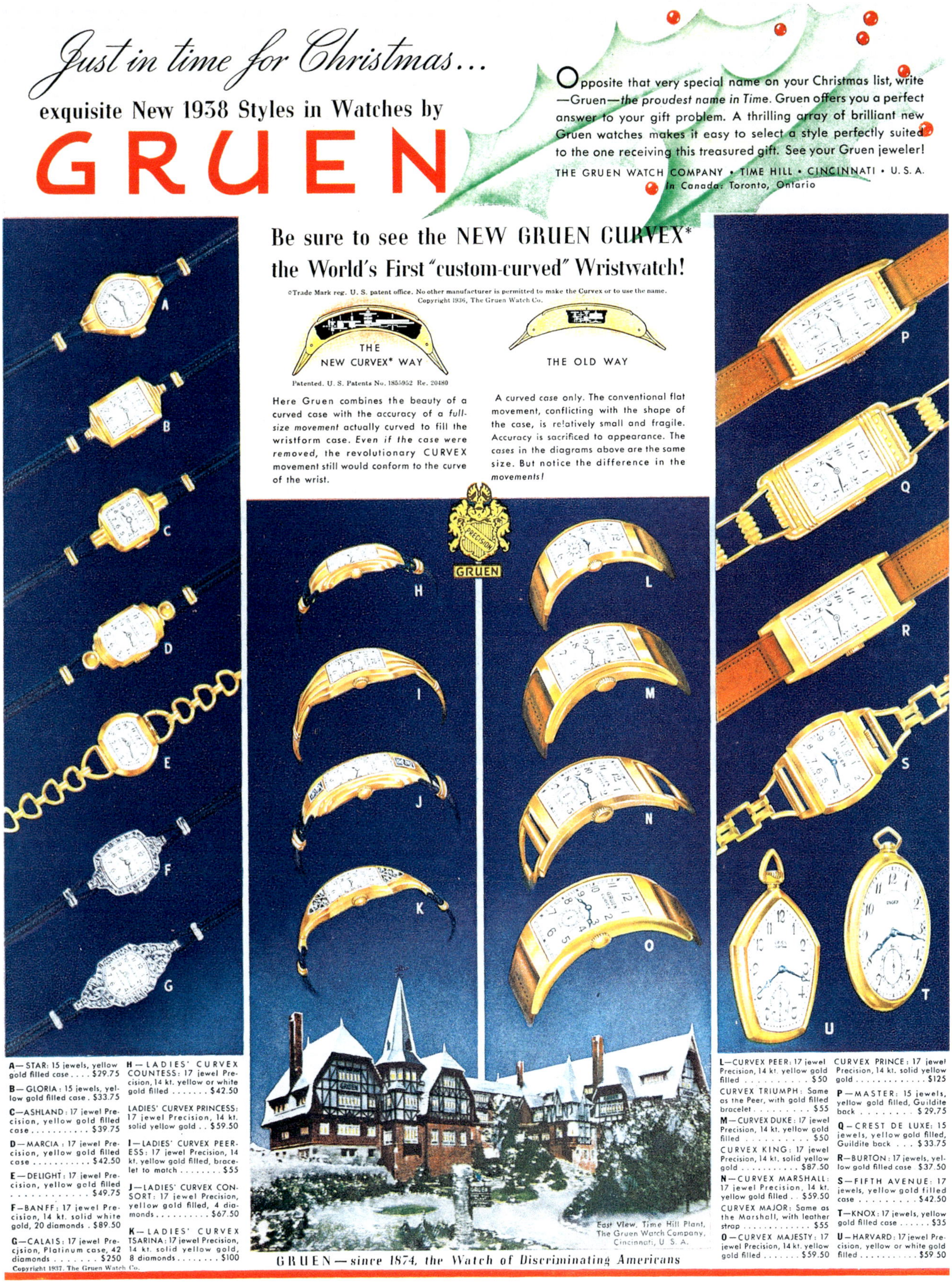
Just in time for Christmas...
exquisite New 1938 Styles in Watches by
GRUEN
Opposite that very special name on your Christmas list, write —Gruen—the proudest name in Time. Gruen offers you a perfect answer to your gift problem. A thrilling array of brilliant new Gruen watches makes it easy to select a style perfectly suited to the one receiving this treasured gift. See your Gruen jeweler!
THE GRUEN WATCH COMPANY • TIME HILL • CINCINNATI • U. S. A.
In Canada: Toronto, Ontario
Be sure to see the NEW GRUEN CURVEX* the World's First "custom-curved" Wristwatch!
*Trade Mark reg. U. S. patent office. No other manufacturer is permitted to make the Curvex or to use the name.
Copyright 1936, The Gruen Watch Co.
THE NEW CURVEX* WAY
THE OLD WAY
Patented. U. S. Patents No. 1855952 Re. 20480
Here Gruen combines the beauty of a curved case with the accuracy of a full-size movement actually curved to fill the wristform case. Even if the case were removed, the revolutionary CURVEX movement still would conform to the curve of the wrist.
A curved case only. The conventional flat movement, conflicting with the shape of the case, is relatively small and fragile. Accuracy is sacrificed to appearance. The cases in the diagrams above are the same size. But notice the difference in the movements!
PRECISION
GRUEN
A
B
C
D
E
F
G
H
I
J
K
L
M
N
O
P
Q
R
S
T
U
A—STAR: 15 jewels, yellow gold filled case $29.75
B—GLORIA: 15 jewels, yellow gold filled case . $33.75
C—ASHLAND: 17 jewel Precision, yellow gold filled case $39.75
D—MARCIA: 17 jewel Precision, yellow gold filled case $42.50
E—DELIGHT: 17 jewel Precision, yellow gold filled $49.75
F—BANFF: 17 jewel Precision, 14 kt. solid white gold, 20 diamonds . $89.50
G—CALAIS: 17 jewel Precision, Platinum case, 42 diamonds $250
H—LADIES' CURVEX COUNTESS: 17 jewel Precision, 14 kt. yellow or white gold filled $42.50
LADIES' CURVEX PRINCESS: 17 jewel Precision, 14 kt. solid yellow gold . . $59.50
I—LADIES' CURVEX PEERESS: 17 jewel Precision, 14 kt. yellow gold filled, bracelet to match $55
J—LADIES' CURVEX CONSORT: 17 jewel Precision, yellow gold filled, 4 diamonds $67.50
K—LADIES' CURVEX TSARINA: 17 jewel Precision, 14 kt. solid yellow gold, 8 diamonds $100
Copyright 1937, The Gruen Watch Co.
East View, Time Hill Plant, The Gruen Watch Company, Cincinnati, U. S. A.
GRUEN—since 1874, the Watch of Discriminating Americans
L—CURVEX PEER: 17 jewel Precision, 14 kt. yellow gold filled $50
CURVEX TRIUMPH: Same as the Peer, with gold filled bracelet $55
M—CURVEX DUKE: 17 jewel Precision, 14 kt. yellow gold filled $50
CURVEX KING: 17 jewel Precision, 14 kt. solid yellow gold $87.50
N—CURVEX MARSHALL: 17 jewel Precision, 14 kt. yellow gold filled . . $59.50
CURVEX MAJOR: Same as the Marshall, with leather strap $55
O—CURVEX MAJESTY: 17 jewel Precision, 14 kt. yellow gold filled $59.50
CURVEX PRINCE: 17 jewel Precision, 14 kt. solid yellow gold $125
P—MASTER: 15 jewels, yellow gold filled, Guildite back $29.75
Q—CREST DE LUXE: 15 jewels, yellow gold filled, Guildite back . . . $33.75
R—BURTON: 17 jewels, yellow gold filled case $37.50
S—FIFTH AVENUE: 17 jewels, yellow gold filled case $42.50
T—KNOX: 17 jewels, yellow gold filled case $35
U—HARVARD: 17 jewel Precision, yellow or white gold filled $59.50

Gruen, 1937

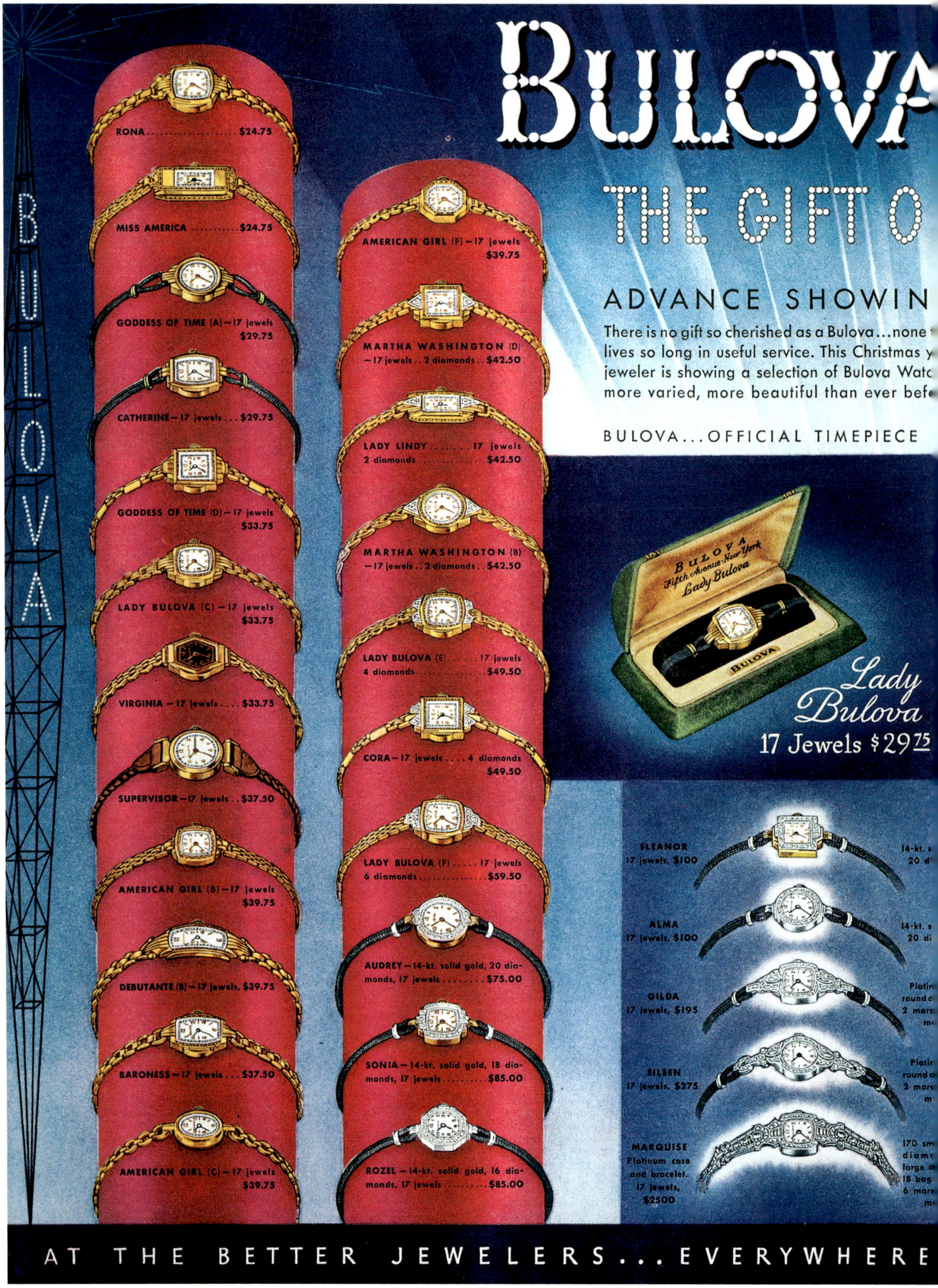
BULOV
THE GIFT O
ADVANCE SHOWIN
There is no gift so cherished as a Bulova...none
lives so long in useful service. This Christmas y
jeweler is showing a selection of Bulova Watc
more varied, more beautiful than ever bef
BULOVA...OFFICIAL TIMEPIECE
BULOVA
RONA.................$24.75
MISS AMERICA..........$24.75
GODDESS OF TIME (A)–17 jewels $29.75
CATHERINE–17 jewels...$29.75
GODDESS OF TIME (D)–17 jewels $33.75
LADY BULOVA (C)–17 jewels $33.75
VIRGINIA–17 jewels....$33.75
SUPERVISOR–17 jewels..$37.50
AMERICAN GIRL (B)–17 jewels $39.75
DEBUTANTE (B)–17 jewels, $39.75
BARONESS–17 jewels....$37.50
AMERICAN GIRL (C)–17 jewels $39.75
AMERICAN GIRL (F)–17 jewels $39.75
MARTHA WASHINGTON (D) –17 jewels..2 diamonds..$42.50
LADY LINDY.......17 jewels 2 diamonds..........$42.50
MARTHA WASHINGTON (B) –17 jewels..2 diamonds..$42.50
LADY BULOVA (E).....17 jewels 4 diamonds..........$49.50
CORA–17 jewels.....4 diamonds $49.50
LADY BULOVA (F).....17 jewels 6 diamonds..........$59.50
AUDREY–14-kt. solid gold, 20 diamonds, 17 jewels........$75.00
SONIA–14-kt. solid gold, 18 diamonds, 17 jewels.........$85.00
ROZEL–14-kt. solid gold, 16 diamonds, 17 jewels.........$85.00
BULOVA Fifth Avenue New York Lady Bulova
BULOVA
Lady Bulova
17 Jewels $29.75
ELEANOR 17 jewels, $100
ALMA 17 jewels, $100
GILDA 17 jewels, $195
EILEEN 17 jewels, $275
MARQUISE Platinum case and bracelet. 17 jewels, $2500
AT THE BETTER JEWELERS...EVERYWHERE

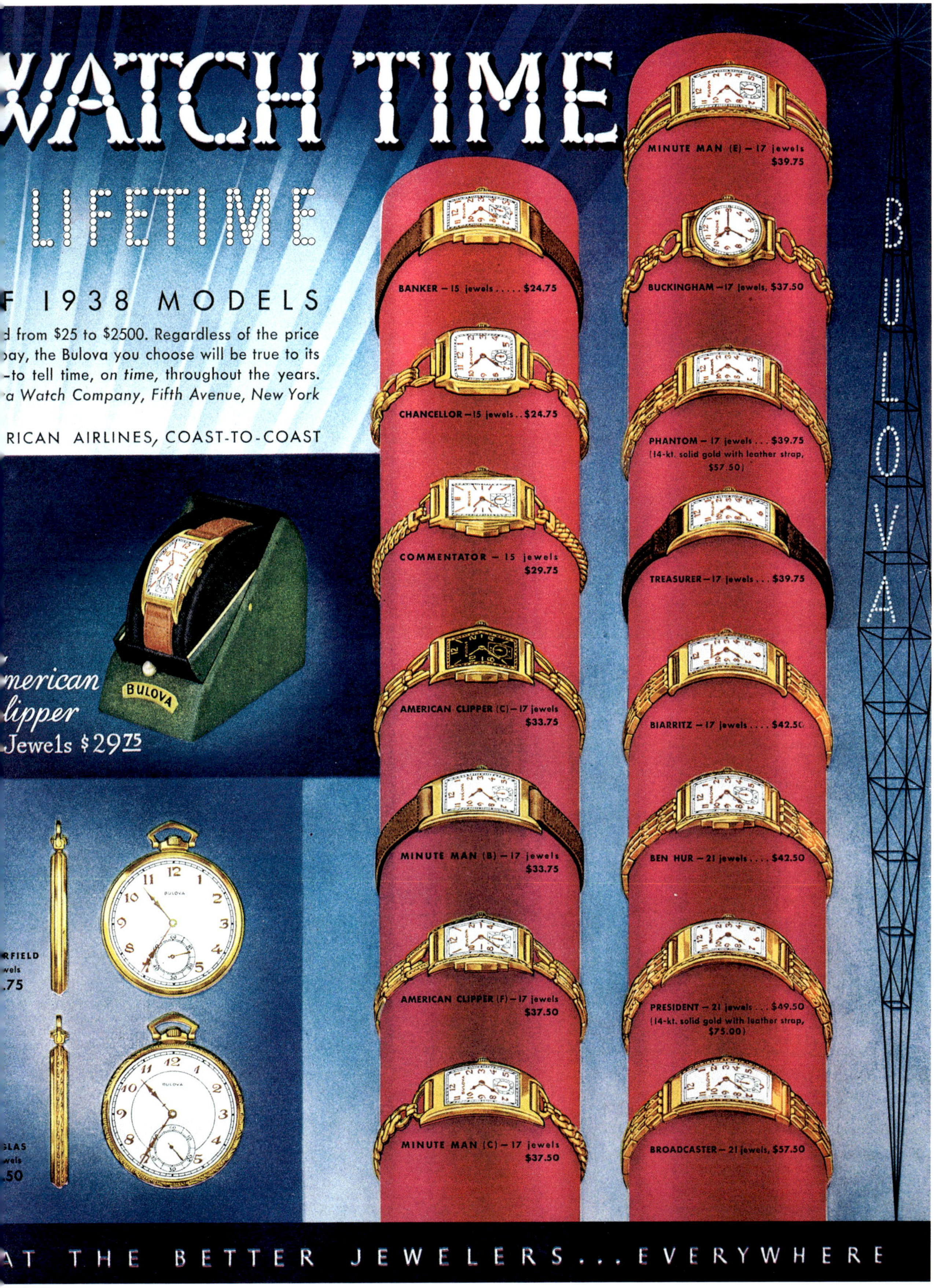
WATCH TIME
LIFETIME
F 1938 MODELS
d from $25 to $2500. Regardless of the price
pay, the Bulova you choose will be true to its
-to tell time, on time, throughout the years.
a Watch Company, Fifth Avenue, New York
RICAN AIRLINES, COAST-TO-COAST
BULOVA
merican
lipper
Jewels $29.75
RFIELD
wels
.75
GLAS
wels
.50
BANKER – 15 jewels $24.75
CHANCELLOR – 15 jewels . . $24.75
COMMENTATOR – 15 jewels $29.75
AMERICAN CLIPPER (C) – 17 jewels $33.75
MINUTE MAN (B) – 17 jewels $33.75
AMERICAN CLIPPER (F) – 17 jewels $37.50
MINUTE MAN (C) – 17 jewels $37.50
MINUTE MAN (E) – 17 jewels $39.75
BUCKINGHAM – 17 jewels, $37.50
PHANTOM – 17 jewels . . . $39.75 (14-kt. solid gold with leather strap, $57.50)
TREASURER – 17 jewels . . . $39.75
BIARRITZ – 17 jewels $42.50
BEN HUR – 21 jewels $42.50
PRESIDENT – 21 jewels . . . $49.50 (14-kt. solid gold with leather strap, $75.00)
BROADCASTER – 21 jewels, $57.50
BULOVA
AT THE BETTER JEWELERS . . . EVERYWHERE

Bulova, 1937

EDISON MAZDA LAMPS
GENERAL ELECTRIC

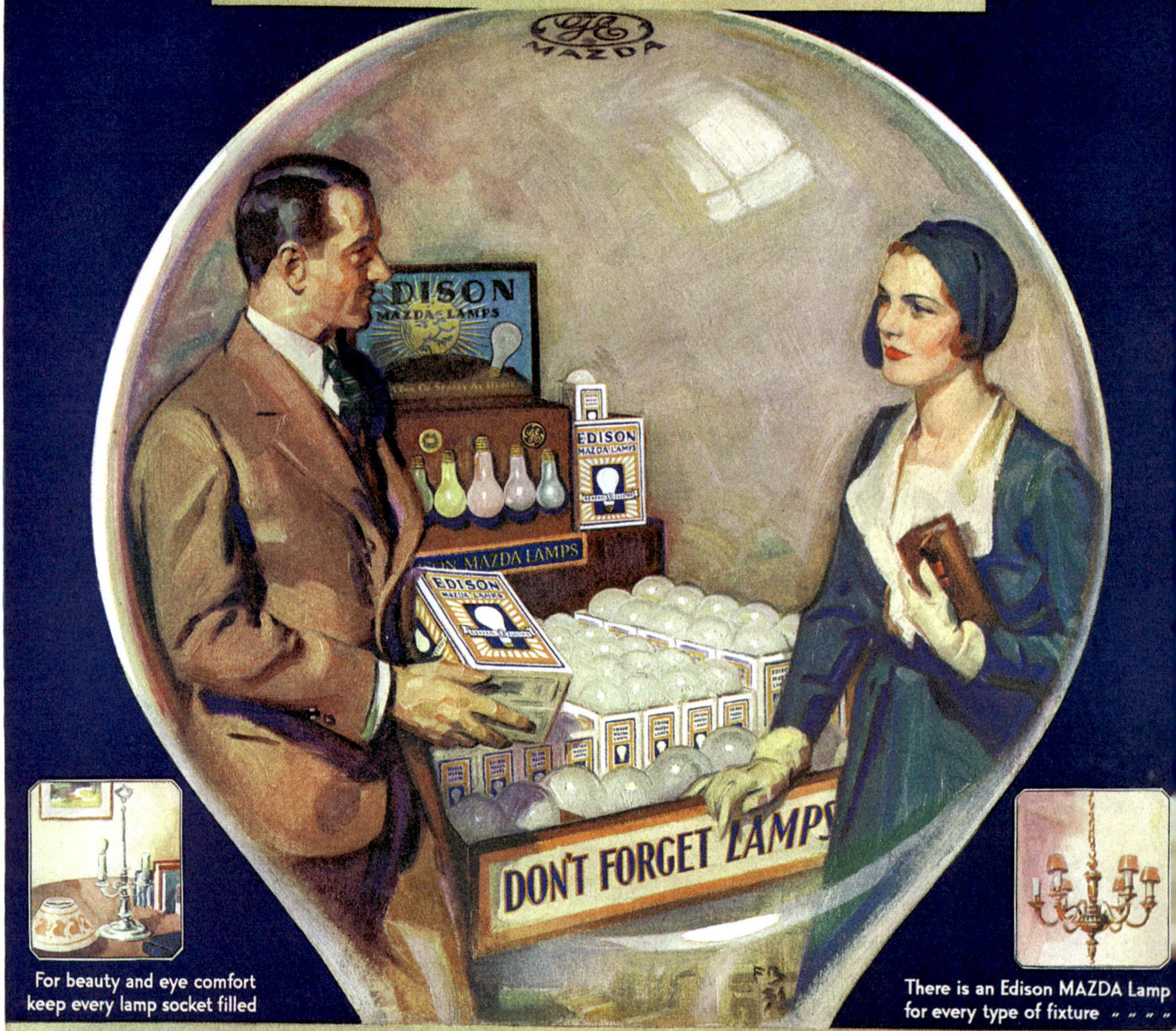

DON'T FORGET LAMPS
Take home a carton today for convenience and good lighting

WHEN you buy Edison MAZDA* Lamps, you get a General Electric product, improved by twenty-five years of research.

Edison MAZDA Lamps have the quality that assures full value of the current consumed. They are nationally advertised, and there is a progressive Edison MAZ Lamp dealer in your neighborhood.

When buying lamps, always look f the name EDISON on the carton and t marks MAZDA and GE on the bulb.

***MAZDA—the mark of a research service**

Join us in The General Electric Program, broadcast every Saturday Evening on a Nation-wide N.B.C. Network · Edison Lamp Works of General Electric, Nela Park, Cleveland, O

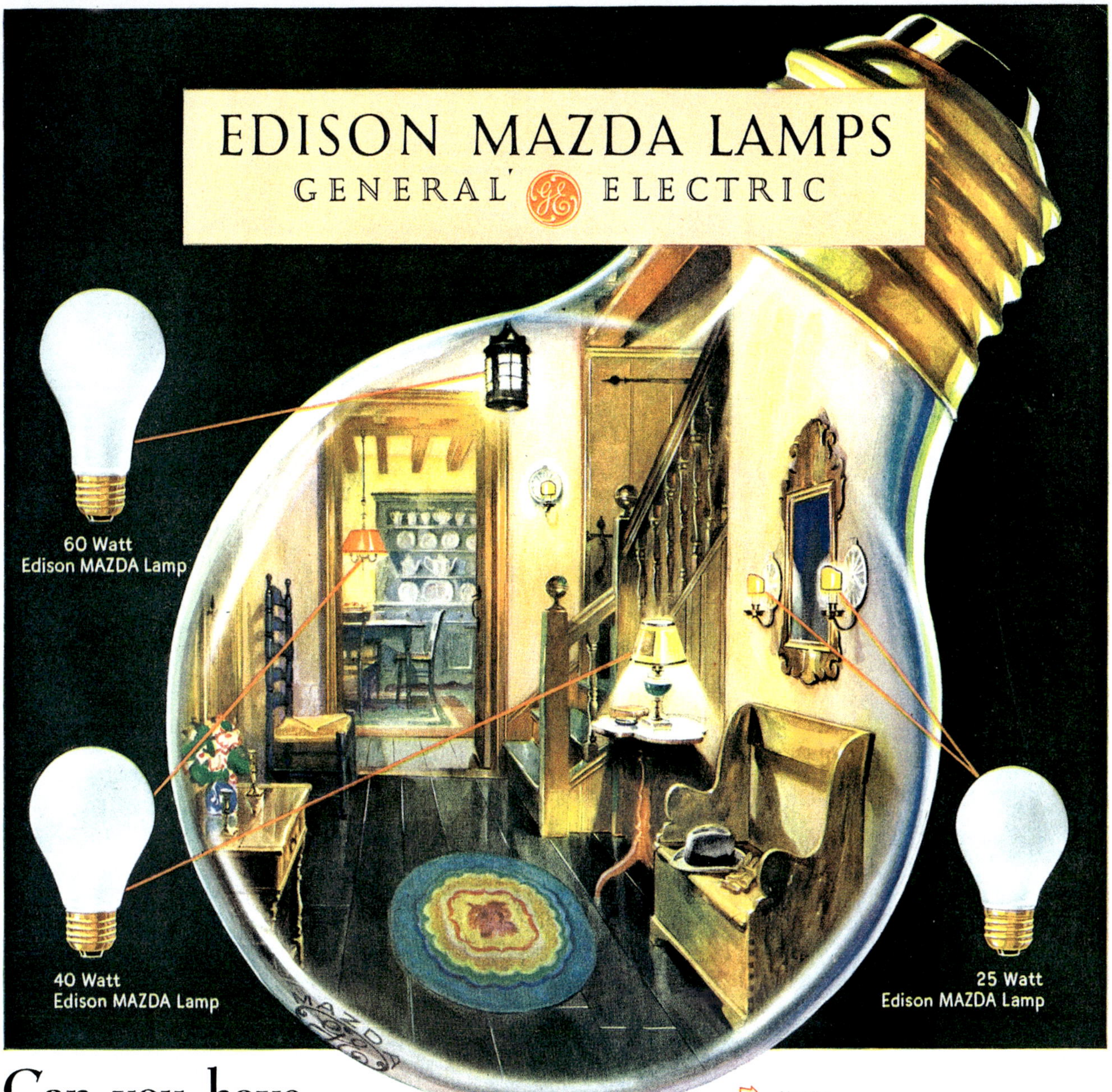

Can you have the RIGHT light in your hall?

Is there a ceiling fixture for general illumination?
Is the stairway well lighted, to prevent missteps?
Is there good light at the mirror?
Does the light in your hall show it at its best?

THE FIRST IMPRESSION of your home will be formed as your guest enters the hall. A favorable first impression will be likely to influence later impressions.

Every hall should be equipped with a ceiling fixture to provide general illumination. The stairway should be well lighted. Dimness there may cause accidents. The importance of good light upon the stairs is emphasized if there are elderly people or small children in your home.

Callers will wish to make use of the hall mirror. A shaded lamp on each side of it will produce the most satisfactory light.

Use Edison MAZDA* Lamps for good lighting throughout your home. Their high quality assures *full value of the current consumed.*

When buying lamps, always look for the name EDISON on the carton and the marks MAZDA and GE on the bulb.

*MAZDA—*the mark of a research service*

MARKS OF QUALITY

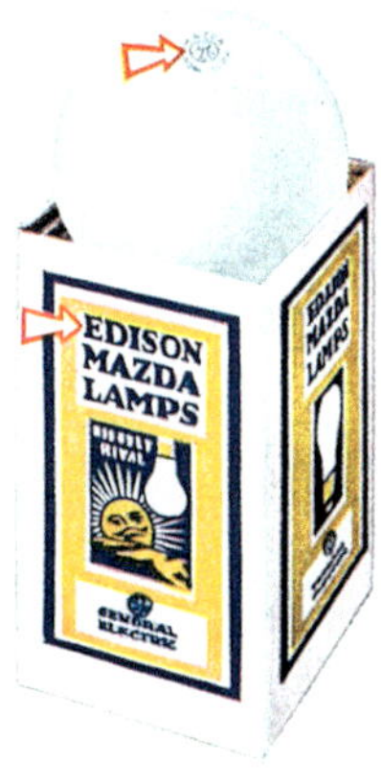

Free booklet tells how to light your home throughout

Few homes have enough light where it is needed. We have prepared a useful illustrated booklet which explains how best to light every room in your home. The coupon will bring you a free copy.

EDISON LAMP WORKS S9
Nela Park, Cleveland, Ohio

Please send me the booklet entitled "How to Light Your Home."

Name..........

Address..........

....

General Electric, 1931 ◄▲

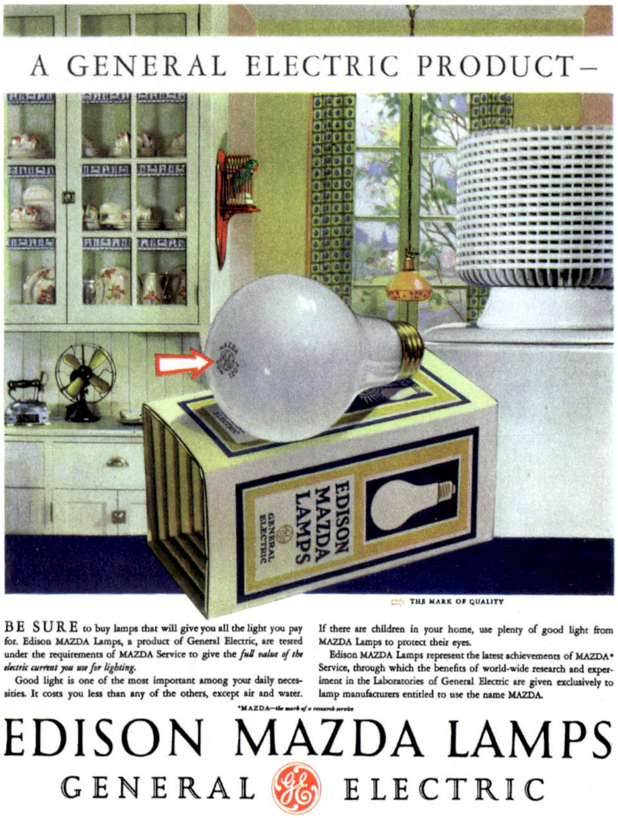

General Electric, 1930

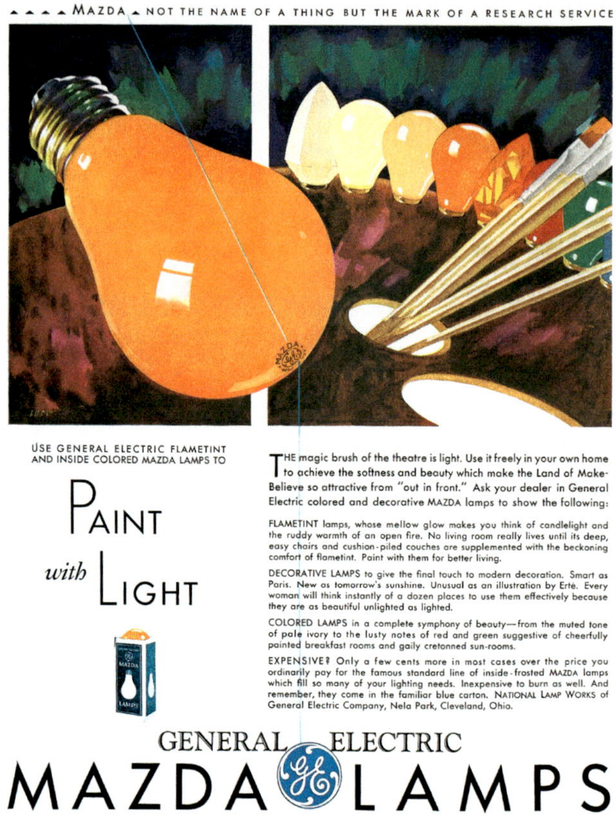

General Electric, 1930

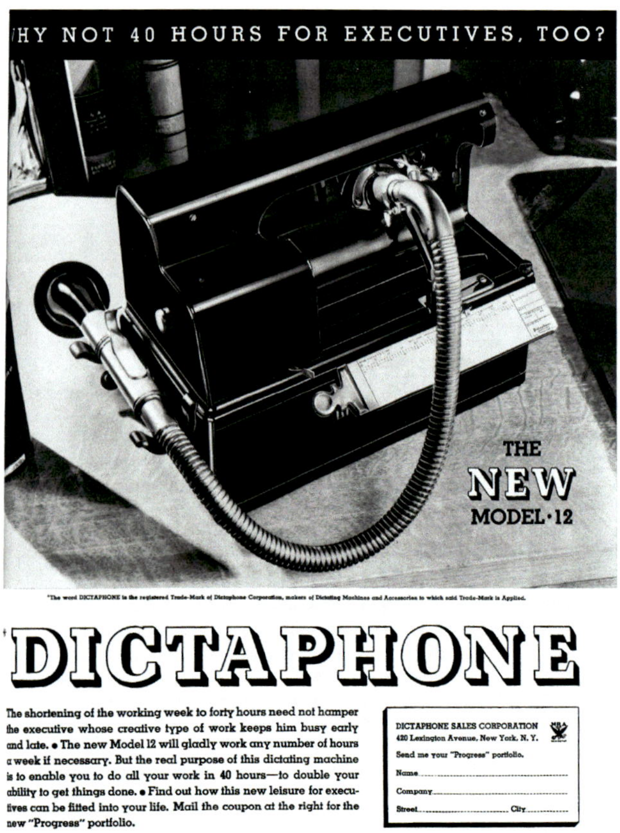

Dictaphone, 1934

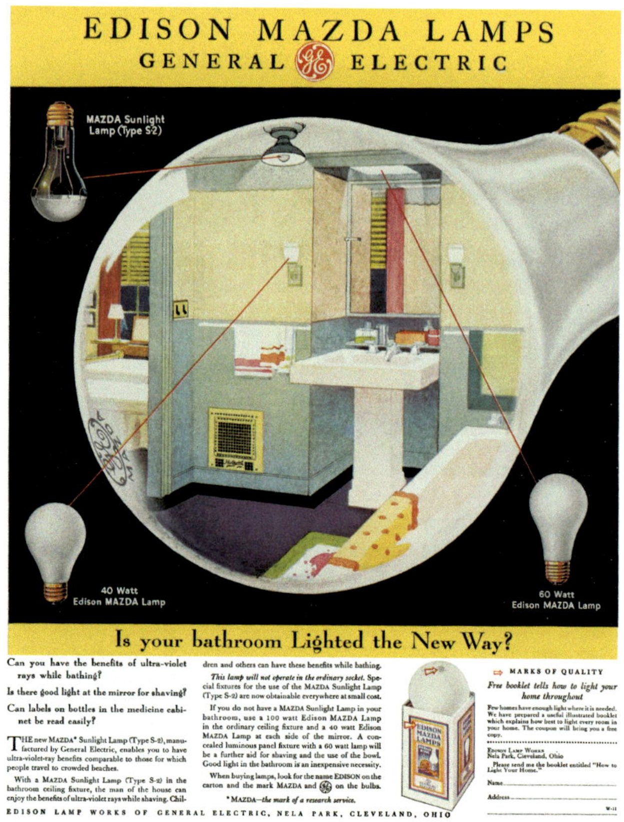

General Electric, 1931

▸ *General Electric, 1937*

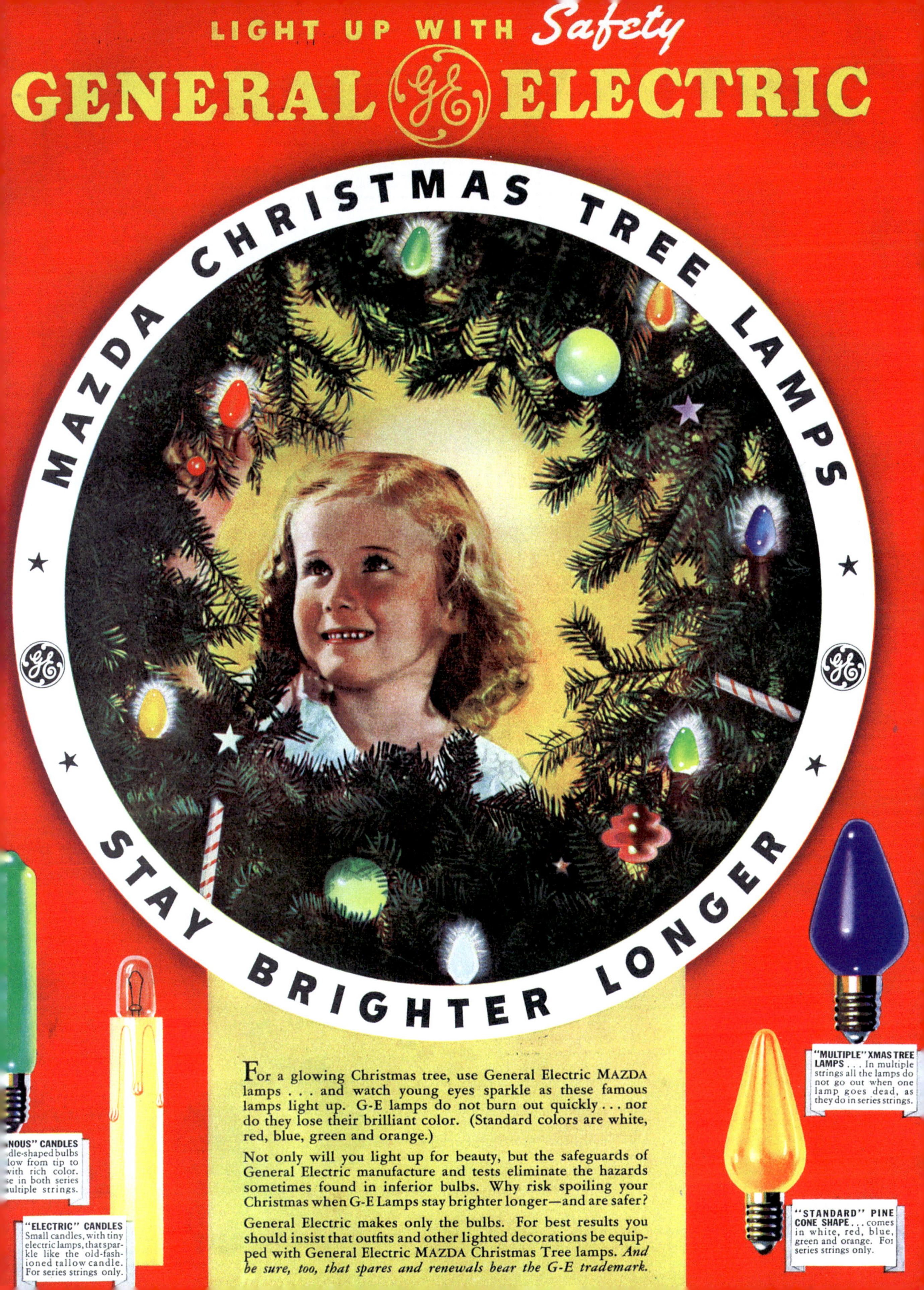

LIGHT UP WITH Safety
GENERAL ELECTRIC
MAZDA CHRISTMAS TREE LAMPS
STAY BRIGHTER LONGER
For a glowing Christmas tree, use General Electric MAZDA lamps . . . and watch young eyes sparkle as these famous lamps light up. G-E lamps do not burn out quickly . . . nor do they lose their brilliant color. (Standard colors are white, red, blue, green and orange.)
Not only will you light up for beauty, but the safeguards of General Electric manufacture and tests eliminate the hazards sometimes found in inferior bulbs. Why risk spoiling your Christmas when G-E Lamps stay brighter longer—and are safer?
General Electric makes only the bulbs. For best results you should insist that outfits and other lighted decorations be equipped with General Electric MAZDA Christmas Tree lamps. *And be sure, too, that spares and renewals bear the G-E trademark.*
NOUS" CANDLES dle-shaped bulbs low from tip to vith rich color. e in both series ultiple strings.
"ELECTRIC" CANDLES Small candles, with tiny electric lamps, that sparkle like the old-fashioned tallow candle. For series strings only.
"MULTIPLE" XMAS TREE LAMPS . . . In multiple strings all the lamps do not go out when one lamp goes dead, as they do in series strings.
"STANDARD" PINE CONE SHAPE . . . comes in white, red, blue, green and orange. For series strings only.

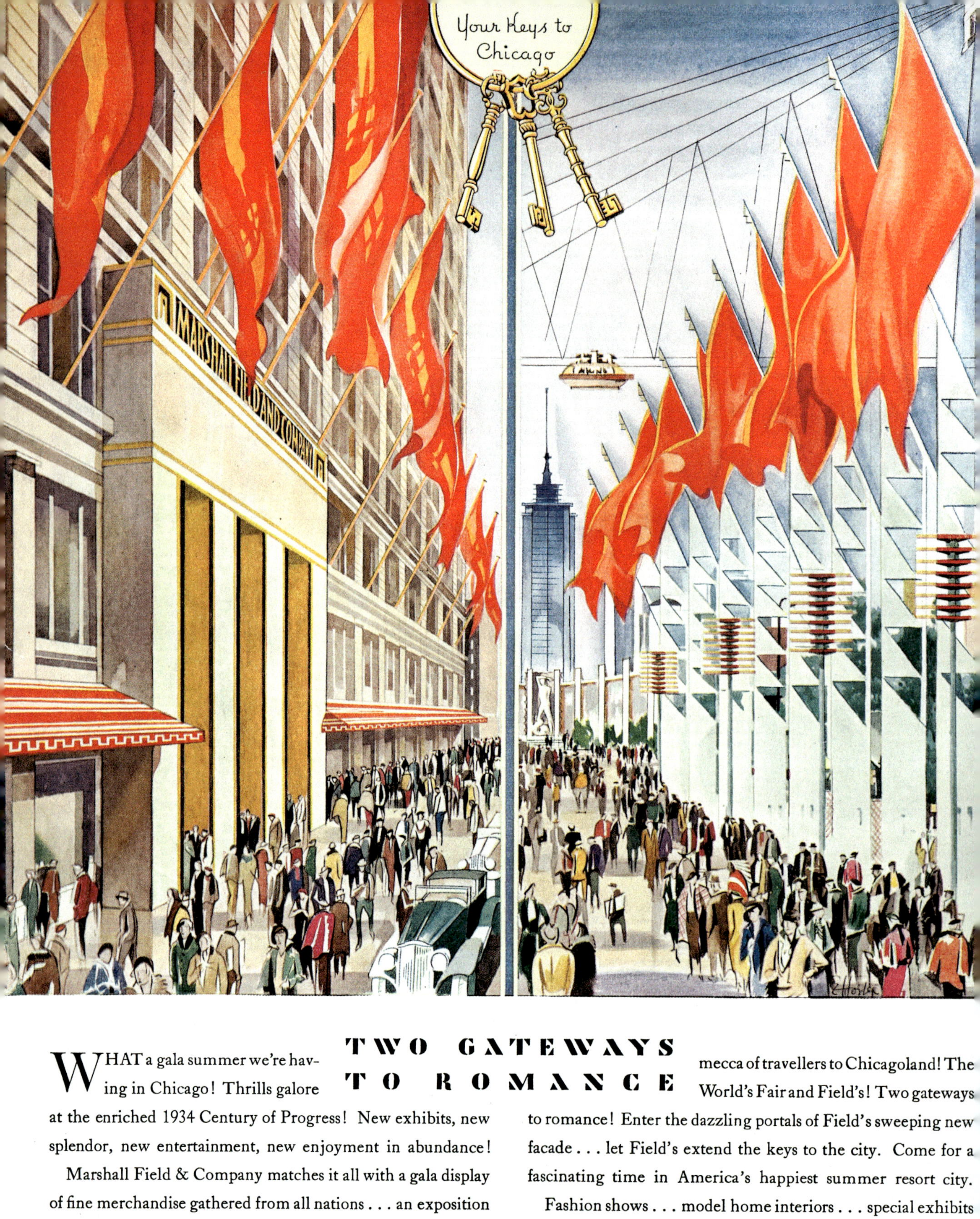

TWO GATEWAYS TO ROMANCE

WHAT a gala summer we're having in Chicago! Thrills galore at the enriched 1934 Century of Progress! New exhibits, new splendor, new entertainment, new enjoyment in abundance!

Marshall Field & Company matches it all with a gala display of fine merchandise gathered from all nations . . . an exposition in itself . . . the art and handicraft of far-flung enterprise *concentrated* within 67 acres of floor space at Field's, favorite mecca of travellers to Chicagoland! The World's Fair and Field's! Two gateways to romance! Enter the dazzling portals of Field's sweeping new facade . . . let Field's extend the keys to the city. Come for a fascinating time in America's happiest summer resort city.

Fashion shows . . . model home interiors . . . special exhibits . . . a place for your luncheon rendezvous . . . to you and your friends we extend this personal invitation to meet at Field's.

Marshall + Field + and + Company + Retail + Chicago

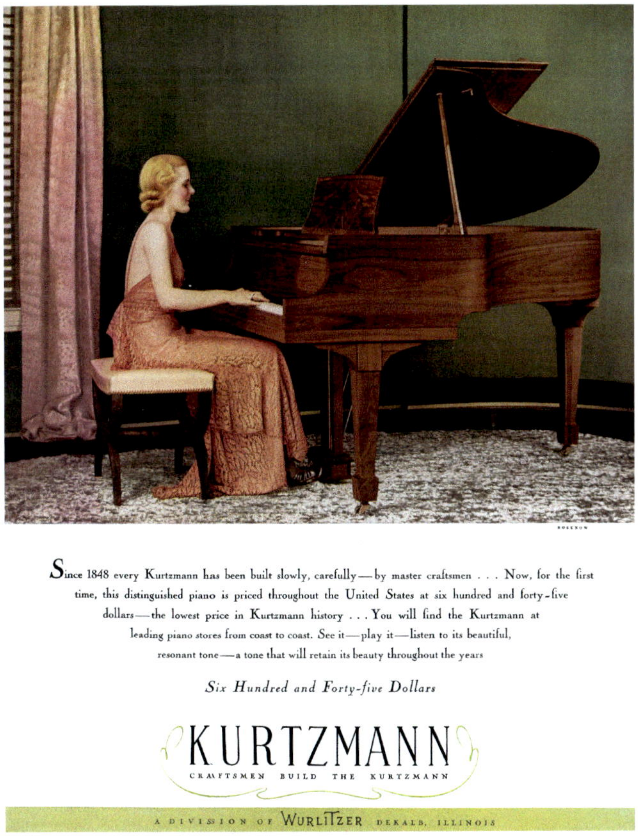

Kurtzmann Piano, 1935

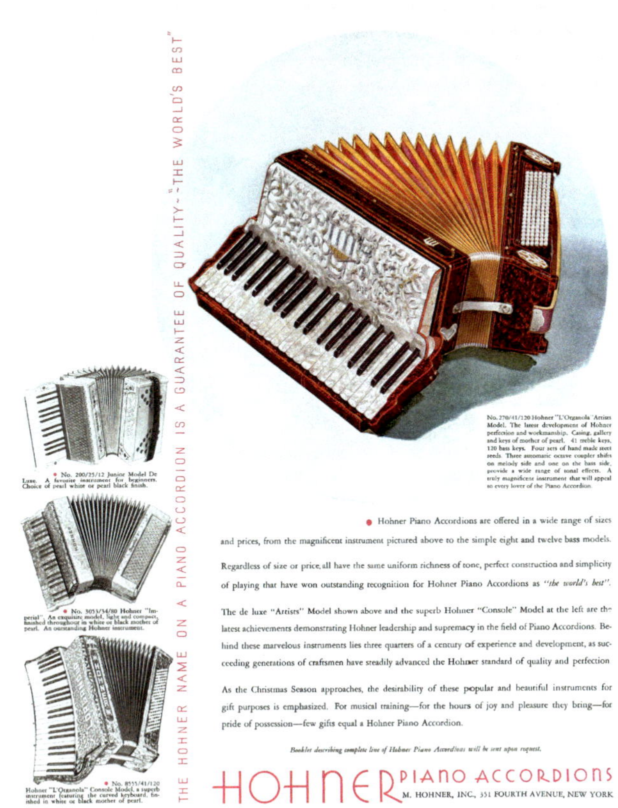

Hohner Accordions, 1934

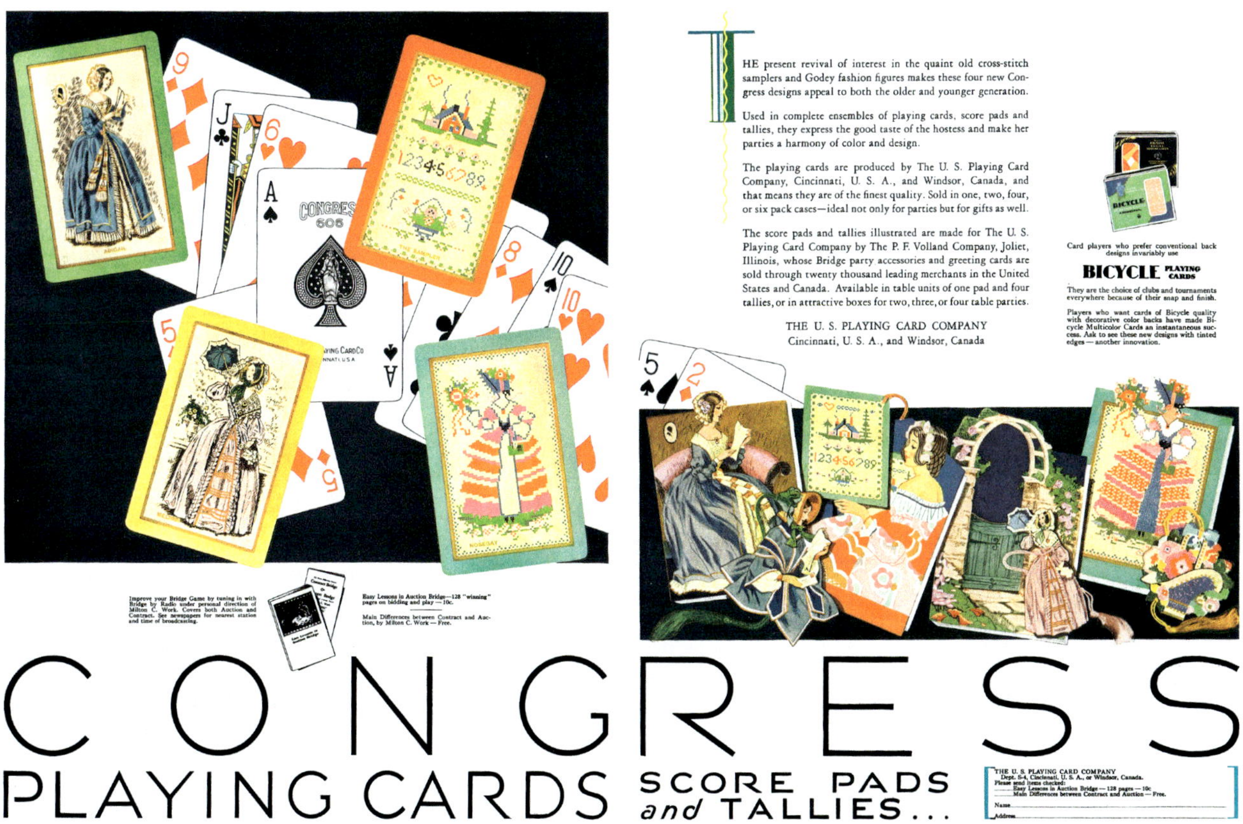

Gateways, 1934 ◄ *Congress Playing Cards, 1930*

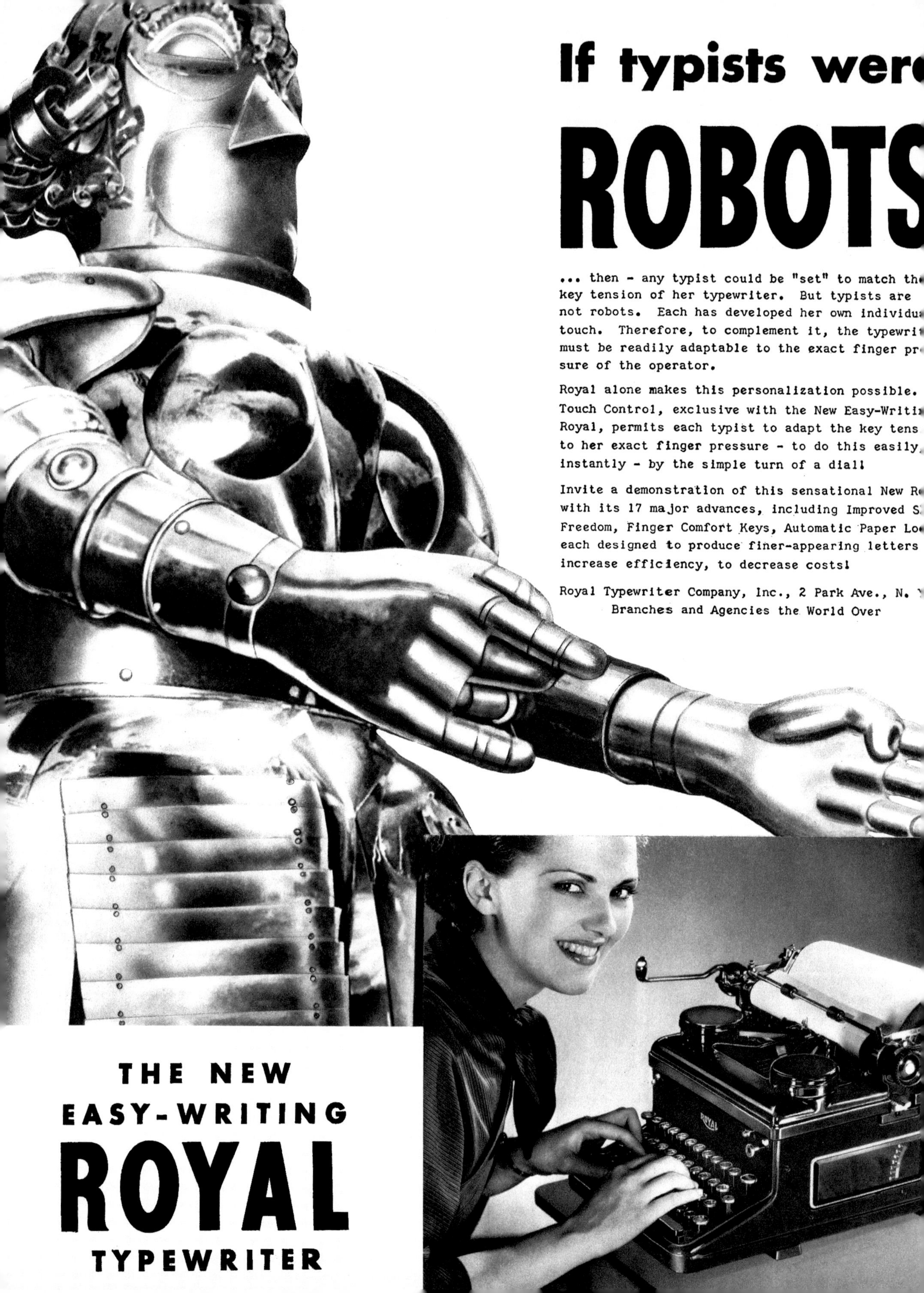
If typists were
ROBOTS
... then - any typist could be "set" to match th key tension of her typewriter. But typists are not robots. Each has developed her own individu touch. Therefore, to complement it, the typewri must be readily adaptable to the exact finger pr sure of the operator.
Royal alone makes this personalization possible. Touch Control, exclusive with the New Easy-Writi Royal, permits each typist to adapt the key tens to her exact finger pressure - to do this easily, instantly - by the simple turn of a dial!
Invite a demonstration of this sensational New R with its 17 major advances, including Improved S Freedom, Finger Comfort Keys, Automatic Paper Lo each designed to produce finer-appearing letters increase efficiency, to decrease costs!
Royal Typewriter Company, Inc., 2 Park Ave., N.
Branches and Agencies the World Over
THE NEW
EASY-WRITING
ROYAL
TYPEWRITER
ROYAL

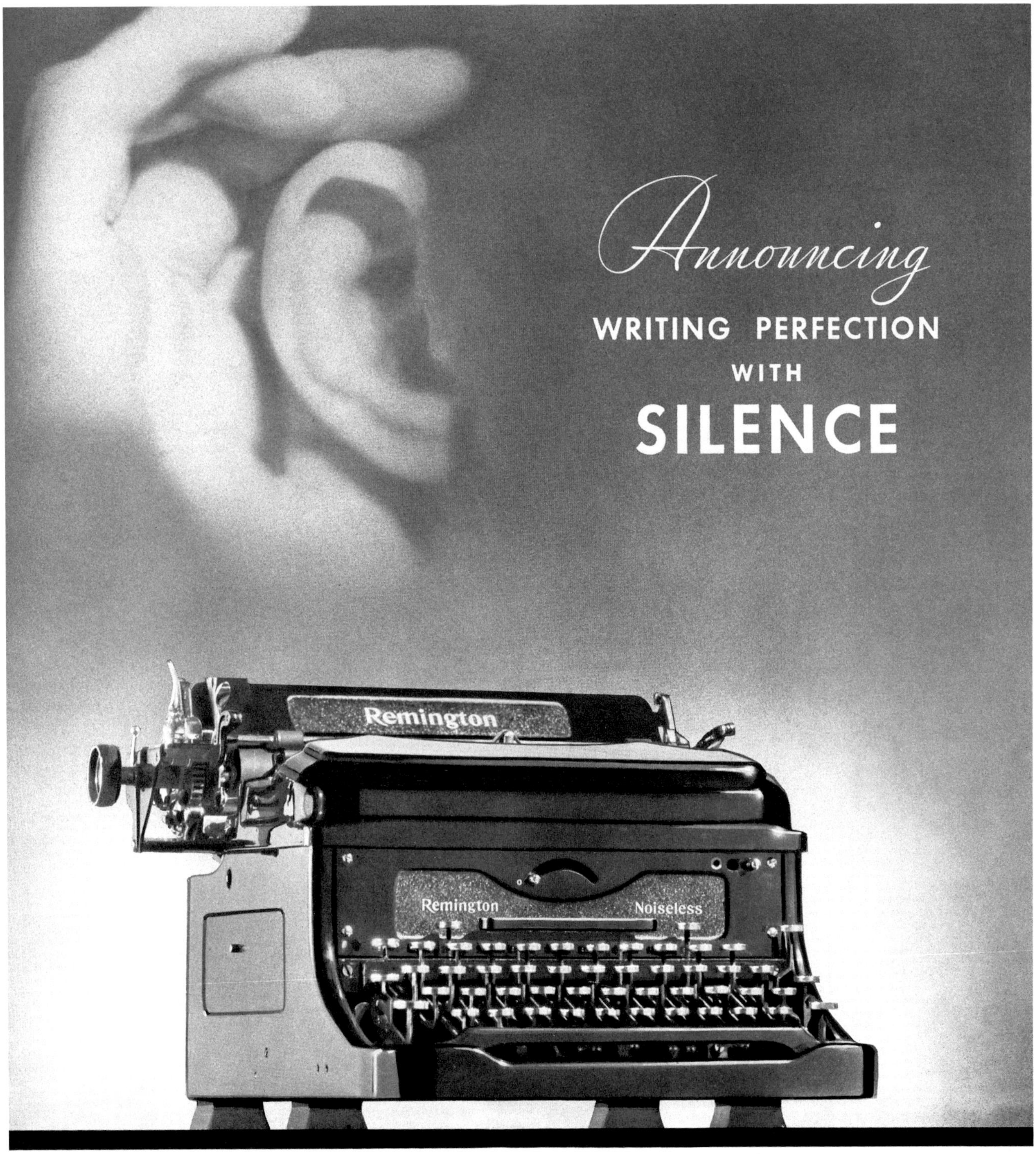

The **NEW** *Remington Noiseless* is the climax of 60 years of typewriter experience. Its writing perfection is the result of dozens of Remington's pioneering developments. Its silence is the result of 24 years' refinement of the noiseless typewriter principle. Combining every known technical improvement into one superlative writing machine, this typewriter incorporates many new operator conveniences as well as new writing efficiency . . . To head stenographers, to secretaries, to executives: We invite you to try this new machine at your leisure. May we also suggest the exchange of your present typewriter for *writing perfection with silence.* Look for Remington Rand in your telephone book. Or, write the Typewriter Division, Remington Rand Inc., Buffalo, New York.

Royal Typewriter, 1935 ◄

Remington Typewriter, 1934

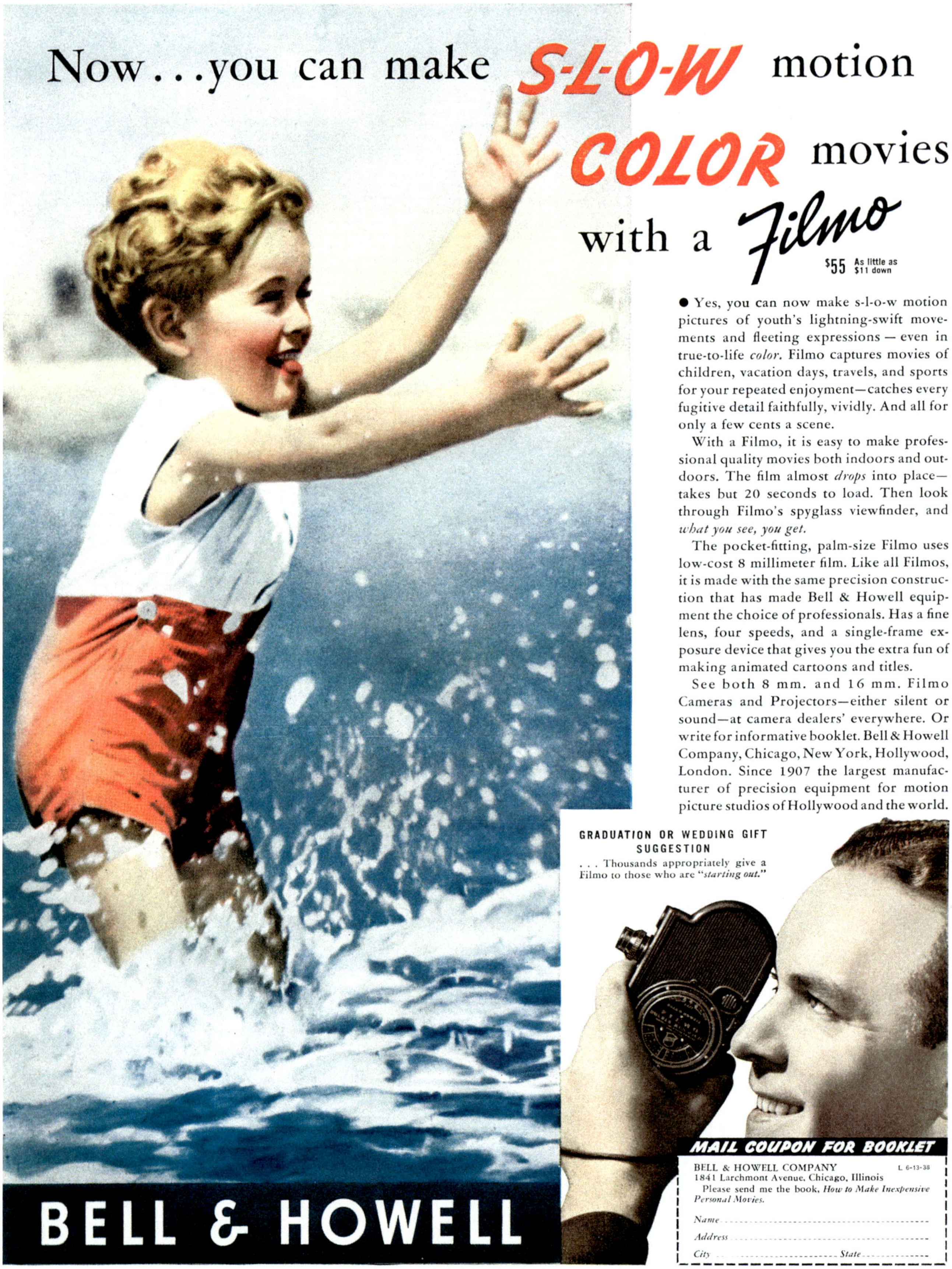

Bell & Howell, 1938

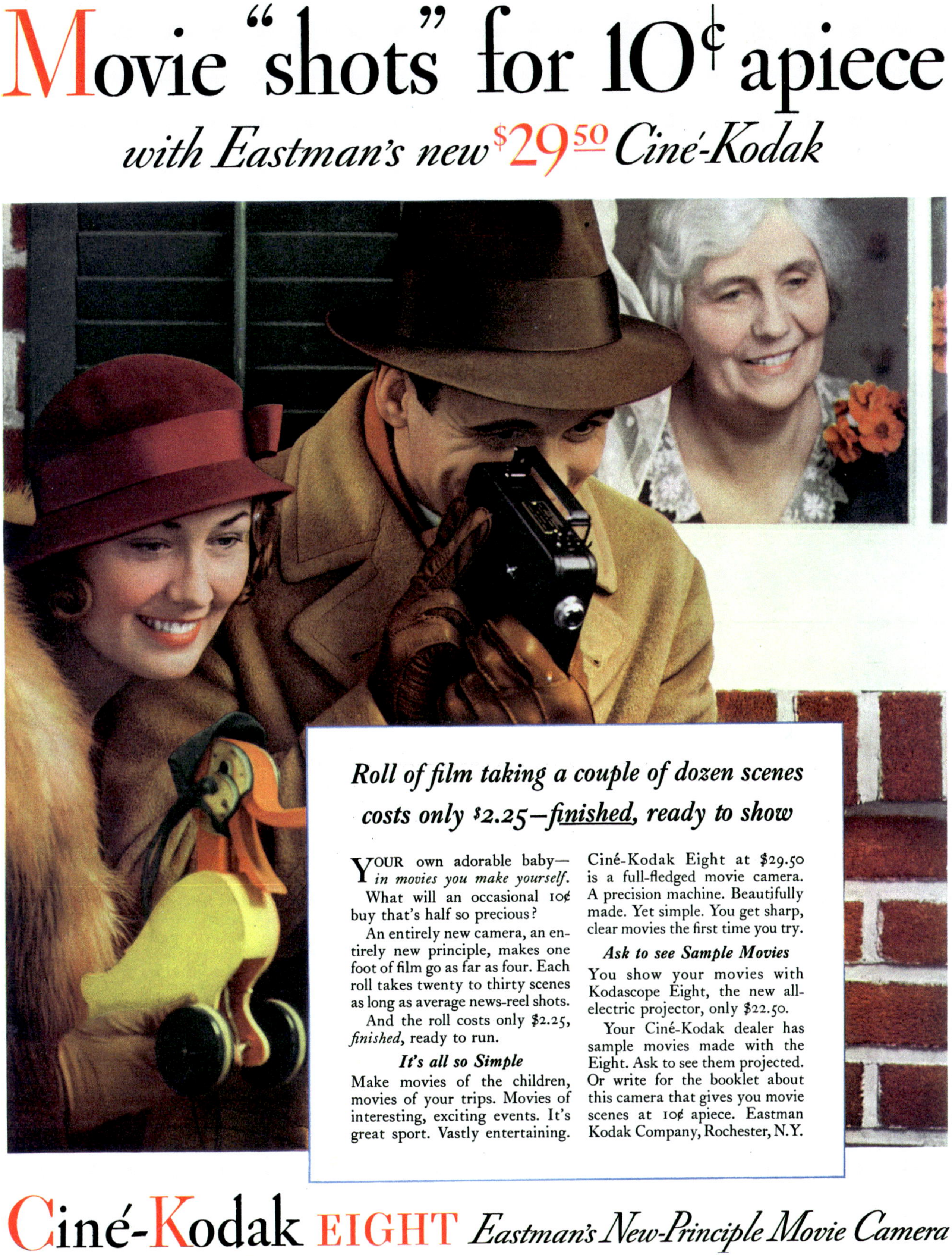

Ciné-Kodak, 1933

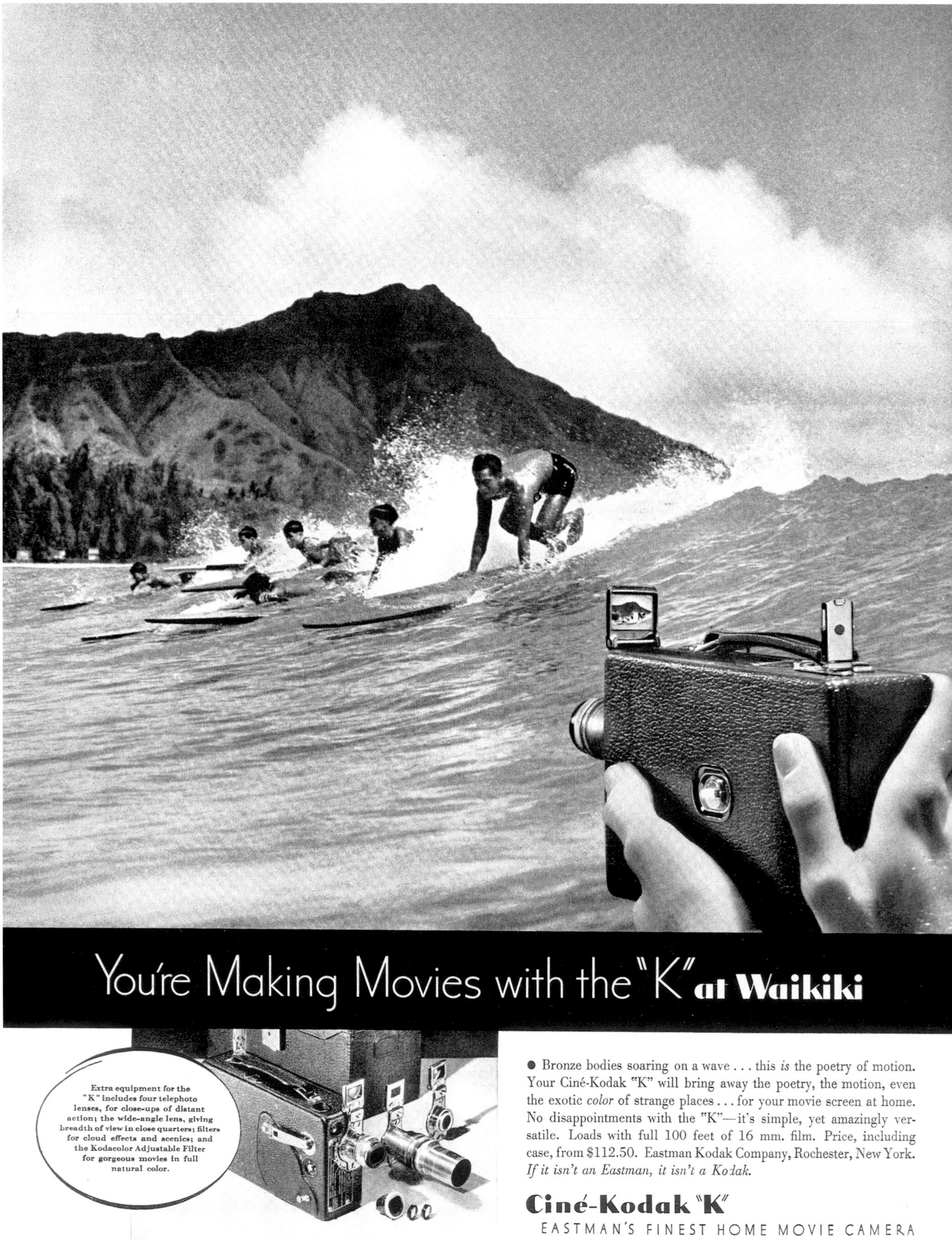

Ciné-Kodak, 1934

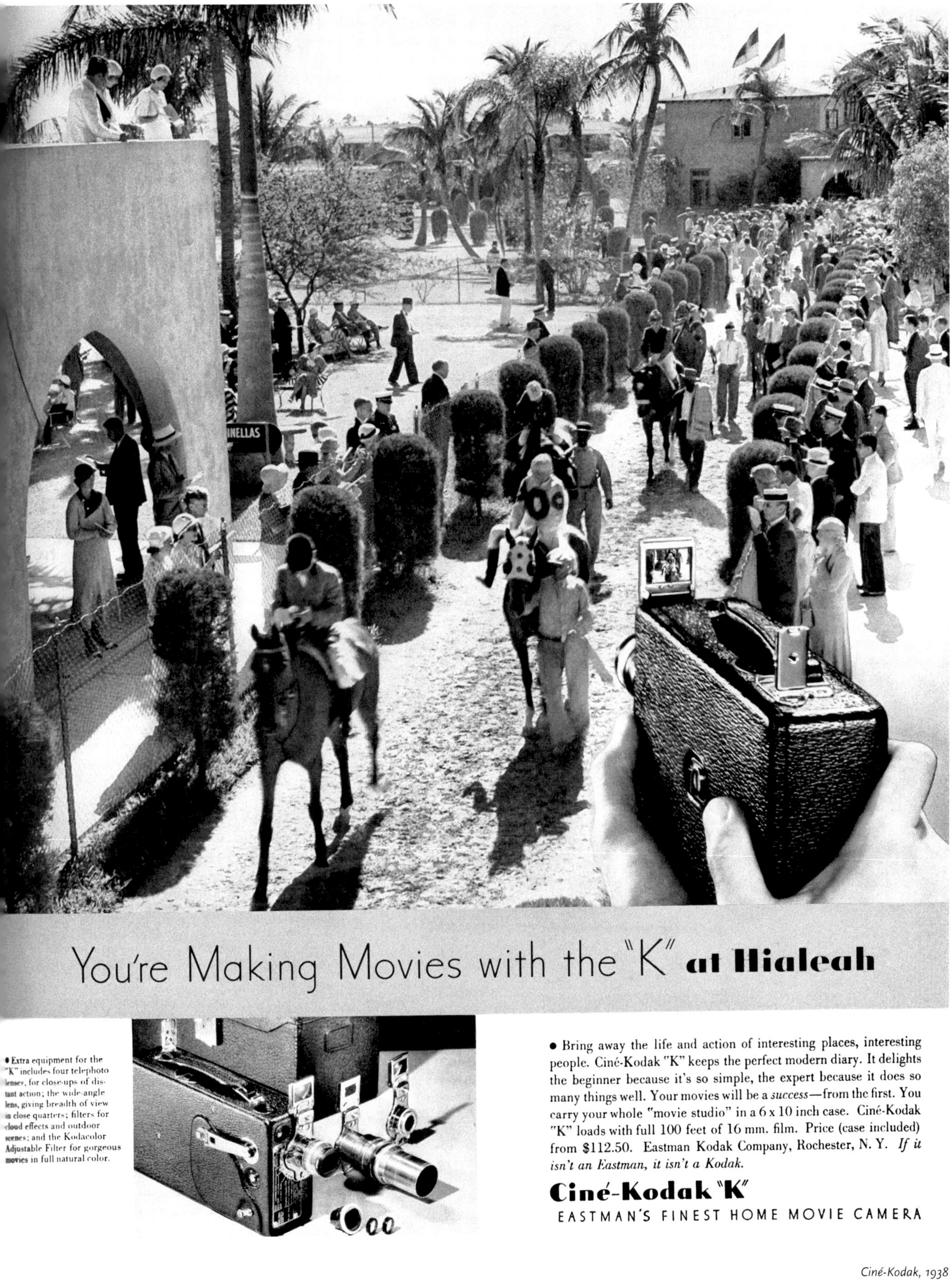

Ciné-Kodak, 1938

THE READYSET TRAVELER

From the unbeaten track . . . from the originality of stylists and camera designers, comes the Readyset Traveler—unquestionably the most outstanding and practical innovation in camera creation of this beauty-conscious day.

In its distinctive specially-woven repp covering, colorful striping, platinum finish, and mechanical rightness there is a cosmopolitan air . . . an expression of the modern spirit that appeals to all who travel—at home or afar. For the Traveler looks like custom-made luggage . . . and *is* luggage—luggage to pack full of pictures.

The Traveler is a certified picture-taker. One you can count on for clear sharp pictures always.

You'll be proud to own, or give as a gift, the colorful, smart Traveler. For the thrill of its possession is surpassed only by the delight in its remarkable picture-taking ability. Ask to see it when you buy your next roll of film.

No. 1 Readyset Traveler—$13.00
(2¼ x 3¼ Pictures)

No. 1A Readyset Traveler—$16.00
(2½ x 4¼ Pictures)

Available
in four different color stripings

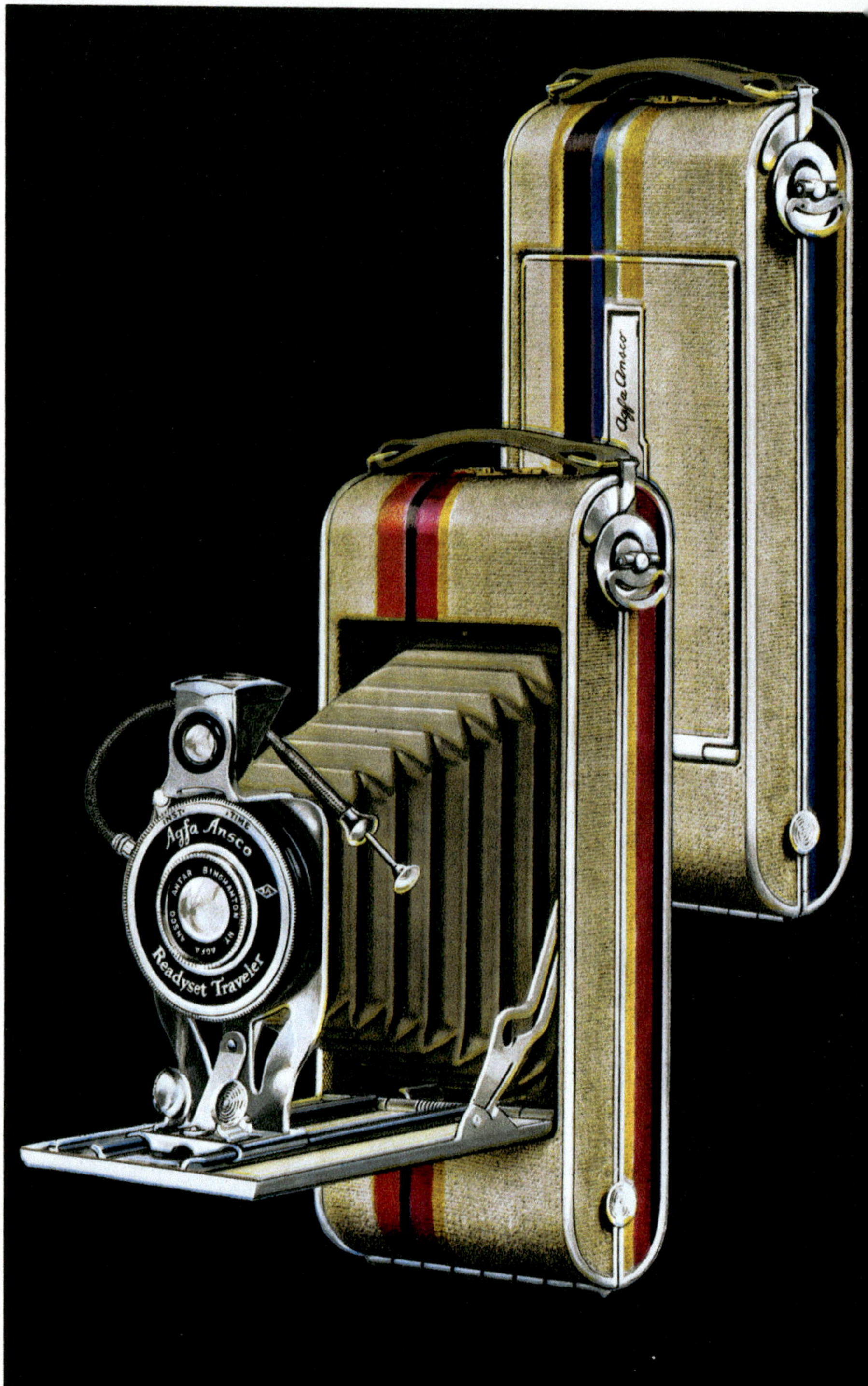

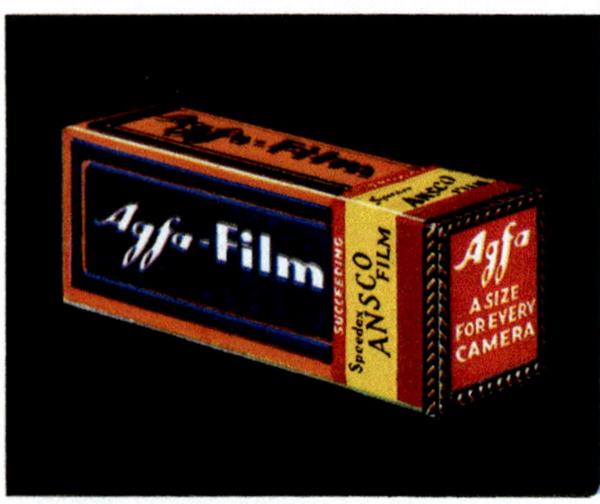

And the Traveler is one of the famous Agfa Ansco Readyset cameras . . . as nearly automatic as cameras can be and yet insure perfect pictures. No focusing, no shutter adjustments—just "Open, aim, shoot." As simple as that.

Agfa film—*the all-weather film*—takes good pictures anywhere . . . under the sun, or under a cloud. A size for every camera.

READYSE
TRAVELE
BY AGFA ANSC

AGFA ANSCO OF BINGHAMTON,
Agfa Ansco Ltd., 204 King Street East, Toronto, C

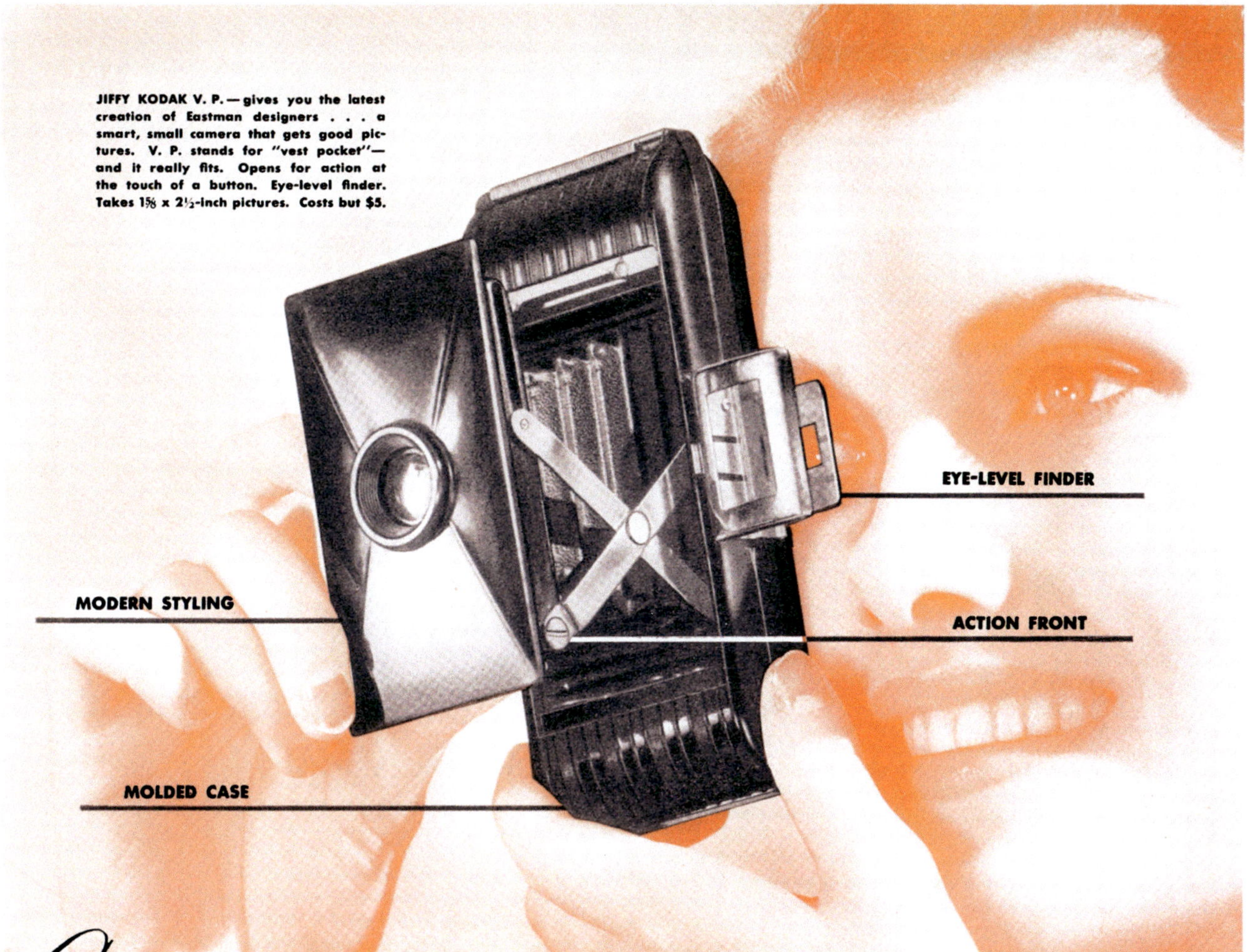

Check these new Kodaks against your old camera

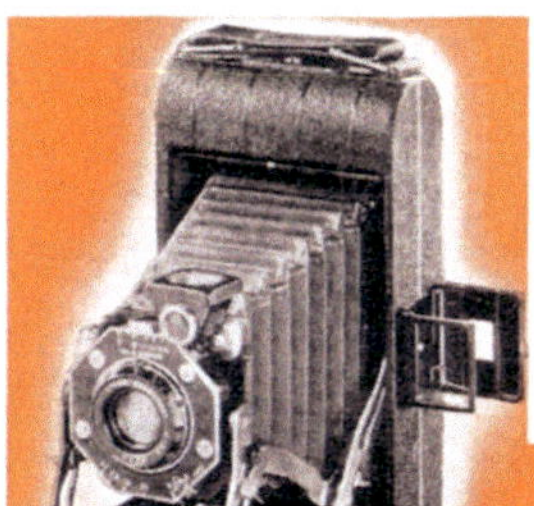

KODAK SIX-20 *(below)*—America's most popular fine camera — rich in appointments, with etched side panels and enameled parts. Its keen *f*.6.3 lens makes snapshots at night with "SS" Film and Photoflood bulbs...its 1/100-second shutter gets children "on the go." Both eye-level and reflecting finders. For 2¼ x 3¼-inch pictures, $17.50. Other models from $14.

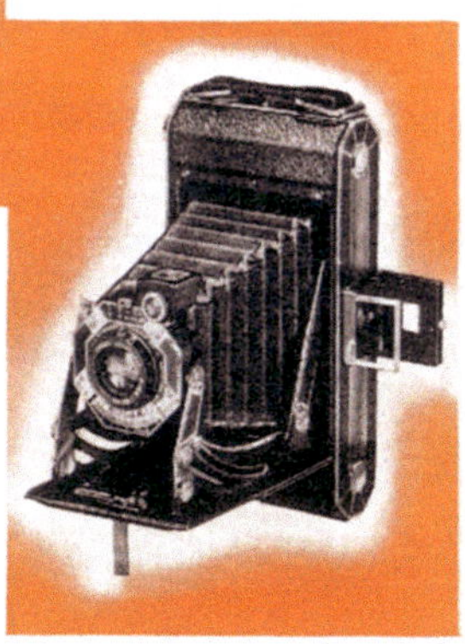

KODAK JUNIOR SIX-20, *f*.6.3 *(above)*—is offered at a remarkably low price for such fine lens and shutter equipment. The Kodak Anastigmat *f*.6.3 lets you make snapshots when you'd ordinarily put your camera away . . on dull days . . in the rain . . AT NIGHT with Kodak "SS" Film and Photoflood bulbs. Has both eye-level and reflecting finders. Three shutter speeds. Makes 2¼ x 3¼-inch pictures. Costs only $13.50. Other models, $10 up.

LIKE ANY OTHER SPORT, picture taking depends a lot on the equipment. Yet many people are still using cameras that were back numbers years ago.

Old models simply don't measure up to 1935 standards. Put yourself behind one of these new Kodaks and you boost your skill about 100%.

Lenses and shutters are better than you could ever before buy at the price. There's more convenience all around. Just look at the features.

Picture this modern world with a modern Kodak—this week-end. Your dealer has the camera you want. Kodaks from $5 up; Brownies as low as $1 . . . What else will bring so much lasting enjoyment?. . . Eastman Kodak Company, Rochester, N. Y. . . . *Only Eastman makes the Kodak.*

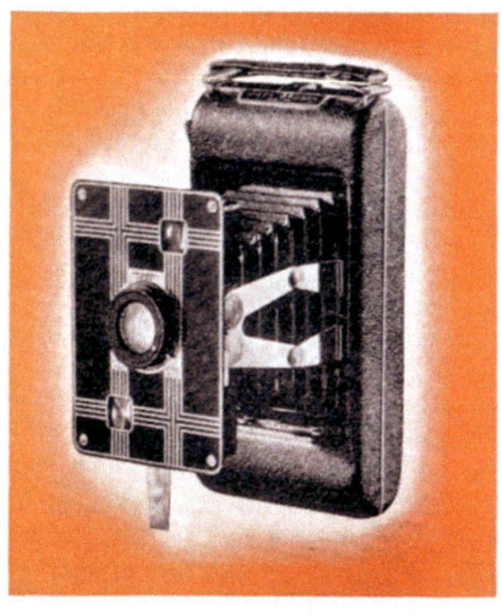

JIFFY KODAK—It works so fast it had to be called "Jiffy." Touch a button—"Pop"—it opens. Touch another—"Click"—it gets the picture. Focuses for near and distant subjects. There's extra smartness in its etched metal front and leather-like finish. Jiffy Six-20, for 2¼ x 3¼-inch pictures, $8. Jiffy Six-16, for 2½ x 4¼-inch pictures, $9.

Agfa Ansco, 1935 ◄ *Kodak, 1935*

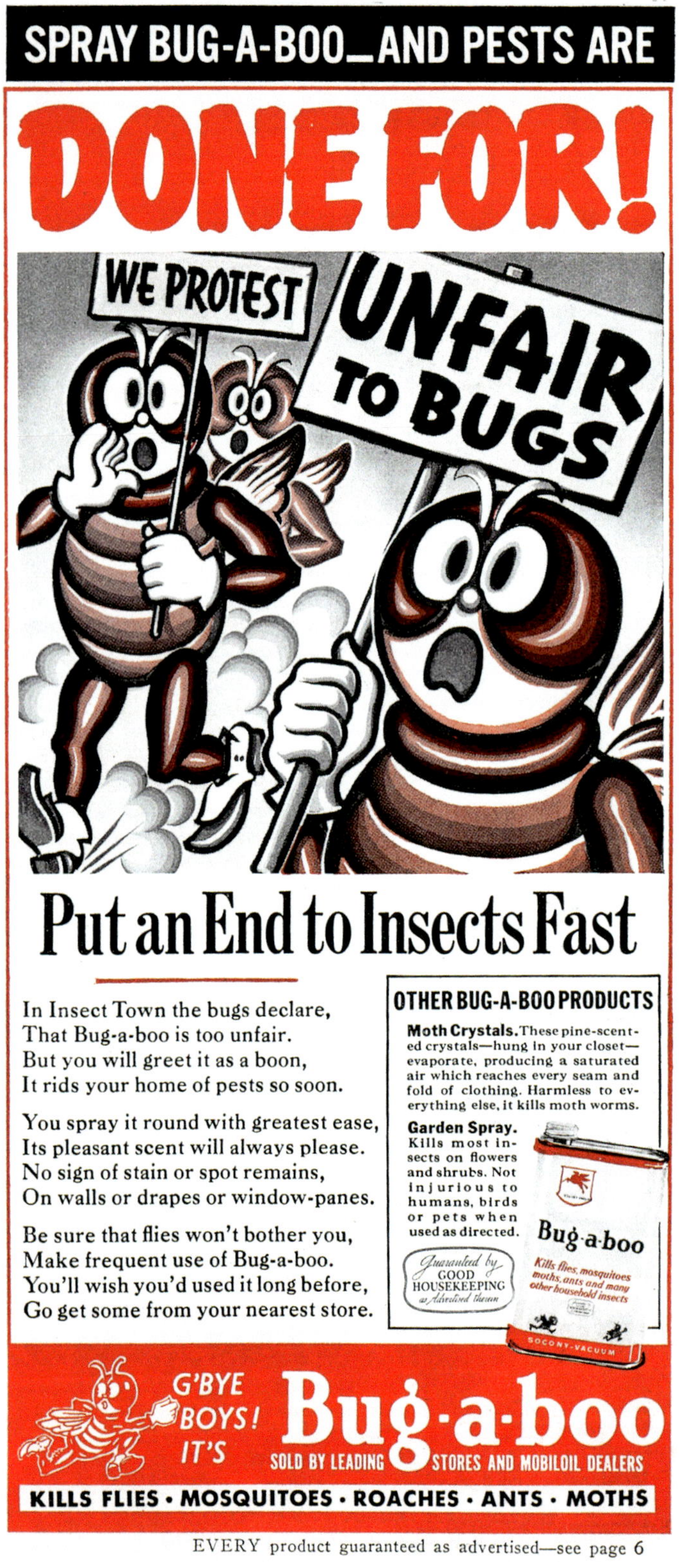

Bug-A-Boo, 1938

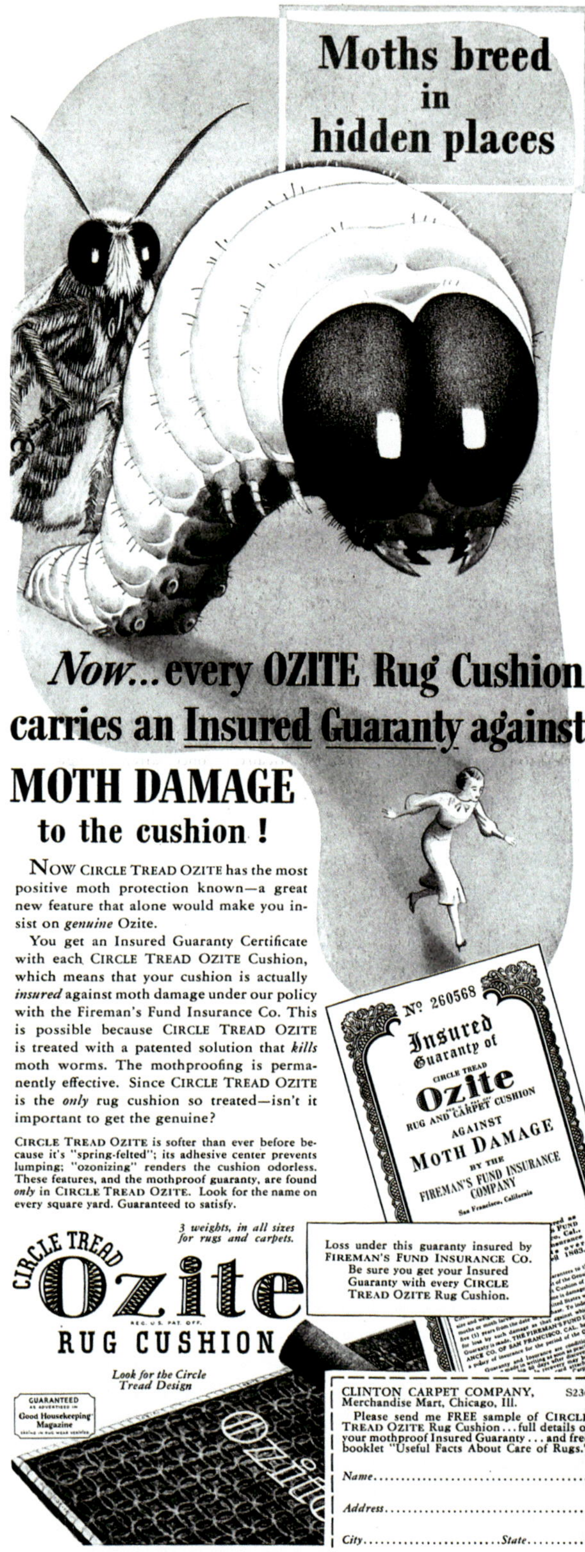

Ozite Rug Cushion, 1930

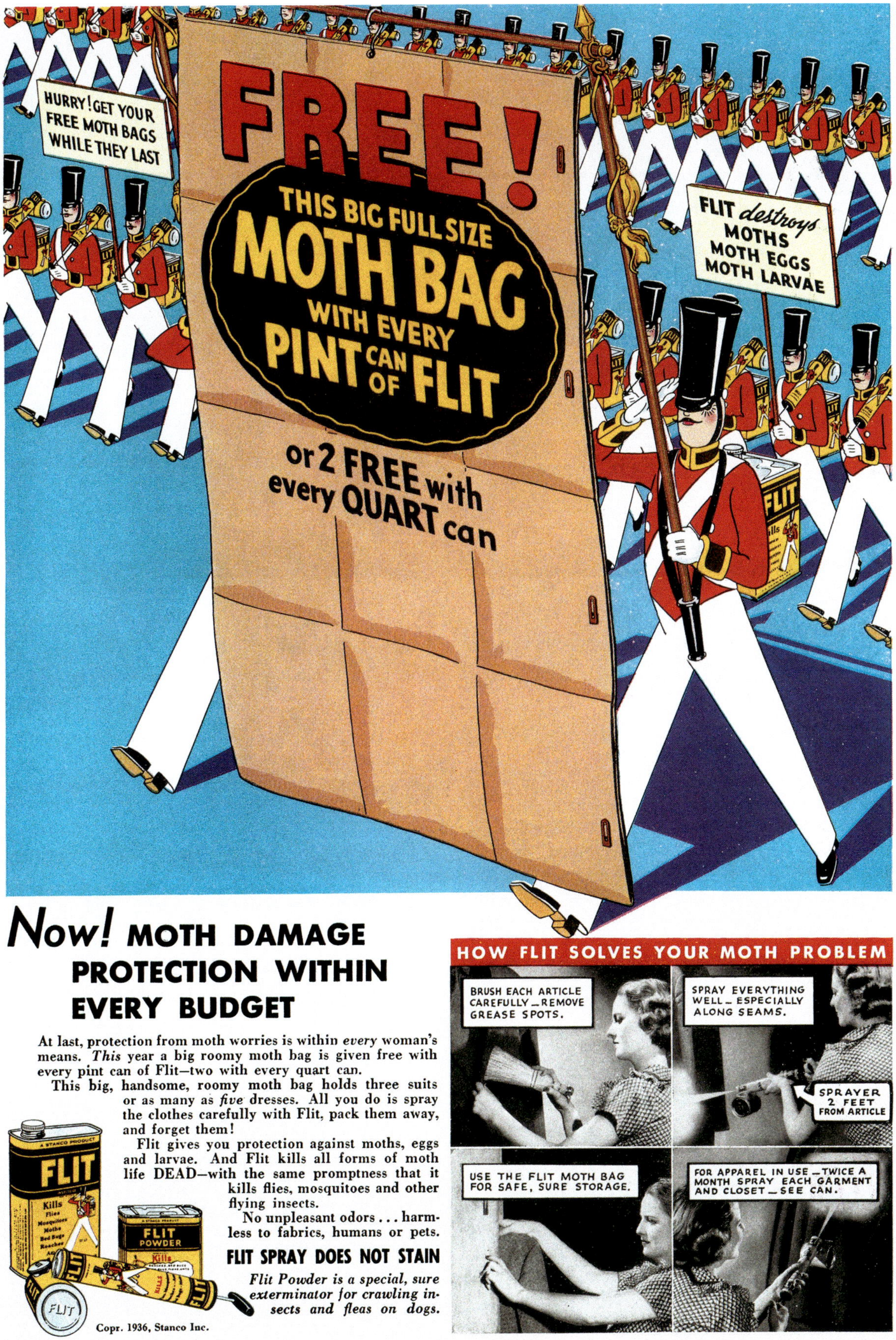
HURRY! GET YOUR FREE MOTH BAGS WHILE THEY LAST
FREE!
THIS BIG FULL SIZE MOTH BAG WITH EVERY PINT CAN OF FLIT
or 2 FREE with every QUART can
FLIT destroys MOTHS MOTH EGGS MOTH LARVAE
Now! MOTH DAMAGE PROTECTION WITHIN EVERY BUDGET
At last, protection from moth worries is within every woman's means. This year a big roomy moth bag is given free with every pint can of Flit—two with every quart can.
This big, handsome, roomy moth bag holds three suits or as many as five dresses. All you do is spray the clothes carefully with Flit, pack them away, and forget them!
Flit gives you protection against moths, eggs and larvae. And Flit kills all forms of moth life DEAD—with the same promptness that it kills flies, mosquitoes and other flying insects.
No unpleasant odors . . . harmless to fabrics, humans or pets.
FLIT SPRAY DOES NOT STAIN
Flit Powder is a special, sure exterminator for crawling insects and fleas on dogs.
Copr. 1936, Stanco Inc.
HOW FLIT SOLVES YOUR MOTH PROBLEM
BRUSH EACH ARTICLE CAREFULLY—REMOVE GREASE SPOTS.
SPRAY EVERYTHING WELL—ESPECIALLY ALONG SEAMS.
SPRAYER 2 FEET FROM ARTICLE
USE THE FLIT MOTH BAG FOR SAFE, SURE STORAGE.
FOR APPAREL IN USE—TWICE A MONTH SPRAY EACH GARMENT AND CLOSET—SEE CAN.

Flit, 1936

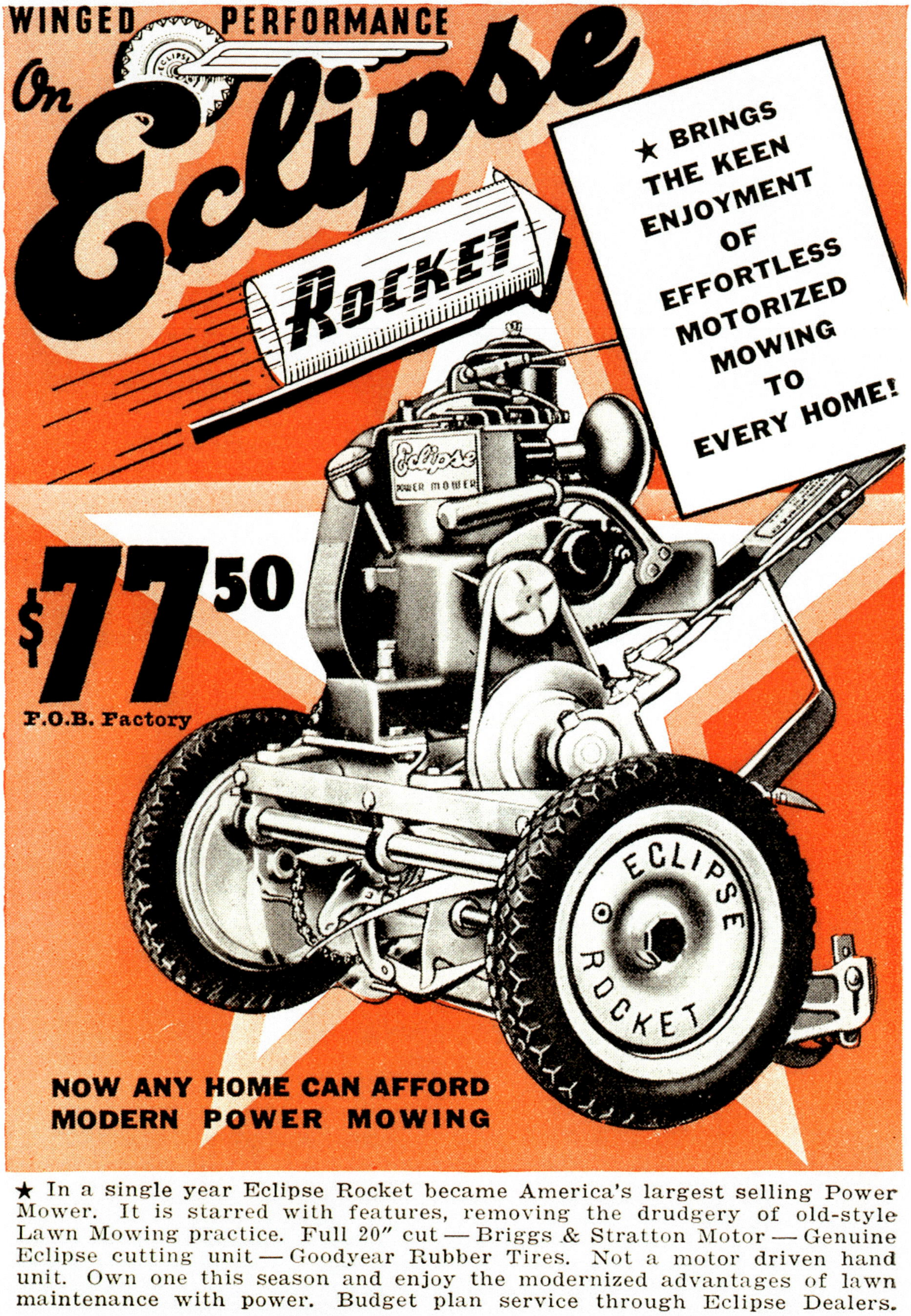

Eclipse Mower, 1939

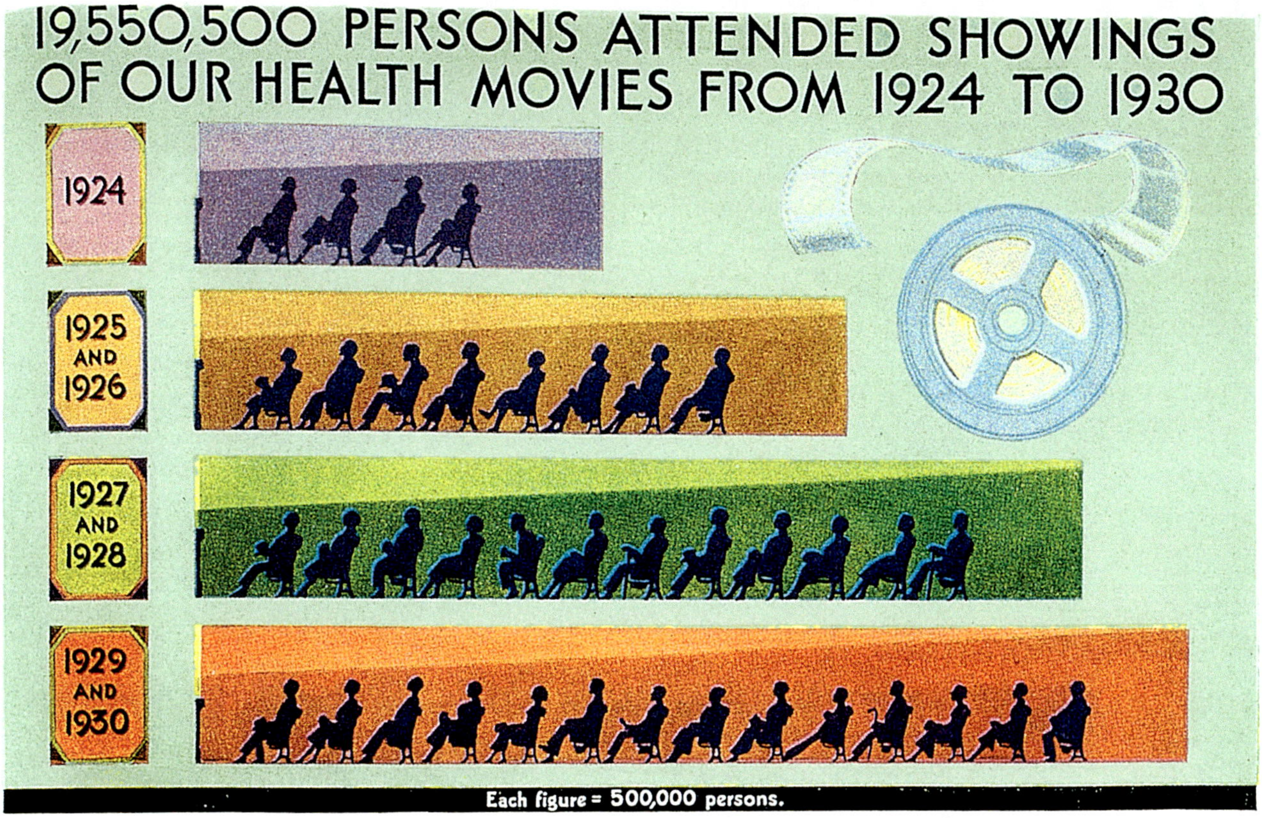

Courtesy of Metropolitan Life Insurance Company—Four-color process, half-tone engraving, 133 screen

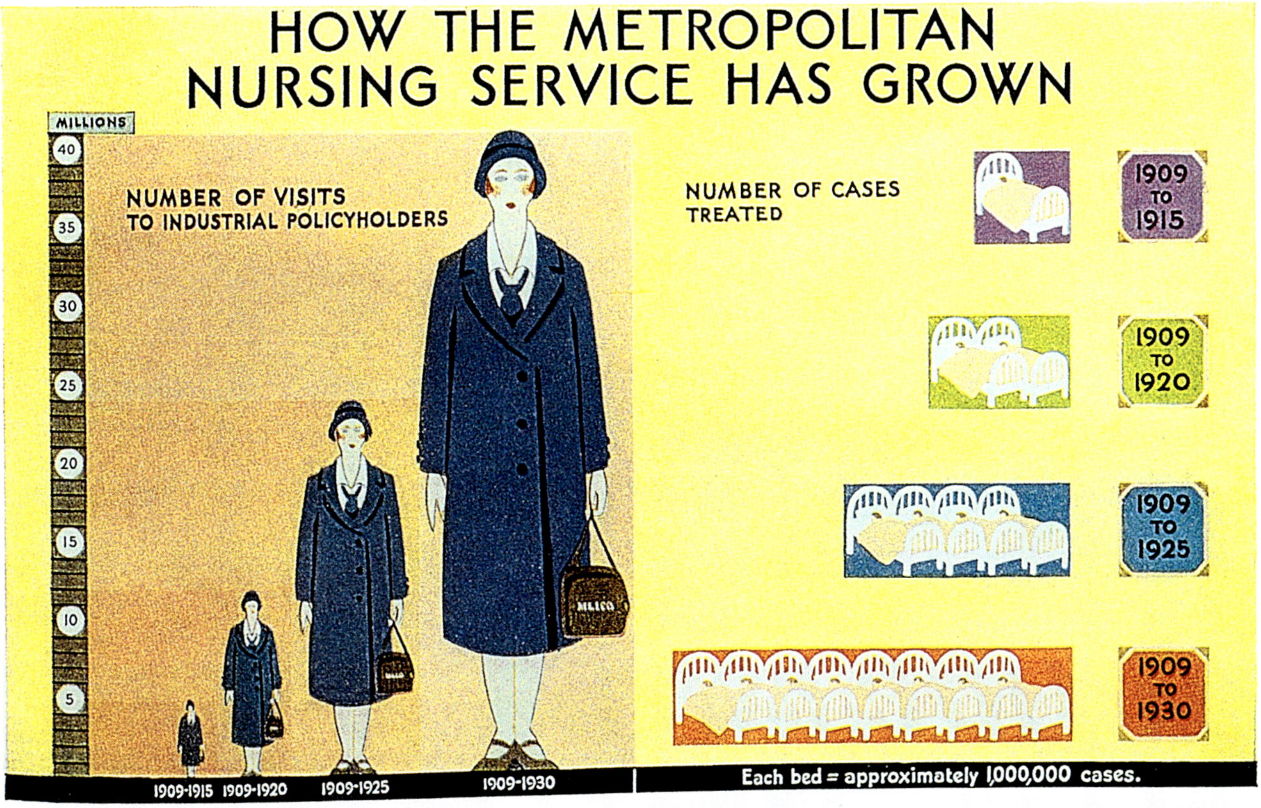

FOR PRINTERS — NUMBER 76 —

Metropolitan Life Insurance, 1932

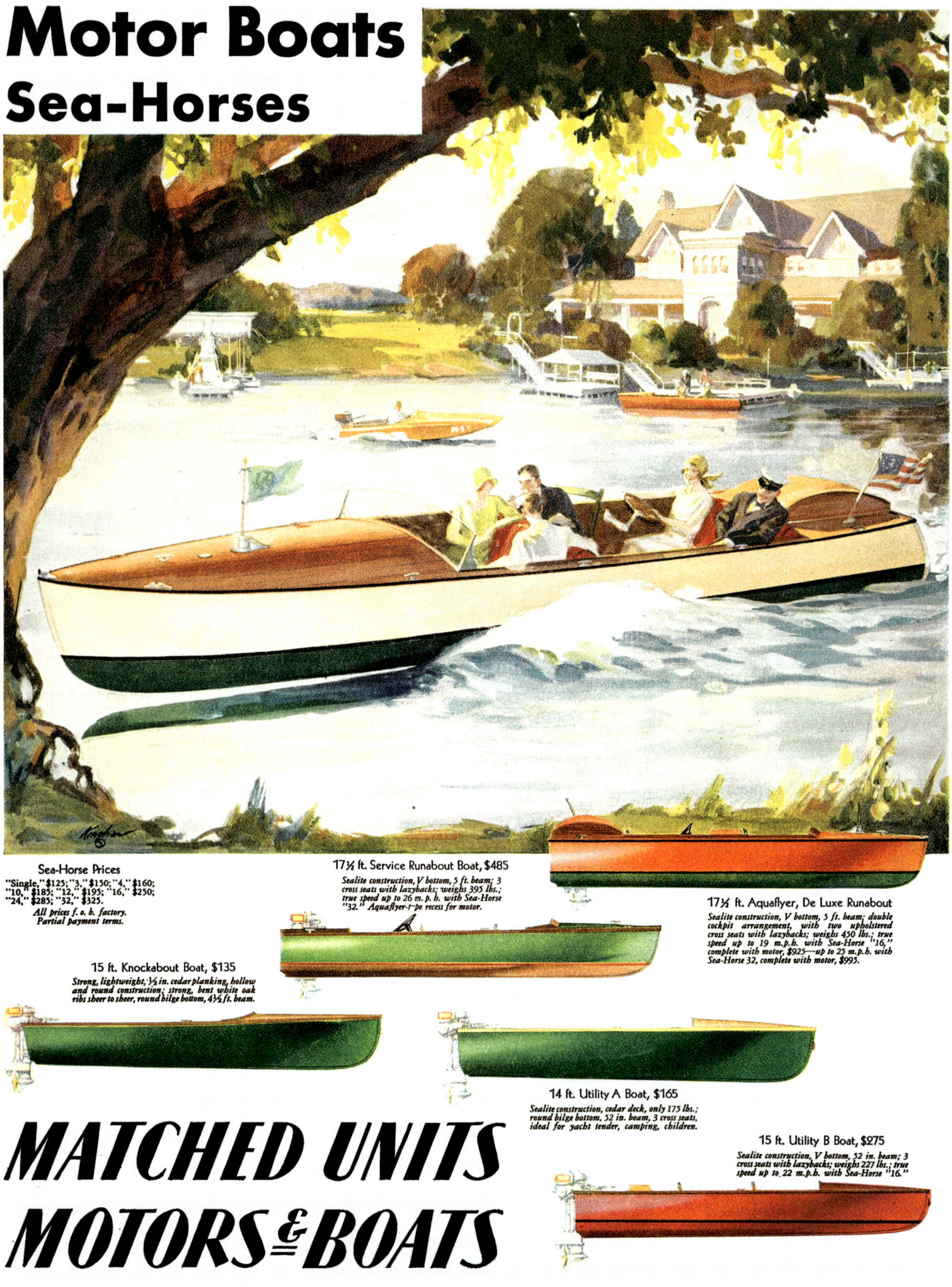

Matched Units Motors & Boats, 1930

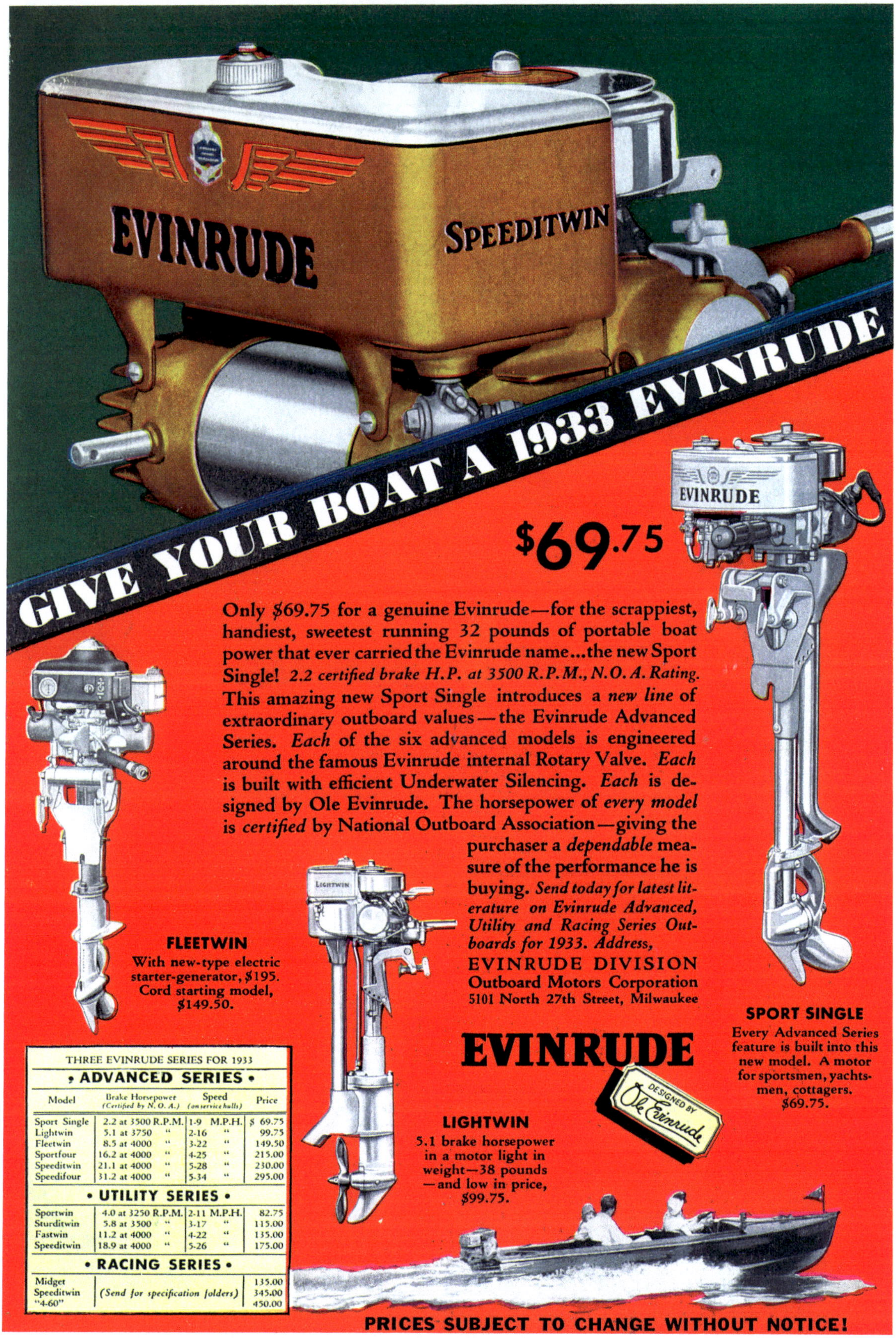

Evinrude, 1933

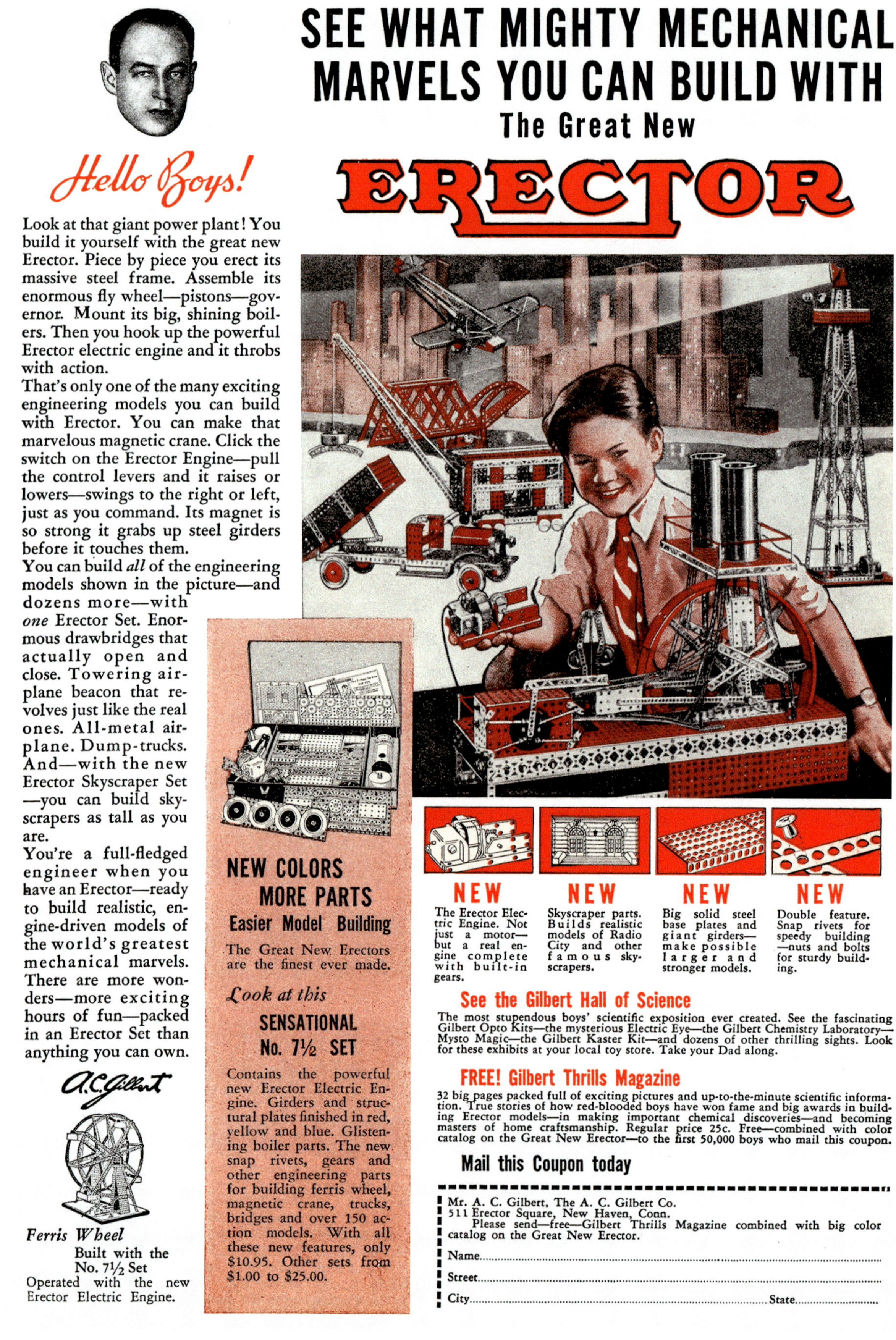

Erector, 1935

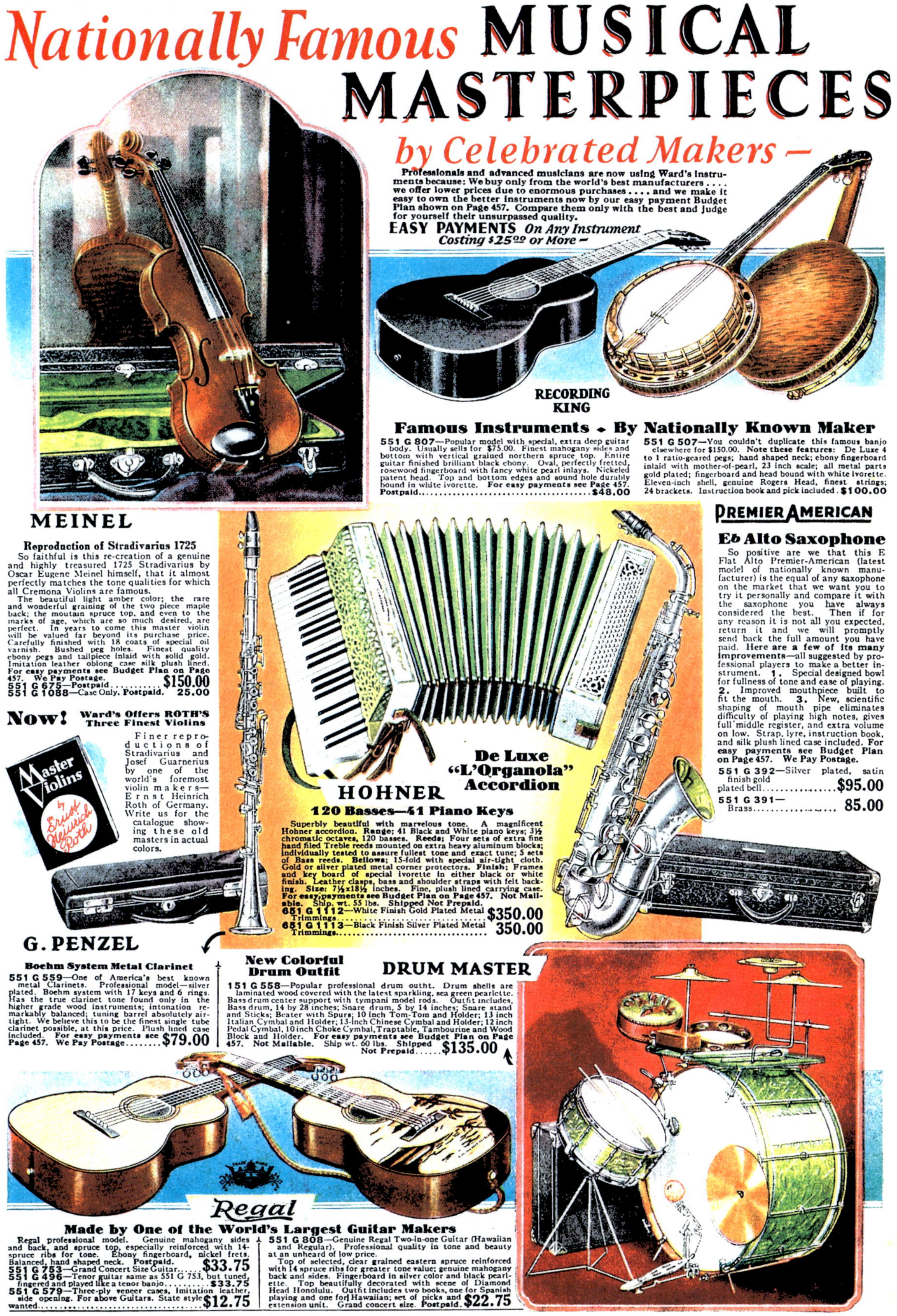

Musical Materpieces, 1931

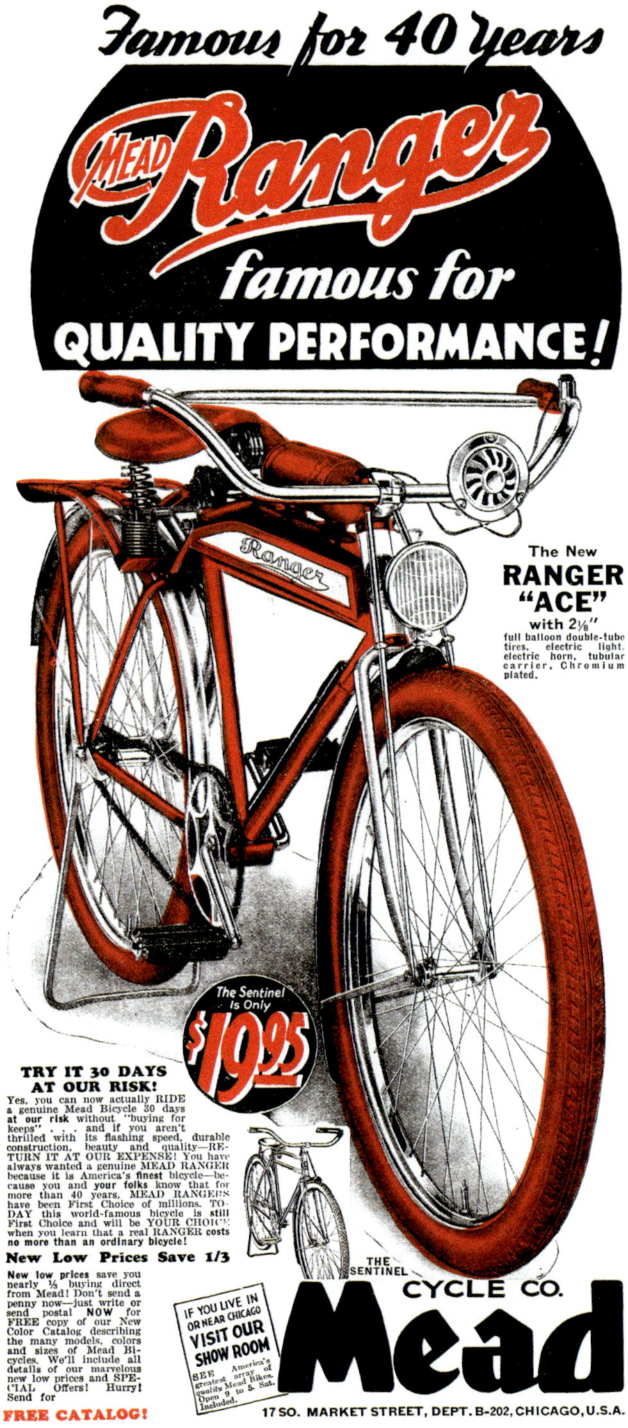

Mead Cycle Co., 1935

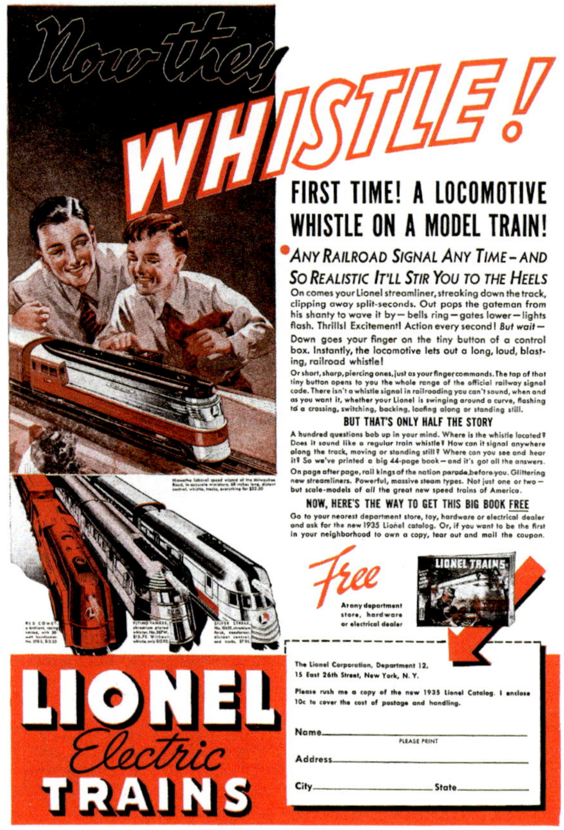

Lionel Electric Trains, 1935

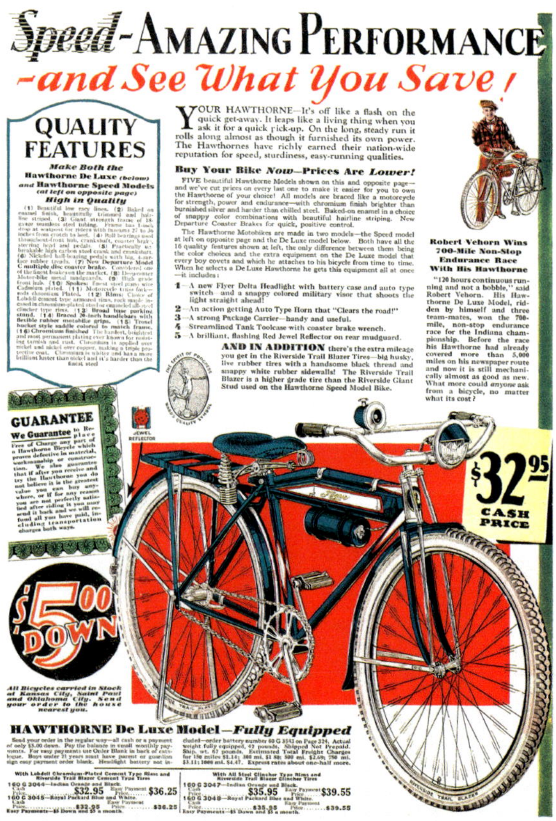

Hawthorne Bicycle, 1930

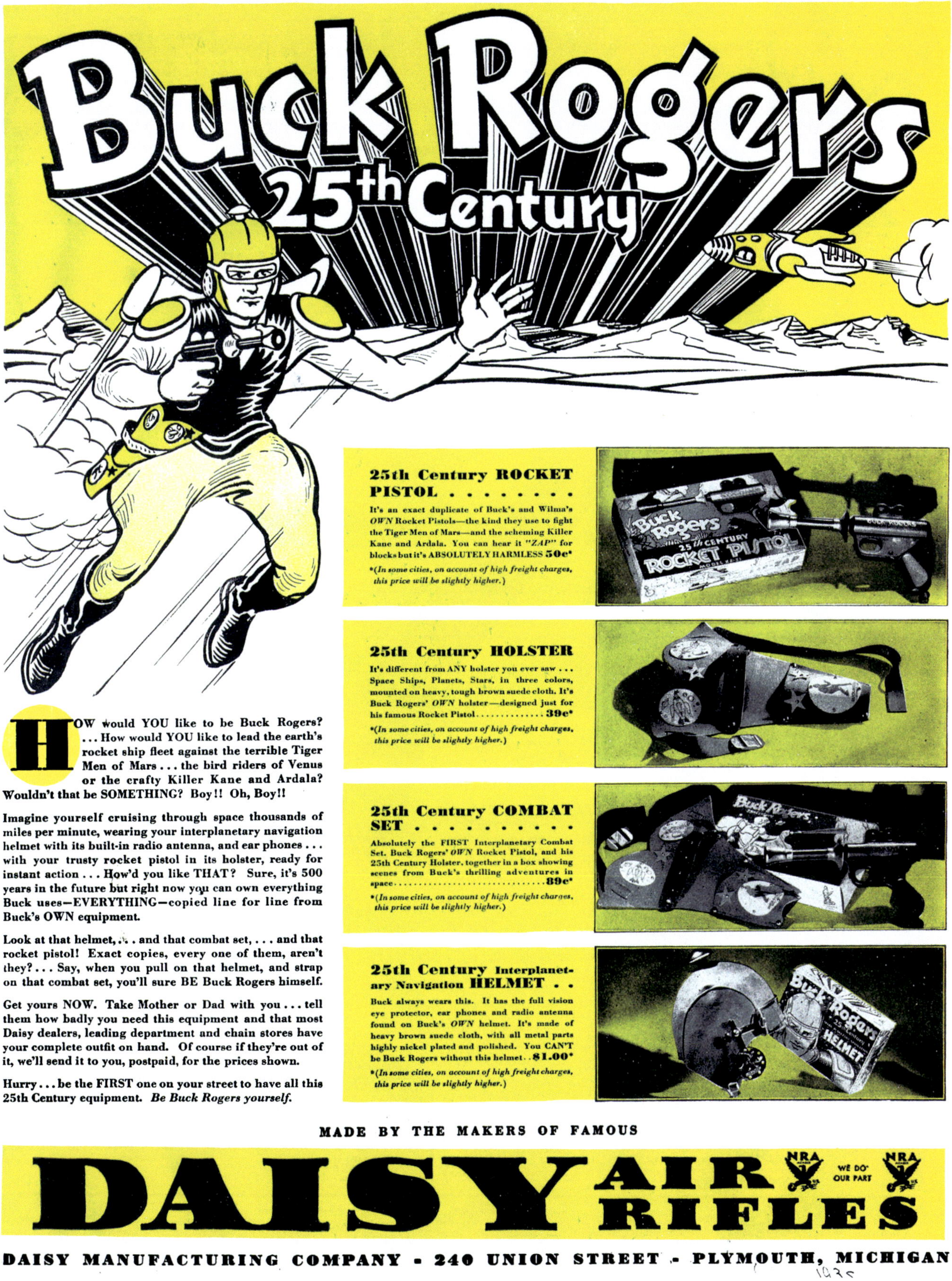

Daisy Air Rifles, 1935

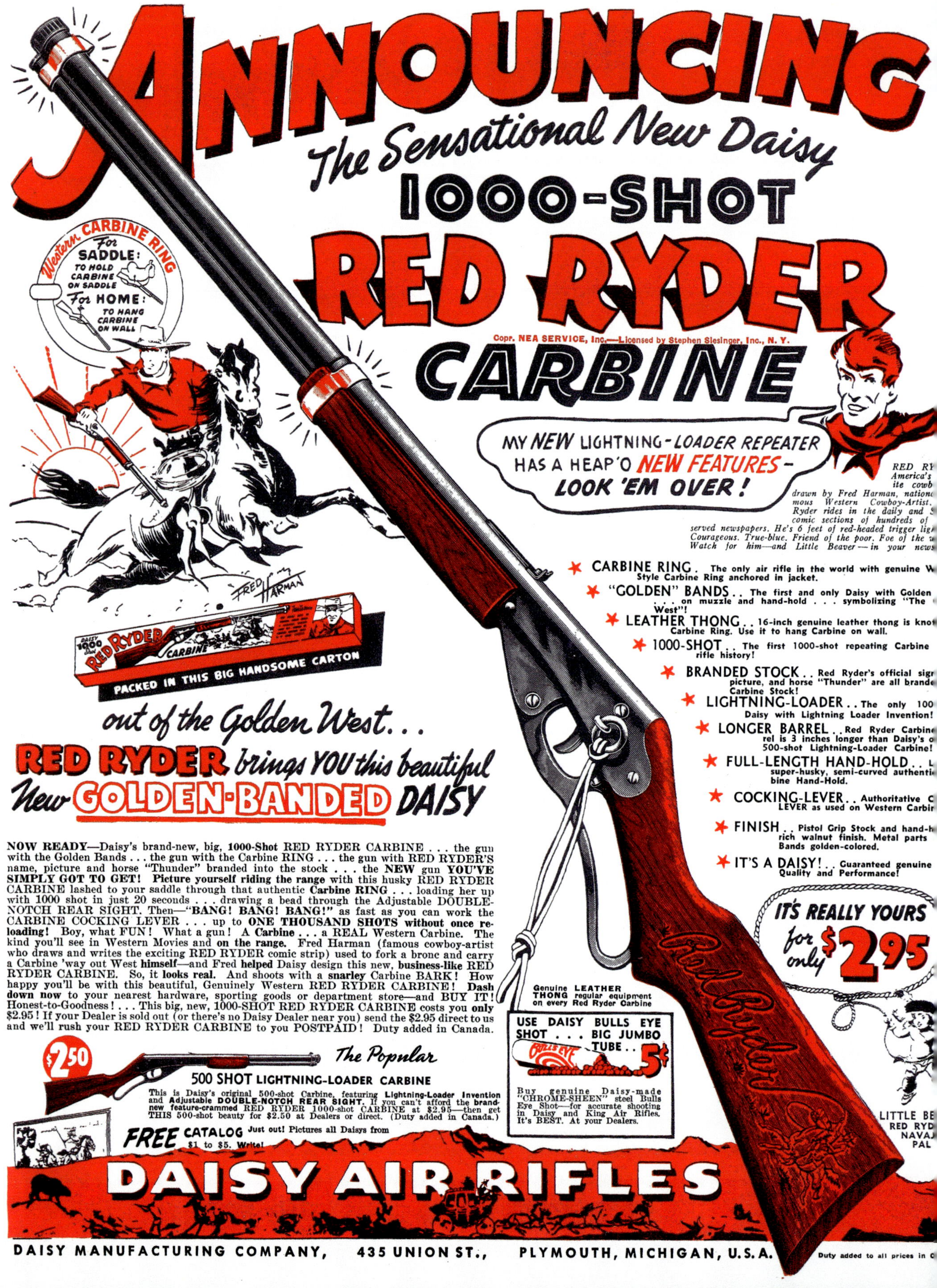

ANNOUNCING
The Sensational New Daisy
1000-SHOT
RED RYDER
Copr. NEA SERVICE, Inc.—Licensed by Stephen Slesinger, Inc., N. Y.
CARBINE
MY NEW LIGHTNING-LOADER REPEATER HAS A HEAP'O NEW FEATURES- LOOK 'EM OVER!
RED RY America's ite cowb drawn by Fred Harman, nationa mous Western Cowboy-Artist. Ryder rides in the daily and S comic sections of hundreds of served newspapers. He's 6 feet of red-headed trigger lig Courageous. True-blue. Friend of the poor. Foe of the w Watch for him—and Little Beaver — in your news
Western CARBINE RING
For SADDLE: TO HOLD CARBINE ON SADDLE
For HOME: TO HANG CARBINE ON WALL
FRED HARMAN
PACKED IN THIS BIG HANDSOME CARTON
★ CARBINE RING. The only air rifle in the world with genuine W Style Carbine Ring anchored in jacket.
★ "GOLDEN" BANDS.. The first and only Daisy with Golden . . . on muzzle and hand-hold . . . symbolizing "The West"!
★ LEATHER THONG.. 16-inch genuine leather thong is knot Carbine Ring. Use it to hang Carbine on wall.
★ 1000-SHOT.. The first 1000-shot repeating Carbine rifle history!
★ BRANDED STOCK.. Red Ryder's official sign picture, and horse "Thunder" are all brande Carbine Stock!
★ LIGHTNING-LOADER.. The only 100 Daisy with Lightning Loader Invention!
★ LONGER BARREL.. Red Ryder Carbine rel is 3 inches longer than Daisy's o 500-shot Lightning-Loader Carbine!
★ FULL-LENGTH HAND-HOLD.. L super-husky, semi-curved authenti bine Hand-Hold.
★ COCKING-LEVER.. Authoritative C LEVER as used on Western Carbir
★ FINISH.. Pistol Grip Stock and hand-h rich walnut finish. Metal parts Bands golden-colored.
★ IT'S A DAISY!.. Guaranteed genuine Quality and Performance!
out of the Golden West...
RED RYDER brings YOU this beautiful New GOLDEN-BANDED DAISY
NOW READY—Daisy's brand-new, big, 1000-Shot RED RYDER CARBINE . . . the gun with the Golden Bands . . . the gun with the Carbine RING . . . the gun with RED RYDER'S name, picture and horse "Thunder" branded into the stock . . . the NEW gun YOU'VE SIMPLY GOT TO GET! Picture yourself riding the range with this husky RED RYDER CARBINE lashed to your saddle through that authentic Carbine RING . . . loading her up with 1000 shot in just 20 seconds . . . drawing a bead through the Adjustable DOUBLE-NOTCH REAR SIGHT. Then—"BANG! BANG! BANG!" as fast as you can work the CARBINE COCKING LEVER . . . up to ONE THOUSAND SHOTS without once re-loading! Boy, what FUN! What a gun! A Carbine . . . a REAL Western Carbine. The kind you'll see in Western Movies and on the range. Fred Harman (famous cowboy-artist who draws and writes the exciting RED RYDER comic strip) used to fork a bronc and carry a Carbine 'way out West himself—and Fred helped Daisy design this new, business-like RED RYDER CARBINE. So, it looks real. And shoots with a snarley Carbine BARK! How happy you'll be with this beautiful, Genuinely Western RED RYDER CARBINE! Dash down now to your nearest hardware, sporting goods or department store—and BUY IT! Honest-to-Goodness! . . . This big, new, 1000-SHOT RED RYDER CARBINE costs you only $2.95! If your Dealer is sold out (or there's no Daisy Dealer near you) send the $2.95 direct to us and we'll rush your RED RYDER CARBINE to you POSTPAID! Duty added in Canada.
Genuine LEATHER THONG regular equipment on every Red Ryder Carbine
IT'S REALLY YOURS for only $2.95
USE DAISY BULLS EYE SHOT . . . BIG JUMBO TUBE . . 5¢
BULLS EYE
Buy genuine Daisy-made "CHROME-SHEEN" steel Bulls Eye Shot—for accurate shooting in Daisy and King Air Rifles. It's BEST. At your Dealers.
Red Ryder
LITTLE BE RED RYD NAVAJ PAL
$2.50
The Popular
500 SHOT LIGHTNING-LOADER CARBINE
This is Daisy's original 500-shot Carbine, featuring Lightning-Loader Invention and Adjustable DOUBLE-NOTCH REAR SIGHT. If you can't afford the brand-new feature-crammed RED RYDER 1000-shot CARBINE at $2.95—then get THIS 500-shot beauty for $2.50 at Dealers or direct. (Duty added in Canada.)
FREE CATALOG Just out! Pictures all Daisys from $1 to $5. Write!
DAISY AIR RIFLES
DAISY MANUFACTURING COMPANY, 435 UNION ST., PLYMOUTH, MICHIGAN, U.S.A.
Duty added to all prices in C

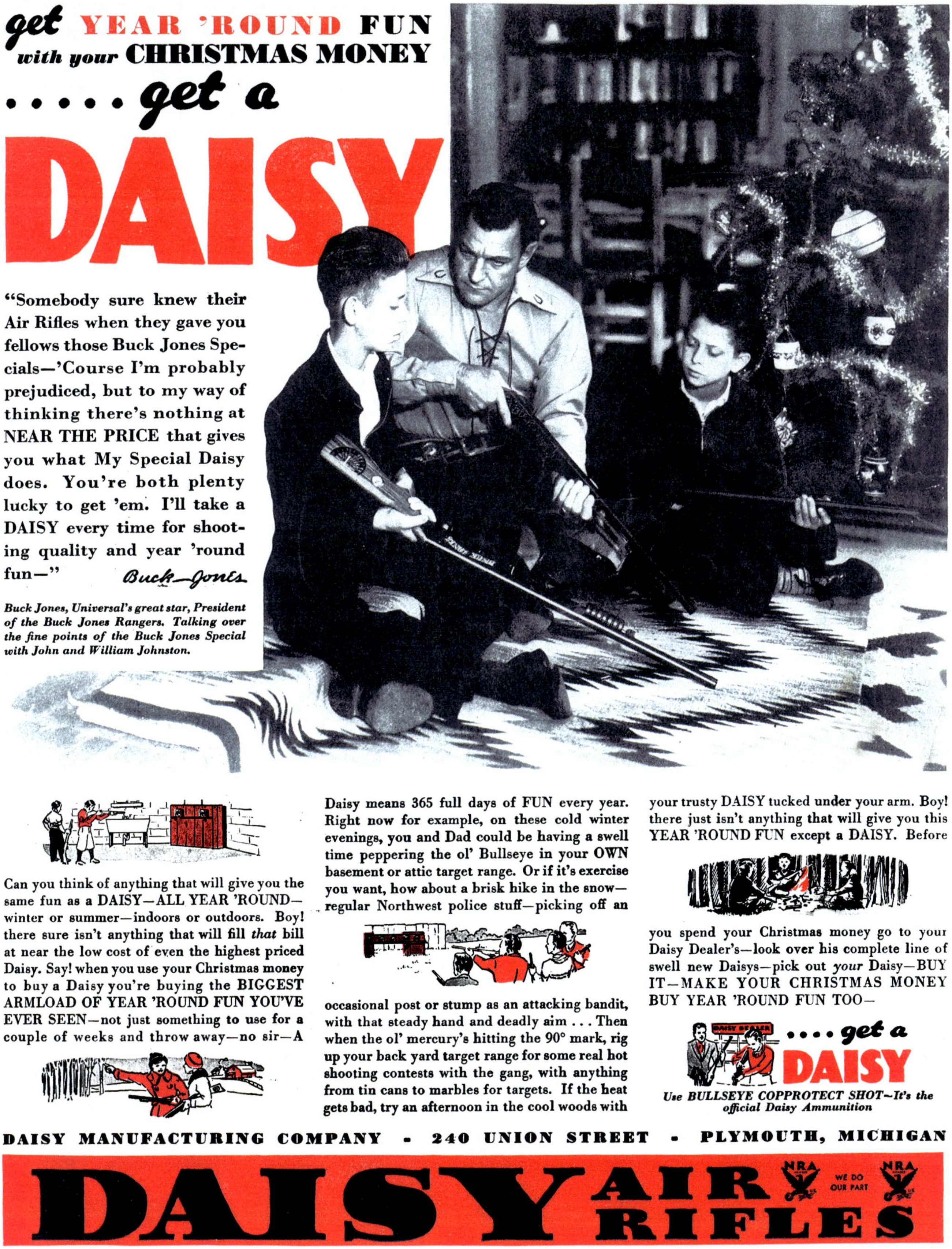

Daisy Air Rifles, 1939 ◂

Daisy Air Rifles, 1935

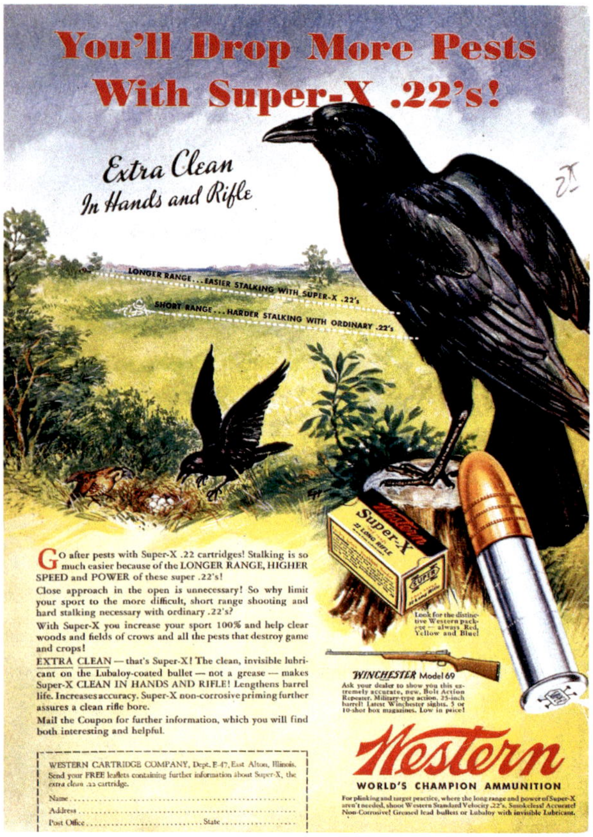

Western Ammunition, 1935

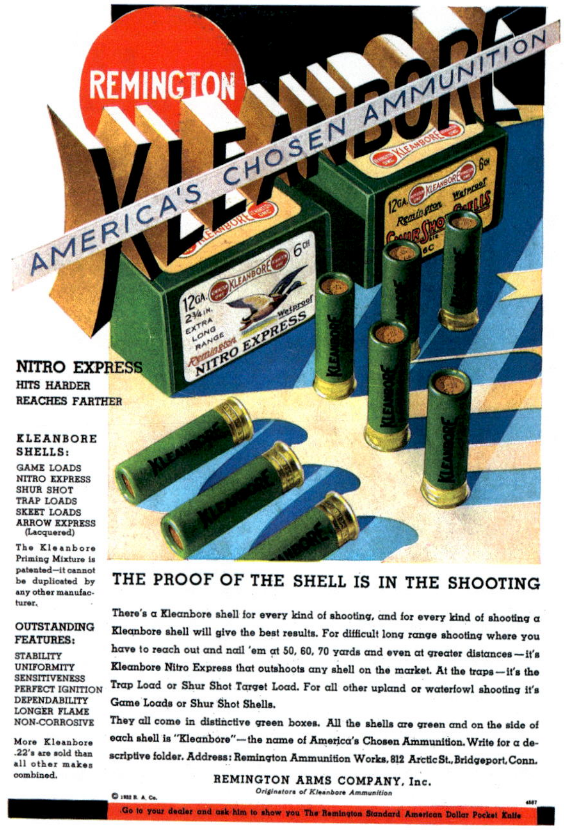

Remington Arms Co., 1932

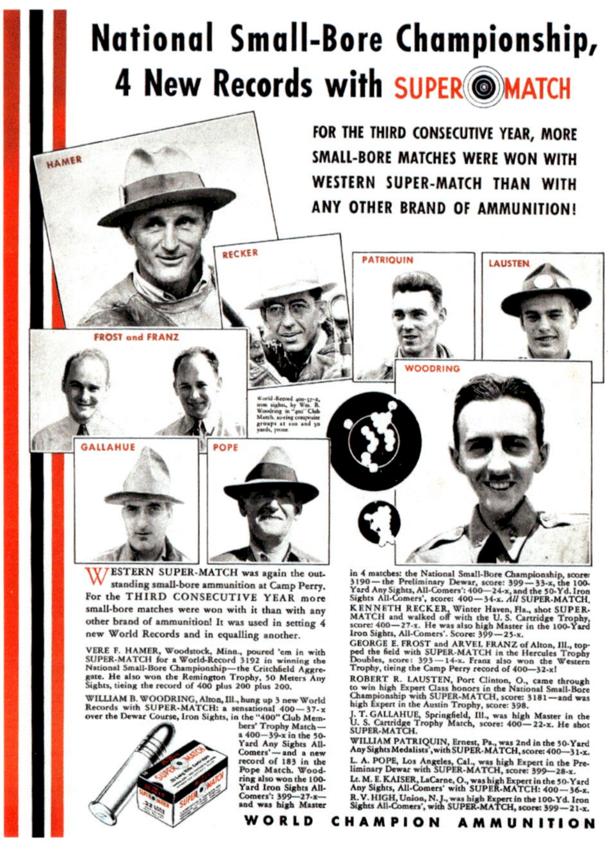

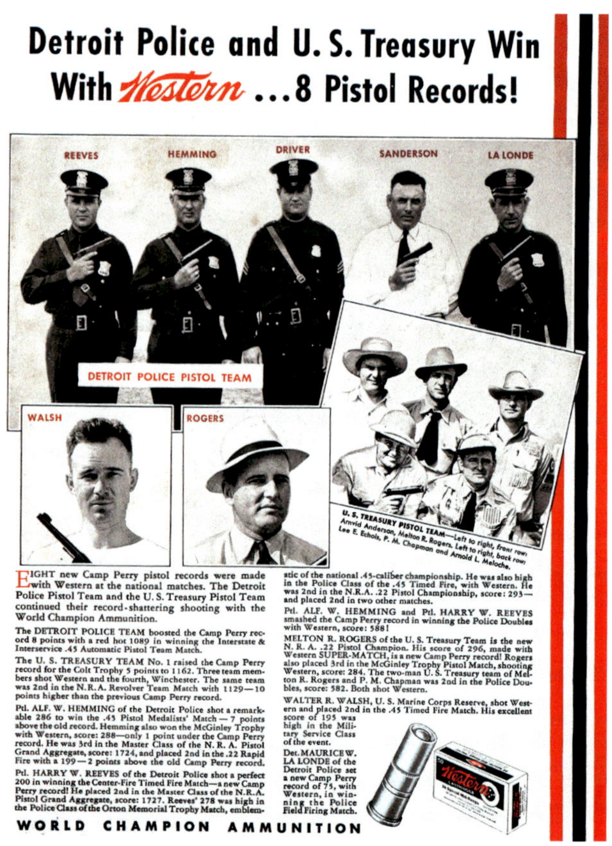

Western Ammunition, 1939

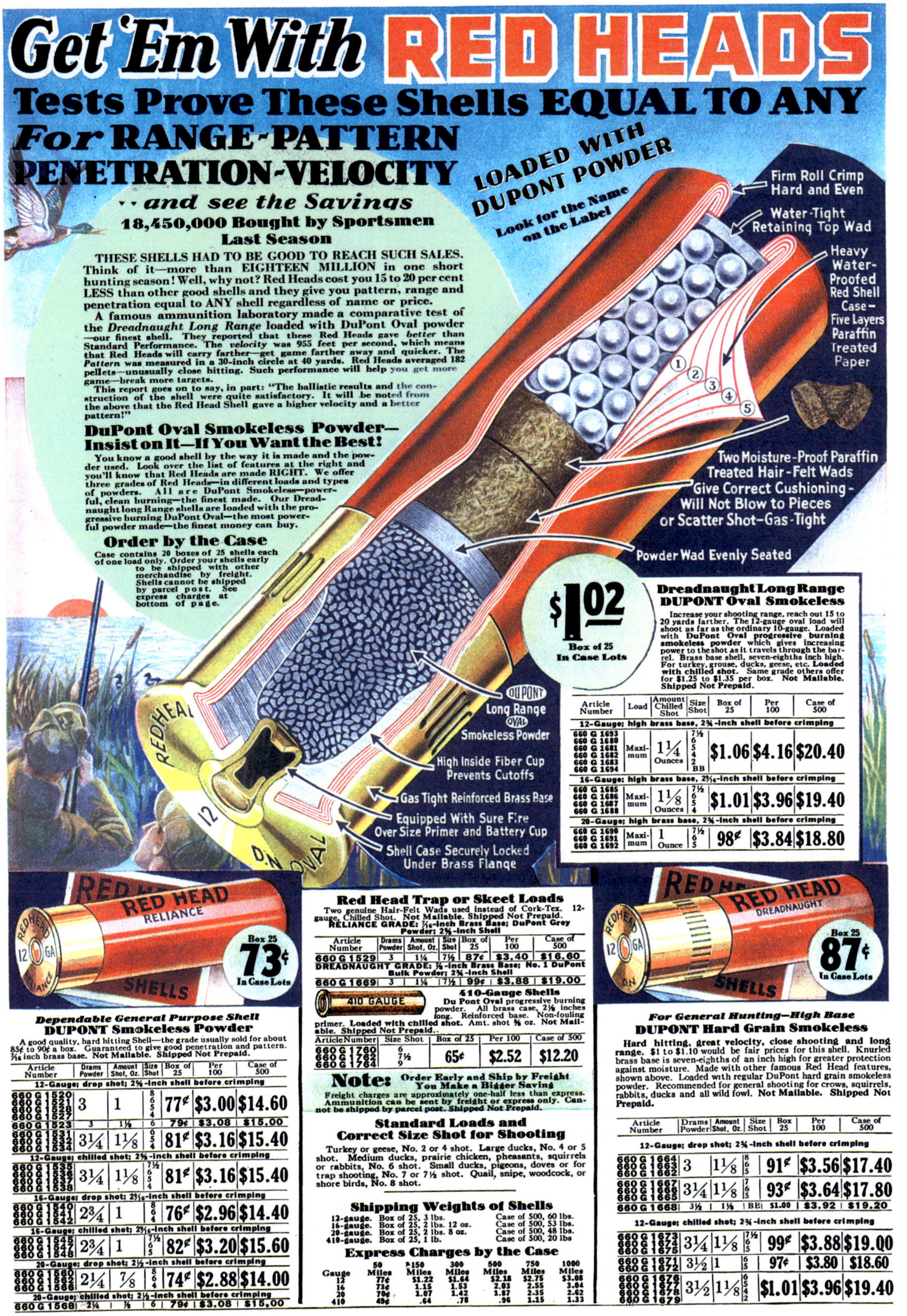

Get 'Em With RED HEADS

Tests Prove These Shells EQUAL TO ANY For RANGE-PATTERN PENETRATION-VELOCITY

.. and see the Savings

18,450,000 Bought by Sportsmen Last Season

THESE SHELLS HAD TO BE GOOD TO REACH SUCH SALES. Think of it—more than EIGHTEEN MILLION in one short hunting season! Well, why not? Red Heads cost you 15 to 20 per cent LESS than other good shells and they give you pattern, range and penetration equal to ANY shell regardless of name or price.

A famous ammunition laboratory made a comparative test of the *Dreadnaught Long Range* loaded with DuPont Oval powder—our finest shell. They reported that these Red Heads gave *better* than Standard Performance. The *velocity* was 955 feet per second, which means that Red Heads will carry farther—get game farther away and quicker. The *Pattern* was measured in a 30-inch circle at 40 yards. Red Heads averaged 182 pellets—unusually close hitting. Such performance will help you get more game—break more targets.

This report goes on to say, in part: "The ballistic results and the construction of the shell were quite satisfactory. It will be noted from the above that the Red Head Shell gave a higher velocity and a better pattern!"

DuPont Oval Smokeless Powder—Insist on It—If You Want the Best!

You know a good shell by the way it is made and the powder used. Look over the list of features at the right and you'll know that Red Heads are made RIGHT. We offer three grades of Red Heads—in different loads and types of powders. All are DuPont Smokeless—powerful, clean burning—the finest made. Our Dreadnaught long Range shells are loaded with the progressive burning DuPont Oval—the most powerful powder made—the finest money can buy.

Order by the Case

Case contains 20 boxes of 25 shells each of one load only. Order your shells early to be shipped with other merchandise by freight. Shells cannot be shipped by parcel post. See express charges at bottom of page.

LOADED WITH DUPONT POWDER

Look for the Name on the Label

Firm Roll Crimp Hard and Even

Water-Tight Retaining Top Wad

Heavy Water-Proofed Red Shell Case—Five Layers Paraffin Treated Paper

Two Moisture-Proof Paraffin Treated Hair-Felt Wads Give Correct Cushioning—Will Not Blow to Pieces or Scatter Shot—Gas-Tight

Powder Wad Evenly Seated

DUPONT Long Range OVAL Smokeless Powder

High Inside Fiber Cup Prevents Cutoffs

Gas Tight Reinforced Brass Base

Equipped With Sure Fire Over Size Primer and Battery Cup

Shell Case Securely Locked Under Brass Flange

$1.02 Box of 25 In Case Lots

Dreadnaught Long Range DUPONT Oval Smokeless

Increase your shooting range, reach out 15 to 20 yards farther. The 12-gauge oval load will shoot as far as the ordinary 10-gauge. Loaded with **DuPont Oval progressive burning smokeless powder** which gives increasing power to the shot as it travels through the barrel. Brass base shell, seven-eighths inch high. For turkey, grouse, ducks, geese, etc. **Loaded with chilled shot.** Same grade others offer for $1.25 to $1.35 per box. **Not Mailable. Shipped Not Prepaid.**

Article Number	Load	Amount Chilled Shot	Size Shot	Box of 25	Per 100	Case of 500
12-Gauge; high brass base, 2¾-inch shell before crimping						
660 G 1693 660 G 1680 660 G 1681 660 G 1682 660 G 1683 660 G 1694	Maximum	1¼ Ounces	7½ 6 5 4 2 BB	$1.06	$4.16	$20.40
16-Gauge; high brass base, 2⁹⁄₁₆-inch shell before crimping						
660 G 1685 660 G 1686 660 G 1687 660 G 1688	Maximum	1⅛ Ounces	7½ 6 5 4	$1.01	$3.96	$19.40
20-Gauge; high brass base, 2¾-inch shell before crimping						
660 G 1690 660 G 1691 660 G 1692	Maximum	1 Ounce	7½ 6 5	98¢	$3.84	$18.80

RED HEAD RELIANCE SHELLS — Box 25 **73¢** In Case Lots

Dependable General Purpose Shell
DUPONT Smokeless Powder

A good quality, hard hitting Shell—the grade usually sold for about 85¢ to 90¢ a box. Guaranteed to give good penetration and pattern. 7⁄16 inch brass base. Not Mailable. Shipped Not Prepaid.

Article Number	Drams Powder	Amount Shot, Oz.	Size Shot	Box of 25	Per 100	Case of 500
12-Gauge; drop shot; 2⅝-inch shell before crimping						
660 G 1520 660 G 1521 660 G 1528 660 G 1527	3	1	8 6 5 4	77¢	$3.00	$14.60
660 G 1523	3	1⅛	6	79¢	$3.08	$15.00
660 G 1531 660 G 1532 660 G 1534	3¼	1⅛	6 5 4	81¢	$3.16	$15.40
12-Gauge; chilled shot; 2⅝-inch shell before crimping						
660 G 1535 660 G 1536 660 G 1537 660 G 1538	3¼	1⅛	7½ 6 5 4	81¢	$3.16	$15.40
16-Gauge; drop shot; 2⁹⁄₁₆-inch shell before crimping						
660 G 1540 660 G 1541 660 G 1542	2¾	1	8 6 4	76¢	$2.96	$14.40
16-Gauge; chilled shot; 2⁹⁄₁₆-inch shell before crimping						
660 G 1545 660 G 1547 660 G 1548	2¾	1	7½ 6 5	82¢	$3.20	$15.60
20-Gauge; drop shot; 2½-inch shell before crimping						
660 G 1560 660 G 1562 660 G 1566	2¼	⅞	8 6 4	74¢	$2.88	$14.00
20-Gauge; chilled shot; 2½-inch shell before crimping						
660 G 1568	2¼	⅞	6	79¢	$3.08	$15.00

Red Head Trap or Skeet Loads

Two genuine Hair-Felt Wads used instead of Cork-Tex. 12-gauge, Chilled Shot. Not Mailable. Shipped Not Prepaid.

Article Number	Drams Powder	Amount Shot, Oz.	Size Shot	Box of 25	Per 100	Case of 500
RELIANCE GRADE: 7⁄16-inch Brass Base; DuPont Grey Powder; 2⅝-inch Shell						
660 G 1529	3	1¼	7½	87¢	$3.40	$16.60
DREADNAUGHT GRADE: ⅞-inch Brass Base; No. 1 DuPont Bulk Powder; 2¾-inch Shell						
660 G 1669	3	1¼	7½	99¢	$3.88	$19.00

410 GAUGE

410-Gauge Shells

Du Pont Oval progressive burning powder. All brass case, 2⅛ inches long. Reinforced base. Non-fouling primer. **Loaded with chilled shot.** Amt. shot ⅜ oz. Not Mailable. Shipped Not Prepaid.

Article Number	Size Shot	Box of 25	Per 100	Case of 500
660 G 1760 660 G 1762 660 G 1764	6 7½ 9	65¢	$2.52	$12.20

Note: Order Early and Ship by Freight You Make a Bigger Saving

Freight charges are approximately one-half less than express. Ammunition can be sent by freight or express only. Cannot be shipped by parcel post. Shipped Not Prepaid.

Standard Loads and Correct Size Shot for Shooting

Turkey or geese, No. 2 or 4 shot. Large ducks, No. 4 or 5 shot. Medium ducks, prairie chicken, pheasants, squirrels or rabbits, No. 6 shot. Small ducks, pigeons, doves or for trap shooting, No. 7 or 7½ shot. Quail, snipe, woodcock, or shore birds, No. 8 shot.

Shipping Weights of Shells

12-gauge.	Box of 25, 3 lbs.	Case of 500, 60 lbs.
16-gauge.	Box of 25, 2 lbs. 12 oz.	Case of 500, 53 lbs.
20-gauge.	Box of 25, 2 lbs. 8 oz.	Case of 500, 48 lbs.
410-gauge.	Box of 25, 1 lb.	Case of 500, 20 lbs

Express Charges by the Case

Gauge	50 Miles	150 Miles	300 Miles	500 Miles	750 Miles	1000 Miles
12	77¢	$1.22	$1.64	$2.18	$2.75	$3.08
16	73¢	1.15	1.53	2.03	2.55	3.04
20	70¢	1.07	1.42	1.87	2.35	2.62
410	49¢	.64	.78	.96	1.15	1.33

RED HEAD DREADNAUGHT SHELLS — Box 25 **87¢** In Case Lots

For General Hunting—High Base
DUPONT Hard Grain Smokeless

Hard hitting, great velocity, close shooting and long range. $1 to $1.10 would be fair prices for this shell. Knurled brass base is seven-eighths of an inch high for greater protection against moisture. Made with other famous Red Head features, shown above. Loaded with regular DuPont hard grain smokeless powder. Recommended for general shooting for crows, squirrels, rabbits, ducks and all wild fowl. **Not Mailable. Shipped Not Prepaid.**

Article Number	Drams Powder	Amount Shot, Oz.	Size Shot	Box 25	Per 100	Case of 500
12-Gauge; drop shot; 2¾-inch shell before crimping						
660 G 1664 660 G 1663 660 G 1662	3	1⅛	8 6 5	91¢	$3.56	$17.40
660 G 1667 660 G 1666 660 G 1665	3¼	1⅛	7 6 5	93¢	$3.64	$17.80
660 G 1668	3½	1⅛	BB	$1.00	$3.92	$19.20
12-Gauge; chilled shot; 2¾-inch shell before crimping						
660 G 1673 660 G 1674 660 G 1675	3¼	1⅛	7½ 6 5	99¢	$3.88	$19.00
660 G 1671 660 G 1672	3½	1	6 5	97¢	$3.80	$18.60
660 G 1676 660 G 1677 660 G 1678 660 G 1679	3½	1⅛	6 5 4 2	$1.01	$3.96	$19.40

Red Heads Ammunition, 1931

SPORS PRESENTS A POPULAR Tested Seller

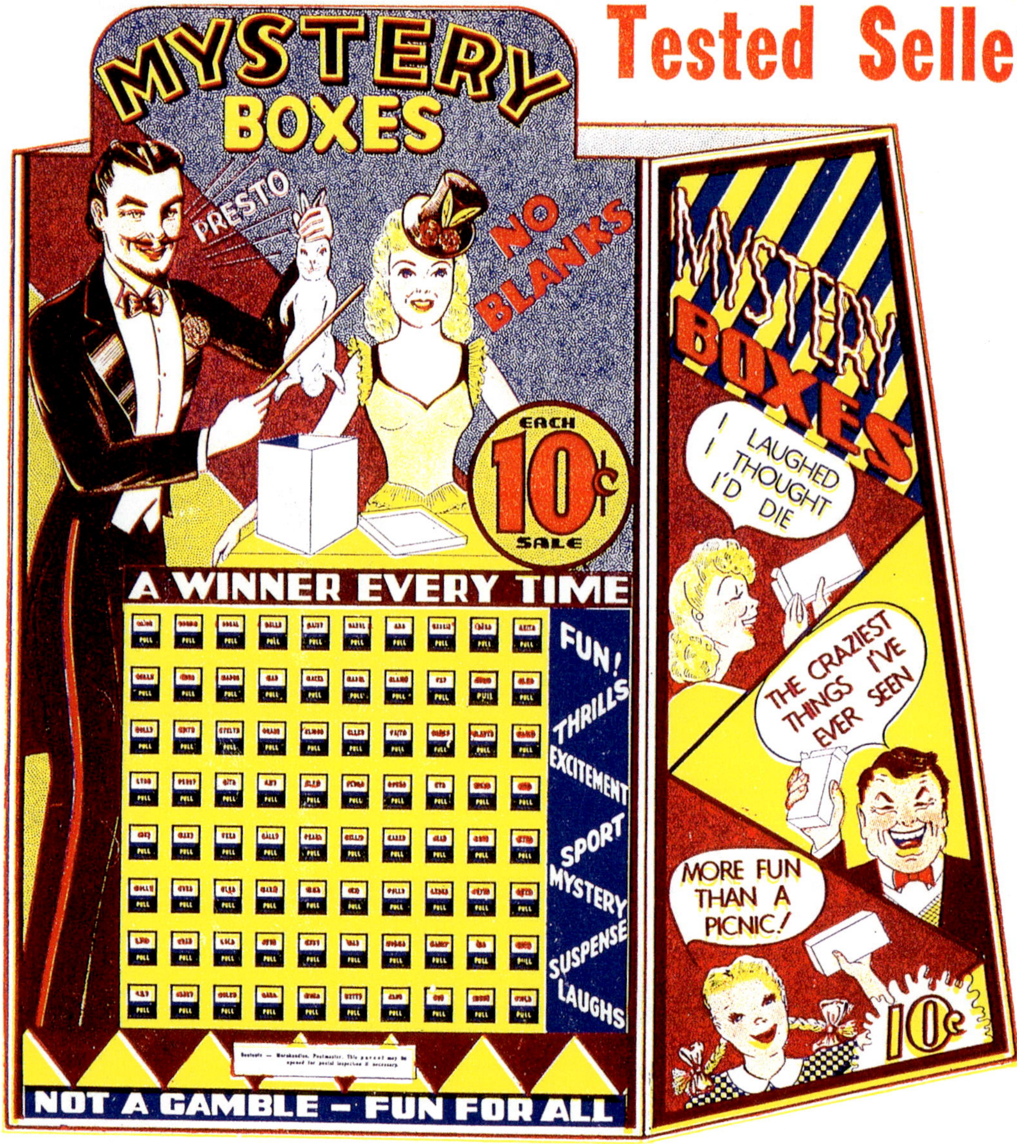

NEWS!

There's big news in the making for selling! Spors Mystery box merchandise display! Designed by us for today's opportunities. These powerful, attention compelling displays should set a standard of high earnings and easy sales.

MYSTERY BOXES as illustrated are now being shown. Many orders for single deals are bringing repeat orders, one after another for five, ten, yes even fifty in some cases. Just six sales a day, grosses you nearly $77.00 in a week. Part time selling should pay you proportionally well.

And remember back of every "Mystery Box" is the Spors Guarantee of Satisfaction.

PROSPECTS EVERYWHERE

• •

Operators Of:

Amusement Places	Taverns
Drug Stores	Barber Shops
Liquor Stores	Clubs
Pool Halls	Fairs
	Picnics
	Church Bazaars

BEAUTIFULLY DESIGNED

No. D1. Mystery Box Deal. It is made up of a beautiful, eye catching three color cabinet which contains 80 numbered surprises to be sold at 10c a sale. Brings in $8. Shipped express or freight. Weighs about 22 lbs.

Sells To Dealers $6.00 Cost You $3.95 -- Lots of 10 $38.50

MAKE QUICK SALES --- SURPRISES CHANGED FREQUENTLY

National Carbon Co., 1932

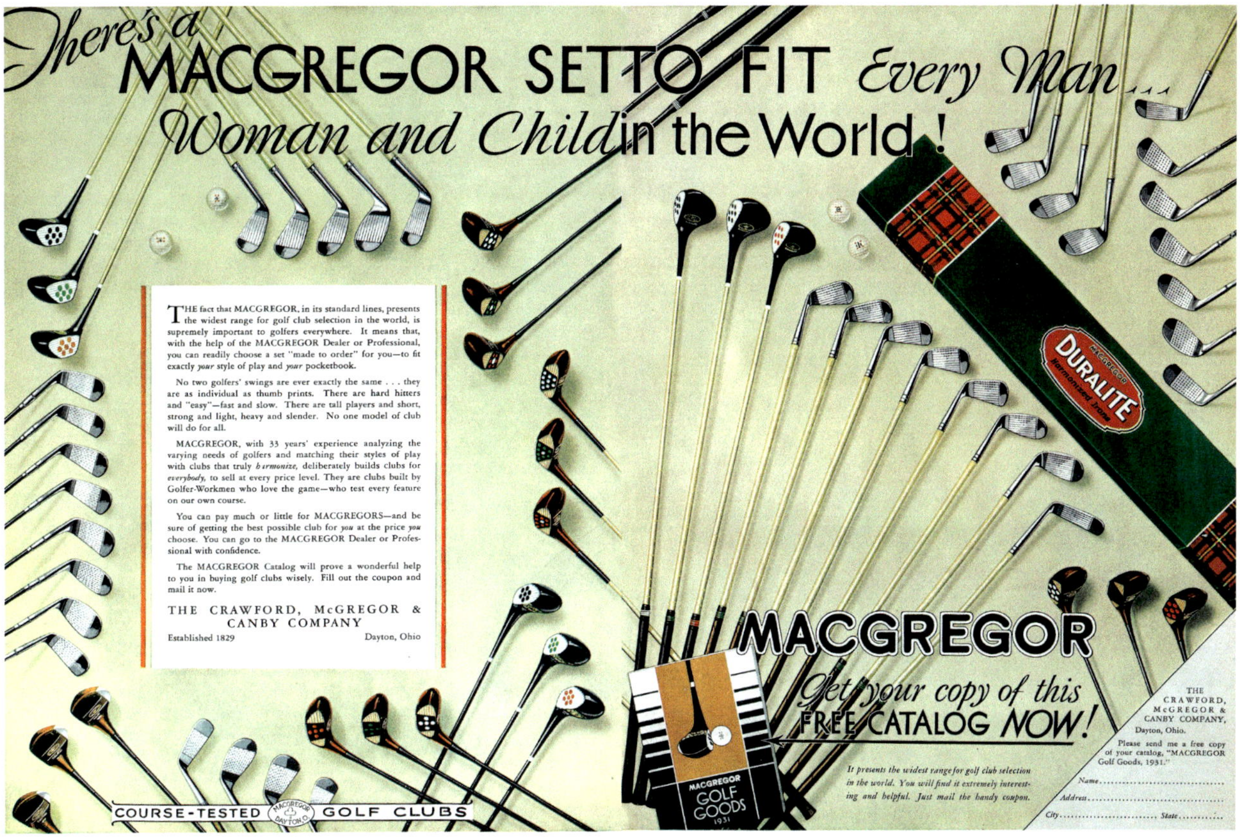

Macgregor, 1931

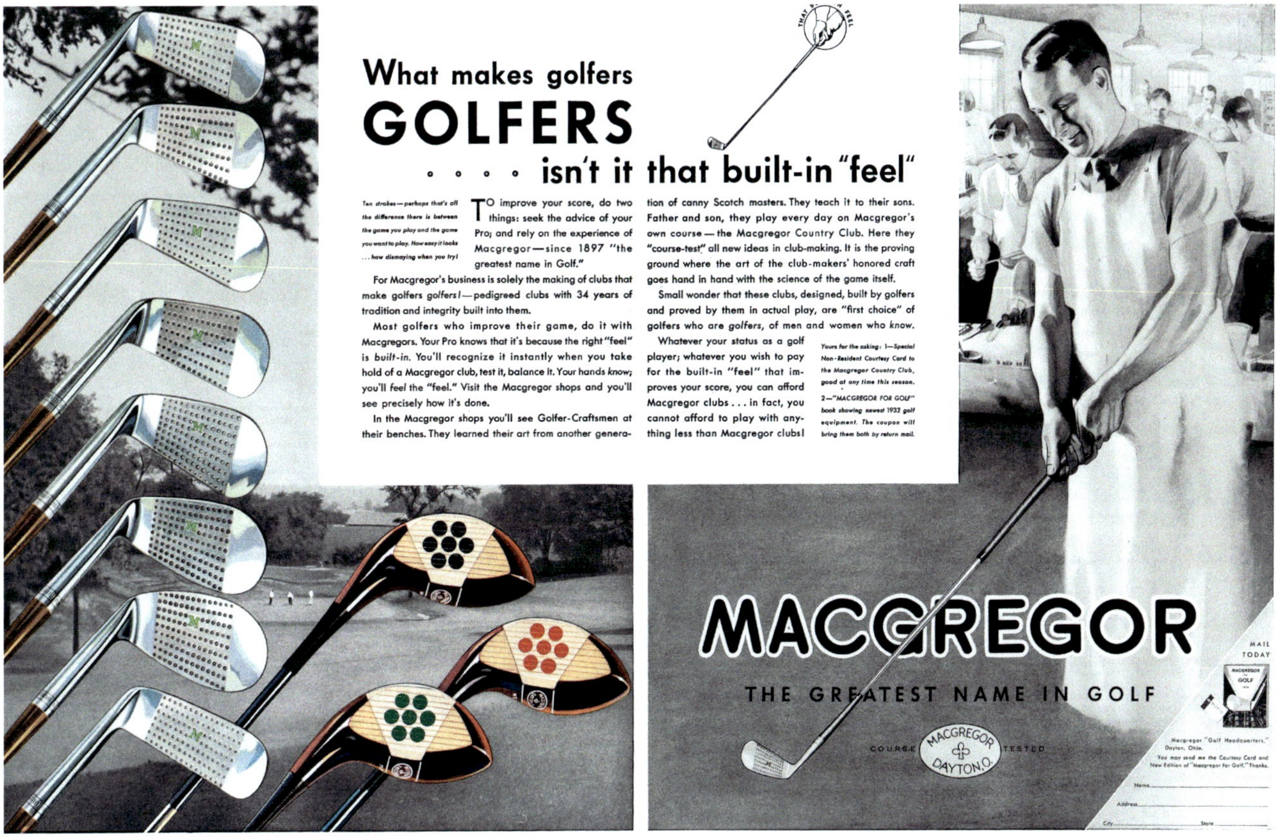

Macgregor, 1932

He took his girl swimming and gave her Athlete's Foot

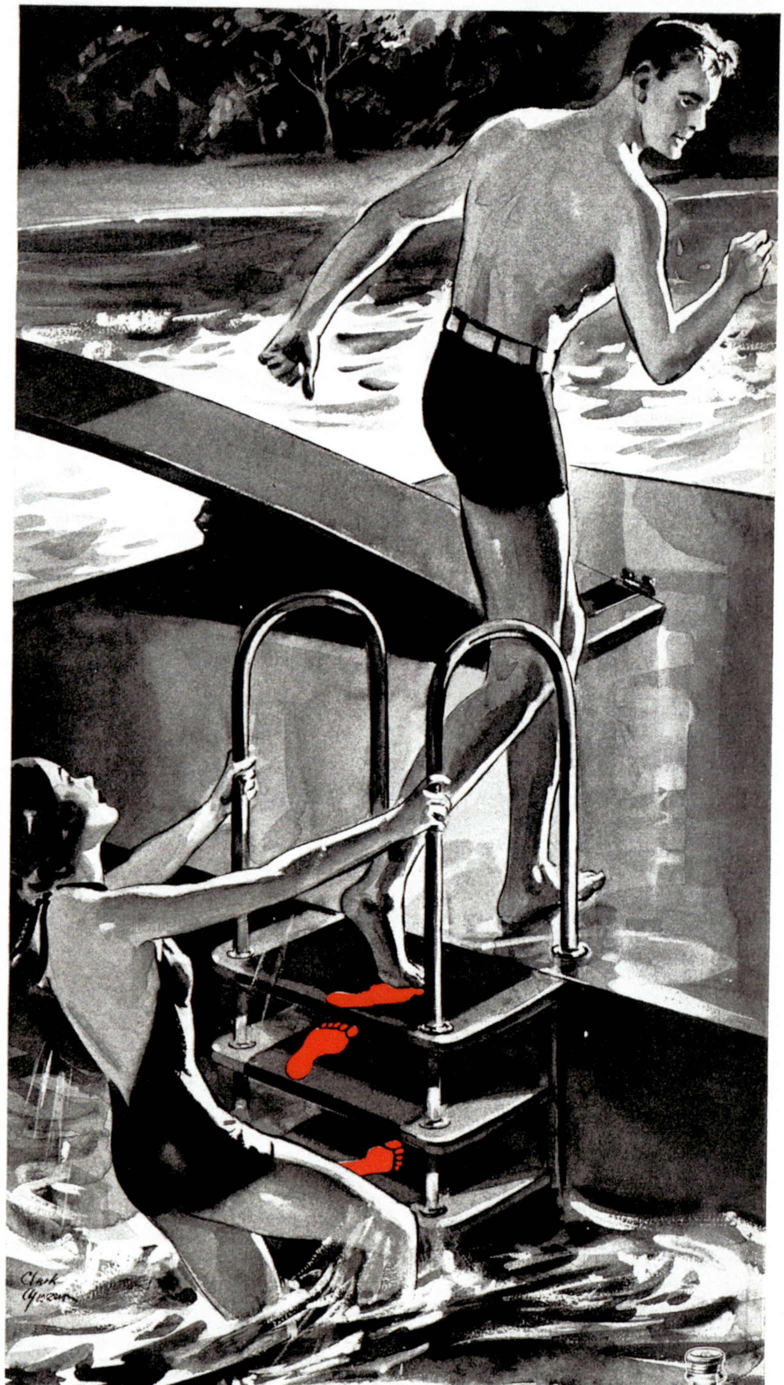

HE WAS A ★ CARRIER

NO ONE is safe in the company of a victim of Athlete's Foot, when their bare feet tread the same surfaces.

For a single carrier of Athlete's Foot—a woman, child or man—may infect scores of other people who are so luckless as to follow in the bath house at the beach, in the shower or locker-room at the club, on the edge of a swimming pool, or even in the family bathroom.

Red skin is the mark of the Carrier

If you suspect you have a case of Athlete's Foot, you may be in danger as grave to yourself as to others who may contract it from you; use Absorbine Jr. promptly.

Don't take chances. Examine the skin between your toes. If it looks red, itches, stings or burns, you'll welcome the cooling, soothing relief brought by applications of Absorbine Jr. You may save yourself a lot of painful trouble.

For Athlete's Foot is caused by an insidious fungus that digs and bores deeper into the skin, when neglected—resulting in unwholesome whiteness and moistness, peeling skin, cracks and painful rawness.

Absorbine Jr. destroys the fungus

Even in advanced stages, Absorbine Jr. relieves the condition and helps to soothe and heal the damaged tissues. If, however, you feel your case is really serious, by all means consult your doctor in addition to the use of Absorbine Jr., morning and night.

When you buy, insist upon genuine Absorbine Jr. and accept no imitations offered as being "just as good." This famous remedy has been tested and proved for its ability to kill the fungus when reached, a fungus so stubborn that infected socks must be boiled 20 minutes to destroy it.

Absorbine Jr. is economical to use because it takes so little to bring relief. Also wonderful for the bites of insects, such as mosquitoes and jiggers. At all druggists, $1.25 a bottle. For free sample, write W. F. Young, Inc., 362 Lyman Street, Springfield, Massachusetts.

★ "Carrier" is the medical term for a person who carries infection. People infected with Athlete's Foot are "carriers." And at least one-half of all adults suffer from it (Athlete's Foot) at some time, according to the U. S. Public Health Service. They spread the disease wherever they tread barefoot.

ABSORBINE JR.

Relieves sore muscles, muscular aches, bruises, sprains and Sunburn

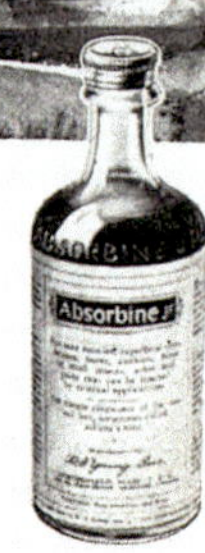

Absorbine Jr., 1937

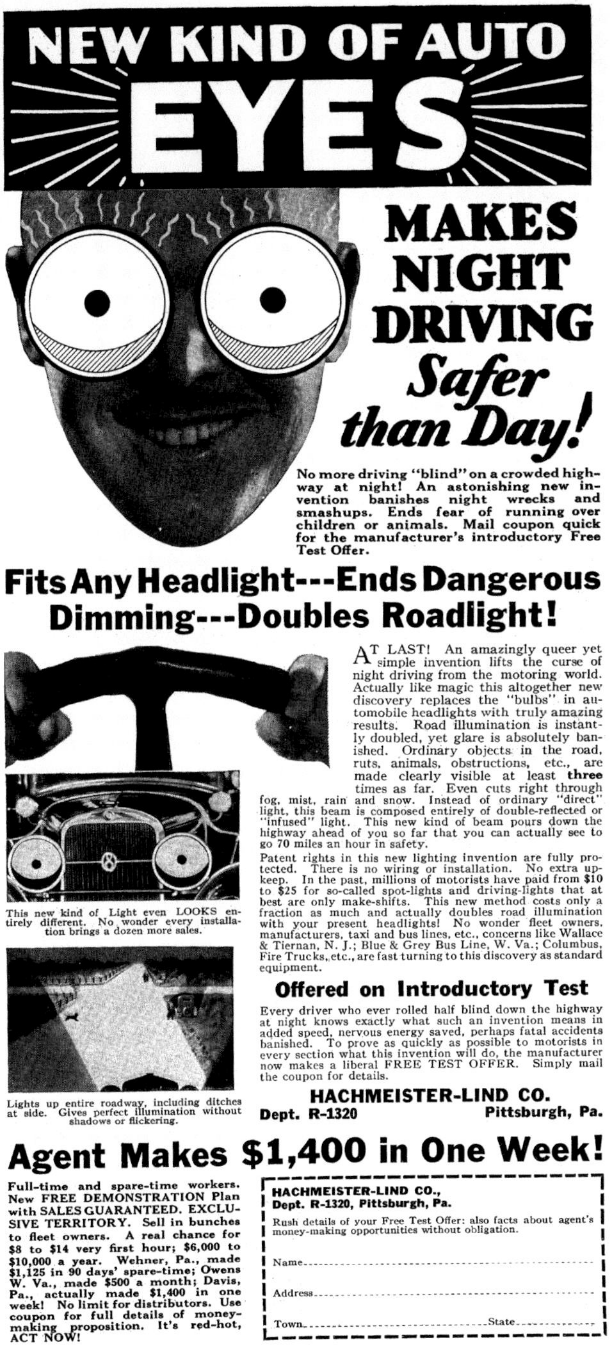

Hachmeister-Lind Co., 1931

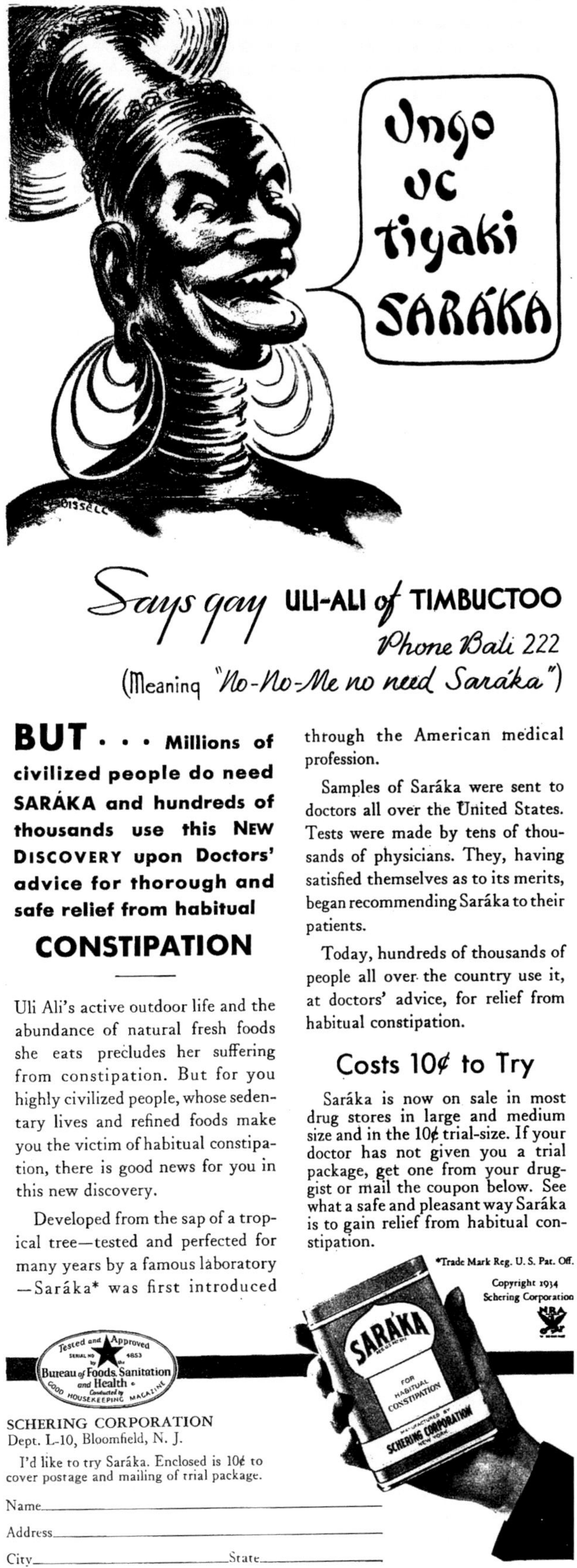

Saráka, 1934

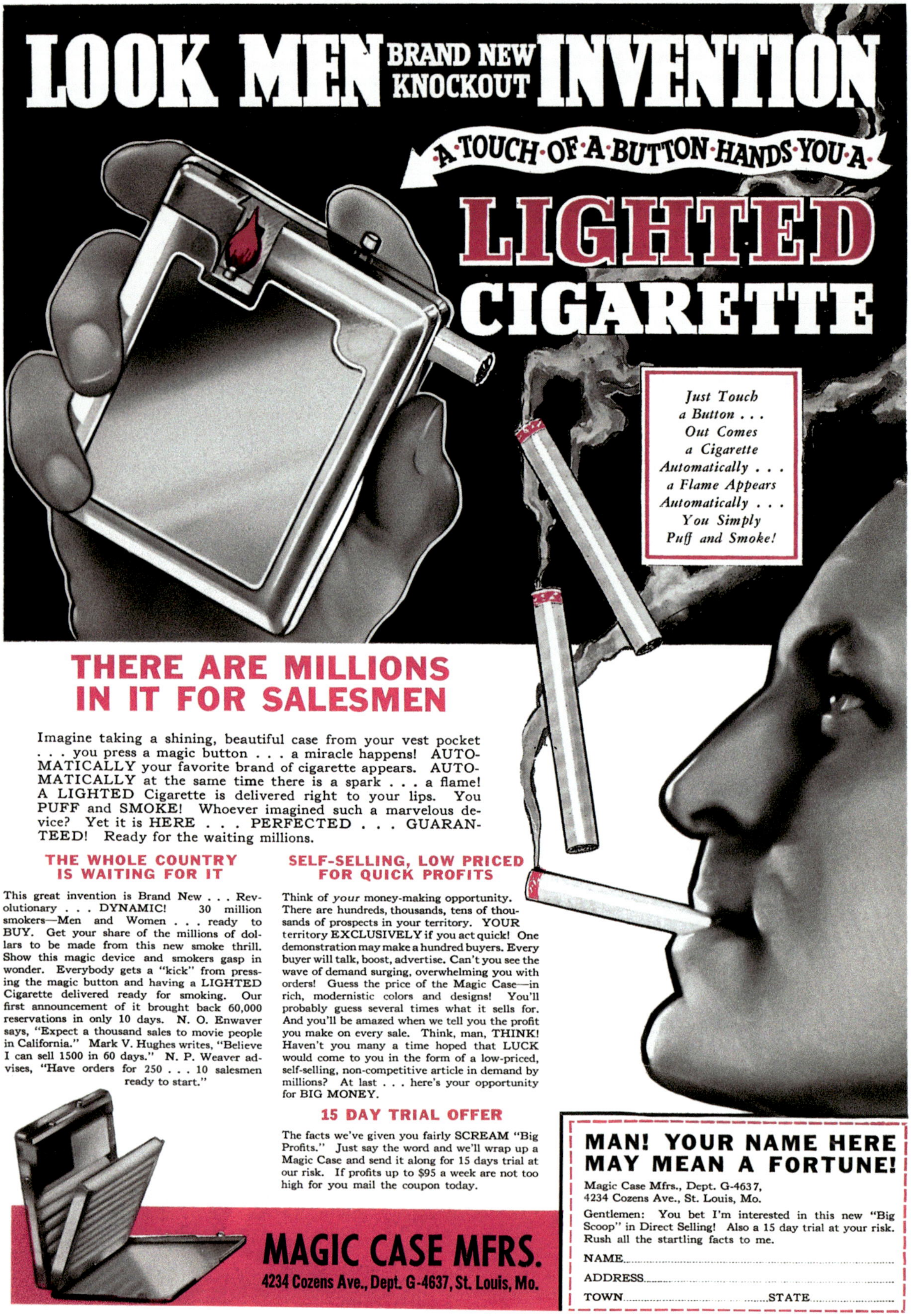

Magic Case Mfrs., 1933

▸ *Jim Brown, 1931*

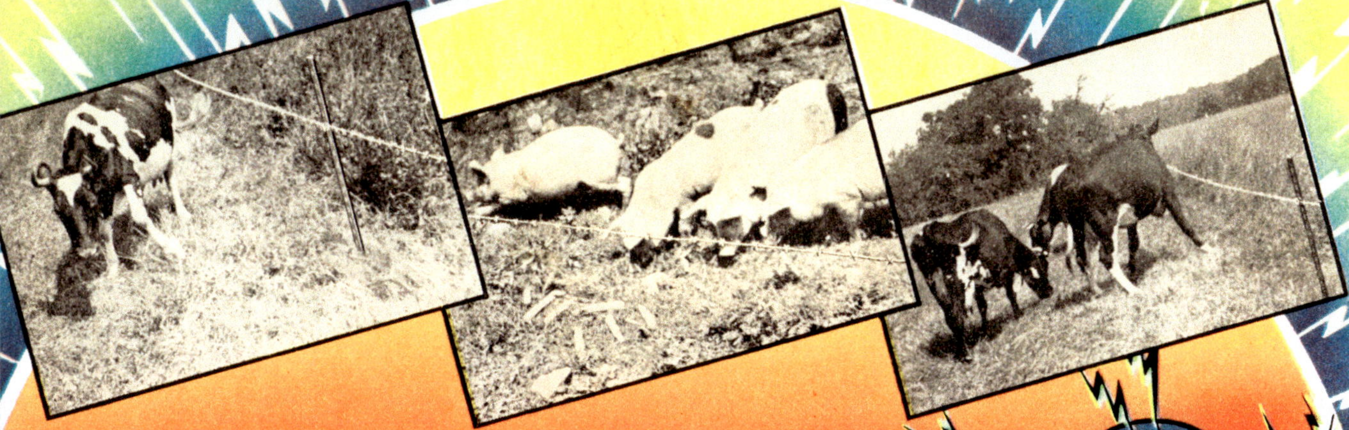

"THE MAGIC FENCE DEVIL"

Jim Brown's **NEW ONE-WIRE**

ELECTRIC FENCE

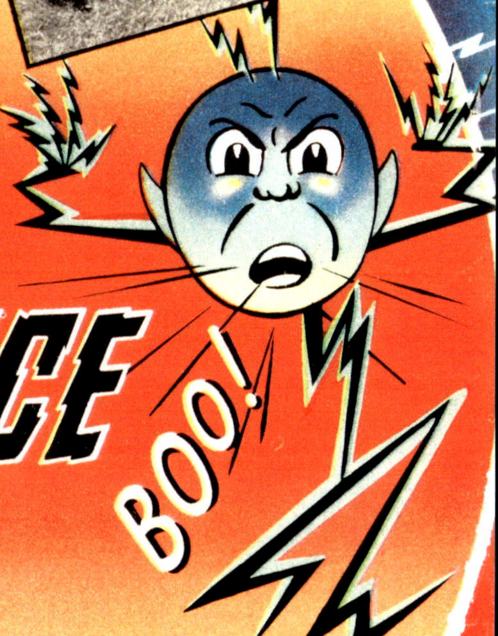

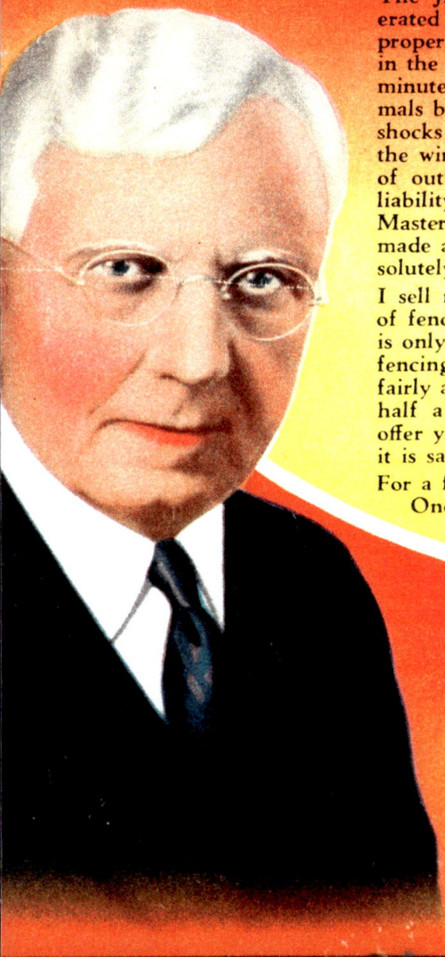

The Jim Brown Fence-Master is a battery operated unit which when attached to a wire and properly grounded generates an electric current in the wire at the rate of about 80 impulses per minute. This slight shock or sting scares animals but doesn't injure them. After one or two shocks they become "educated" and don't touch the wire. The successful operation of this type of outfit clearly depends upon its absolute reliability. I claim that the Jim Brown Fence-Master is the most reliable outfit of its kind made and because it is battery operated it is absolutely safe.

I sell more different kinds and sizes and styles of fencing than anyone else in the country. It is only natural, therefore, that I include Electric fencing as part of my line. Since I have dealt fairly and squarely with my customers for nearly half a century, you can be sure that when I offer you an Electric Fence it is because I know it is safe, economical and reliable.

For a full description and prices of Jim Brown's One-Wire Electric Fence, read pages 40 and 41 of this catalog.

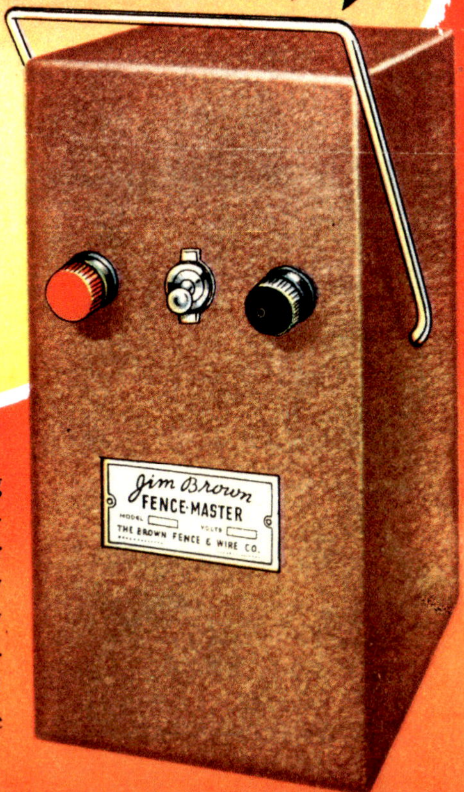

I believe that Electric Fencing has a place in farming operations as temporary fencing for hogging down corn, or for any other purpose where a quickly erected temporary fence is important. See pages 40 and 41 for full particulars about the Jim Brown Fence Master.

THE BROWN FENCE & WIRE CO. CLEVELAND, OHIO. MEMPHIS, TENN.

And the winner is...

Clean as a Whistle

If the sinister rubber glove was not enough, then surely the threatening surgical instruments would suffice in scaring consumers into thinking twice about using anything but the best to complete their personal regime. This aggressive marketing of a hygienic product played on the country's obsession with sanitation that had begun earlier in the century. While the nature of "toilet tissue illness" is never directly stated, the message is clear. Use Scott® Tissue, or face the surgeon's knife.

Nicht nur sauber, sondern rein

Sollte der scheußliche Gummihandschuh nicht reichen, dann würden die Furcht einflößenden Chirurgeninstrumente die Verbraucher bestimmt davon überzeugen, ihrem Allerwertesten nur mit einem Spitzenprodukt zu Leibe zu rücken. Diese aggressive Werbung für ein Hygieneprodukt konnte auf eine amerikanische Obsession hinsichtlich der Körperpflege bauen, die schon früher eingesetzt hatte. Der wahre Charakter der geheimnisvollen „Toilettenpapier-Krankheit" bleibt zwar im Dunkeln, doch die Botschaft ist eindeutig: Nimm Klopapier von Scott oder sag dem OP-Tisch guten Tag.

Propre comme un sou neuf

Si les sinistres gants en caoutchouc ne suffisaient pas, la menace des instruments chirurgicaux devait achever de terrifier le consommateur qui aurait envisagé d'utiliser autre chose que le meilleur pour son hygiène intime. Cette campagne de choc pour du papier hygiénique exploitait l'obsession nationale pour la santé publique qui s'était développée plus tôt au début du siècle. Si la nature de « la maladie du papier toilette » n'est jamais explicite, le message est clair : utilisez Scott® Tissue, ou bien préparez-vous à passer sur le billard.

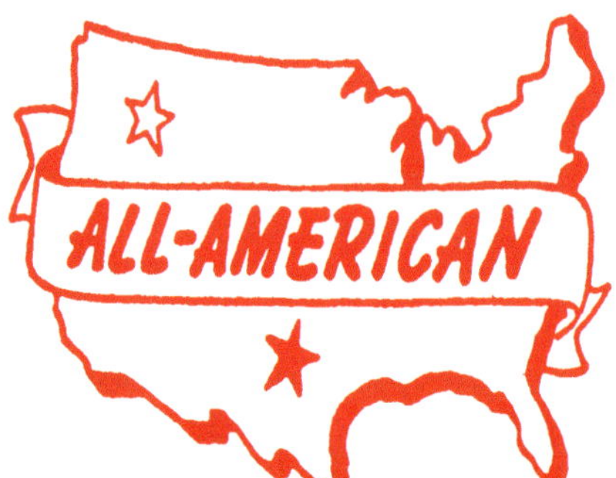

Scott Tissues, 1931

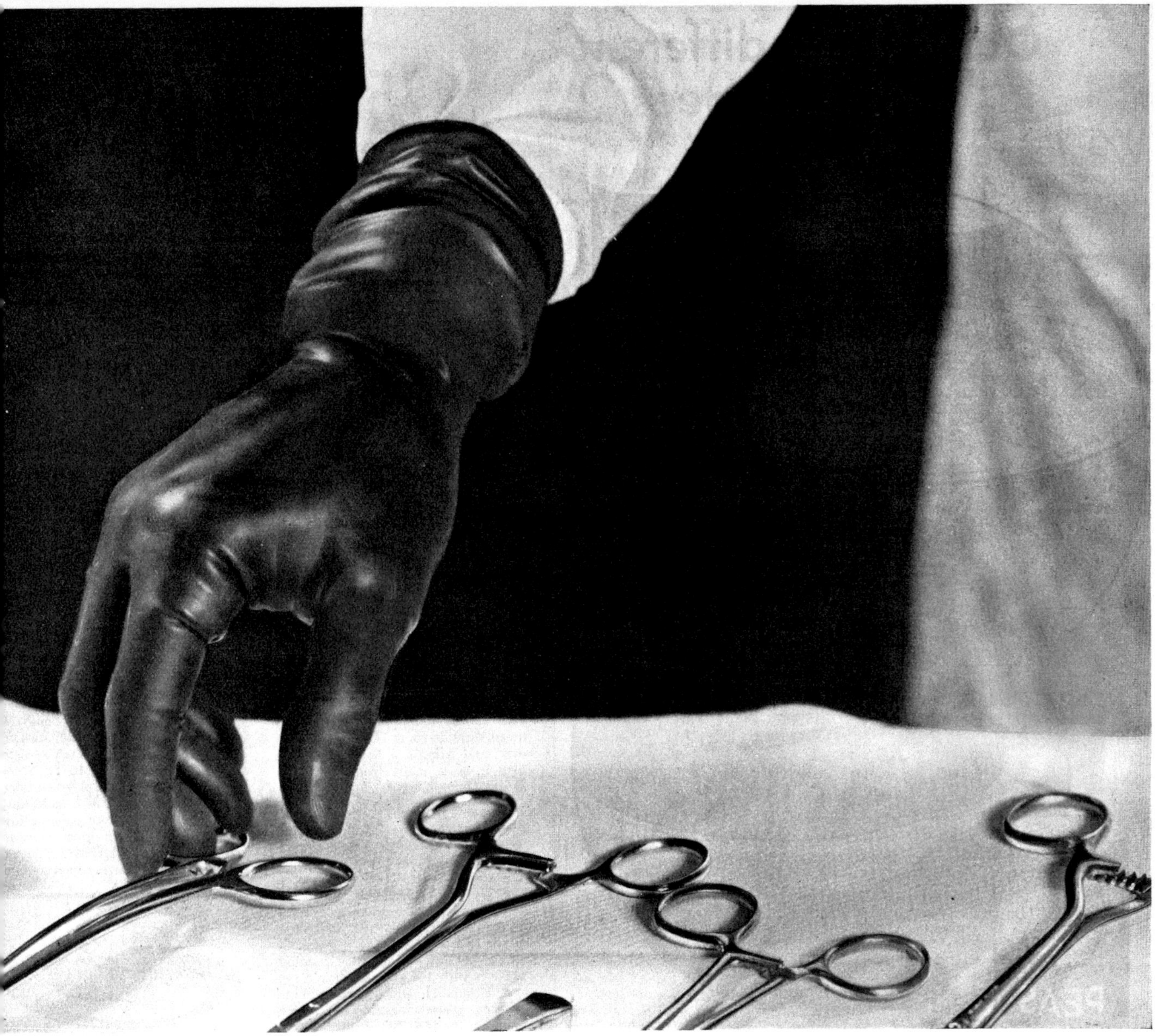

. . . often the only relief from toilet tissue illness

THE annual reports issued by public ·itals show an astonishing percentage of ·l cases . . . many of which require surgical ment.

·ysicians who specialize in ailments of this estimate that 65 per cent of all men and ·en over 40 suffer from some form of rectal ss.

·any of these cases are directly traceable to in- ·r toilet tissue. Harsh, chemically impure toi- ·ssue—made from reclaimed waste material. · a safety precaution millions of women are ·pping their bathrooms with the tissues that ·ors and hospitals approve for safety—Scot- ·ue and Waldorf.

These two health tissues are made only from fresh new materials, specially processed to obtain an extremely soft, cloth-like texture. They are *twice as absorbent* as ordinary kinds.

Without this degree of absorbency, thorough hygiene is impossible.

You can rely on Scott Tissues to protect your family's health—just as doctors and hospitals rely on them to protect the health of their patients.

Eliminate a needless risk. Ask for ScotTissue or Waldorf when you order. They cost no more than inferior tissues. Scott Paper Company, Chester, Pa. In Canada, Scott Paper Co., Ltd., Toronto, Ont.

SCOTTISSUE, *an extremely soft, pure white, absorbent roll containing 1,000 sheets*

2 *for* 25¢
Price for U. S. only

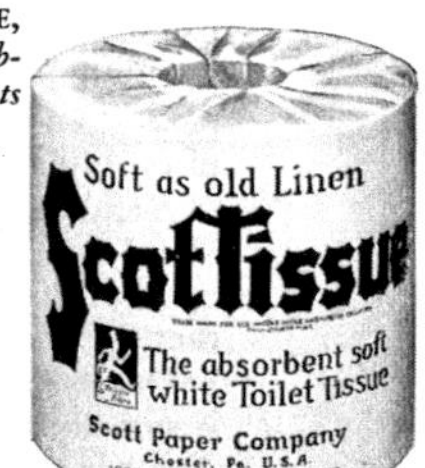

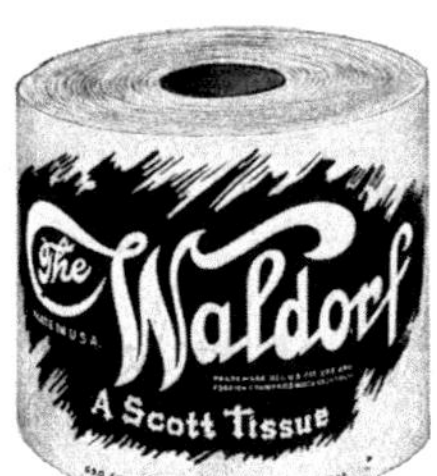

WALDORF, *soft and absorbent, yet inexpensive. Any family can afford this fine tissue* 3 *for* 20¢
Price for U. S. only

·octors, Hospitals, Health Authorities approve Scott Tissues for Safety

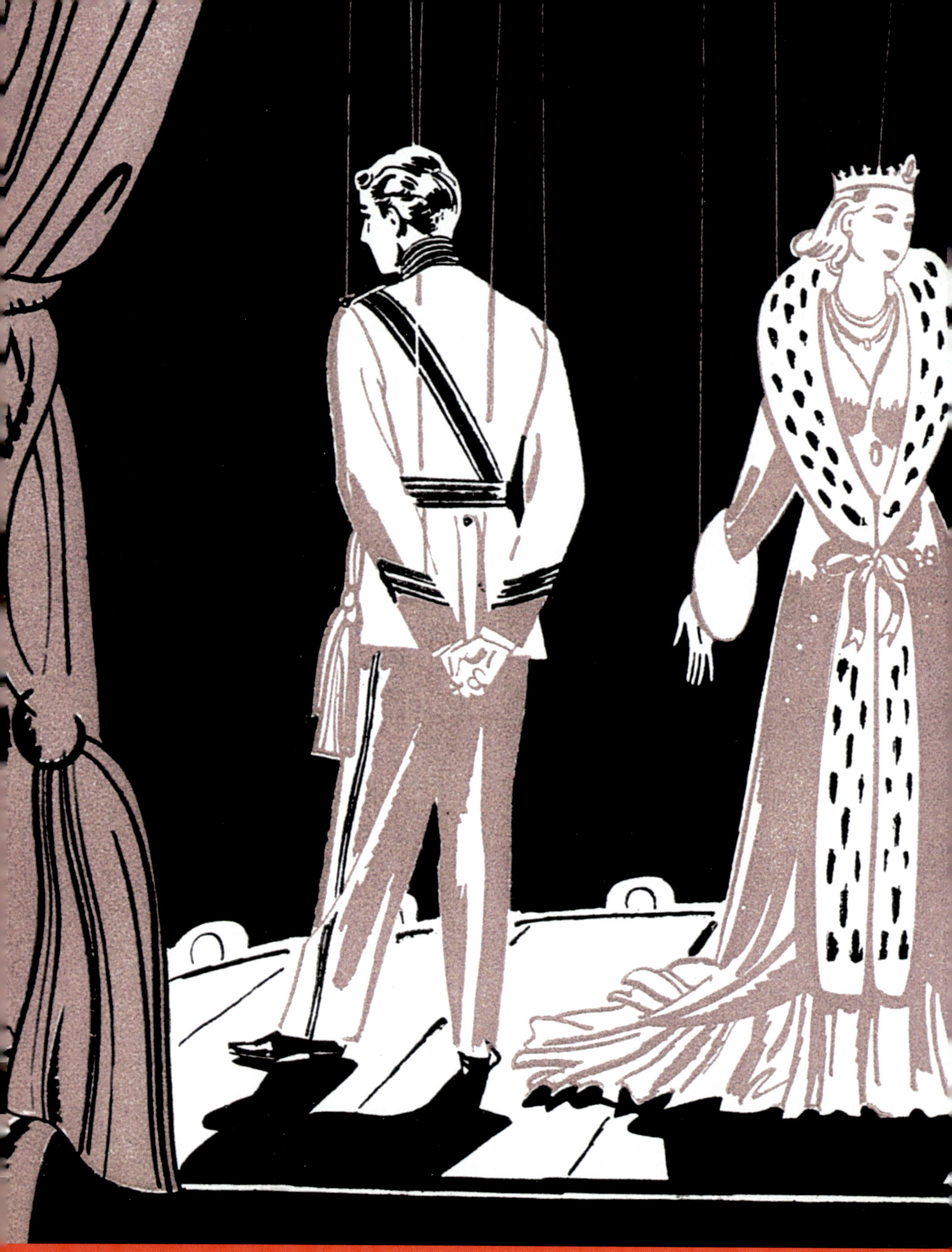

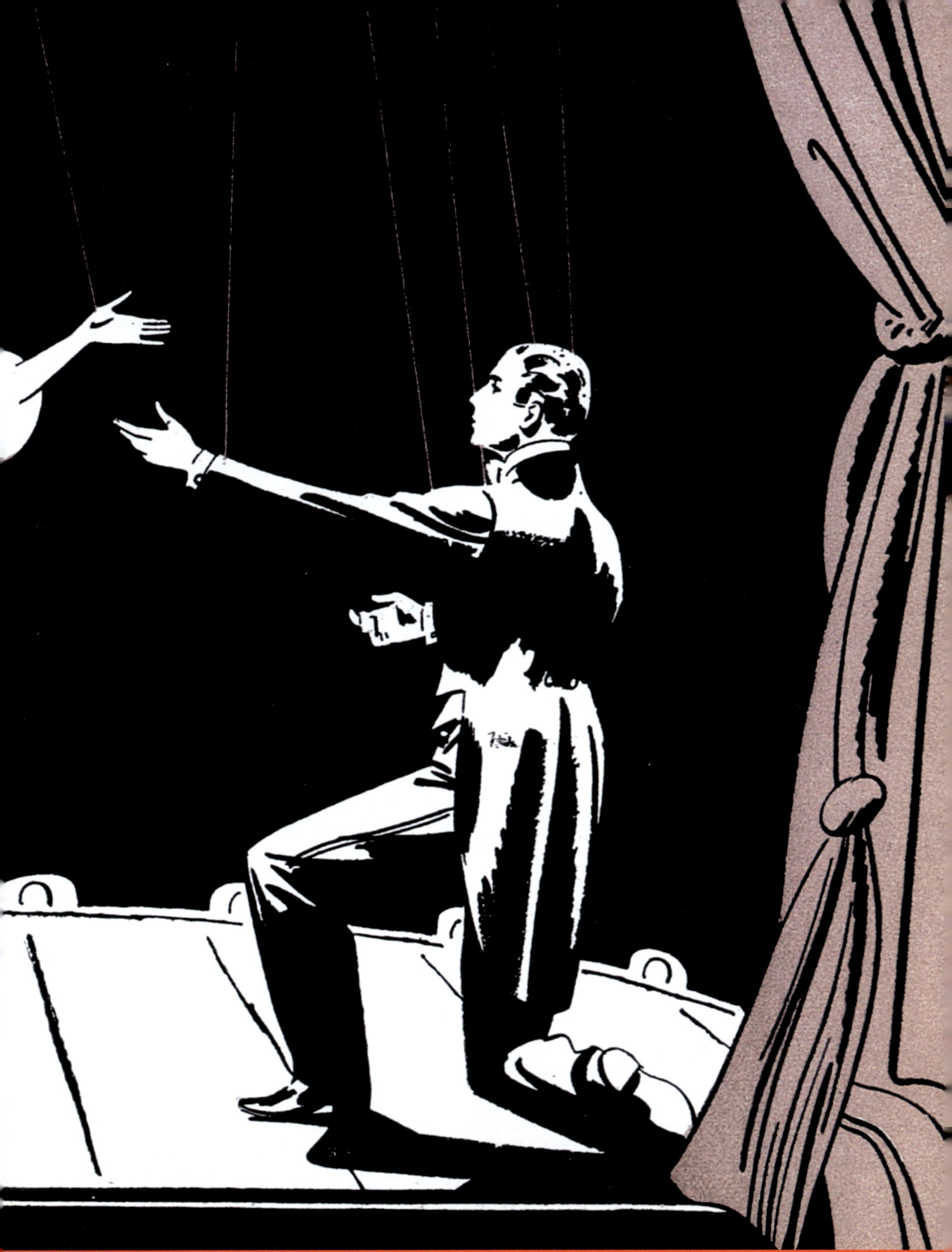

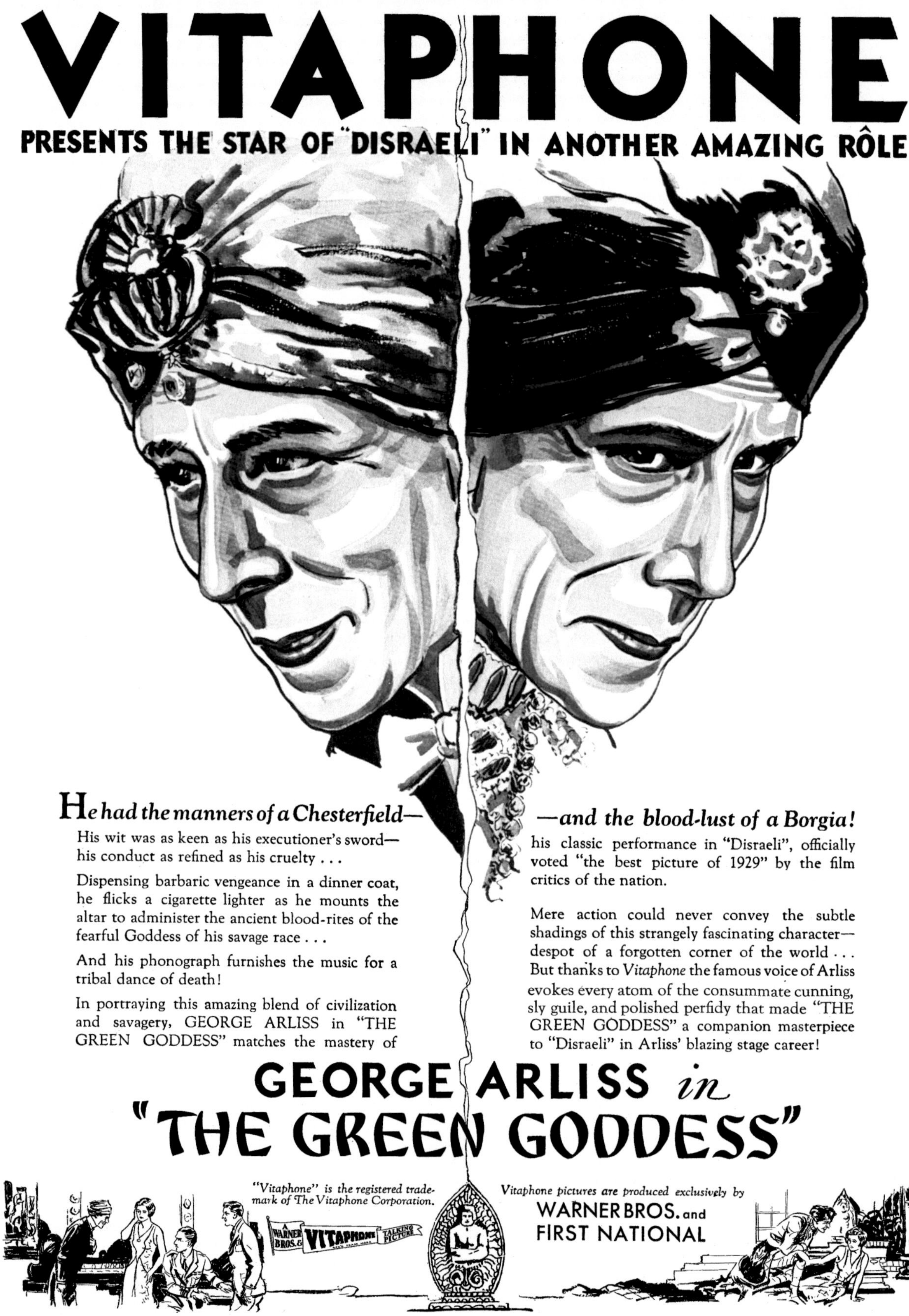

A Princess Marries 1938 ◂◂ *The Green Goddess, 1930* ▸ *Under A Texas Moon, 1930*

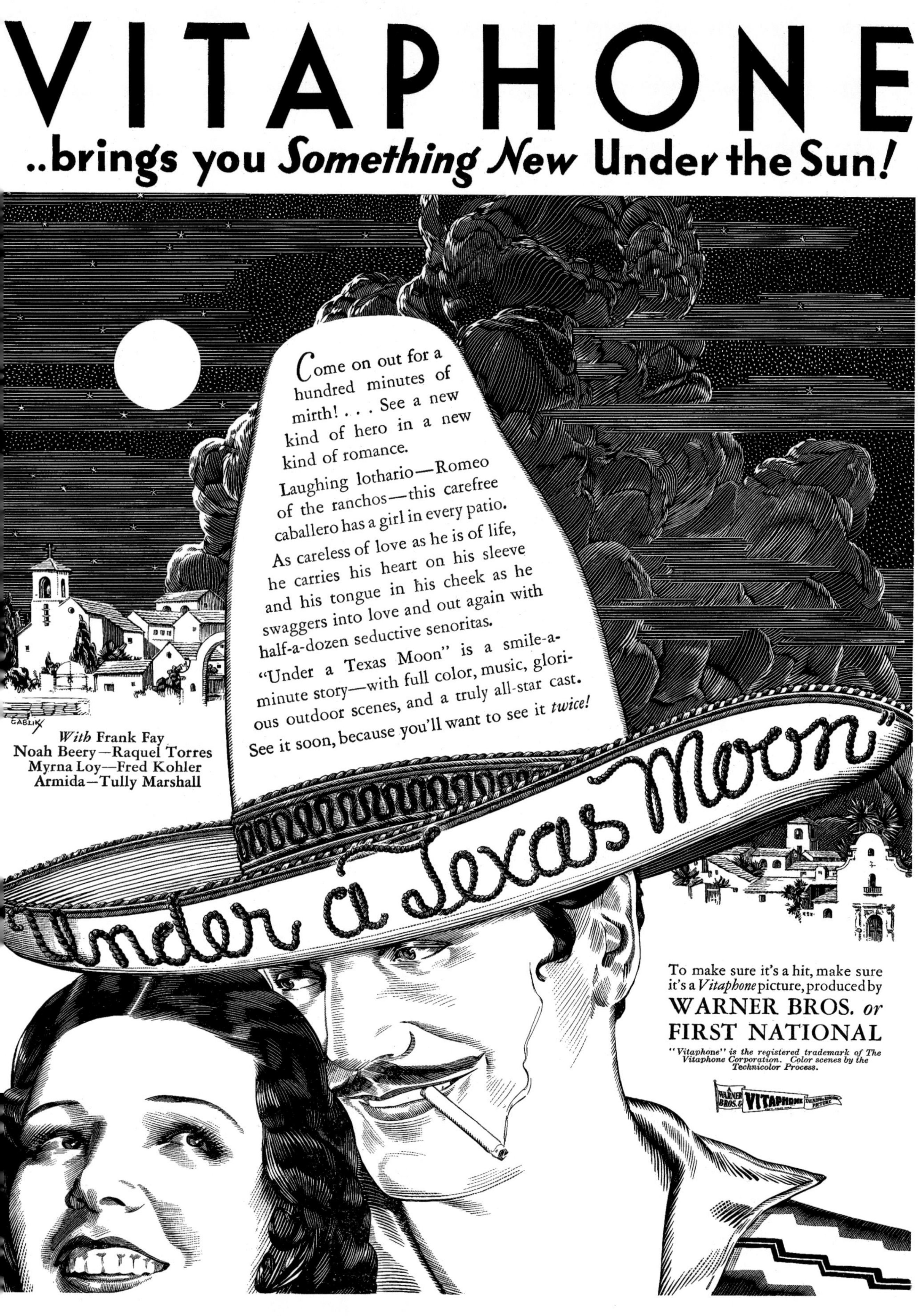
VITAPHONE
..brings you Something New Under the Sun!
Come on out for a hundred minutes of mirth! . . . See a new kind of hero in a new kind of romance.
Laughing lothario—Romeo of the ranchos—this carefree caballero has a girl in every patio. As careless of love as he is of life, he carries his heart on his sleeve and his tongue in his cheek as he swaggers into love and out again with half-a-dozen seductive senoritas.
"Under a Texas Moon" is a smile-a-minute story—with full color, music, glorious outdoor scenes, and a truly all-star cast. See it soon, because you'll want to see it twice!
"Under a Texas Moon"
GABLIK
With Frank Fay
Noah Beery—Raquel Torres
Myrna Loy—Fred Kohler
Armida—Tully Marshall
To make sure it's a hit, make sure it's a Vitaphone picture, produced by
WARNER BROS. or FIRST NATIONAL
"Vitaphone" is the registered trademark of The Vitaphone Corporation. Color scenes by the Technicolor Process.
A WARNER BROS. & VITAPHONE TALKING & SINGING PICTURE

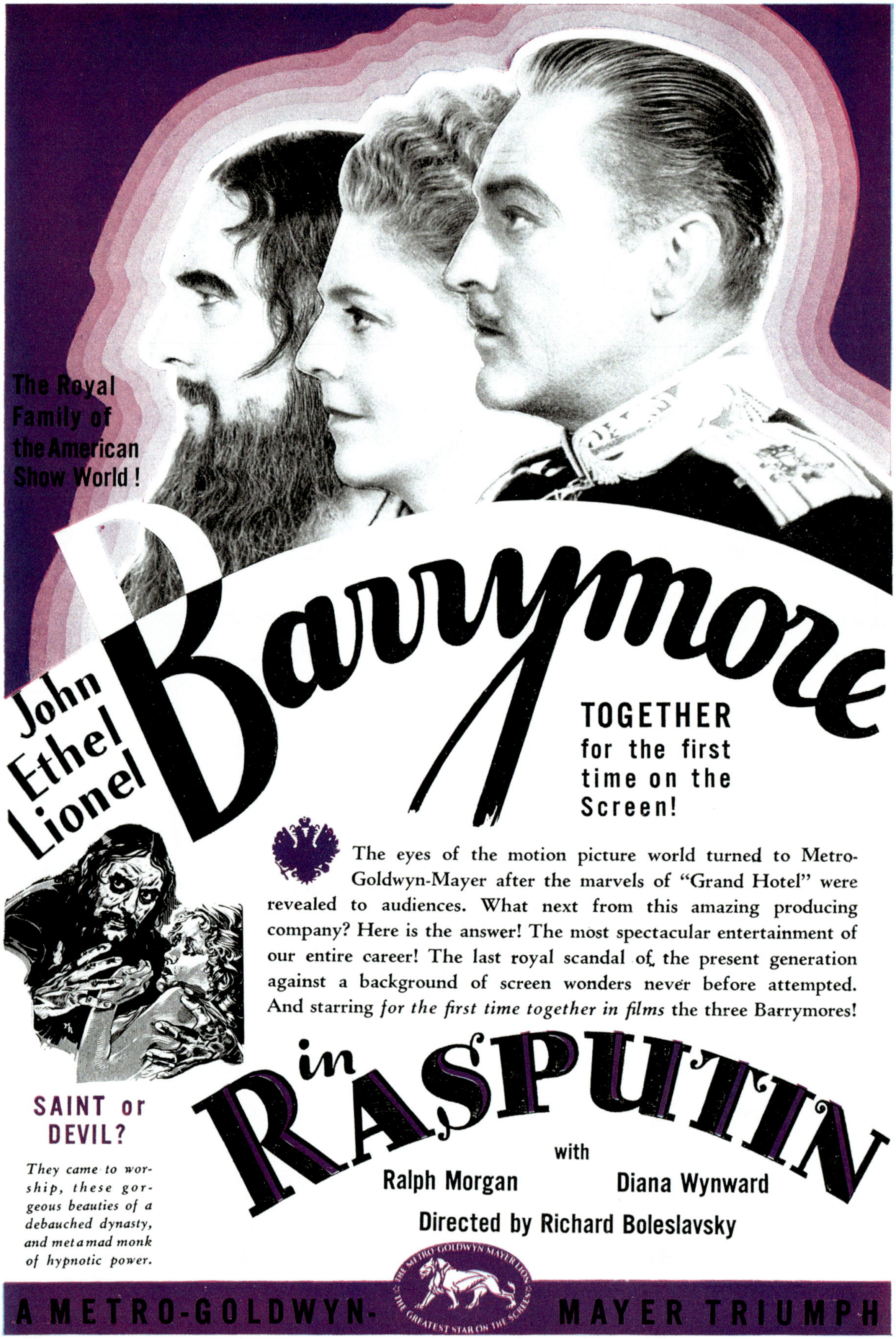

Rasputin, 1932

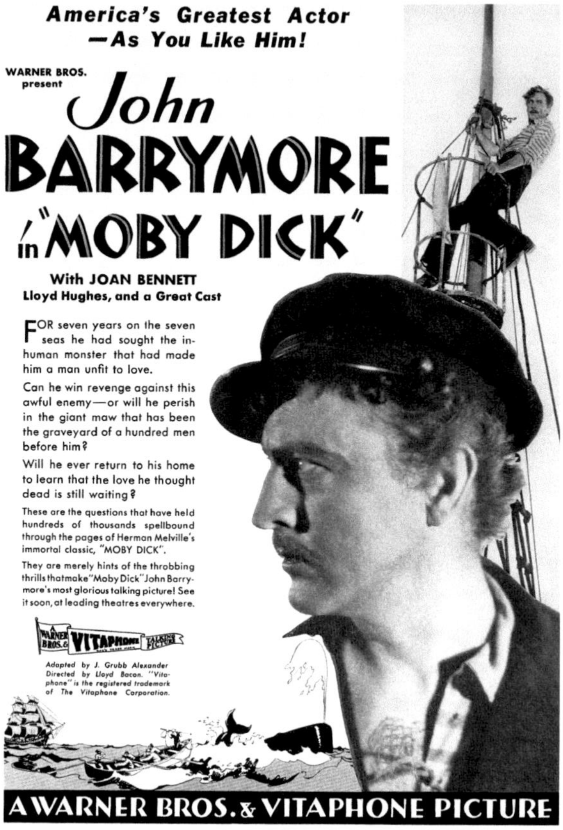

Moby Dick, 1930

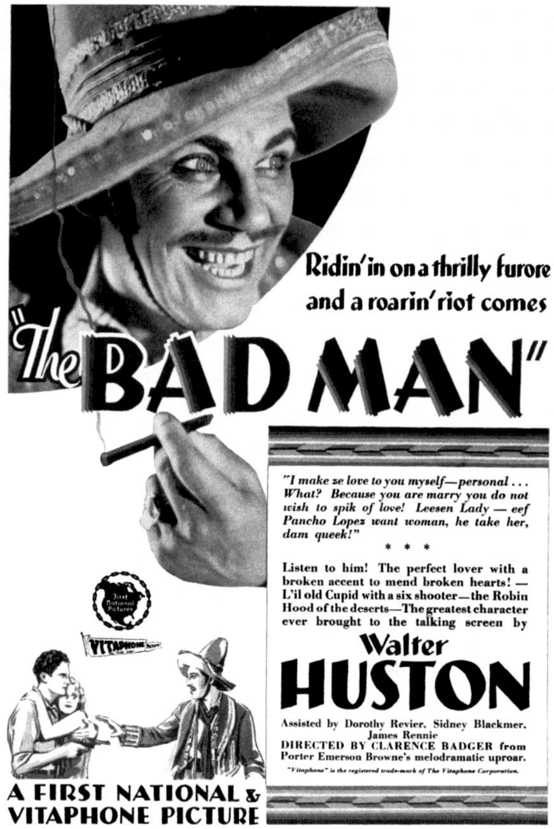

The Badman, 1930

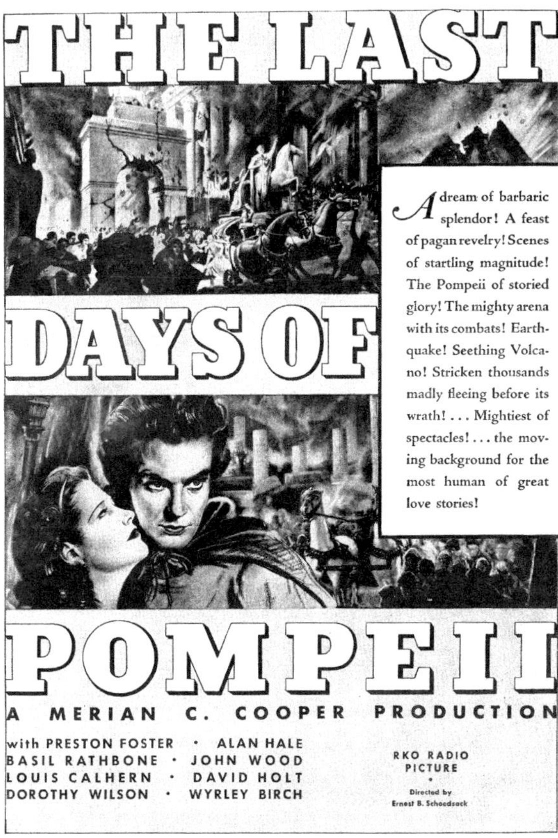

The Last Days Of Pompeii, 1935

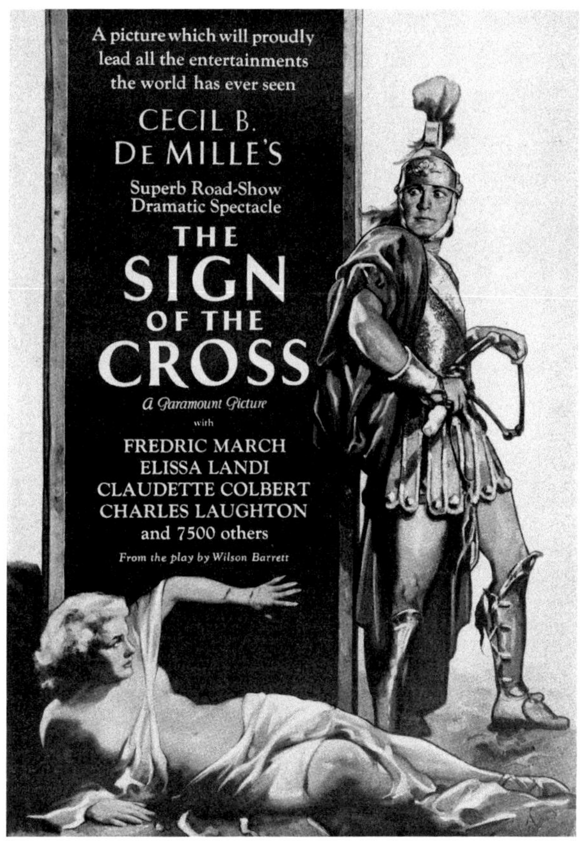

The Sign Of The Cross, 1933

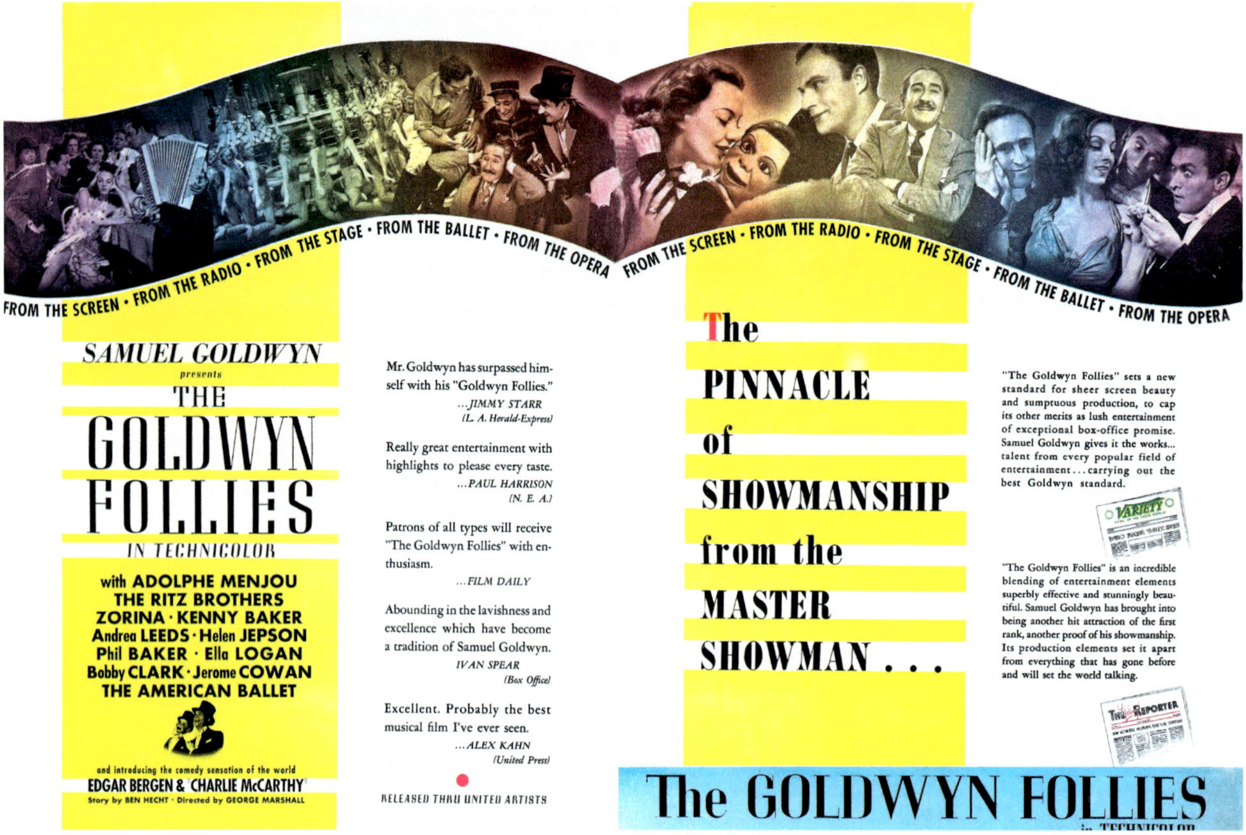

The Goldwyn Follies, 1938

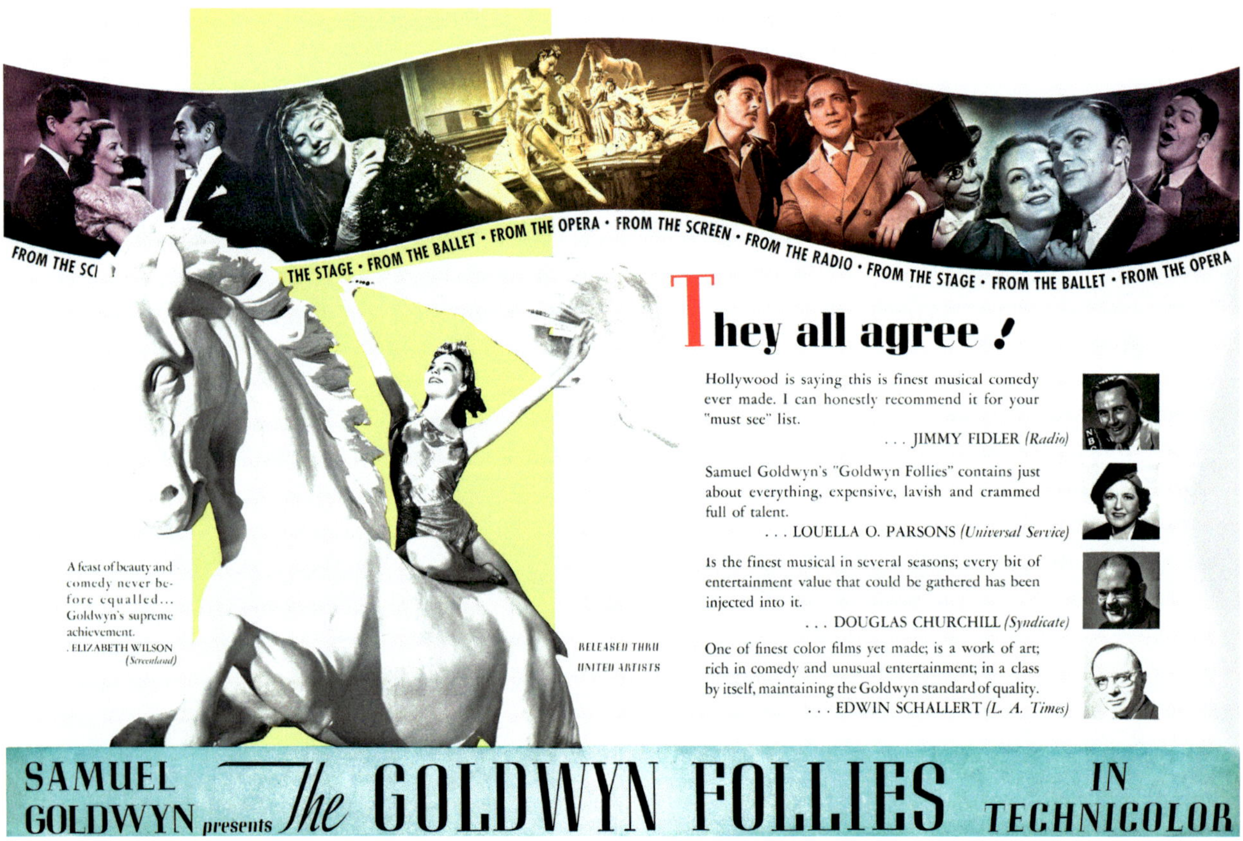

The Goldwyn Follies, 1938

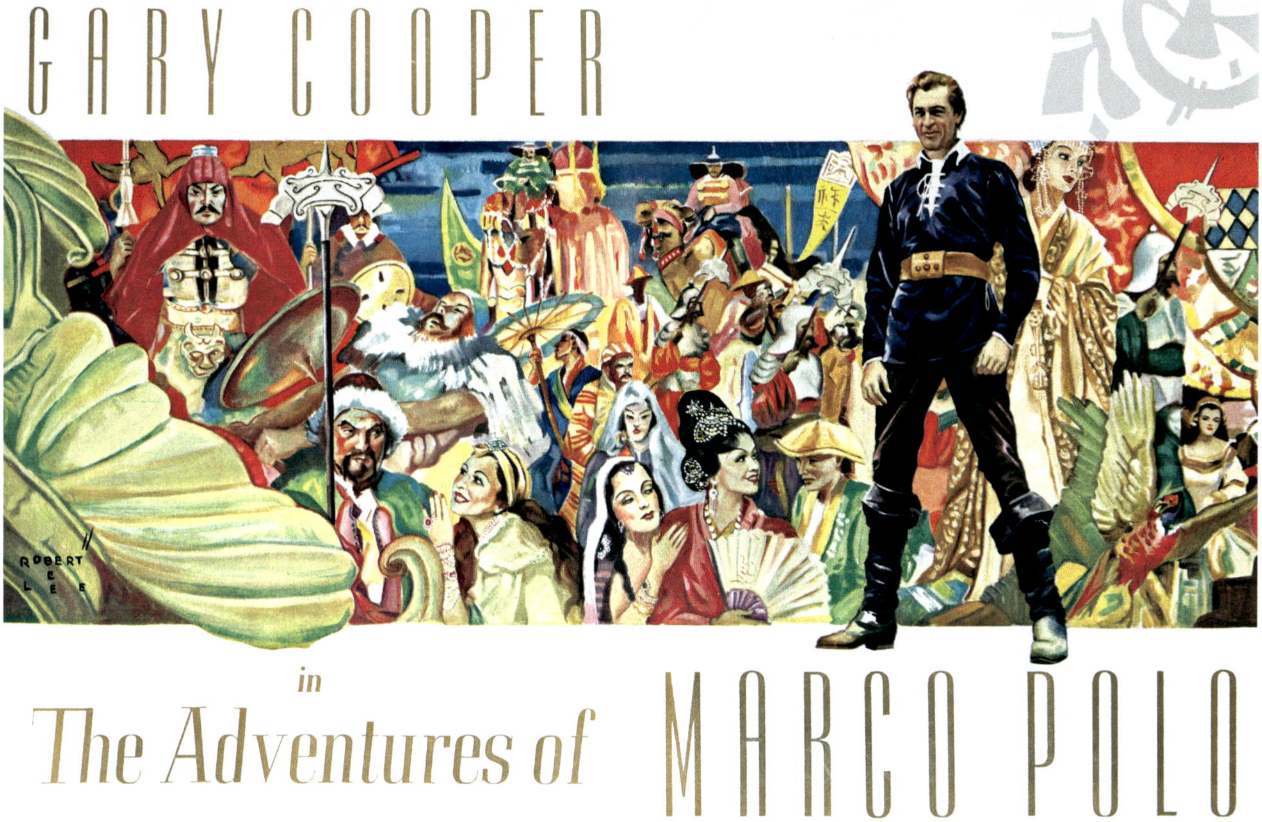

Marco Polo, 1938

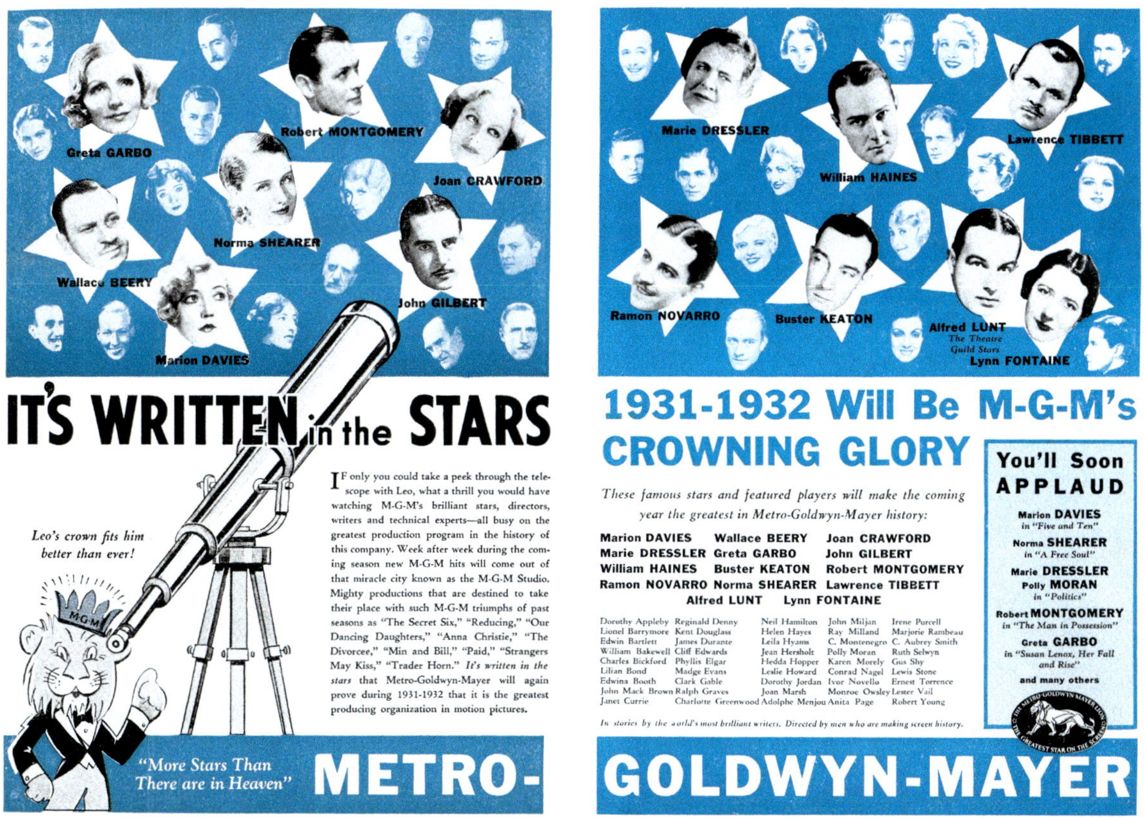

Metro-Goldwyn-Mayer, 1931

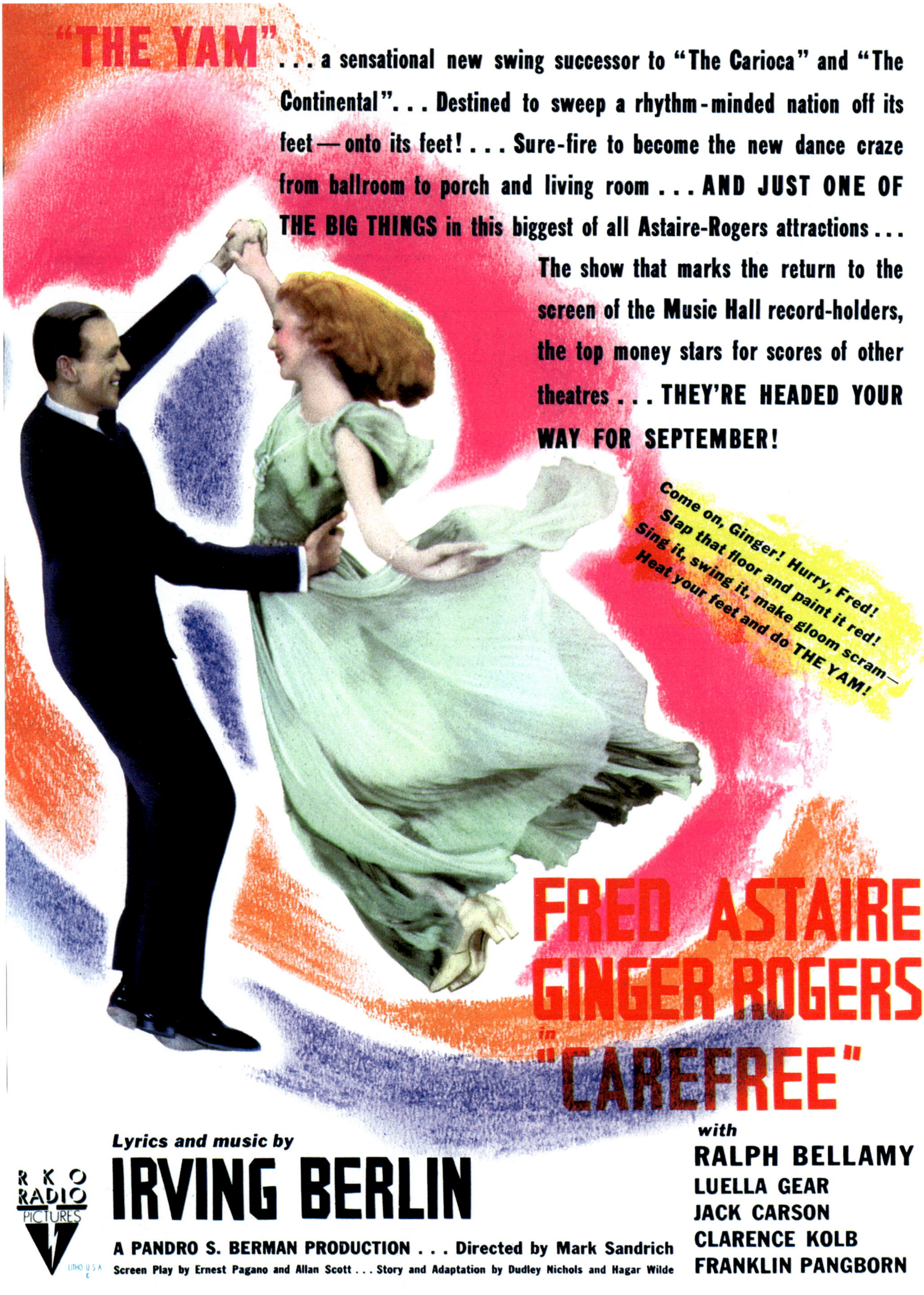
"THE YAM" . . . a sensational new swing successor to "The Carioca" and "The Continental". . . Destined to sweep a rhythm-minded nation off its feet — onto its feet! . . . Sure-fire to become the new dance craze from ballroom to porch and living room . . . AND JUST ONE OF THE BIG THINGS in this biggest of all Astaire-Rogers attractions . . . The show that marks the return to the screen of the Music Hall record-holders, the top money stars for scores of other theatres . . . THEY'RE HEADED YOUR WAY FOR SEPTEMBER!
Come on, Ginger! Hurry, Fred!
Slap that floor and paint it red!
Sing it, swing it, make gloom scram—
Heat your feet and do THE YAM!
FRED ASTAIRE
GINGER ROGERS
in
"CAREFREE"
with
RALPH BELLAMY
LUELLA GEAR
JACK CARSON
CLARENCE KOLB
FRANKLIN PANGBORN
Lyrics and music by
IRVING BERLIN
RKO RADIO PICTURES
A PANDRO S. BERMAN PRODUCTION . . . Directed by Mark Sandrich
Screen Play by Ernest Pagano and Allan Scott . . . Story and Adaptation by Dudley Nichols and Hagar Wilde
LITHO U.S.A.

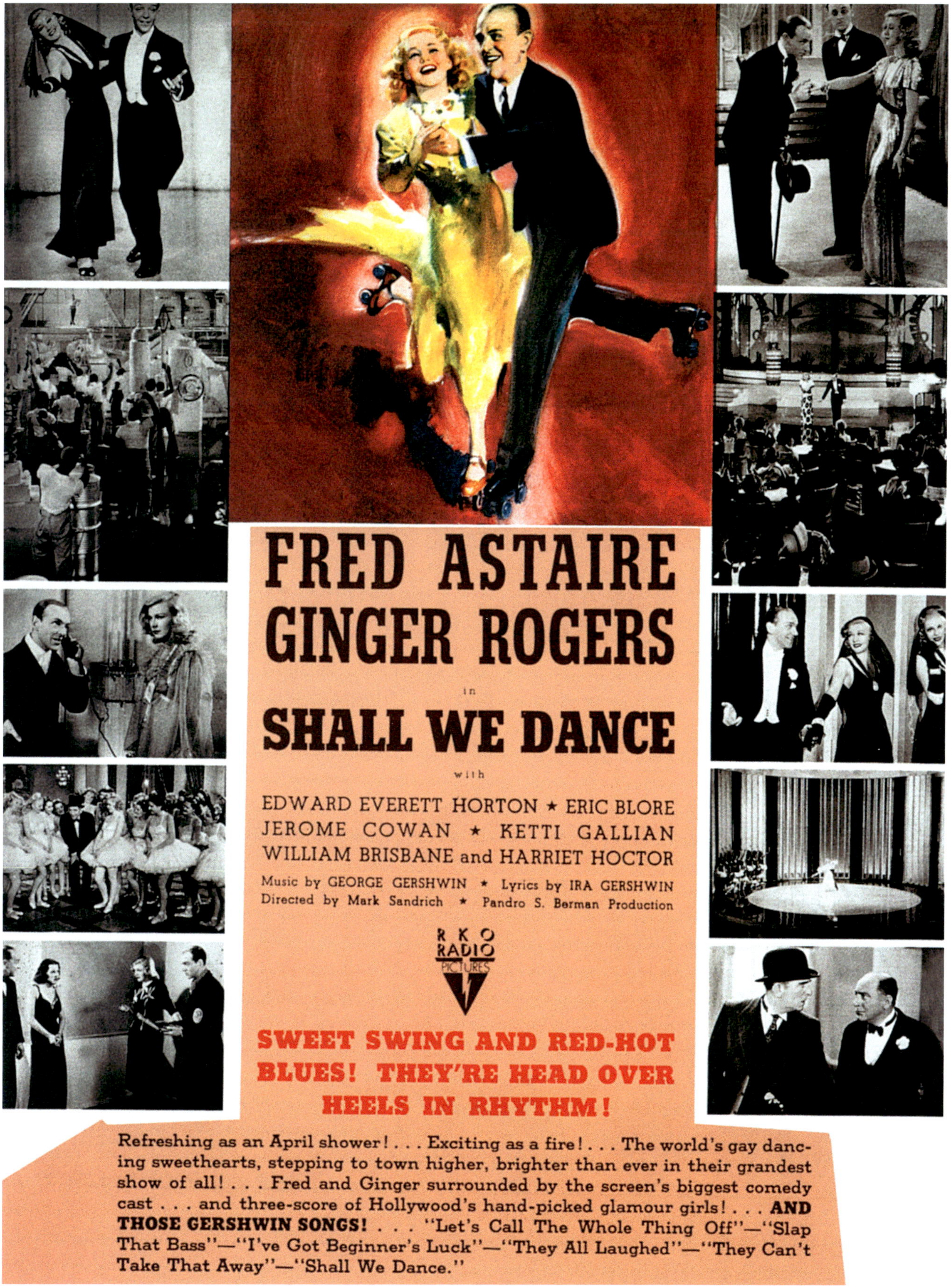

Carefree, 1938 ◄

Shall We Dance, 1937

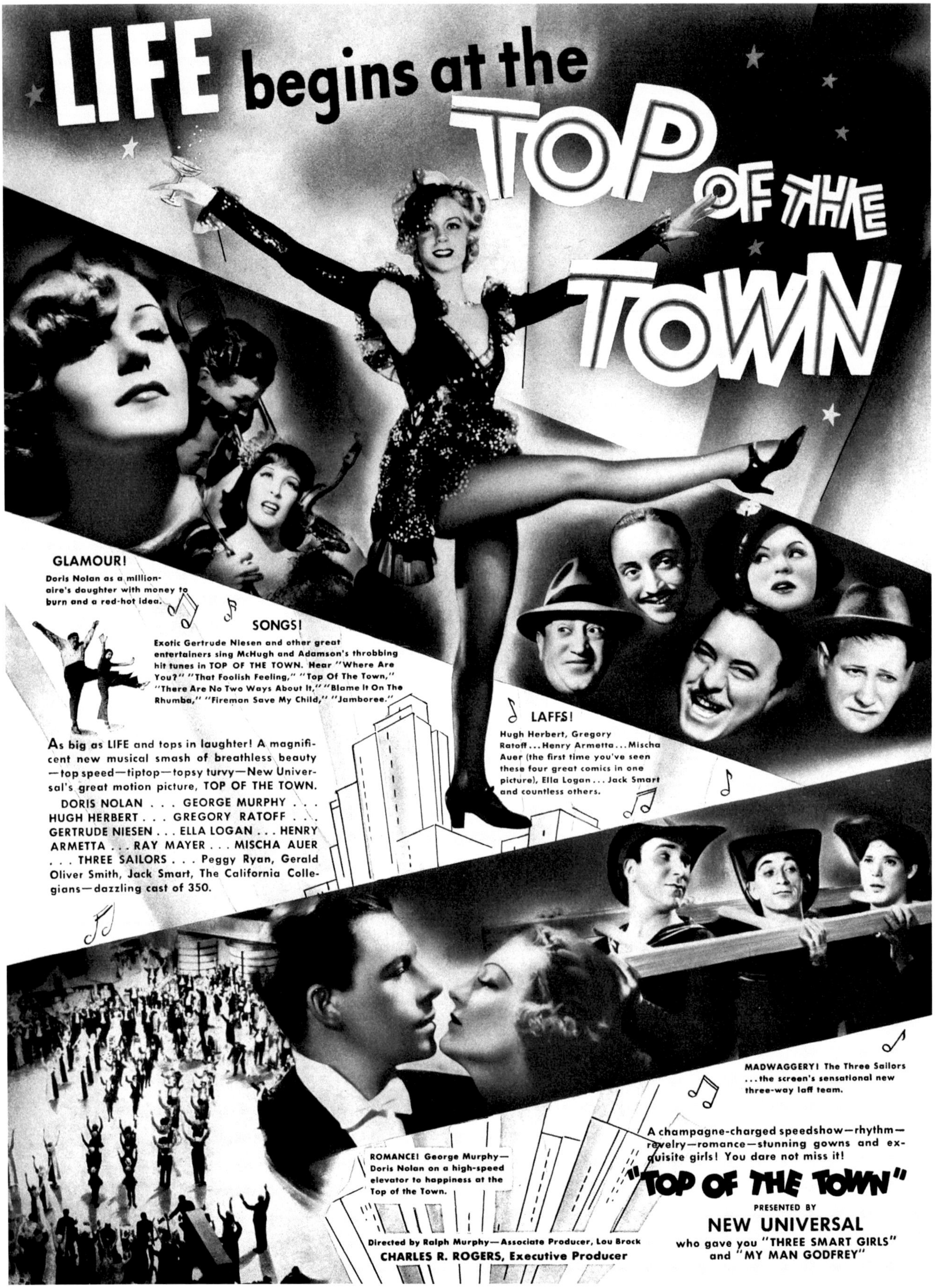

Top Of The Town, 1937

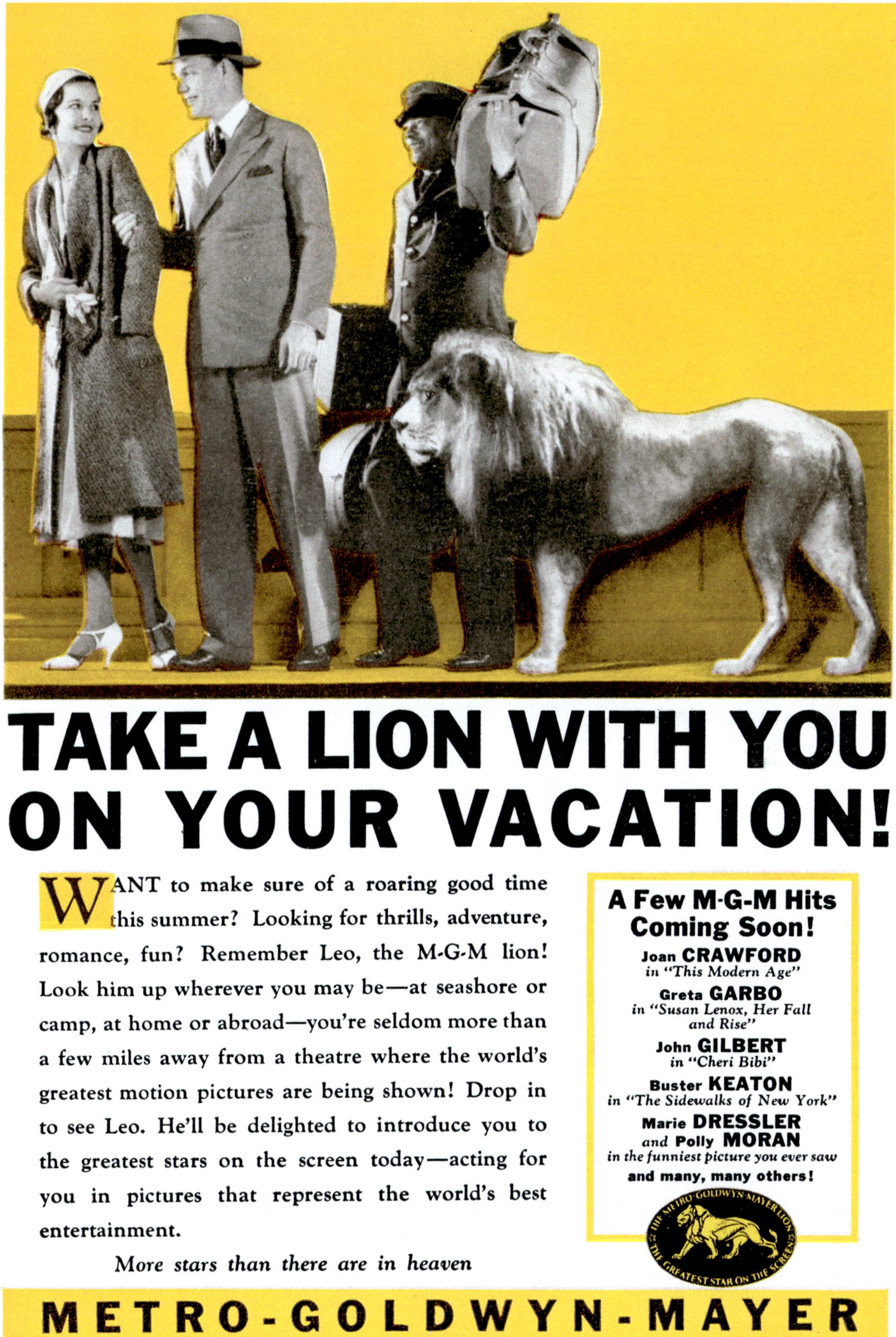

Metro-Goldwyn-Mayer, 1931

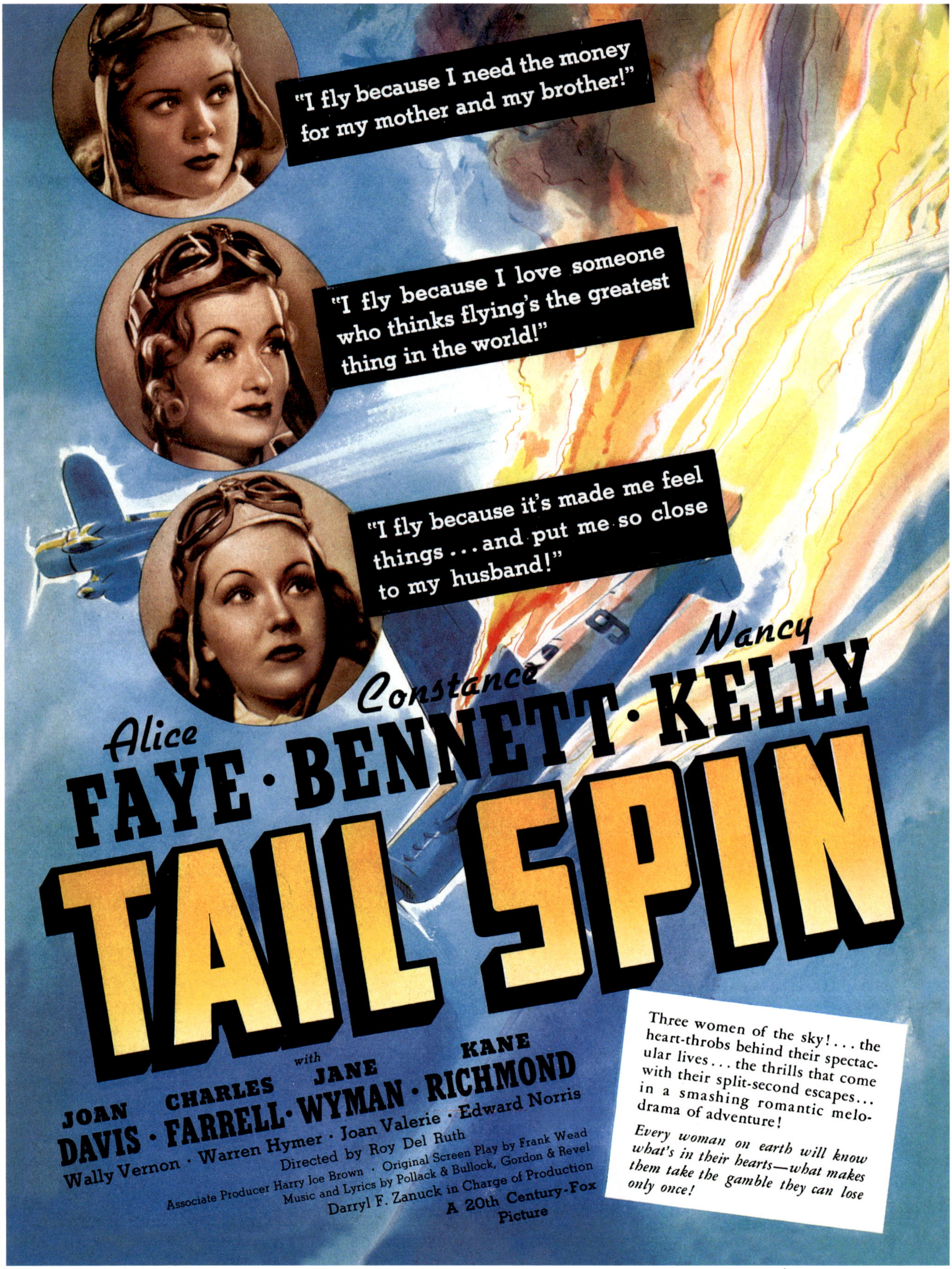

Tail Spin, 1939

▸ *Men With Wings*, 1938

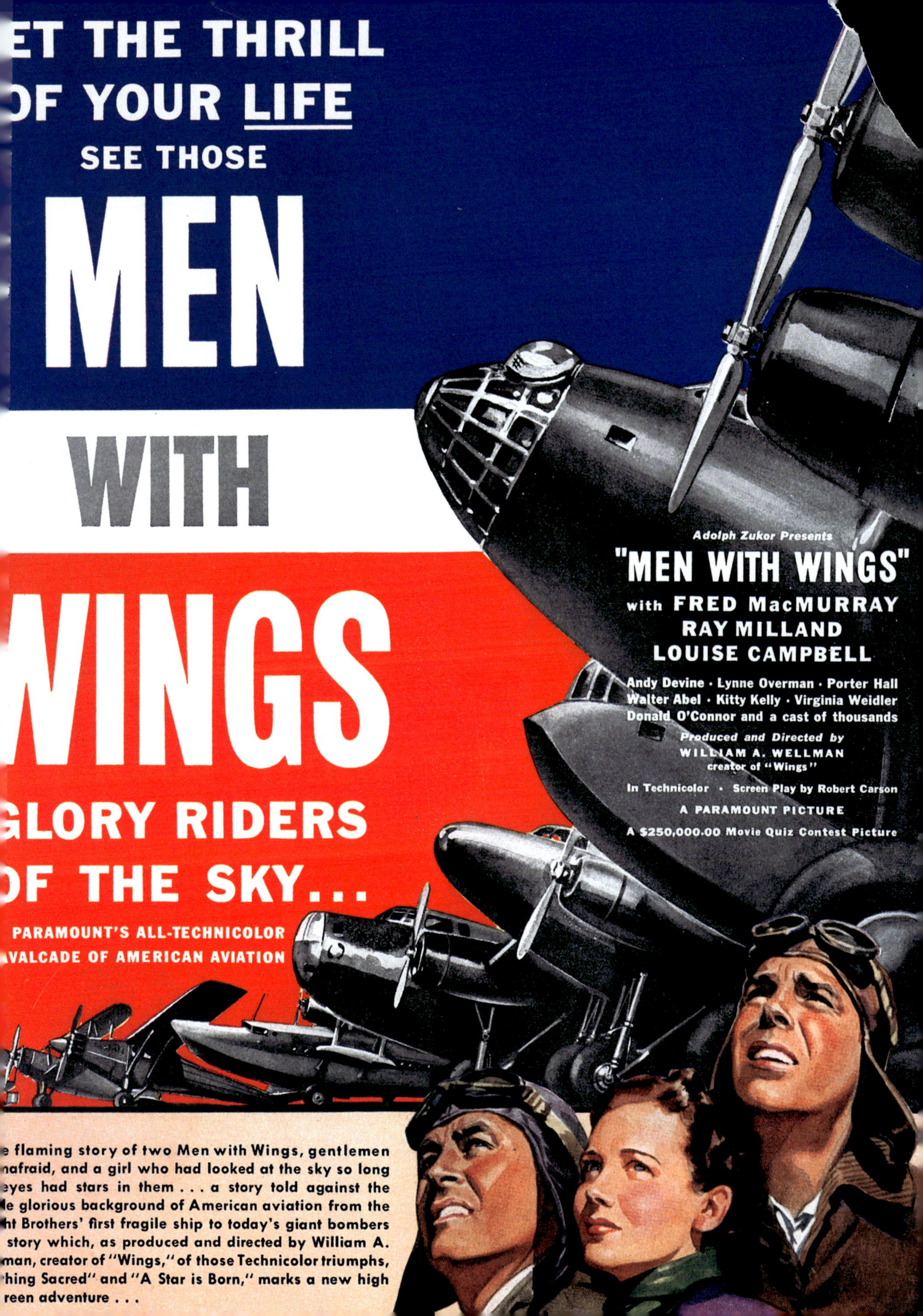
ET THE THRILL
OF YOUR LIFE
SEE THOSE
MEN
WITH
WINGS
GLORY RIDERS
OF THE SKY...
PARAMOUNT'S ALL-TECHNICOLOR
VALCADE OF AMERICAN AVIATION
Adolph Zukor Presents
"MEN WITH WINGS"
with FRED MacMURRAY
RAY MILLAND
LOUISE CAMPBELL
Andy Devine · Lynne Overman · Porter Hall
Walter Abel · Kitty Kelly · Virginia Weidler
Donald O'Connor and a cast of thousands
Produced and Directed by
WILLIAM A. WELLMAN
creator of "Wings"
In Technicolor · Screen Play by Robert Carson
A PARAMOUNT PICTURE
A $250,000.00 Movie Quiz Contest Picture
e flaming story of two Men with Wings, gentlemen
nafraid, and a girl who had looked at the sky so long
eyes had stars in them . . . a story told against the
e glorious background of American aviation from the
ht Brothers' first fragile ship to today's giant bombers
story which, as produced and directed by William A.
man, creator of "Wings," of those Technicolor triumphs,
hing Sacred" and "A Star is Born," marks a new high
reen adventure . . .

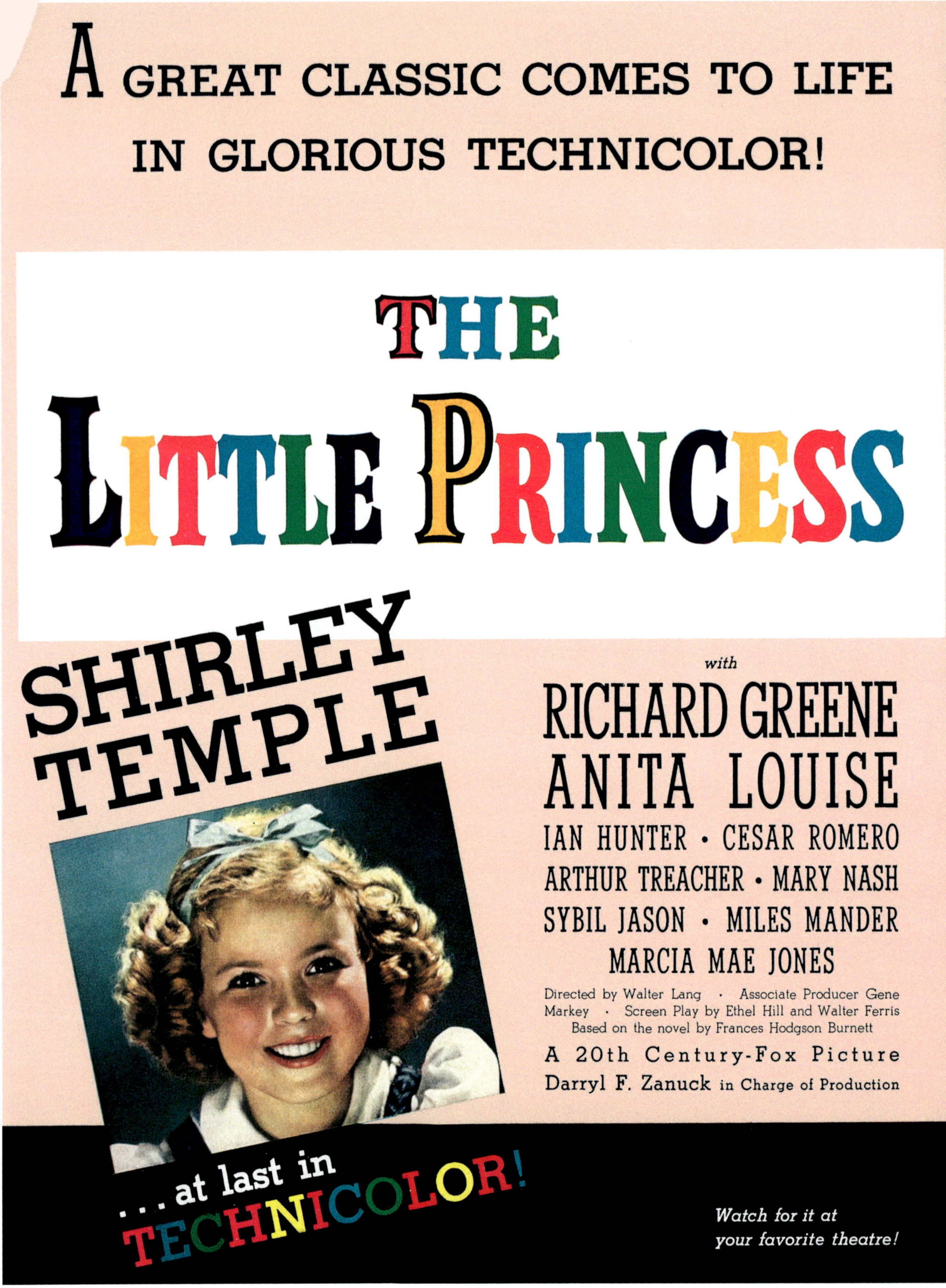

The Little Princess, 1939

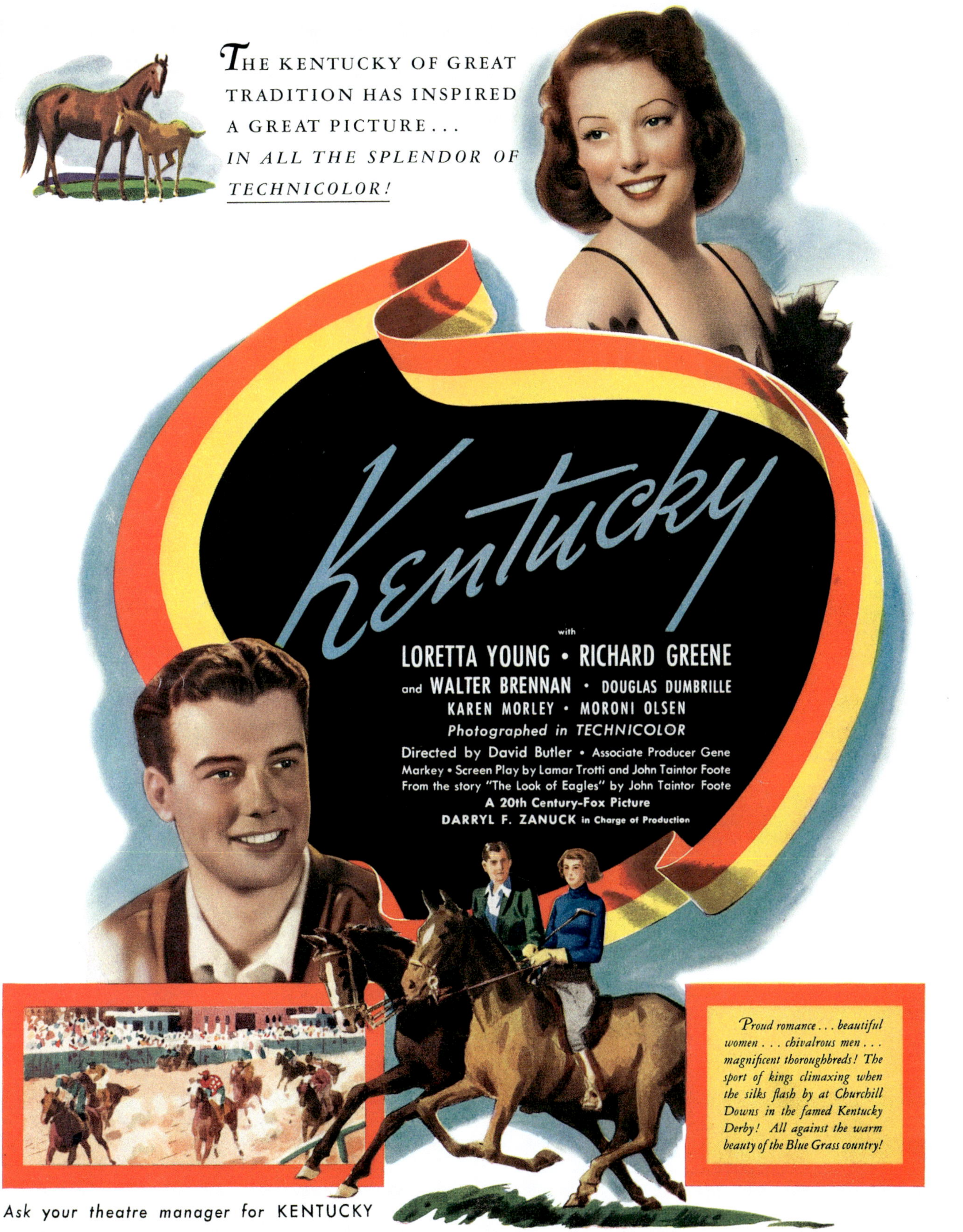

Kentucky, 1939

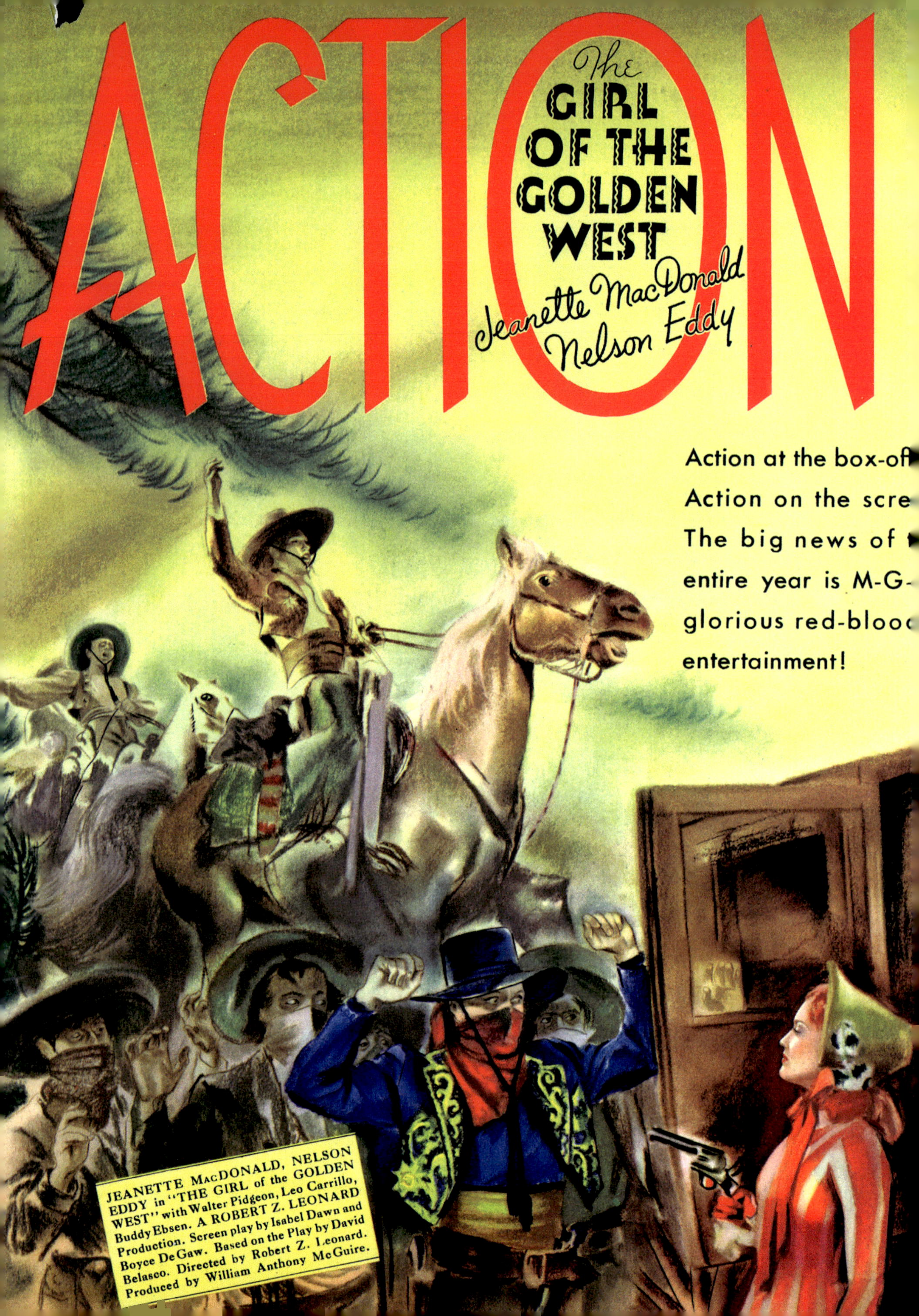
ACTION
The GIRL OF THE GOLDEN WEST
Jeanette MacDonald
Nelson Eddy
Action at the box-of
Action on the scre
The big news of
entire year is M-G-
glorious red-bloo
entertainment!
JEANETTE MacDONALD, NELSON EDDY in "THE GIRL of the GOLDEN WEST" with Walter Pidgeon, Leo Carrillo, Buddy Ebsen. A ROBERT Z. LEONARD Production. Screen play by Isabel Dawn and Boyce DeGaw. Based on the Play by David Belasco. Directed by Robert Z. Leonard. Produced by William Anthony McGuire.

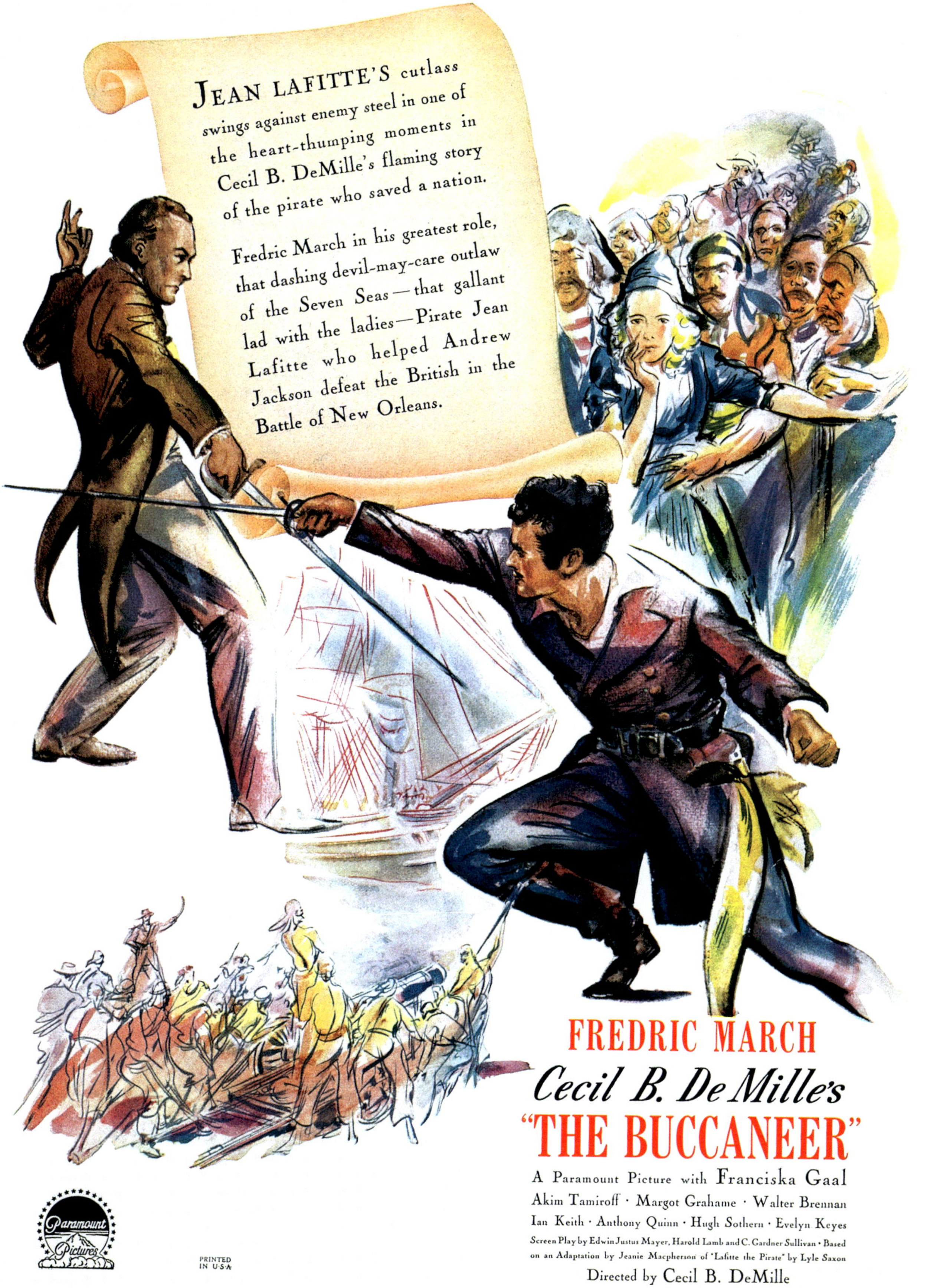

The Girl Of The Golden West, 1938 ◂

The Buccaneer, 1938

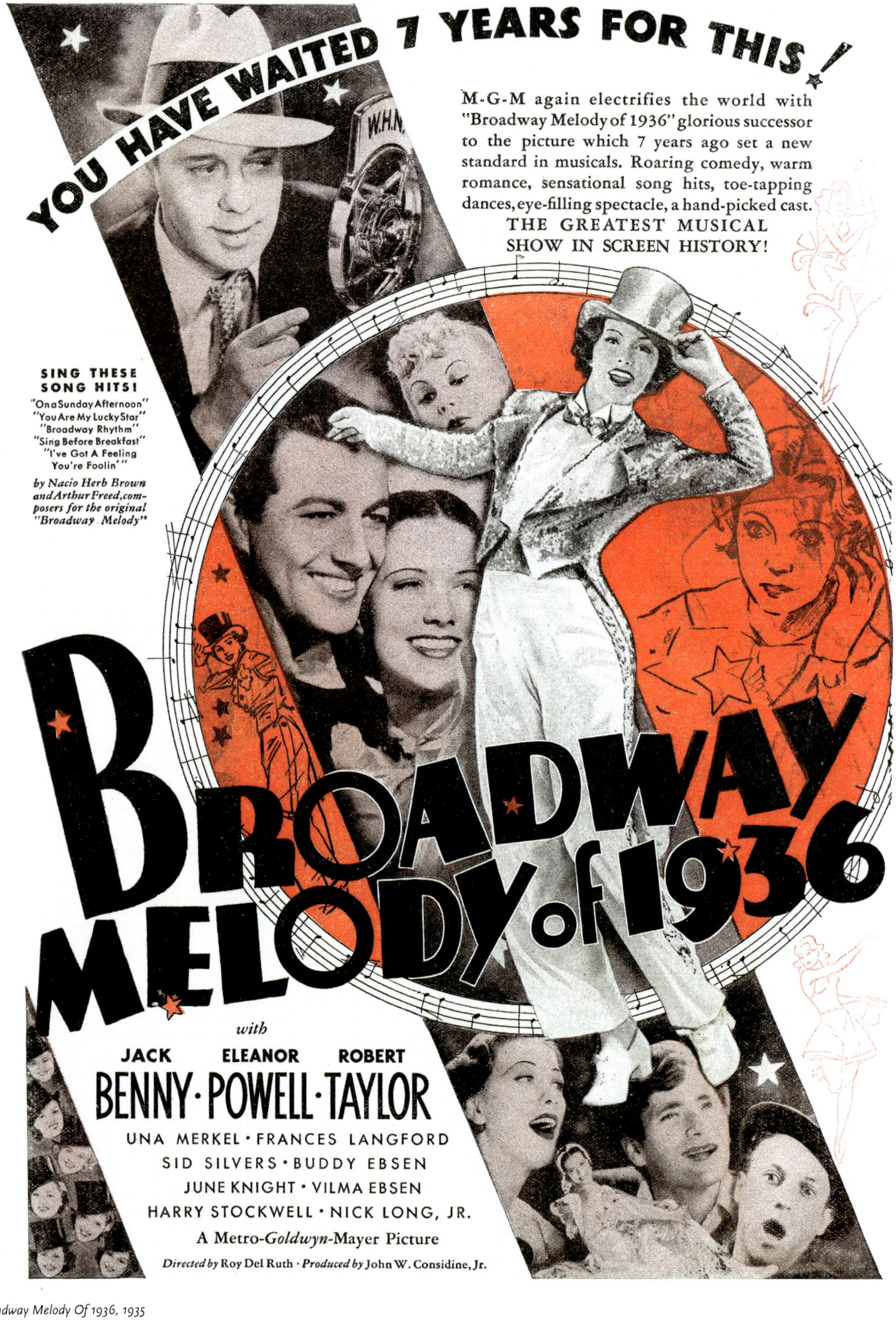

Broadway Melody Of 1936, 1935

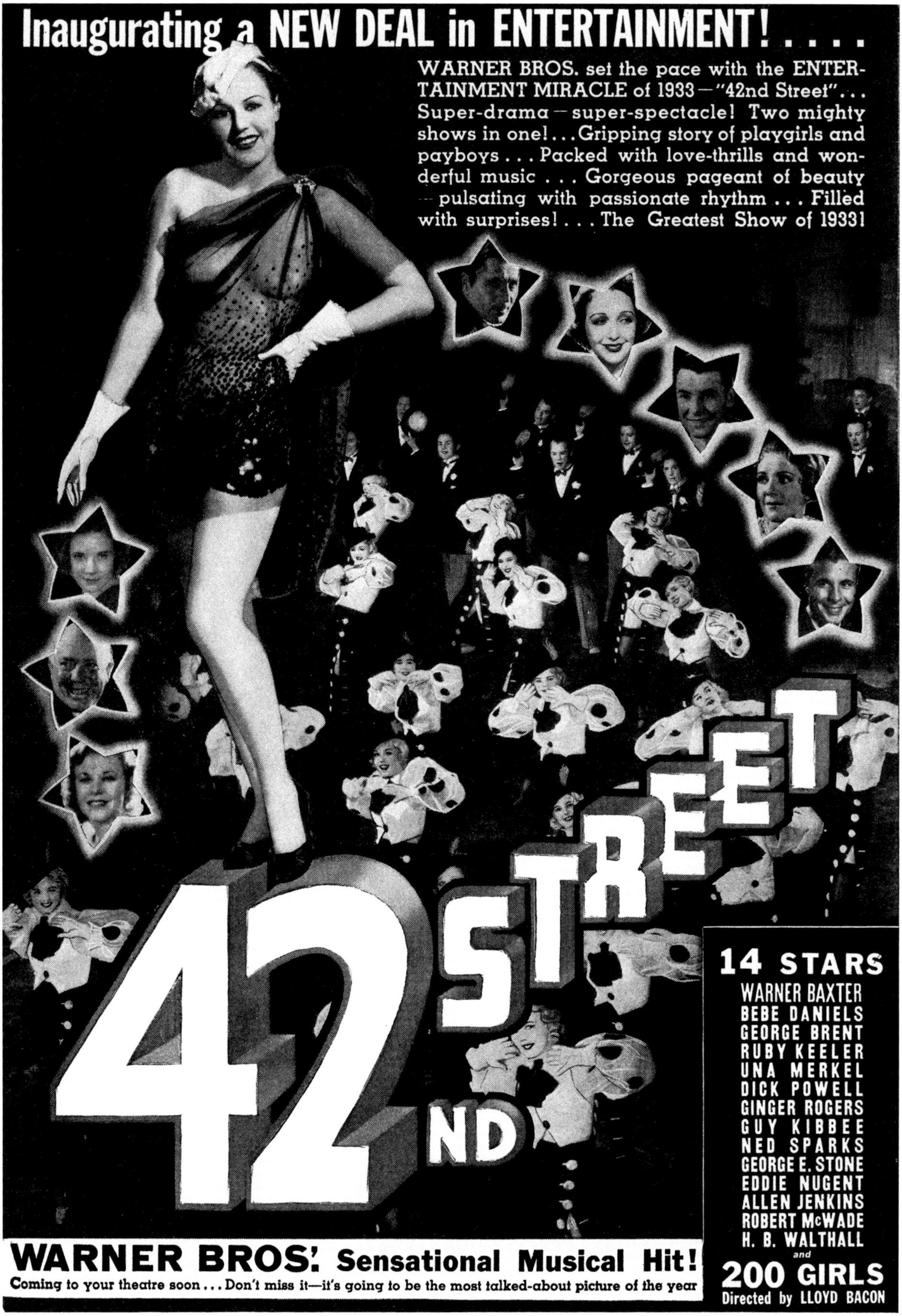

42nd Street, 1933

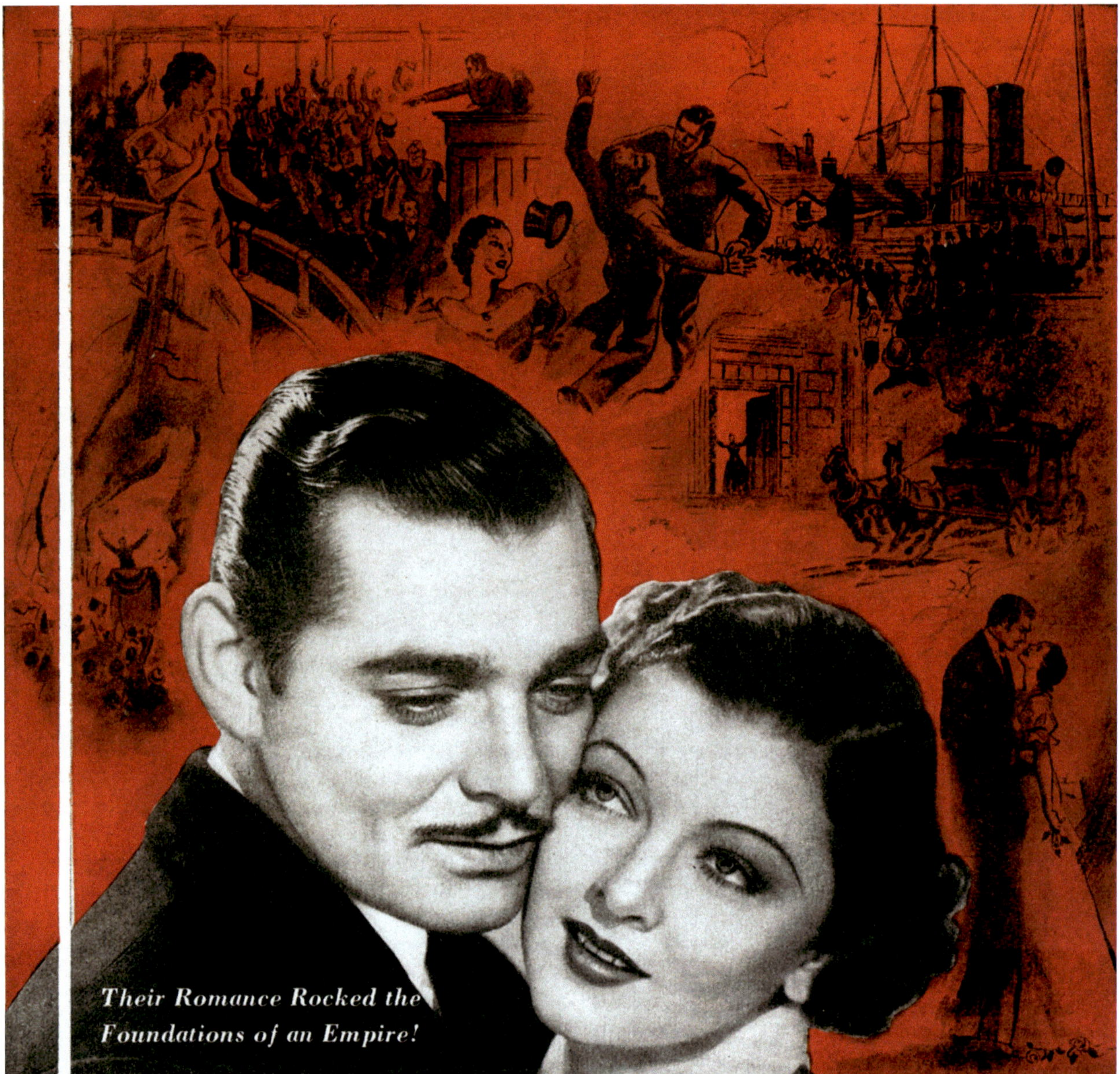

THE MOST *Powerful* LOVE STORY EVER FILMED!

...Of a Patriot Who Lost a Country When He Found a Woman

You thought "San Francisco" was exciting—but wait! You'll be thrilled to your finger-tips when this mighty drama comes thundering from the screen. A fiery romance with your two favorite stars!... CLARK GABLE—courageous, masterful leader of a fighting nation . . . MYRNA LOY—the bewitching beauty in whose arms he forgot the pain of leadership . . .

Answering the call of millions of picture-goers M-G-M has brought them together in the most dramatic heart-stabbing love story of our time!

CLARK GABLE • MYRNA LOY

IN

PARNELL

A Metro-Goldwyn-Mayer production based on the great stage play that thrilled Broadway for months, with EDNA MAY OLIVER, BILLIE BURKE, and a great M-G-M cast. Directed and produced by John Stahl.

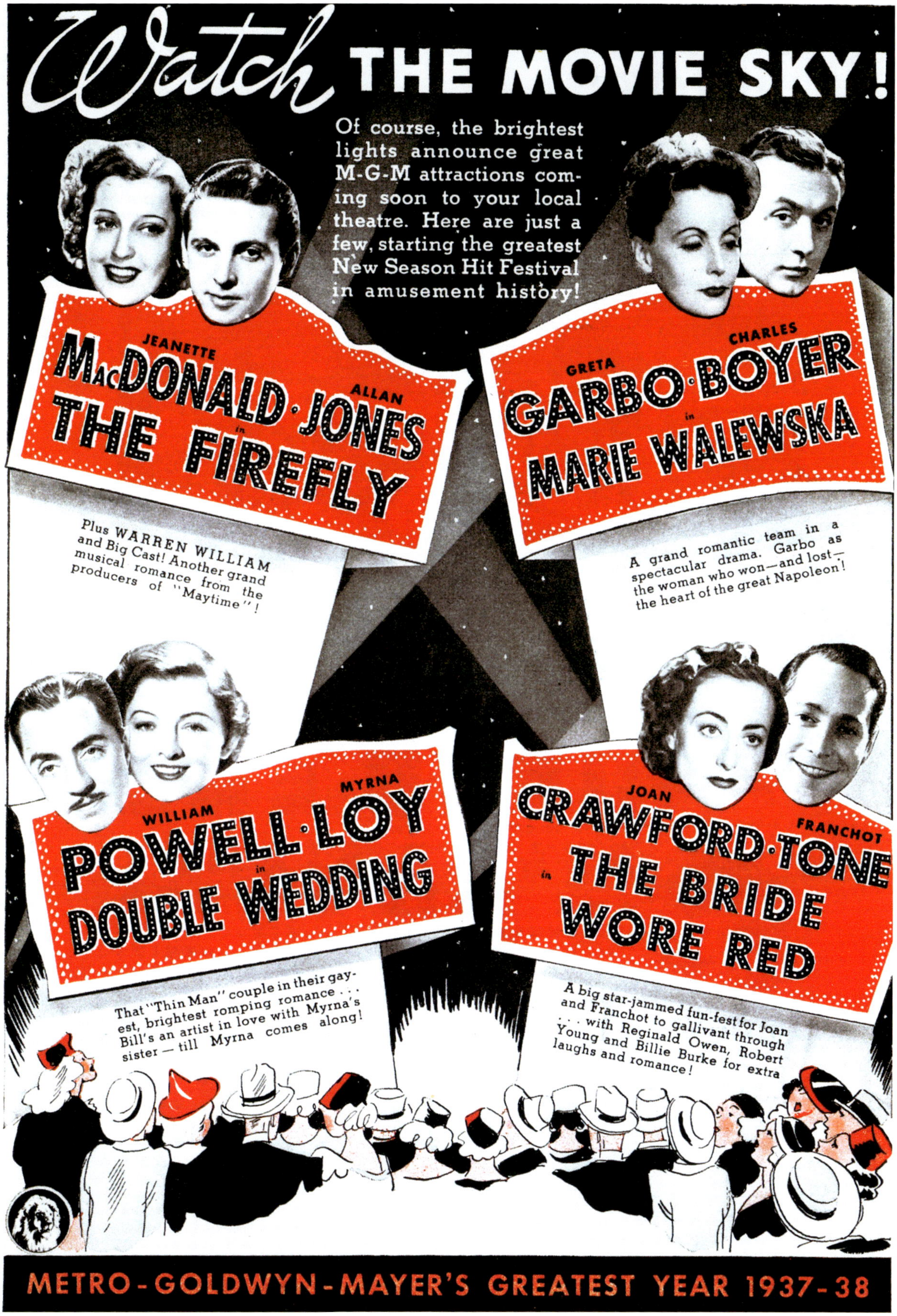

Parnell, 1937 ◂

Metro-Goldwyn-Mayer, 1937

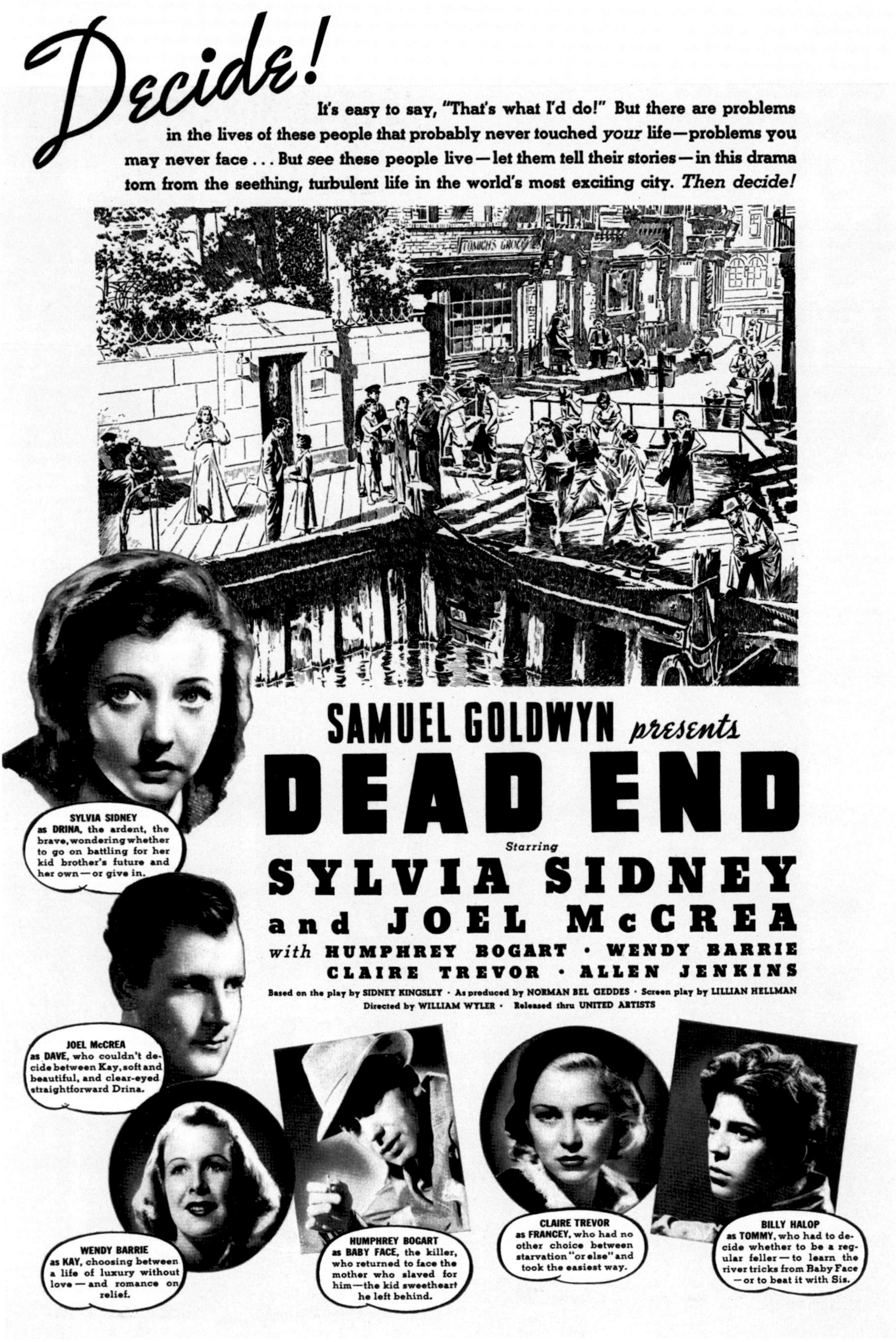

Dead End, 1937

▸ *Gold Diggers Of 1933*, 1933

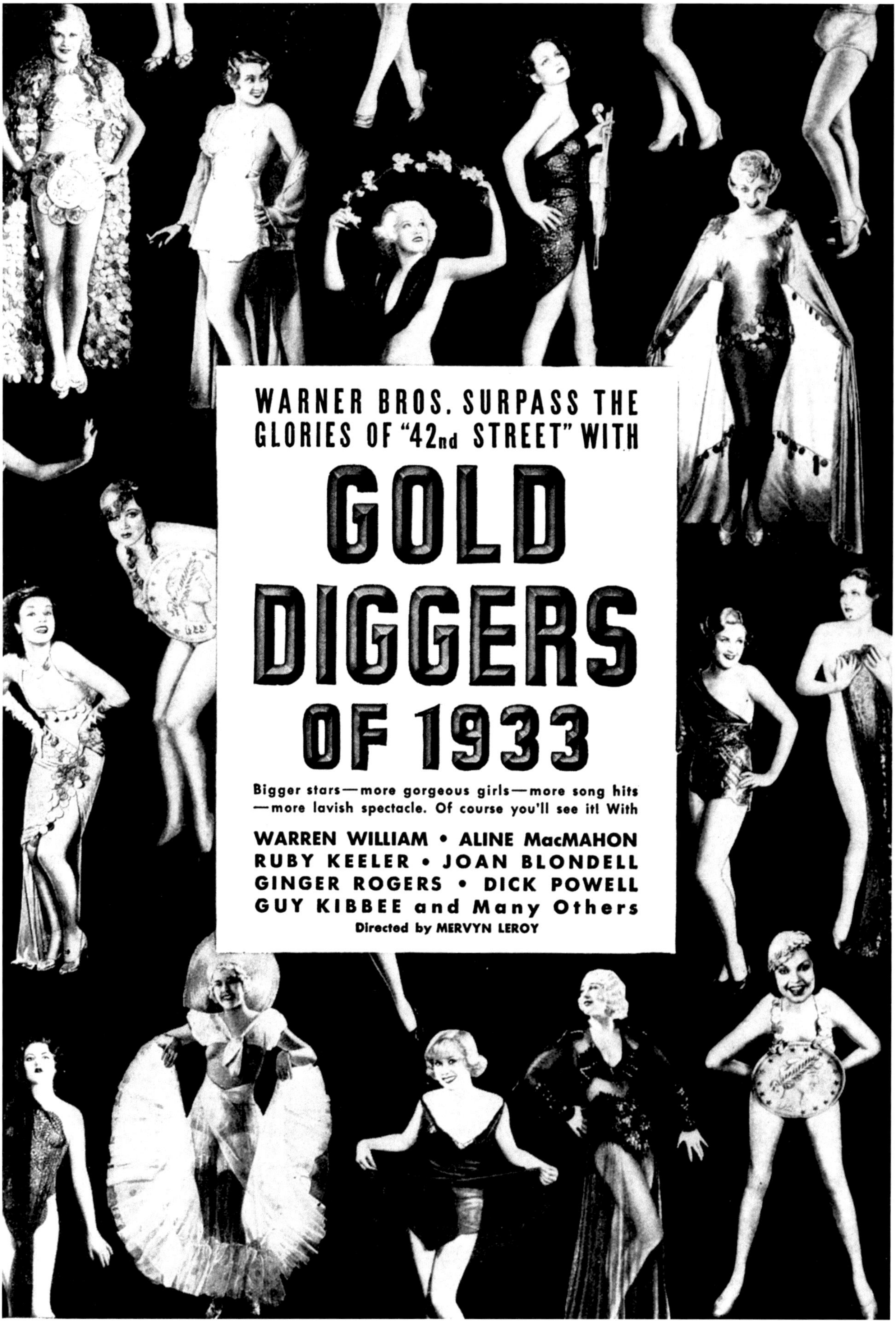
WARNER BROS. SURPASS THE GLORIES OF "42nd STREET" WITH
GOLD DIGGERS OF 1933
Bigger stars—more gorgeous girls—more song hits—more lavish spectacle. Of course you'll see it! With
WARREN WILLIAM • ALINE MacMAHON
RUBY KEELER • JOAN BLONDELL
GINGER ROGERS • DICK POWELL
GUY KIBBEE and Many Others
Directed by MERVYN LEROY

MARLENE DIETRIC

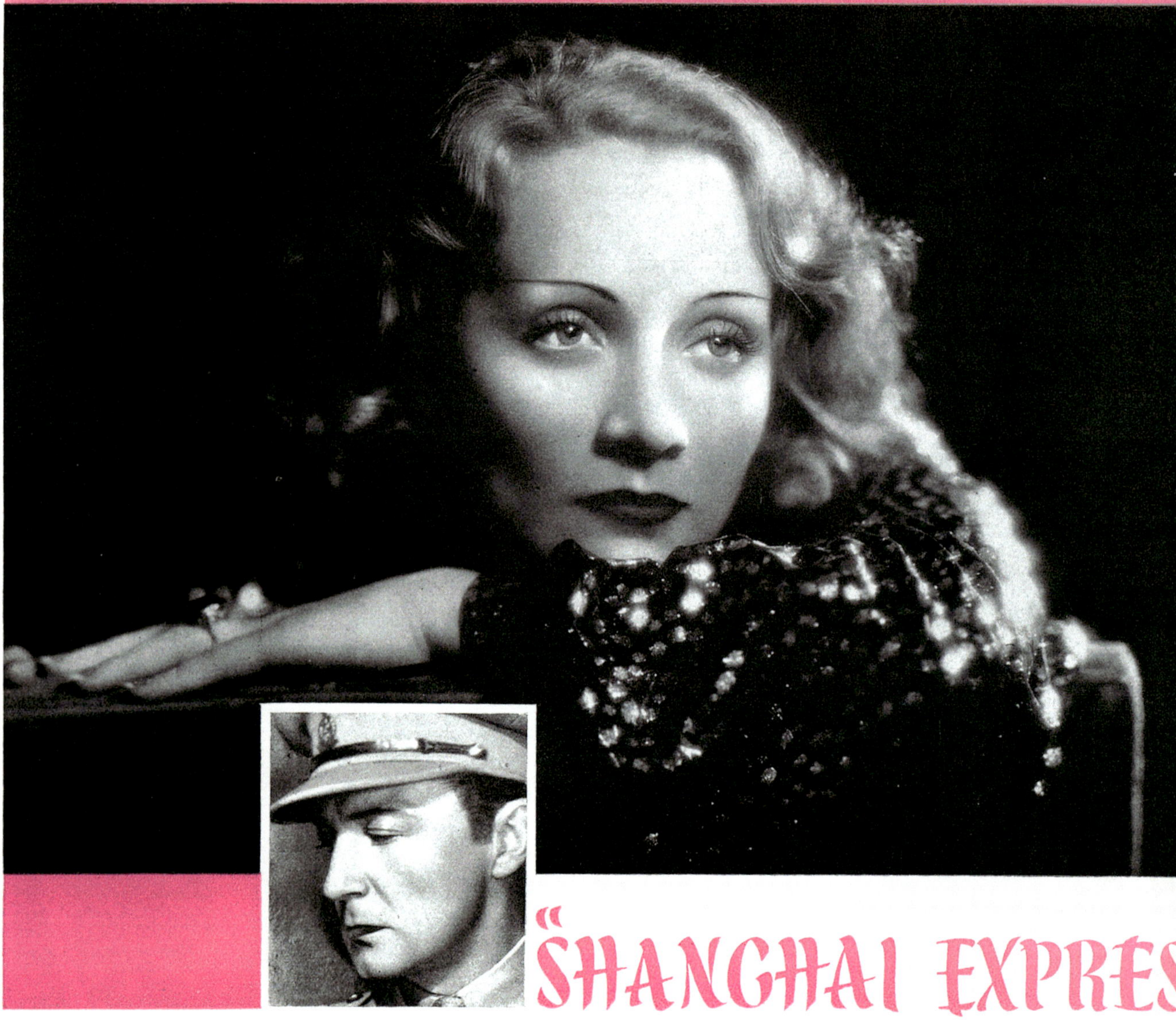

"SHANGHAI EXPRES

All men desired her, this ravishing, mysterious creature whose scarlet life held many men—whose Love only one had ever known! Parted, they meet again, on the Shanghai Express—seething with intrigue, desire, hatred—hurtling through the night with a dead man at the throttle . . . *Marlene Dietrich,* with an irresistible new warmth! The lover who comes back, *Clive Brook!* The year's greatest melodrama, *"Shanghai Express!"* See it—you'll live a thrilling new adventure in a night. And when the picture's over and you're home once more, you'll realize again how true it is when you say, *"If it's a Paramount Picture it's the best show in town!"*

with CLIVE BROOK
Anna May Wong, Warner Oland and Eugene Pallette. Directed by JOSEF VON STERNBERG

Paramount Pictures

PARAMOUNT PUBLIX CORP. ADOLPH ZUKOR, PRES. PARAMOUNT BLDG., N. Y

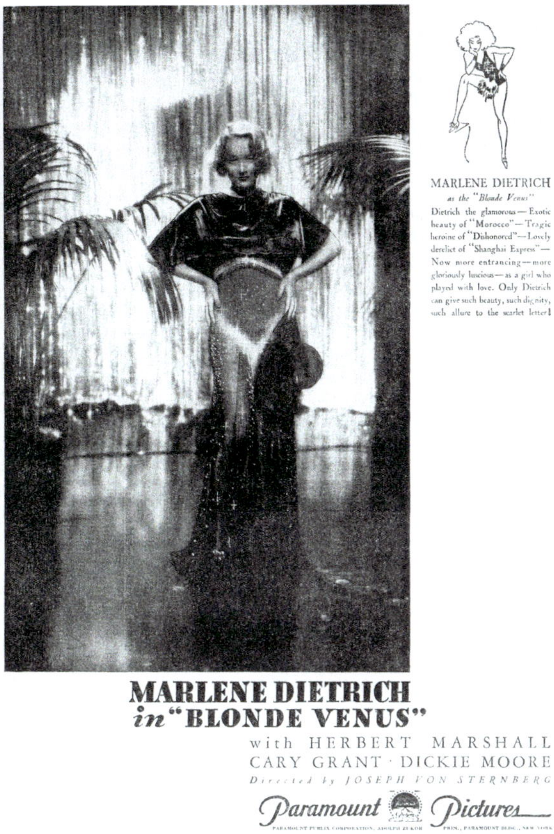

Blonde Venus, 1932

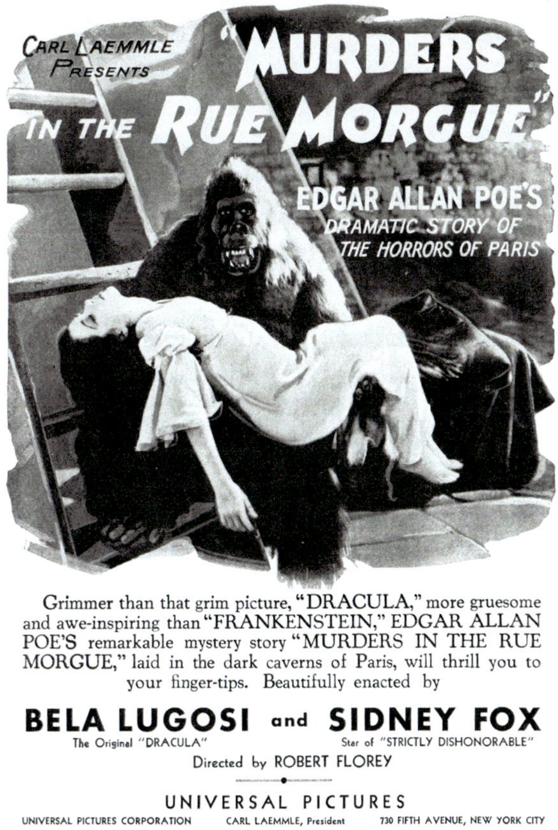

Murders In The Rue Morgue, 1932

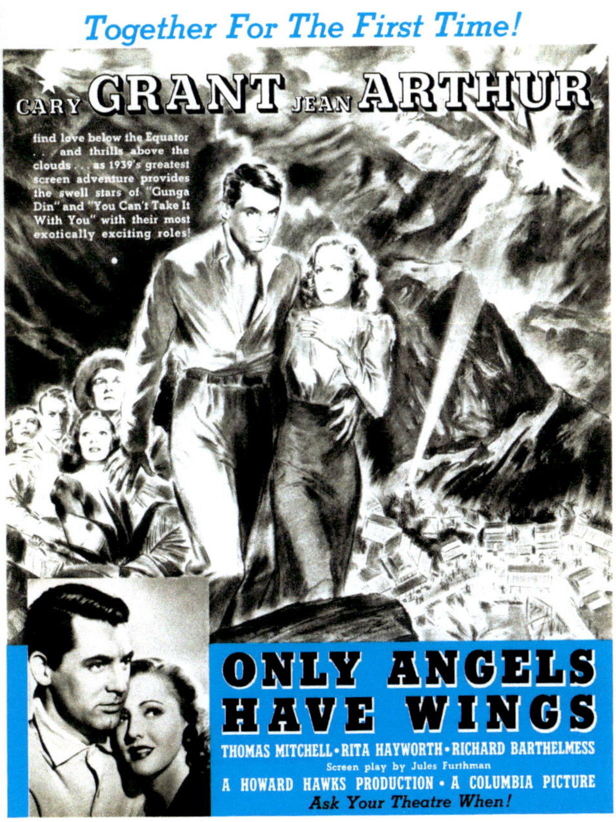

Shanghai Express, 1932 ◂ Only Angels Have Wings, 1939

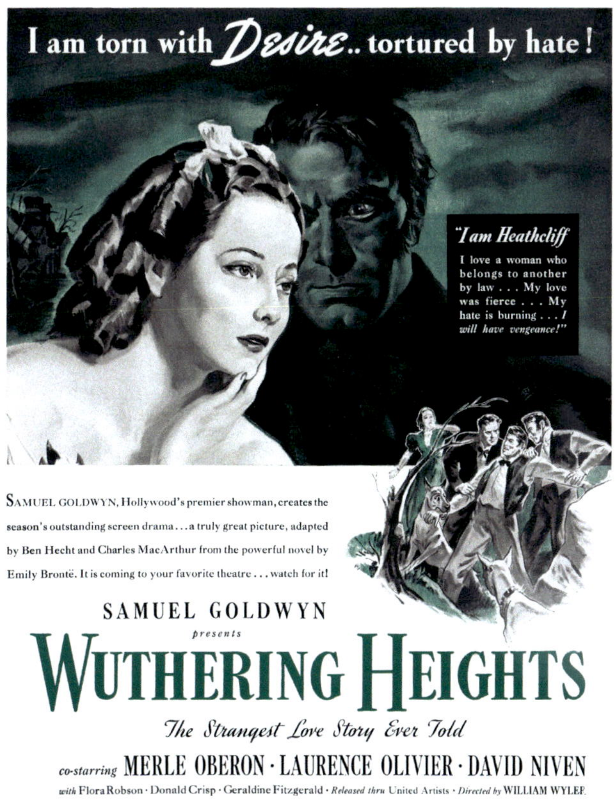

Wuthering Heights, 1939

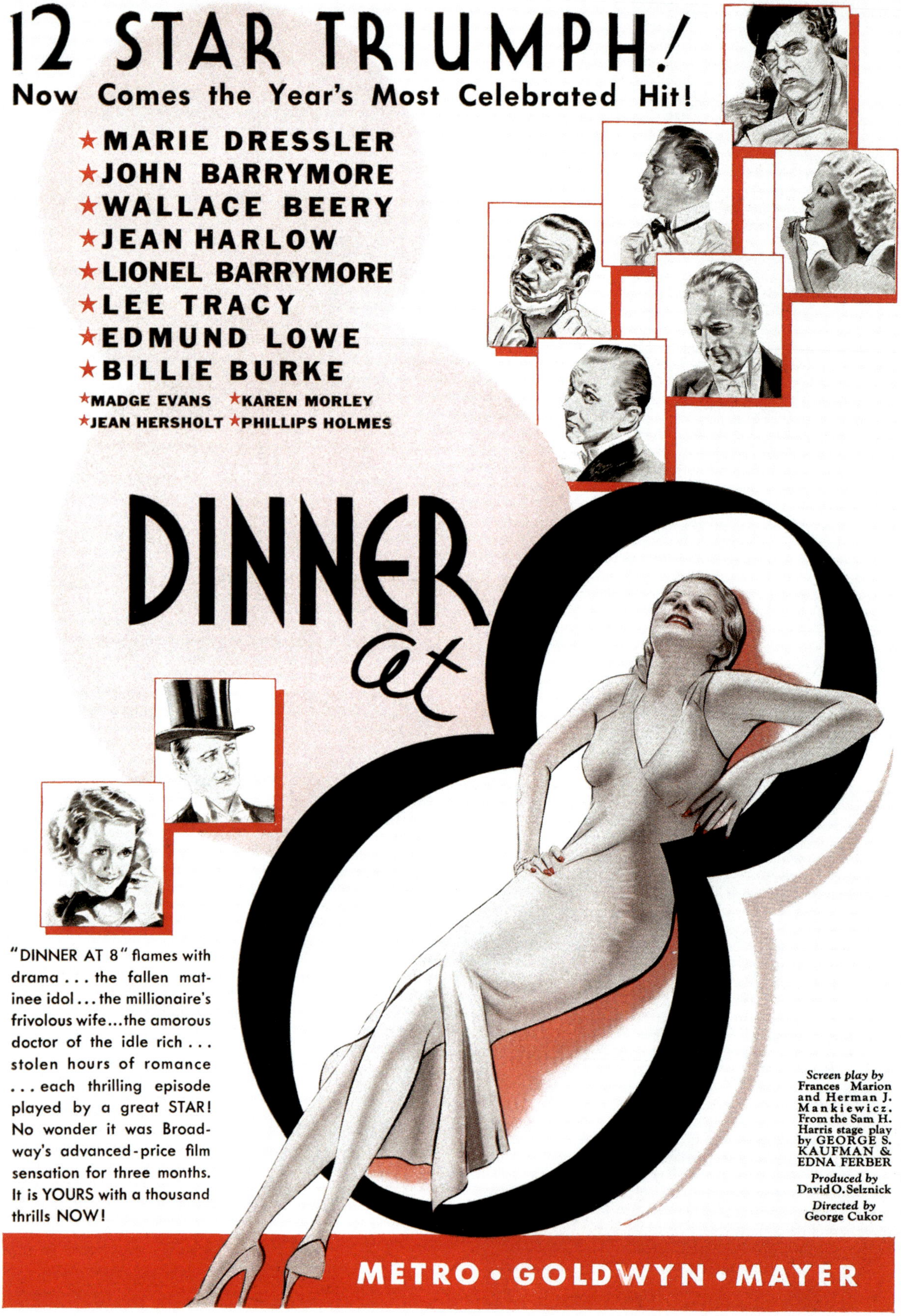

Dinner At 8, 1933

► *Mannequin, 1938*

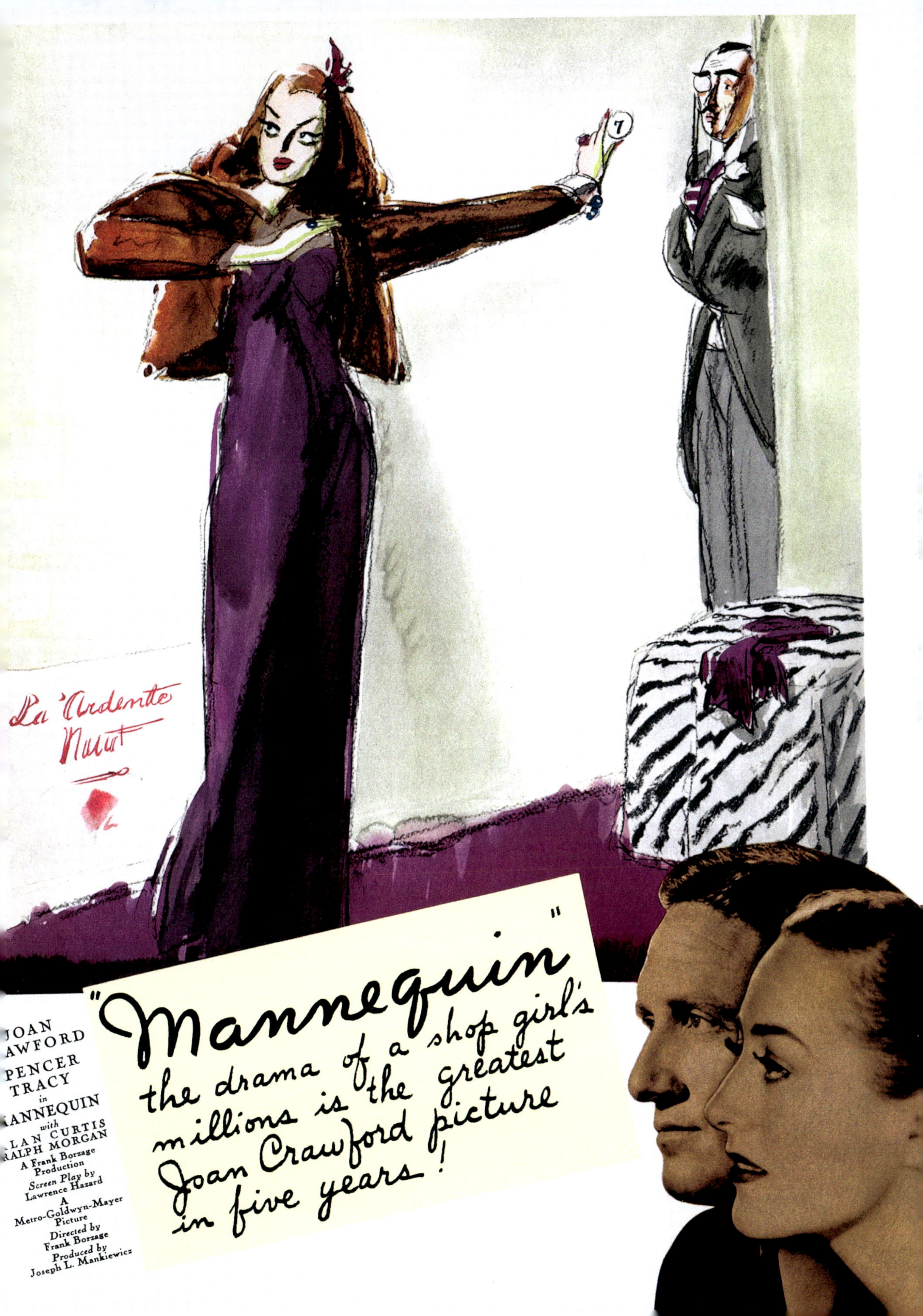
"Mannequin"
the drama of a shop girl's millions is the greatest Joan Crawford picture in five years!
JOAN
AWFORD
PENCER
TRACY
in
ANNEQUIN
with
LAN CURTIS
RALPH MORGAN
A Frank Borzage Production
Screen Play by Lawrence Hazard
A Metro-Goldwyn-Mayer Picture
Directed by Frank Borzage
Produced by Joseph L. Mankiewicz

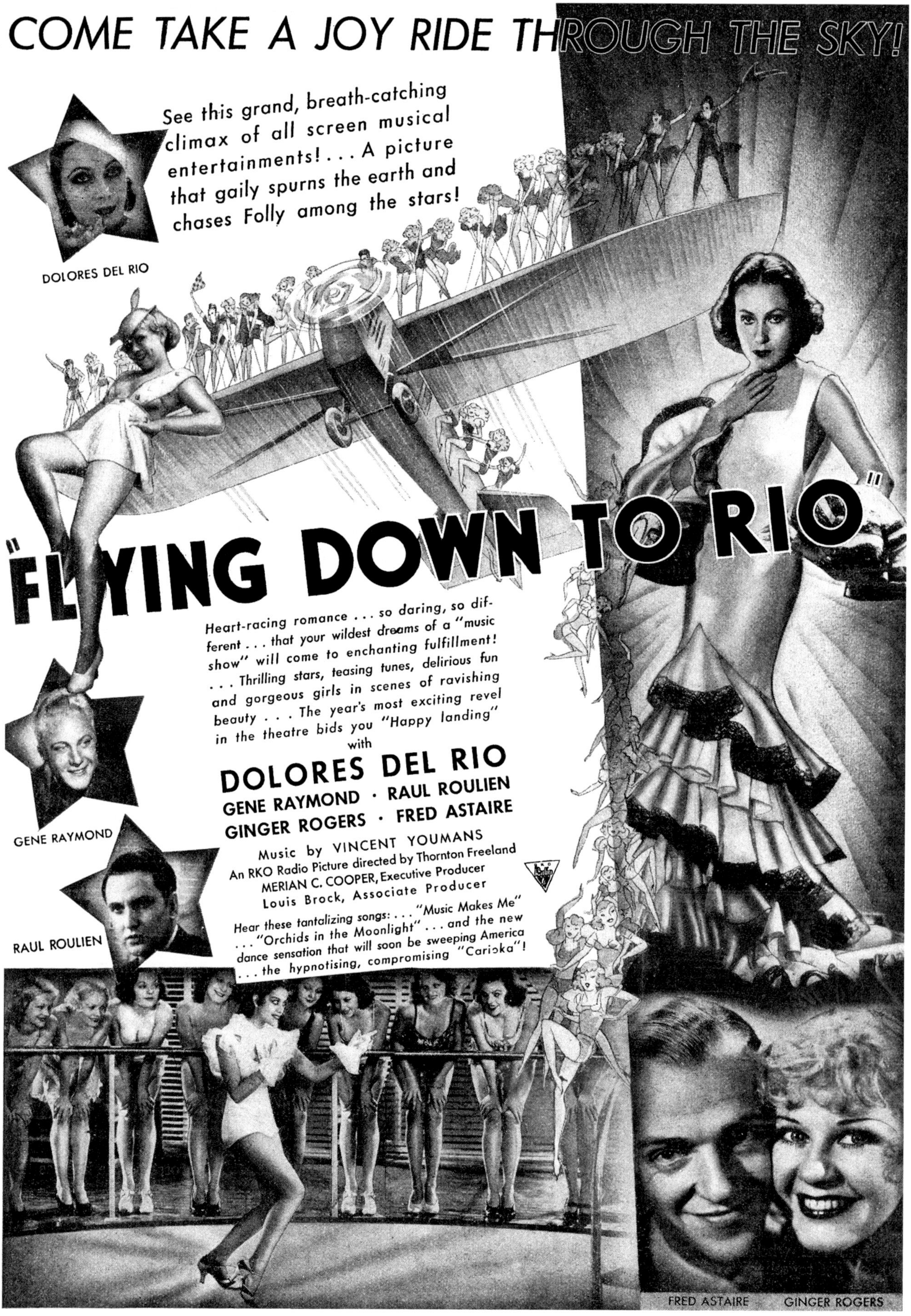
COME TAKE A JOY RIDE THROUGH THE SKY!
See this grand, breath-catching climax of all screen musical entertainments! . . . A picture that gaily spurns the earth and chases Folly among the stars!
DOLORES DEL RIO
"FLYING DOWN TO RIO"
Heart-racing romance . . . so daring, so different . . . that your wildest dreams of a "music show" will come to enchanting fulfillment! . . . Thrilling stars, teasing tunes, delirious fun and gorgeous girls in scenes of ravishing beauty . . . The year's most exciting revel in the theatre bids you "Happy landing"
with
DOLORES DEL RIO
GENE RAYMOND · RAUL ROULIEN
GINGER ROGERS · FRED ASTAIRE
Music by VINCENT YOUMANS
An RKO Radio Picture directed by Thornton Freeland
MERIAN C. COOPER, Executive Producer
Louis Brock, Associate Producer
Hear these tantalizing songs: . . . "Music Makes Me" . . . "Orchids in the Moonlight" . . . and the new dance sensation that will soon be sweeping America . . . the hypnotising, compromising "Carioka"!
GENE RAYMOND
RAUL ROULIEN
FRED ASTAIRE
GINGER ROGERS

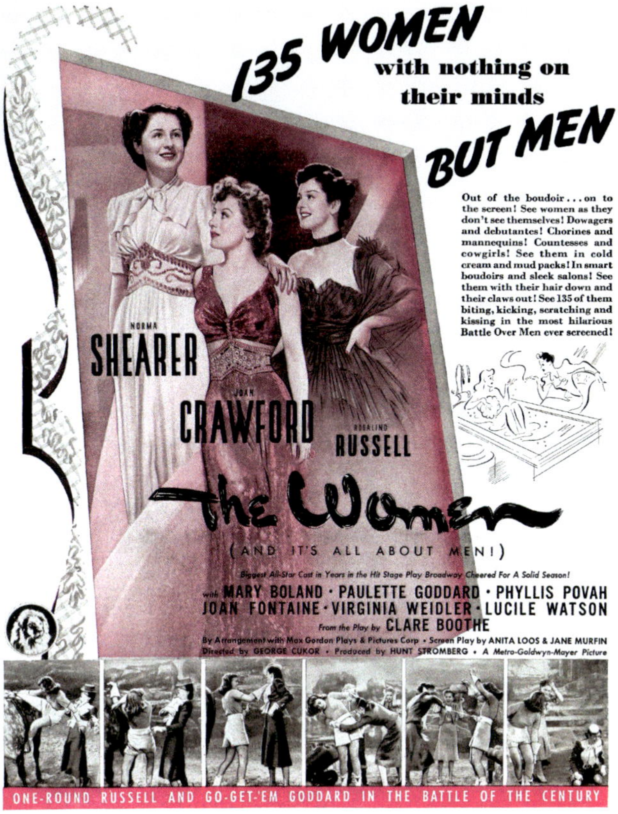

The Women, 1939

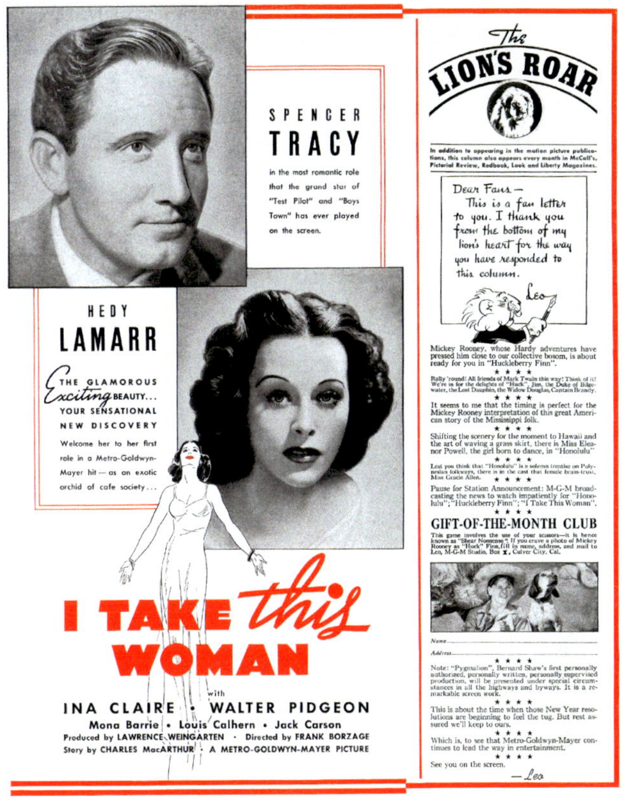

I Take This Woman, 1939

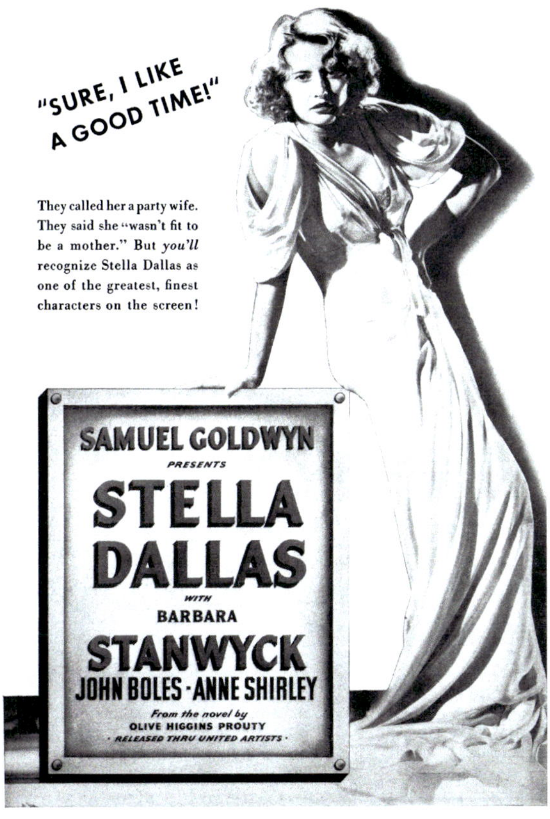

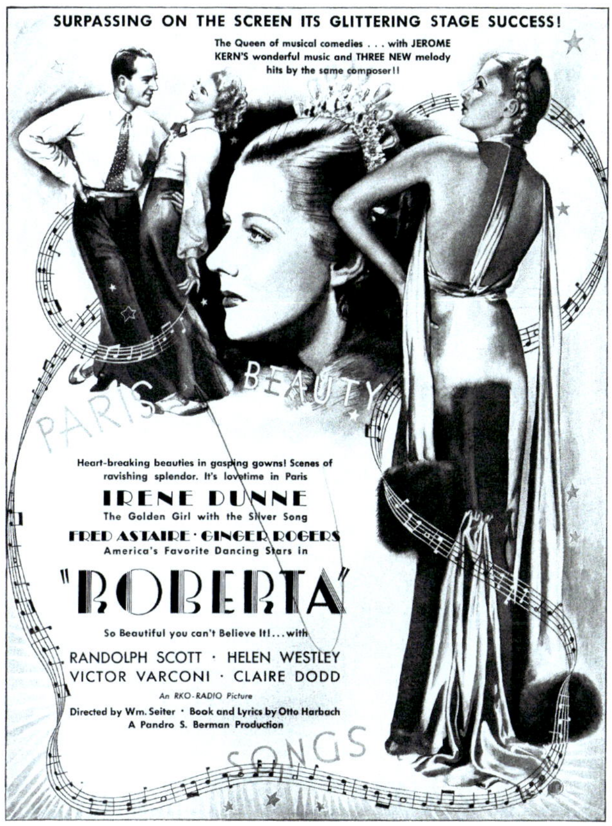

Flying Down To Rio, 1933 ◂ *Stella Dallas, 1937*

Roberta, 1935

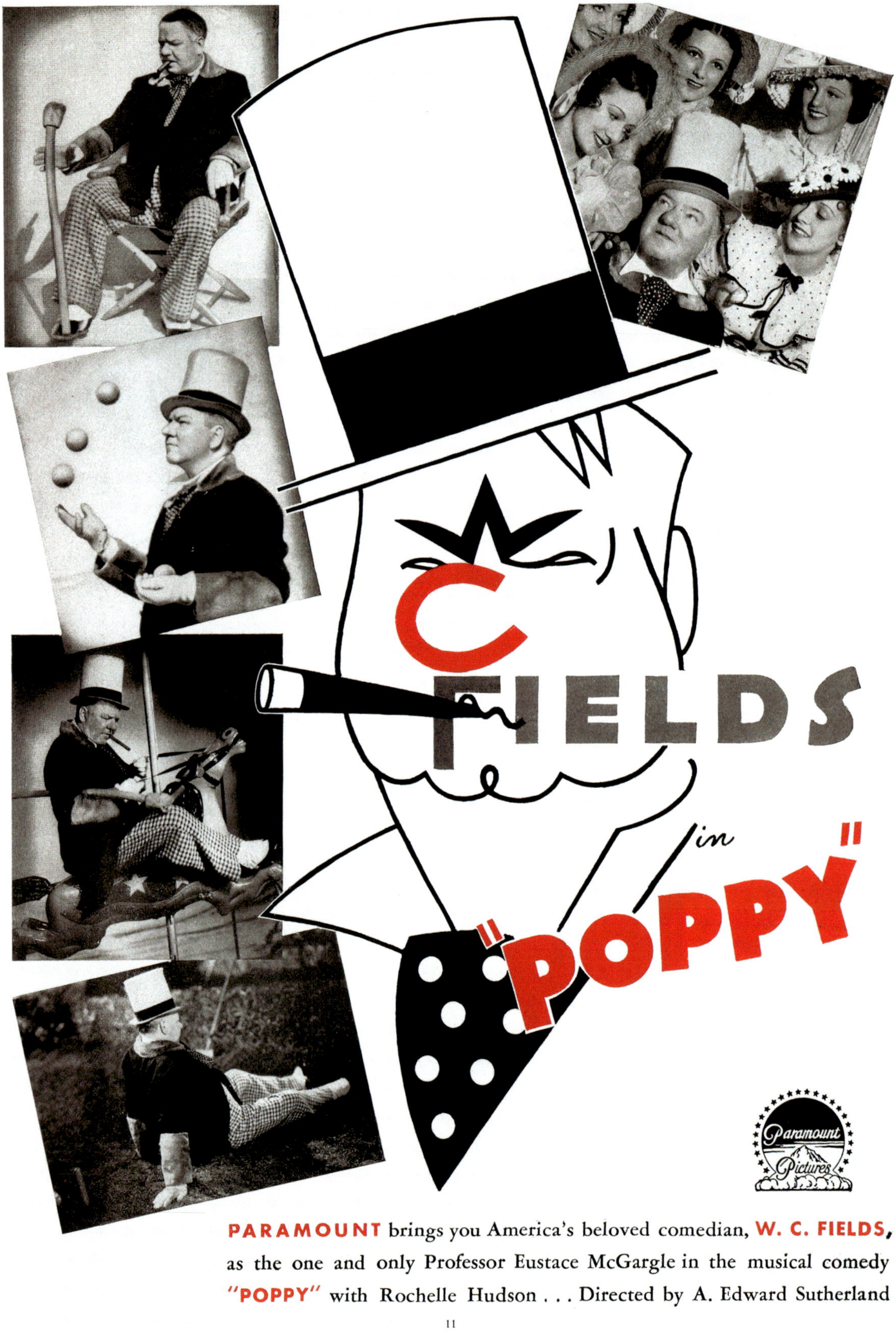

Poppy, 1936

► *A Princess Marries*, 1938

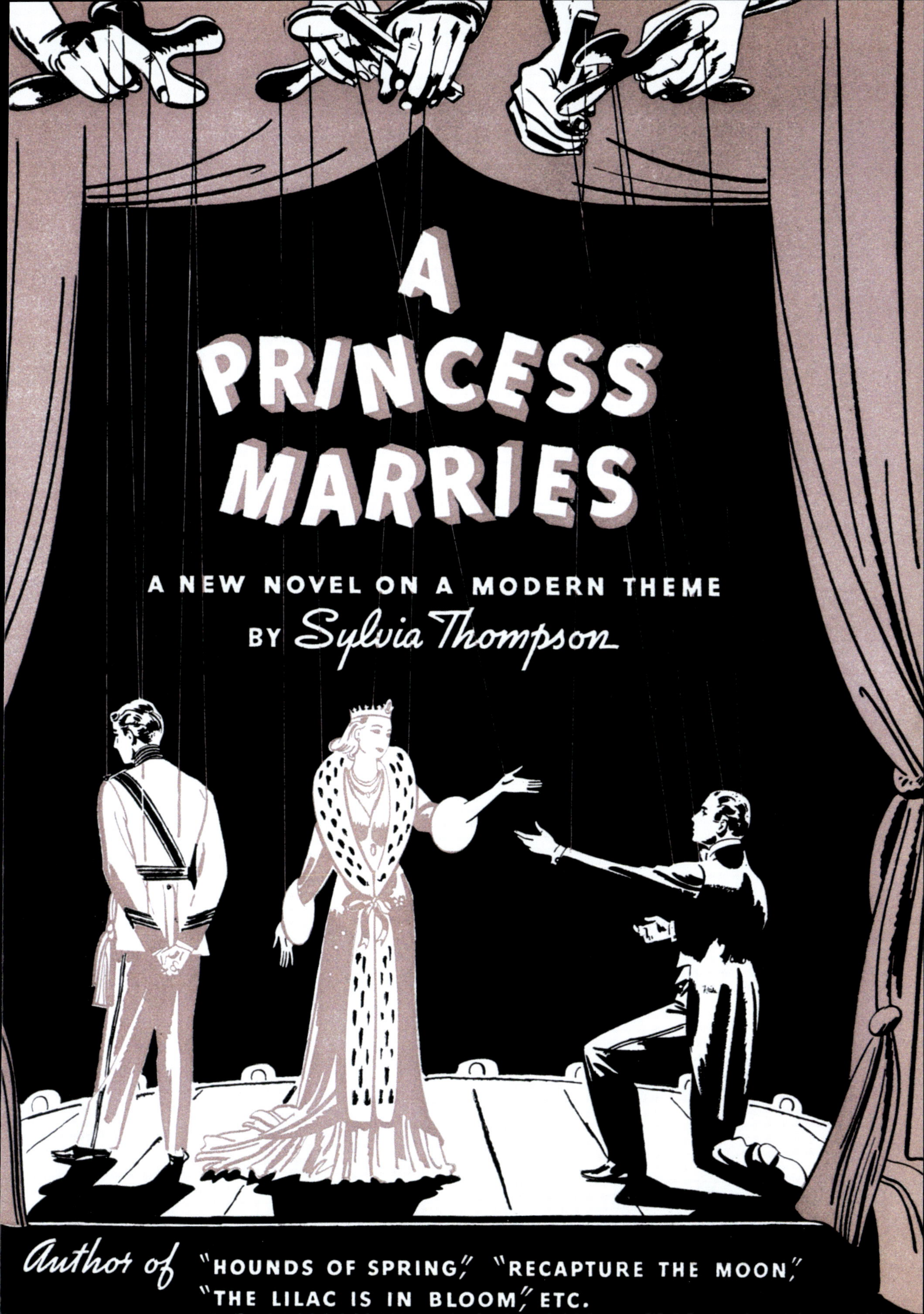
A PRINCESS MARRIES
A NEW NOVEL ON A MODERN THEME
BY Sylvia Thompson
Author of "HOUNDS OF SPRING," "RECAPTURE THE MOON,"
"THE LILAC IS IN BLOOM," ETC.

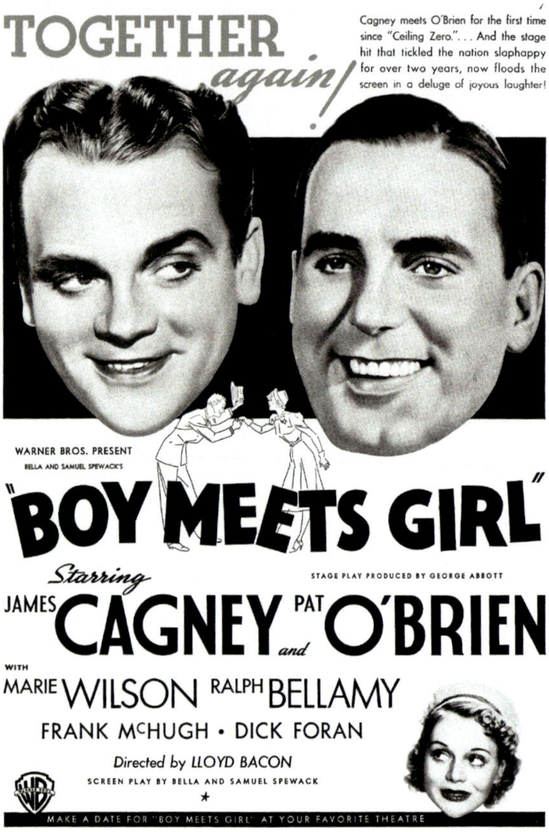

Boy Meets Girl, 1938

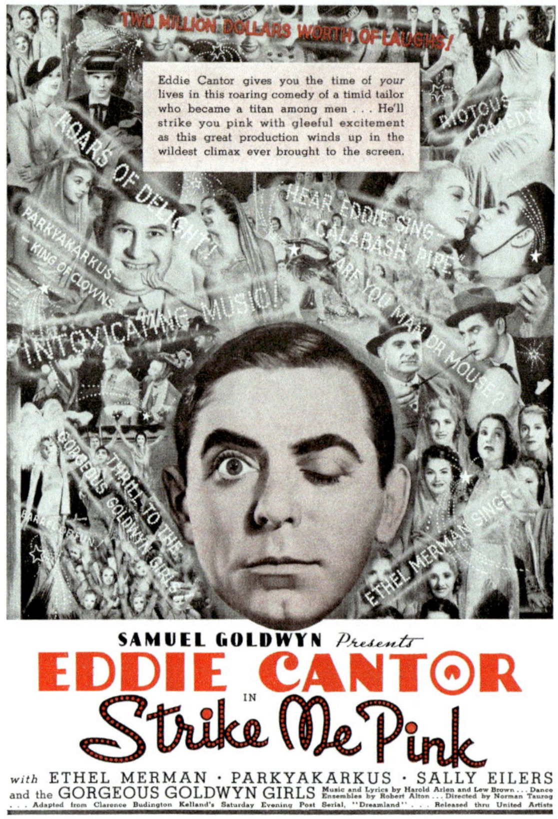

Strike Me Pink, 1936

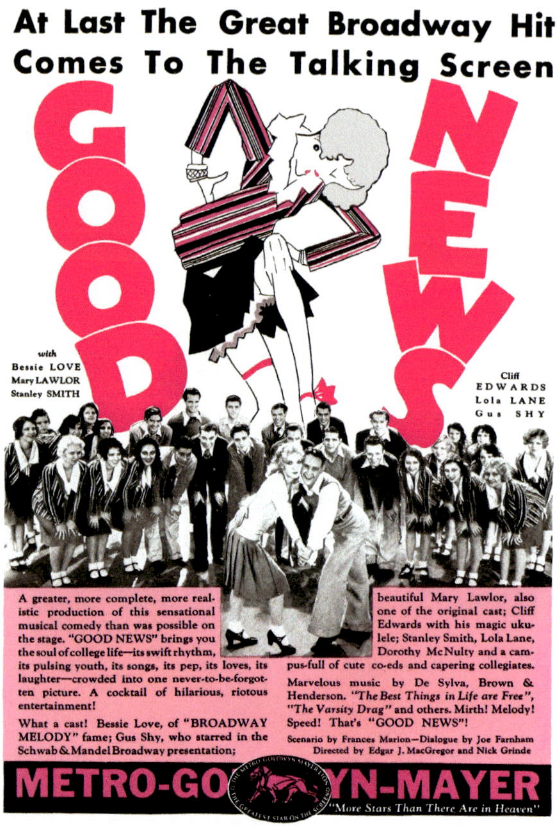

Good News, 1930

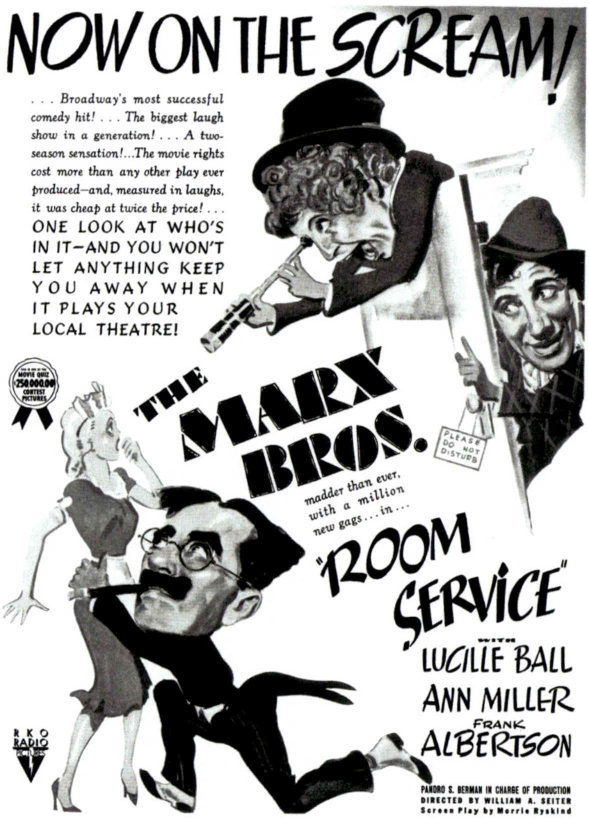

Room Service, 1938

▸ Paramount, 1931

THE NIGHT ANGEL

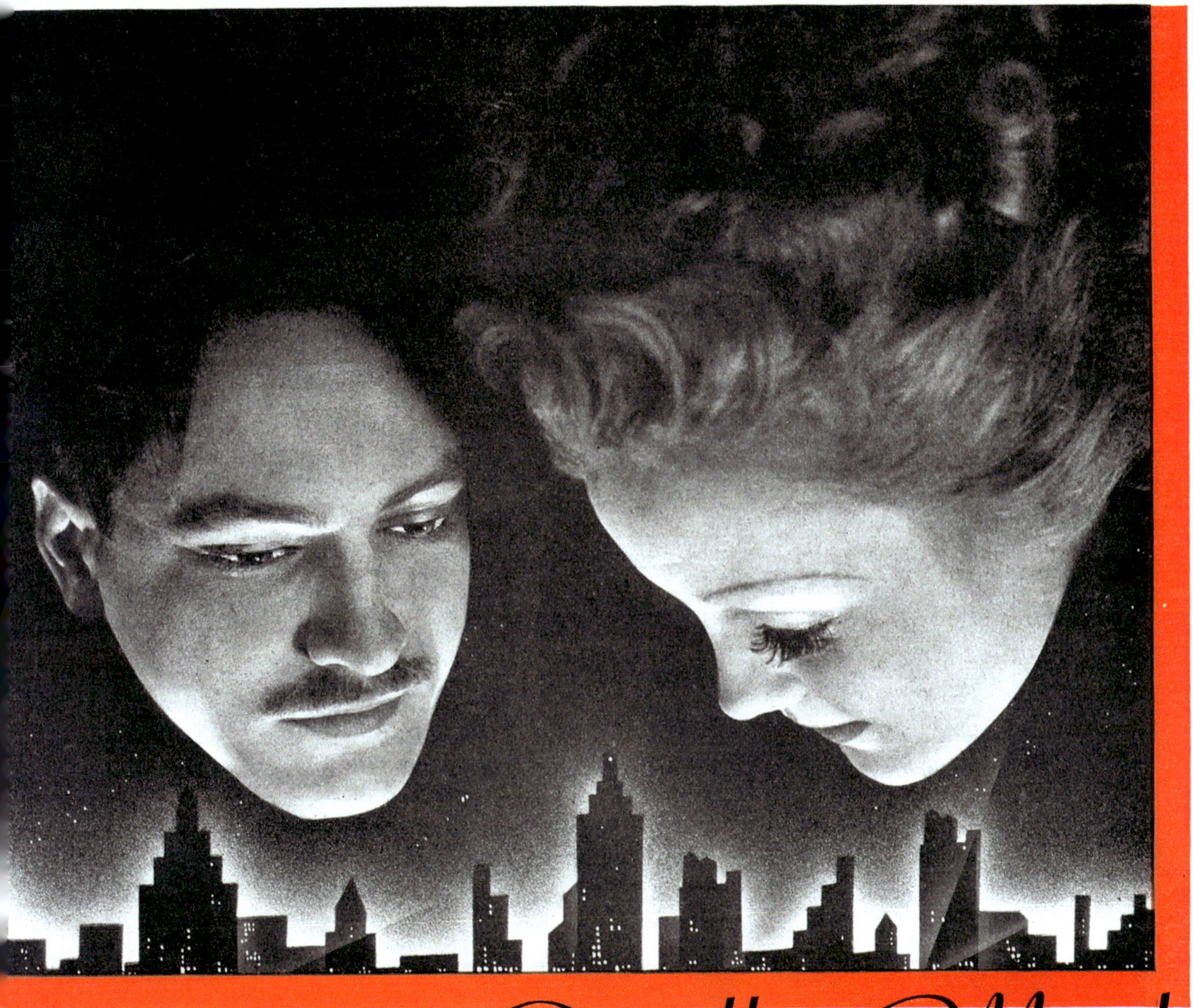

NANCY Carroll FREDRIC March

YOU may think your life is confined by scenes all too familiar and that for you thrills and adventure lie only beyond the horizon. But you'll forget all that and drink deeply of life and love when in your own theatre you witness Paramount's great production, "THE NIGHT ANGEL." A powerful drama of fierce hates and intense love, laid in a setting strange and colorful. And so produced by Paramount as to breathe actuality. See it—*and live! "If it's a Paramount Picture it's the best show in town!"*

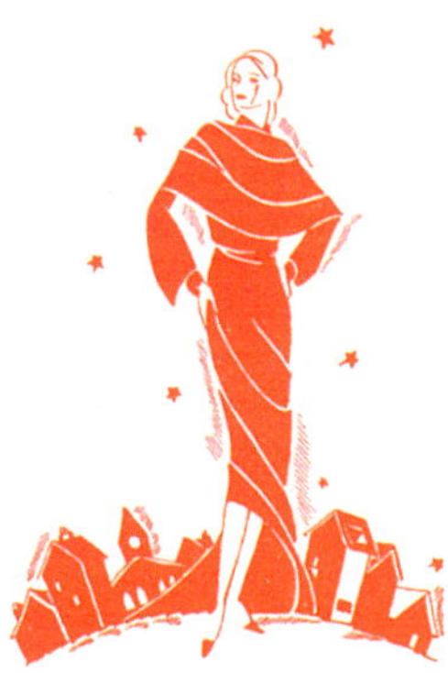

With Phoebe Foster. Written and directed by Edmund Goulding.

TRADE MARK

Paramount Pictures

PARAMOUNT PUBLIX CORPORATION, ADOLPH ZUKOR, PRES., PARAMOUNT BLDG., N. Y.

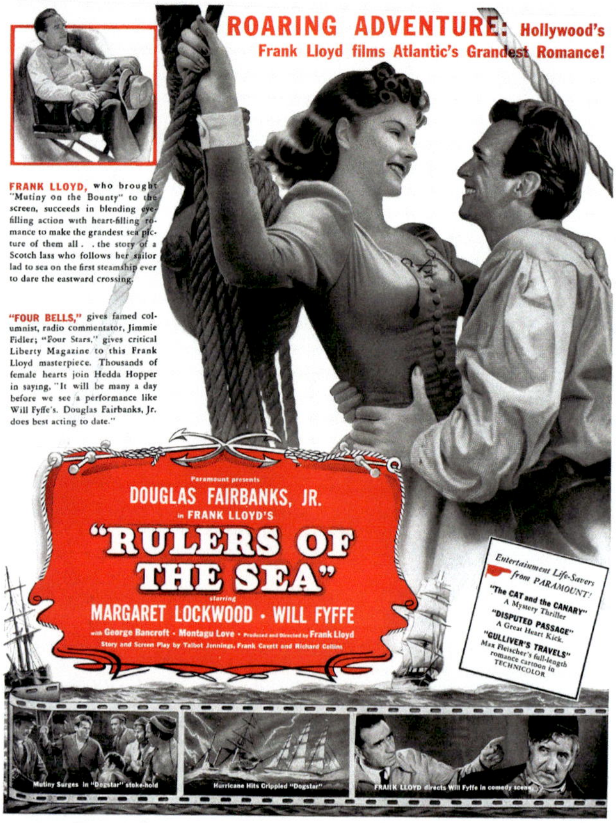

Rulers Of The Sea, 1939

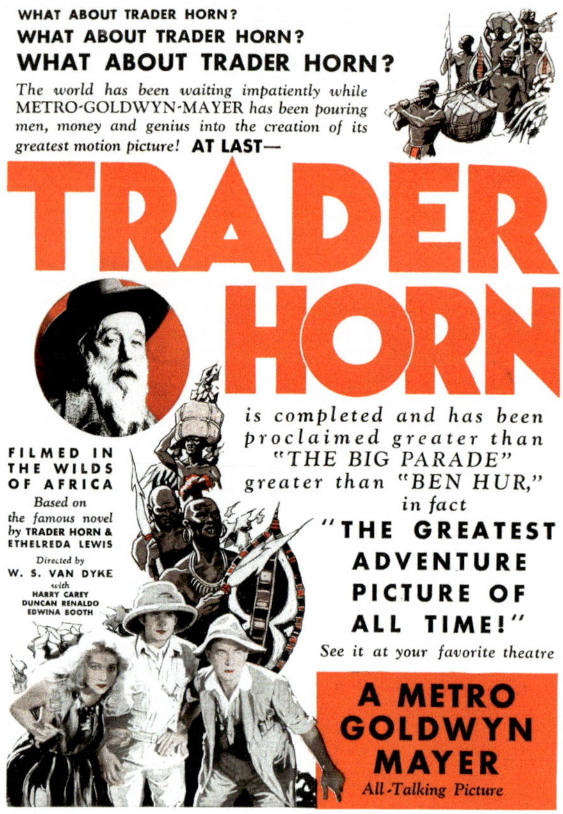

Trader Horn, 1931

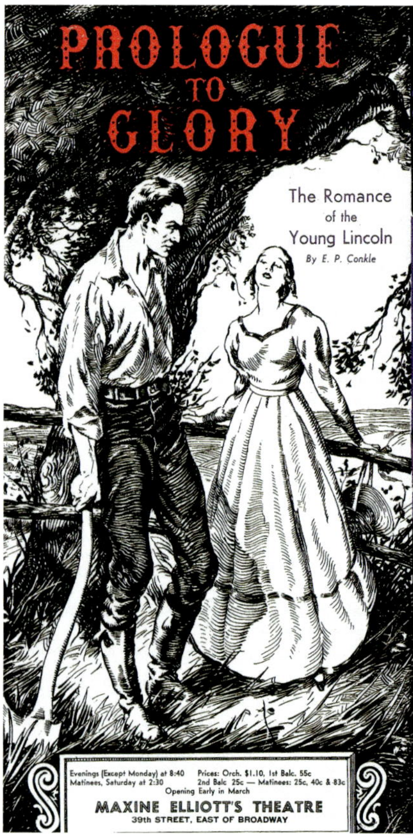

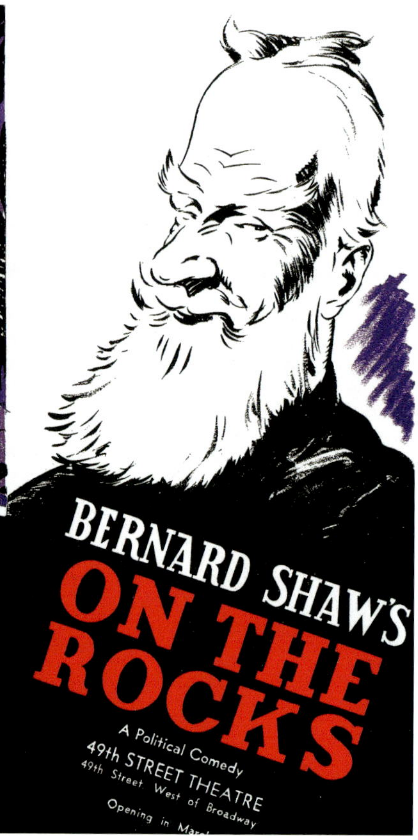

Prologue to Glory, 1938; Haiti, 1938; On the Rocks, 1933

► *Stanley And Livingstone, 1939*

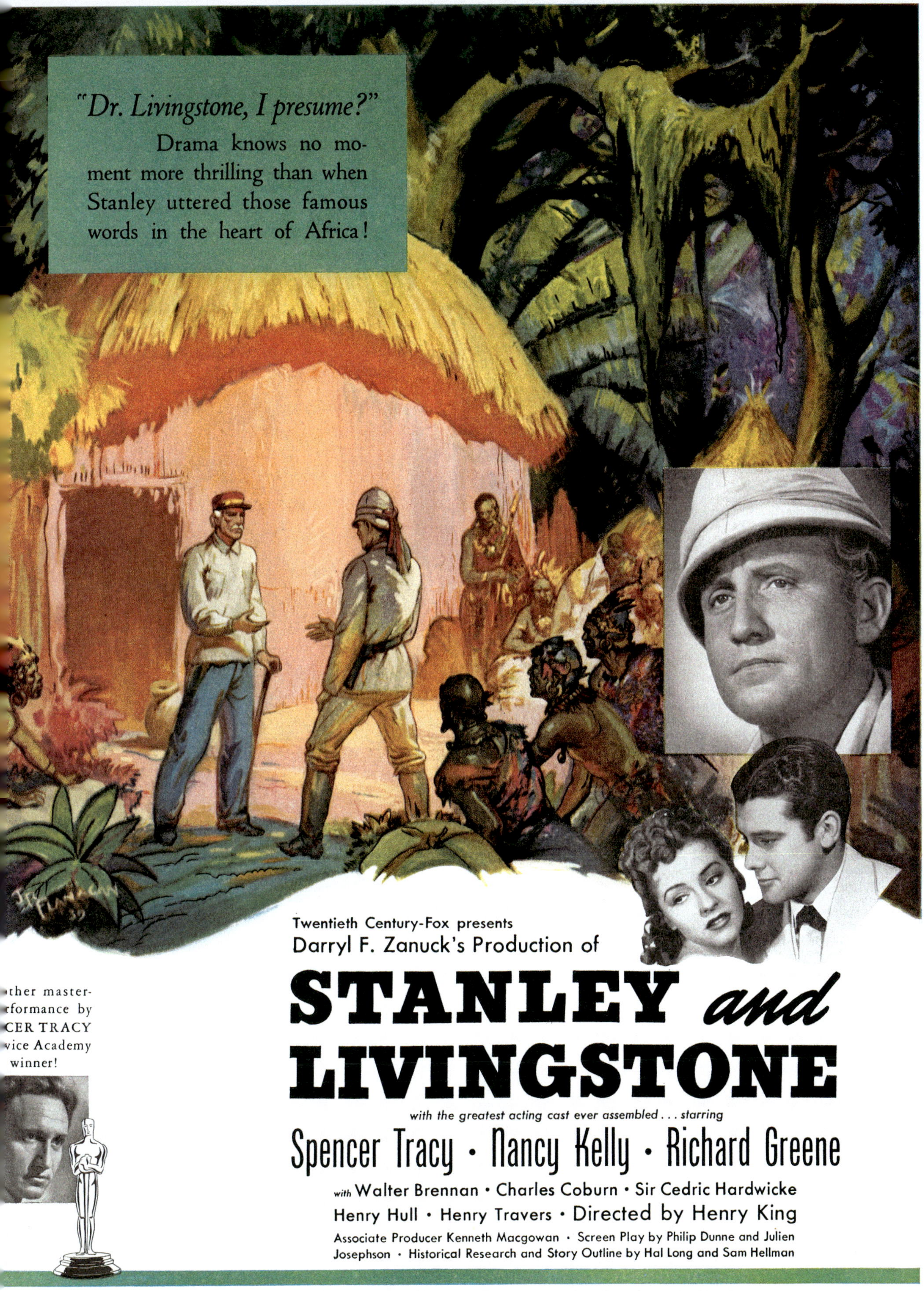
"Dr. Livingstone, I presume?"
Drama knows no moment more thrilling than when Stanley uttered those famous words in the heart of Africa!
Twentieth Century-Fox presents
Darryl F. Zanuck's Production of
STANLEY and LIVINGSTONE
with the greatest acting cast ever assembled . . . starring
Spencer Tracy • Nancy Kelly • Richard Greene
with Walter Brennan • Charles Coburn • Sir Cedric Hardwicke
Henry Hull • Henry Travers • Directed by Henry King
Associate Producer Kenneth Macgowan • Screen Play by Philip Dunne and Julien Josephson • Historical Research and Story Outline by Hal Long and Sam Hellman
ther master-
rformance by
CER TRACY
vice Academy
winner!

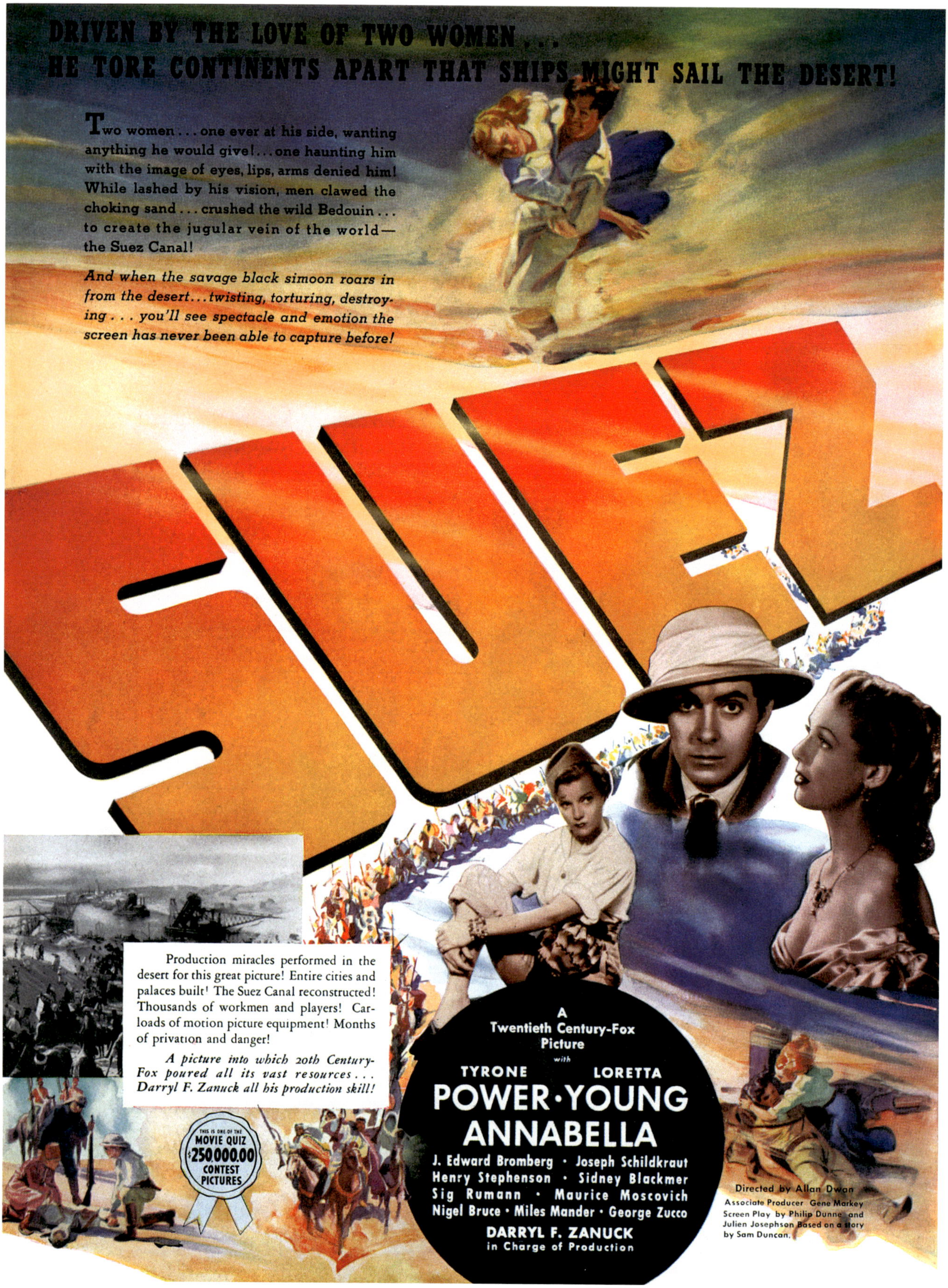
DRIVEN BY THE LOVE OF TWO WOMEN . . .
HE TORE CONTINENTS APART THAT SHIPS MIGHT SAIL THE DESERT!
Two women . . . one ever at his side, wanting anything he would give! . . . one haunting him with the image of eyes, lips, arms denied him! While lashed by his vision, men clawed the choking sand . . . crushed the wild Bedouin . . . to create the jugular vein of the world—the Suez Canal!
And when the savage black simoon roars in from the desert . . . twisting, torturing, destroying . . . you'll see spectacle and emotion the screen has never been able to capture before!
SUEZ
Production miracles performed in the desert for this great picture! Entire cities and palaces built! The Suez Canal reconstructed! Thousands of workmen and players! Carloads of motion picture equipment! Months of privation and danger!
A picture into which 20th Century-Fox poured all its vast resources . . . Darryl F. Zanuck all his production skill!
THIS IS ONE OF THE MOVIE QUIZ $250,000.00 CONTEST PICTURES
A Twentieth Century-Fox Picture
with
TYRONE POWER · LORETTA YOUNG
ANNABELLA
J. Edward Bromberg · Joseph Schildkraut
Henry Stephenson · Sidney Blackmer
Sig Rumann · Maurice Moscovich
Nigel Bruce · Miles Mander · George Zucco
DARRYL F. ZANUCK in Charge of Production
Directed by Allan Dwan
Associate Producer Gene Markey
Screen Play by Philip Dunne and Julien Josephson Based on a story by Sam Duncan.

Suez, 1938

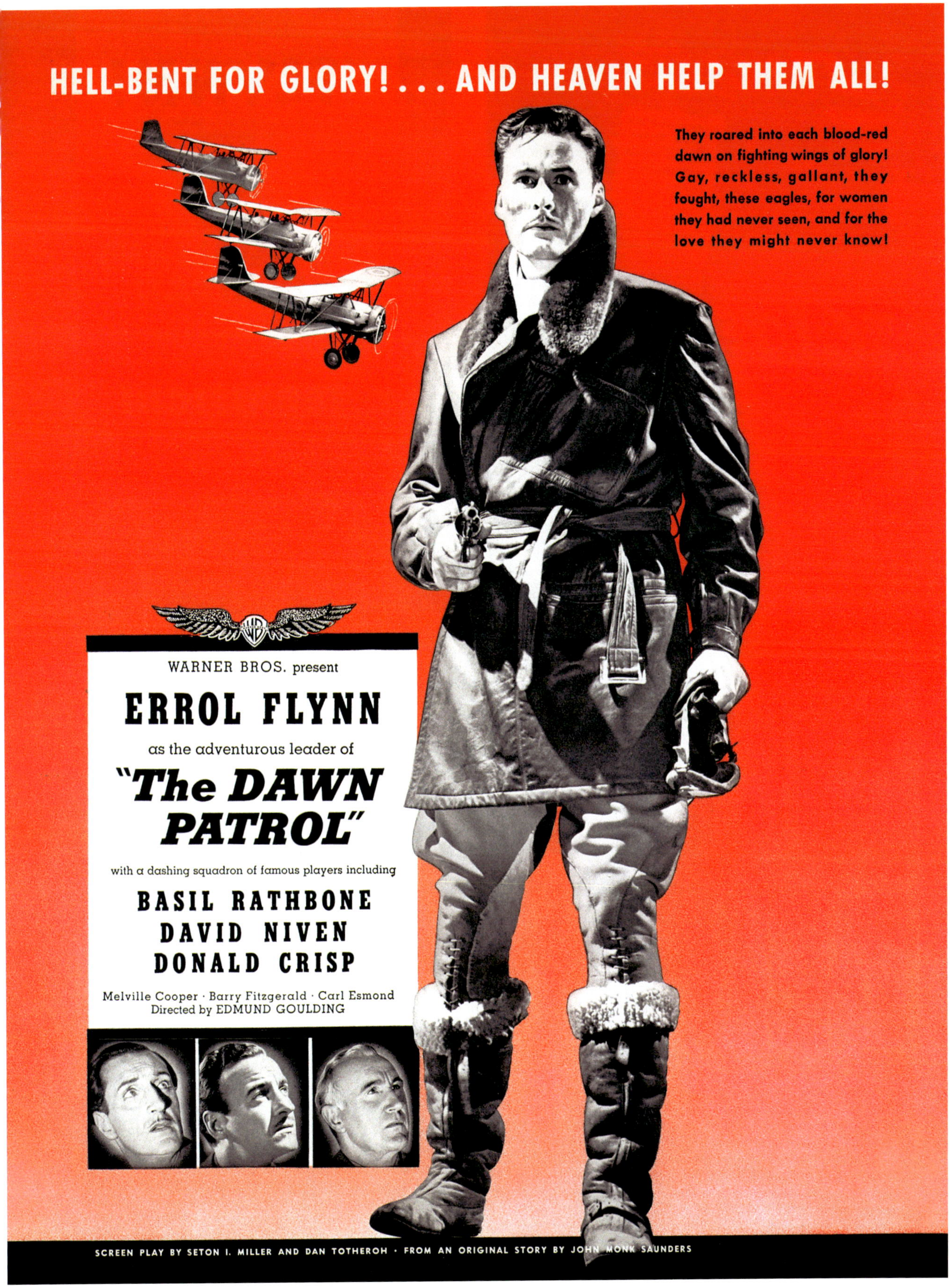

The Dawn Patrol, 1939

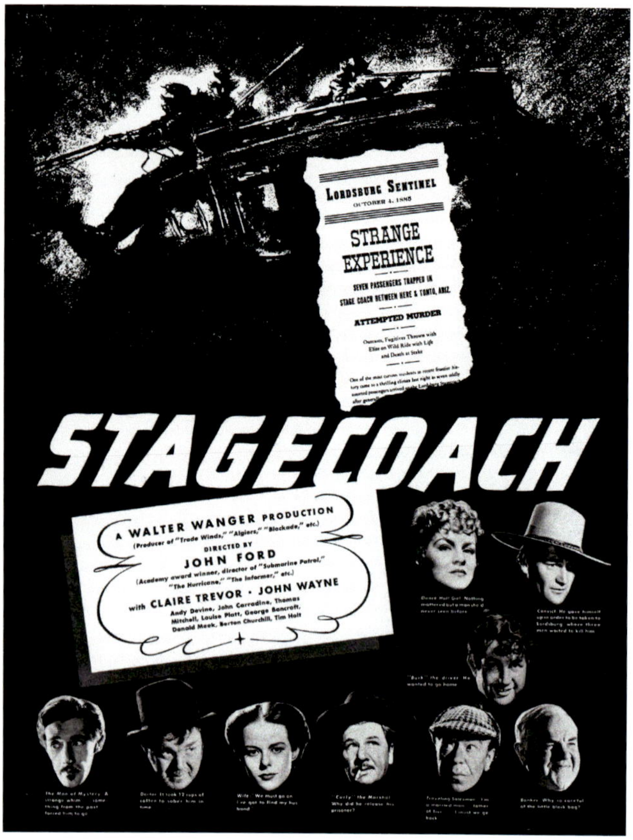

Stagecoach, 1939

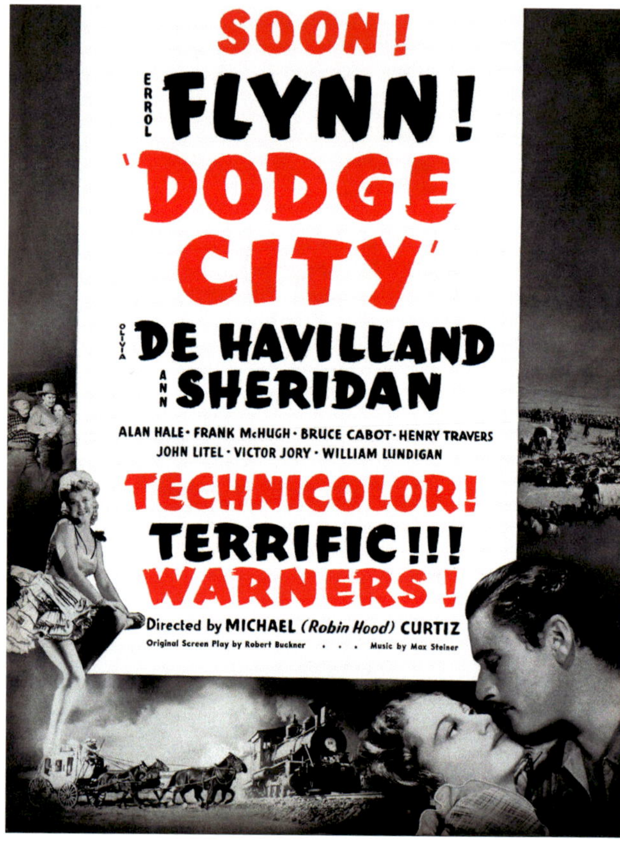

Dodge City, 1939

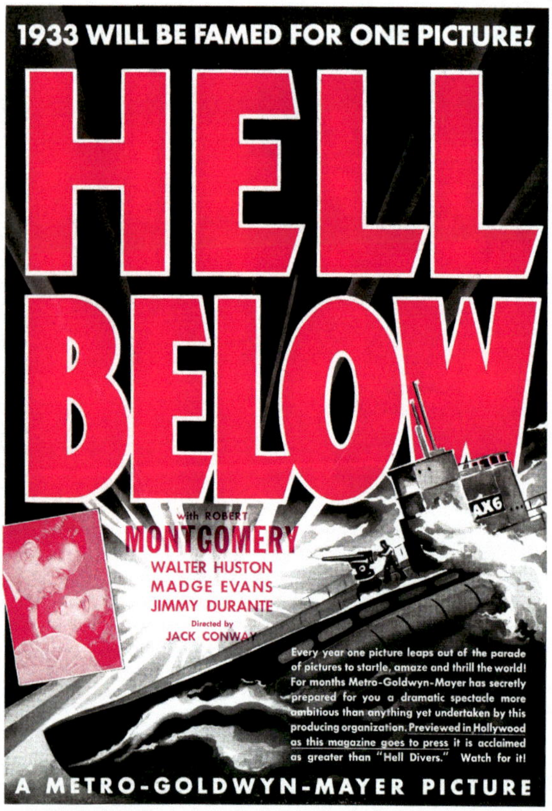

Hell Below, 1933

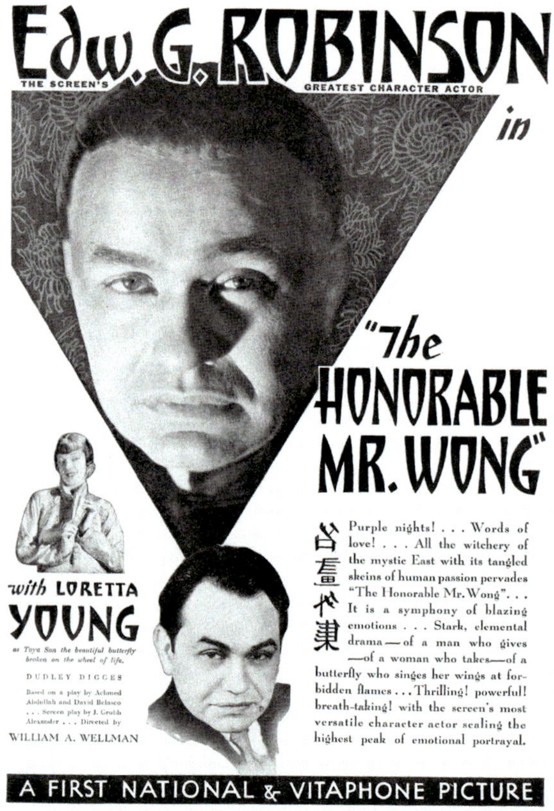

The Honorable Mr. Wong, 1932

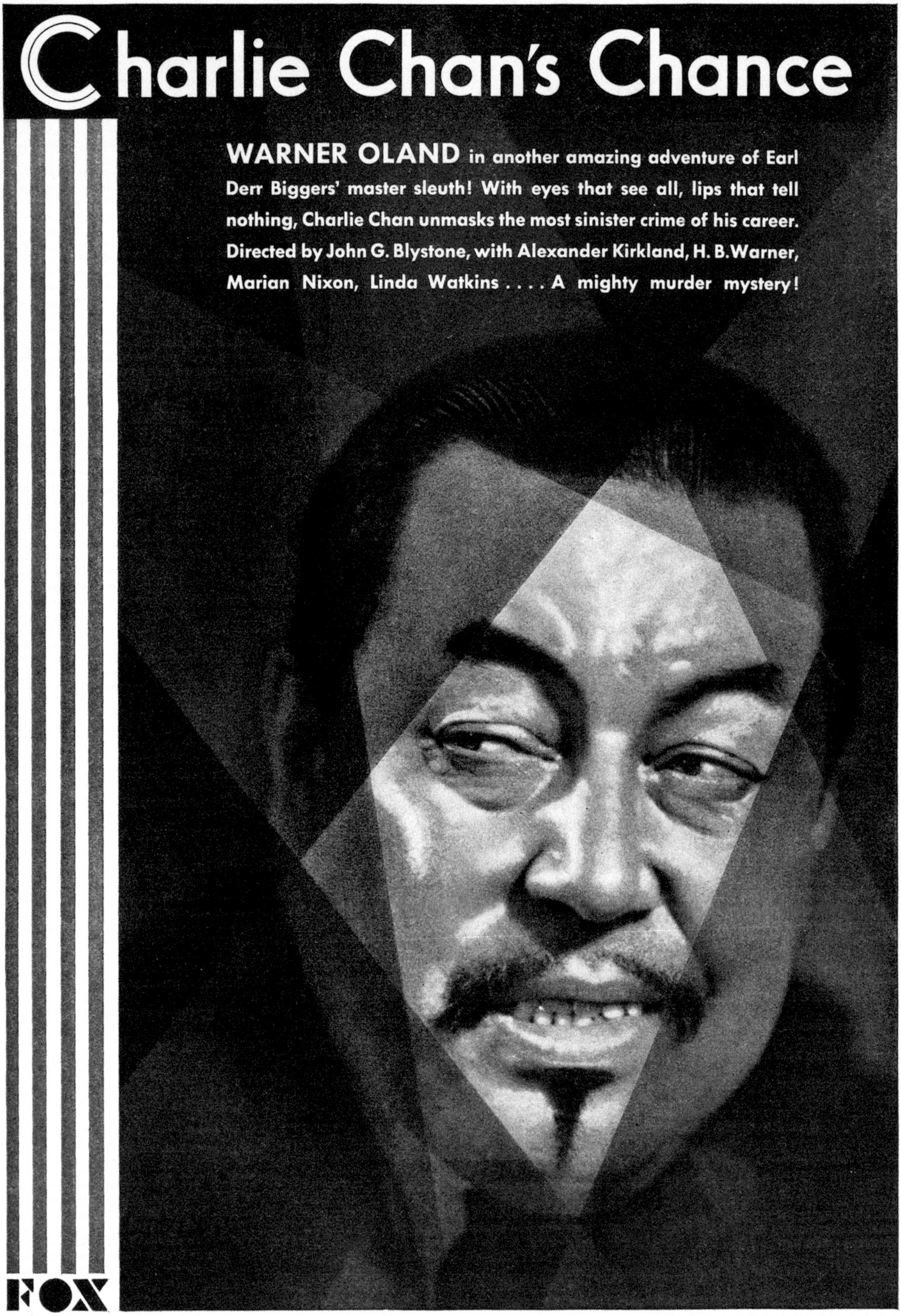

Charlie Chan, 1932

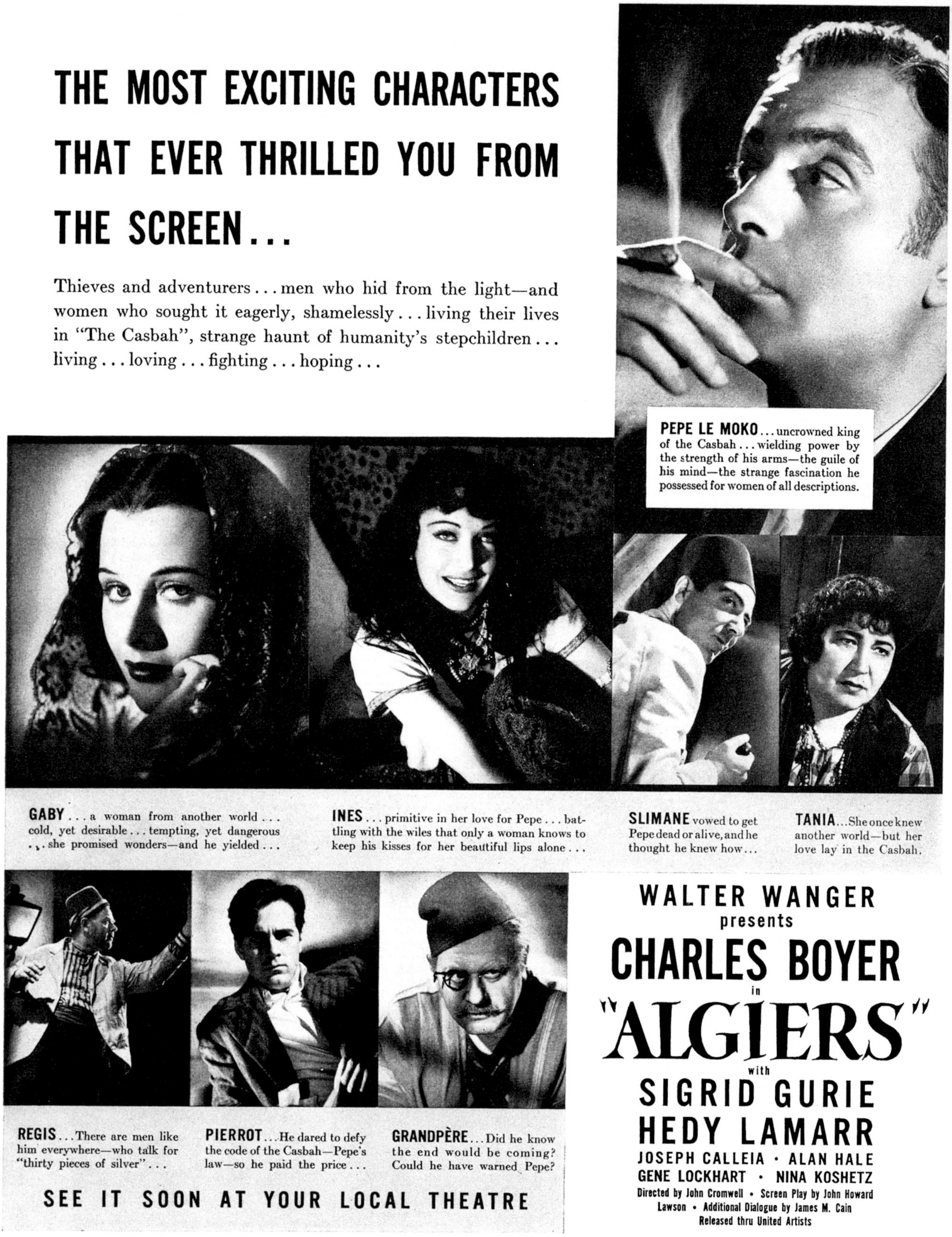

Algiers, 1938

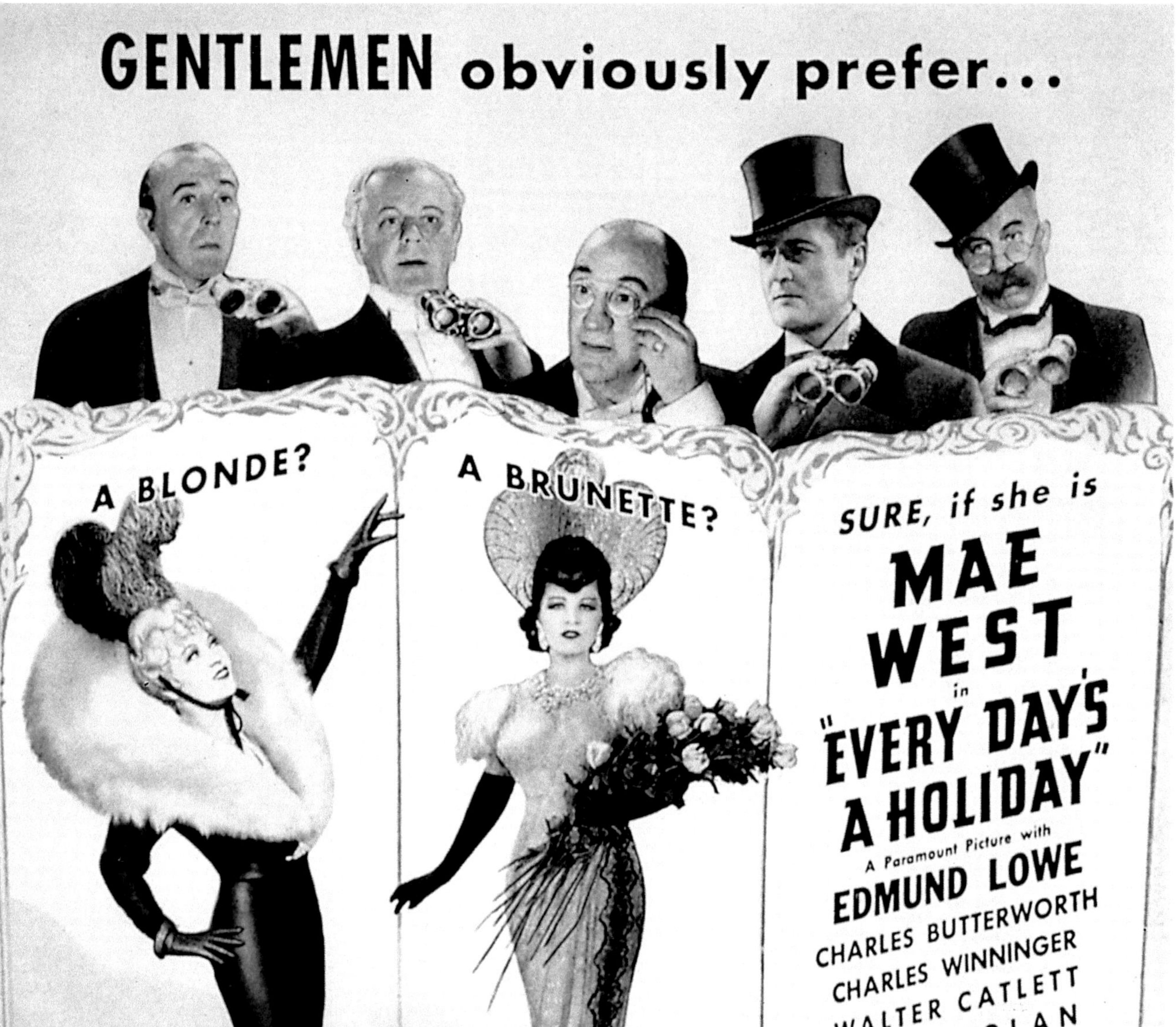

Every Day's A Holiday, 1937

TOGETHER AGAIN
in another M-G-M *hit!*

Ever since beautiful Joan Crawford and Bob Montgomery appeared together in "Our Blushing Brides" and "Untamed" we've been swamped with requests to co-star them again. You'll be delighted with the result.

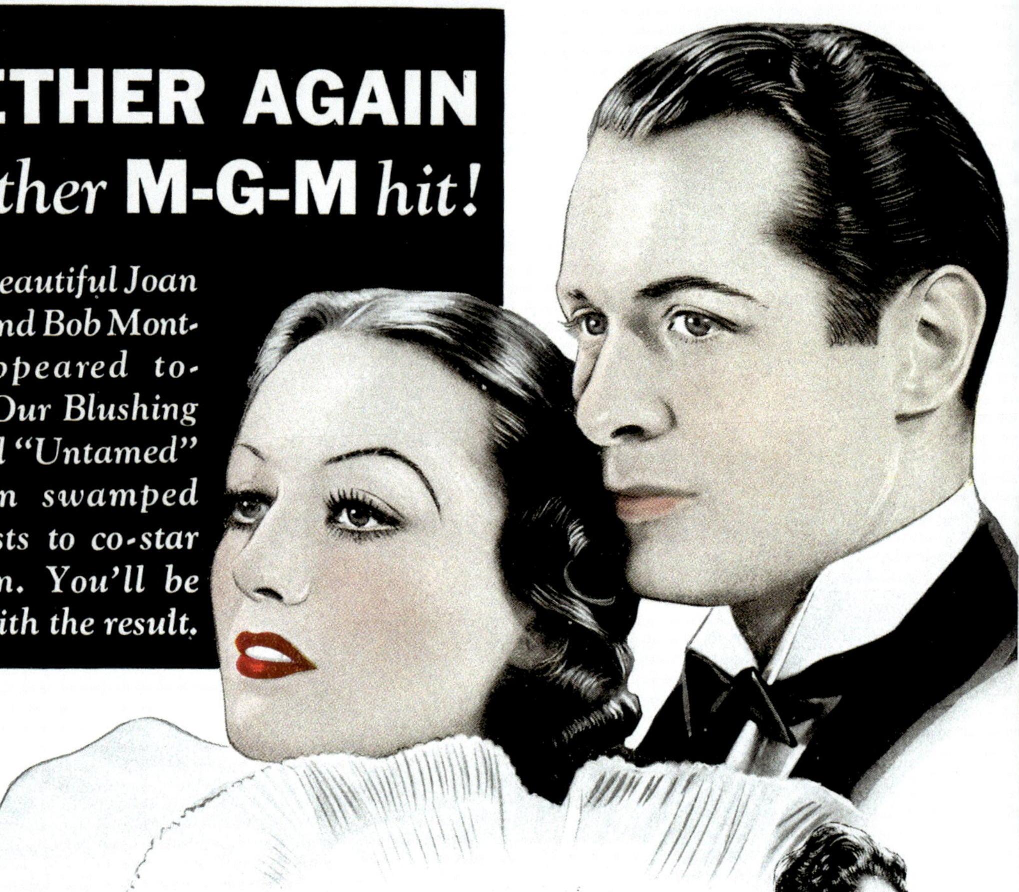

Joan
CRAWFORD
Robert
MONTGOMERY

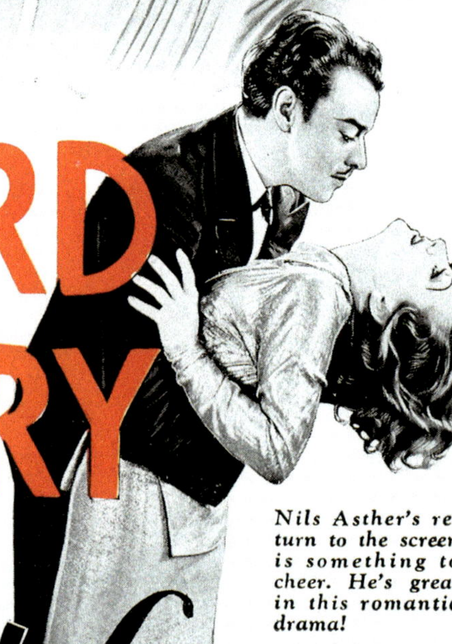

Nils Asther's return to the screen is something to cheer. He's great in this romantic drama!

in CLARENCE BROWN'S *production*

Letty Lynton

Beautiful Joan Crawford gives what many critics believe to be the most impressive performance of her career. Faced by her former lover and her husband-to-be she takes a course which leads to the very brink of tragedy. Once again Joan Crawford mingles tears and laughter, heart-throbs and thrills—again she captures the hearts of millions of her screen admirers! You'll compare it with the most thrilling picture you've ever seen!

with

NILS ASTHER
MAY ROBSON
LEWIS STONE

From the novel by Marie Belloc Lowndes

ARS GRATIA ARTIS

METRO-GOLDWYN-MAYER

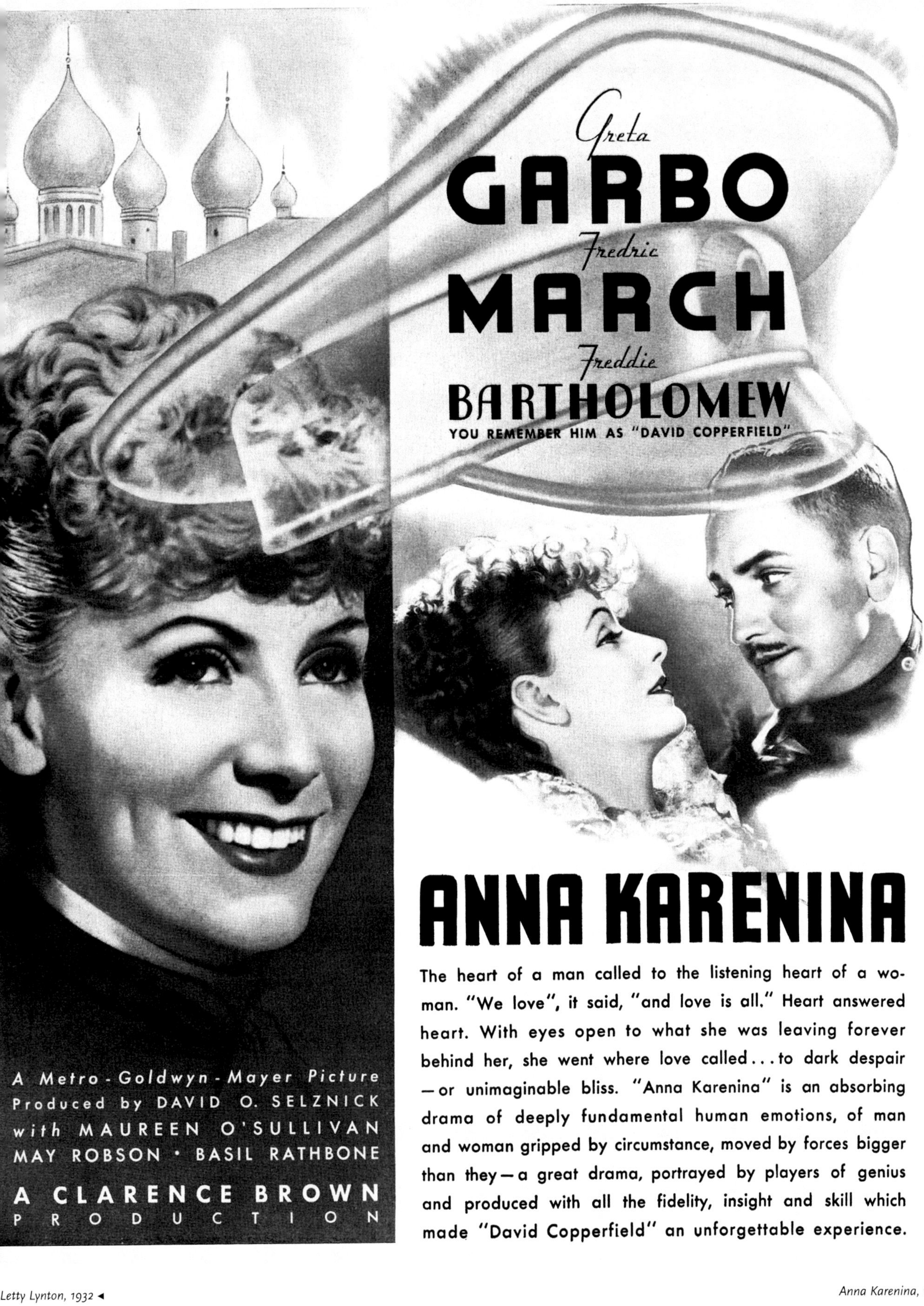

Letty Lynton, 1932 ◄

Anna Karenina, 1935

And the winner is...

Some Liked It Sinful

Pre-Code Hollywood offered a variety of provocative films that provided more than just a titillating taste of the day's rapidly loosening sexual mores. By 1930, the Motion Picture Producers and Distributors of America (MPPDA) bowed to pressure from religious groups and the Federal government to clean up the nipples, the couples in bed together, the exposed navels. Under the direction of president Will Hays, the major studios agreed to a system of self-censorship. By 1934 the Hays Code was in effect, and films like *Illicit* were a thing of the past. It was not until 1968 that Americans were again treated to snippets of cinematic sin.

Manche mögen's heiß

Vor den Tagen der Selbstzensur ging es in vielen Hollywoodfilmen drauf, drunter und drüber – sie boten ein Spiegelbild der sich rapide lockernden Moralvorstellungen jener Jahre. Anfang der Dreißiger die Motion Picture Producers and Distributors of America (MPPDA) beugten sich schließlich der Forderung von Bundesregierung und verschiedenen religiösen Organisationen, in Sachen Nippel, Pärchen im Lotterbett und blanke Bauchnabel aufzuräumen. Unter der Leitung des MPPDA-Präsidenten Will Hays stimmten die großen Studios einem System der Selbstzensur. 1934 trat der Hays Code in Kraft, und Filme wie *Illicit* gehörten der Vergangenheit an. Erst 1968 sollten die Amerikaner wieder Sündiges auf der Leinwand sehen dürfen.

Certains l'aimaient sulfureux.

Dans les années 20, Hollywood produisit de nombreux films provocants qui offraient plus qu'un aperçu émoustillant de la libération des mœurs. A partir de 1930, des groupes religieux et le gouvernement fédéral s'insurgèrent contre ces images de plus en plus torrides s'étalant sur les écrans. La MPPDA (Motion Pictures Producers and Distributors of America) finit par céder à la pression et consentit à faire le ménage dans une industrie cinématographique perçue comme moralement corrompue. Adieu les seins nus, les couples montrés au lit, les nombrils à l'air ! Sous la direction de Will Hays, président de la MPPDA, les principaux studios acceptèrent un système d'autocensure et la création d'une « Légion de la décence ». Dès 1934, le Production Code, également appelé « Hays Code », entra en vigueur et des films comme *Illicit* furent bannis. Il fallut attendre 1968 pour que les Américains aient à nouveau le droit d'entrevoir des fragments de péchés sur pellicule.

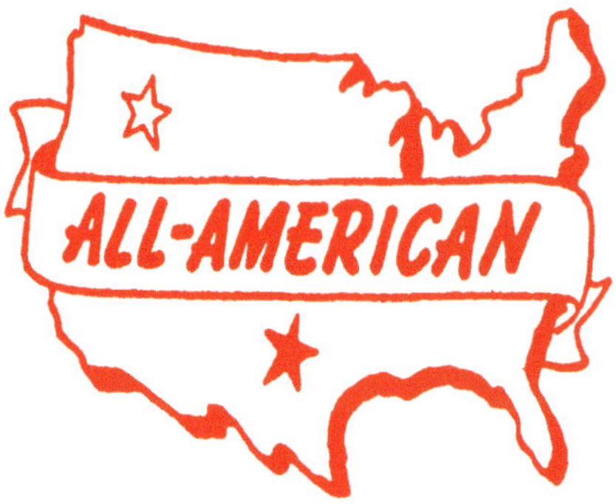

Illicit, 1931

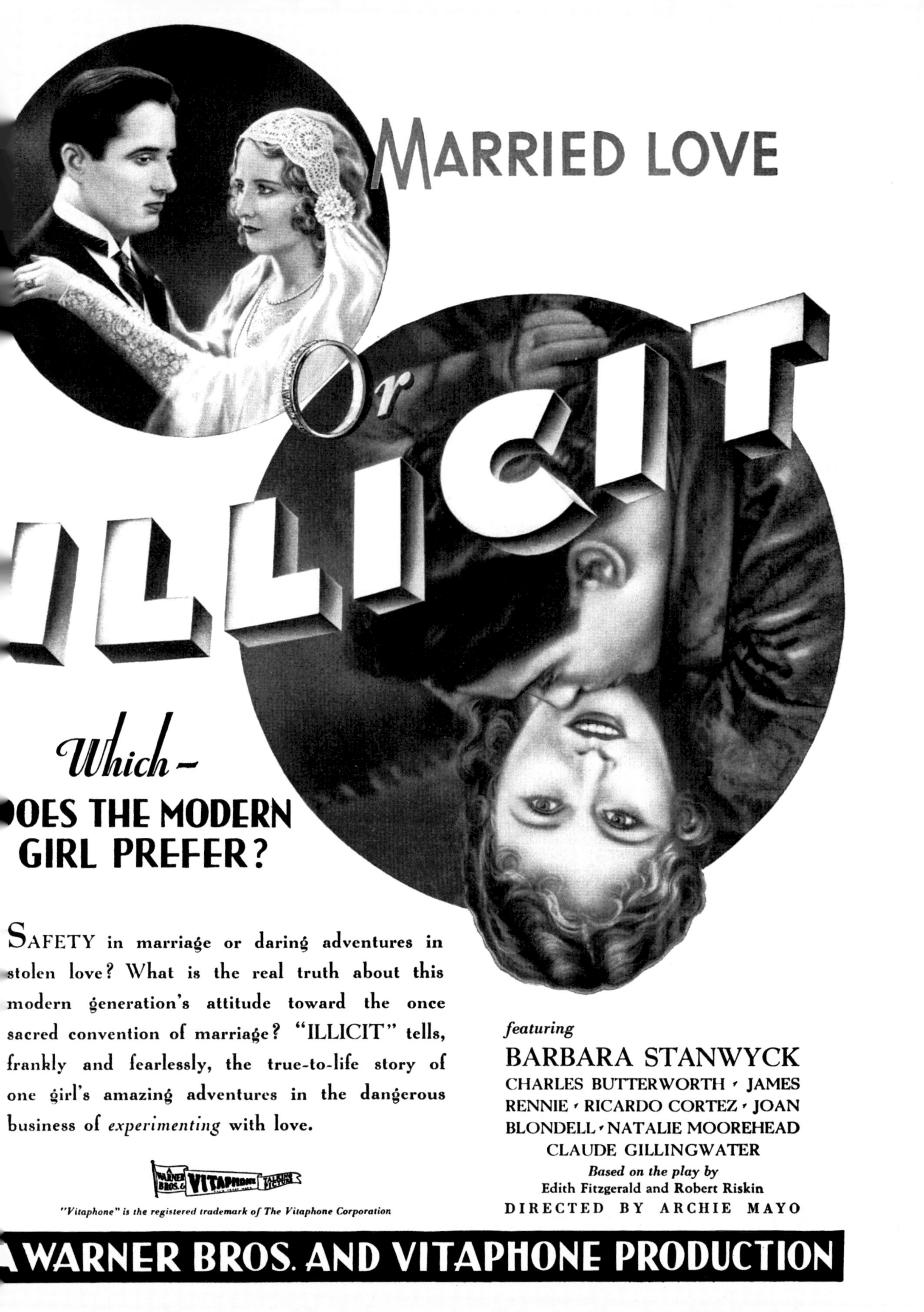
MARRIED LOVE
Or
ILLICIT
Which –
OES THE MODERN
GIRL PREFER?
SAFETY in marriage or daring adventures in stolen love? What is the real truth about this modern generation's attitude toward the once sacred convention of marriage? "ILLICIT" tells, frankly and fearlessly, the true-to-life story of one girl's amazing adventures in the dangerous business of *experimenting* with love.
"Vitaphone" is the registered trademark of The Vitaphone Corporation
featuring
BARBARA STANWYCK
CHARLES BUTTERWORTH · JAMES RENNIE · RICARDO CORTEZ · JOAN BLONDELL · NATALIE MOOREHEAD
CLAUDE GILLINGWATER
Based on the play by
Edith Fitzgerald and Robert Riskin
DIRECTED BY ARCHIE MAYO
WARNER BROS. AND VITAPHONE PRODUCTION

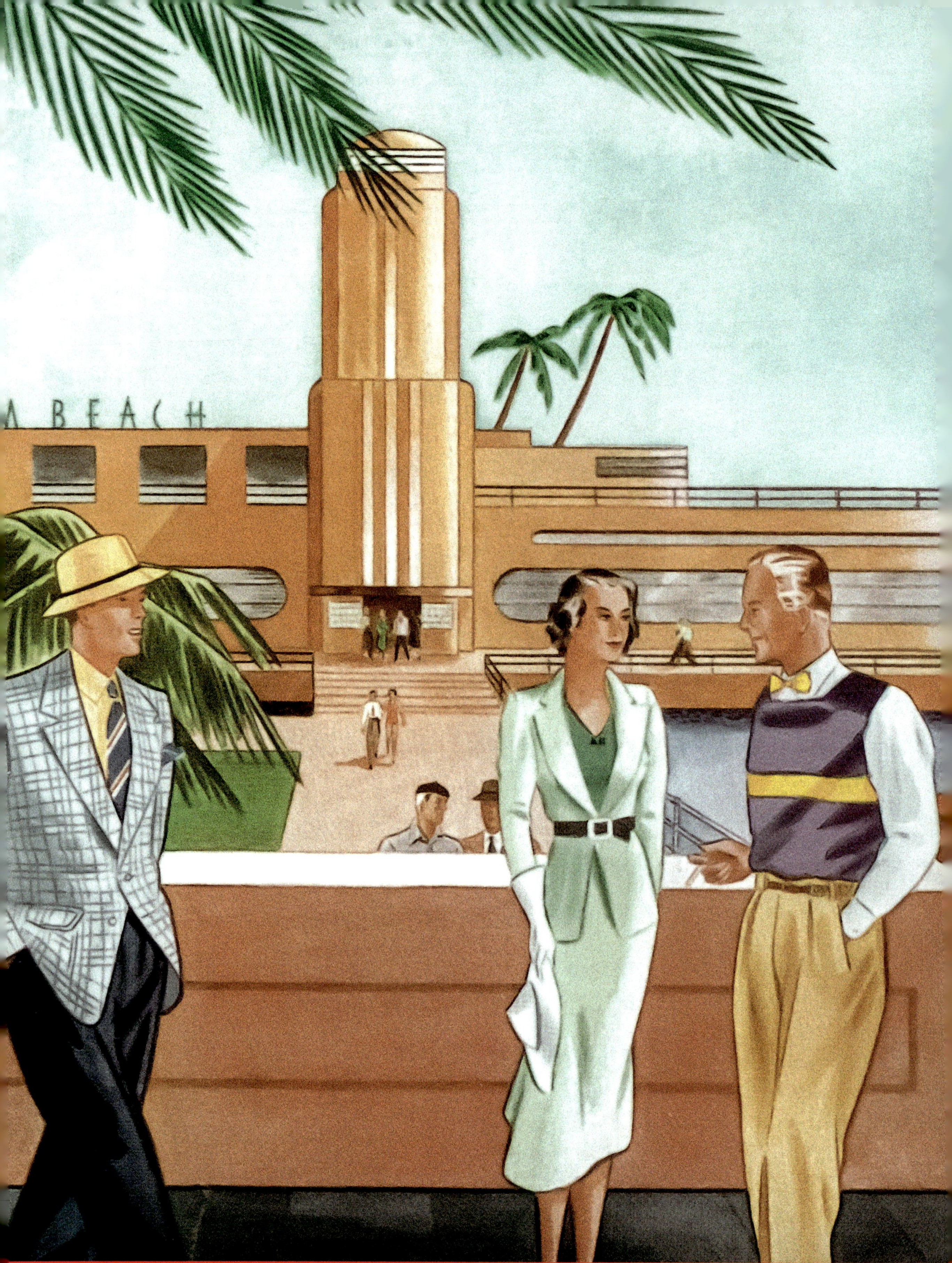
BEACH

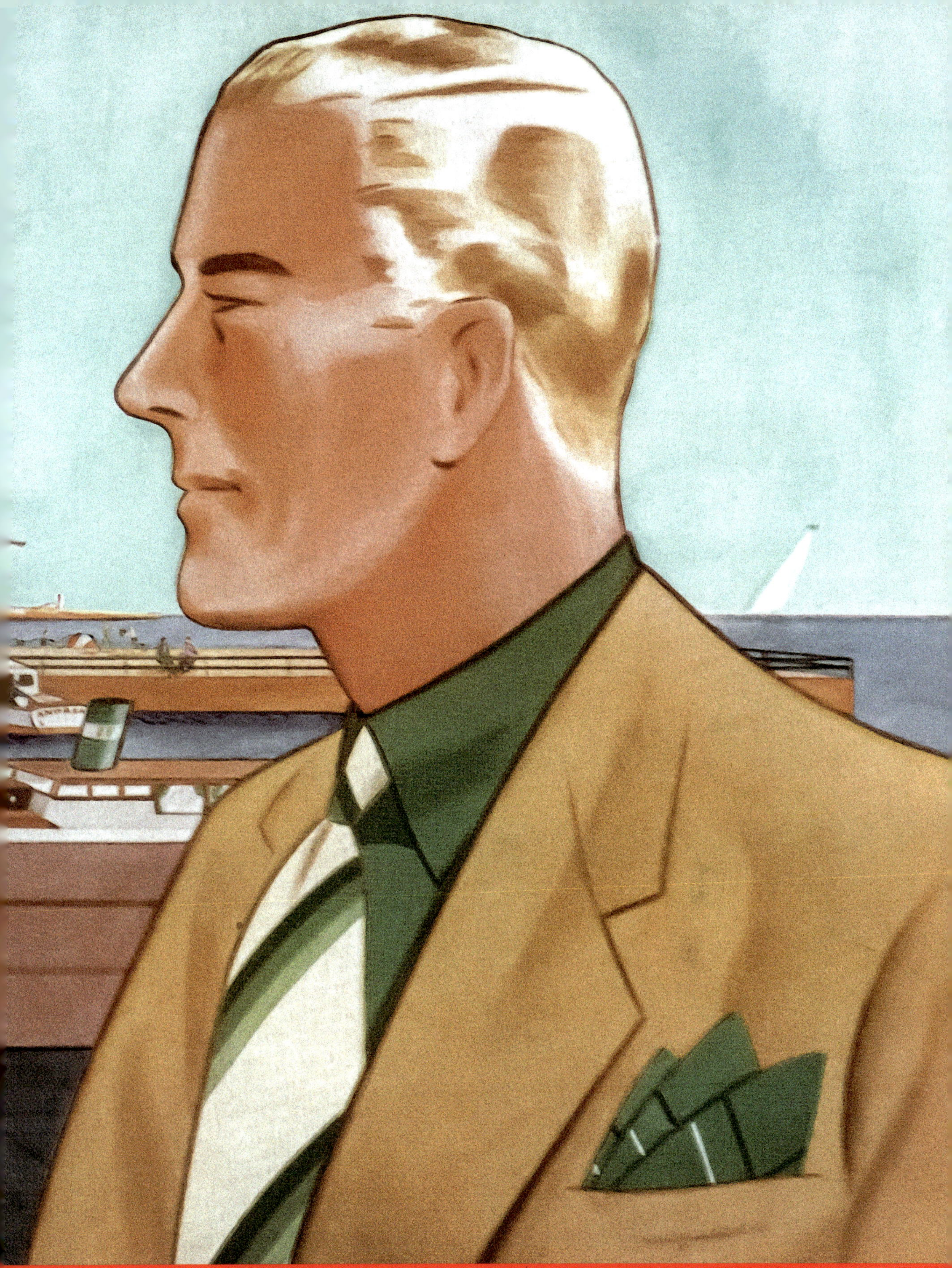

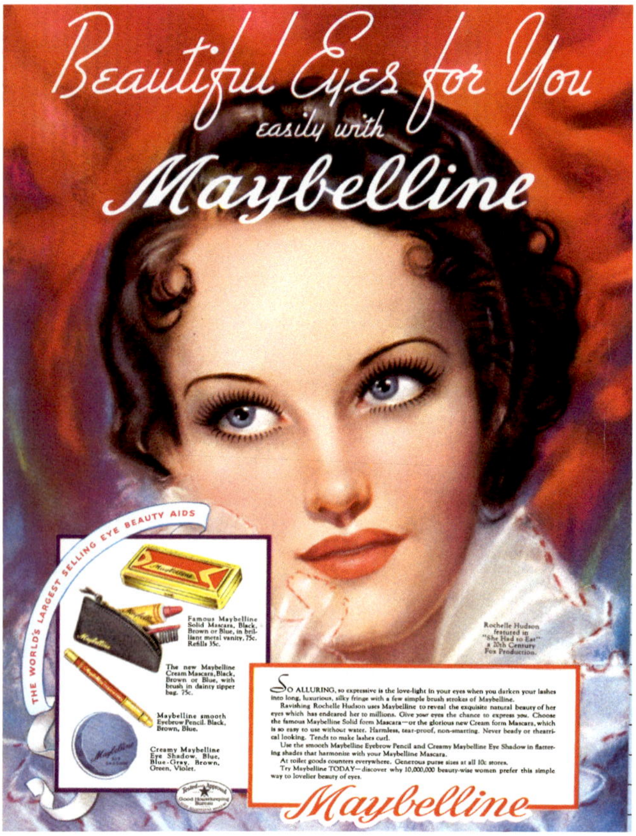

Maybelline, 1937

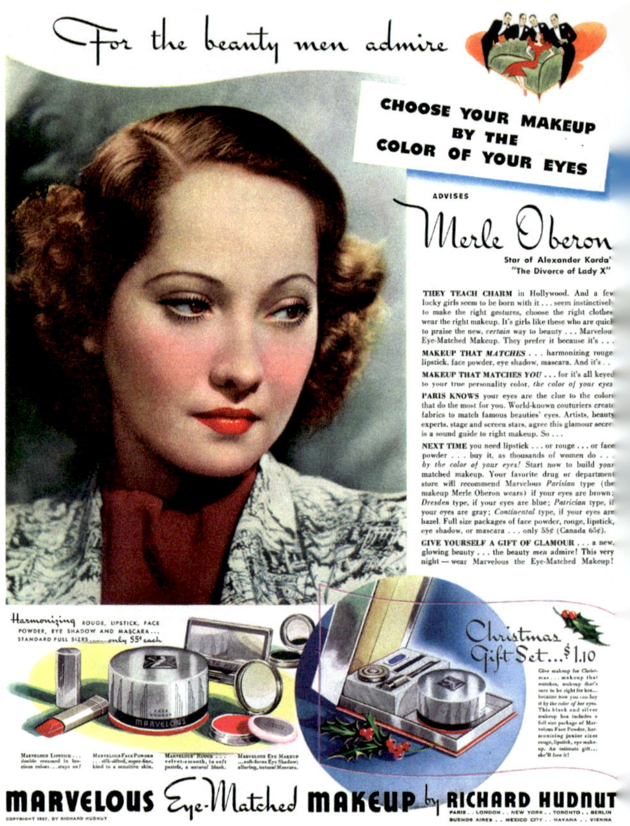

Richard Hudnut Makeup, 1937

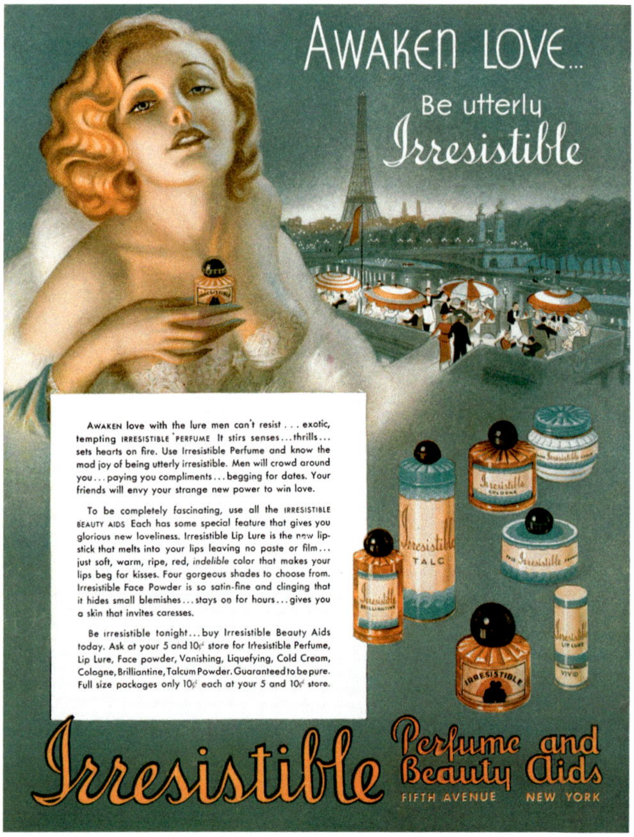

The Weisbaum Bros., 1937 ◄◄ Irresistible Perfume, 1935

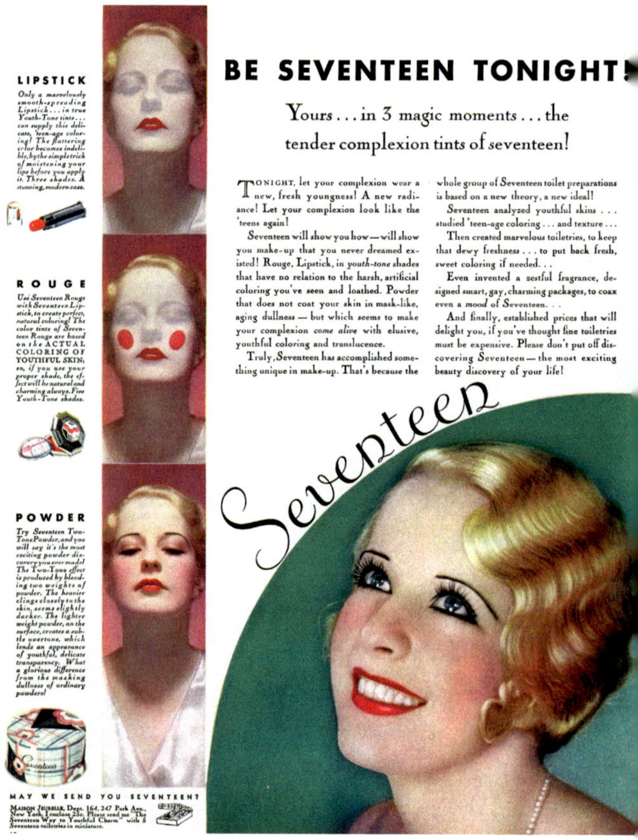

Seventeen, 1932

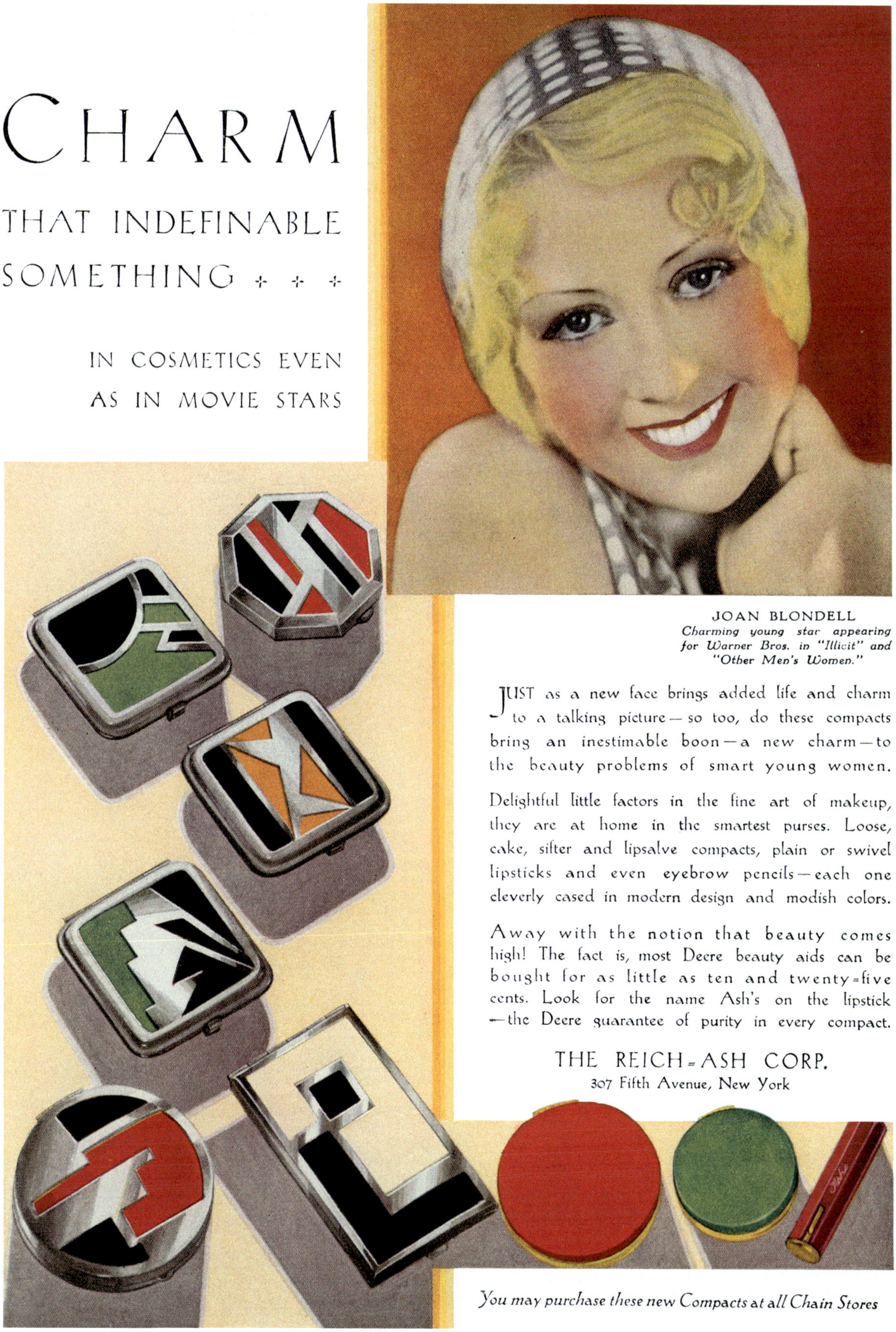

Reich-Ash Co., 1931

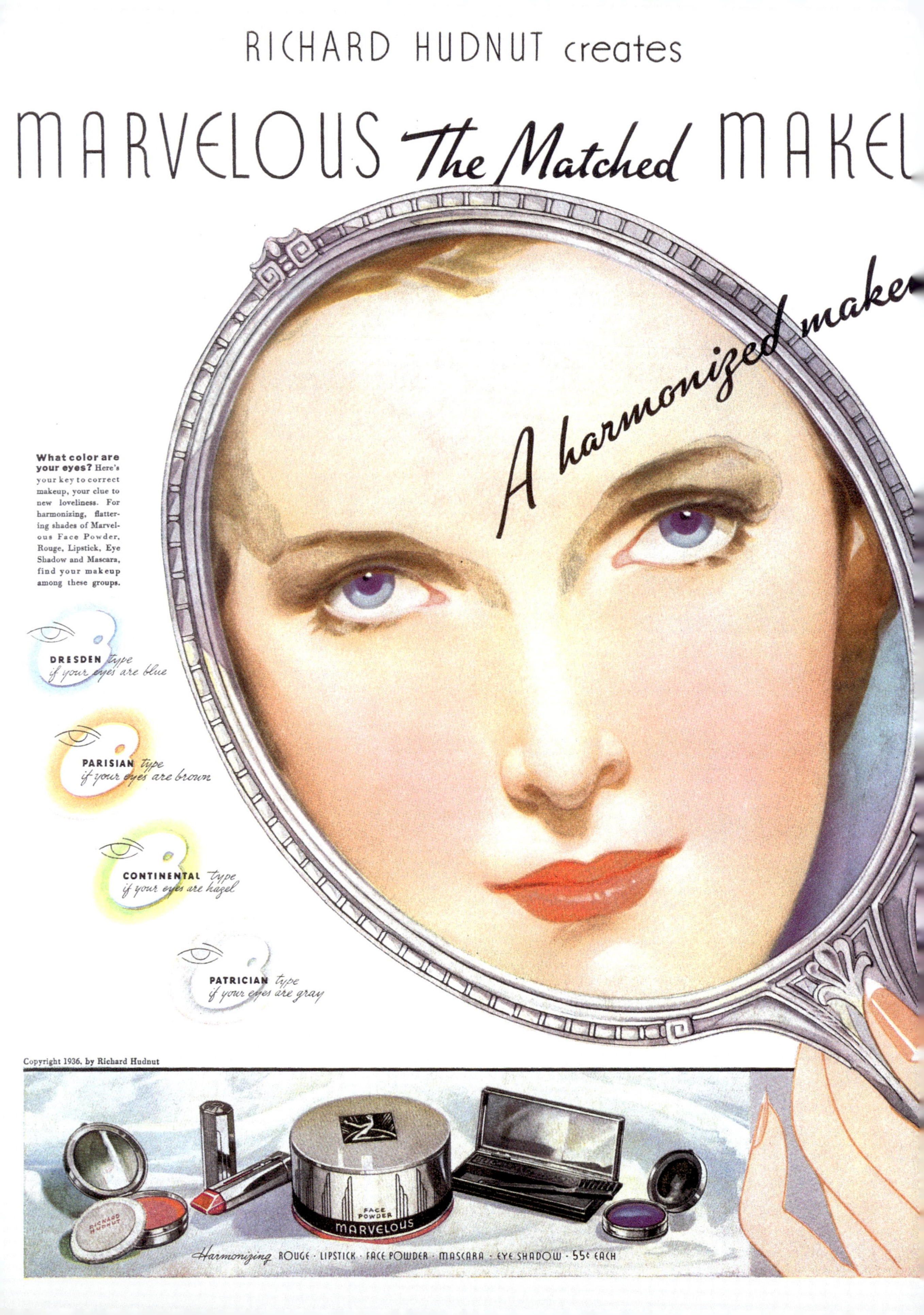
RICHARD HUDNUT creates
MARVELOUS The Matched MAKE
A harmonized make
What color are your eyes? Here's your key to correct makeup, your clue to new loveliness. For harmonizing, flattering shades of Marvelous Face Powder, Rouge, Lipstick, Eye Shadow and Mascara, find your makeup among these groups.
DRESDEN type if your eyes are blue
PARISIAN type if your eyes are brown
CONTINENTAL type if your eyes are hazel
PATRICIAN type if your eyes are gray
Copyright 1936, by Richard Hudnut
RICHARD HUDNUT
FACE POWDER
MARVELOUS
Harmonizing ROUGE · LIPSTICK · FACE POWDER · MASCARA · EYE SHADOW · 55¢ EACH

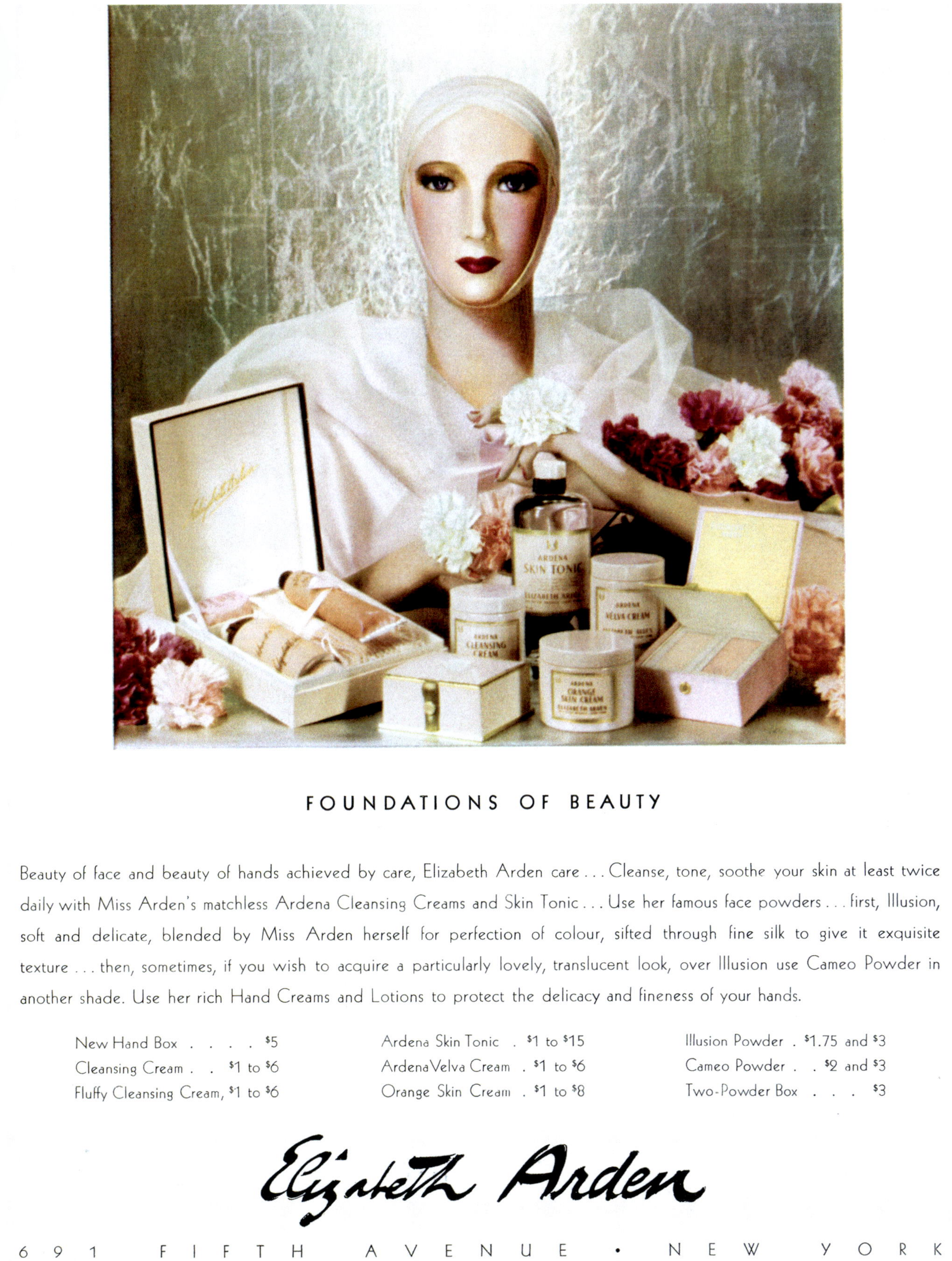

Richard Hudnut Makeup, 1936 ◂

Elizabeth Arden, 1939

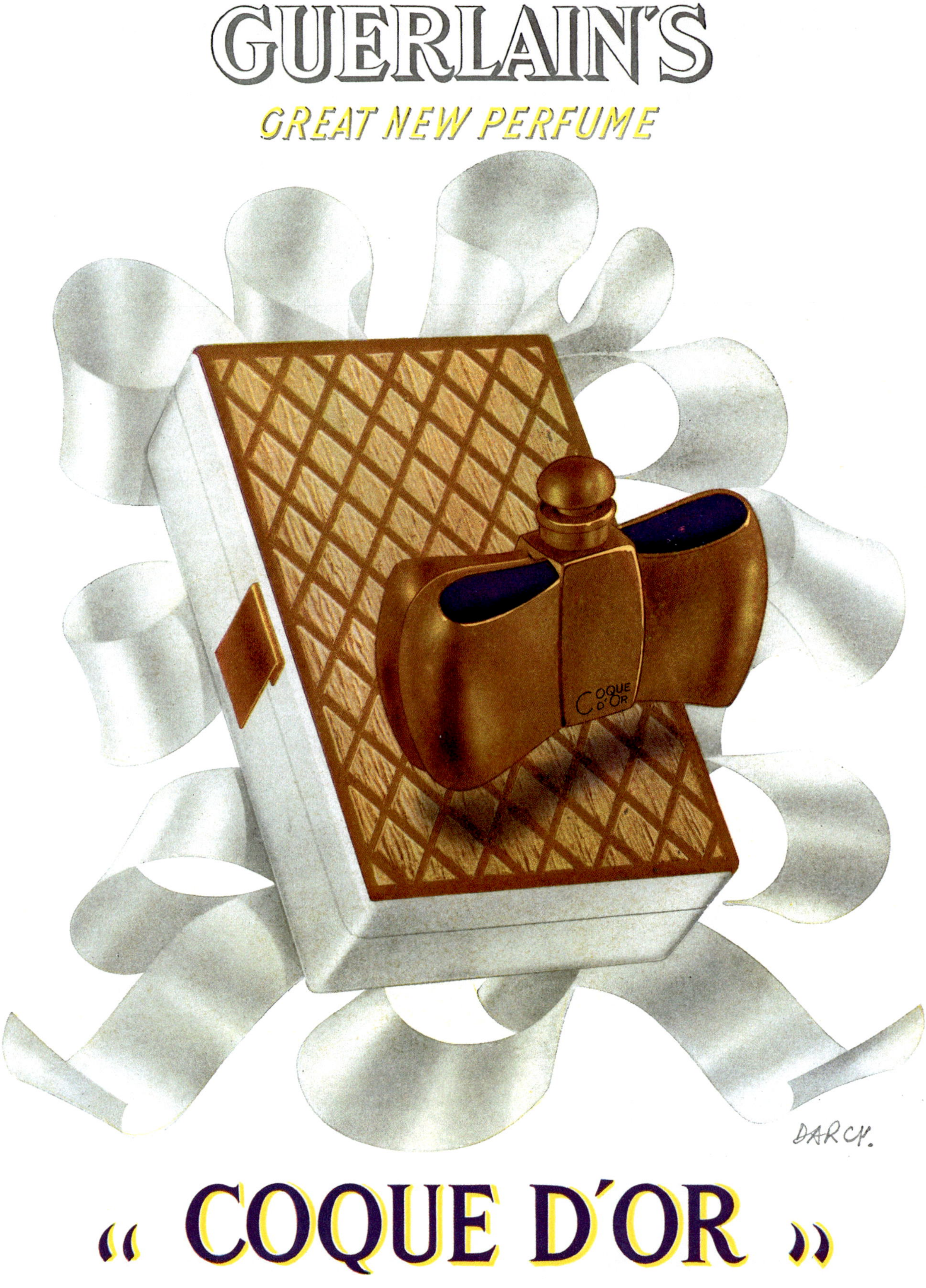

Guerlain, 1939

► Guerlain, 1938

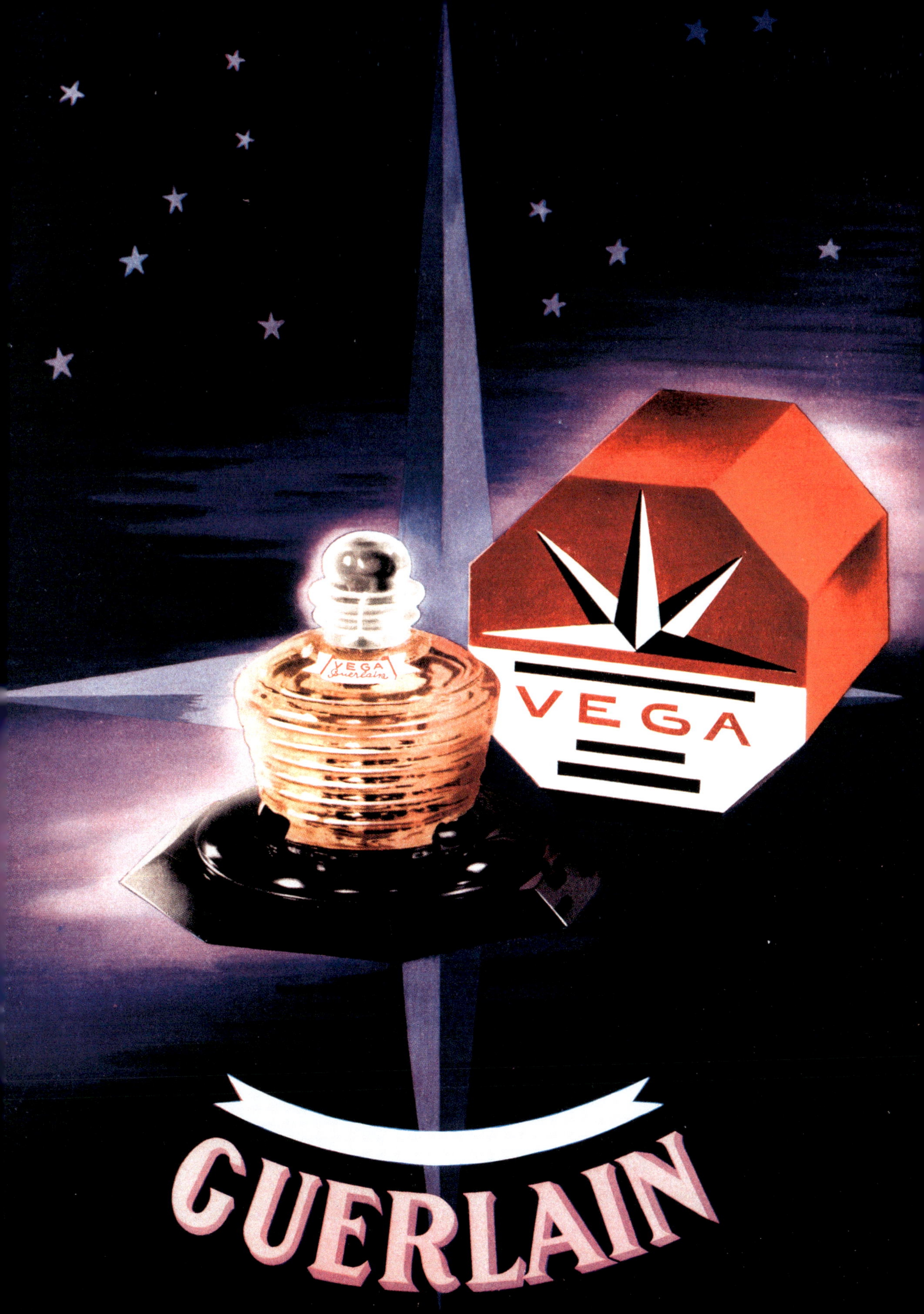
VEGA
Guerlain
VEGA
GUERLAIN

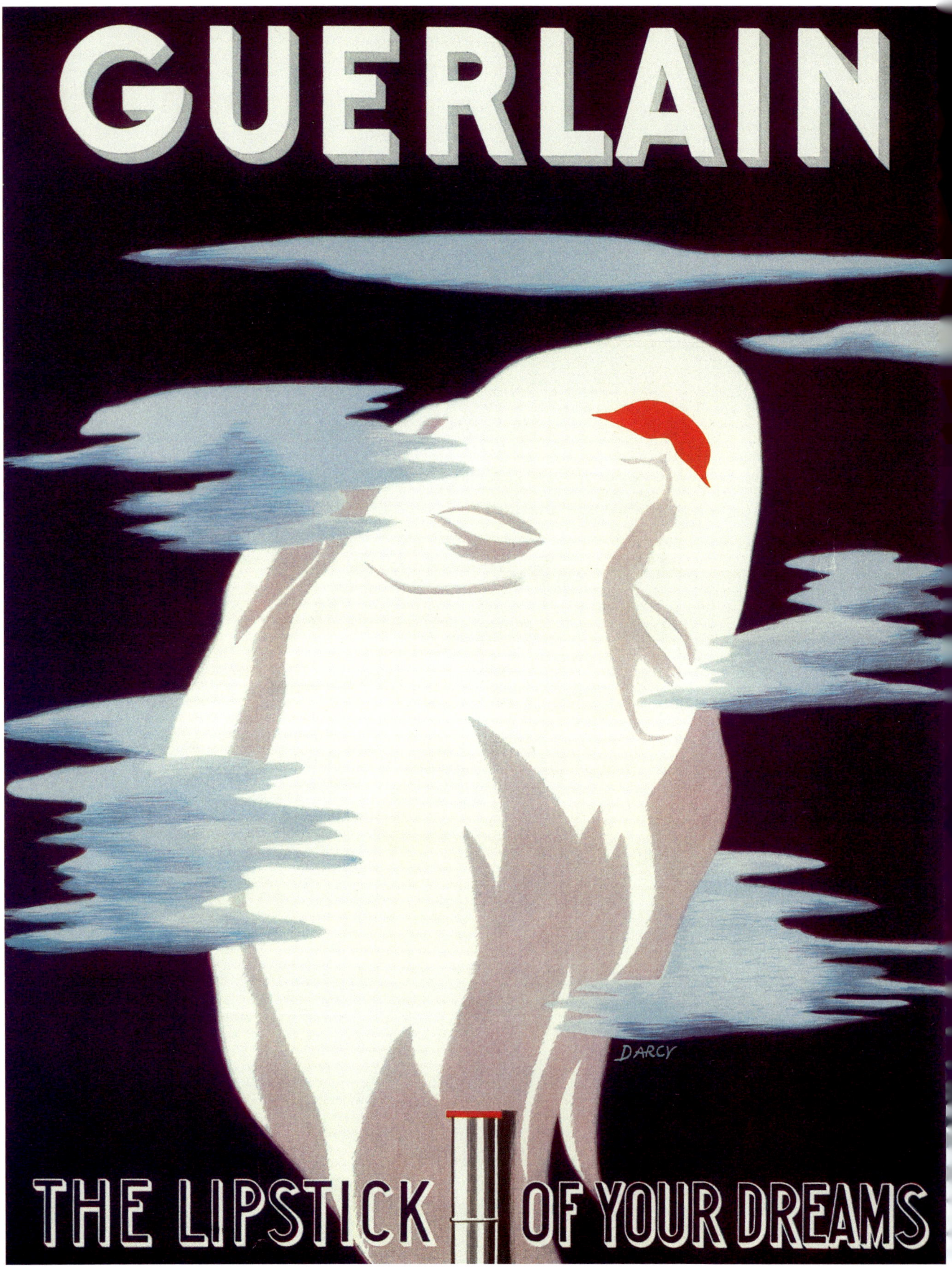

Guerlain, 1938

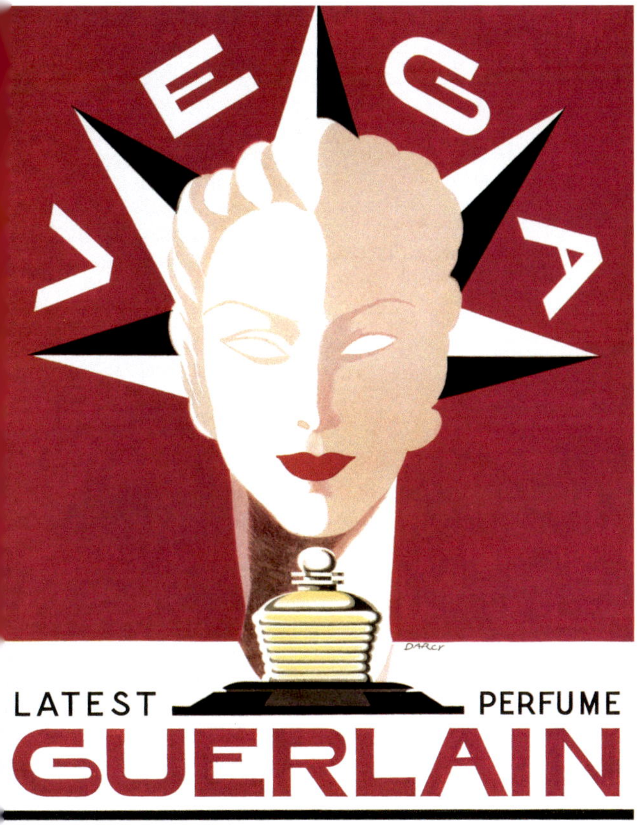

Guerlain, 1937

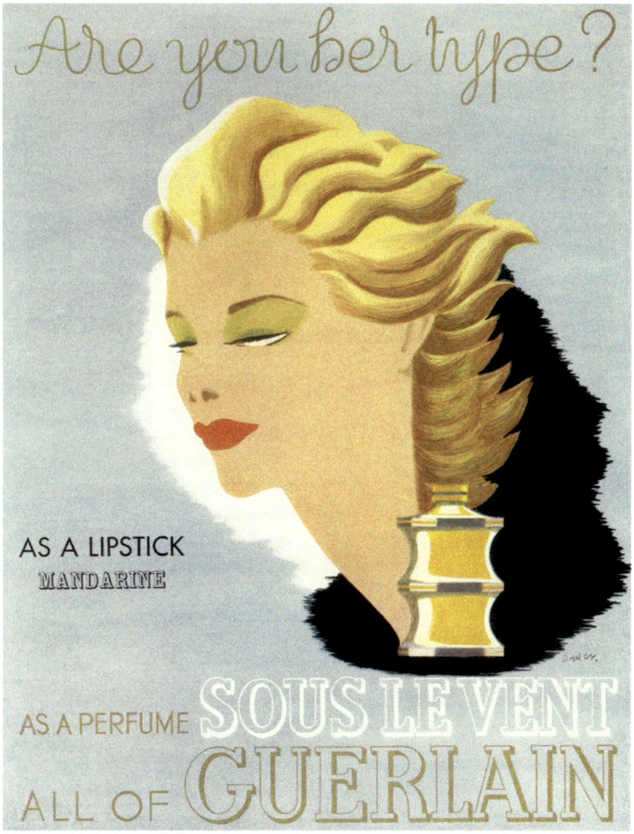

Guerlain, 1938

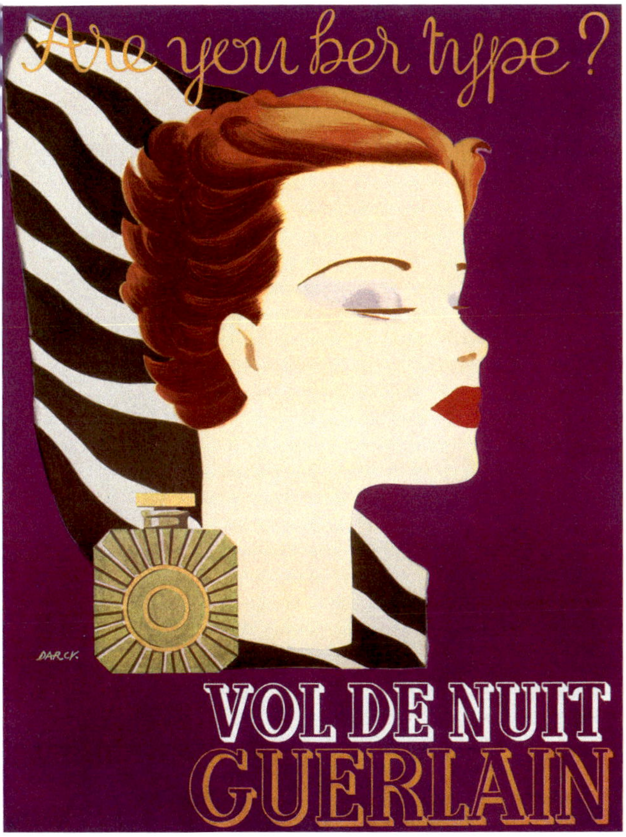

Guerlain, 1938

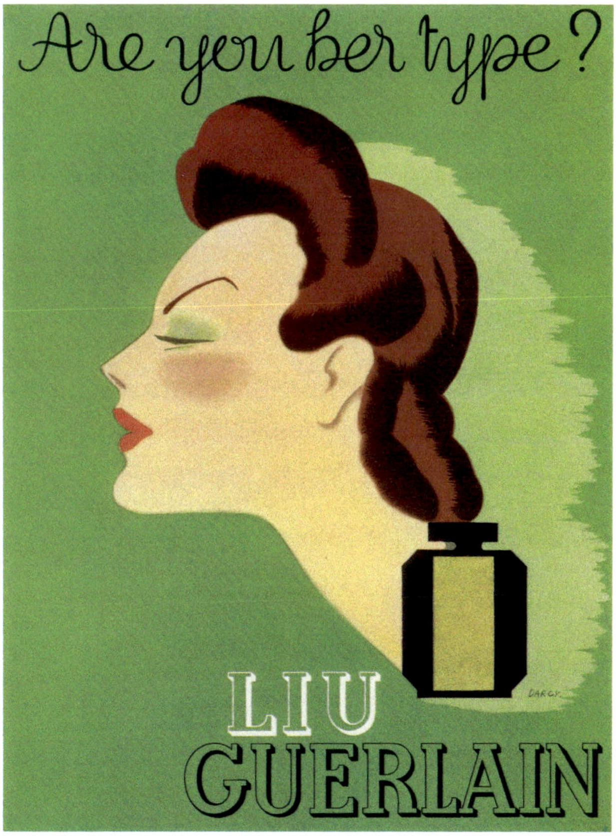

Guerlain, 1937

►► *McCall's, 1934*

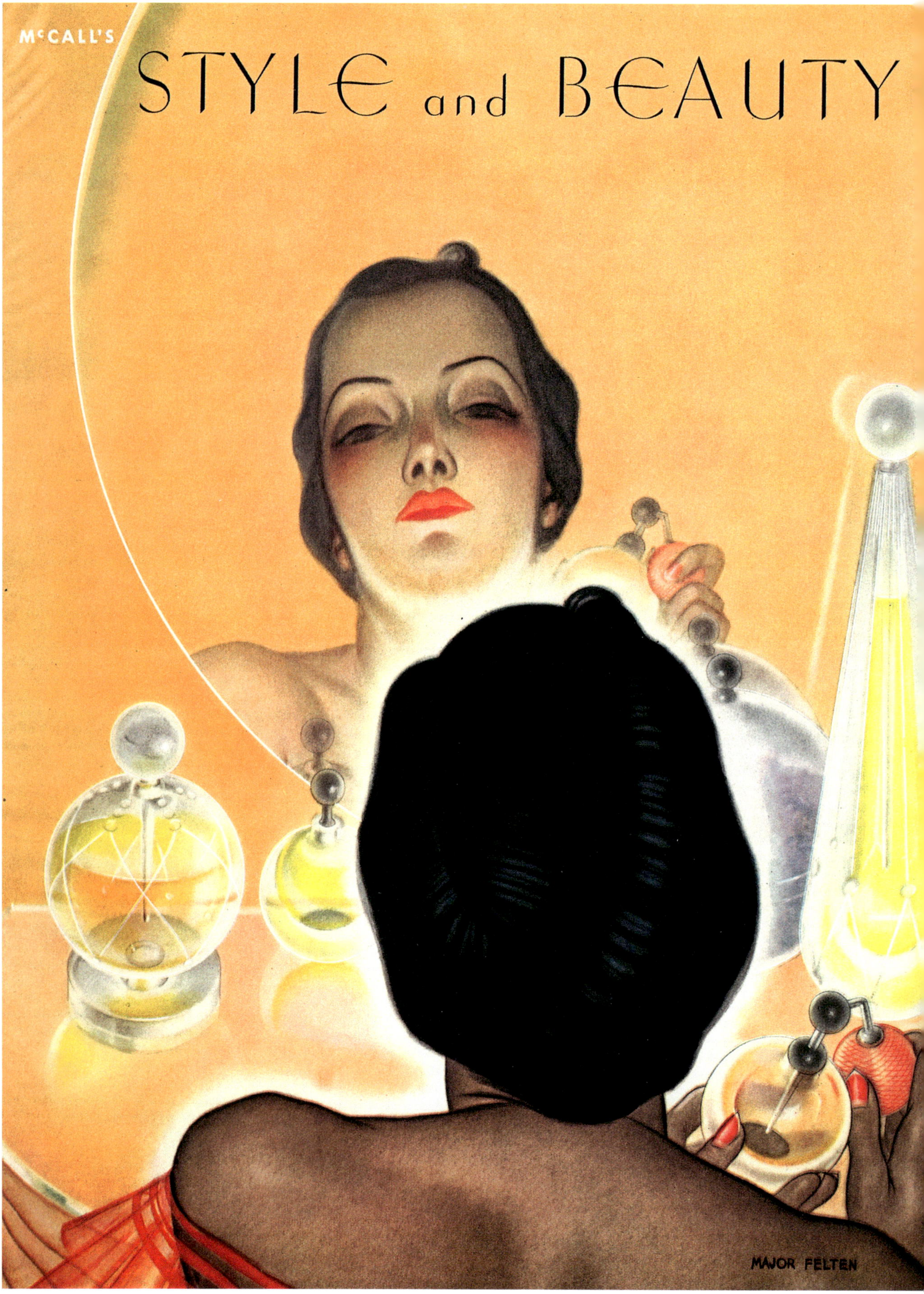
McCALL'S
STYLE and BEAUTY
MAJOR FELTEN

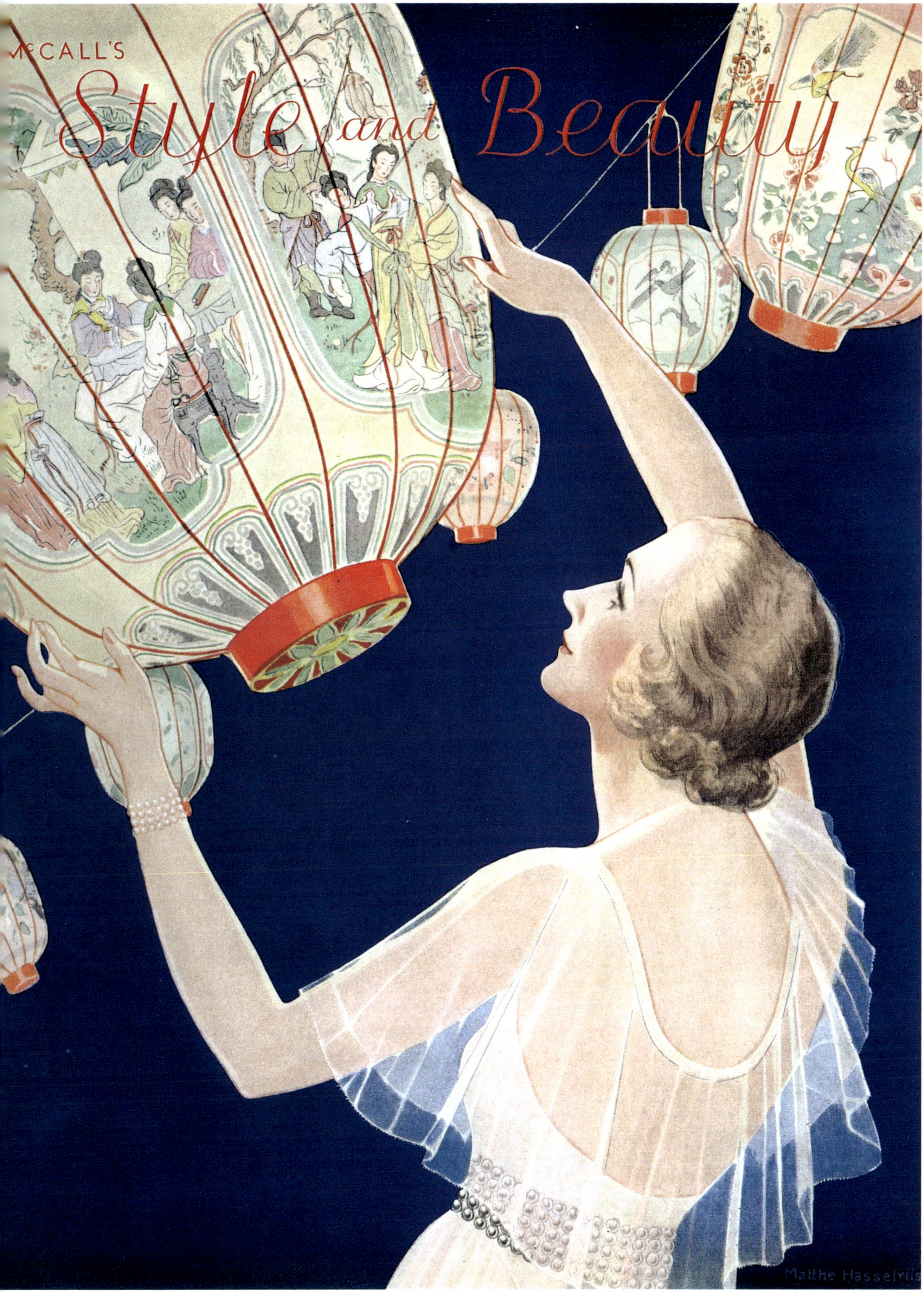
McCALL'S
Style and Beauty
Matthe Hasselriis

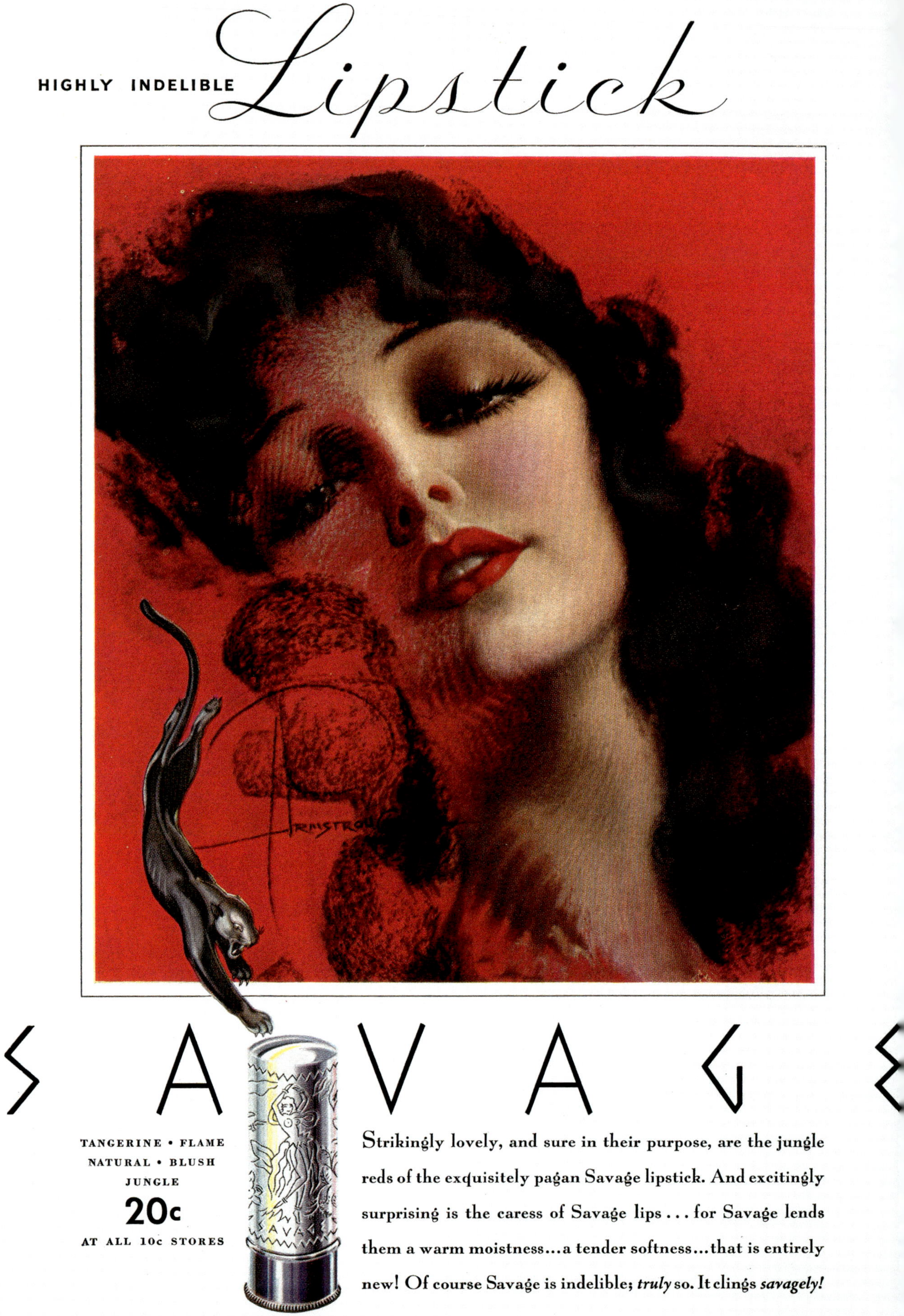
HIGHLY INDELIBLE Lipstick
SAVAGE
TANGERINE • FLAME
NATURAL • BLUSH
JUNGLE
20c
AT ALL 10c STORES
Strikingly lovely, and sure in their purpose, are the jungle reds of the exquisitely pagan Savage lipstick. And excitingly surprising is the caress of Savage lips . . . for Savage lends them a warm moistness...a tender softness...that is entirely new! Of course Savage is indelible; truly so. It clings savagely!

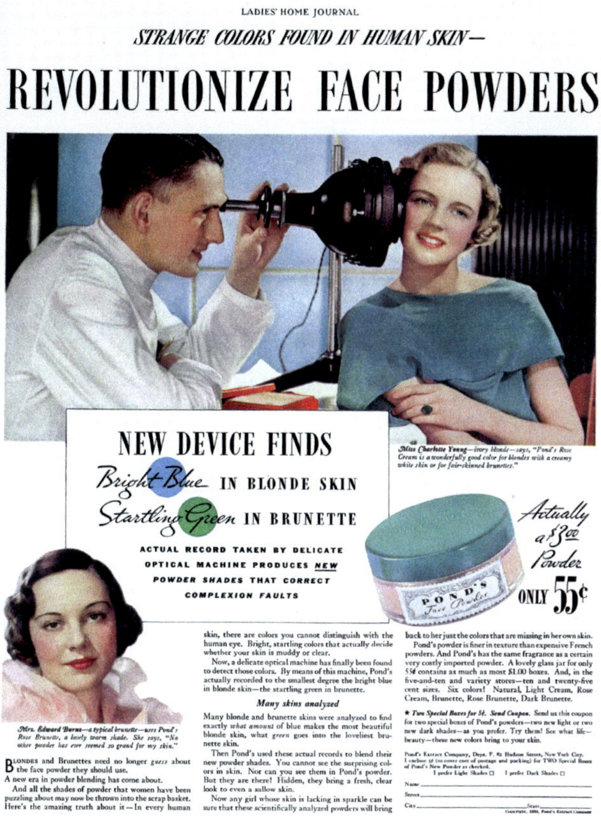

Pond's, 1934

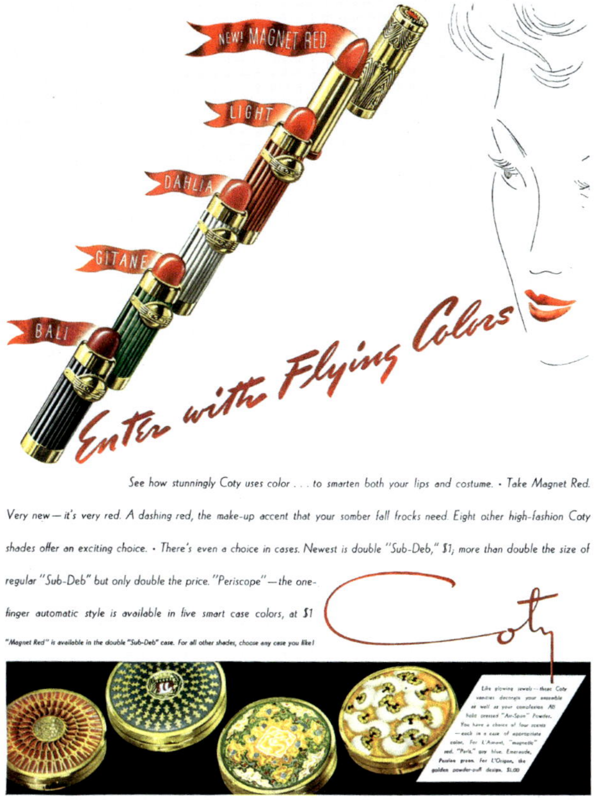

Coty, 1939

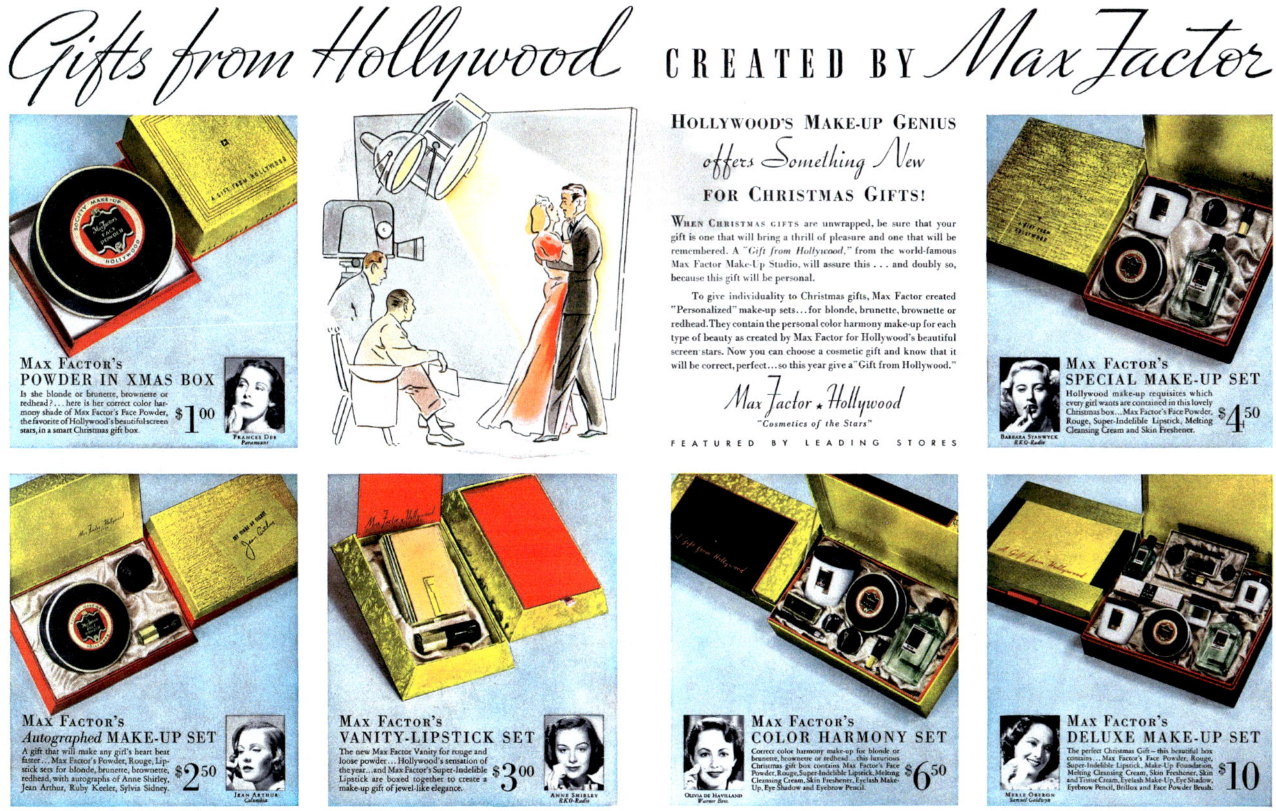

McCall's, 1933 ◄◄ Savage Lipstick, 1937 ◄

Max Factor, 1937

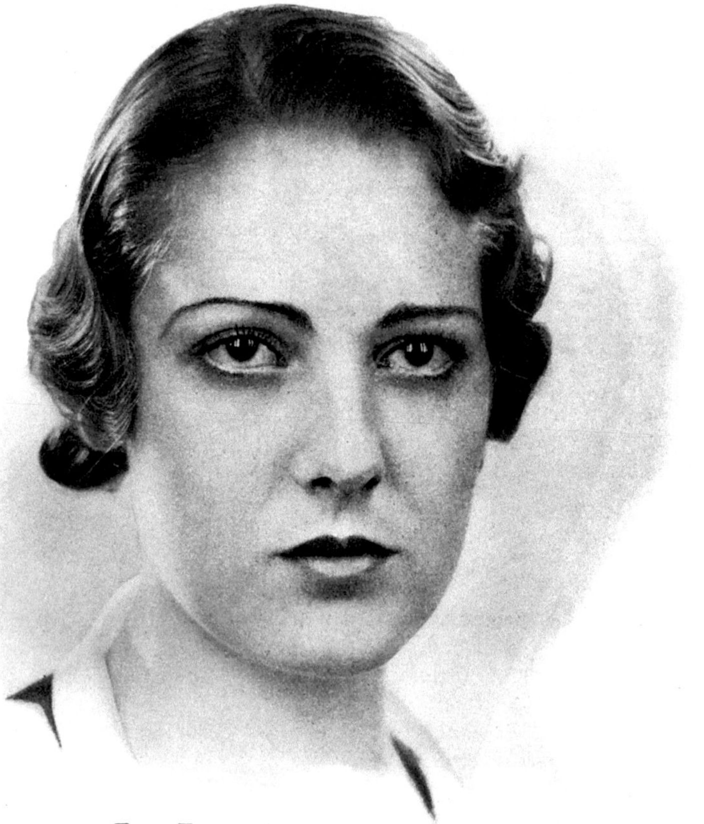

"Why wasn't I born a man?"

[The age-old cry of the sex destined to bear most of the world's troubles]

WHERE is the woman who has not, at some period in her life, used these very words? They sound like a complaint, but they are really a protest—a protest against those burdens of life which are wholly woman's.

Some of them still think—

Why do women use poisonous antiseptics in their desire for personal hygiene and surgical cleanliness? Of course they *do not need* to resort to poisons for this purpose, but many women still *think* they must!

If they would consult their own doctors they would find that cresol and carbolic acid have been displaced by a new, safe, non-poisonous antiseptic-germicide of great power, called *Zonite.*

Zonite is in a class by itself. No other non-poisonous antiseptic has one-quarter its germ-killing strength. Even when compared with the poisons, Zonite stands out supreme. It is far more powerful than any dilution of cresol or carbolic acid that can be safely allowed on the human body.

Women of the independent, enlightened type all over the world are today using Zonite for exclusively feminine purposes—undoubtedly more of them than are using any other germicide. They realize that Zonite is a genuine *personal antiseptic* for use on the body—not a disinfectant for tubs, buckets and staircases.

Zonite holds no poison-threat

Women all around you are using Zonite. Have *you* introduced it to your own special circle? Remember, Zonite is as safe as pure water. No injury to sensitive tissues with Zonite. No fear of accidental poisoning!

Zonite comes in two forms. The liquid is 30¢, 60¢ and $1.00. Zonite Suppositories are $1.00 a dozen. These dainty white cones provide a *continuing* antiseptic action. Many women use both.

"Facts for Women"—Sent by mail

This much-discussed booklet gives clear, concise information on the whole subject. Frank, authoritative, important. Send for it right away. Zonite Products Corporation, Chrysler Building, New York, N. Y.

ZONITE PRODUCTS CORPORATION MC-35
Chrysler Building, New York, N. Y.
Please send me free copy of the booklet or booklets checked below.
☐ Facts for Women ☐ Use of Antiseptics in the Home
NAME..
(Please print name)
ADDRESS...
CITY..................................STATE............
(In Canada: Sainte Therese, P. Q.)

Zonite, 1933

▸ *Kotex, 1937*

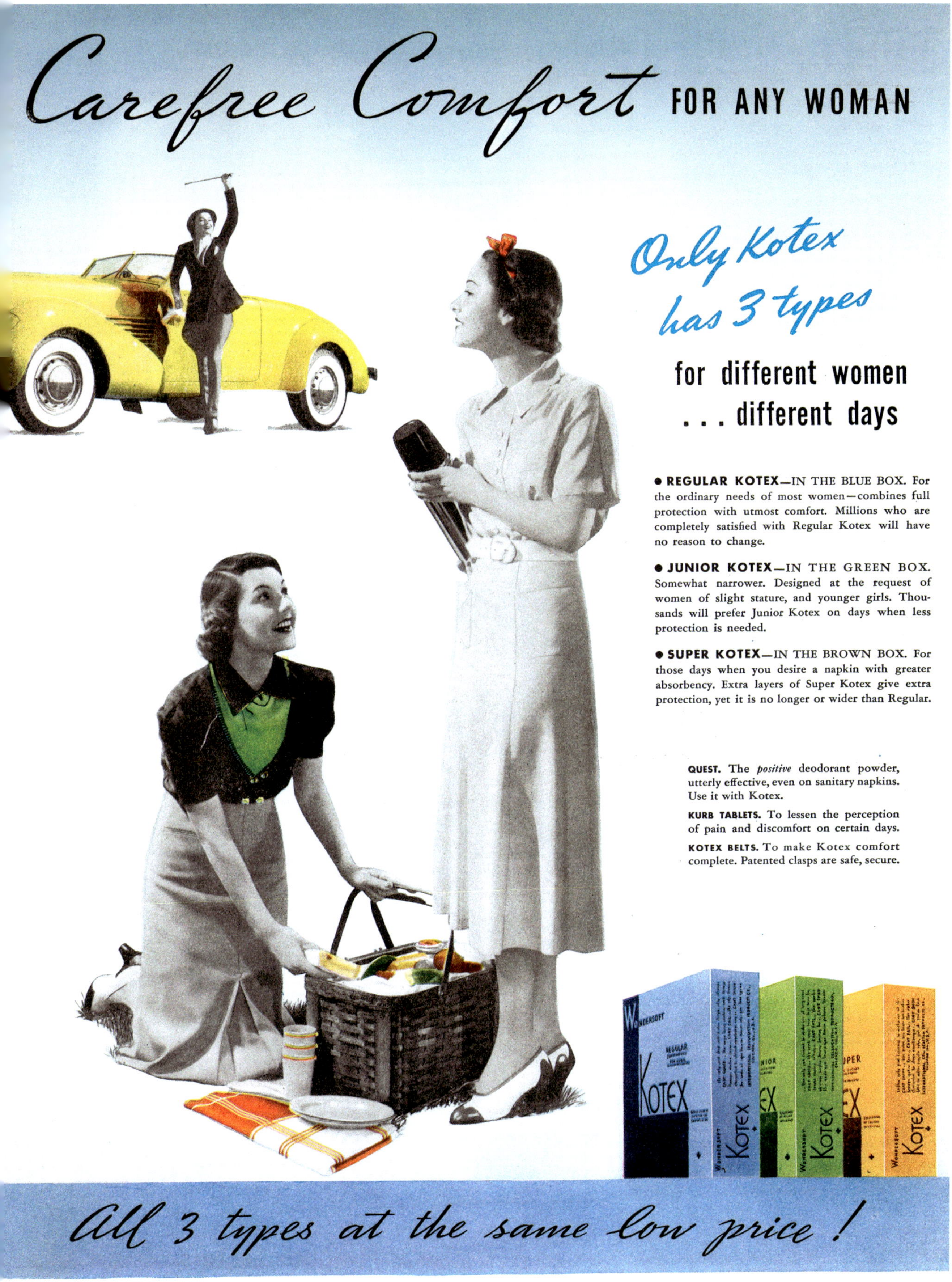
Carefree Comfort FOR ANY WOMAN
Only Kotex has 3 types
for different women
. . . different days
• REGULAR KOTEX—IN THE BLUE BOX. For the ordinary needs of most women—combines full protection with utmost comfort. Millions who are completely satisfied with Regular Kotex will have no reason to change.
• JUNIOR KOTEX—IN THE GREEN BOX. Somewhat narrower. Designed at the request of women of slight stature, and younger girls. Thousands will prefer Junior Kotex on days when less protection is needed.
• SUPER KOTEX—IN THE BROWN BOX. For those days when you desire a napkin with greater absorbency. Extra layers of Super Kotex give extra protection, yet it is no longer or wider than Regular.
QUEST. The *positive* deodorant powder, utterly effective, even on sanitary napkins. Use it with Kotex.
KURB TABLETS. To lessen the perception of pain and discomfort on certain days.
KOTEX BELTS. To make Kotex comfort complete. Patented clasps are safe, secure.
KOTEX
Kotex
Kotex
Kotex
All 3 types at the same low price!

GIBBS IMPORTED FRENCH WIGS

Prices subject to change without notice

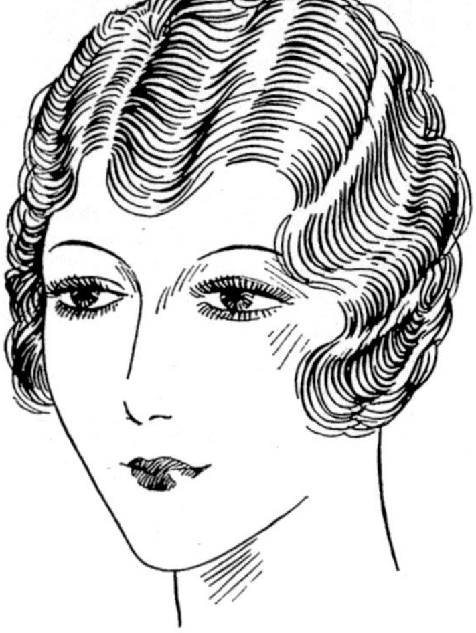

No. 5H212

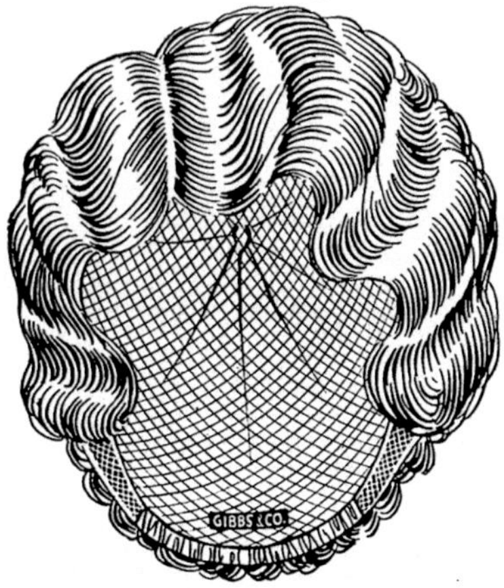

No. 5H223 and 5H224

No. 5H212—French Imported Bobbed Wig. Hand drawn parting made of natural wavy cut hair. All ventilated. Adjustable to fit any head. Very effective and much in demand.

No. 5H223—Natural colors only. French Imported Bobbed wig of natural wavy cut hair. No blondes or drabs. Curls in back.

No. 5H224—Bobbed wig with long hair in back. Natural shades only. Same as 5H223, with bun in back.

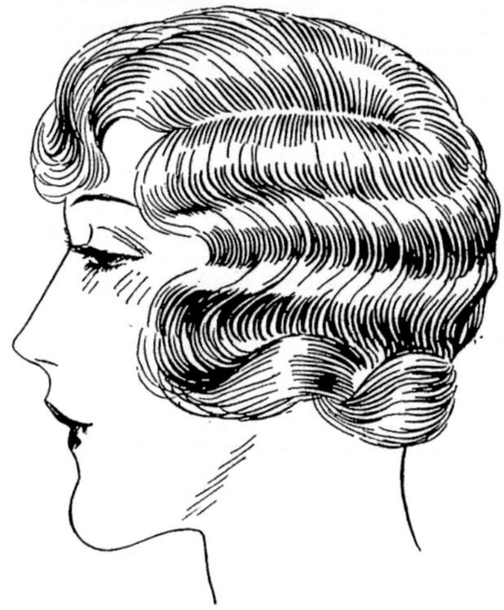

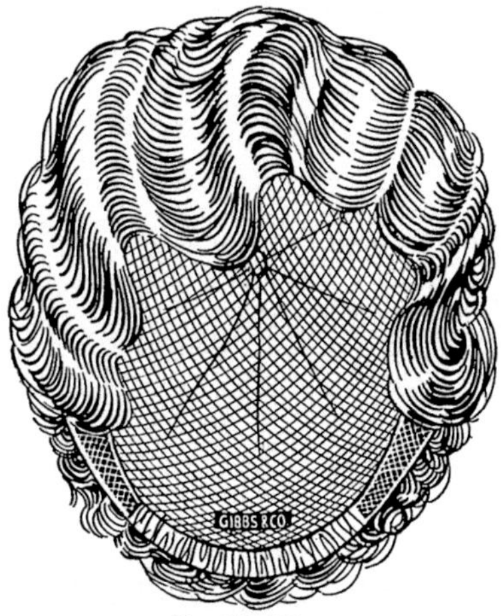

No. 5H211

No. 5H211—Bobbed wig with long hair in back, about 16″. Gives the appearance of a full grown head of hair. Available in natural shades only. The illustration shows its effective style.

No. 5H238—The finest piece of its kind brought into this country. Semi-long wig, about shoulder length. Finest Moravian cut hair, naturally wavy. In natural shades only.

PINLET CLUSTER

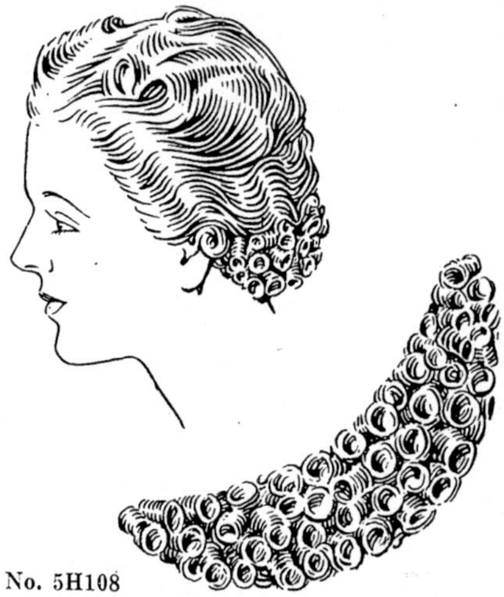

No. 5H108

An attractive headdress for the back of the head. Made of 1½ ounces of natural curly hair. A style that is much in demand.

GIBBS DOUBLE SWIRL

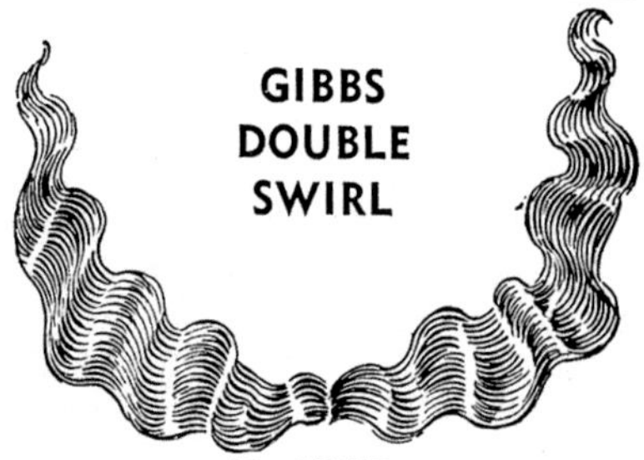

No. 5H118

This hair is invisibly joined so that it may be worn twice around the head, giving the appearance of being one's own hair. Becoming when worn either flat, waved or braided.

GIBBS BISCUIT COILS

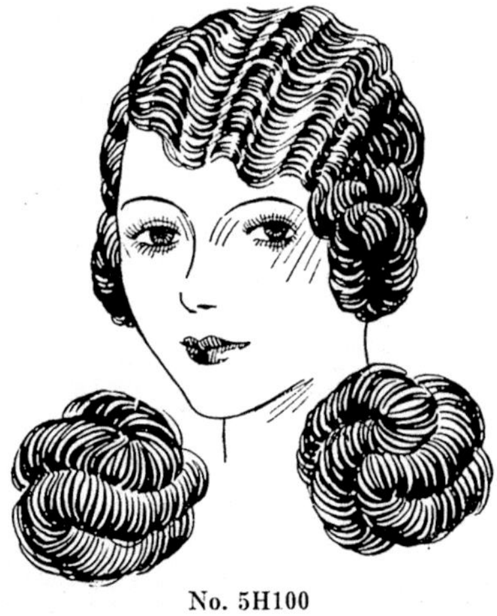

No. 5H100

These pieces are made so that they can be used not only as coils but as side waves. This is done by unbraiding the coil and marcelling the pieces. The two coils weigh 1½ ounces and are made of 18-inch hair.

MIGNONETTE CURLS

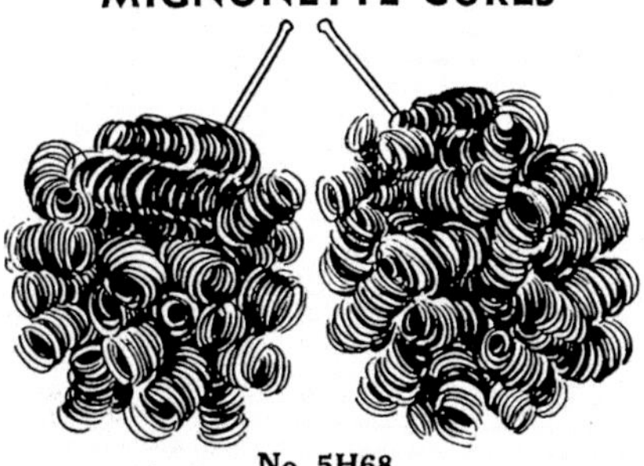

No. 5H68

These can be worn either over the ears or as a cluster in the back.

GIBBS PIN CURLS

No. 5H74

Small curls to be worn at the temples. (Not illustrated.)

WHEN ORDERING HAIR GOODS

• When a perfect match is desired, always send a sample, cut from above the ear, in a separate envelope, plainly marked with your name and address. We specialize in matching difficult shades, and both you and your customers can be assured of perfect satisfaction.

FOR COMPLETE HAIR GOODS PRICES SEE PAGE 126

Gibbs French Wigs, 1935

► *Listerine, 1931*

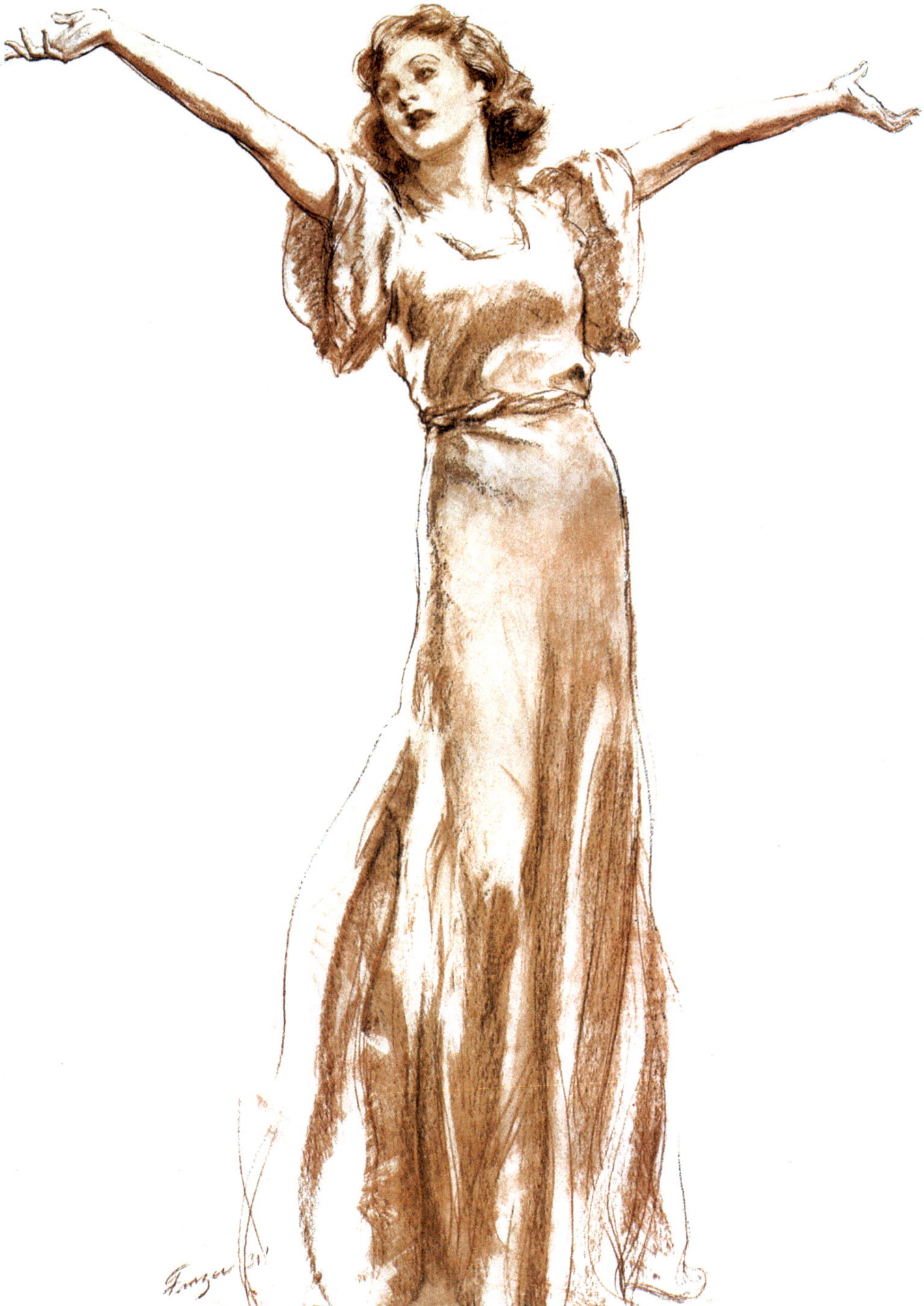

YOU 5,000,000 WOMEN WHO WANT TO GET MARRIED:

How's Your Breath Today?

5,000,000 young women become of marriageable age this year . . . How many of them, we wonder, will make the grade? One thing is certain; they can't expect to attract and hold men if they have halitosis (unpleasant breath). It nullifies every other charm. Everyone is likely to have halitosis at one time or another. When that time comes, you won't realize it, because halitosis does not announce itself to its victim. Why risk offending, when Listerine will put you on the safe side? Simply rinse the mouth with it. Every morning and every night, and between times before meeting others. Listerine instantly halts fermentation, the cause of 90% of mouth odors; then gets rid of the odors themselves. The breath becomes sweet and agreeable. Lambert Pharmacal Co., St. Louis, Mo.

USE LISTERINE BEFORE ALL SOCIAL ENGAGEMENTS

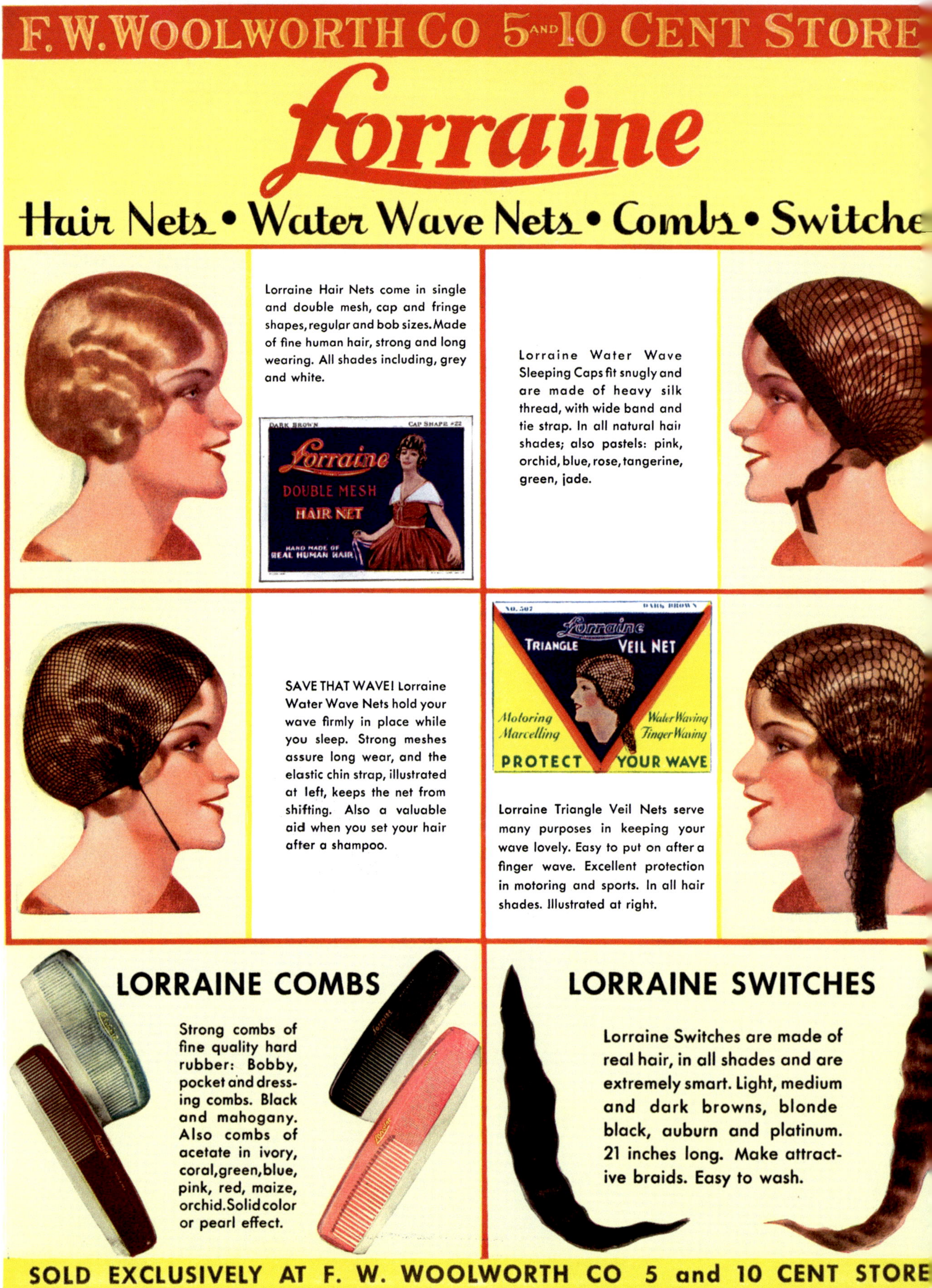
F. W. WOOLWORTH CO 5 AND 10 CENT STORE
Lorraine
Hair Nets • Water Wave Nets • Combs • Switche
Lorraine Hair Nets come in single and double mesh, cap and fringe shapes, regular and bob sizes. Made of fine human hair, strong and long wearing. All shades including, grey and white.
DARK BROWN
CAP SHAPE #22
Lorraine
DOUBLE MESH
HAIR NET
HAND MADE OF REAL HUMAN HAIR
Lorraine Water Wave Sleeping Caps fit snugly and are made of heavy silk thread, with wide band and tie strap. In all natural hair shades; also pastels: pink, orchid, blue, rose, tangerine, green, jade.
SAVE THAT WAVE! Lorraine Water Wave Nets hold your wave firmly in place while you sleep. Strong meshes assure long wear, and the elastic chin strap, illustrated at left, keeps the net from shifting. Also a valuable aid when you set your hair after a shampoo.
NO. 507
DARK BROWN
Lorraine
TRIANGLE
VEIL NET
Motoring
Marcelling
Water Waving
Finger Waving
PROTECT
YOUR WAVE
Lorraine Triangle Veil Nets serve many purposes in keeping your wave lovely. Easy to put on after a finger wave. Excellent protection in motoring and sports. In all hair shades. Illustrated at right.
LORRAINE COMBS
Strong combs of fine quality hard rubber: Bobby, pocket and dressing combs. Black and mahogany. Also combs of acetate in ivory, coral, green, blue, pink, red, maize, orchid. Solid color or pearl effect.
LORRAINE SWITCHES
Lorraine Switches are made of real hair, in all shades and are extremely smart. Light, medium and dark browns, blonde black, auburn and platinum. 21 inches long. Make attractive braids. Easy to wash.
SOLD EXCLUSIVELY AT F. W. WOOLWORTH CO 5 and 10 CENT STORE

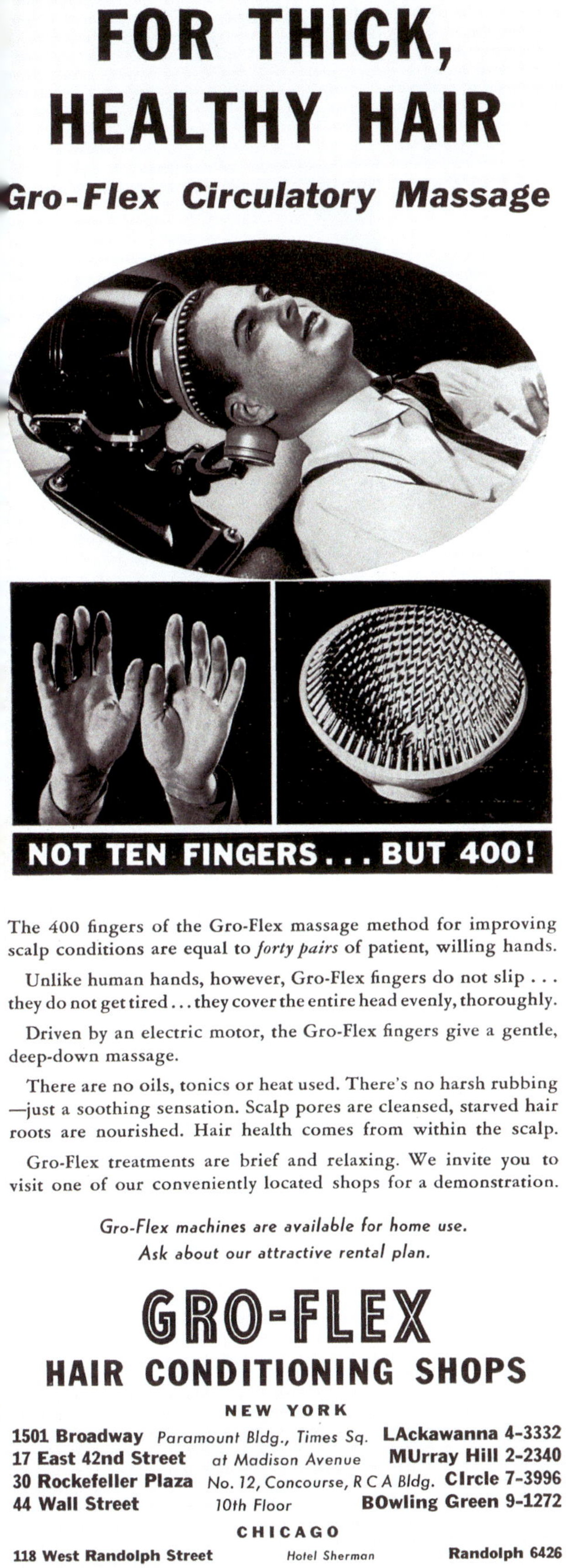

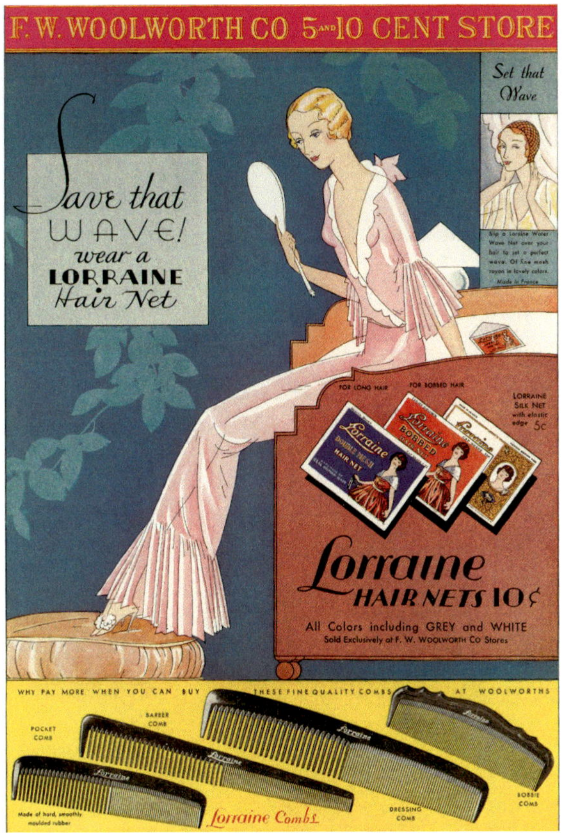

Lorraine, 1932

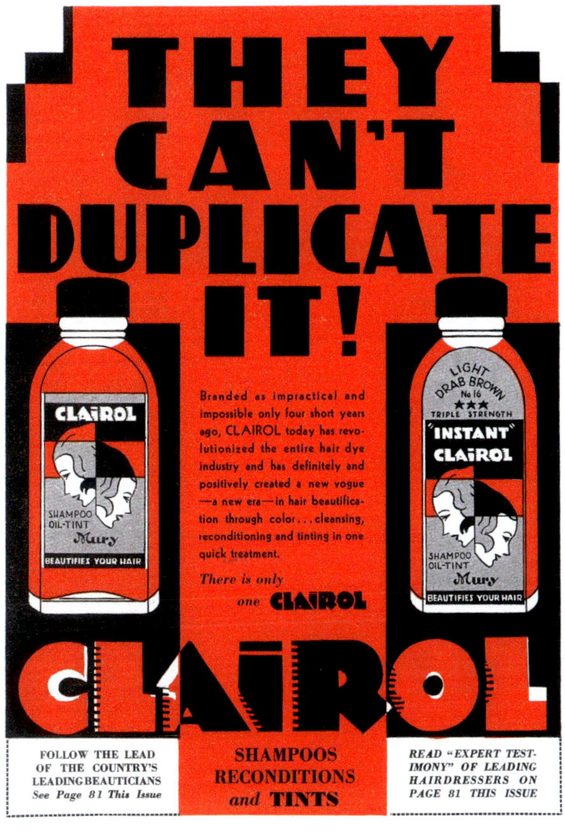

Lorraine, 1935 ◄ Gro-Flex, 1935

Clairol, 1936

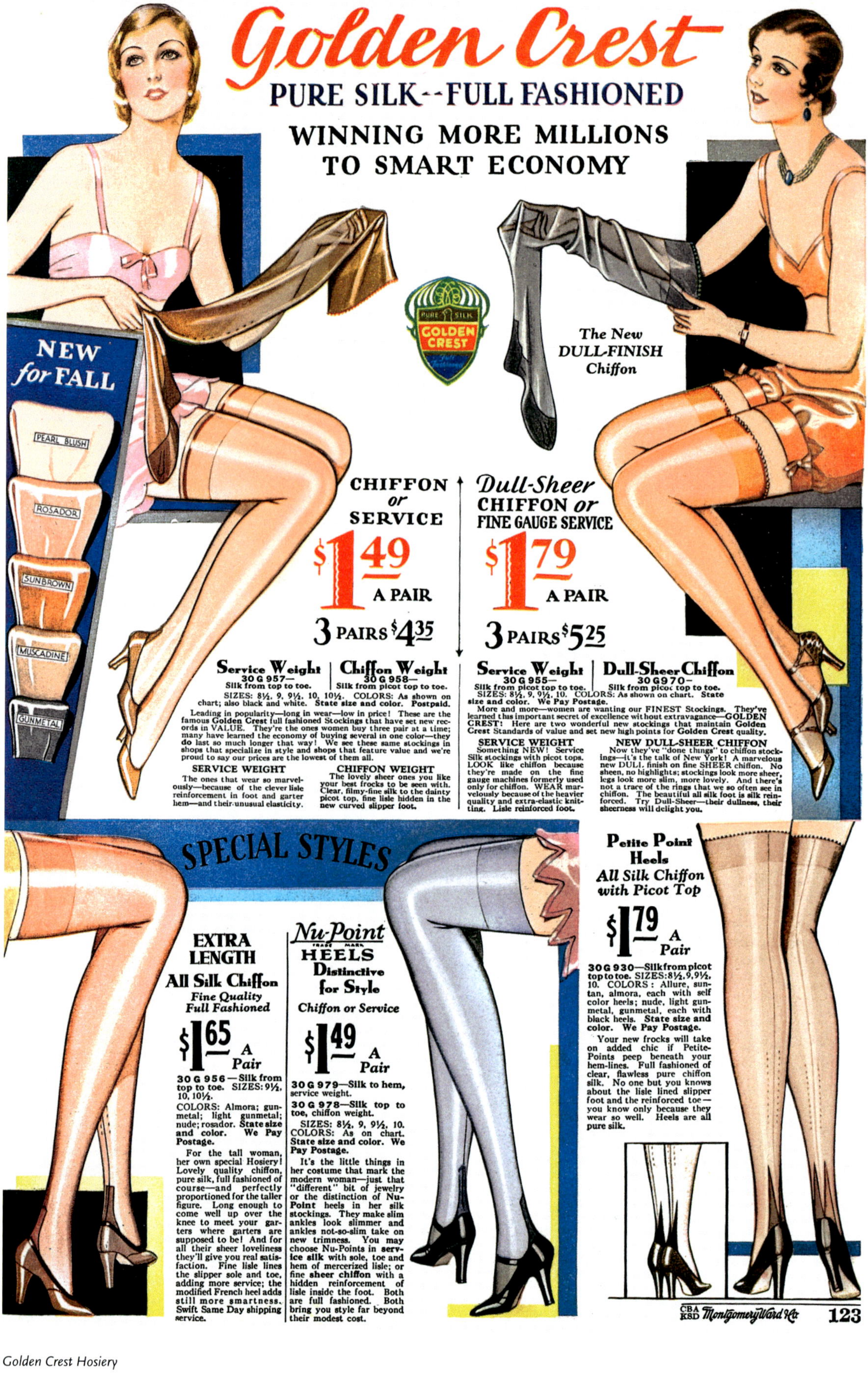

Golden Crest Hosiery

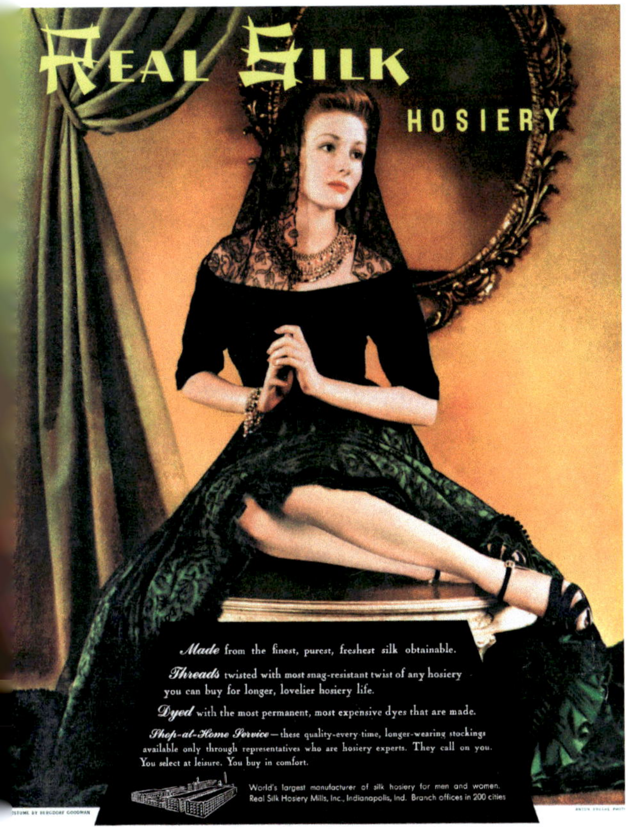

Real Silk Hosiery, 1939

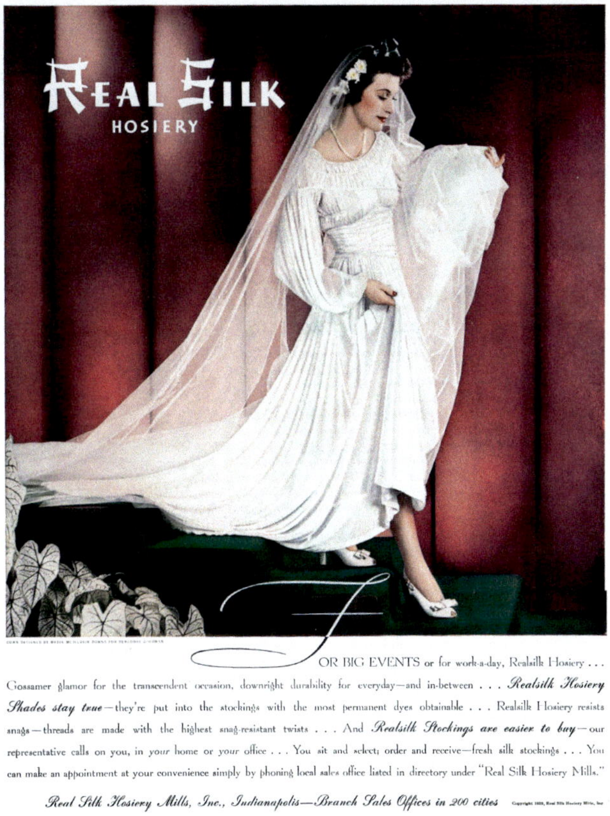

Real Silk Hosiery, 1939

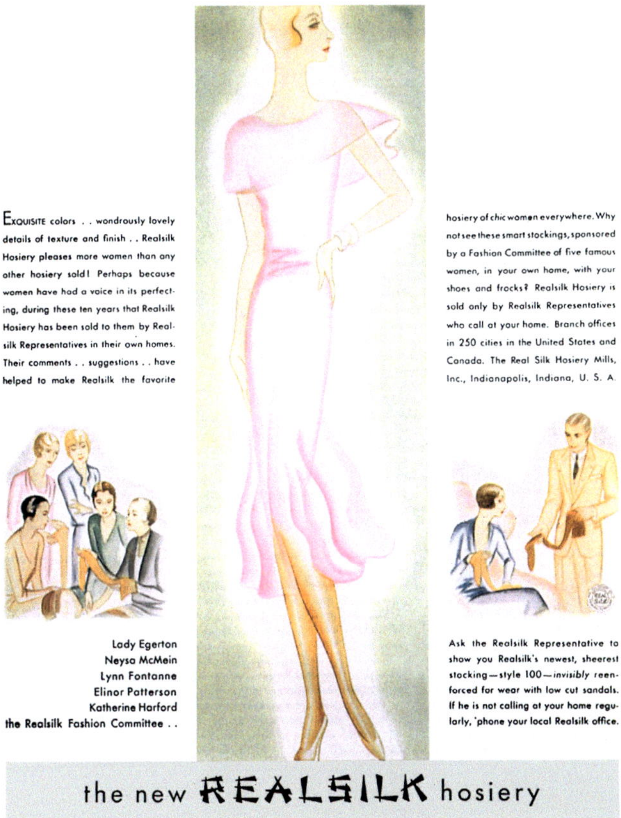

Real Silk Hosiery, 1930

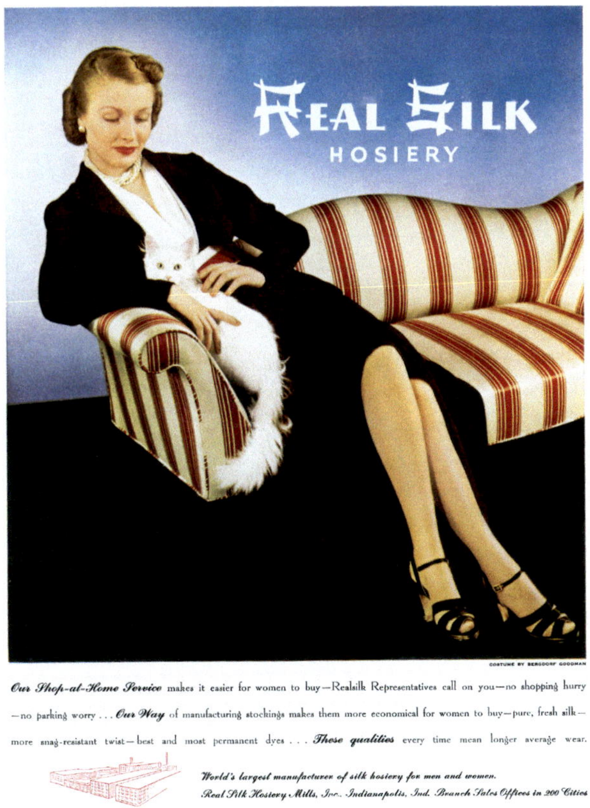

Real Silk Hosiery, 1939

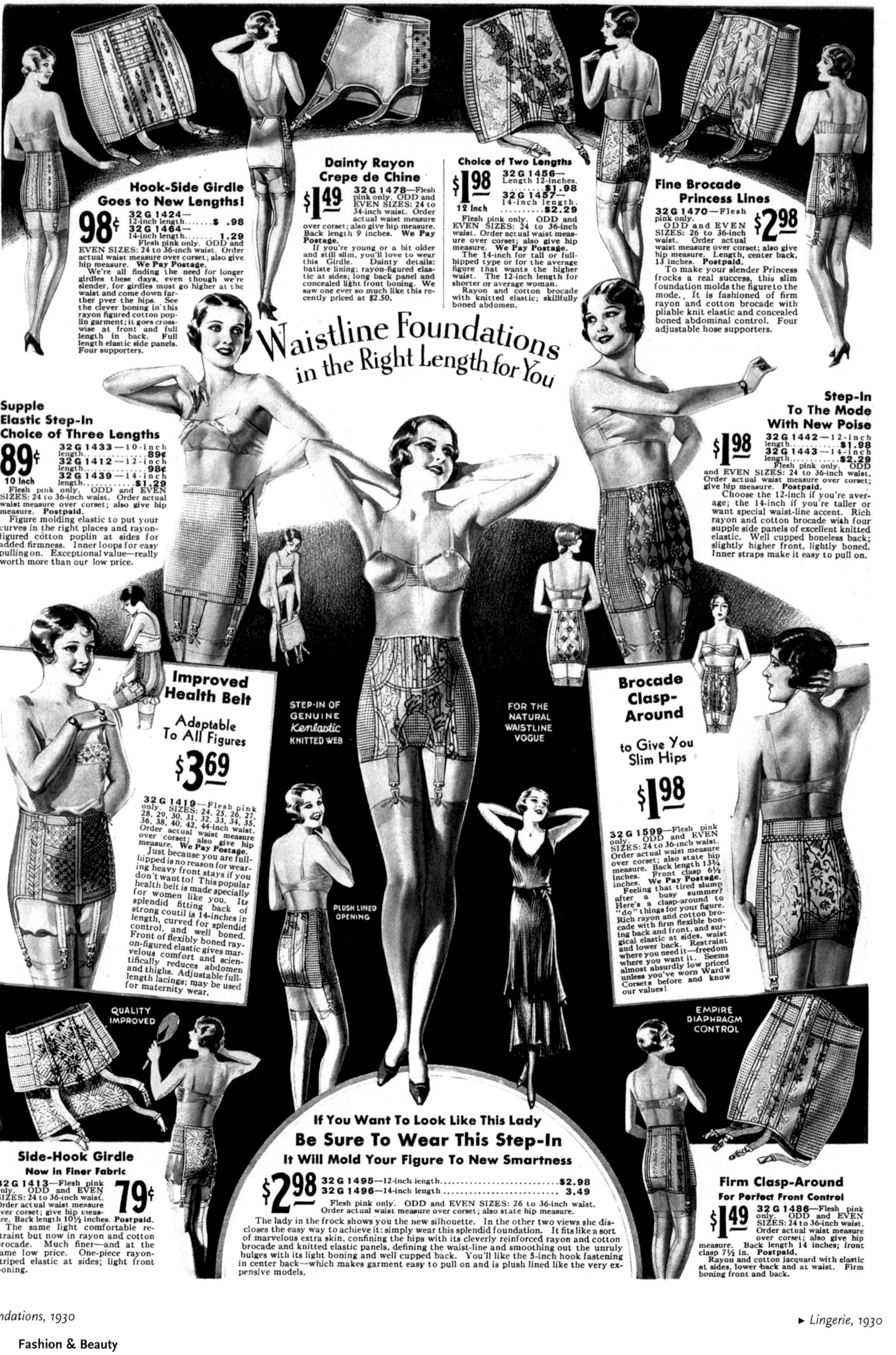

Foundations, 1930

► *Lingerie, 1930*

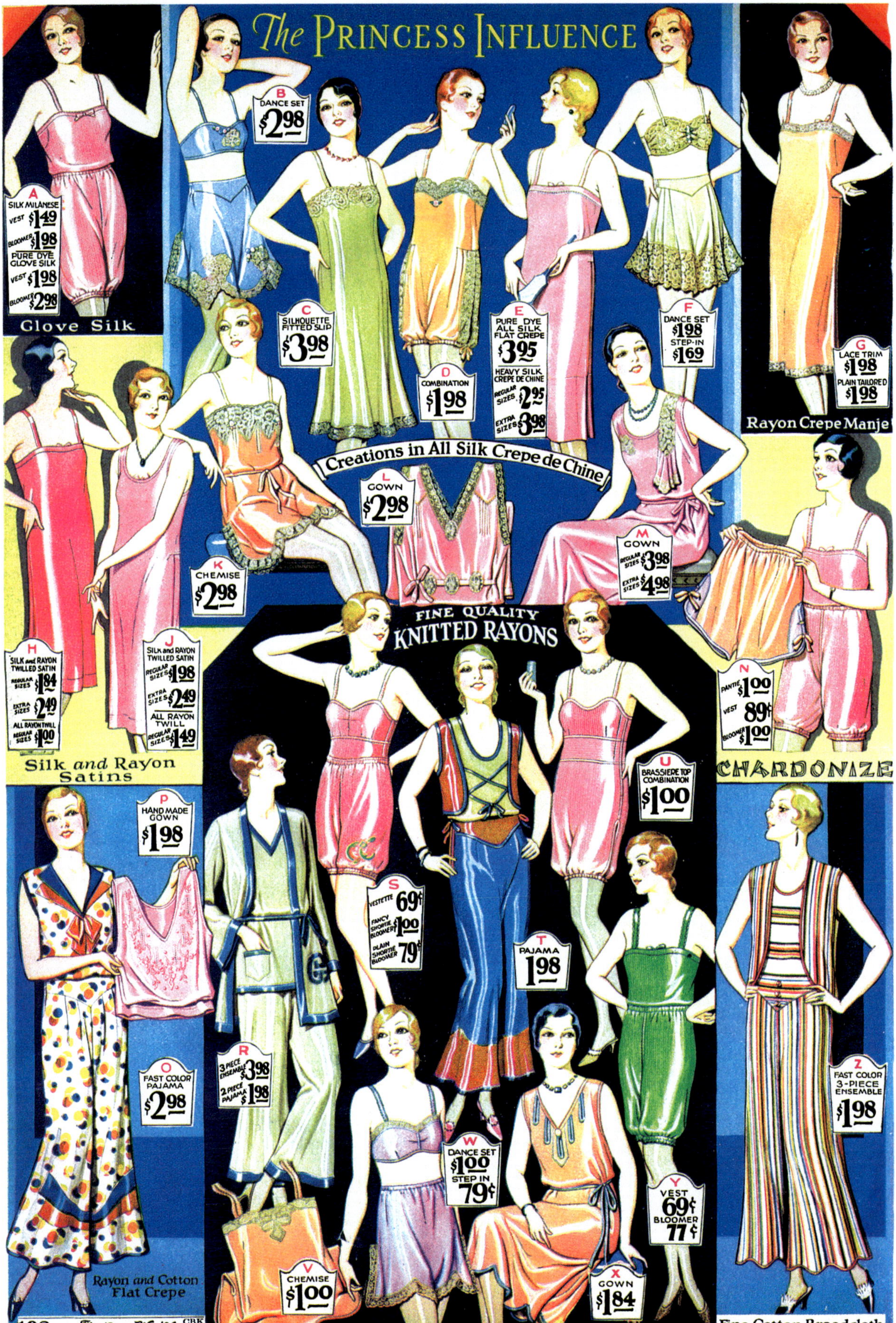
The PRINCESS INFLUENCE
A
SILK MILANESE
VEST $1.49
BLOOMER $1.98
PURE DYE GLOVE SILK
VEST $1.98
BLOOMER $2.98
Glove Silk
B
DANCE SET
$2.98
C
SILHOUETTE FITTED SLIP
$3.98
D
COMBINATION
$1.98
E
PURE DYE ALL SILK FLAT CREPE
$3.95
HEAVY SILK CREPE DE CHINE
REGULAR SIZES $2.95
EXTRA SIZES $3.98
F
DANCE SET
$1.98
STEP-IN
$1.69
G
LACE TRIM
$1.98
PLAIN TAILORED
$1.98
Rayon Crepe Manje
Creations in All Silk Crepe de Chine
L
GOWN
$2.98
K
CHEMISE
$2.98
M
GOWN
REGULAR SIZES $3.98
EXTRA SIZES $4.98
H
SILK and RAYON TWILLED SATIN
REGULAR SIZES $1.84
EXTRA SIZES $2.49
ALL RAYON TWILL
REGULAR SIZES $1.00
J
SILK and RAYON TWILLED SATIN
REGULAR SIZES $1.98
EXTRA SIZES $2.49
ALL RAYON TWILL
REGULAR SIZES $1.49
Silk and Rayon Satins
FINE QUALITY
KNITTED RAYONS
N
PANTIE $1.00
VEST 89¢
BLOOMER $1.00
CHARDONIZE
P
HAND MADE GOWN
$1.98
U
BRASSIERE TOP COMBINATION
$1.00
S
VESTETTE 69¢
FANCY SHORTIE BLOOMER $1.00
PLAIN SHORTIE BLOOMER 79¢
T
PAJAMA
1.98
R
3 PIECE ENSEMBLE $3.98
2 PIECE PAJAMA $1.98
O
FAST COLOR PAJAMA
$2.98
Z
FAST COLOR 3-PIECE ENSEMBLE
$1.98
W
DANCE SET
$1.00
STEP IN
79¢
Y
VEST
69¢
BLOOMER
77¢
V
CHEMISE
$1.00
X
GOWN
$1.84
Rayon and Cotton Flat Crepe
Fine Cotton Broadcloth

MUNSING Wear presents Foundette

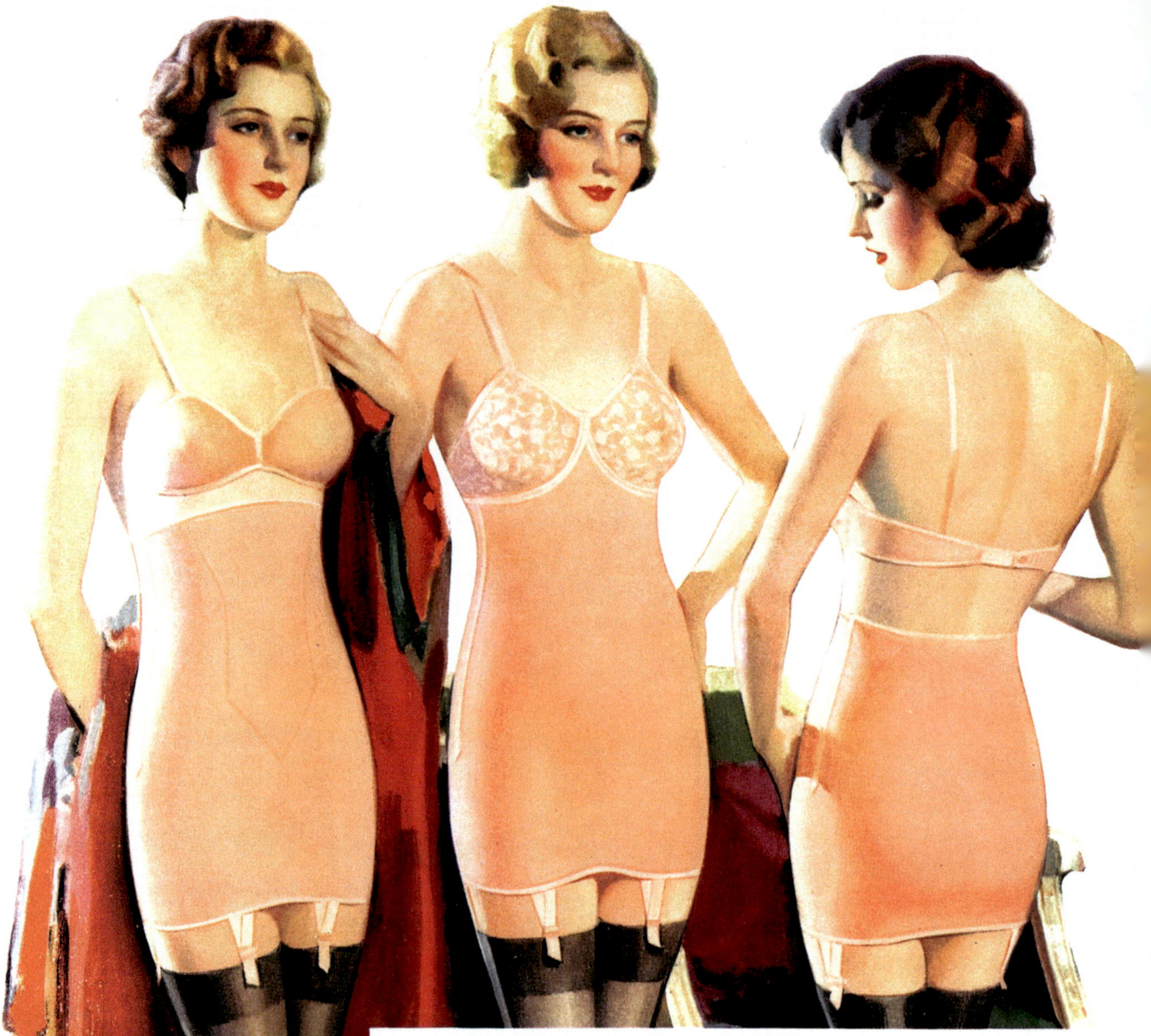

Brand New Foundation Garments of a Bra New Fabric, Invented by MUNSINGWEAR

YOU'VE never seen step-in girdles and foundation garments quite like these . . . for nothing like them has ever been created! Foundettes slim the hips, trim the waist, flatten the diaphragm and smooth the silhouette into smart and lovely lines. Yet, you've never worn anything quite so comfortable! Fashioned of specially processed two-way-stretch fabric...invented by Munsingwear...F dettes will wash marvelously and wear v derfully. They won't pull away from seams or ravel back or curl. You'll like M singwear Foundettes for slimmer figures. they're priced for slimmer purses. See t new Foundettes at a Munsingwear de near you. Munsingwear, Minneapolis.

Munsingwear makes all styles of smart undergarments in all types of fabrics. For men, women and children.

UNDERWEAR · WATERWEAR · HOSIERY
SLEEPING AND LOUNGING GARMENTS · KNIT COATS
PULL-ONS · FOUNDATION GARMENTS

LET MUNSINGWEAR COVER YOU WITH SATISFACTIO

You *can* lose that bulge if *you send us the coupon below*

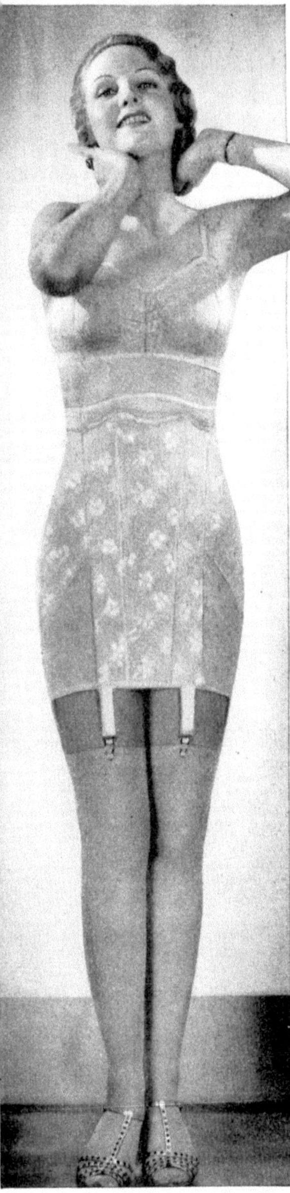

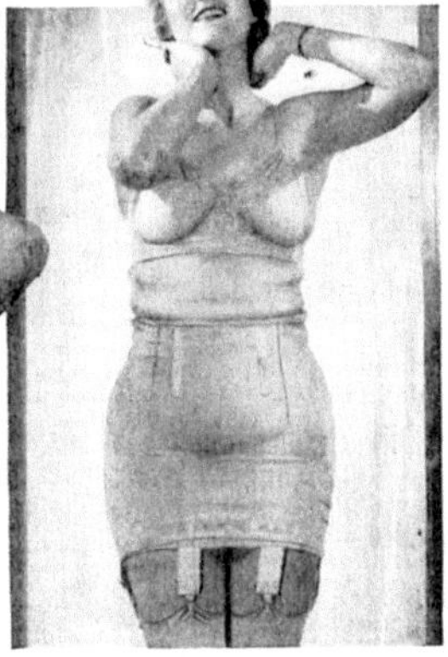

Above, note the startling proof of the sagging of the whole figure in the ordinary corset. At left, the same woman photographed the very same day in her Spencer. Observe how much longer and slimmer all the lines of her figure look.

YOU have a figure problem . . . Why not find out about a Spencer now?

It is human nature to put things off. Women often write us saying that they had intended to ask our advice about some unlovely bulge but put it off from month to month. Then some discomfort forced them to send in the coupon for advice about their figure problem. When they experience the blissful comfort of a Spencer designed exclusively for them, they invariably exclaim, "Why didn't I find out about a Spencer long ago?"

Have a Spencer designed to give needed support for tired muscles and smooth away every bulge. Your Spencer will effectively correct any figure fault because every section, every line is designed, cut and made to solve your figure problem and yours only. Spencers are light and flexible yet *every Spencer is guaranteed to keep its lovely lines so long as it is worn!*

Have a figure analysis—free

Have you ever had a Spencer Corsetiere make a study of your figure? At any time most convenient for you an intelligent woman, trained in the Spencer designer's methods of figure analysis, will call at your home. Do not delay. A study of your figure will cost you nothing. Stop experimenting. Prices depend on materials selected. A wide range to suit every purse.

Send for interesting free booklet "Your Figure Problem"

Look in your telephone book under "Spencer Corsetiere" and call your nearest corsetiere or send us the coupon below for booklet. This will not obligate you in any way.

Copyright, 1937, Spencer Corset Co., Inc.

Write Anne Spencer

for personal advice FREE on figure faults checked here.

November, 1937

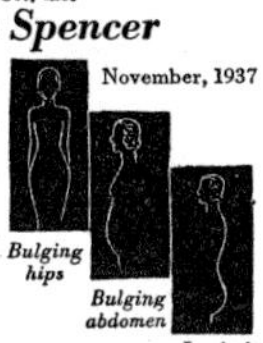

Bulging hips

Bulging abdomen

Lordosis backline

Anne Spencer,
Spencer Corset Co., Inc.,
135 Derby Avenue,
New Haven, Connecticut.

Do You Want to Make Money?

Ambitious women may find business openings as corsetieres in every state. We train you. If interested, check here . . . . . ☐

Name__________

Address__________

Also made in Canada and England at Rock Island, Quebec, and 4 & 5 Old Bond St., London, W. I.

SPENCER ***INDIVIDUALLY DESIGNED*** **CORSETS**

"I had a problem with ugly bulges

until I sent the Spencer coupon below"

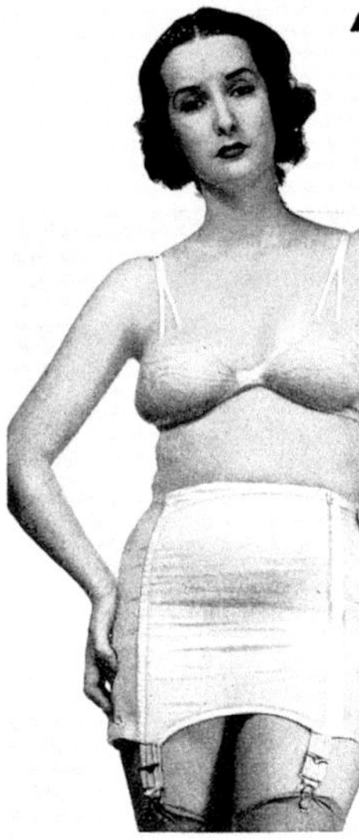

Above: Note the bulging of the hips and abdomen in the ordinary corset. At right the same woman in her Spencer. Hips are slenderized and the abdominal bulge is gone.

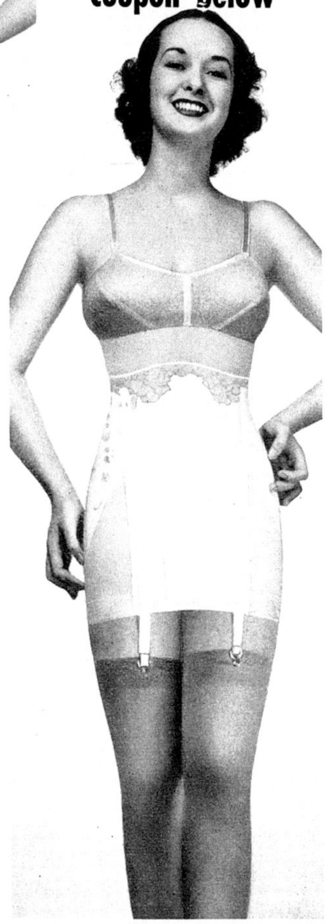

"I've lost inches in my Spencer"

Are your hips a problem? Are you troubled with a bulging abdomen or a "spare-tire" of flesh around the waist line? Then follow the example of the young woman in the photograph and find out what a Spencer can do for you.

Your Spencer corset and brassiere will effectively correct any figure fault because every section, every line is designed, cut and made to solve your figure problem and yours only. Spencers are light and flexible yet *every Spencer is guaranteed to keep its lovely lines as long as it is worn!*

Have a figure analysis—free

At any convenient time, a Spencer Corsetiere, trained in the Spencer designer's methods of figure analysis, will call at your home. A study of your figure will cost you nothing. Stop experimenting. Prices depend on materials selected. A wide range to suit every purse.

Send for interesting free booklet "Your Figure Problem"

Look in your telephone book under "Spencer Corsetiere" and call your nearest corsetiere or send us the coupon below for booklet. This will not obligate you in any way.

Copyright, 1939, Spencer Corset Co., Inc.

Write Anne Spencer

for personal advice FREE on figure faults checked here.

May 8, 1939

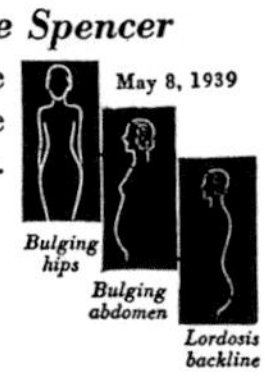

Bulging hips

Bulging abdomen

Lordosis backline

Anne Spencer,
Spencer Corset Co., Inc.
133 Derby Avenue,
New Haven, Connecticut.

Do You Want to Make Money?

Ambitious women may find business openings as corsetieres in every state. We train you. If interested, check here . . . . . ☐

Name__________

Address__________

Also made in Canada and England at Rock Island, Quebec, and 4 & 5 Old Bond St., London, W. I.

SPENCER ***INDIVIDUALLY DESIGNED*** **CORSETS**

Munsing Wear, 1933 ◄ *Spencer Corsets, 1937*

Spencer Corset, 1939

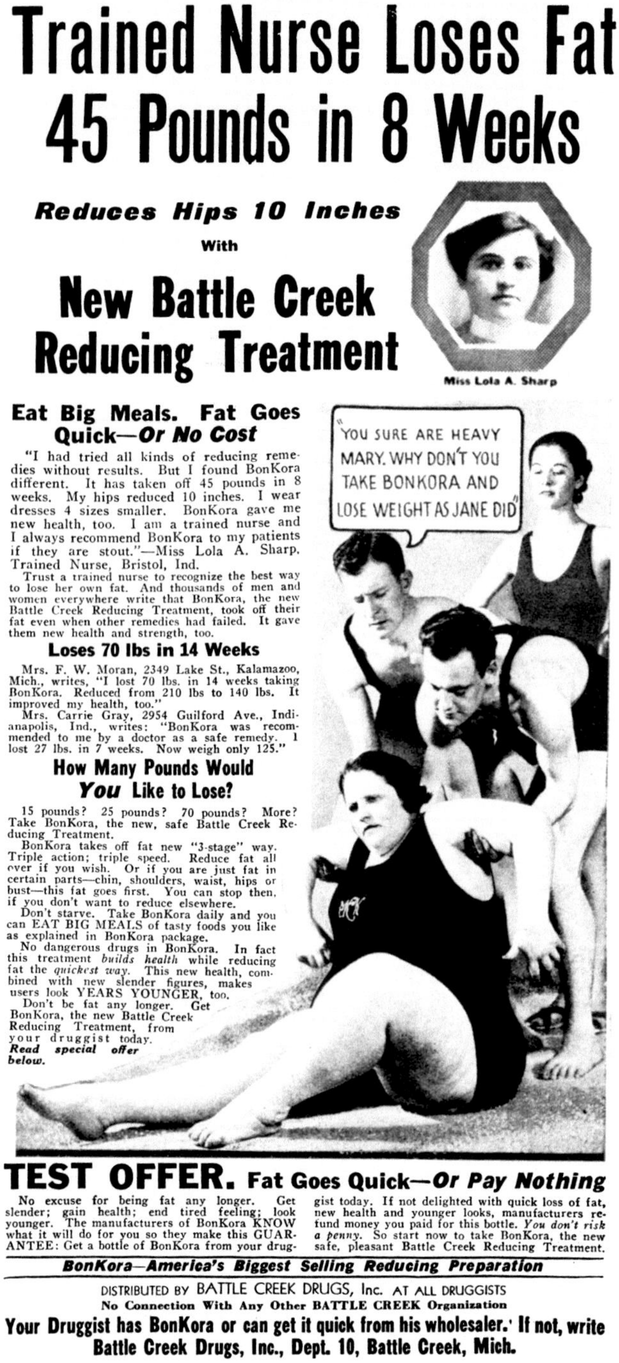

Battle Creek Drugs, 1933

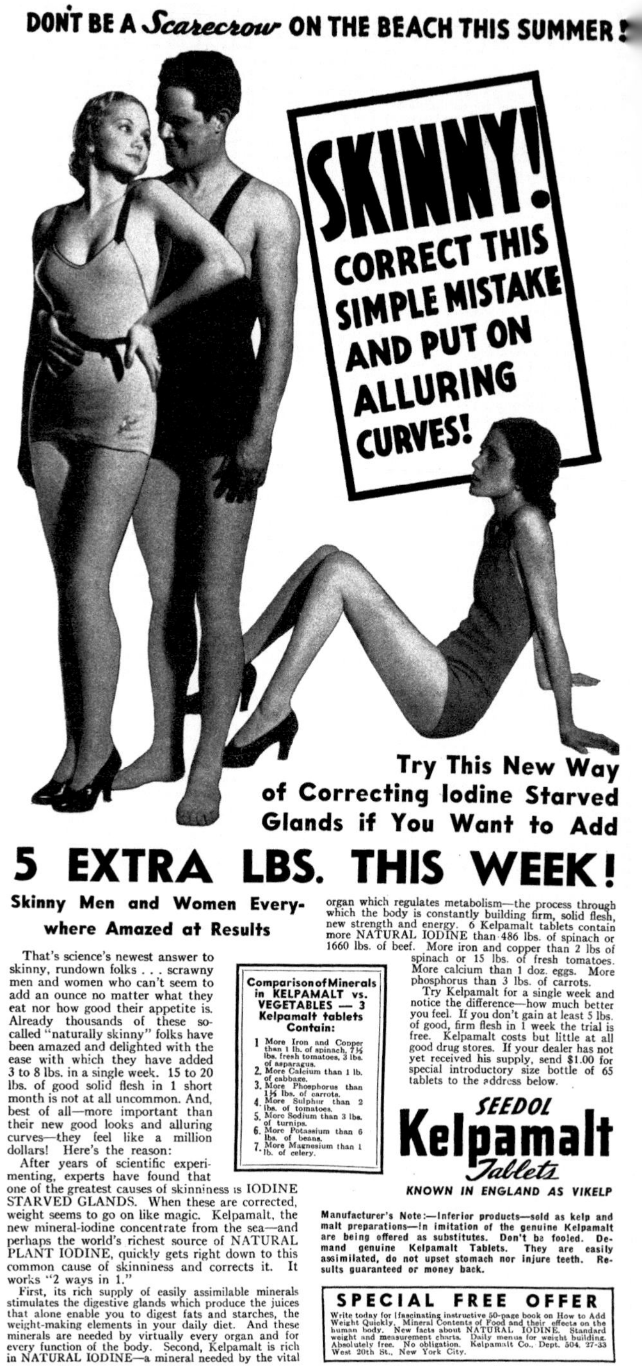

Kelpamalt, 1935

▸ Fabrics

SILVANIA Prints

Tubfast—Thrifty

17¢ A Yard

New cotton Prints as cheerful as a sunny morning, as tubfast as hard wear demands, and a lower price than seems possible!

16 G 3205—Width 36 inches. Patterns as shown. **Order by article number and state pattern number. We Pay Postage.**

GLORIO

Famous Tubfast Prints

38¢ A Yard

One of the best-known "buys" at Ward's—our fine-textured, smartly patterned Glorio Prints. Well-mercerized, amazingly durable—and every year growing more fashionably important! Prim frocks, pajamas, or dress-up rompers. Tubfast cotton.

16 G 3756—Width 36 in. Patterns as shown. **Order by article number and state pattern number Postpaid.**

PINNACLE Tubfast PRINTS

Bright Flower Tints

23¢ A Yard

For that pert afternoon dress or daughter's newest frock, you must have the latest Pinnacle Print! Fast-color cotton.

16 G 3209—Width 36 inches. Patterns as shown. **Order by article number and state pattern number. We Pay Postage.**

PERCALE

Fast to Sun or Tub

17¢ A Yard Postpaid

The always useful Percale, with same fast dyes as in higher priced fabrics.

16 G 3410—Width 36 inches. COLORS: As shown. **State color.**

16 G 3411—Same width and quality as above. **White only. Yard...14¢**

PINNACLE

Fast Color Cloth

23¢ A Yard Postpaid

Charming colors for both tiny frocks and grown-up ones. Fast to sun or suds!

16 G 3412—Width 36 inches. COLORS: As shown. **State color.**

16 G 3413—Same width and quality as above. **White only.........19¢**

BRIGHT COTTONS are the VOGUE

They're Serviceable and Thrift-Priced

LEVIATHAN CHAMBRAY

A Big Seller A Huge Value

12¢ A Yard

Well-named is this Leviathan Chambray! We sold over a million yards last year. Big value any way you look at it—a superior quality in sturdy cotton yarns, a fascinating choice of colors, a price that is a real surprise. Lots of those bright smocks, house dresses and cute playsuits you see are of this same Ward's chambray.

16 G 3115—Width 36 inches. COLORS: As shown. Order by article number and state pattern number. Postpaid.

GINGHAM

A Yard-Wide Thrift

15¢ A Yard

Just as practical as it is wide! Bright checks for cover-all aprons—gay plaids for small folks' things. With all the new interest in Gingham, you can't do without this at our economy price.

16 G 3124—Width 36 inches. **Order by article number and state pattern number. We Pay Postage.**

APRON GINGHAM

Better Grade at Small Cost

11¢ A Yard

You can't compare this Gingham with others—so low its close-marked price, so tremendously useful are its neat checks.

16 G 3107—Width 32 inches. COLORS: As shown. State color.

Firm CHAMBRAY Shirting

Ward's Countryside Quality

14¢ A Yard

A famous quality at Ward's famous price. Shirts, house-dresses, play-suits of this closely woven soil resisting Chambray will wear and keep its good appearance.

16 G 3270—Width 28 inches. **Order by article number and state pattern number. Postpaid.**

Guaranteed Fast Colors

Fast Color ZEPHYR GINGHAM—Our Finest

Fully Mercerized—Beautifully Soft-Spun

31¢ A Yard

Now that gingham has started going to all the best places, women are demanding the BEST—our own permanent-finish ZEPHYR. A fine yarn Gingham beautifully mercerized and sheer. Guaranteed fast color of course. Patterns from grown-up plaids down to the tiniest of baby-checks.

16 G 3161—Width 32 inches. **Order by article number and state pattern number. We Pay Postage.**

Famous AMOSKEAG 19000 Range Gingham

A TUBFAST FABRIC THAT YOU'LL LIKE

For Frocks—Aprons—Curtains

17¢ A Yard

A Gingham for a dozen things, in a quality famous for generations—Plaids for play, checks for cheerful curtains, soft shades for street. A big gingham value that brings you a saving with every yard.

16 G 3129—Width 32 inches. PATTERNS: As shown. **Order by article number and state pattern number. We Pay Postage.**

Style and Beauty

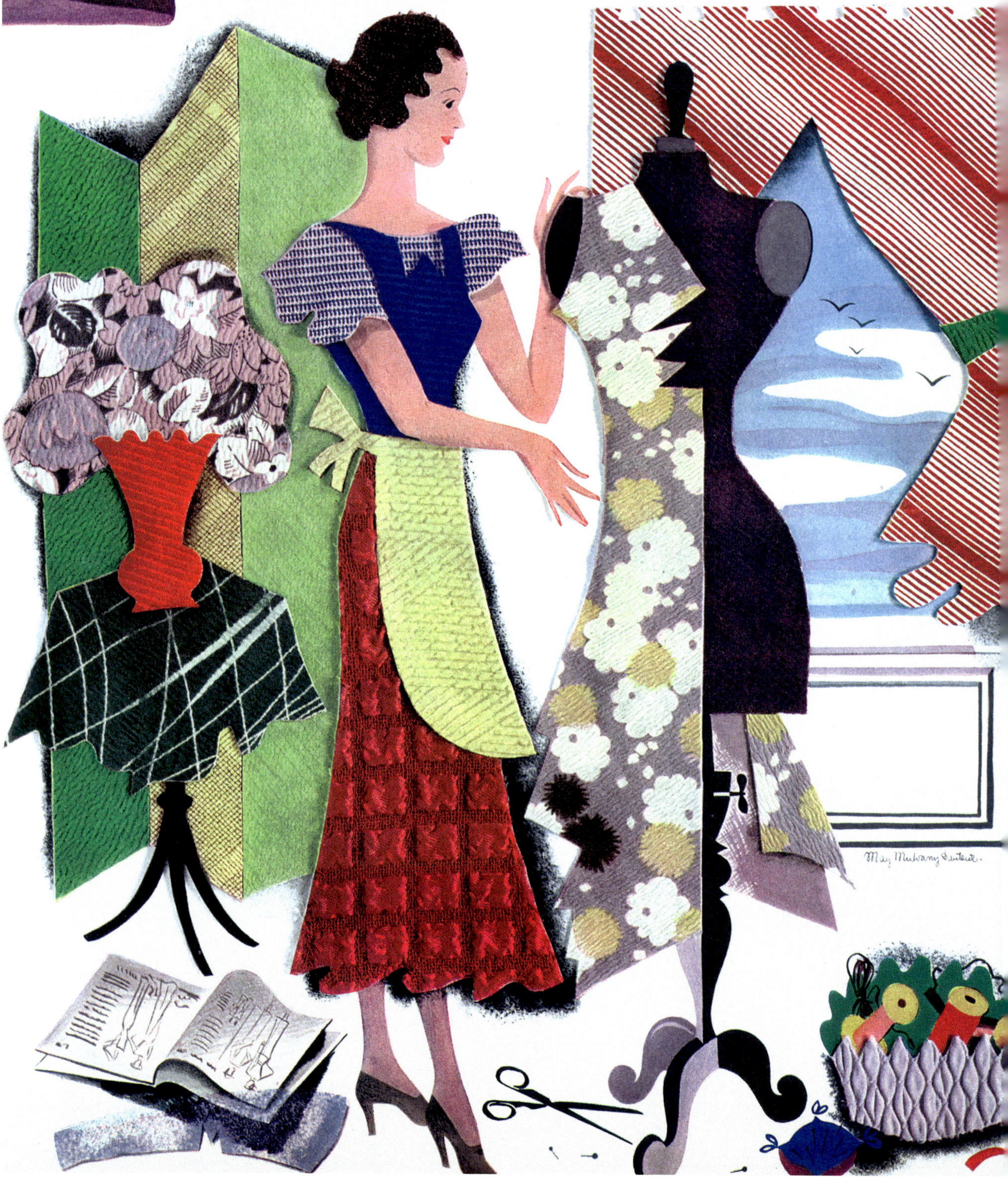

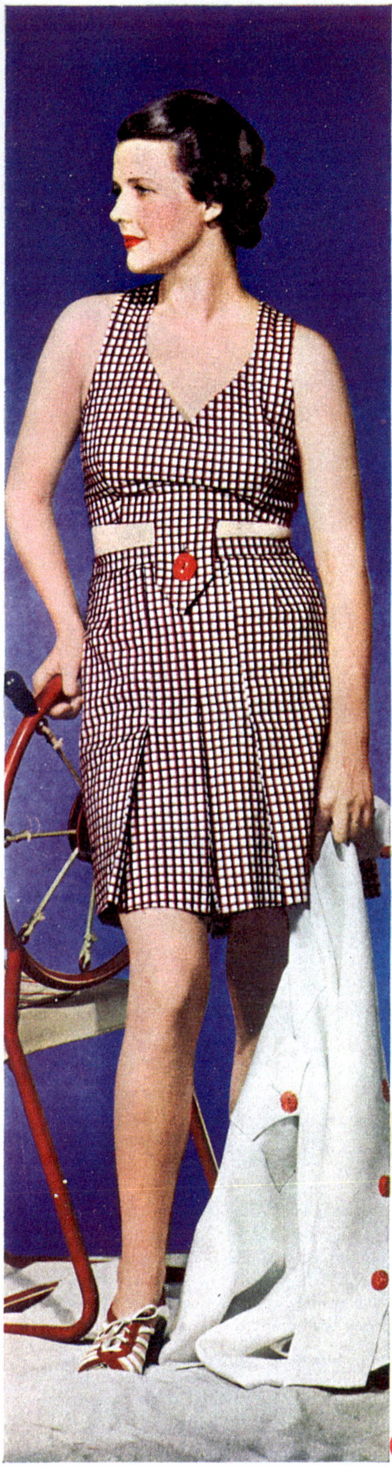

SIMPLICITY PATTERN 1776—15c complete. Shorts with button-on top, of seersucker gingham. Separate wrap-around skirt of white linen tweed.

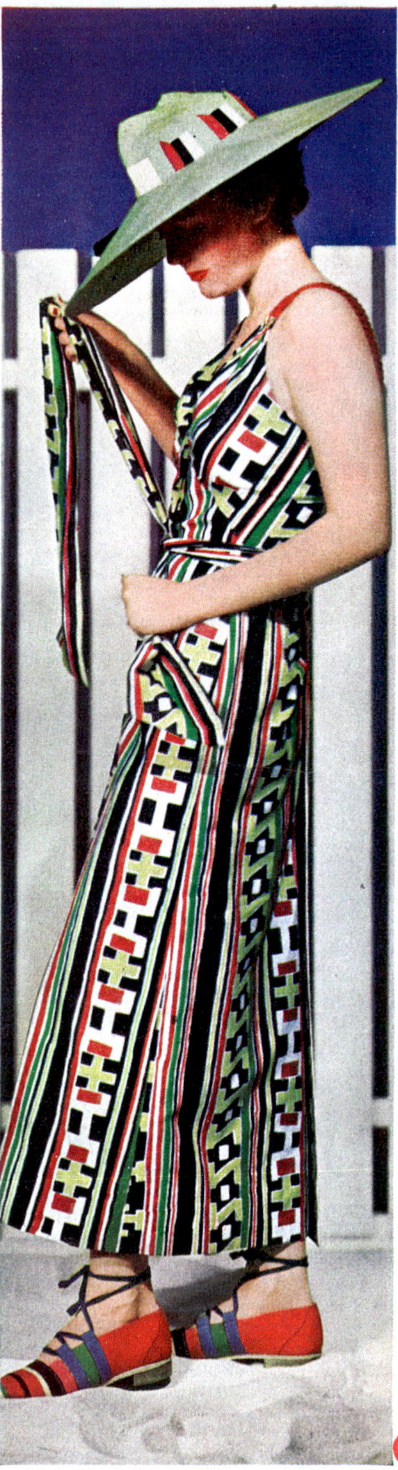

SIMPLICITY PATTERN 1773—15c complete. Tie-around and bareback play-dress of bright cotton-print with amusing laundry rope suspenders.

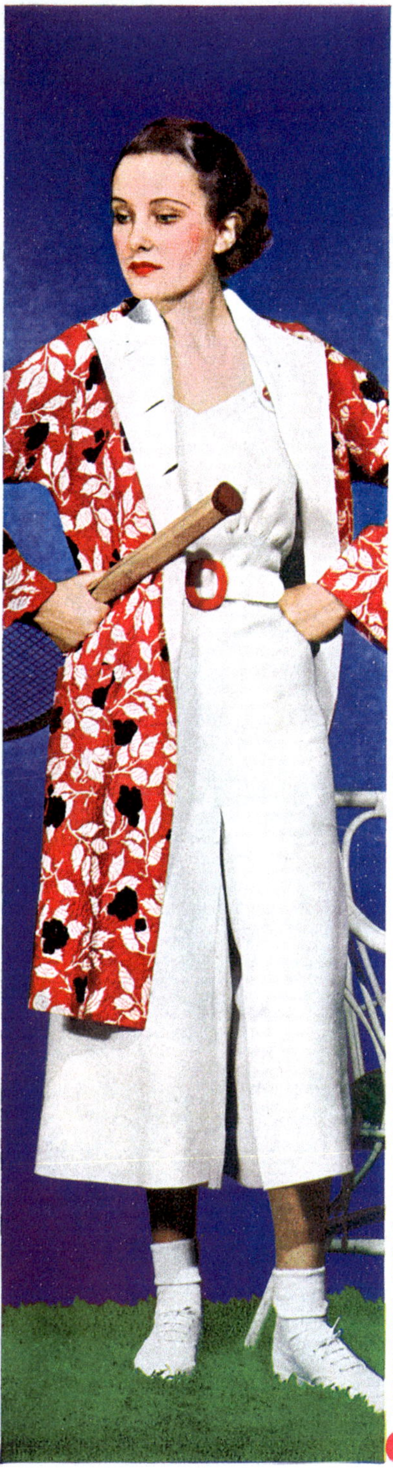

SIMPLICITY CUSTOMODE PATTERN 8217—25c complete. Divided-skirt, white linen sports dress and quilted cotton coat faced with the linen.

Patterns

Preview these play-clothes, made up with Simplicity Patterns, in the better stores that sell the patterns . . . you'll find these stores clear across the country. And remember, in any event—"you're always in style when you dress with Simplicity."

McCall's, 1933 ◂

Simplicity Patterns, 1935

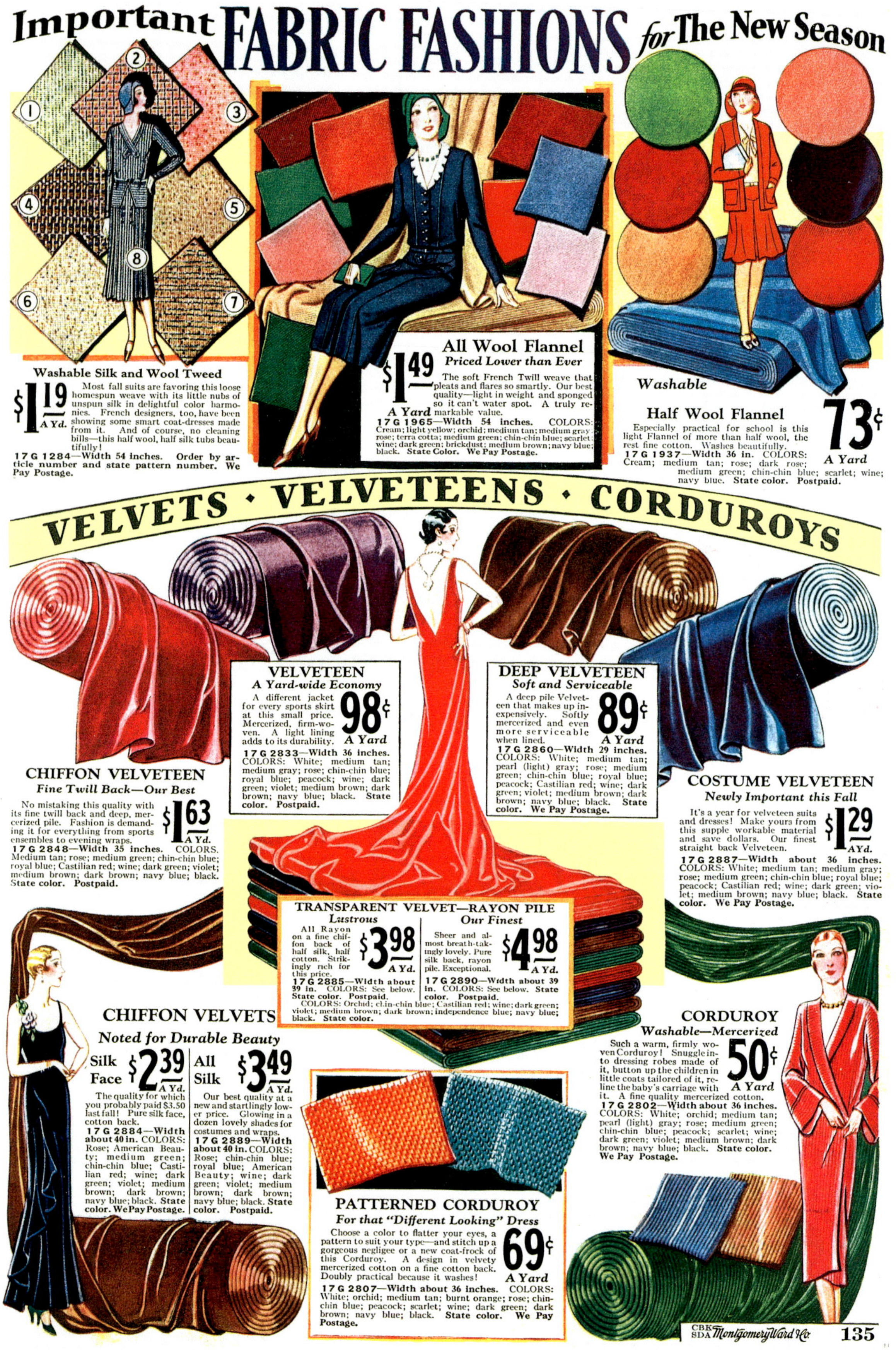
Important FABRIC FASHIONS for The New Season
1
2
3
4
5
6
7
8
Washable Silk and Wool Tweed
$1.19 A Yd.
Most fall suits are favoring this loose homespun weave with its little nubs of unspun silk in delightful color harmonies. French designers, too, have been showing some smart coat-dresses made from it. And of course, no cleaning bills—this half wool, half silk tubs beautifully!
17 G 1284—Width 54 inches. Order by article number and state pattern number. We Pay Postage.
All Wool Flannel
Priced Lower than Ever
$1.49 A Yard
The soft French Twill weave that pleats and flares so smartly. Our best quality—light in weight and sponged so it can't water spot. A truly remarkable value.
17 G 1965—Width 54 inches. COLORS: Cream; light yellow; orchid; medium tan; medium gray; rose; terra cotta; medium green; chin-chin blue; scarlet; wine; dark green; brickdust; medium brown; navy blue; black. State Color. We Pay Postage.
Washable
Half Wool Flannel
73¢ A Yard
Especially practical for school is this light Flannel of more than half wool, the rest fine cotton. Washes beautifully.
17 G 1937—Width 36 in. COLORS: Cream; medium tan; rose; dark rose; medium green; chin-chin blue; scarlet; wine; navy blue. State color. Postpaid.
VELVETS · VELVETEENS · CORDUROYS
VELVETEEN
A Yard-wide Economy
98¢ A Yard
A different jacket for every sports skirt at this small price. Mercerized, firm-woven. A light lining adds to its durability.
17 G 2833—Width 36 inches. COLORS: White; medium tan; medium gray; rose; chin-chin blue; royal blue; peacock; wine; dark green; violet; medium brown; dark brown; navy blue; black. State color. Postpaid.
DEEP VELVETEEN
Soft and Serviceable
89¢ A Yard
A deep pile Velveteen that makes up inexpensively. Softly mercerized and even more serviceable when lined.
17 G 2860—Width 29 inches. COLORS: White; medium tan; pearl (light) gray; rose; medium green; chin-chin blue; royal blue; peacock; Castilian red; wine; dark green; violet; medium brown; dark brown; navy blue; black. State color. We Pay Postage.
CHIFFON VELVETEEN
Fine Twill Back—Our Best
$1.63 A Yd.
No mistaking this quality with its fine twill back and deep, mercerized pile. Fashion is demanding it for everything from sports ensembles to evening wraps.
17 G 2848—Width 35 inches. COLORS. Medium tan; rose; medium green; chin-chin blue; royal blue; Castilian red; wine; dark green; violet; medium brown; dark brown; navy blue; black. State color. Postpaid.
COSTUME VELVETEEN
Newly Important this Fall
$1.29 A Yd.
It's a year for velveteen suits and dresses! Make yours from this supple workable material and save dollars. Our finest straight back Velveteen.
17 G 2887—Width about 36 inches. COLORS: White; medium tan; medium gray; rose; medium green; chin-chin blue; royal blue; peacock; Castilian red; wine; dark green; violet; medium brown; navy blue; black. State color. We Pay Postage.
TRANSPARENT VELVET—RAYON PILE
Lustrous
$3.98 A Yd.
All Rayon on a fine chiffon back of half silk, half cotton. Strikingly rich for this price.
17 G 2885—Width about 39 in. COLORS: See below. State color. Postpaid.
Our Finest
$4.98 A Yd.
Sheer and almost breath-takingly lovely. Pure silk back, rayon pile. Exceptional.
17 G 2890—Width about 39 in. COLORS: See below. State color. Postpaid.
COLORS: Orchid; chin-chin blue; Castilian red; wine; dark green; violet; medium brown; dark brown; independence blue; navy blue; black. State color.
CHIFFON VELVETS
Noted for Durable Beauty
Silk Face $2.39 A Yd.
The quality for which you probably paid $3.50 last fall! Pure silk face, cotton back.
17 G 2884—Width about 40 in. COLORS: Rose; American Beauty; medium green; chin-chin blue; Castilian red; wine; dark green; violet; medium brown; dark brown; navy blue; black. State color. We Pay Postage.
All Silk $3.49 A Yd.
Our best quality at a new and startlingly lower price. Glowing in a dozen lovely shades for costumes and wraps.
17 G 2889—Width about 40 in. COLORS: Rose; chin-chin blue; royal blue; American Beauty; wine; dark green; violet; medium brown; dark brown; navy blue; black. State color. Postpaid.
CORDUROY
Washable—Mercerized
50¢ A Yard
Such a warm, firmly woven Corduroy! Snuggle into dressing robes made of it, button up the children in little coats tailored of it, reline the baby's carriage with it. A fine quality mercerized cotton.
17 G 2802—Width about 36 inches. COLORS: White; orchid; medium tan; pearl (light) gray; rose; medium green; chin-chin blue; peacock; scarlet; wine; dark green; violet; medium brown; dark brown; navy blue; black. State color. We Pay Postage.
PATTERNED CORDUROY
For that "Different Looking" Dress
69¢ A Yard
Choose a color to flatter your eyes, a pattern to suit your type—and stitch up a gorgeous negligee or a new coat-frock of this Corduroy. A design in velvety mercerized cotton on a fine cotton back. Doubly practical because it washes!
17 G 2807—Width about 36 inches. COLORS: White; orchid; medium tan; burnt orange; rose; chin-chin blue; peacock; scarlet; wine; dark green; dark brown; navy blue; black. State color. We Pay Postage.
CBK SDA Montgomery Ward & Co. 135

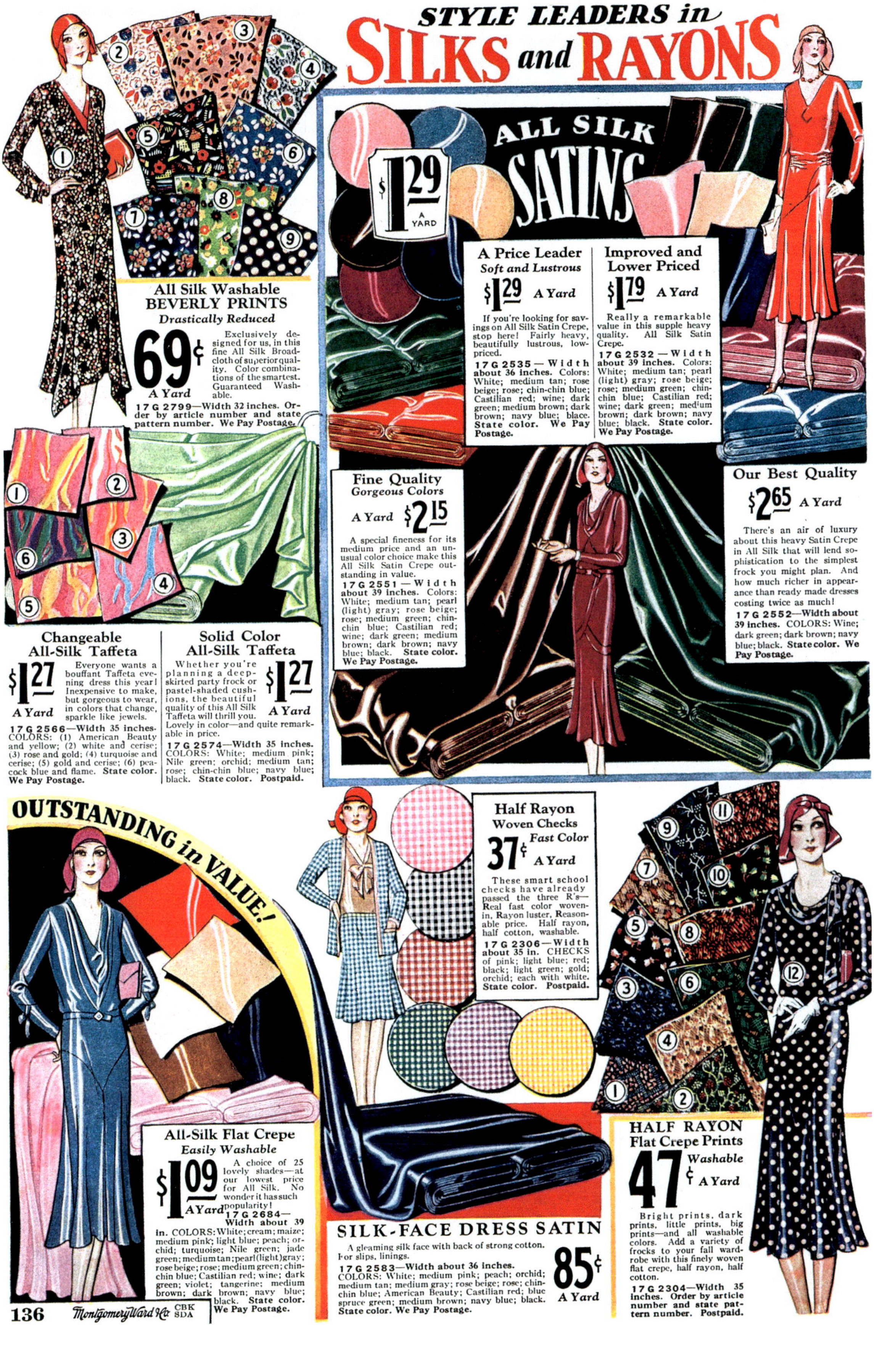

STYLE LEADERS in
SILKS and RAYONS

ALL SILK SATINS

$1.29 A YARD

A Price Leader
Soft and Lustrous

$1.29 A Yard

If you're looking for savings on All Silk Satin Crepe, stop here! Fairly heavy, beautifully lustrous, low-priced.

17 G 2535—Width about 36 inches. Colors: White; medium tan; rose beige; rose; chin-chin blue; Castilian red; wine; dark green; medium brown; dark brown; navy blue; black. **State color. We Pay Postage.**

Improved and Lower Priced

$1.79 A Yard

Really a remarkable value in this supple heavy quality. All Silk Satin Crepe.

17 G 2532—Width about 39 inches. Colors: White; medium tan; pearl (light) gray; rose beige; rose; medium green; chin-chin blue; Castilian red; wine; dark green; medium brown; dark brown; navy blue; black. **State color. We Pay Postage.**

All Silk Washable BEVERLY PRINTS
Drastically Reduced

69¢ A Yard

Exclusively designed for us, in this fine All Silk Broadcloth of superior quality. Color combinations of the smartest. Guaranteed Washable.

17 G 2799—Width 32 inches. Order by article number and state pattern number. We Pay Postage.

Fine Quality
Gorgeous Colors

A Yard $2.15

A special fineness for its medium price and an unusual color choice make this All Silk Satin Crepe outstanding in value.

17 G 2551—Width about 39 inches. Colors: White; medium tan; pearl (light) gray; rose beige; rose; medium green; chin-chin blue; Castilian red; wine; dark green; medium brown; dark brown; navy blue; black. **State color. We Pay Postage.**

Our Best Quality

$2.65 A Yard

There's an air of luxury about this heavy Satin Crepe in All Silk that will lend sophistication to the simplest frock you might plan. And how much richer in appearance than ready made dresses costing twice as much!

17 G 2552—Width about 39 inches. COLORS: Wine; dark green; dark brown; navy blue; black. **State color. We Pay Postage.**

Changeable All-Silk Taffeta

$1.27 A Yard

Everyone wants a bouffant Taffeta evening dress this year! Inexpensive to make, but gorgeous to wear, in colors that change, sparkle like jewels.

17 G 2566—Width 35 inches. COLORS: (1) American Beauty and yellow; (2) white and cerise; (3) rose and gold; (4) turquoise and cerise; (5) gold and cerise; (6) peacock blue and flame. **State color. We Pay Postage.**

Solid Color All-Silk Taffeta

$1.27 A Yard

Whether you're planning a deep-skirted party frock or pastel-shaded cushions, the beautiful quality of this All Silk Taffeta will thrill you. Lovely in color—and quite remarkable in price.

17 G 2574—Width 35 inches. COLORS: White; medium pink; Nile green; orchid; medium tan; rose; chin-chin blue; navy blue; black. **State color. Postpaid.**

OUTSTANDING in VALUE!

Half Rayon Woven Checks

37¢ *Fast Color* A Yard

These smart school checks have already passed the three R's—Real fast color woven-in, Rayon luster, Reasonable price. Half rayon, half cotton, washable.

17 G 2306—Width about 35 in. CHECKS of pink; light blue; red; black; light green; gold; orchid; each with white. **State color. Postpaid.**

All-Silk Flat Crepe
Easily Washable

$1.09 A Yard

A choice of 25 lovely shades—at our lowest price for All Silk. No wonder it has such popularity!

17 G 2684—Width about 39 in. COLORS: White; cream; maize; medium pink; light blue; peach; orchid; turquoise; Nile green; jade green; medium tan; pearl (light) gray; rose beige; rose; medium green; chin-chin blue; Castilian red; wine; dark green; violet; tangerine; medium brown; dark brown; navy blue; black. **State color. We Pay Postage.**

SILK-FACE DRESS SATIN

A gleaming silk face with back of strong cotton. For slips, linings.

17 G 2583—Width about 36 inches. COLORS: White; medium pink; peach; orchid; medium tan; medium gray; rose beige; rose; chin-chin blue; American Beauty; Castilian red; blue spruce green; medium brown; navy blue; black. **State color. We Pay Postage.**

85¢ A Yard

HALF RAYON Flat Crepe Prints

47¢ *Washable* A Yard

Bright prints, dark prints, little prints, big prints—and all washable colors. Add a variety of frocks to your fall wardrobe with this finely woven flat crepe, half rayon, half cotton.

17 G 2304—Width 35 inches. Order by article number and state pattern number. Postpaid.

136 Montgomery Ward Co. CBK SDA

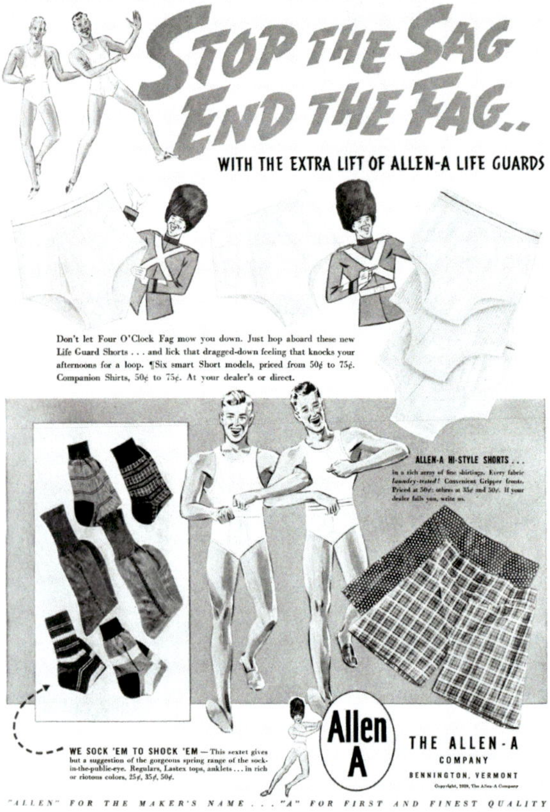

Allen-A Co., 1939

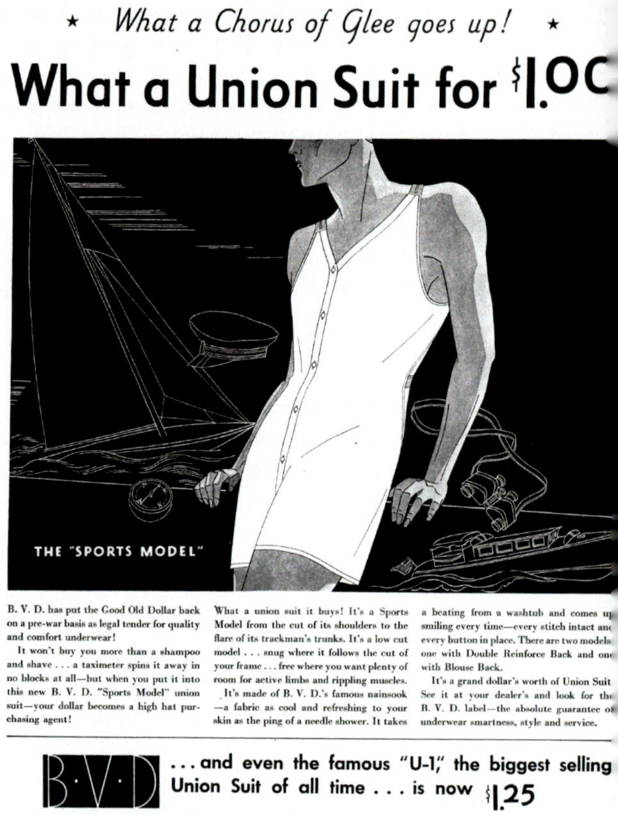

B.V.D., 1931

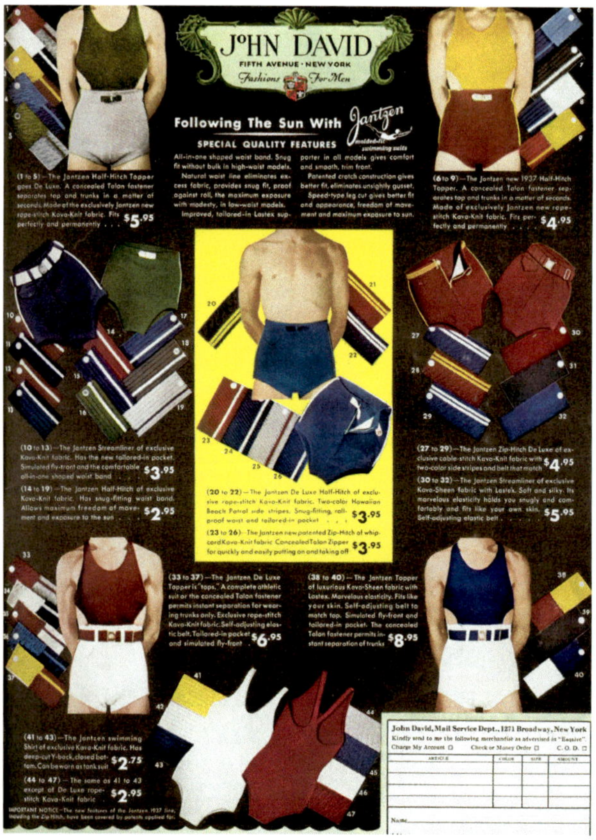

John David, 1937

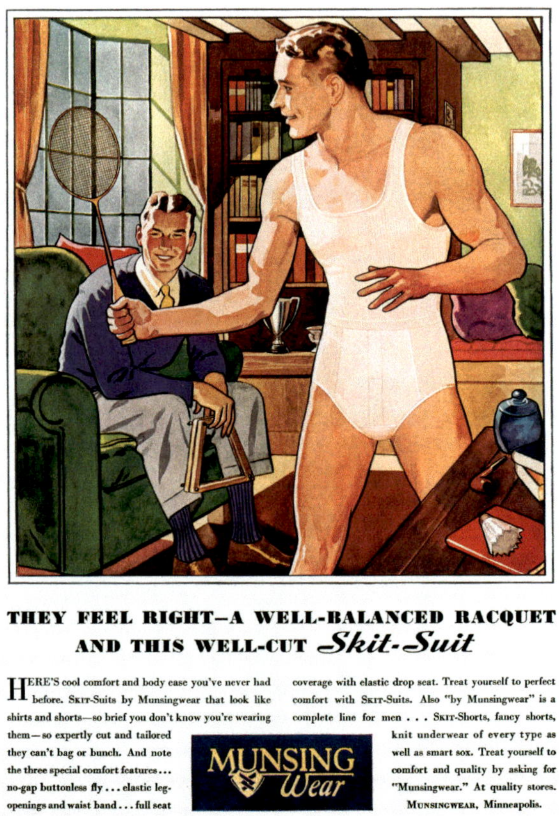

Munsing Wear, 1937

▶ Arrow Shirts, 1938

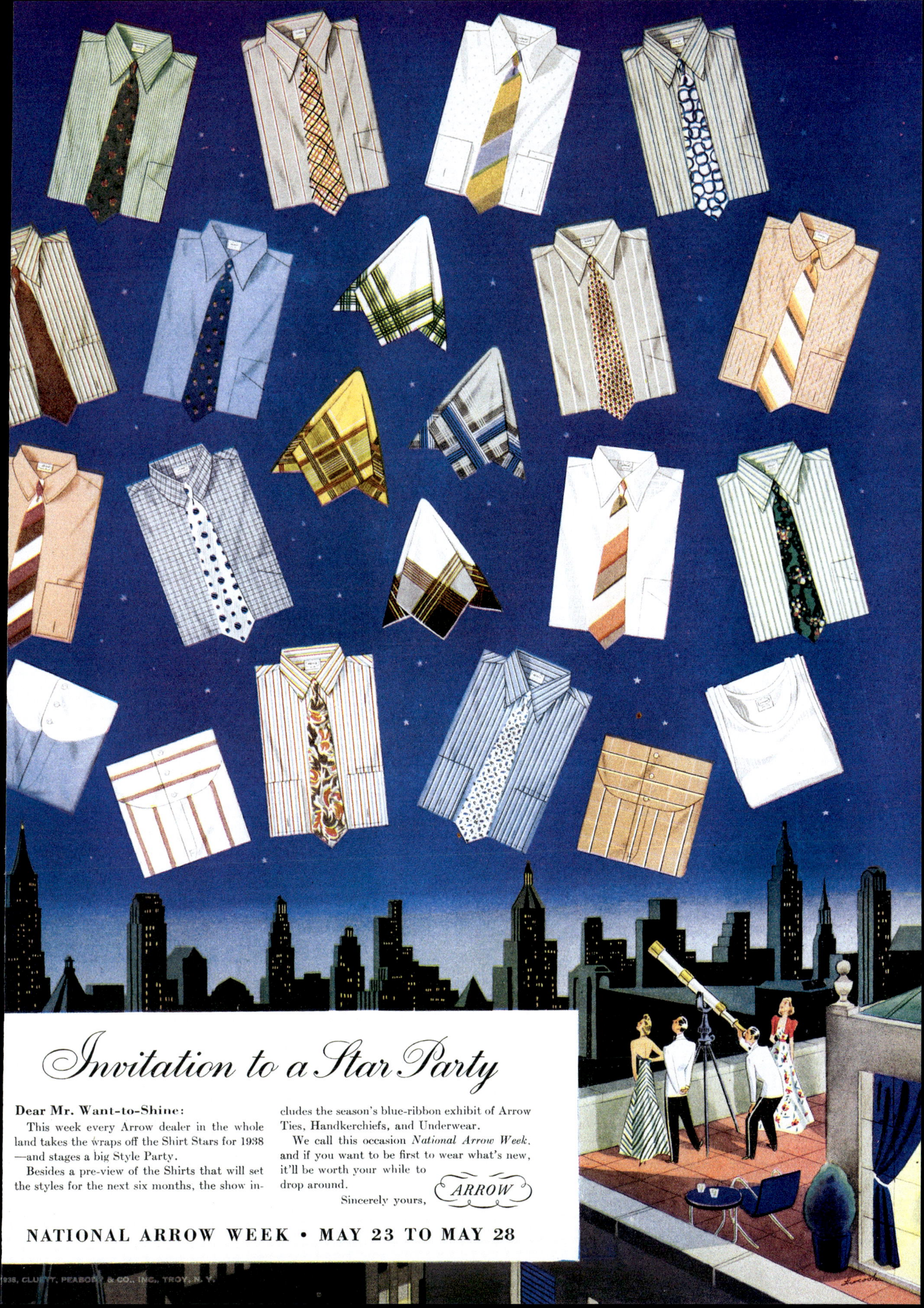
Invitation to a Star Party
Dear Mr. Want-to-Shine:
This week every Arrow dealer in the whole land takes the wraps off the Shirt Stars for 1938—and stages a big Style Party.
Besides a pre-view of the Shirts that will set the styles for the next six months, the show includes the season's blue-ribbon exhibit of Arrow Ties, Handkerchiefs, and Underwear.
We call this occasion *National Arrow Week*, and if you want to be first to wear what's new, it'll be worth your while to drop around.
Sincerely yours,
ARROW
NATIONAL ARROW WEEK • MAY 23 TO MAY 28
1938, CLUETT, PEABODY & CO., INC., TROY, N. Y.

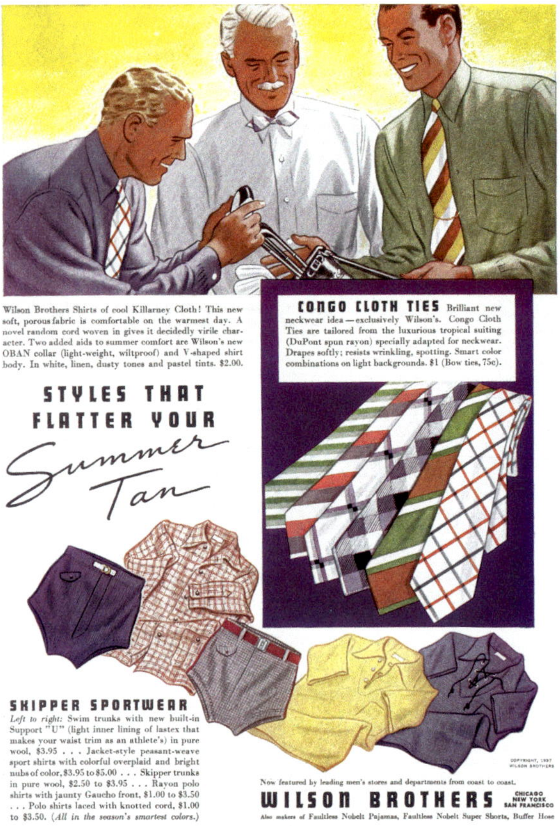

Wilson Brothers, 1937

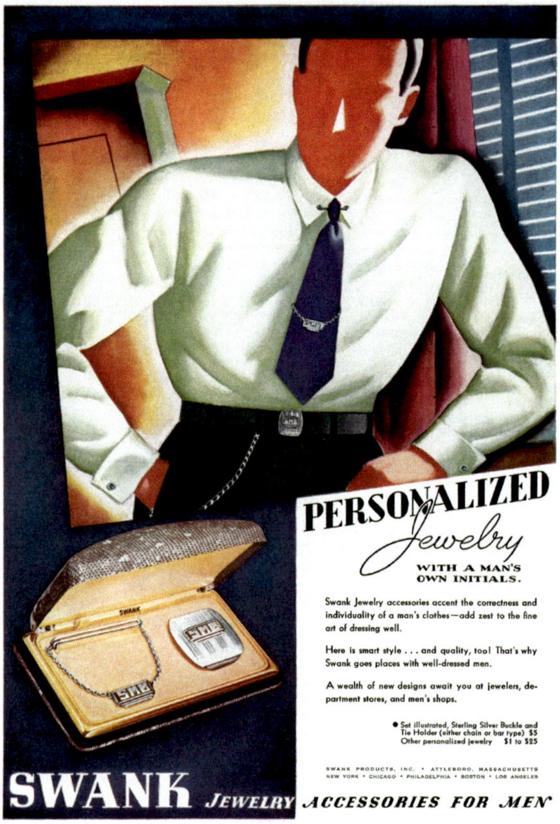

Swank, 1936

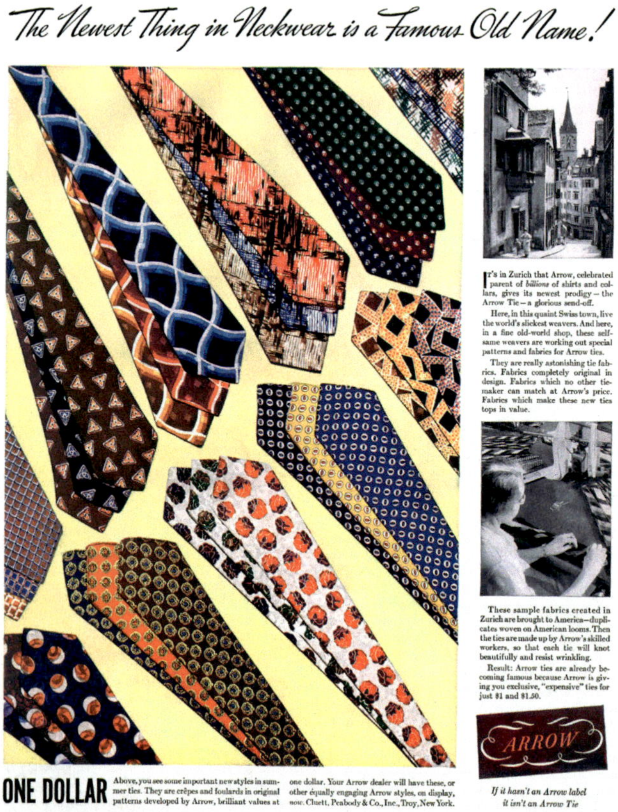

Arrow, 1937

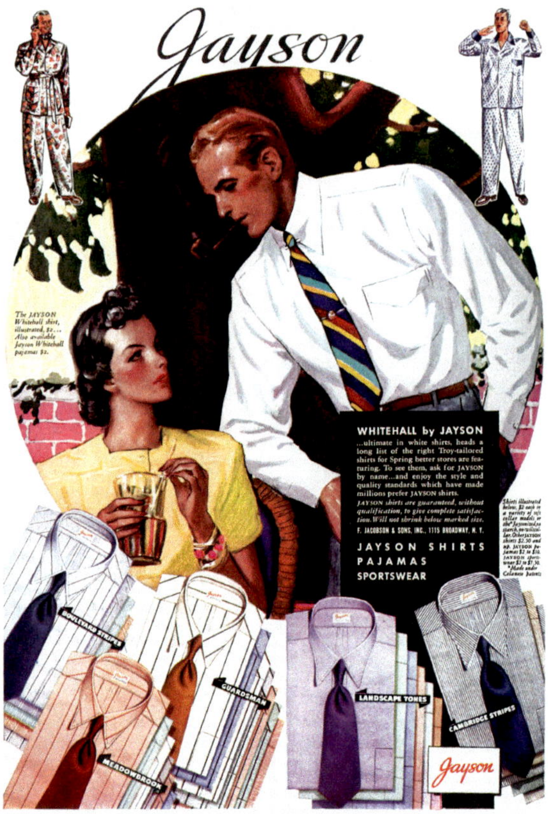

Jayson, 1939

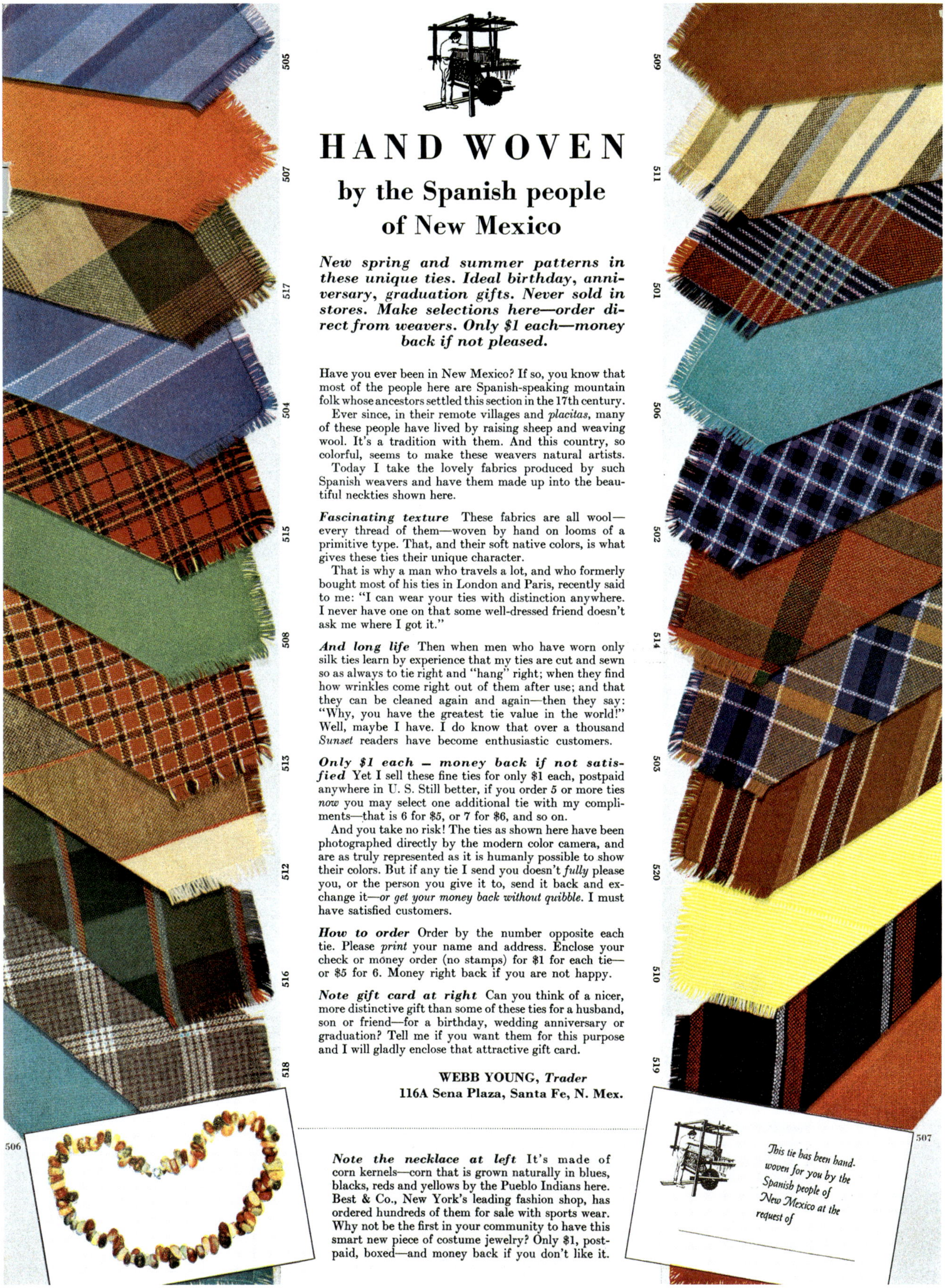

Webb Young, 1939

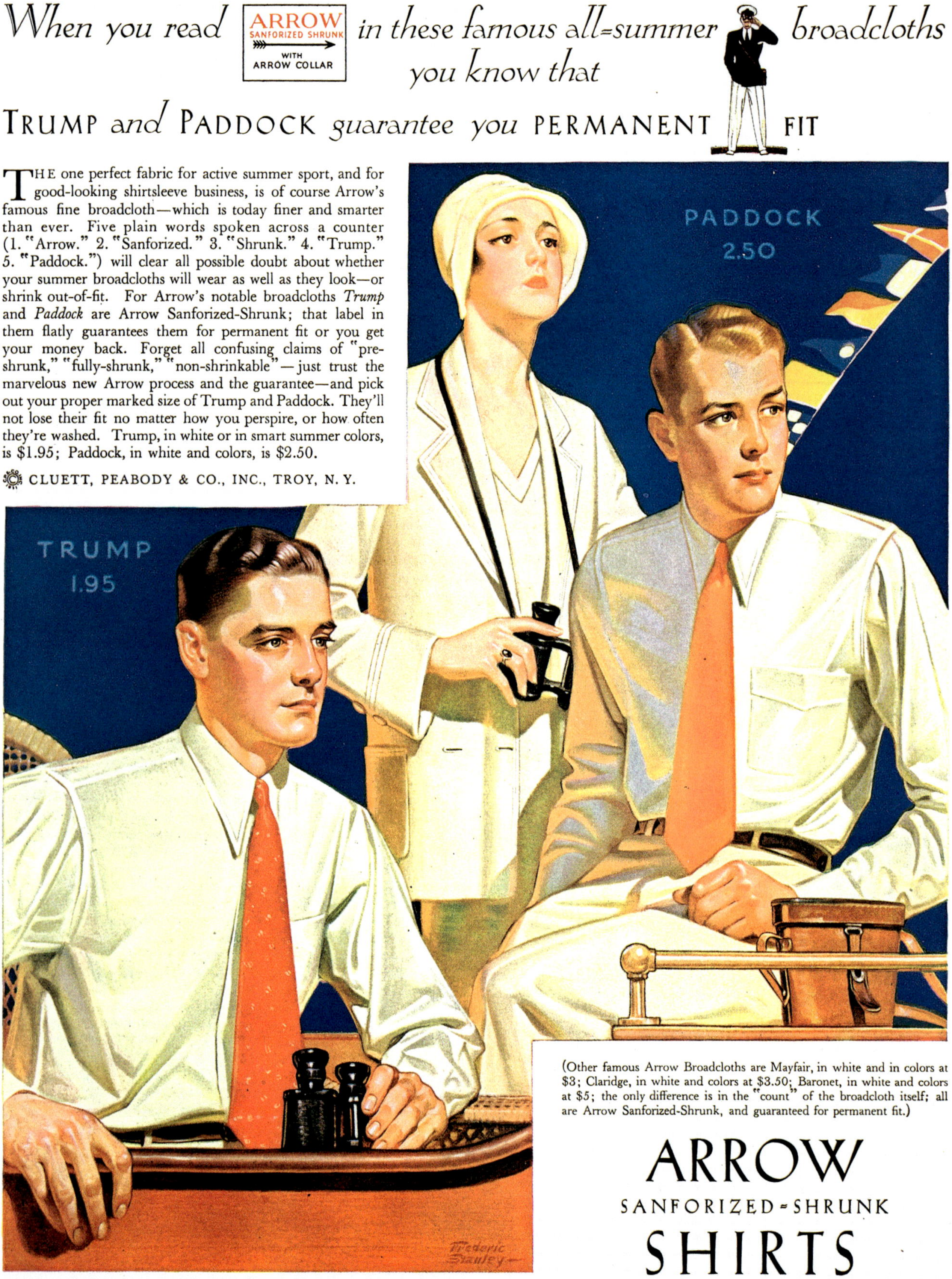
When you read
ARROW
SANFORIZED SHRUNK
WITH ARROW COLLAR
in these famous all-summer broadcloths you know that
TRUMP and PADDOCK guarantee you PERMANENT FIT
THE one perfect fabric for active summer sport, and for good-looking shirtsleeve business, is of course Arrow's famous fine broadcloth—which is today finer and smarter than ever. Five plain words spoken across a counter (1. "Arrow." 2. "Sanforized." 3. "Shrunk." 4. "Trump." 5. "Paddock.") will clear all possible doubt about whether your summer broadcloths will wear as well as they look—or shrink out-of-fit. For Arrow's notable broadcloths *Trump* and *Paddock* are Arrow Sanforized-Shrunk; that label in them flatly guarantees them for permanent fit or you get your money back. Forget all confusing claims of "pre-shrunk," "fully-shrunk," "non-shrinkable"—just trust the marvelous new Arrow process and the guarantee—and pick out your proper marked size of Trump and Paddock. They'll not lose their fit no matter how you perspire, or how often they're washed. Trump, in white or in smart summer colors, is $1.95; Paddock, in white and colors, is $2.50.
CLUETT, PEABODY & CO., INC., TROY, N. Y.
PADDOCK
2.50
TRUMP
1.95
(Other famous Arrow Broadcloths are Mayfair, in white and in colors at $3; Claridge, in white and colors at $3.50; Baronet, in white and colors at $5; the only difference is in the "count" of the broadcloth itself; all are Arrow Sanforized-Shrunk, and guaranteed for permanent fit.)
Frederic Stanley
ARROW
SANFORIZED-SHRUNK
SHIRTS

▲▶ *Arrow*, 1931

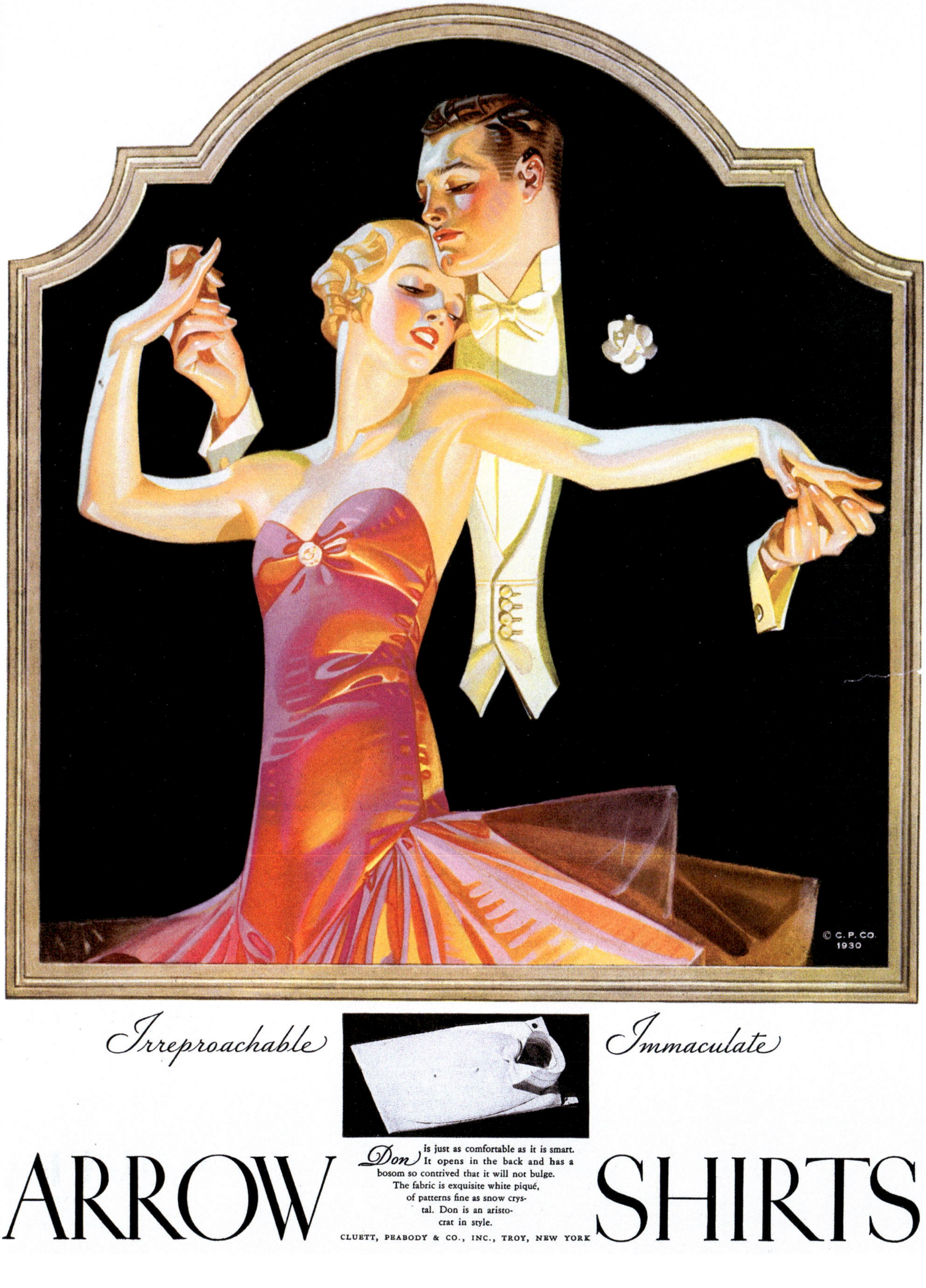
© C. P. CO. 1930
Irreproachable
Immaculate
ARROW
Don is just as comfortable as it is smart. It opens in the back and has a bosom so contrived that it will not bulge. The fabric is exquisite white piqué, of patterns fine as snow crystal. Don is an aristocrat in style.
CLUETT, PEABODY & CO., INC., TROY, NEW YORK
SHIRTS

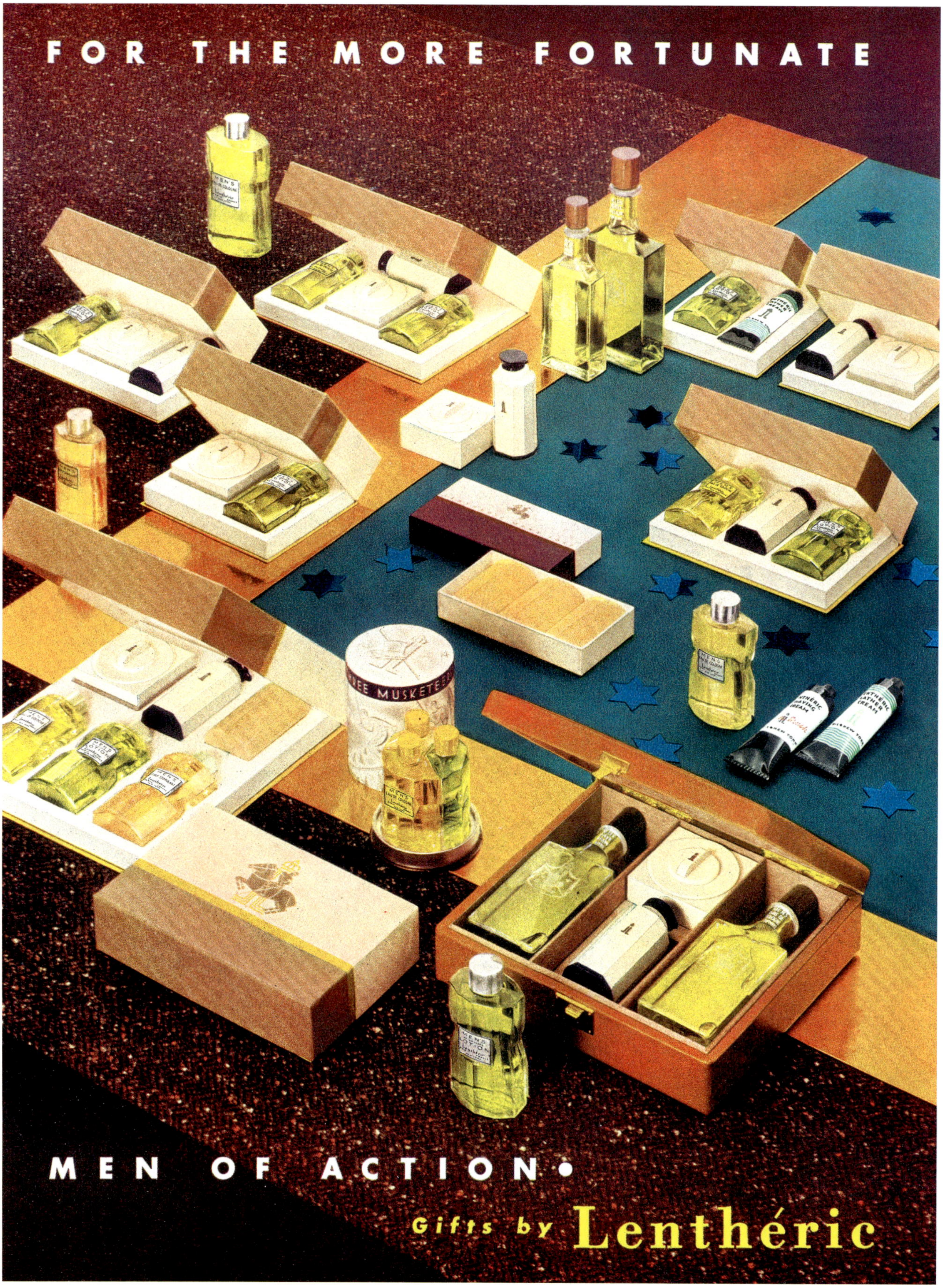

Lentheric, 1938

▸ *Williams, 1937*

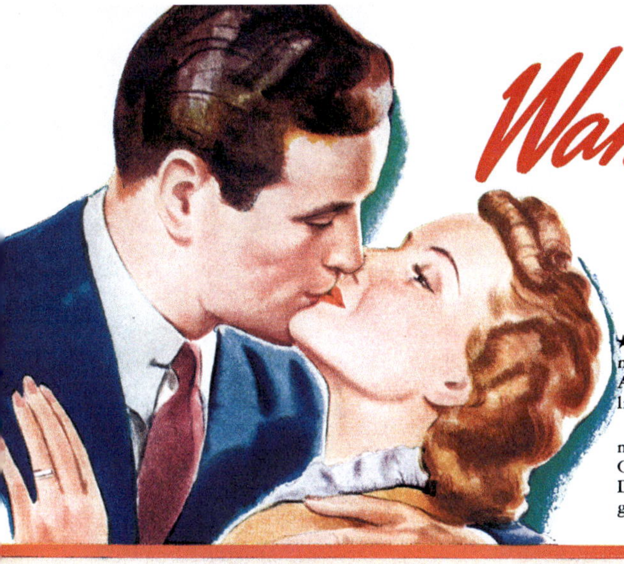

Want a Hug and Kiss for Christmas

★ What'll *you* have for Christmas? A mumbled thanks—or a big hug and kiss? All ladies who vote for the latter please line up at the Williams gift counter.

Smart, yes . . . also useful and essentially masculine—welcome in any home on Christmas morning. This year be certain. Don't take chances on not satisfying—give that man of yours a gift he can USE!

Men, for nearly 100 years, have sworn by these Williams shaving products. You can get them now in any of these handsome Gift Packages.

Please attend to this business early, while stores are still well stocked and buying is fun. Save yourself weary footsteps and endless hunting—get HIM a Williams Gift Set!

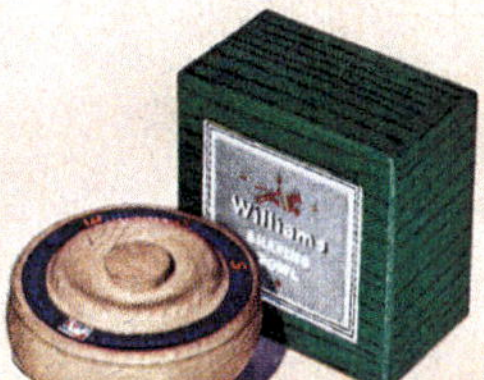

$1

GENUINE WILLIAMS SHAVING BOWL. Contains the famous Williams Shaving Cake in an attractive bowl of dark natural wood. Long lasting, too.

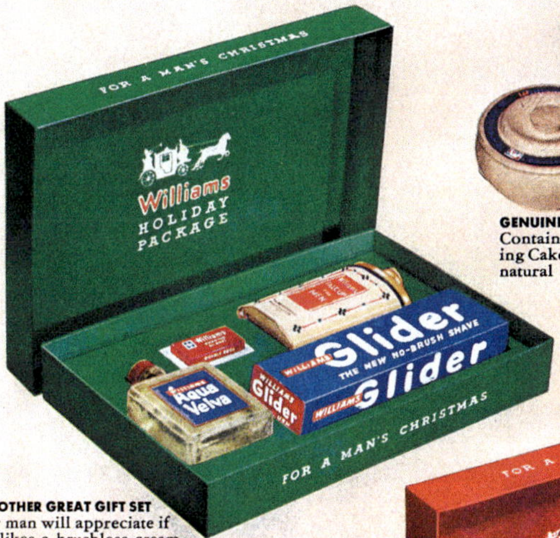

ANOTHER GREAT GIFT SET any man will appreciate if he likes a brushless cream. Featuring Glider—Williams "No-Brush" Shave Cream. Also contains: a 5-ounce bottle of Aqua Velva, Williams Talcum for Men, Williams Razor Blades.

COMPLETE FOR $1

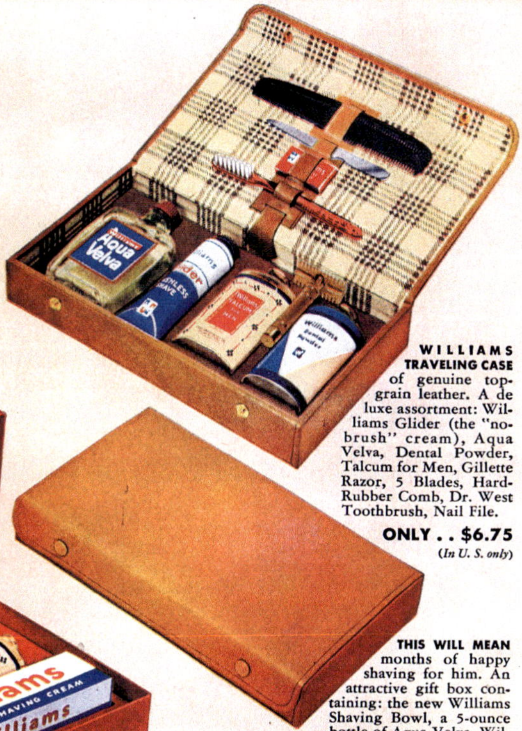

WILLIAMS TRAVELING CASE of genuine top-grain leather. A de luxe assortment: Williams Glider (the "no-brush" cream), Aqua Velva, Dental Powder, Talcum for Men, Gillette Razor, 5 Blades, Hard-Rubber Comb, Dr. West Toothbrush, Nail File.

ONLY . . $6.75

(In U. S. only)

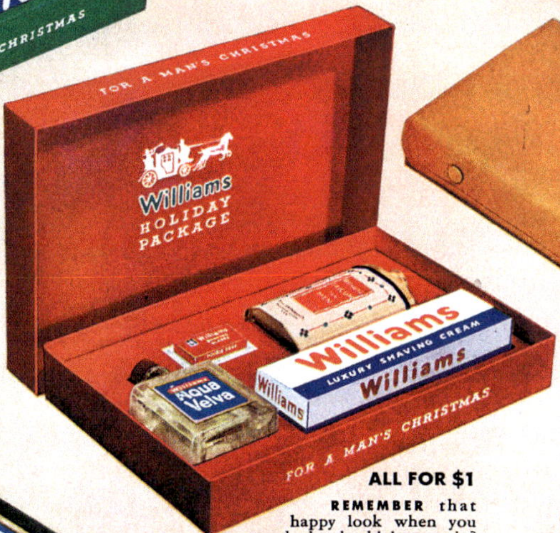

ALL FOR $1

REMEMBER that happy look when you served the huckleberry pie? Get a return performance with this inexpensive Holiday Package. Contains: Williams Shaving Cream, a 5-ounce bottle of Aqua Velva, Williams Talcum for Men, 5 Williams Razor Blades.

THIS WILL MEAN months of happy shaving for him. An attractive gift box containing: the new Williams Shaving Bowl, a 5-ounce bottle of Aqua Velva, Williams Talcum for Men, Williams Eau de Cologne.

YOURS FOR $1.50

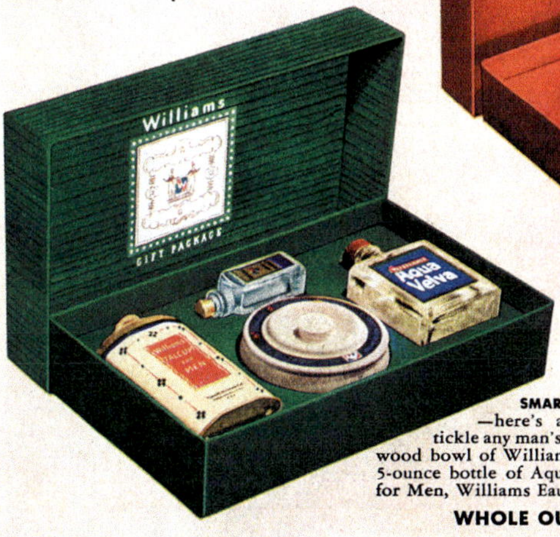

SMART . . . USEFUL . . . COMPLETE —here's a shaving outfit that will tickle any man's fancy. An exquisite natural-wood bowl of Williams famous Shaving Cake, a 5-ounce bottle of Aqua Velva, Williams Talcum for Men, Williams Eau de Cologne.

WHOLE OUTFIT ONLY . . . $1.50

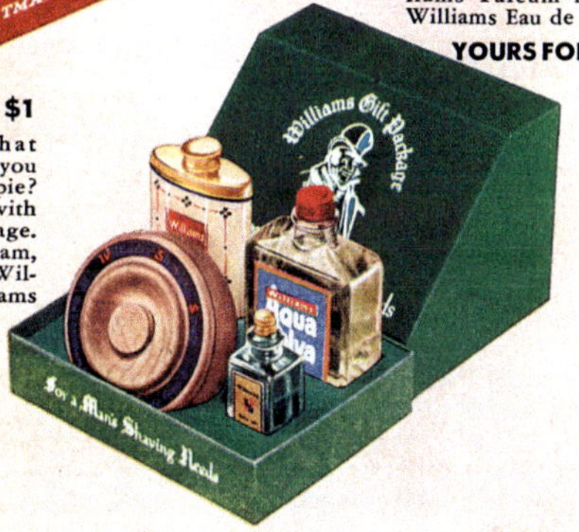

Gifts for Gentlemen by Williams

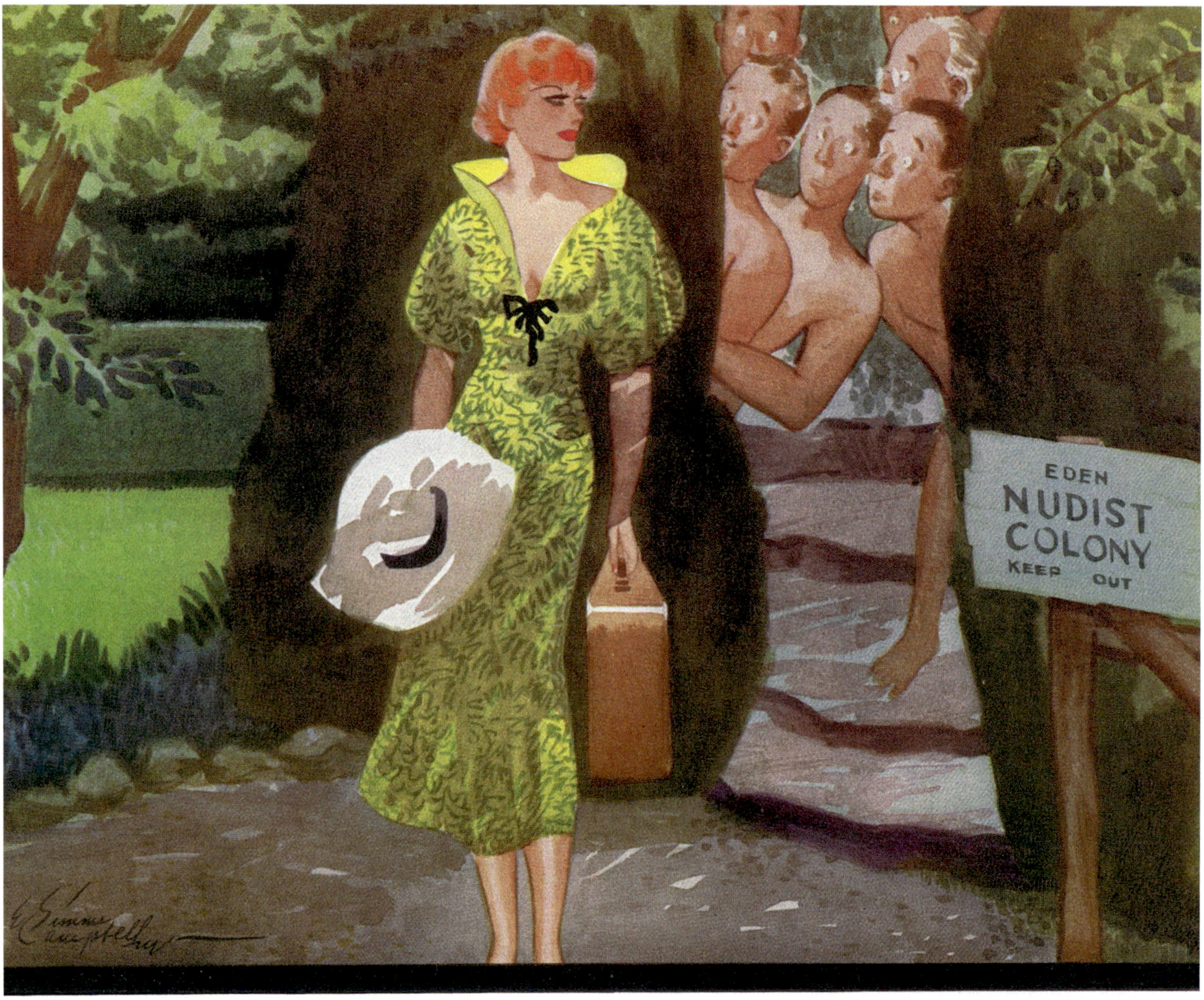

"Sure I'm leaving—I can't get used to men without Hart Schaffner & Marx clothes!"

THIS is a free country. If these gentlemen think they're going to enjoy life better without clothes—that's their business. But as long as most men have to wear clothes—that's our business!

And candor certainly compels us to admit that—much as we admire the American male—he looks a lot better *with* smart clothes than without them; and smart clothes naturally mean Hart Schaffner & Marx clothes! So no matter if you're trying to impress blonde, brunette or boss, take a lesson from the little lady above; drop in today and inspect the great collection of new, up-to-the-minute styles now on display at your local Hart Schaffner & Marx dealer!

★ The growing demand by well dressed men for a plainer back sport suit was a feature of the Palm Beach season. According to Robert Surrey, famed Hart Schaffner & Marx style scout, it gained momentum as fashion leaders moved northward with Spring through Augusta, Aiken, Pinehurst and the Virginia fox hunting country. This beltless model, the Ascot, with gussets at the shoulder for freedom of movement and the new side vents, has become a prime favorite at all the smart country clubs.

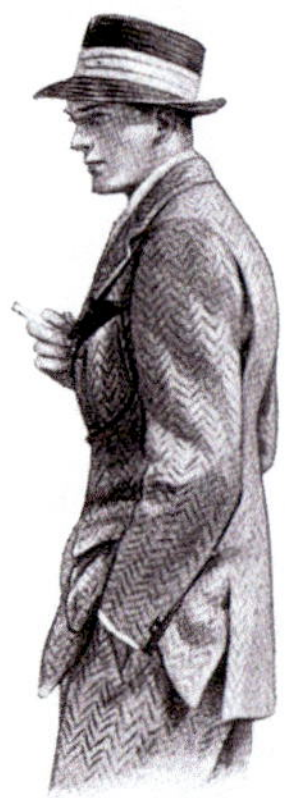

HART SCHAFFNER & MARX

THE TRUMPETER LABEL

A SMALL THING TO LOOK FOR ... A BIG THING TO FIND

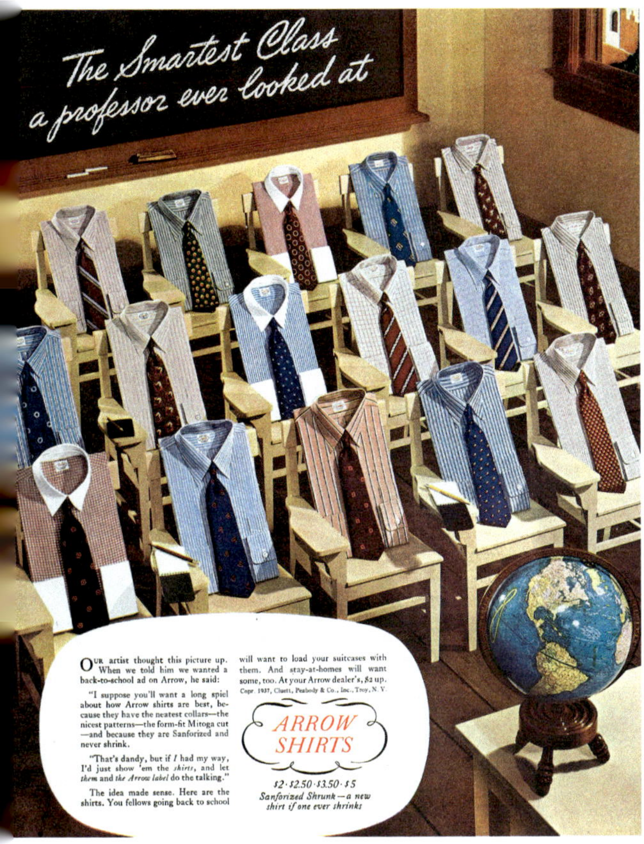

Arrow, 1937

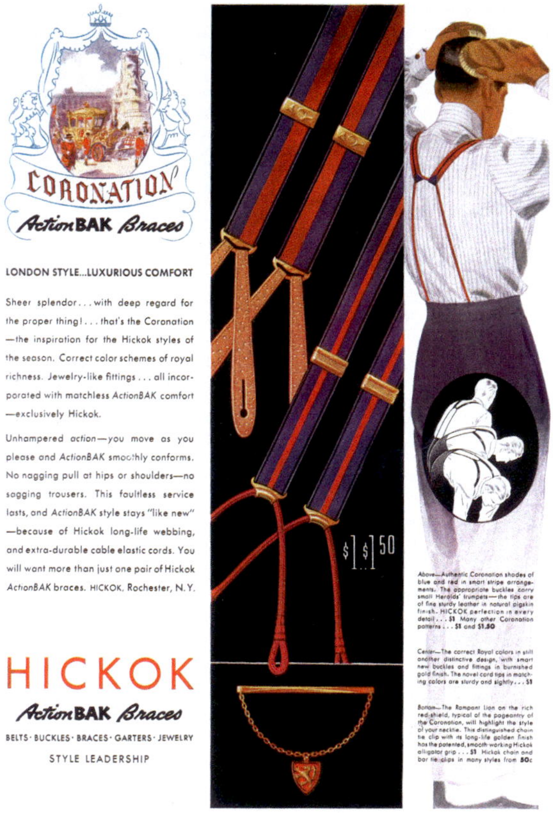

Hickok, 1937

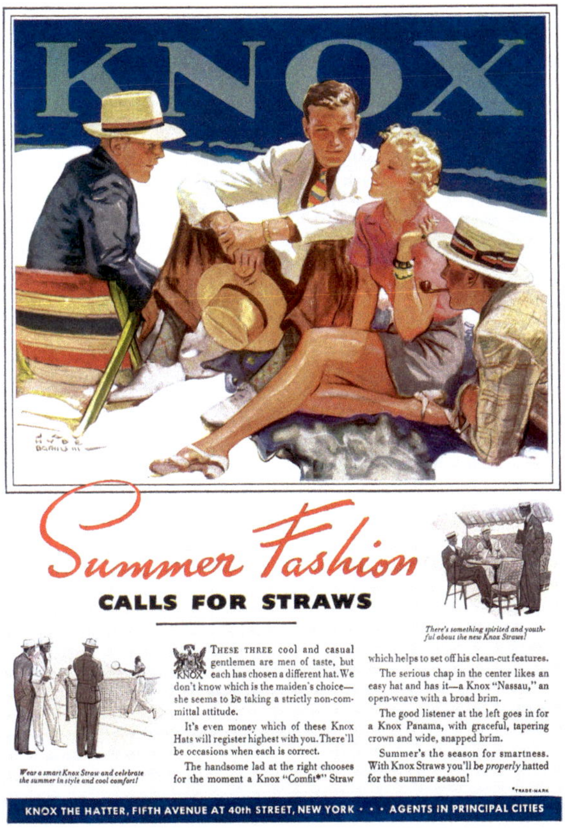

Hart Schaffner & Marx, 1936 ◂ Knox, 1937

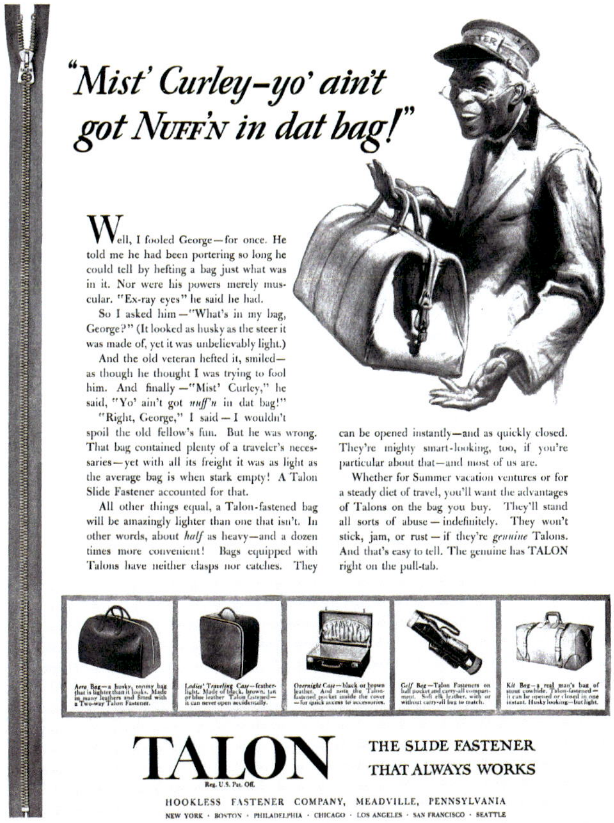

Talon, 1931

COLOR

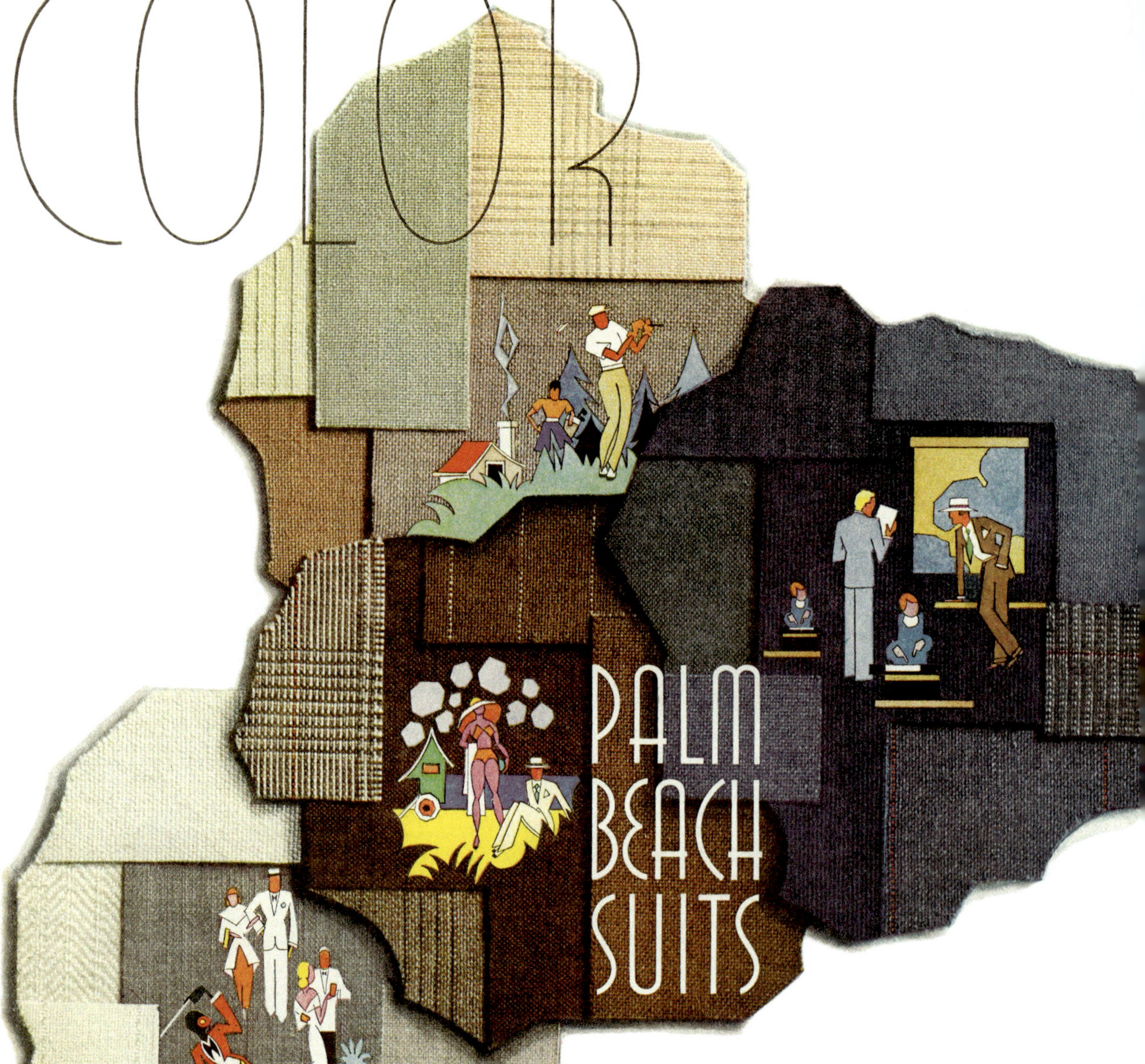

HANS FLATO

It's very old fashioned to think that Palm Beach means a light color ● Palm Beach is the name of the most popular summer suit in the world: *The suit that lets your body breathe* ● You can have it in blue or brown or gray or white—in fact, a whole world of colors and patterns. ● The cloth is made by the famous GOODALL mills—by no one else—and is tailored by GOODALL experts into the smartest washable suits of the season ● You'll know you're getting the genuine when you see the trade marked label in the garment. Suits $17.75—Slacks $5.50—Dinner Formal $20.00. Goodall Company, Cincinnati, Ohio.

$17.75

TAILORED BY GOO
Palm Beac
FROM THE GENUINE

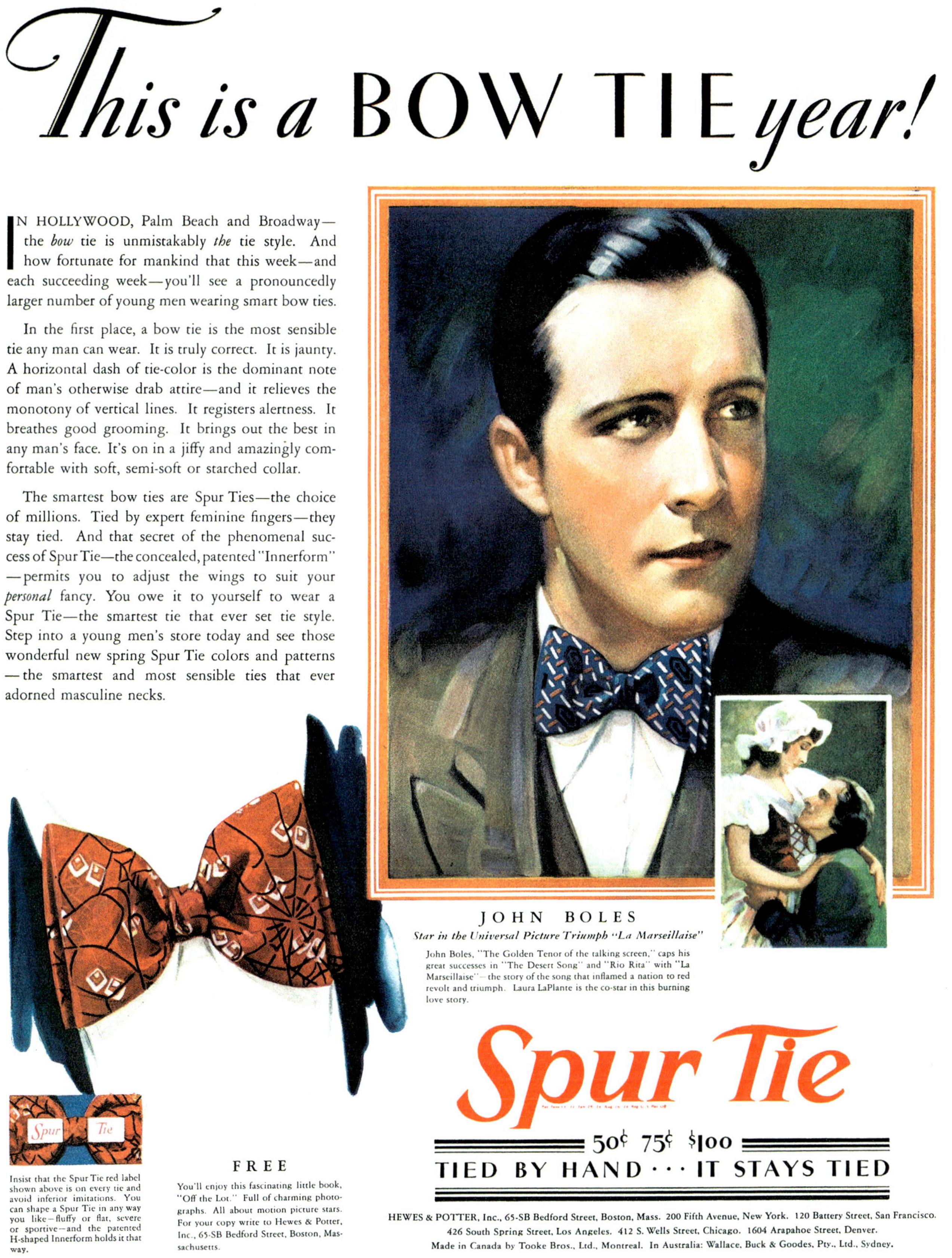

Palm Beach Suits, 1938 ◂

Spur Tie, 1930

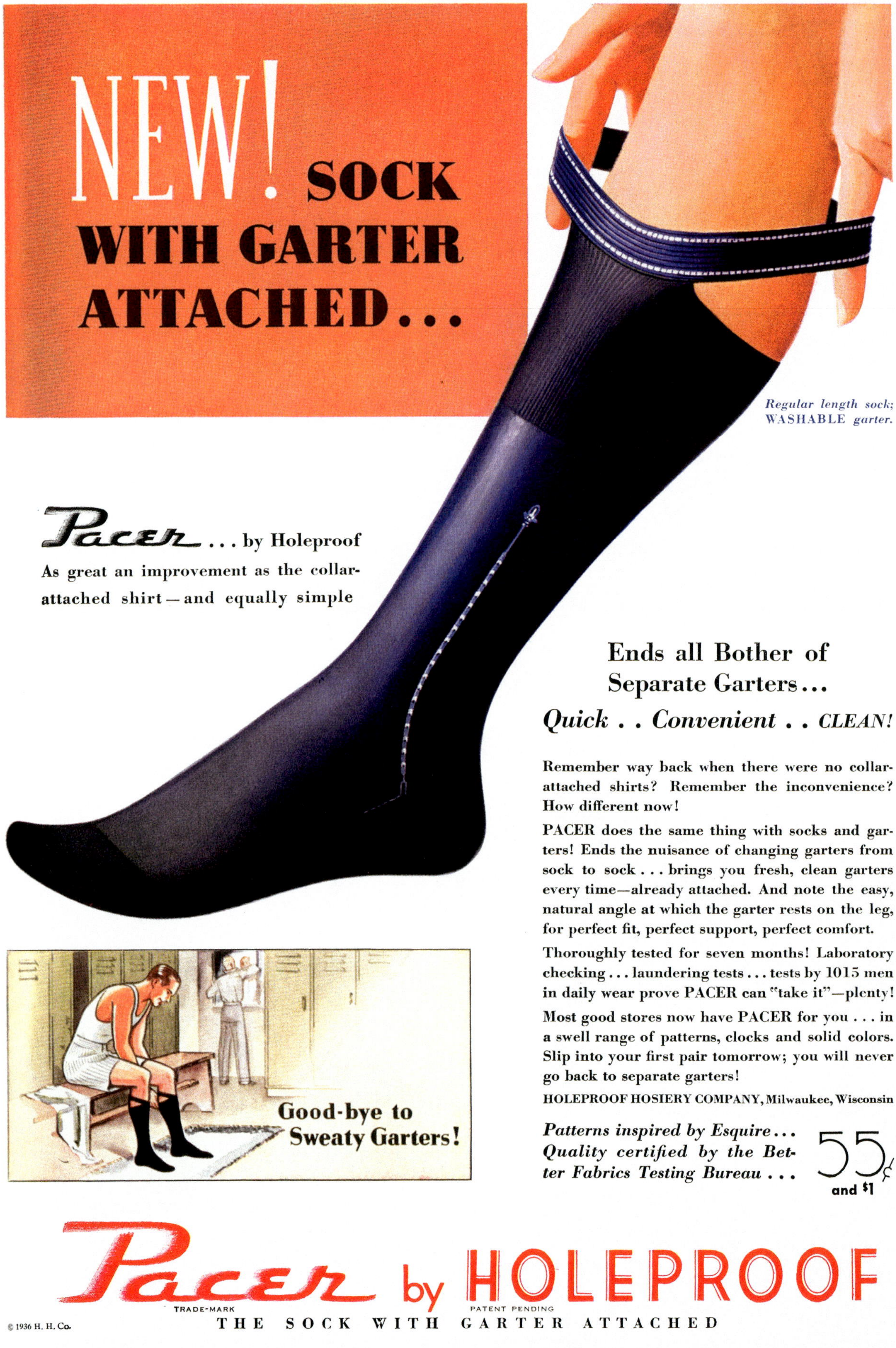

NEW! SOCK WITH GARTER ATTACHED...
Regular length sock; WASHABLE garter.
Pacer ... by Holeproof
As great an improvement as the collar-attached shirt—and equally simple
Ends all Bother of Separate Garters...
Quick .. Convenient .. CLEAN!
Remember way back when there were no collar-attached shirts? Remember the inconvenience? How different now!
PACER does the same thing with socks and garters! Ends the nuisance of changing garters from sock to sock ... brings you fresh, clean garters every time—already attached. And note the easy, natural angle at which the garter rests on the leg, for perfect fit, perfect support, perfect comfort.
Thoroughly tested for seven months! Laboratory checking ... laundering tests ... tests by 1015 men in daily wear prove PACER can "take it"—plenty!
Most good stores now have PACER for you ... in a swell range of patterns, clocks and solid colors. Slip into your first pair tomorrow; you will never go back to separate garters!
HOLEPROOF HOSIERY COMPANY, Milwaukee, Wisconsin
Good-bye to Sweaty Garters!
Patterns inspired by Esquire ... Quality certified by the Better Fabrics Testing Bureau ...
55¢ and $1
Pacer by HOLEPROOF
TRADE-MARK
PATENT PENDING
THE SOCK WITH GARTER ATTACHED
© 1936 H. H. Co.

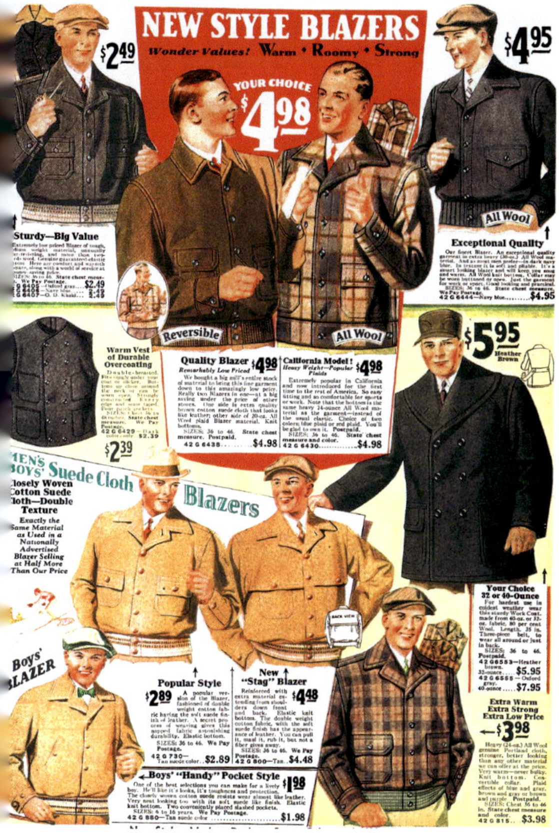

Blazers, 1931

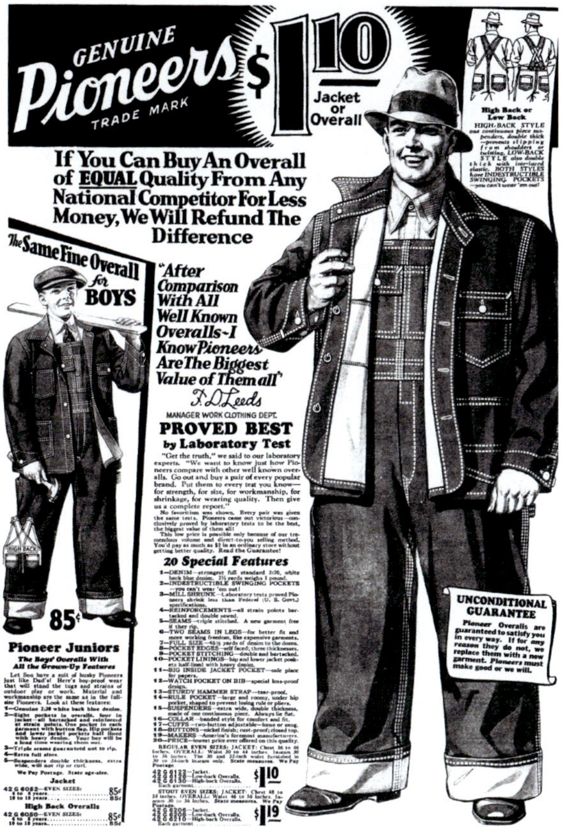

Pioneers, 1930

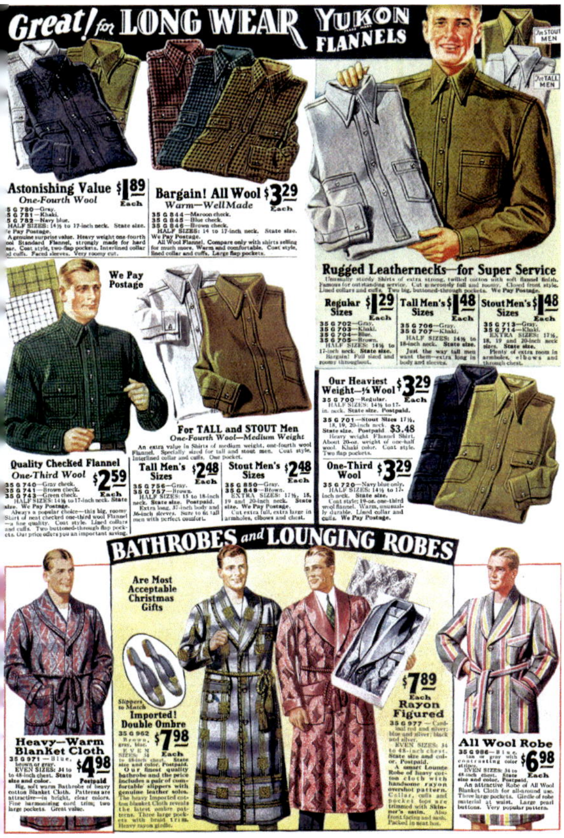

Pacer, 1936 ◂ Yukon Flannels, 1931

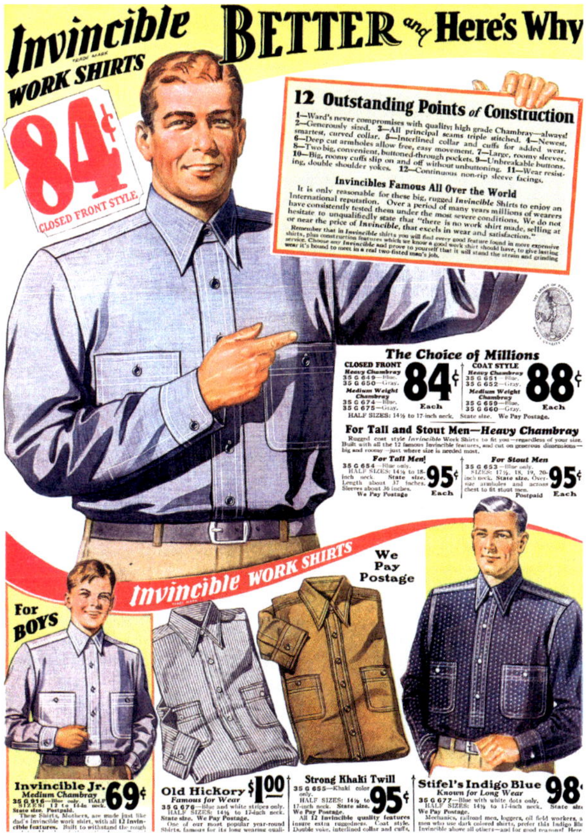

Work Shirts, 1931

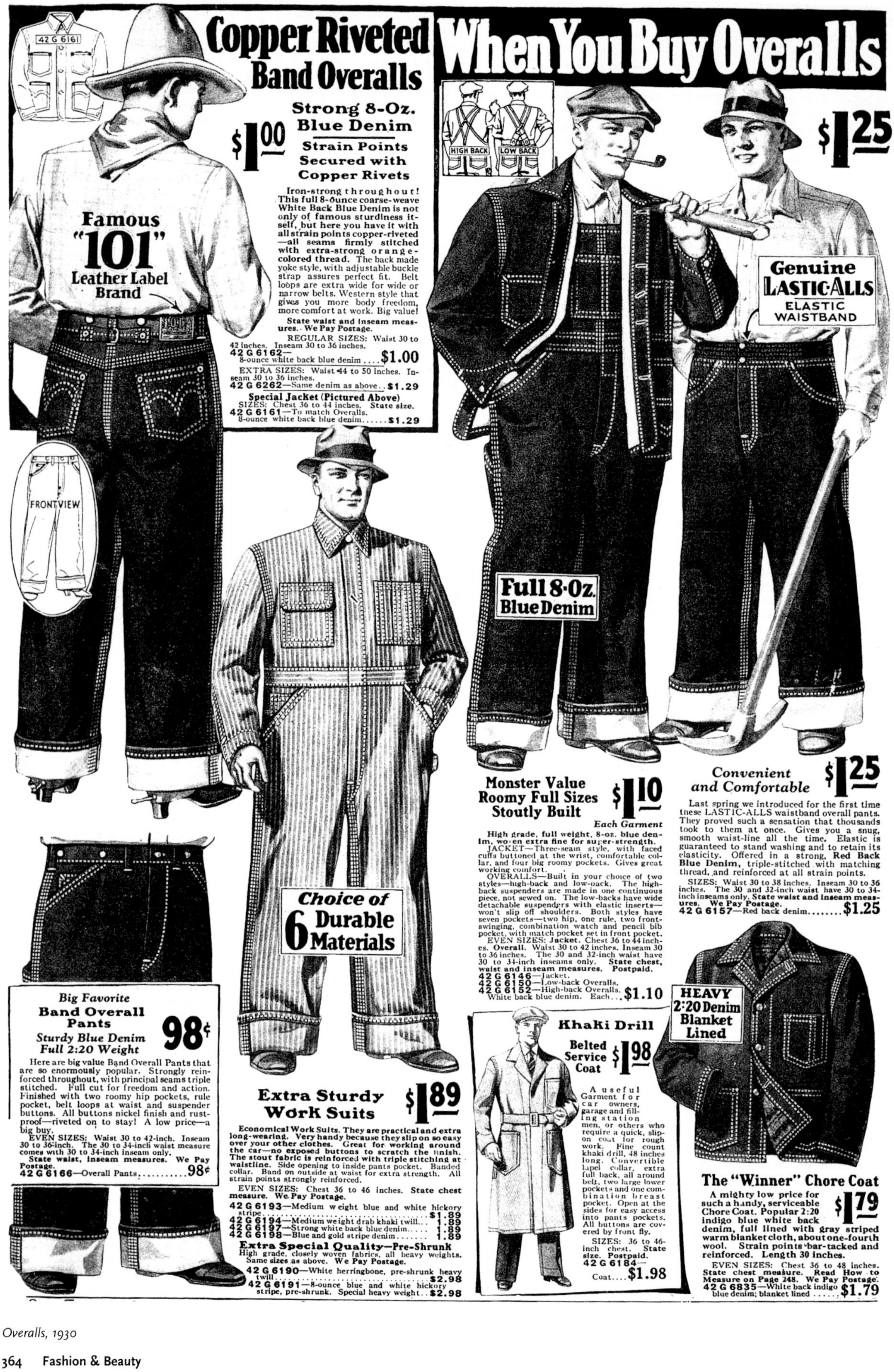

Overalls, 1930

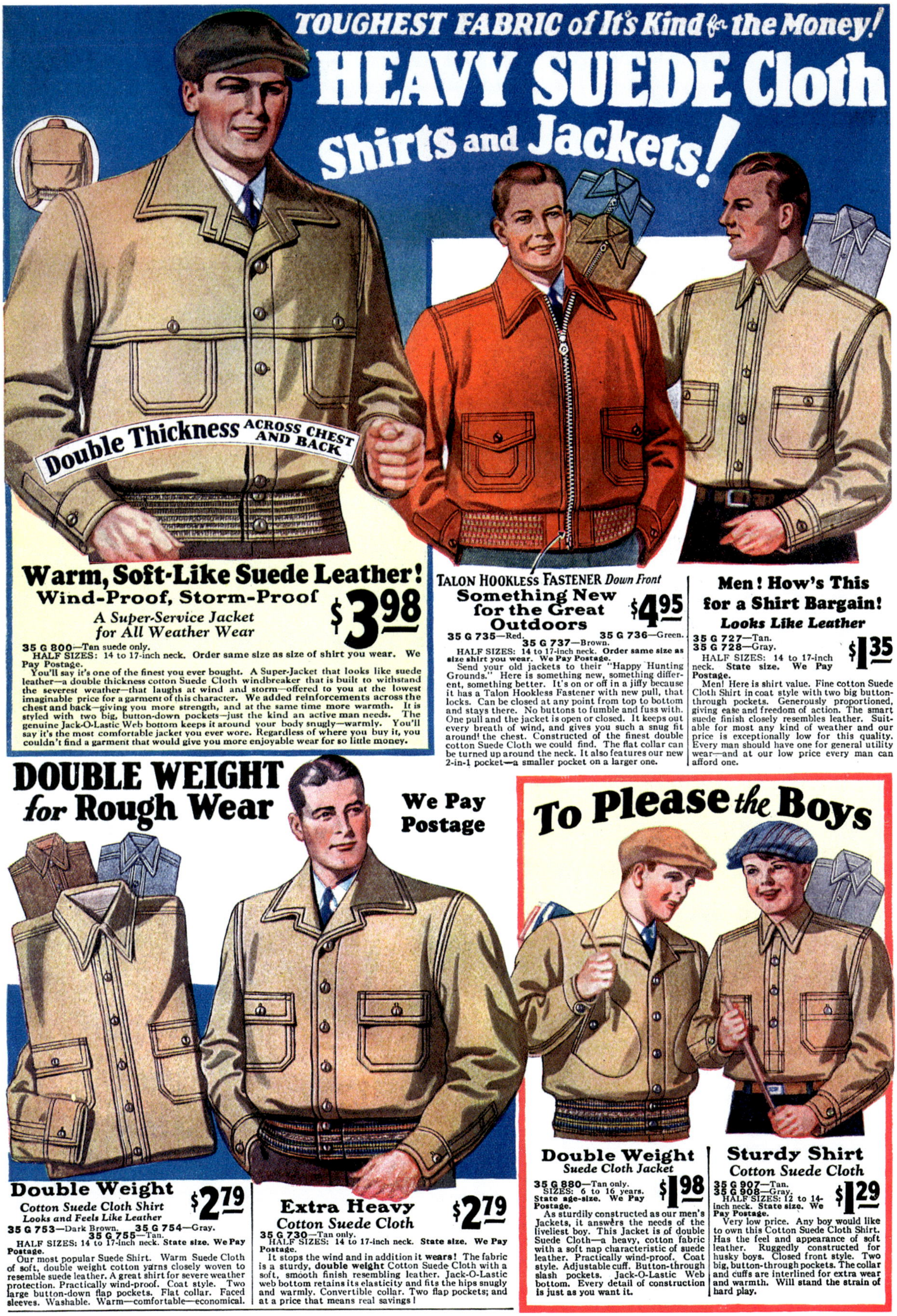

Men's Wear, 1931

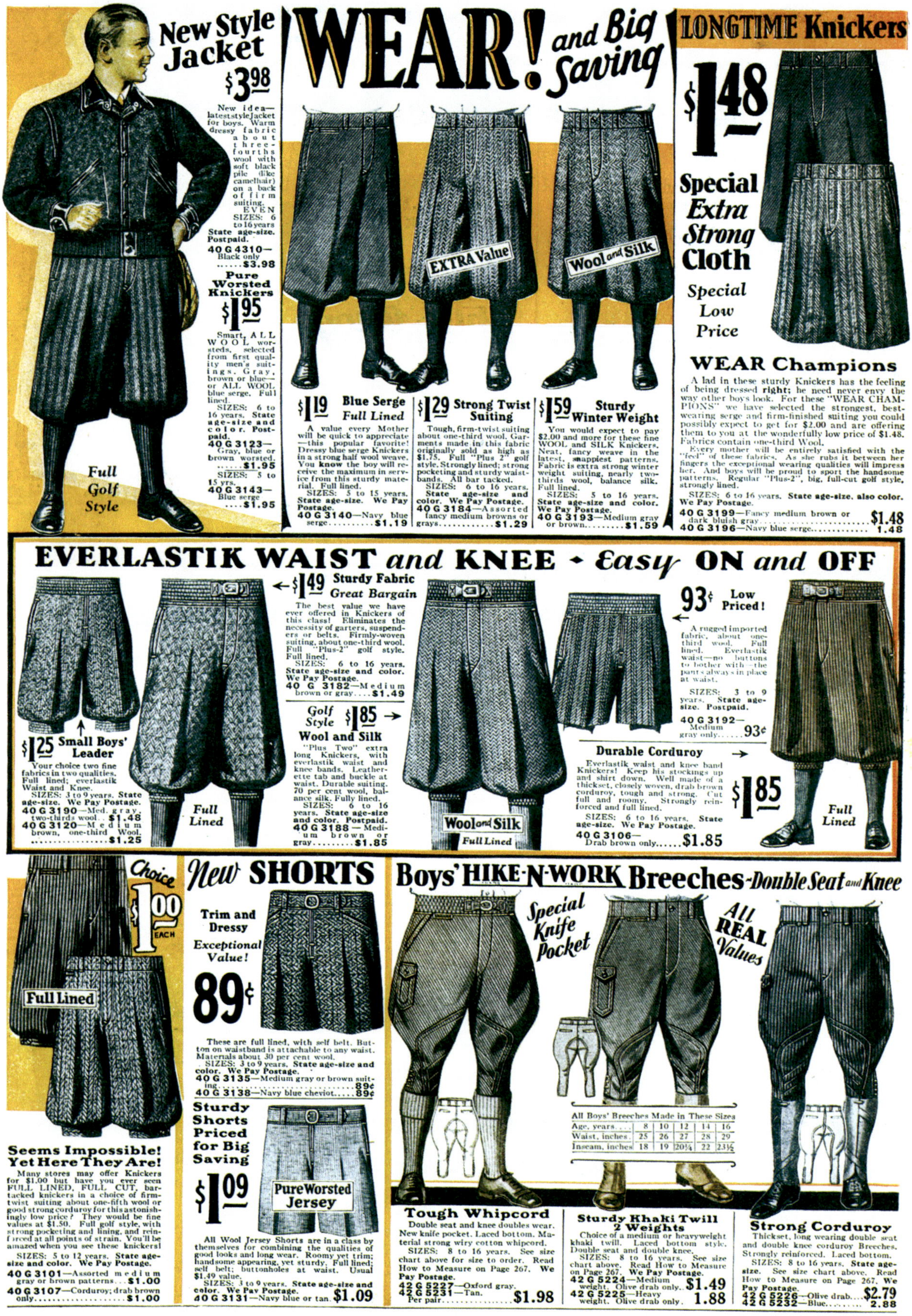

Knickers, 1931

► *Men's Hats, 1930*

MEN'S CAPS
Newest Fabrics and Patterns

Without Inbands

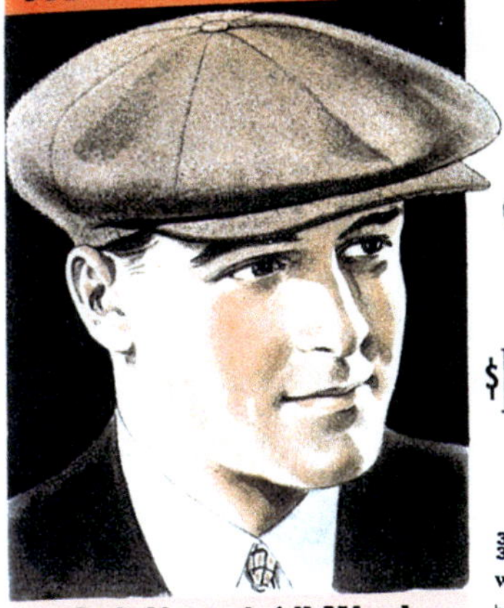

Soft Napped All Wool
Resembles Camel Hair
Dressy—Rich Looking

$1.75

39 G 650—Medium gray.
39 G 651—Tan.
SIZES: 6¾, 6⅞, 7, 7⅛, 7¼, 7⅜, 7½, 7⅝, 7¾. **State size.** Read How to Measure on Page 247. **We Pay Postage.**

The featured style and material for 1931—promises popularity far excelling anything in recent years! All Wool. Just the Cap for early Fall wear. A perfect match for a camel hair coat.

Hand shaped and hand blocked. Made in the popular 8-4 style. Silk-faced satin lining. Full leather sweatband. Unbreakable visor.

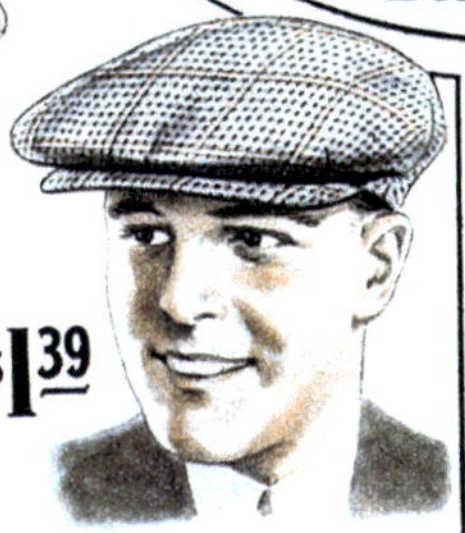

$1.39

Adjustable Style
39 G 623—Fancy bluish-gray plaid.
39 G 625—Fancy tan plaid.
SIZES: Adjustable from 6¾ to 7½. **We Pay Postage.**

Will fit any head. Simply adjust buckle in front. Tailored of a swagger plaid material about two-thirds wool—very sturdy. Silk-faced satin lining. Genuine leather sweatband in front. Unbreakable visor.

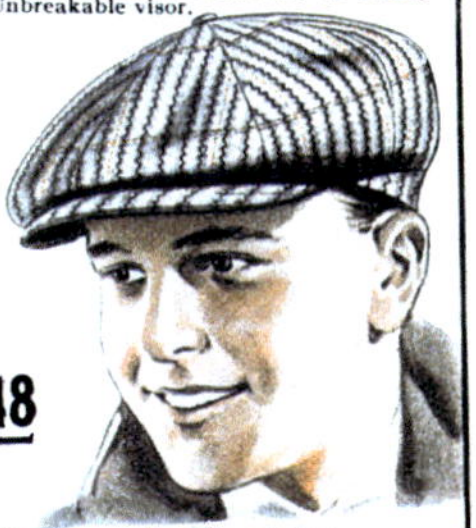

$1.48

Peppy Collegiate
39 G 631—Light gray. **39 G 635**—Tan.
ALL SIZES: 6½ to 7½. **State size. Postpaid.**

New Fall patterns and colors. Fashioned of fine fabrics, about two-thirds wool, in 8-4 style and fully lined with attractive rayon-faced material. Full leather sweatband; unbreakable visor.

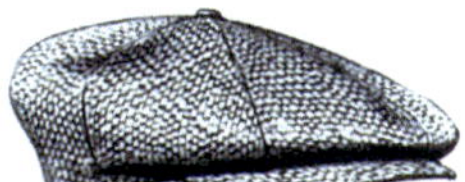

$1.00

All Wool Tweed
39 G 633—Medium gray.
39 G 634—Tan.
SIZES: 6¾ to 7¾. Read How to Measure on Page 247. **State size. We Pay Postage.**

A wonderful Cap for **$1.00**. Carefully made in 8-4 style of All Wool tweeds. Unbreakable visor. Leather sweatband in front. Full lined

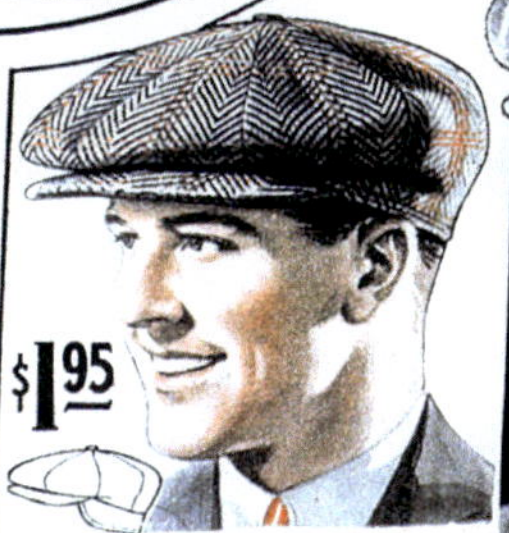

$1.95

Our Finest Cap
39 G 647—Gray.
39 G 649—Medium brown.
SIZES: 6¾ to 7¾. **State size.** Read How to Measure on Page 247. **We Pay Postage.**

Hand shaped of very fine All Wool material. Patterns perfectly matched. Lined with lustrous silk-faced satin. Unbreakable visor. Sanitary lined inband.

With Inbands

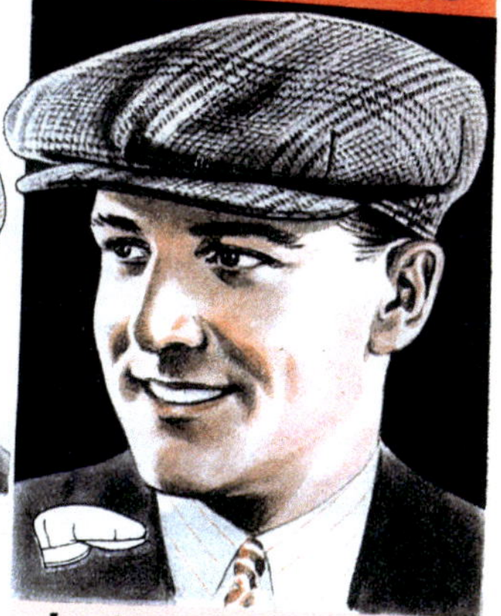

Leader Value—All Wool
Sateen Lined

$1.39

39 G 606—Fancy medium brown plaid.
39 G 608—Fancy medium gray plaid.
SIZES: 6¾, 6⅞, 7, 7⅛, 7¼, 7⅜, 7½, 7⅝, 7¾. **State size.** Read How to Measure on Page 247. **We Pay Postage.**

Again we offer our Big Feature Cap value for men. Only **$1.39**—but the equal in quality, tailoring and style to most **$2** caps. Hand shaped and hand blocked, by one of the country's foremost cap makers. Fine All Wool top coating material. Stylish one-piece top with warm inband for cold weather. Sateen lined. Unbreakable visor.

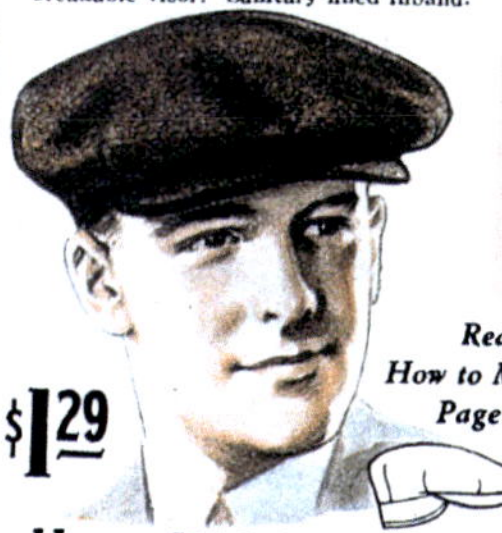

$1.29

Read How to Measure Page 247

Heavy Weight All Wool
39 G 617—Dark brown.
39 G 621—Dark gray.
SIZES: 6¾, 6⅞, 7, 7⅛, 7¼, 7⅜, 7½, 7⅝, 7¾.

Fine All Wool overcoating material, an extra heavy winter weight. Sateen lining. Warm inband. Unbreakable visor. **State size. Postpaid.**

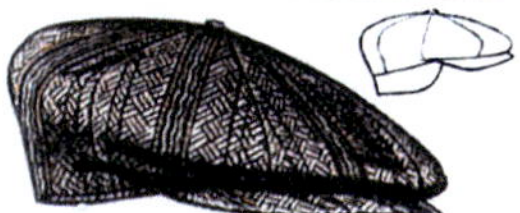

Big Value!

89¢

39 G 609—Medium gray.
39 G 611—Brown.
SIZES: 6¾, 6⅞, 7, 7⅛, 7¼, 7⅜, 7½. **State size. We Pay Postage.**

Exceptional bargain! About two-thirds wool, balance silk. Warm inband to cover ears. Full cotton twill lined. Unbreakable visor.

Special Offer — CHOICE $1.00 Each

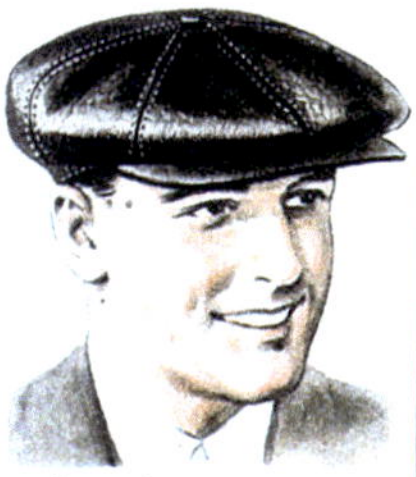

Genuine Leather
39 G 721—Black.
39 G 723—Brown.

$1.49

SIZES: 6¾, 6⅞, 7, 7⅛, 7¼, 7⅜, 7½, 7⅝, 7¾. **State size.** Read How to Measure, Page 247. **Postpaid.**

A genuine sheepskin leather Cap—built to stand rough wear. Great for every man, but particularly for men wearing leather coats. Made in the 8-4 style. Warm lined inband pulls down over ears. Full flannel lined. Unbreakable visor. Entire cap is strong, durable—sure to give several seasons' wear. Rushed to you by Ward's speedy service!

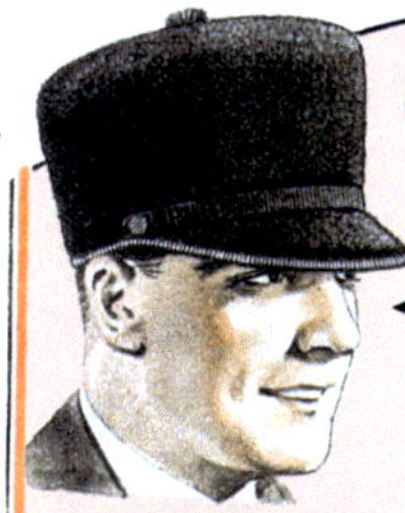

← The Genuine "Scotch" Cap
39 G 729—
Navy blue only... **$1.00**
SIZES: 6¾, 6⅞, 7, 7⅛, 7¼, 7⅜, 7½, 7⅝, 7¾. **State size. We Pay Postage.**

A big bargain leader in a popular Cap. Heavy weight All Wool. The genuine original "Scotch" Cap—famous for complete protection against cold. Full flannel lined. Unbreakable visor. Warm inband that pulls well down over the ears in cold weather. Speedy Same Day shipping service.

Corduroy "Tie-Top" →
39 G 733—Tan.
39 G 734—
Navy blue........ **$1.00**
SIZES: 6¾, 6⅞, 7, 7⅛, 7¼, 7⅜, 7½, 7⅝, 7¾. **State size.** Be sure to read How to Measure on Page 247. **We Pay Postage.**

The ace of $1 Corduroy Cap values. Fur lined inband and tie top of double thickness to pull down over ears in cold weather. Full lined with chamois-like cloth. Extra quality at a money saving price.

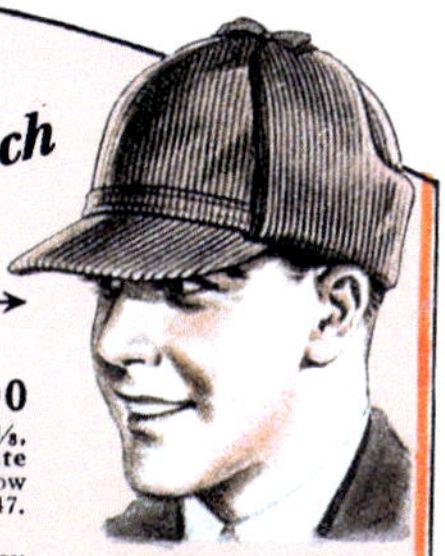

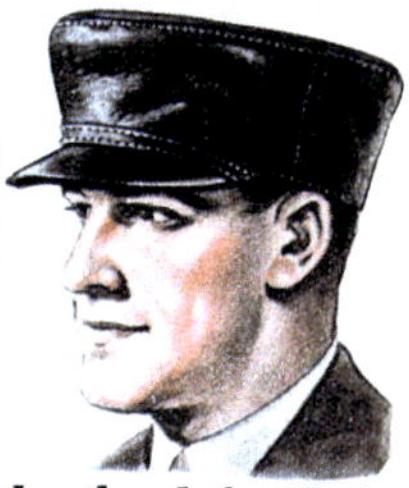

Leather Judge Style

$1.49

39 G 711—Black.
39 G 715—Brown.
SIZES: 6¾, 6⅞, 7, 7⅛, 7¼, 7⅜, 7½, 7⅝, 7¾. **State size.** Be sure to read How to Measure, Page 247. **We Pay Postage.**

Popular Judge style Cap of genuine sheepskin leather—tough, durable and pliable.

Full flannel lined. Unbreakable visor. Warm inband to protect the ears in cold weather.

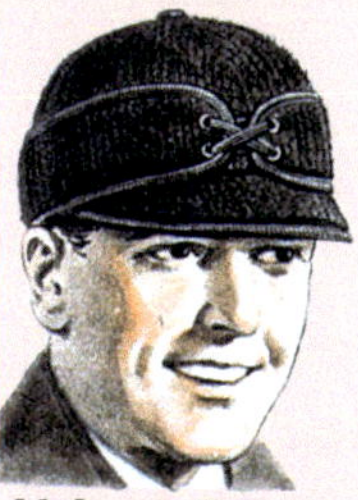

Mohawk Knit Wool
39 G 759—Navy blue.
39 G 761—Gray........ **$1.00**
SIZES: 6¾, 6⅞, 7, 7⅛, 7¼, 7⅜, 7½. **State size. Postpaid.**

A new, warm Cap of All Wool Mohawk knit. All Wool lining. Unbreakable visor. Great for men who work outdoors. Outside pulldown to cover ears in cold weather.

Leather Helmet
All Wool Lined

39 G 704—
Black leather.
39 G 705—
Brown leather. **$1.00**
SIZES: 6¾, 6⅞, 7, 7⅛, 7¼, 7⅜, 7½. **State size. We Pay Postage.**

Big value! A genuine sheepskin leather Helmet far superior to most helmets priced near one dollar. Months of hard wear prove its real quality. The leather is soft and pliable, yet very durable. Full lined with thick warm All Wool flannel.

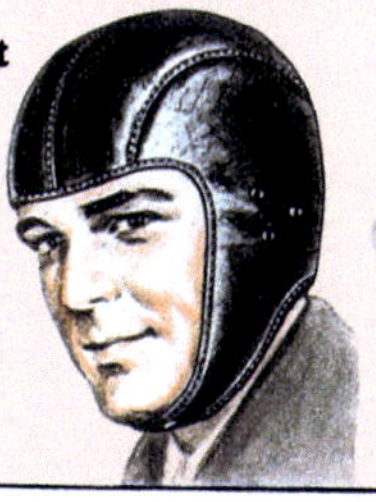

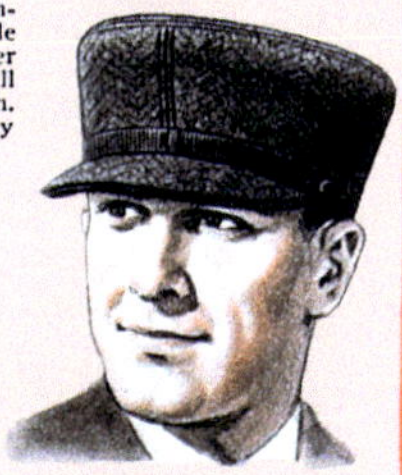

Wool Judge Cap
39 G 725—
Assorted colors...... **$1.00**
SIZES: 6¾, 6⅞, 7, 7⅛, 7¼, 7⅜, 7½. **State size. Postpaid.**

Assorted fine heavy All Wool overcoating. Full lined with strong cotton twill. Lined inband. Unbreakable visor

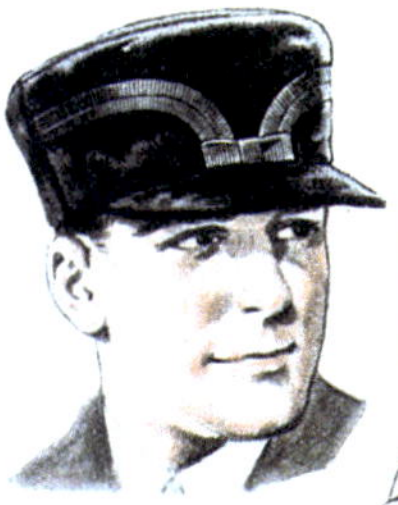

Silk Pile Plush

$1.69

39 G 753—Black only.
SIZES: 6¾, 6⅞, 7, 7⅛, 7¼, 7⅜, 7½, 7⅝, 7¾. **State size.** Read How to Measure on Page 247. **We Pay Postage.**

Heavy Silk pile plush. Full sateen lined, hand blocked and has an unbreakable visor. Warm lined inside band. An unusually good quality Cap.

39 G 751—Same as above except medium weight plush..... **$1.29**

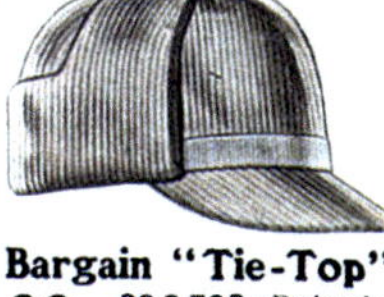

Bargain "Tie-Top"

69¢

39 G 703—Drab only.
SIZES: 6¾, 6⅞, 7, 7⅛, 7¼, 7⅜, 7½. **State size.** Read How to Measure on Page 247. **Postpaid.**

A low priced thick set corduroy Cap that wears well. Full lined with warm lining. Unbreakable visor.

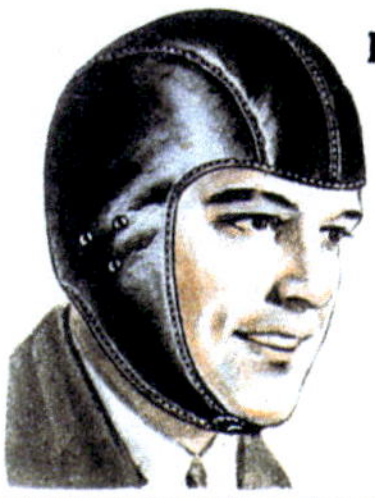

Horsehide Helmet

$1.49

39 G 755—
Black.
39 G 757—
Brown.
SIZES: 6¾ to 7½. **State size.** Read How to Measure on Page 247. **Postpaid.**

Men—match your leather coat with this durable genuine horsehide Helmet. You'll be a long, long time wearing it out too, because horsehide is the strongest leather used in clothing. Full lined with warm wool cloth. Adjustable snap fastens under chin. Keeps the entire head warm. Ventilation eyelets for ears. The workmanship is sturdy enough to last as long as the leather!

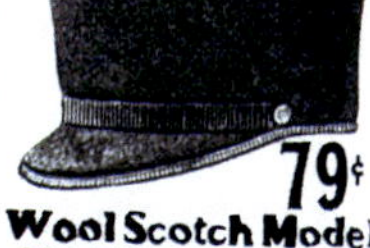

79¢

Wool Scotch Model
39 G 719—Navy blue only.
SIZES: 6¾, 6⅞, 7, 7⅛, 7¼, 7⅜, 7½. **State size.**

"Scotch" model of All Wool Melton, full lined with part wool felt. Warm inband. Unbreakable visor. **Postpaid.**

Served With
BYRD Expedition

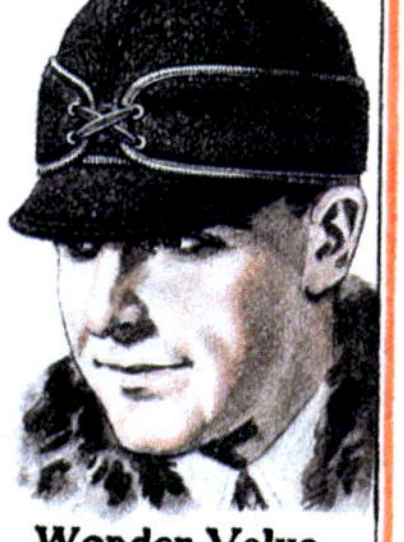

Wonder Value

89¢

39 G 731—Dark blue Melton cloth.
39 G 732—Drab brown corduroy.
39 G 735—Dark blue corduroy.
SIZES: 6¾ to 7¾. **State size. Served at the North and South Pole!** Warm and long wearing. Full lined with warm red flannel. Outside slide band. Unbreakable visor. **Postpaid.**

C.M.O. STYLE-LEADERS FOR 1938!

SEE PAGES 274 TO 318 FOR OTHER BARGAINS IN MEN AND BOYS' WEAR

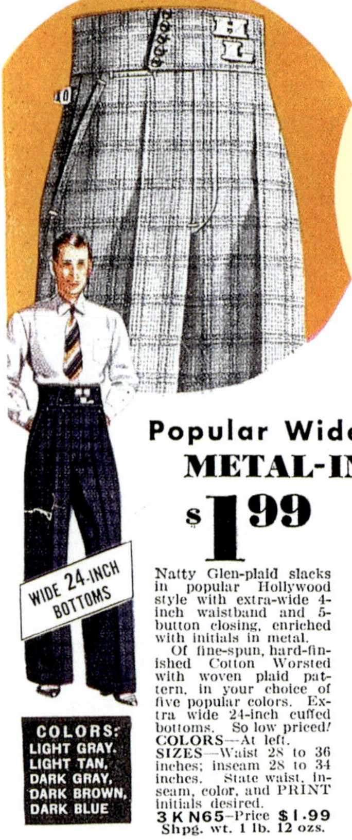

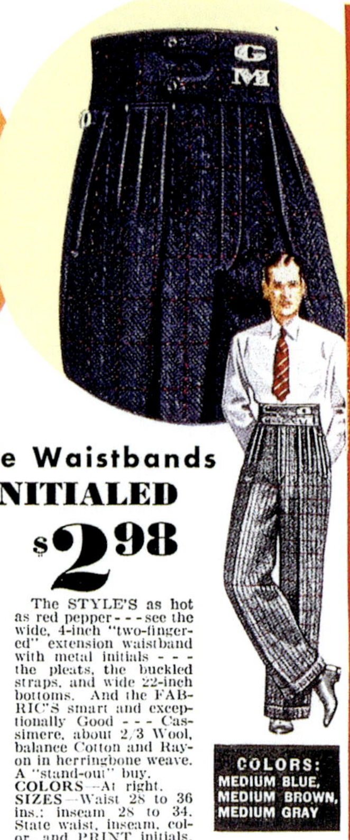

Popular Wide Waistbands
METAL-INITIALED

$1.99

Natty Glen-plaid slacks in popular Hollywood style with extra-wide 4-inch waistband and 5-button closing, enriched with initials in metal.

Of fine-spun, hard-finished Cotton Worsted with woven plaid pattern, in your choice of five popular colors. Extra wide 24-inch cuffed bottoms. So low priced!
COLORS—At left.
SIZES—Waist 28 to 36 inches; inseam 28 to 34 inches. State waist, inseam, color, and PRINT initials desired.
3 K N65—Price **$1.99**
Shpg. wt. 1 lb. 12 ozs.

$2.98

The STYLE'S as hot as red pepper - - - see the wide, 4-inch "two-fingered" extension waistband with metal initials - - - the pleats, the buckled straps, and wide 22-inch bottoms. And the FABRIC'S smart and exceptionally Good - - - Cassimere, about 2/3 Wool, balance Cotton and Rayon in herringbone weave. A "stand-out" buy.
COLORS—At right.
SIZES—Waist 28 to 36 ins.; inseam 28 to 34. State waist, inseam, color, and PRINT initials.
3 K N28—Price **$2.98**
Shpg. wt. 2 lbs.

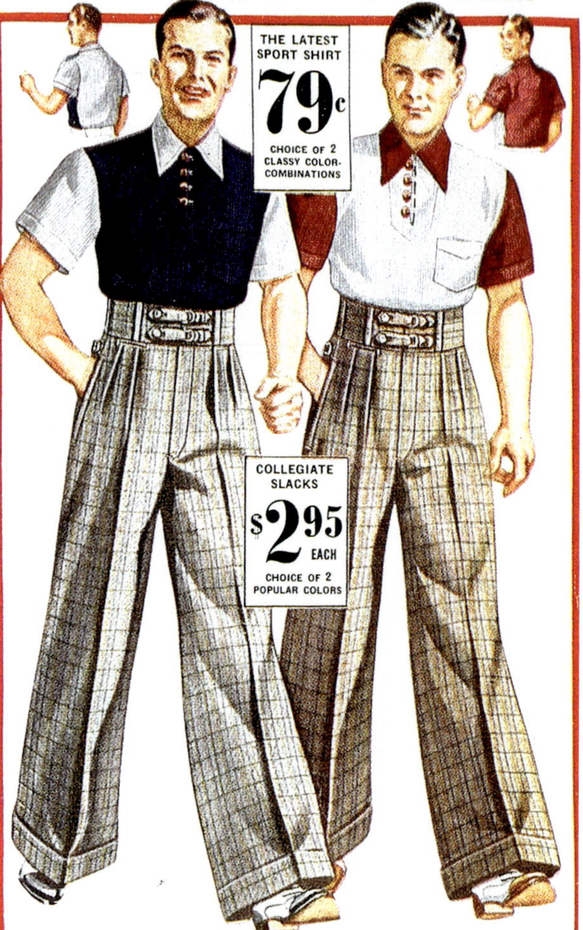

"Swellegant" newest collegiate-style slacks with pleats, and wide 3-inch waistband with ring-decorated straps fastening with buttons. Of Fine Flannel, about 1/3 Wool, balance Cotton and Rayon, with smart 3-tone windowpane pattern. 22-inch bottoms. Excellent value!
COLORS—Light-gray, or Light-tan. State waist, inseam, and color.
3 K N30—SIZES—Waist 28 to 36 ins.; inseam 29 to 34. Price **$2.95**
Shpg. wt. 1 lb. 12 ozs.

A "rah-rah" shirt - - - the most dapper you'll see on the campus. Back, sleeves, and collar in one shade; front contrasting-colored. Of Fine Quality Knitted Combed Cotton Jersey. A "beaut!"
COLORS—Navy-with-gray, or Gray-with-maroon. State color and size.
3 K V15—SMALL fits chest 34-36 ins.; MEDIUM 37-40; LARGE 41-44 . . . **79c**
Shpg. wt. 8 ozs.

INITIALS MONOGRAMMED
WITHOUT EXTRA CHARGE

WE WILL EMBROIDER ANY 2 OR 3 LETTERS ON SHIRTS SHOWN BELOW

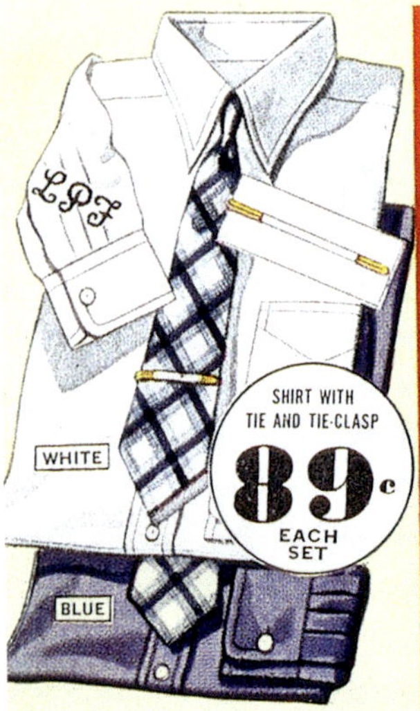

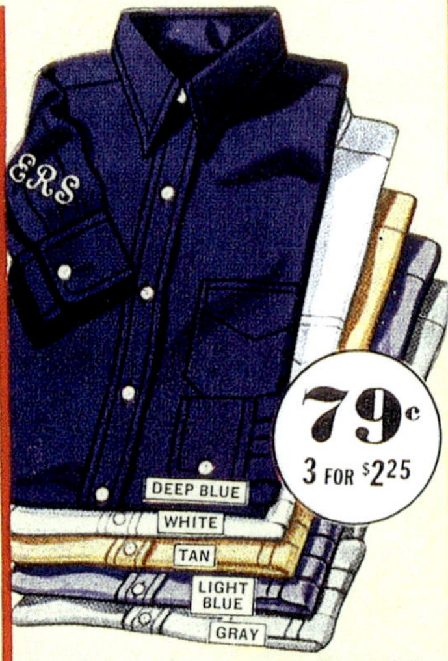

SPECIAL VALUE!

An outstanding bargain in a set con-
sisting of one monogrammed Good Qual-
ity, fast-color Cotton Broadcloth shirt,
A neat-looking tie, and a tie-clasp with
mother-of-pearl top. Immense value!
COLORS—White, or Blue; harmonizing
plaid tie as pictured or similar. State
color and size. PRINT initials.
Neck Sizes—14-14½-15-15½-16-16½-17.
3 K U40—Money-saving price, Set **89c**
Shpg. wt. 12 ozs.

SANFORIZED-SHRUNK

It sets the pace in outstanding value. "Quality" features you'd never expect in a shirt priced so low - - - ***"Sanforizing"*** and embroidered initials. Of Fast-color Good Quality Cotton Broadcloth. Very well made, with pleats in sleeves and back. COLORS—As named on picture. PRINT your initials. State color and size.
NECK SIZES—14-14½-15-15½-16-16½-17.
3 K U36—**3 for $2.25**. Each **79c**
Shpg. wt. 10 ozs. each.

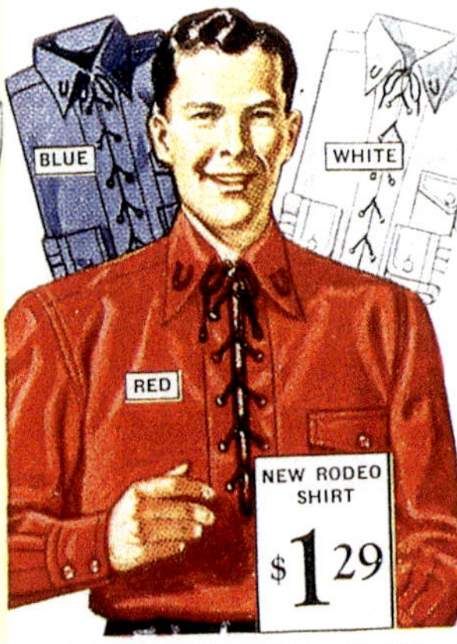

Embroidered horseshoes on the collar, and cord lacings through the 12 eyelets, make this slipover shirt so delightfully "horsey." Of Good Quality Cotton Broadcloth.
COLORS—Copen-blue, Red, White.
3 K U35—SIZES—SMALL, MED., LARGE.
Shpg. wt. 12 ozs.

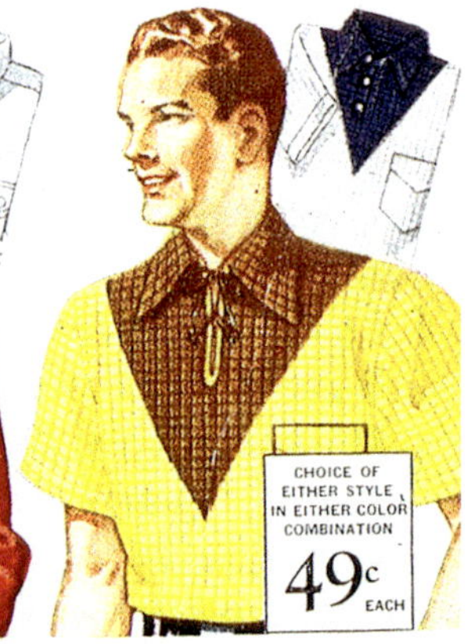

Cool, easily-laundered shirts in two snappy styles. Of Cotton, mesh-knit.
COLORS—White-with-navy, or Yellow-with-brown. State color, size.
SIZES—SMALL, MEDIUM, or LARGE.
Shpg. wt. 8 ozs. each.
3 K V21—3-BUTTON CLOSING **49c**
3 K V4—4 EYELETS, LACED **49c**

CHICAGO MAIL ORDER COMPANY - CHICAGO

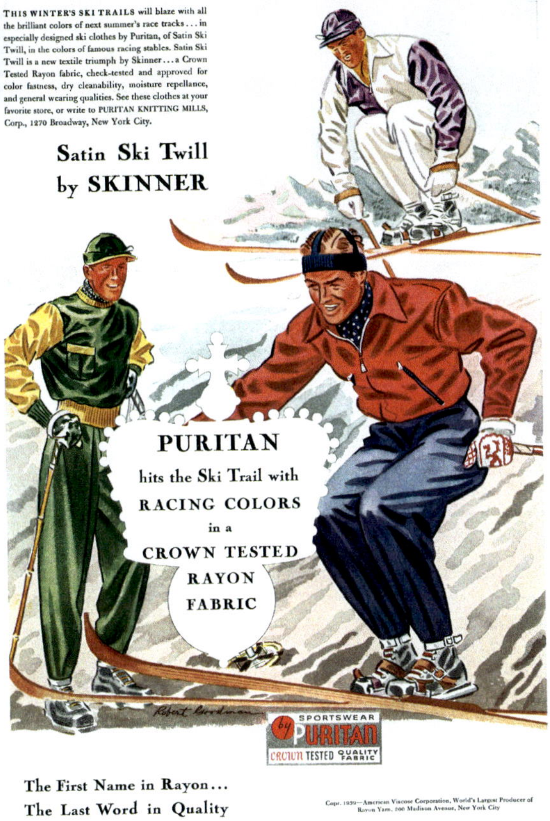

Puritan Sportswear, 1939

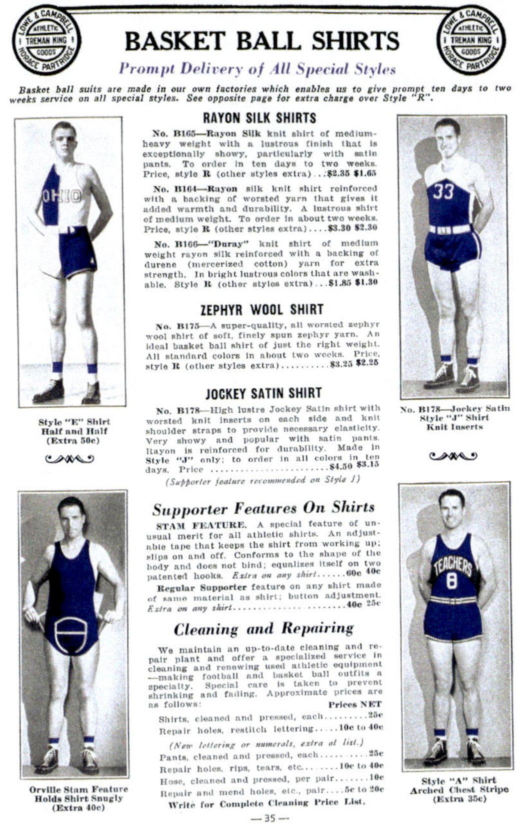

BASKET BALL SHIRTS

Prompt Delivery of All Special Styles

Basket ball suits are made in our own factories which enables us to give prompt ten days to two weeks service on all special styles. See opposite page for extra charge over Style "R".

RAYON SILK SHIRTS

No. B165—Rayon Silk knit shirt of medium-heavy weight with a lustrous finish that is exceptionally showy, particularly with satin pants. To order in ten days to two weeks. Price, style **R** (other styles extra) . . . **$2.35 $1.65**

No. B164—Rayon silk knit shirt reinforced with a backing of worsted yarn that gives it added warmth and durability. A lustrous shirt of medium weight. To order in about two weeks. Price, style **R** (other styles extra) **$3.30 $2.30**

No. B166—"Duray" knit shirt of medium weight rayon silk reinforced with a backing of durene (mercerized cotton) yarn for extra strength. In bright lustrous colors that are washable. Style **R** (other styles extra) . . . **$1.85 $1.30**

ZEPHYR WOOL SHIRT

No. B175—A super-quality, all worsted zephyr wool shirt of soft, finely spun zephyr yarn. An ideal basket ball shirt of just the right weight. All standard colors in about two weeks. Price, style **R** (other styles extra) **$3.25 $2.25**

JOCKEY SATIN SHIRT

No. B178—High lustre Jockey Satin shirt with worsted knit inserts on each side and knit shoulder straps to provide necessary elasticity. Very showy and popular with satin pants. Rayon is reinforced for durability. Made in **Style "J"** only; to order in all colors in ten days. Price **$4.50 $3.15**

(Supporter feature recommended on Style J)

Supporter Features On Shirts

STAM FEATURE. A special feature of unusual merit for all athletic shirts. An adjustable tape that keeps the shirt from working up; slips on and off. Conforms to the shape of the body and does not bind; equalizes itself on two patented hooks. *Extra on any shirt* **60c 40c**

Regular Supporter feature on any shirt made of same material as shirt; button adjustment. *Extra on any shirt* **40c 25c**

Cleaning and Repairing

We maintain an up-to-date cleaning and repair plant and offer a specialized service in cleaning and renewing used athletic equipment—making football and basket ball outfits a specialty. Special care is taken to prevent shrinking and fading. Approximate prices are as follows: **Prices NET**

Shirts, cleaned and pressed, each **25c**
Repair holes, restitch lettering . . . . . **10c to 40c**
(New lettering or numerals, extra at list.)
Pants, cleaned and pressed, each **25c**
Repair holes, rips, tears, etc. . . . . **10c to 40c**
Hose, cleaned and pressed, per pair **10c**
Repair and mend holes, etc., pair . . . . **5c to 20c**

Write for Complete Cleaning Price List.

Style "E" Shirt Half and Half (Extra 50c)

No. B178—Jockey Satin Style "J" Shirt Knit Inserts

Orville Stam Feature Holds Shirt Snugly (Extra 40c)

Style "A" Shirt Arched Chest Stripe (Extra 35c)

— 35 —

Basket Ball Shirts

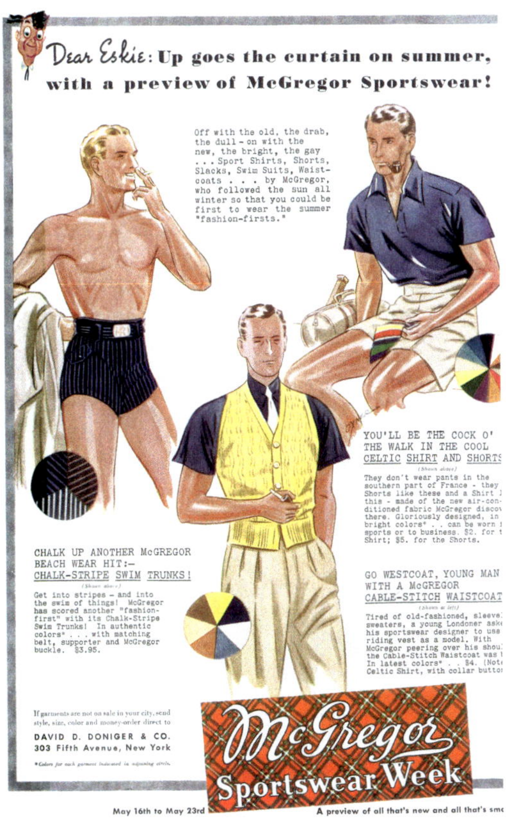

Men's Wear, 1938 ◂ *McGregor Sportswear, 1936*

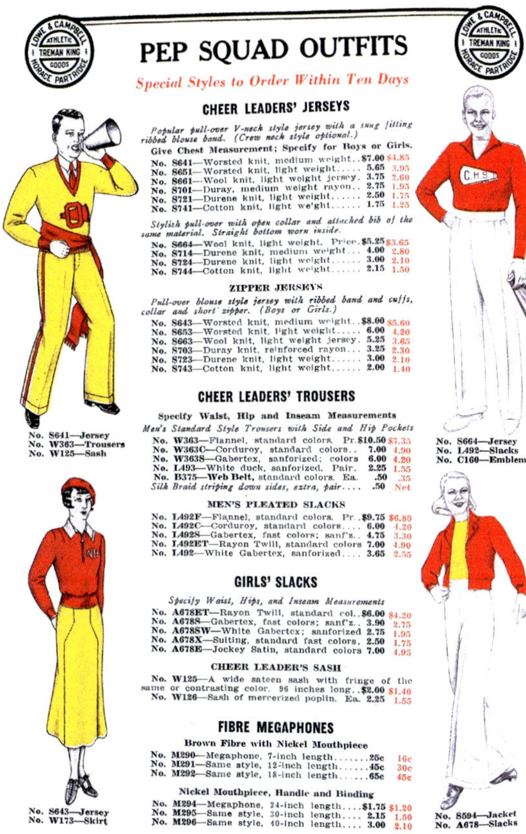

PEP SQUAD OUTFITS

Special Styles to Order Within Ten Days

CHEER LEADERS' JERSEYS

Popular pull-over V-neck style jersey with a snug fitting ribbed blouse band. (Crew neck style optional.)

Give Chest Measurement; Specify for Boys or Girls.

No. S641—Worsted knit, medium weight . . **$7.00** $4.85
No. S651—Worsted knit, light weight **5.65** 3.95
No. S661—Wool knit, light weight jersey. **3.75** 2.60
No. S701—Duray, medium weight rayon . . **2.75** 1.95
No. S721—Durene knit, light weight **2.50** 1.75
No. S741—Cotton knit, light we'ght **1.75** 1.25

Stylish pull-over with open collar and attached bib of the same material. Straight bottom worn inside.

No. S664—Wool knit, light weight. Price . **$5.25** $3.65
No. S714—Durene knit, medium weight . . . **4.00** 2.80
No. S724—Durene knit, light weight **3.00** 2.10
No. S744—Cotton knit, light weight **2.15** 1.50

ZIPPER JERSEYS

Pull-over blouse style jersey with ribbed band and cuffs, collar and short zipper. (Boys or Girls.)

No. S643—Worsted knit, medium weight . . **$8.00** $5.60
No. S653—Worsted knit, light weight **6.00** 4.20
No. S663—Wool knit, light weight jersey. **5.25** 3.65
No. S703—Duray knit, reinforced rayon . . . **3.25** 2.30
No. S723—Durene knit, light weight **3.00** 2.10
No. S743—Cotton knit, light weight **2.00** 1.40

CHEER LEADERS' TROUSERS

Specify Waist, Hip and Inseam Measurements

Men's Standard Style Trousers with Side and Hip Pockets

No. W363—Flannel, standard colors. Pr. **$10.50** $7.35
No. W363C—Corduroy, standard colors . . **7.00** 4.90
No. W363S—Gabertex, sanforized; colors **6.00** 4.20
No. L493—White duck, sanforized. Pair. **2.25** 1.55
No. B375—Web Belt, standard colors. Ea. **.50** .35
Silk Braid striping down sides, extra, pair . . . . **.50** Net

MEN'S PLEATED SLACKS

No. L492F—Flannel, standard colors. Pr. . **$9.75** $6.80
No. L492C—Corduroy, standard colors **6.00** 4.20
No. L492S—Gabertex, fast colors; sanf'z. . **4.75** 3.30
No. L492ET—Rayon Twill, standard colors **7.00** 4.90
No. L492—White Gabertex, sanforized **3.65** 2.55

GIRLS' SLACKS

Specify Waist, Hips, and Inseam Measurements

No. A678ET—Rayon Twill, standard col. . **$6.00** $4.20
No. A678S—Gabertex, fast colors; sanf'z. . **3.90** 2.75
No. A678SW—White Gabertex; sanforized **2.75** 1.95
No. A678X—Suiting, standard fast colors. **2.50** 1.75
No. A678E—Jockey Satin, standard colors **7.00** 4.95

CHEER LEADER'S SASH

No. W125—A wide sateen sash with fringe of the same or contrasting color. 96 inches long . . **$2.00** $1.40
No. W126—Sash of mercerized poplin. Ea. **2.25** 1.55

FIBRE MEGAPHONES

Brown Fibre with Nickel Mouthpiece

No. M290—Megaphone, 7-inch length **25c** 16c
No. M291—Same style, 12-inch length **45c** 30c
No. M292—Same style, 18-inch length **65c** 45c

Nickel Mouthpiece, Handle and Binding

No. M294—Megaphone, 24-inch length **$1.75** $1.20
No. M295—Same style, 30-inch length **2.15** 1.50
No. M296—Same style, 40-inch length **3.00** 2.10

No. S641—Jersey
No. W363—Trousers
No. W125—Sash

No. S664—Jersey
No. L492—Slacks
No. C160—Emblem

No. S643—Jersey
No. W173—Skirt

No. S594—Jacket
No. A678—Slacks

Pep Squad Outfits

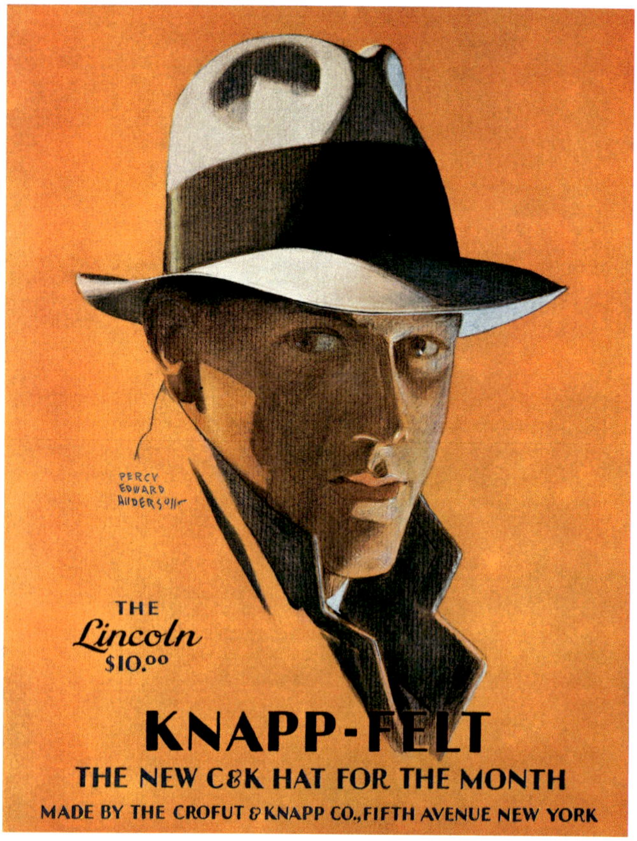

Knapp-Felt, 1930

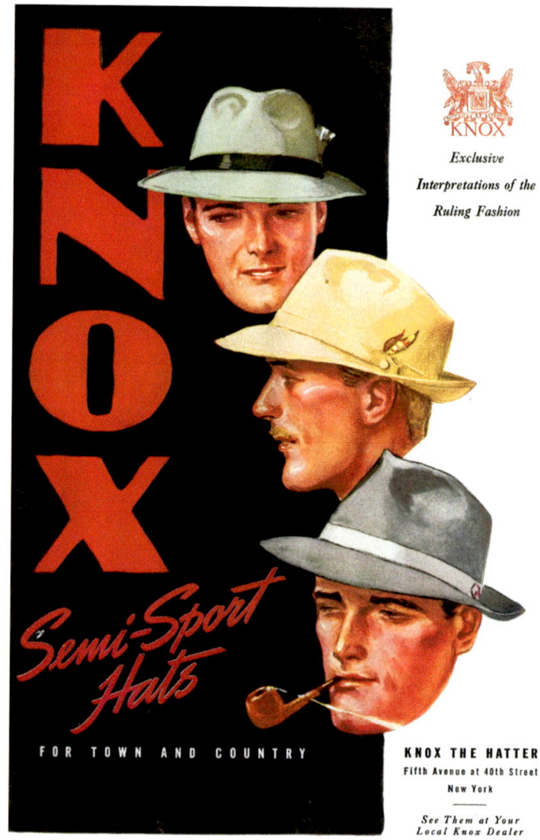

Knox Hats, 1939

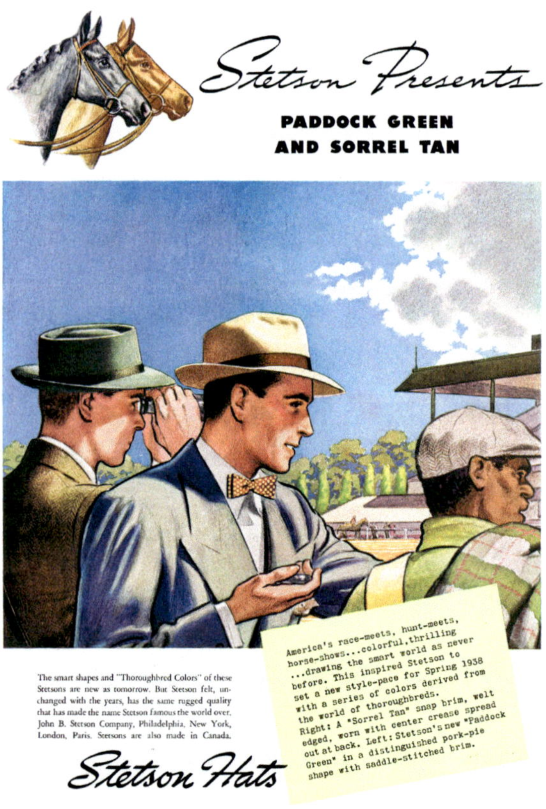

Stetson Hats, 1938

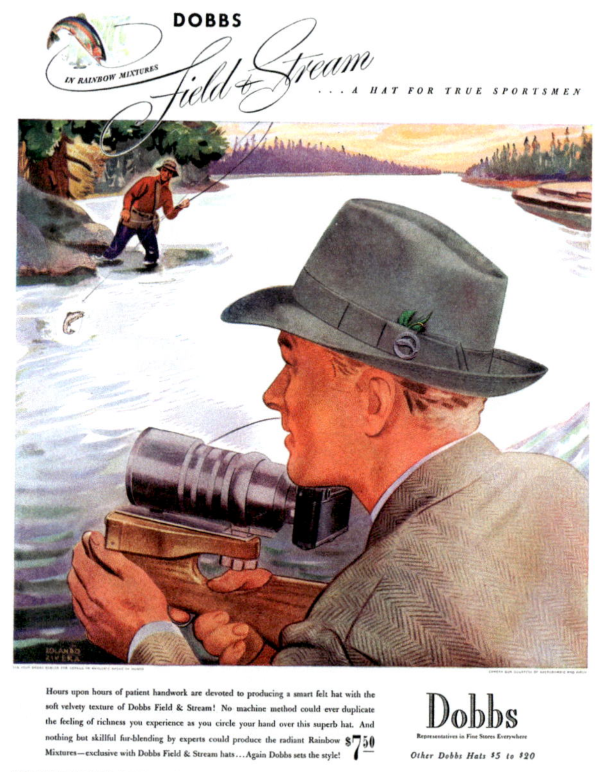

Dobbs Hats, 1939

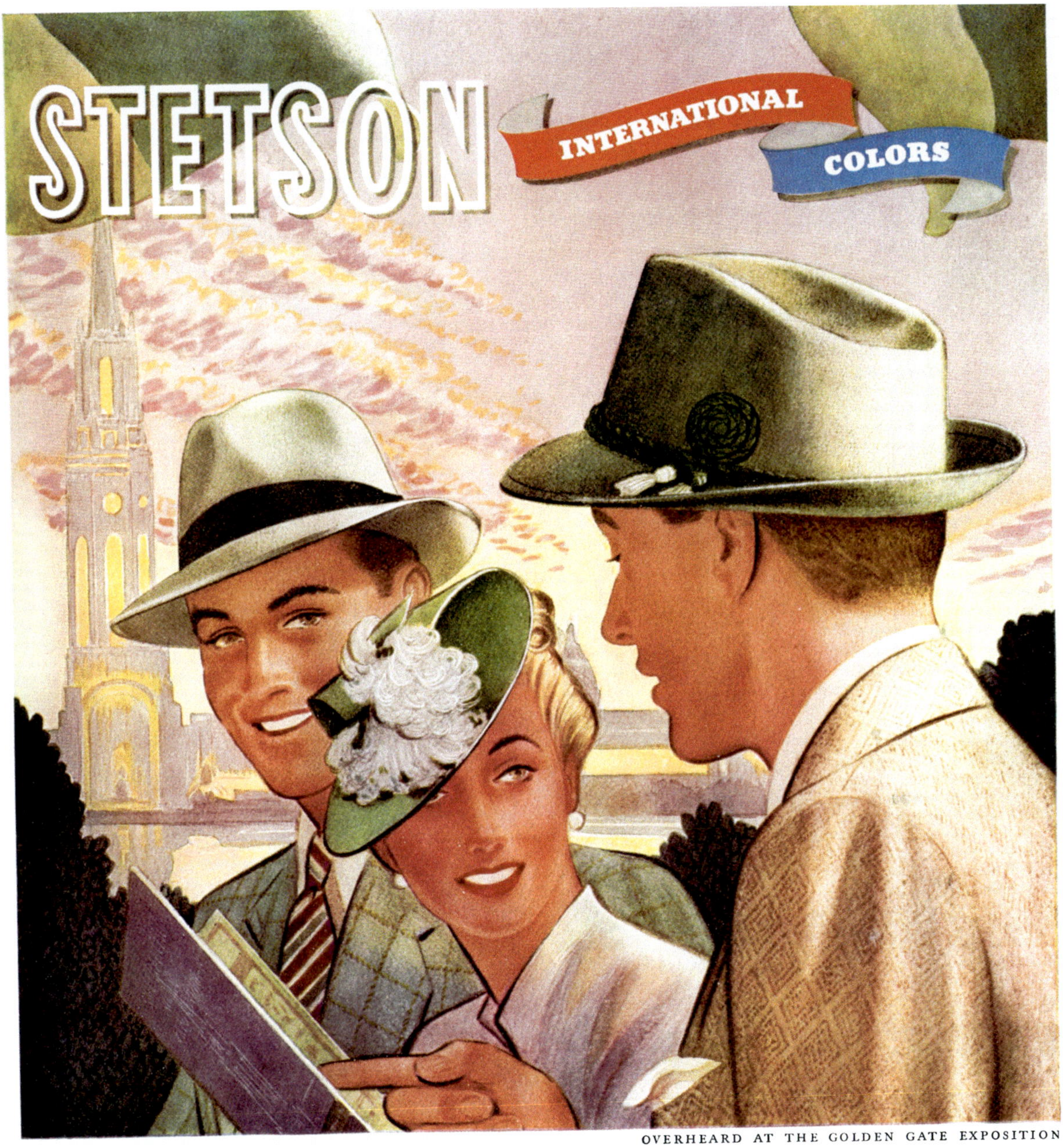

OVERHEARD AT THE GOLDEN GATE EXPOSITION

"Pretend you're not looking!"

JANET: Here come the cameramen! They must think you boys are distinguished international visitors.

PETE: Nice compliment, Janet. But I get it—it must be our new Stetsons.

JANET: Ah-hah! So that's how you suddenly got that continental air!

BILL: Sure! It's a trick Stetson does with their new International Colors!

PETE: *Didn't I tell you*, Bill? Faint hat never won fair lady!

STETSONS ARE PRICED $5 to $40

STETSONS MADE IN CANADA, FROM $5.50 • JOHN B. STETSON COMPANY, PHILADELPHIA, NEW YORK, LONDON, PARIS

Stetson, 1939

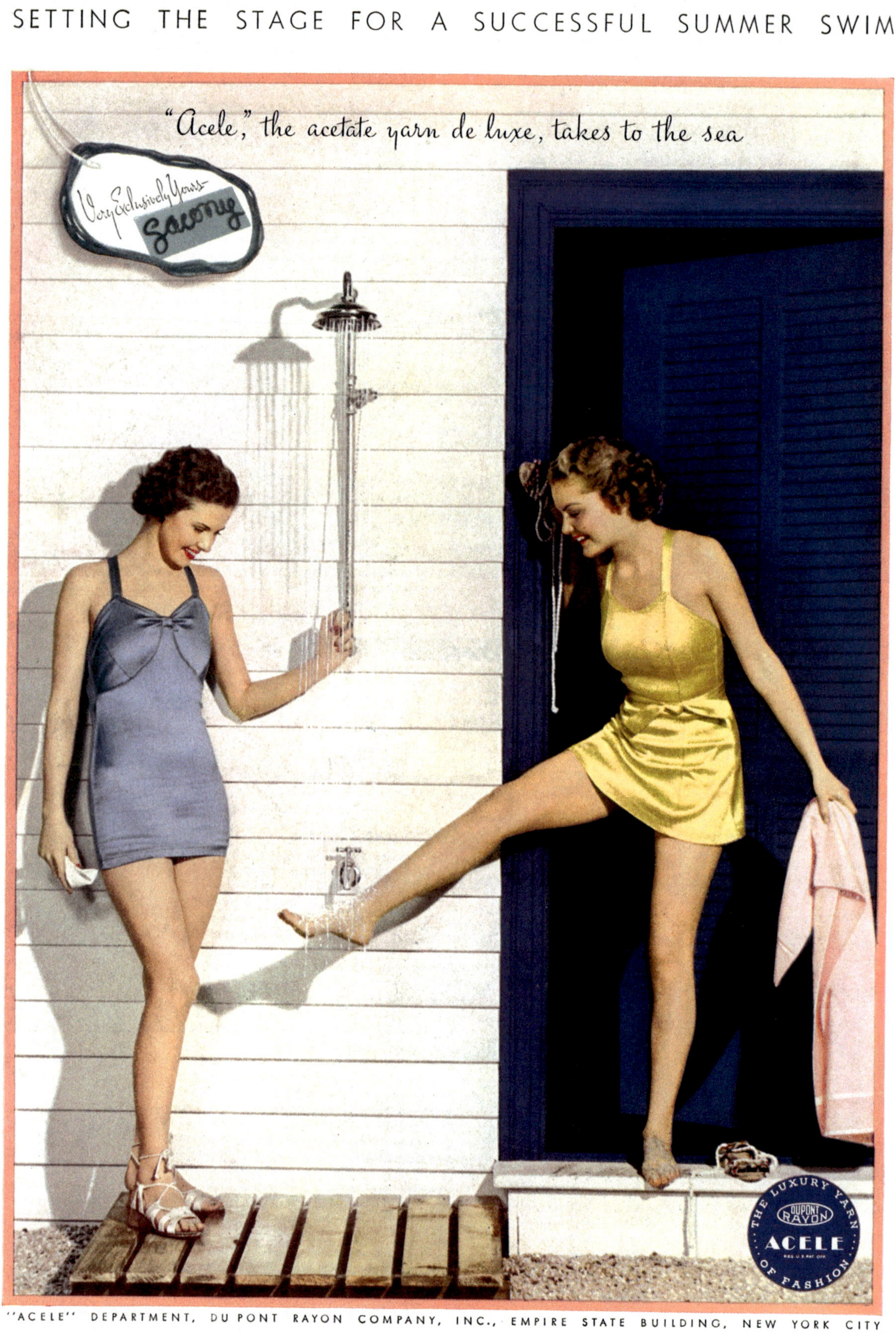
SETTING THE STAGE FOR A SUCCESSFUL SUMMER SWIM
"Acele," the acetate yarn de luxe, takes to the sea
Very Exclusively Yours—
Saxony
THE LUXURY YARN OF FASHION
DUPONT RAYON
ACELE
"ACELE" DEPARTMENT, DU PONT RAYON COMPANY, INC., EMPIRE STATE BUILDING, NEW YORK CITY

Acele, 1936

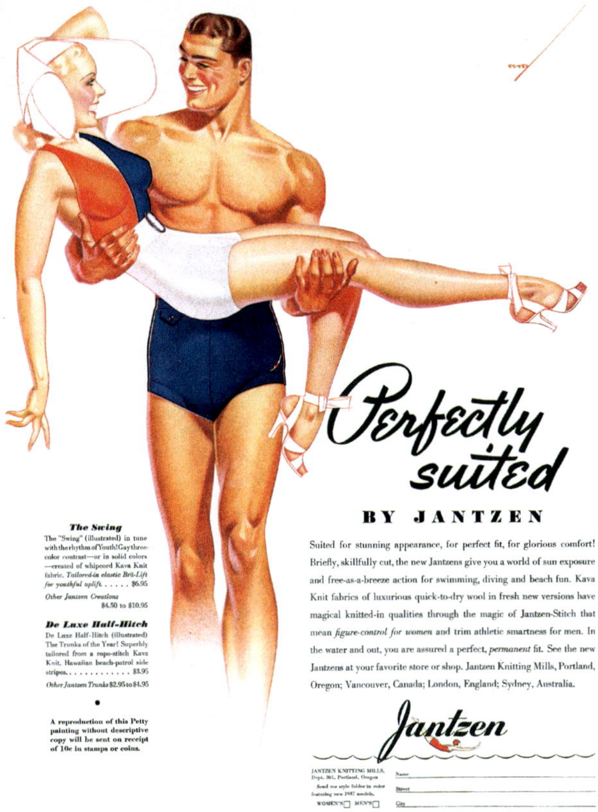

Jantzen, 1937

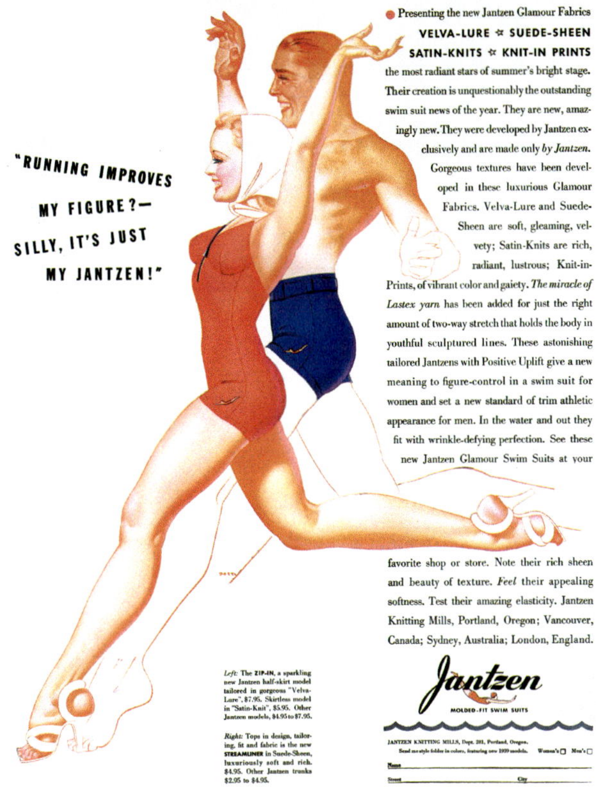

Jantzen, 1939

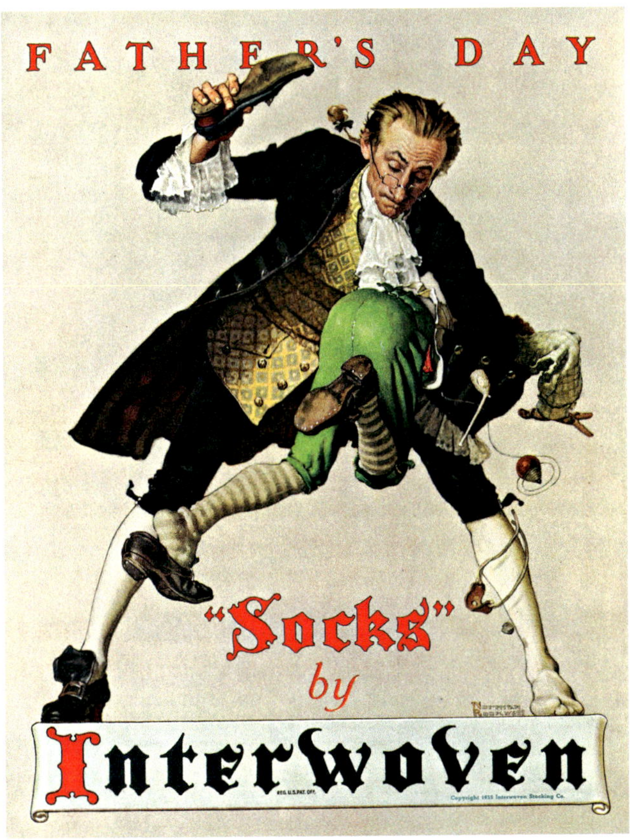

Interwoven, 1935

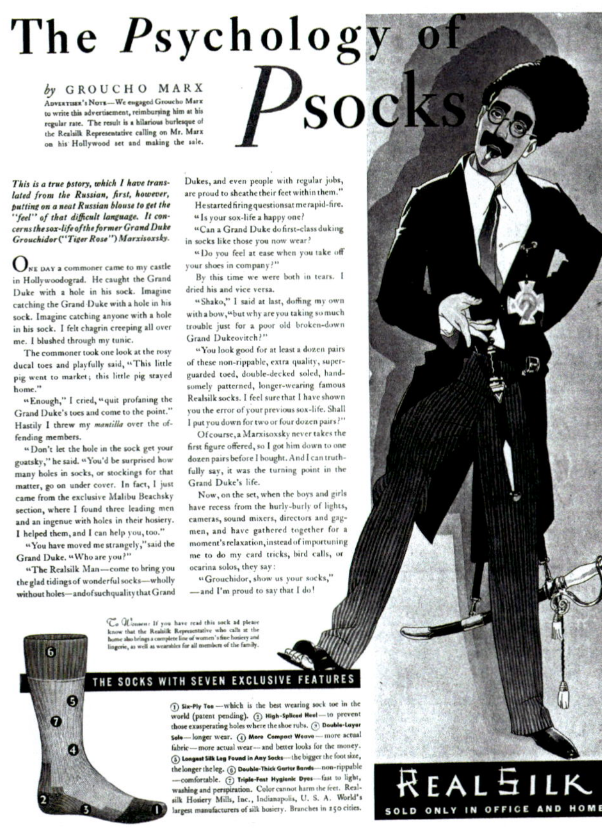

Real Silk, 1932

▸▸ Kiddies Play Suits, 1930

Give Him A Young America TRADE MARK

FRUIT-OF-THE-LOOM Wash Suits

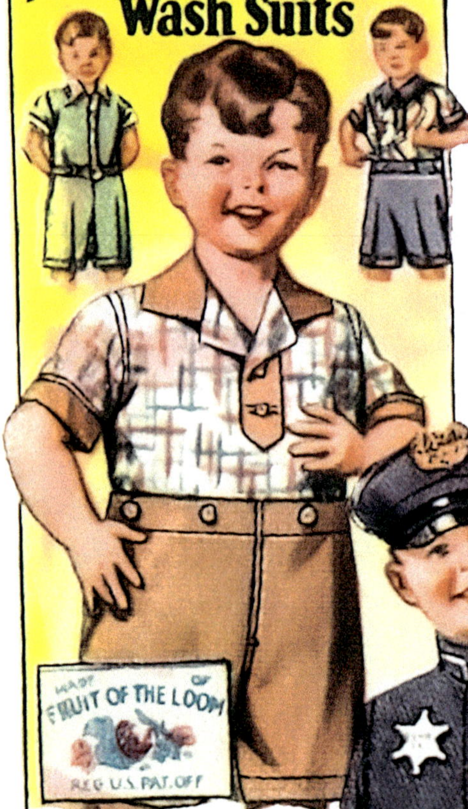

Sold by Mail Only by Ward's, With Label in Suits

$1.00 Each

State Second and Third Choice

SIZES: 2 to 8 years. State age-size. We Pay Postage.
40 G 3704 — Blues, tans and greens, combination trim. All same or similar to styles shown. Each... **$1.00**

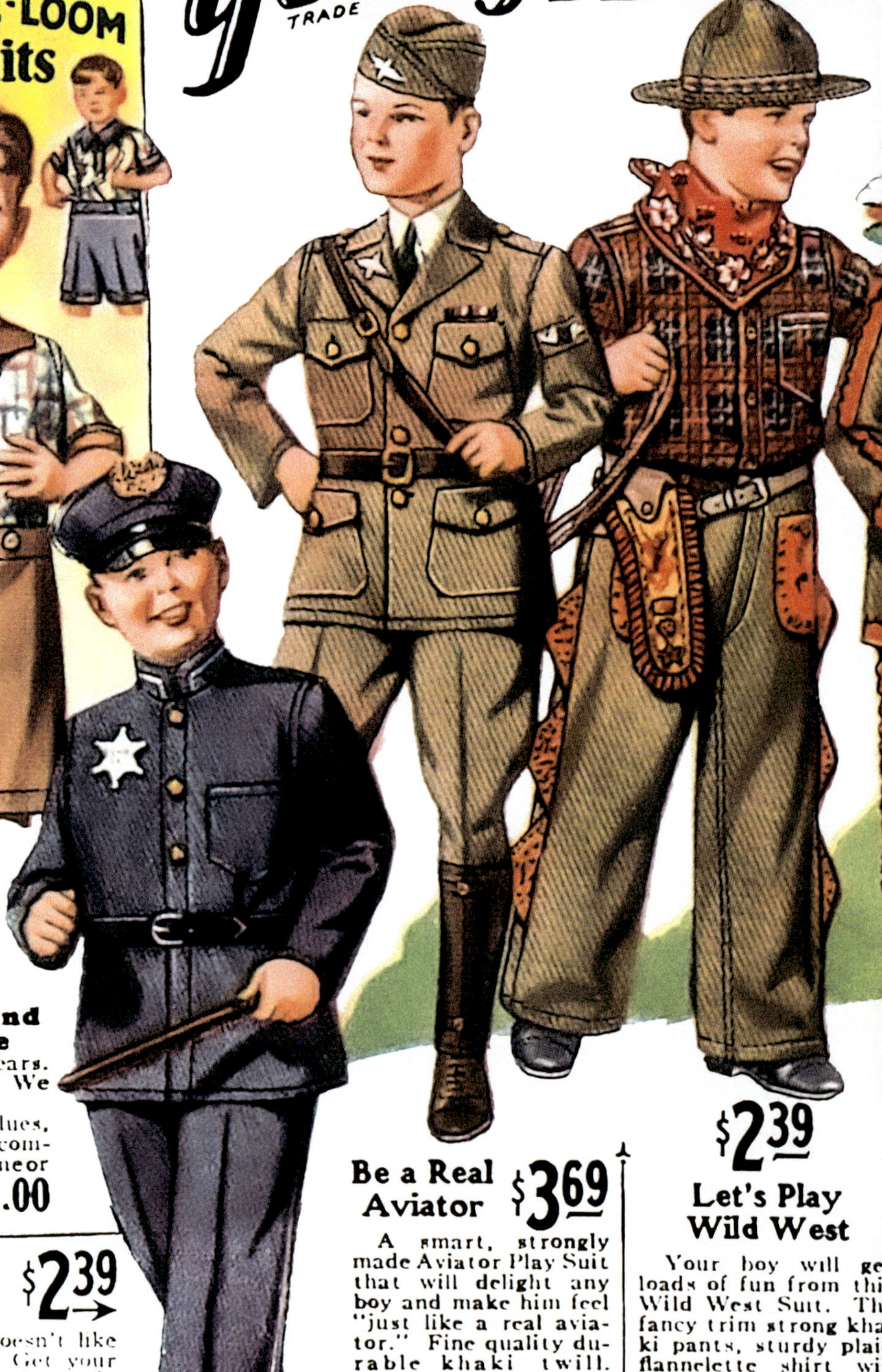

Stop! I Am the Law! $2.39 →

What little boy doesn't like to play policeman? Get your boy this strongly made outfit consisting of jacket, long pants and cap of navy blue drill, belt, billie and detachable star. Chief badge on cap. A Play Suit that will save his better clothes.
EVEN SIZES: 4 to 14 years. State age-size. Postpaid.
40 G 4120— Blue only........ **$2.39**

Be a Real Aviator $3.69

A smart, strongly made Aviator Play Suit that will delight any boy and make him feel "just like a real aviator." Fine quality durable khaki twill. Smartly tailored coat, trim breeches, overseas hat, imitation leather Sam Brown belt, puttees, and two nickeled pins with wings. **Postpaid.**
EVEN SIZES: 4 to 16 yrs. State age-size.
40 G 4136 . $3.69

$2.39 Let's Play Wild West

Your boy will get loads of fun from this Wild West Suit. The fancy trim strong khaki pants, sturdy plaid flannelette shirt will stand rough wear. Included in this outfit are hat, lariat, extra large toy pistol and holster and bandanna handkerchief.
EVEN SIZES: 4 to 14 years. Stage age-size. Postpaid.
40 G 4104 . $2.39

Blue denim........65¢
42 G 5919—
Tan khaki jean........85¢

...ay Suit

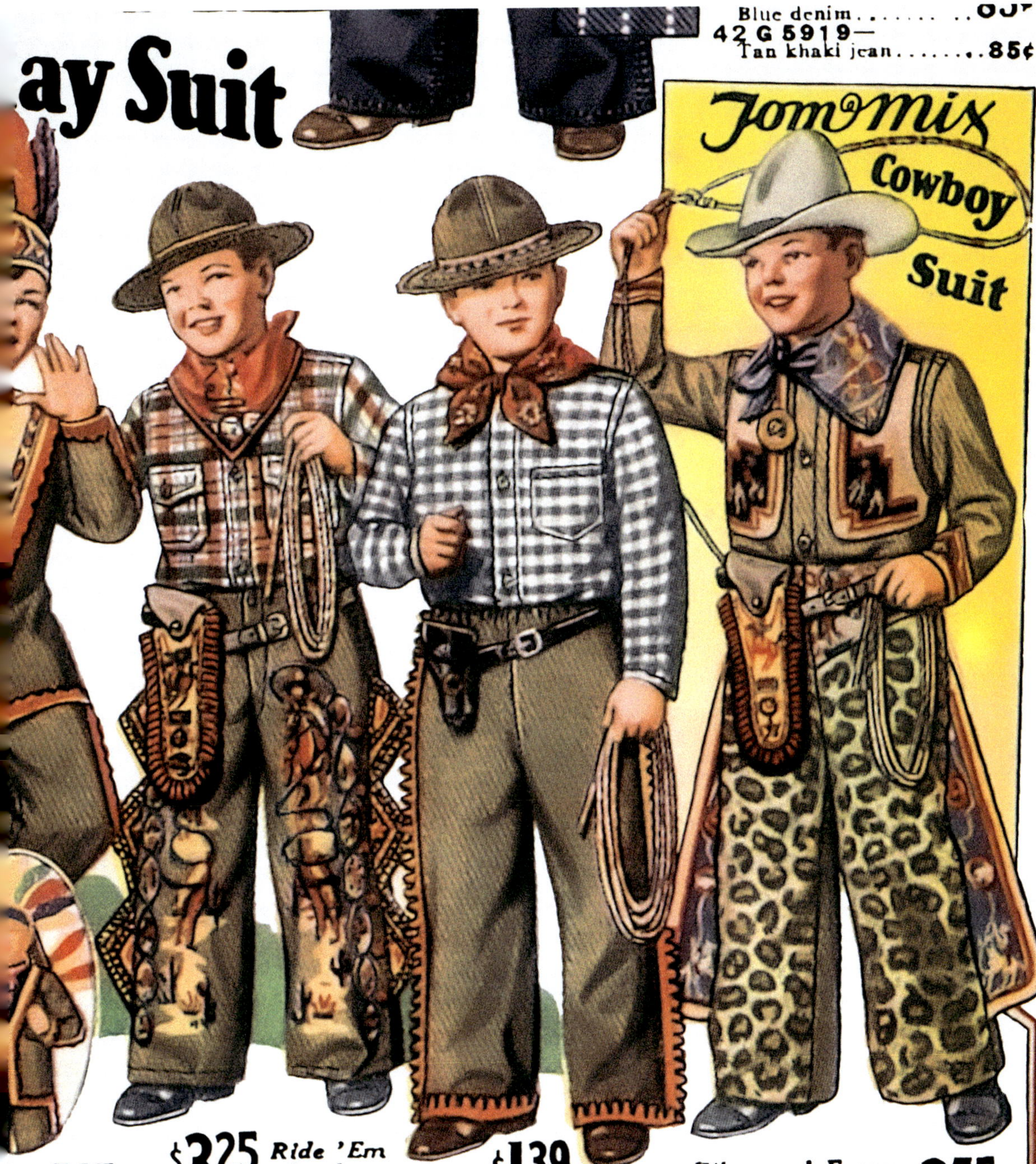

$1.65

...trimmings ...this good ...khaki In-...fit. Head-...welve highly ...thers. The ...of lighter ...aki. Post-

...SIZES: 4 to ... Tan only. ...-size.
...32 $1.65

...SIZES: 4 to ... Tan only. ...e-size.
...24....95¢

$3.25 *Ride 'Em Cowboy*

Just Off the Ranch

A new Cowboy Outfit **sold by mail only by Ward's.** Sure to please every real boy. Pants made of extra heavy khaki, with bright painted trimmings. Heavy flannelette assorted plaid shirts. Extra large toy gun with trimly painted holster. Every item pictured included.

EVEN SIZES: 4 to 14 years. **State age-size. We Pay Postage.**
40 G 4106 $3.25

$1.39

7-Piece Cowboy Suit

For only $1.39 you get a Cowboy Suit that will please your boy and help keep his better clothes for dress wear. Long pants of durable khaki have imitation leather fringing. Waist is strong cotton flannel in colorful checked patterns. Big value.

EVEN SIZES: 4 to 14 years. **State age-size. We Pay Postage.**
40 G 4102 $1.39

Whoopee! Every Boy Wants This Tom Mix Suit $3.75

Genuine Tom Mix Cowboy Outfit. Just what every boy wants when he plays wild west or rodeo. Outfit is strong khaki twill, with chaps of cotton flannel. Fast-color painted decorations on the imitation leather chest plates and chap trimmings. Wool felt Carlsbad Junior hat; lariat; toy pistol and holster (large size); fancy painted large size neckerchief; and autographed picture of Tom Mix.

EVEN SIZES: 4 to 14 yrs. **State age-size. Postpaid.**
40 G 4142...... $3.75

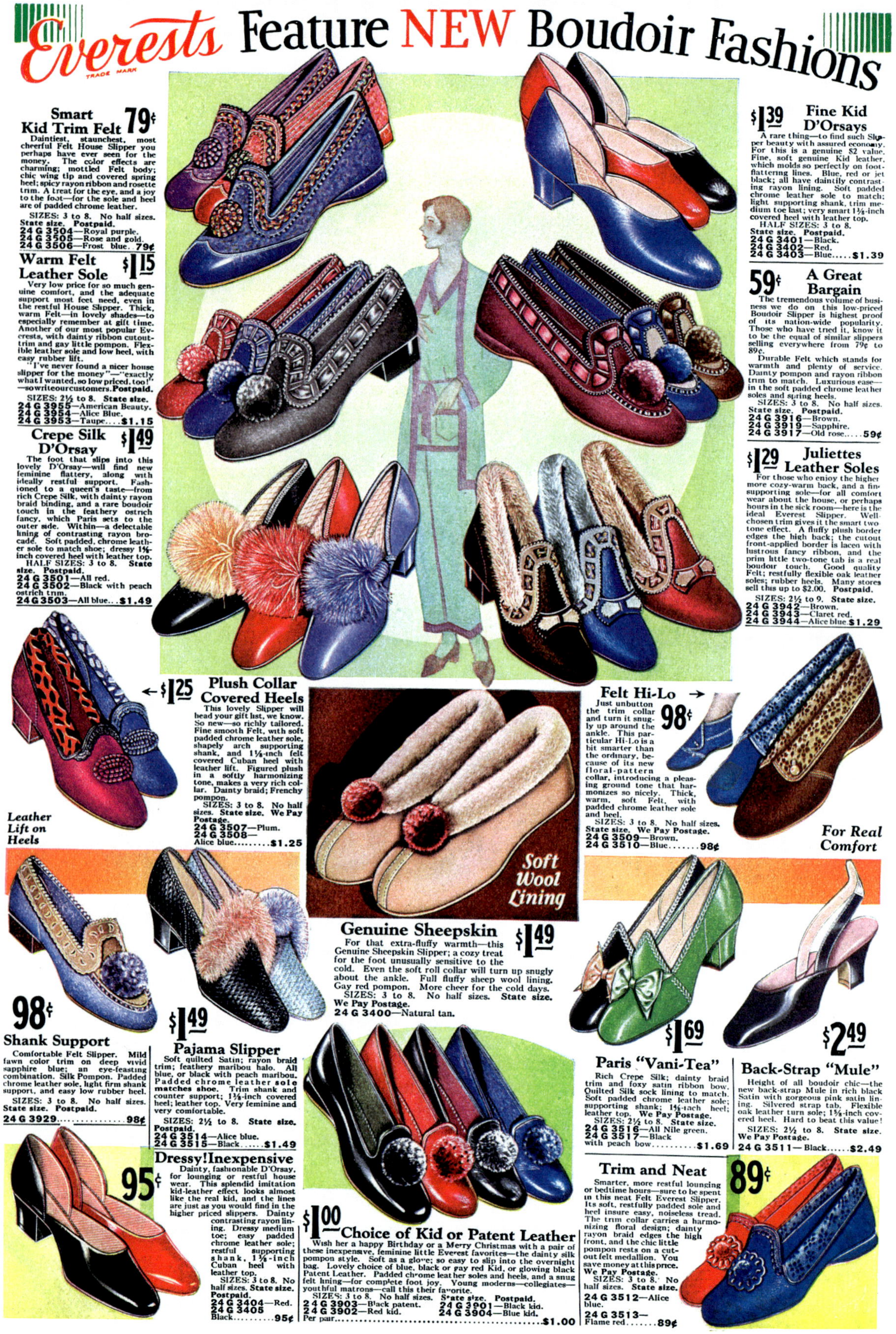

Everests Feature NEW Boudoir Fashions

TRADE MARK

Smart Kid Trim Felt 79¢

Daintiest, staunchest, most cheerful Felt House Slipper you perhaps have ever seen for the money. The color effects are charming; mottled Felt body; chic wing tip and covered spring heel; spicy rayon ribbon and rosette trim. A treat for the eye, and a joy to the foot—for the sole and heel are of padded chrome leather.

SIZES: 3 to 8. No half sizes. State size. **Postpaid.**
24 G 3504—Royal purple.
24 G 3505—Rose and gold.
24 G 3506—Frost blue. **79¢**

Warm Felt Leather Sole $1.15

Very low price for so much genuine comfort, and the adequate support most feet need, even in the restful House Slipper. Thick, warm Felt—in lovely shades—to especially remember at gift time. Another of our most popular Everests, with dainty ribbon cutout-trim and gay little pompon. Flexible leather sole and low heel, with easy rubber lift.

"I've never found a nicer house slipper for the money"—"exactly what I wanted, so low priced, too!"—so write our customers. **Postpaid.**

SIZES: 2½ to 8. **State size.**
24 G 3955—American Beauty.
24 G 3954—Alice Blue.
24 G 3953—Taupe.... **$1.15**

Crepe Silk D'Orsay $1.49

The foot that slips into this lovely D'Orsay—will find new feminine flattery, along with ideally restful support. Fashioned to a queen's taste—from rich Crepe Silk, with dainty rayon braid binding, and a rare boudoir touch in the feathery ostrich fancy, which Paris sets to the outer side. Within—a delectable lining of contrasting rayon brocade. Soft padded, chrome leather sole to match shoe; dressy 1⅝-inch covered heel with leather top.

HALF SIZES: 3 to 8. **State size. Postpaid.**
24 G 3501—All red.
24 G 3502—Black with peach ostrich trim.
24 G 3503—All blue... **$1.49**

$1.39 Fine Kid D'Orsays

A rare thing—to find such Slipper beauty with assured economy. For this is a genuine $2 value. Fine, soft genuine Kid leather, which molds so perfectly on foot-flattering lines. Blue, red or jet black; all have daintily contrasting rayon lining. Soft padded chrome leather sole to match; light supporting shank, trim medium toe last; very smart 1⅜-inch covered heel with leather top.

HALF SIZES: 3 to 8. **State size. Postpaid.**
24 G 3401—Black.
24 G 3402—Red.
24 G 3403—Blue..... **$1.39**

59¢ A Great Bargain

The tremendous volume of business we do on this low-priced Boudoir Slipper is highest proof of its nation-wide popularity. Those who have tried it, know it to be the equal of similar slippers selling everywhere from 79¢ to 89¢.

Durable Felt which stands for warmth and plenty of service. Dainty pompon and rayon ribbon trim to match. Luxurious ease—in the soft padded chrome leather soles and spring heels.

SIZES: 3 to 8. No half sizes. **State size. Postpaid.**
24 G 3916—Brown.
24 G 3919—Sapphire.
24 G 3917—Old rose..... **59¢**

$1.29 Juliettes Leather Soles

For those who enjoy the higher more cozy-warm back, and a firm supporting sole—for all comfort wear about the house, or perhaps hours in the sick room—here is the ideal Everest Slipper. Well-chosen trim gives it the smart two-tone effect. A fluffy plush border edges the high back; the cutout front-applied border is laced with lustrous fancy ribbon, and the prim little two-tone tab is a real boudoir touch. Good quality Felt; restfully flexible oak leather soles; rubber heels. Many stores sell this up to $2.00. **Postpaid.**

SIZES: 2½ to 9. **State size.**
24 G 3942—Brown.
24 G 3943—Claret red.
24 G 3944—Alice blue. **$1.29**

← $1.25 Plush Collar Covered Heels

This lovely Slipper will head your gift list, we know. So new—so richly tailored. Fine smooth Felt, with soft padded chrome leather sole, shapely arch supporting shank, and 1⅛-inch felt covered Cuban heel with leather lift. Figured plush in a softly harmonizing tone, makes a very rich collar. Dainty braid; Frenchy pompon.

SIZES: 3 to 8. No half sizes. **State size. We Pay Postage.**
24 G 3507—Plum.
24 G 3508—Alice blue......... **$1.25**

Leather Lift on Heels

Soft Wool Lining

Genuine Sheepskin $1.49

For that extra-fluffy warmth—this Genuine Sheepskin Slipper; a cozy treat for the foot unusually sensitive to the cold. Even the soft roll collar will turn up snugly about the ankle. Full fluffy sheep wool lining. Gay red pompon. More cheer for the cold days.

SIZES: 3 to 8. No half sizes. **State size. We Pay Postage.**
24 G 3400—Natural tan.

Felt Hi-Lo → 98¢

Just unbutton the trim collar and turn it snugly up around the ankle. This particular Hi-Lo is a bit smarter than the ordinary, because of its new floral-pattern collar, introducing a pleasing ground tone that harmonizes so nicely. Thick, warm, soft Felt, with padded chrome leather sole and heel.

SIZES: 3 to 8. No half sizes. **State size. We Pay Postage.**
24 G 3509—Brown.
24 G 3510—Blue....... **98¢**

For Real Comfort

98¢ Shank Support

Comfortable Felt Slipper. Mild fawn color trim on deep vivid sapphire blue; an eye-feasting combination. Silk Pompon. Padded chrome leather sole, light firm shank support, and easy low rubber heel.

SIZES: 3 to 8. No half sizes. **State size. Postpaid.**
24 G 3929............... **98¢**

$1.49 Pajama Slipper

Soft quilted Satin; rayon braid trim; feathery maribou halo. All blue, or black with peach maribou. Padded chrome leather **sole matches shoe.** Trim shank and counter support; 1⅜-inch covered heel; leather top. Very feminine and very comfortable.

SIZES: 2½ to 8. **State size. Postpaid.**
24 G 3514—Alice blue.
24 G 3515—Black...... **$1.49**

95¢ Dressy! Inexpensive

Dainty, fashionable D'Orsay, for lounging or restful house wear. This splendid imitation kid-leather effect looks almost like the real kid, and the lines are just as you would find in the higher priced slippers. Dainty contrasting rayon lining. Dressy medium toe; easy padded chrome leather sole; restful supporting shank, 1⅜-inch Cuban heel with leather top.

SIZES: 3 to 8. No half sizes. **State size. Postpaid.**
24 G 3404—Red.
24 G 3405 Black........... **95¢**

$1.00 Choice of Kid or Patent Leather

Wish her a happy Birthday or a Merry Christmas with a pair of these inexpensive, feminine little Everest favorites—the dainty silk pompon style. Soft as a glove; so easy to slip into the overnight bag. Lovely choice of blue, black or gay red Kid, or glowing black Patent Leather. Padded chrome leather soles and heels, and a snug felt lining—for complete foot joy. Young moderns—collegiates—youthful matrons—call this their favorite.

SIZES: 3 to 8. No half sizes. **State size. Postpaid.**
24 G 3903—Black patent.
24 G 3902—Red kid.
24 G 3901—Black kid.
24 G 3904—Blue kid.
Per pair.................................... **$1.00**

$1.69 Paris "Vani-Tea"

Rich Crepe Silk; dainty braid trim and foxy satin ribbon bow. Quilted Silk sock lining to match. Soft padded chrome leather sole; supporting shank; 1⅝-inch heel; leather top. **We Pay Postage.**

SIZES: 2½ to 8. **State size.**
24 G 3516—All Nile green.
24 G 3517—Black with peach bow........... **$1.69**

$2.49 Back-Strap "Mule"

Height of all boudoir chic—the new back-strap Mule in rich black Satin with gorgeous pink satin lining. Silvered strap tab. Flexible oak leather turn sole; 1⅝-inch covered heel. Hard to beat this value!

SIZES: 2½ to 8. **State size. We Pay Postage.**
24 G 3511—Black...... **$2.49**

Trim and Neat 89¢

Smarter, more restful lounging or bedtime hours—sure to be spent in this neat Felt Everest Slipper. Its soft, restfully padded sole and heel insure easy, noiseless tread. The trim collar carries a harmonizing floral design; dainty rayon braid edges the high front, and the chic little pompon rests on a cutout felt medallion. You save money at this price. **We Pay Postage.**

SIZES: 3 to 8. No half sizes. **State size.**
24 G 3512—Alice blue.
24 G 3513—Flame red....... **89¢**

Shoes, 1930

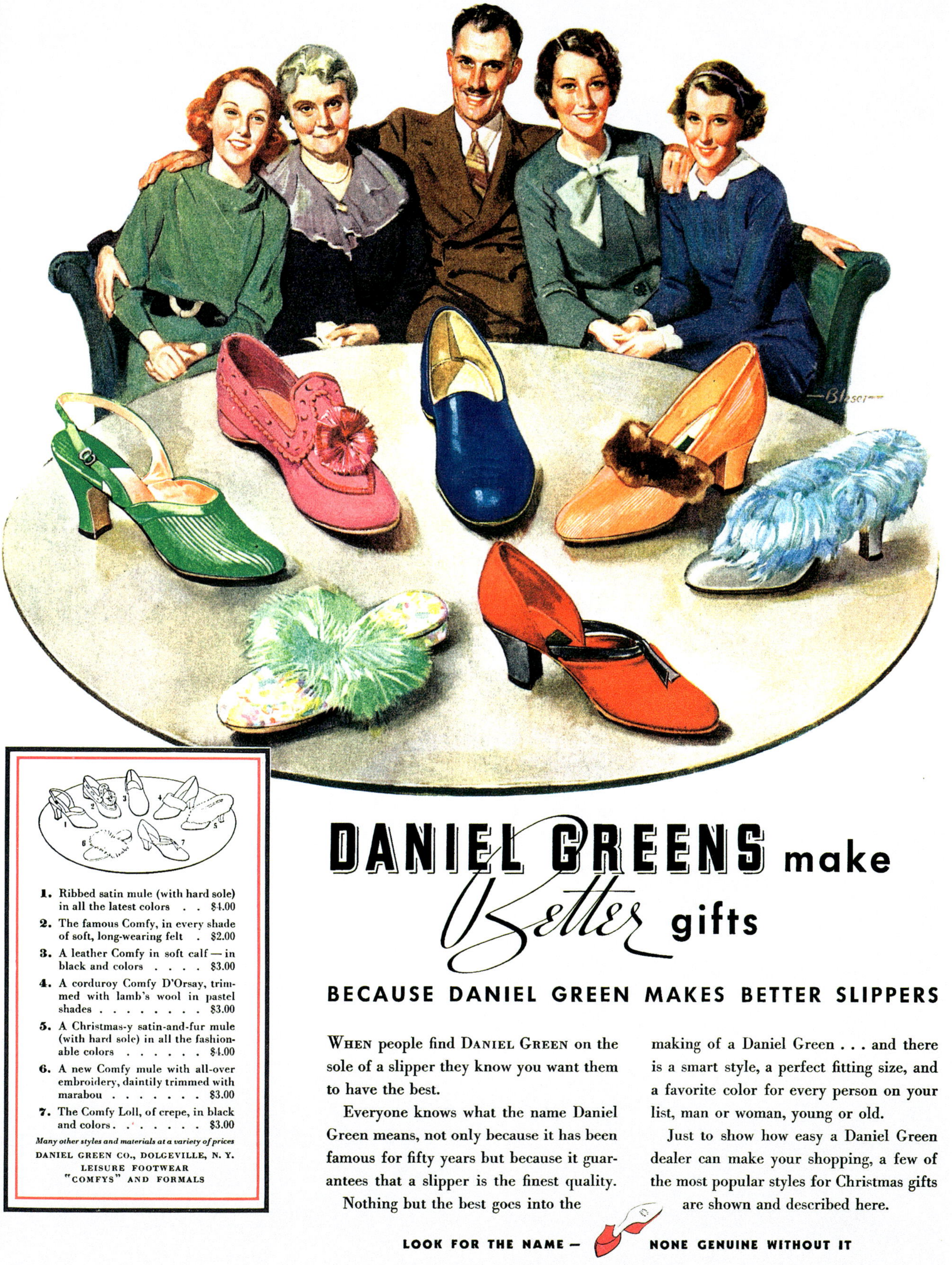

Daniel Greens Shoes, 1935

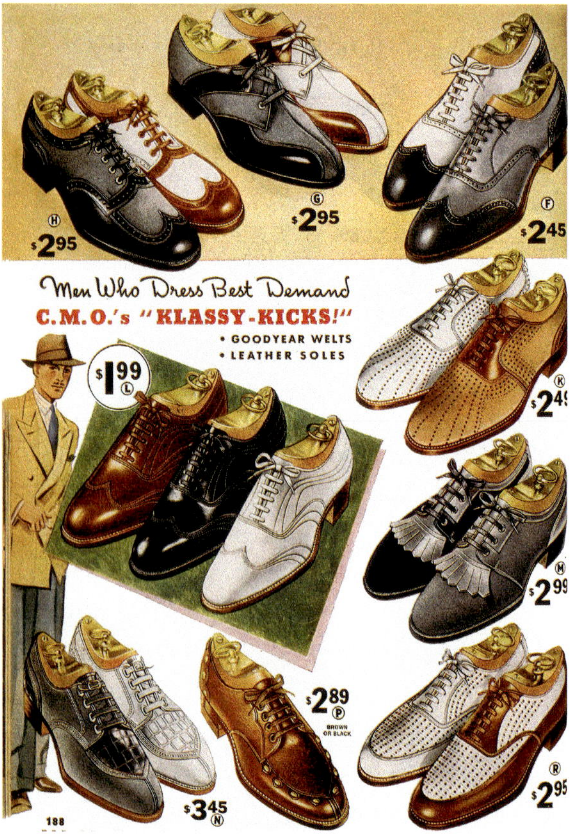

Klassy Kicks, 1933

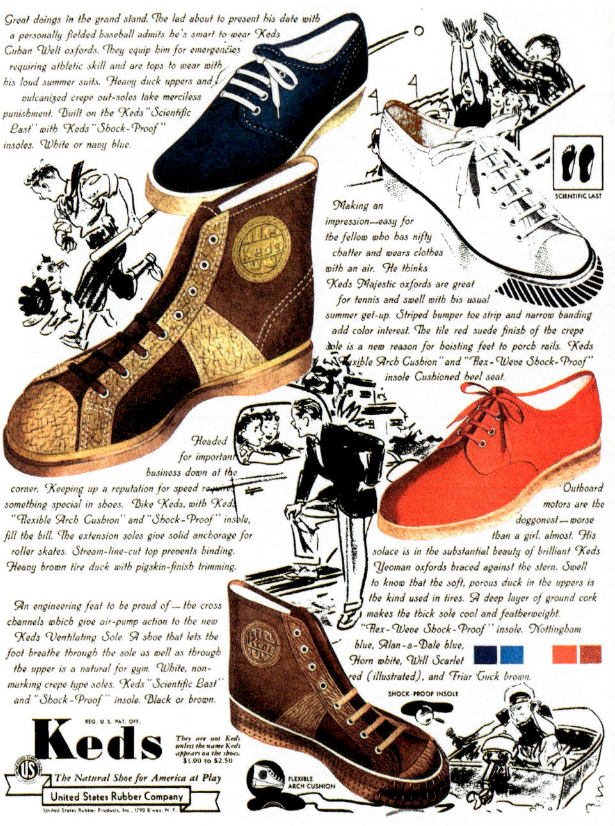

Keds, 1937

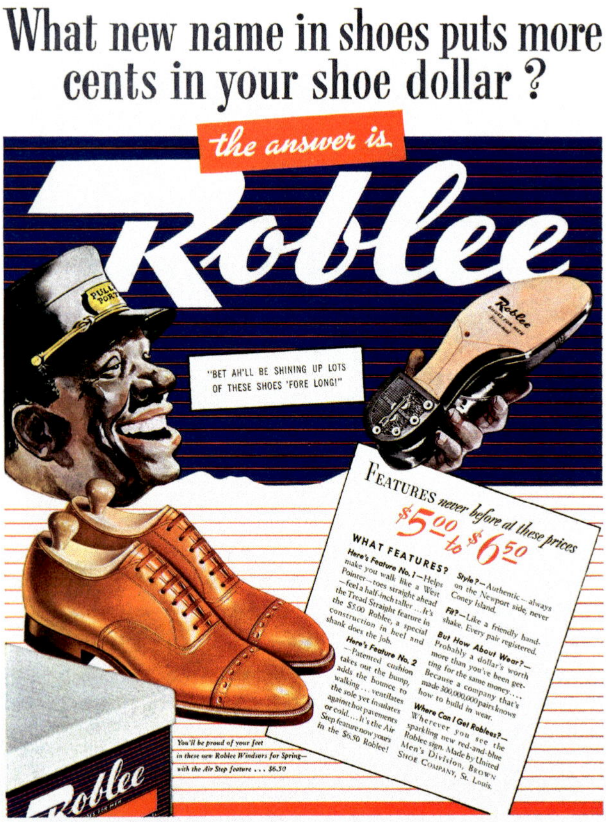

Roblee, 1939

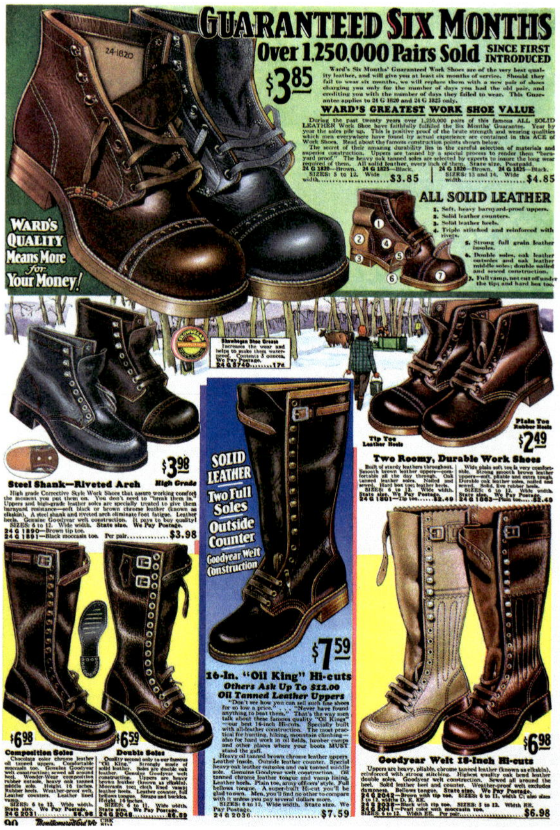

Boots, 1930

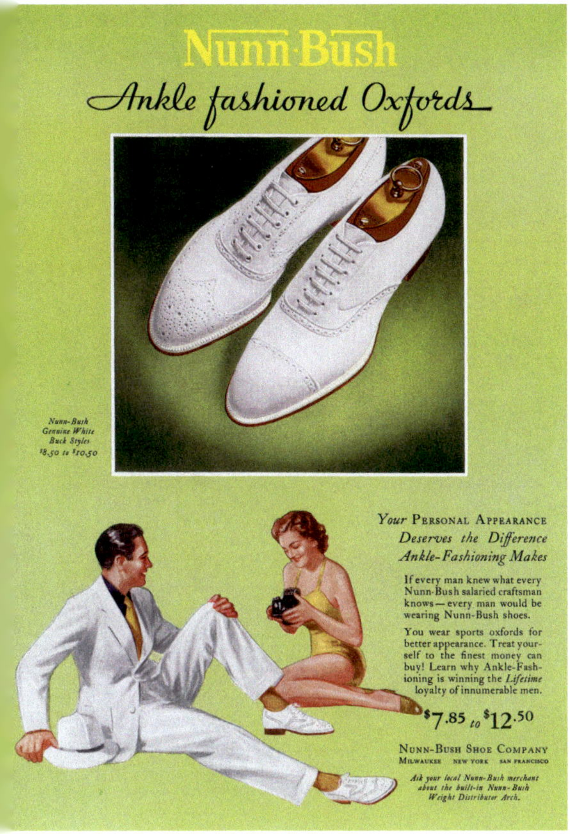

Nunn-Busch, 1937

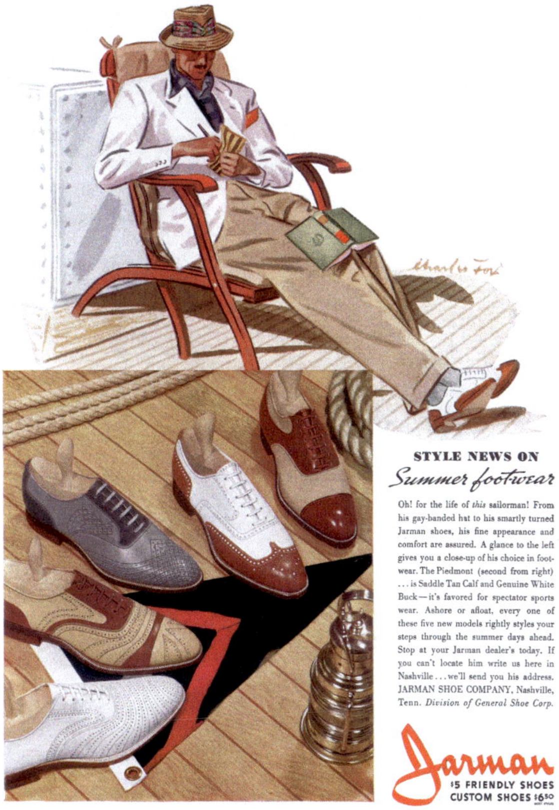

Jarman Shoes, 1937

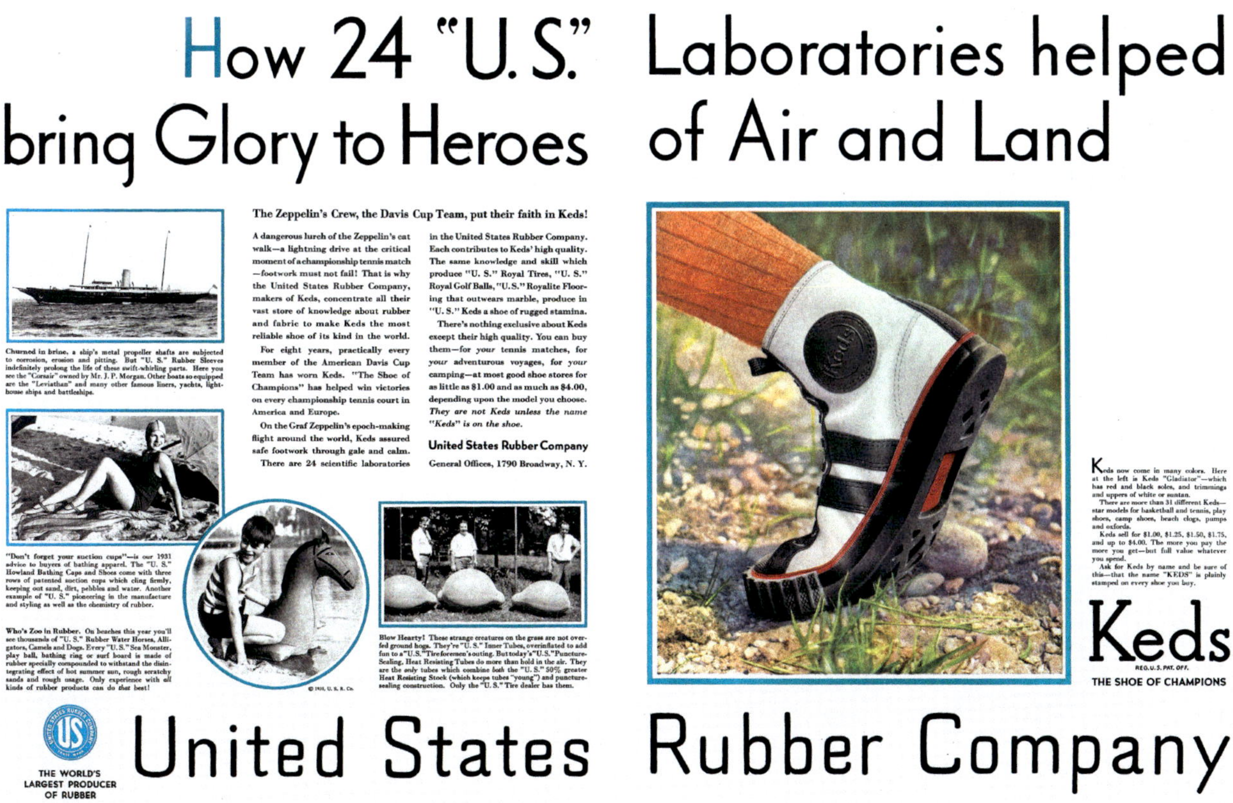

U.S. Rubber Co., 1931

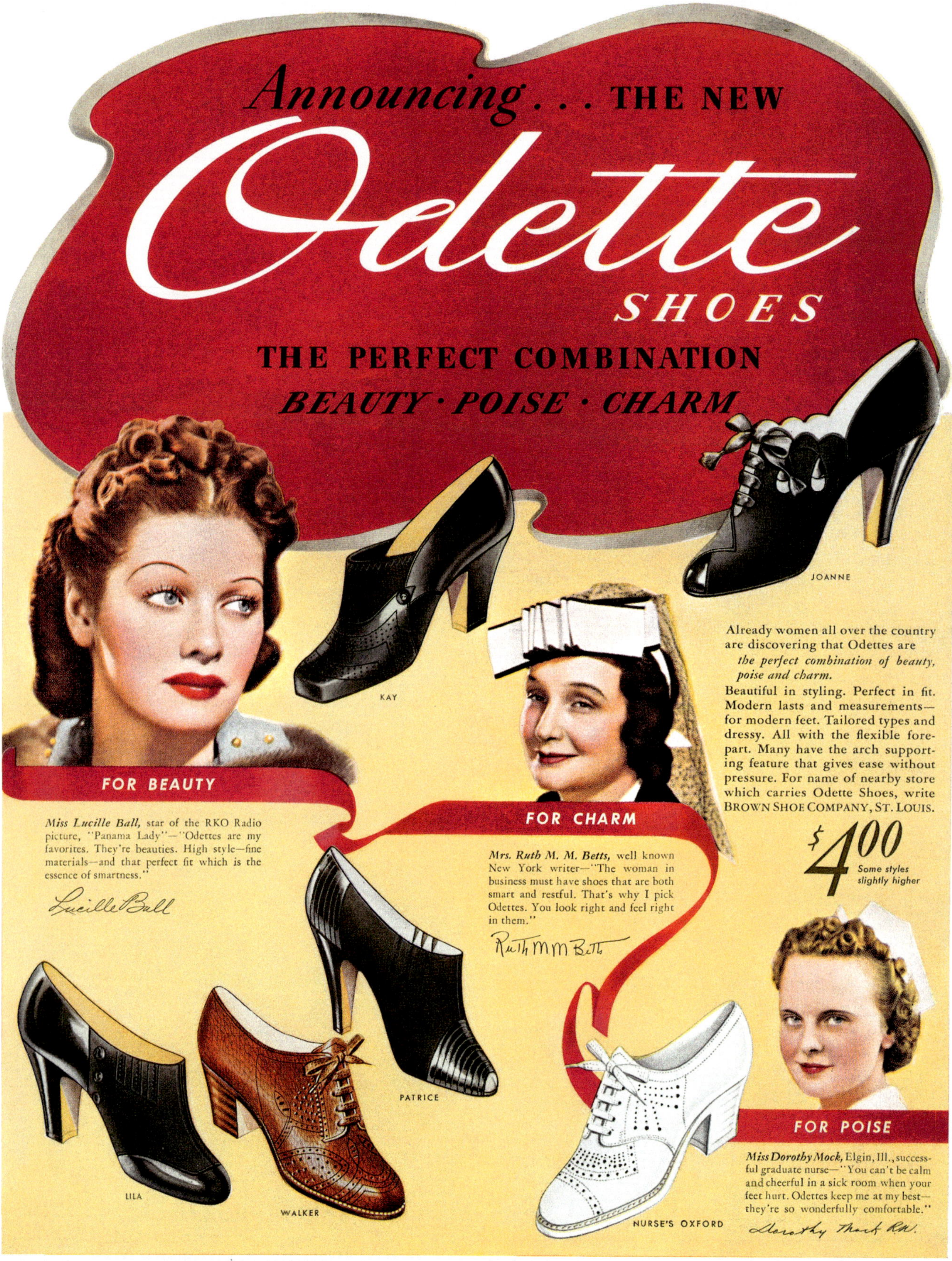

Odette Shoes, 1939

▸ *Shoes, 1931*

Again! Newest Styles . . Lowest Prices

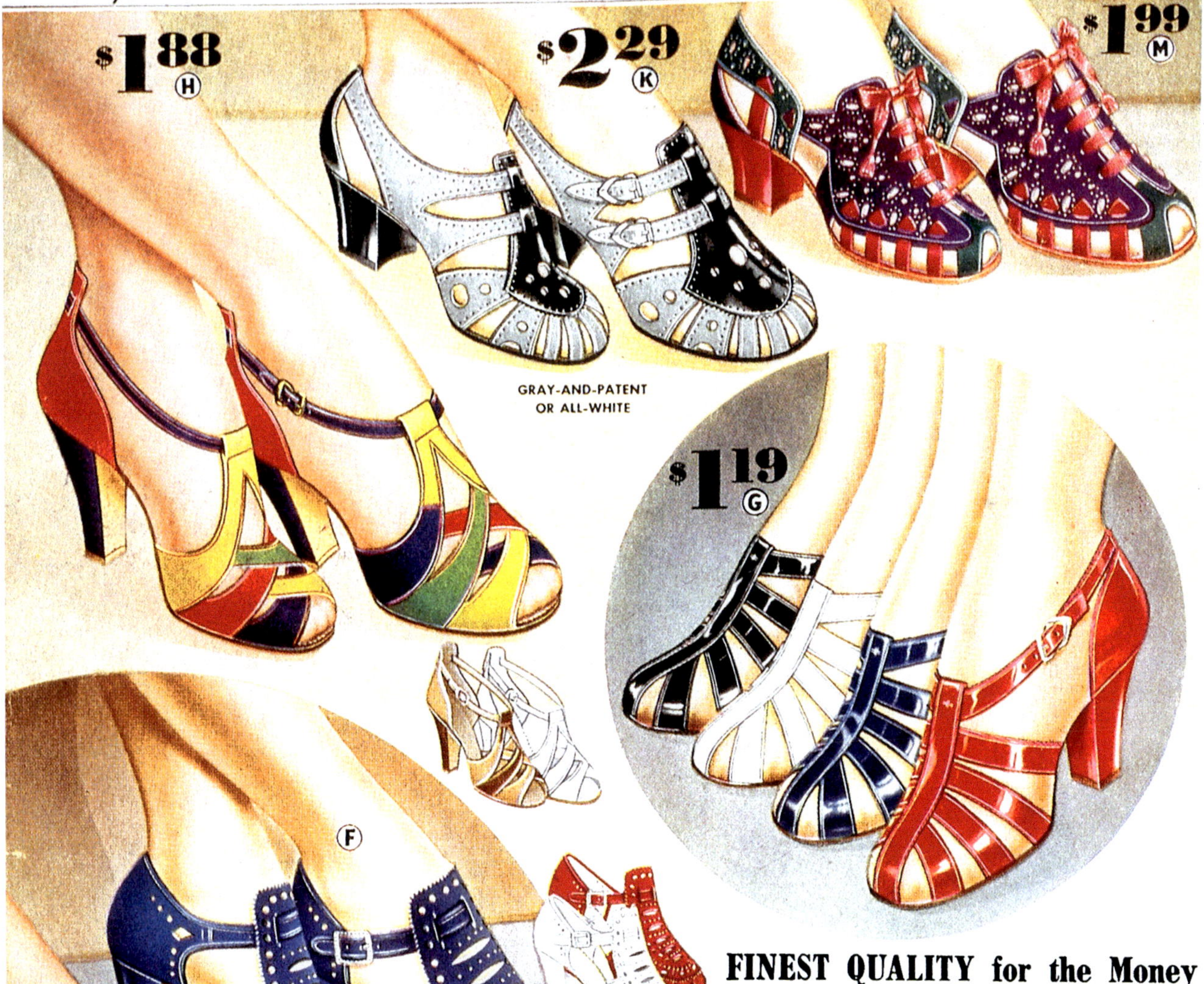

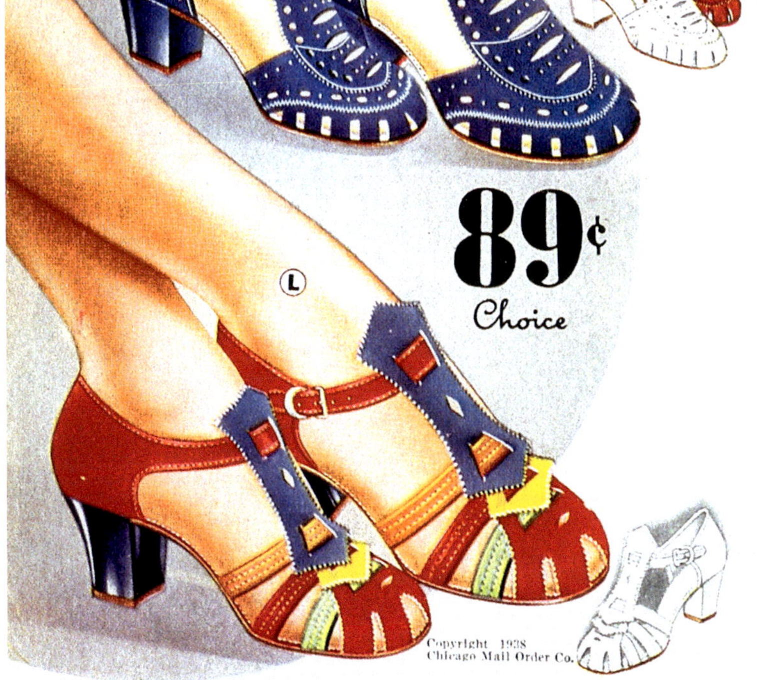

FINEST QUALITY for the Money

(F) Value too big for words! High-styled, stunningly cut-out models - - - Good Quality footwear - - - for a price that's lower than low! Made of Arrabuk, a chic, sturdy, suede-like shoe-fabric, with an extra good quality leather sole, and voguish, sensible 1⅝-inch heel. **SIZES**—2½ to 8; wide widths. State color, size, all numbers in your shoe. Price. . **89c**
Shpg. wt. 1 lb. 2 ozs.
3 J 909—BLUE **3 J 910**—RED
3 J 908—WHITE

(H) Heart's desire of the fashion-loving! - - - this newest "Wish-bone" sandal! Adorable, open-toe. Good Quality model, priced low! Made of the leathers below, with an extra good quality leather sole. 2⅝-in. spike heel. **SIZES**—3 to 9; wide widths. State color, size, numbers in your shoe. Price **$1.88**
Shpg. wt. 1 lb. 2 ozs.
3 J 783—MULTI-COLOR SUEDE.
3 J 784—BEIGE OMBRE SUEDE.
3 J 785—WHITE PATENT.

(L) An attention-gripping low price for such style-alert, Good Quality slippers! Cleverly cut out and saw-edge-trimmed front-strap models of Arrabuk, a sturdy, suedelike shoe-fabric. Extra good quality leather sole! 1⅞-inch heels. De luxe value! Buy two pairs! **SIZES**—2½ to 8; wide widths. State color, size, numbers printed in your shoe. **89c**
Shpg. wt. 1 lb.
3 J 913—MULTI-COLOR
3 J 914—WHITE

(G) Style-stars that will shine bright in 1938! Dramatically low in price! Good Quality, cool sandals, artfully, and almost entirely composed of straps! Of Extra Good Imitation patent leather. Extra good leather sole. 2-in. heel. **SIZES**—2½ to 8; wide widths. State color, size, all numbers in your shoe. . **$1.19**
Shpg. wt. 1 lb.
3 J 883—RED **3 J 884**—BLUE
3 J 882—WHITE
3 J 885—BLACK

(K) One of the smartest shoes on earth! Darling two-strap models with open quarters and cutouts. Extra Good, including their leather sole! 1⅜-inch heel. Bargains! **SIZES**—2½ to 8; wide widths. State color, size, nos. printed in your shoe. . . . **$2.29**
Shpg. wt. 1 lb. 2 ozs.
3 J 1062—GRAY SUEDE LEATHER WITH BLACK PATENT LEATHER
3 J 1063—ALL-WHITE BUCK-EFFECT LEATHER

(M) Nothing newer! Nothing more decorative has ever touched your foot! A Good Quality, elaborately cutout model of chic Rough Leather, with spearhead bands of shiny patent leather! Extra good leather sole. 1⅝-inch heel. A-1 value! **SIZES**—2½ to 8; wide widths. State color, size, and numbers in your shoe. . . **$1.99**
Shpg. wt. 1 lb. 2 ozs.
3 J 826—MULTI-COLOR
3 J 827—BEIGE OMBRE
3 J 828—ALL-WHITE

And the winner is...

Americans Wanted More

In the midst of the Depression, when depleted wallets were the norm, people were looking for more of everything—more money, more food, more woman. Gone was the flat-chested flapper of the previous decade. Many American women subscribed to a new standard of beauty, perhaps inspired by full-figured movie icons like Mae West. The mere sentiment of selling extra pounds to wome was unique to the time. By decade's end standards of beauty took another turn, and the lean, mean look became the ideal for the remainder of the century.

Darf's auch etwas mehr sein?

Während der Depression, als Schmalhans Küchenmeister war, hätte es für die Amerikaner von allem etwas mehr sein dürfen – meh Geld, reichhaltigeres Essen, üppigere Frauen. Der flachbrüstige Flapper-Look war passé. Viele amerikanische Frauen folgten dem neuen Schönheitsideal, das durch kurvenreiche Filmstars wie Mae West verkörpert wurde. Schon die bloße Idee, Frauen mit zusätzlichen Pfunde zu beglücken, dürfte einmalig sein. Als der Krieg und die damit verbundene Rationierung drohten, änderte sich das Schönheitsideal erneut, und für den Rest des Jahrhunderts war der ranke und schlanke Look angesagt.

Toujours plus !

En pleine Dépression, alors que la plupart des bourses étaient vides, les Américains en voulaient toujours plus : plus d'argent, plus de nourriture, plus de féminité. Adieu les garçonnes à la poitrine plate des années folles ! De nombreuses Américaines adoptèrent les nouveaux canons de la beauté, sans doute inspirés par de plantureuses idoles de cinéma comme Mae West. Si le modèle de cette publicité pour une formule miracle pour grossir n'a rien d'un Rubens, vendre des kilos supplémentaires aux femmes était propre à cette époque. A la fin de la décennie, marquée par la menace de la guerre et le rationnement, les critères de beauté changèrent à nouveau et la silhouette svelte redevint l'idéal féminin jusqu'à la fin du siècle.

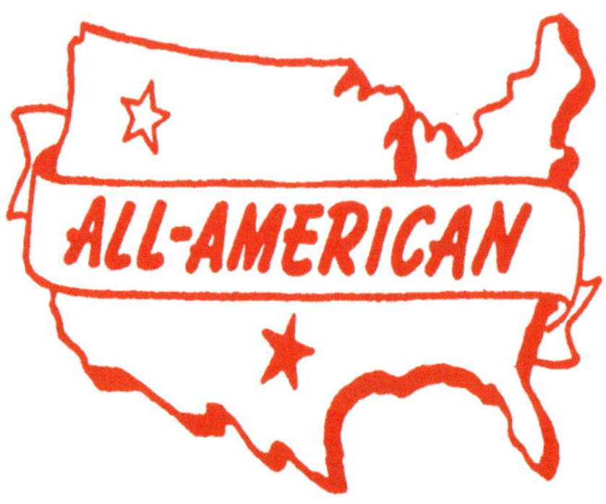

Ironized Yeast Co., 1935

I HAVE PLENTY OF DATES SINCE I'VE PUT ON 10 POUNDS

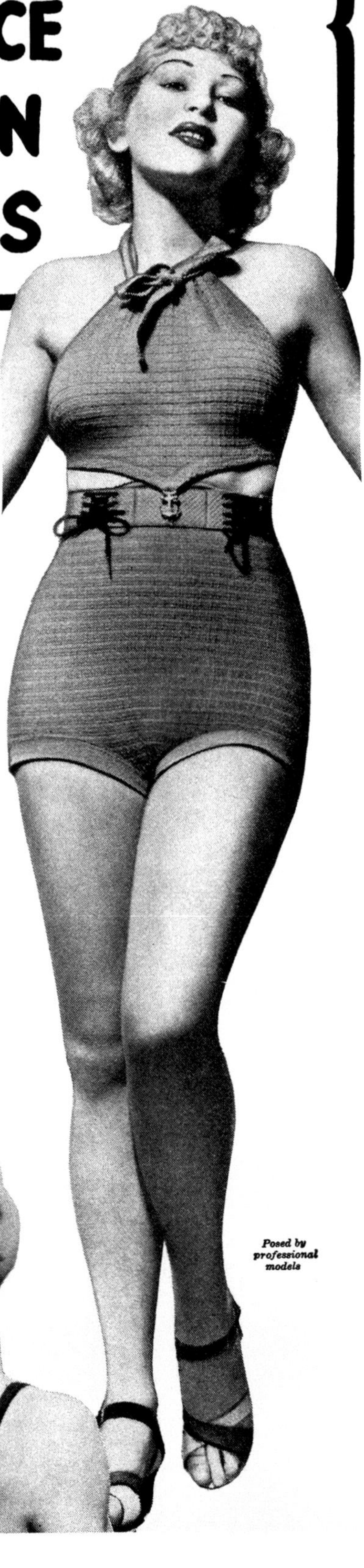

Skinny? New easy way adds 5 to 15 lbs. *quick*

DOCTORS for years have prescribed yeast to build up health. But now with this new yeast discovery in little tablets you get far greater results — health, and also solid, attractive flesh—*and in a far shorter time!*

Not only are thousands quickly gaining beauty-bringing pounds, but also clear, radiant skin, freedom from indigestion, constipation and nervousness, glorious new pep.

This amazing new product, Ironized Yeast, is made from special *brewers' ale yeast* imported from Europe—the richest yeast known —which by a new process is concentrated 7 times—*made 7 times more powerful.*

But that is not all! This rich yeast is then ironized with 3 special kinds of iron.

Day after day, as you take Ironized Yeast tablets, watch flat chest develop, skinny limbs round out attractively, skin clear to beauty—you're an entirely new person.

Results guaranteed

No matter how skinny and weak you may be, this marvelous new Ironized Yeast should build you up in a few short weeks as it has thousands. If you are not delighted with the results of the very first package, your money instantly refunded.

Special FREE offer!

To start you building up your health right away, we make this absolutely FREE offer. Purchase a package of Ironized Yeast tablets at once, cut out the seal on the box and mail it to us with a clipping of this paragraph. We will send you a fascinating new book on health, "New Facts About Your Body," by a well-known authority. Remember, results are guaranteed with the very first package — *or your money refunded.* At all druggists. Ironized Yeast Company, Inc., Dept. 128, Atlanta, Ga.

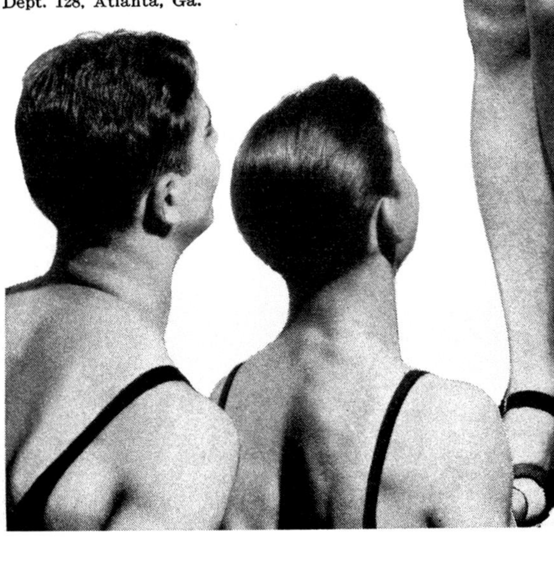

Posed by professional models

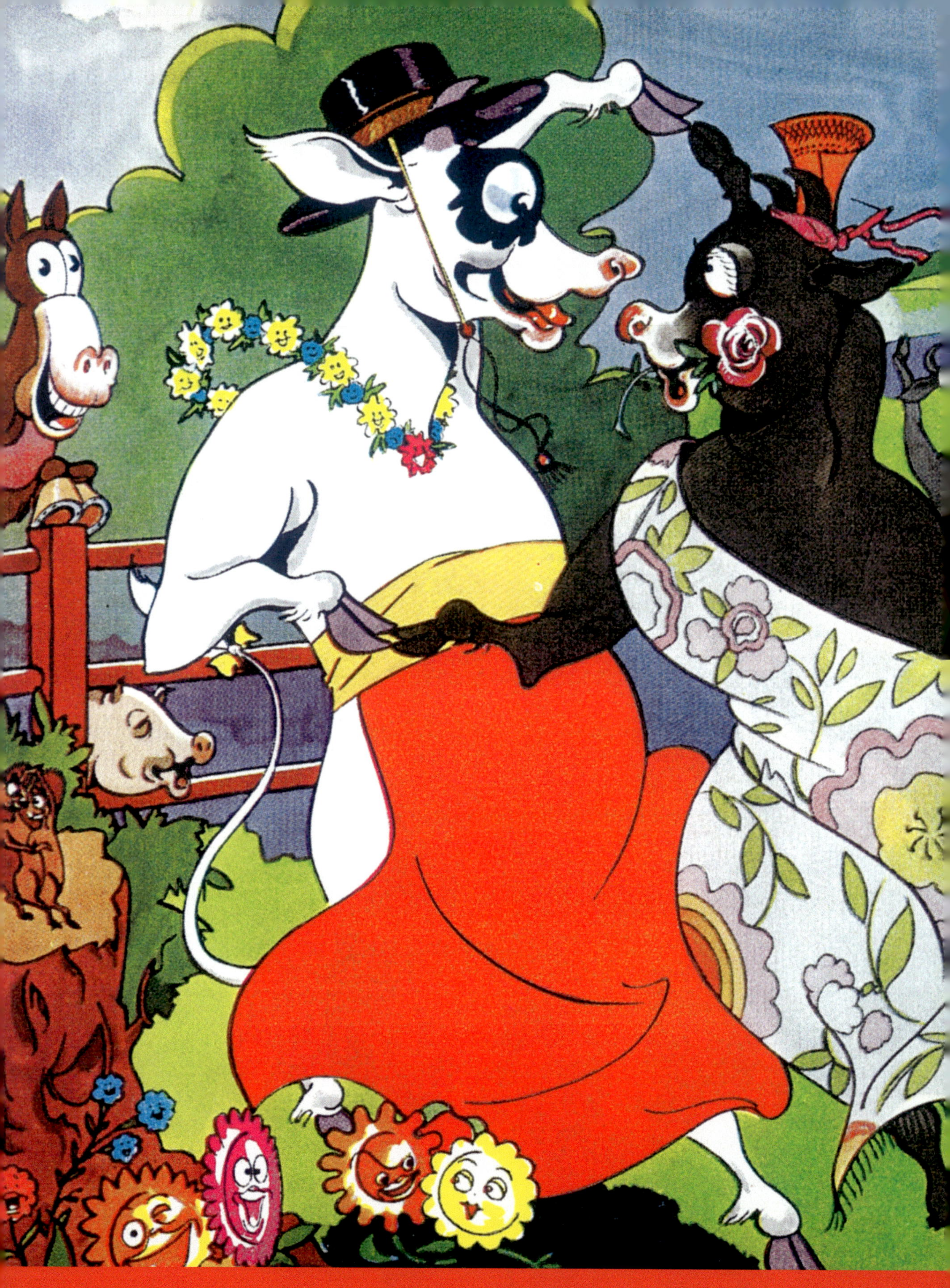

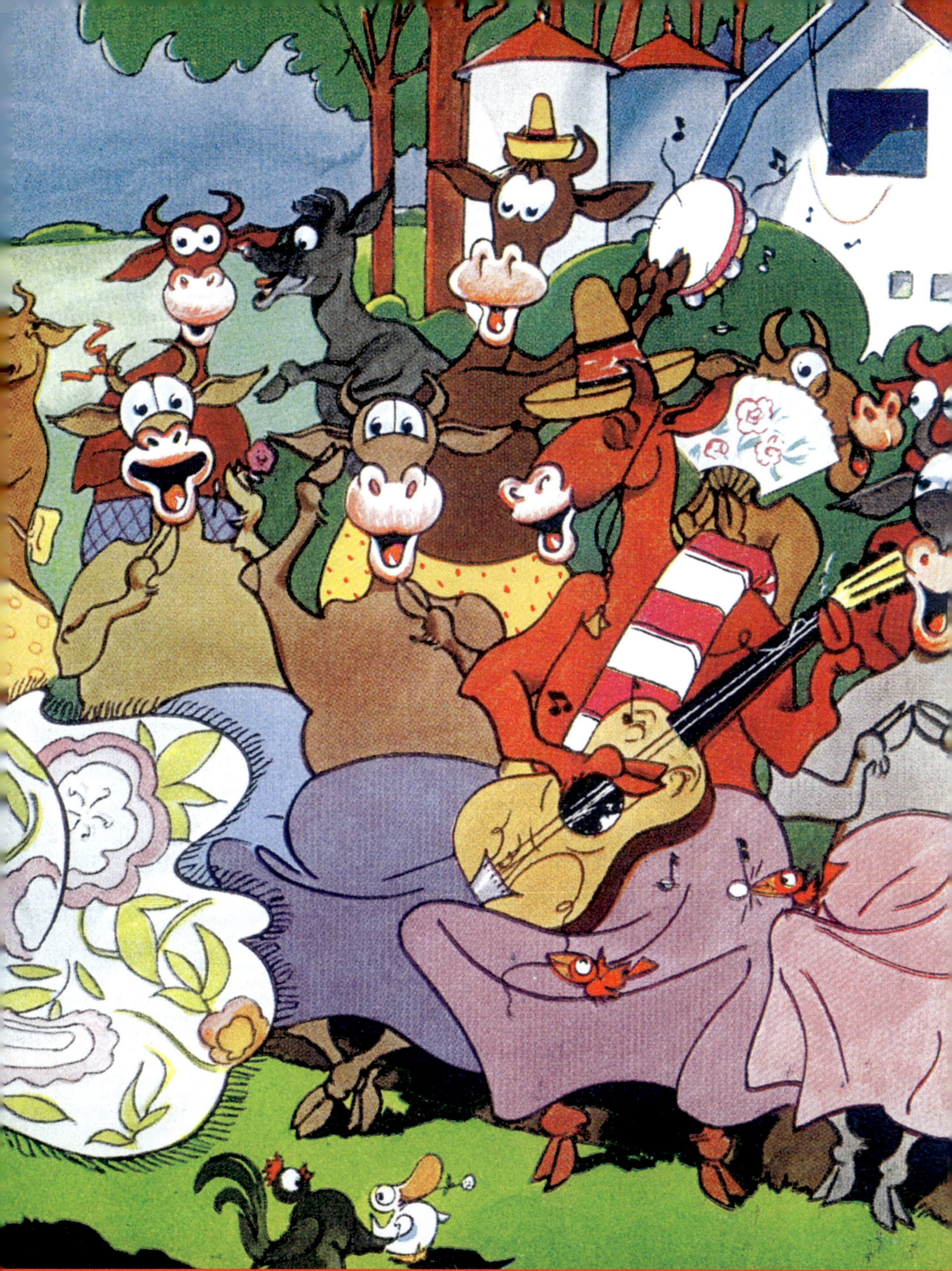

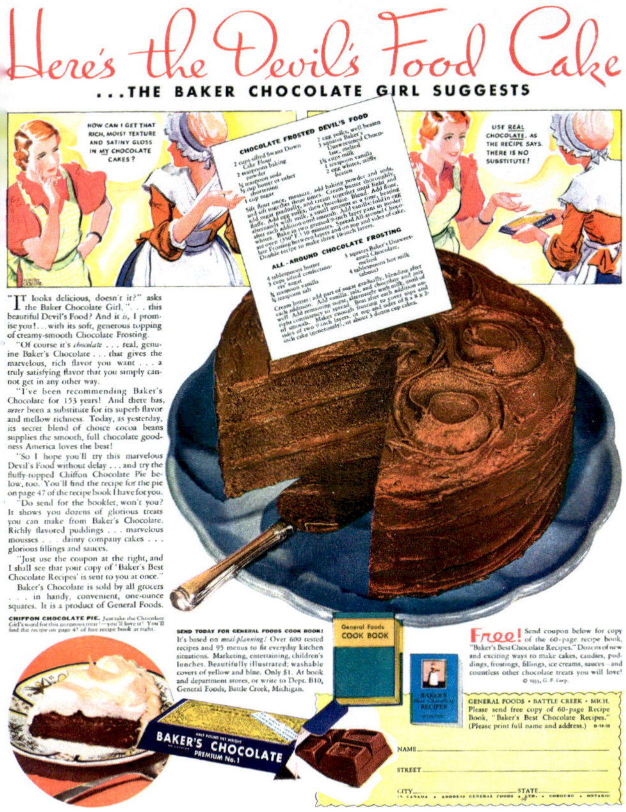

Baker's Chocolate, 1933

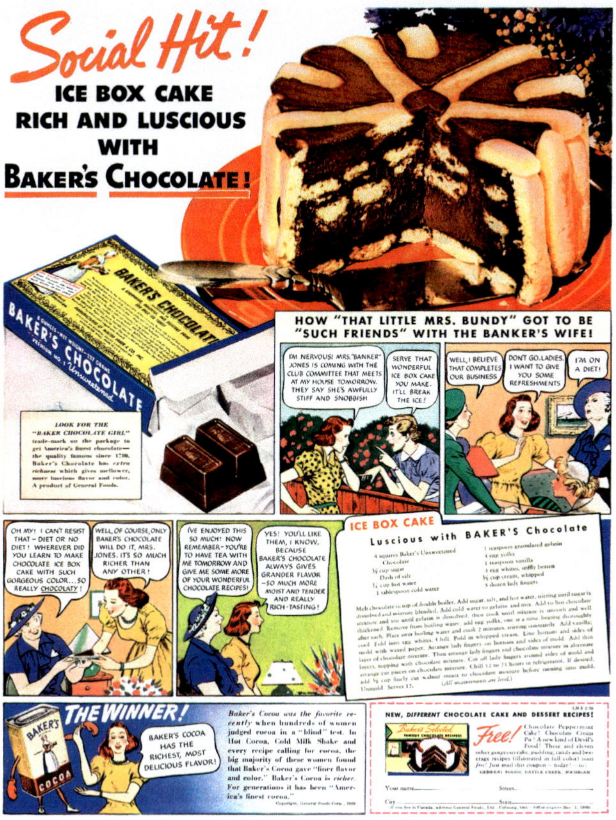

Baker's Chocolate, 1938

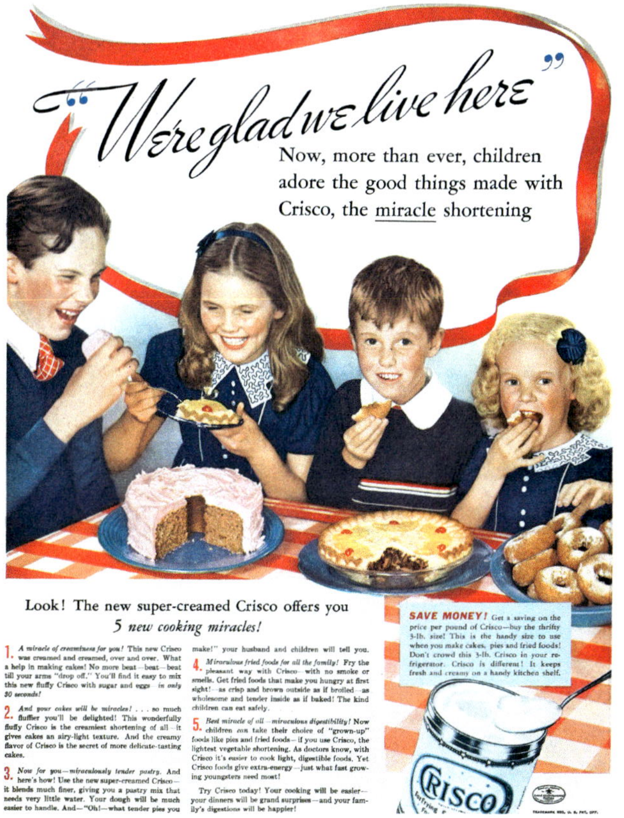

Swift's Brookfield Butter, 1934 ◄◄ Sperry Flour, 1939 ◄ Crisco, 1937

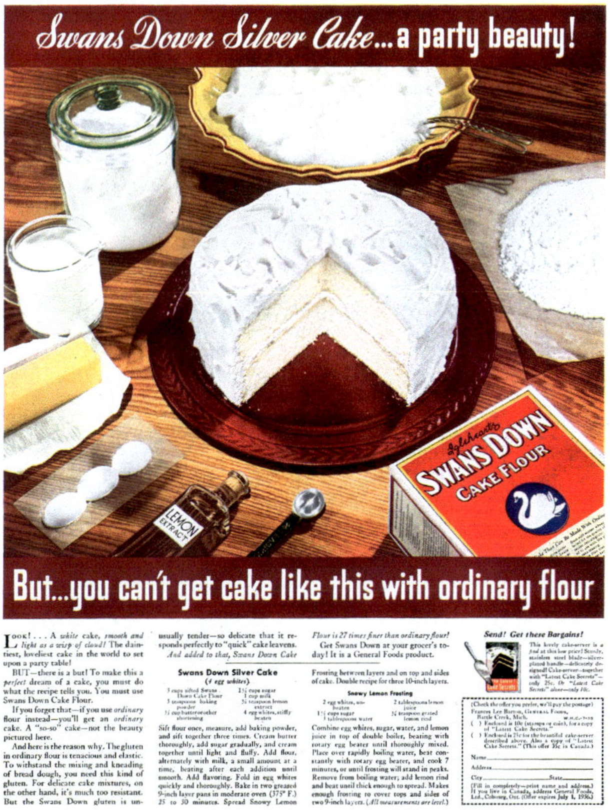

Swans Down Cake Flour, 1935

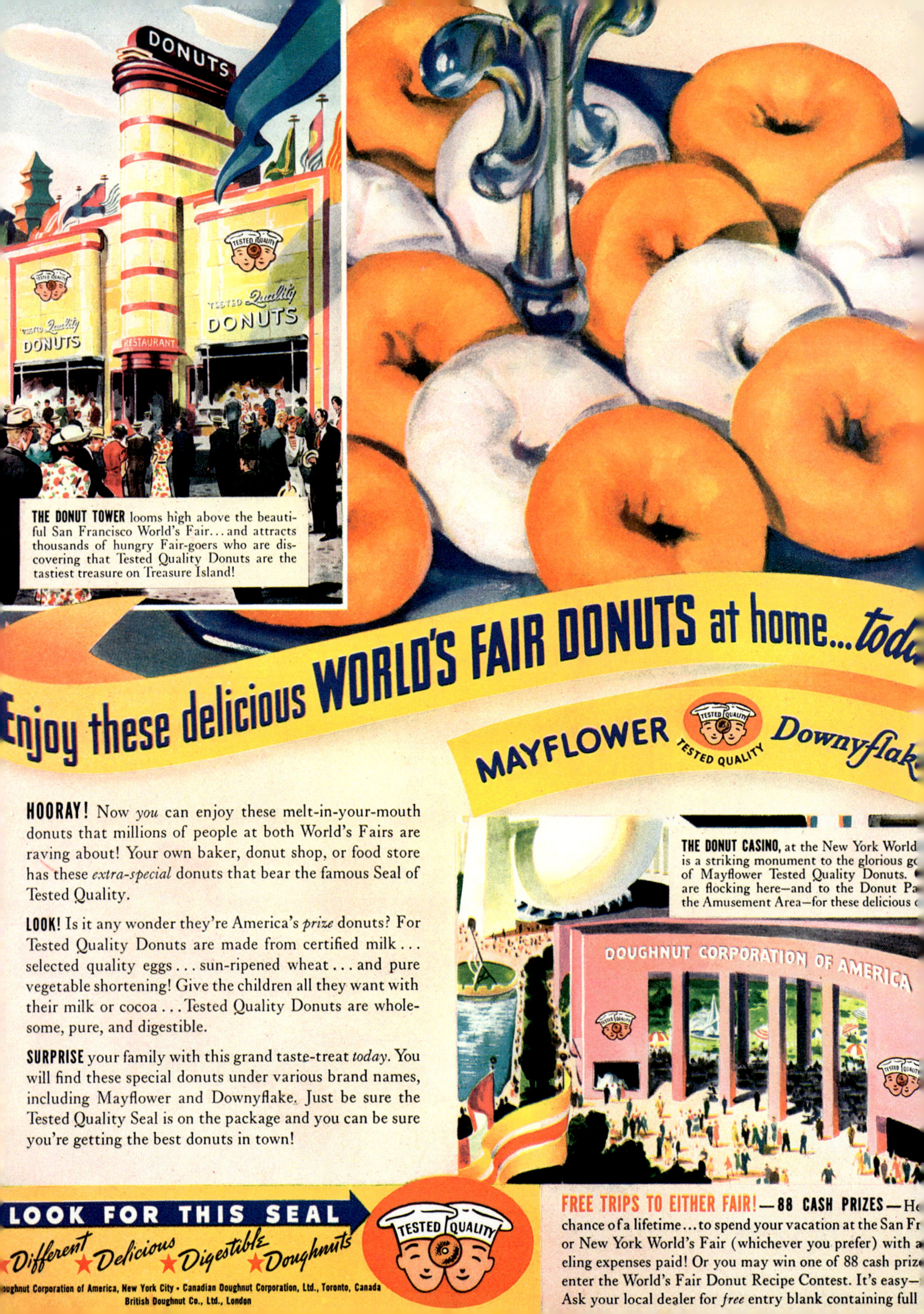
DONUTS
TESTED QUALITY
Tested Quality DONUTS
RESTAURANT
Tested Quality DONUTS
THE DONUT TOWER looms high above the beautiful San Francisco World's Fair... and attracts thousands of hungry Fair-goers who are discovering that Tested Quality Donuts are the tastiest treasure on Treasure Island!
Enjoy these delicious WORLD'S FAIR DONUTS at home...toda
MAYFLOWER
TESTED QUALITY
TESTED QUALITY
Downyflak
HOORAY! Now you can enjoy these melt-in-your-mouth donuts that millions of people at both World's Fairs are raving about! Your own baker, donut shop, or food store has these extra-special donuts that bear the famous Seal of Tested Quality.
LOOK! Is it any wonder they're America's prize donuts? For Tested Quality Donuts are made from certified milk... selected quality eggs... sun-ripened wheat... and pure vegetable shortening! Give the children all they want with their milk or cocoa... Tested Quality Donuts are wholesome, pure, and digestible.
SURPRISE your family with this grand taste-treat today. You will find these special donuts under various brand names, including Mayflower and Downyflake. Just be sure the Tested Quality Seal is on the package and you can be sure you're getting the best donuts in town!
THE DONUT CASINO, at the New York World
is a striking monument to the glorious g
of Mayflower Tested Quality Donuts.
are flocking here—and to the Donut Pa
the Amusement Area—for these delicious
DOUGHNUT CORPORATION OF AMERICA
LOOK FOR THIS SEAL
Different ★ Delicious ★ Digestible ★ Doughnuts
TESTED QUALITY
oughnut Corporation of America, New York City • Canadian Doughnut Corporation, Ltd., Toronto, Canada
British Doughnut Co., Ltd., London
FREE TRIPS TO EITHER FAIR!—88 CASH PRIZES—He
chance of a lifetime... to spend your vacation at the San Fr
or New York World's Fair (whichever you prefer) with a
eling expenses paid! Or you may win one of 88 cash priz
enter the World's Fair Donut Recipe Contest. It's easy—
Ask your local dealer for free entry blank containing full

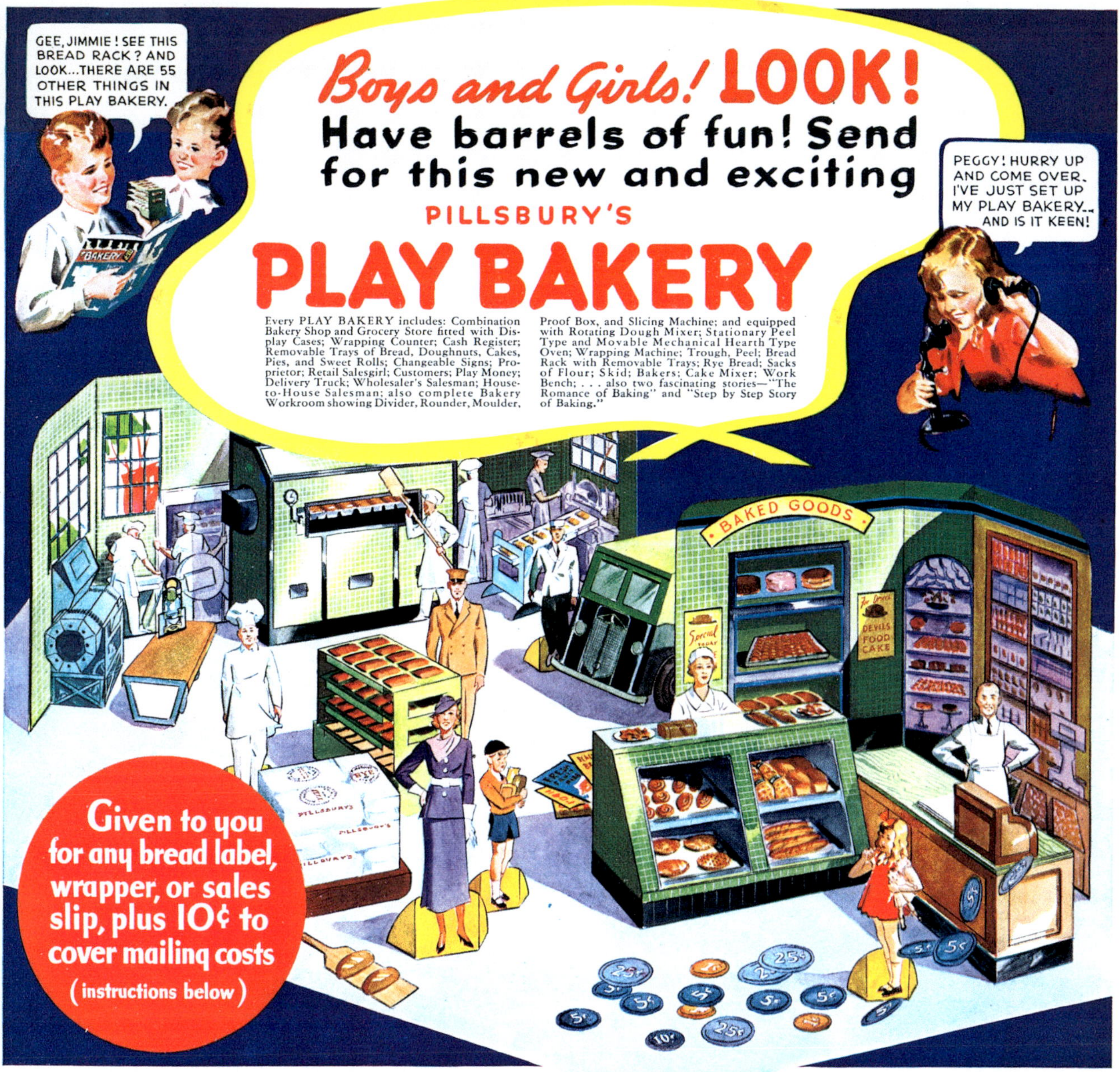

Comes to you all ready to press out and set up. No cutting or pasting. Complete instructions with each Bakery. 56 different pieces. Everything you need to play Wholesale Baker—Retail Baker—and House-to-House Baker. A thrilling and realistic trip through Bakeryland. You can actually turn the dough mixer, put loaves of bread in the oven, haul baked goods in the truck, put cakes, doughnuts, bread and pies in the display cases and take them out again just as real bakers do. You have never seen anything like it. Be the first in your neighborhood to have this fascinating Play Bakery. *Send for yours TODAY!*

USE THIS HANDY COUPON

Pillsbury Flour Mills Company, P. O. Box 511
Minneapolis, Minnesota

Please send me a PLAY BAKERY. I enclose a wrapper (label, or sales slip) taken from a loaf of baker's bread, and 10c in coin.

NAME ....

ADDRESS ....

CITY ....

HERE'S HOW YOU GET IT!

Buy a loaf of any baker's bread (any kind). Send the label, or brand name cut from wrapper, or the sales slip, with 10c (in coin, not stamps) and your name and address to Pillsbury Flour Mills Company, Box 511, Minneapolis, Minnesota. Your Play Bakery will be mailed promptly, and postpaid. This offer is good in the U. S. A. only, and expires October 15, 1936.

To parents This unusual offer is made for two reasons:

First, to induce you to buy and serve the delicious bread made for you by the modern baker—to induce you to find out how the baker saves you time and money, how he gives you and your children the vigor that comes from the rich, quick nourishment of baked foods.

Second, to bring to your children a new and exciting form of amusement that will keep them happy and occupied for hours at a time. Besides being real fun for children of all ages, this Play Bakery will help them to learn many interesting facts about modern commercial baking—one of our oldest and most essential industries.

To teachers Teachers who are interested in the project method of education are invited to avail themselves of this opportunity to procure, for their classroom use, an authentic presentation of the equipment and methods used in the production and sale of commercially baked foods.

IT PAYS TO PATRONIZE YOUR BAKER

Donuts, 1939 ◄

Pillsbury, 1936

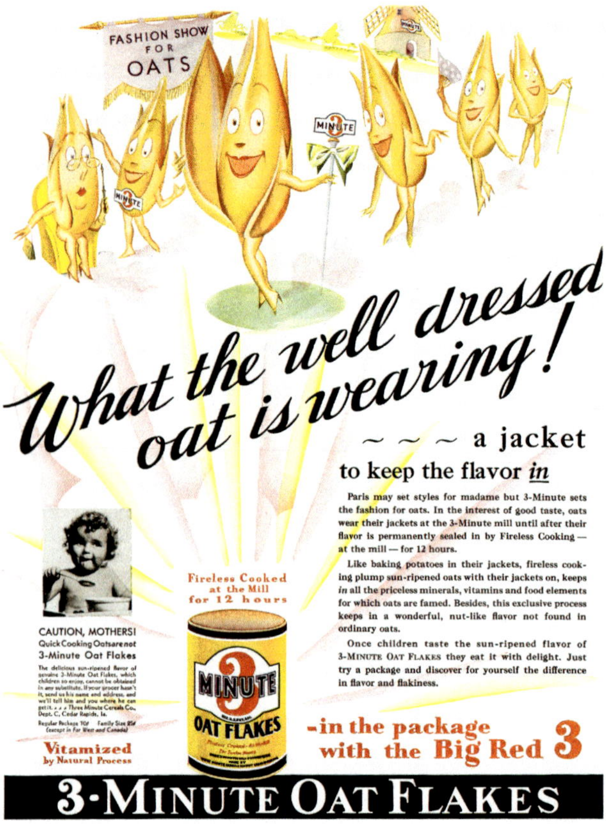

3-Minute Oat Flakes, 1931

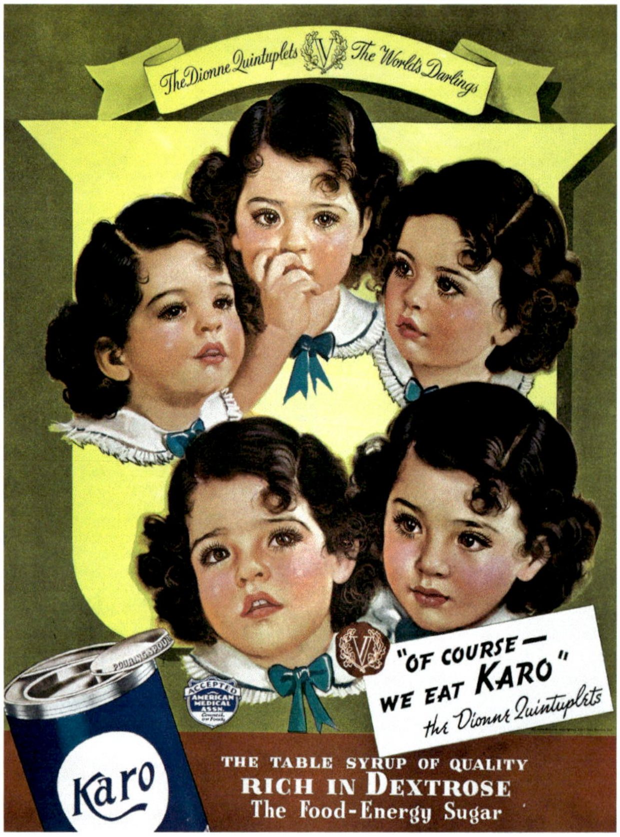

Karo, 1937

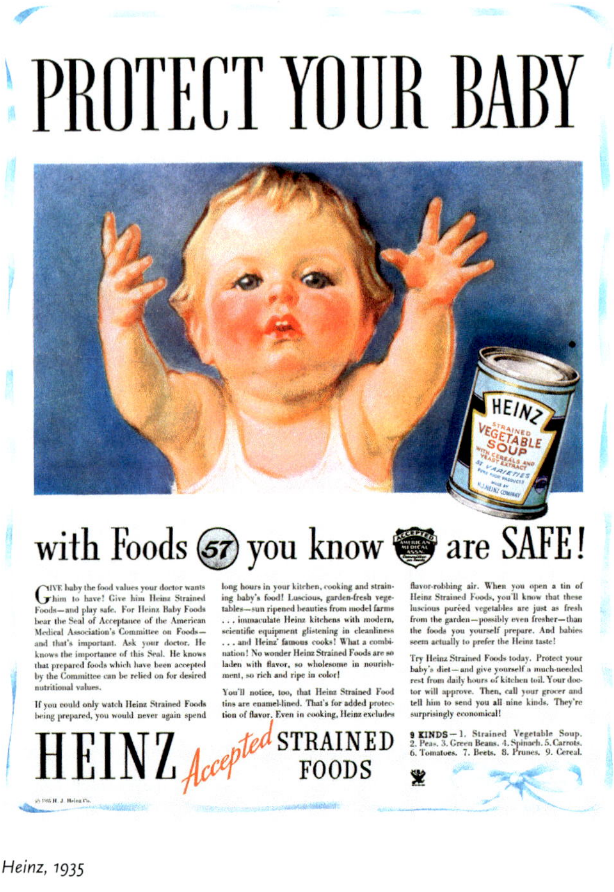

Heinz, 1935

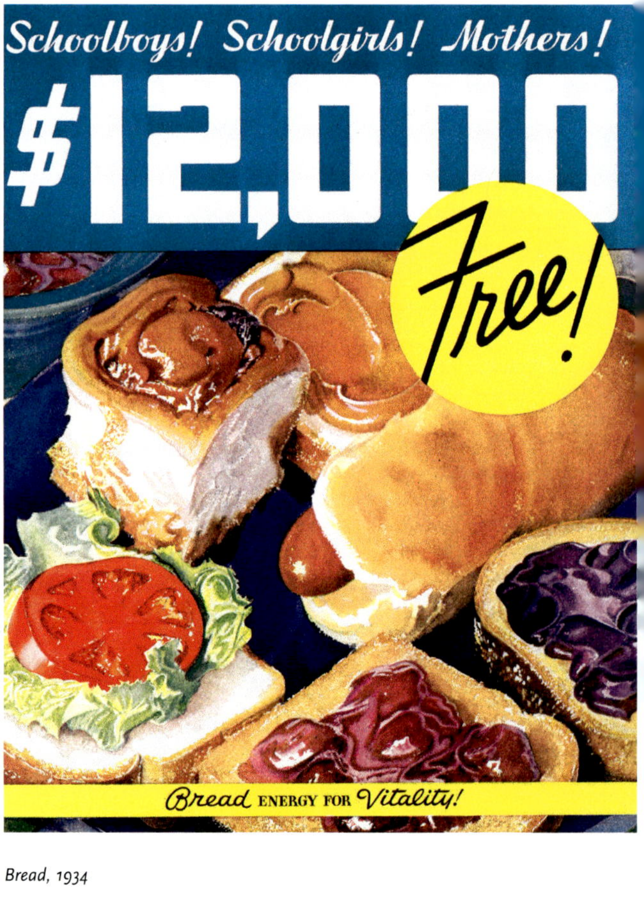

Bread, 1934

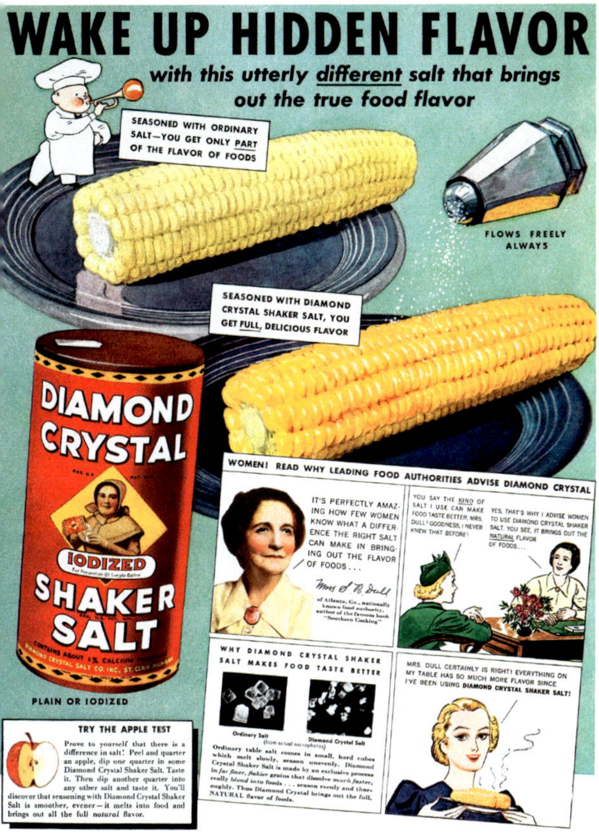

Diamond Crystal Salt, 1937

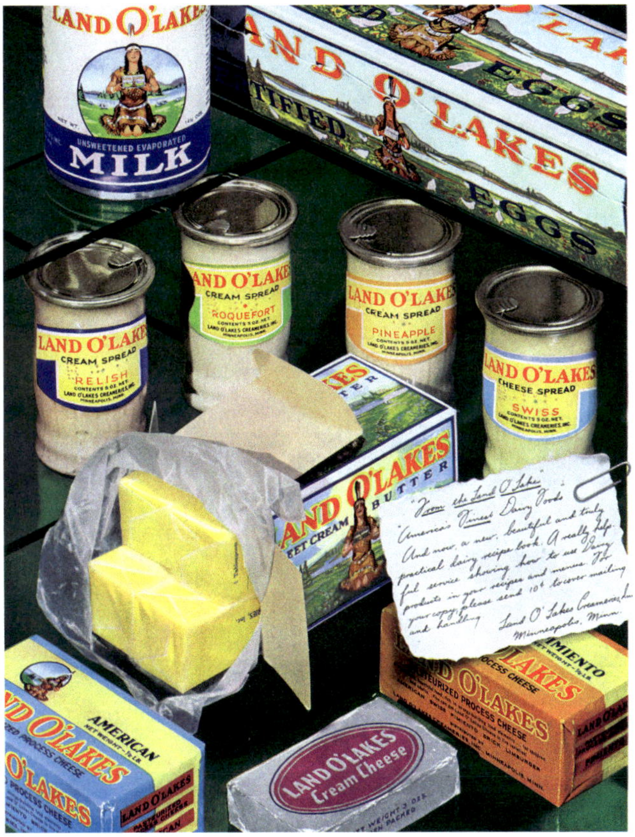

Land O' Lakes, 1935

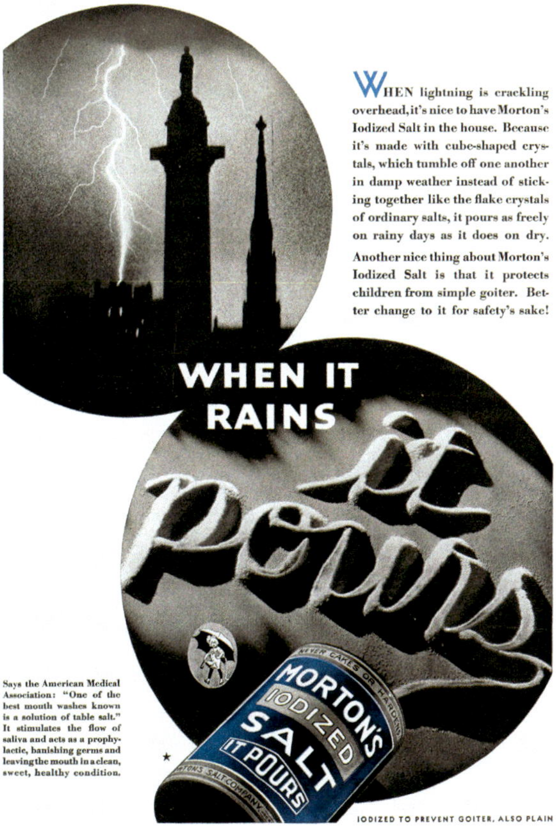

Morton's Salt, 1930

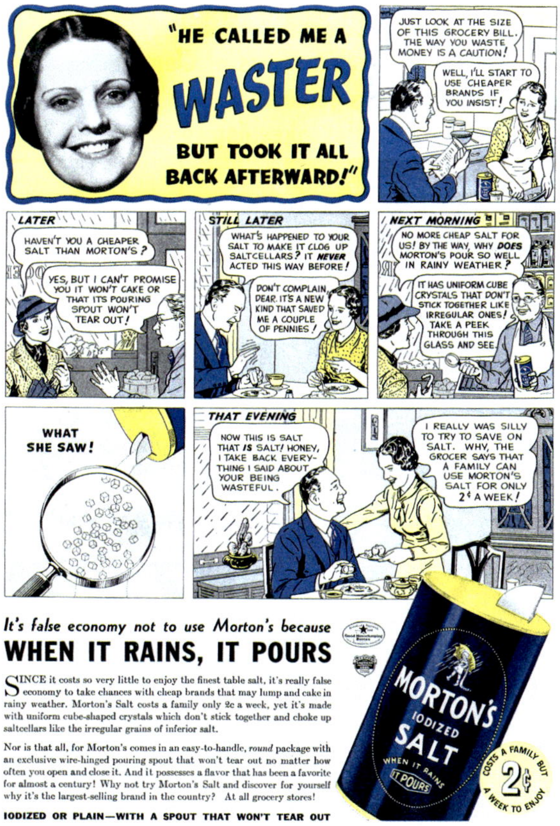

Morton's Salt, 1938

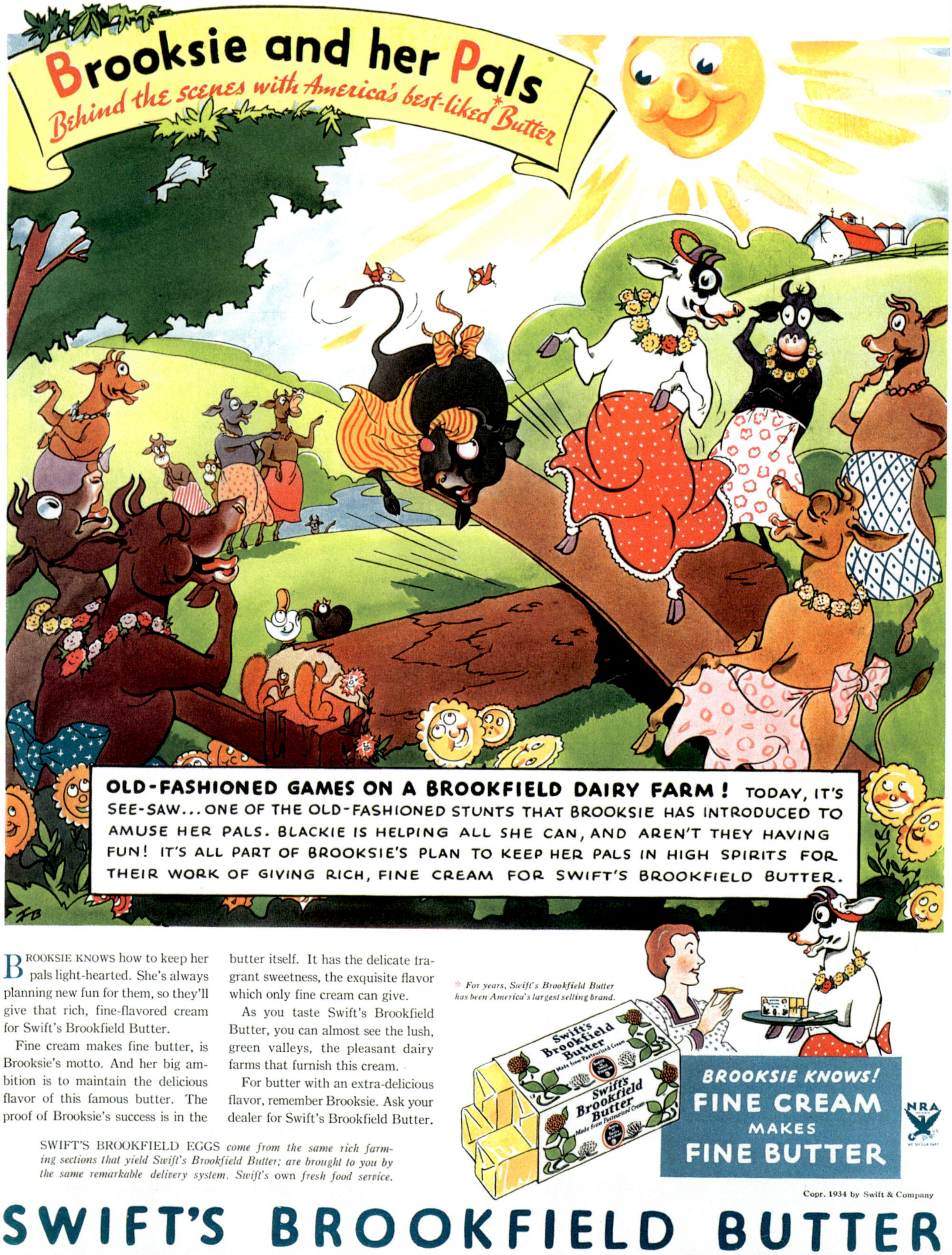

Swift's Brookfield Butter, 1934

► *Bordon's*, 1939

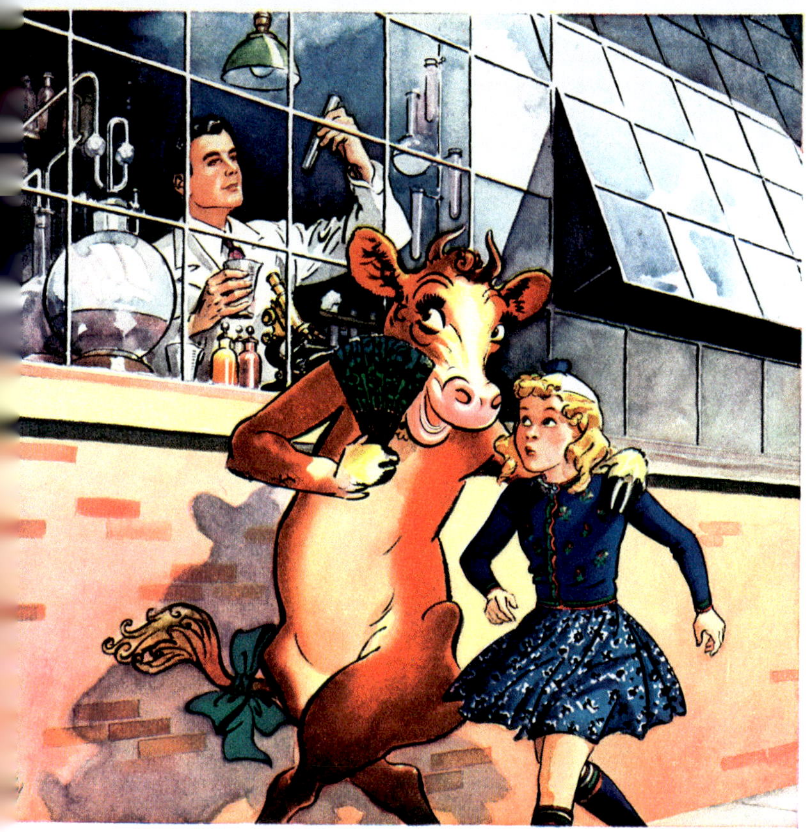

"Don't look now—but that man is crazy about me!"

:y about *you*, Elsie?" said the Little Girl doubt-
ılly. "He looks more to me as if he were in love
those tubes and bottles and things."

that's just *his* way of caring for me," mooed
e Borden Cow. "You see, he's one of Borden's
cientists. So instead of sending me flowers or
he makes wonderful tests and fills out heaps of
–all about *me!*"

e," puzzled the Little Girl. "And is that what
call being *romantic?*"

aps not," admitted Elsie. "But it certainly keeps
ealthy. And by keeping me in the pink, he
e give better milk and cream—which in turn
etter things to eat, like *Borden's Ice Cream*."

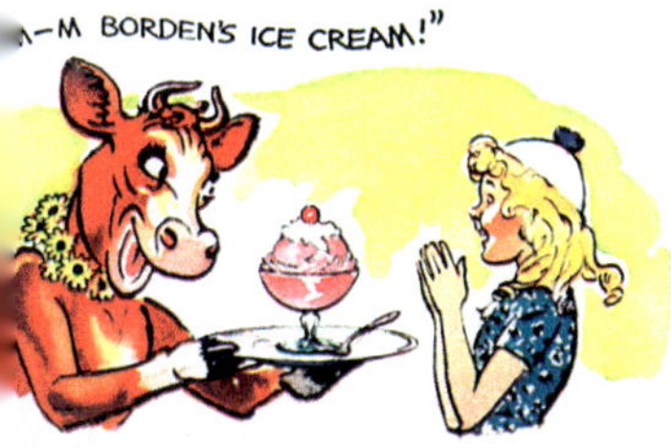

ly, that *is* better!" cried the Little Girl. "Better
ything else I can think of!"

s of *other* good things to eat," explained Elsie,
we their goodness to the attention Borden ex-
e forever showering on me and mine. Look at
le delightful family of *Borden's Fine Cheeses!*"

"*My* favorite cheese-food of all is *Borden's Chateau*," put in the Little Girl.

"It's such a great favorite with everyone," nodded Elsie, "that lots of people have tried to copy its wonder-

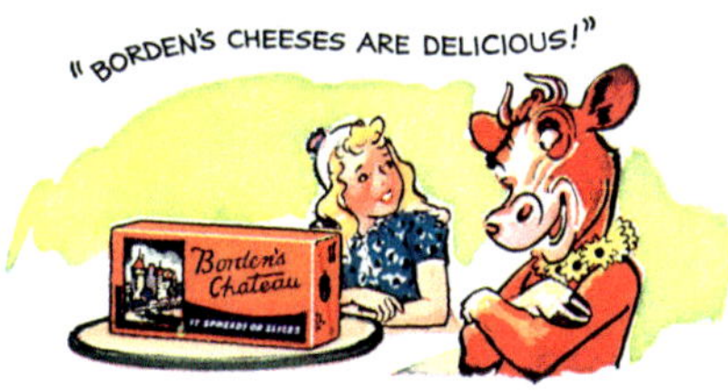

ful flavor. They can't, though—for only Borden knows how to give it that flavor with fine, costly, aged cheese. By the way, do you believe in *magic?*"

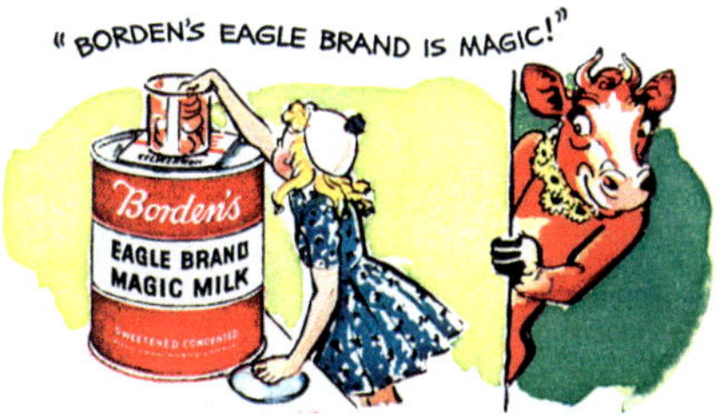

"Why—is *he* going to *do* some?" the Little Girl gasped, looking in again at the Borden Scientist.

"He's doing some all the time," Elsie replied. "And he helps your mother do another kind of magic right in your kitchen—with *Borden's Eagle Brand Sweetened Condensed Milk*. That helps her make perfectly scrumptious cookies, candies, and cake frostings—*in almost no time* . . . I'll bet your mother makes nice cream soups and mashed potatoes, too . . ."

"Sure she does," the Little Girl answered positively: "she makes them better than anybody in the world!"

"Then I know she makes them with *Borden's Irradiated Evaporated Milk*," smiled Elsie, "for that has a particularly fresh, natural flavor—a special goodness it owes to Borden's scientific watchfulness and care.

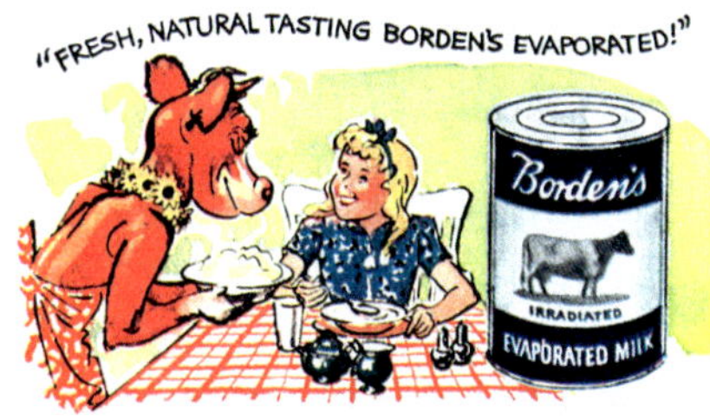

It's this very special Borden care that has always persuaded your mother and daddy to choose *Borden's Milk* for you to drink!"

"If that's what makes it taste so good," said the Little Girl, "then I'm sorry it's only milk and things made from milk that get cared for by you Borden people."

Elsie looked pleased. "It isn't only those," she confessed. "There are some Borden things that have nothing to do with my milk—but they're just as good as they can be, too. *Borden's None Such Mince Meat*, for instance. Mmm—you never tasted spicier, juicier,

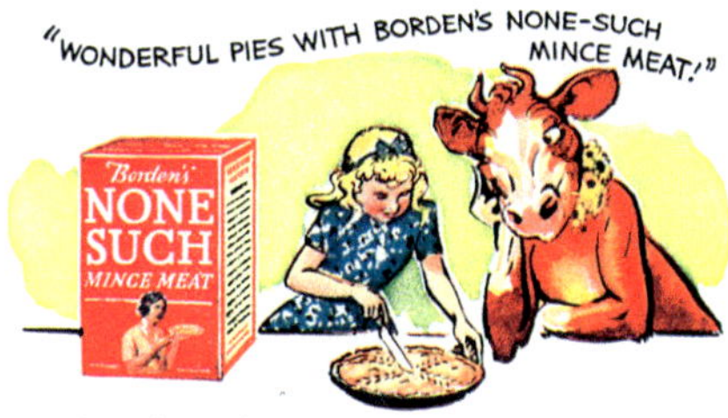

grander mince pies than that makes! So you see, it's really Borden's extra carefulness and skill with *any* food bearing their name that makes the big difference . . . that makes folks confident whenever they buy any food that—'if it's Borden's it's GOT to be good!' "

Borden uses milk from more than 100,000 dairy farms . . . more than 27,500 Borden employees work in partnership with 47,000 owner-stockholders, to provide the best of dairy products, to guard the goodness of all Borden foods, and to bring them to your home.

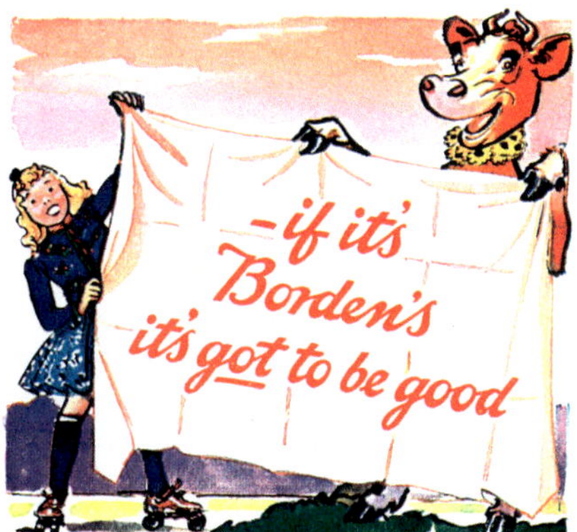

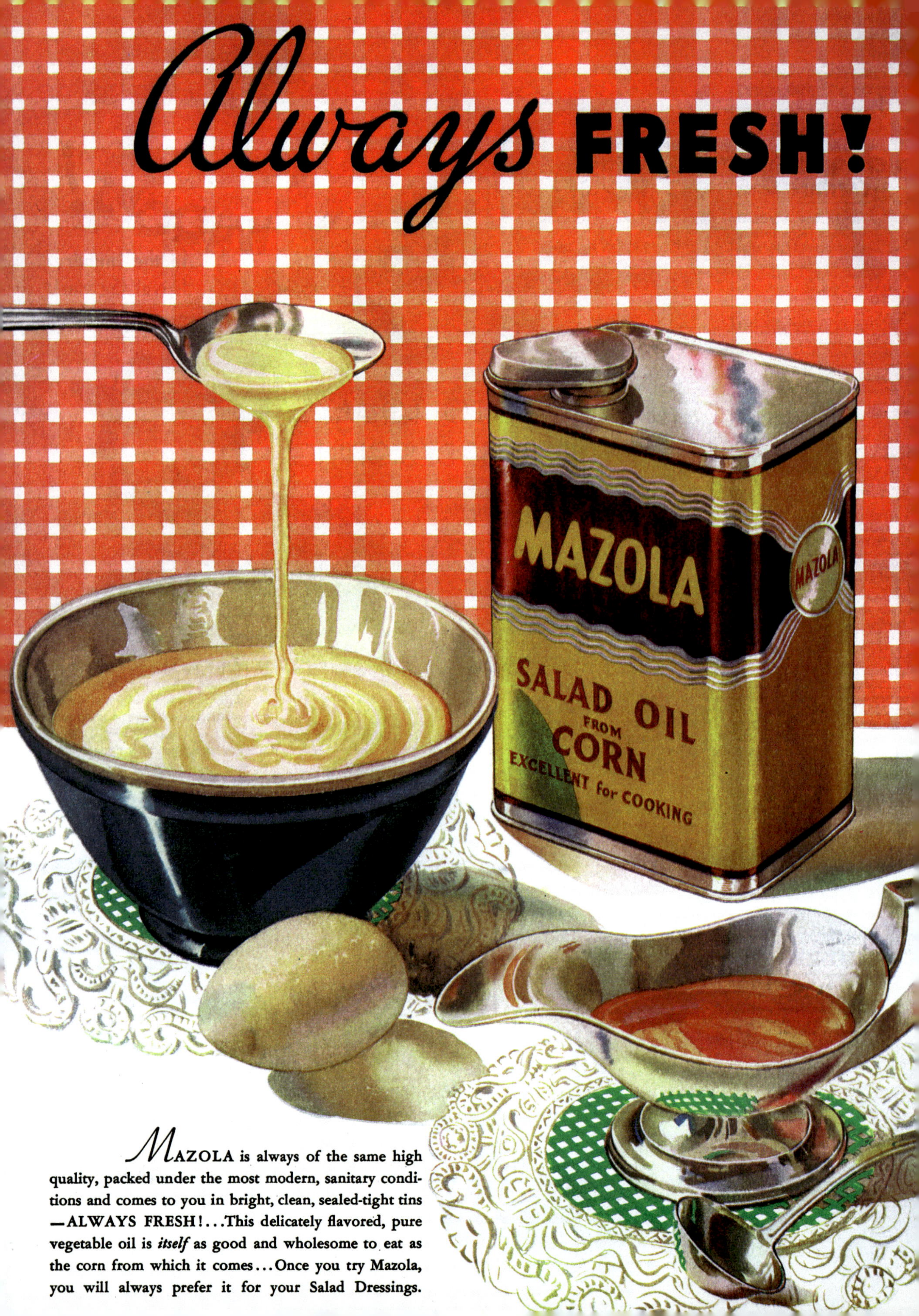
Always FRESH!
MAZOLA
MAZOLA
SALAD OIL FROM CORN
EXCELLENT for COOKING
MAZOLA is always of the same high quality, packed under the most modern, sanitary conditions and comes to you in bright, clean, sealed-tight tins —ALWAYS FRESH!...This delicately flavored, pure vegetable oil is *itself* as good and wholesome to eat as the corn from which it comes...Once you try Mazola, you will always prefer it for your Salad Dressings.

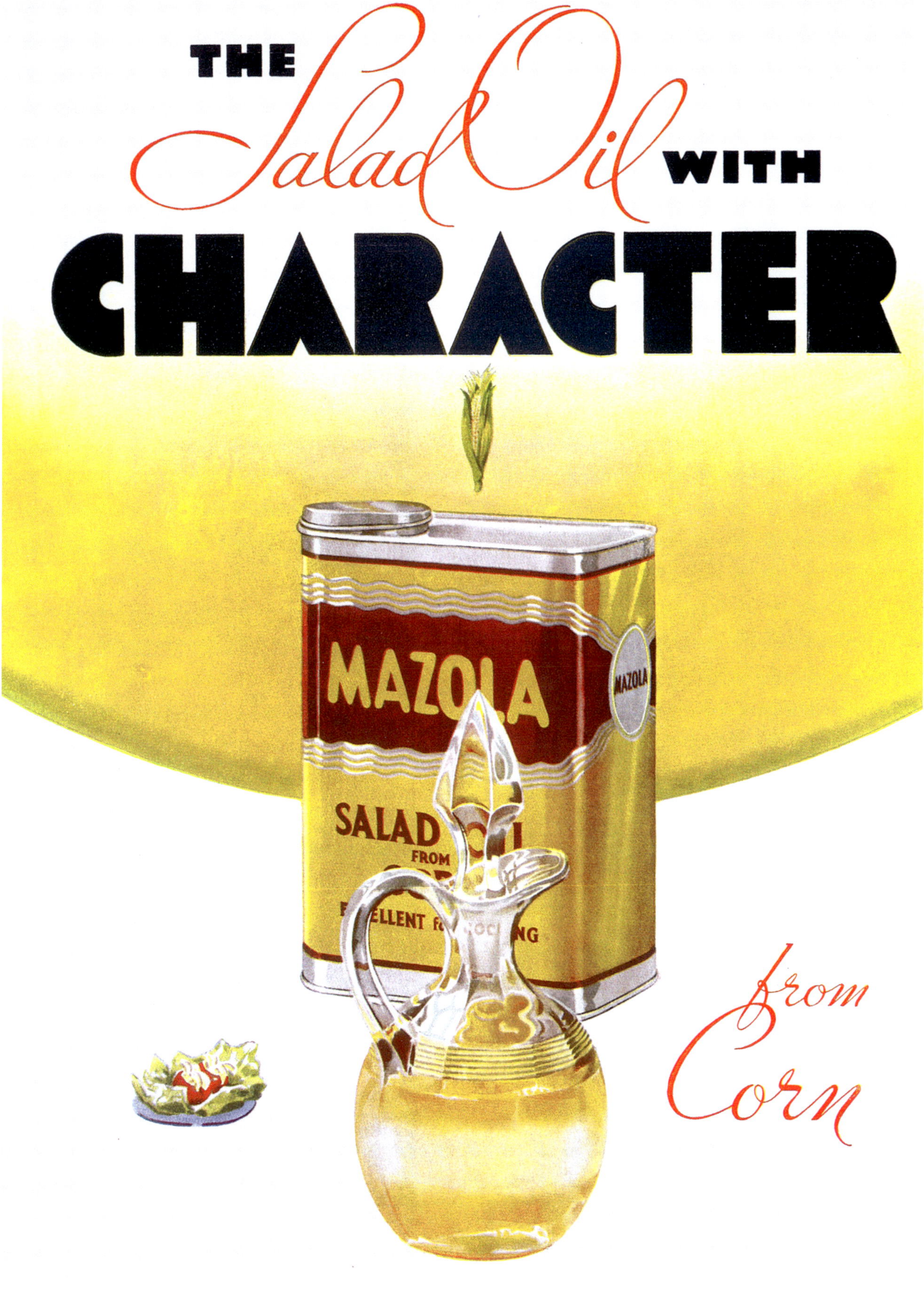

Mazola Salad Oil, 1935 ◂

Mazola Salad Oil, 1936

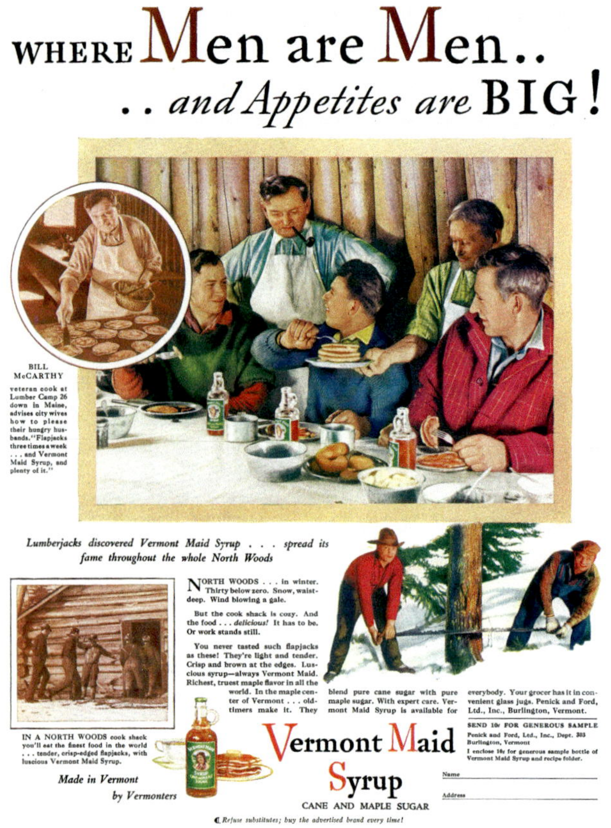

Vermont Maid Syrup, 1931

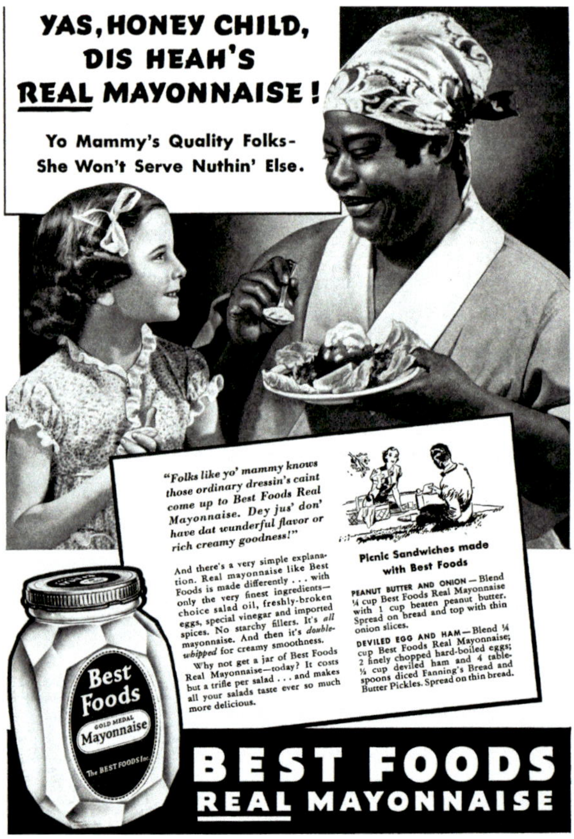

Best Foods, 1936

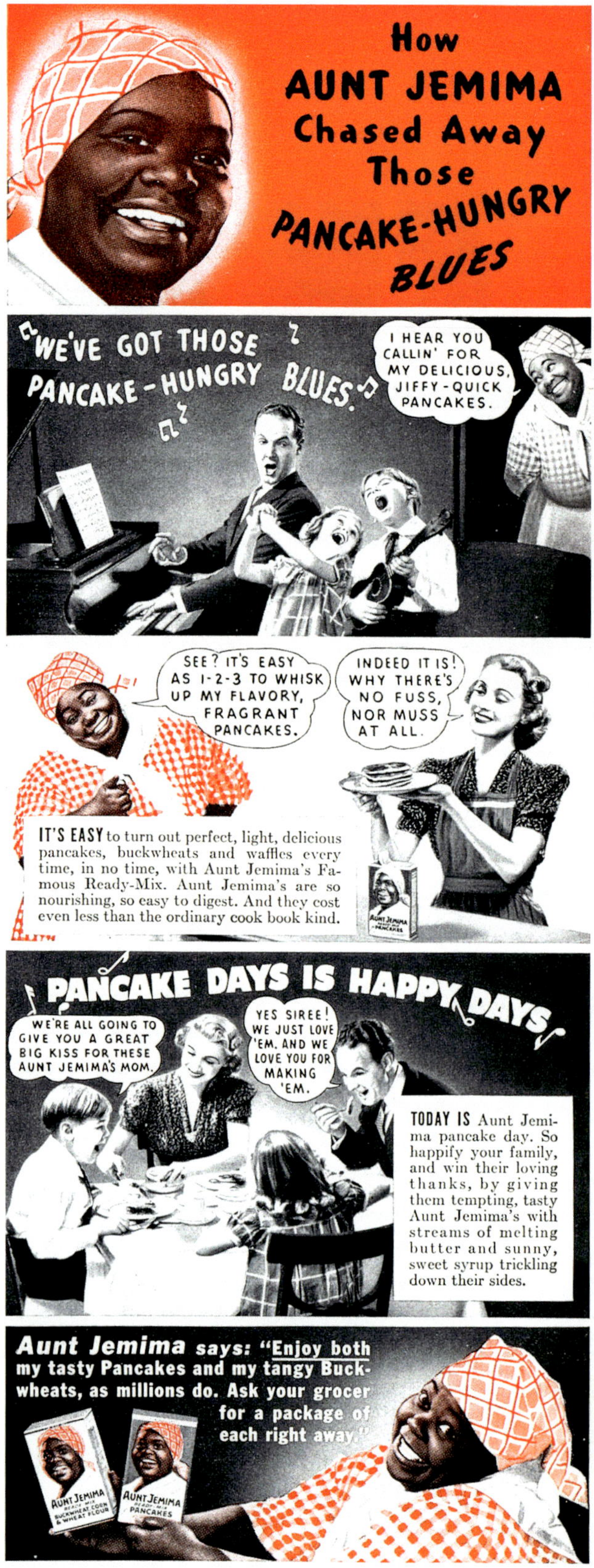

Aunt Jemima, 1939

▸ *Aunt Jemima, 1935*

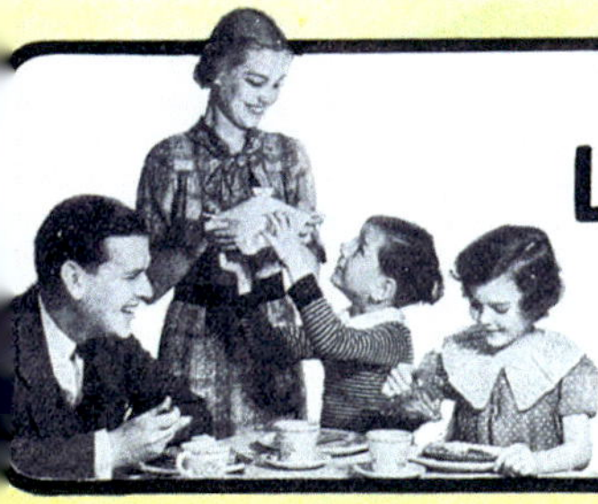

LET OL' AUNTIE SING A SONG IN YO' KITCHEN

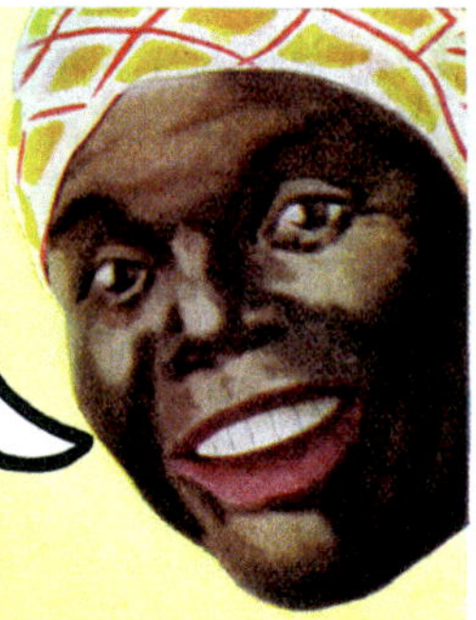

Make meal-time an adventure with

AUNT JEMIMA'S MAGIC MENU

HAM 'N' WAFFLES, SOUTHERN STYLE

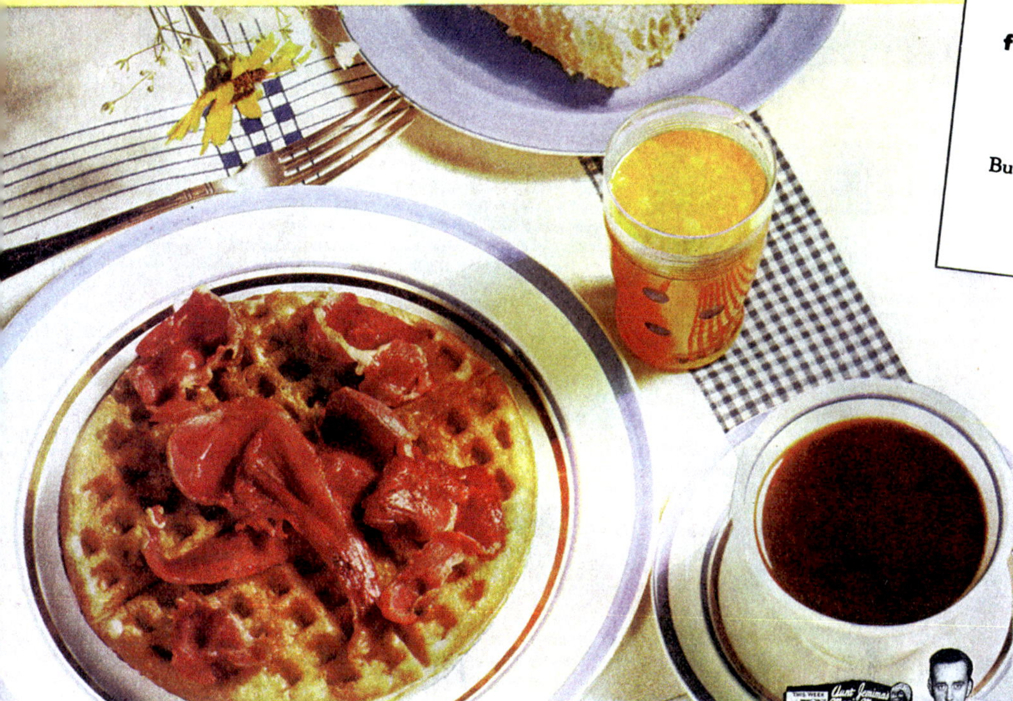

MENU

for Ham 'n' Waffle Breakfast

Chilled Fruit Juice
Aunt Jemima Waffles
Butter Honey or Syrup
Frizzled Ham
Coffee

Directions for making

AUNT JEMIMA WAFFLES

1 Mix milk or water with equal amounts of Aunt Jemima Pancake Flour according to package recipe.

2 Have waffle iron just hot enough. To test, put a drop of water on iron. If it goes right up in a puff of steam, iron is too hot. If it bounces around a second before evaporating, iron is hot enough.

3 Grease iron very lightly. Don't pour grease on. Spread it thinly with pad or brush.

4 Pour batter into iron. Let bake until a golden brown.

ODAY you can make the same light, fluffy, soul-satisfying waffles that were the talk the Old South—with Aunt Jemima's ret recipe. Four different flours, with other redients—all ready to mix with milk or ter. Not a single thing to prepare.

t's so easy for you to get them light and ll-done because Aunt Jemima's special blend rantees far more fluffiness than ordinary ad or biscuit flour. For Aunt Jemima's contains only about half the amount of gluten of ordinary flour. And gluten is the taffy-like substance in flour that resists heat and slows up the baking process.

That's why, with about half the gluten of ordinary flour, Aunt Jemima's come out so perfectly done, so tender, fluffy and light in the few short minutes waffles are on the fire. And note this, ladies, an Aunt Jemima waffle, a square of butter and 1½ ounces of syrup are only 382 calories. Yet standard diets permit a total of 2,000 to 4,000 calories in the three daily meals. So enjoy the zest, the old-time tang of Ham 'n' Waffles, Southern style. There's a heap of good living in this easy-to-prepare meal.

Your grocer will deliver any of the ingredients you need for it, complete with simple, printed directions. So phone your order now.

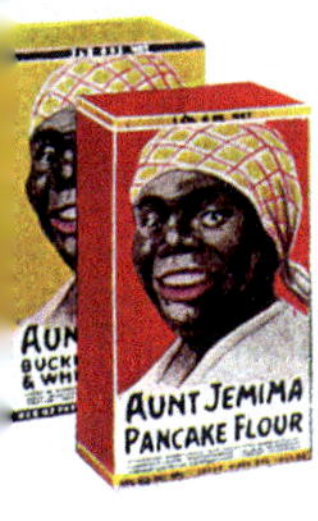

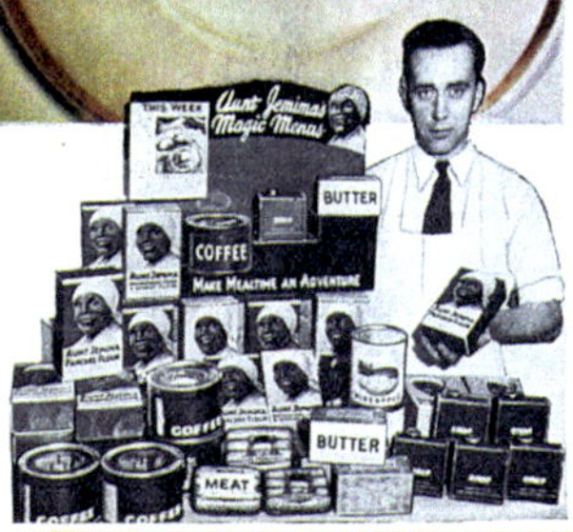

Any ingredients for the Magic Menu shown above, with printed, easy directions, are supplied by all grocers showing this display. A wonderfully easy meal to prepare, with the special waffle blend that guarantees far more fluffiness.

FREE WITH 1 BOX-TOP **Aunt Jemima's Album of Secret Recipes**

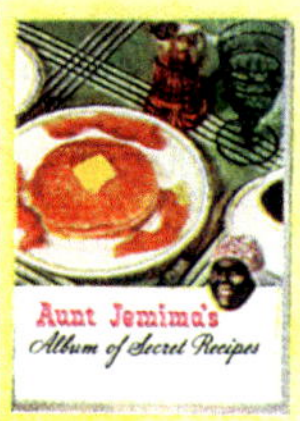

A wonderful new 36-page cook-book, illustrated in full colors, with 64 Aunt Jemima recipes and 22 complete menus. Simple, easy directions that save steps, time and energy. Mail coupon for this booklet today and use it to thrill the family with bright, new and interesting meals. Send 1 Box-Top from either Aunt Jemima's Pancake Flour or Aunt Jemima's Buckwheat, to The Quaker Oats Co., Dept. L1, Box 1083, Chicago, Illinois.

Name__________

Address__________

City__________ State__________

AUNT JEMIMA

Pancake Flour *in the red package . . .* **Buckwheat** *in the yellow package*

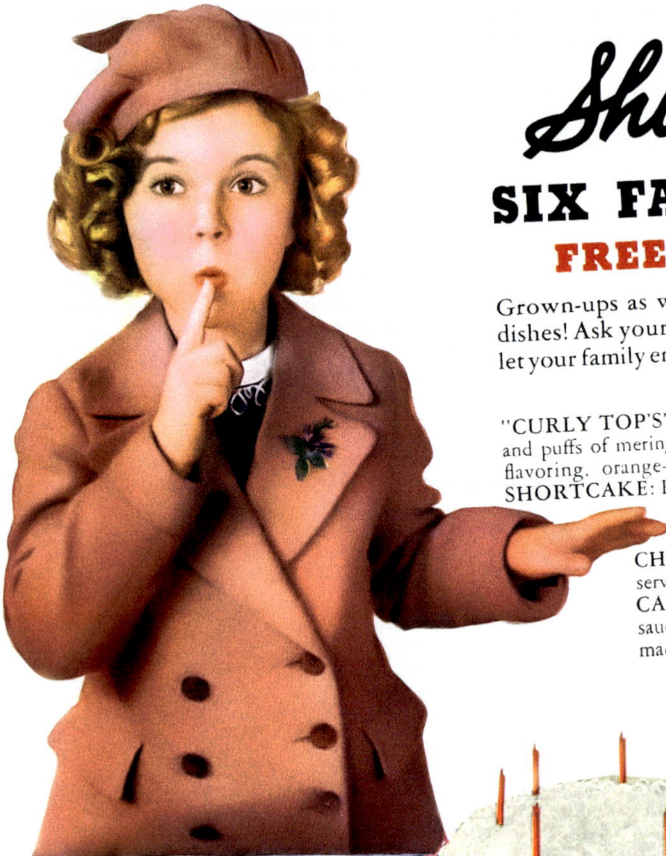

Shirley Temple's
SIX FAVORITE DESSERTS
FREE AT YOUR GROCER'S!

Grown-ups as well as little Shirley, love these original, tempting dishes! Ask your grocer for this clever set of six different recipes and let your family enjoy the same desserts often served in Shirley's home.

Top Row:

"CURLY TOP'S" FAVORITE: Apple sauce custard with peanut-butter crumbs and puffs of meringue. SHIRLEY'S 7th BIRTHDAY CAKE: Orange juice flavoring, orange-custard filling, and cocoanut frosting. HOLLYWOOD SHORTCAKE: Fluffy-light gingerbread, fresh strawberries and whipped cream.

Bottom Row:

CHOCOLATE "PUDDING-TART": Real Rocky Road pudding served in a flaky pastry shell. "POOR LITTLE RICH GIRL" CAKE: An ice cream "sandwich", made with cake and chocolate sauce. STUDIO-LUNCH COOKIES: Inexpensive, crisp cakes made of "sugar and spice and everything nice."

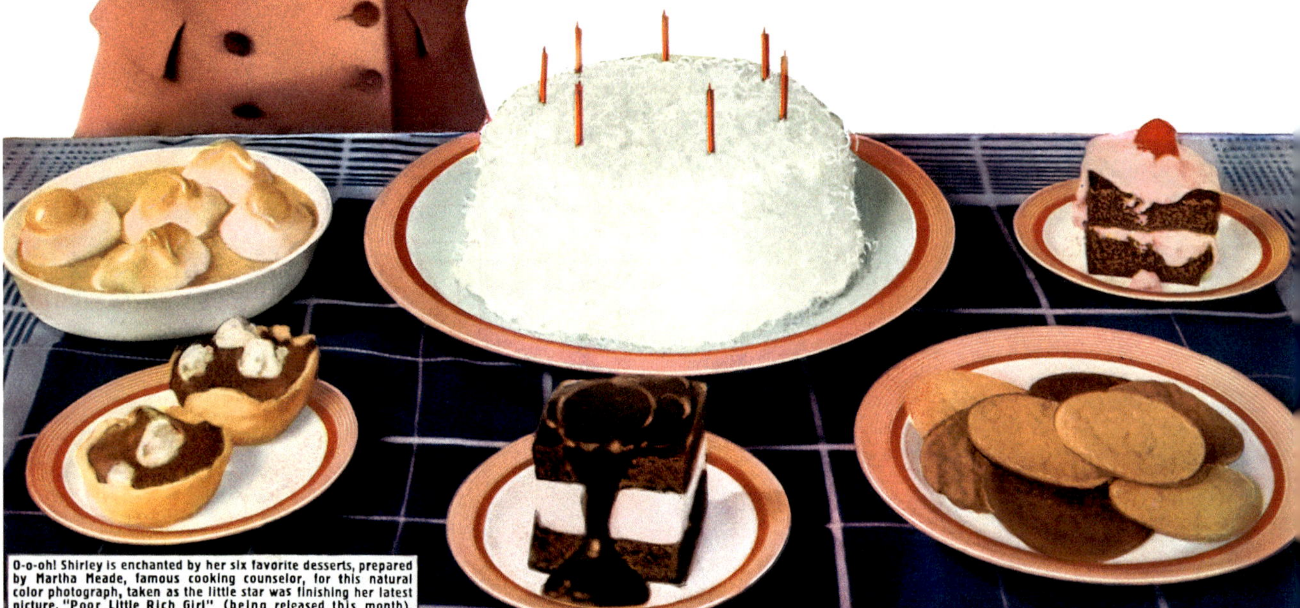

O-o-oh! Shirley is enchanted by her six favorite desserts, prepared by Martha Meade, famous cooking counselor, for this natural color photograph, taken as the little star was finishing her latest picture, "Poor Little Rich Girl" (being released this month).

TO MAKE THESE DESSERTS EXACTLY AS SHIRLEY TEMPLE PREFERS THEM, BE SURE YOU USE DRIFTED SNOW, THE "HOME-PERFECTED" FLOUR

Get your copy of Shirley Temple's favorite desserts from your grocer before they're all gone!

Because they're the choice of a world famous star, don't think these desserts are difficult or costly. You'll make them perfectly by using Drifted Snow "Home-Perfected" Flour. Variation in flour quality causes one-half of all baking failures. To save you from this, Drifted Snow Flour is tested by Sperry's staff of 117 Western homemakers, living in many states. Only flour which they find gives uniform results under all conditions is sold as Drifted Snow "Home-Perfected" Flour. That's why it will give you better baking, save you from failures and waste.

Remember, everybody will want Shirley Temple's desserts. Get your copy free at your grocer's and order a sack of Drifted Snow "Home-Perfected" Flour. Then you can make these dishes just the way the little star loves them.

DRIFTED SNOW "Home Perfected" FLOUR

36 more recipes!

In addition to the Shirley Temple desserts, Sperry offers you Martha Meade's popular "Six-of-a Kind" book of 36 recipes. It's packed FREE in every sack of Drifted Snow Flour.

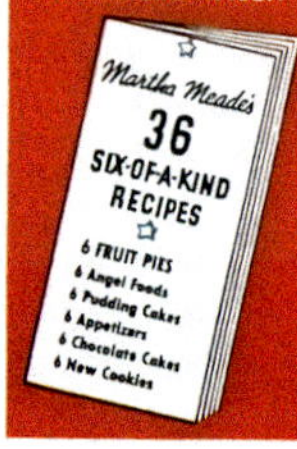

LOOK FOR THIS DISPLAY AT YOUR GROCER'S!

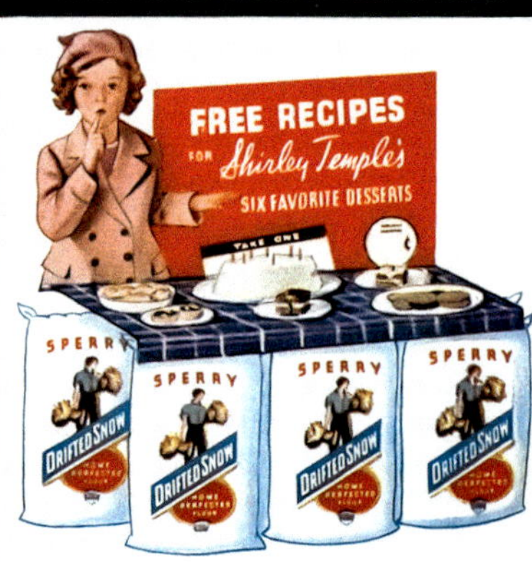

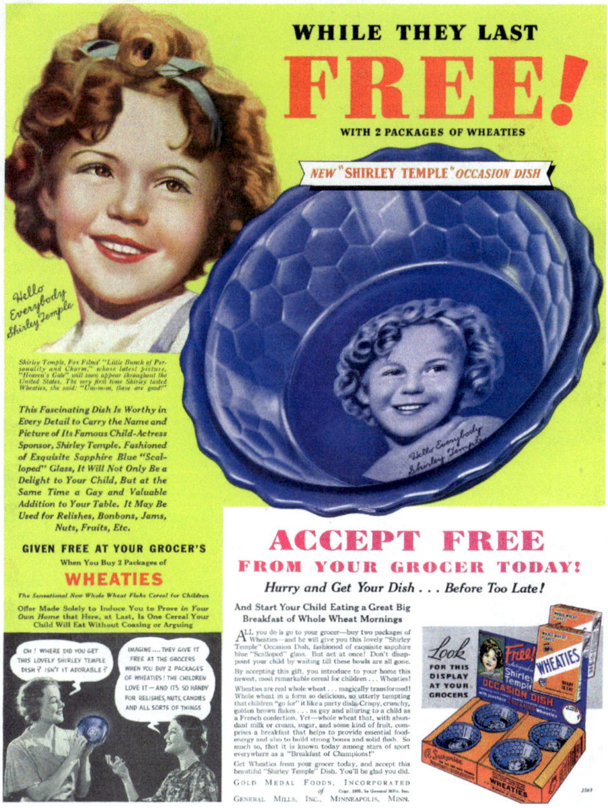

Wheaties, 1935

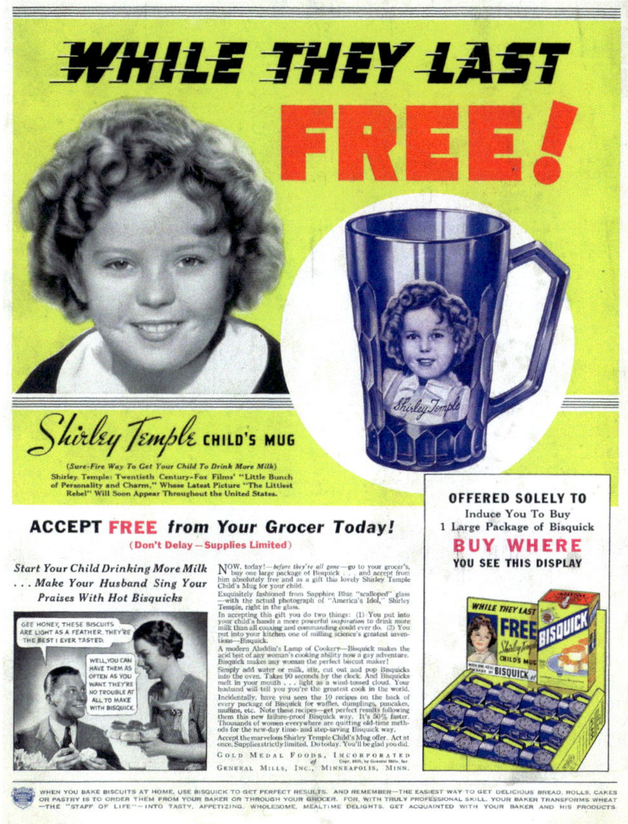

Bisquick, 1935

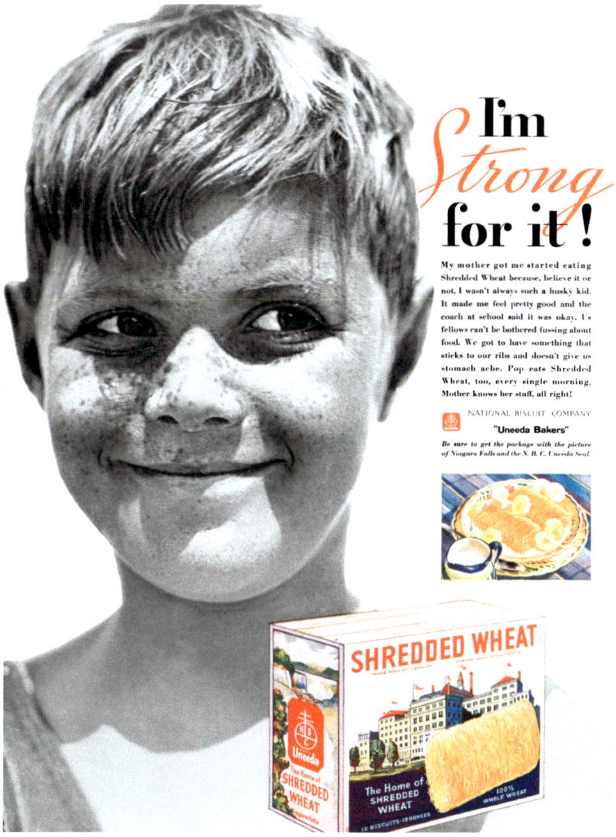

Sperry Flour, 1936 ◂ Shredded Wheat, 1934

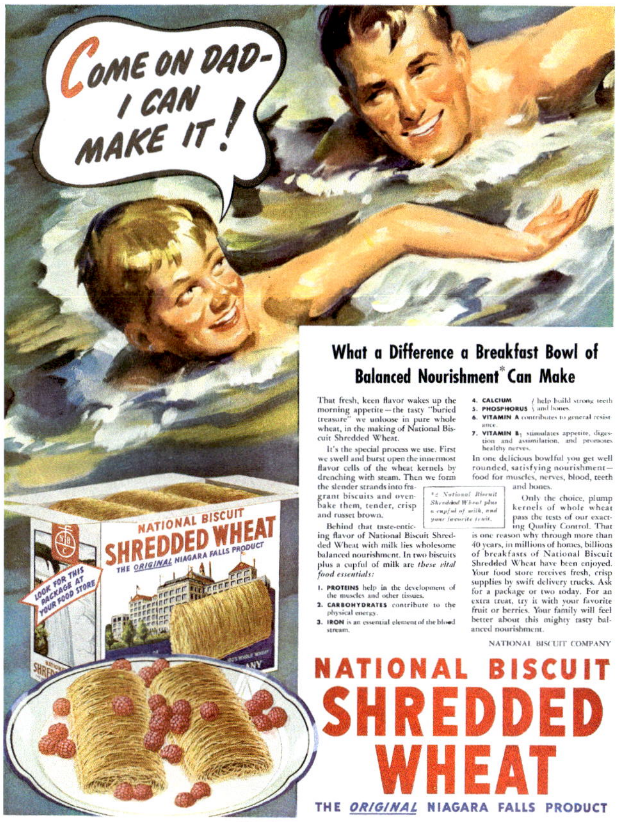

Shredded Wheat, 1939

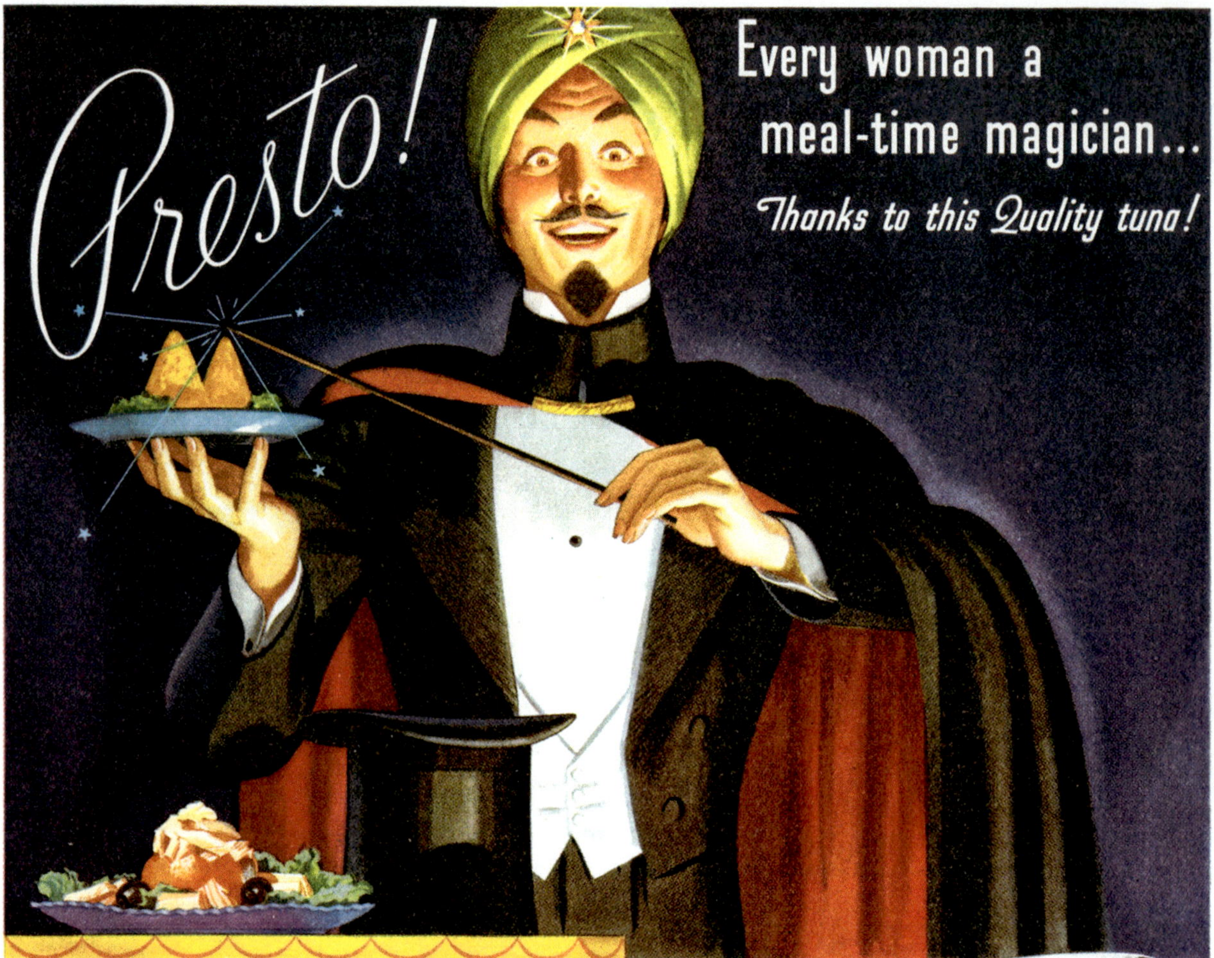

THERE'S many a magic culinary triumph you can "pull out of the hat"... if you use this superior quality tuna!

For remember . . . there's no halfway quality in tuna! It's either delicious, tender, and rich in food value . . . or it isn't! A tuna salad, a tuna cocktail, tuna en casserole is either a brilliant success or a dismal failure!

So, take no chances; insist upon the tuna whose quality America has relied on for 27 years. Only the tender *light* meat is packed. Containing Vitamins "A" and "D", and Iodine, that effective preventive of nutritional goiter, it's a "rich" food but not a heavy food; easy to digest; quick to assimilate.

Some like it HOT, some like it COLD! Serve tuna several times a week, the year round. Cocktails, hors d'oeuvres, salads, sandwiches, creamed tuna, tuna en casserole, tuna croquettes; what other single food offers such a variety of uses!

Van Camp Sea Food Co., Inc., Terminal Island, Calif.

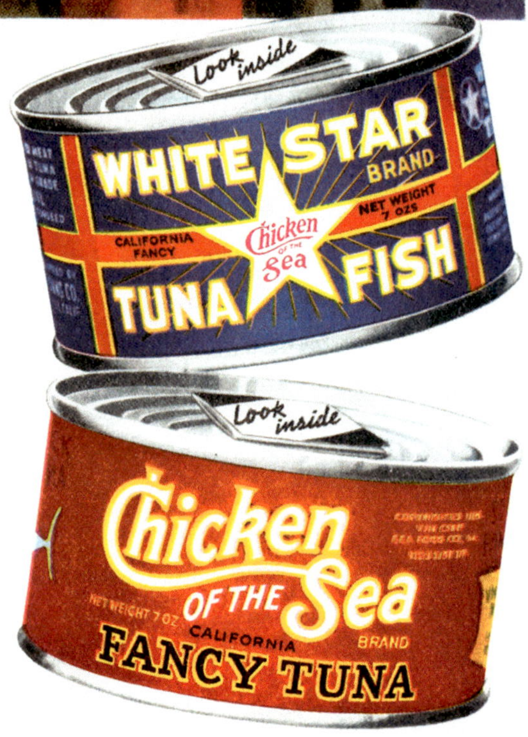

NEW!

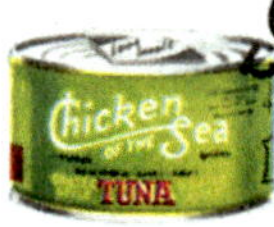

It's Grated!

And, here is this famous tuna in a new style . . . grated! Much more convenient . . . and economical . . . for many tuna recipes, especially salads and sandwiches. No mincing, no shredding, no flaking; use it just as it comes from the can!

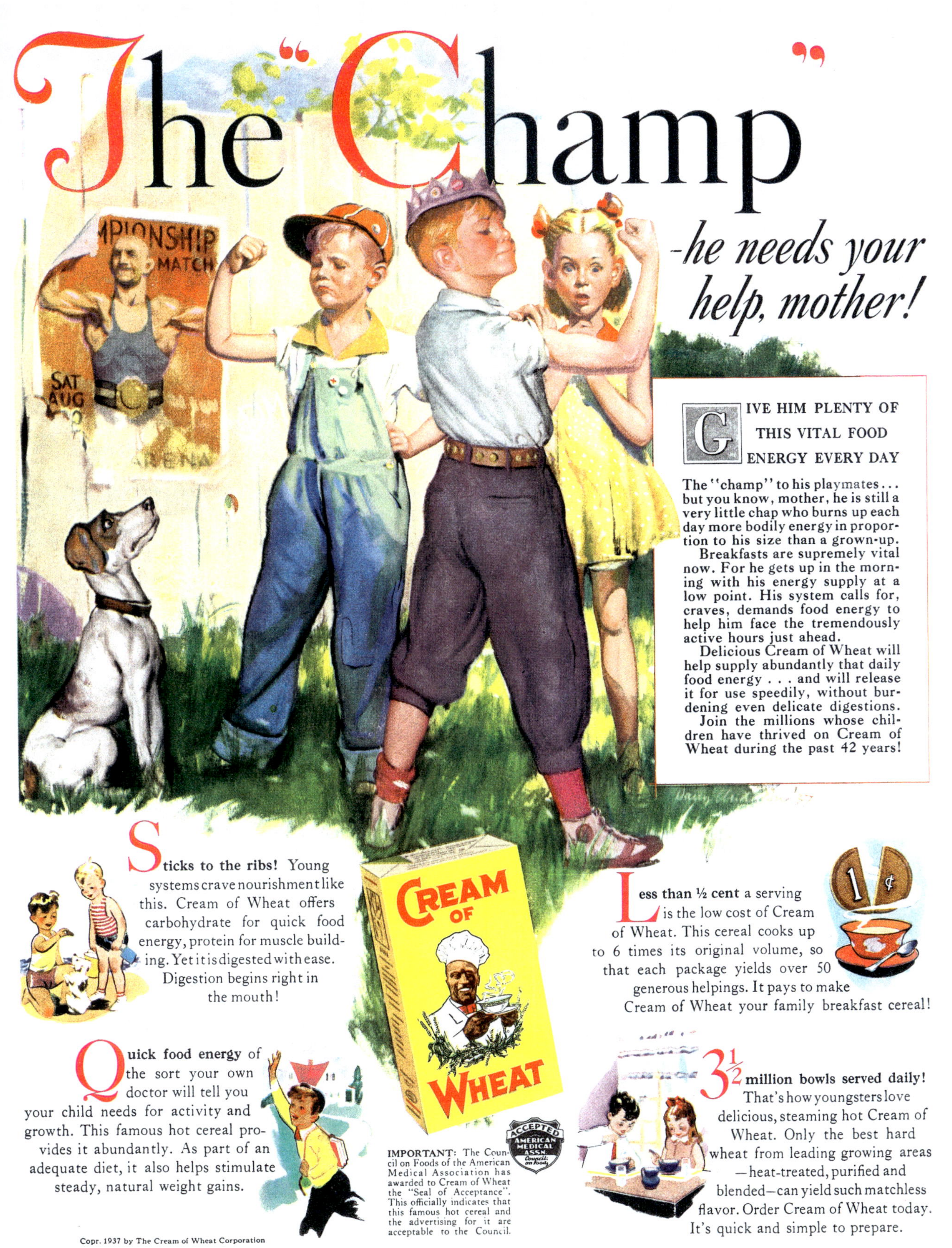

White Star Tuna, 1939 ◄

Cream Of Wheat, 1937

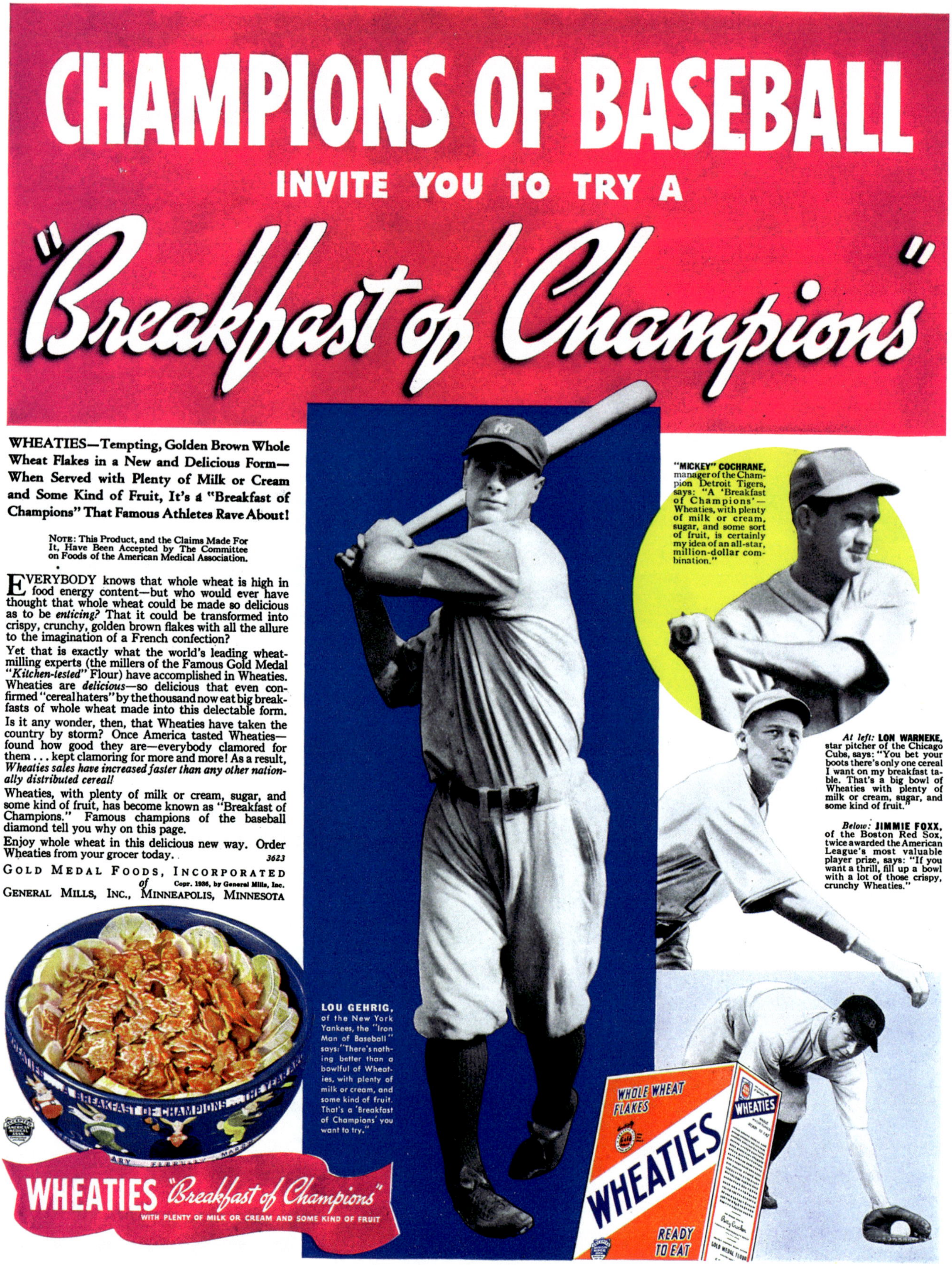

Wheaties, 1936

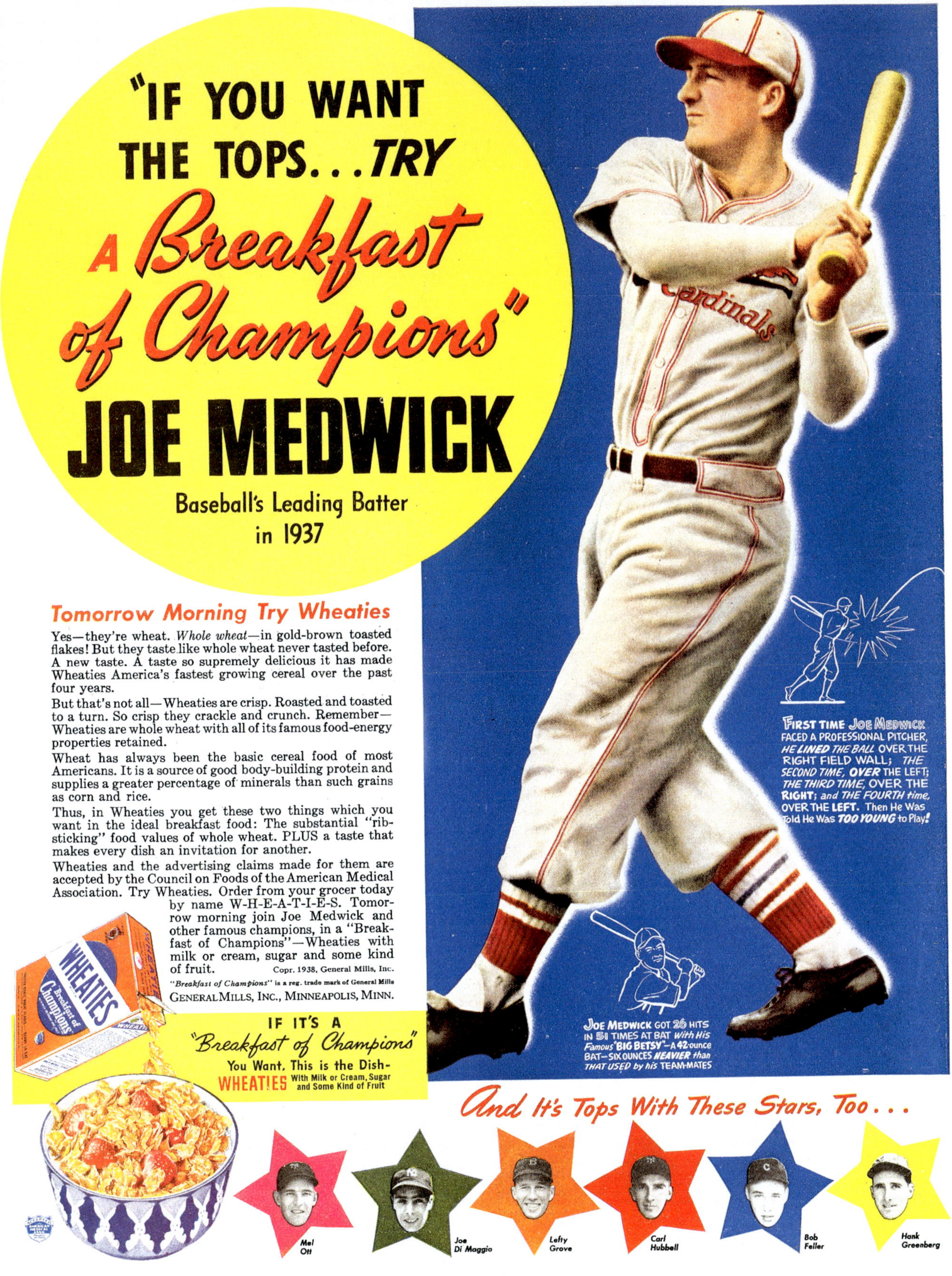

Wheaties, 1938

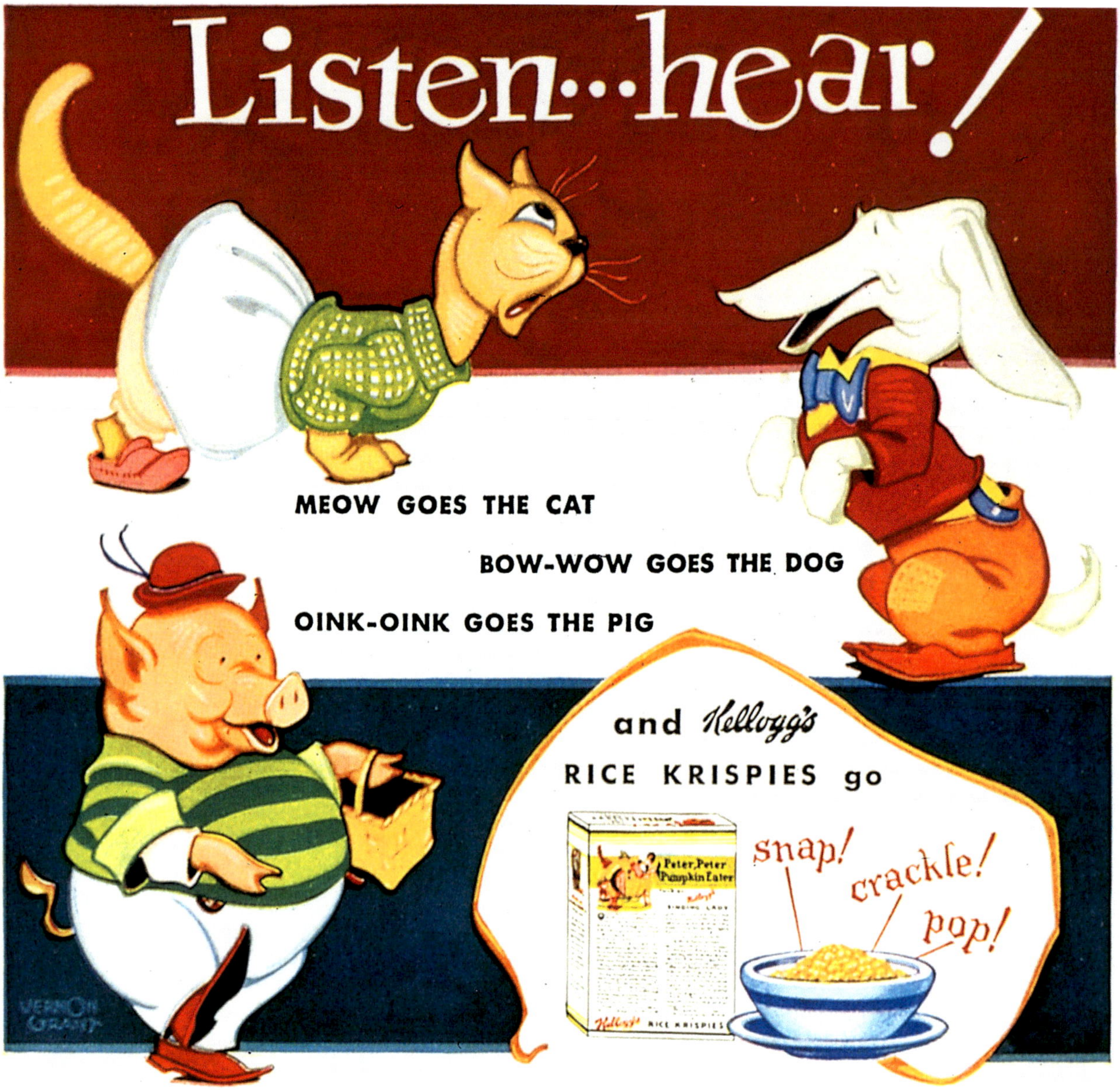

You may wonder why Kellogg's Rice Krispies crackle in milk or cream. That is a secret that Kellogg will always keep, but the crunchy crispness and delicious flavor of Rice Krispies is always yours to enjoy.

Adults as well as children welcome the sound of Kellogg's Rice Krispies and their unusual goodness. Nourishing and easy to digest. Extra delicious with fruits or honey added. When Rice Krispies are eaten at the nursery supper or for a bedtime snack, they promote restful sleep.

Grocers everywhere sell Rice Krispies. The WAXTITE bag inside the red-and-green package keeps them oven-fresh. Easy to prepare. Economical too. Many generous servings for a few cents. Made by Kellogg in Battle Creek.

•

LOOK! **On the back of every package of Kellogg's Rice Krispies is a delightful Mother Goose story as told by Kellogg's Singing Lady. New stories appear constantly, and children all over the country eagerly look for them. The more Rice Krispies you buy the more stories you get.**

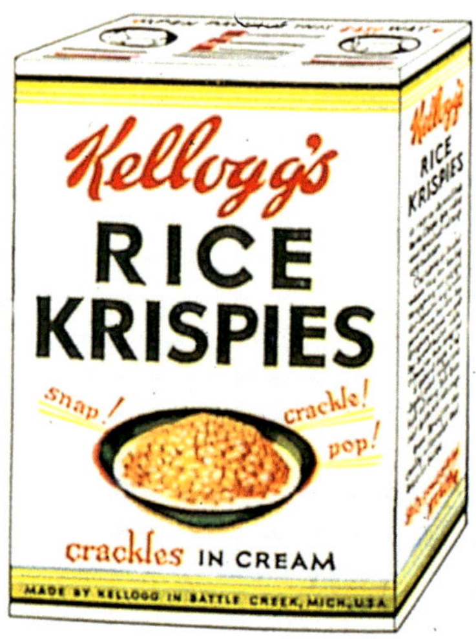

Kellogg's RICE KRISPIES

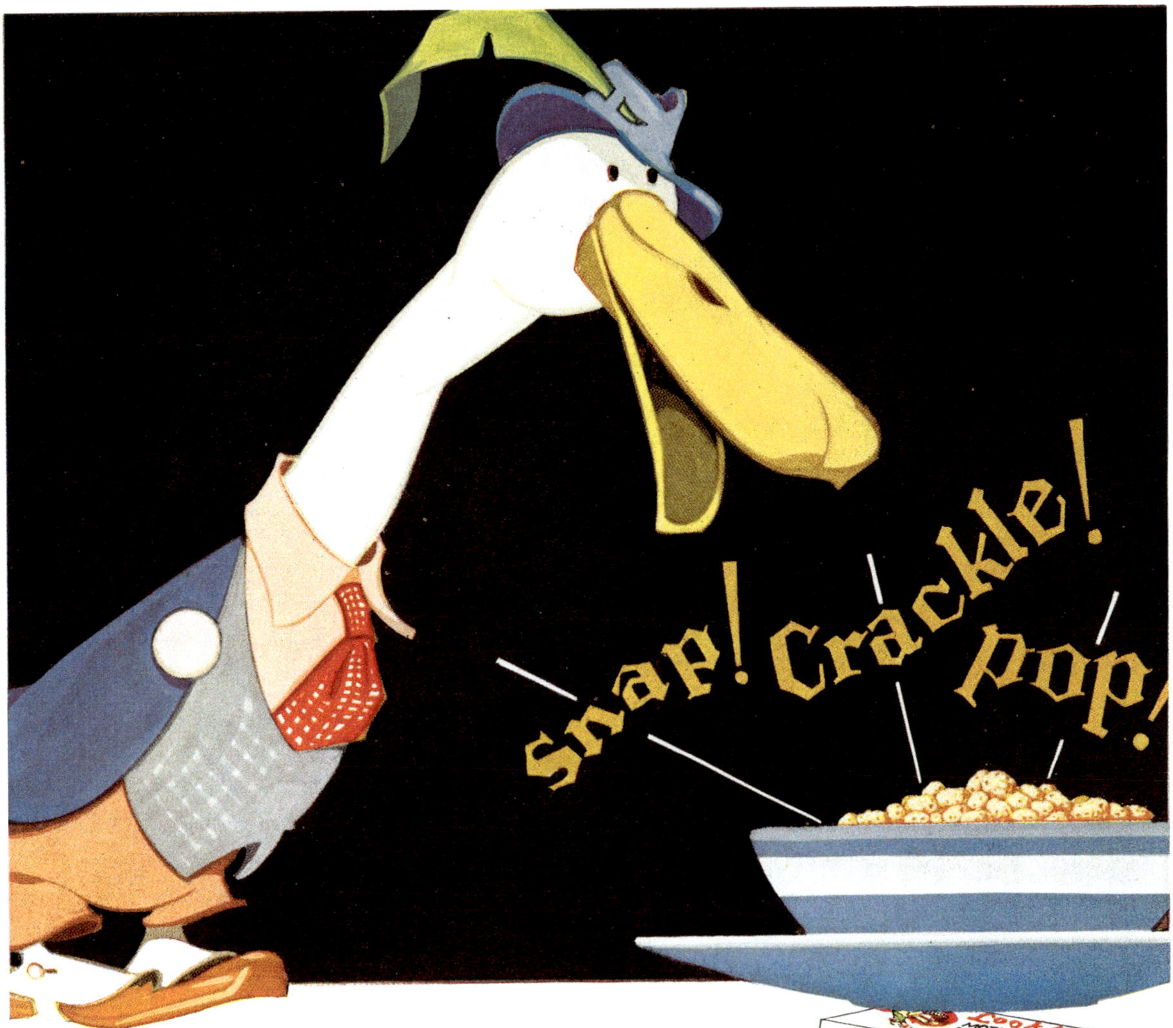

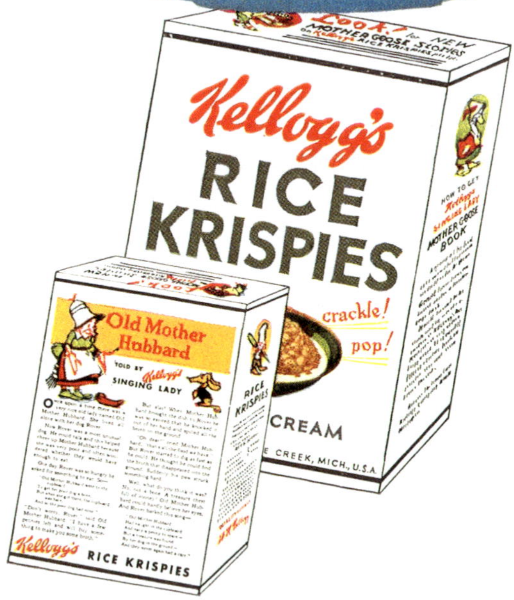

SURPRISED? Yes indeed, everybody is surprised when they first hear Kellogg's Rice Krispies crackling out loud in milk or cream. A crisp, cheery call that seems to say—"Listen . . . . get hungry!"

Serve Rice Krispies any time and you'll enjoy them. And when children eat Rice Krispies at supper, or you have a bowlful for a bedtime snack, they promote sound sleep.

Rice Krispies are nourishing and easy to digest. Extra delicious with fruits or honey added. Sold by grocers everywhere. The WAXTITE bag inside the package keeps them oven-fresh. Made by Kellogg in Battle Creek. Quality guaranteed.

SOMETHING EXTRA! On the back of every package of Kellogg's Rice Krispies is a Mother Goose story as told by Kellogg's Singing Lady. Children love these stories, and since new ones are constantly appearing, the more Rice Krispies you buy, the more stories you get.

Kellogg's RICE KRISPIES

Rice Krispies, 1935 ◄▲

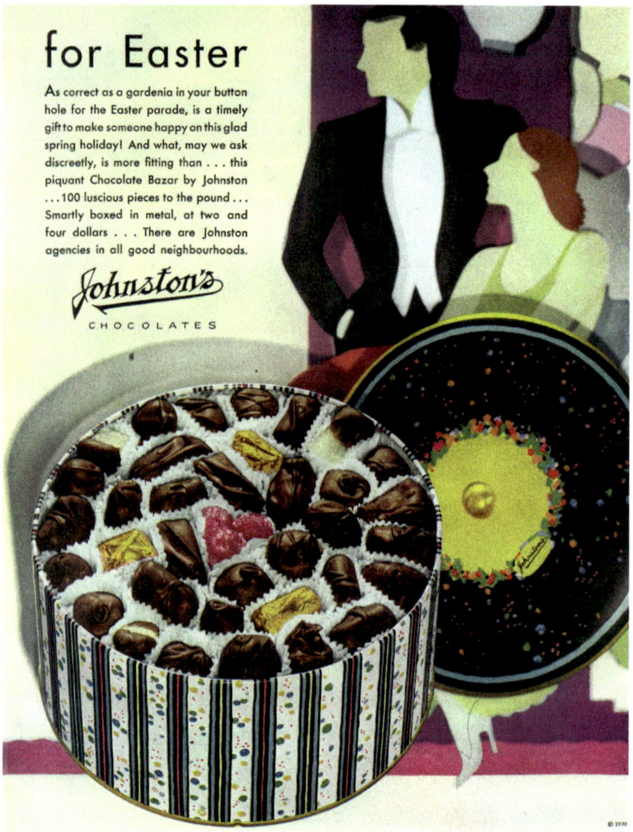

Johnston's Chocolates, 1930

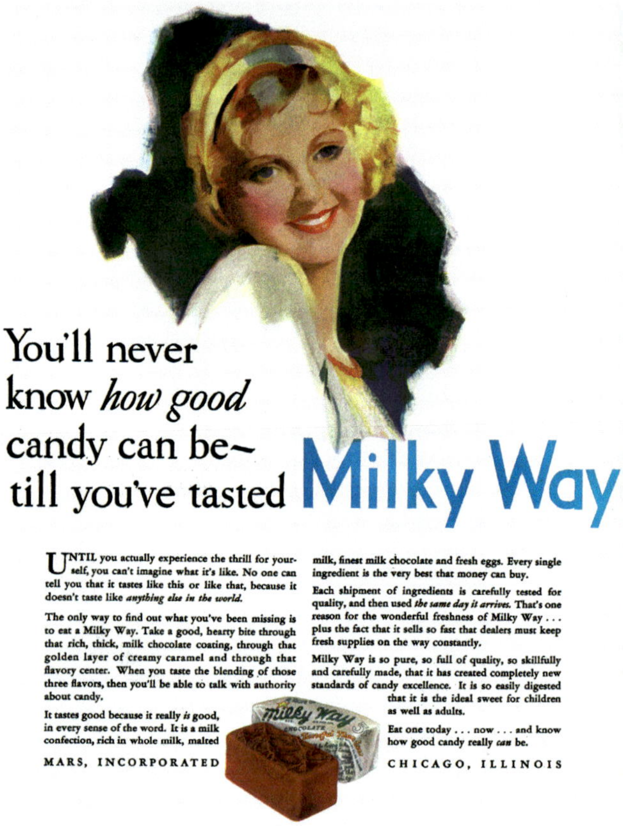

Milky Way, 1931

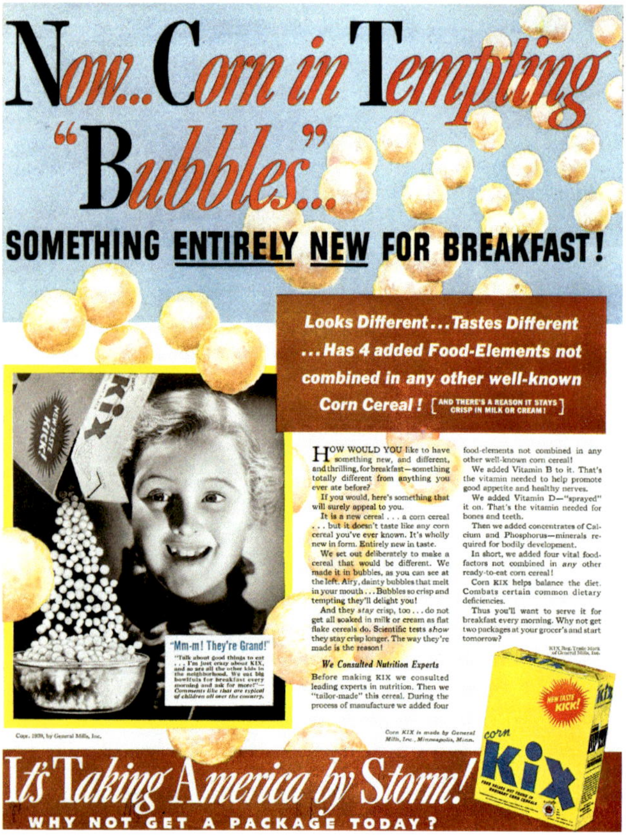

Kix, 1939

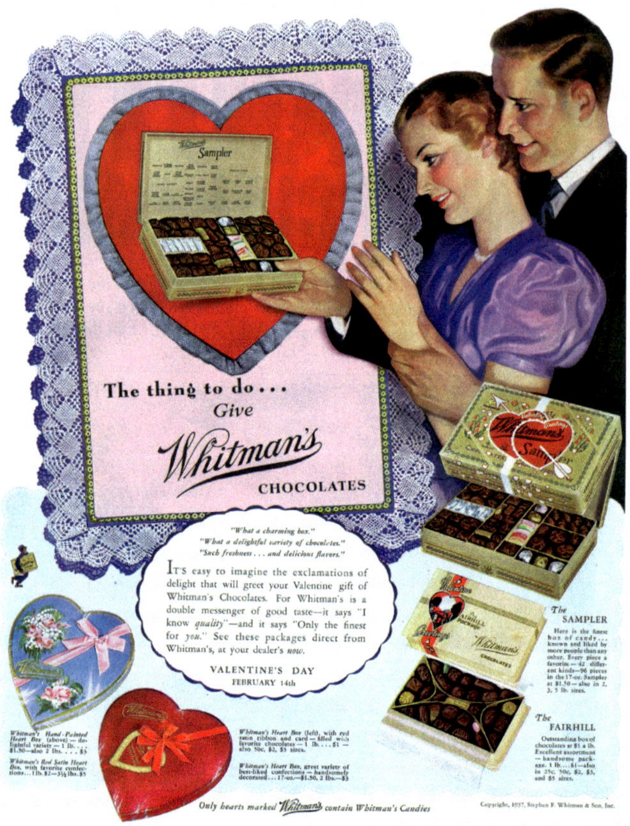

Whitman's Chocolates, 1937

► *Nabisco, 1938*

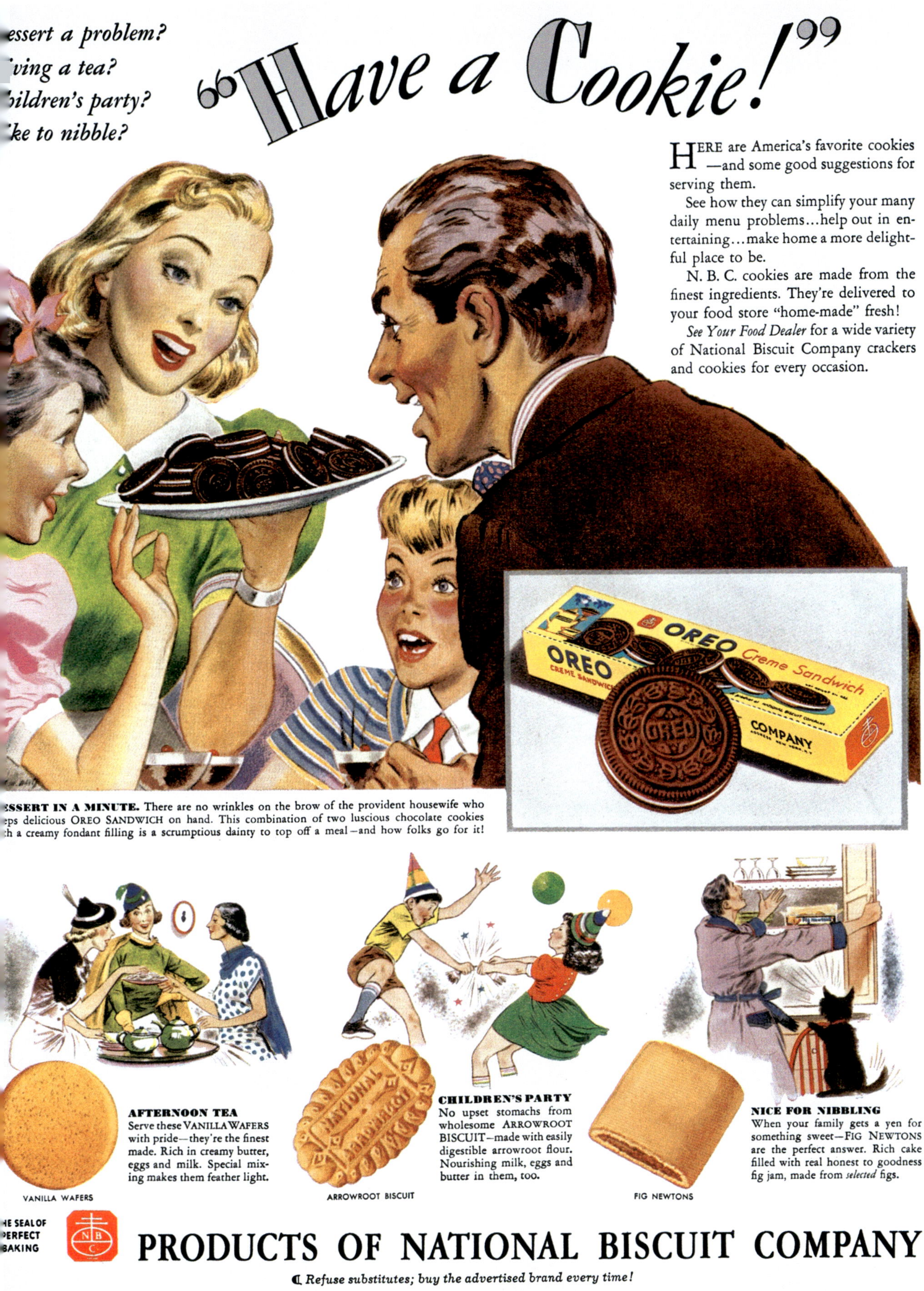

essert a problem?
ving a tea?
ildren's party?
ke to nibble?
"Have a Cookie!"
HERE are America's favorite cookies—and some good suggestions for serving them.
See how they can simplify your many daily menu problems...help out in entertaining...make home a more delightful place to be.
N. B. C. cookies are made from the finest ingredients. They're delivered to your food store "home-made" fresh!
See Your Food Dealer for a wide variety of National Biscuit Company crackers and cookies for every occasion.
OREO Creme Sandwich
OREO
COMPANY
SSERT IN A MINUTE. There are no wrinkles on the brow of the provident housewife who eps delicious OREO SANDWICH on hand. This combination of two luscious chocolate cookies h a creamy fondant filling is a scrumptious dainty to top off a meal—and how folks go for it!
AFTERNOON TEA
Serve these VANILLA WAFERS with pride—they're the finest made. Rich in creamy butter, eggs and milk. Special mixing makes them feather light.
VANILLA WAFERS
NATIONAL ARROWROOT
CHILDREN'S PARTY
No upset stomachs from wholesome ARROWROOT BISCUIT—made with easily digestible arrowroot flour. Nourishing milk, eggs and butter in them, too.
ARROWROOT BISCUIT
FIG NEWTONS
NICE FOR NIBBLING
When your family gets a yen for something sweet—FIG NEWTONS are the perfect answer. Rich cake filled with real honest to goodness fig jam, made from selected figs.
HE SEAL OF
ERFECT
BAKING
N B C
PRODUCTS OF NATIONAL BISCUIT COMPANY
Refuse substitutes; buy the advertised brand every time!

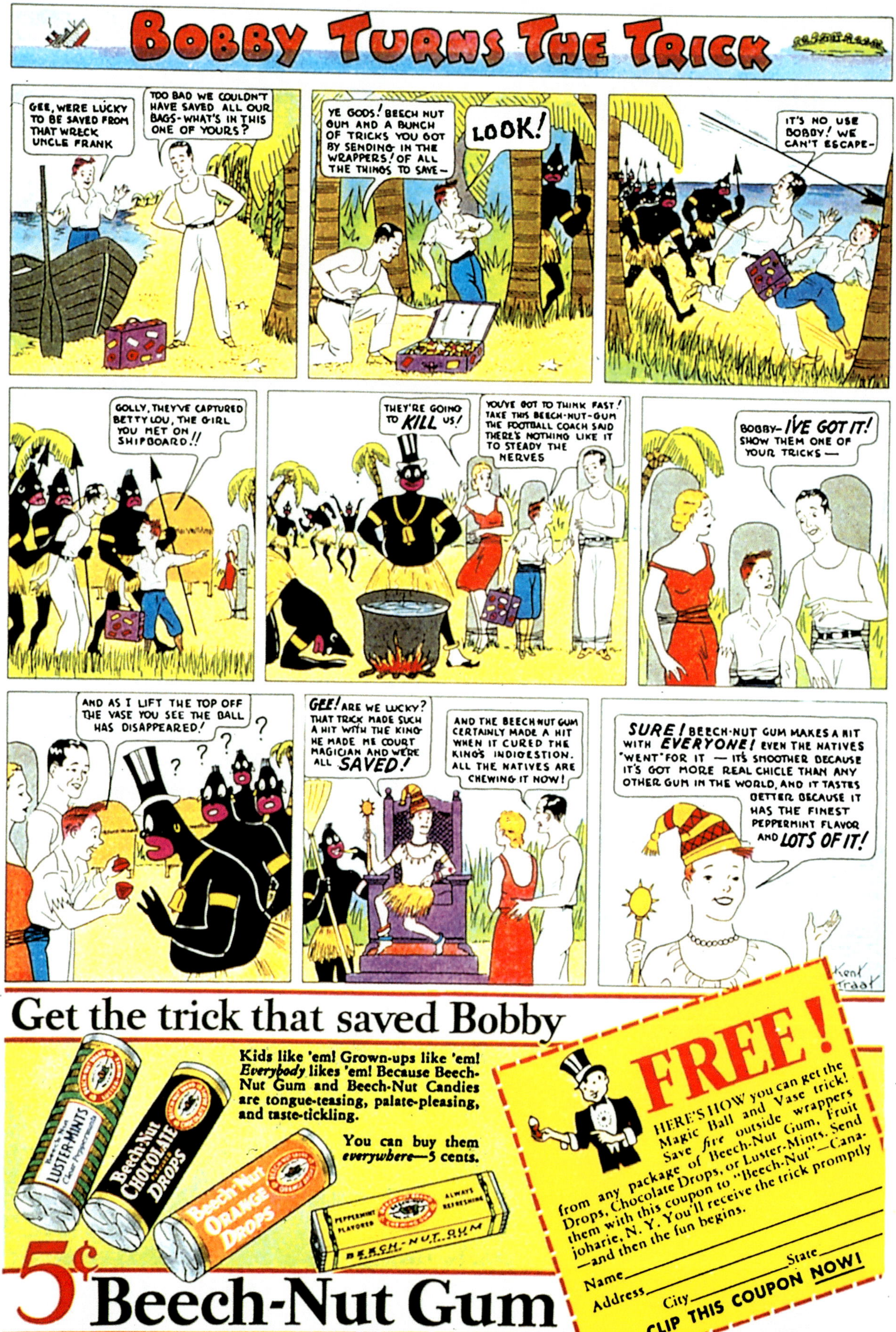
BOBBY TURNS THE TRICK
GEE, WERE LUCKY TO BE SAVED FROM THAT WRECK UNCLE FRANK
TOO BAD WE COULDN'T HAVE SAVED ALL OUR BAGS - WHAT'S IN THIS ONE OF YOURS?
YE GODS! BEECH NUT GUM AND A BUNCH OF TRICKS YOU GOT BY SENDING IN THE WRAPPERS! OF ALL THE THINGS TO SAVE -
LOOK!
IT'S NO USE BOBBY! WE CAN'T ESCAPE -
GOLLY, THEY'VE CAPTURED BETTY LOU, THE GIRL YOU MET ON SHIPBOARD!!
THEY'RE GOING TO KILL US!
YOU'VE GOT TO THINK FAST! TAKE THIS BEECH-NUT-GUM THE FOOTBALL COACH SAID THERE'S NOTHING LIKE IT TO STEADY THE NERVES
BOBBY - I'VE GOT IT! SHOW THEM ONE OF YOUR TRICKS -
AND AS I LIFT THE TOP OFF THE VASE YOU SEE THE BALL HAS DISAPPEARED!
? ? ? ? ?
GEE! ARE WE LUCKY? THAT TRICK MADE SUCH A HIT WITH THE KING HE MADE ME COURT MAGICIAN AND WE'RE ALL SAVED!
AND THE BEECH-NUT GUM CERTAINLY MADE A HIT WHEN IT CURED THE KING'S INDIGESTION. ALL THE NATIVES ARE CHEWING IT NOW!
SURE! BEECH-NUT GUM MAKES A HIT WITH EVERYONE! EVEN THE NATIVES "WENT" FOR IT — IT'S SMOOTHER BECAUSE IT'S GOT MORE REAL CHICLE THAN ANY OTHER GUM IN THE WORLD, AND IT TASTES BETTER BECAUSE IT HAS THE FINEST PEPPERMINT FLAVOR AND LOTS OF IT!
Kent Traat
Get the trick that saved Bobby
Kids like 'em! Grown-ups like 'em! Everybody likes 'em! Because Beech-Nut Gum and Beech-Nut Candies are tongue-teasing, palate-pleasing, and taste-tickling.
You can buy them everywhere—5 cents.
Beech-Nut LUSTER-MINTS
Beech-Nut CHOCOLATE DROPS
Beech-Nut ORANGE DROPS
PEPPERMINT FLAVORED
ALWAYS REFRESHING
BEECH-NUT GUM
FREE!
HERE'S HOW you can get the Magic Ball and Vase trick! Save five outside wrappers from any package of Beech-Nut Gum, Fruit Drops, Chocolate Drops, or Luster-Mints. Send them with this coupon to "Beech-Nut"—Canajoharie, N. Y. You'll receive the trick promptly —and then the fun begins.
Name
Address
City
State
CLIP THIS COUPON NOW!
5¢ Beech-Nut Gum

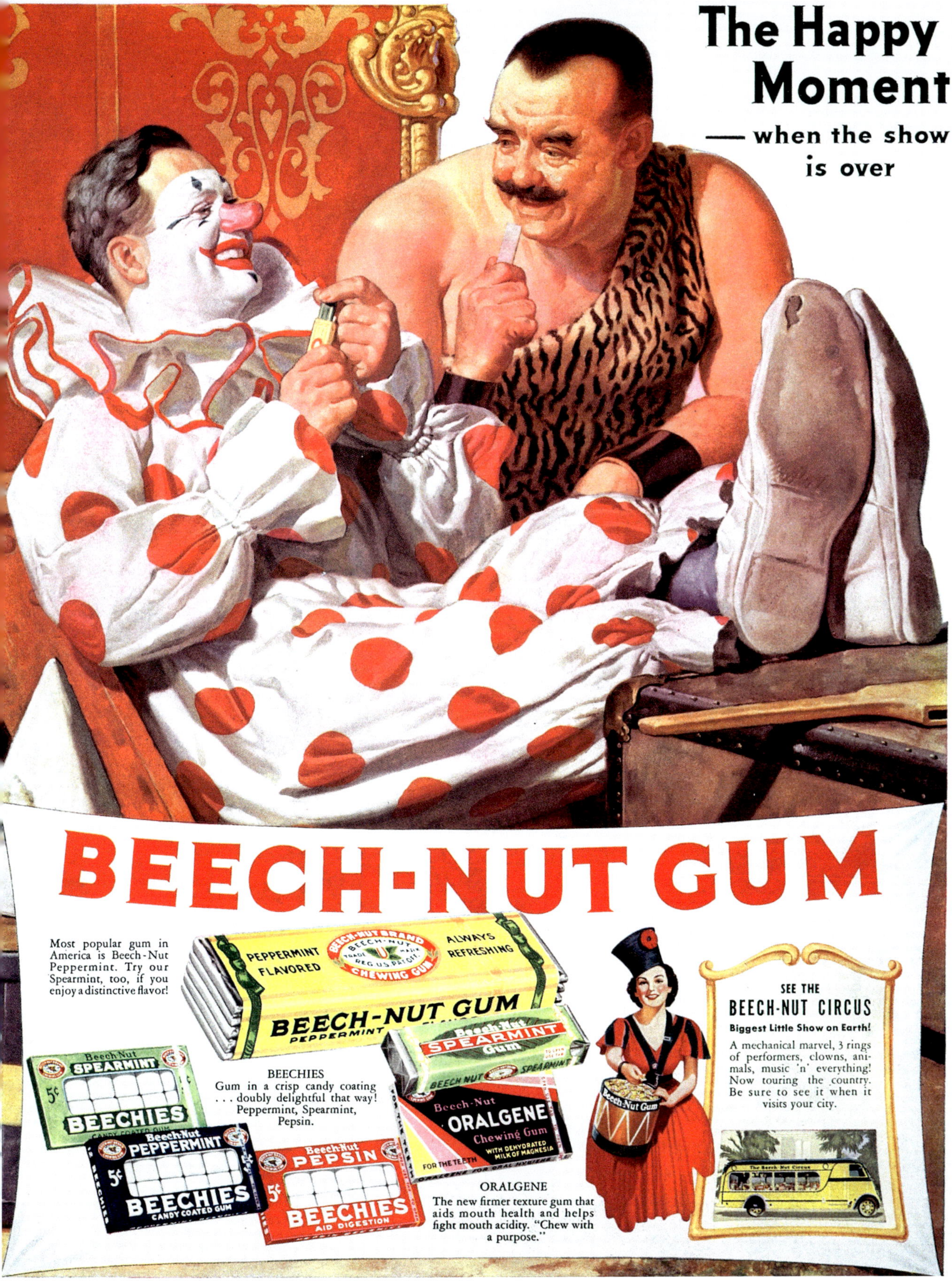

Beech-Nut Gum, 1932 ◄

Beech-Nut Gum, 1937

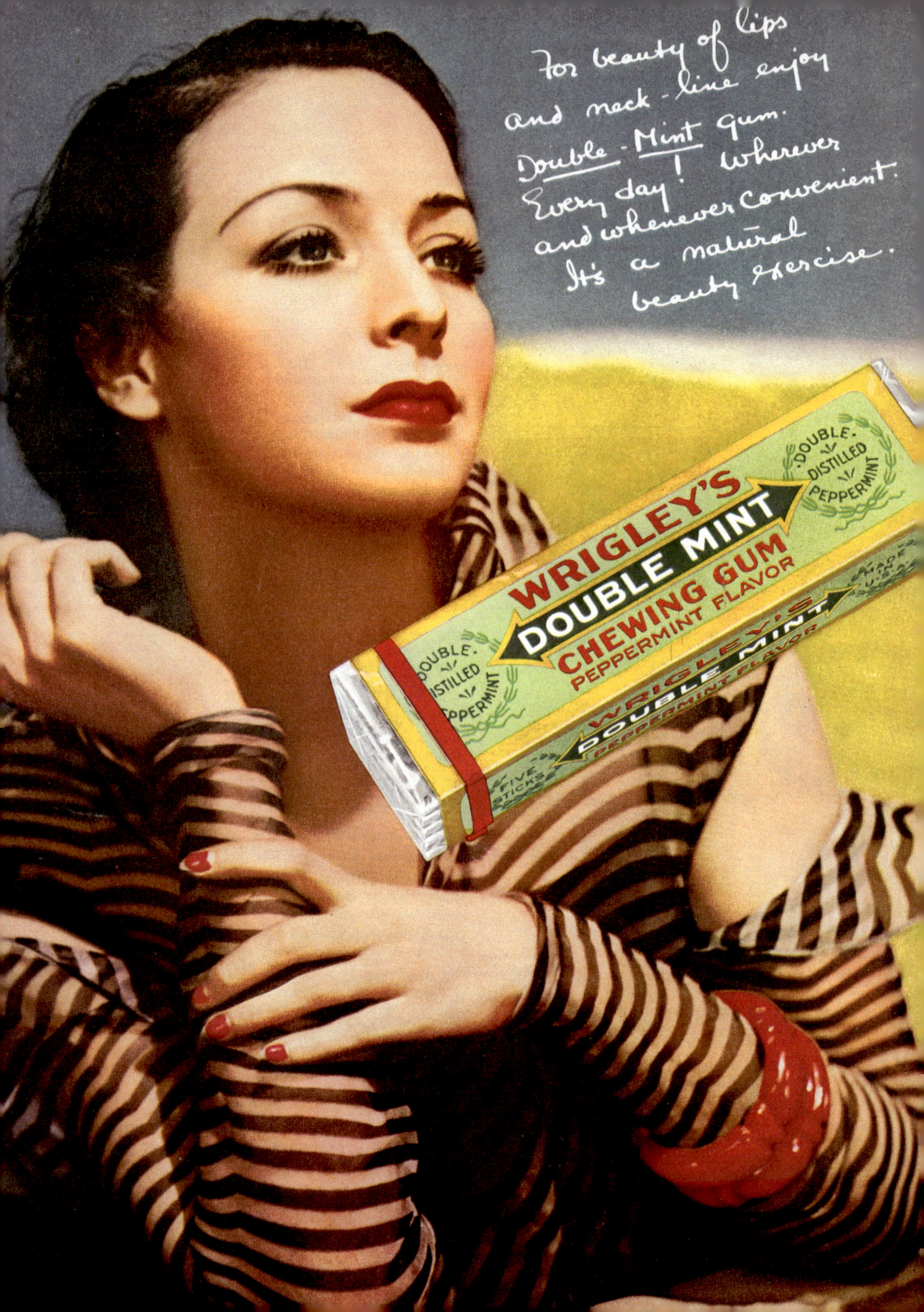
For beauty of lips
and neck-line enjoy
Double-Mint gum.
Every day! Wherever
and whenever convenient.
It's a natural
beauty exercise.
WRIGLEY'S
DOUBLE MINT
CHEWING GUM
PEPPERMINT FLAVOR
DOUBLE DISTILLED PEPPERMINT
DOUBLE DISTILLED PEPPERMINT
WRIGLEY'S
DOUBLE MINT
PEPPERMINT FLAVOR
FIVE STICKS
MADE IN U.S.A.

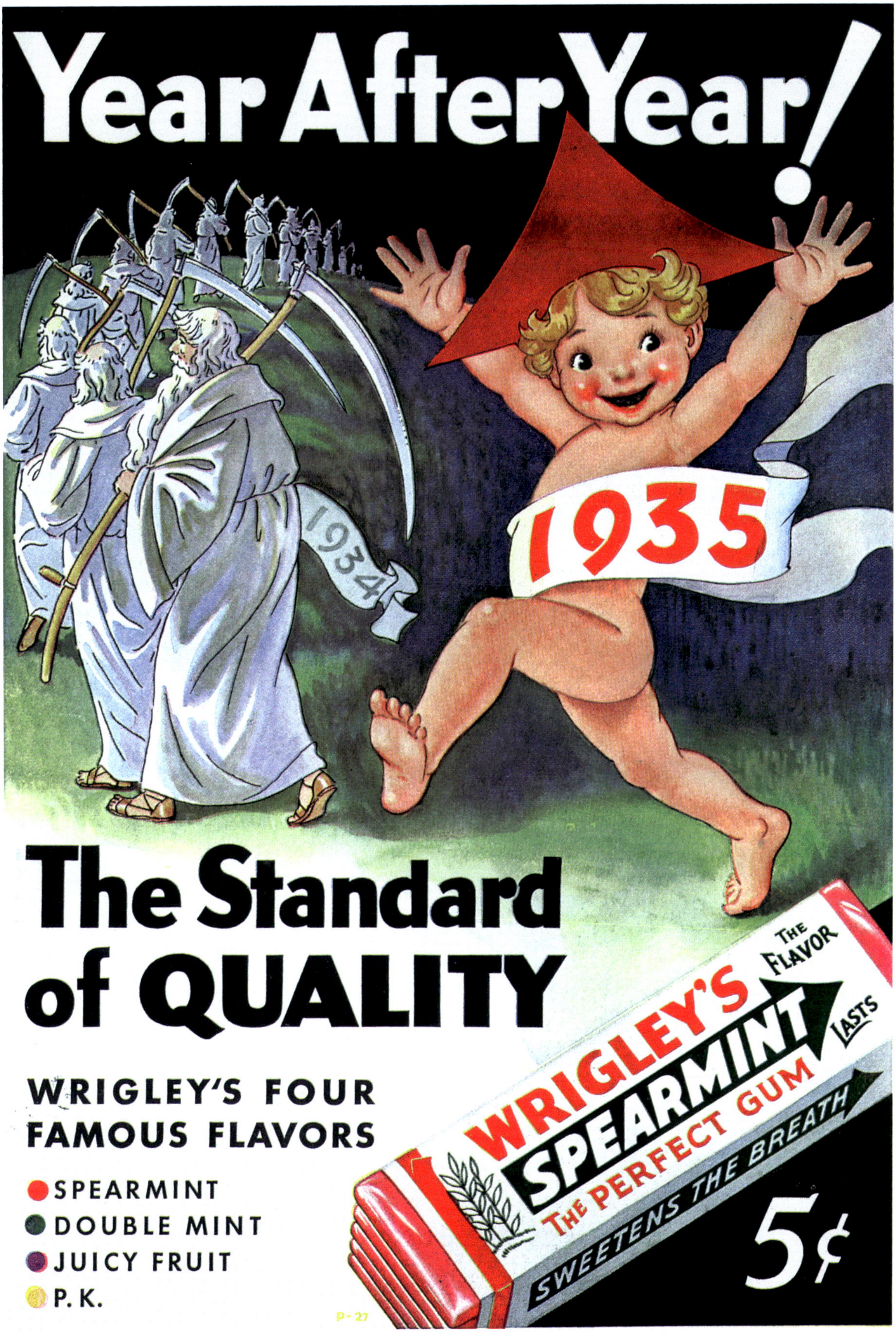

Wrigley's Gum, 1935 ◄▲

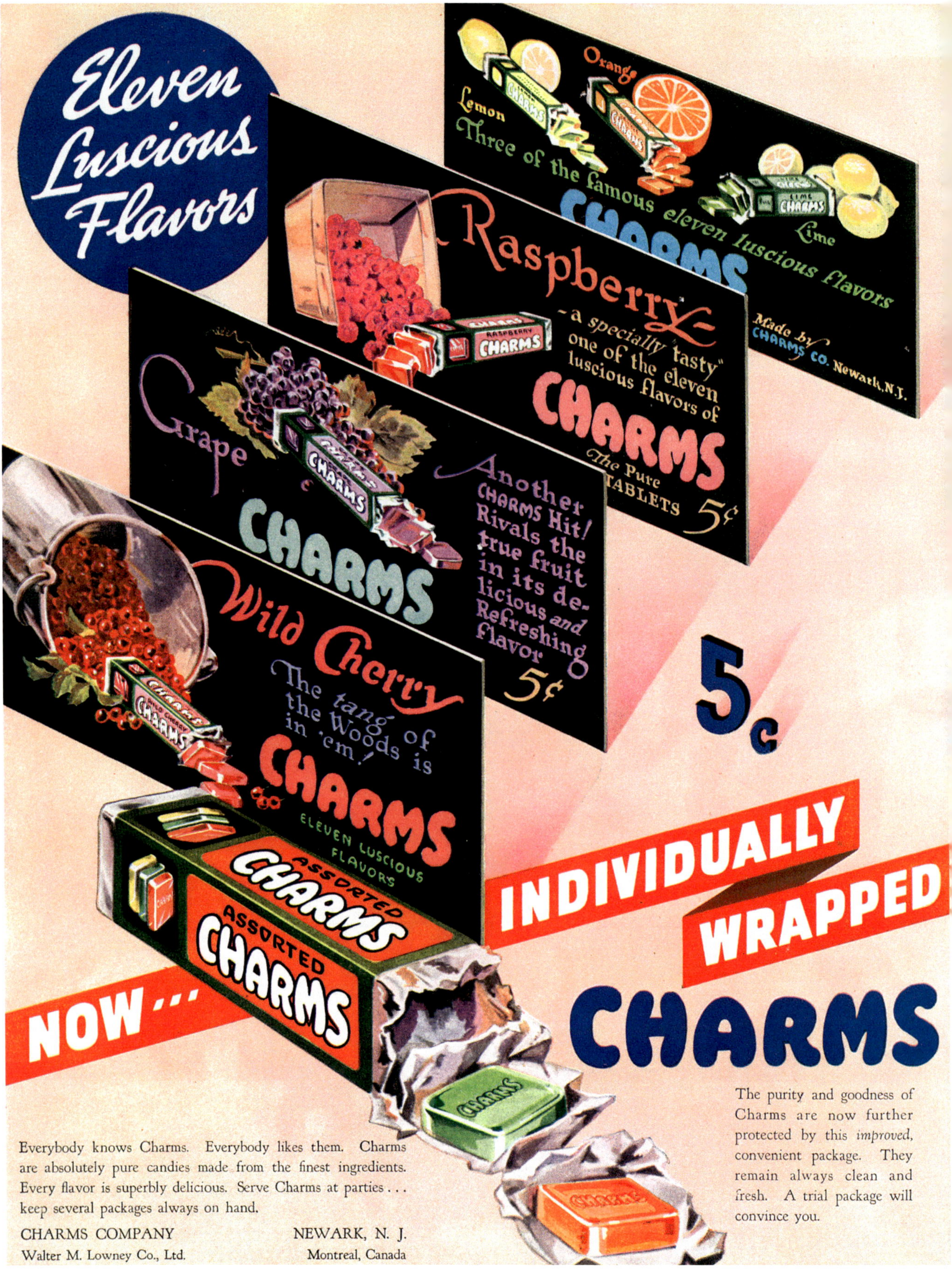
Eleven Luscious Flavors
Orange
Lemon
Three of the famous eleven luscious flavors
CHARMS
Lime
Made by CHARMS CO. Newark, N.J.
Raspberry
– a specially "tasty" one of the eleven luscious flavors of
CHARMS
The Pure TABLETS 5¢
Grape
CHARMS
Another CHARMS Hit! Rivals the true fruit in its delicious and Refreshing flavor
5¢
Wild Cherry
The tang of the Woods is in 'em!
CHARMS
ELEVEN LUSCIOUS FLAVORS
5c
ASSORTED CHARMS
NOW . . .
INDIVIDUALLY WRAPPED
CHARMS
Everybody knows Charms. Everybody likes them. Charms are absolutely pure candies made from the finest ingredients. Every flavor is superbly delicious. Serve Charms at parties . . . keep several packages always on hand.
CHARMS COMPANY NEWARK, N. J.
Walter M. Lowney Co., Ltd. Montreal, Canada
The purity and goodness of Charms are now further protected by this *improved*, convenient package. They remain always clean and fresh. A trial package will convince you.

Charms, 1937

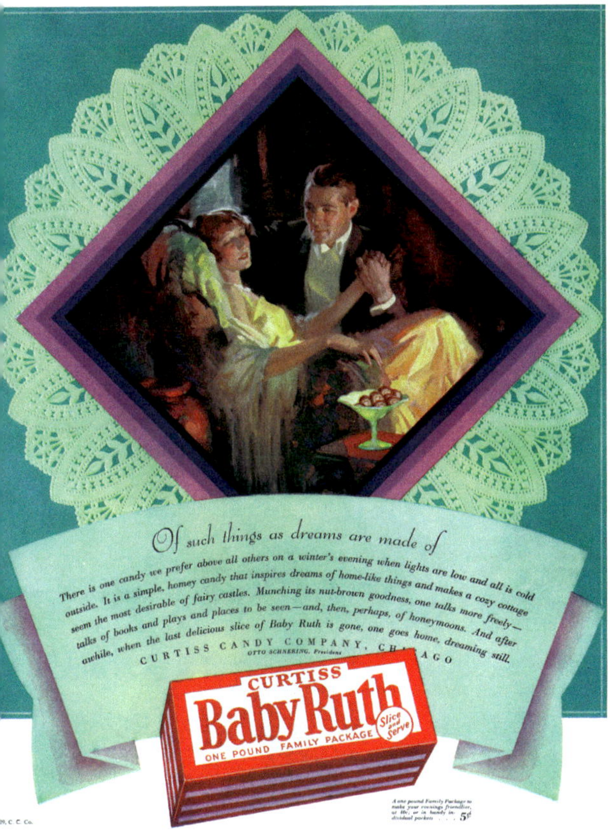

Baby Ruth, 1939

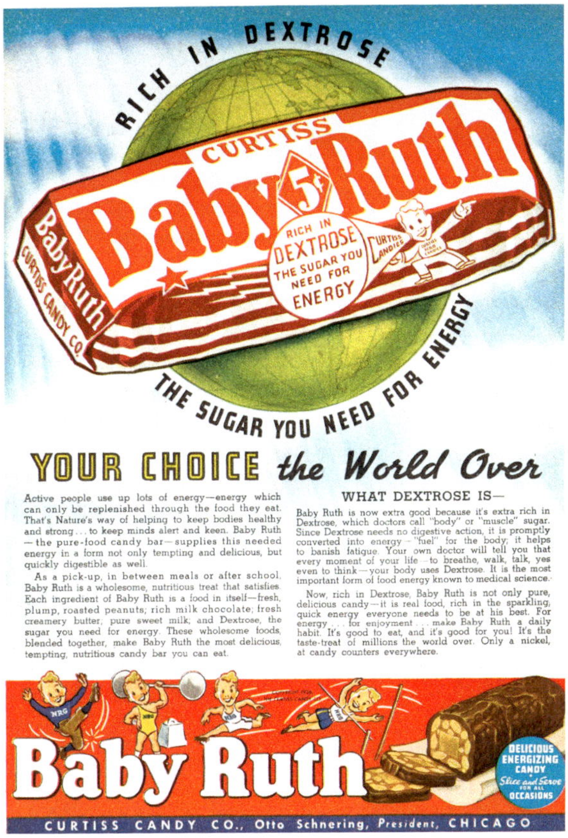

Baby Ruth, 1937

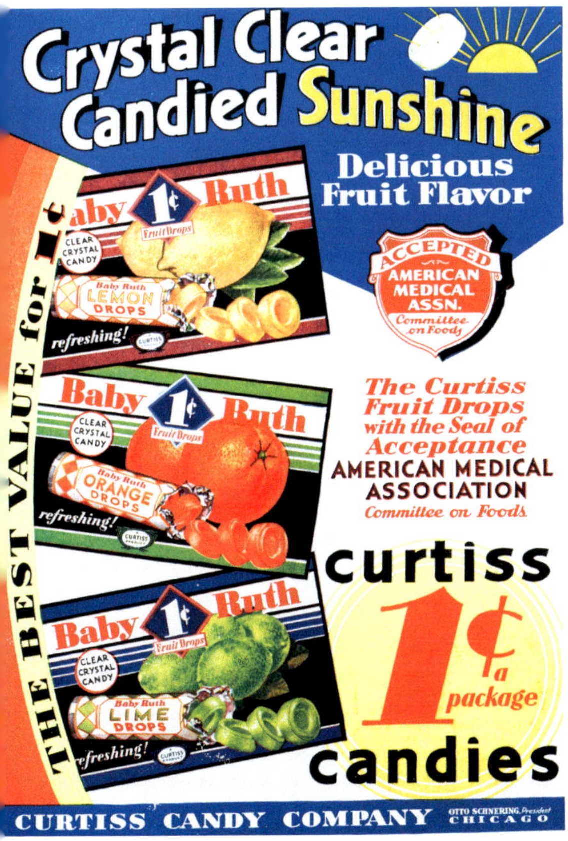

Curtiss Candy Co., 1933

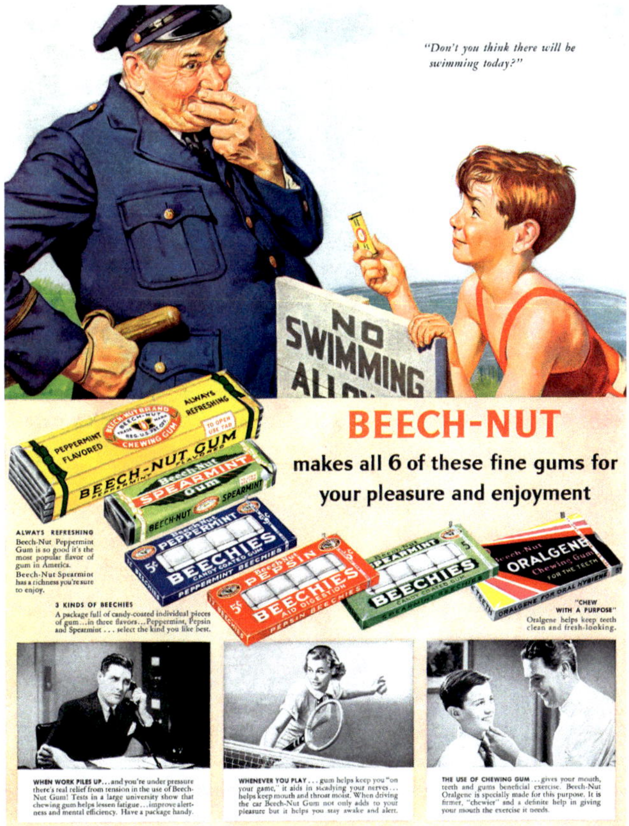

Beech-Nut Gum, 1938

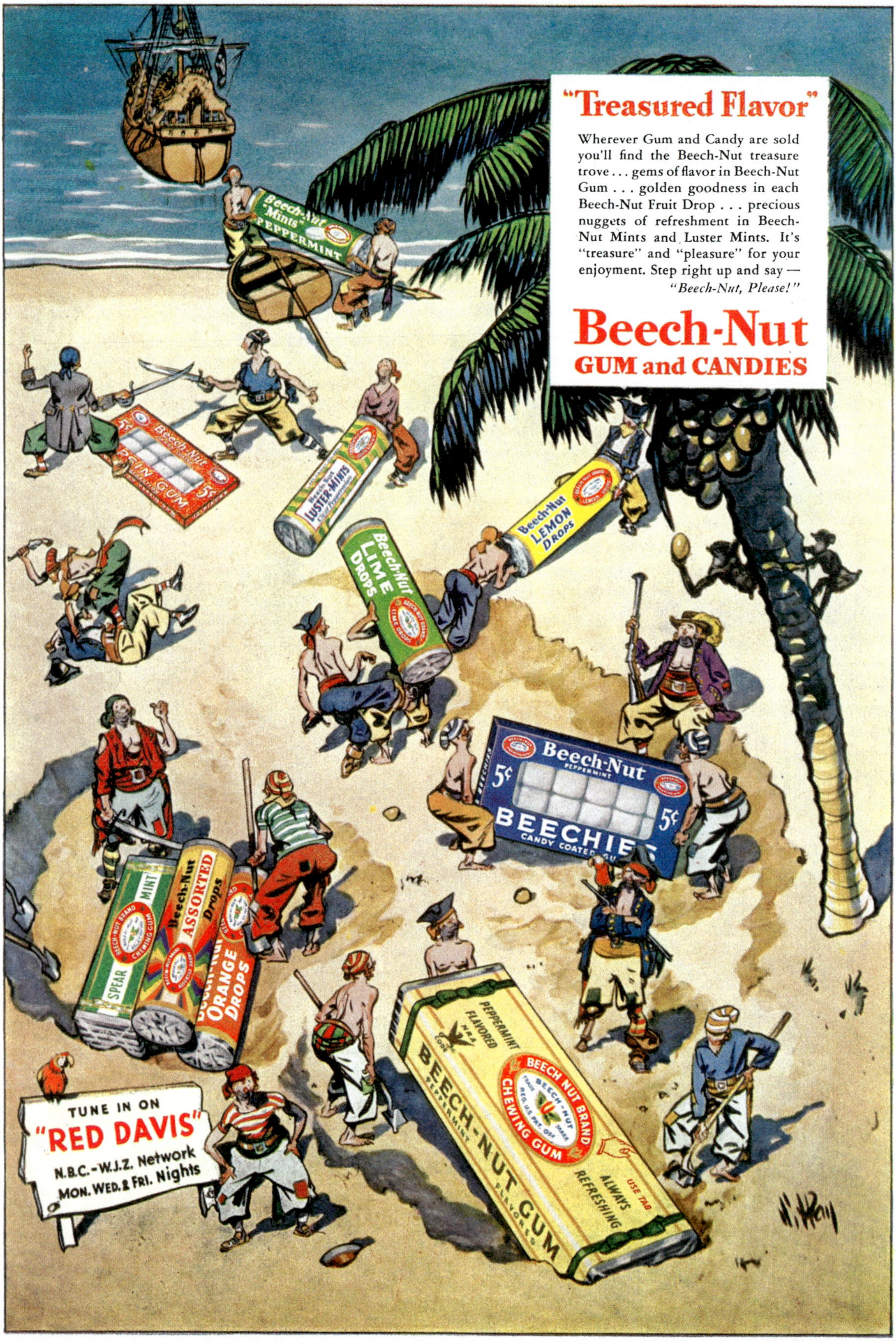

Beech-Nut Gum, 1935

▸ Tempters Gum, 1935

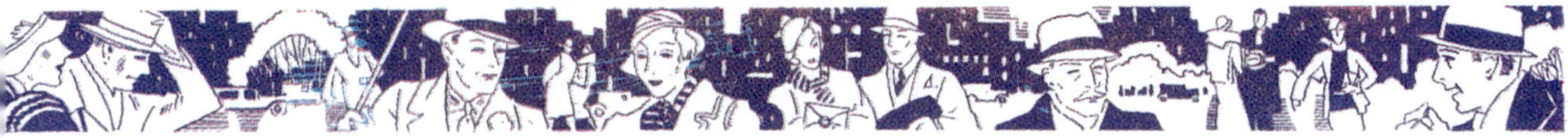

The delicious candy coating is the secret of Tempters goodness. At your first delightful bite you are greeted by a burst of full flavor—fresh and delicate, with all the new-made tastiness sealed up tight in the candy coating. Each gay color is a different flavor—peppermint, spearmint, cinnamon, wintergreen, tutti frutti. Try any or all of them today.

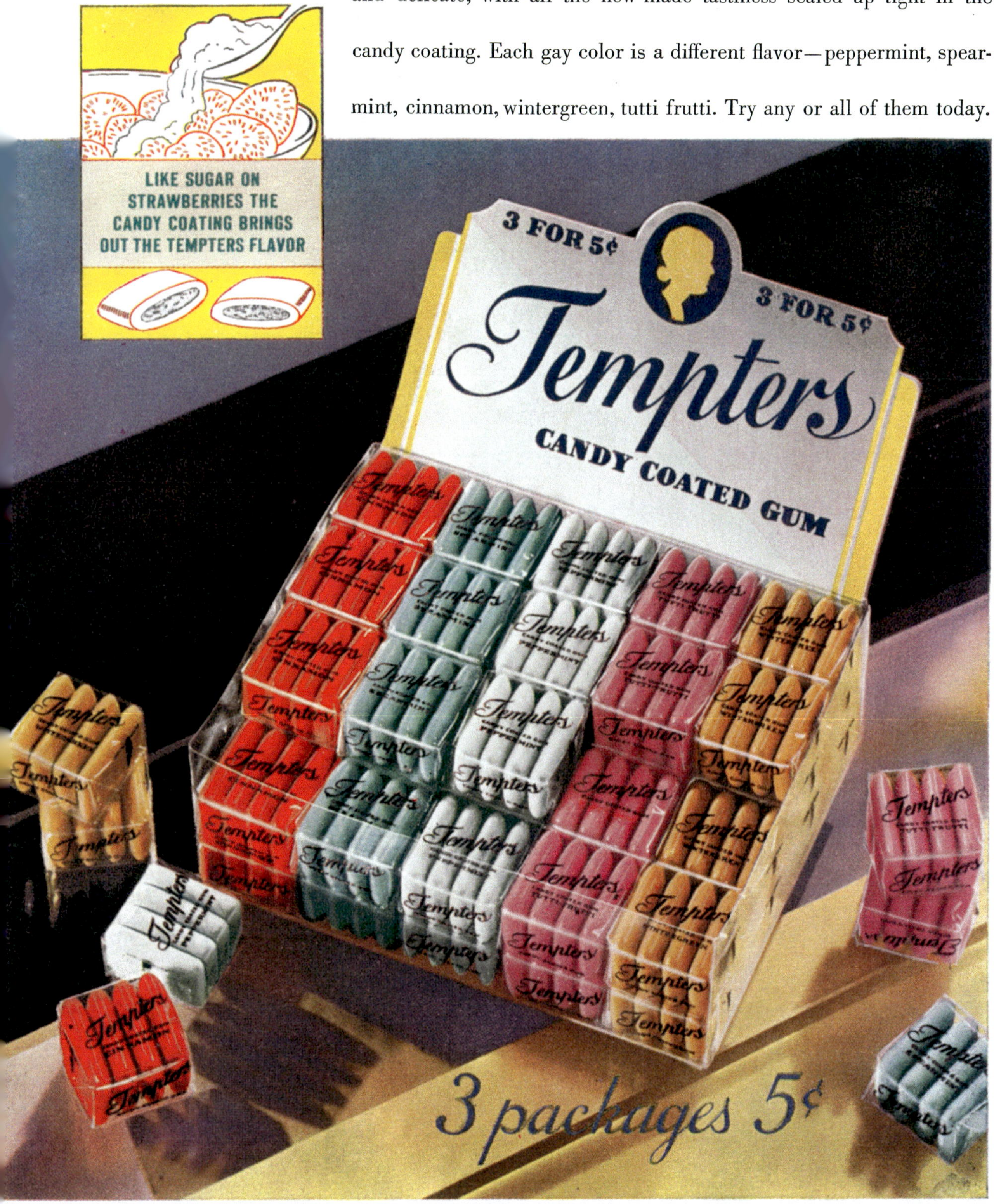

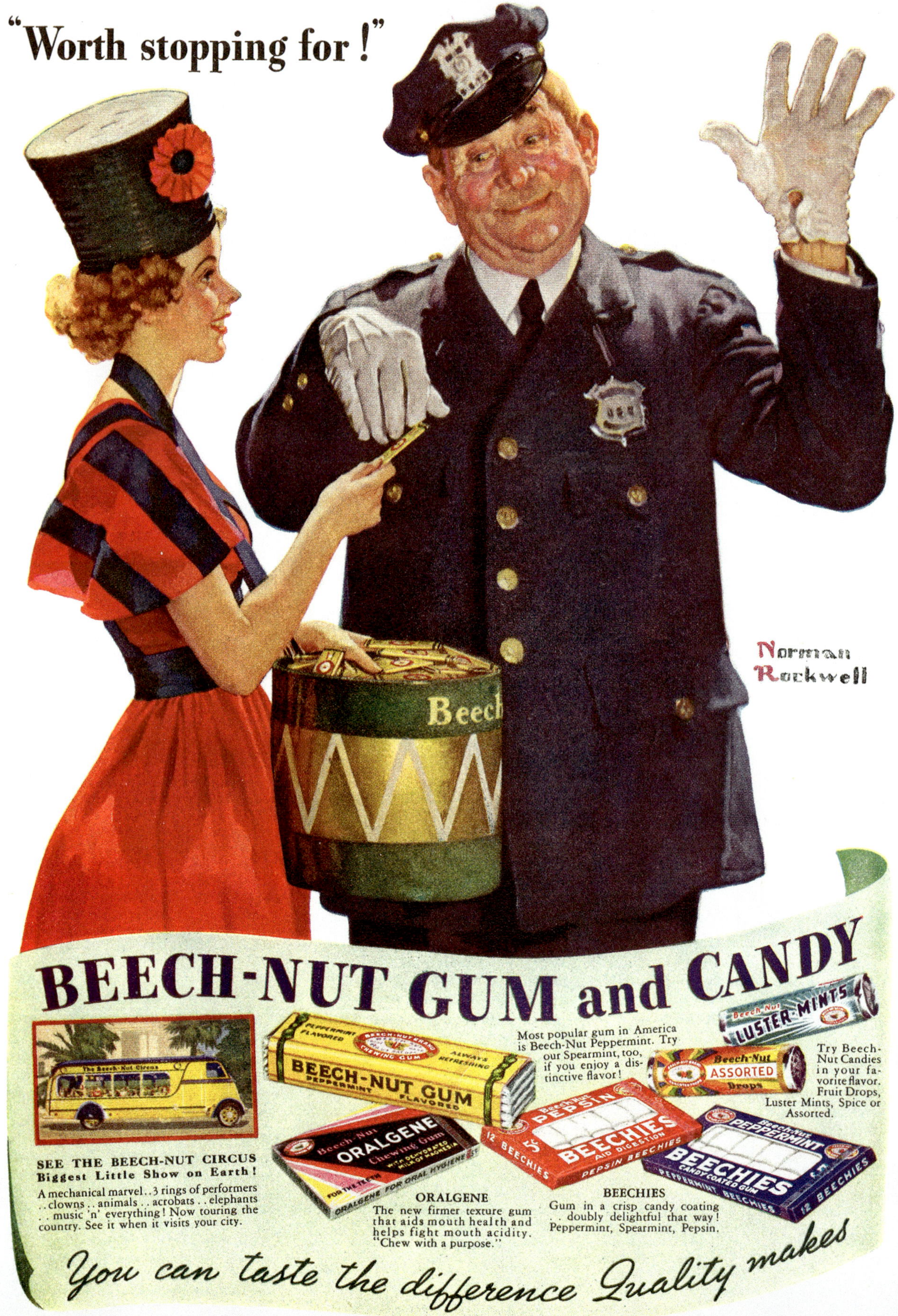

"Worth stopping for!"
Norman Rockwell
BEECH-NUT GUM and CANDY
SEE THE BEECH-NUT CIRCUS
Biggest Little Show on Earth!
A mechanical marvel..3 rings of performers ..clowns..animals..acrobats..elephants ..music 'n' everything! Now touring the country. See it when it visits your city.
Most popular gum in America is Beech-Nut Peppermint. Try our Spearmint, too, if you enjoy a distinctive flavor!
Try Beech-Nut Candies in your favorite flavor. Fruit Drops, Luster Mints, Spice or Assorted.
ORALGENE
The new firmer texture gum that aids mouth health and helps fight mouth acidity. "Chew with a purpose."
BEECHIES
Gum in a crisp candy coating .. doubly delightful that way! Peppermint, Spearmint, Pepsin.
You can taste the difference Quality makes

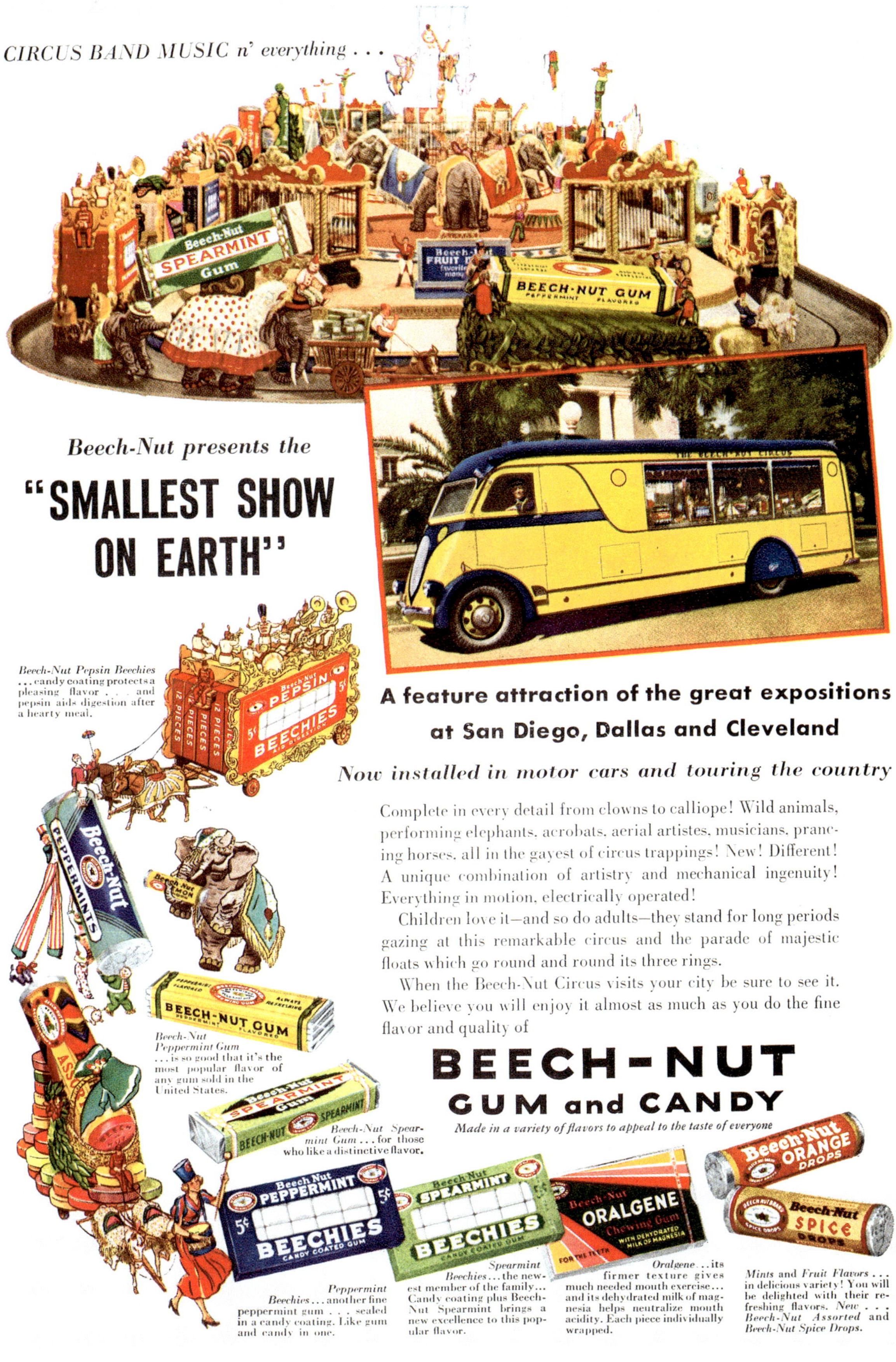

Beech-Nut Gum & Candy, 1937 ◄

Beech-Nut Gum & Candy, 1936

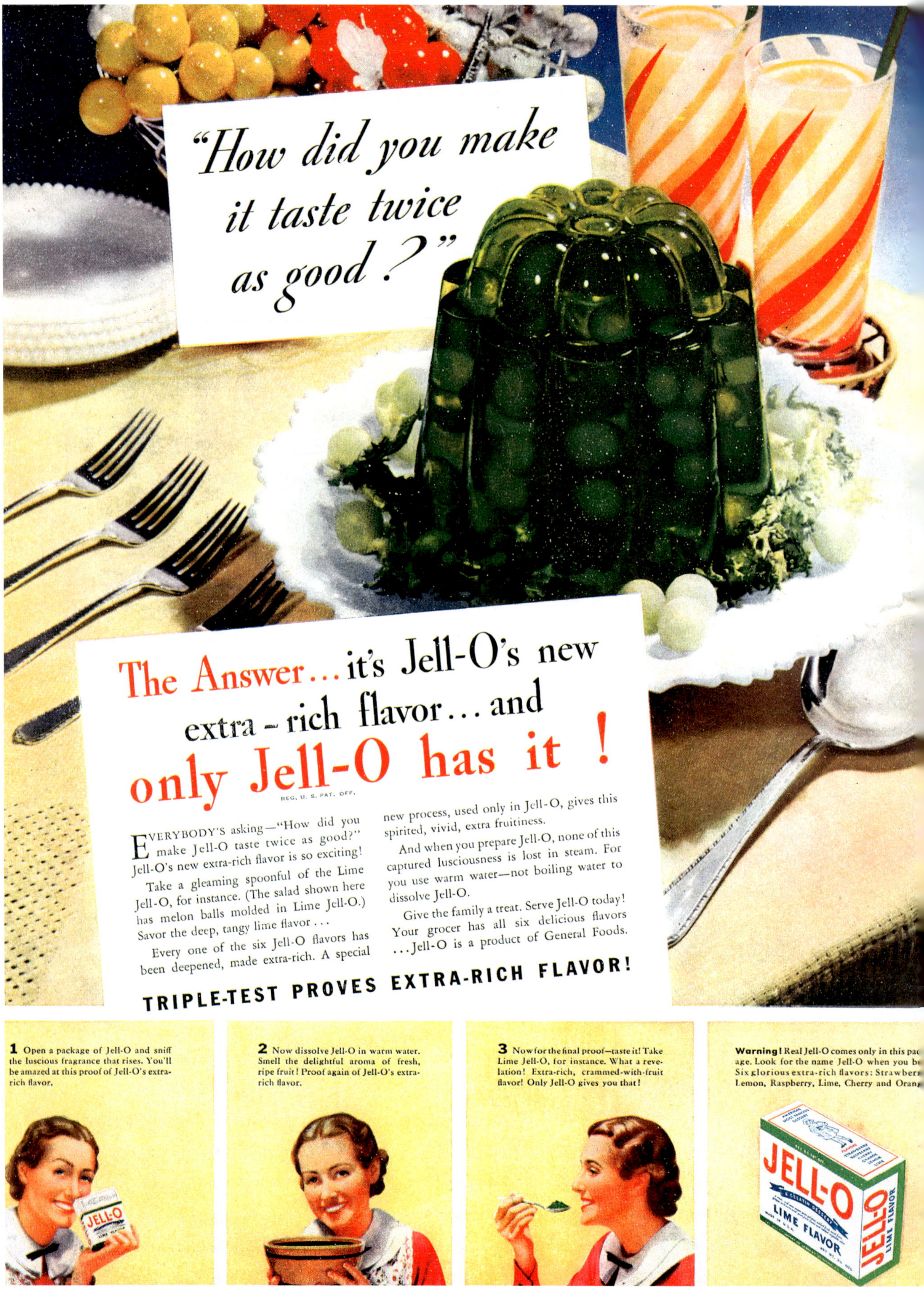

"How did you make it taste twice as good?"
The Answer... it's Jell-O's new extra-rich flavor... and only Jell-O has it!
REG. U. S. PAT. OFF.
EVERYBODY'S asking—"How did you make Jell-O taste twice as good?" Jell-O's new extra-rich flavor is so exciting!
Take a gleaming spoonful of the Lime Jell-O, for instance. (The salad shown here has melon balls molded in Lime Jell-O.) Savor the deep, tangy lime flavor . . .
Every one of the six Jell-O flavors has been deepened, made extra-rich. A special new process, used only in Jell-O, gives this spirited, vivid, extra fruitiness.
And when you prepare Jell-O, none of this captured lusciousness is lost in steam. For you use warm water—not boiling water to dissolve Jell-O.
Give the family a treat. Serve Jell-O today! Your grocer has all six delicious flavors . . . Jell-O is a product of General Foods.
TRIPLE-TEST PROVES EXTRA-RICH FLAVOR!
1 Open a package of Jell-O and sniff the luscious fragrance that rises. You'll be amazed at this proof of Jell-O's extra-rich flavor.
2 Now dissolve Jell-O in warm water. Smell the delightful aroma of fresh, ripe fruit! Proof again of Jell-O's extra-rich flavor.
3 Now for the final proof—taste it! Take Lime Jell-O, for instance. What a revelation! Extra-rich, crammed-with-fruit flavor! Only Jell-O gives you that!
Warning! Real Jell-O comes only in this pac age. Look for the name Jell-O when you b Six glorious extra-rich flavors: Strawberr Lemon, Raspberry, Lime, Cherry and Oran
JELL-O
LIME FLAVOR

How does it SMELL... *when you mix it?*

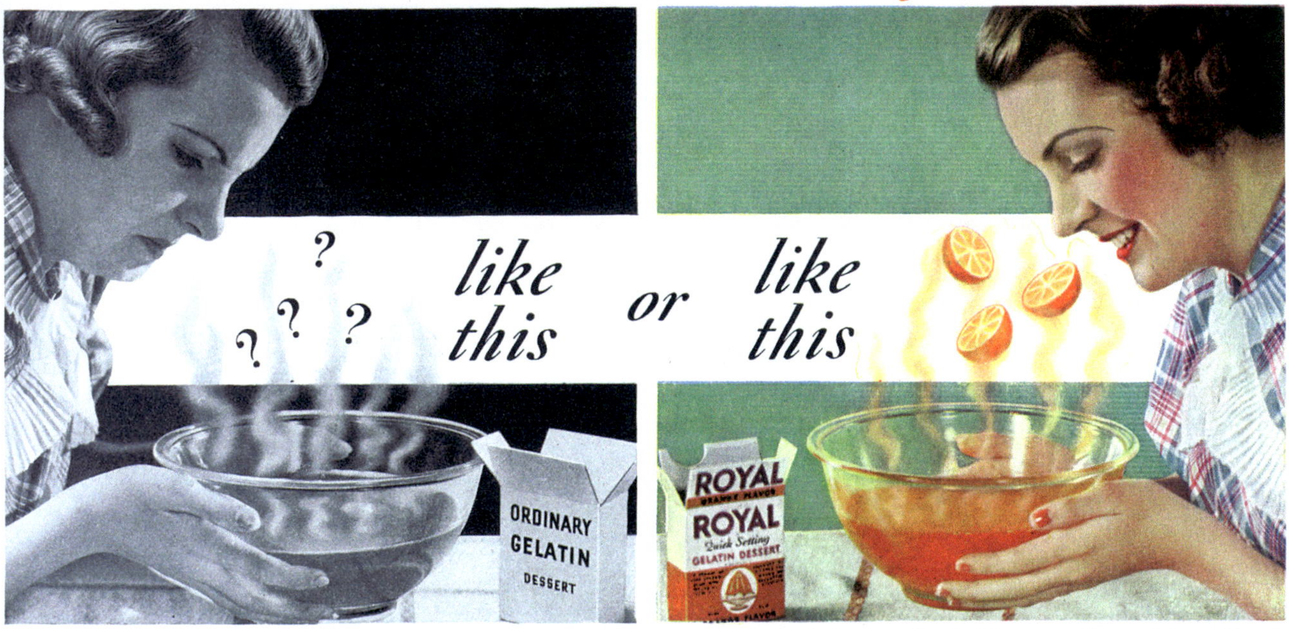

Smell your gelatin as you add hot water. With ordinary gelatin desserts, the odor is unpleasant.

But Royal has just the fragrance of fruit. Royal Orange smells like oranges, ripe and juicy.

THIS TEST ***tells you instantly why millions of women have changed to Royal Gelatin***

You can actually smell the difference in gelatin desserts. Just try it for yourself.

As you add the hot water to your gelatin, bend over the bowl and take a whiff of the rising vapor.

With ordinary gelatin desserts, you'll notice an unpleasant smell. But with Royal Gelatin you'll get just the delightful fragrance of fruit. The sweet aroma of raspberry or strawberry . . . the refreshing odor of lemon or lime.

This test tells you why millions of women are changing to Royal . . . why the sale of this high-quality gelatin has more than doubled in a year.

And the flavor of Royal is as delicious as its aroma. Royal Orange has the same refreshing tang you get in the actual juice of the fruit.

Seven pure fruit flavors: Lime, Lemon, Orange, Pineapple, Raspberry, Cherry, Strawberry. And the new Royal Gelatin Aspic, unsweetened, for delicious jellied meats and salads.

FREE COOK BOOK—Send for *"Royal Desserts,"* a beautiful booklet containing over 100 tempting, delicious recipes. Address: ROYAL GELATIN, Product of Standard Brands Incorporated, Dept. G-23, 691 Washington Street, New York City.

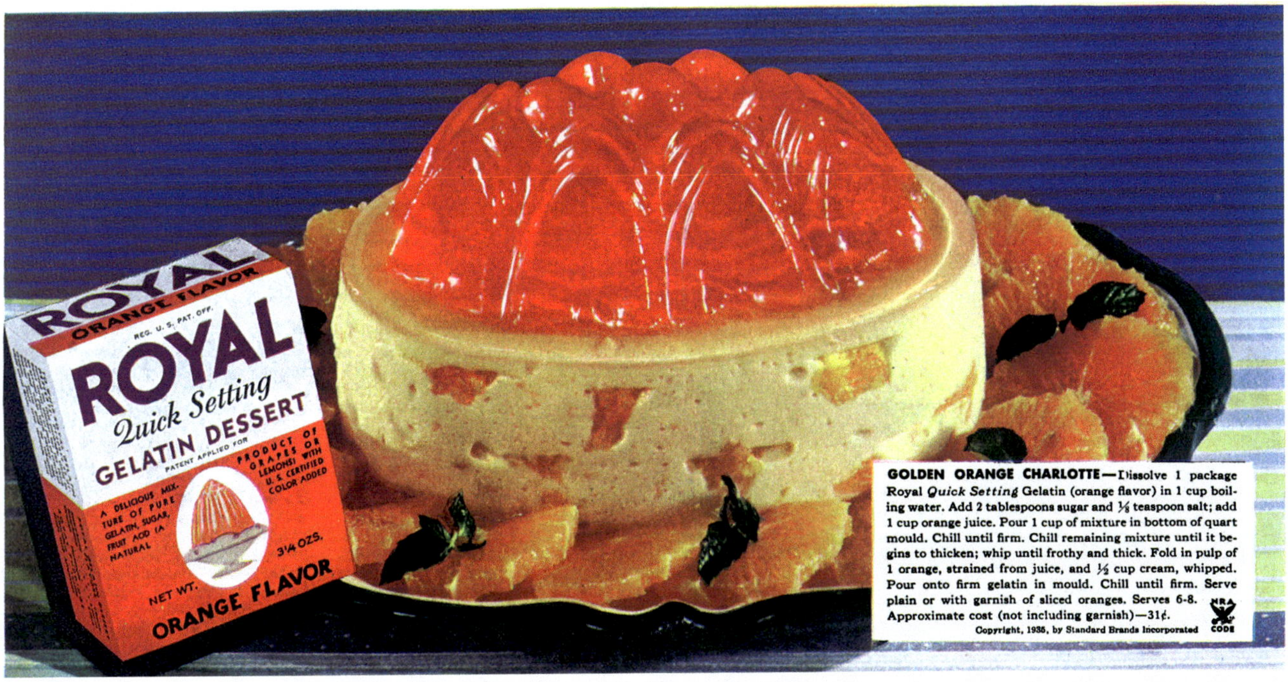

GOLDEN ORANGE CHARLOTTE—Dissolve 1 package Royal *Quick Setting* Gelatin (orange flavor) in 1 cup boiling water. Add 2 tablespoons sugar and ⅛ teaspoon salt; add 1 cup orange juice. Pour 1 cup of mixture in bottom of quart mould. Chill until firm. Chill remaining mixture until it begins to thicken; whip until frothy and thick. Fold in pulp of 1 orange, strained from juice, and ½ cup cream, whipped. Pour onto firm gelatin in mould. Chill until firm. Serve plain or with garnish of sliced oranges. Serves 6-8. Approximate cost (not including garnish)—31¢.

NRA CODE

Jell-O, 1935 ◄

Royal Gelatin, 1937

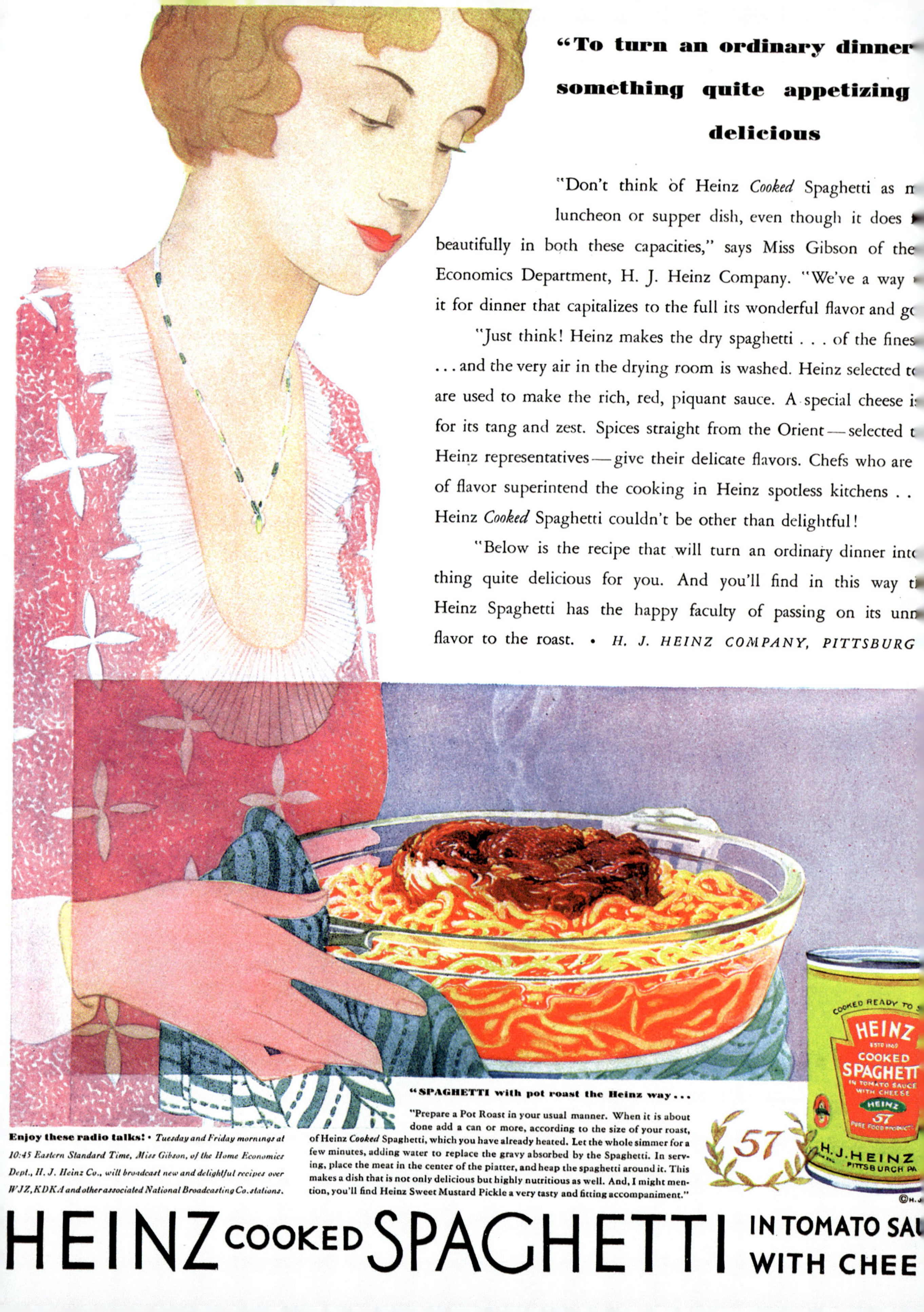
"To turn an ordinary dinner
something quite appetizing
delicious
"Don't think of Heinz Cooked Spaghetti as
luncheon or supper dish, even though it does
beautifully in both these capacities," says Miss Gibson of the
Economics Department, H. J. Heinz Company. "We've a way
it for dinner that capitalizes to the full its wonderful flavor and
"Just think! Heinz makes the dry spaghetti . . . of the fines
. . . and the very air in the drying room is washed. Heinz selected
are used to make the rich, red, piquant sauce. A special cheese
for its tang and zest. Spices straight from the Orient—selected
Heinz representatives—give their delicate flavors. Chefs who are
of flavor superintend the cooking in Heinz spotless kitchens . .
Heinz Cooked Spaghetti couldn't be other than delightful!
"Below is the recipe that will turn an ordinary dinner int
thing quite delicious for you. And you'll find in this way
Heinz Spaghetti has the happy faculty of passing on its un
flavor to the roast. • H. J. HEINZ COMPANY, PITTSBURG
"SPAGHETTI with pot roast the Heinz way . . .
"Prepare a Pot Roast in your usual manner. When it is about done add a can or more, according to the size of your roast, of Heinz Cooked Spaghetti, which you have already heated. Let the whole simmer for a few minutes, adding water to replace the gravy absorbed by the Spaghetti. In serving, place the meat in the center of the platter, and heap the spaghetti around it. This makes a dish that is not only delicious but highly nutritious as well. And, I might mention, you'll find Heinz Sweet Mustard Pickle a very tasty and fitting accompaniment."
Enjoy these radio talks! • Tuesday and Friday mornings at 10:45 Eastern Standard Time, Miss Gibson, of the Home Economics Dept., H. J. Heinz Co., will broadcast new and delightful recipes over WJZ, KDKA and other associated National Broadcasting Co. stations.
HEINZ
COOKED
SPAGHETT
IN TOMATO SAUCE WITH CHEESE
HEINZ 57
PURE FOOD PRODUCTS
H. J. HEINZ
PITTSBURGH PA
57
HEINZ COOKED SPAGHETTI
IN TOMATO SA
WITH CHEE

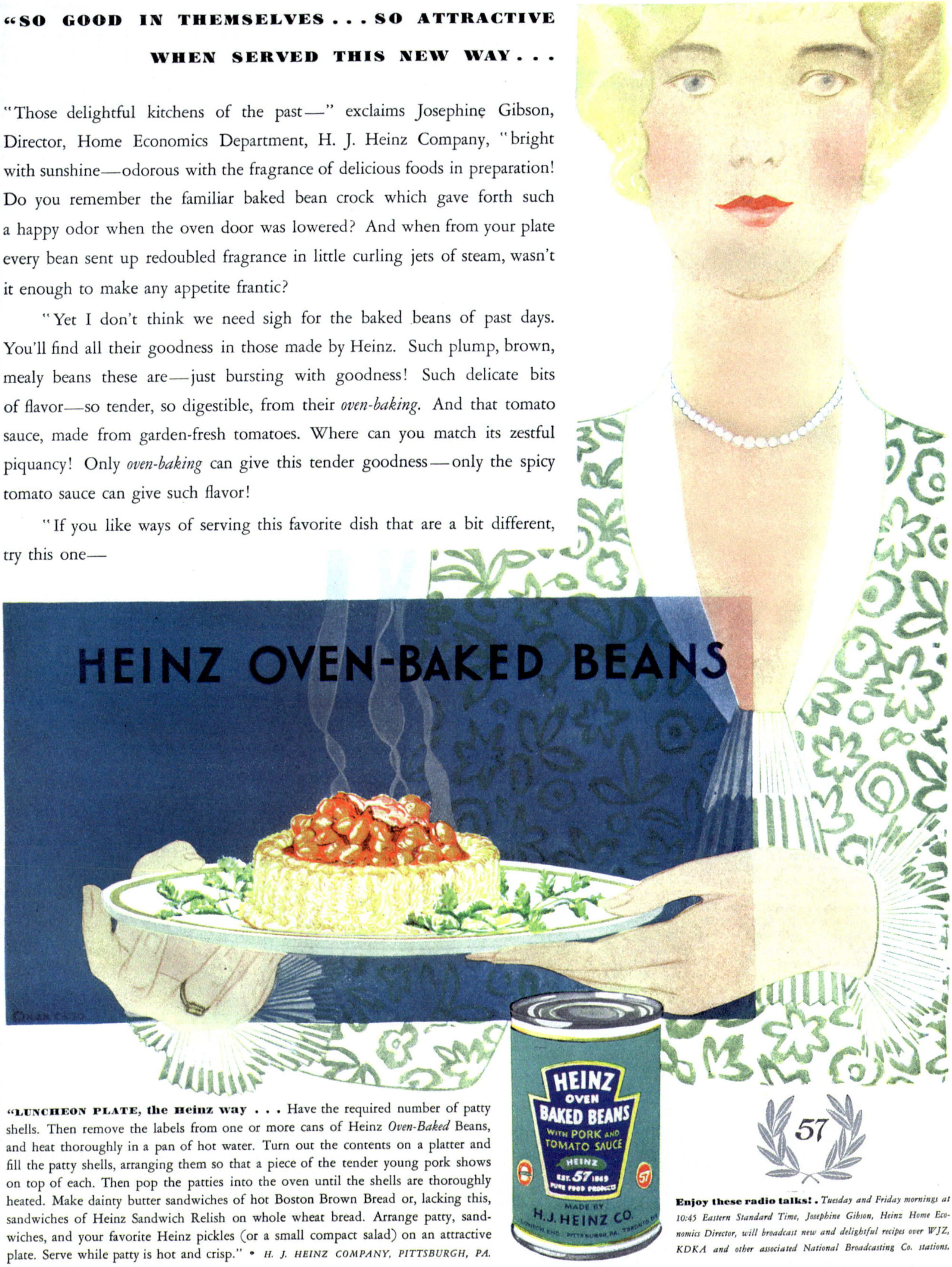

Heinz Spaghetti, 1930 ◂

Heinz Baked Beans, 1930

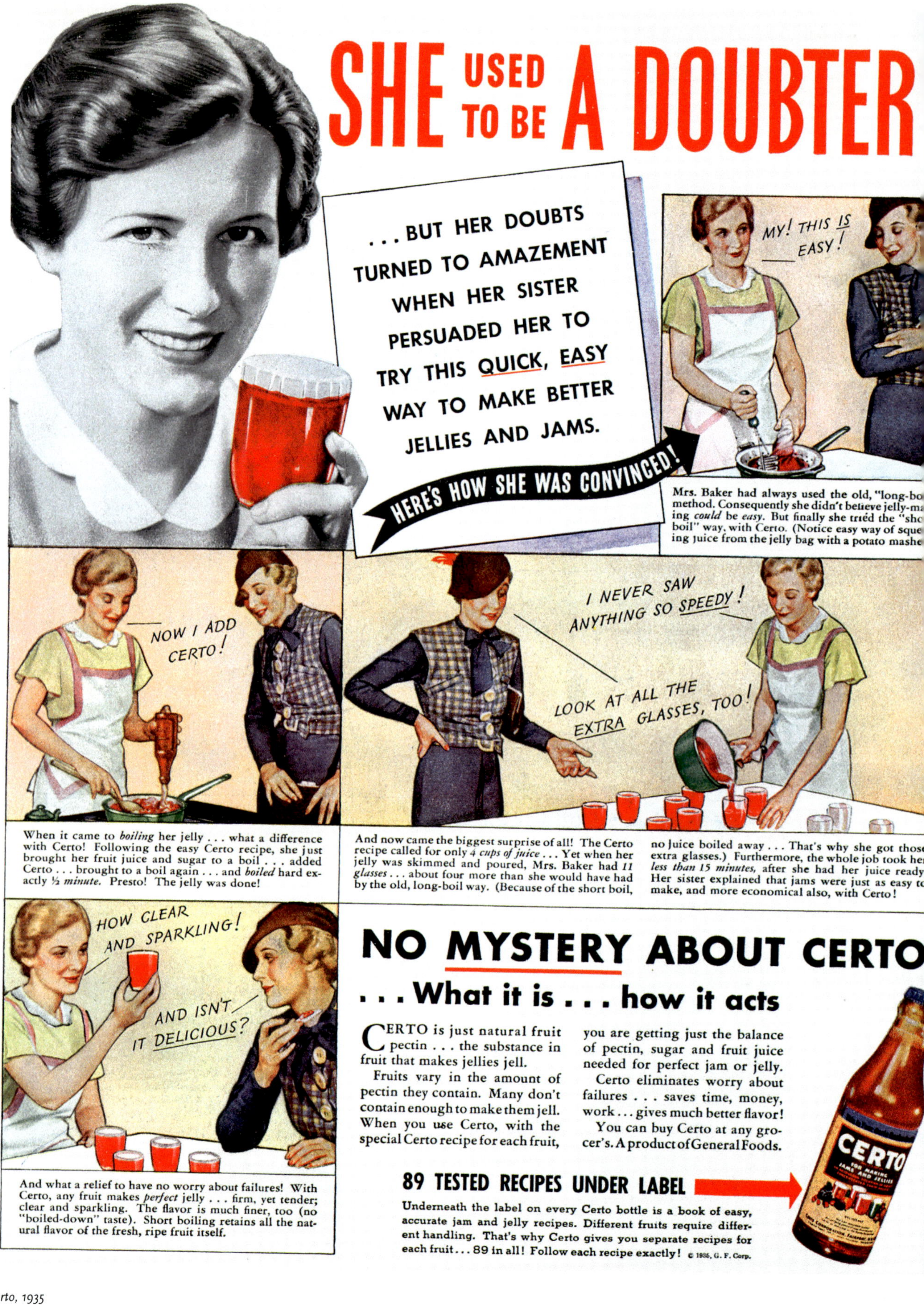
SHE USED TO BE A DOUBTER
. . . BUT HER DOUBTS TURNED TO AMAZEMENT WHEN HER SISTER PERSUADED HER TO TRY THIS QUICK, EASY WAY TO MAKE BETTER JELLIES AND JAMS.
HERE'S HOW SHE WAS CONVINCED!
MY! THIS IS EASY!
Mrs. Baker had always used the old, "long-bo method. Consequently she didn't believe jelly-ma ing could be easy. But finally she tried the "sho boil" way, with Certo. (Notice easy way of sque ing juice from the jelly bag with a potato mashe
NOW I ADD CERTO!
When it came to boiling her jelly . . . what a difference with Certo! Following the easy Certo recipe, she just brought her fruit juice and sugar to a boil . . . added Certo . . . brought to a boil again . . . and boiled hard exactly ½ minute. Presto! The jelly was done!
I NEVER SAW ANYTHING SO SPEEDY!
LOOK AT ALL THE EXTRA GLASSES, TOO!
And now came the biggest surprise of all! The Certo recipe called for only 4 cups of juice . . . Yet when her jelly was skimmed and poured, Mrs. Baker had 11 glasses . . . about four more than she would have had by the old, long-boil way. (Because of the short boil, no juice boiled away . . . That's why she got those extra glasses.) Furthermore, the whole job took her less than 15 minutes, after she had her juice ready. Her sister explained that jams were just as easy to make, and more economical also, with Certo!
HOW CLEAR AND SPARKLING!
AND ISN'T IT DELICIOUS?
And what a relief to have no worry about failures! With Certo, any fruit makes perfect jelly . . . firm, yet tender; clear and sparkling. The flavor is much finer, too (no "boiled-down" taste). Short boiling retains all the natural flavor of the fresh, ripe fruit itself.
NO MYSTERY ABOUT CERTO
. . . What it is . . . how it acts
CERTO is just natural fruit pectin . . . the substance in fruit that makes jellies jell.
Fruits vary in the amount of pectin they contain. Many don't contain enough to make them jell. When you use Certo, with the special Certo recipe for each fruit, you are getting just the balance of pectin, sugar and fruit juice needed for perfect jam or jelly.
Certo eliminates worry about failures . . . saves time, money, work . . . gives much better flavor!
You can buy Certo at any grocer's. A product of General Foods.
89 TESTED RECIPES UNDER LABEL
Underneath the label on every Certo bottle is a book of easy, accurate jam and jelly recipes. Different fruits require different handling. That's why Certo gives you separate recipes for each fruit . . . 89 in all! Follow each recipe exactly!
© 1935, G. F. Corp.
CERTO

Certo, 1935

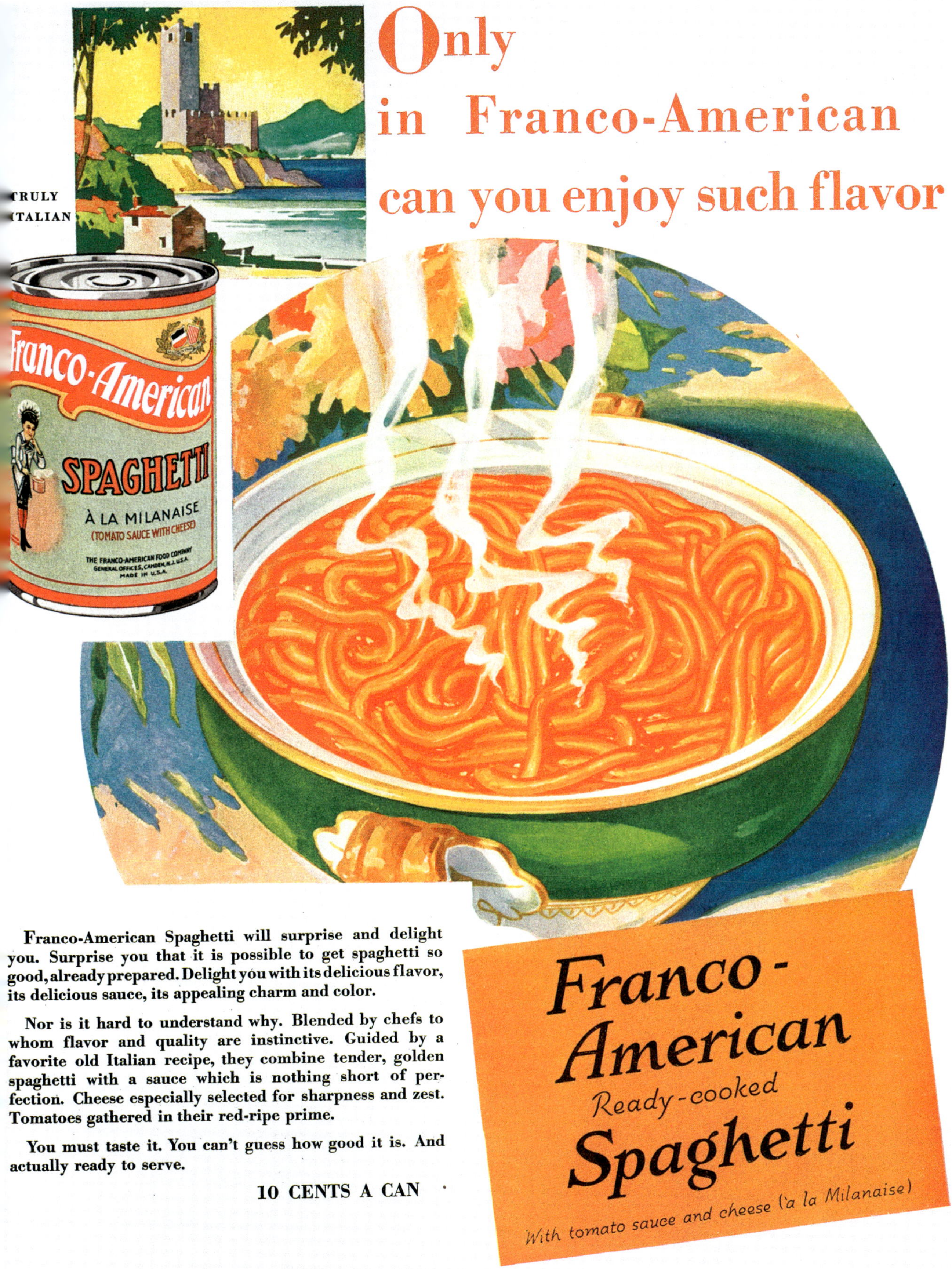

Franco-American Spaghetti, 1932

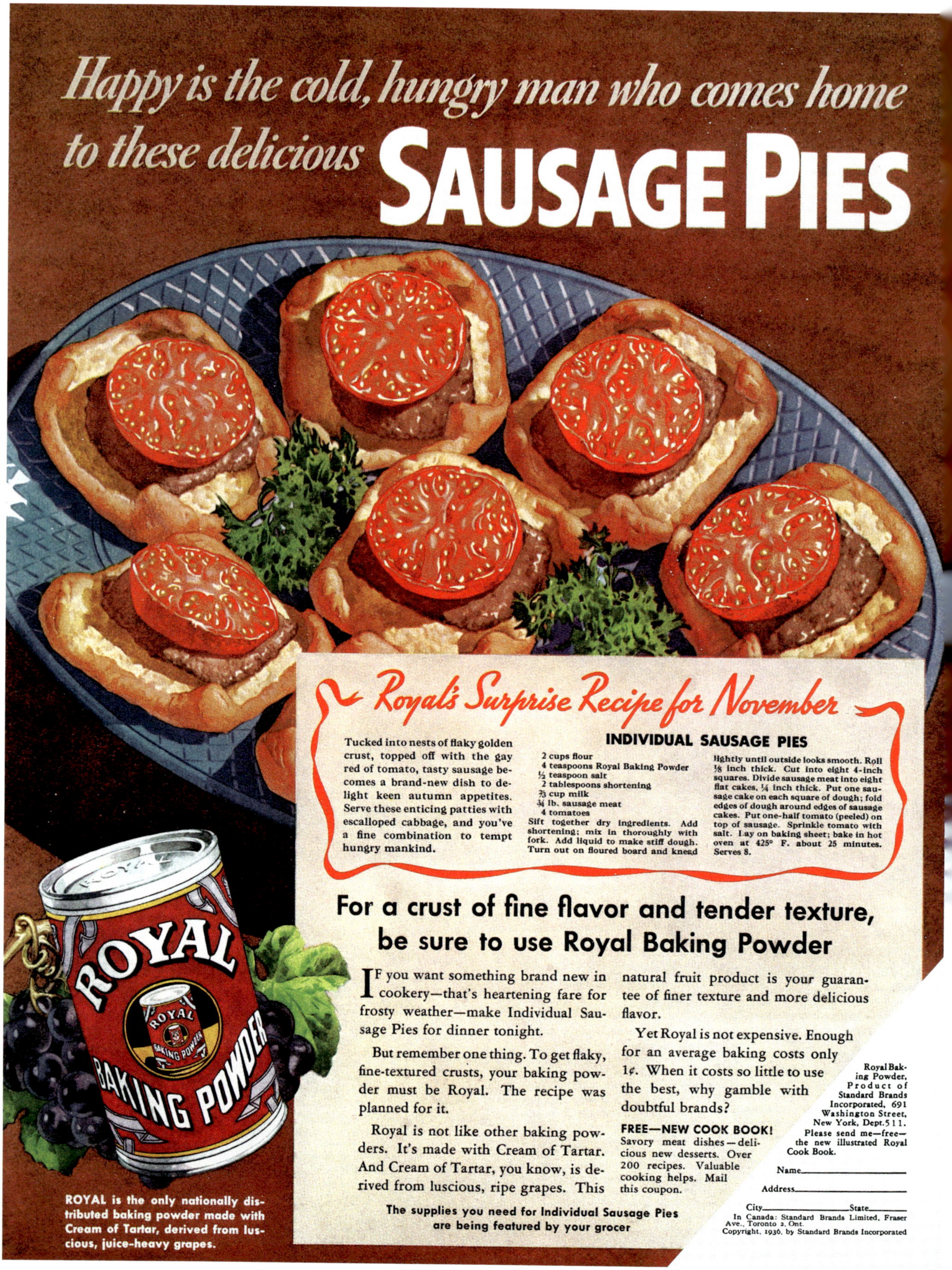

Royal Baking Powder, 1936

► *Parade of Progress, 1939*

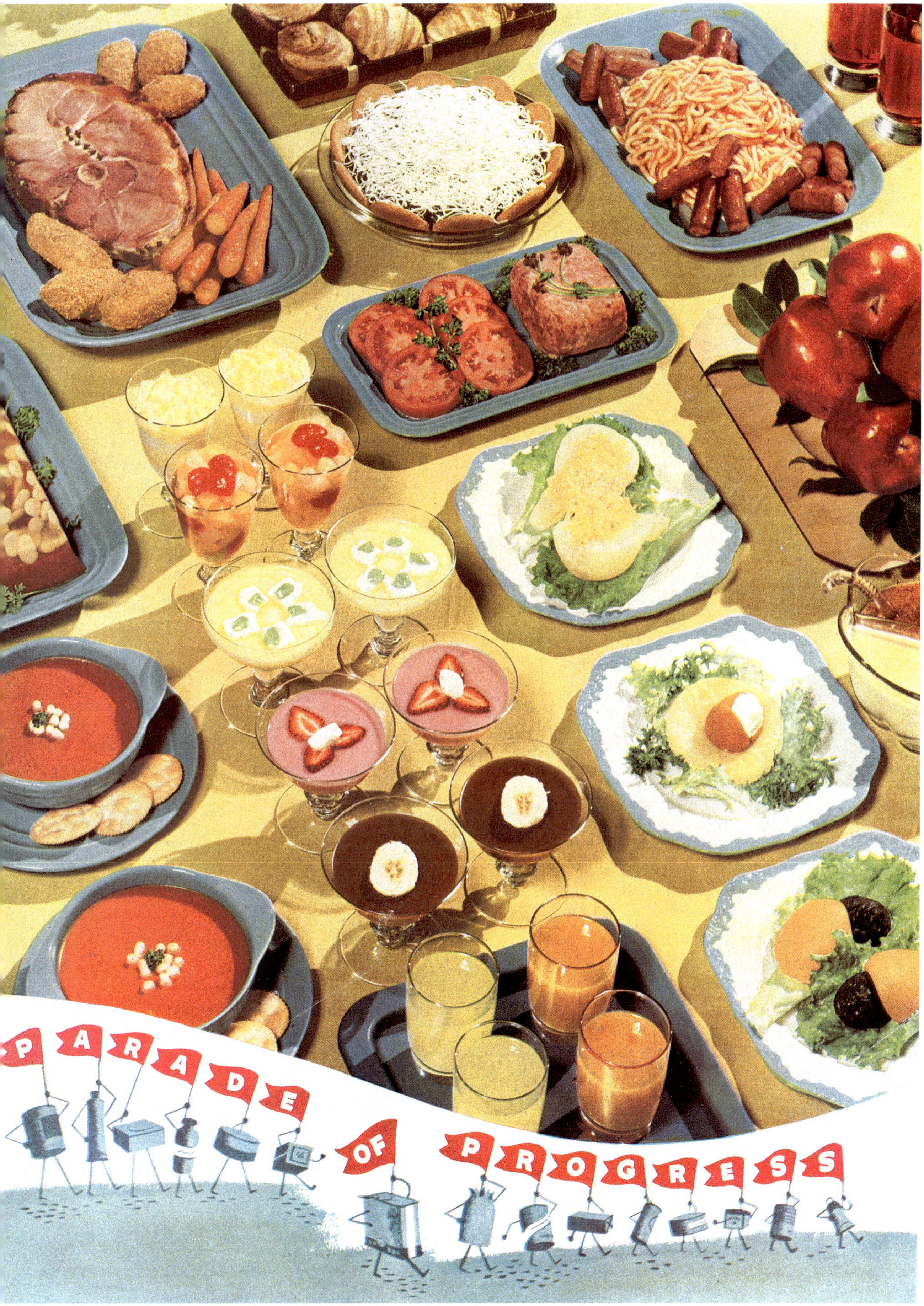
PARADE OF PROGRESS

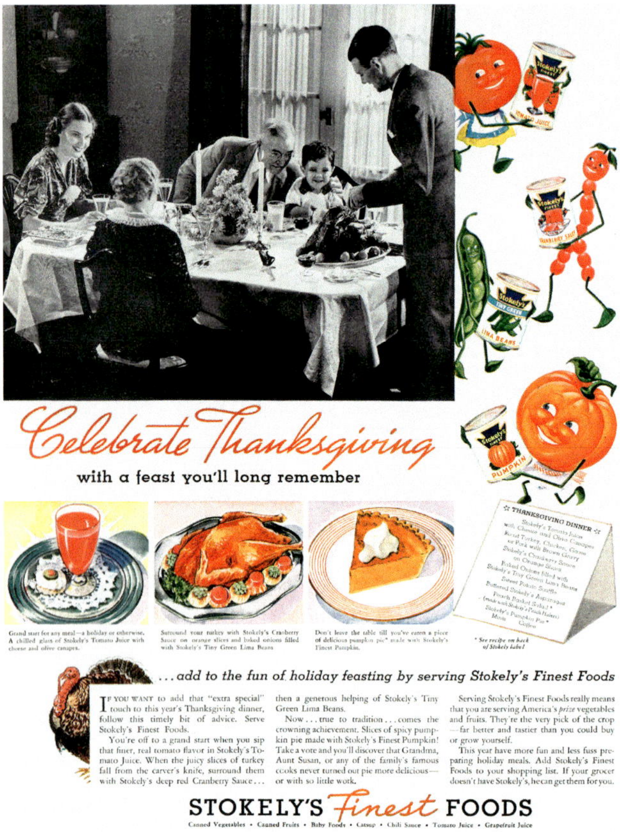

Stokely's Foods, 1937

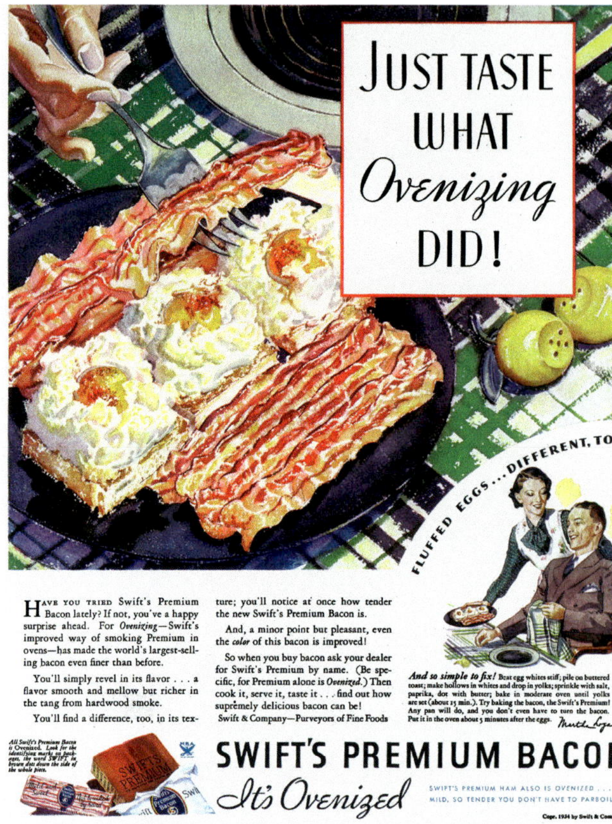

Swift's Premium Meats, 1934

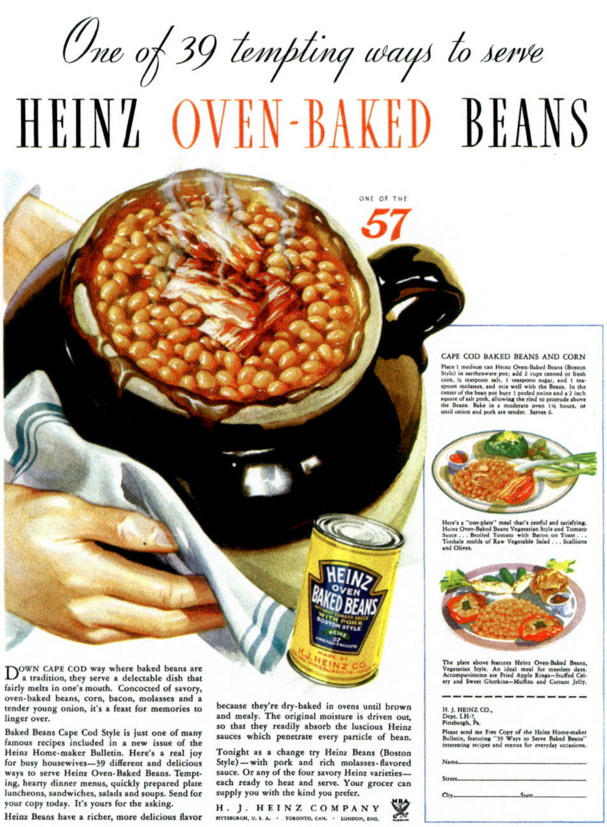

Heinz Baked Beans, 1934

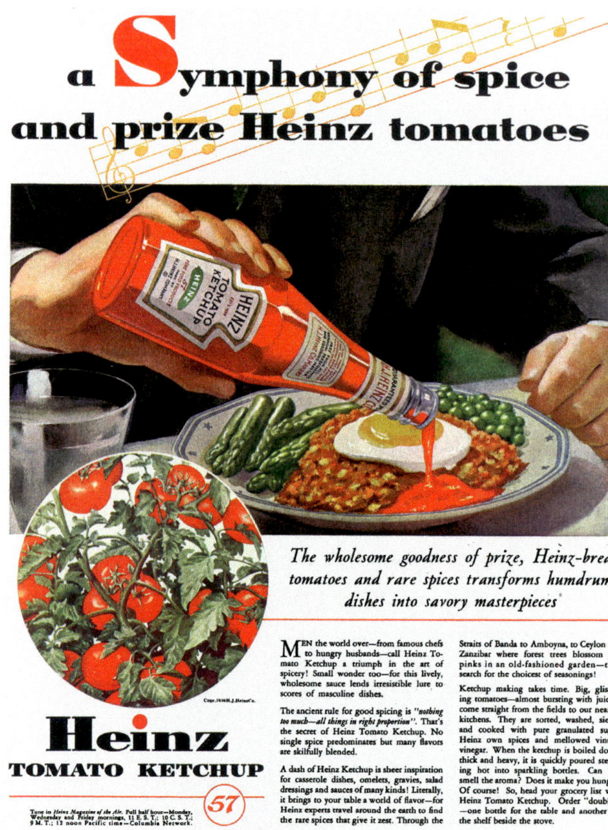

Heinz Ketchup, 1936

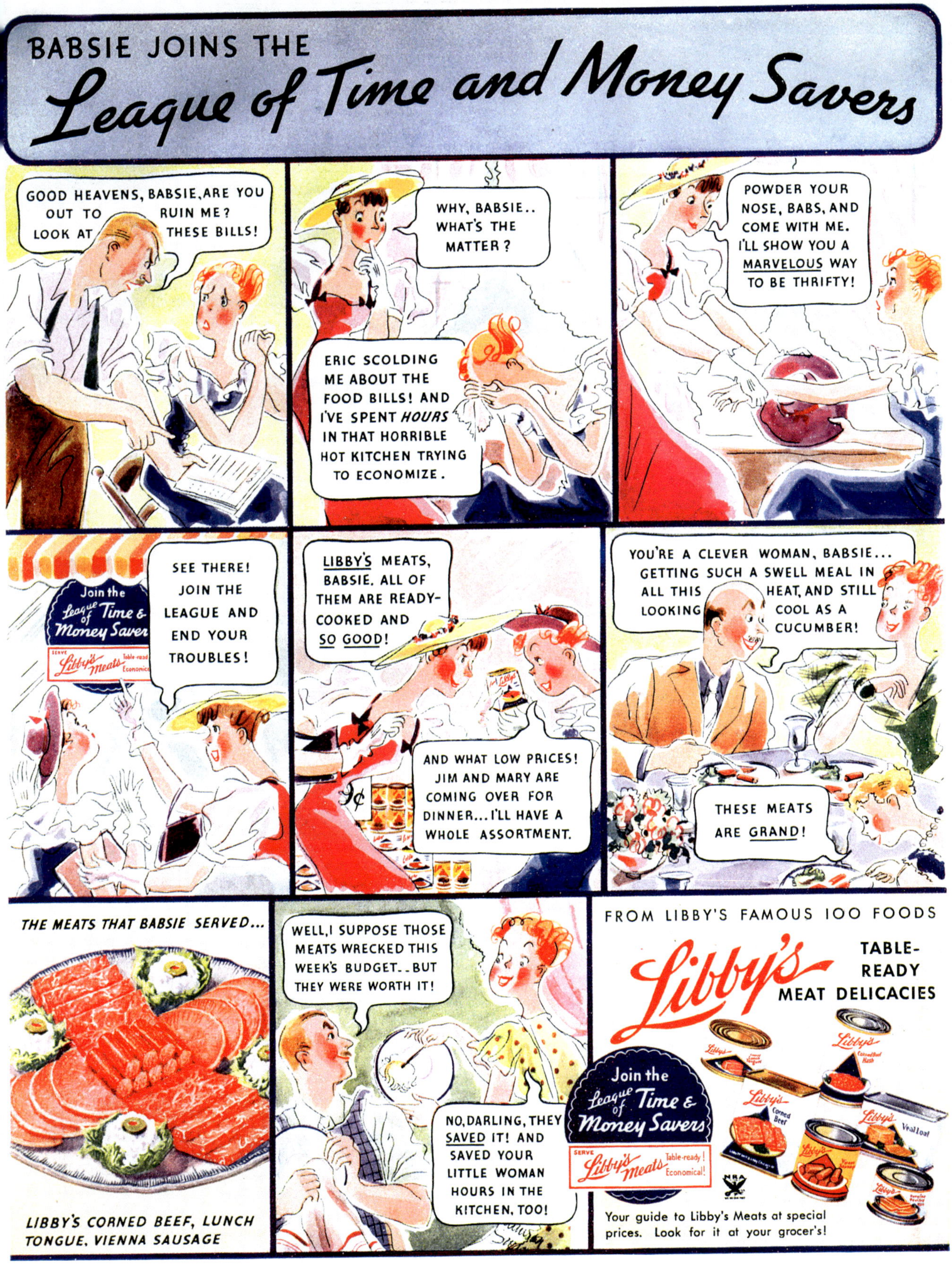

Libby's Meats, 1935

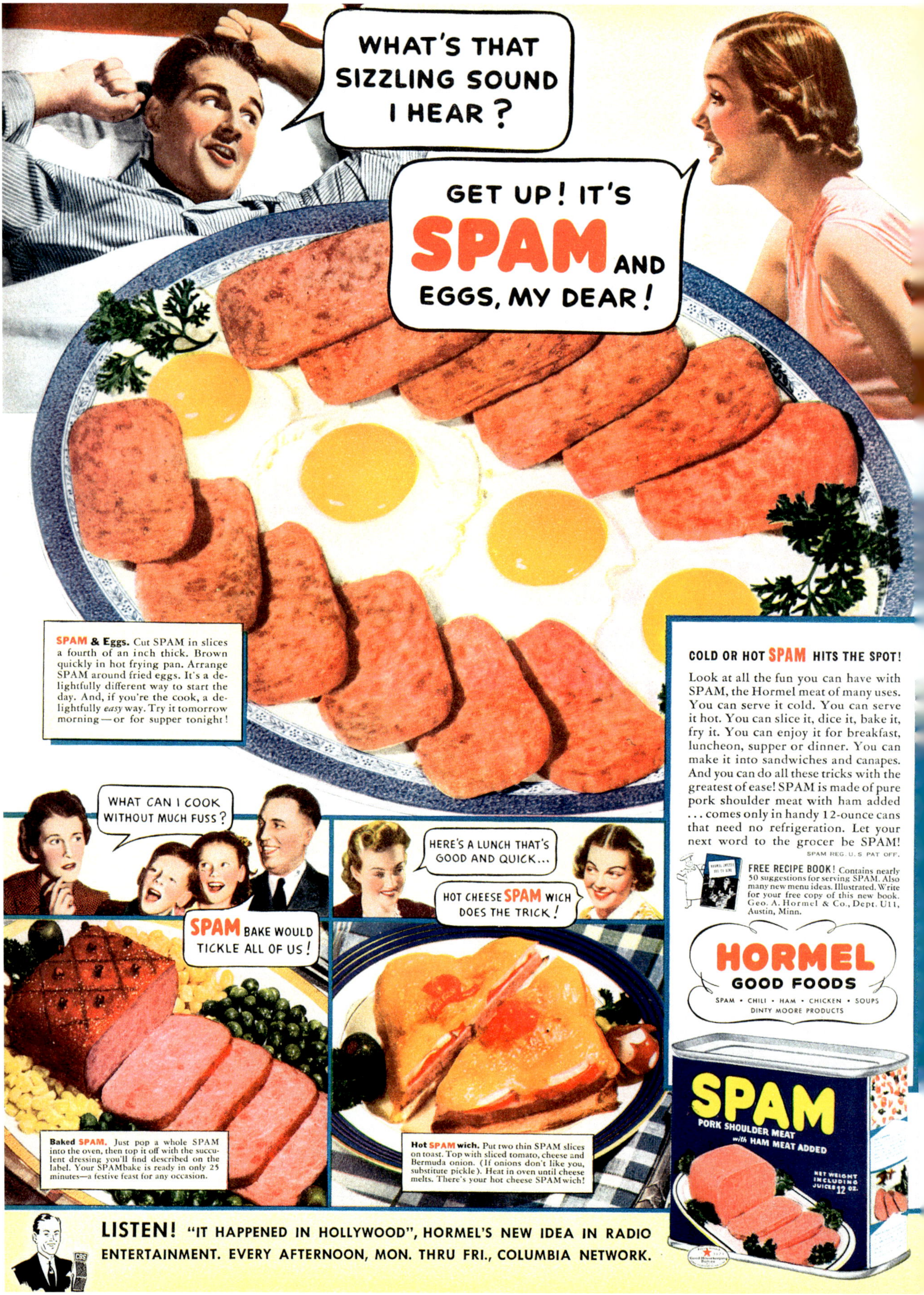

WHAT'S THAT SIZZLING SOUND I HEAR?
GET UP! IT'S SPAM AND EGGS, MY DEAR!
SPAM & Eggs. Cut SPAM in slices a fourth of an inch thick. Brown quickly in hot frying pan. Arrange SPAM around fried eggs. It's a delightfully different way to start the day. And, if you're the cook, a delightfully *easy* way. Try it tomorrow morning—or for supper tonight!
COLD OR HOT SPAM HITS THE SPOT!
Look at all the fun you can have with SPAM, the Hormel meat of many uses. You can serve it cold. You can serve it hot. You can slice it, dice it, bake it, fry it. You can enjoy it for breakfast, luncheon, supper or dinner. You can make it into sandwiches and canapes. And you can do all these tricks with the greatest of ease! SPAM is made of pure pork shoulder meat with ham added . . . comes only in handy 12-ounce cans that need no refrigeration. Let your next word to the grocer be SPAM!
SPAM REG. U. S. PAT. OFF.
FREE RECIPE BOOK! Contains nearly 50 suggestions for serving SPAM. Also many new menu ideas. Illustrated. Write for your free copy of this new book. Geo. A. Hormel & Co., Dept. U11, Austin, Minn.
WHAT CAN I COOK WITHOUT MUCH FUSS?
SPAM BAKE WOULD TICKLE ALL OF US!
HERE'S A LUNCH THAT'S GOOD AND QUICK...
HOT CHEESE SPAM WICH DOES THE TRICK!
HORMEL GOOD FOODS
SPAM • CHILI • HAM • CHICKEN • SOUPS
DINTY MOORE PRODUCTS
Baked SPAM. Just pop a whole SPAM into the oven, then top it off with the succulent dressing you'll find described on the label. Your SPAMbake is ready in only 25 minutes—a festive feast for any occasion.
Hot SPAM wich. Put two thin SPAM slices on toast. Top with sliced tomato, cheese and Bermuda onion. (If onions don't like you, substitute pickle). Heat in oven until cheese melts. There's your hot cheese SPAM wich!
SPAM
PORK SHOULDER MEAT with HAM MEAT ADDED
NET WEIGHT INCLUDING JUICES 12 OZ.
CBS
LISTEN! "IT HAPPENED IN HOLLYWOOD", HORMEL'S NEW IDEA IN RADIO ENTERTAINMENT. EVERY AFTERNOON, MON. THRU FRI., COLUMBIA NETWORK.

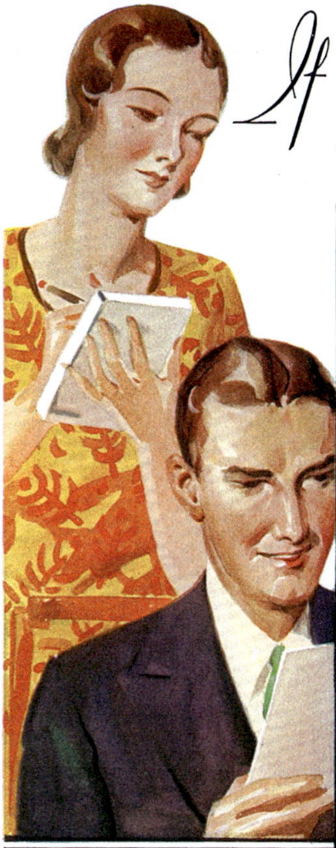

If home menus were **PRINTED** *these dishes would have French names*

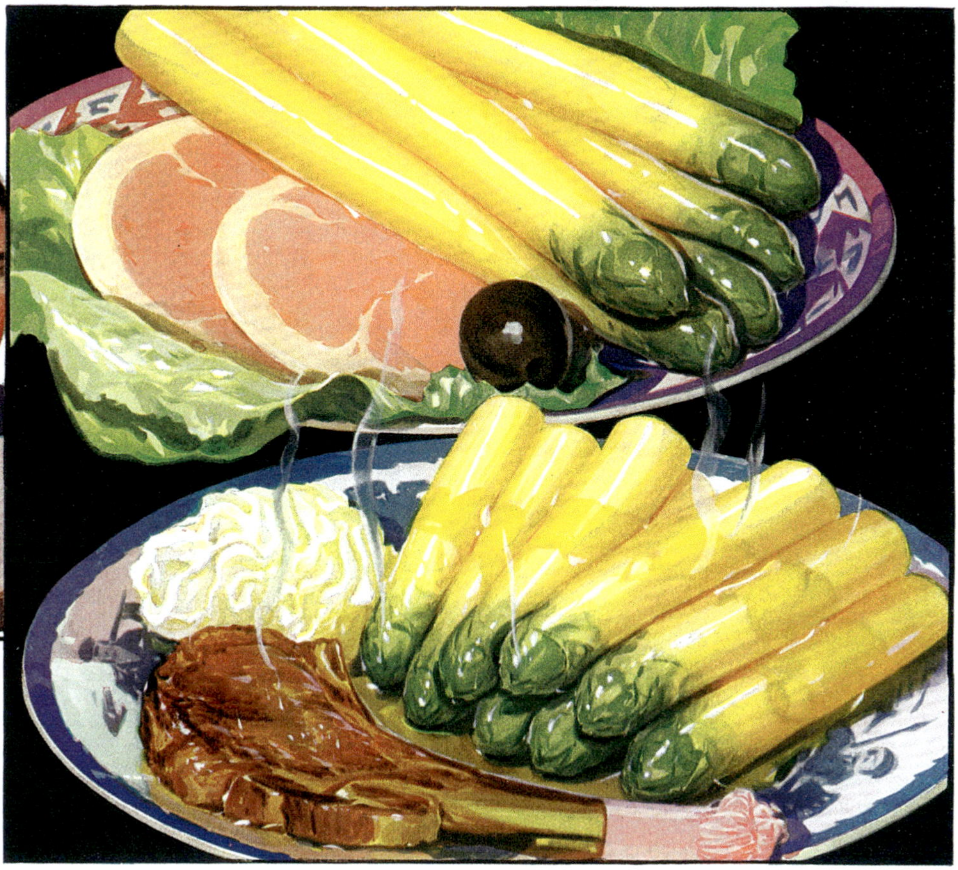

SERVE this enticing hot dish at home—and it is called "asparagus." But downtown—on the printed menu of the *maître d'hôtel,* it is "Asparagus *Polonaise.*"

Yes, it's the same simple dish you may serve at home, but—the *maître d'hôtel* appreciates *the better-touch* that asparagus gives the menu, and he names his enticing asparagus dishes accordingly.

Well, why not use the same method at home—except the printed menu? Try this: serve Asparagus *Polonaise* tomorrow for dinner. And *c-a-l-l* it Asparagus *Polonaise;* get the family to call it Asparagus *Polonaise.* And note the effect of your good salesmanship on the appetites of everybody at the table.

Asparagus Polonaise

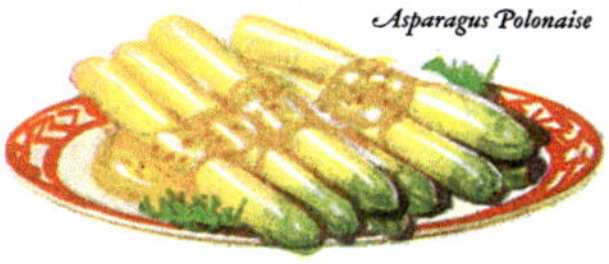

Here's the recipe: Turn California Canned Asparagus into a saucepan and heat, using the liquid in the can. Allow 6 to 8 spears for each service. While this is heating, melt 2 tablespoons of butter in a frying pan, and add ½ cup of soft bread crumbs. Fry until a golden, appetizing brown, then add ¼ teaspoon of salt. Remove from the fire, add a chopped, hard-cooked egg, and pour over the asparagus, near the tips. This recipe will make a real asparagus treat for four persons.

How very easy it is! Really, it's remarkable how many *better-touch* dishes you can make with asparagus. And it's surely a delight to see how enthusiastically the family will welcome them.

Nor need you ever hesitate to serve asparagus—in breakfast omelets, in luncheon salads, or as hot dinner dishes—for asparagus is a non-fattening delicacy. It fits any diet. It fits every appetite. And that's all the more reason why you should have a supply always on your pantry shelf—both tips and long spears.

California Canned Asparagus is not only a wonderful day-round delicacy, but it is a most convenient food to use.

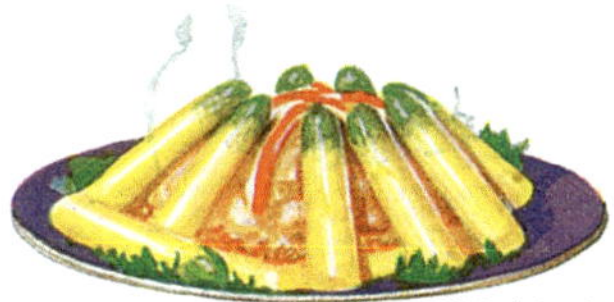

Tips with Chicken à la King

It is ready to serve just as it comes from the can—with all its tender freshness kept intact for your table.

Remember this, too—you serve all of the asparagus you buy. There's nothing to cut away—therefore, nothing to throw away. Even the liquid in the can is an excellent stock to use with soups.

And now there's a new asparagus recipe book—"This Business of Tempting Appetites"—containing dozens of different asparagus dishes to help you keep your menus worthy of your cooking skill. Write for your copy tonight. It's free, of course!

Canners League, Asparagus Section, Dept. 482
800 Adam Grant Bldg., San Francisco, Calif.

Please send me free of charge, the new recipe book, "This Business of Tempting Appetites."

Name ____________________

Address ____________________

City ______________ State ________

CALIFORNIA CANNED
Asparagus
The World's Most Popular Salad and Vegetable Delicacy

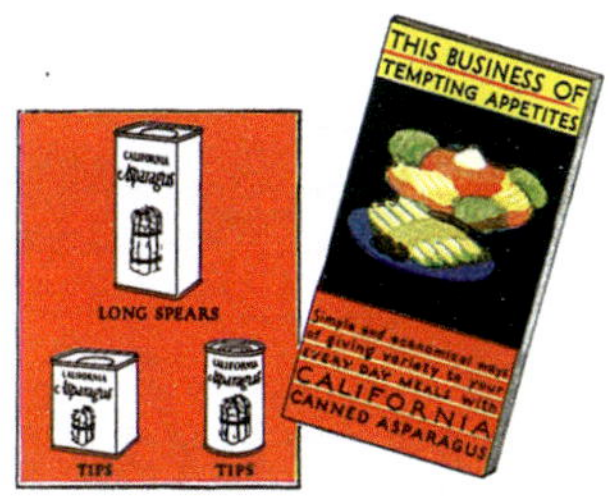

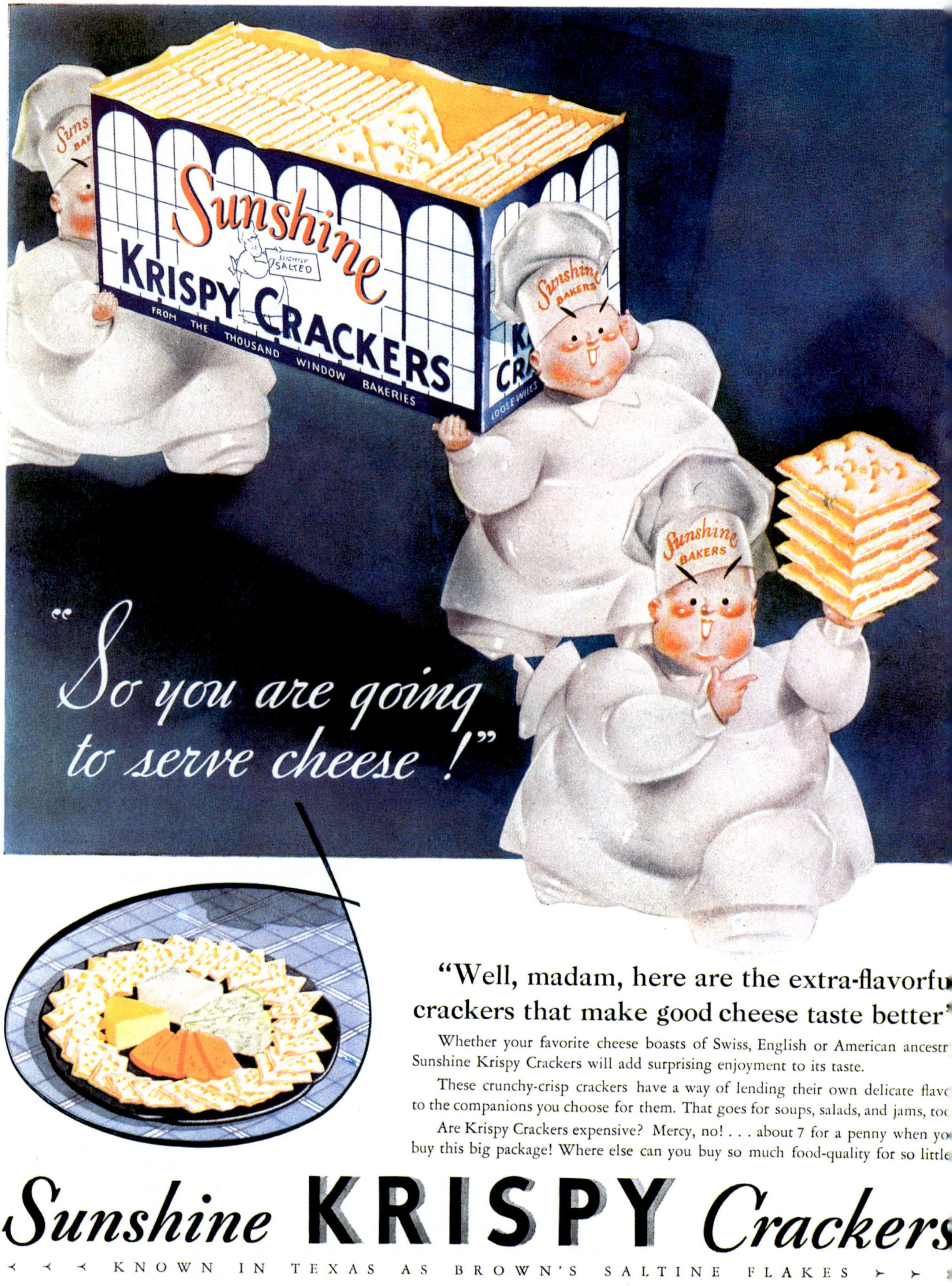
Sunshine
KRISPY CRACKERS
SLIGHTLY SALTED
FROM THE THOUSAND WINDOW BAKERIES
LOOSE-WILES
Sunshine BAKERS
"So you are going to serve cheese!"
"Well, madam, here are the extra-flavorfu
crackers that make good cheese taste better'
Whether your favorite cheese boasts of Swiss, English or American ancestr
Sunshine Krispy Crackers will add surprising enjoyment to its taste.
These crunchy-crisp crackers have a way of lending their own delicate flavo
to the companions you choose for them. That goes for soups, salads, and jams, too
Are Krispy Crackers expensive? Mercy, no! . . . about 7 for a penny when yo
buy this big package! Where else can you buy so much food-quality for so little
Sunshine KRISPY Crackers
KNOWN IN TEXAS AS BROWN'S SALTINE FLAKES

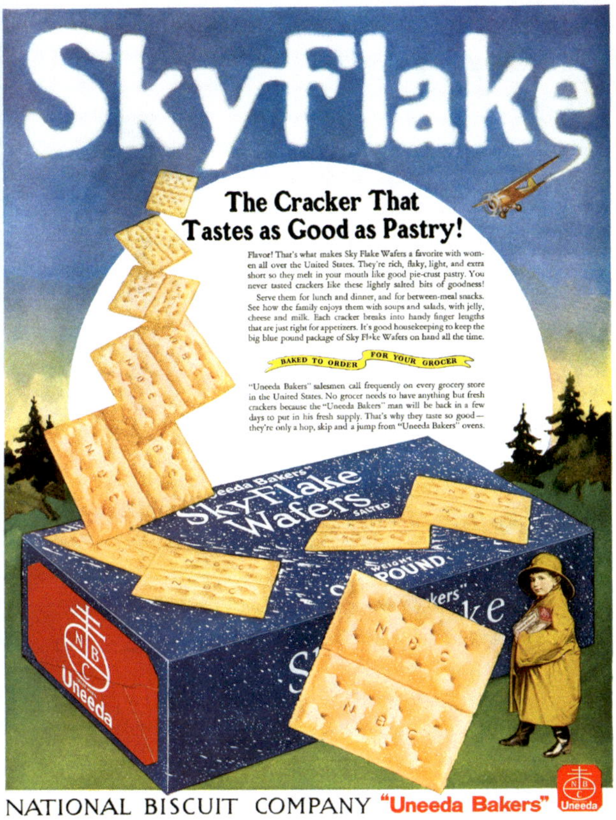

National Biscuit Co., 1934

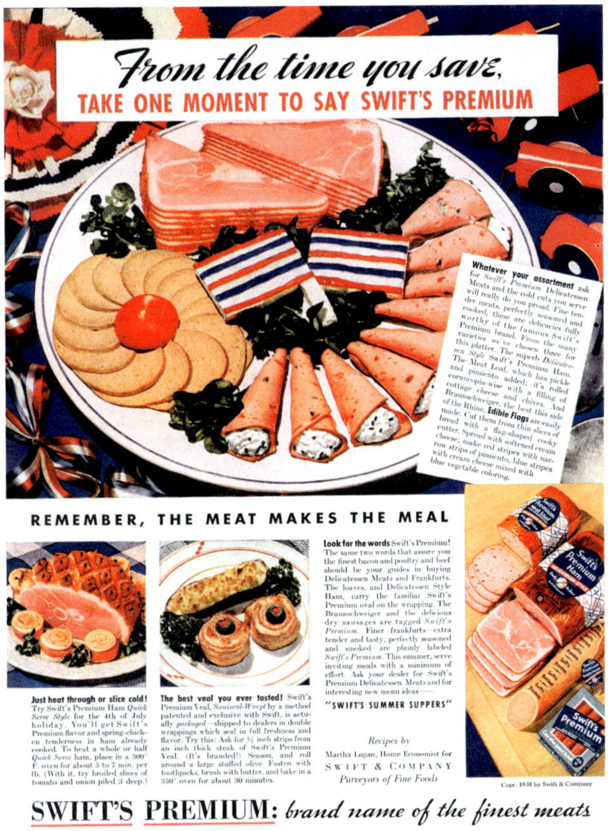

Swift's Premium Meats, 1938

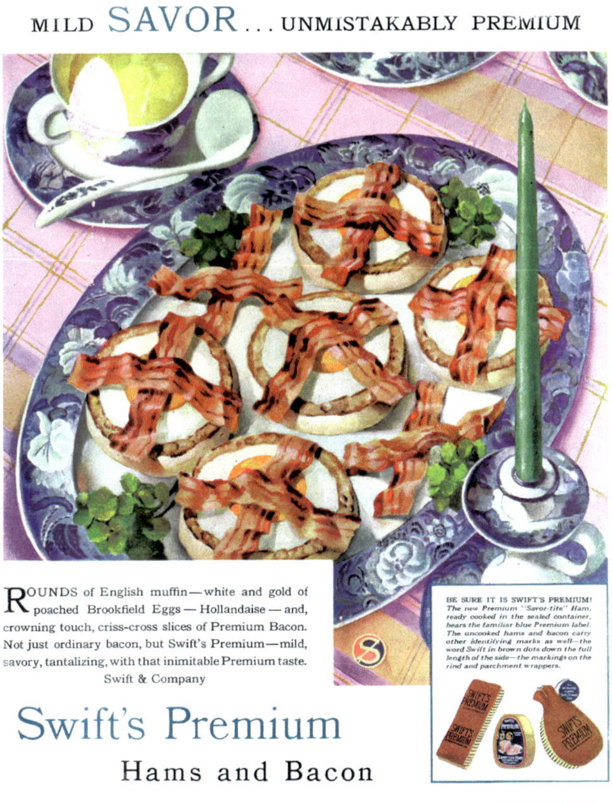

Sunshine Crackers, 1935 ◂ Swift's Premium Meats, 1930

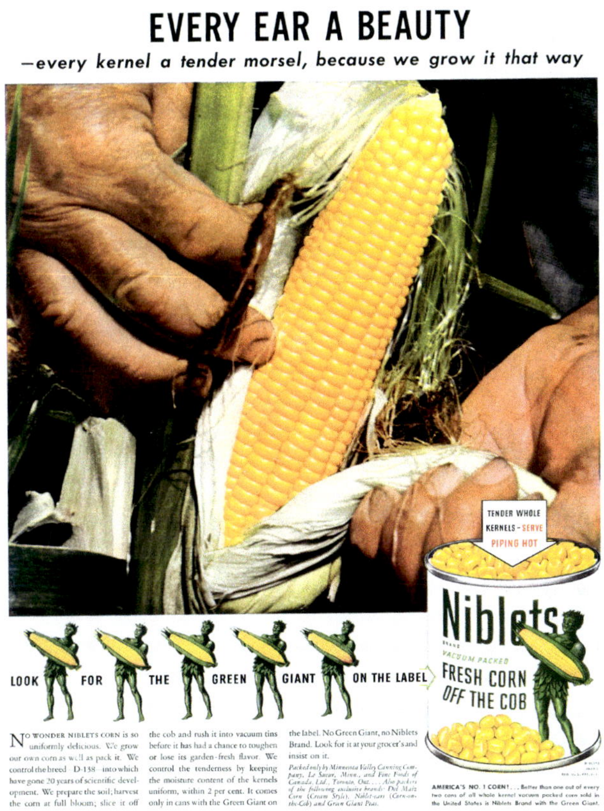

Niblets, 1939

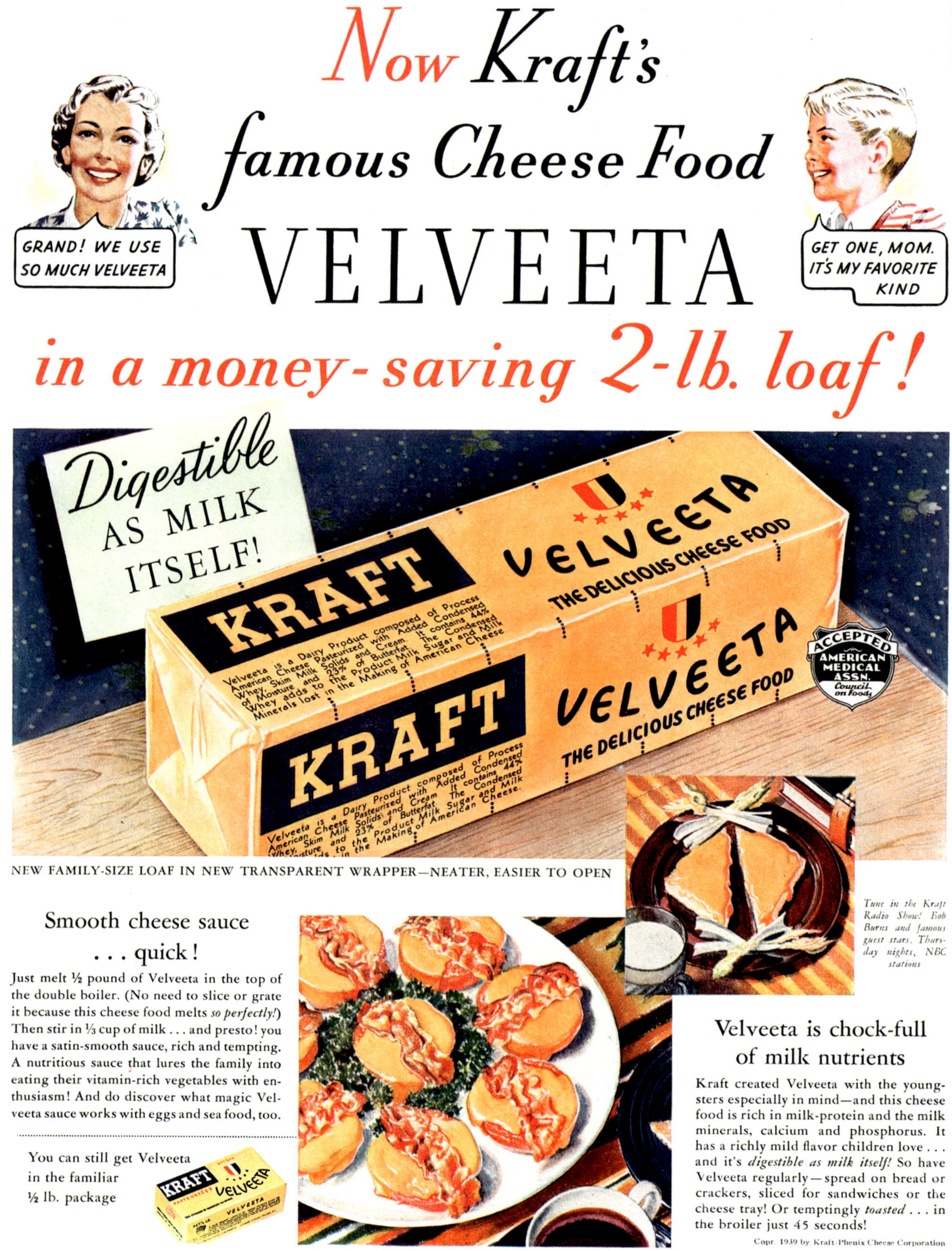

Velveeta, 1939

▸ *Ritz Cracker, 1937* ▸▸ *Planter's Peanuts, 1930*

There's RITZ... one friend I always recognize!

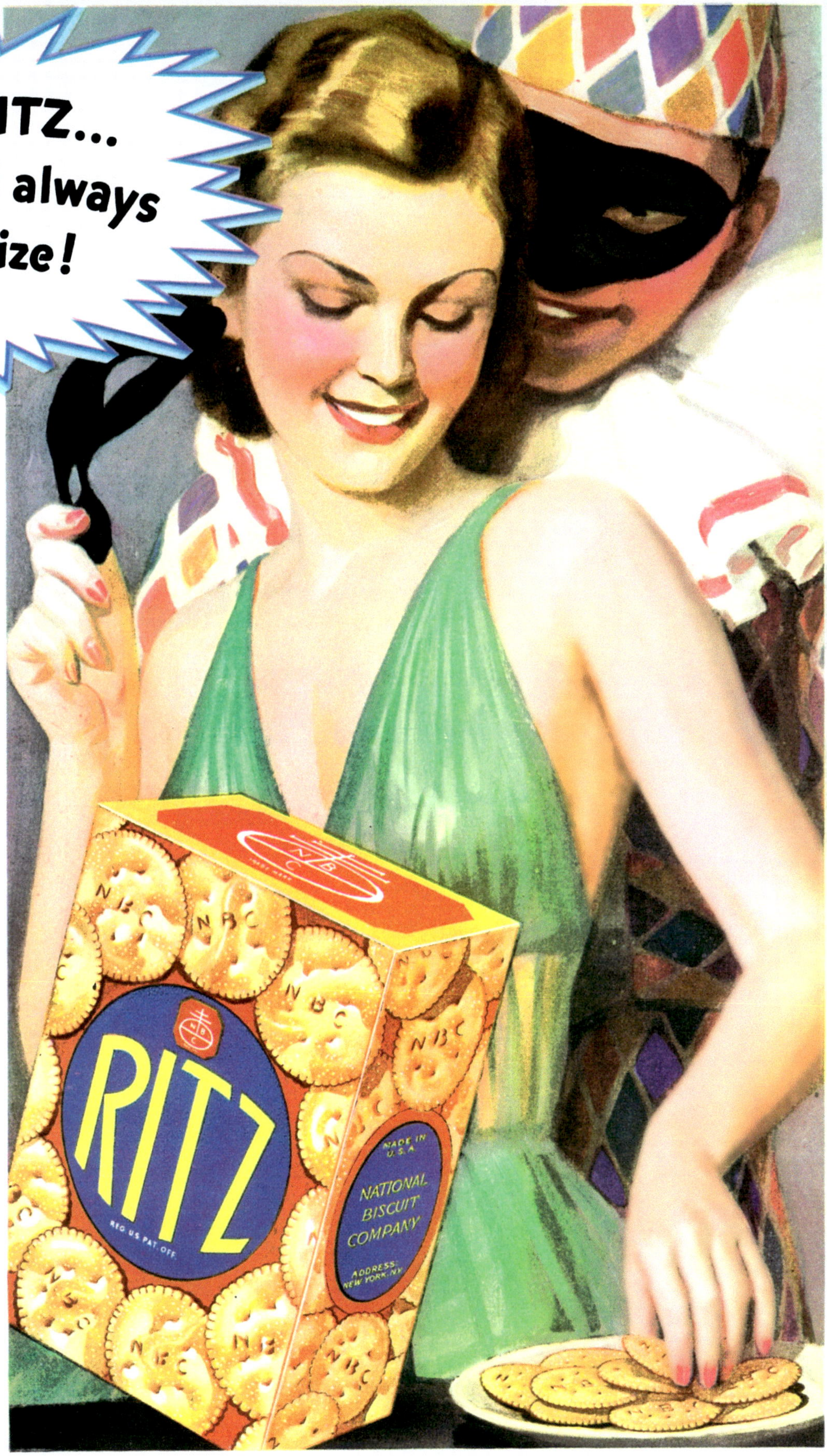

›er party suggestions

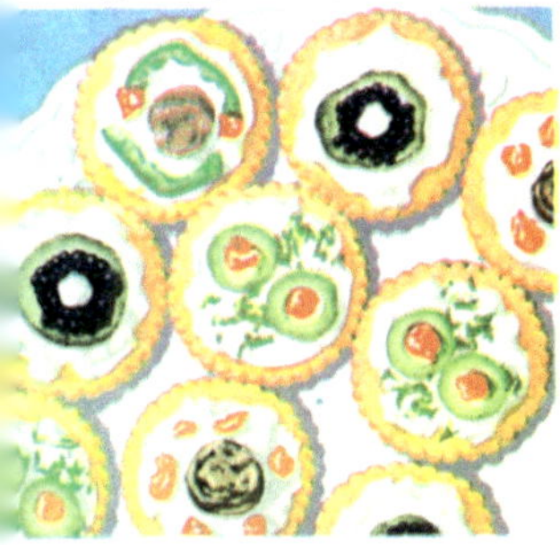

PPETIZERS that make any occasion
Spread Ritz with cream cheese softened
m. Top with (1) anchovy fillets, garnish
of pimiento; (2) olive rings filled with
› with pearl onion; (3) slices of stuffed
nish with parsley. Ritz exciting nut-like
ıkes these canapes really distinctive.

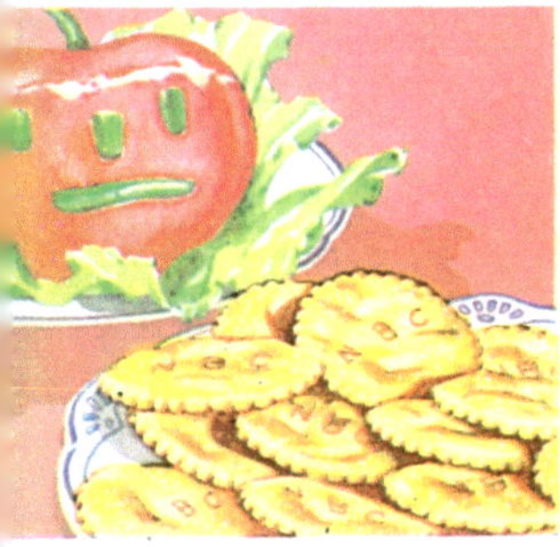

TO MASQUERADE served with
Ritz means more fun for Hallowe'en.
ıt firm tomatoes and fill with chopped
nd pecans, mixed with mayonnaise. Make
eyes, nose, mouth—insert green pepper.
›er for stem. Serve on lettuce with Ritz.

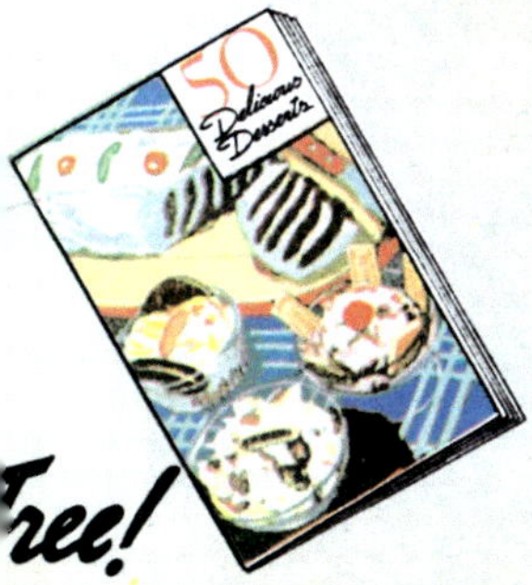

ree!

ascinating book "50 Delicious Desserts"
th delectable, easy-to-make recipes that
add a festive touch to party menus.
te National Biscuit Company, 449 West
Street, Dept. 102, New York City.

THE SEAL OF PERFECT BAKING — *Ritz is a product of* NATIONAL BISCUIT COMPANY

PLANTERS

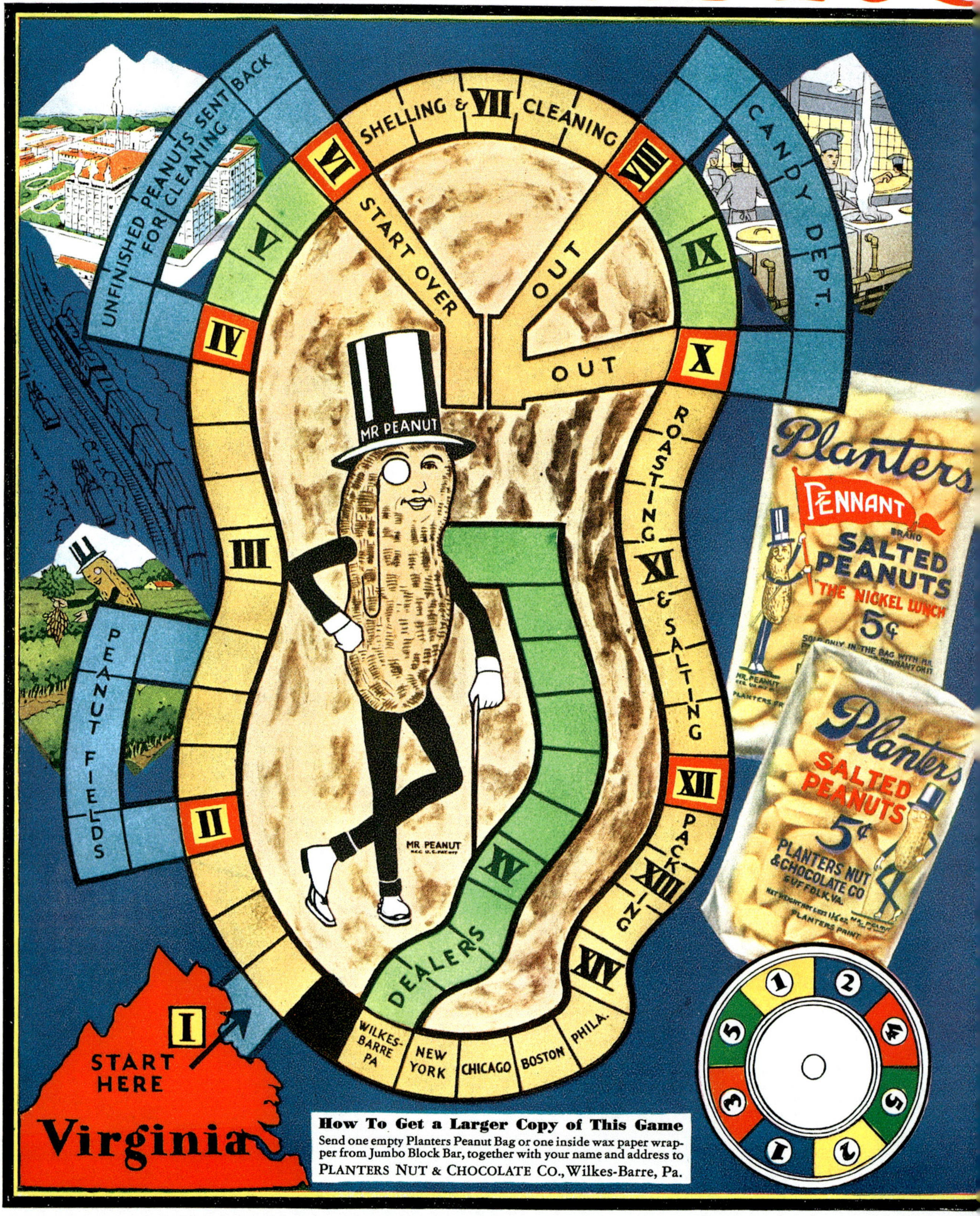

UNFINISHED PEANUTS SENT BACK FOR CLEANING
SHELLING & VII CLEANING
CANDY DEPT.
START OVER
OUT
OUT
MR PEANUT
MR PEANUT
ROASTING
XI
& SALTING
PACKING
XIII
XIV
PEANUT FIELDS
DEALERS
XV
WILKES-BARRE PA
NEW YORK
CHICAGO
BOSTON
PHILA.
I
II
III
IV
V
VI
VIII
IX
X
XII
START HERE
Virginia
Planters
PENNANT BRAND
SALTED PEANUTS
THE NICKEL LUNCH
5¢
Planters
SALTED PEANUTS
5¢
PLANTERS NUT & CHOCOLATE CO
SUFFOLK, VA.
1
2
4
5
2
1
3
5
How To Get a Larger Copy of This Game
Send one empty Planters Peanut Bag or one inside wax paper wrapper from Jumbo Block Bar, together with your name and address to PLANTERS NUT & CHOCOLATE CO., Wilkes-Barre, Pa.

PEANUTS

DIRECTIONS.

Two, three, or four persons may play, each player using three counters of the same color, red, blue, yellow or green. (Each counter represents a lot of peanuts.)

After a counter is entered, as later described, it is moved forward on the path around the Peanut, the number of spaces indicated by the count which is secured by spinning the arrow on the counter. Only one counter may occupy any one space at any time, with the exception of the entering place, the State of Virginia.

A counter may be captured by a player who received a count which takes him to a space on which an opponent's man is located. Captured counter must start over again. Player making the capture can count ten spaces forward with any of his counters.

If the space to which a player counts in safety zones is occupied by another counter, he may either take the space directly behind that space or lose his turn, as he may choose.

VA.

I. The start of the game is from Virginia, because the finest and most flavory peanuts (the kind Planters uses) come from there. To start, the player must have a FIVE because the Roman symbol for FIVE is V, which also stands for Virginia. Virginia Peanuts are the only ones that may become Planters Salted Peanuts. V-five is also the price of Planters Bag of Peanuts.

II. FIELD INSPECTOR. If the player passes the inspector's space it means that the peanuts are well grown and may be gathered and sent on to the Factories. If the player stops on the inspector's space he must detour through the Path marked Peanut Fields, meaning that they cannot be gathered and shipped to Planters until they are fully matured.

III. Upon farmers' wagons and upon railroad cars, the matured peanuts travel to Planters factories at SUFFOLK, VIRGINIA, Charleston, South Carolina, and San Francisco, California.

IV. RECEIVING INSPECTOR. If the player passes the inspector at the Receiving Department of the Factories they go straight on into the receiving rooms, if the player stops on the inspector's space it means that the raw peanuts were not properly cleaned and bagged. They must detour through a cleaning process before they can enter the factory, (Section colored blue).

V. This is a SAFETY ZONE called PLANTERS. You can easily remember this by saying to yourself: "When I get to Planters Peanuts I am safe." Any counter which is in this section cannot be captured.

VI. RAW PEANUT INSPECTOR. If a player passes this inspector he can proceed straight into the Manufacturing Department. If he can stop at the Inspector's Space, it means that the peanuts are not of the right quality for Planters Products. The counter drops down the Chute and is OUT. However, he may start over again by getting a five.

VII. The players are going through the FACTORIES where the wonderful machinery shells and skins the roasted peanuts.

VIII. ROASTED PEANUT INSPECTOR. If the player passes this inspector, it means that he can go straight on to the next process. If the player stops on the Inspector's space, it means that some imperfection has been discovered that could not be seen when the peanut was in the shell. Out the player goes with that counter and IT CANNOT RETURN TO THE GAME, for no imperfect peanuts can be used for Planters Salted Peanuts.

If a player moving from Process VII gets a 2, it means that it must go to the Candy Department and in continuing will not go out if gets a number 1, but will remain on VII and with the next number will move the counter into the Candy Department. In order to go out, must land on VIII without stopping at the blank space before VIII.

IX. This is a SAFETY ZONE like V. Remember, when you get to PLANTERS you are safe.

X. CANDY INSPECTOR. This Inspection applies only to pieces that have gone to the Candy Department. If these players pass the Inspector's space it means that they are perfect and can go down to the wrapping and shipping Processes. If they stop on the Inspector's space it means that something has been found wrong and OUT THEY GO. They cannot return to the game, as no imperfect candies are allowed to reach the Customer.

XI. This process represents roasting and salting for the Big Peanuts. This is an important process and accounts for much of the wonderful flavor and crispness of Planters Salted Peanuts. For the Candy Peanuts this section represents many processes such as Chocolate Coating, Peanut Bar Making, etc.

XII. FINAL INSPECTOR. It's hard luck to go this far and be thrown out for good, but that's what happens to all Planters Products that can't pass the Final Inspector. If the players pass this space they can go to the packing and wrapping processes.

XIII. Here Planters Salted Peanuts are packed in the familiar glass jars from which they are sold in the even more familiar Glassine Bags. Here, too, Planters Peanut Candies are wrapped in wax paper and sealed to keep them fresh.

XIV. From the Factories Planters Products are shipped to the big branch offices at Wilkes-Barre, Pa., New York, Chicago, Boston, Philadelphia. (XV)

XV. From the Branch Offices they go to the hundreds of thousands of dealers all over this great country.

HERE let us present to you MR. PEANUT, who greets you with a smile. We are sure you will enjoy knowing him and will like him for his good qualities. The Player who has two counters first reaching Goal wins the game.

Play
the NEW GAME

[Thousands everywhere are enjoying it!]

PLANTERS PEANUT PARTY

LAY cardboard underneath the page on the left, read the directions on this page, and the note at the bottom of this page—if you want a larger copy of the game, send one empty Planters Peanut bag or one inside wrapper from Jumbo Block Bar to Planters Nut & Chocolate Co., Wilkes-Barre, Pa.

PLANTERS rule as a favorite everywhere, because they are the choice of the world's finest peanut crops. Big, luscious golden nuggets selected from the finest *Virginia* plantations. Salted and roasted by the one and only PLANTERS process in the giant plants at Suffolk, Virginia, the heart of the peanut country. Look for Mr. Peanut on the glassine bag, and you are sure of getting the genuine nickel lunch of supremely fine PLANTERS PEANUTS.

PLANTERS NUT & CHOCOLATE CO.

SUFFOLK, VA. WILKES-BARRE, PA.
SAN FRANCISCO
TORONTO, CAN.

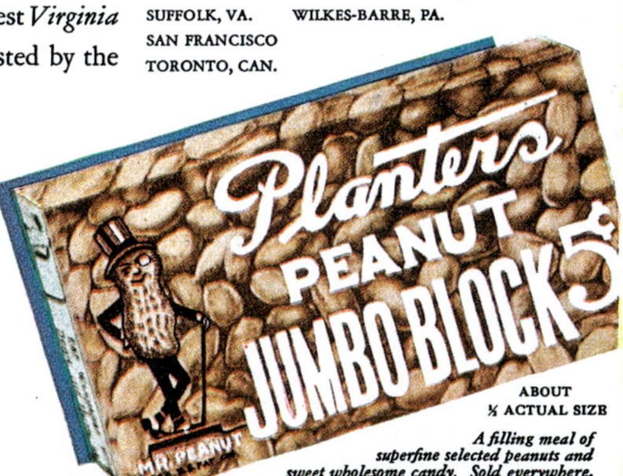

ABOUT ½ ACTUAL SIZE

A filling meal of superfine selected peanuts and sweet wholesome candy. Sold everywhere.

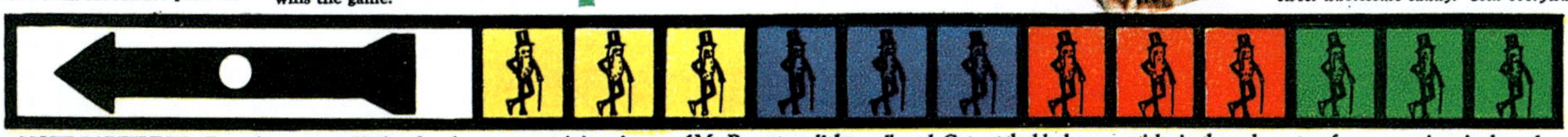

NOTE CAREFULLY—Paste the arrow and little colored squares containing pictures of Mr. Peanut, on light cardboard. Cut out the black arrow, stick pin through center of arrow, passing pin through center of colored circle so arrow will spin as an indicator. Use the little colored squares as movable pieces, or men, in playing the game.

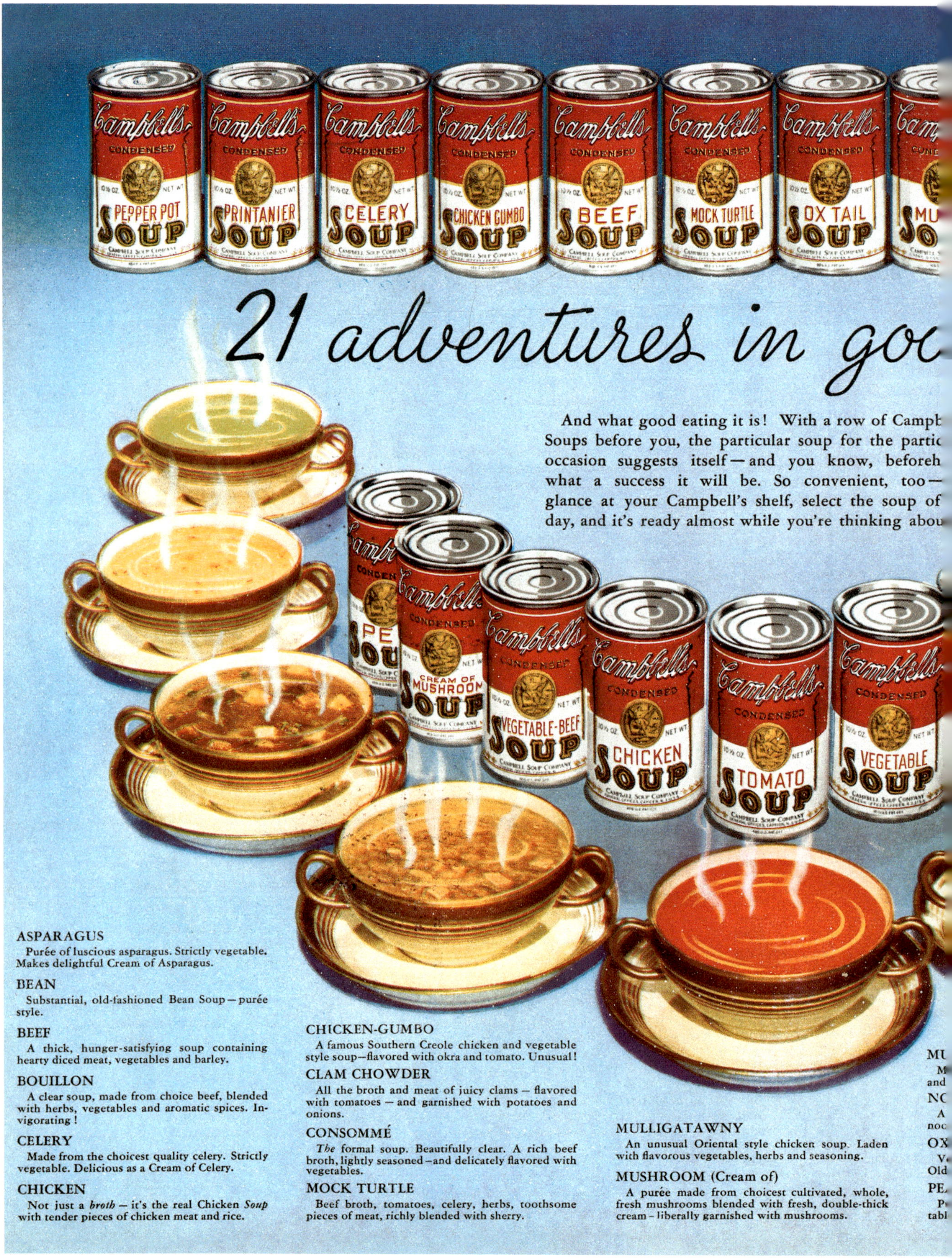

Campbell's Soup, 1936

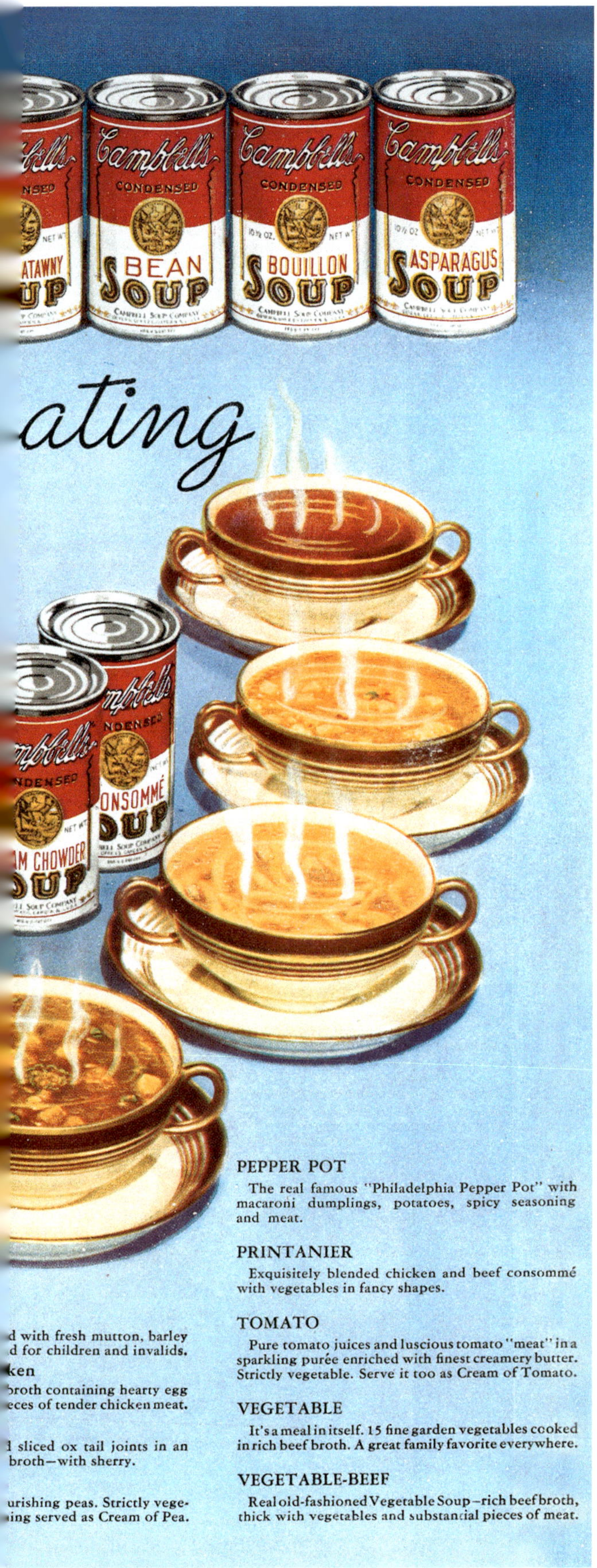

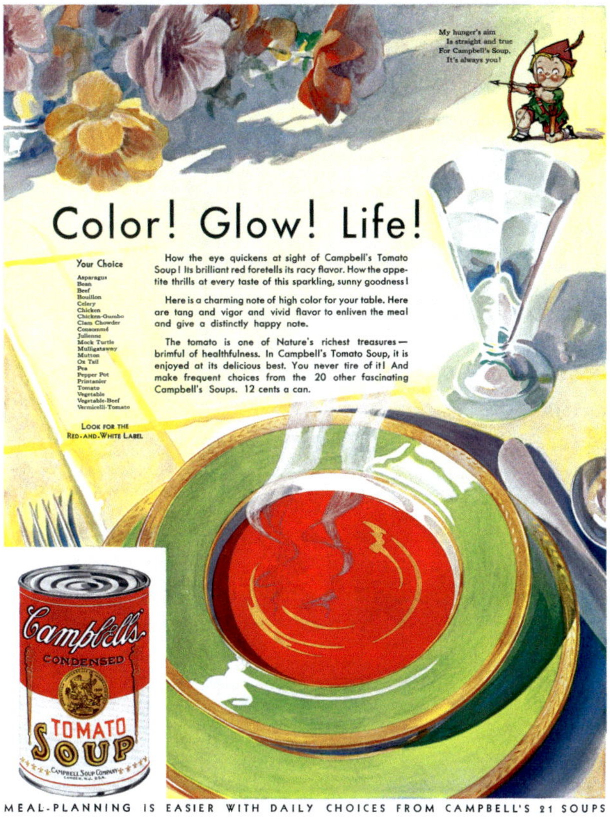

Campbell's Soup, 1931

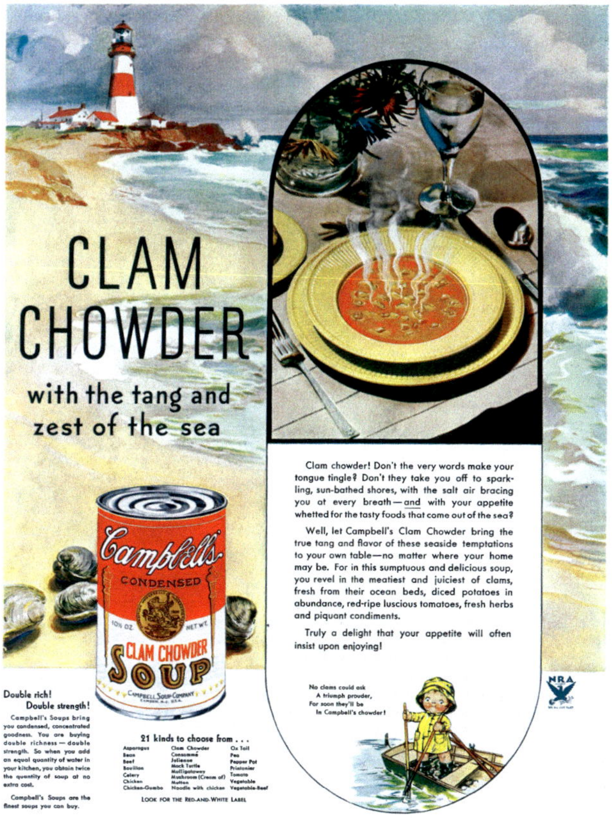

Campbell's Soup, 1934

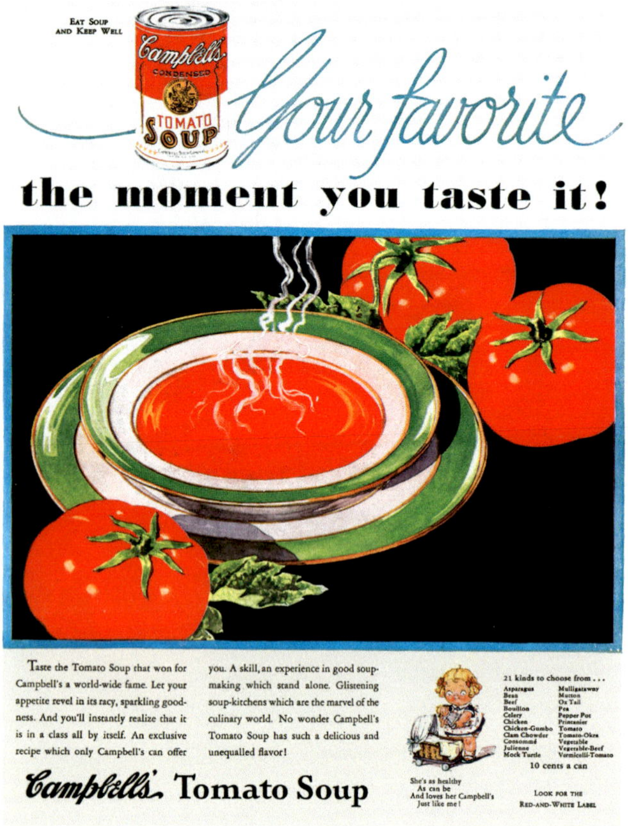

Campbell's Soup, 1933

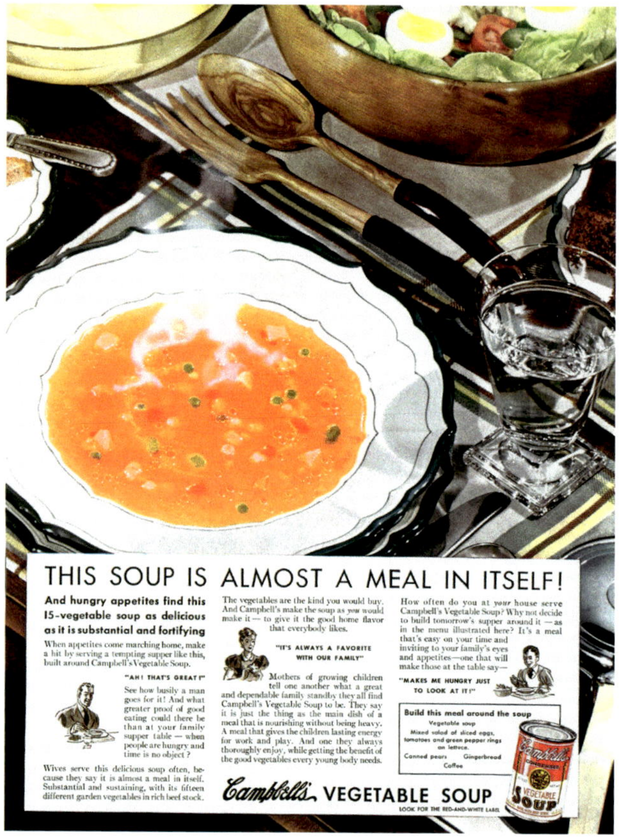

Campbell's Soup, 1939

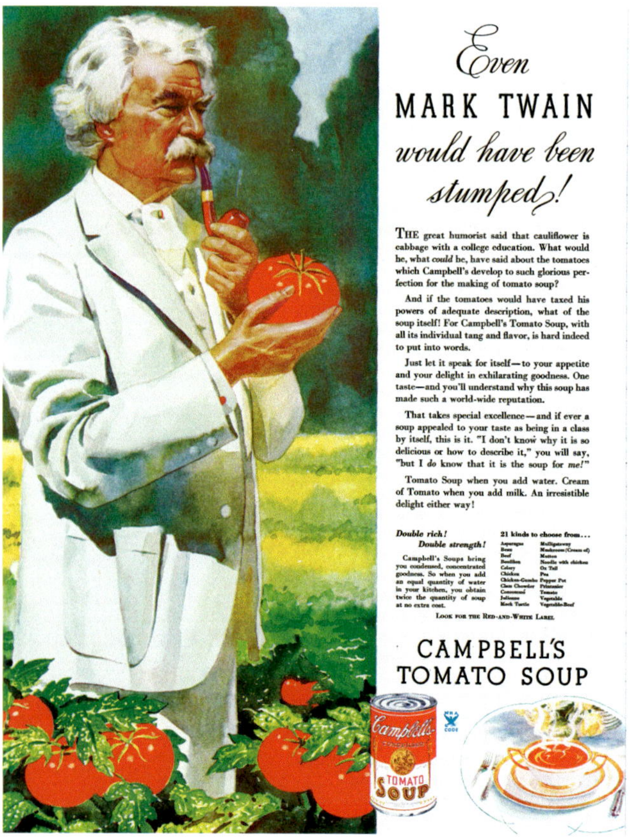

Campbell's Soup, 1934

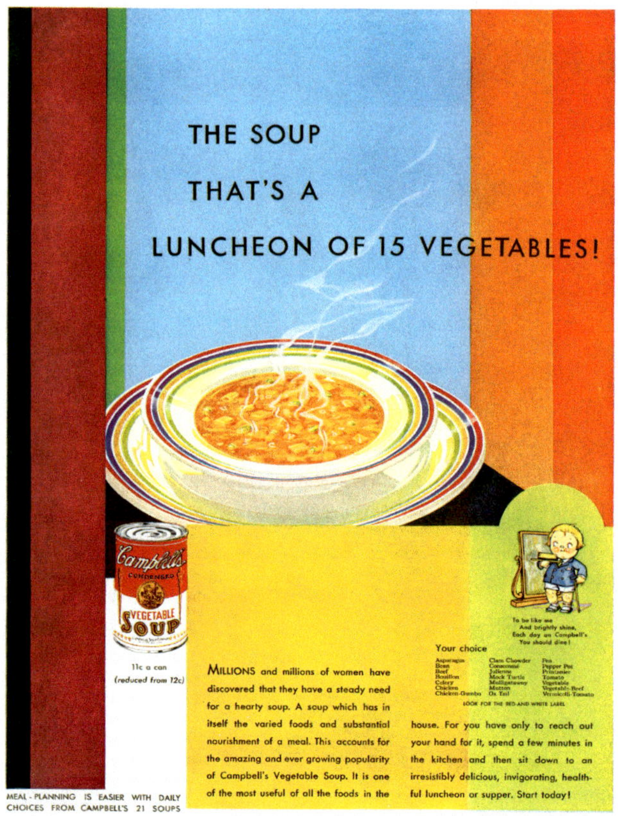

Campbell's Soup, 1931

▸ *Campbell's Soup, 1935*

EVERYWHERE...

....the sunny, sparkling favorite!

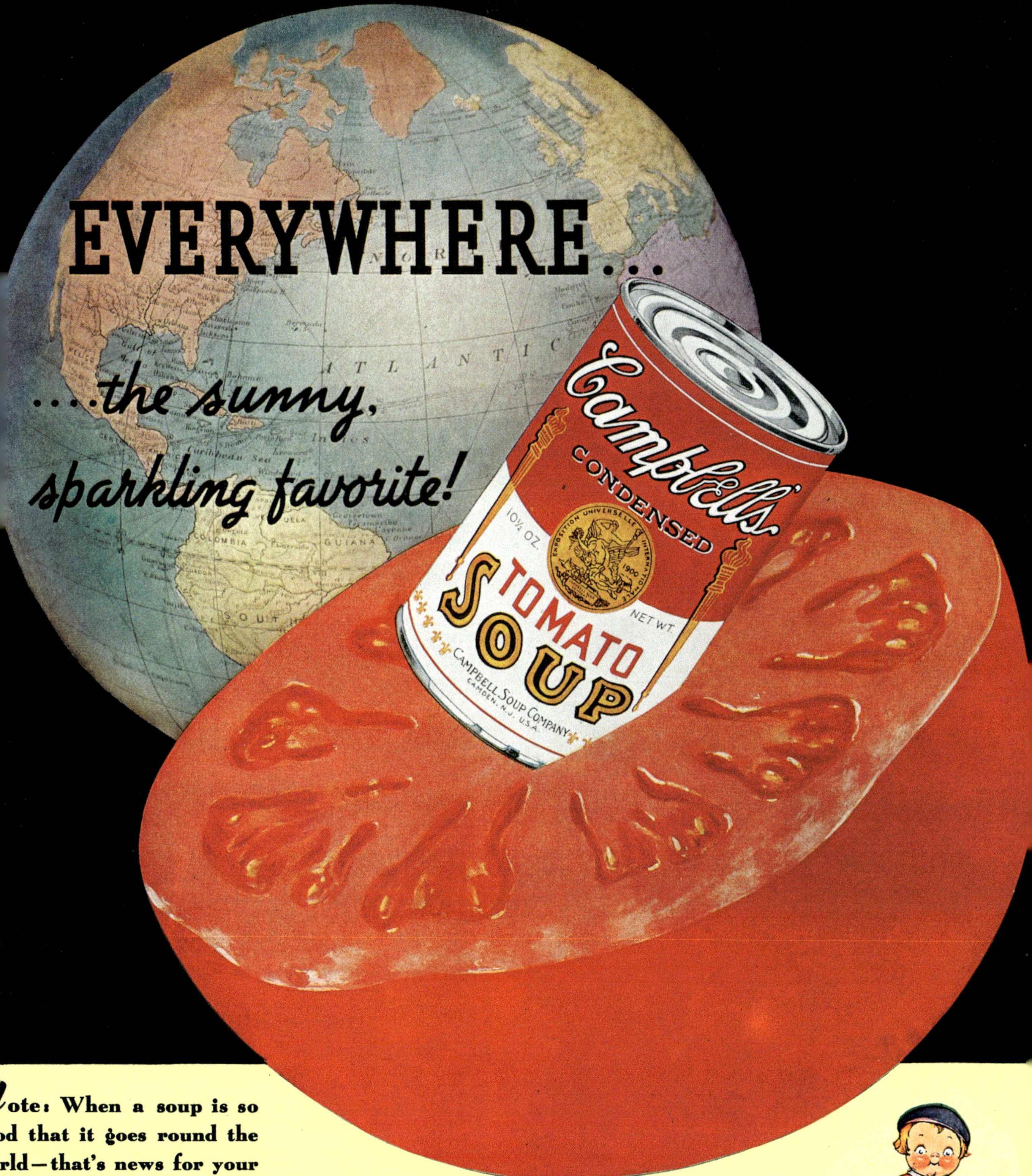

ote: When a soup is so od that it goes round the rld—that's news for your petite.)

Many a traveler to foreign shores has come back with winkling eye and a merry story about discovering pbell's Tomato Soup in some far off corner of the n. And no wonder, for its deliciousness, its tang and have made friends for it everywhere. It is far and away *world's most popular soup.*

And this is why: For over a quarter of a century, choice atoes have been specially bred for it in Campbell's hothouses and gardens. Fine, sweet table butter is used to make it still smoother and even more nourishing. The most skillful seasoning adds the final exquisite touch. And, following Campbell's special recipe, internationally known chefs bring this greatest of soups to such perfection that every time you eat it you will say there is not another tomato soup like it.

News is news. But tasting says it all so much better. Why not serve Campbell's Tomato Soup tomorrow?

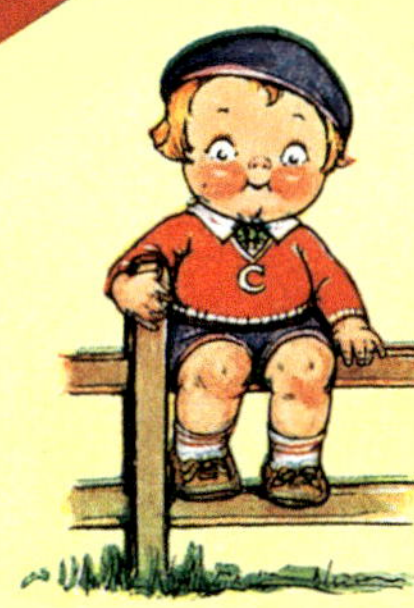

The wish I wish
This very minute
Is for a plate
With Campbell's in it!

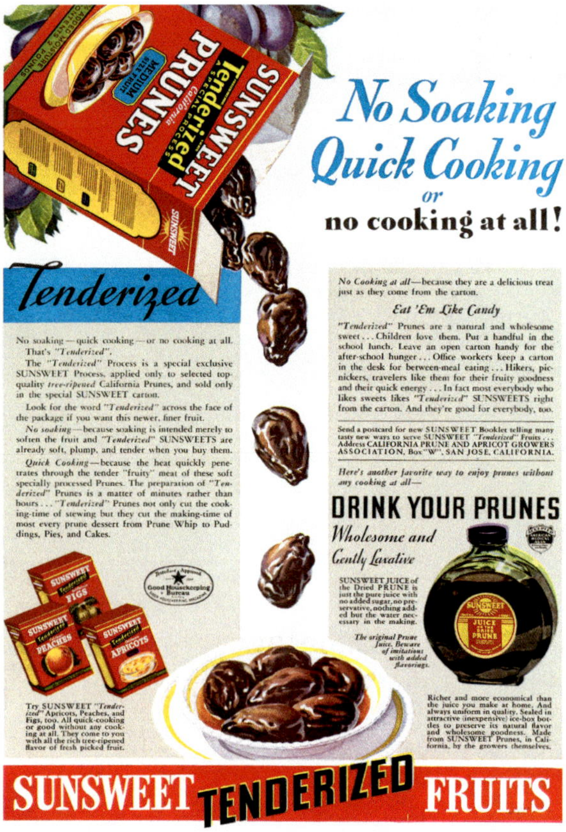

Sunsweet Prunes, 1934

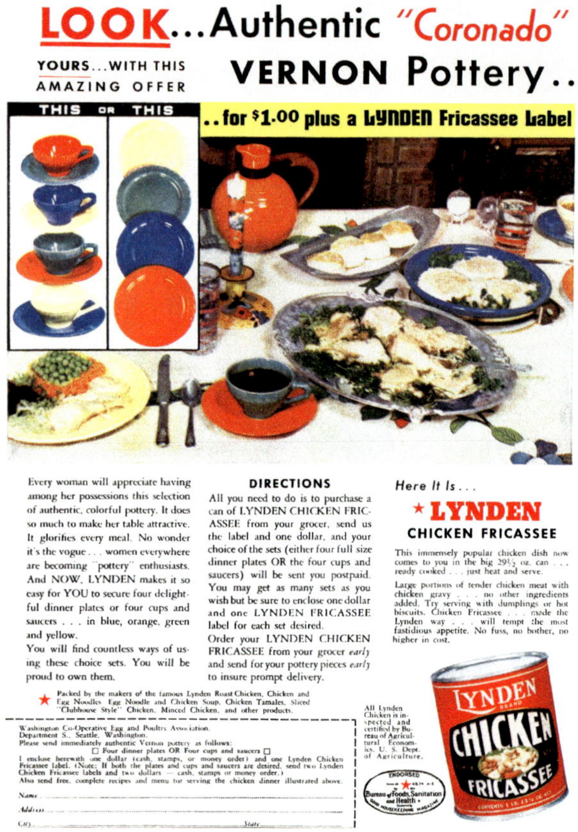

Lynden Chicken Fricassee, 1938

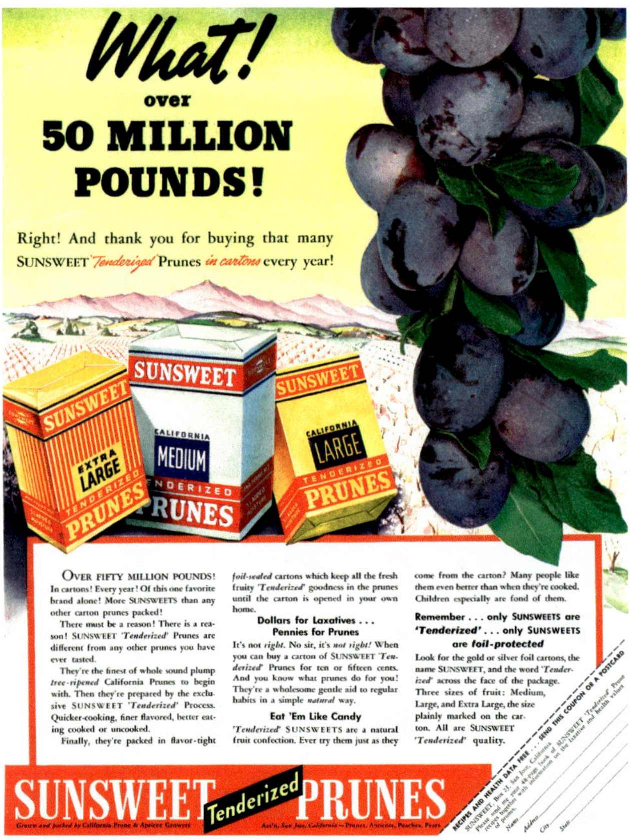

Sunsweet Prunes, 1938

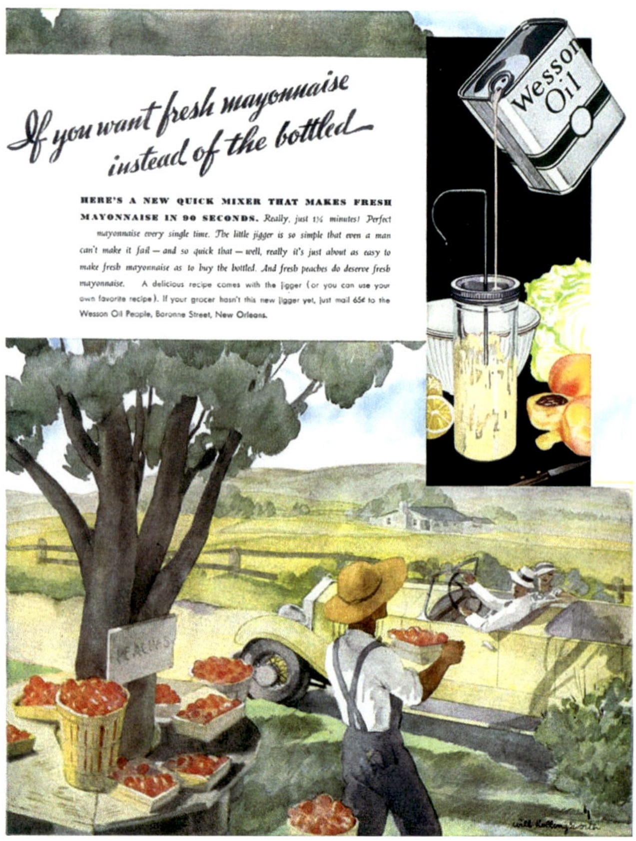

Wessen Oil, 1934

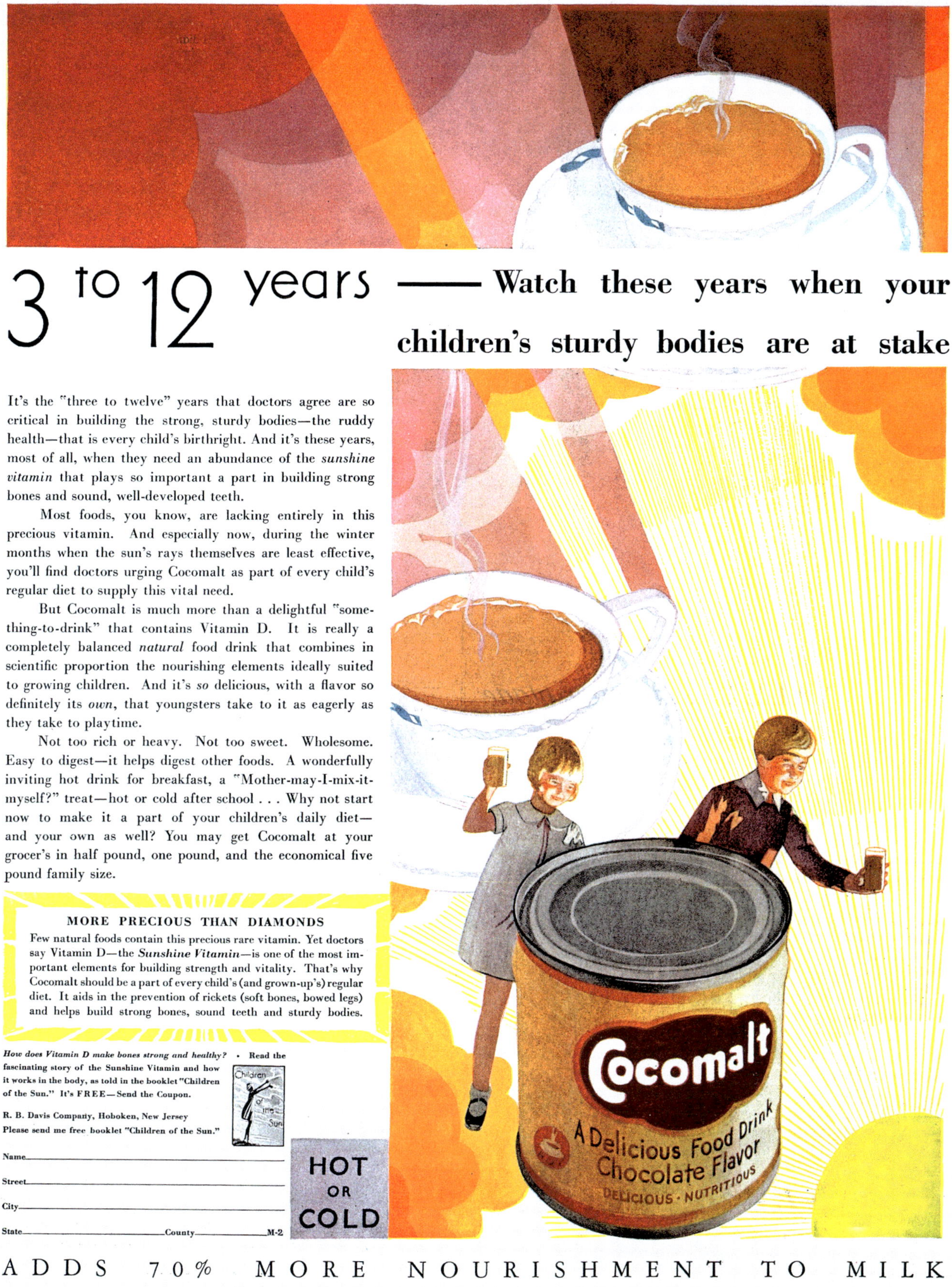

Cocomalt, 1930

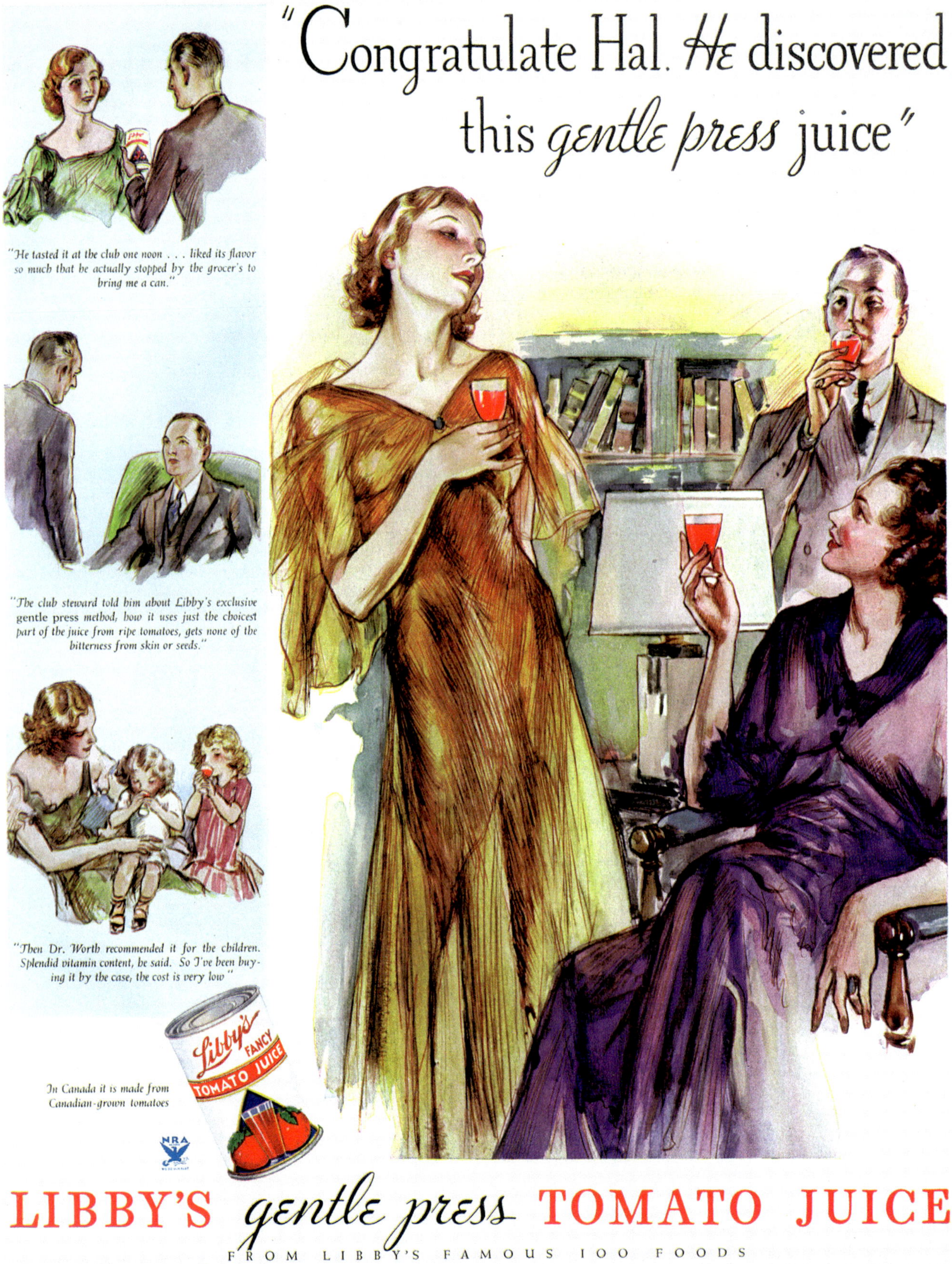

Libby's, 1934

► Libby's, 1938

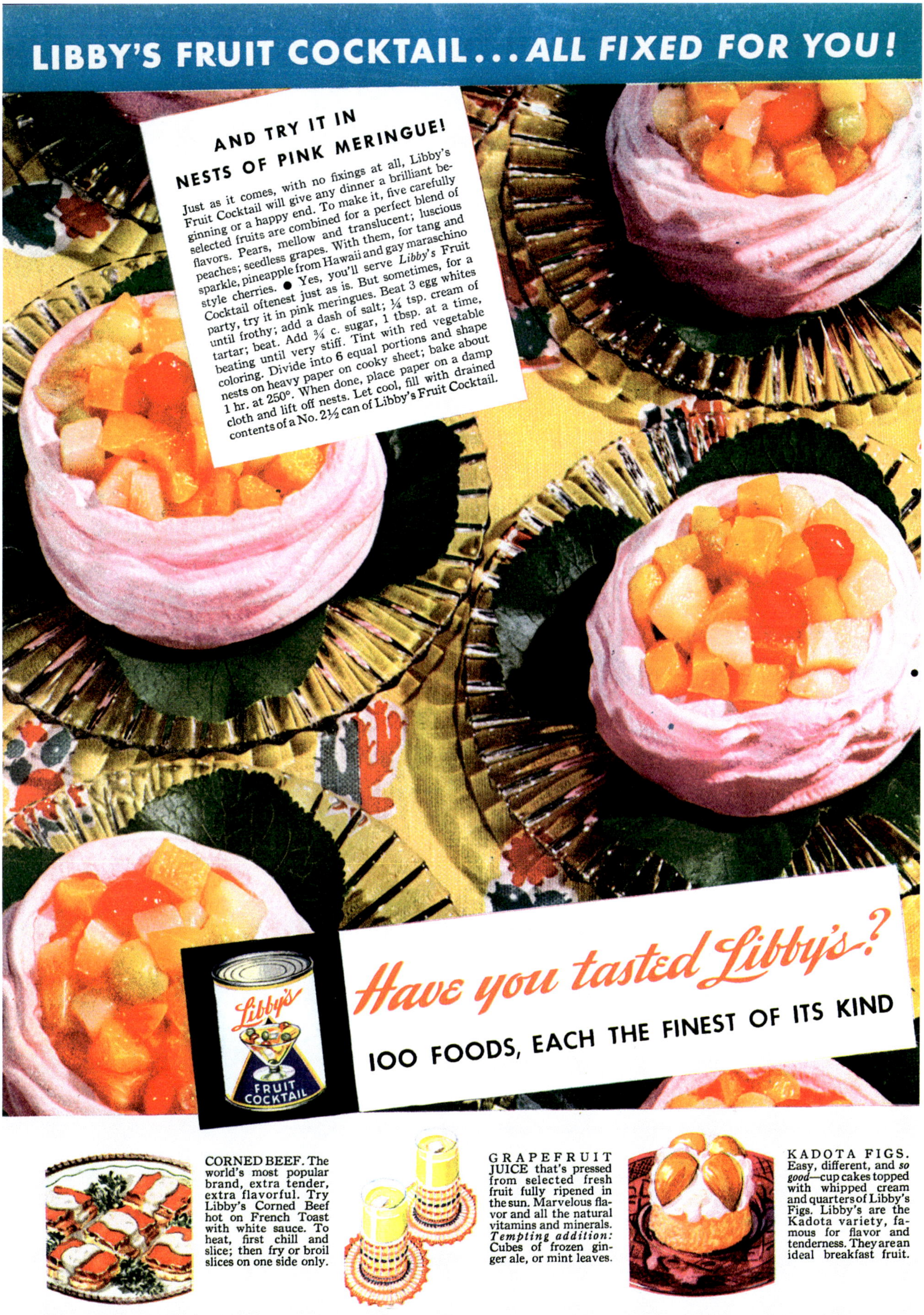
LIBBY'S FRUIT COCKTAIL . . . ALL FIXED FOR YOU!
AND TRY IT IN NESTS OF PINK MERINGUE!
Just as it comes, with no fixings at all, Libby's Fruit Cocktail will give any dinner a brilliant beginning or a happy end. To make it, five carefully selected fruits are combined for a perfect blend of flavors. Pears, mellow and translucent; luscious peaches; seedless grapes. With them, for tang and sparkle, pineapple from Hawaii and gay maraschino style cherries. ● Yes, you'll serve Libby's Fruit Cocktail oftenest just as is. But sometimes, for a party, try it in pink meringues. Beat 3 egg whites until frothy; add a dash of salt; ¼ tsp. cream of tartar; beat. Add ¾ c. sugar, 1 tbsp. at a time, beating until very stiff. Tint with red vegetable coloring. Divide into 6 equal portions and shape nests on heavy paper on cooky sheet; bake about 1 hr. at 250°. When done, place paper on a damp cloth and lift off nests. Let cool, fill with drained contents of a No. 2½ can of Libby's Fruit Cocktail.
Libby's
FRUIT COCKTAIL
Have you tasted Libby's?
100 FOODS, EACH THE FINEST OF ITS KIND
CORNED BEEF. The world's most popular brand, extra tender, extra flavorful. Try Libby's Corned Beef hot on French Toast with white sauce. To heat, first chill and slice; then fry or broil slices on one side only.
GRAPEFRUIT JUICE that's pressed from selected fresh fruit fully ripened in the sun. Marvelous flavor and all the natural vitamins and minerals. Tempting addition: Cubes of frozen ginger ale, or mint leaves.
KADOTA FIGS. Easy, different, and so good—cup cakes topped with whipped cream and quarters of Libby's Figs. Libby's are the Kadota variety, famous for flavor and tenderness. They are an ideal breakfast fruit.

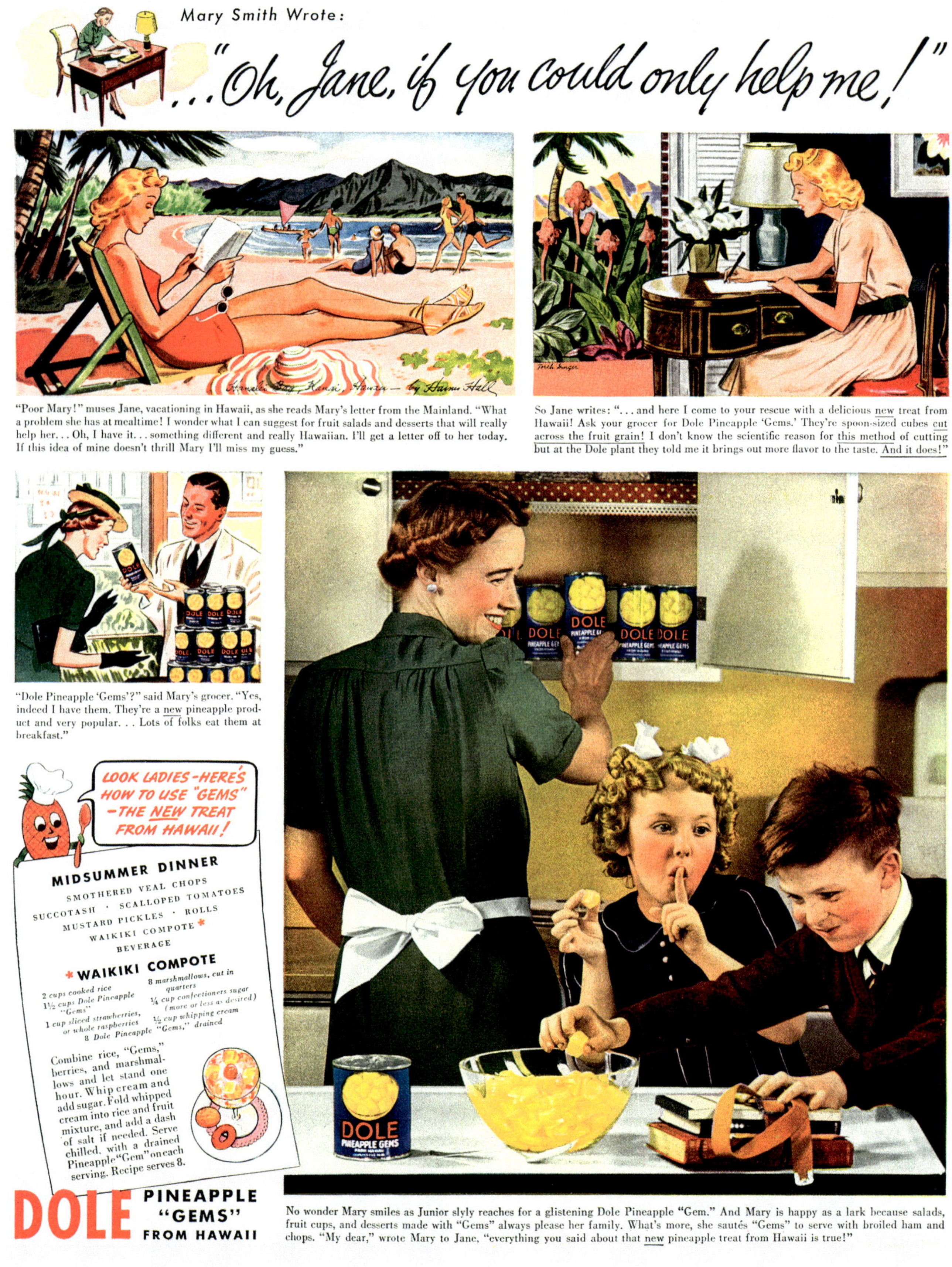

Dole Pineapple, 1939

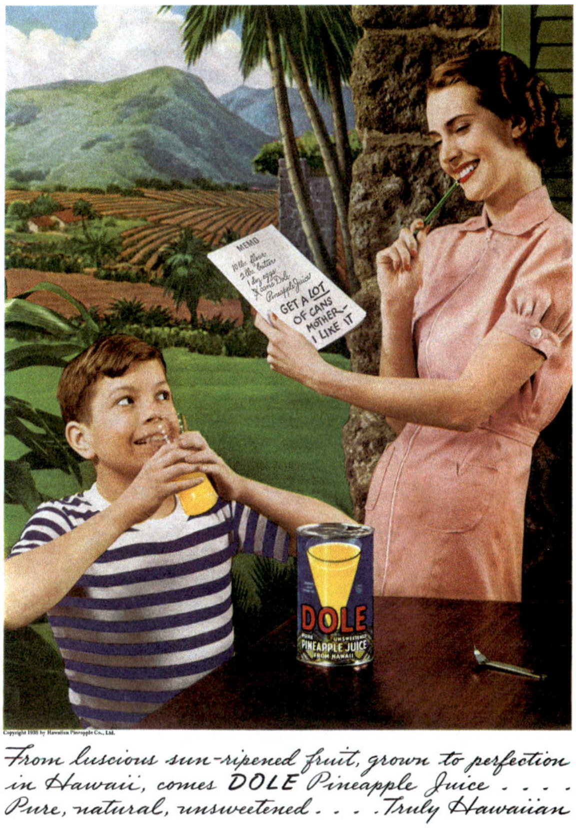

Dole Pineapple, 1938

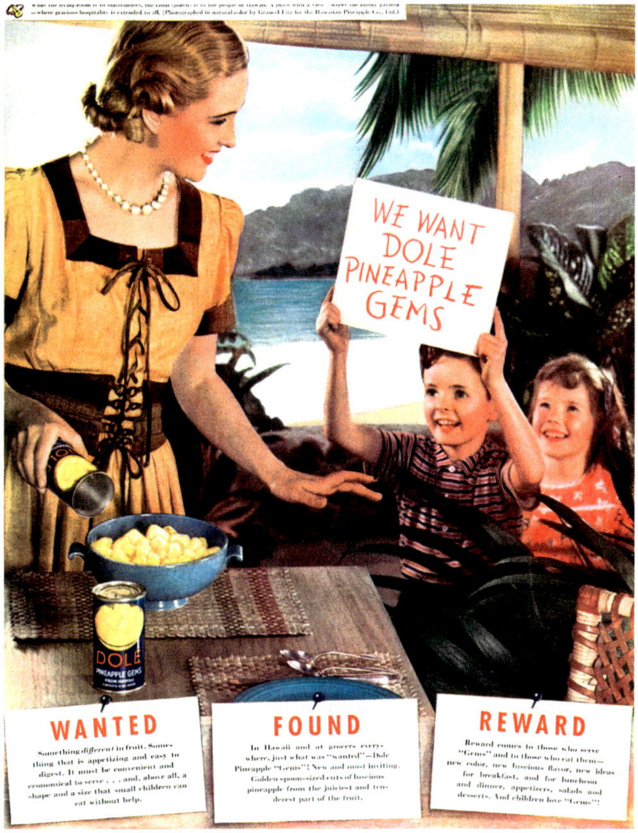

Dole Pineapple, 1931

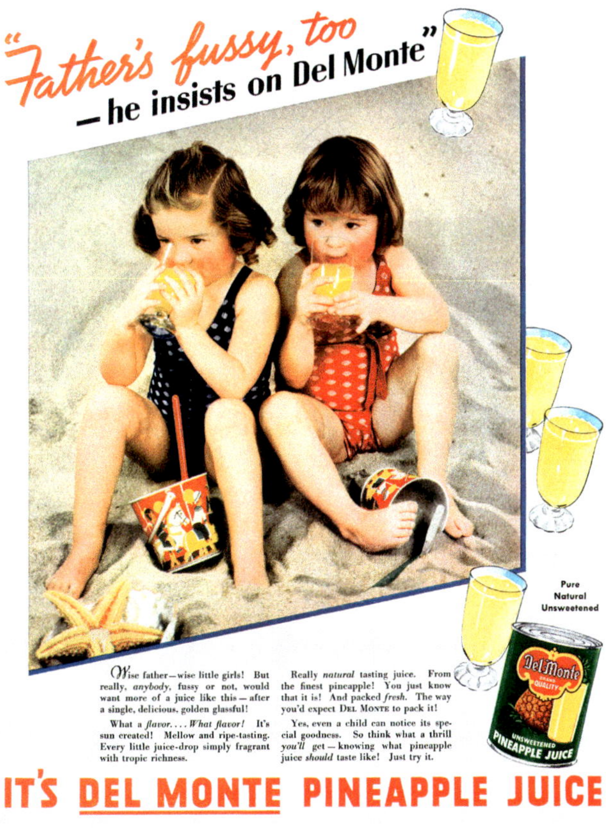

Del Monte, 1937

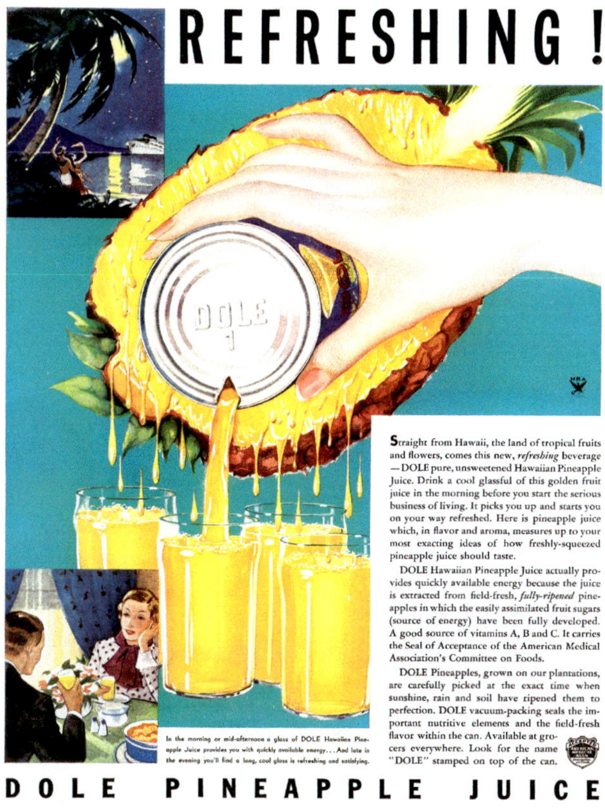

Dole Pineapple, 1934

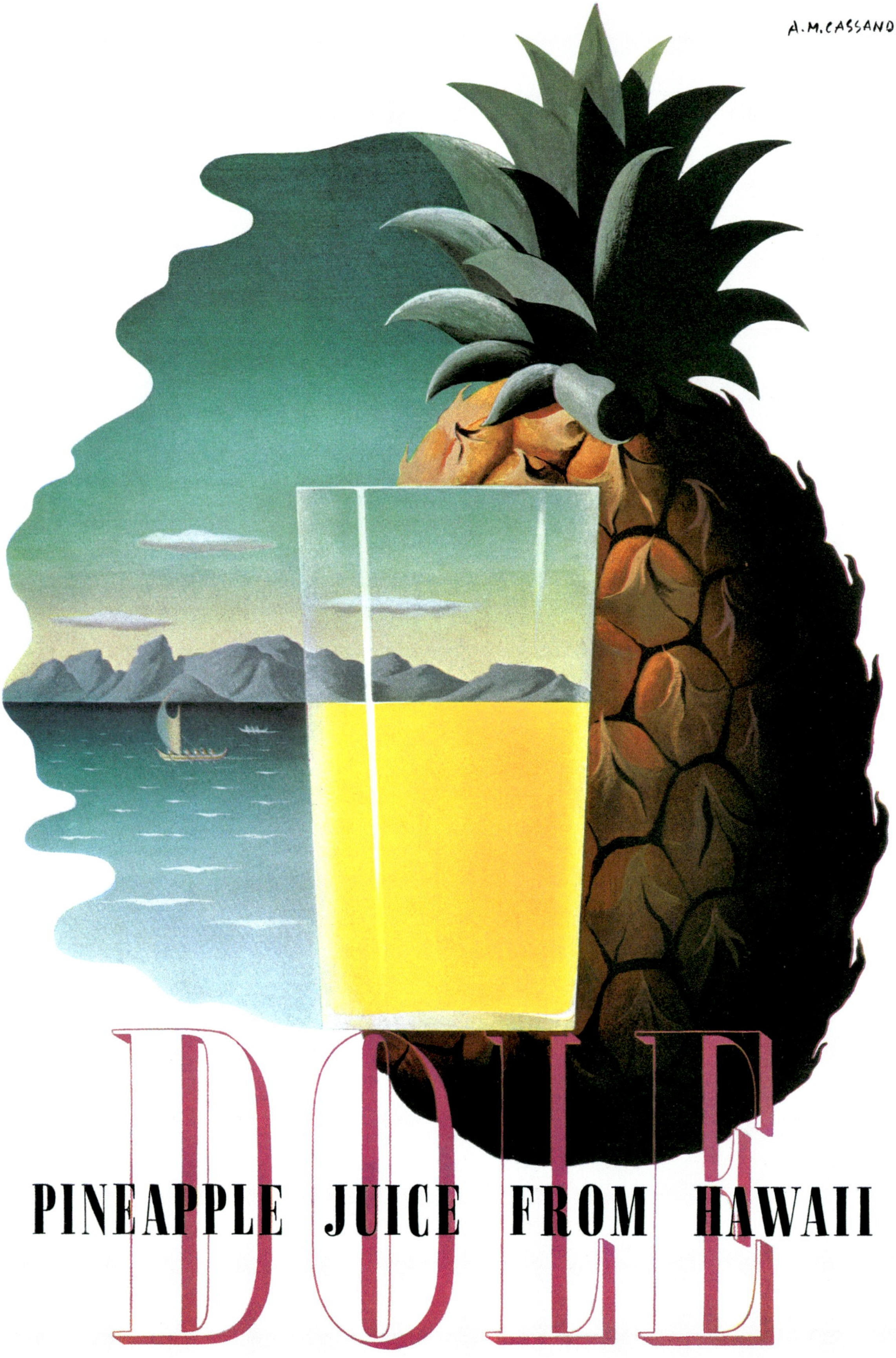

Dole Pineapple, 1937

▸ *Dole Pineapple, 1938*

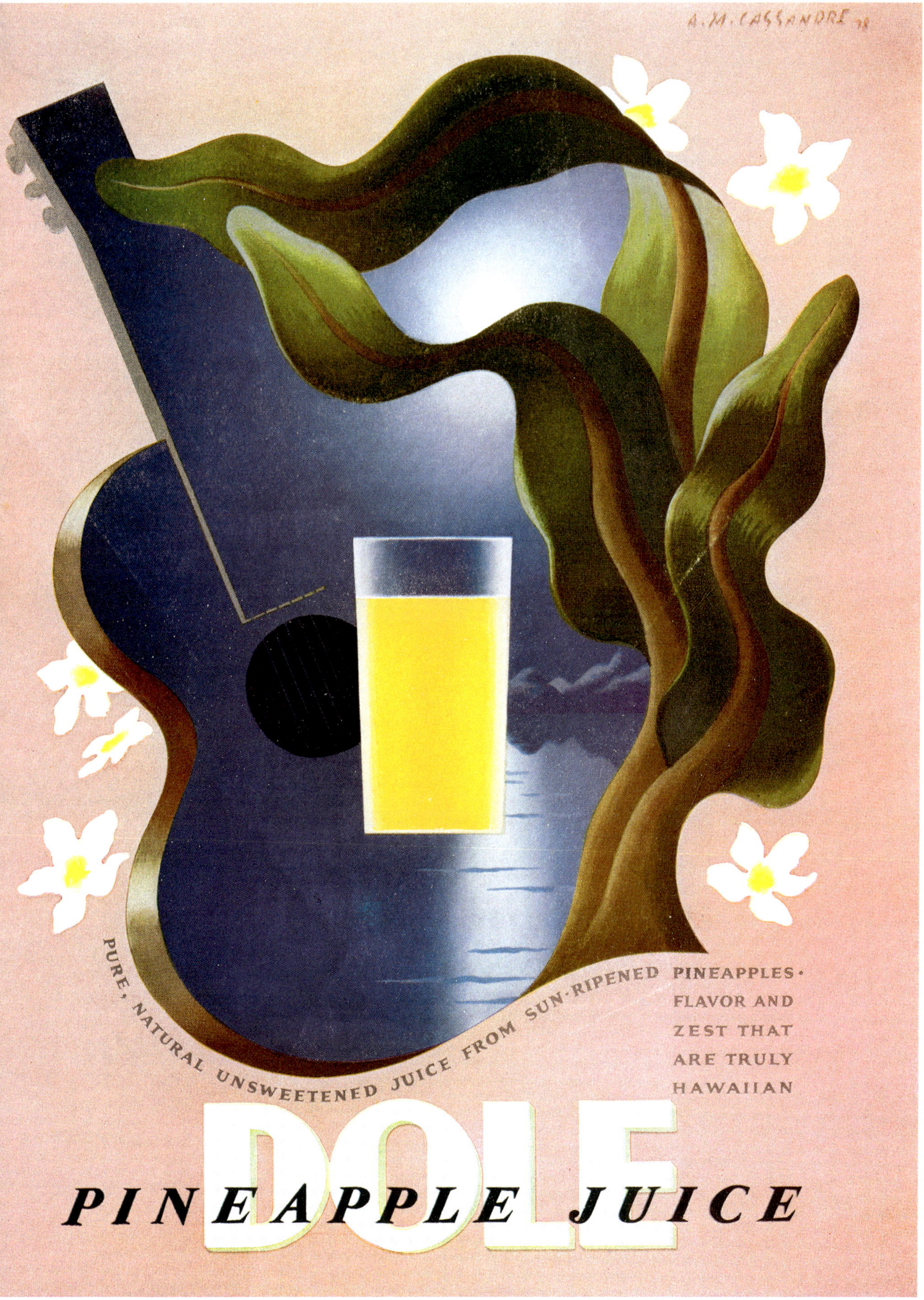
A.M. CASSANDRE 38
PURE, NATURAL UNSWEETENED JUICE FROM SUN-RIPENED PINEAPPLES·
FLAVOR AND ZEST THAT ARE TRULY HAWAIIAN
DOLE
PINEAPPLE JUICE

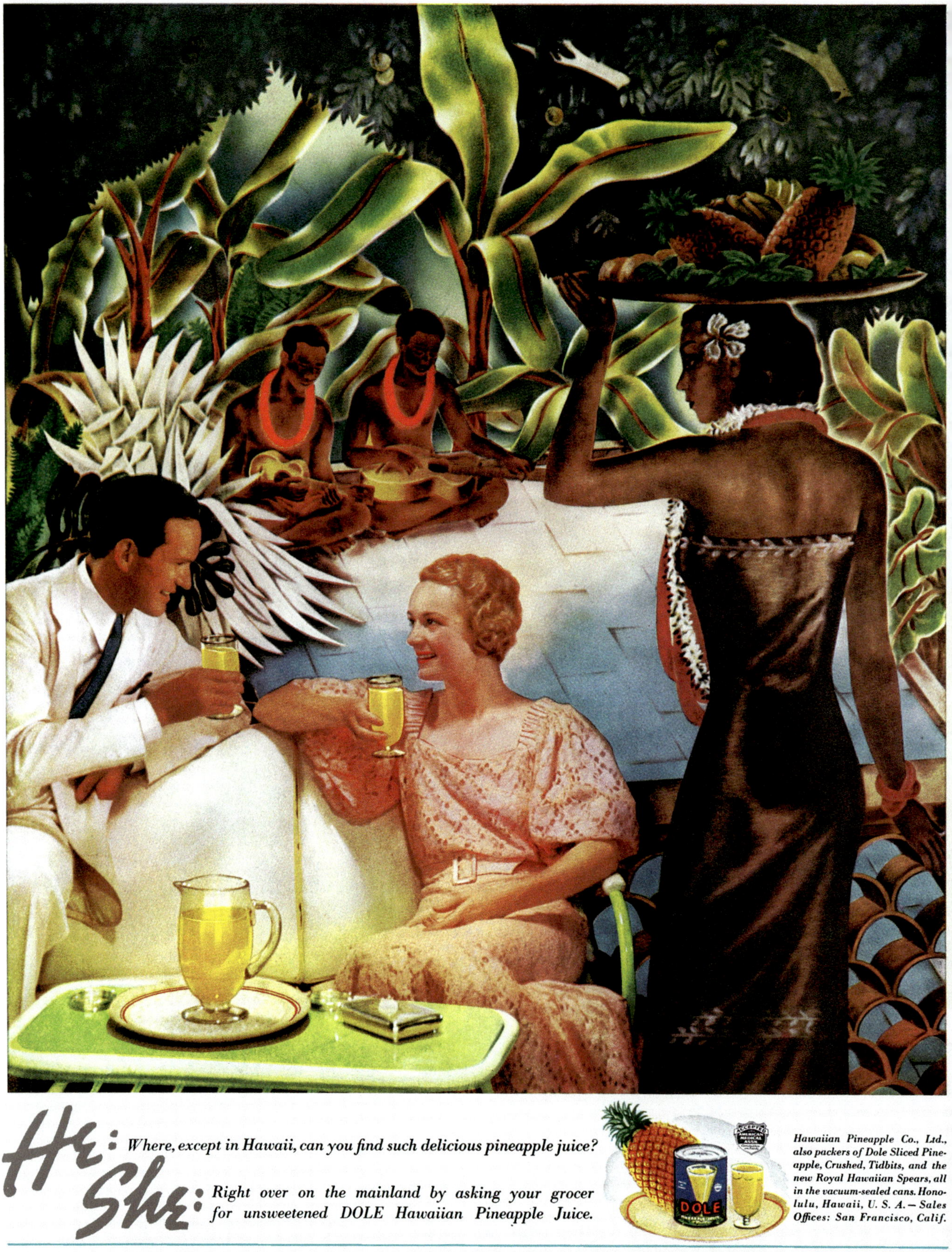

Dole Pineapple, 1937

▸ *Dole Pineapple, 1934*

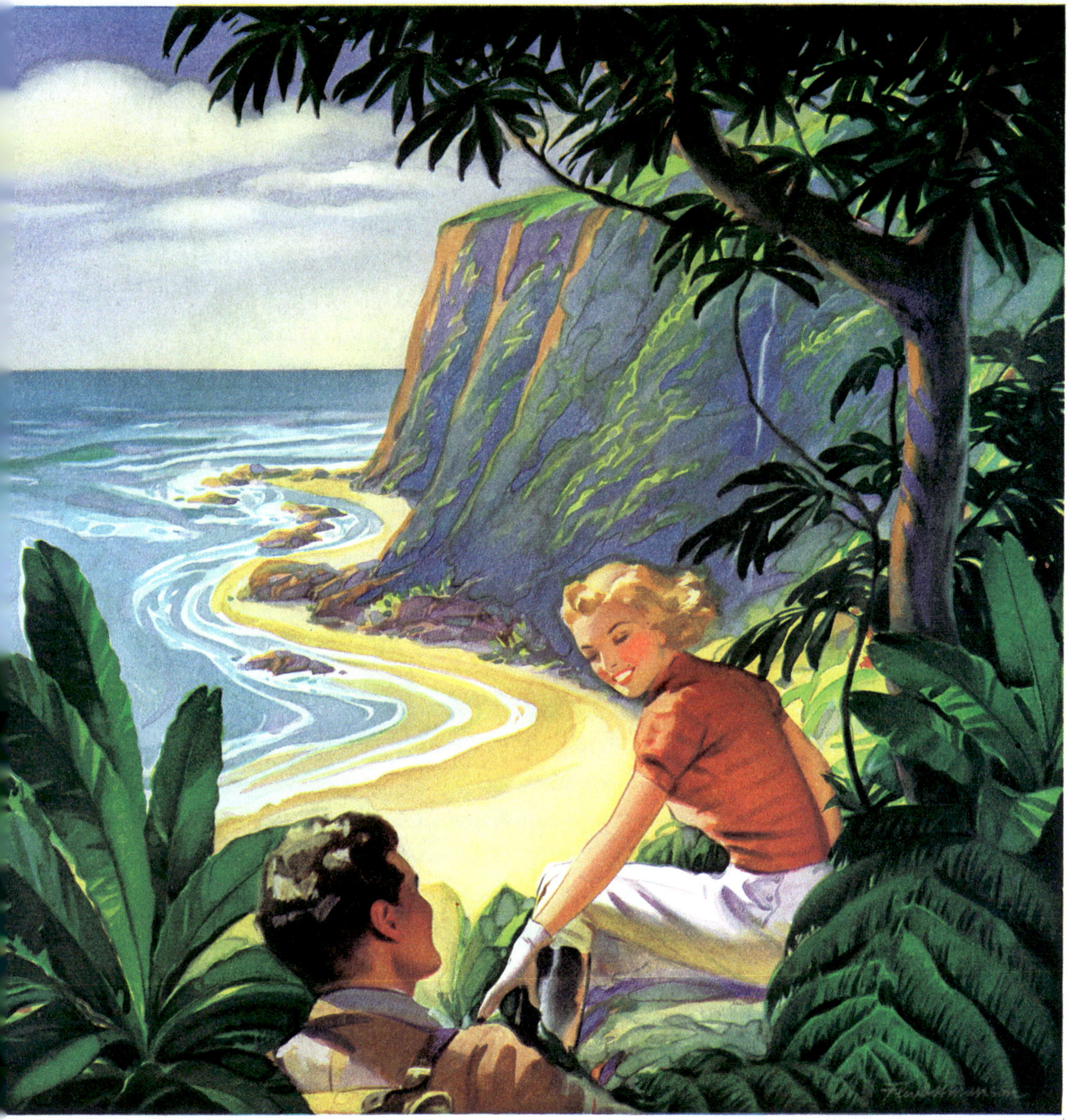

m these happy islands . . . a pure, golden juice to delight your taste

these incredibly beautiful islands of Hawaii ›d with the romance and joy of distant ages ‹'ll find that pure, unsweetened Hawaiian ›eapple Juice has long increased the delight living. The finest Hawaiian pineapples are LE-grown. In a modern plant, with every › in the juicing process rigidly controlled, pure, unsweetened juice is extracted from

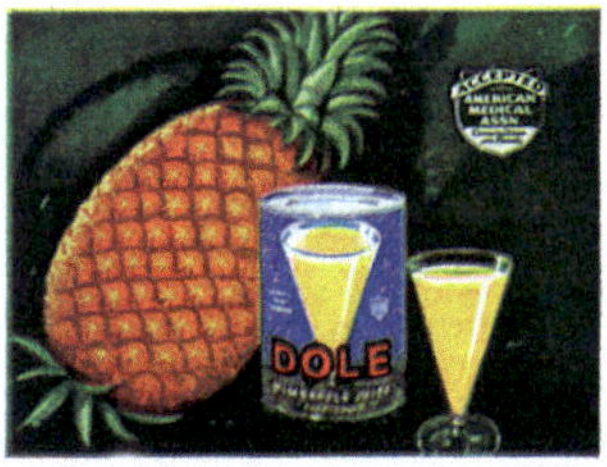

these luscious pineapples and swiftly vacuum-packed in sanitary cans for your protection. Lift your own glass of cool golden DOLE Pineapple Juice and say, as they do in the Islands, "Aloha Nui!"..."A Toast of Friendship and Delight"... A Toast of good cheer and refreshing goodness! Hawaiian Pineapple Co., Ltd., Honolulu, Hawaii. Sales Offices: 215 Market Street, San Francisco.

OLE PINEAPPLE JUICE

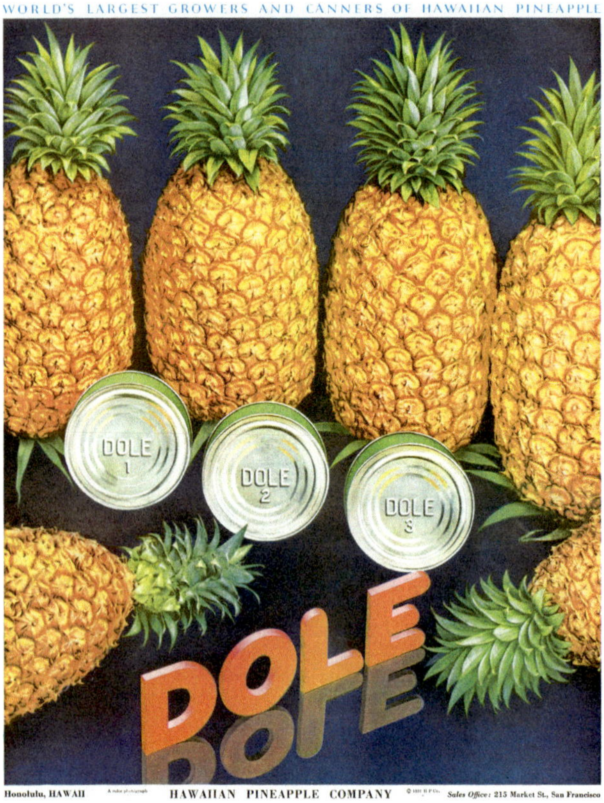

Dole Pineapple, 1939

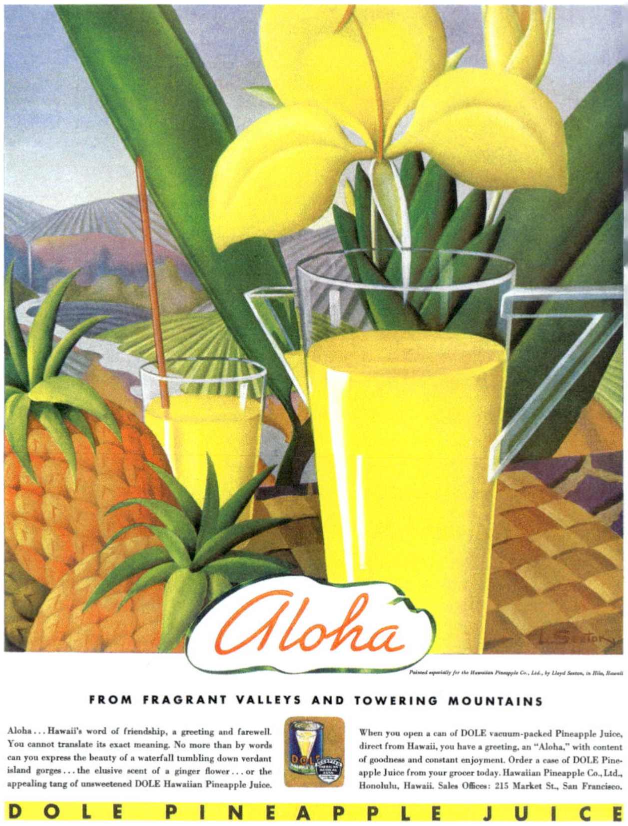

Dole Pineapple, 1935

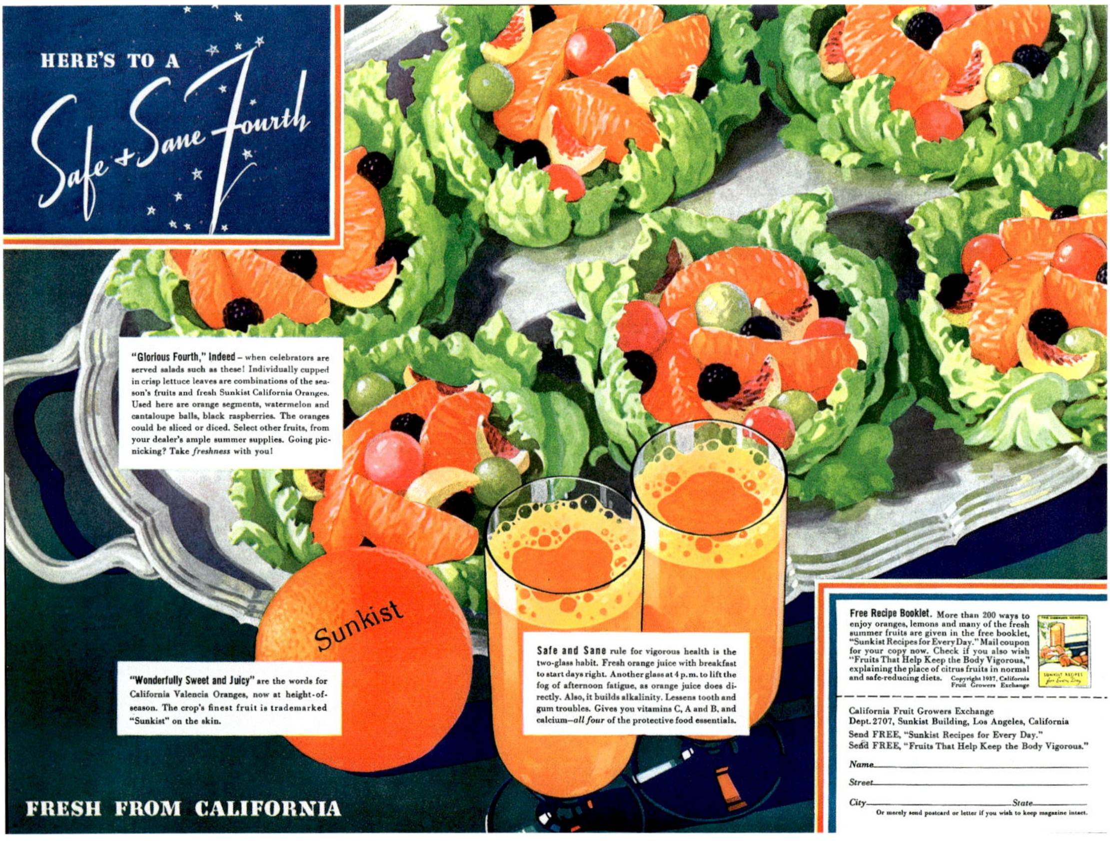

Sunkist Oranges, 1937

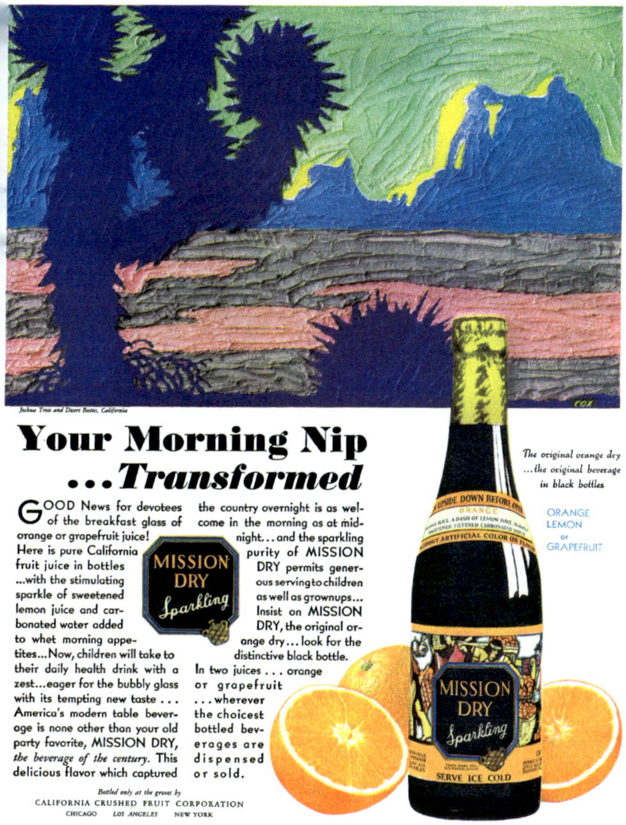

Mission Dry, 1930

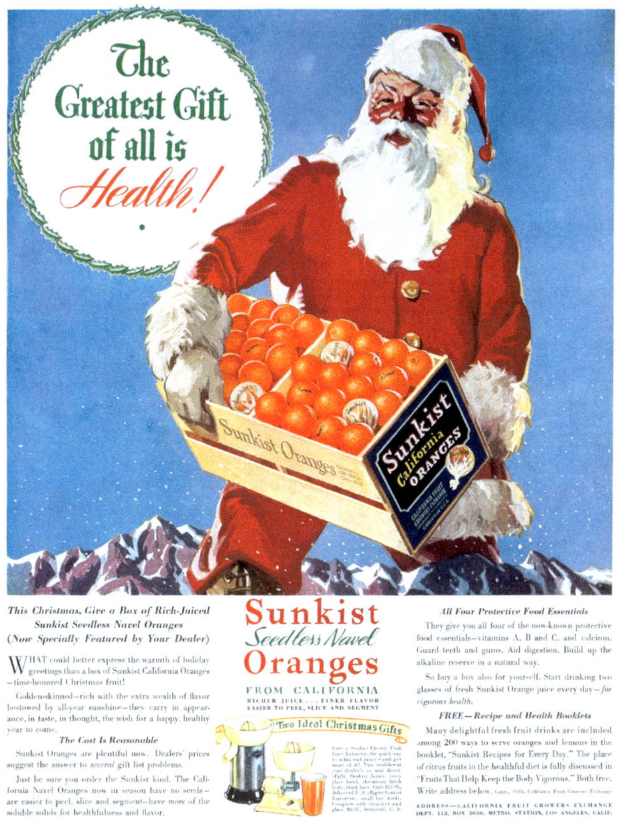

Sunkist Oranges, 1935

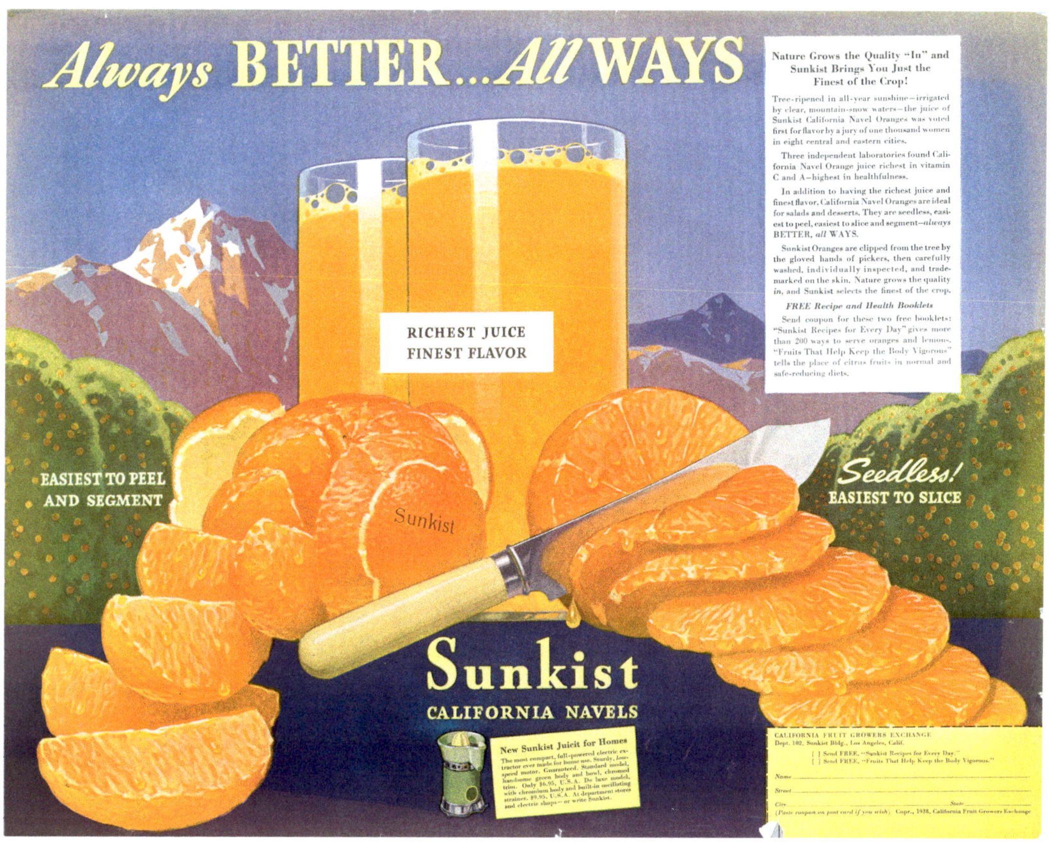

Sunkist Oranges, 1938

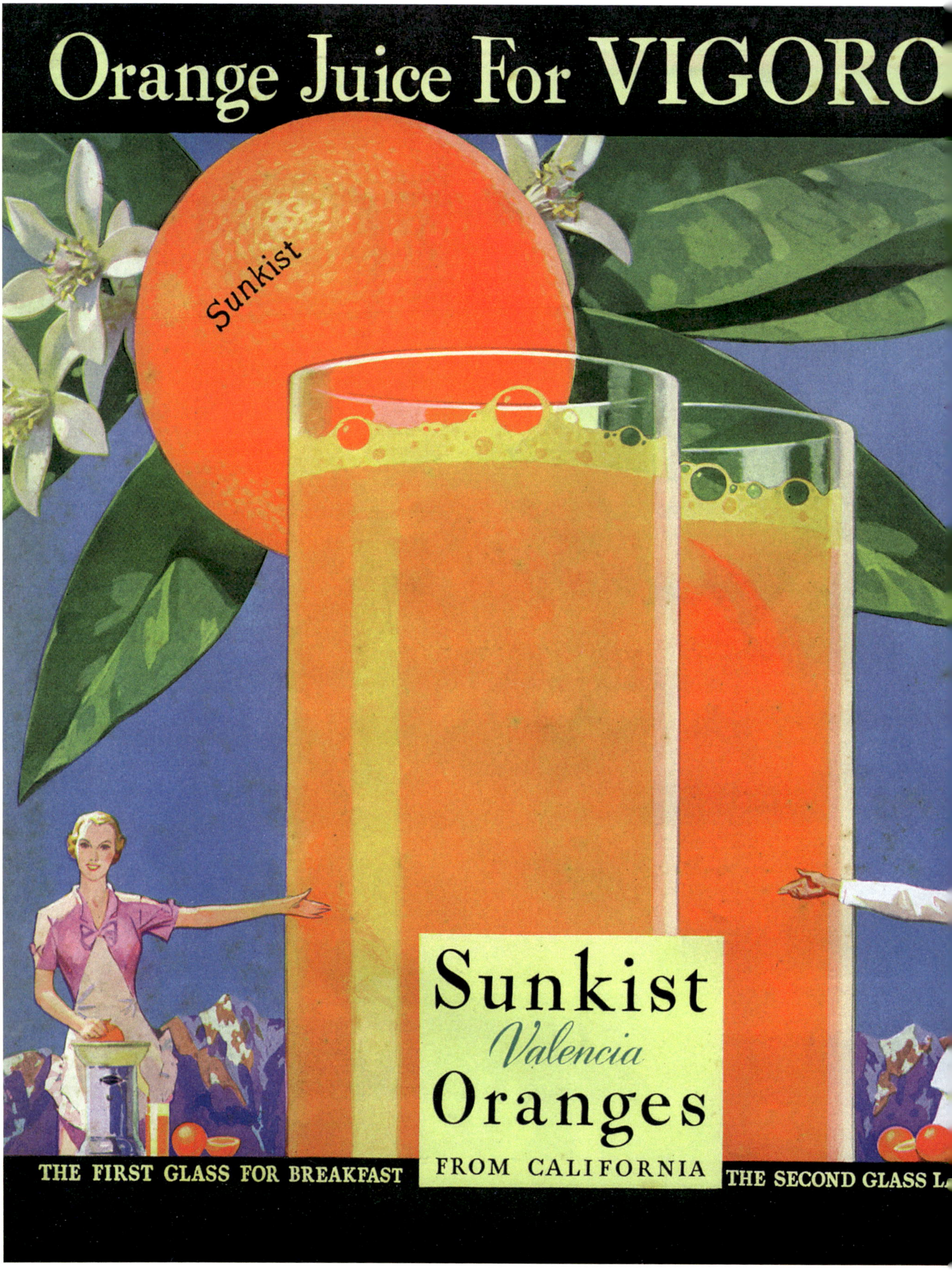

Sunkist Oranges, 1935

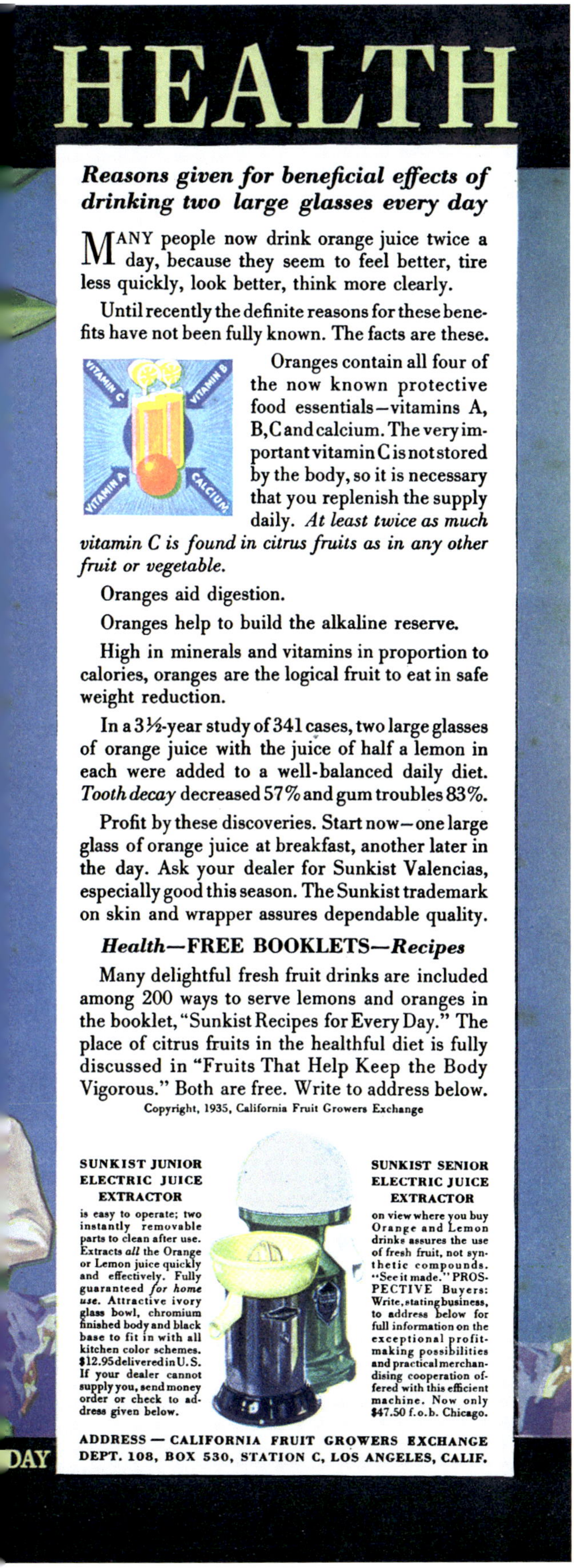

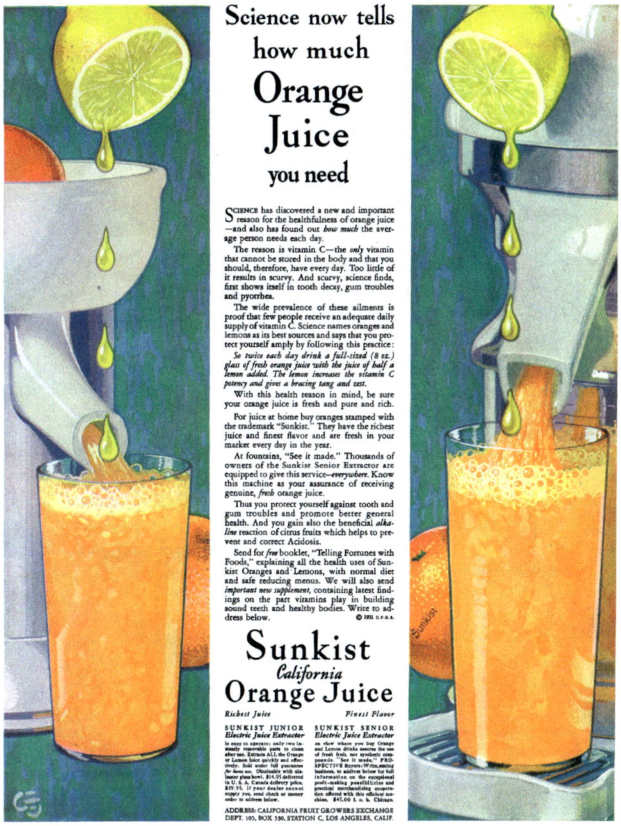

Sunkist Orange Juice, 1931

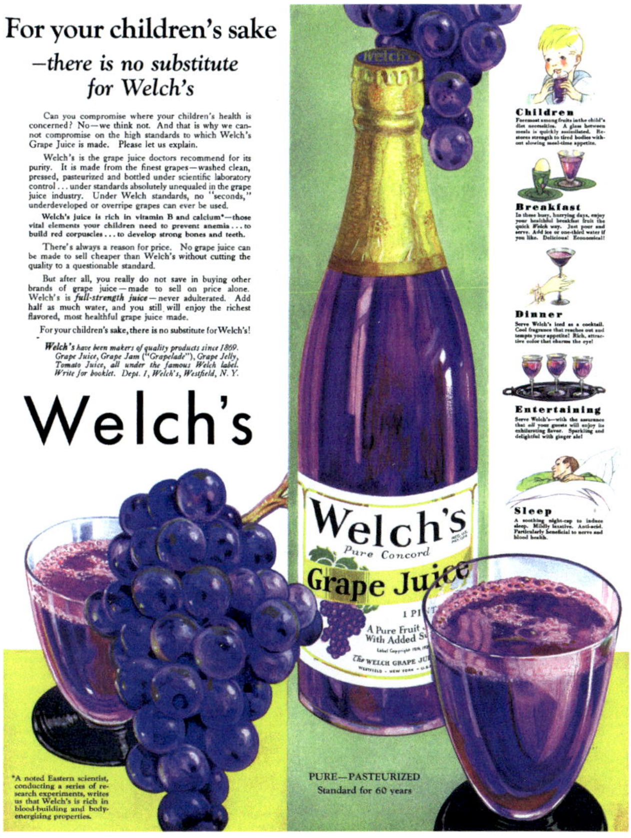

Welch's Grape Juice, 1932

Golly, Mis' Mari

FOLKS JUS' CAN'T HELP HAVIN' A FRIENDLY FEELIN' FOR DIS HEAH COFFEE!

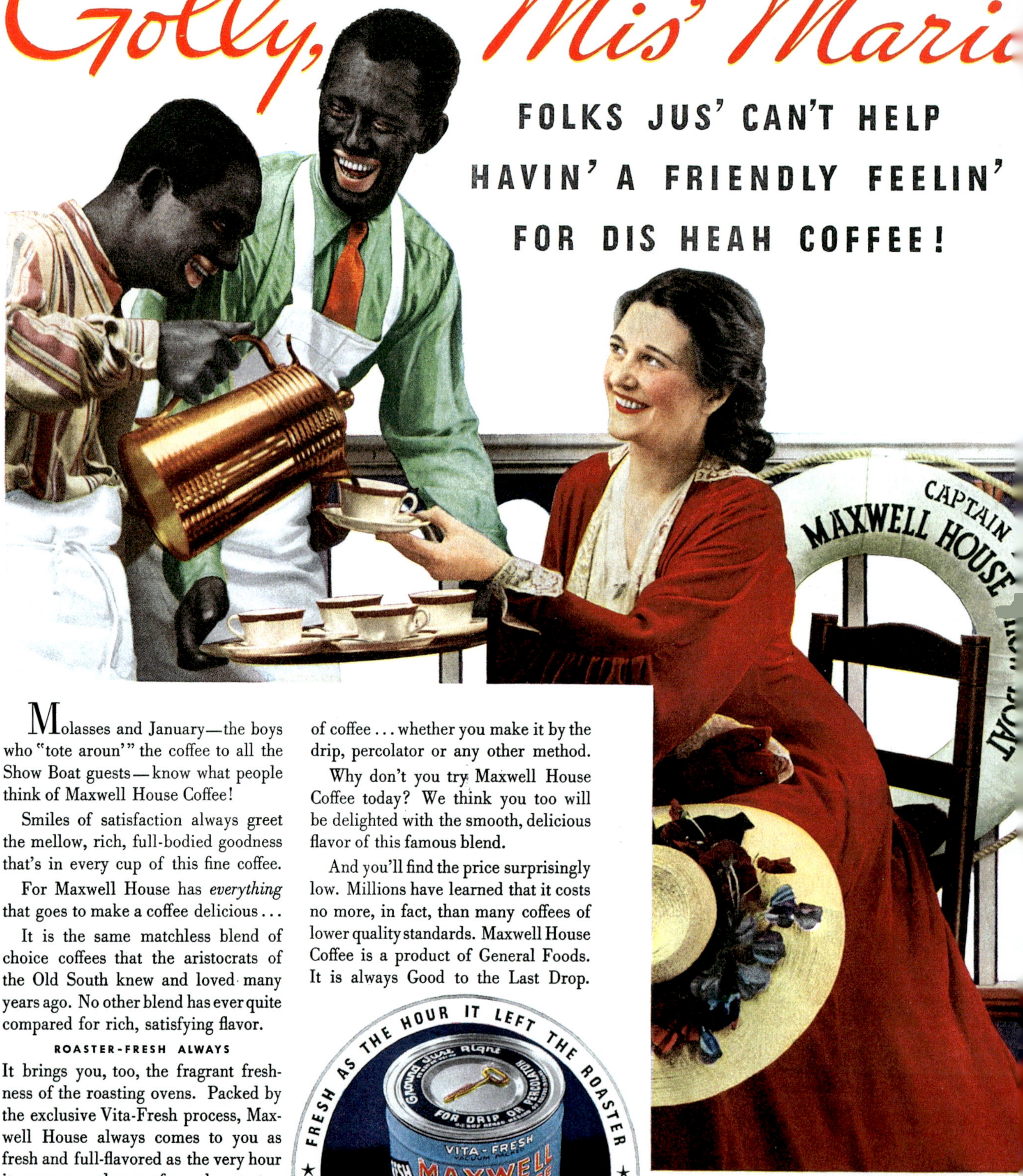

Molasses and January—the boys who "tote aroun'" the coffee to all the Show Boat guests—know what people think of Maxwell House Coffee!

Smiles of satisfaction always greet the mellow, rich, full-bodied goodness that's in every cup of this fine coffee.

For Maxwell House has *everything* that goes to make a coffee delicious...

It is the same matchless blend of choice coffees that the aristocrats of the Old South knew and loved many years ago. No other blend has ever quite compared for rich, satisfying flavor.

ROASTER-FRESH ALWAYS

It brings you, too, the fragrant freshness of the roasting ovens. Packed by the exclusive Vita-Fresh process, Maxwell House always comes to you as fresh and full-flavored as the very hour it was scooped warm from the roaster. And no coffee can be fresher than that!

And it is ground by a newly developed process that assures you perfect uniformity and delicious flavor in every cup of coffee... whether you make it by the drip, percolator or any other method.

Why don't you try Maxwell House Coffee today? We think you too will be delighted with the smooth, delicious flavor of this famous blend.

And you'll find the price surprisingly low. Millions have learned that it costs no more, in fact, than many coffees of lower quality standards. Maxwell House Coffee is a product of General Foods. It is always Good to the Last Drop.

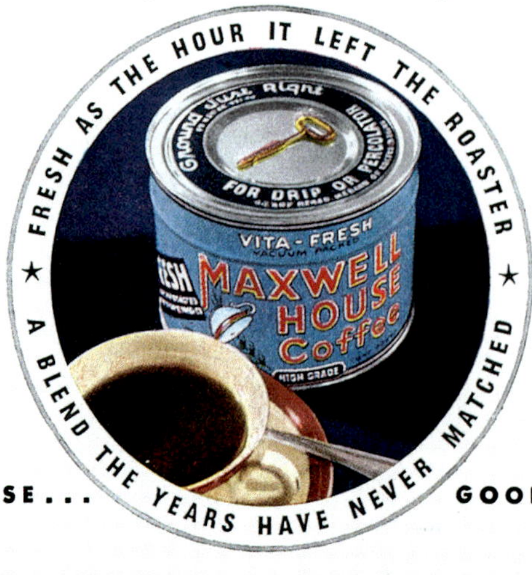

MOLASSES AND JANUARY stop their fun-making long enough to "another cup of coffee" for Maria, Captain Henry's sister. Hear stars of the Maxwell House Show Boat—one of radio's greatest sh every Thursday night. Hear, also, the lovely voices of Lanny Ross, A Hanshaw, Conrad Thibault and Mary Lou, and the glorious music Voorhees and his Show Boat Band. A full hour of gorgeous enterta —every Thursday night! N.B.C. Coast-to-Coast hook-up. ©G.F.Co

MAXWELL HOUSE... GOOD TO THE LAST DROP

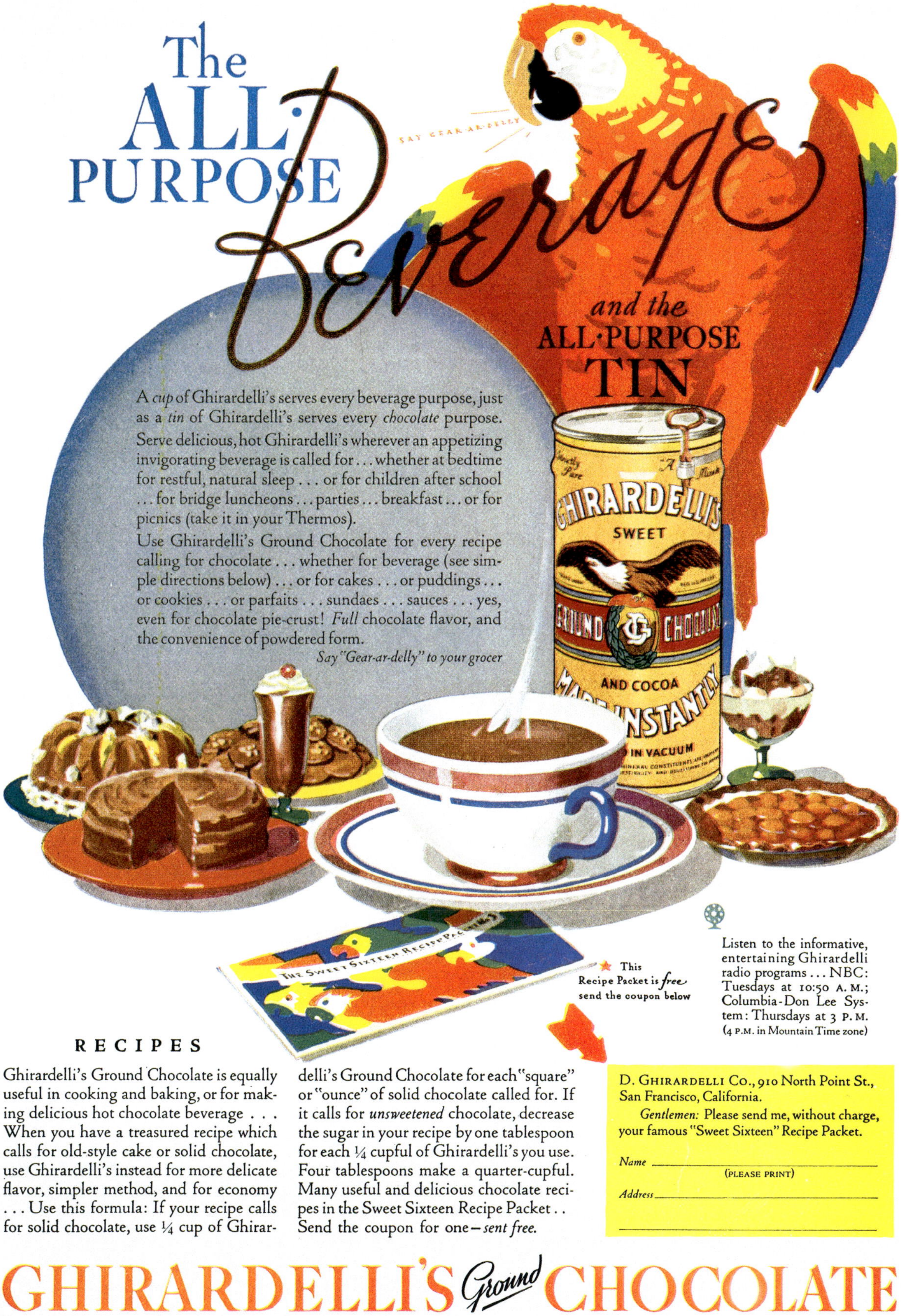

Ghirardelli's Chocolate, 1932

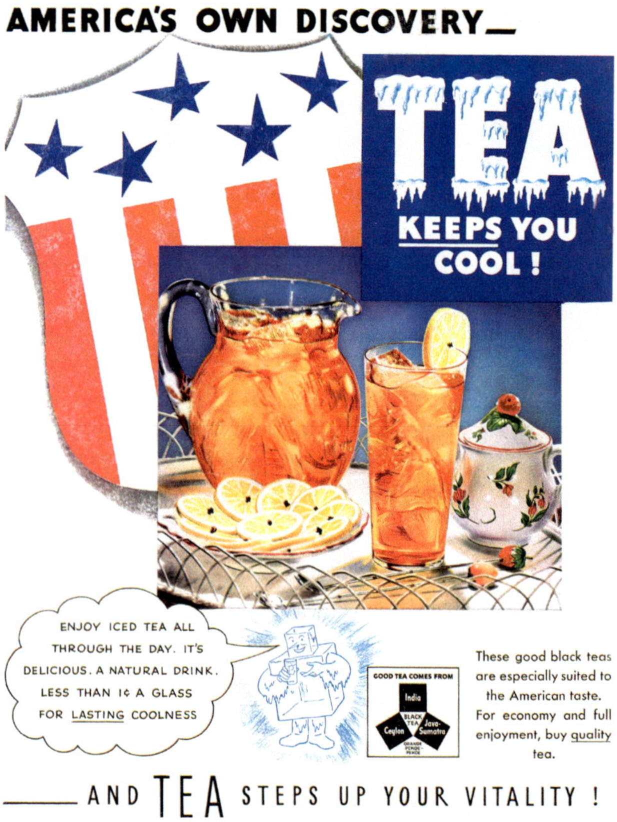

Tea, 1938

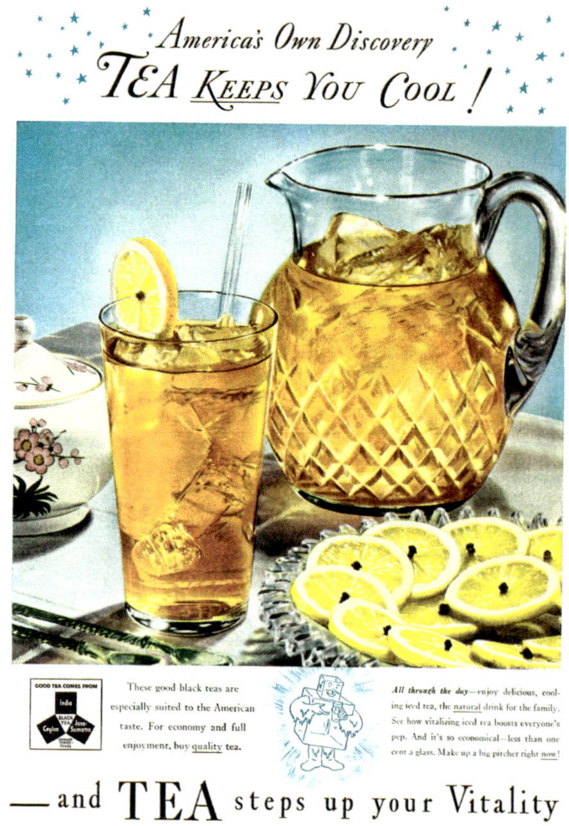

Tea, 1938

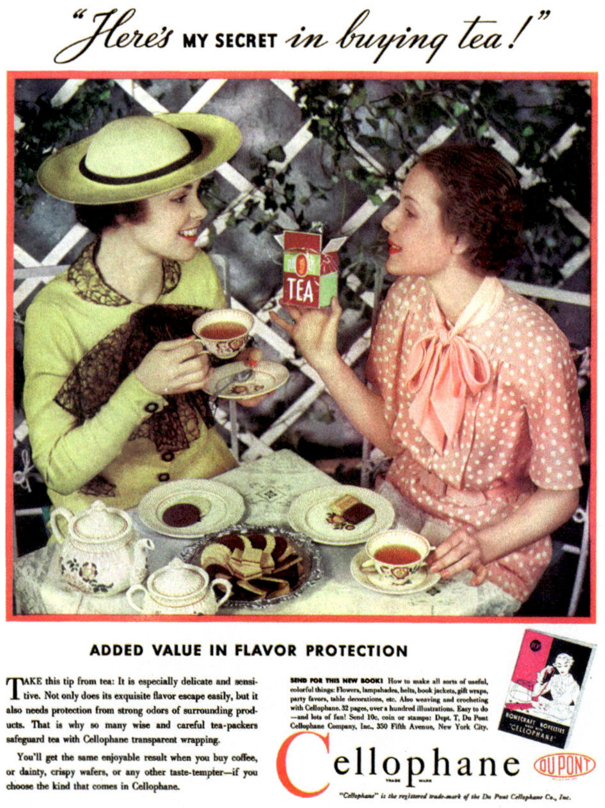

Cellophane, 1935

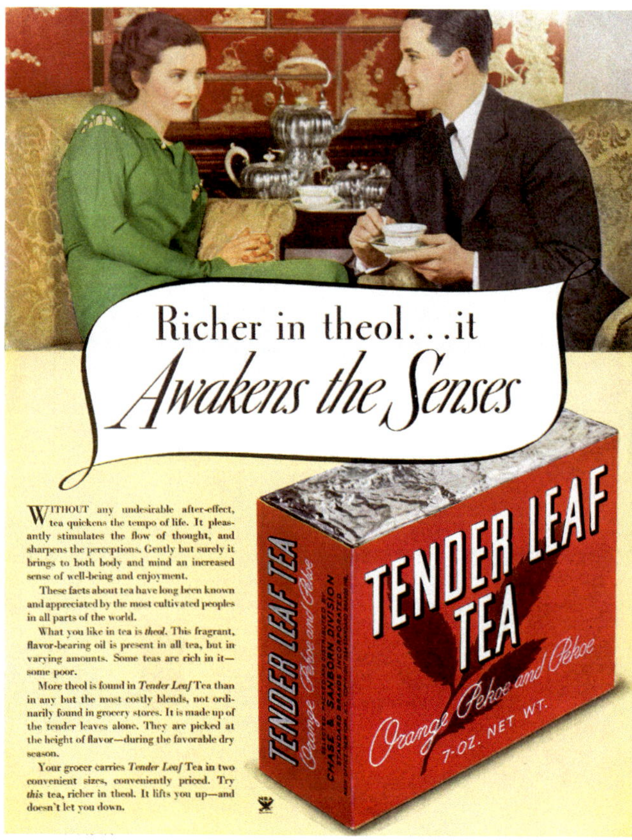

Tender Leaf Tea, 1934

▸ Lipton's Tea, 1938

ho says it's the world's greatest tea?

VHEN anything is said to be "the world's greatest," it should stand ıdy to defend that title.

Lipton's presents the following evidence support its reputation as "the world's ɔst delicious tea."

• • •

One indication that Lipton's must be ırticularly good is the fact that it has ɛ largest sale in the world. *It's an ıtstanding favorite with the men and ɔmen of America—and of six other eat tea-loving nations.*

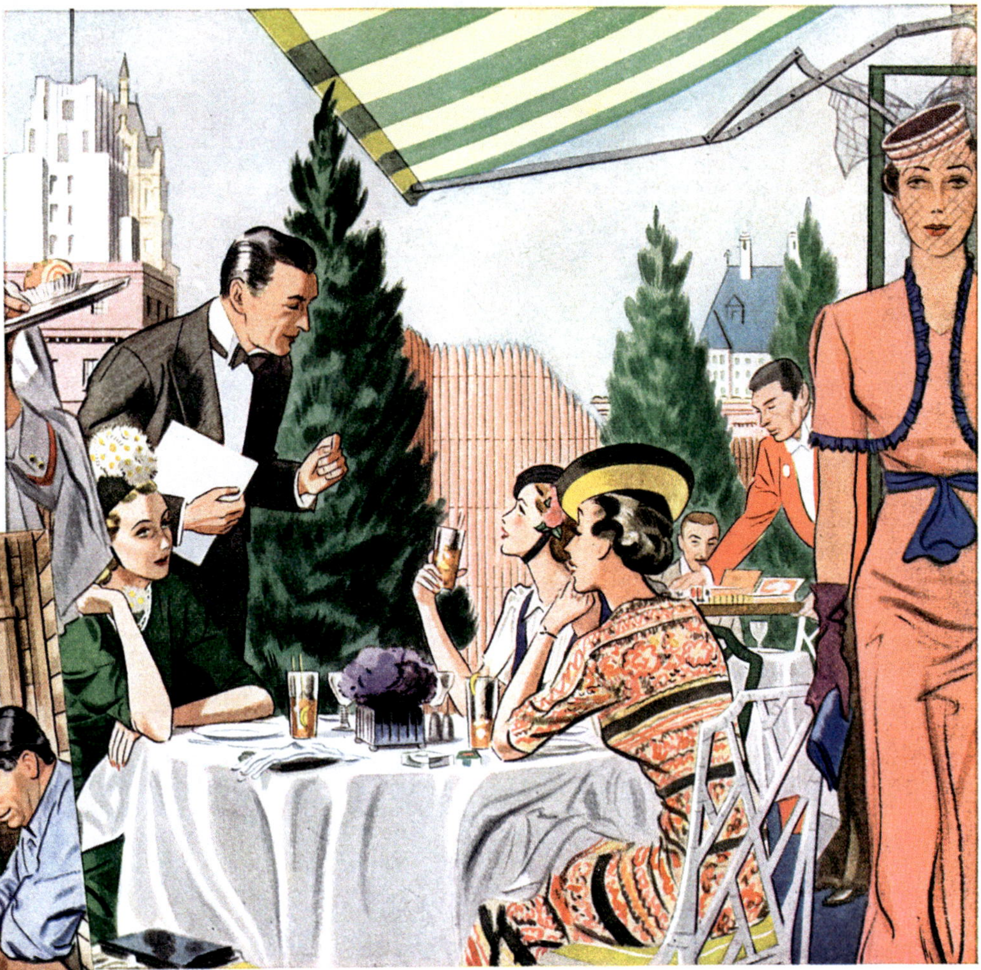

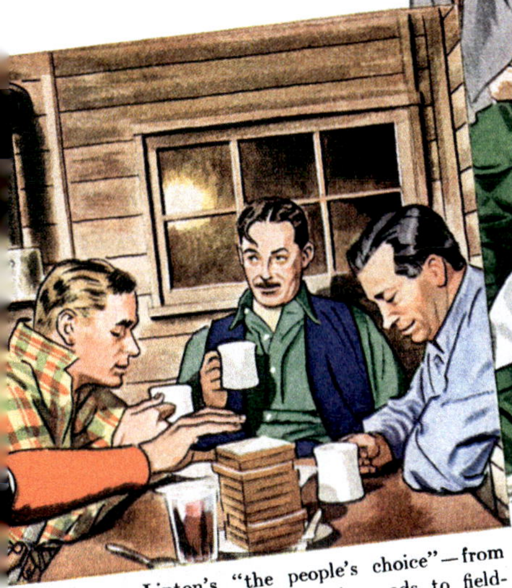

1. Not only is Lipton's "the people's choice"—from lumberjacks in the Canadian north woods to field-workers "down under" in Australia—but it is a tea upon which royal honors have been bestowed.

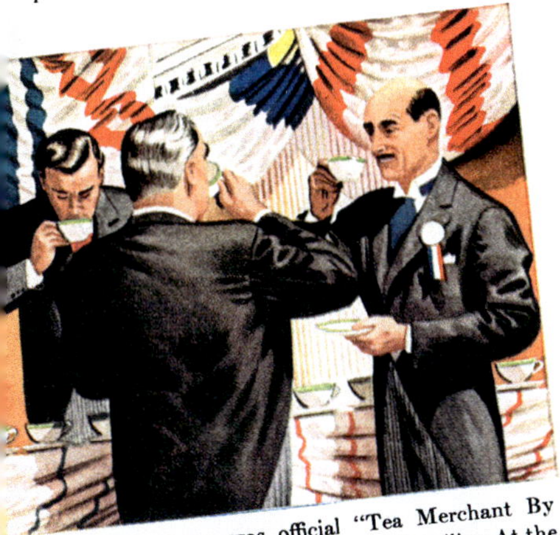

2. Sir Thomas Lipton was official "Tea Merchant By Appointment" to three different Royal Families. At the Tea Exposition of Ceylon and India, the tea from Lipton's own gardens was awarded the Gold Medal as the "Choicest Tea Grown." Lipton's Tea has carried off top honors at five great World's Fairs!

LIPTON'S TEA

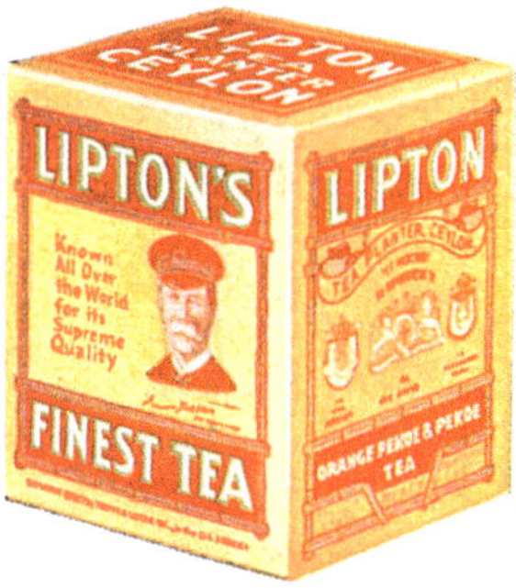

3. But the most convincing evidence is to be found in the cup of Lipton's you make for yourself. As the boiling water releases the enticing aroma...as you look into the clear tempting color . . . as that incomparable flavor warms you and delights you . . . you will say "This *is* the finest tea I've ever tasted!"

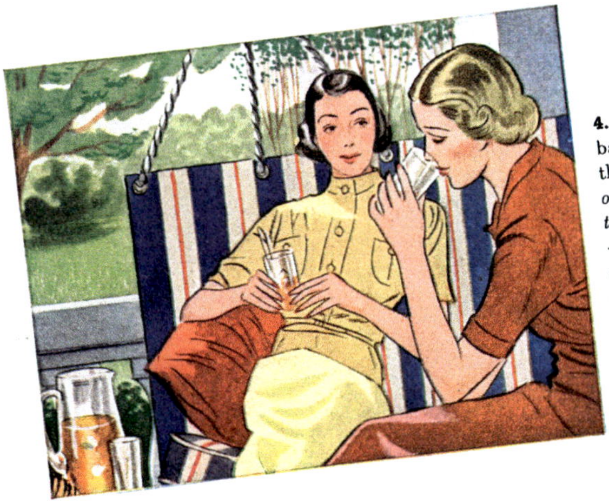

4. Price? Fortunately, it is no barrier to *your* enjoyment of this grand tea. Anyone, *everyone*, can afford the best, because *tea—even a tea as fine as Lipton's tea—costs less than any other beverage except water!* Order a package of Lipton's Tea from your grocer today.

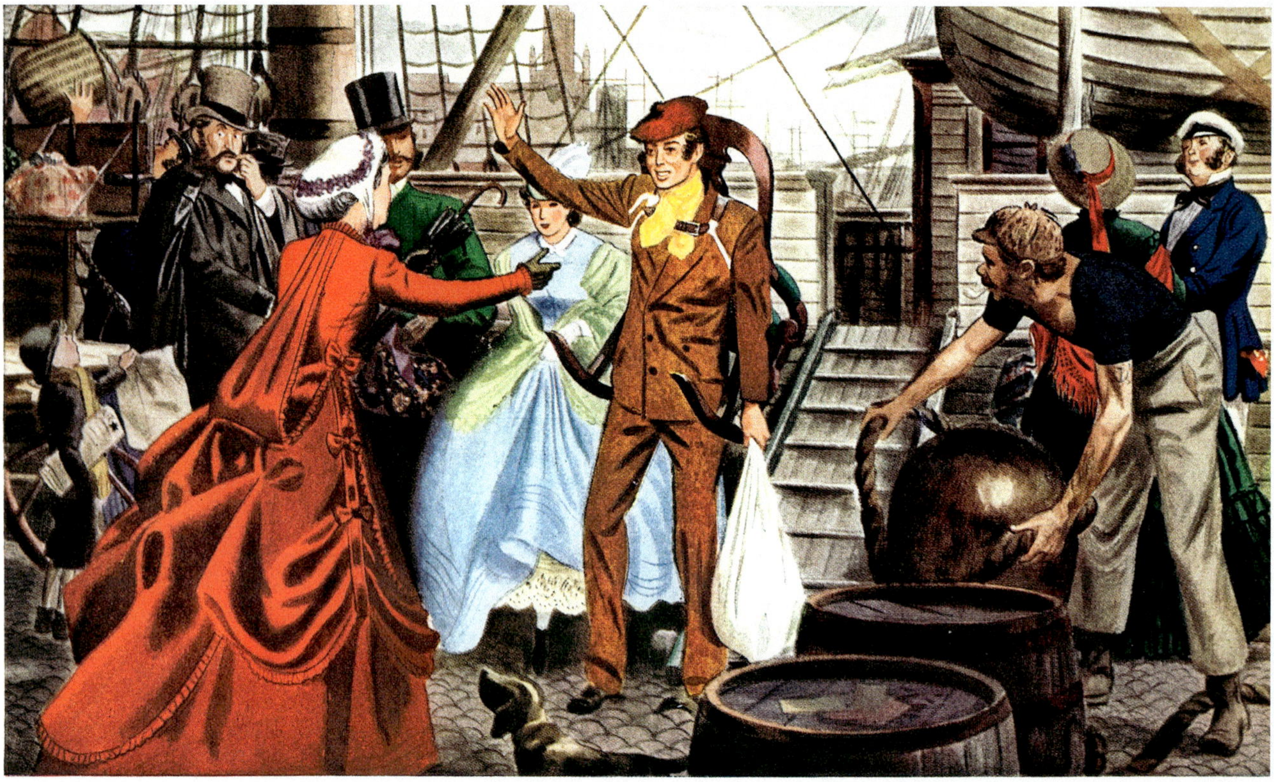

With £100, a sack of flour, and a rocking chair

DID YOU know that the famous Sir Thomas Lipton—international sportsman and "Tea Merchant By Appointment" to three different Royal Families—began life without title or fortune?

. . .

Born in Glasgow of Irish parents, he came to America at 17, had jobs in Virginia and New Orleans. When he went home to start a business of his own, he had a hundred pounds in money, a sack of flour, and a rocking chair for his mother.

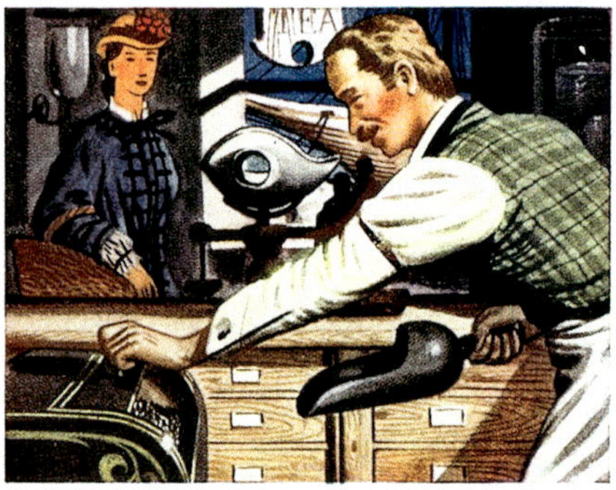

1. The young merchant with the up-and-coming American ideas soon had a chain of fine provision shops. He sent to America for bacon, to Denmark for butter. And every time he opened the black-and-gold tea canisters, he wondered where to go for finer tea.

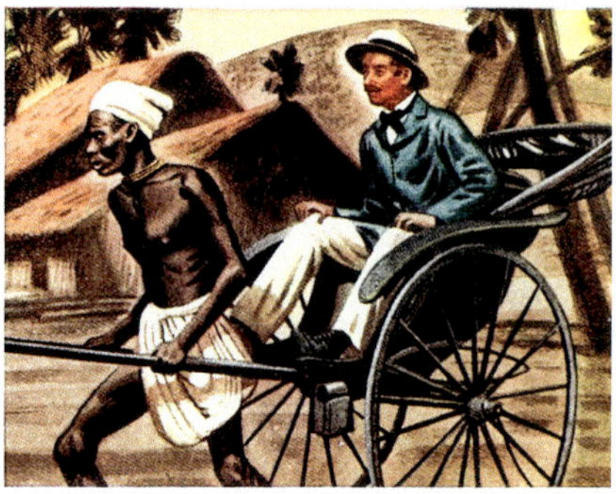

2. At last he found that finer tea. It grew up in the hills on the Isle of Ceylon, and it had a remarkably rich, deeper flavor—an unmatched aroma. Straightway, he bought plantations on those remote plateaus, began the scientific cultivation of tea.

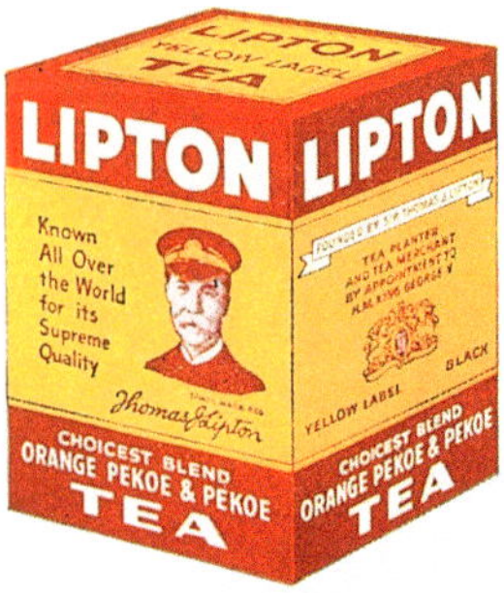

—"PEPS YOU UP!"

LIPTON'S TEA

3. With superb varieties from his own gardens as a basis, the eager planter perfected the blend to which he gave his name. Lipton's Tea won medals at five World Fairs; today it is the favorite of seven nations—including ours.

A luxury? Yes!—*but not in price!* No beverage except water costs as little as tea . . . even tea as fine as Lipton's! So get a package today. Pour freshly boiling water over the delicate aromatic leaves. Steep three to five minutes. Then taste the most delicious and reviving drink that Nature offers! Tea at its wonderful best—Lipton's Tea.

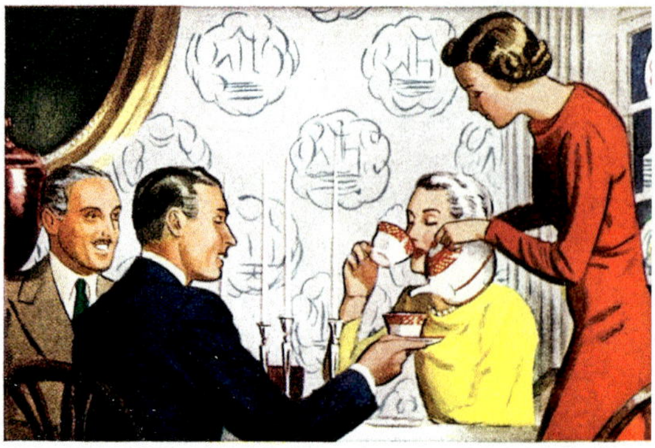

Lipton's Tea, 1939

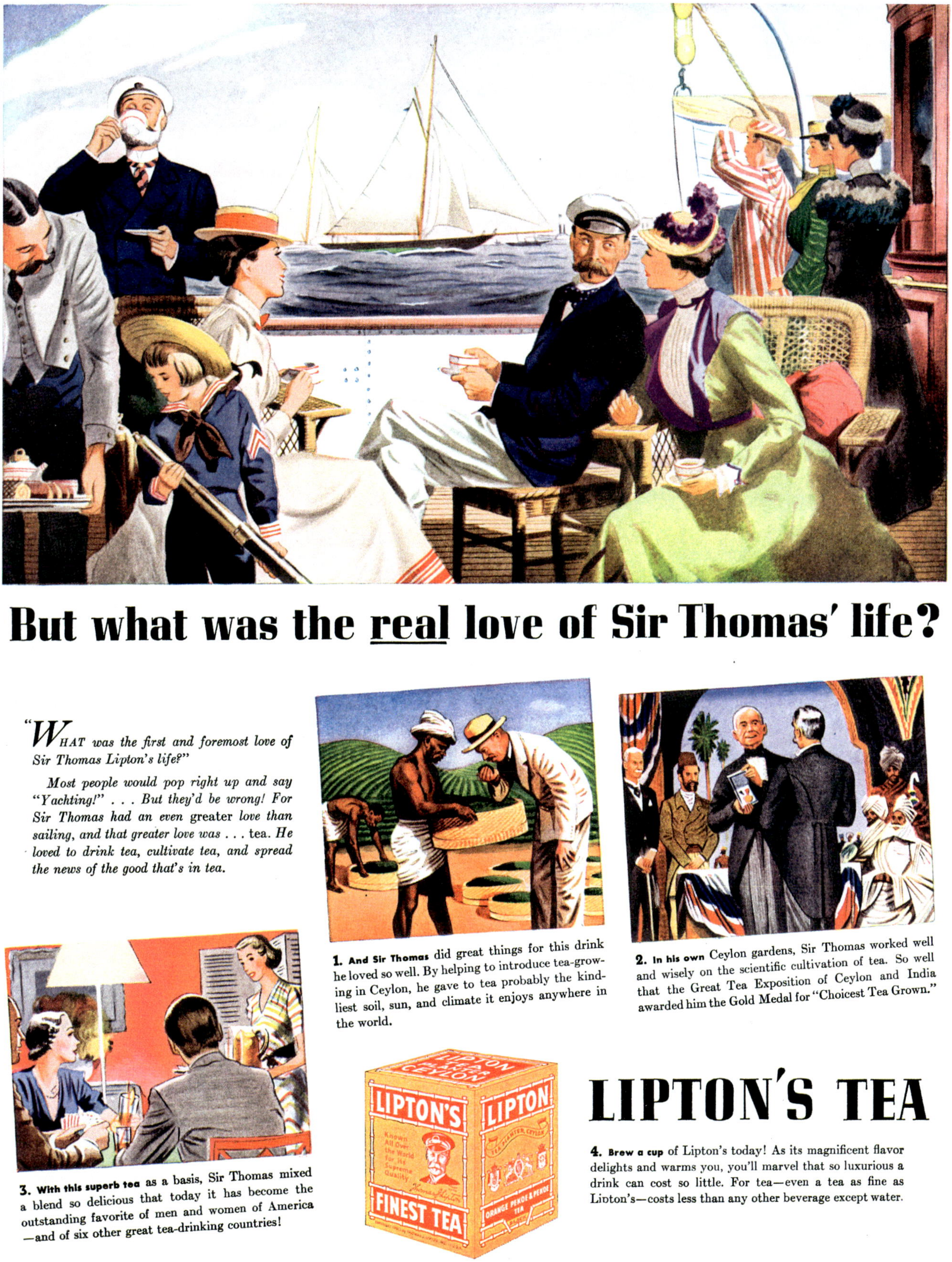

Lipton's Tea, 1938

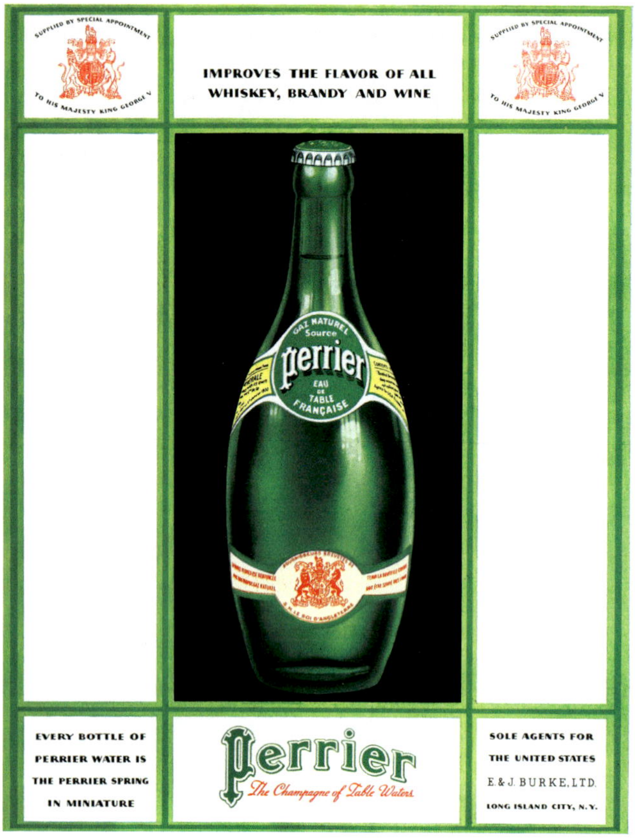

Perrier, 1934

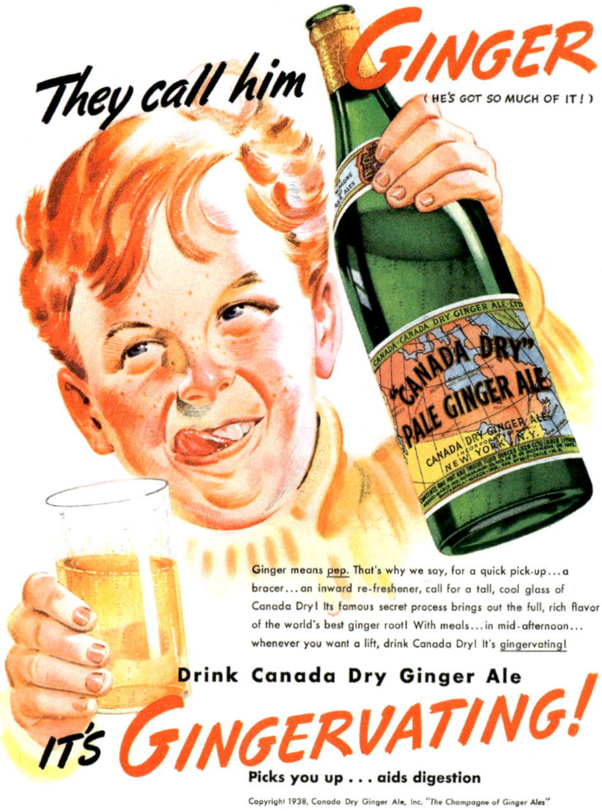

Canada Dry Ginger Ale, 1938

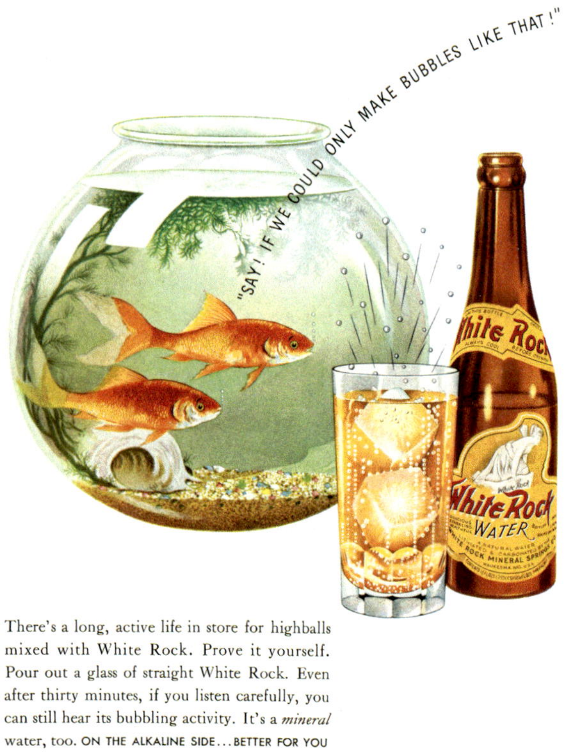

White Rock Water, 1938

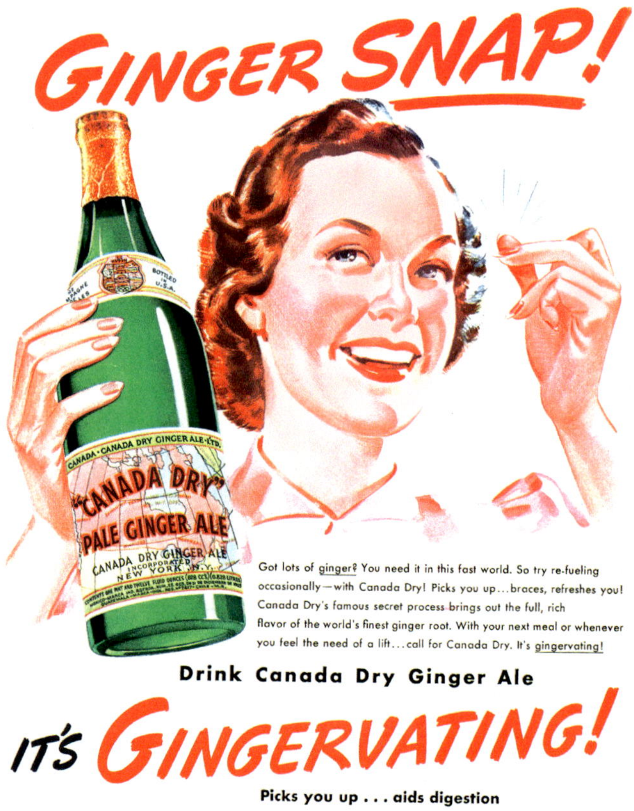

Canada Dry Ginger Ale, 1939

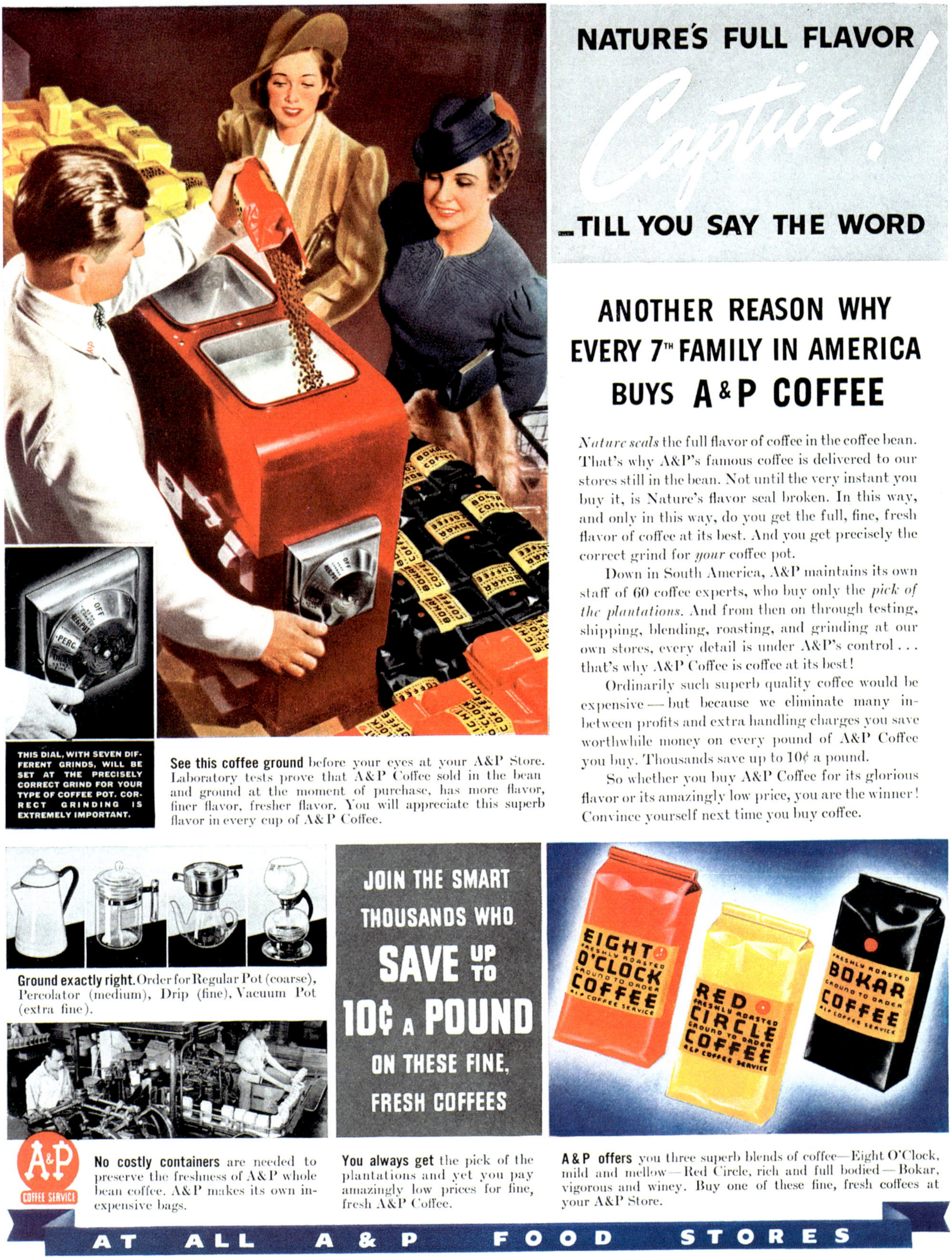

A&P Coffee, 1939

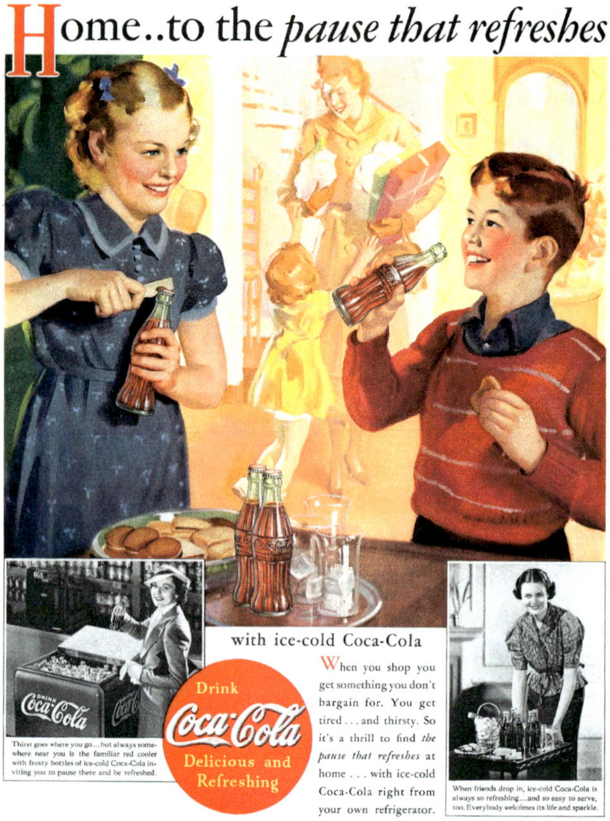

Coca-Cola, 1937

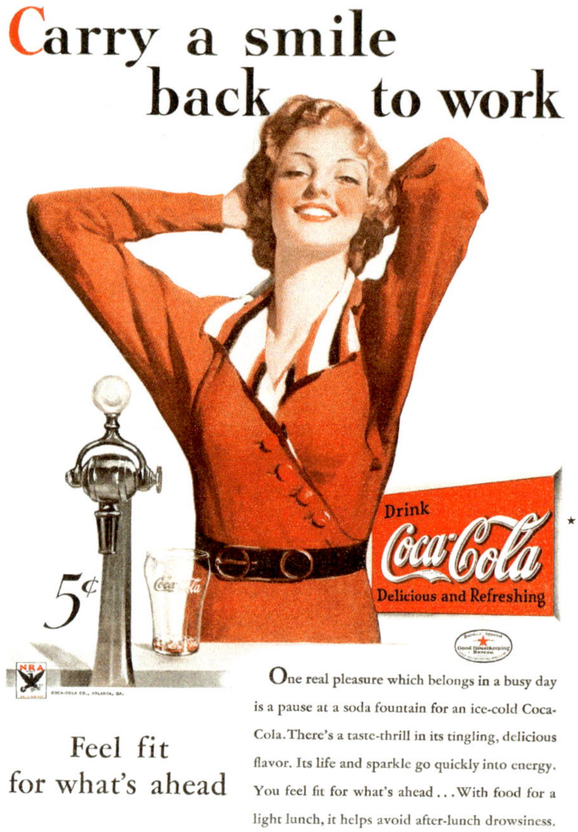

Coca-Cola, 1934

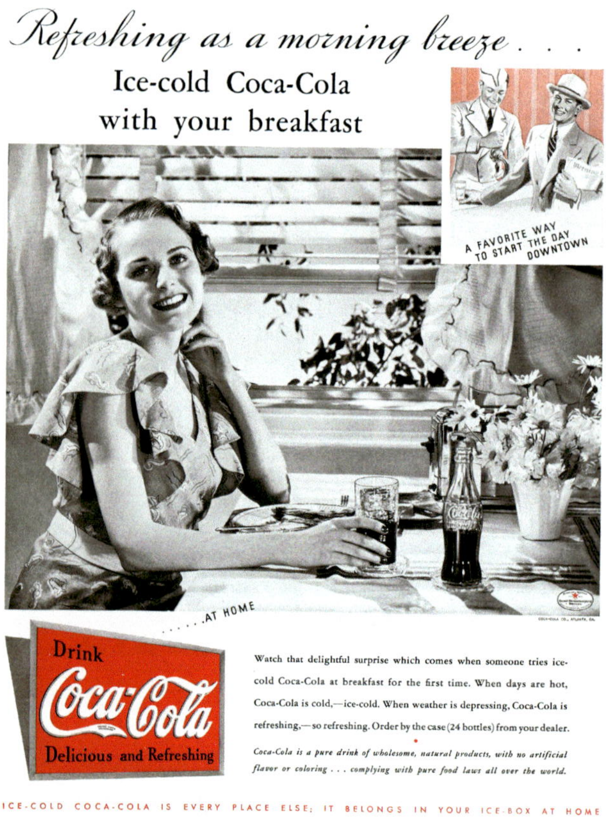

Coca-Cola, 1935

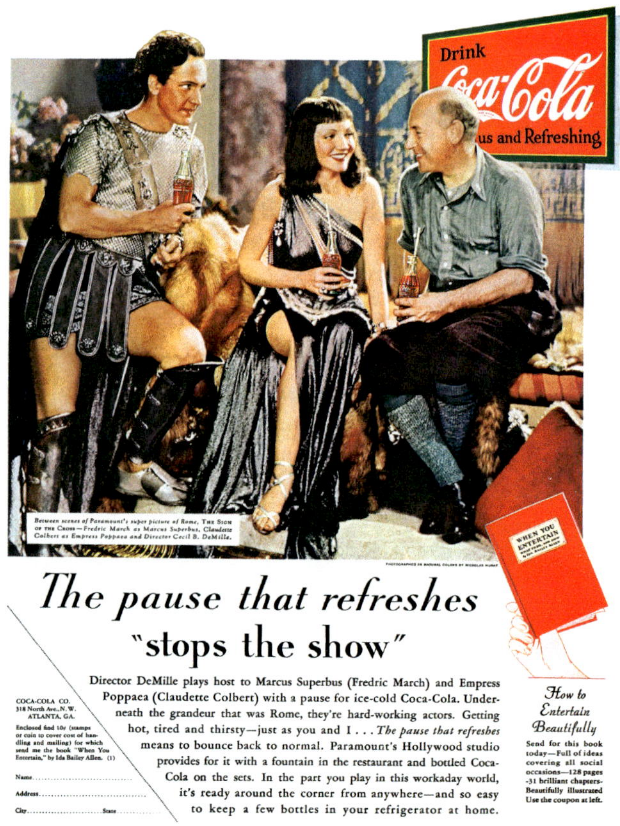

Coca-Cola, 1933

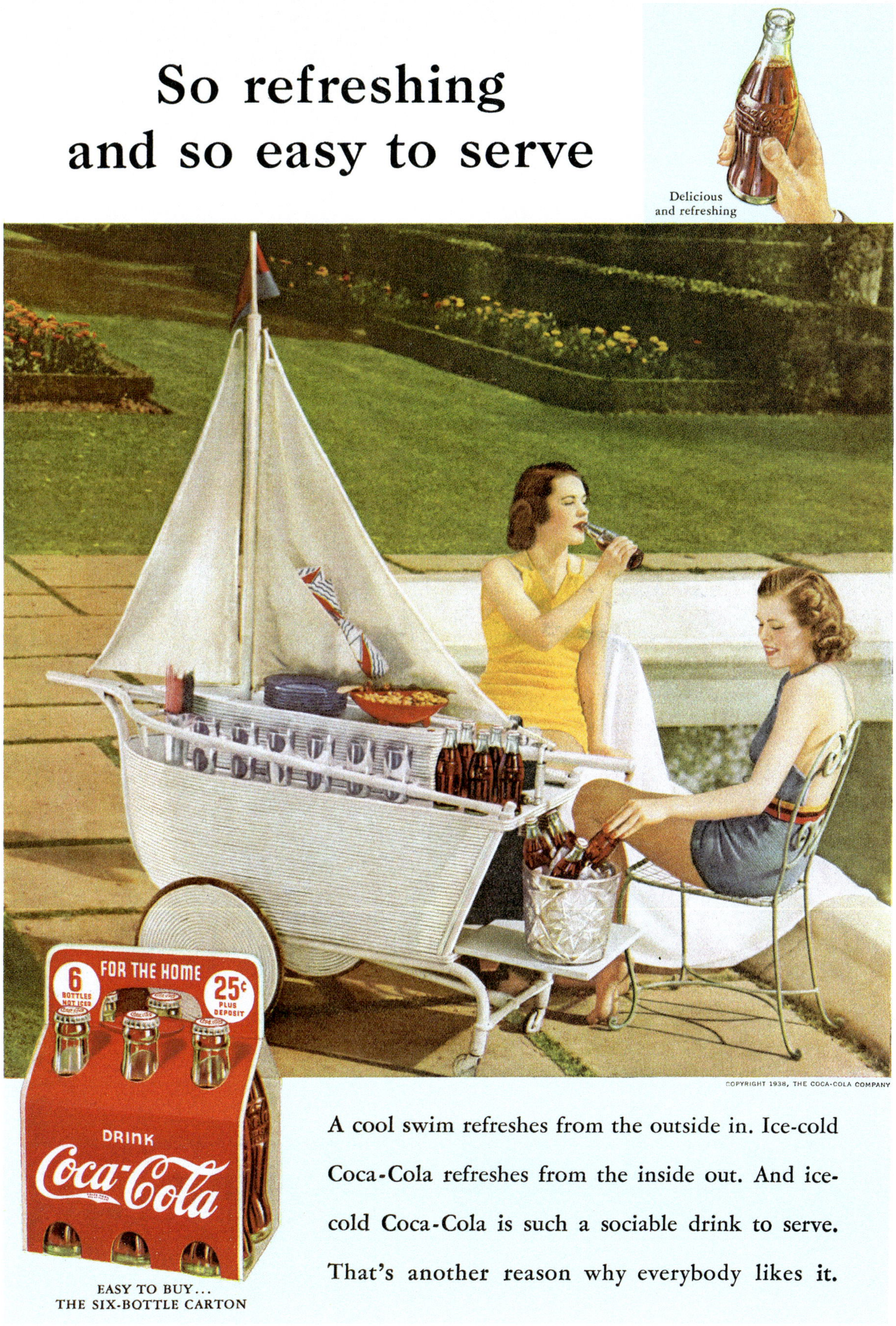

Coca-Cola, 1938

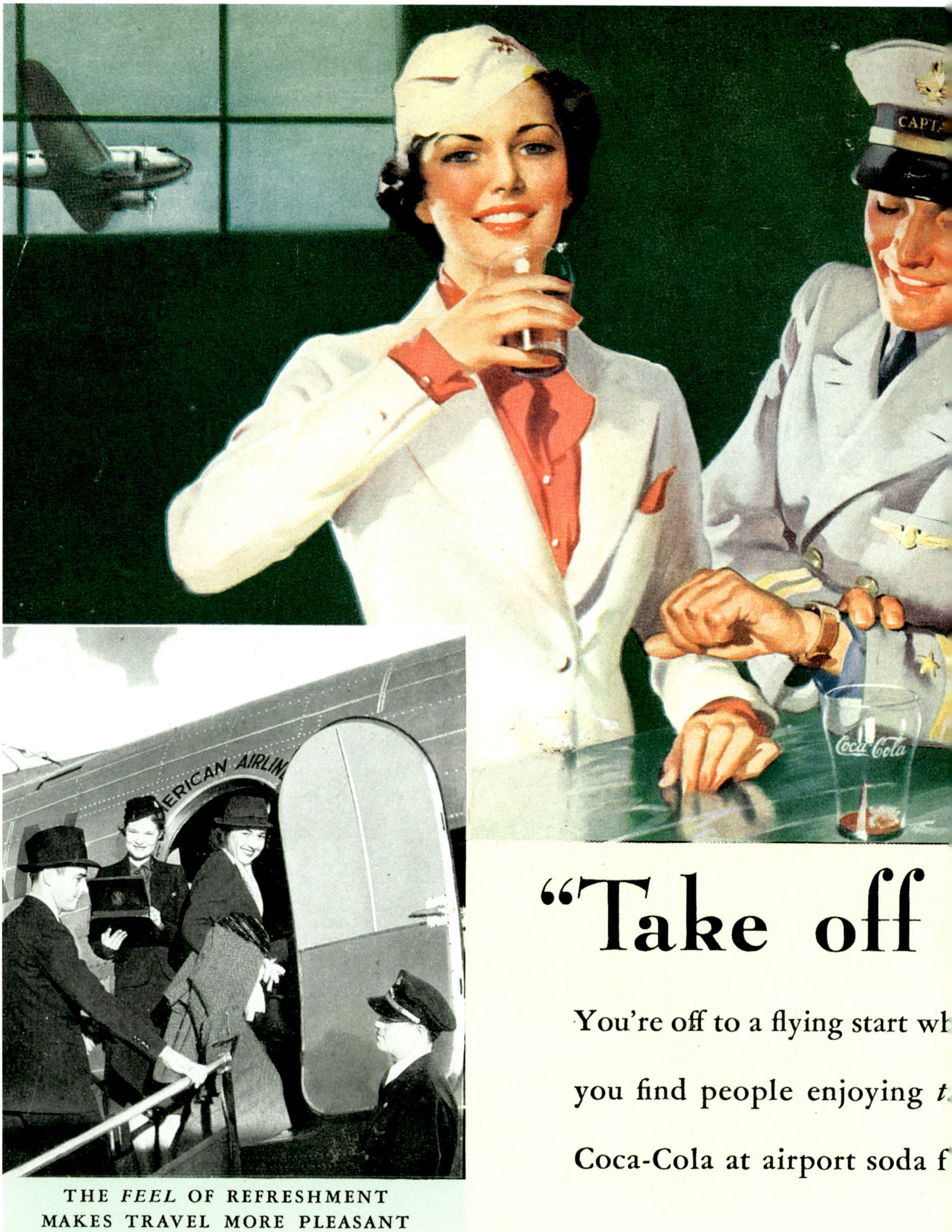

Coca-Cola, 1938

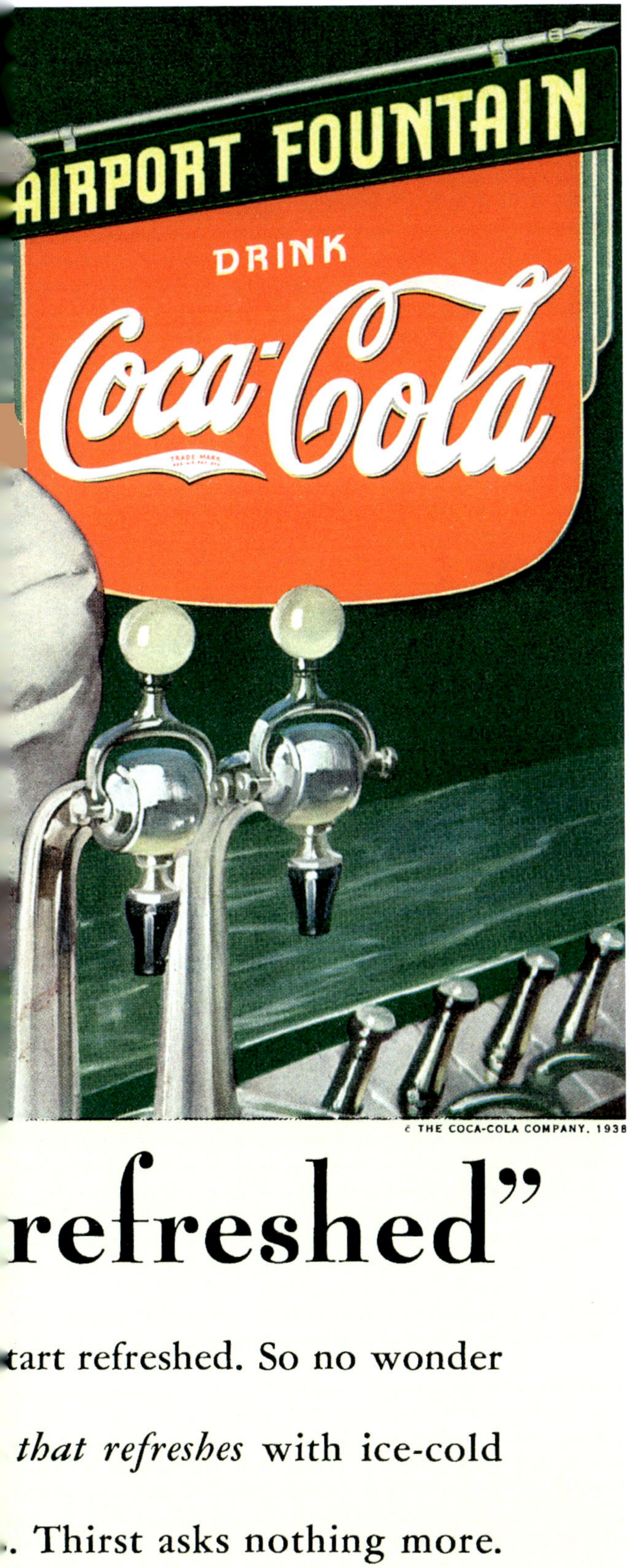

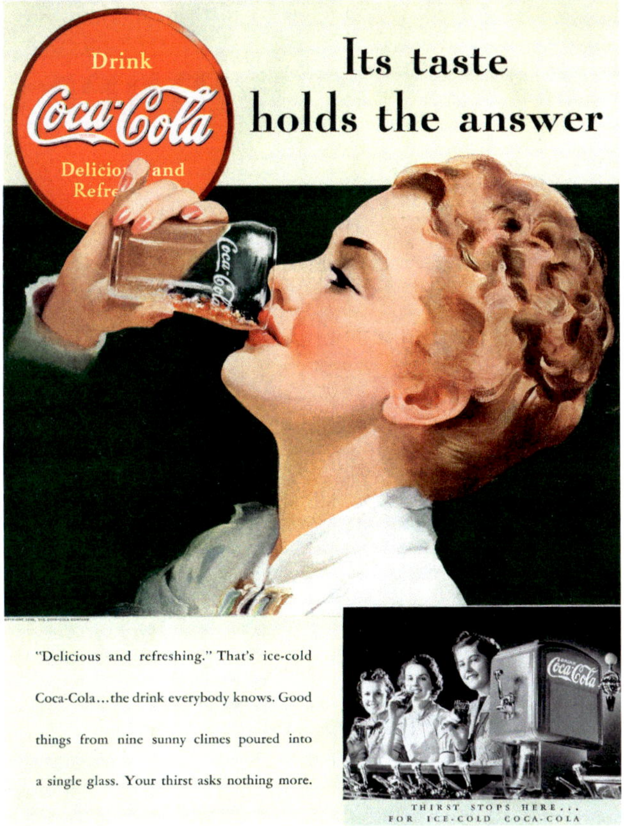

Coca-Cola, 1939

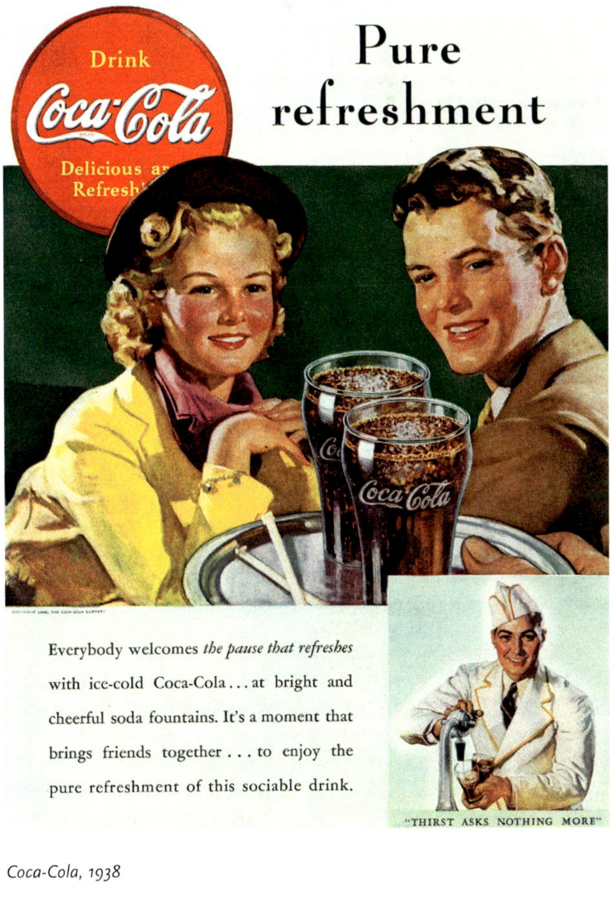

Coca-Cola, 1938

And the winner is...

Coffee, Tea, or Mam-my

Long before decaf coffee became an American staple, Sanka® was offering "the mister" a 97 % caffeine-free beverage. In marketing this product as a luxury item—a popular advertising strategy—black stereotypes were exploited to appeal to a more elitist consumer. Discomforting as this ad may be, little has changed in today's mainstream advertising mix.

Kaffee, Tee und Kulleraugen

Lange bevor die Amerikaner entkoffeinierten Kaffee zu einem ihrer Grundnahrungsmittel machten, bot die Firma Sanka dem weißen Herrn und Meister einen zu 97 % koffeinfreien Kaffee an. Um einer elitären Klientel dieses Produkt als Luxusgut anzudienen – eine populäre Werbestrategie –, bediente man sich rassistischer Stereotypen. So unangenehm einem diese Anzeige nun erscheinen mag, viel hat sich bis heute nicht geändert.

Café, thé ou nounou ?

Bien avant que le café décaféiné ne devienne un produit de base pour les Américains, Sanka® proposait déjà une boisson à 97 % sans caféine. Pour commercialiser ce produit comme article de luxe (une stratégie publicitaire fréquemment utilisée), les Noirs étaient exploités comme stéréotypes pour cibler un consommateur plus élitiste. Aussi dérangeante que soit cette affiche aujourd'hui, les recettes des publicités grand public n'ont guère changé depuis.

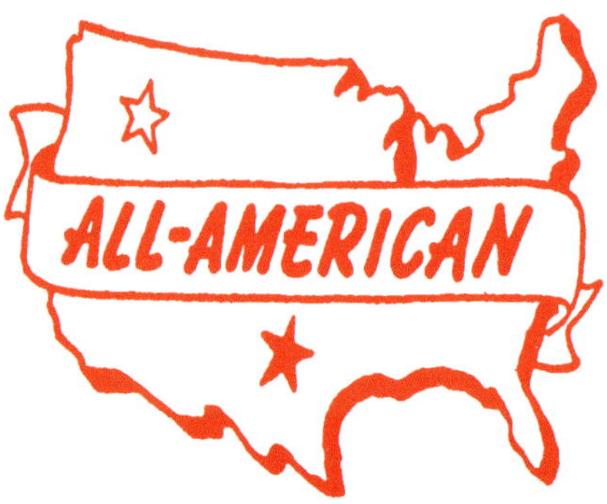

Sanka Coffee, 1933

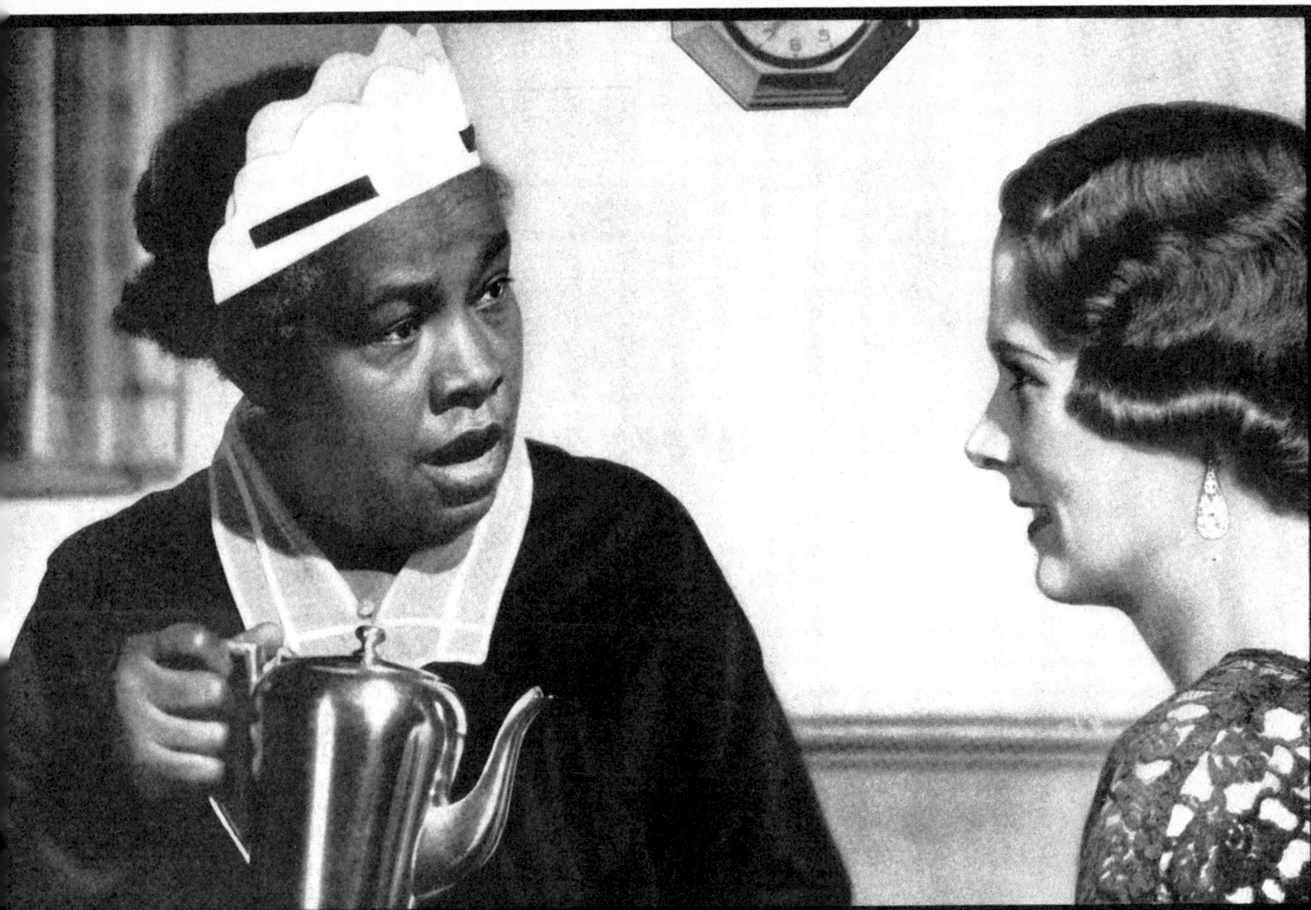

"You ain't goin' to let the Mister rink coffee <u>at</u> <u>night</u>, is you?"

HAPS you're in the same boat as "the ister." Perhaps the caffein in coffee keeps ake, too.

, you can now enjoy coffee at any hour— leep the sleep of the just! . . . How? By ng Sanka Coffee.

Real *coffee—and* real *sleep!*

Coffee is real coffee—with 97% of the removed. No fear of sleeplessness, indi- n, jumpy nerves. But, you may ask, does einated coffee taste as good as other coffees? bit! The only thing caffein ever added fee was regrets. It isn't even responsible for that cheery glow. That comes from coffee's own steaming warmth and bracing flavor.

Sanka Coffee is a blend of the choicest Central and South American coffees—roasted to the peak of brown perfection. You prepare it as you've always prepared coffee—boil, percolate or drip. You delight in the same appetizing aroma—the same rich, satisfying flavor.

For proof—make the night-test!

To prove it, drink your first cup of Sanka Coffee at night. Next morning you'll know, from actual experience, that you've discovered a delicious coffee you can enjoy morning, noon *and* night—without regret!

Packed in vacuum-sealed cans, Sanka Coffee comes to you as fresh and fragrant as the day it was roasted. Your grocer sells it—ground or in the bean—with the guarantee of absolute satisfaction or your money back. Or send in the coupon and 10¢ for a sample can. Sanka Coffee is a product of General Foods. Get a pound to-day.

Sanka Coffee has been accepted by the Committee on Foods of the American Medical Association with the statement: "Sanka Coffee . . . is free from caffein effect and can be used when other coffee has been forbidden."

anka Coffee

L COFFEE • 97% CAFFEIN-FREE • *DRINK IT • AND SLEEP!*

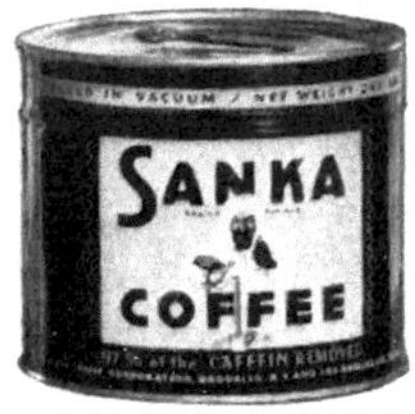

General Foods, Battle Creek, Mich. L.H.J.—4-33

Enclosed find 10¢ in stamps to cover the cost of mailing and packing, for which please send me a ¼-lb. sample can of Sanka Coffee.

Name ____________________

Street ____________________

City ____________ *State* ______

This offer not good in Canada

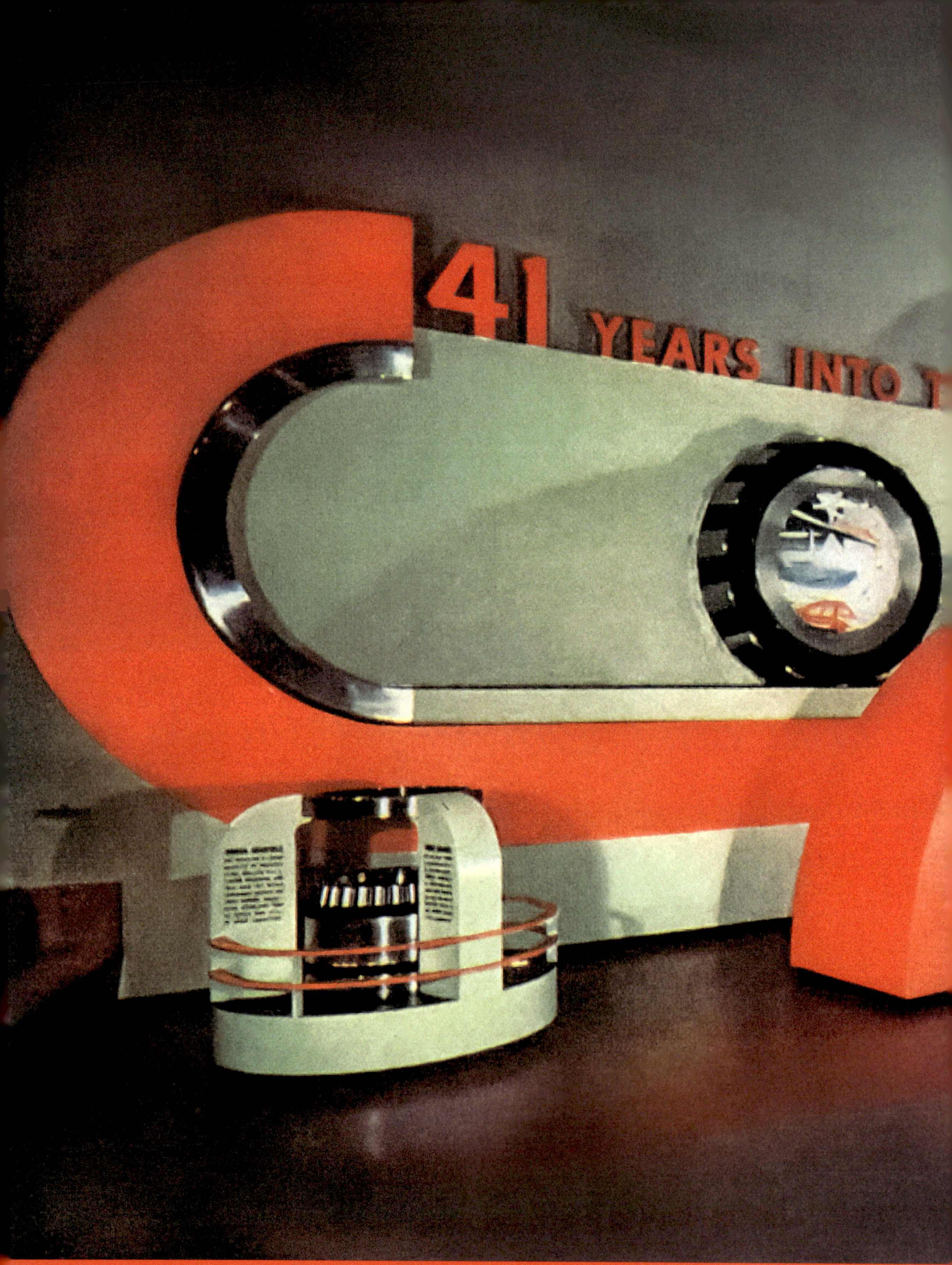
41
YEARS INTO

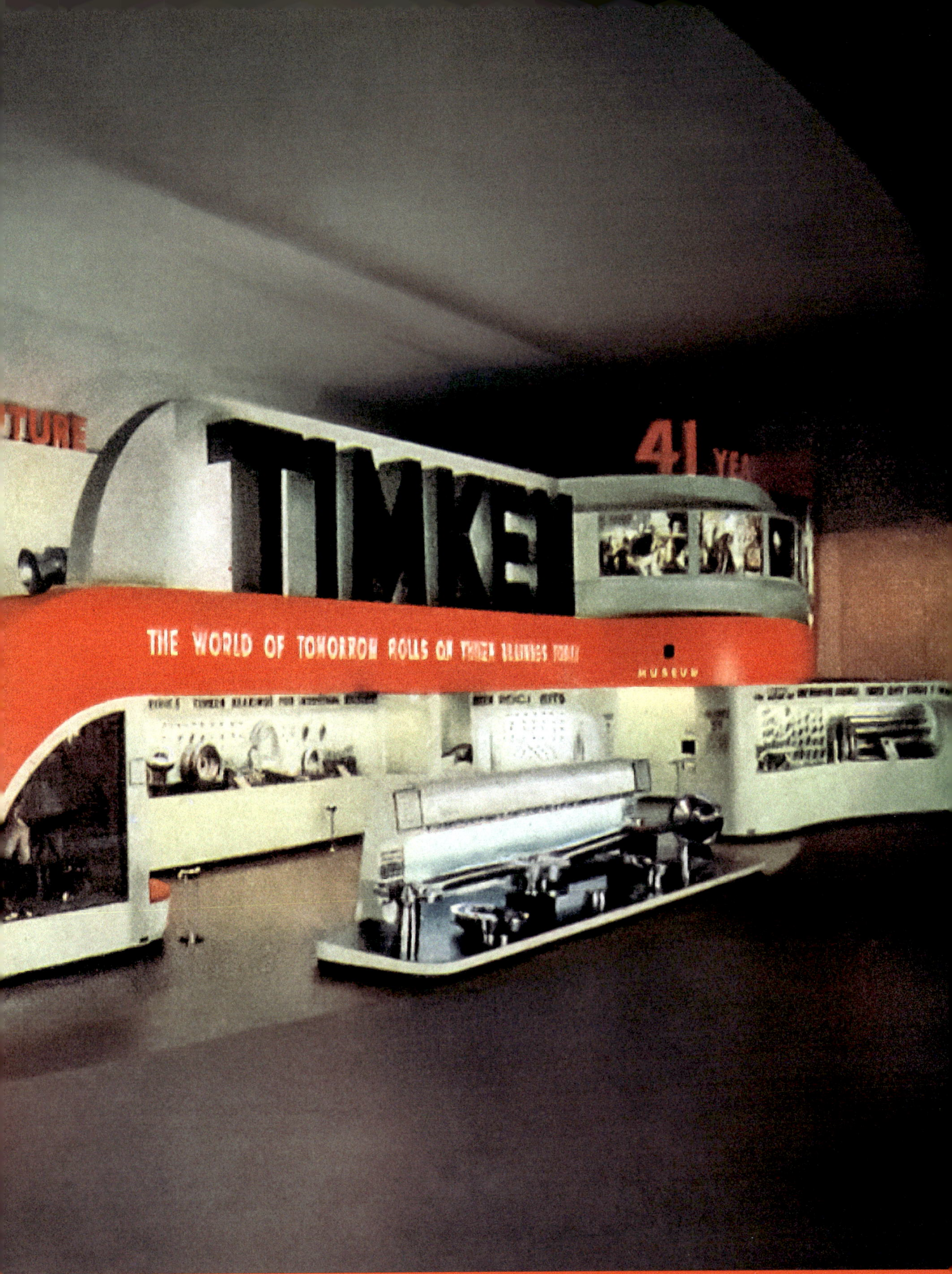
TIMKEN
THE WORLD OF TOMORROW ROLLS ON

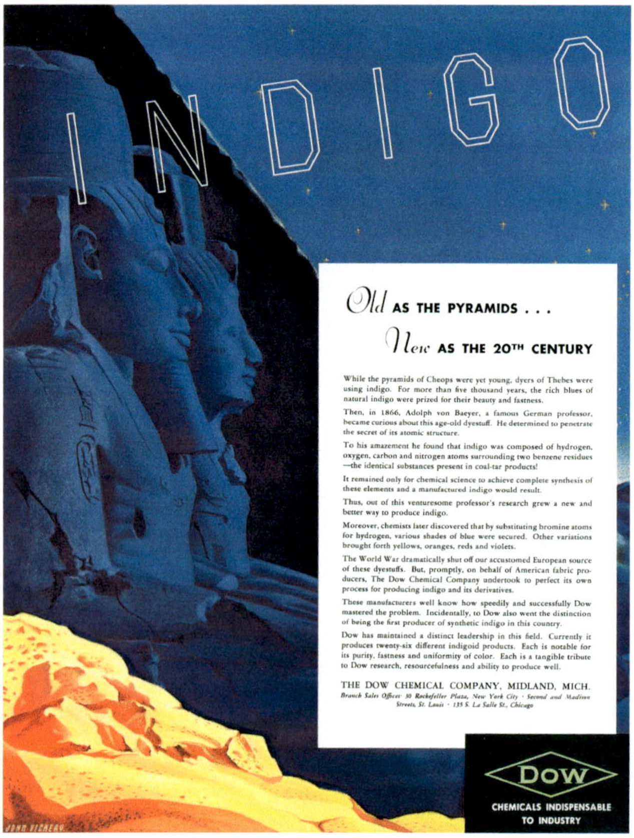

Dow Chemicals, 1937

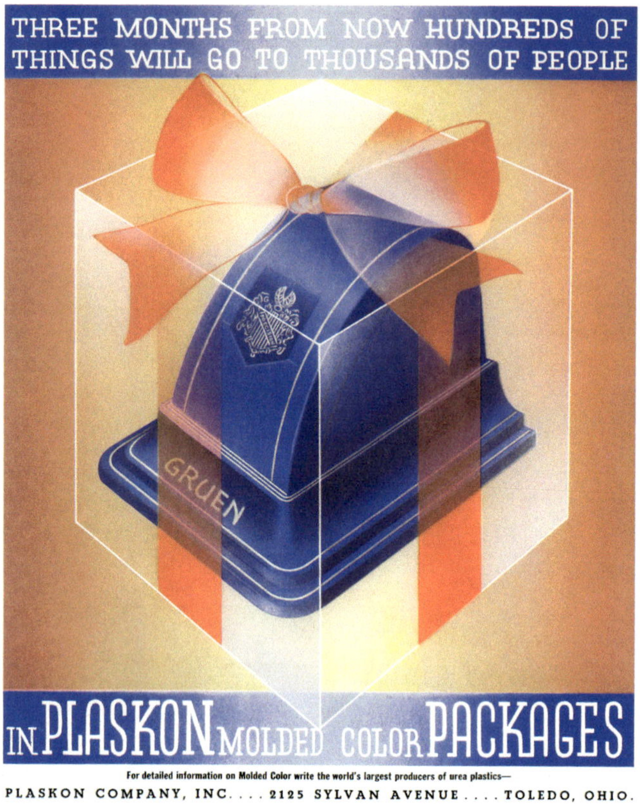

Plaskon Co.

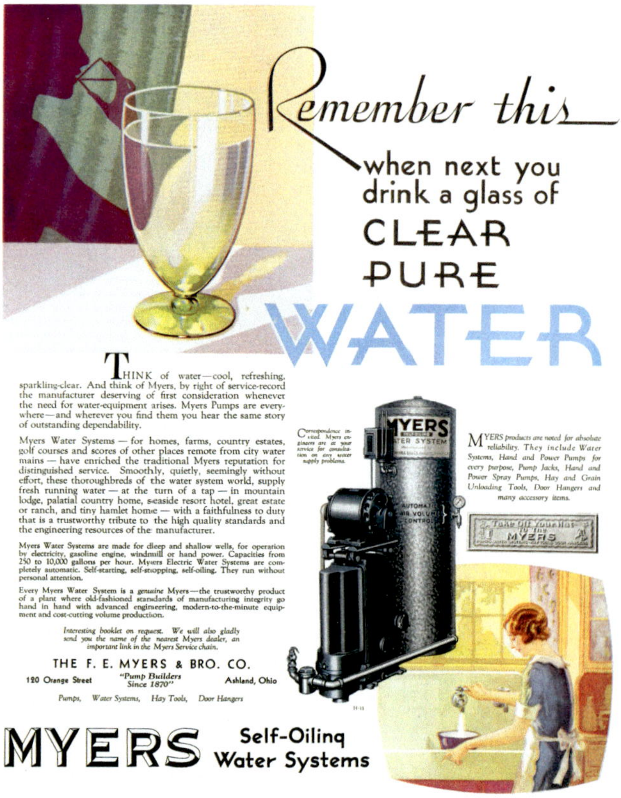

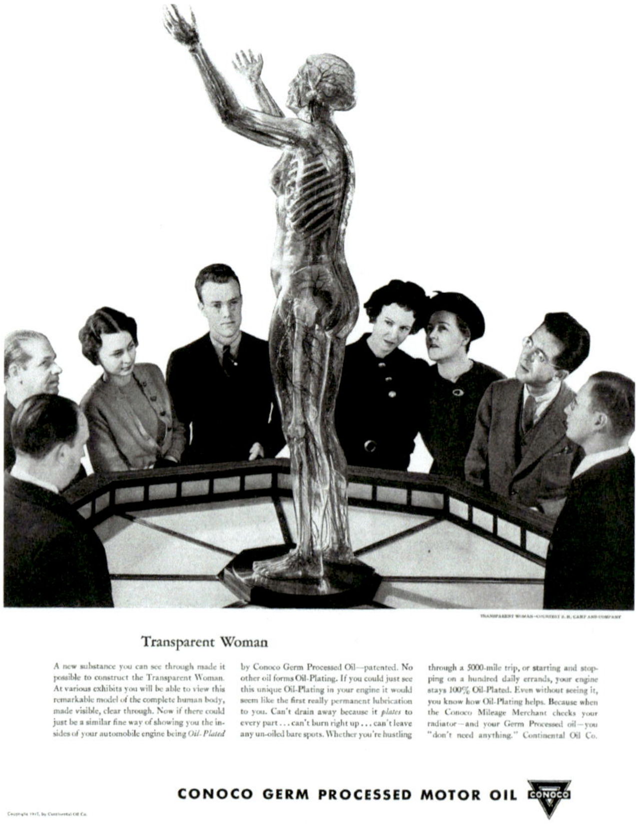

Timken, 1939 ◂◂ *Myers Water Systems, 1932*

Conoco, 1937

▸ *National Cash Register, 1933*

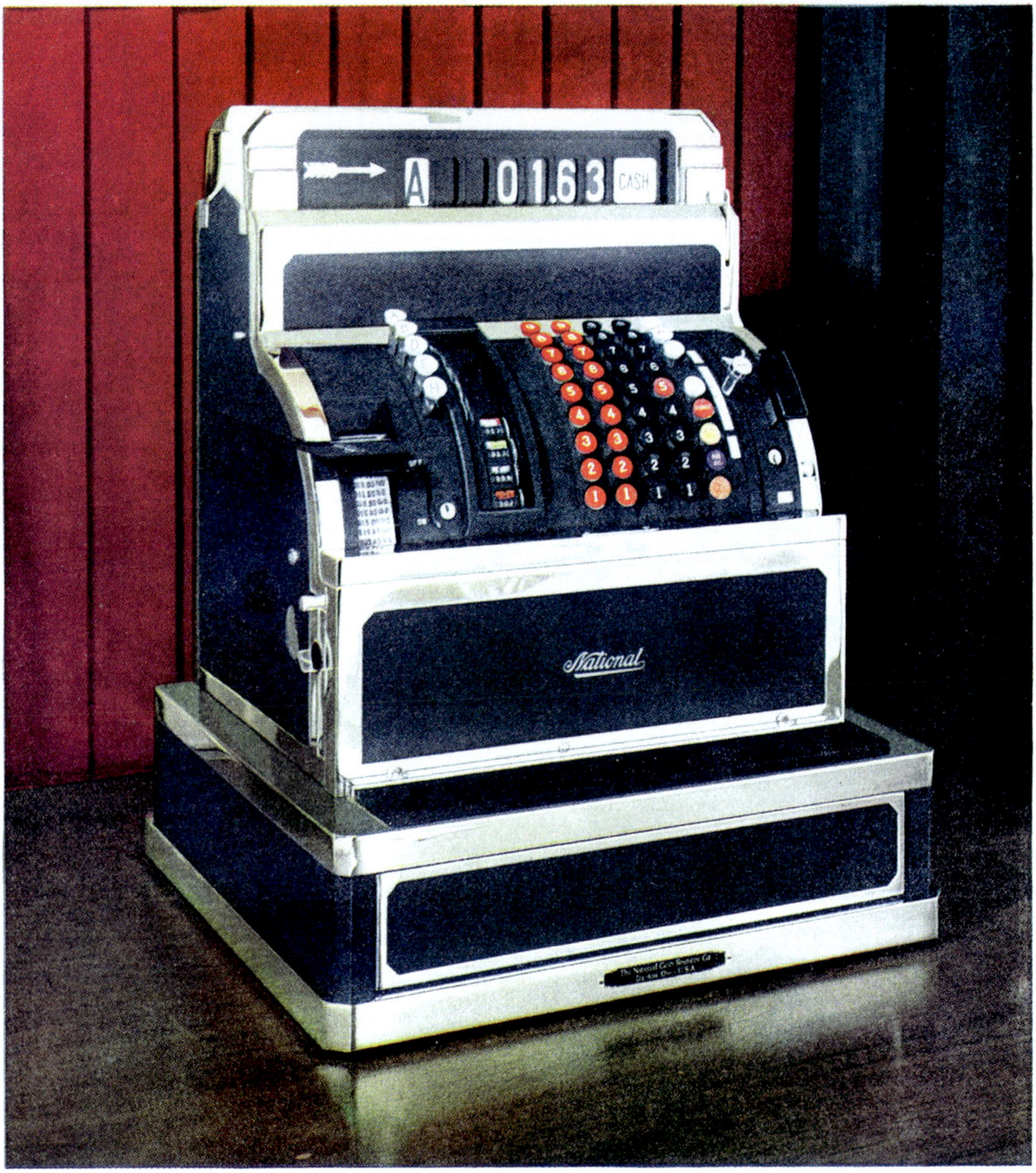

NATIONAL CASH REGISTER COMPANY ANTICIPATED THE NEW NEEDS OF THESE CHANGING TIMES. ● NOT BY ANY MAGIC OF MIND OR
'TERN OF PALMISTRY. BUT BY VIRTUE OF 50 YEARS' EXPERIENCE FEELING THE PULSE BEATS OF A THOUSAND DIFFERENT TYPES OF BUSINESS. ●
'IONAL ENGINEERS HAVE DEVELOPED NEW CASH REGISTERS, ACCOUNTING MACHINES AND SYSTEMS THAT WILL RECORD AMERICA'S RETURN
DOING-BUSINESS-AT-A-PROFIT. ● THESE NEW PRODUCTS ARE THE RESULT OF A MAJOR INVESTMENT IN RESEARCH, NEW TOOLS, NEW DIES,
V SALES IDEAS, NEW SERVICE PLANS. ● FOR MONTHS, OUR PLANTS HAVE BEEN WORKING FULL BLAST, BUILDING THESE MACHINES WHOSE
:AINS" PROVIDE THE ADDED INFORMATION TODAY'S BUSINESS MAN MUST HAVE, BE HE A MANUFACTURER, A BARBER, A RETAILER, OR A
OT-BLACK. ● THE NATIONAL CASH REGISTER COMPANY IS PROUD OF THE CONTRIBUTION IT IS AGAIN ABLE TO OFFER AMERICAN BUSINESS.

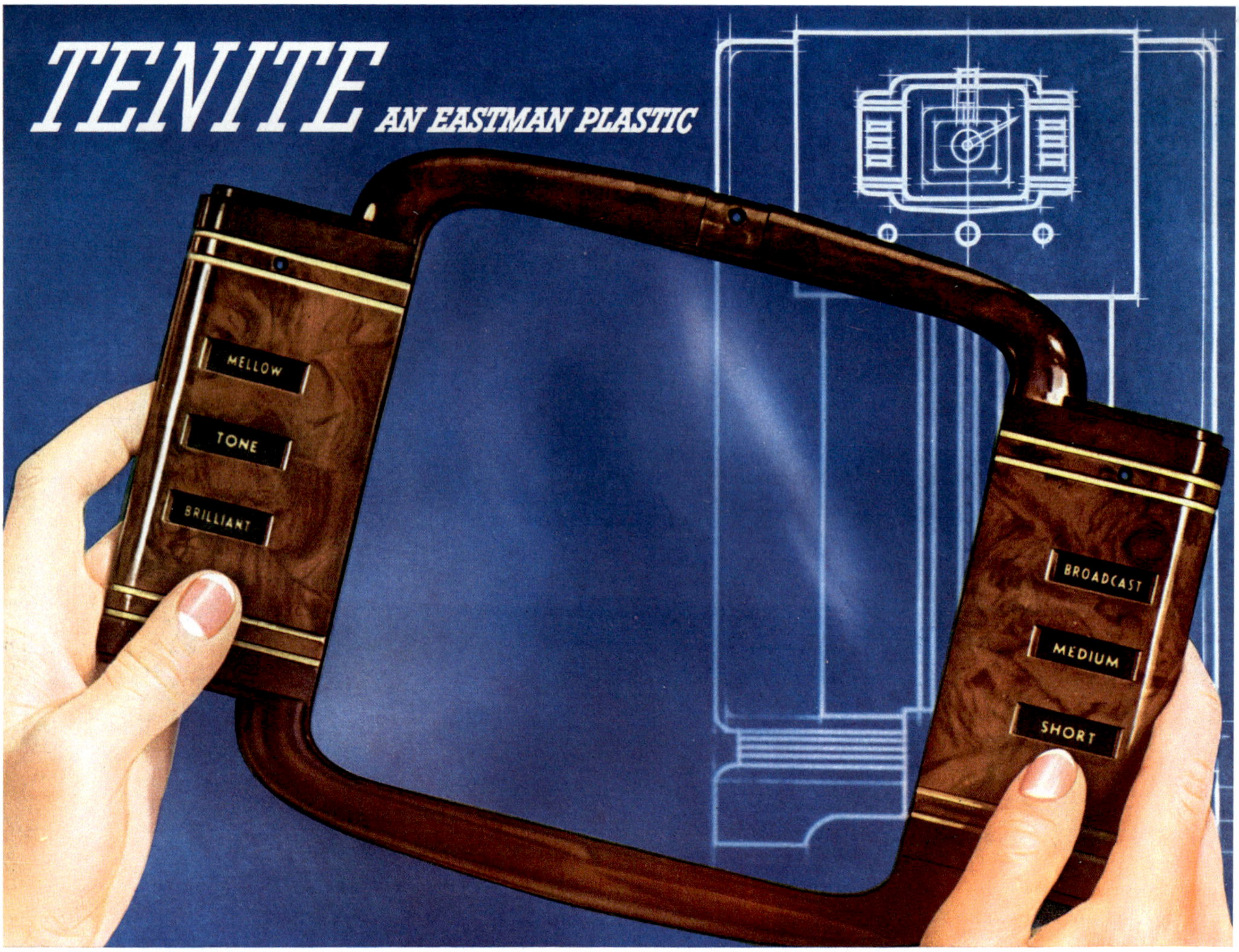

A PROBLEM OLD AS GLASS

. . . AS SOLVED FOR RCA VICTOR

SINCE glass was first made, craftsmen have sought simple ways of framing it or attaching it to other materials securely, without strain.

A method newly found by plastic molders is to cast directly around glass a frame of Tenite. Tenite-framed glass is in effect one piece—an air-tight, dust-tight, vibration-proof unit which can readily be fastened to wood or metal.

Outstanding examples of this new plastic art, here illustrated, are the Tenite frames molded around the dial glasses of 1938 RCA Victor radios.

Sound manufacturing economies and added sales appeal mark the success of this application. Neither wood nor metal could have duplicated Tenite's perfect union with glass, its lustrous beauty, its flexibility of design or its low assembly cost.

Tenite offers industry more than a new grip on glass. Many manufacturers are finding that their products can be molded of Tenite more economically than they can be cast or machined from any other material. For reasons of beauty, serviceability and cost, Tenite is displacing wood, metal and rubber in a wide variety of everyday uses—steering wheels, door knobs, combs, pencils, buttons, toys, typewriter keys, fish baits, goggles.

TENITE BOOK ON REQUEST

Tenite is a tough, practically unbreakable plastic made of Eastman cellulose acetate, in all colors—plain, variegated, transparent, opaque. Custom molders will gladly tell you about its suitability for your product. Or write us direct for a 52-page book on Tenite and its uses.

TENNESSEE EASTMAN CORPORATION
KINGSPORT, TENN.
(*SUBSIDIARY OF EASTMAN KODAK COMPANY*)

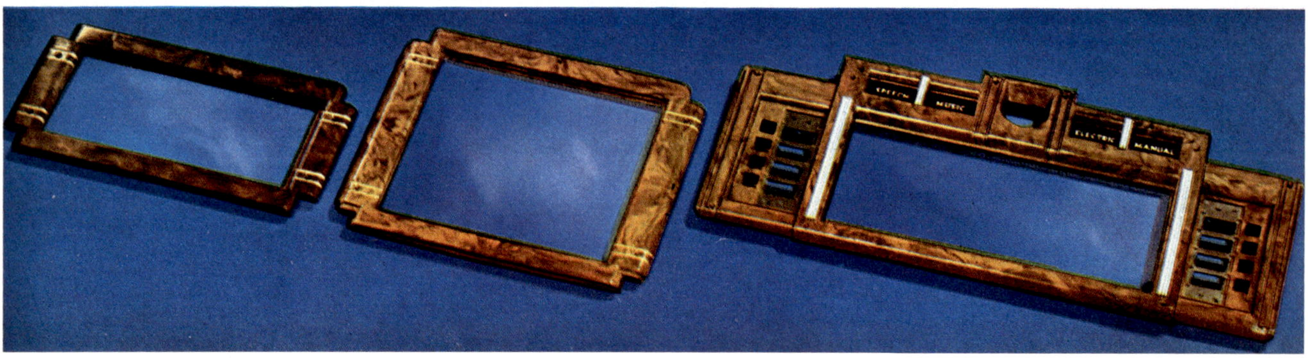

Tenite Plastic, 1937

▸ *Tenite Plastic, 1939*

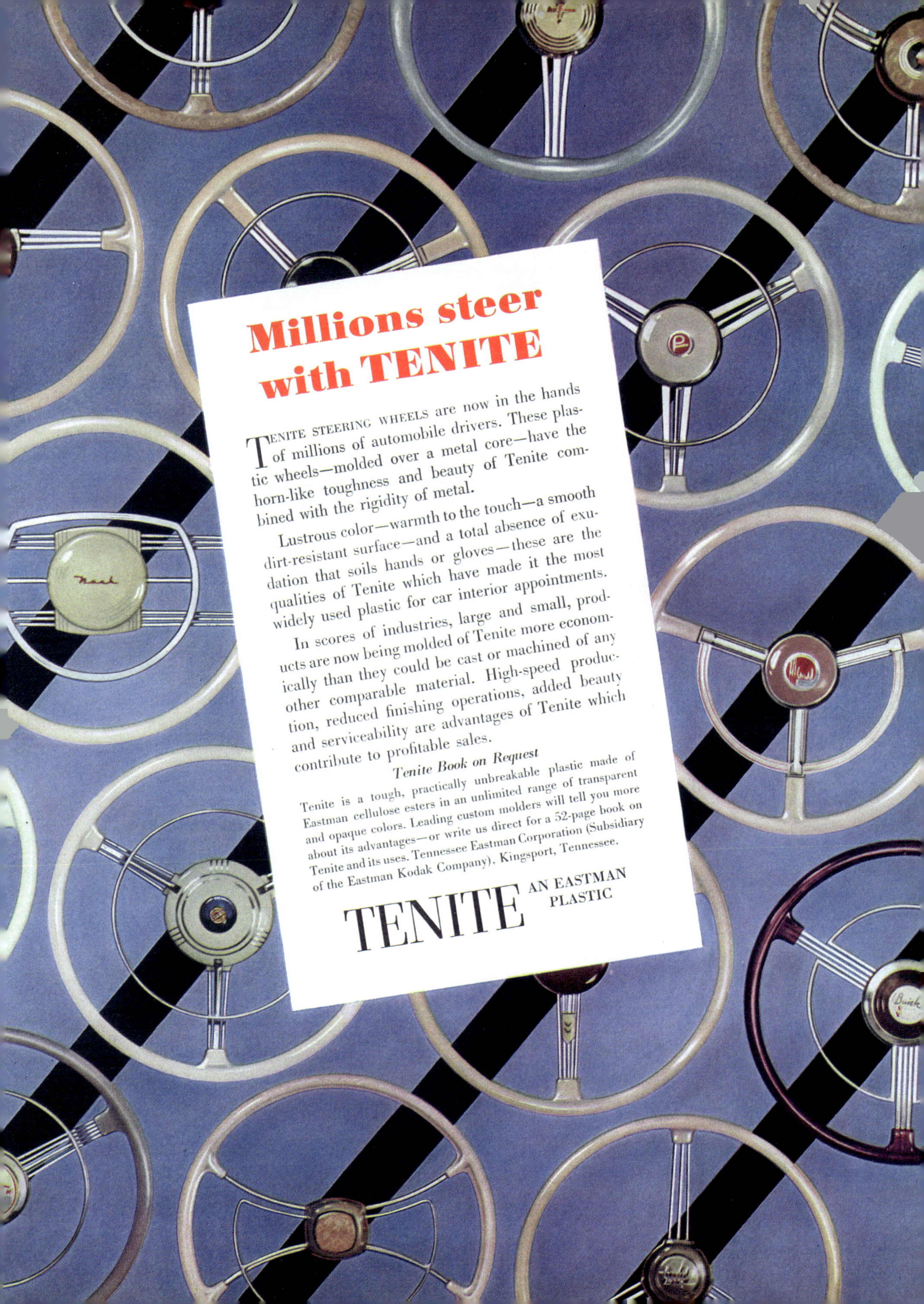

Millions steer with TENITE
TENITE STEERING WHEELS are now in the hands of millions of automobile drivers. These plastic wheels—molded over a metal core—have the horn-like toughness and beauty of Tenite combined with the rigidity of metal.
Lustrous color—warmth to the touch—a smooth dirt-resistant surface—and a total absence of exudation that soils hands or gloves—these are the qualities of Tenite which have made it the most widely used plastic for car interior appointments.
In scores of industries, large and small, products are now being molded of Tenite more economically than they could be cast or machined of any other comparable material. High-speed production, reduced finishing operations, added beauty and serviceability are advantages of Tenite which contribute to profitable sales.
Tenite Book on Request
Tenite is a tough, practically unbreakable plastic made of Eastman cellulose esters in an unlimited range of transparent and opaque colors. Leading custom molders will tell you more about its advantages—or write us direct for a 52-page book on Tenite and its uses. Tennessee Eastman Corporation (Subsidiary of the Eastman Kodak Company), Kingsport, Tennessee.
TENITE
AN EASTMAN PLASTIC

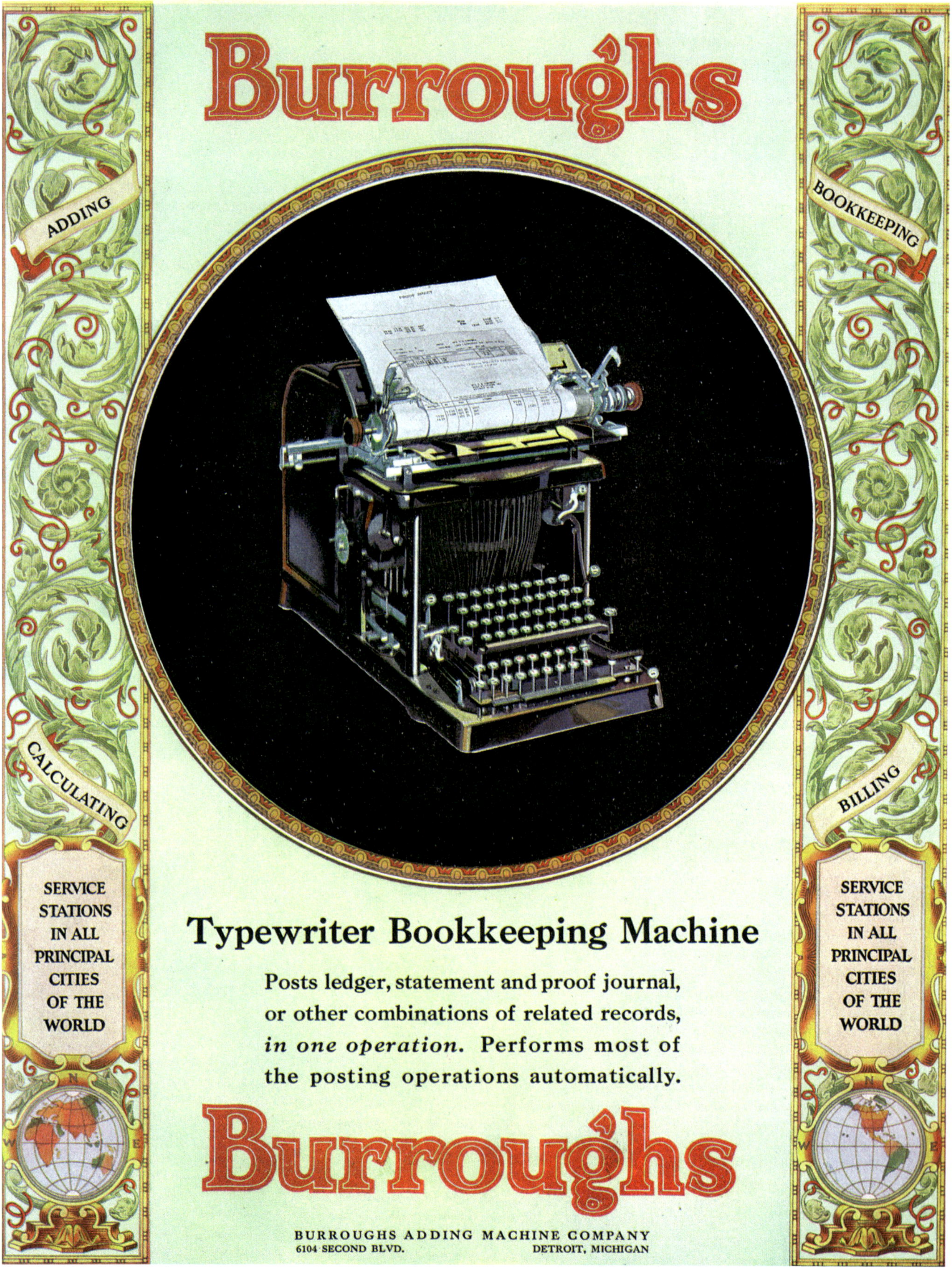

Burroughs Adding Machine Co., 1930

▸ *NCR Co., 1930*

REGISTERS *and* MACHINES

'or *your* business

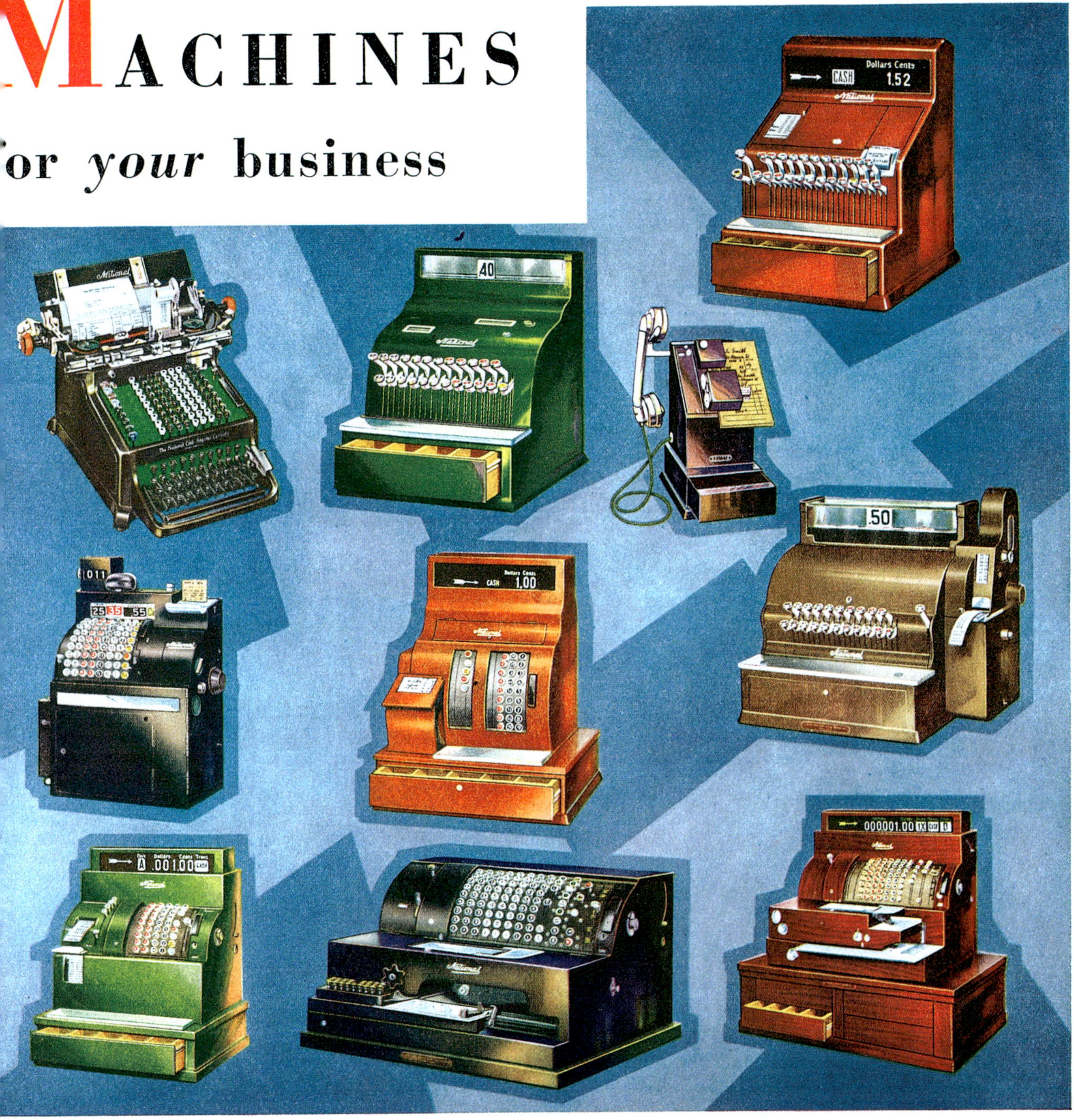

riced at $60, $75, $95, $100, $115, $125, $150, $175, $200, $225, $250, $275, $300, $325, $350 and up in the U. S. A.

REGISTER COMPANY

EGISTERS AND ACCOUNTING MACHINES

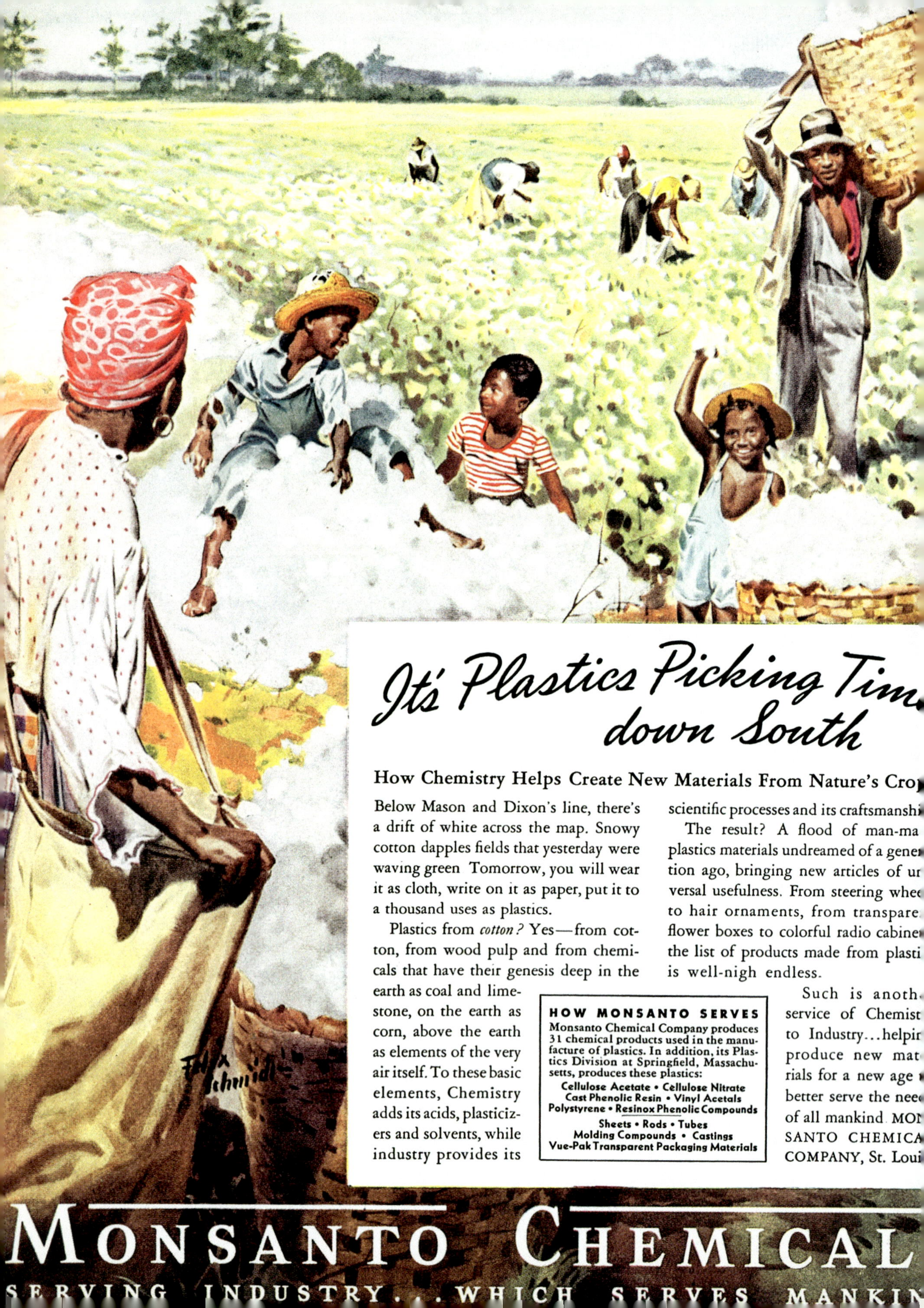
It's Plastics Picking Tim
down South
How Chemistry Helps Create New Materials From Nature's Cro
Below Mason and Dixon's line, there's a drift of white across the map. Snowy cotton dapples fields that yesterday were waving green Tomorrow, you will wear it as cloth, write on it as paper, put it to a thousand uses as plastics.
Plastics from *cotton?* Yes—from cotton, from wood pulp and from chemicals that have their genesis deep in the earth as coal and limestone, on the earth as corn, above the earth as elements of the very air itself. To these basic elements, Chemistry adds its acids, plasticizers and solvents, while industry provides its scientific processes and its craftsmanshi
The result? A flood of man-ma plastics materials undreamed of a gener tion ago, bringing new articles of ur versal usefulness. From steering whee to hair ornaments, from transpare flower boxes to colorful radio cabine the list of products made from plasti is well-nigh endless.
Such is anoth service of Chemist to Industry...helpir produce new mat rials for a new age better serve the nee of all mankind. MON SANTO CHEMICA COMPANY, St. Loui
HOW MONSANTO SERVES
Monsanto Chemical Company produces 31 chemical products used in the manufacture of plastics. In addition, its Plastics Division at Springfield, Massachusetts, produces these plastics:
Cellulose Acetate • Cellulose Nitrate
Cast Phenolic Resin • Vinyl Acetals
Polystyrene • Resinox Phenolic Compounds
Sheets • Rods • Tubes
Molding Compounds • Castings
Vue-Pak Transparent Packaging Materials
MONSANTO CHEMICAL
SERVING INDUSTRY... WHICH SERVES MANKIN

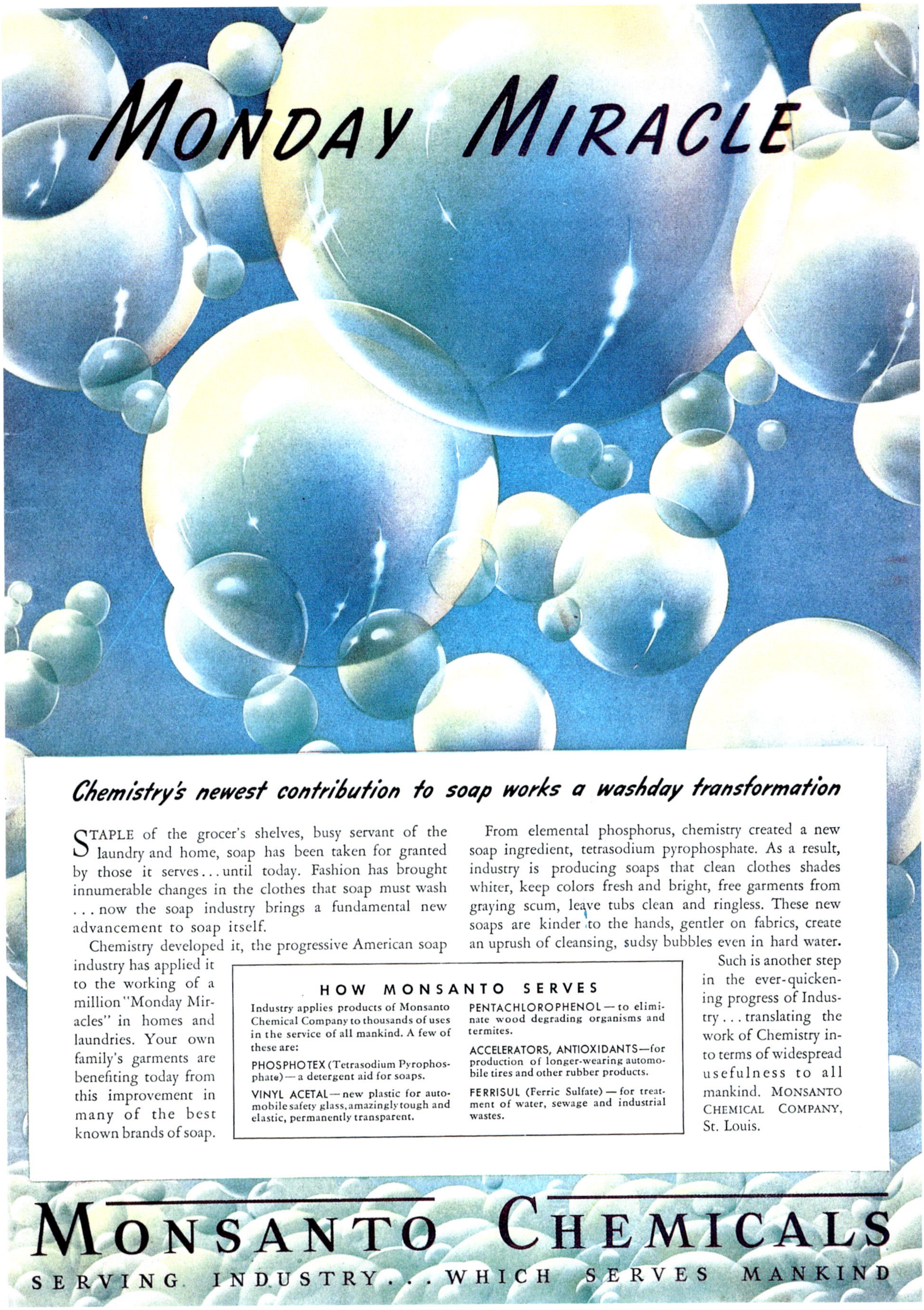

Monsanto Chemicals, 1939 ◄▲

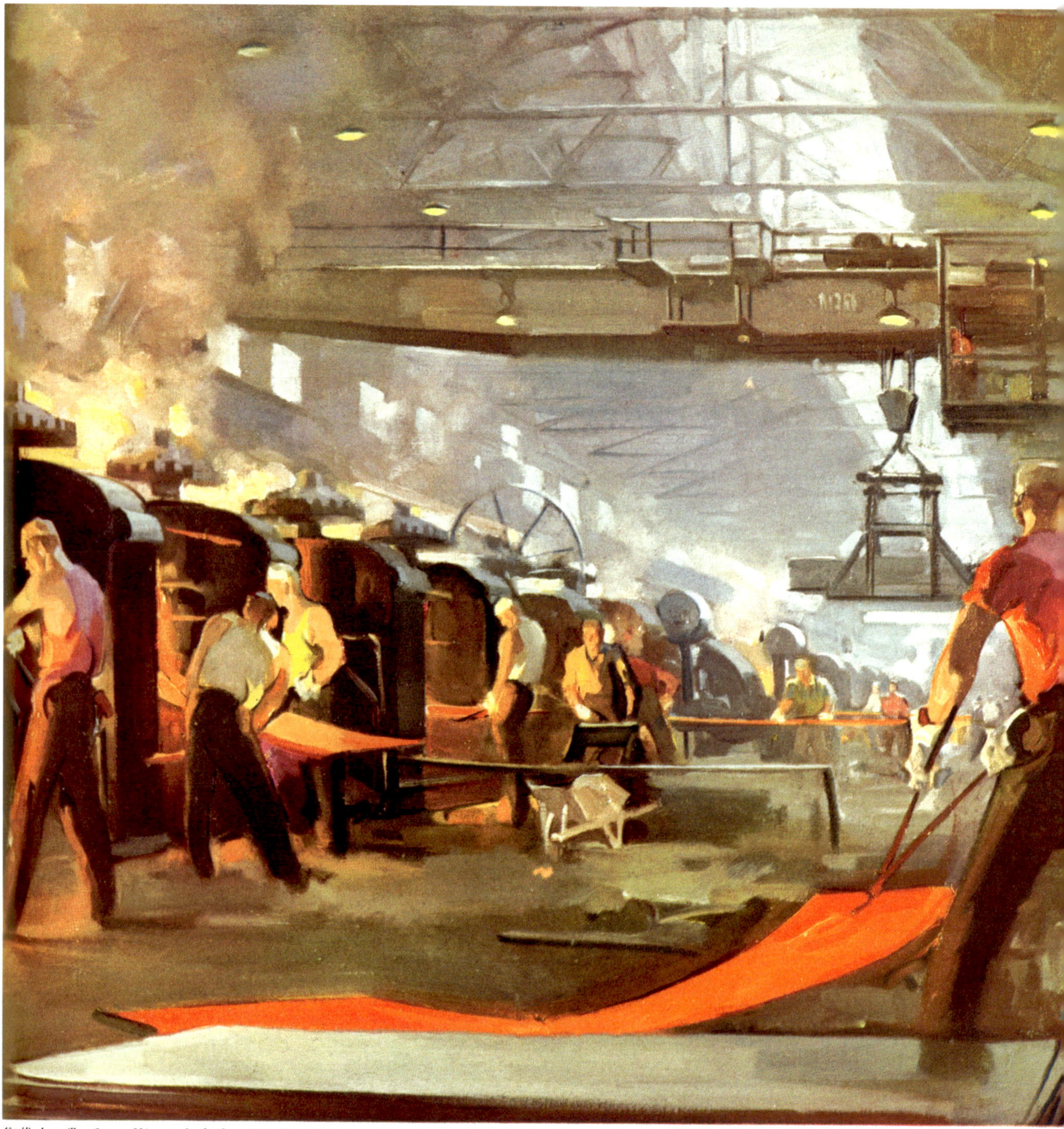

A Republic sheet mill at Canton, Ohio—one of a far flung chain of Republic plants, strategically located and efficiently organized to provide the special steels that are playing an important part in America's industrial development.

IMPROVING PRODUCTS AND PROFITS

In hundreds of manufacturing plants, newer and better metals, introduced by Republic, have replaced old materials, accepted for generations as "the best that could be produced for the purpose."

And you would expect Republic to lead in the development of new steels for new uses. The entire organization is young, aggressive, facing forward, looking ahead . . . eager to work with any manufacturer or fabricator who is anxious to improve his product and his profits.

Republic is already the world's largest producer of alloys . . . and has the greatest capacity for the production of Enduro, the stainless steel now used so widely. The making of pipe has been revolutionized through Republic's electric weld process. And Republic's Toncan Iron is saving millions of dollars in the fight against rust.

Republic is alert to the changed production and merchandising conditions of today . . and is ever ready to help industry meet them.

REPUBLIC STEEL CORPORATION

GENERAL OFFICES YOUNGSTOWN, OHIO

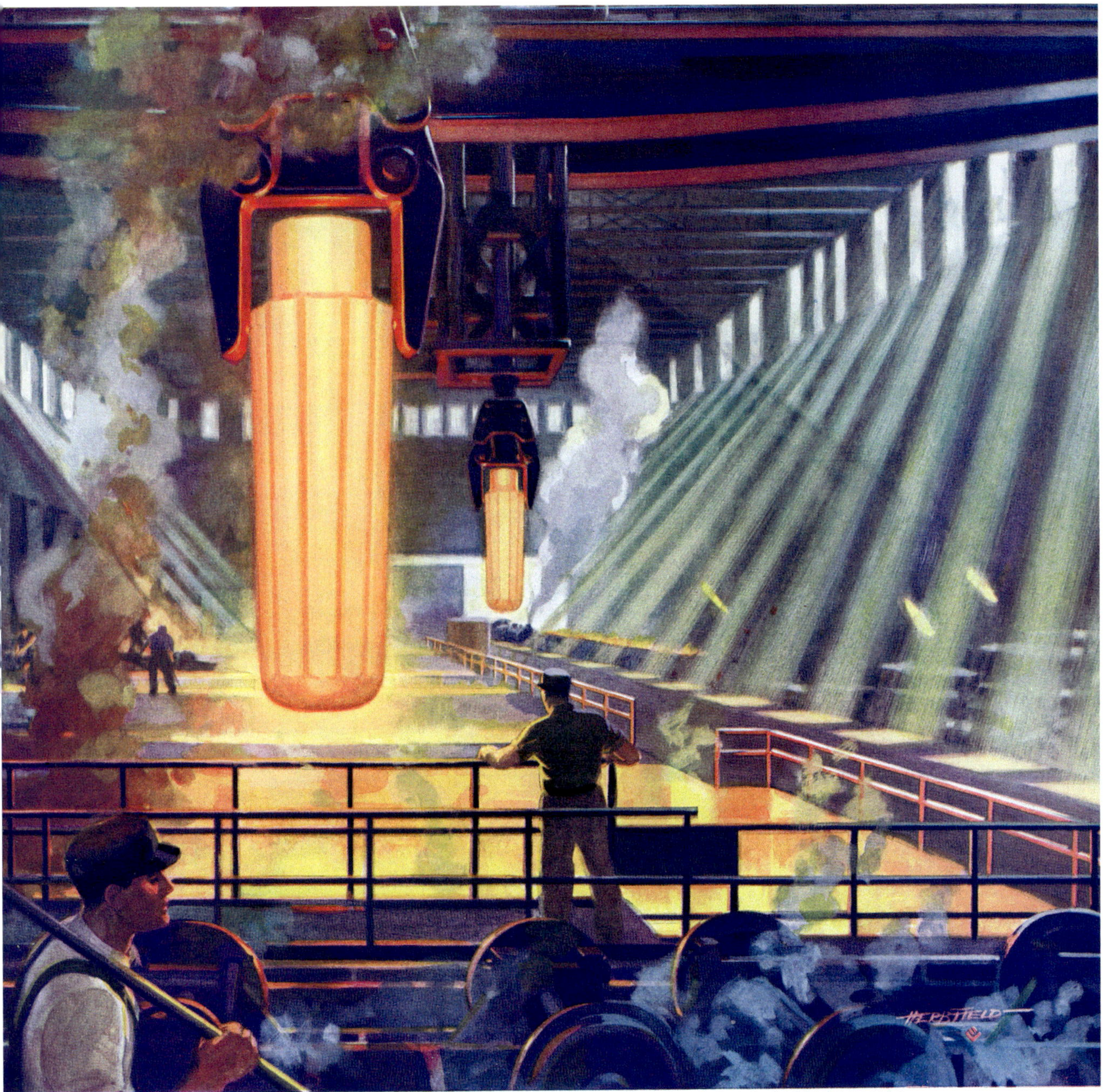

The entire Republic organization is young, aggressive, alert to the changed production and merchandising conditions of today—and ready to help industry to meet them

KEEPING A STRIDE AHEAD

• Republic's service to industry goes far beyond the meeting of mere tonnage requirements. • It lies in the constant development of new steels for new uses—in constructive, technical help to fabricators, manufacturers, architects and engineers—in new ideas, new products, new ways of doing things. • Republic has always had the courage to pioneer—the ability to keep a full stride ahead. That spirit carried along by a young, aggressive organization has made Republic the world's largest producer of alloy steels. • It is responsible for Enduro, the perfected stainless steel, for Toncan, the rust-resisting iron—for "electric weld" pipe, the Agathon alloys and Republic's other modern metals. • Republic representatives are easy to reach. You will find them alert, progressive—ready to be of service.

REPUBLIC STEEL CORPORATION

GENERAL OFFICES · YOUNGSTOWN, OHIO

ALLOY AND CARBON STEELS • TONCAN IRON • STAINLESS STEEL • PIPE AND TUBULAR PRODUCTS • BARS AND SHAPES • HOT AND COLD ROLLED STRIP PLATES • BLACK, BLUE ANNEALED AND GALVANIZED SHEETS • SPECIAL FINISH SHEETS • TIN PLATE • NUTS, BOLTS, RIVETS, ETC. • WIRE PRODUCTS • DIE ROLLED PRODUCTS

Republic Steel Co., 1933 ◄▲

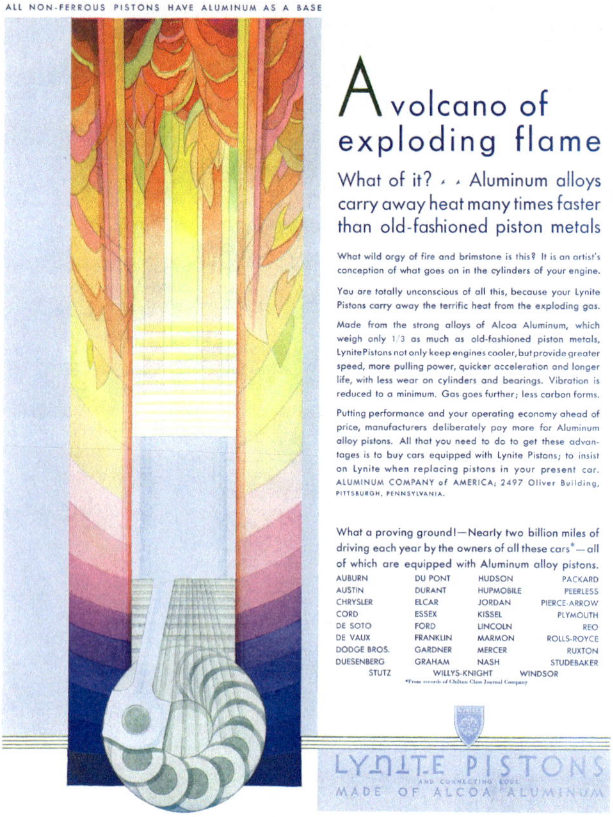

Alcoa Aluminum, 1931

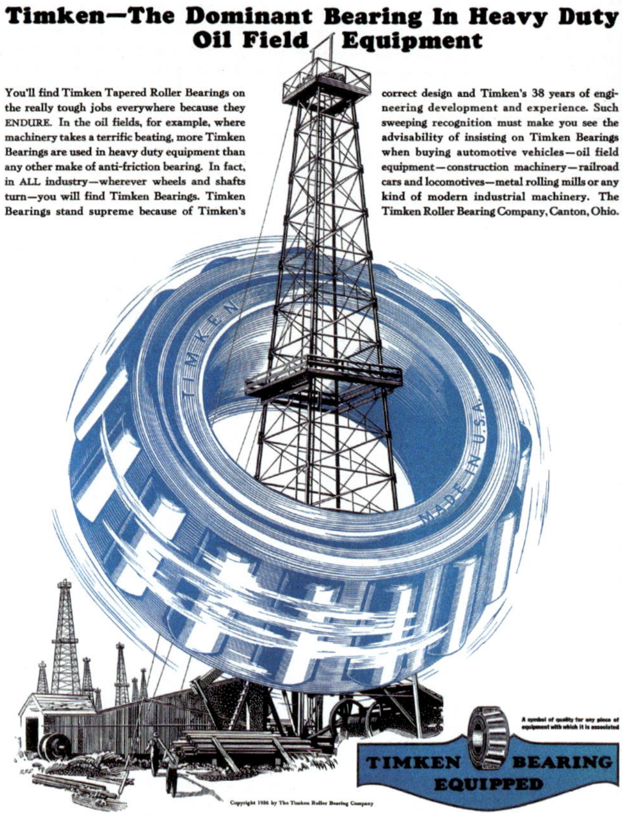

Timken, 1934

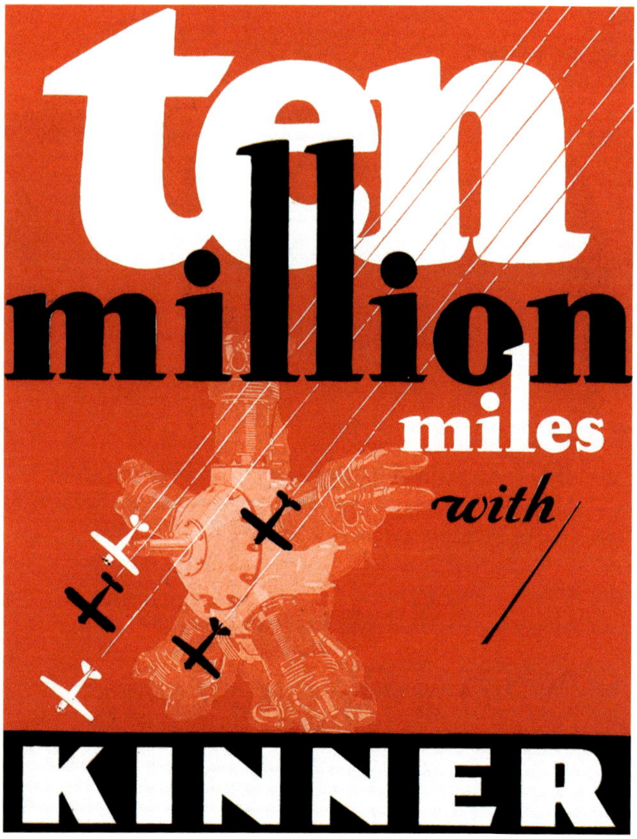

Kinner, 1930

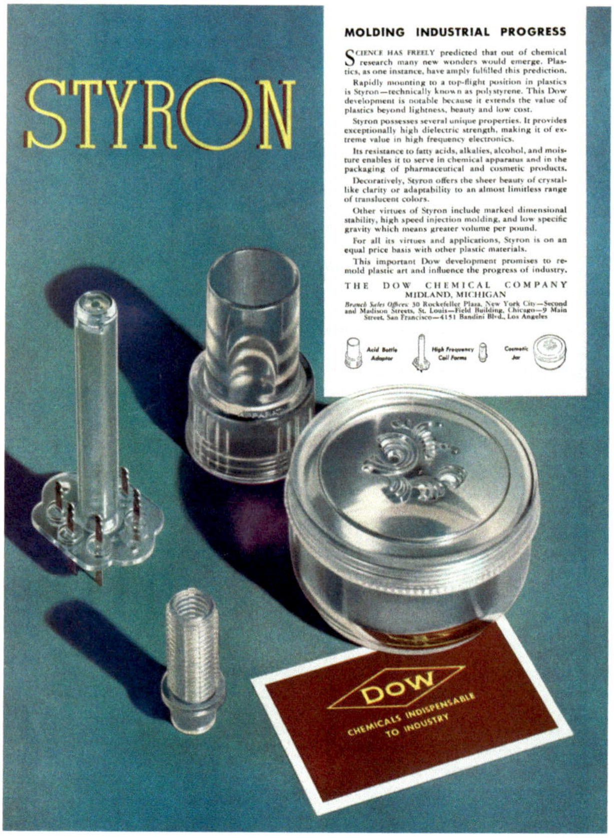

Dow Chemicals, 1939

▸ *Alcoa Aluminum, 1931*

NON-FERROUS PISTONS HAVE ALUMINUM AS A BASE

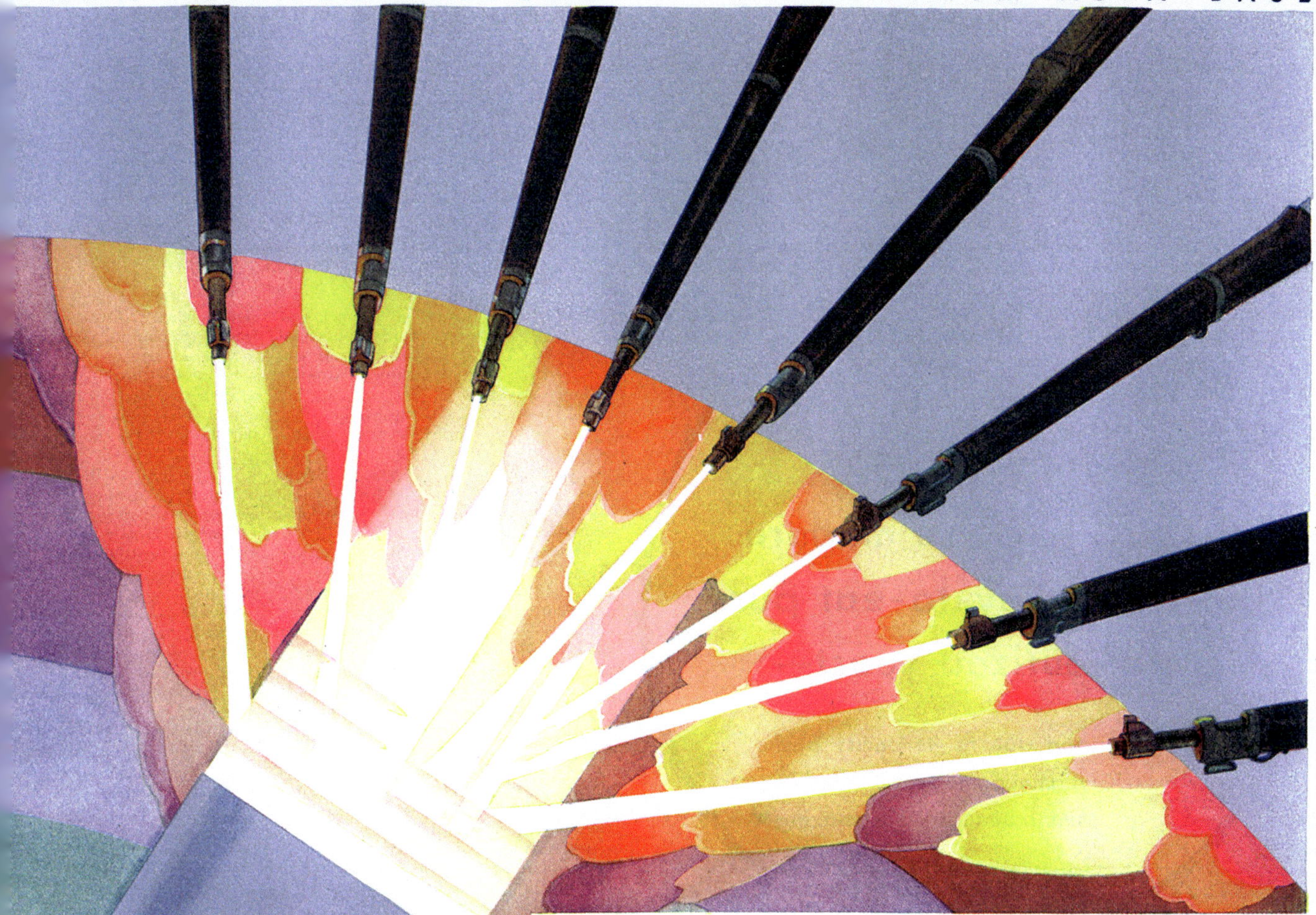

TOUGH-Aluminum Alloy Pistons face a firing squad hundreds of times a minute and *Live*

"Load"—"Ready"—"Aim"—"Fire"—Like a command to a firing squad, your foot on the throttle gives the signal. A wall of exploding flame hits the pistons—but Lynite Pistons are not made to be "killed in action." They are just naturally *tough.*

But mere toughness is not enough. Lynite Pistons are made of light, strong alloys of Alcoa Aluminum, which weigh only ⅓ as much as old-fashioned piston material, and conduct heat many times faster. There lies the difference—*such a difference* that manufacturers, placing performance and your operating economy ahead of price, deliberately pay more for aluminum alloy pistons to give you advantages like these: longer piston life; cooler engines; less carbon; reduced vibration; less wear on bearings and cylinders.

Buy cars equipped with aluminum alloy pistons and you get more performance for your automobile dollar. When replacing pistons in your present car be sure to specify Lynite Pistons made of the light, strong alloys of Alcoa Aluminum. ALUMINUM COMPANY of AMERICA; 2497 Oliver Building, PITTSBURGH, PENNA.

LYNITE
REG. U. S. PAT. OFF.

What a proving ground! Nearly 2 Billion miles of driving each year by owners of these cars* equipped with aluminum alloy pistons.

AUBURN	ESSEX	NASH
AUSTIN	FORD	PACKARD
CHRYSLER	FRANKLIN	PEERLESS
CORD	GRAHAM	PIERCE-ARROW
DE SOTO	HUDSON	PLYMOUTH
DE VAUX	HUPMOBILE	REO
DODGE BROS.	JORDAN	ROLLS-ROYCE
DUESENBERG	LINCOLN	STUDEBAKER
DU PONT	MARMON	STUTZ
DURANT		WILLYS-KNIGHT

*From Automotive Industries

LYNITE PISTONS
AND CONNECTING RODS
MADE OF ALCOA ALUMINUM

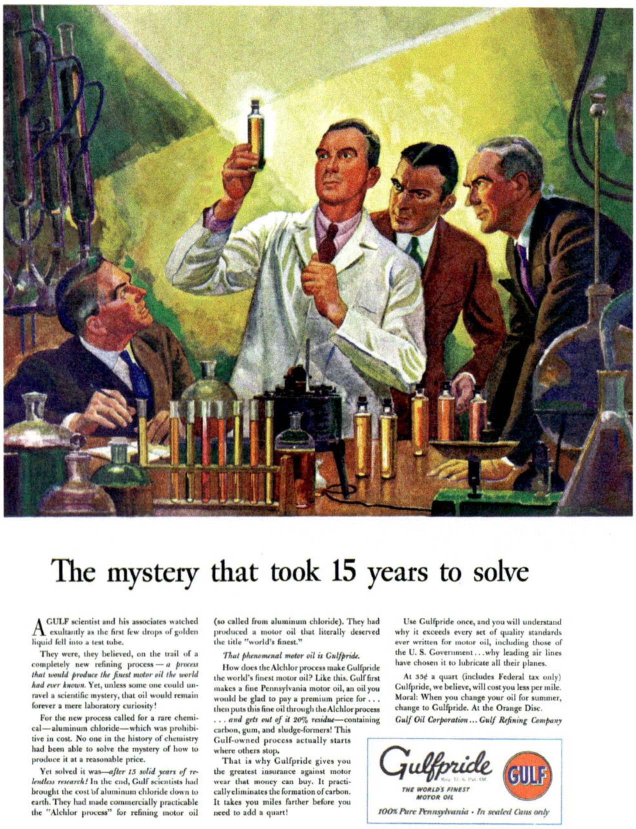

Gulf Refining Co., 1937

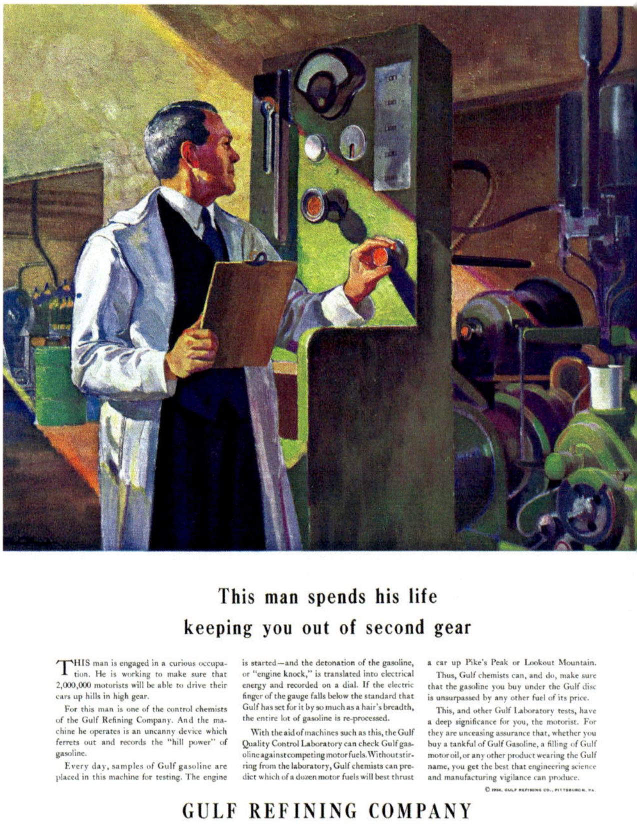

Gulf Refining Co., 1934

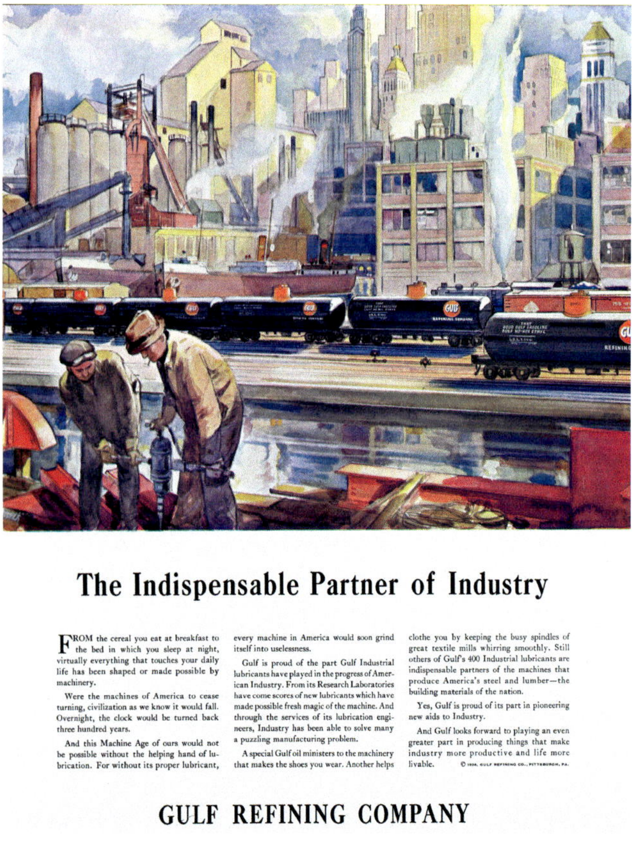

Gulf Refining Co., 1934

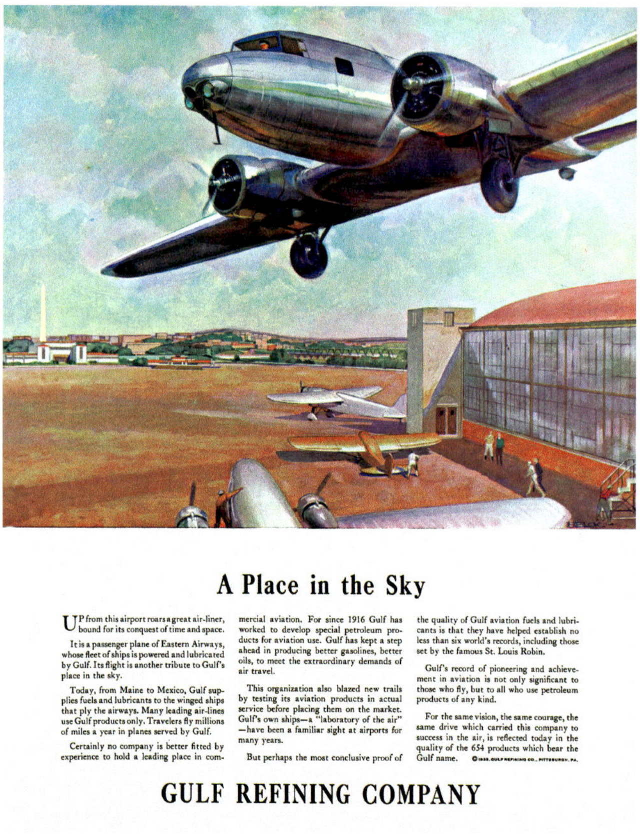

Gulf Refining Co., 1935

▸ Gulf Refining Co., 1935

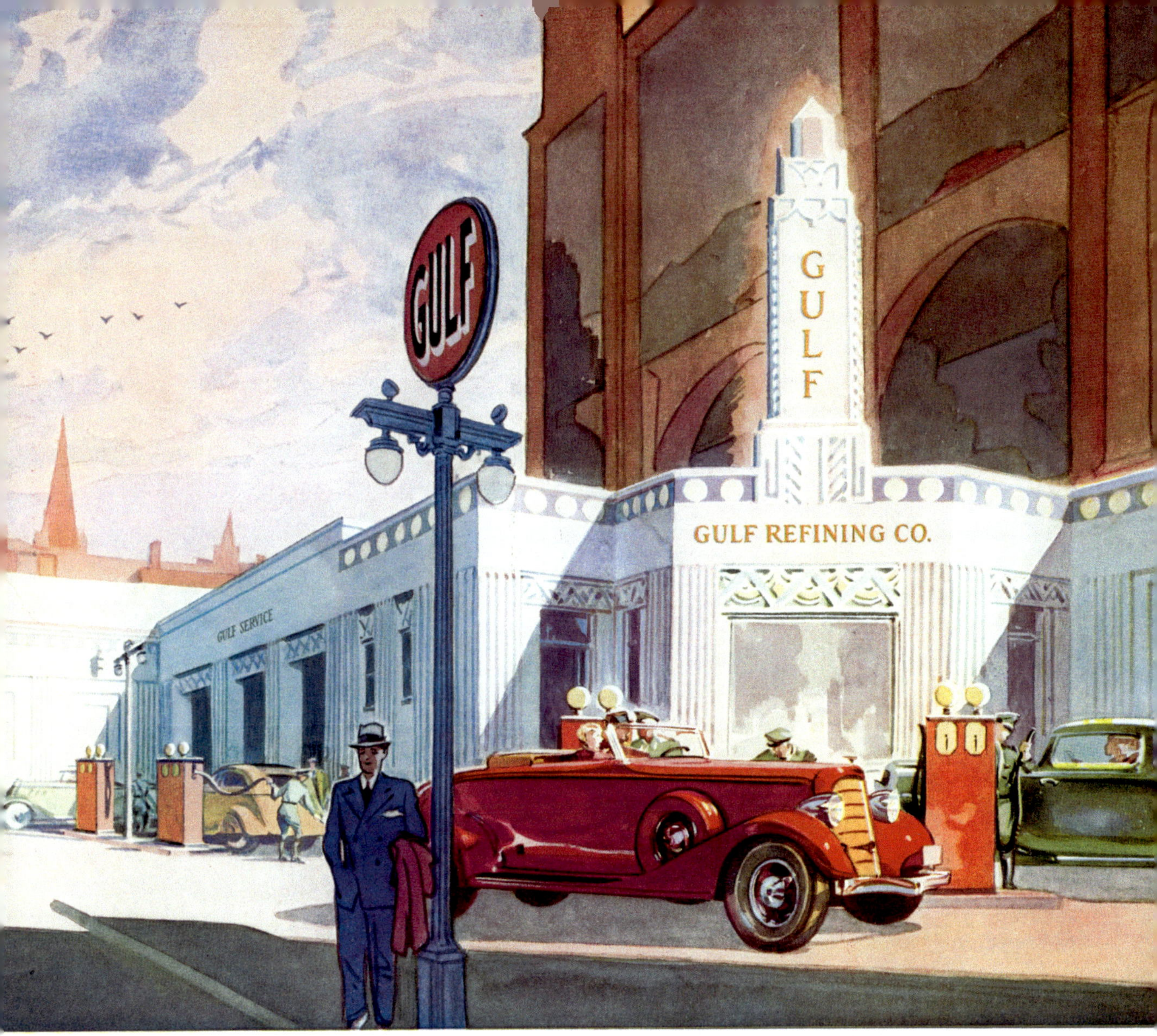

Mile-stone on a road that has no end

ON a downtown corner in a well-known Eastern city is a new and significant building.

It is a service station—one of the most complete and luxurious that may be found anywhere in America. Its beauty is unusual. Yet its significance lies in the fact that here, in stone and steel, is a prediction.

For this service station is an indication of what tomorrow may bring to the highways of America. It offers new and thoughtful conveniences to the travelling public. It is a milestone on the road toward the day when major service stations may be, in effect, depots of travel rather than ports of call.

Gulf believes that motoring is still in a stage of comparative infancy. It believes in its increasing importance in the American scene. And as this form of transportation grows in magnitude, the scope, comforts and facilities of service stations must broaden with it.

With this in mind, Gulf is constantly studying traffic flow and traffic trends, to the end of offering still other small but important comforts to road-weary motorists.

For Gulf believes that good service is only the beginning of better service. It is an evolutionary process which, because of the very nature of the industry we serve, can have no end.

GULF REFINING COMPANY

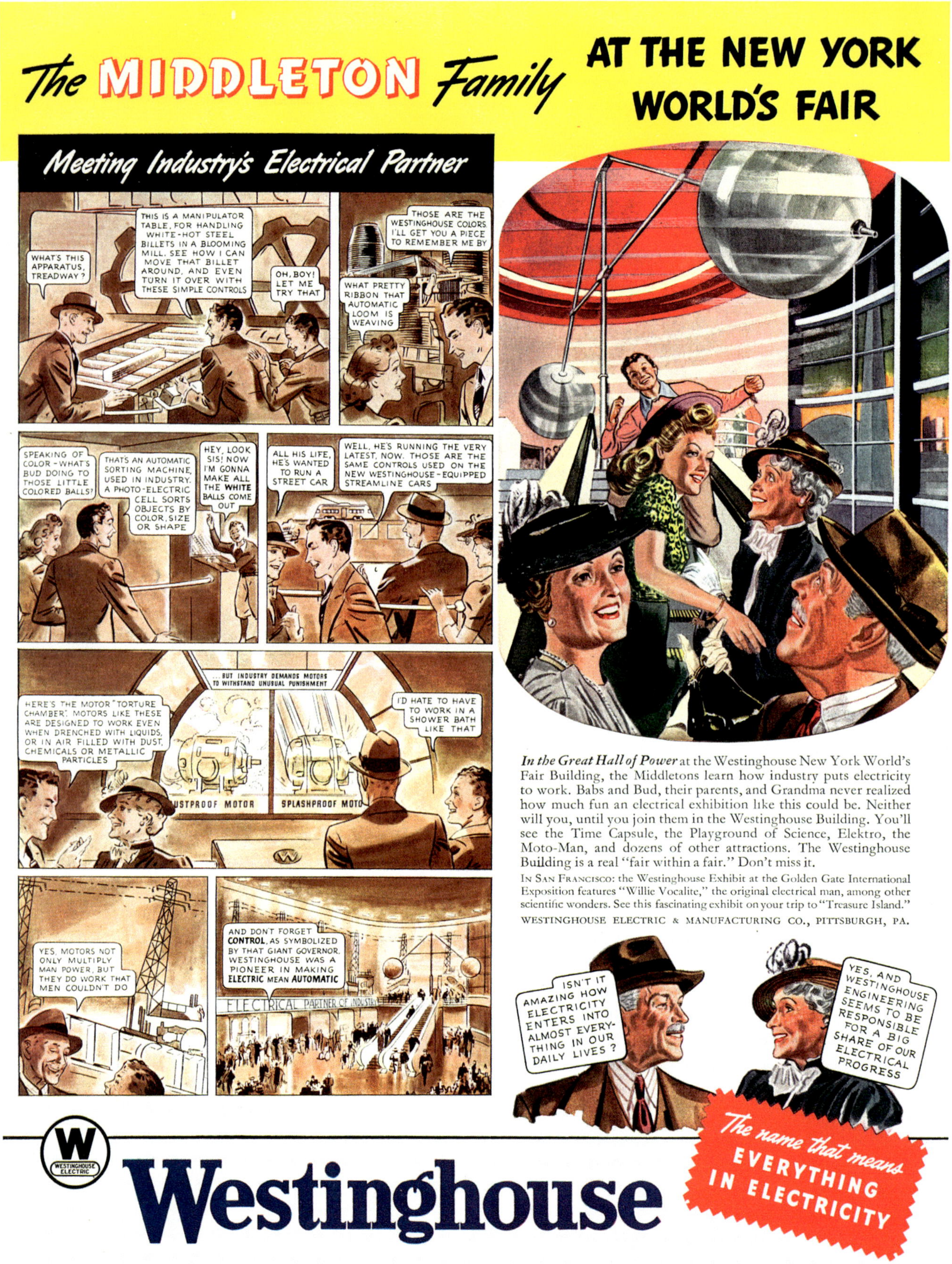

Westinghouse, 1939

► *Oldsmobile, 1930*

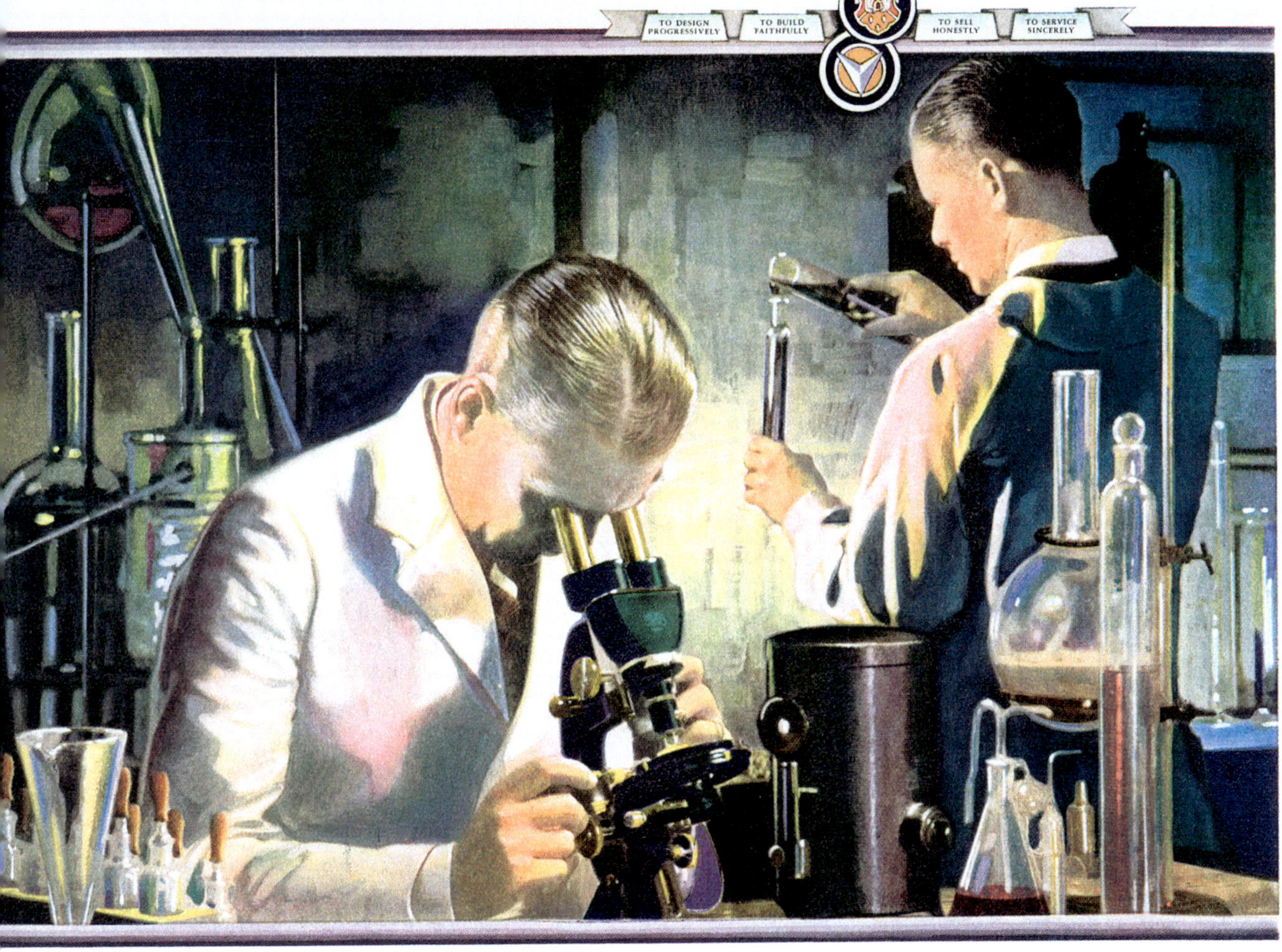

The Scientist, too, Adds His Skill in Building These Fine Cars

'ew people realize the important part science plays in guarding the quality of Oldsmobile and Viking.

/irtually every bit of material is subjected to rigid chem- or physical tests before it is specified for use in these , and again during the manufacturing process.

The equipment of these scientific laboratories includes ices for testing the hardness of metal . . . devices to prove esistance to twisting . . . devices to measure its compressi- y . . . devices to check tensile strength.

There are microscopes to show the grain size and distri- on in metal. There are camera attachments to photo- h microstructure for close inspection. There is full ipment for both quantitative and qualitative chemical lyses. In short, Oldsmobile-Viking scientists have at r disposal complete, modern laboratory apparatus for ırate, efficient chemical and metallurgical control work.

These extensive laboratories are maintained for only one purpose—to make sure that everything that goes into Oldsmobile or Viking meets the exacting standards of science.

Such care is consistent with the Oldsmobile-Viking principle of safeguarding quality. More than that, it is a fundamental step in maintaining to the letter the four responsibilities Olds Motor Works recognizes toward every owner . . . to design progressively; to manufacture faithfully; to sell honestly; to service sincerely . . . four responsibilities which provide firm assurance to the public that both Oldsmobile and Viking are fine, dependable automobiles.

OLDSMOBILE SIX
VIKING EIGHT

PRODUCTS OF GENERAL MOTORS

J&L STEEL

JALCOLD

A TINPLATE FOR SEVERE TREATMEN

A notable example of Jones & Laughlin product development

This cold rolled special purpose plate is Jones & Laughlin's latest and greatest advance in twenty-four years of making high quality tin plate. The cold reducing mill on which Jalcold is rolled is shown in the illustration. It employs a balanced combination of pressure, speed and tension, all of which factors are closely regulated by means of highly sensitive, mechanical and electrical controls. Careful choice as to the chemical analy the steel used, and the rolling on this most modern improved mill, produce a plate which is more unifor gauge, has a smoother surface and a greater adaptab for severe drawing operations than any tin plate p ously produced. Jalcold Tin Plate should be spec for exacting requirements demanding these qual

JONES & LAUGHLIN STEEL CORPORATION

AMERICAN IRON AND STEEL WORKS

JONES & LAUGHLIN BUILDING, PITTSBURGH, PENNSYLVANIA

J & L STEEL PRODUCTS . . . *Open Hearth and Bessemer Steel*

Billets, Sheet Bars, Skelp . . . Hot Rolled Bars, Plates, Shapes, Strip and Sheets . . . Light Weight Channels . . . Railroad Spikes and Tie Plates . . . Bars for Concrete Reinforcement . . . Forgi . . . Jalcase Steel . . . Cold Finished Steel . . . Steel Piling . . . Junior Beams . . . Fabricated Structural Work . . . Standard Pipe . . . Seamless Oil Country Tubular Products . . . Hot Rolled S Boiler Tubes . . . Seamless and Welded Mechanical Tubing . . . Wire Rods and Wire Products . . . Tin Plate and Black Sheets . . . Coke By-Products

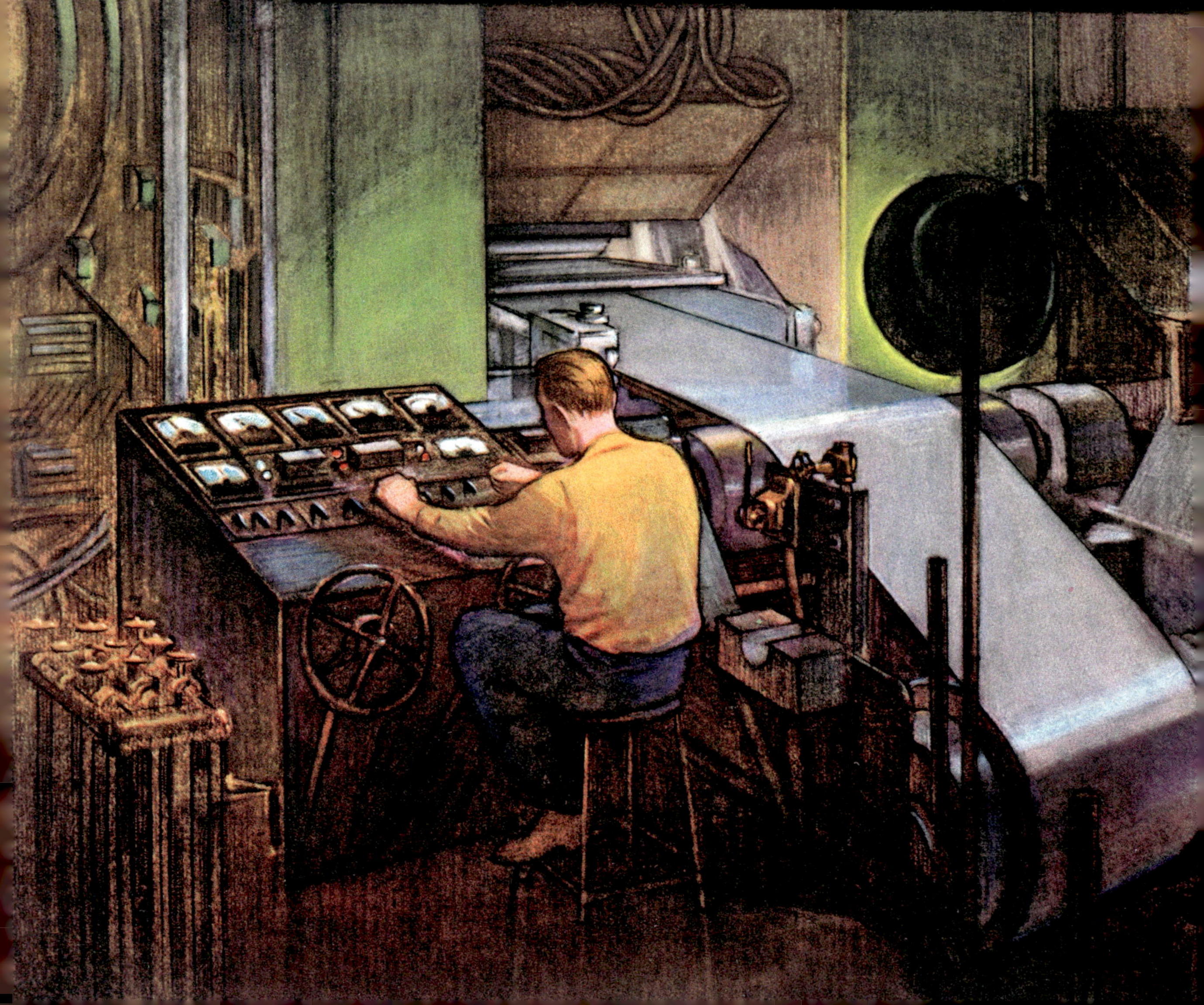

"To save time is to lengthen life—"

"ACCELERATION, rather than structural change, is the key to an understanding of our recent economic developments."

—From the report of President Hoover's Committee on Recent Economic Changes

THE PLOD of the ox-cart. The jog trot of the horse and buggy. The rush of the high-powered motor car. The zoom of the airplane. Acceleration. *Faster* speed all the time. ✓ Speed and more speed in production, transportation, communication, and as a result, more wealth, more happiness, and yes, more leisure for us all. ✓ Scientific research has been the pacemaker of this faster, yet more leisurely, existence. At a steadily increasing rate it is giving us hundreds of inventions and improvements which speed up work, save time and money, revolutionize life and labor in the modern age. ✓ Conceive how much time modern electric lighting has saved the American people—not to mention the billion dollars a year in lighting bills saved by the repeatedly improved efficiency of the Mazda lamp. Think of the extraordinary democratization of entertainment and education made possible by the radio tube! ✓ Both these benefits to the public owe much to the steady flow of discovery and invention from General Electric laboratories. So do the X-ray and cathode-ray tubes, the calorizing of steel, atomic-hydrogen welding, the generation of power for home and industry at steadily lower costs. ✓ The G-E monogram is a symbol of research. Every product bearing this monogram represents to-day and will represent to-morrow the highest standard of electrical correctness and dependability.

JOIN US IN THE GENERAL ELECTRIC HOUR, BROADCAST EVERY SATURDAY AT 9 P. M., E. S. T., ON A NATION-WIDE N. B. C. NETWORK

For the Home—General Electric and its associated companies manufacture a complete line of electric products including G-E Mazda and G-E Edison Mazda lamps, G-E refrigerators, G-E fans, G-E vacuum cleaners, G-E wiring systems, Edison Hotpoint heating appliances, and G-E motors for other household electric products.

For Industry—Several thousand electric products and appliances, including generating and distributing apparatus, motors, electric heating apparatus, street lights, floodlights, traffic lights, airport lights, Cooper Hewitt lights, Victor X-ray apparatus, motion-picture apparatus, electric locomotives and equipment, and street-car equipment.

GENERAL ELECTRIC

General Electric, 1930

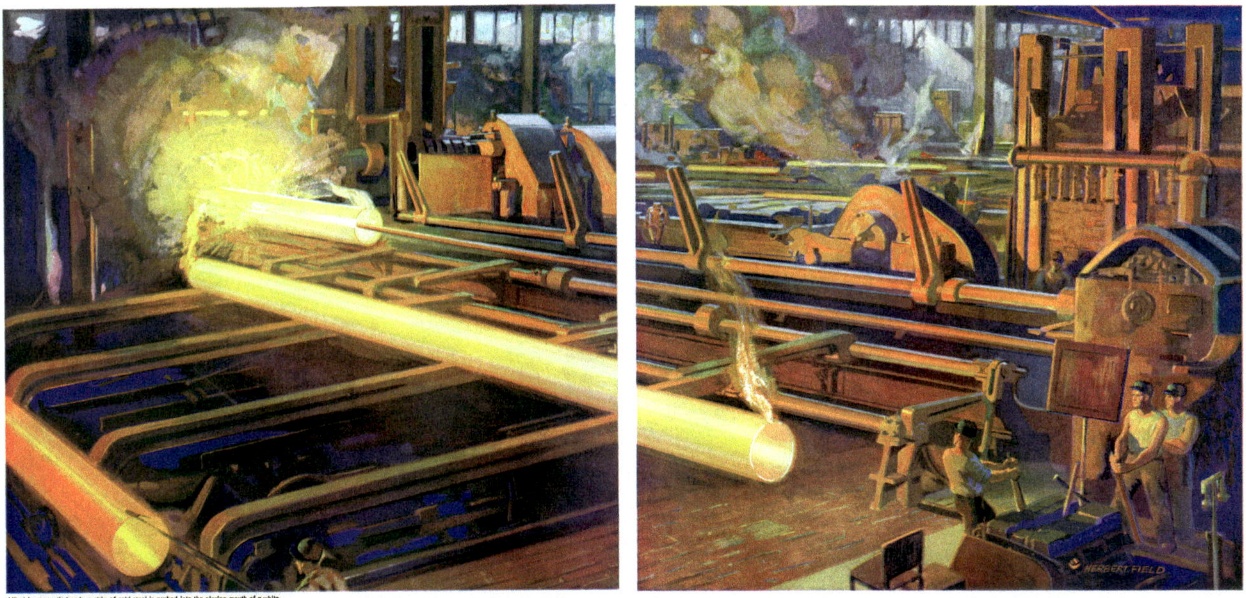

Lifted by magnetic hands, a strip of cold steel is pushed into the glaring mouth of a white hot furnace. Masked men, moving like automatons, drag it out again—blinding hot—hurling off a million tiny meteors of steel. Shaped—reheated—welded, amid a crackling symphony of noises, it rolls down the skids for finishing, cutting, threading, testing, shipping.

. . A MIGHTY SPECTACLE OF STEEL

Picturesque and awe inspiring is this mighty spectacle of steel—the making of pipe by the "lap-weld" process, which, with the "butt-weld" process, holds an important place in the manufacture of pipe. But Republic, alert to changing trends in industry and never content to let well enough alone, has expended $10,000,000 in acquiring and developing a newer method—faster, more economical and far better in results—the instantaneous Electric Weld. Originally used for welding small tubing and conduit, this process now handles sizes up to sixteen inches. Large users, insisting upon the most rigid standards of quality, have already purchased over four thousand miles of Republic Electric Weld Pipe. Repeat orders, constantly coming in from these original buyers, give tangible evidence of satisfactory service. The pipe of the future will be Electric Weld—and Republic, by its large investment in this revolutionary process, has merely given further evidence of its adoption of a program of continuous improvement and constructive contribution to better products of steel.

REPUBLIC STEEL CORPORATION
HEADQUARTERS: YOUNGSTOWN, OHIO

ALLOY AND CARBON STEELS . TONCAN IRON . STAINLESS STEEL . PIPE AND TUBULAR PRODUCTS . BARS AND SHAPES . HOT AND COLD ROLLED STRIP . COKE . PIG IRON PLATES . BLACK, BLUE ANNEALED AND GALVANIZED SHEETS . SPECIAL FINISH SHEETS . TIN PLATE . NUTS, BOLTS, RIVETS, ETC. . WIRE PRODUCTS . DIE ROLLED PRODUCTS

Jones & Laughlin, 1934 ◂ *Republic Steel Co., 1931*

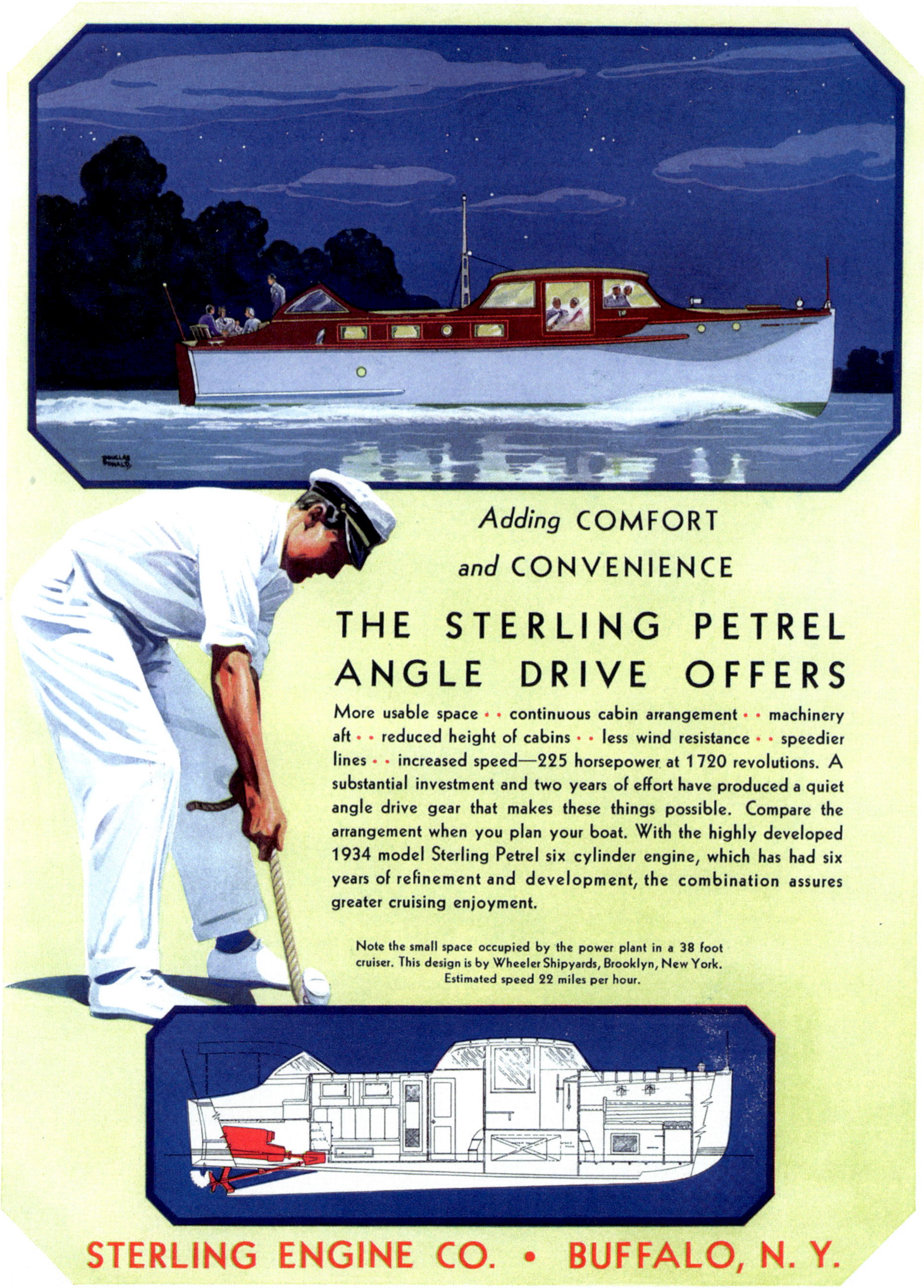

Sterling Engine Co., 1934

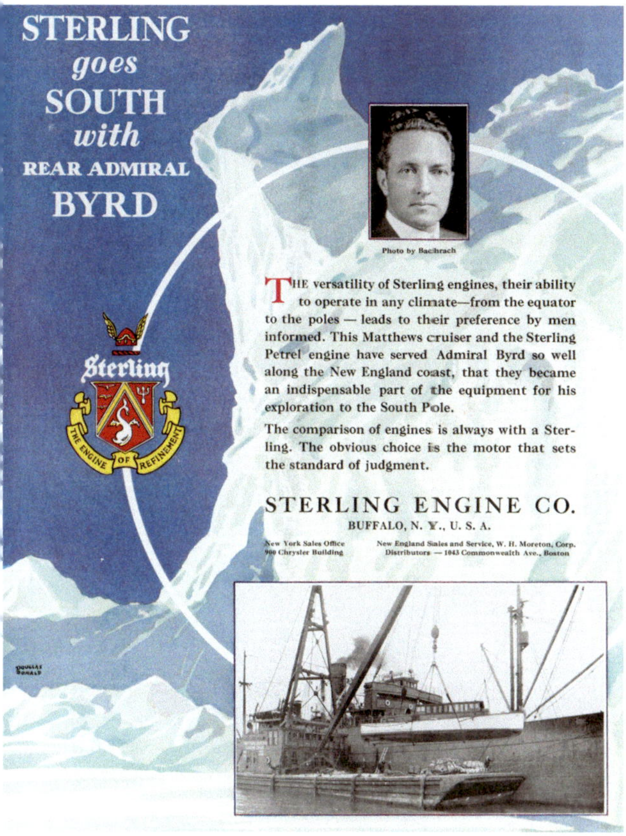

Sterling Engine Co., 1934

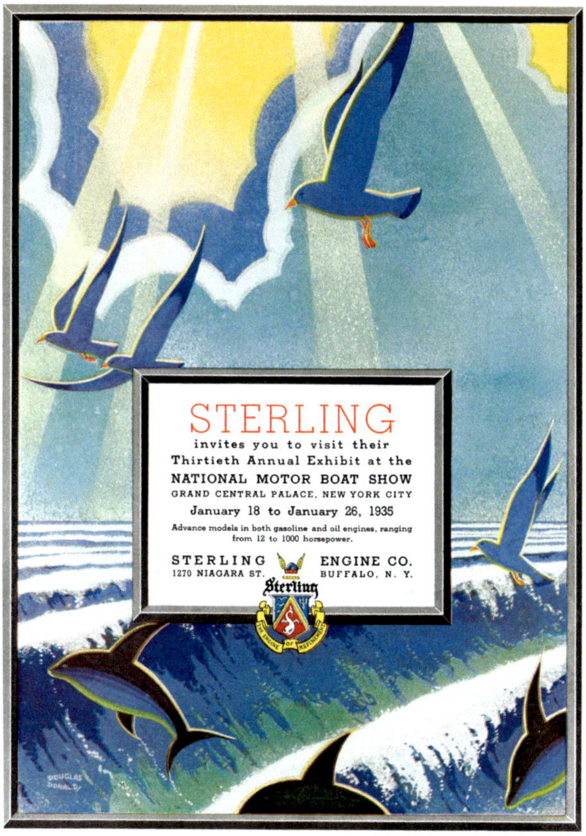

Sterling Engine Co., 1935

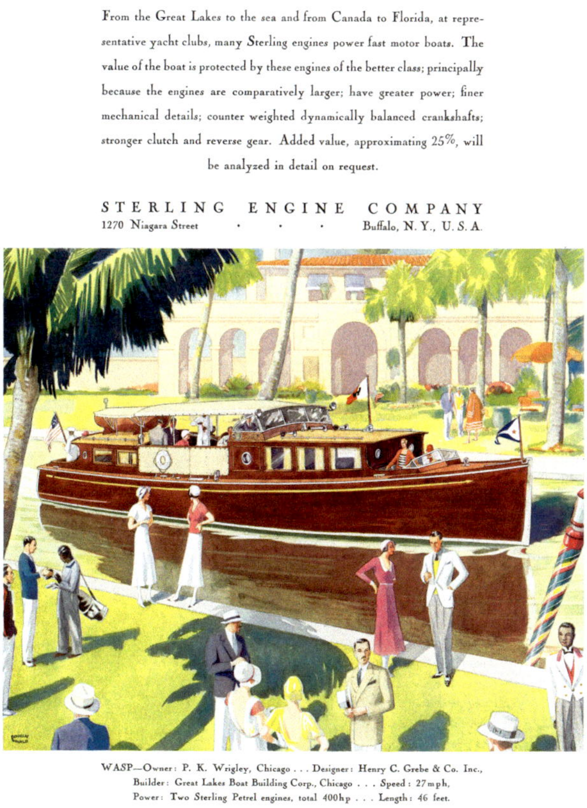

Sterling Engine Co., 1932

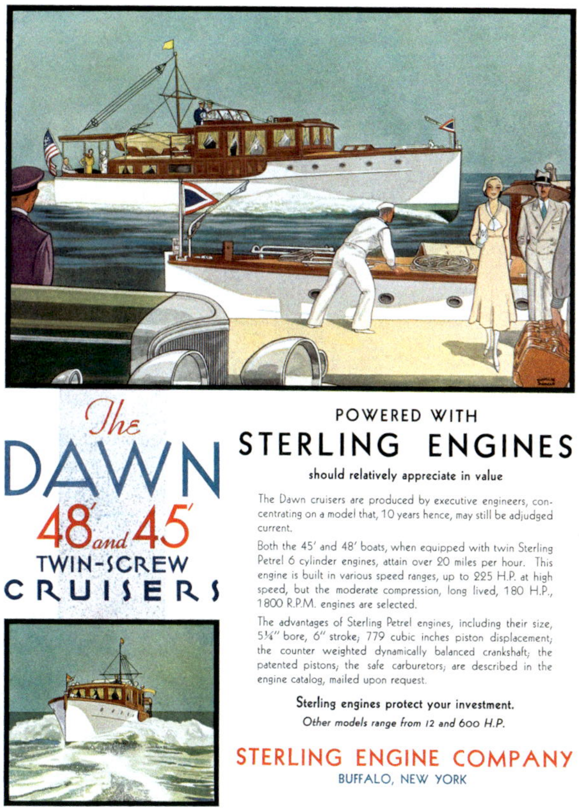

Sterling Engine Co., 1931

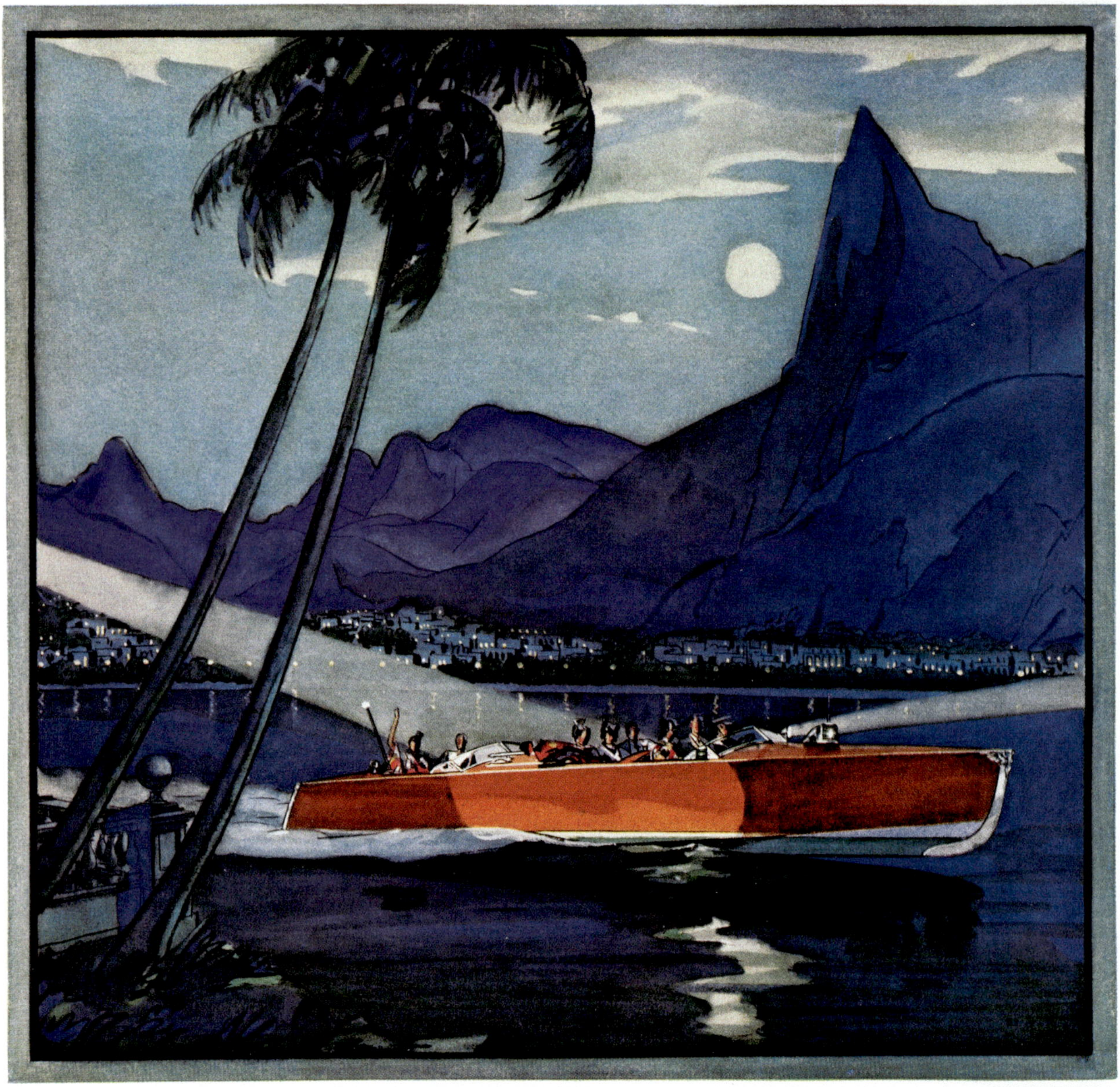

DODGE 28-FT. RUNABOUT — 300 H. P. LYCOMING V-TYPE, 12 CYL. ENGINE — 45 M. P. H. — SEATS 10 — PRICE, F. O. B. WORKS: $4500

FROM moonlight on Rio's Botafogo Crescent to California's golden sunshine - - - - from Palm Beach to the Riviera - - - - wherever sport and romance ride the waters, there you find Dodge Boats - - - - Flashing beauty to give the eye a new delight - - - - fleeting speed to bring new thrills to sportsmen - - - - amazingly low prices well within the reach of thousands who never before could satisfy their wish to own a fine boat - - - - From the 16-foot runabout at $945 to the 45-mile speedster at $4500, Dodge Boats present the utmost in value at the world's lowest prices - - - - Planked with genuine mahogany, the bottoms double planked, with ribs and frames of stout white oak, today's Dodge Fleet excels even the previous craftsmanship of Dodge - - - - The smallest of the fleet makes 30 miles an hour and the largest rides with ease at the racing speed of 45 miles - - - - The Dodge catalog shows and describes all Dodge Boats in 16, 21, 25 and 28 foot lengths, open and closed models - - - - A copy will be sent free on request.

DODGE BOATS

HORACE E. DODGE BOAT & PLANE CORPORATION, Works: Newport News, Va. GENERAL SALES DEPARTMENT: 21 West 46th St., New York City

Dodge Boats, 1930

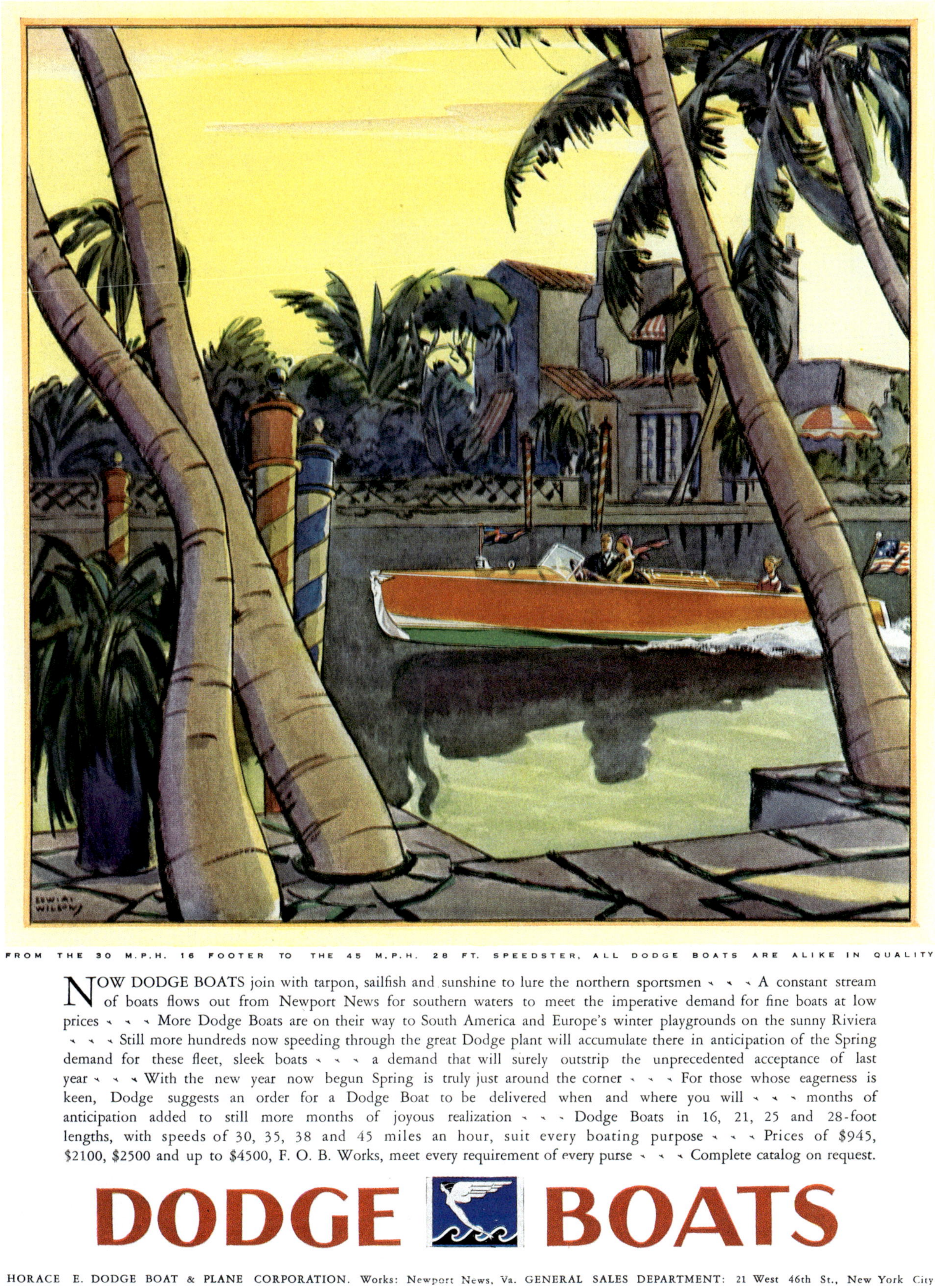

Dodge Boats, 1931

STERLING ENGINES

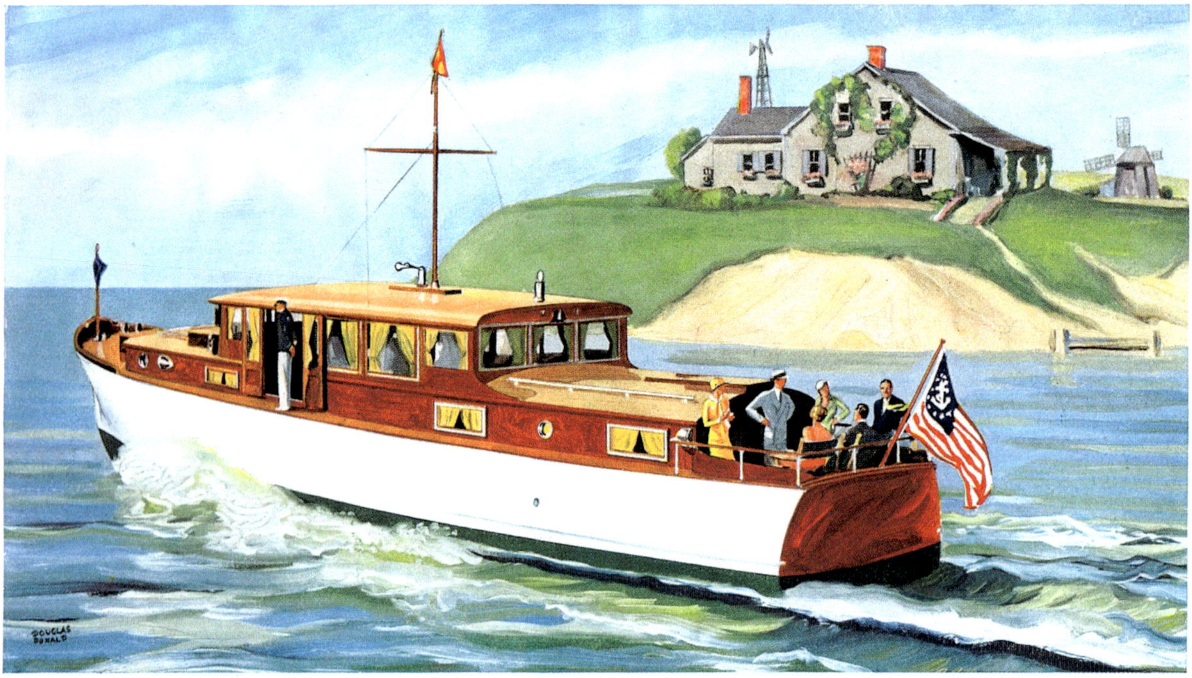

Matthews 46 foot enclosed bridge deck cruiser. Speed with single Sterling Petrel ,20 miles plus; with twin Sterling Petrels, 26 miles.

JUDGE VALUE BY COMPARISON

The Sterling Petrel 180-225 H. P. engine is the better buy for Matthews cruisers. The staunchly built heavily timbered hulls; intended for years of seaworthiness, beautifully refined, require power. Petrel engines contribute years of smooth service with ordinary attention; are more carefully built and longer tested, so that the hazard of "running in" the engine is eliminated. The patented Sterling piston is successful. The engine is lower in height, reducing the center of gravity, but has a long connecting rod, reducing piston side thrust and cylinder wear.

Sterling

THE ENGINE OF REFINEMENT

MODELS FROM 12 TO 565 H. P.

Sterling builds all high powered engines with a counter weighted dynamically balanced crankshaft, accepting a handicap of its added cost, to reduce the forces which otherwise deteriorate an engine. And the Petrel is almost 15% larger than engines of comparative price! Quieter running at less effort, eliminates the need of ever removing the engine from the boat for bearing attention. The additional cost of the Petrel is slight—but more than compensated in desirable attributes, which you are invited to consider. Investigate before you buy.

STERLING ENGINE COMPANY • BUFFALO, N. Y., U. S. A.

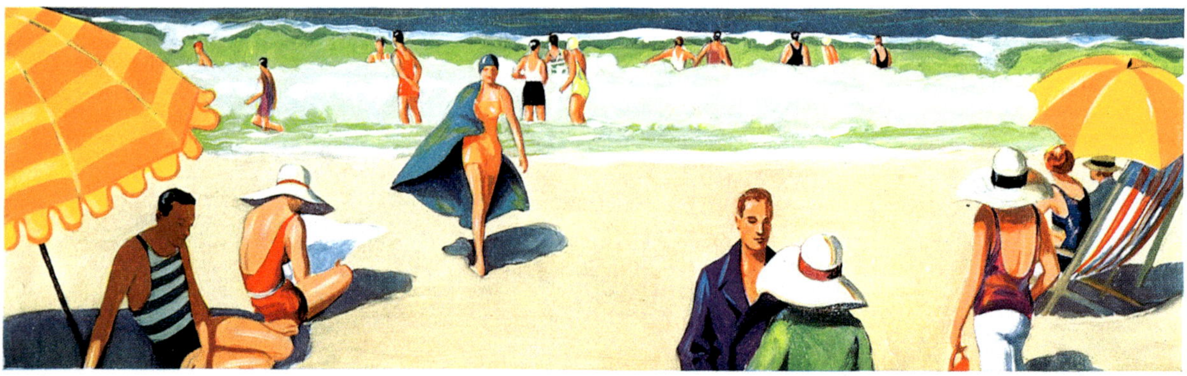

Sterling Engine Co., 1932

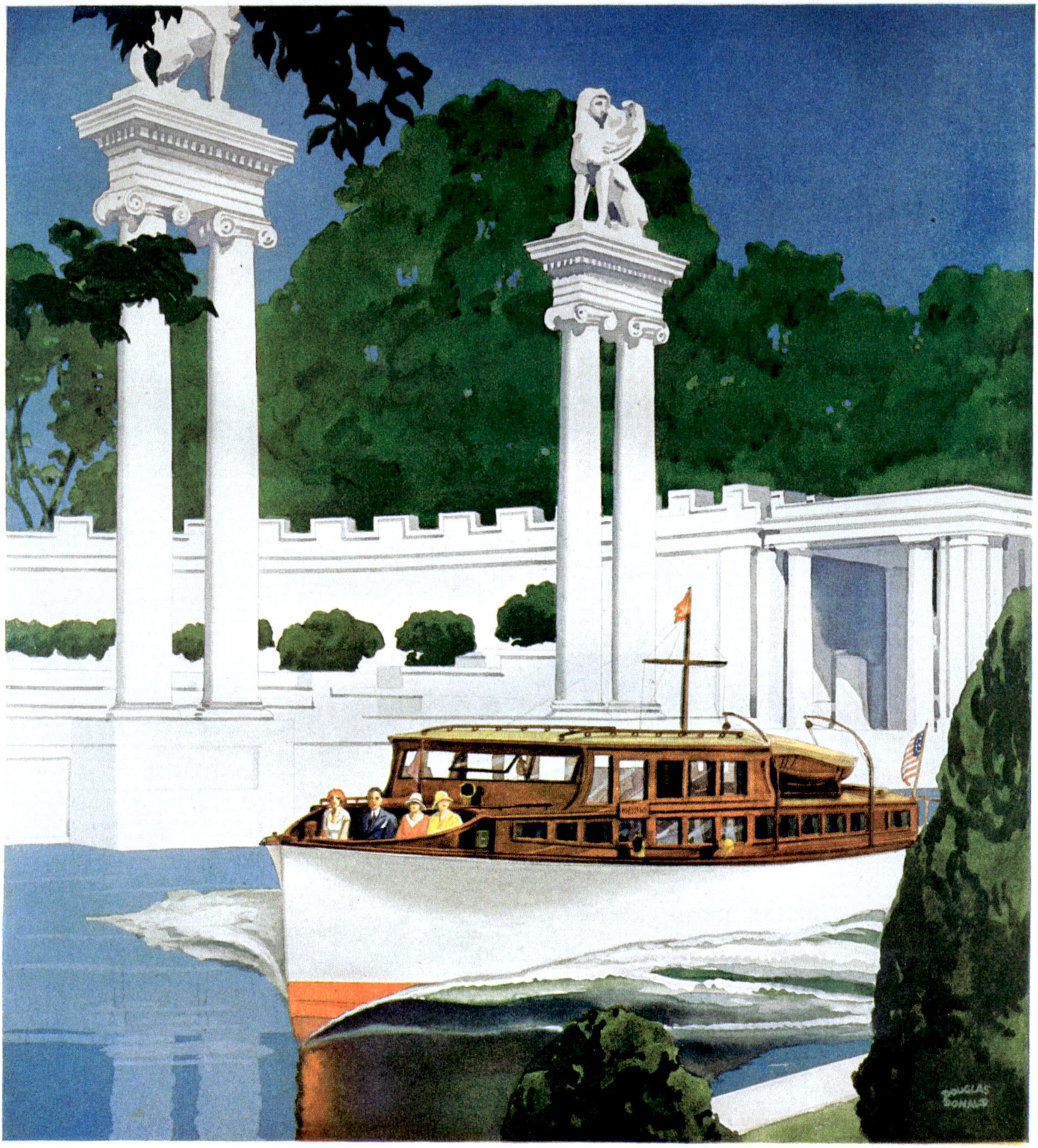

The Record Breaking

FAIRFORM FLYER

56′ Fairform Flyer, built by Huckins Yacht Corp., Jacksonville, Fla. Equipped with twin Dolphin Special 6 cylinder Sterling engines 290 H. P. each, 1950 R. P. M.

Modern in design and speed, equipped with established seasoned engines, the new Fairform Flyer suggests a late afternoon cruise—the antithesis of the lawn party of the 'eighties. Or, perhaps a week end journey of exploration—new scenery, open space, relaxation, and kindred terms, that prepare you for Monday with a feeling of having rediscovered America. . . . .

STERLING ENGINE COMPANY

BUFFALO, NEW YORK, U. S. A.

W. H. Moreton Corp., Distributors, Boston

Bruns, Kimball & Co., Distributors, New York

Sterling Engine Co., 1930

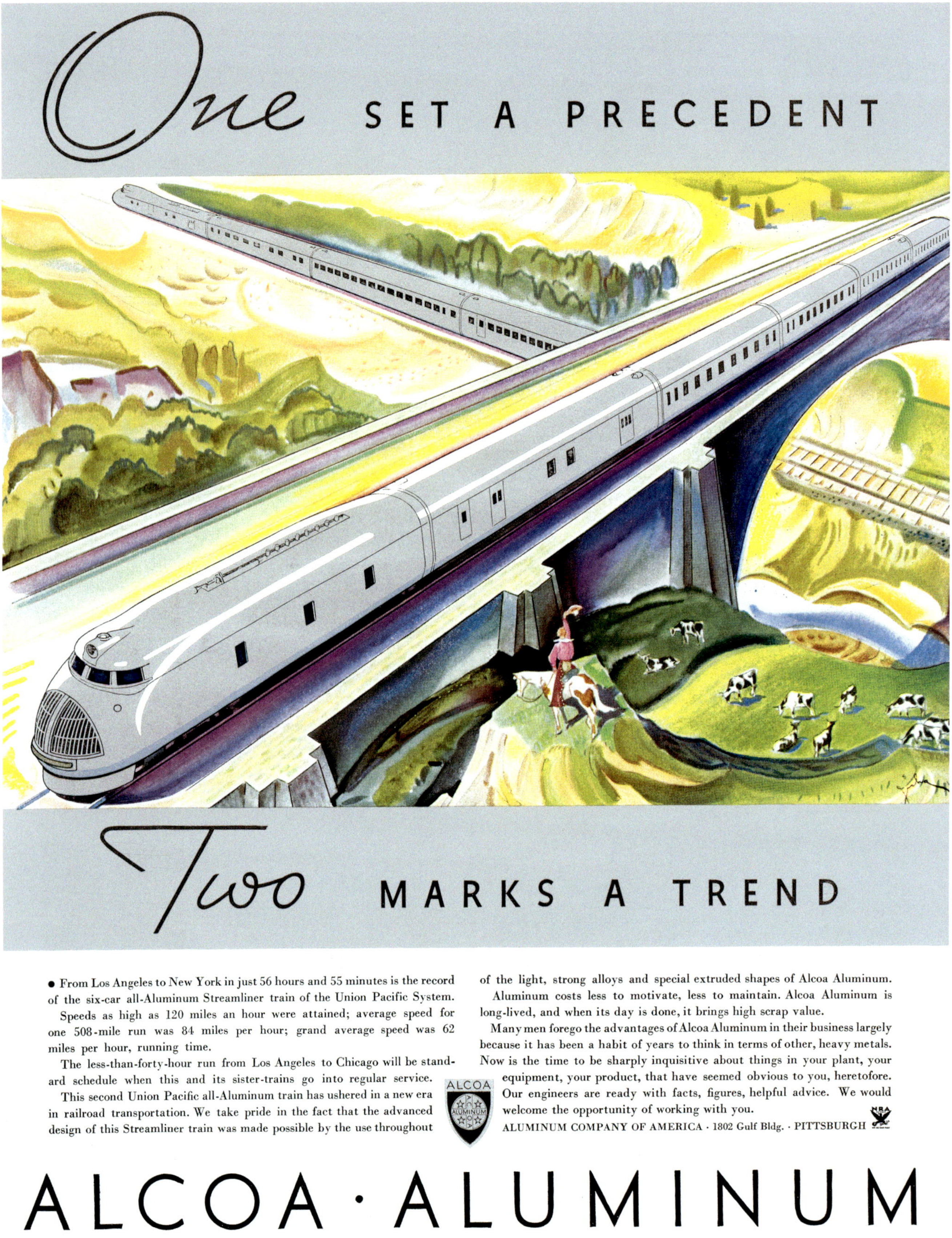

Alcoa Aluminum, 1935

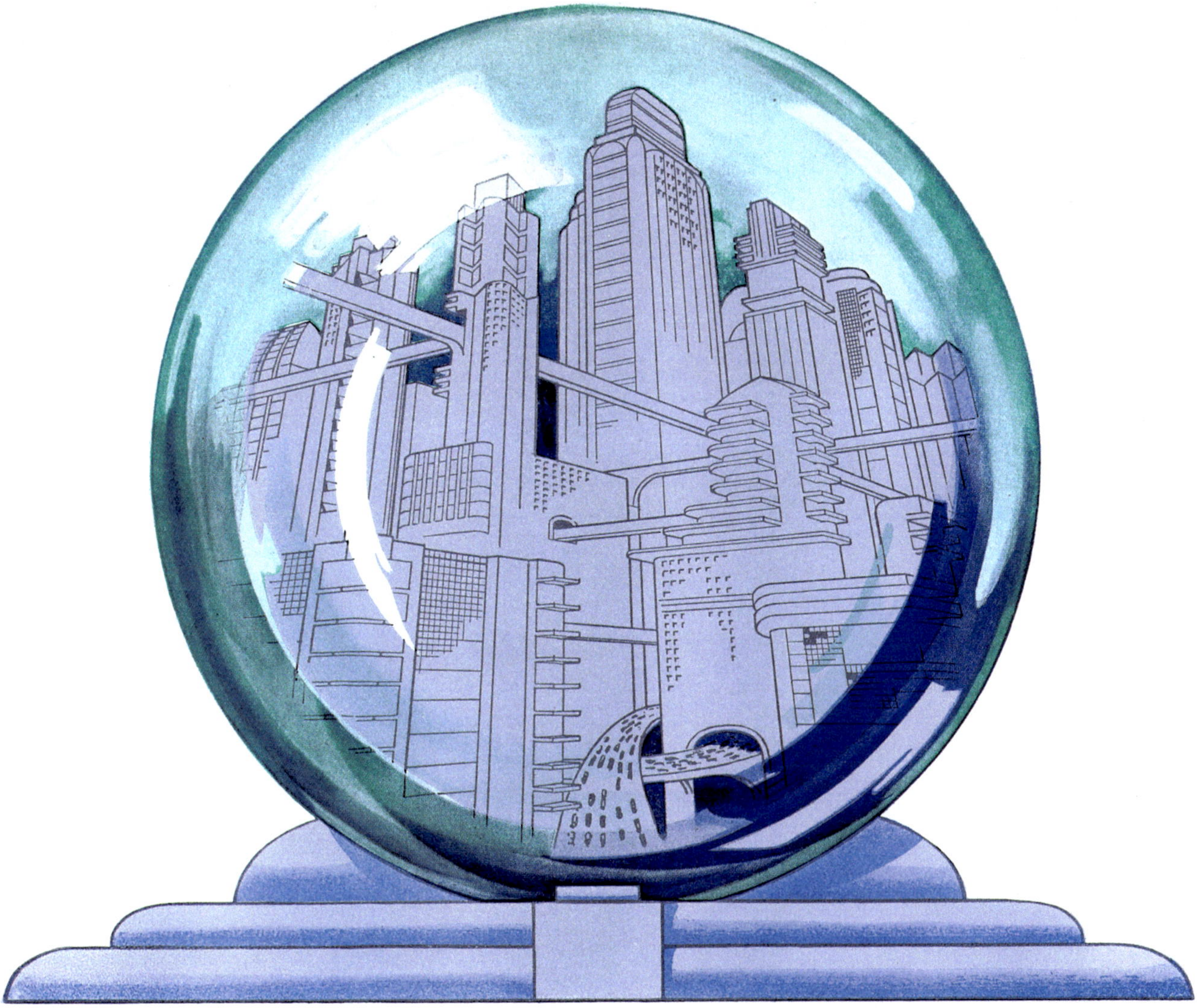

Peer into the Future

Alcoa Aluminum is revealed

a shining symbol of strength . . . light weight . . . enduring beauty

Even as we look, the present passes. A decade slips by and the desire for the stimulating contacts of city life has increased our urban population twice as fast as the country at large.

Crowded metropolitan space demands expansion—but how? Probably through buildings rising tier upon tier; overhead traffic lanes; roof space for aeroplane landings; aerial sidewalks; terraced parks—buildings mounting ever upward.

Peer into the future and Alcoa Aluminum is revealed. Weighing only one-third as much as metals now commonly used, Alcoa Aluminum is destined to play a prominent part in future building development.

Alcoa Aluminum resists corrosion. It need not be painted. It will not streak adjoining surfaces. It can be cast, forged, drawn, extruded, welded and riveted. On the exterior of buildings its beauty is already seen—its light weight and strength utilized. For the interior trim and furnishings of office buildings, stores, and residences its decorative charm is employed. Providing the architect with a metal that lends itself readily to design and fine detail; that insures permanence; that saves handling of unnecessary dead-weight; that cuts cost of erection, Alcoa Aluminum will find ever-increasing use.

In each of our offices we have competent representatives, who are familiar with the decorative and structural uses of each of the special Alcoa Aluminum alloys. The services of these representatives are available to architects. ALUMINUM COMPANY *of* AMERICA; 2497 Oliver Building, PITTSBURGH, PA.

ALCOA ALUMINUM

Alcoa Aluminum, 1931

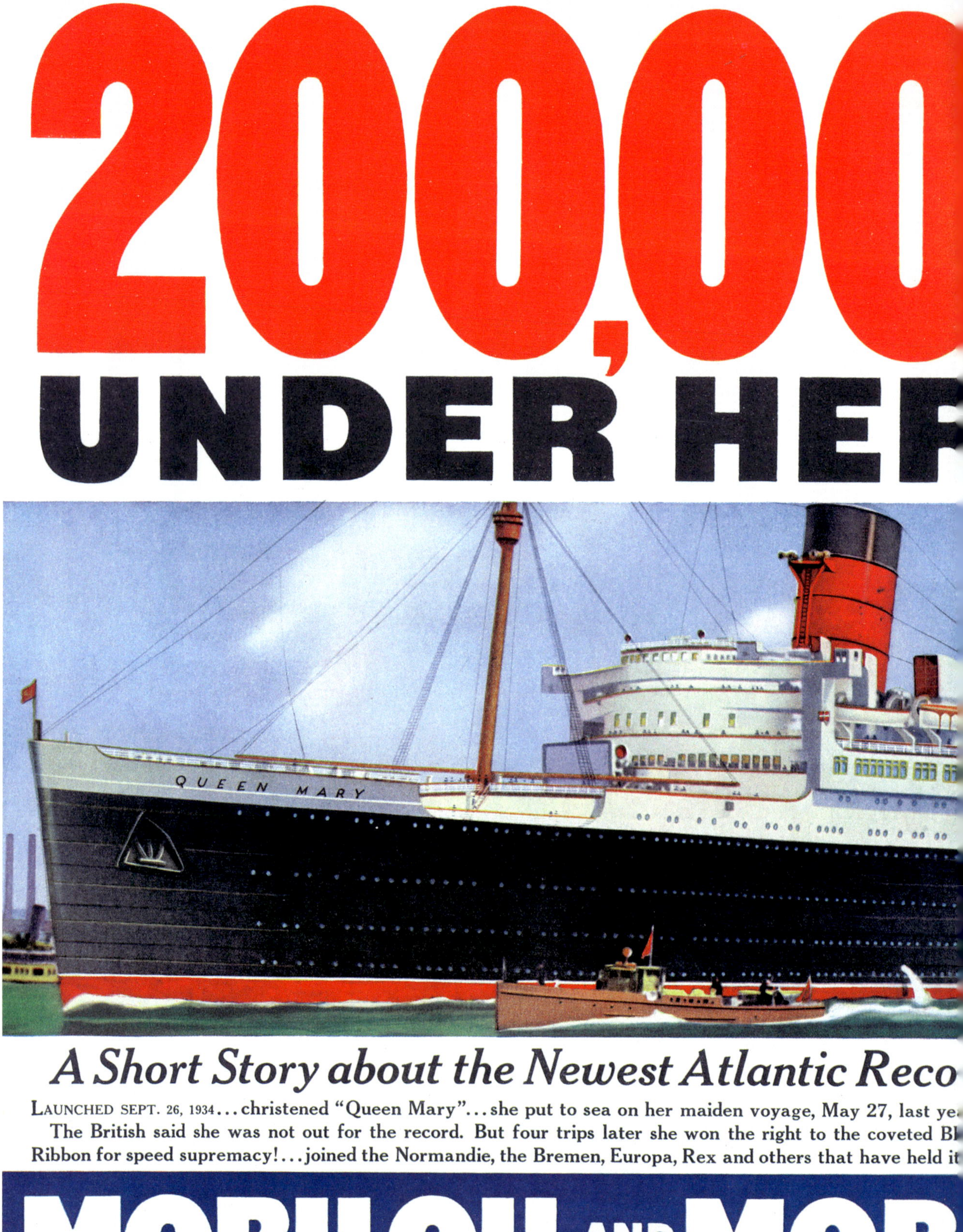
200,00
UNDER HER
QUEEN MARY
A Short Story about the Newest Atlantic Reco
LAUNCHED SEPT. 26, 1934...christened "Queen Mary"...she put to sea on her maiden voyage, May 27, last ye
The British said she was not out for the record. But four trips later she won the right to the coveted Bl
Ribbon for speed supremacy!...joined the Normandie, the Bremen, Europa, Rex and others that have held it
MOBILOIL AND MOB

0H.P

HOOD_

AND SHE RELIES ON THE MAKERS OF MOBILOIL FOR VITAL ENGINE PROTECTION

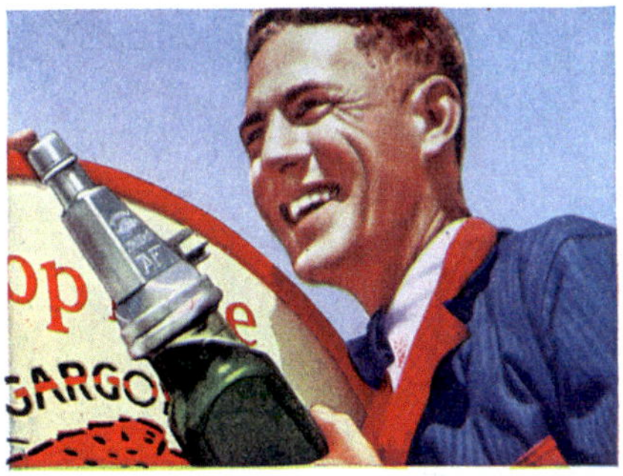

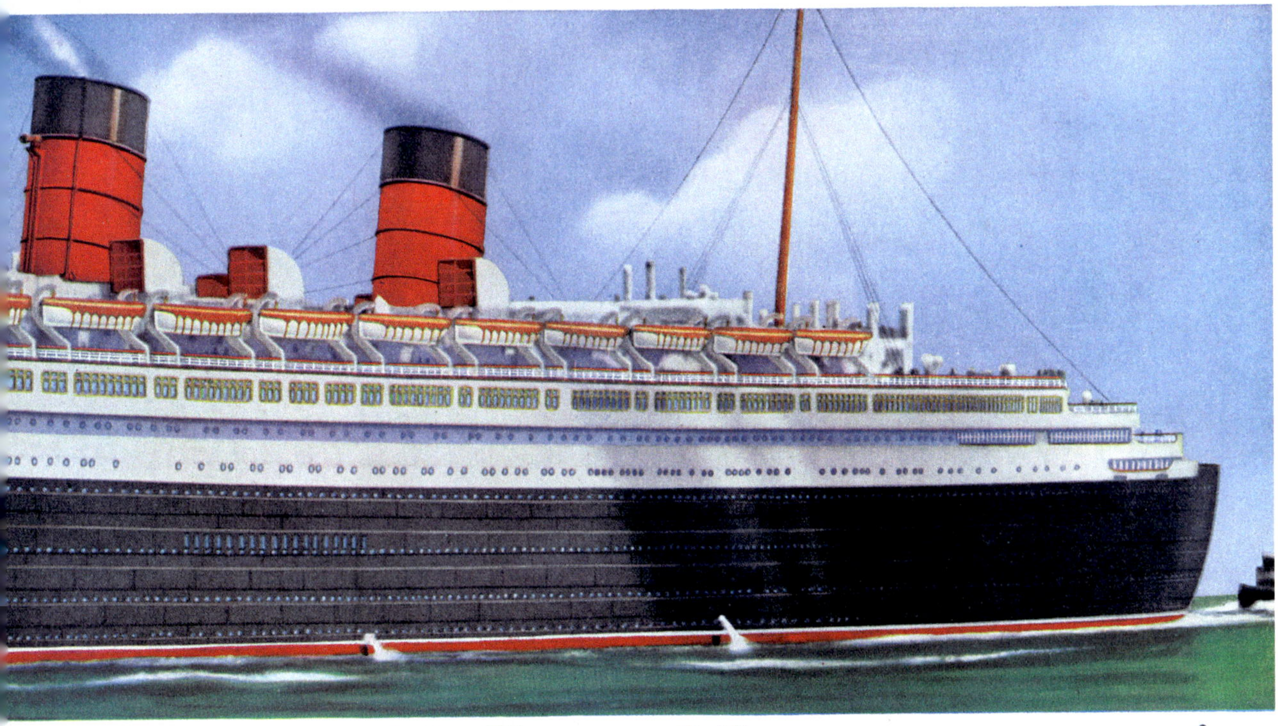

ɔlder.. the World's Finest Oil.. AND YOUR CAR!

hat has this to do with your car? Just this: every North Atlantic record-breaker has been lubricated by
: makers of Mobiloil. Which just about makes Mobiloil the world's Blue Ribbon motor oil, doesn't it?
t does. Mobiloil is the world's largest-selling motor oil today. Use it in your car... and you have the best!

GAS SOCONY-VACUUM OIL COMPANY, INC.

Mobilgas Mobiloil

Socony-Vacuum Oil Co., 1937

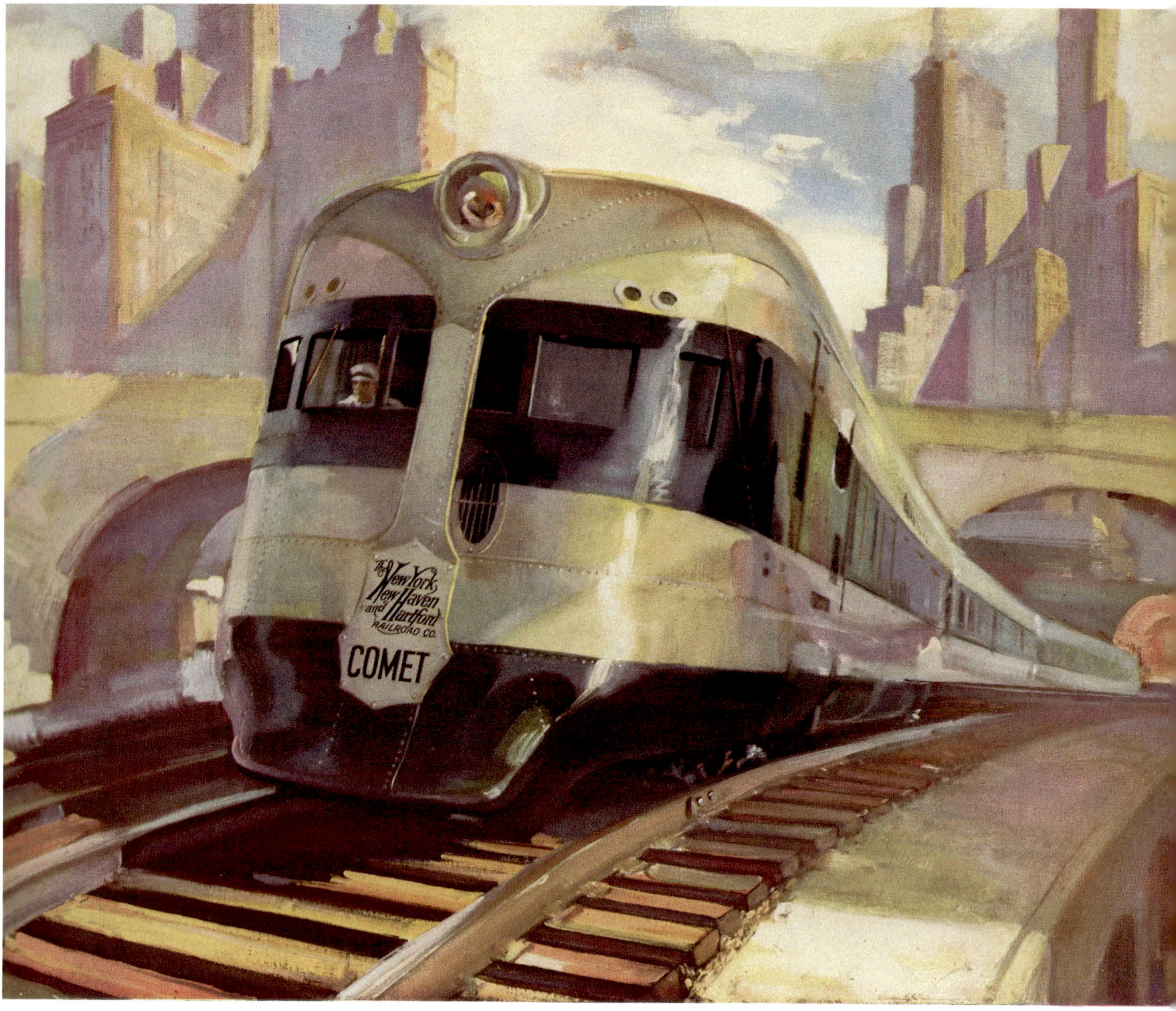

The Railroad Revolution

LAST December, *Fortune* made a prophecy. In the lightweight, streamlined Diesel train, said this publication, lay the genesis of a railroad revolution.

Today—less than one year later—the revolution is in full swing. The Diesel train is fast becoming a familiar part of the American scene. And a silvery symbol of this new era in rail transportation is the New York, New Haven and Hartford's "Comet."

Slipping through space like a meteor through the sky, this new train cuts one-third off the regular time between Boston and Providence. It can travel at a speed of 110 miles an hour, and still have power in reserve.

And every mile "The Comet" clicks off is a tribute to the quality of Gulf products. For its two great Diesel units are now fueled and lubricated exclusively by Gulf.

Perhaps no single organization is better equipped to take a part in the railroad revolution than the Gulf Refining Company. Its experimental work with Diesel engines dates back many years, beginning with the marine engines in Gulf's own great fleet of tankers.

As the Diesel has lost weight and gained horsepower, special fuels and lubricants have been developed to meet each changing condition. And now Gulf scientists are working towards the day when Diesel transportation will demand still more of Gulf.

It is possible, and even probable, that the Diesel train will soon become the ordinary means of high-speed overland travel. But however fast it may develop, Gulf will be ready with the proper fuels and lubricants.

GULF REFINING COMPANY

Gulf Refining Co., 1935

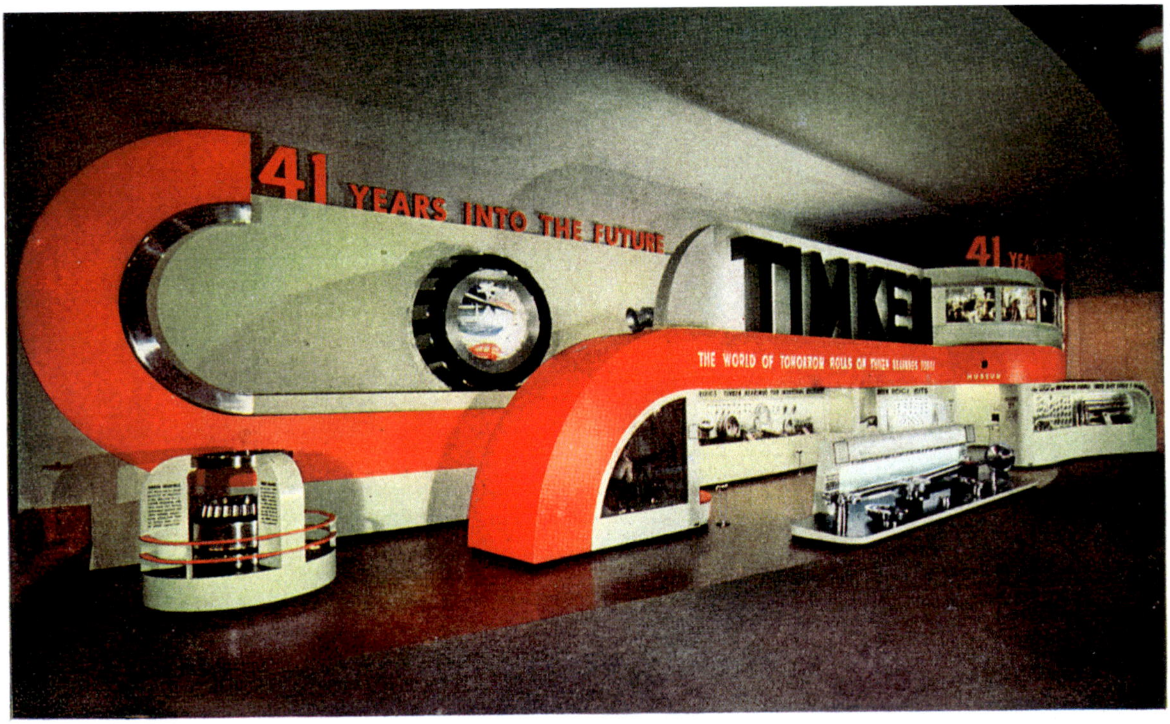

With TIMKEN At The New York World's Fair

INTERESTING HIGHLIGHTS OF THE TIMKEN EXHIBIT

One of the first automobiles to be equipped with TIMKEN Bearings.

A TIMKEN Roll Neck Bearing having a load capacity of nearly three million pounds.

A machine that measures the thickness of a human hair in hundred-thousandths of an inch, as a demonstration of the precision with which TIMKEN Bearings are made.

A diorama showing in miniature the world's largest electric steel furnace — capacity 75 tons of steel per heat.

A TIMKEN Fuel Injection Pump cut away to show the internal mechanism in operation.

The various parts of a TIMKEN Bearing automatically assembling and disassembling to demonstrate the tapered design and construction of the TIMKEN Bearing.

A display dramatizing the Timken Roller Bearing Company's contributions to modern locomotive design—including TIMKEN Locomotive Bearings, main rods, side rods and other reciprocating parts.

And

THE TIMKEN ROLLER SKATERS in a sensational novelty act performed on a platform only nine feet in diameter elevated seven feet above the floor. The skaters perform ten times daily.

The exhibit of TIMKEN Products at the New York World's Fair has been acclaimed one of the outstanding features of this, the greatest show of all time.

Strikingly original in conception, wonderfully beautiful in its gorgeous color scheme and brilliant lighting effects, the Timken Exhibit emphasizes the keynote of the Fair "The World of Tomorrow" in a manner that captivates every visitor. But the Timken Exhibit has other claims to preeminence apart from its originality and beauty. Never before for example, has such a comprehensive display of bearings been seen in one place. Here are shown TIMKEN Bearings ranging from a few ounces in weight to one weighing more than *three tons;* bearings for every possible application in industry and transportation—from automobiles to railroad trains and from precision machine tools to huge steel rolling mills. Equally impressive are the displays of other TIMKEN Products; including TIMKEN Alloy Steels, TIMKEN Alloy and Carbon Steel Seamless Tubing, TIMKEN Rock Bits, and TIMKEN Fuel Injection Equipment for fuel oil burning engines.

Nor is novelty lacking, for as a demonstration of the precision with which TIMKEN Bearings are made there is a machine capable of measuring the thickness of a human hair in hundred-thousandths of an inch! Visitors can measure their own hair on this machine and keep the measurement records for souvenirs. Naturally this is one of the most popular spots in the entire Fair.

All in all the Timken Exhibit is a truly remarkable achievement—an attraction no visitor can afford to miss. You will find it in the Metals Building adjacent to the Trylon and Perisphere.

THE TIMKEN ROLLER BEARING COMPANY, CANTON, OHIO

TIMKEN

TRADE-MARK REG. U. S. PAT. OFF.

Timken, 1939

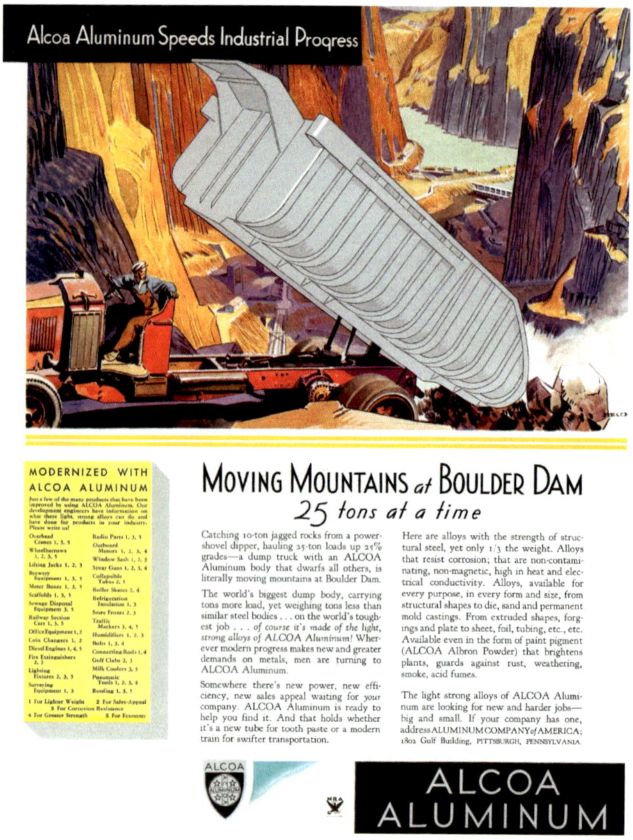

Alcoa Aluminum, 1934

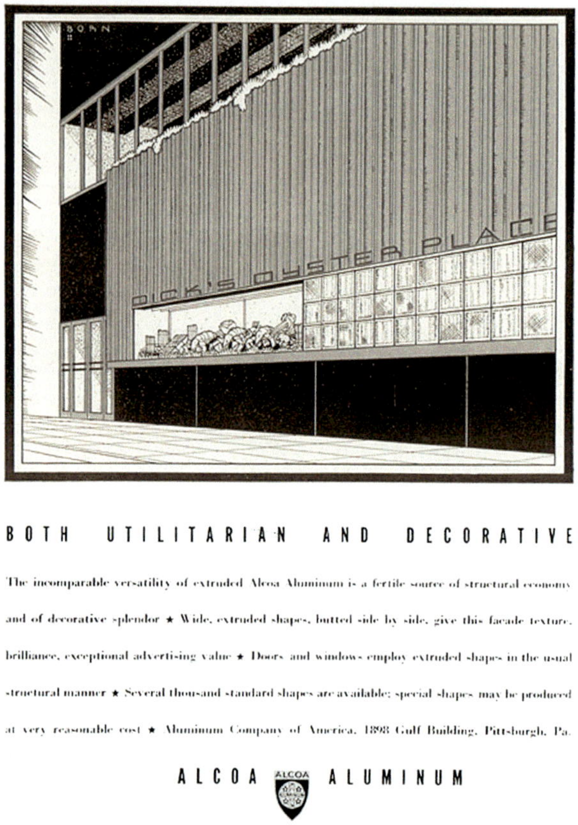

Alcoa Aluminum, 1935

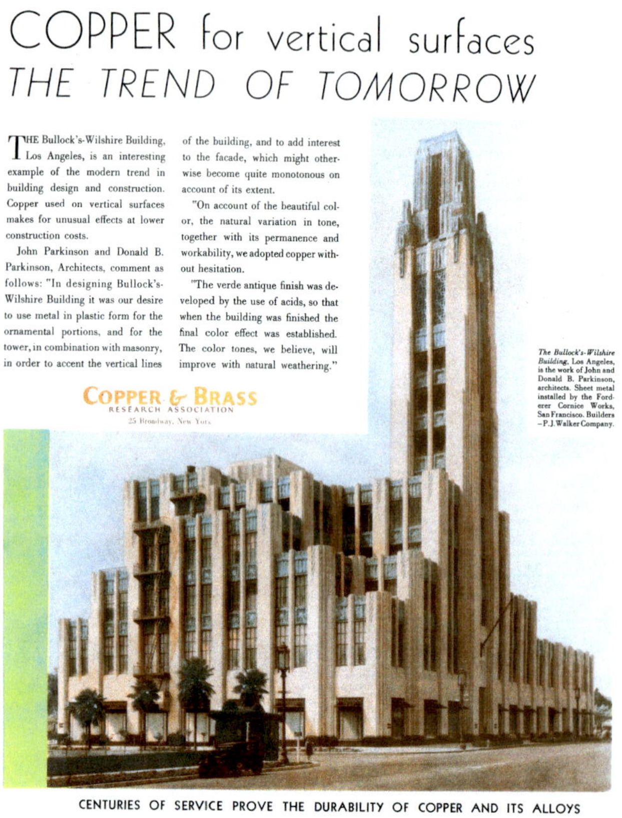

Copper & Brass, 1931

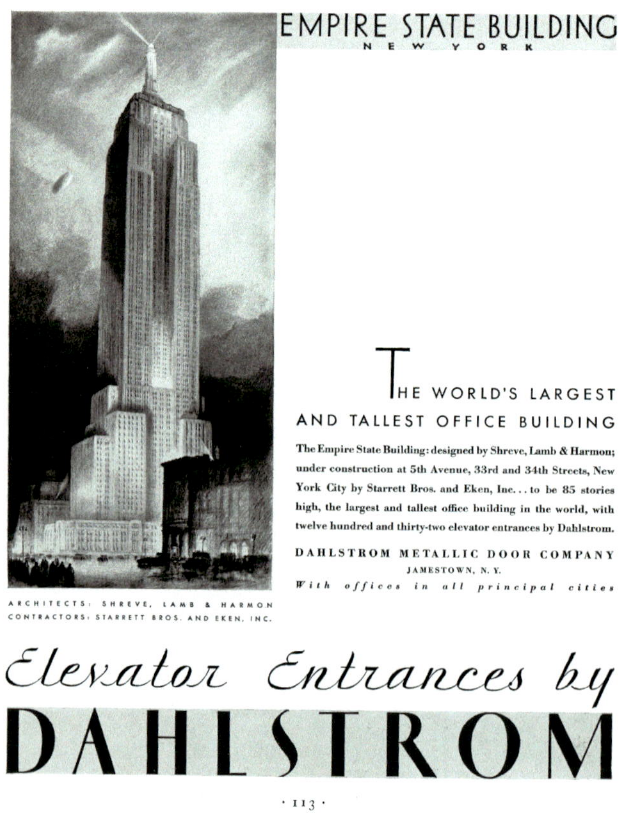

Empire State Building, 1930

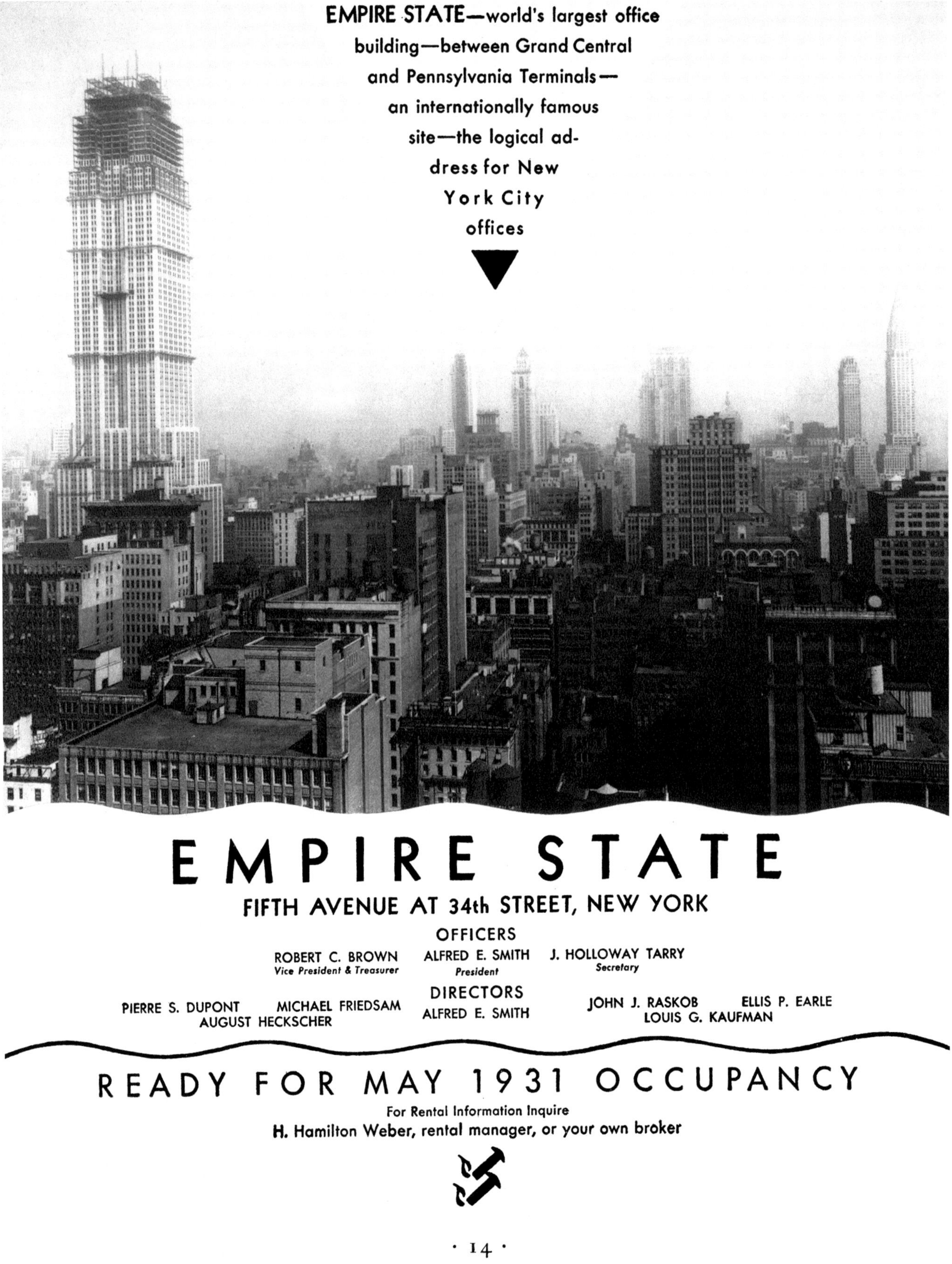

Empire State Building, 1930

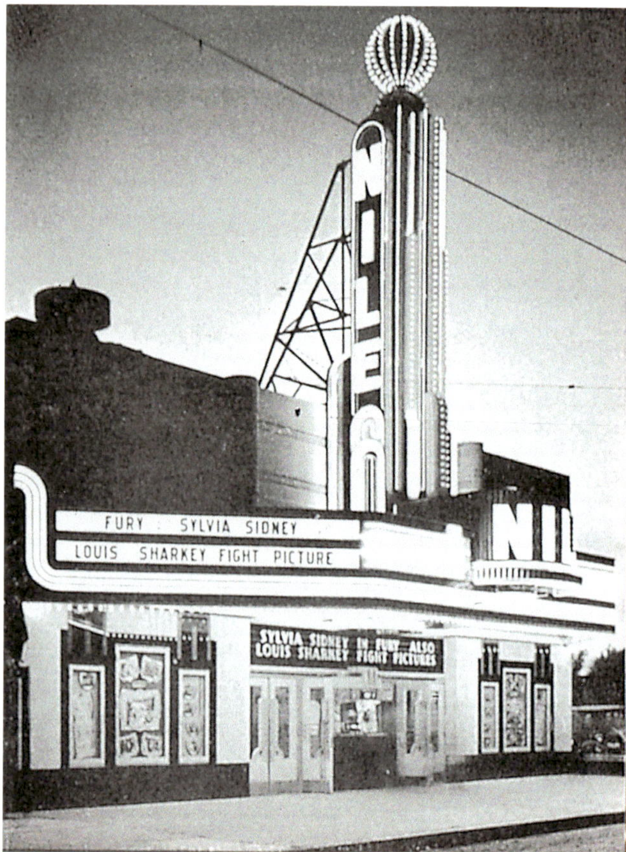

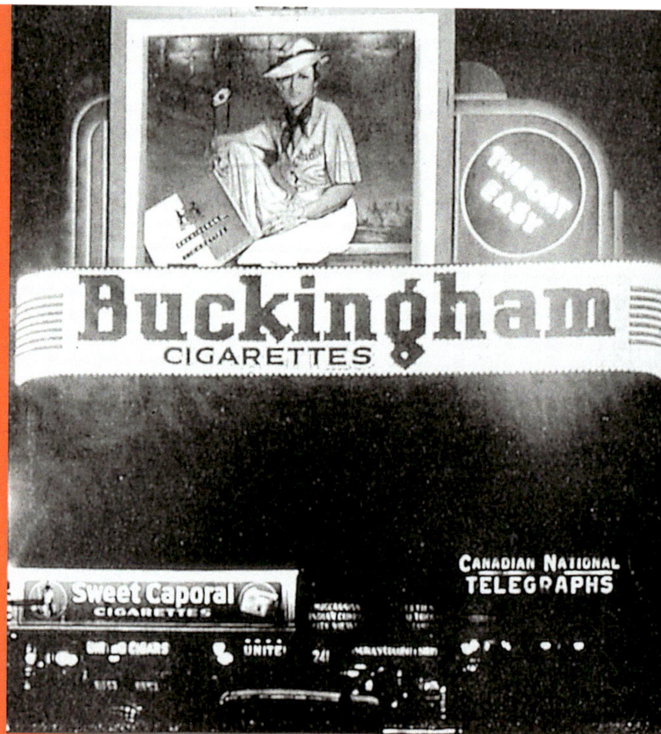

● ABOVE: Animated spectacular 60 x 35 ft. in dimensions, incorporating 1200 ft. of tubing and 4500 bulbs, built in Montreal by Claude Neon General Advertising, Ltd., using 25 Jefferson Transformers.

● LEFT: Novel theatre front in Minneapolis by Vent and Canopy Company, incorporating 30 Jefferson Transformers.

On Unique Spectaculars -- Small Shop Signs -- Anywhere -- Dependability Comes First

The smallest sign is just as important to its owners as the largest. . . . And trouble with any sign takes a slice of your profits to make it right.

That is why so many leading contractors standardize on Jefferson Transformers—use them on every installation of every size. These contractors know that Midpoint Grounded, Balanced Design, pioneered by Jefferson, is unequaled for dependable, efficient and economical operation — that improvement has followed improvement on Jefferson Transformers, each development adding to sturdiness, length of life, economy, or convenience of installation.

Get complete information on the Jefferson Line for all requirements by writing for Bulletin No. 352-LT. JEFFERSON ELECTRIC COMPANY, Bellwood (Suburb of Chicago), Illinois. Canadian Factory: 535 College Street, Toronto.

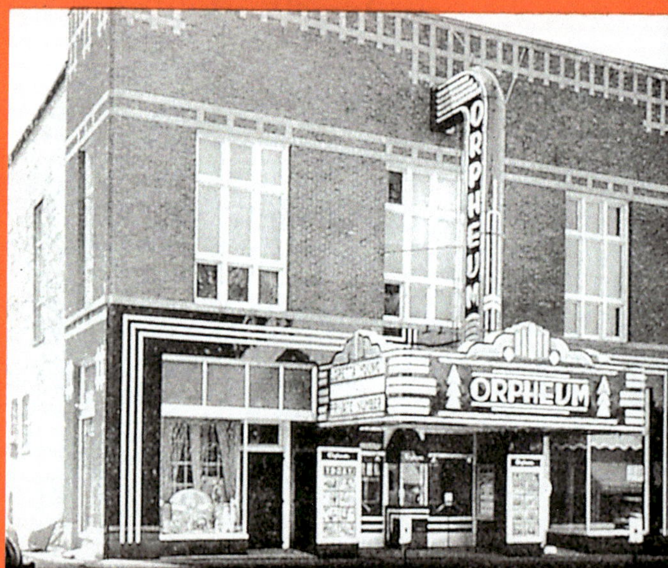

● The Midwest Neon Company, Sioux City, Iowa, built and installed this theatre front at Pipestone, Minn., using 27 Jefferson Transformers.

JEFFERSON *Luminous Tube* Transformers

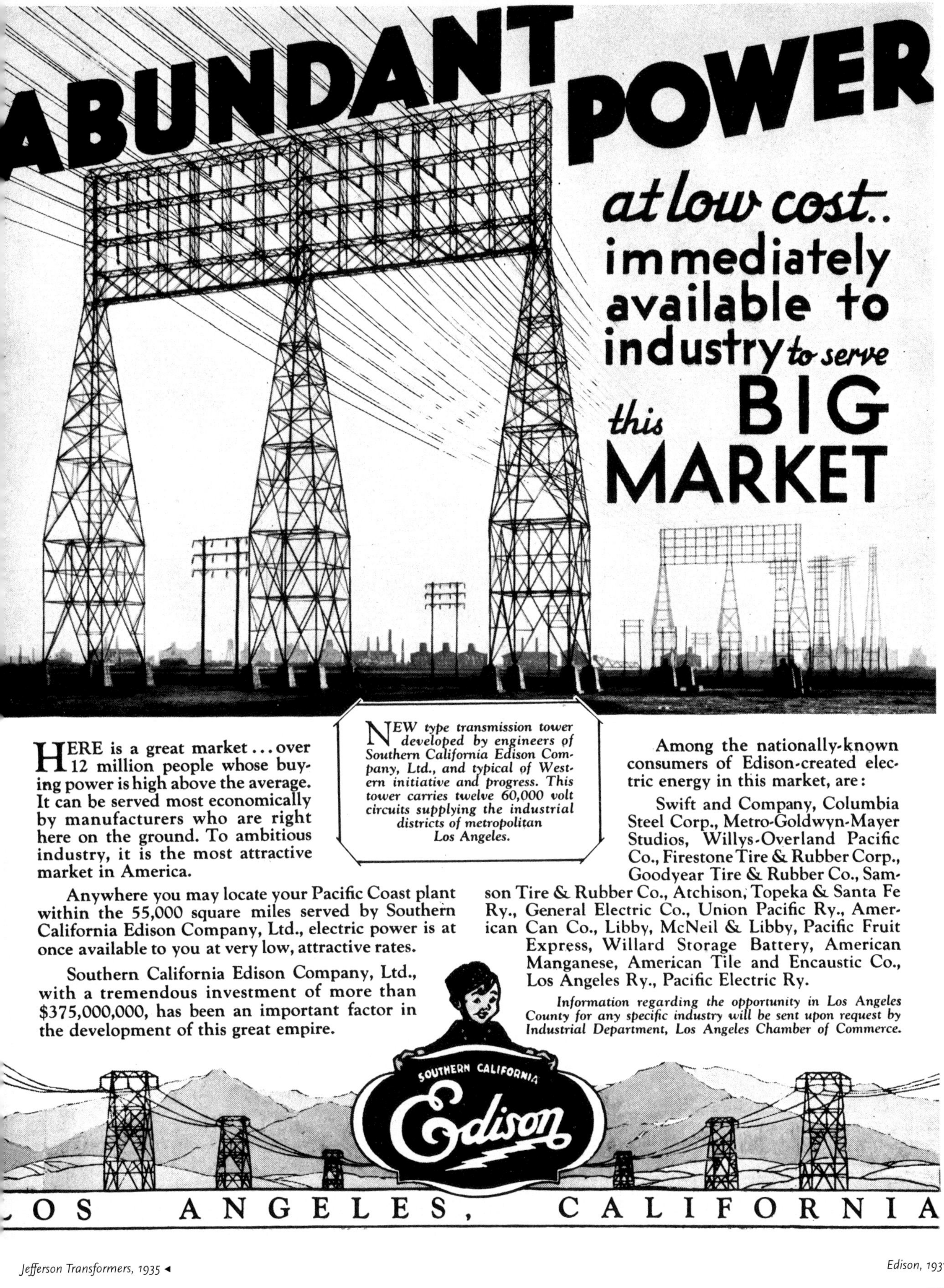

Jefferson Transformers, 1935 ◄

Edison, 1931

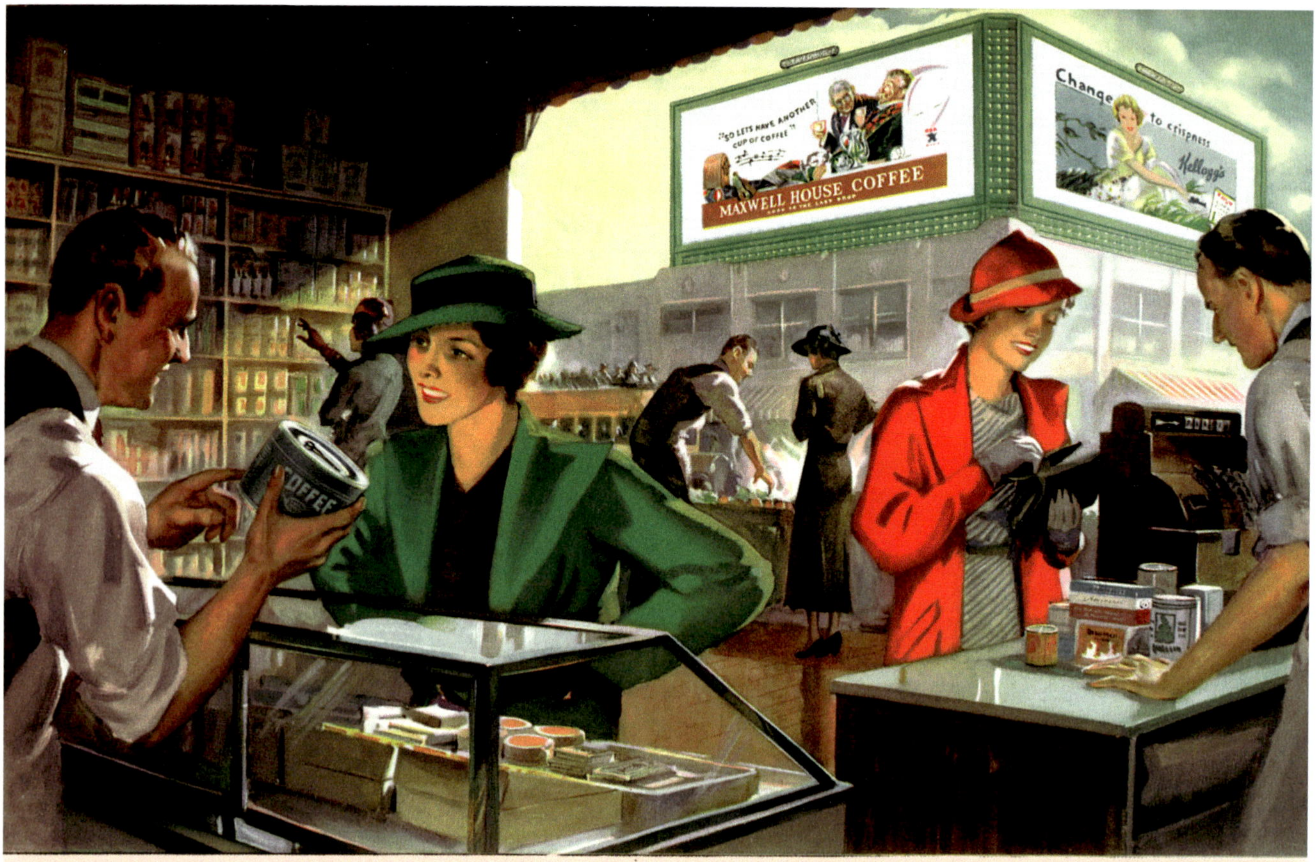

Outdoor Advertising reaches the public when it is on the move...convenient to the point of sale

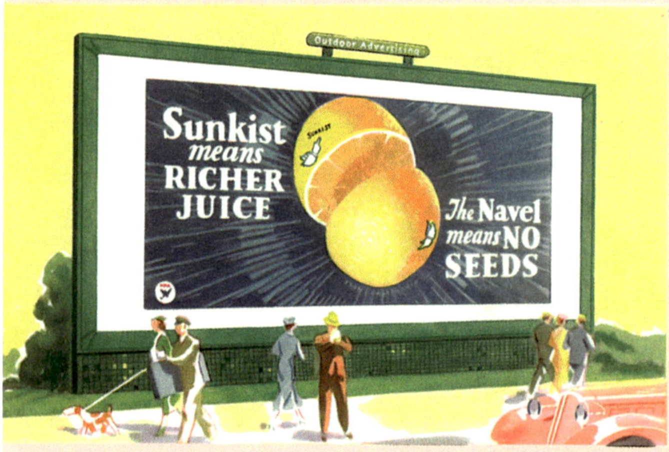

In 1908 the California Fruit Growers' Exchange appropriated $7,000 and began to advertise its Sunkist Oranges. In 1934 this advertiser has *this* to say (in January 15 issue of Sales Management), about Outdoor Advertising:

"We believe that in our poster advertising we link five strong factors in the accomplishment of our marketing program. We use pictures, little text. We reach every Sunkist prospect, since even those who know little English understand pictures and learn to know the trademark. Color, the basic appeal in Sunkist display, tempts the appetite and adds force through the dramatic size of posters."

Outdoor Advertising delivers circulation, according to actual traffic count, to guarantee thorough coverage of any market entered.

It impresses that circulation by dramatic simplicity, dominating size, full color—and with a reiterative persistence that is inescapable.

By exerting this irresistible influence upon prospective buyers when they are out of doors, ready to buy, Outdoor Advertising bridges the gap between advertising read or heard indoors and the point of actual purchase.

As a part of many a sound merchandising plan, Outdoor Advertising has proved its economy, demonstrated its power, built profitable sales. Actual examples of what Outdoor Advertising can do to promote the sale of your product at low cost will be supplied upon request. Investigate now while space is still available.

OUTDOOR ADVERTISING INDUSTRY

OUTDOOR ADVERTISING INCORPORATED

1 PARK AVENUE, NEW YORK • 165 WEST WACKER DRIVE, CHICAGO

ATLANTA • BOSTON • CLEVELAND • HOUSTON • LOS ANGELES • ST. LOUIS • BALTIMORE • CINCINNATI • DETROIT • KANSAS CITY • PHILADELPHIA • SAN FRANCISCO

Outdoor Advertising Industry, 1934

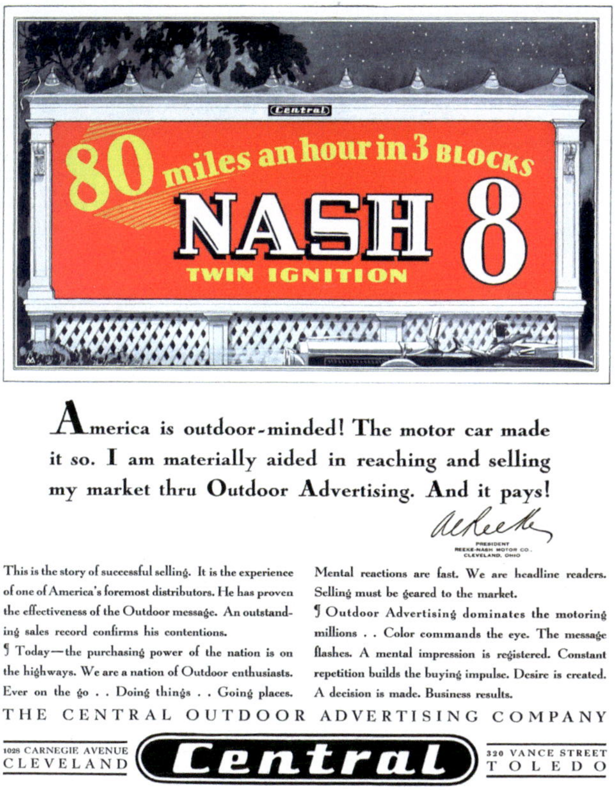

Central Outdoor Advertising Co., 1930

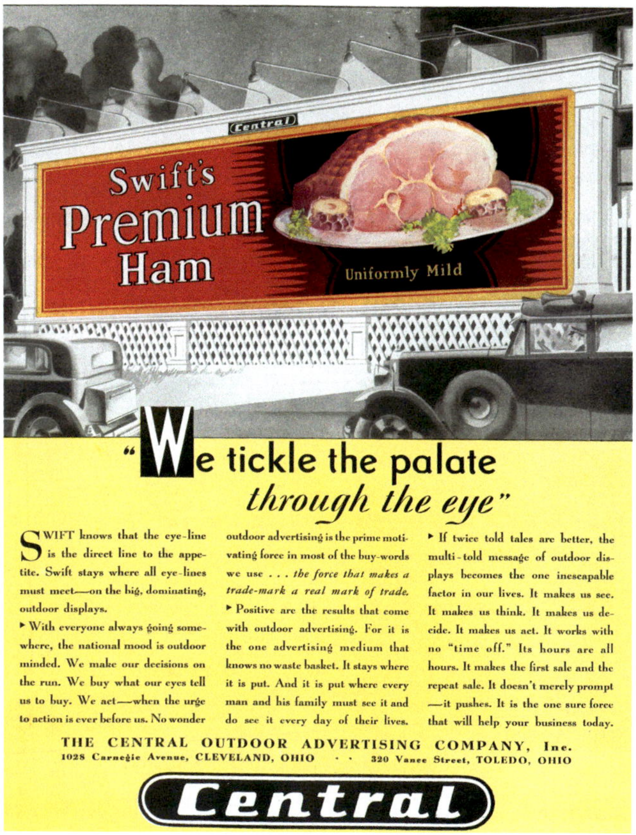

Central Outdoor Advertising Co., 1930

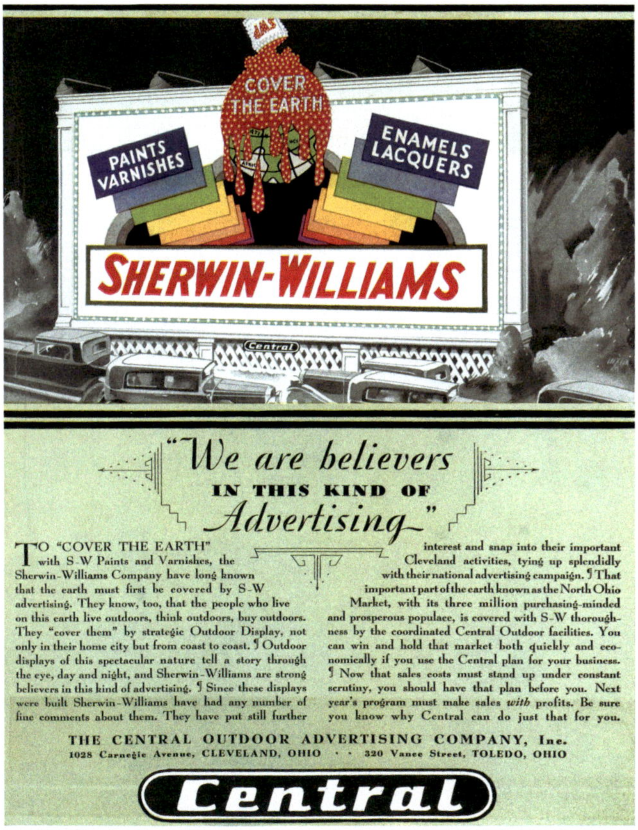

Central Outdoor Advertising Co., 1930

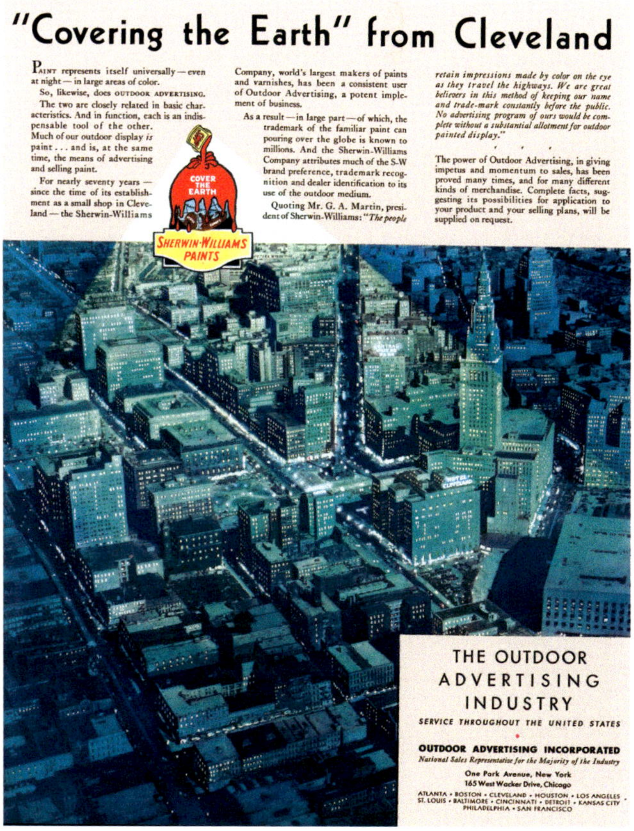

Central Outdoor Advertising Co., 1934

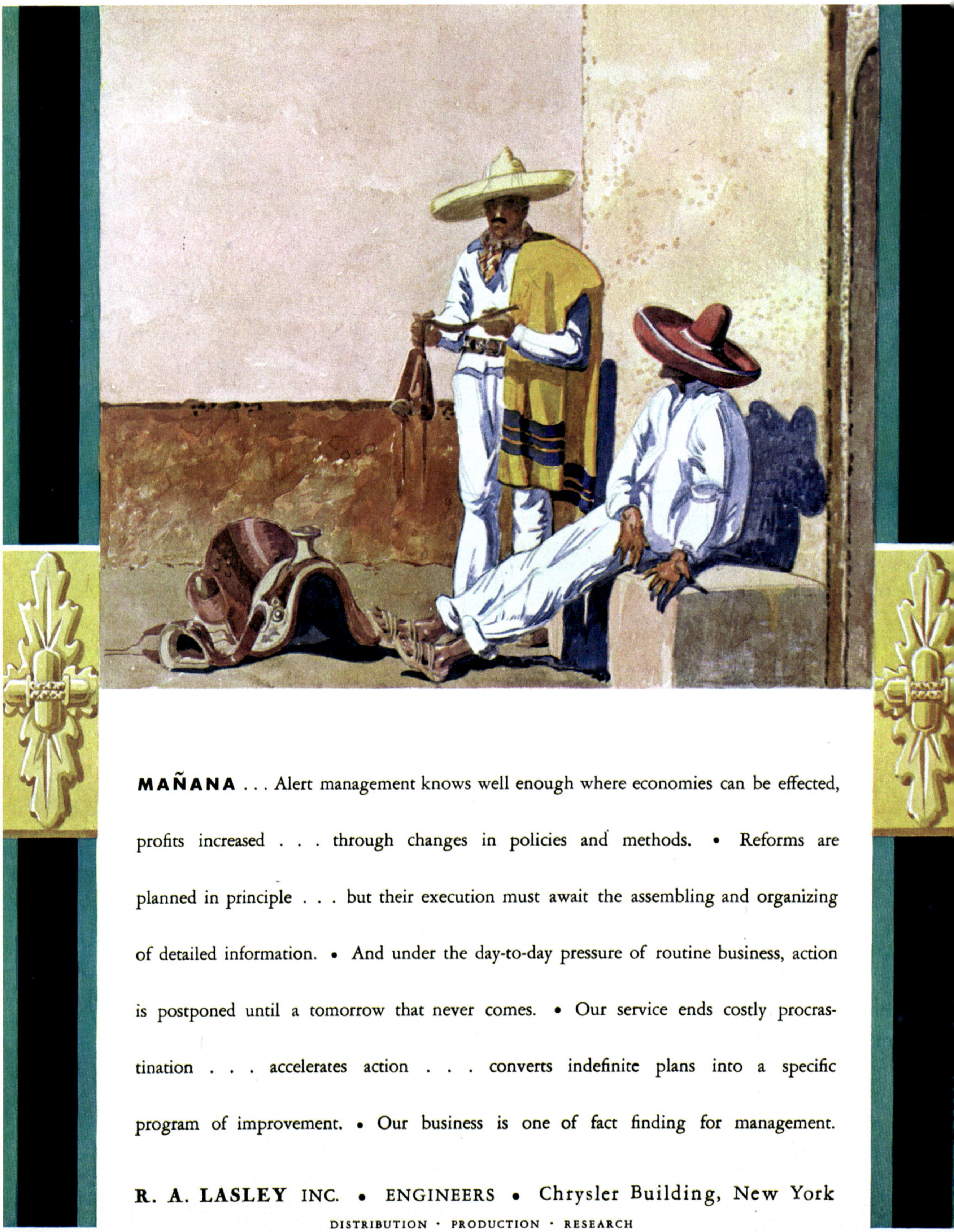

▲► *R. A. Lasley Inc., 1934*

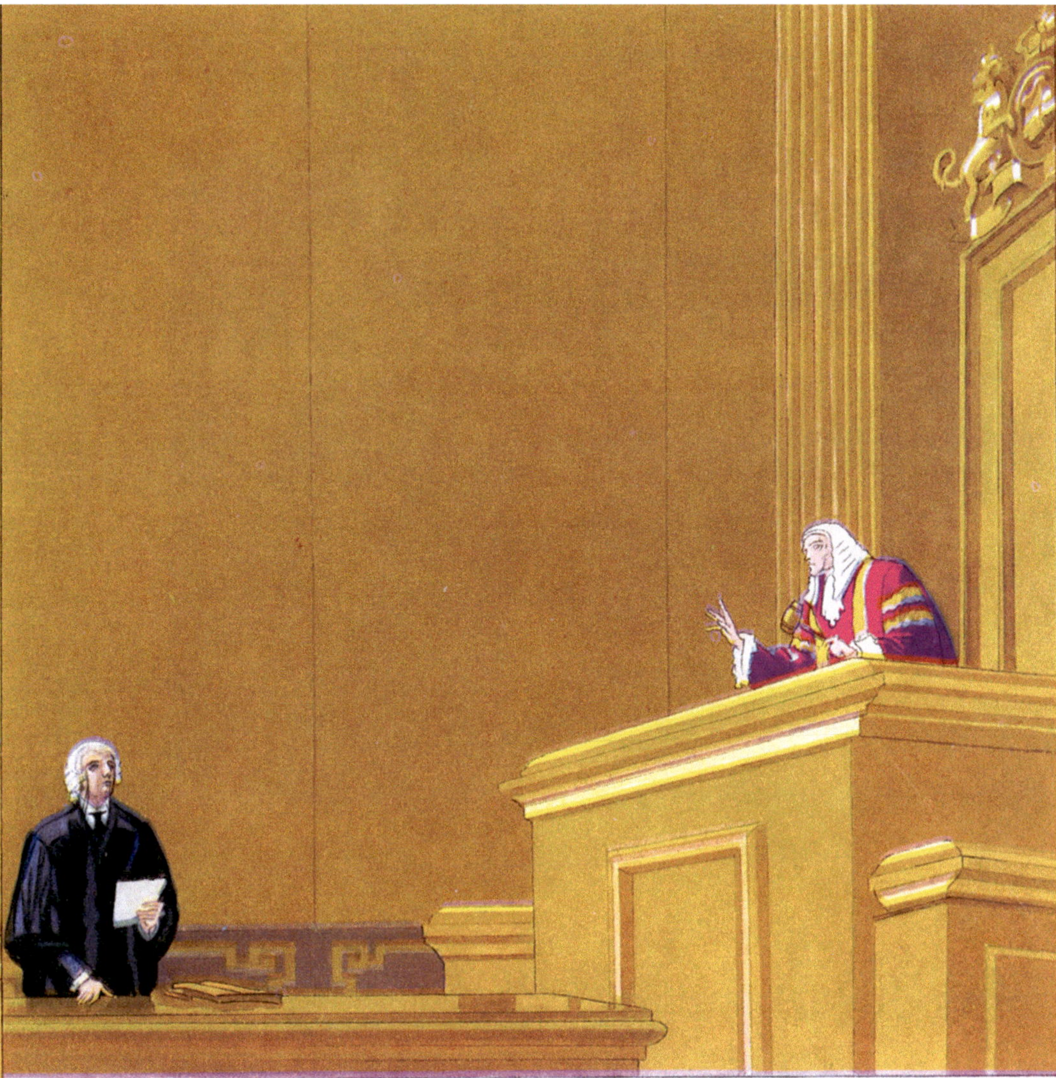

OBJECTION SUSTAINED . . . Objection or no objection, lawyers will continue to ask leading questions • So will business. Business still asks leading questions . . . finds out what it wants to find out . . . proves the point it wishes to prove with market research. Without benefit of independent counsel this evidence forms the record . . . guides production . . . dictates the policy of promotion . . . maps the sales strategy. And oftener than not, misses the mark! • If you want to know what your customers think of you and your product, individually and collectively, and how they came to have these opinions, we can help you. Our business is one of fact finding for management, of asking direct, *not* leading, questions.

R. A. LASLEY INC. • ENGINEERS • Chrysler Building, New York

DISTRIBUTION—PRODUCTION—RESEARCH

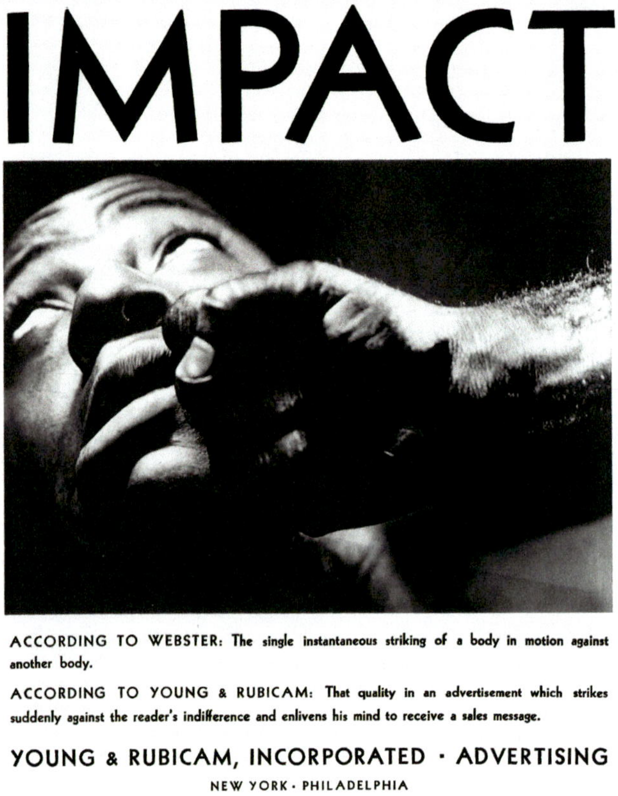

Young & Rubicam, 1930

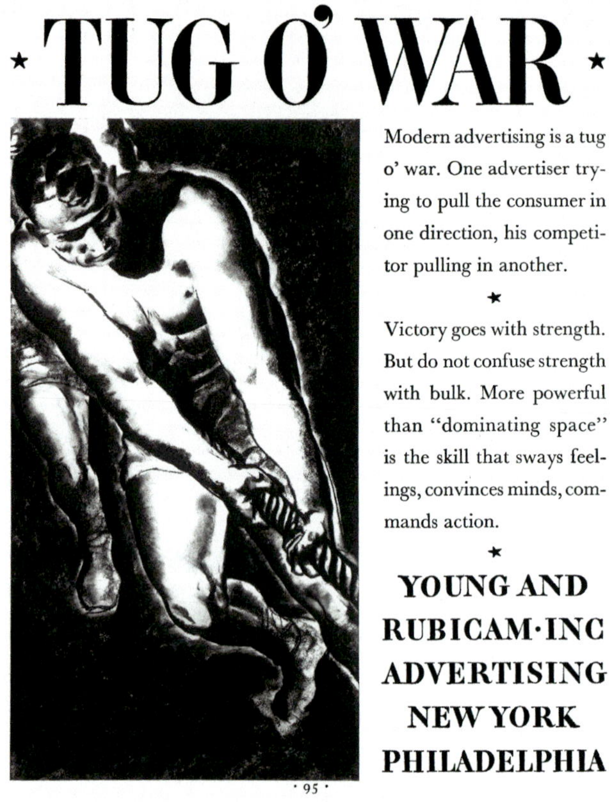

Young & Rubicam, 1930

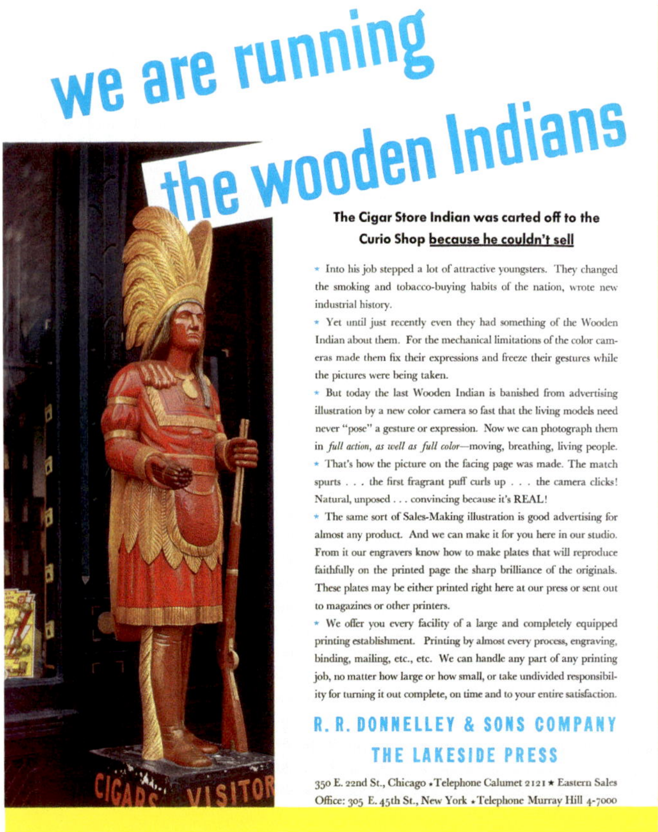

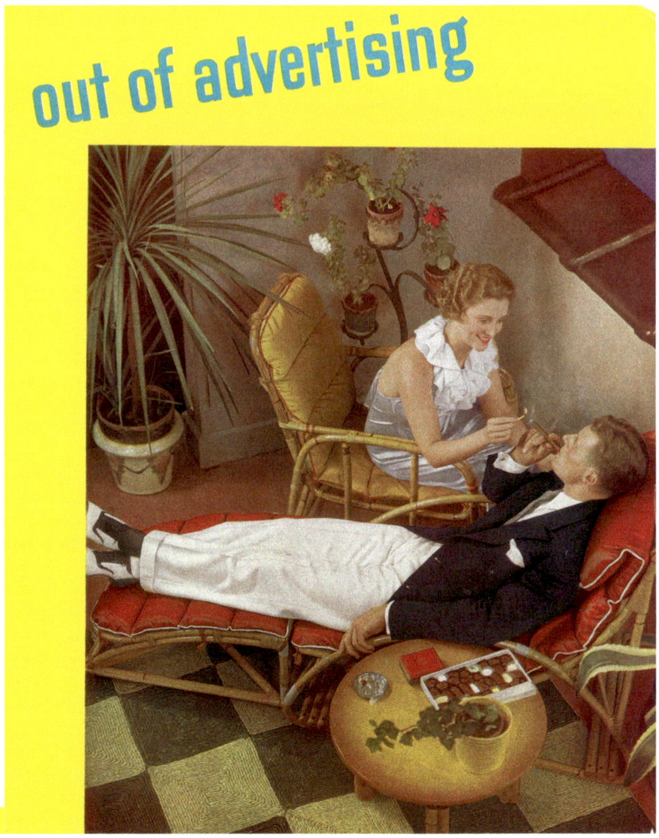

R.R. Donnelley & Sons, 1934

▸ *Frigidaire, 1935*

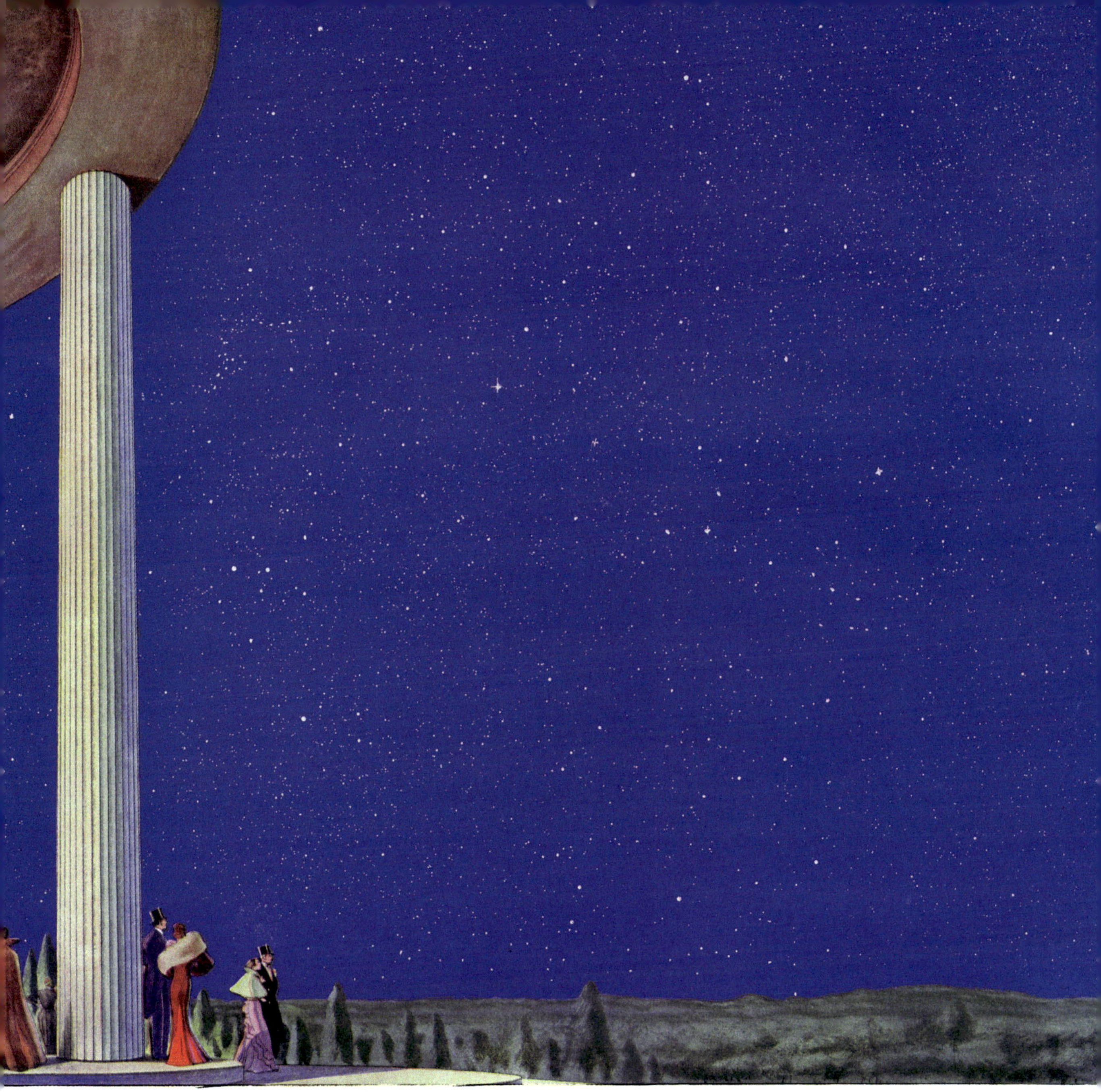

FOURTH MILLION

ᴅᴀʏ three million genuine Frigidaires ve been built and the manufacture of 4th million has begun. Throughout the rld Frigidaire has set the standard for icient automatic refrigeration. Into llions of homes it has brought a higher ne of living—a better standard of health. And constantly, through the years, gidaire has been improved. Benefiting m the suggestions of users, and the engi-ring facilities of General Motors, it has ered better arrangement of food space—snow-white porcelain on steel inside and out, the Cold Control, the Hydrator, light that flashes on at the opening of the door—more ice, automatic ice tray release, automatic reset defrosting, and remarkably low operating cost. In an endless flow, General Motors has added to Frigidaire improvements and conveniences that have set this one make apart from all other refrigerators.

Three million Frigidaires have been built—and the greatest single influence in the choice of Frigidaire by new buyers is the enthusiastic recommendation of its users.

The manufacture of the 4th million has begun. There are sixteen beautiful models that represent further new standards of value—every one equipped with Frigidaire's newest contribution to its future users, the Super Freezer—which provides a *complete refrigeration service* in every model.

The Frigidaire '35's are here. And we are proud of the fact that we can offer them at prices that will make them available to new millions of homes.

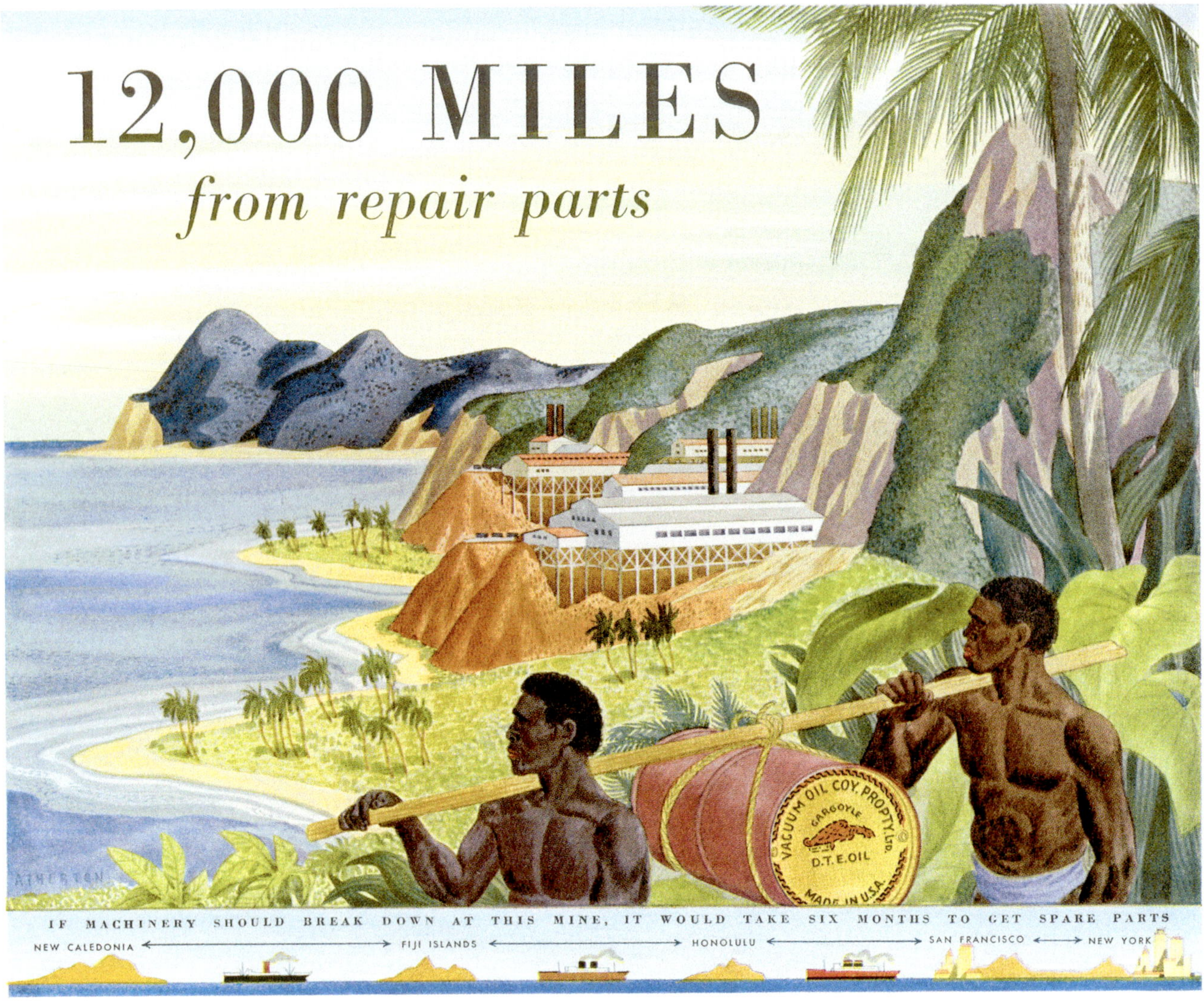

World's most isolated power plant uses Gargoyle Lubricants to safeguard equipment

There are no power consultants on the South Sea island of New Caledonia—no spare parts within 12,000 miles. Should machinery break down in Mutual Chemical Company's chrome mines, operations would come to a halt for at least six months. Lubrication *must be* correct.

So these mines guard against machinery breakdowns by the use of Gargoyle Lubricants.

Gargoyle D. T. E. Oil Extra Heavy used in these Diesel engines and Gargoyle D. T. E. Oil Heavy Medium used in the air compressors, are the grades recommended and used by the engine builders. These are the identical oils that are available for use in your plant—in New York or New Caledonia.

You'll find Gargoyle Lubricants used in industrial plants in every corner of the globe and in most leading plants in world industrial centers. Plants in Manchester, England, and Pittsburgh, Pa., for instance, can obtain spare parts quickly, but even a few hours' interruption might disrupt production schedules. So the same Gargoyle Lubricants keep machinery running smoothly.

Plant operating records, written in every language, prove that the use of Gargoyle Lubricants and Socony-Vacuum engineering service reduces power consumption from 3% to 10%, lowers maintenance and repair expense, speeds up production, insures against breakdowns.

Any Socony-Vacuum representative will be glad to show you how correct lubrication has helped lower unit production costs in leading plants in your own industry.

Socony-Vacuum Corporation, 26 Broadway, New York City. Branches and distributors throughout the world.

SOCONY-VACUUM
CORPORATION

GARGOYLE Lubricating Oils

Socony-Vacuum Co., 1934

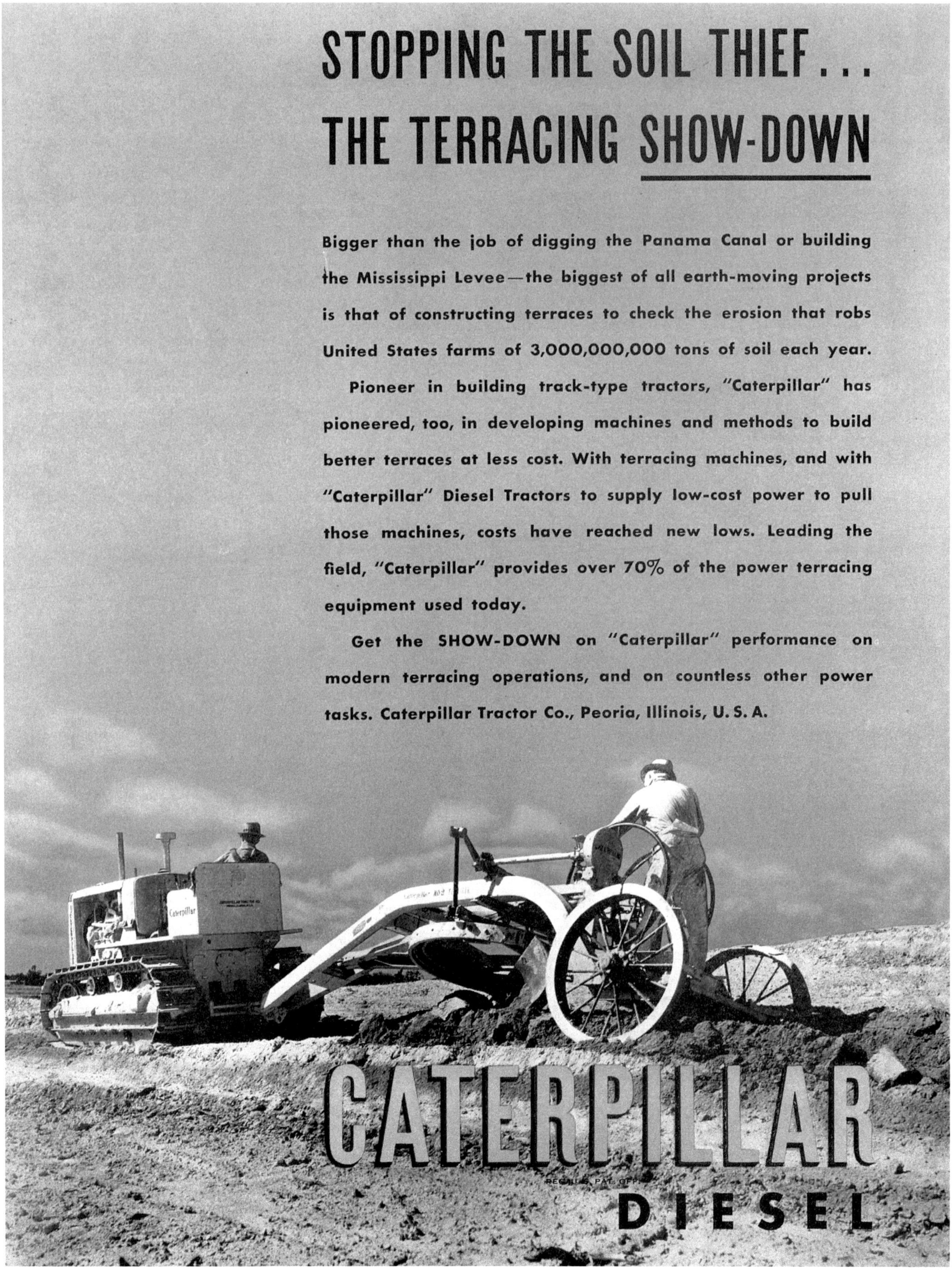

Caterpillar, 1935

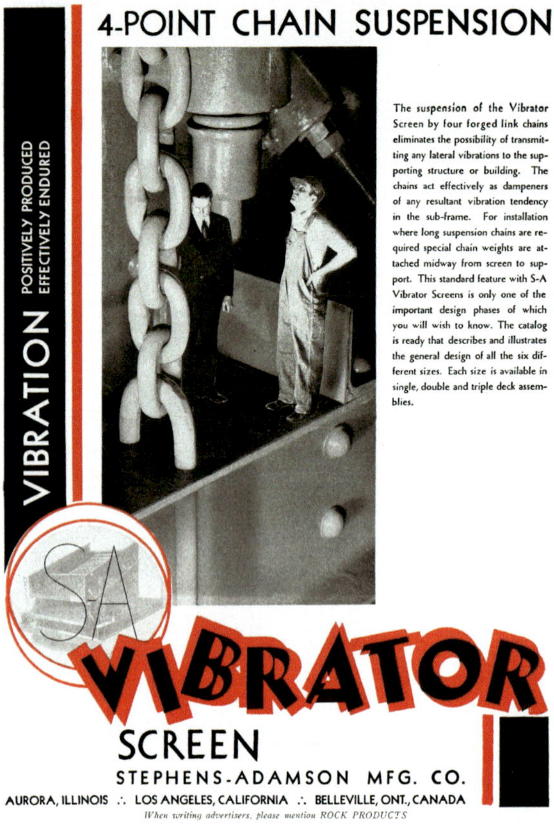

S-A Vibrator Screen, 1930

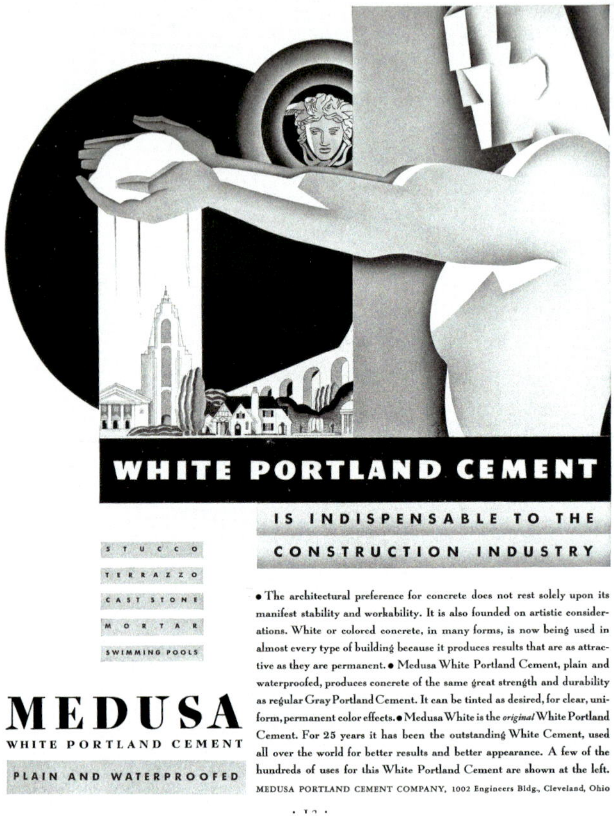

Medusa, 1931

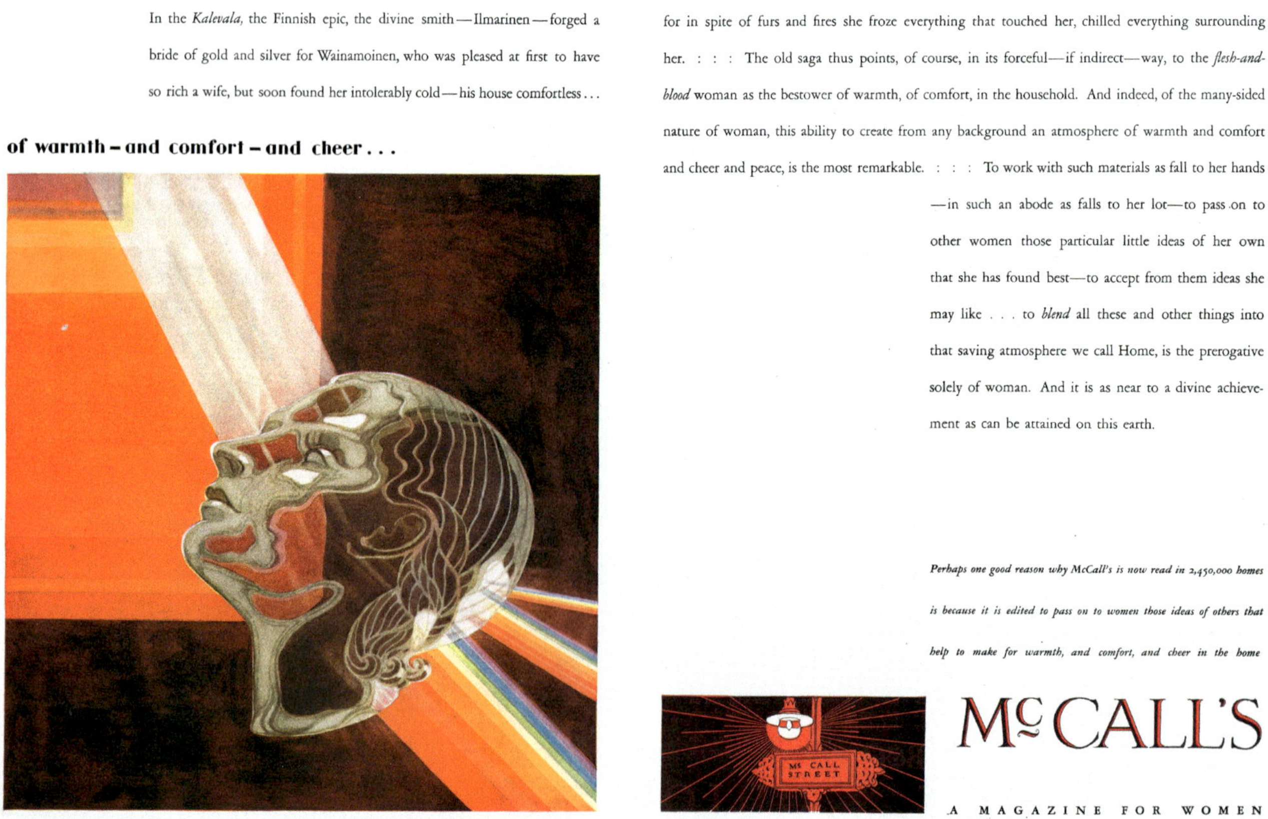

McCall's, 1930

► *Popular Mechanics, 1932* ►► *Philadelphia, 1930*

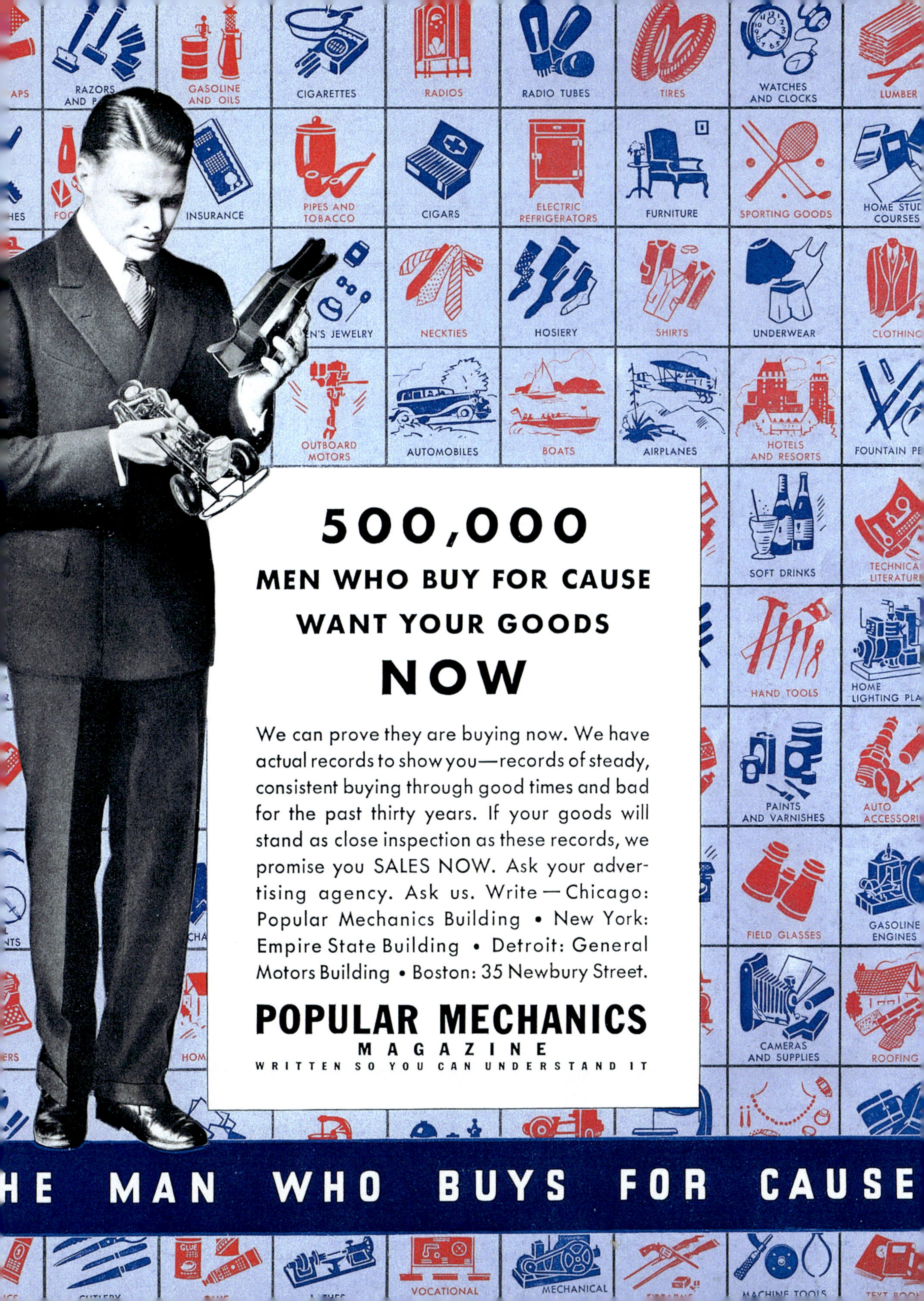

500,000
MEN WHO BUY FOR CAUSE
WANT YOUR GOODS
NOW
We can prove they are buying now. We have actual records to show you—records of steady, consistent buying through good times and bad for the past thirty years. If your goods will stand as close inspection as these records, we promise you SALES NOW. Ask your advertising agency. Ask us. Write—Chicago: Popular Mechanics Building • New York: Empire State Building • Detroit: General Motors Building • Boston: 35 Newbury Street.
POPULAR MECHANICS
MAGAZINE
WRITTEN SO YOU CAN UNDERSTAND IT
HE MAN WHO BUYS FOR CAUSE
GASOLINE AND OILS
CIGARETTES
RADIOS
RADIO TUBES
TIRES
WATCHES AND CLOCKS
LUMBER
INSURANCE
PIPES AND TOBACCO
CIGARS
ELECTRIC REFRIGERATORS
FURNITURE
SPORTING GOODS
NECKTIES
HOSIERY
SHIRTS
UNDERWEAR
OUTBOARD MOTORS
AUTOMOBILES
BOATS
AIRPLANES
HOTELS AND RESORTS
SOFT DRINKS
HAND TOOLS
PAINTS AND VARNISHES
FIELD GLASSES
GASOLINE ENGINES
CAMERAS AND SUPPLIES
ROOFING
VOCATIONAL
MECHANICAL

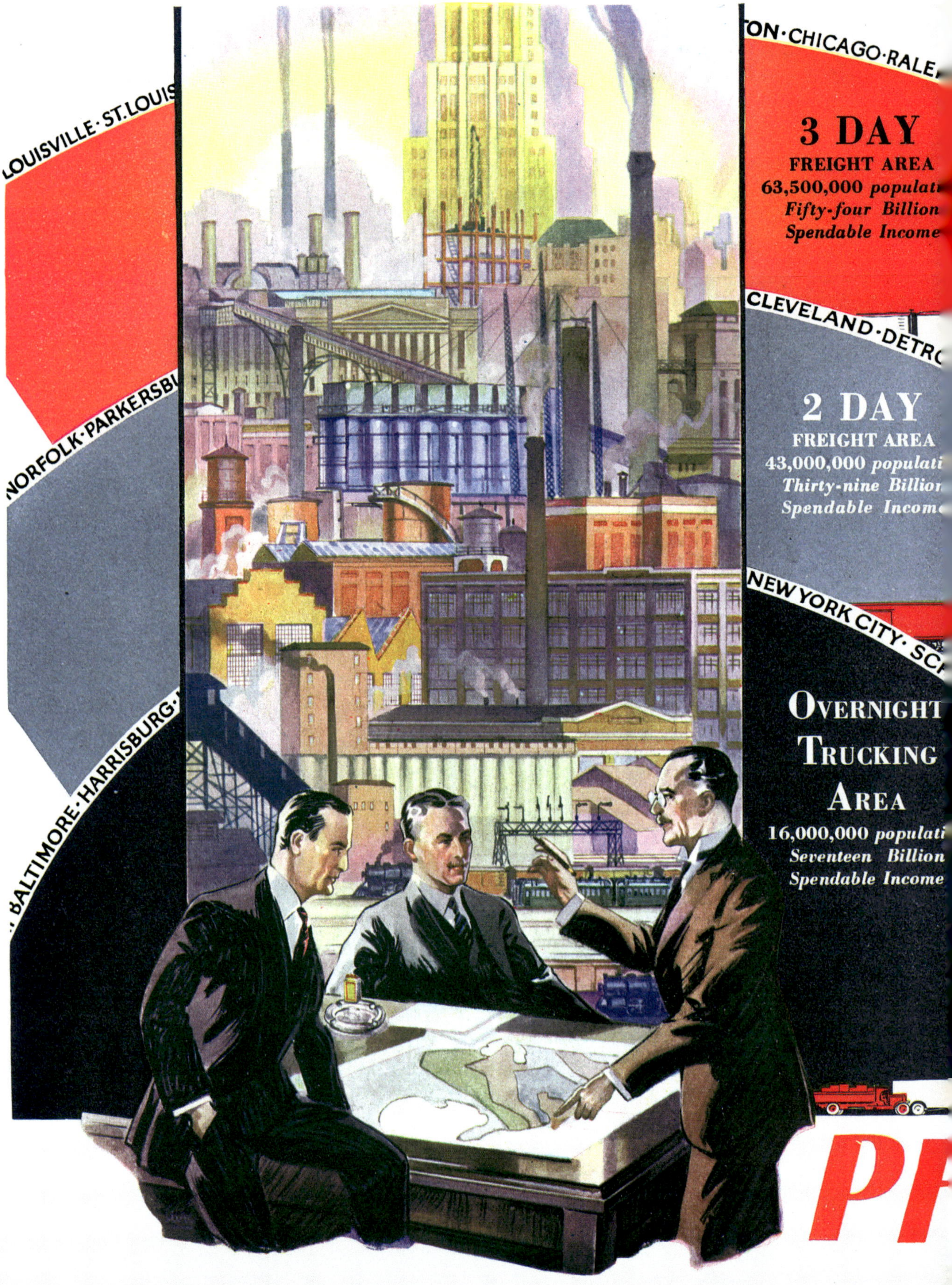

LOUISVILLE·ST.LOUIS
NORFOLK·PARKERSB
BALTIMORE·HARRISBURG·
ON·CHICAGO·RALE
3 DAY
FREIGHT AREA
63,500,000 populati
Fifty-four Billion
Spendable Income
CLEVELAND·DETR
2 DAY
FREIGHT AREA
43,000,000 populati
Thirty-nine Billion
Spendable Income
NEW YORK CITY·SC
OVERNIGHT
TRUCKING
AREA
16,000,000 populati
Seventeen Billion
Spendable Income
PF

ROM

Philadelphia

The Work Shop of the World

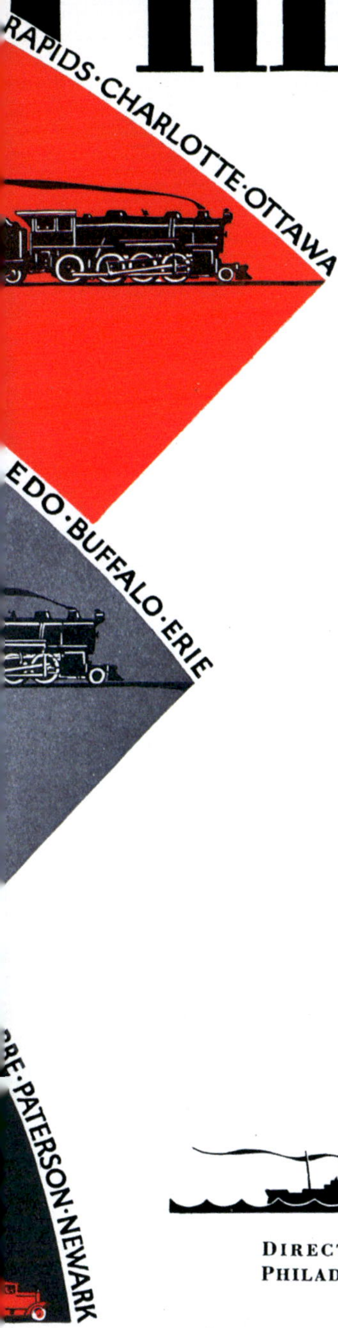

. . . . you can reach more people with less effort than from any other center in the United States. To speed up distribution, locate your plant in Philadelphia. Send for information. Philadelphia Business Progress Association, 1442 Widener Building.

Address Department P for booklet, "Production and Distribution in the Philadelphia Area."

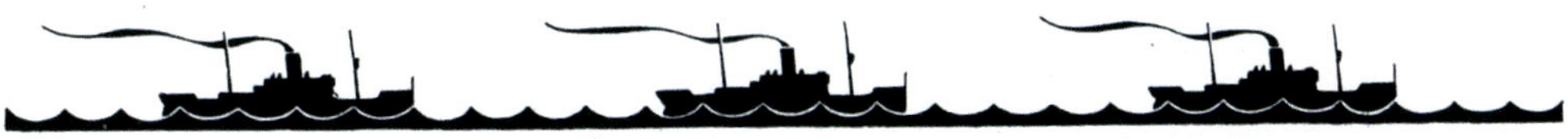

DIRECT SAILINGS (WITHOUT LIGHTERAGE) FROM THE PORT OF PHILADELPHIA TO PRINCIPAL SEA PORT COUNTRIES OF THE WORLD

LADELPHIA

USINESS PROGRESS ASSOCIATION

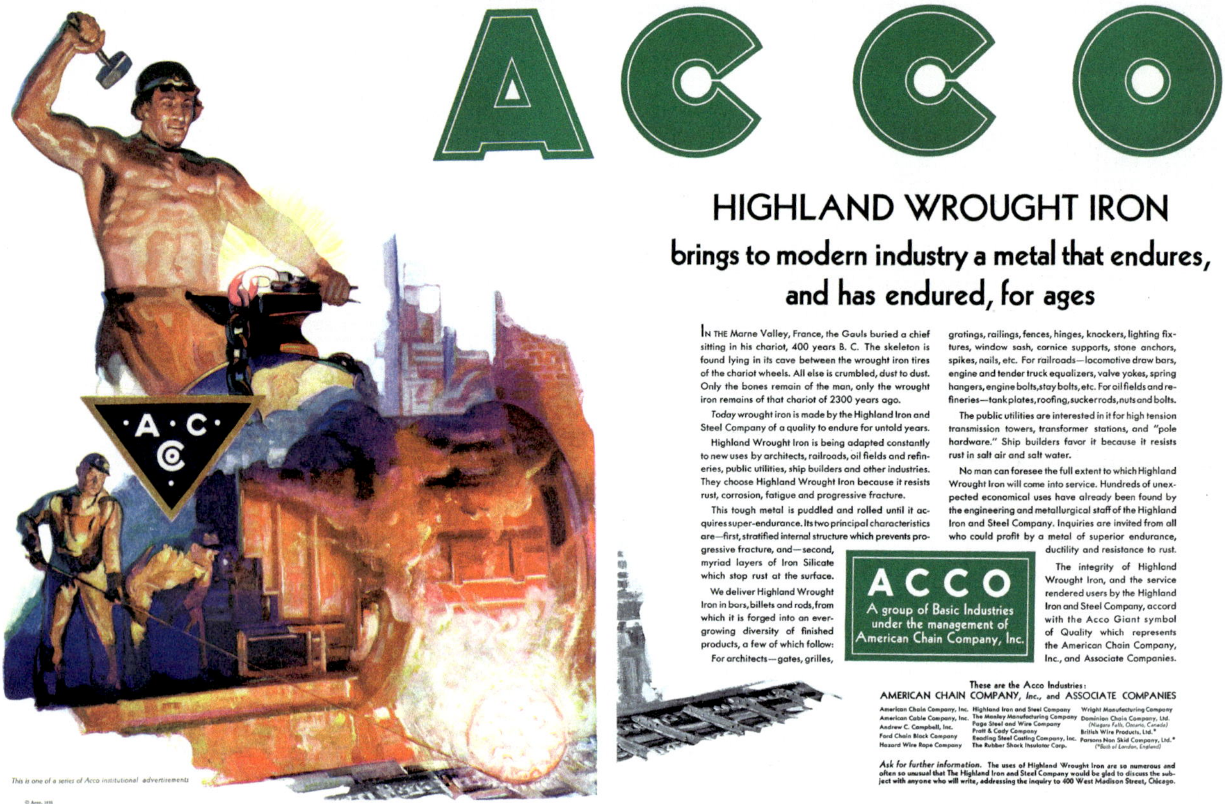

ACCO, 1931

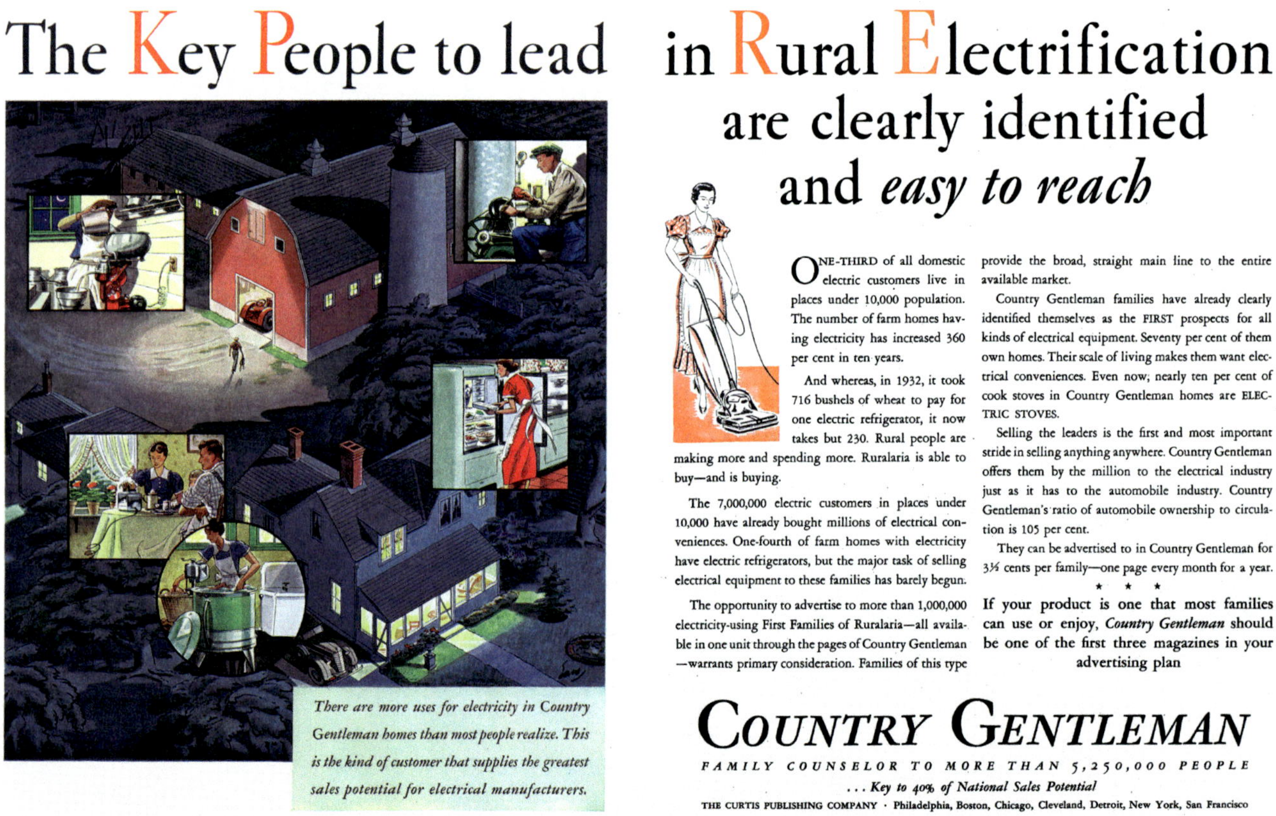

Country Gentleman, 1936

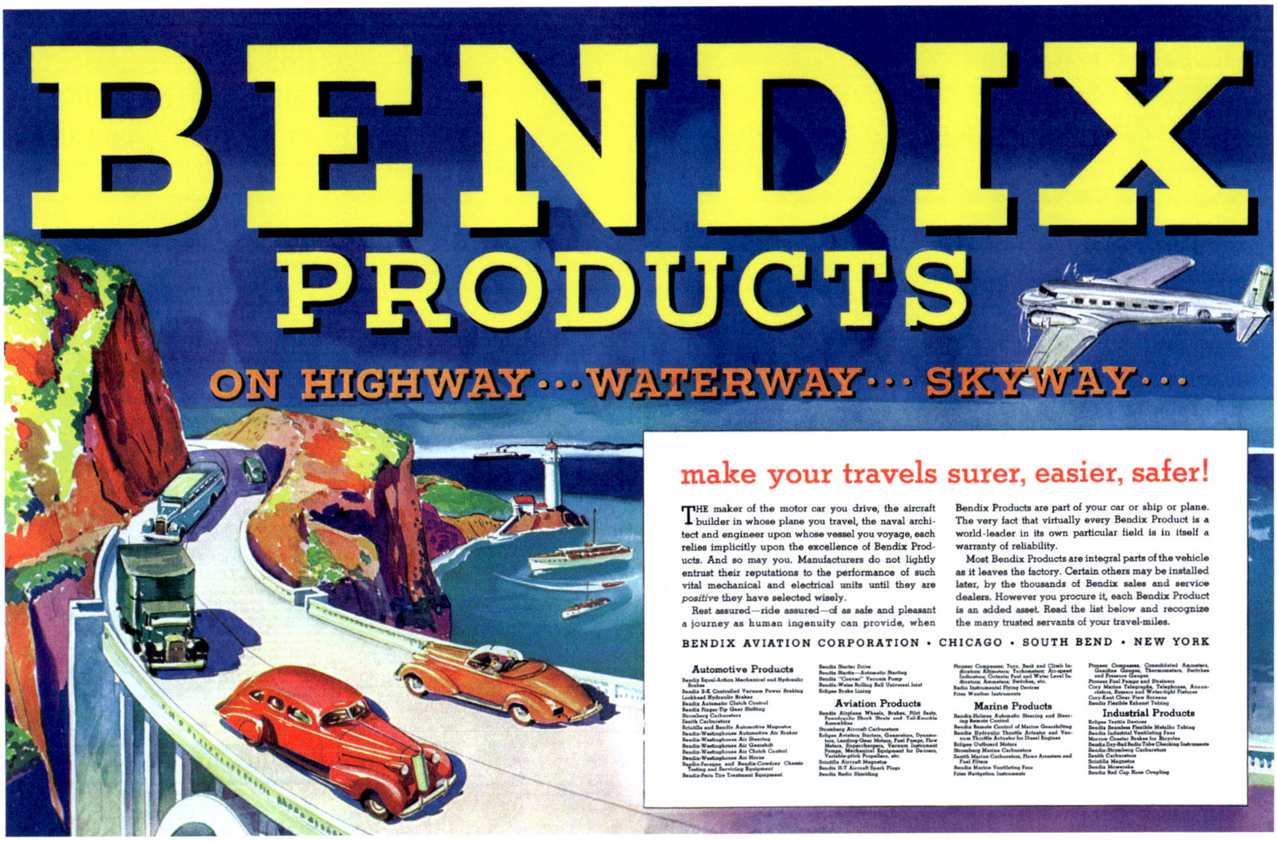

Bendix Products, 1934

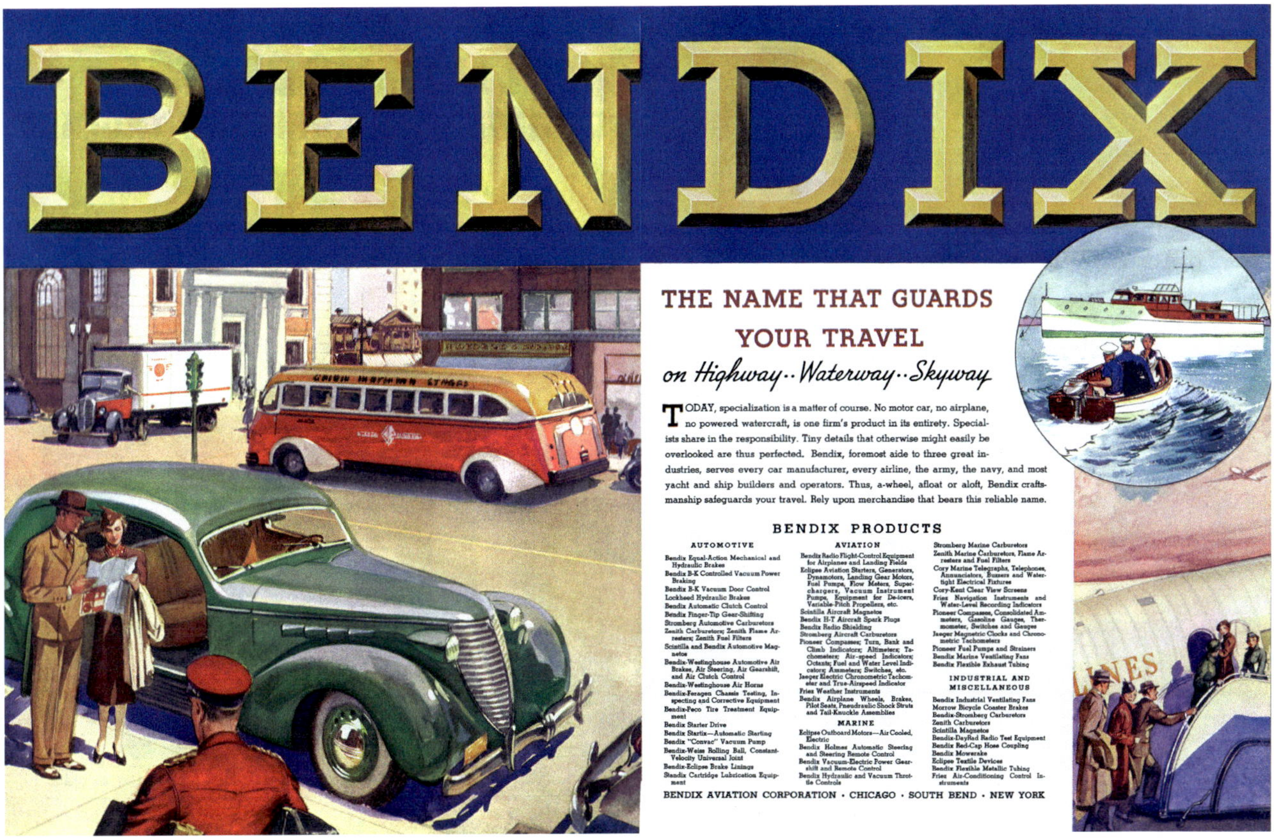

Bendix Products, 1937

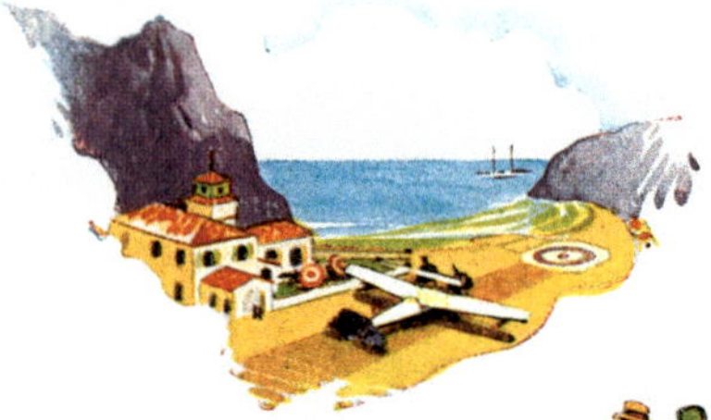

Into the amphibion class with its inherent advantages for transport serv
Douglas has introduced a plane of startling performance . . . and typical Douglas dependabil
It has the ability to alight on water or land closest to the heart of cities, and to
straight to its destination, irrespective of terrain. It has a speed of 150 m.p.h., maneuvers
one motor. It is comfortable . . . quiet, and is custom-finished to accommodate eight or ten. M
we send detailed information? Douglas Aircraft Company, Inc., Santa Monica, Califorr

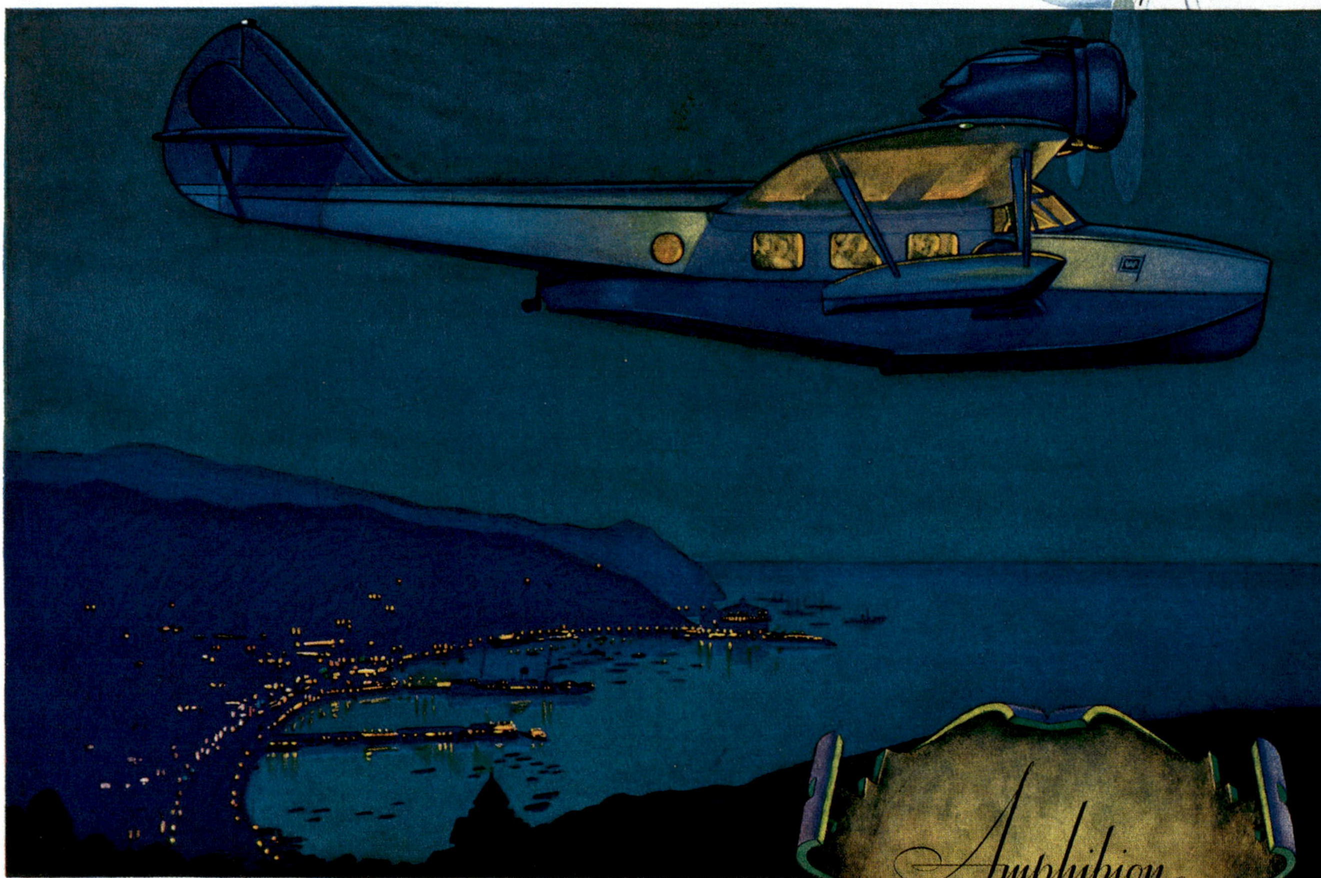

A Douglas Amphibion of the Wilmington-Catalina Airline fleet. The line maintains a 10-trip schedule daily between the Southern California mainland and the island.

Amphibion
CUSTOM BUILT BY
DOUGLAS

FIRST AROUND THE WORLD

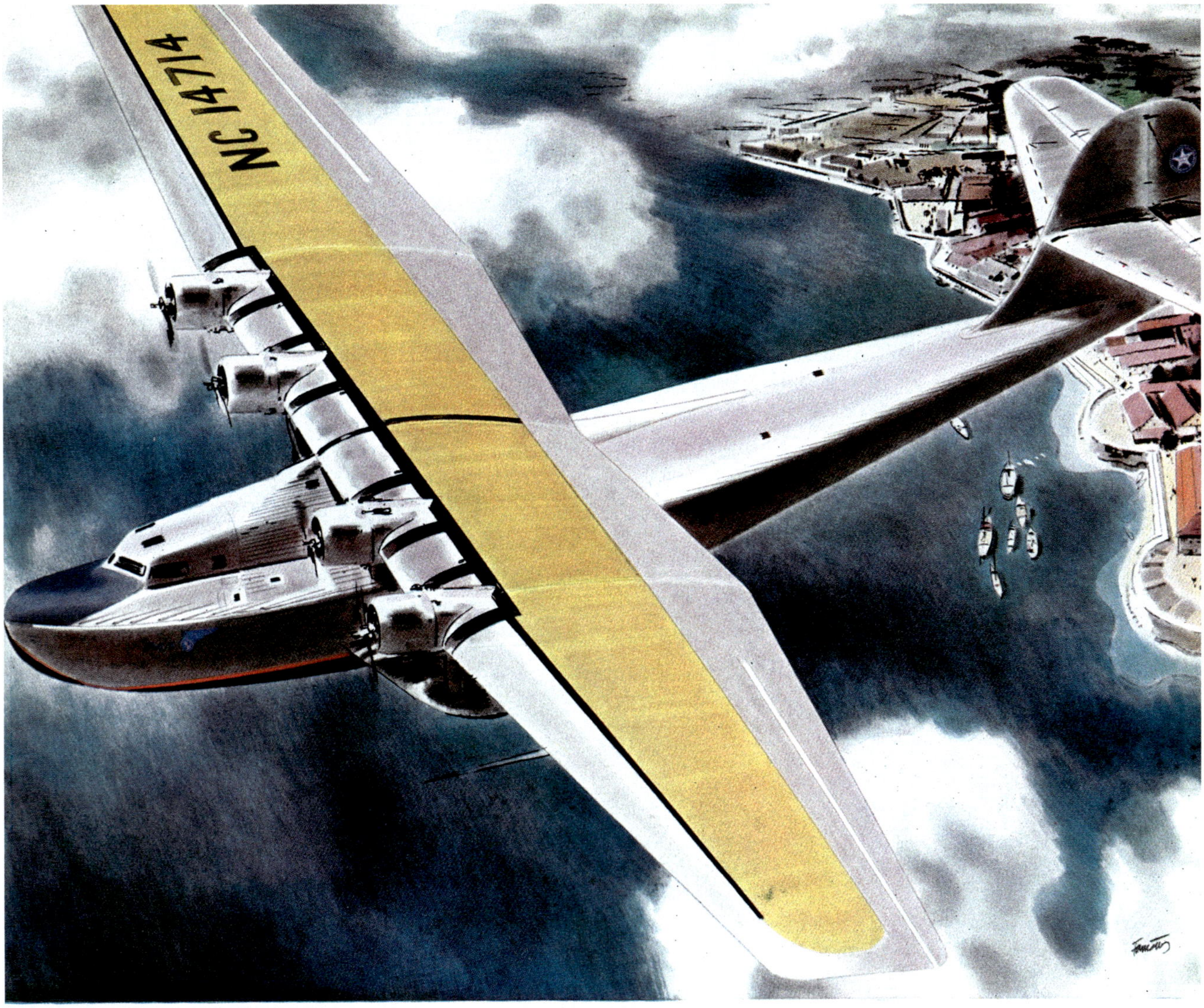

"NEXT STOP.. CHINA!"

HIGH OVER MANILA'S TROPIC SHORES, a modern clipper 3 days out of the Golden Gate clears the mists . . . circles to westward . . . disappears over the horizon, China-bound! No mere flight of fancy, this . . . no imaginative dream of the far distant future!

When this giant 25-ton air-liner roars away on the last leg of the California to the Orient run . . . it will mark the completion of plans and routes studied and charted for years. *It will inaugurate the first scheduled trans-oceanic air service in the world . . . linking the new world with the old!*

To the men of Pan American Airways goes the honor for this thrilling achievement...to the vision and resourcefulness of its engineers and the efficiency of its pilots and navigators.

Already, initial test flights have thrilled the world with the amazing smoothness and the mathematical precision with which they have been accomplished. Already, a chain of bases has been laid across the Pacific at Midway Island, Wake Island and Guam to Manila.

Of fundamental importance, at these bases of supply, are Socony-Vacuum lubricants. Hundreds of barrels of Aero Mobiloil have been transported to the islands, ready to play their part in the regular operation of Pan American's mighty motors!

Thus again, as in the epoch-making flights of the past . . . the Wright brothers' pioneering flights . . . Lindbergh's dash to Paris . . . the U. S. Army 'round-the-world flight . . . and as in the present vast operation of the Deutsche Luft Hansa throughout Europe and South America . . . Socony-Vacuum lubricants have been chosen to perform . . . where *unfailing* performance is vital!

Today, in 63 countries of the world . . . flyers, as well as motorists, mariners and manufacturers, look to Socony-Vacuum for the finest petroleum products that modern methods can produce.

SOCONY-VACUUM OIL COMPANY, INC.

STANDARD OIL OF NEW YORK DIVISION · WHITE STAR DIVISION · LUBRITE DIVISION · WHITE EAGLE DIVISION · WADHAMS OIL COMPANY
MAGNOLIA PETROLEUM COMPANY · GENERAL PETROLEUM CORPORATION OF CALIFORNIA

SOCONY-VACUUM

Douglas Aircraft Co., 1931 ◄

Socony-Vacuum Oil Co., 1935

All

STERLING POWERED

Colossal projects, driven by Sterling engines, completed visions of master engineers, are active testimony to the character of Sterlings. What other marine engine has so qualified industrially, in such an array of imposing and successful applications?

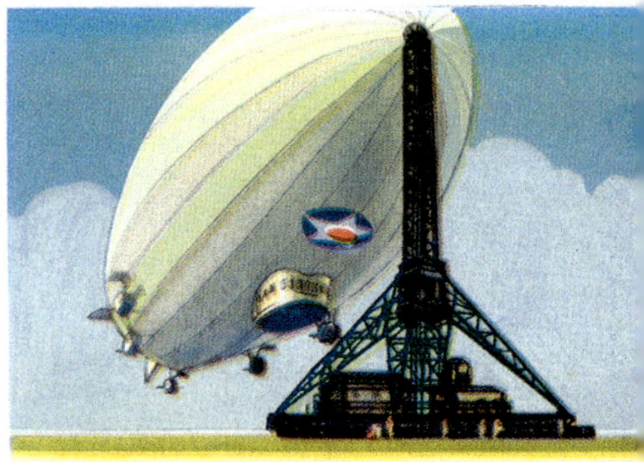

Lakehurst, telescoping mooring mast, Sterling Viking 8 cylinder engine, 565 H.P., 1200 R.P.M.

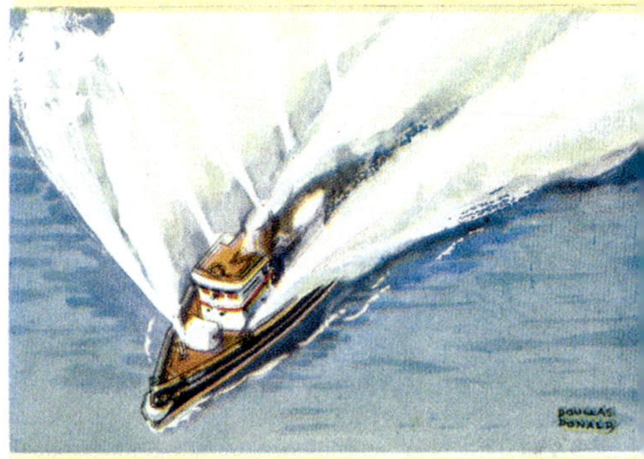

New York City, fireboat, 5 Sterling Viking 8 cylinder engines, total 3000 H.P., 1200 R.P.M.

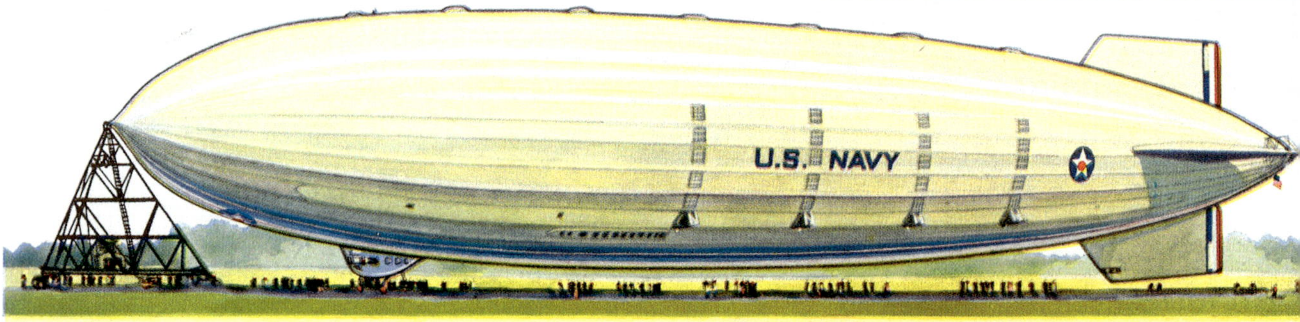

Akron, Ohio, mooring mast, Sterling Dolphin 8 cylinder engine, 240 H.P., 1200 R.P.M.

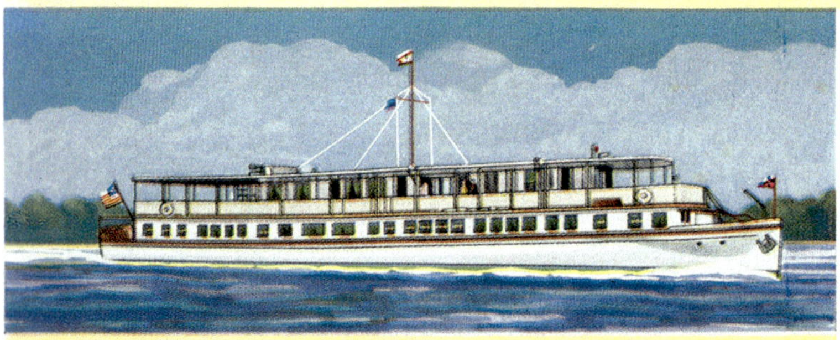

St. Paul, cruising house-boat, 125′ long, 25′ beam, 2 Sterling Petrel reduction gear engines, 180 H.P. each, 600 R.P.M., built by Joseph Dingle Boat Works.

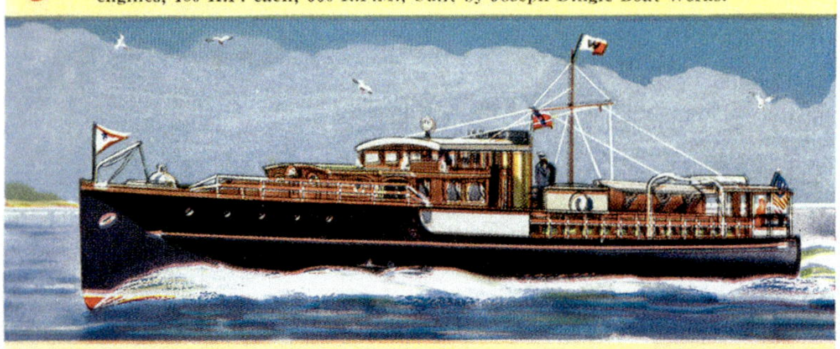

Chicago, WASP, 88′ fast cruiser, designed by Grebe, built by Great Lakes, driven by 2 Sterling Viking 8 cylinder engines, total 1130 H.P.

The Navy mooring masts at Lakehurst, Akron and Sunnyvale; the giant New York City fireboat, only gasoline-electric boat, most powerful fireboat in the world; the great Portland and Tacoma fireboats, and many others; bridges, pumps, generators, locomotives, rail motor cars, all equipped with Sterling engines, all requiring specific technical knowledge, are evidence that Sterling maintains a progressive organization.

Every Sterling model is scientifically engineered and most carefully built. Every model, compared in terms of power and mechanical attributes, typifies 25% greater value. Prices are interestingly low.

STERLING
ENGINE COMPANY
BUFFALO, NEW YORK, U.S.A.

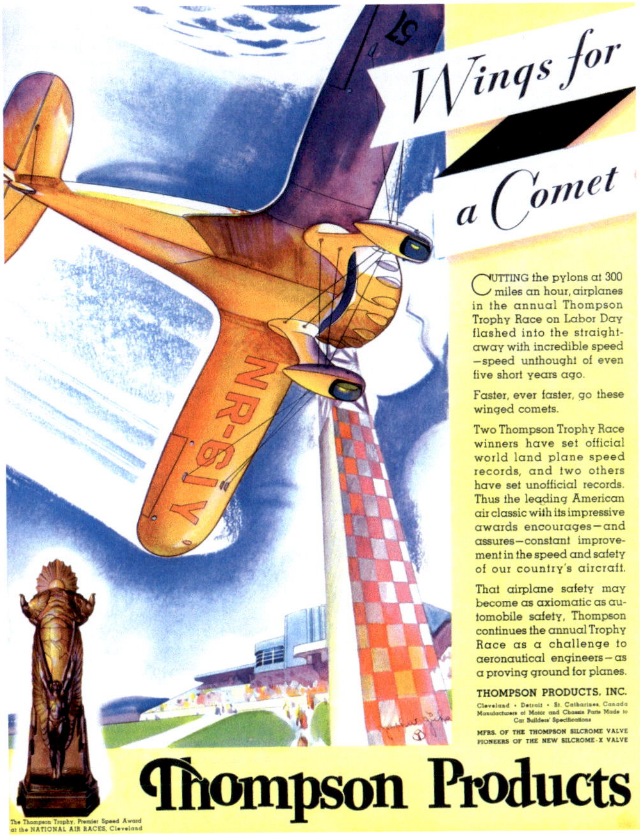

Thompson Products, 1935

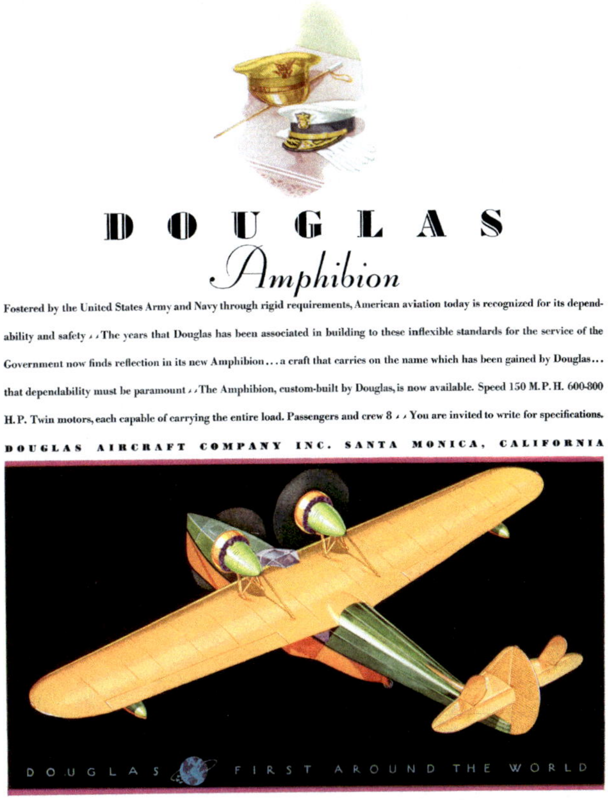

Douglas Aircraft Co., 1931

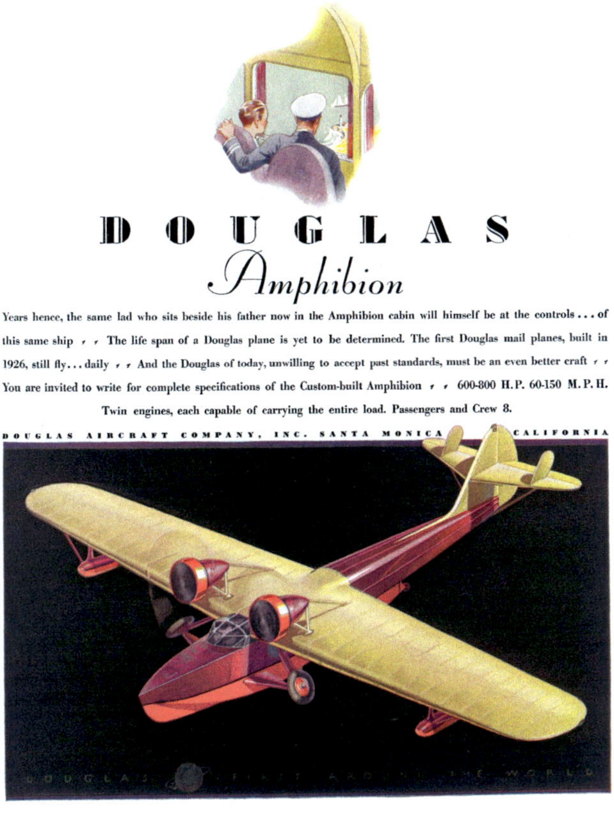

Sterling Engine Co., 1933 ◀ *Douglas Aircraft Co., 1931*

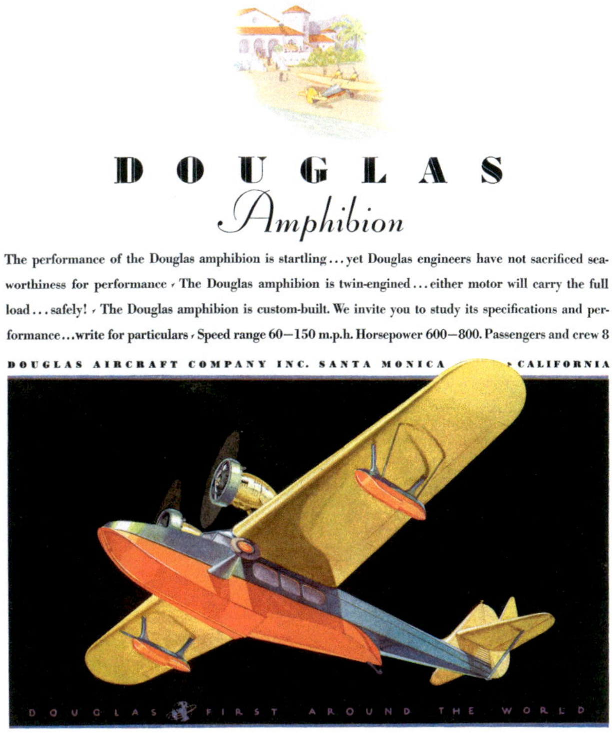

Douglas Aircraft Co., 1931

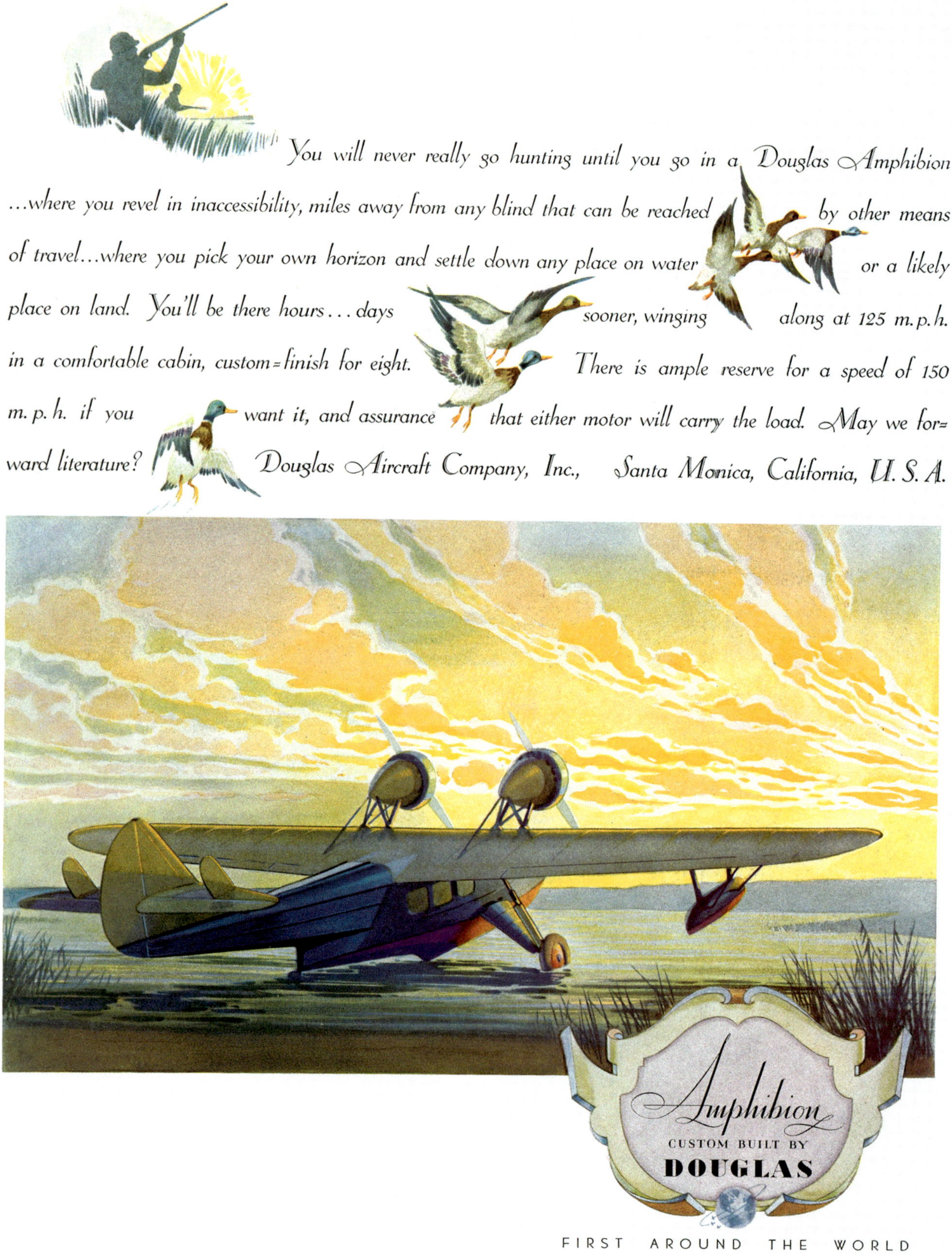

Douglas Aircraft Co., 1931

► *Sterling Engine Co., 1930*

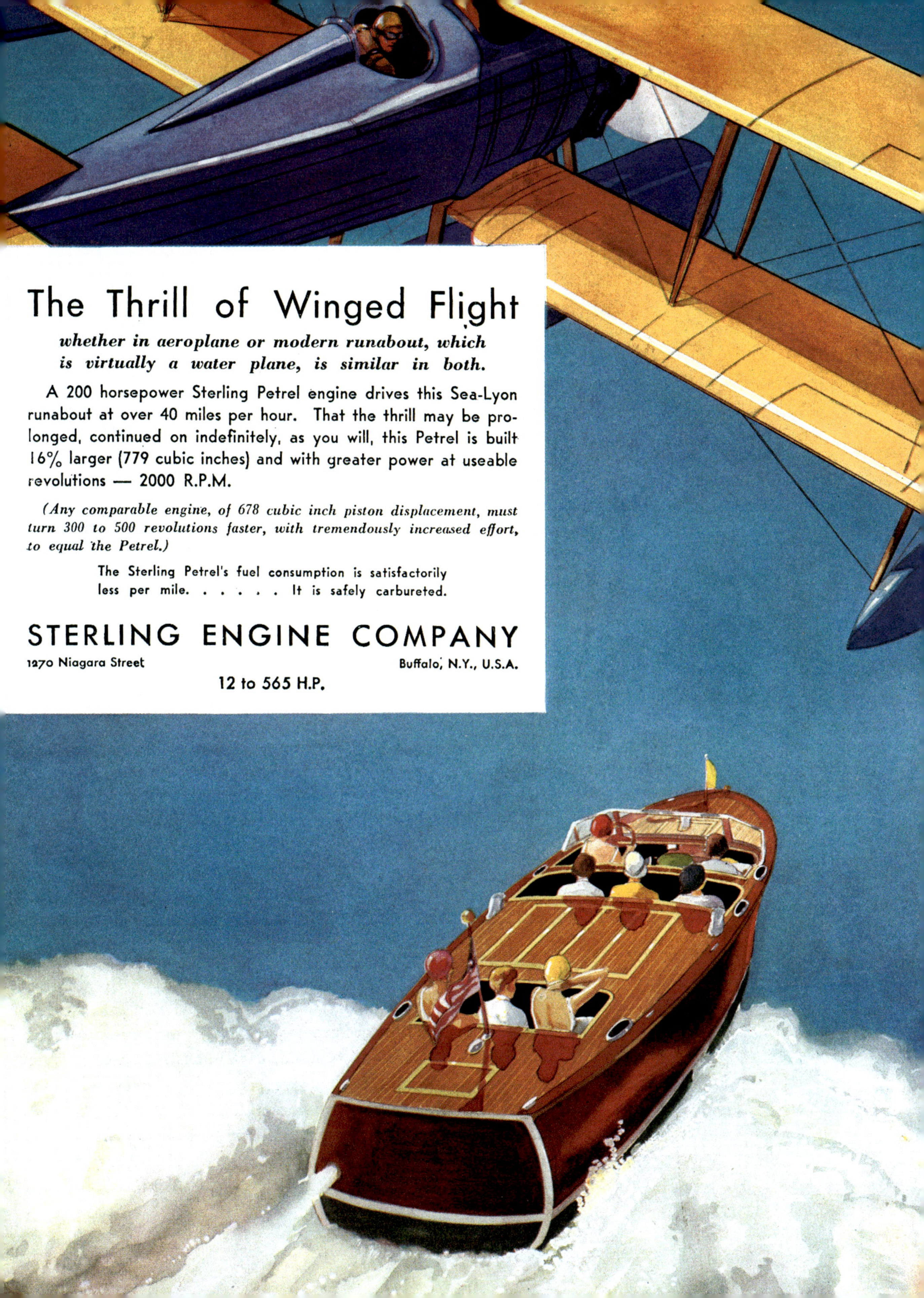
The Thrill of Winged Flight
whether in aeroplane or modern runabout, which is virtually a water plane, is similar in both.
A 200 horsepower Sterling Petrel engine drives this Sea-Lyon runabout at over 40 miles per hour. That the thrill may be prolonged, continued on indefinitely, as you will, this Petrel is built 16% larger (779 cubic inches) and with greater power at useable revolutions — 2000 R.P.M.
(Any comparable engine, of 678 cubic inch piston displacement, must turn 300 to 500 revolutions faster, with tremendously increased effort, to equal the Petrel.)
The Sterling Petrel's fuel consumption is satisfactorily less per mile. . . . . . It is safely carbureted.
STERLING ENGINE COMPANY
1270 Niagara Street
Buffalo, N.Y., U.S.A.
12 to 565 H.P.

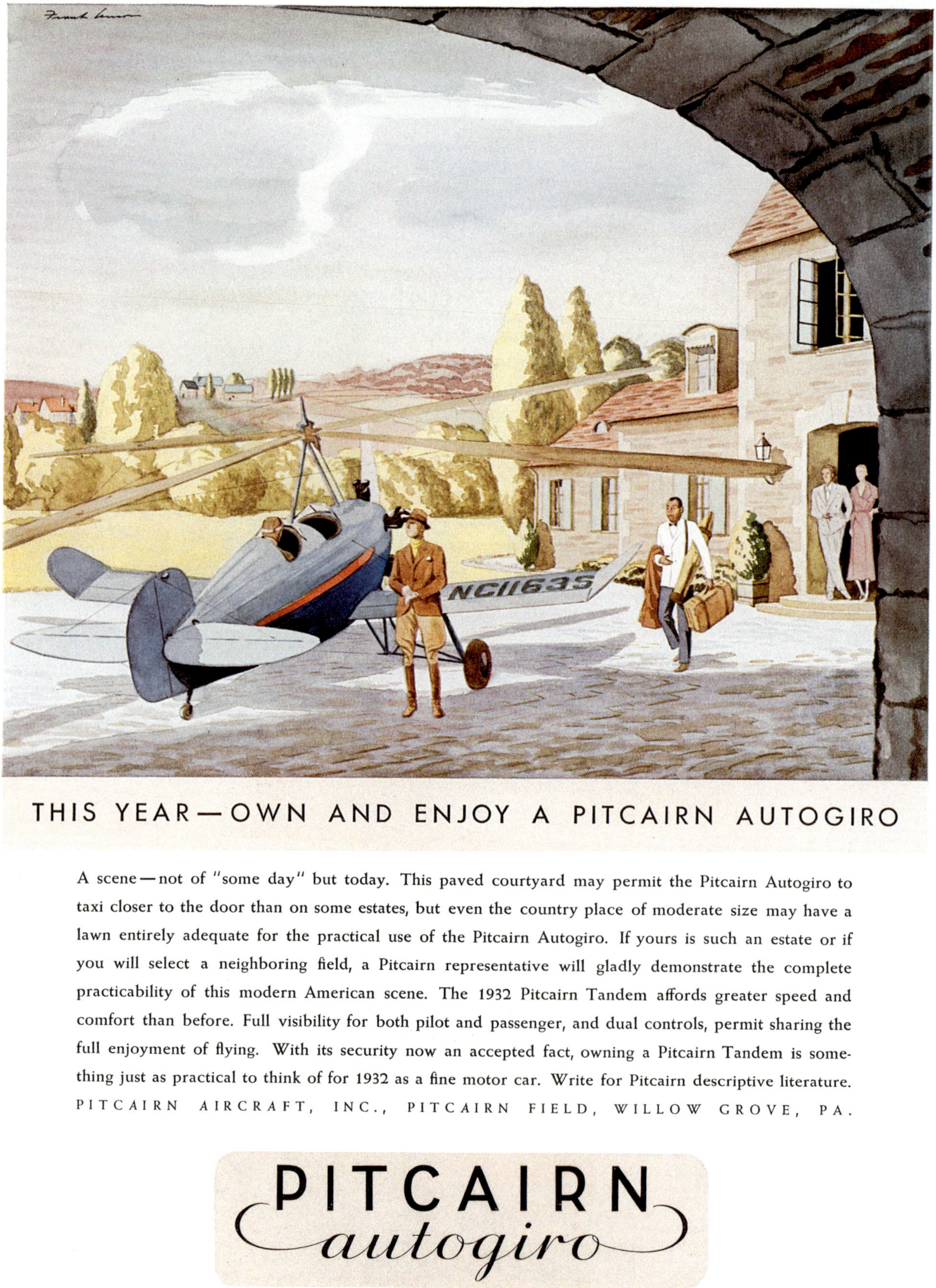

Pitcairn Autogiro, 1932

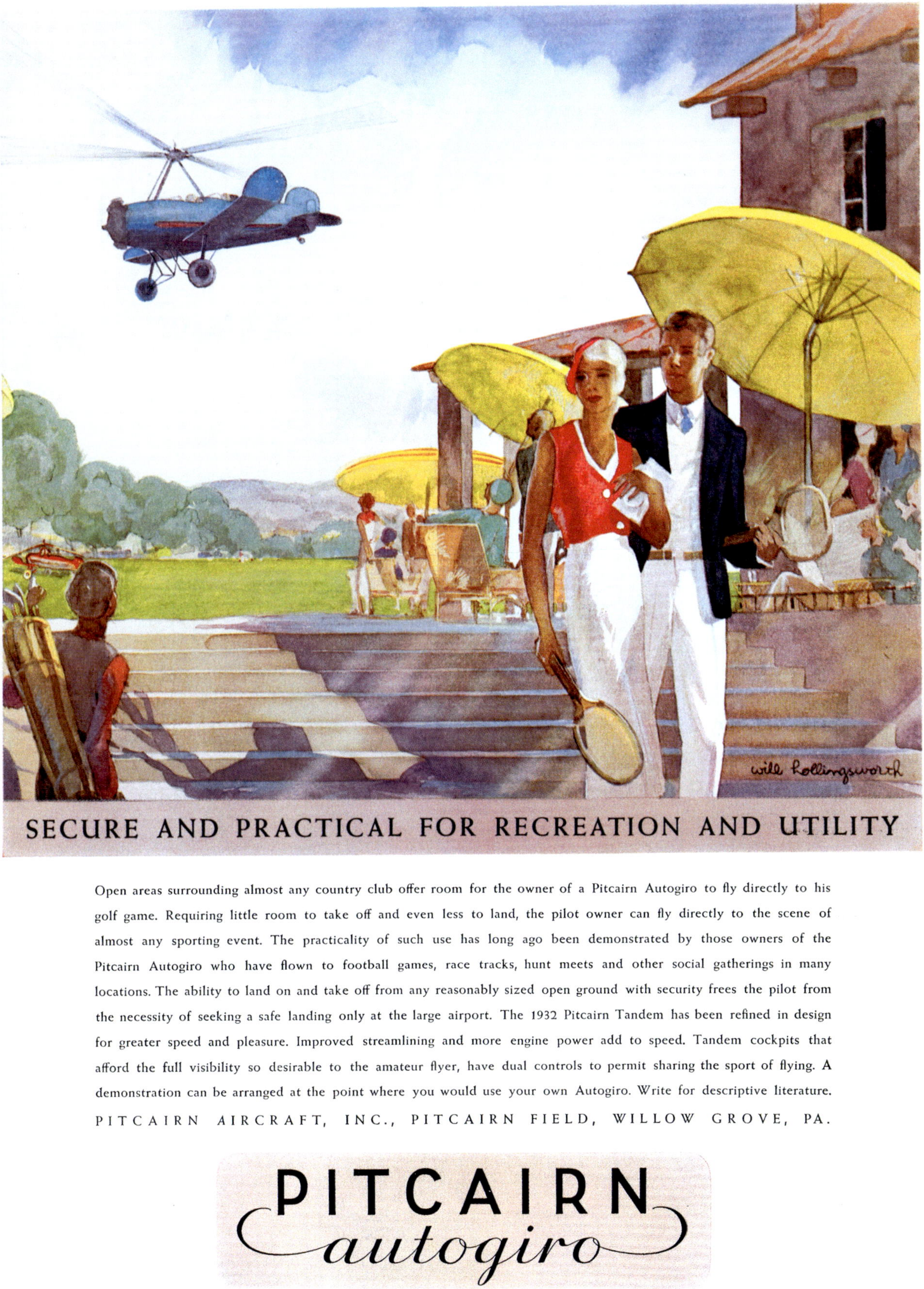

Pitcairn Autogiro, 1931

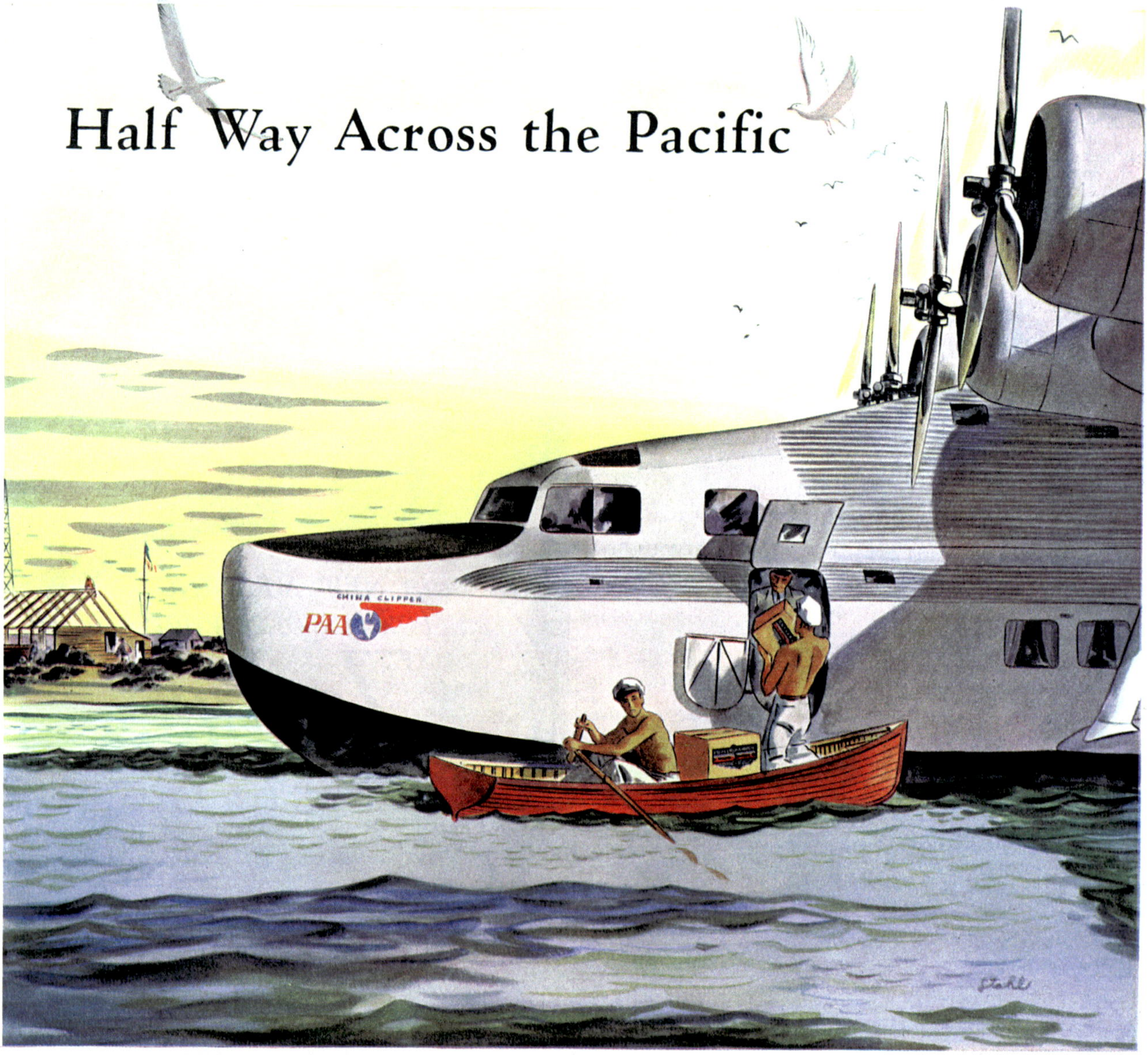

Of course, the Motor Control is Cutler-Hammer

In this electrical age, Motor Control is ever in the vanguard of civilization's onward march, for electric motors now do the back-breaking work wherever men go. Water must be pumped. Air must be moved. Tools must be turned. The needs of the machine shop, homes or hotel on tiny Wake Island, Mid-Pacific station of the Pan-American Airways, are the same as those in your own home town. . . . Being isolated several *thousand* miles from any help, however, makes people very serious about the choice of Motor Control. No one likes the inconvenience, the waste of time, or the repair costs of mechanical troubles, but on Wake Island such troubles could become a near-calamity. So the Motor Control for Wake Island, delivered there on one of the earliest trips of the famous China Clipper, is all *genuine* Cutler-Hammer Motor Control.

CUTLER-HAMMER
MOTOR CONTROL
C-H

Cutler-Hammer Motor Control is an outstanding choice wherever the importance of reliable, trouble-free electric motor performance is recognized. Many factories use Cutler-Hammer Motor Control exclusively . . . specify it by name for every motor or motorized machine purchased and refuse to accept any substitute. A majority of all electric motor builders recommend Cutler-Hammer Motor Control. Leading machinery builders feature it as standard equipment. A host of independent electrical wholesalers carry adequate stocks for your convenience. CUTLER-HAMMER, Inc., *Pioneer Manufacturers of Electric Control Apparatus*, 1259 St. Paul Avenue, Milwaukee, Wisconsin.

Cutler-Hammer, 1938

► *Westinghouse, 1936*

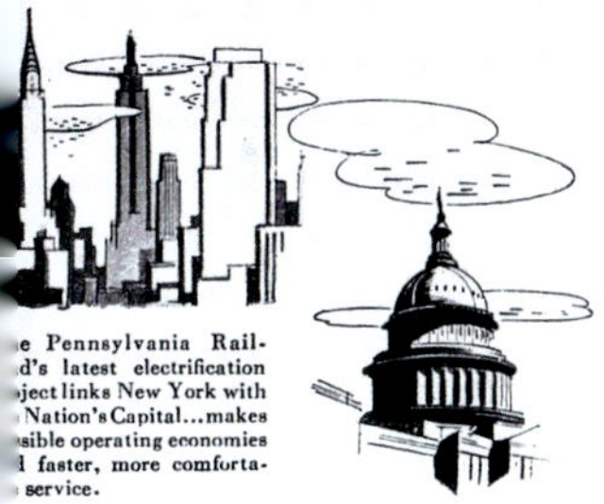

e Pennsylvania Rail-
d's latest electrification
ject links New York with
Nation's Capital...makes
sible operating economies
l faster, more comforta-
service.

WINGS FOR THE IRON HORSE

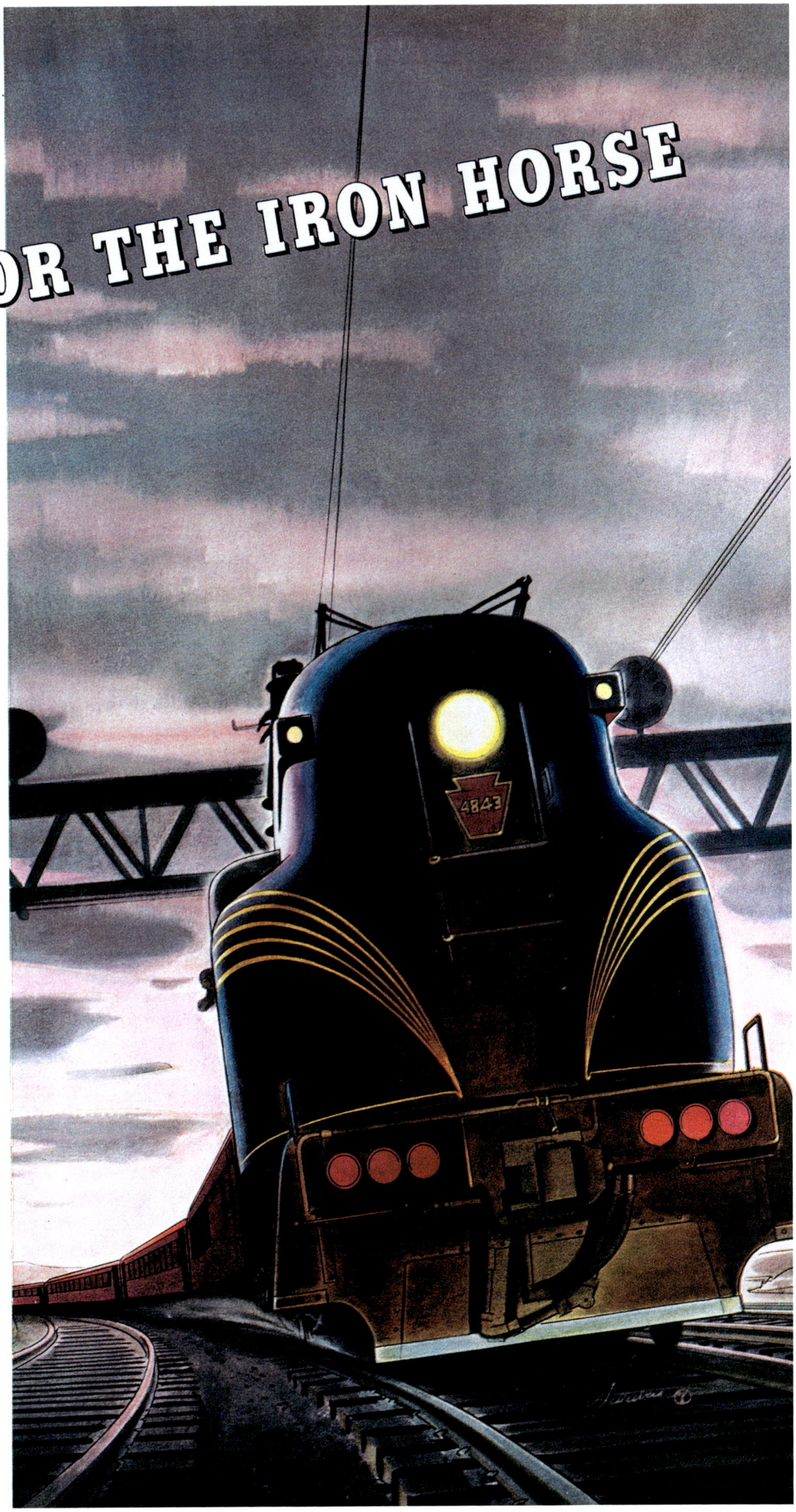

he Pennsylvania Railroad's new ectric highway from New York Washington opens another stir-ng chapter in the annals of trans-ortation. Heretofore railroad ectrification was primarily de-oted to the improvement of termi-al and main line suburban service, tunnel operations, and the haul-ig of heavy freight over steep ountain grades. Today it becomes he new order of railroad modern-ation on major trunk lines... epresents a definite advance in the conomical readjustment of rail-oad facilities to the demands of nodern travel.

In this advance, Westinghouse has layed a major role, consistent with lifelong tradition of co-operation vith the Transportation Industry.

The Westinghouse Electric and Ianufacturing Company was eared on that tradition. Its foun-ler invented and brought to bril-iant fruition the Westinghouse Air Brake. Its first great achieve-nent was the successful promulga-ion of the alternating current ystem... upon which is based the Pennsylvania's system for main ine electrification.

To this great project, Westing-ouse brought the wealth of a half-entury of experience and engi-eering progress. A conspicuous xample of Westinghouse enter-prise on every front where elec-ricity is helping to build a new and better economic civilization. Westinghouse Electric & Manufac-turing Co., East Pittsburgh, Pa.

WESTINGHOUSE W 1886 1936 GOLDEN JUBILEE

50 YEARS OF
GROWTH AND ACHIEVEMENT

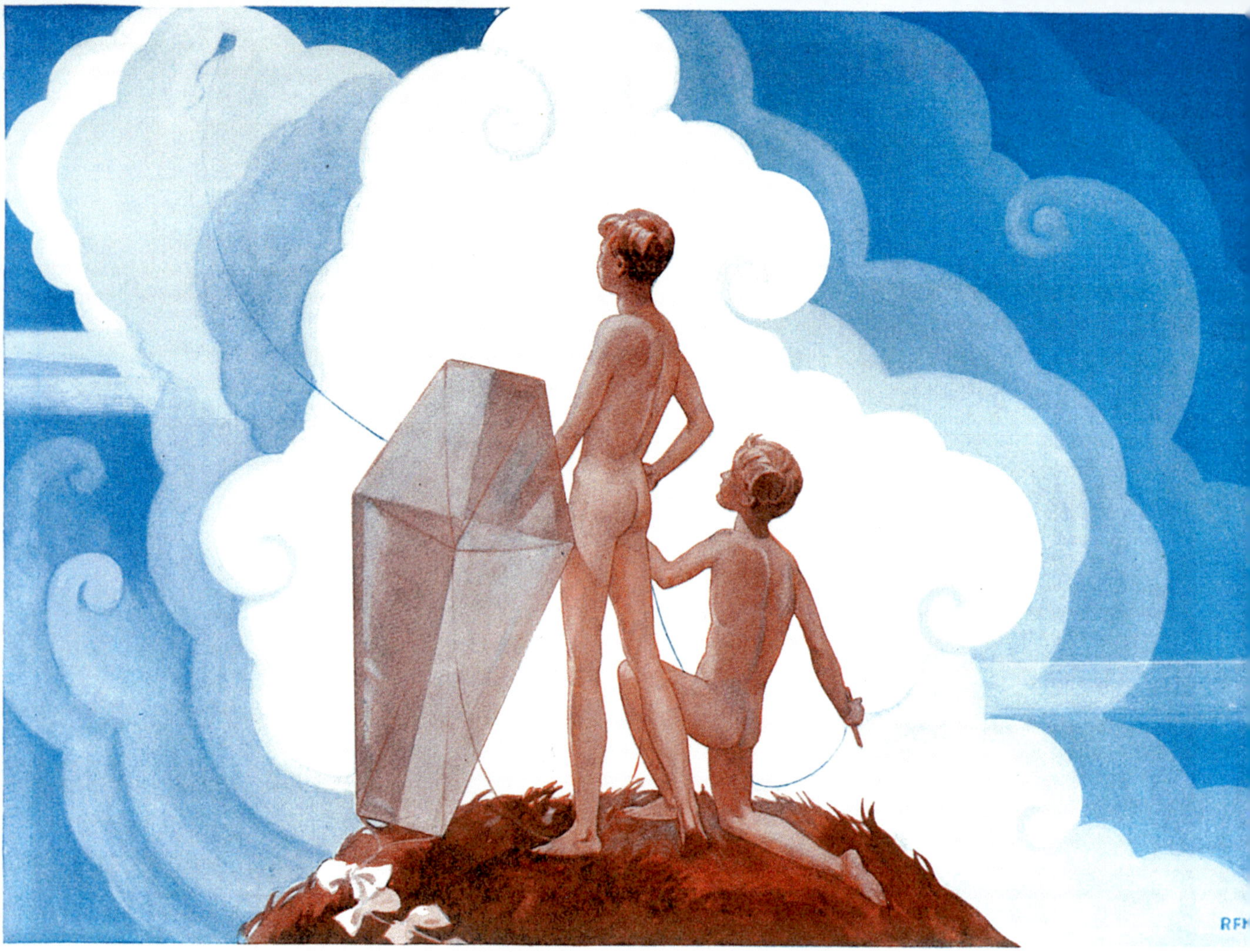

NATURE'S AIR IS BEST

WHEN a new June sun coaxes blossoms from plant and tree . . . when the morning grass glistens with warm dew and puffy snow-white clouds float over a sapphire sky . . . then instinct tells us Nature's air is at its best and all mankind yearns to answer the call of the great outdoors.

Healthful warmth like that of a fine June day—made so by Nature's own formula—is brought to your home through all the winter months by the Holland Vaporaire Heating System.

No longer need any one pay the penalty of obsolete heating methods. No longer need any one live in stifling, stagnant, baked-dry air . . . Holland's simple, compact, electrically-controlled home heating and air-conditioning system warms, humidifies and circulates the air you breathe. You enjoy a refreshing, exhilarating indoor atmosphere.

In winter, a moist balmy current of warmth circulates through every room and keeps the proper temperature constant. The air changes completely every few minutes.

In summer, a power-driven, airplane-type propeller sends zestful, cooling breezes through the whole house—making hot, sultry days and nights comfortable.

Every Holland Vaporaire Heating System is accurately engineered and custom built to fit the exact requirements of the home it serves. One company plans, builds, sells, installs and finances. Responsibility is undivided. Comfort and satisfaction are guaranteed by Holland's written bond.

Get the facts. There's a direct factory branch in your community. Simply telephone. Have a Holland heating engineer call. No obligation . . . Vaporaire Division, HOLLAND FURNACE COMPANY, Holland, Michigan.

FREE HEATING ENGINEERING SERVICE

Holland's Complete Heating Survey is the modern way to heating comfort. Holland Surveys include humidity reading, chimney draft tests, show you how to save fuel and money through proper heat distribution, disclose fire risks, and reveal the reasons some rooms are hard to heat. Have a Complete Heating Survey made by Holland heating engineers without delay. No cost—no obligation.

World's largest installers of home heating systems, operating three large factories and 554 factory branches from coast to coast

HOLLAND VAPORAIRE HEATING

THE ELECTRICALLY CONTROLLED AIR-CONDITIONING SYSTEM FOR WINTER HEATING AND SUMMER COOLING

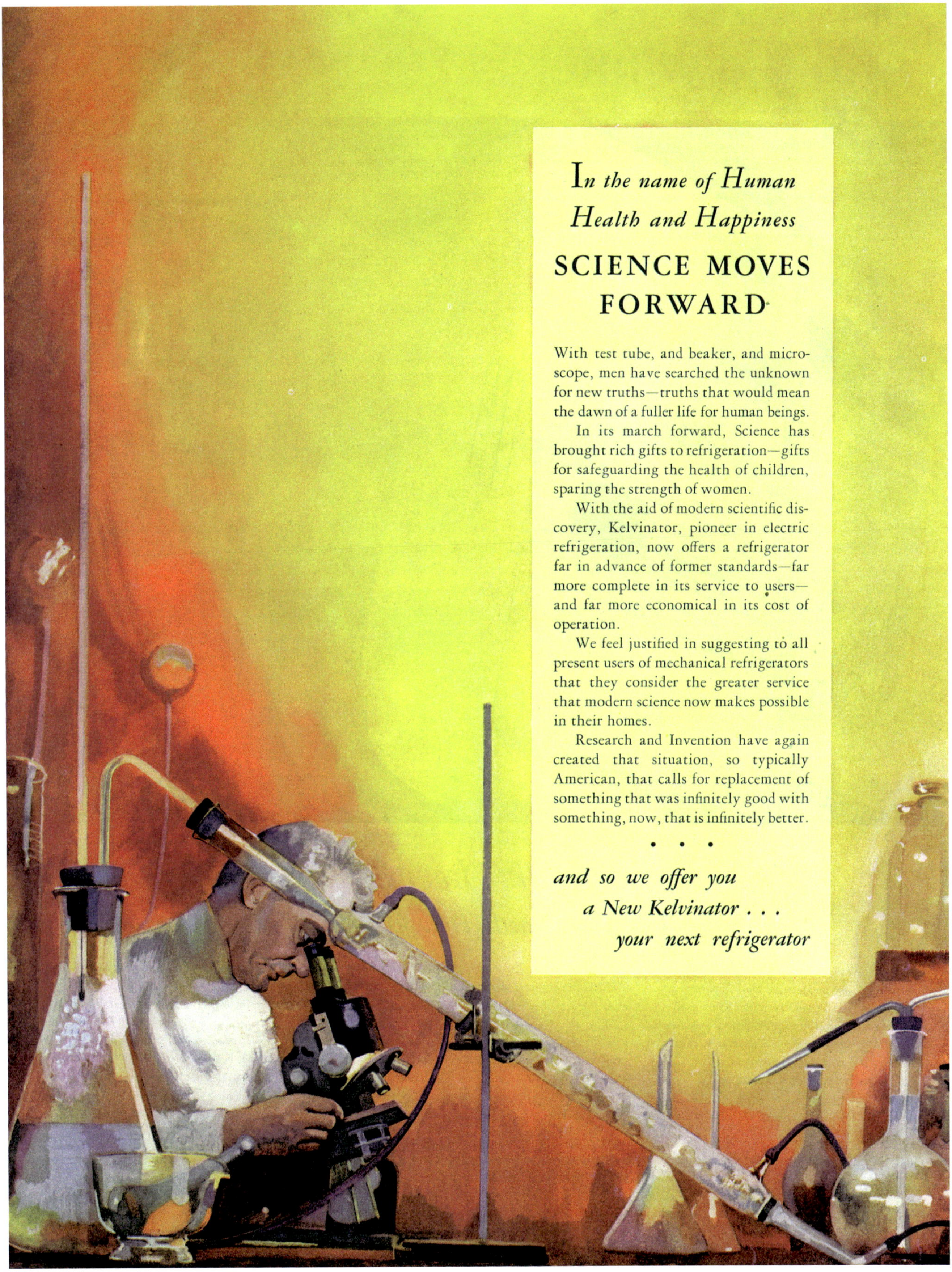

Holland Vaporaire Heating, 1931 ◂

Kelvinator, 1936

And the winner is...

Between World Wars

Long before the shadow of war was cast on the United States, one of the country's first modern peace organizations was lobbying Americans to consider an alternative. Founded in 1936, World Peaceways was instrumental in convincing Franklin D. Roosevelt to stave off involvement in World War II during the 1930s. Their aggressive series of magazine ads, billboards, and radio programs—some featuring babies on butcher blocks or disabled WW-I vets who had been all but forgotten—also reminded the country that, in contemporary warfare, there could be no such thing as a noncombatant US citizen.

Zwischen den Kriegen

Lange bevor düstere Kriegswolken am Horizont aufzogen, versuchte eine der ersten modernen Friedensgruppen des Landes, den Amerikanern Alternativen aufzuzeigen. 1936 gegründet, war World Peaceways maßgeblich daran beteiligt, Franklin D. Roosevelt davon zu überzeugen, das Land aus dem Zweiten Weltkrieg herauszuhalten. Mit aggressiven Reklametafeln, Radiospots und Anzeigen – einige zeigten Babys auf Schlachterblöcken und die schon fast in Vergessenheit geratenen Kriegskrüppel des Ersten Weltkriegs – erinnerten sie die Nation daran, dass es in einem modernen Krieg keine unbeteiligten Zivilisten mehr gibt.

Entre deux guerres mondiales

Bien avant que l'ombre de la guerre ne s'abatte sur les Etats-Unis, l'une des premières organisations pacifistes américaines faisait campagne contre l'éventualité d'un conflit armé. Fondée en 1936, World Peaceways contribua à convaincre Franklin D. Roosevelt de retarder l'intervention de son pays dans la Seconde Guerre mondiale. Ses campagnes de choc dans les magazines, sur les panneaux d'affichage ou à la radio (certaines montrant des bébés sur des tables de boucher ou des soldats de la Grande Guerre revenus infirmes, puis oubliés) rappelèrent également aux citoyens américains que, dans la guerre moderne, il n'y avait pas de non-combattants.

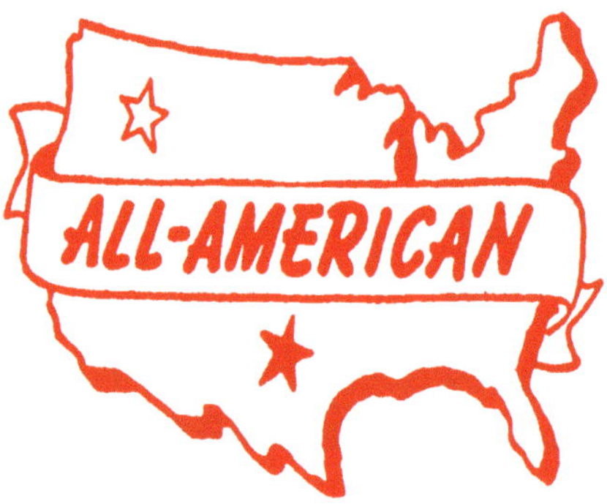

World Peaceways, 1935

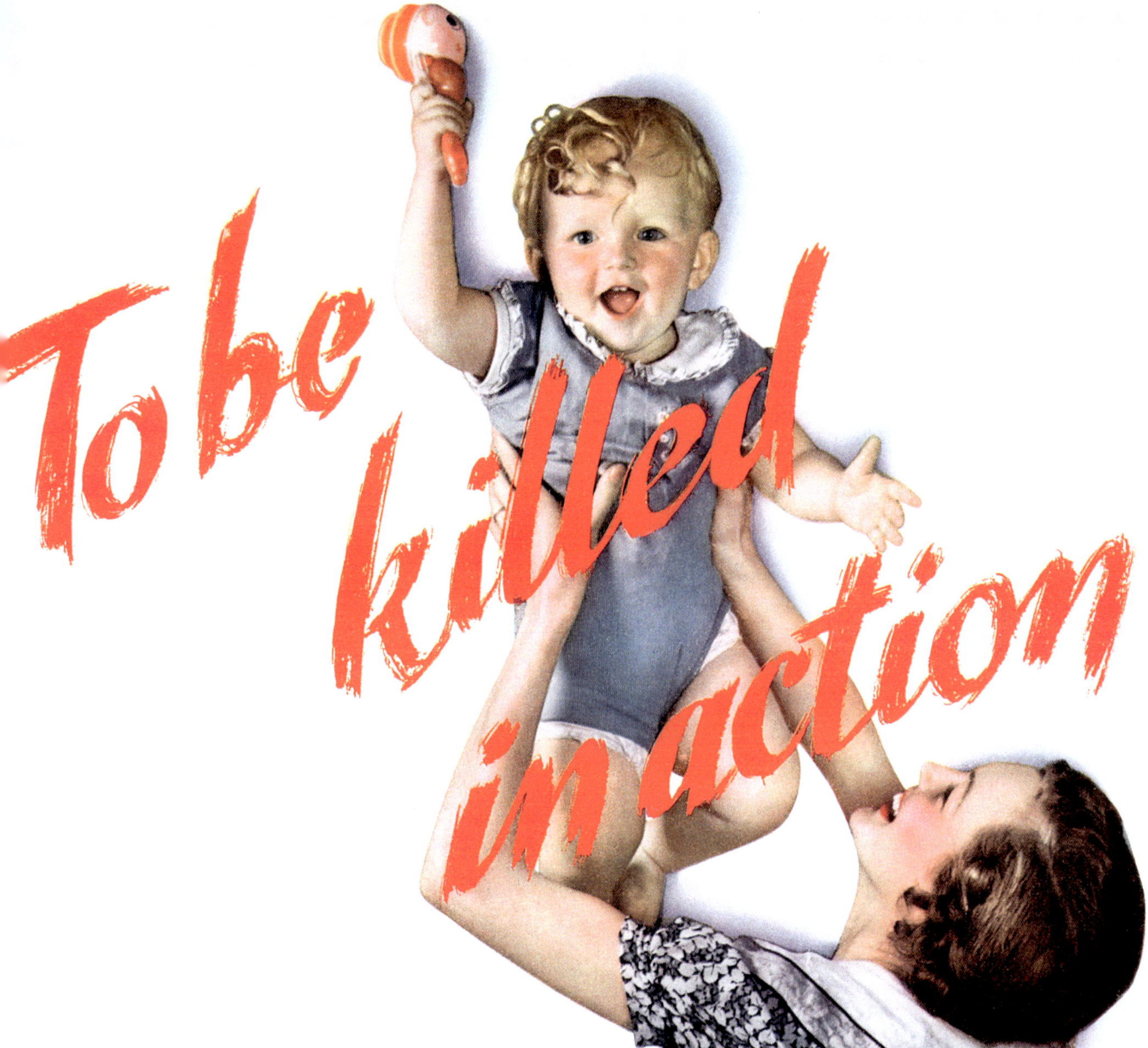

He's going to grow up to go to war?

No—he's never going to grow up at all. If another war comes, he and his mother and thousands upon thousands like them are going to "die in action."

"Impossible!" you say. "They're non-combatants." Don't be silly—there'll be no such thing as non-combatants in the next war.

Wide-cruising submarines, and bombing planes will laugh at front lines. Gas—gas so powerful that one drop on your skin will kill you—will not be particular whose skin it touches. There will be no haven, no sanctuary, no safety. *Everyone* will suffer.

And for what? *Glory*—where was it in the last war?

Victory—where was it in the last peace?

With that cruel lesson still fresh in mind, is another war to be forced upon us—a war infinitely more horrible, more futile, and more lasting in its harm than the last?

That is for you to decide!

What to do about it

Hysterical protests won't avert another war, any more than will "preparedness."

Civilization must build its own defense out of human reason and intelligence, properly organized and applied.

To every reasonable and intelligent man and woman in America goes the responsibility of doing his or her share to avert the coming war.

World Peaceways offers a practical plan of how you *can* help. Write for it. There is no obligation involved in your inquiry, except the obligation to your conscience and to your conviction that *there must be no more wars.* World Peaceways, Inc., 103 Park Avenue, New York City.

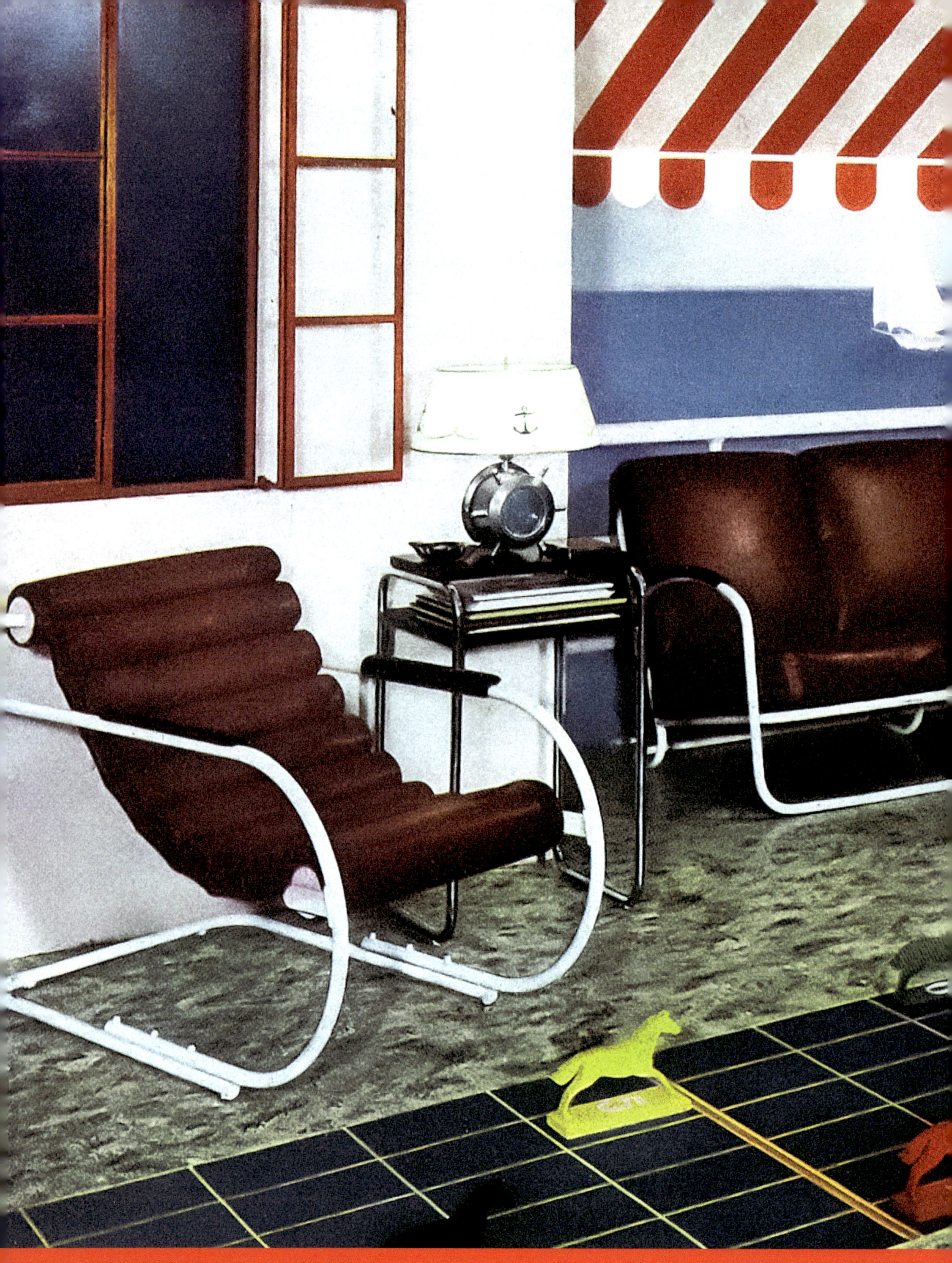

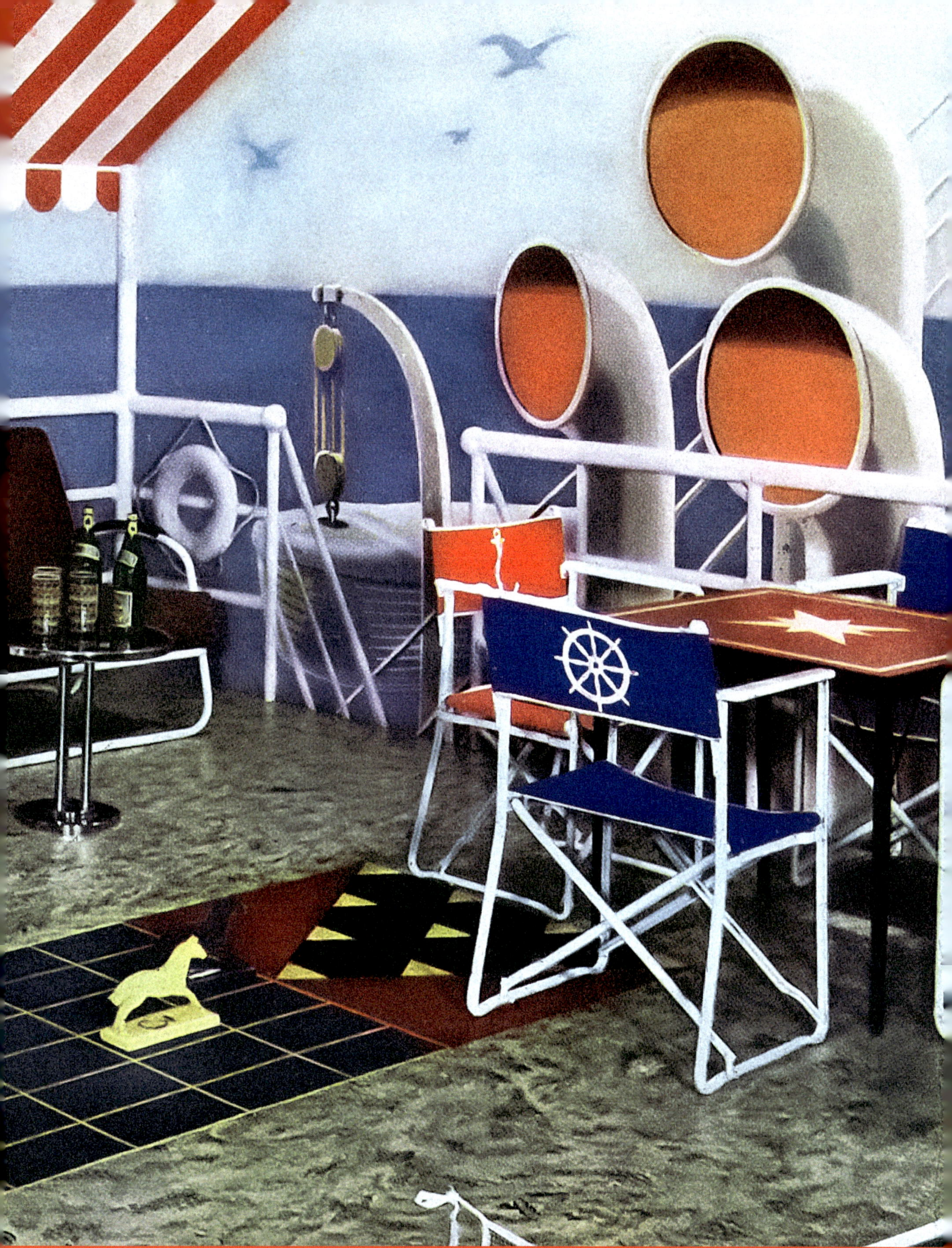

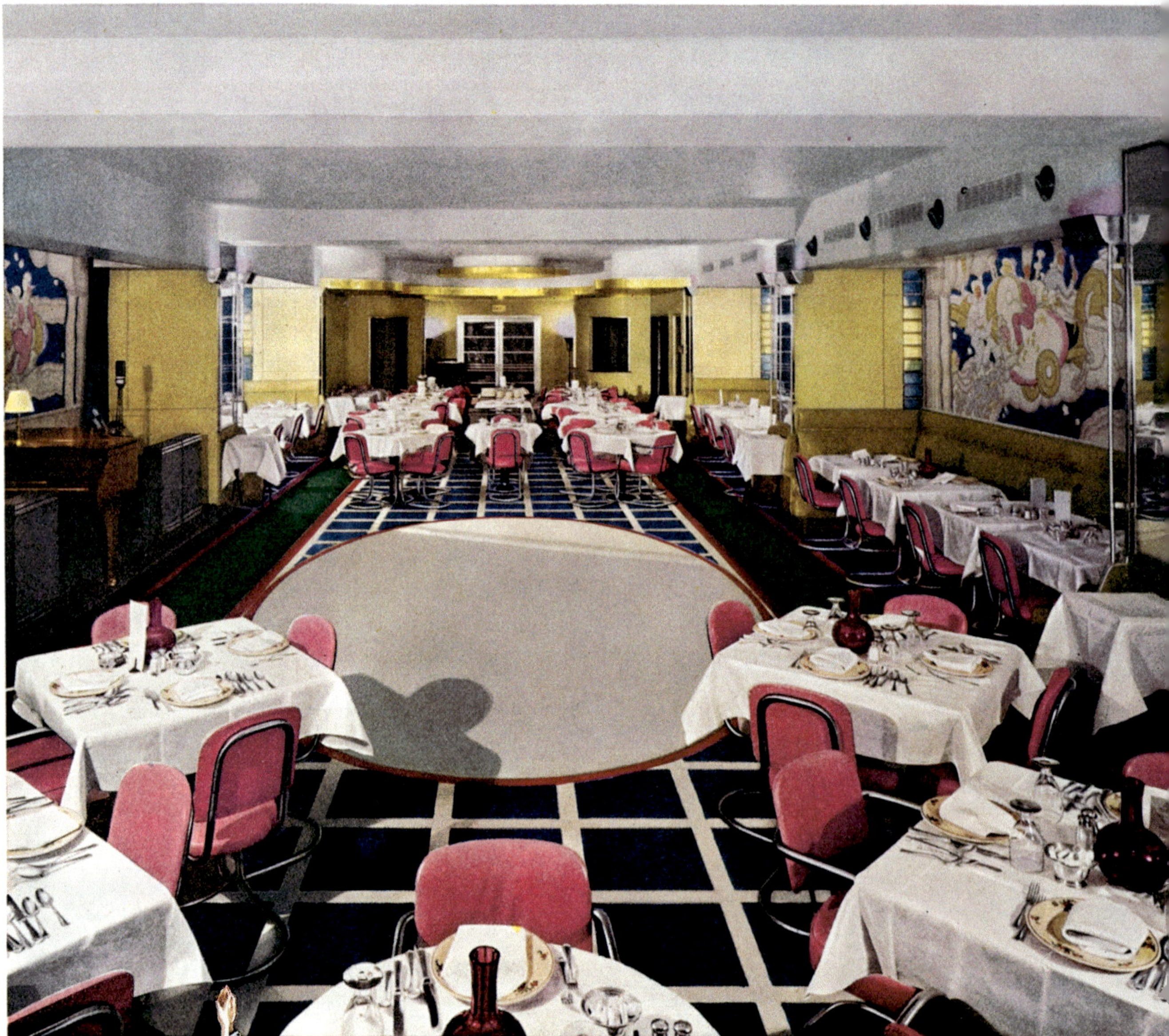

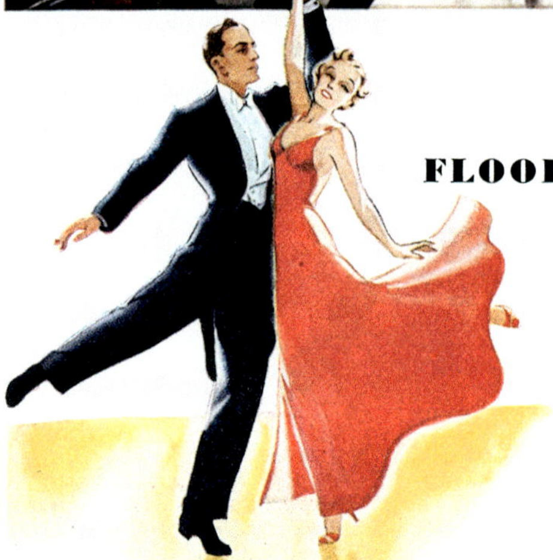

THE AMBASSADOR HOTEL, Washington, D. C., has spread color and comfort underfoot with this special designed Armstrong's Linoleum Floor in cadet blue, ruby, and white. Trimly tailored and cemented in place over cushio ing felt, such a floor also offers the advantage of lowered maintenance costs, and satisfactory service over many year

FLOOR SHOWMANSHIP has made the Ambassador Hotel a famous rendezvous at th Nation's Capital. For the gay Armstrong's Linoleum Floor has been an irresistible invitation to th smart set who dine here nightly. It's been two years now since this Armstrong Floor started welcom ing guests to the Ambassador. Yet, despite the unusually severe wear, this floor looks as fresh as th day it was installed. This is just another practical example of the service you can expect fror Armstrong's Linoleum in your own place of business. An example, too, of how you can now hav floors specially designed to match any decorative motif. Such floors put showmanship into a busines interior. And put a real saving into your pocket, for they cut maintenance costs to a minimum. As your local merchant to give you all the facts and figures of these better floors for better business

Write for Free Book, "Better Floors for Better Business." Illustrates all types of business interiors that have put floors on the sales force. Armstrong Cork Products Company, Floor Division, 3709 Liberty St., Lancaster, Pa. (Makers of cork products since 1860)

ARMSTRONG'S LINOLEUM FLOORS

Custom-Laid or Standard Designs

PLAIN • INLAID • EMBOSSED • JASPÉ • LINOTILE • CORK TILE • ACCOTILE • RUBBER TILE • ARMSTRONG'S LINOWALL *and* ARMSTRONG'S QUAKER RUG

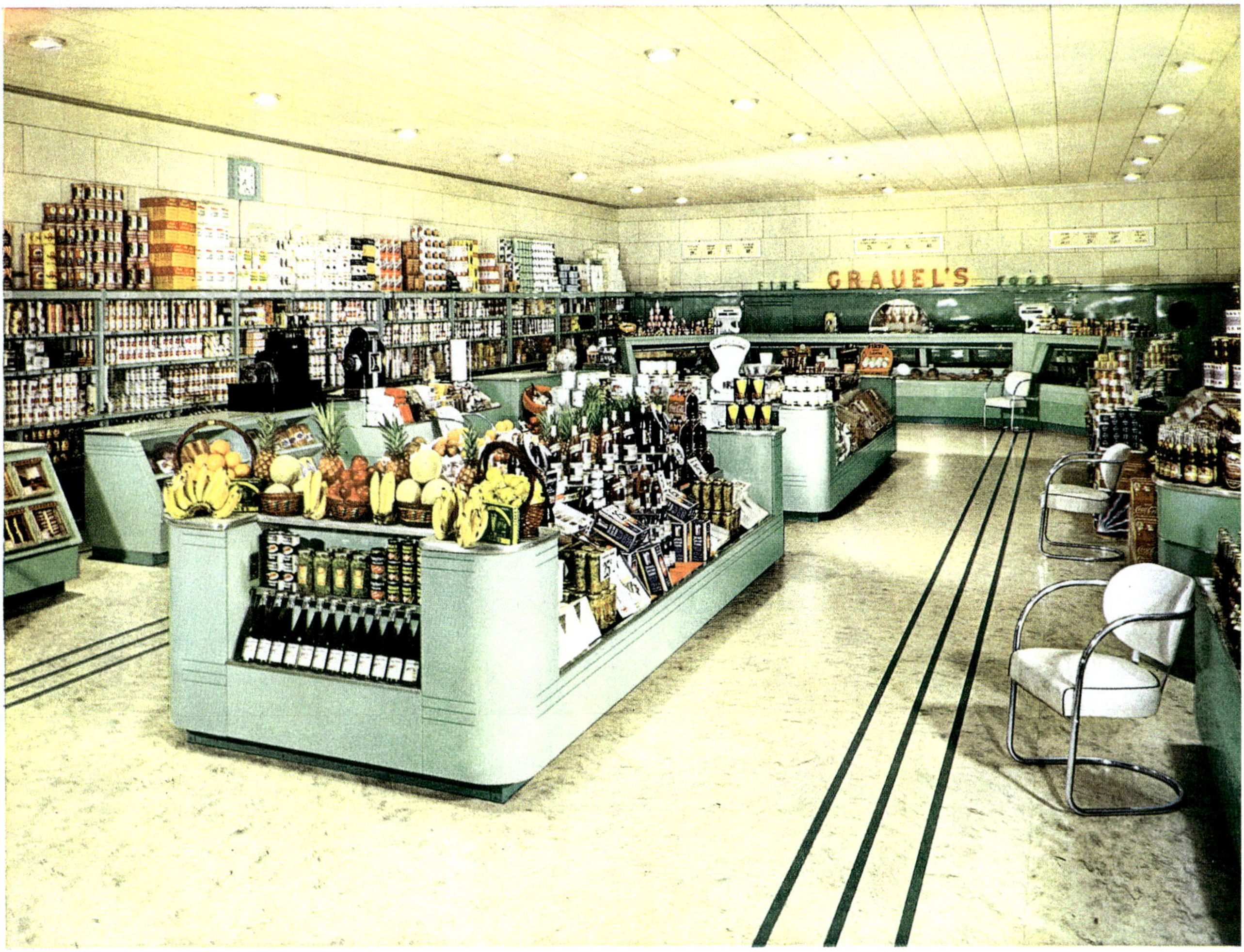

FAMOUS FOR FINE FOOD, Grauel's Market, Baltimore, is also becoming famous for its fine, trade-attracting floor—a special design in Armstrong's Linoleum installed by John R. Livezey, designed by J. P. Pfeiffer & Son, Baltimore (Marbelle No. 03 with strips of jade green). Table and counter tops are also Armstrong's Marbelle Linoleum.

BUY-APPEAL FROM THE FLOOR UP is the plan of this modern market. "Despite keen competition, this plan is paying attractive trade dividends," enthusiastically reports Mr. Harry Grauel, the proprietor. "Folks like the fine, spick-and-span appearance of my Armstrong Floor. It has eye-appeal and *buy*-appeal. It's my best silent salesman!" Mr. Grauel will also tell you that Armstrong's Linoleum Floors, when trimly and properly cemented in place over felt, can take street-floor traffic, that such floors cut cleaning to a minimum, and do away with expensive floor refinishing. When the photograph above was taken, this floor hadn't been washed, waxed, or polished in a month, although it had received a daily sweeping. You see it reproduced just as the camera caught it—no tracks, traffic lanes, or scuff marks. Your local linoleum merchant can demonstrate two other big virtues of modern Armstrong Floors . . . cushioning comfort underfoot, and a price that should appeal to any careful business executive. Let him tell you the whole story of floors that put showmanship in selling.

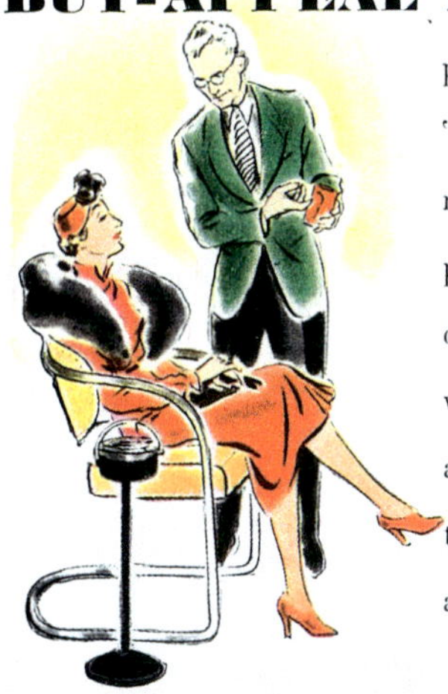

WE'LL SEND YOU a most helpful portfolio of different business interiors if you write for "Better Floors for Better Business." It also brings you the wear, care, and cost story in concise, quick-reference form. No charge (40¢ outside U. S. A.). Armstrong Cork Products Company, Floor Division, 3711 Clay Street, Lancaster, Pennsylvania. (Makers of cork products since 1860)

ARMSTRONG'S LINOLEUM FLOORS

Custom-Laid or Standard Designs

PLAIN • INLAID • EMBOSSED • JASPÉ • LINOTILE • CORK TILE • ACCOTILE • RUBBER TILE • ARMSTRONG'S LINOWALL and ARMSTRONG'S QUAKER RUGS

Armstrong's Linoleum Floors, 1934 ◄◄

◄▲ *Armstrong's Linoleum Floors, 1937*

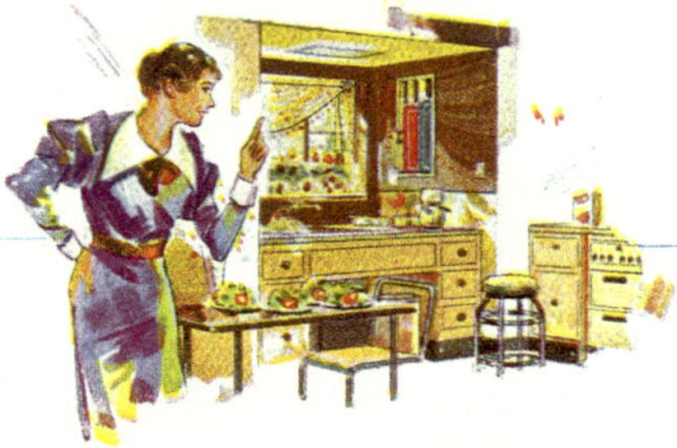

This kitchen smiles with a bright Armstrong's Straight Line Inlaid Linoleum Floor, No. 14240, making a foundation of charm for the modern fixtures. Sparkling, washable walls are Armstrong's Linowall No. 723. Note the well lighted sink, the niche for trays, the recessed cupboard that saves space. And to keep milady presentable is the make-up mirror. Complete specifications sent upon request. Remodel your kitchen today. *Insist on a permanent job cemented over felt—the most satisfactory way to install linoleum on wood floors.*

"LOOK PLEASANT, KITCHEN!..

... guests are about to arrive. And you know how guests are these days... they simply *won't* stay in the living-room, the way guests used to! The very first time I come out here, the whole mad pack will be on my heels ... But let them come. *What of it*, Kitchen? Aren't you about the nicest-looking room in my whole house? And easy on the feet, too, because of this linoleum-over-felt floor. And aren't you the easiest of all rooms to clean up, after everyone has gone home? Indeed you are! Thanks to your smooth Armstrong's Linoleum Floor, that doesn't hang on to dust and dirt and won't spot ... and your washable walls of Armstrong's Linowall ... always glistening ... always looking as though I spend most of my life washing and scrubbing them. But I don't, do I, Kitchen? That's our secret—yours and mine—and that man's at the linoleum store. The one that told me all about Armstrong's Linoleum and Linowall, and helped me choose just the right pattern!

"There's the bell! They're here. Kitchen, look pleasant!"

A brand-new booklet: "The Care of Modern Floors." It describes the simplest, most inexpensive methods of taking care of linoleum and other types of resilient floors. Every good housekeeper needs this book. Sent free. Armstrong Cork Products Company, Floor Division, 3604 College Avenue, Lancaster, Pa. (Makers of cork products since 1860)

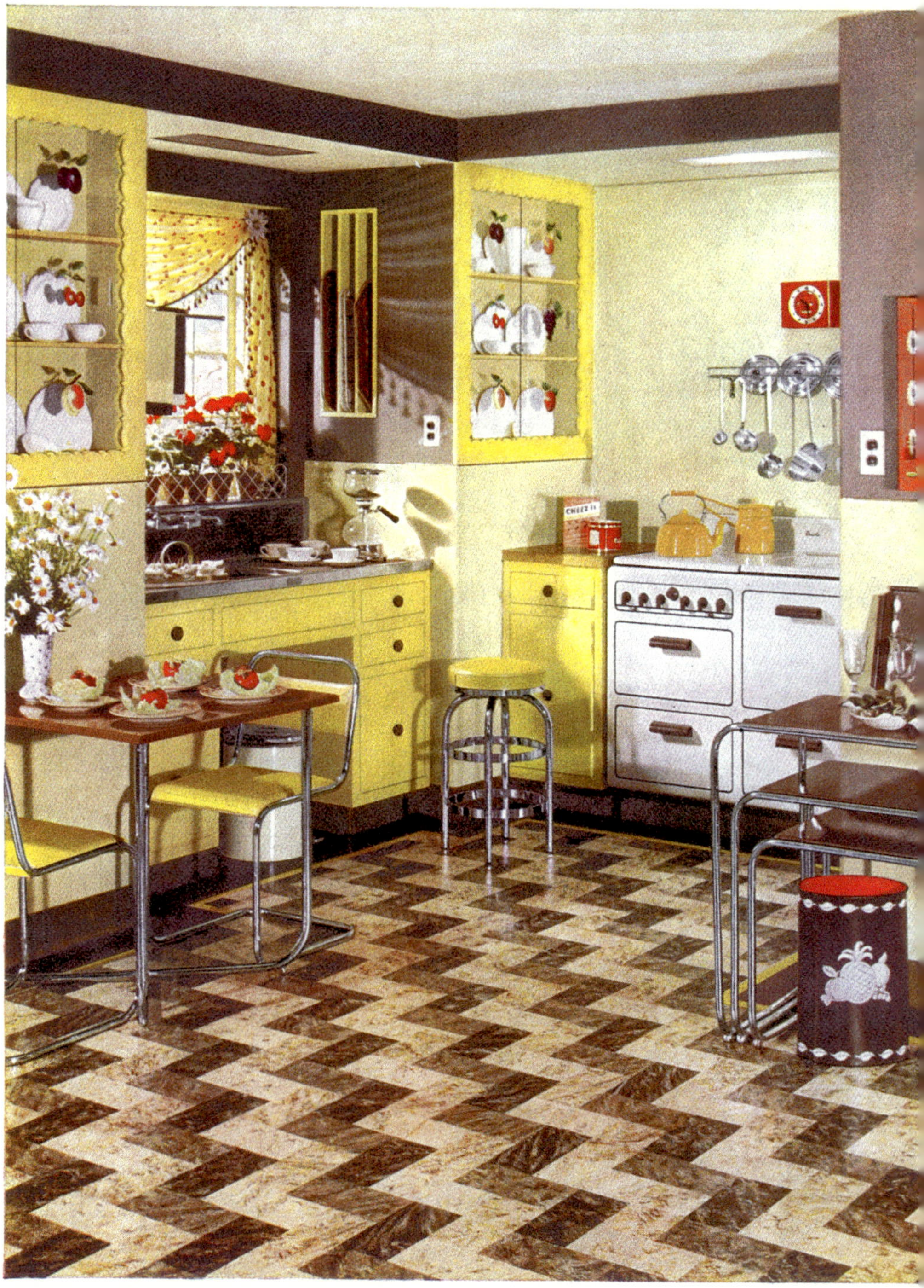

ARMSTRONG'S LINOLEUM FLOORS

ARMSTRONG CORK

for every room in the house

PLAIN • INLAID • EMBOSSED • JASPÉ • PRINTED • ARMSTRONG'S QUAKER RUGS *and* ARMSTRONG'S LINOWA

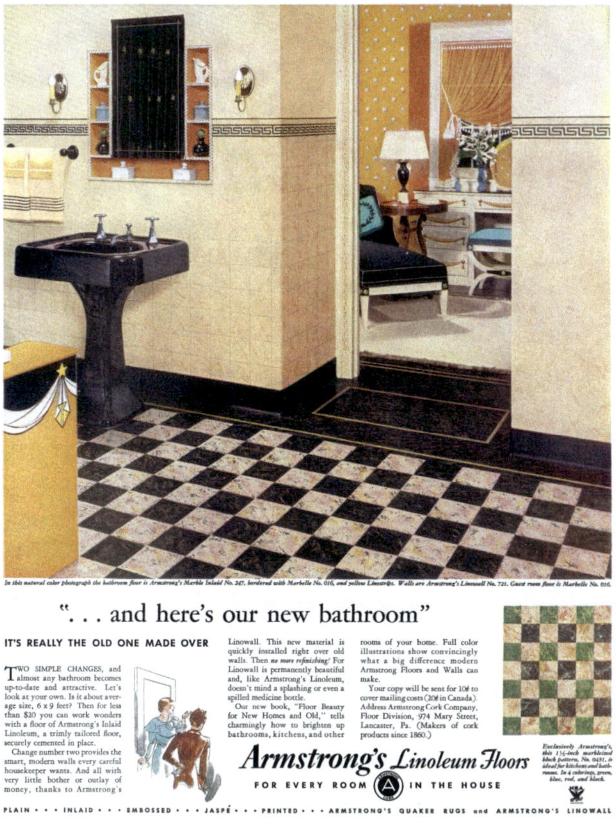

Armstrong's Linoleum Floors, 1934

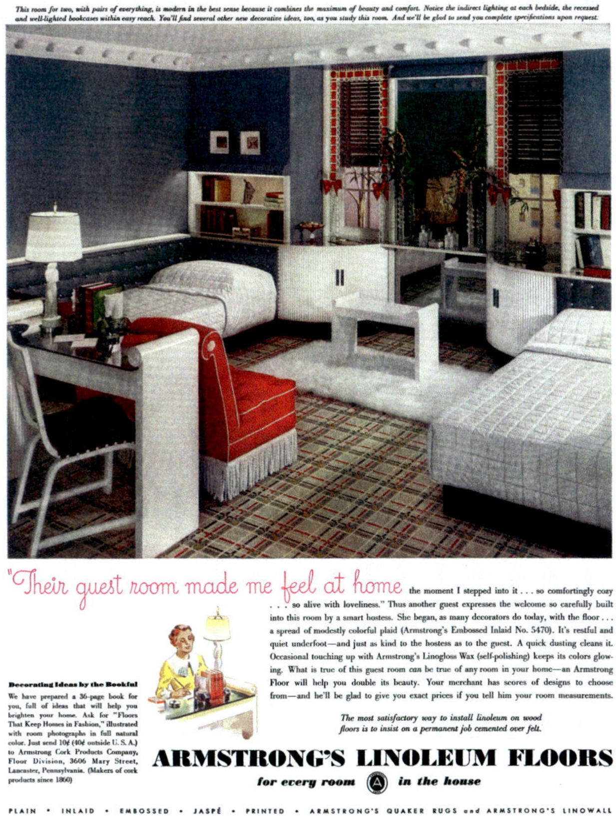

Armstrong's Linoleum Floors, 1936

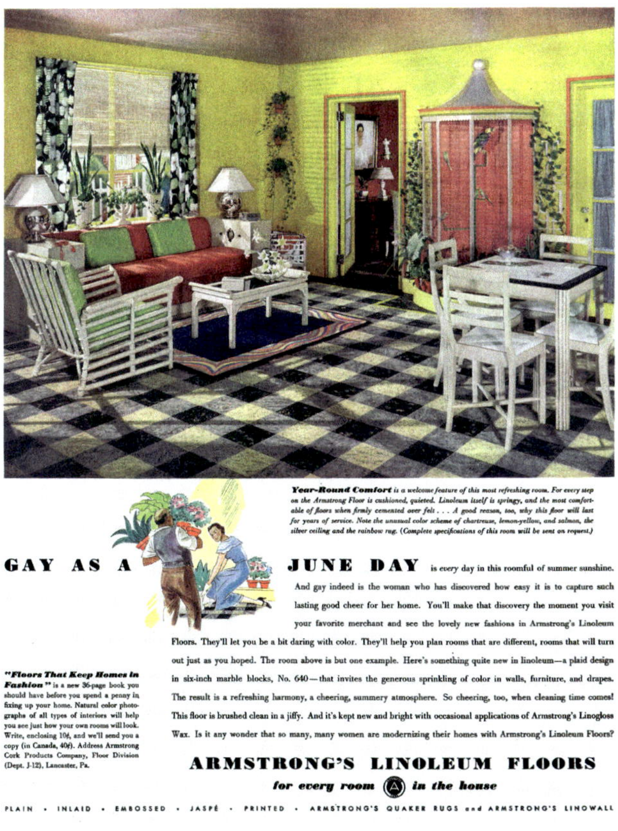

Armstrong's Linoleum Floors, 1936 ◄ *Armstrong's Linoleum Floors, 1935*

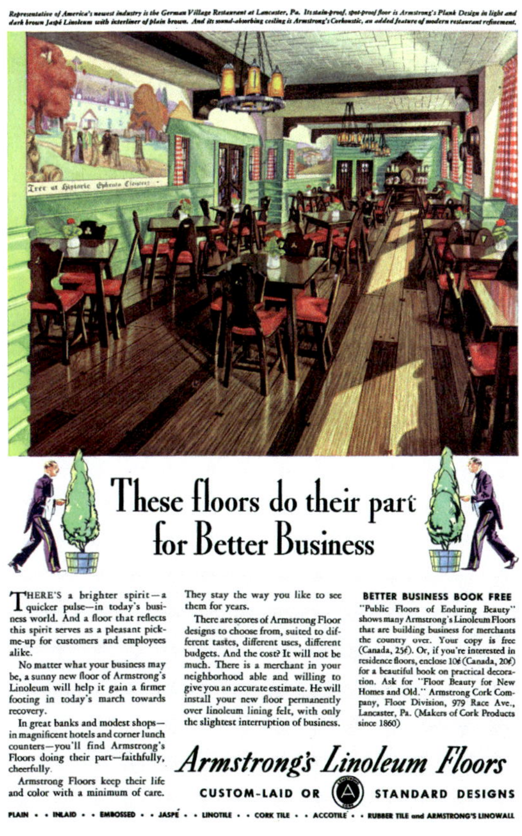

Armstrong's Linoleum Floors, 1934 ►► *Armstrong's Linoleum Floors, 1932*

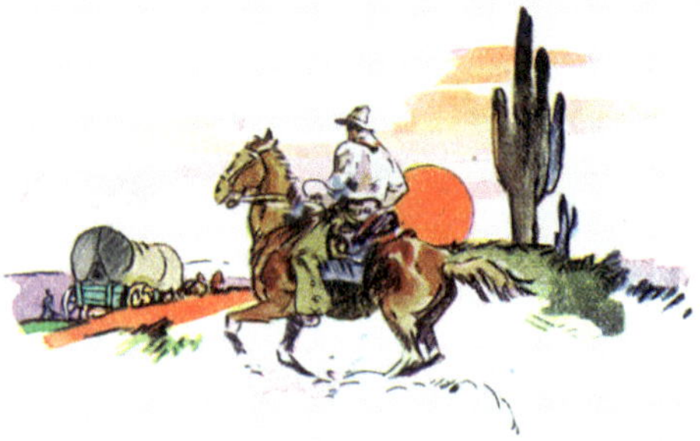

Go West, young man. right in your own room

AN ARMSTRONG FLOOR WILL HELP YOU DO I

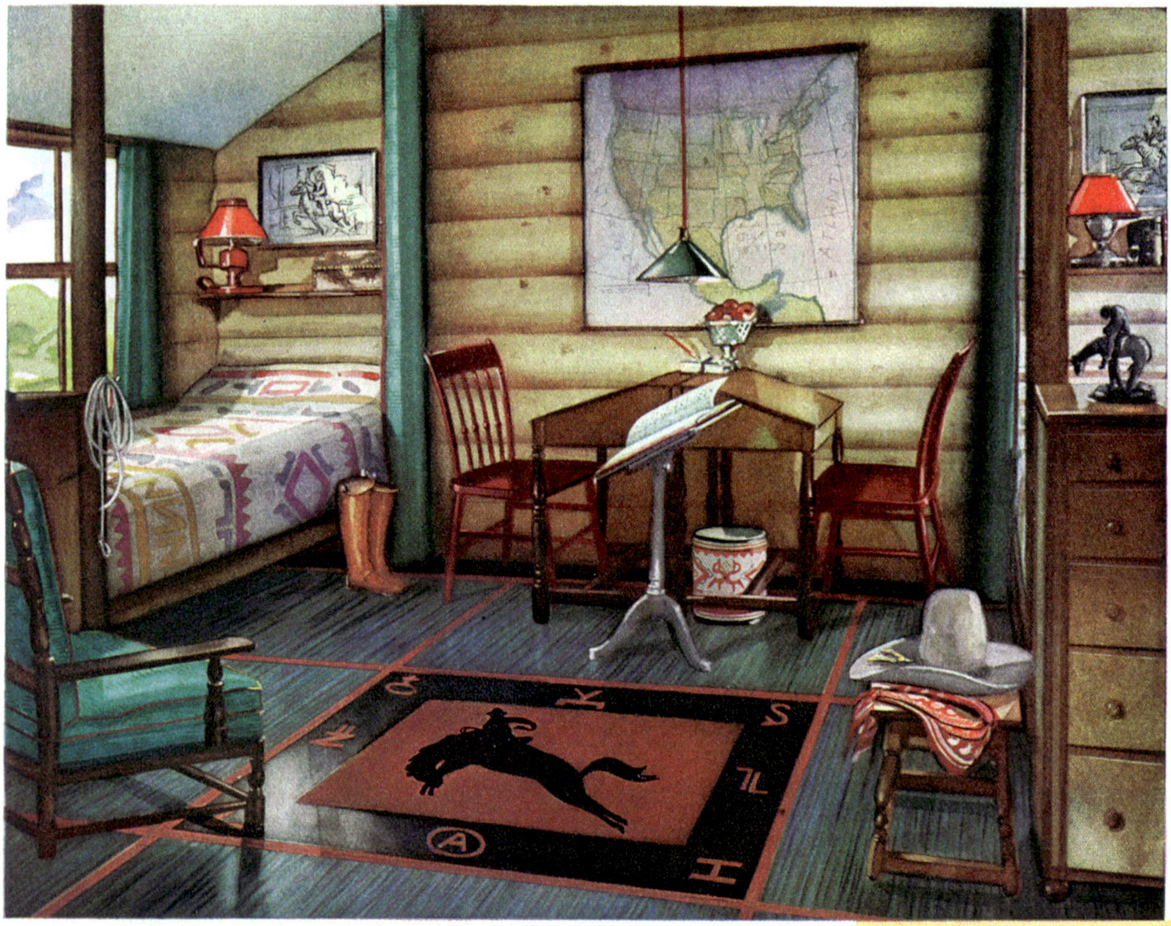

This western thril help any youth to sa dreams and ride 'e Somehow lessons ge lot easier in a roo this. And playtime become packed with venture—adventure t red-blooded dad wi to share. Try it . . Armstrong's Heathe No. 012, in a var floor designs. We' your local mercha the exact Armstrong that fits both your ro your pocketboo

Armstrong's (A) Product

HOW will you have your "West"? Wild and woolly . . . or with all the swank and smartness of a dude ranch? It's yours, pardner, without leaving your home. Just let your imagination ride along with us on a scouting trip through Idea Land.

First we'll spread a swatch of wind-swept prairie for our floor. (It's Heather Jaspé Linoleum—"brand-new and very low in price," the merchant will tell you.) We'll put Broncho Bill himself right in the middle of it—an easy trick with plain colors of Armstrong's Linoleum.

Now—whoopee-ee!—you're in the saddle for a round-up of all the rest of the things you want in your home-made West. Say, that floor *does* start you off with a snap! That's the way Armstrong Floors are. Thoroughbreds. Full of spirit. Real inspirations in planning any interior.

When you tell this tale to the foreman of your ranch, be sure to mention that Armstrong Floors are *thrifty* floors. Their first cost has no fancy trimmings—and there'll be no extras for fixing them up as the years roll by. Another thing to remember—cementing over linoleum lining felt insures long service as well as foot-cushioning comfort. And yes, say something about cleaning ease! That's always a welcome feature of an Armstrong's Linoleum Floor.

By the way, complete plans of this ranch are yours if you'll say, "Send them on." Add, "I'd also like a copy of the 'Home Decorator's Idea Book,'" and twenty-eight more smart room ideas will come your way. Just enclose 10¢ to cover cost of mailing (in Canada, 20¢). Address Armstrong Cork Company, Floor Division, 954 Mary Street, Lancaster, Pennsylvania. (Makers of cork products since 1860)

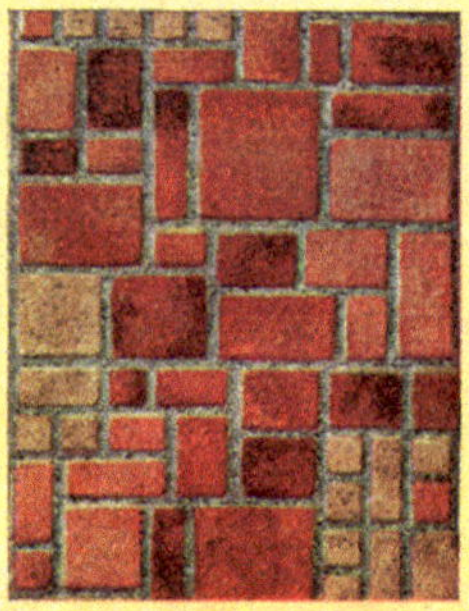

AND, SPEAKING OF THRIFT . . .

Today you can buy mo Armstrong's Linoleum fo your money than in man many years. And never h the quality been better the designs more beautif At the left—another new o —Shaded Embossed No. 535

Armstrong's Linoleum Floors

FOR EVERY ROOM IN THE HOUSE

PLAIN · · · INLAID · · · EMBOSSED · · · JASPÉ · · · LINOFLOR · · PRINTED · · · *and* ARMSTRONG'S QUAKER R

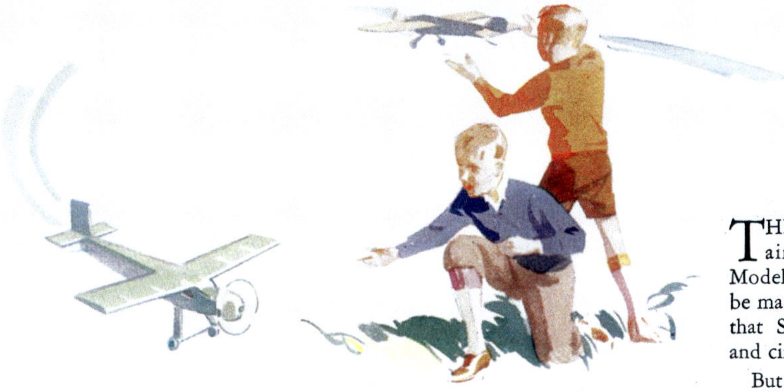

APPY LANDINGS

for young airmen who haven't won their wings

THESE are adventurous days for air-minded young America. Models to be built. Test flights to be made. Maps to be studied. And that Saturday afternoon air meet and circus!

But even intrepid aviators must have an airport. So Flight Commander (that's mother, of course) does some very special planning. The closet becomes a chart room. The bed a handy storehouse. A little more magic—and the floor is just the happiest landing field a busy boy could wish for.

It won't tell tales on him for one thing—the Accolac-Processed surface is spot-proof, stain-proof. It's built for hard service—every color inlaid. It helps quiet noise, soften footsteps. And it's springy and warm, too—cemented firmly in place over linoleum lining felt.

The happiest part of this Armstrong floor is its pleasing design. This is just one of innumerable motifs you can plan with Armstrong's Linoleum. Some, called Linosets, come all ready for quick installation. Others can be worked out in plain, or marble, or Jaspé linoleum to suit your fancy. Your local linoleum, furniture, or department store merchant will tell you the whole story of these Armstrong Floors of individual design.

Plans for this room free

In the meantime, our Bureau of Interior Decoration would like to send you complete working plans for this young airman's room—color scheme, furniture details, floor plan. Plus a bookful of other equally unusual interiors called "New Ideas in Home Decoration." Just send 10¢ to cover mailing. Address Armstrong Cork Company, Floor Division, 339 Lincoln Ave., Lancaster, Pennsylvania. (Makers of cork products since 1860.)

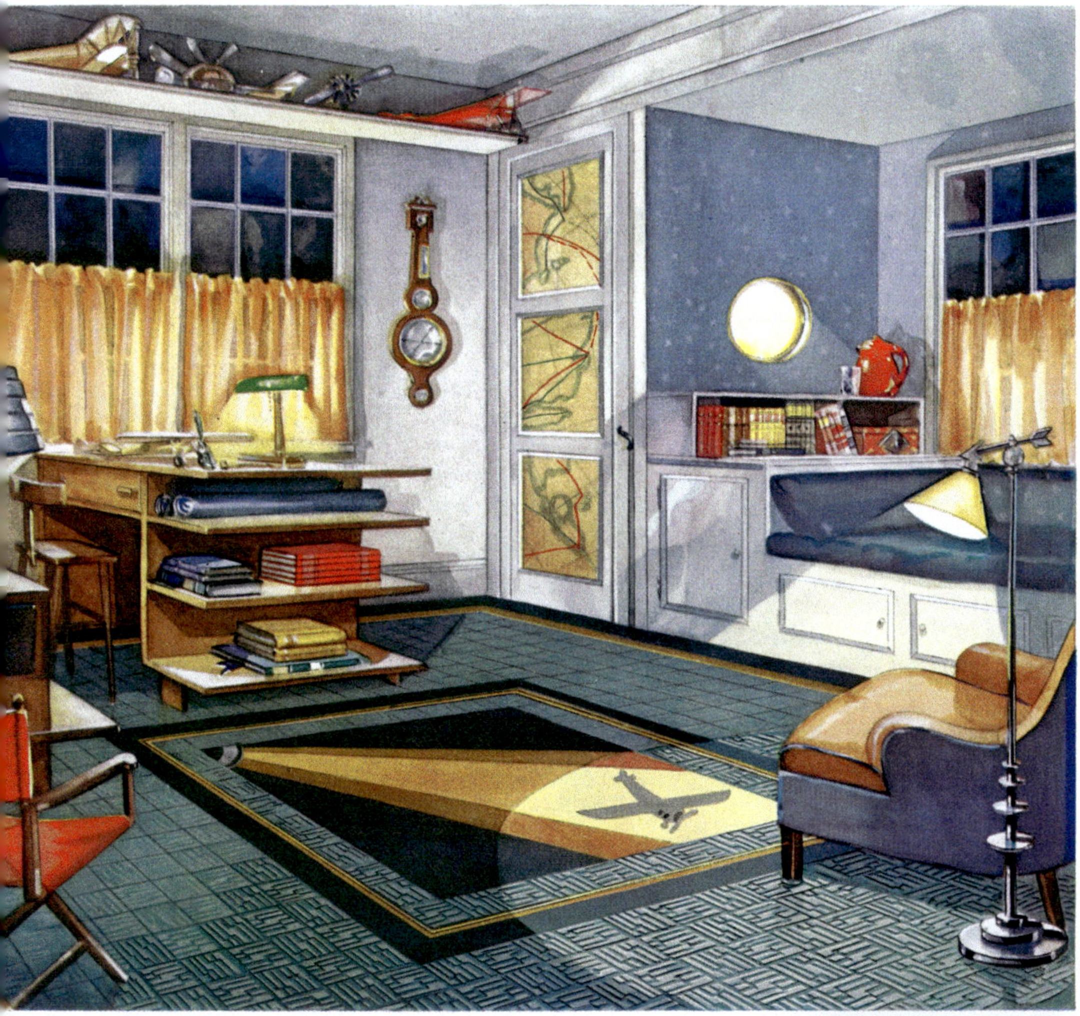

Some day a very lucky son of a very famous flyer may have a room like this. At least we hope he'll have as happy a landing place for his imaginary flights as the Armstrong's Linoleum Floor shown. Embossed Inlaid No. 3221 forms the field, while plain blue, tan, and yellow linoleum are used for the center inset design. Two designs below are: left, Linoset No. 2; right, Jaspé No. 010.

Armstrong's (A) Product

rmstrong's Linoleum Floors

for every room in the house

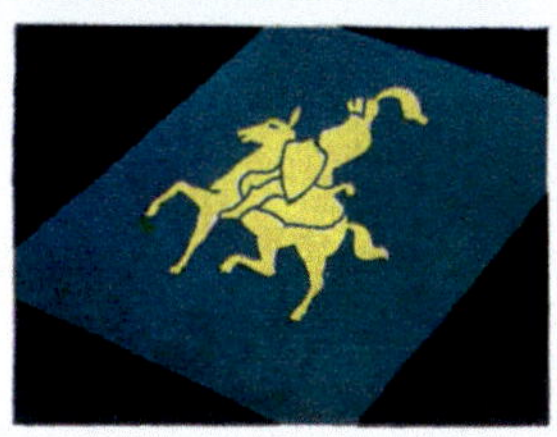

IN ⁝ INLAID ⁝ EMBOSSED · · · JASPÉ ⁝ PRINTED ⁝ *and* ARMSTRONG'S QUAKER RUGS

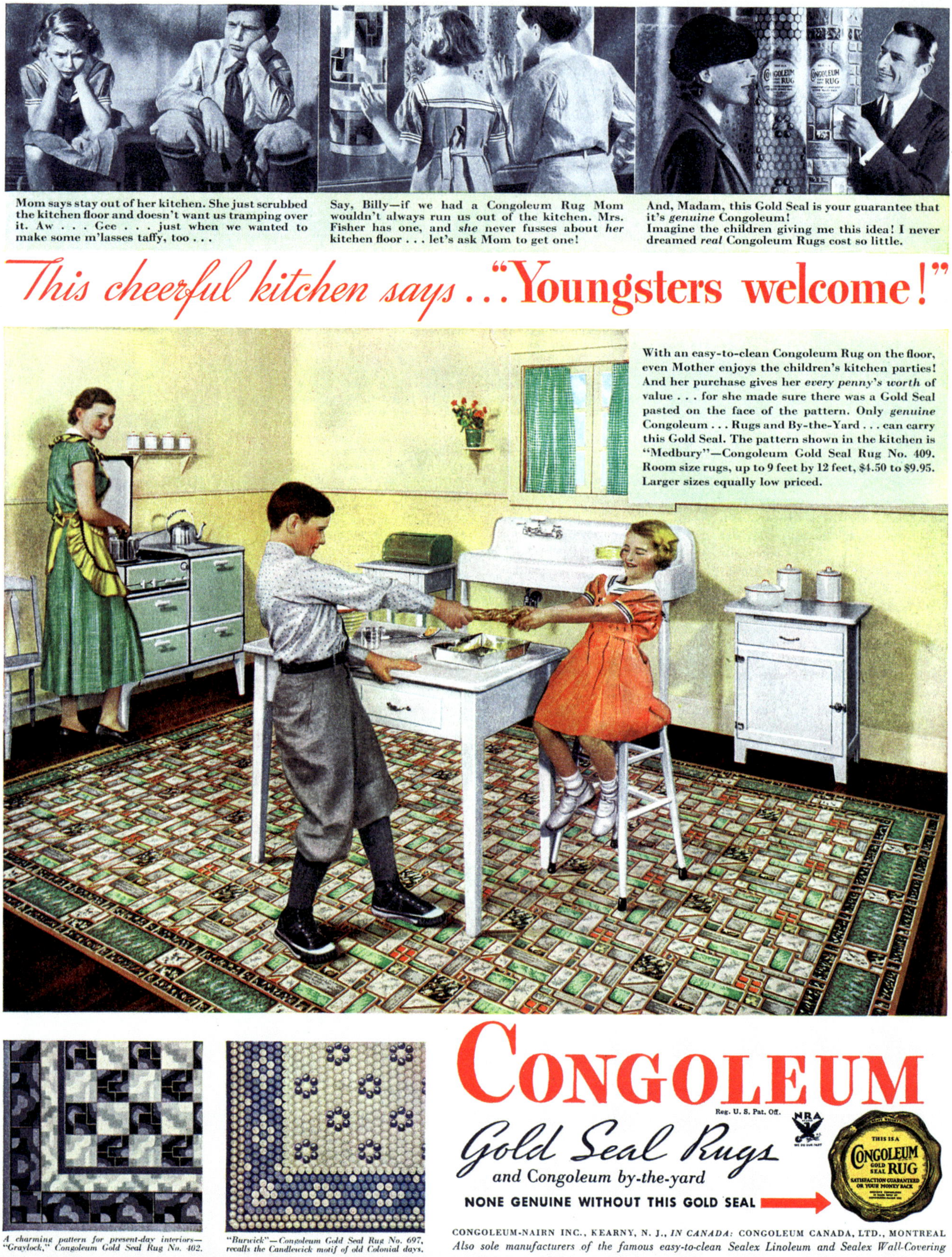

Armstrong's Linoleum Floors, 1931 ◂◂ *Congoleum, 1935*

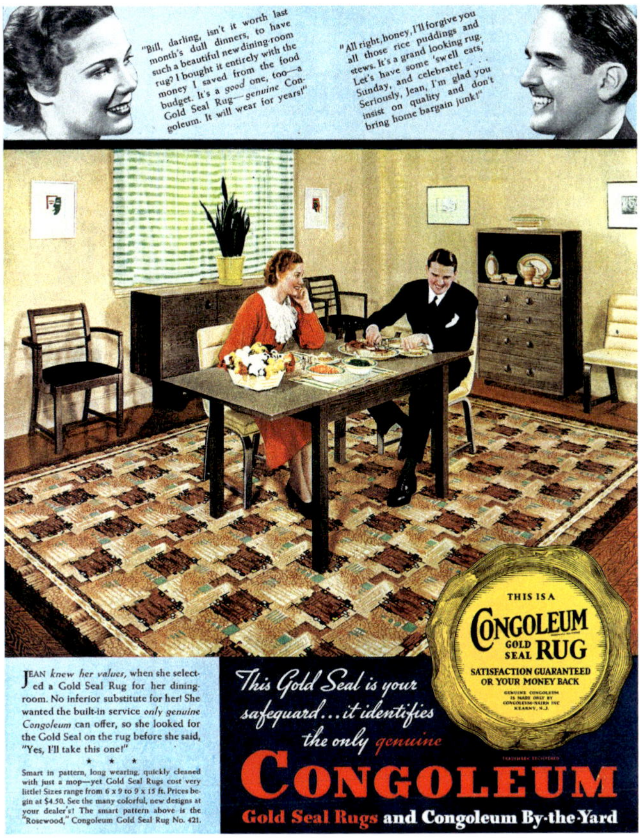

Congoleum, 1936

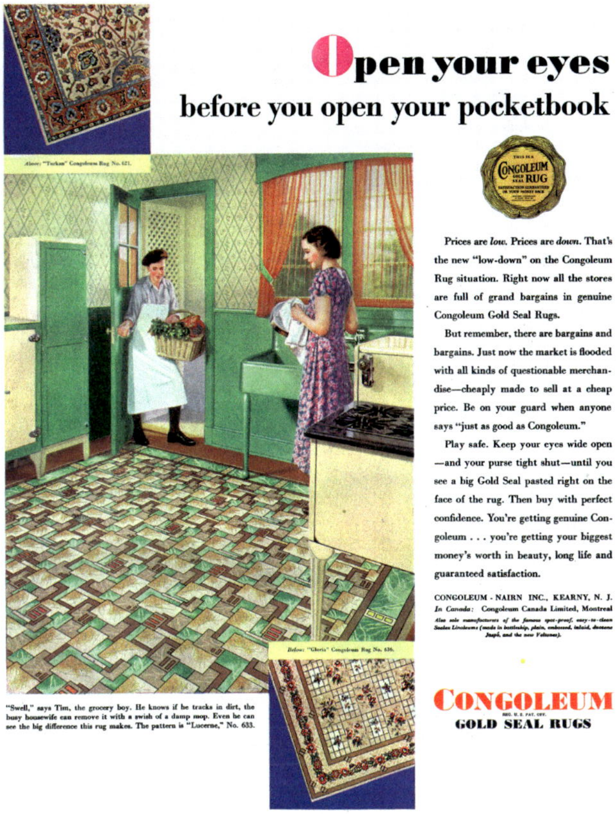

Congoleum, 1932

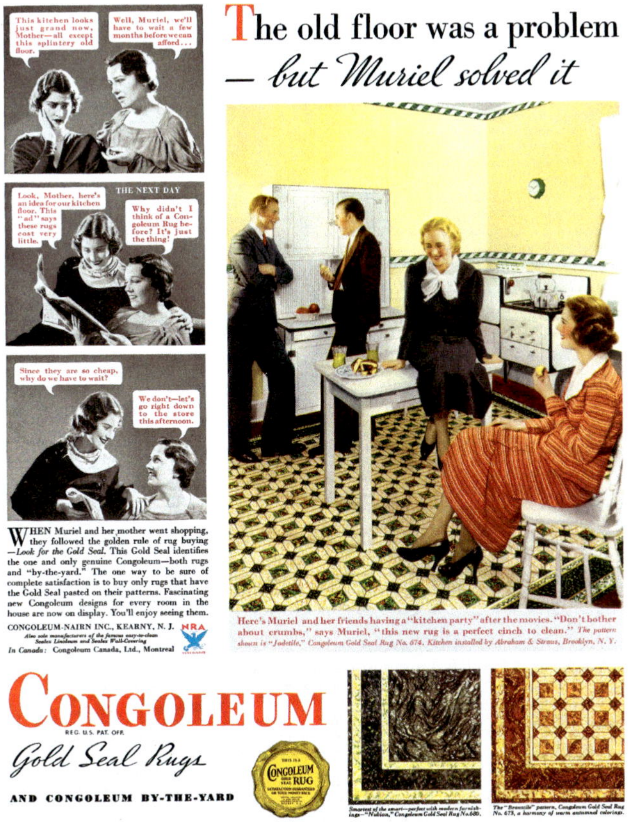

Congoleum, 1934

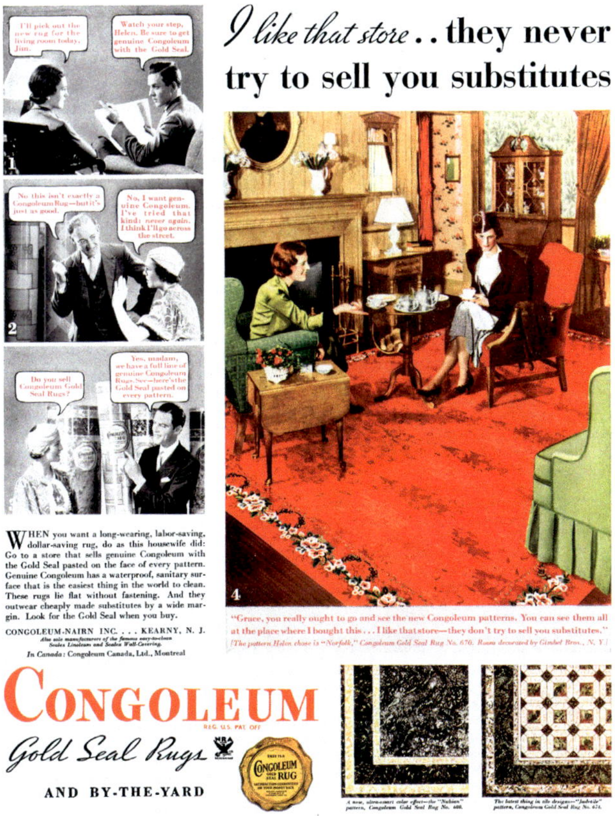

Congoleum, 1934

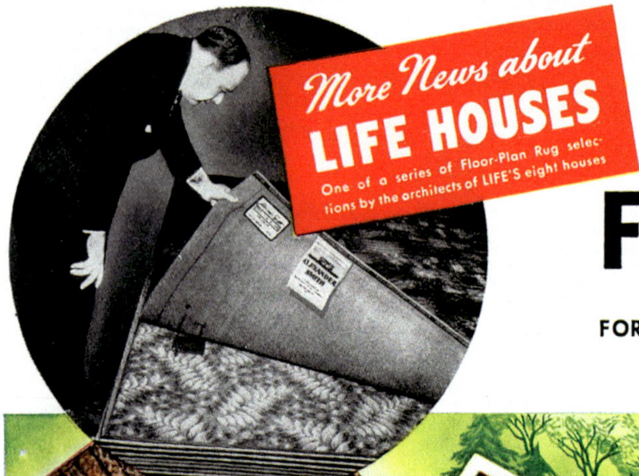

Architect ROYAL BARRY WILLS chose these

ALEXANDER SMITH FLOOR-PLAN RUGS

(TRADE MARK)

FOR HIS $5000-$6000 INCOME LIFE HOUSE

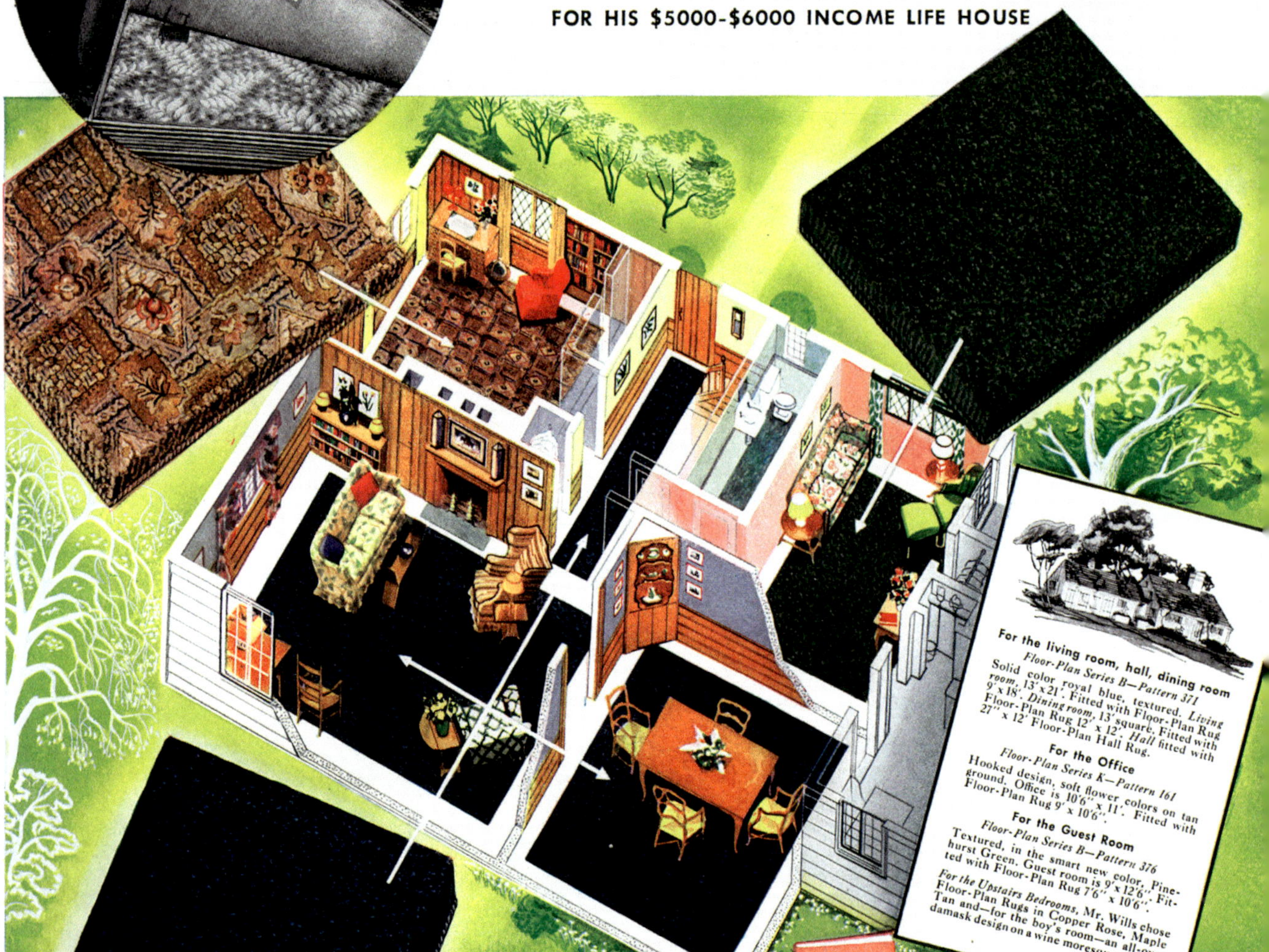

Mr. Wills had to choose rugs for *eight* rooms, each room of a *different size*, each with a *different color scheme*. Yet, he reports, he had no difficulty finding eight Alexander Smith Floor-Plan Rugs in *just* the colors, textures and patterns he wanted, and in the *exact* sizes he wanted. The cross-section shows his selections for the downstairs rooms. Equally important, the cost was *well within* the furnishings budget of a $5000-$6000 income family!

No matter what the type of your house, the size or shape of your rooms, or the size of your budget, you can solve *your* rug problem just as easily merely by going to your favorite store and asking to see *Alexander Smith* Floor-Plan Rugs. Look for the gold label with the Good Housekeeping Guaranty.

ALEXANDER SMITH

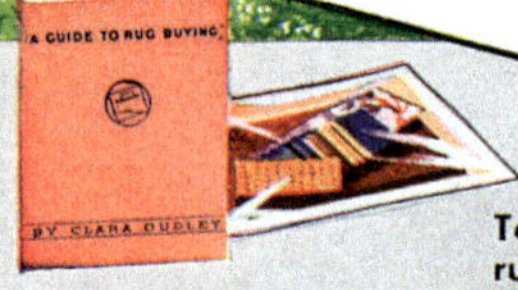

FREE!

To help you choose new rugs for your own home

The selections of LIFE'S architects, together with Clara Dudley's famous "Guide to Rug Buying" will be sent FREE on receipt of coupon below. If you would like a Color Scheme Kit (samples of rug, wallpaper, drapery and upholstery fabrics) indicate on coupon color of your room and enclose 10c in stamps or coin.

Alexander Smith & Sons Carpet Co., 295 Fifth Avenue, New York

☐ Please send me *FREE*, list of Floor-Plan Rug selections of LIFE'S architects, and Clara Dudley's "Guide to Rug Buying."

☐ I also enclose 10c for which please send me a Clara Dudley Floor-Plan Rug Color Scheme Kit for a room in which the prevailing color (walls, furniture or draperies) is ______________

NAME ______________________________
PRINT NAME AND ADDRESS

ADDRESS ______________________________ L-4

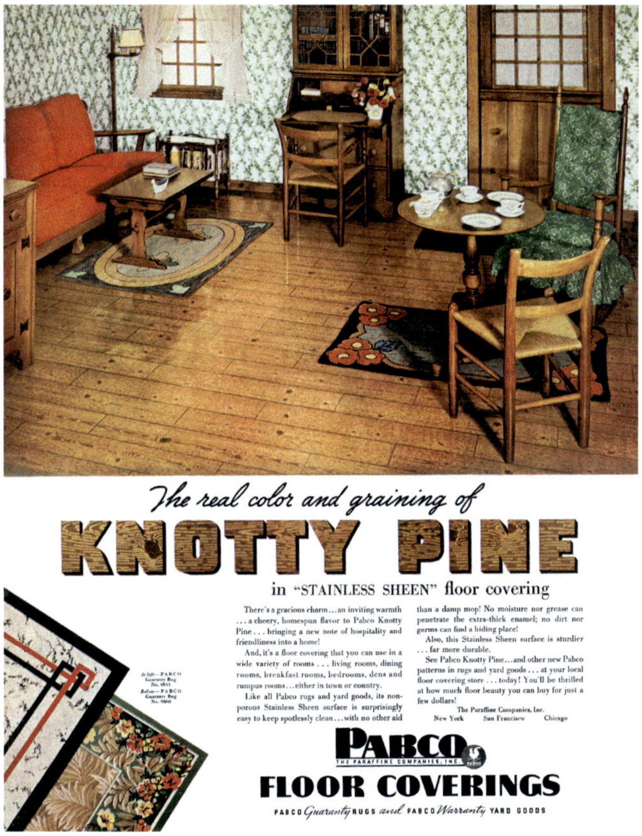

Pabco Floor Coverings, 1938

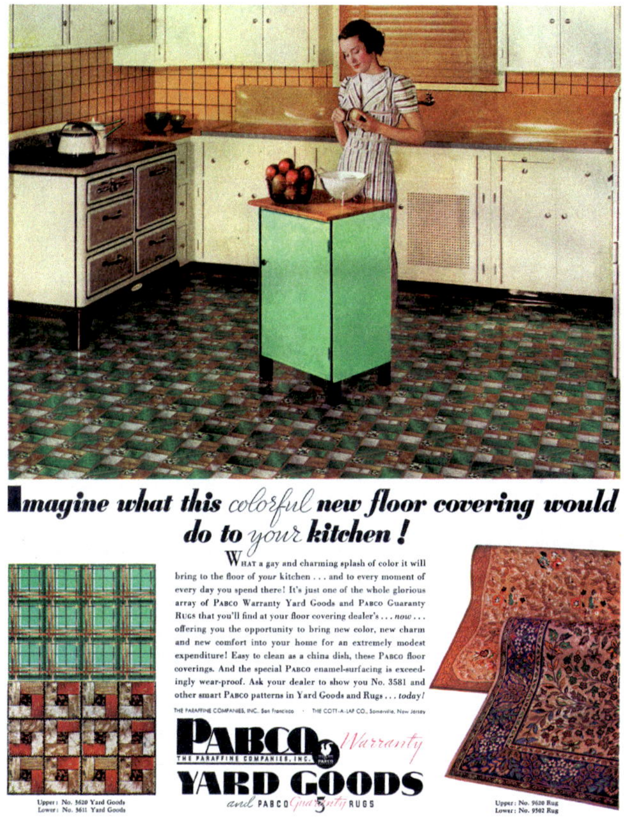

Pabco, 1936

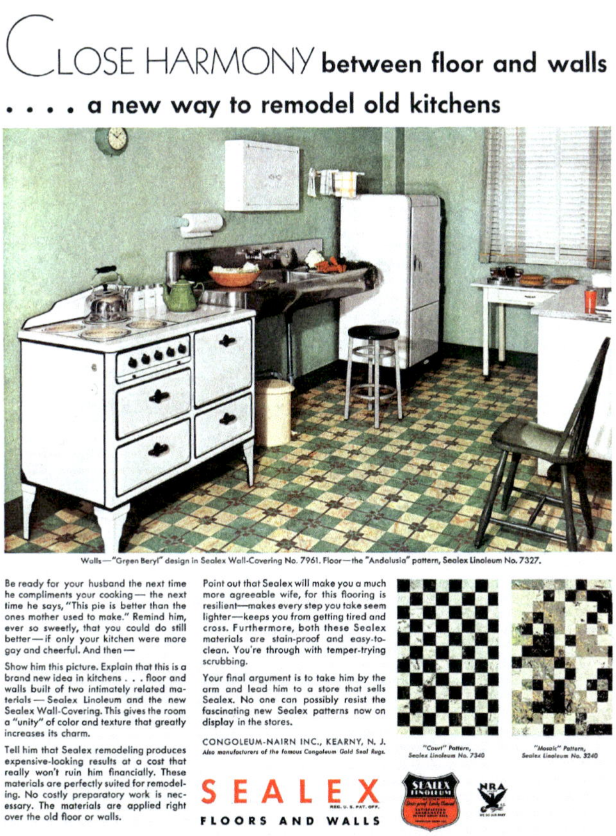

Alexander Smith, 1939 ◂ Sealex, 1933

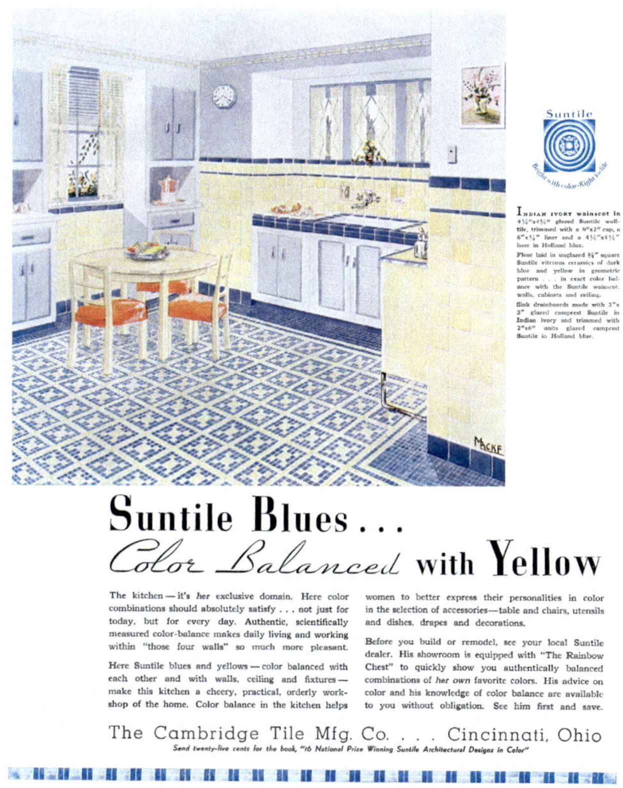

Cambridge Tile Co., 1937

▸▸ Axminster Rugs, 1931

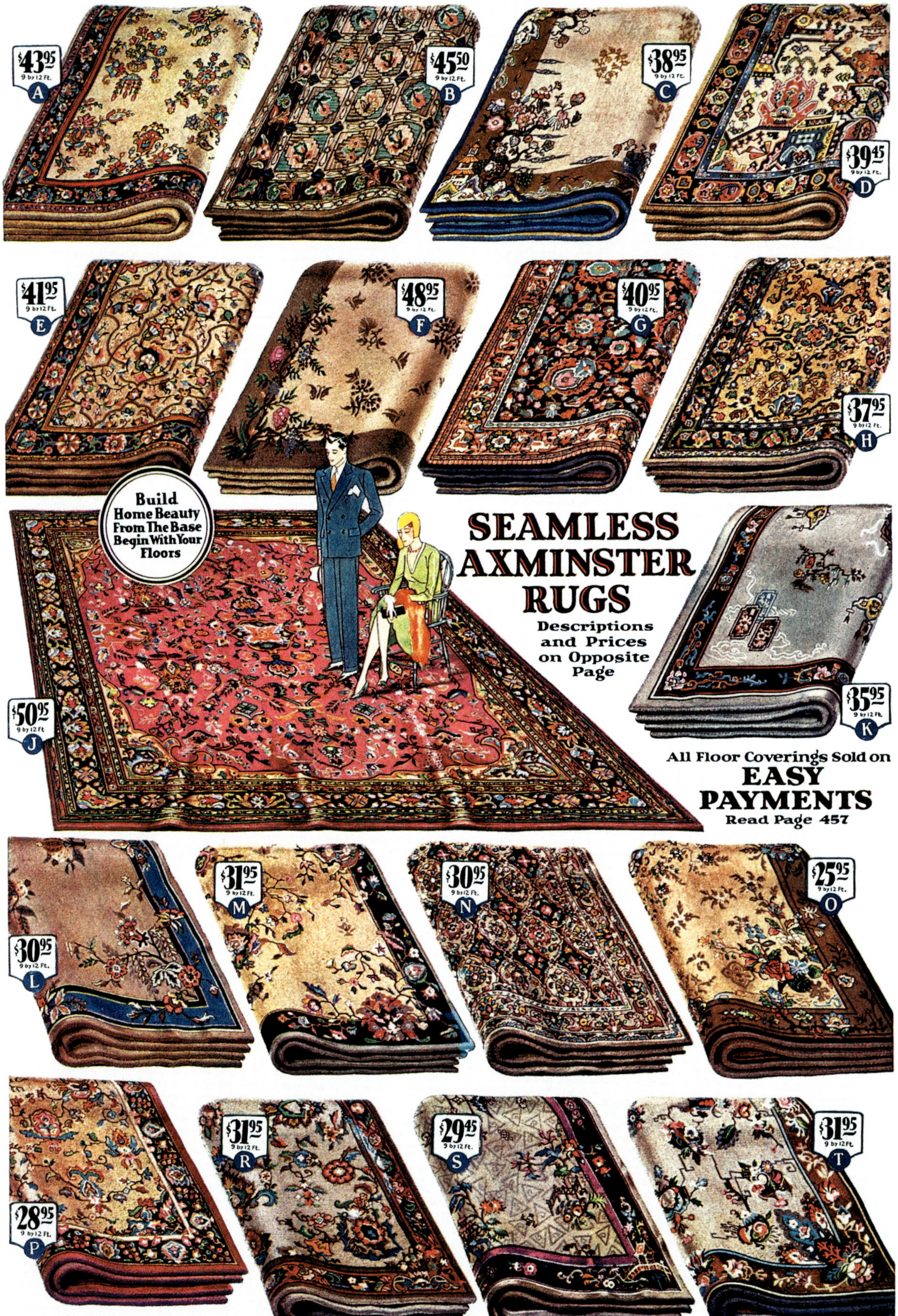

$43.95 9 by 12 Ft. A
$45.50 9 by 12 Ft. B
$38.95 9 by 12 Ft. C
$39.45 9 by 12 Ft. D
$41.95 9 by 12 Ft. E
$48.95 9 by 12 Ft. F
$40.95 9 by 12 Ft. G
$37.95 9 by 12 Ft. H
Build Home Beauty From The Base Begin With Your Floors
SEAMLESS AXMINSTER RUGS
Descriptions and Prices on Opposite Page
$50.95 9 by 12 Ft. J
$35.95 9 by 12 Ft. K
All Floor Coverings Sold on EASY PAYMENTS
Read Page 457
$30.95 9 by 12 Ft. L
$31.95 9 by 12 Ft. M
$30.95 9 by 12 Ft. N
$25.95 9 by 12 Ft. O
$28.95 9 by 12 Ft. P
$31.95 9 by 12 Ft. R
$29.45 9 by 12 Ft. S
$31.95 9 by 12 Ft. T

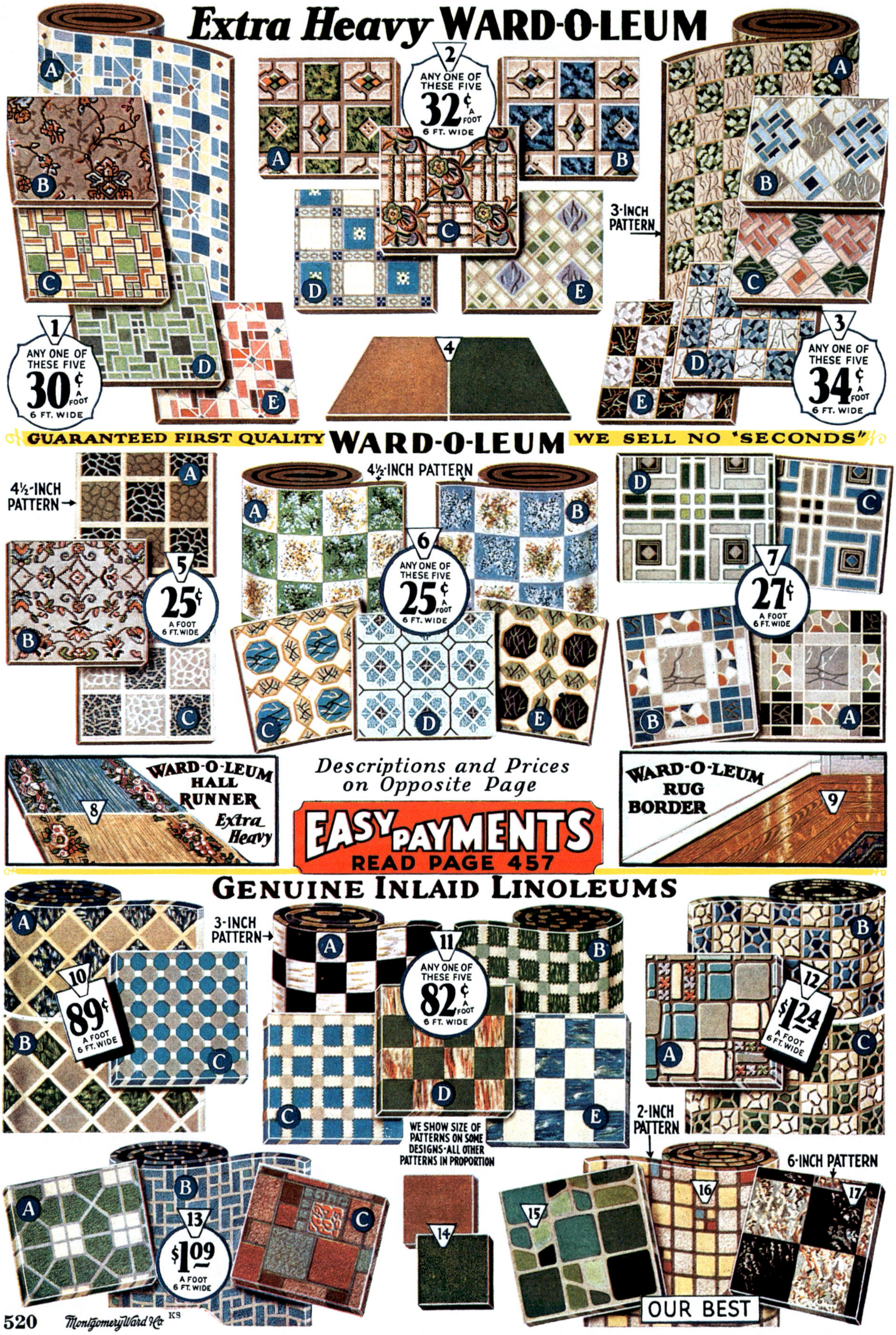

Extra Heavy WARD-O-LEUM
A
B
C
D
E
1
ANY ONE OF THESE FIVE 30¢ A FOOT 6 FT. WIDE
2
ANY ONE OF THESE FIVE 32¢ A FOOT 6 FT. WIDE
3-INCH PATTERN
3
ANY ONE OF THESE FIVE 34¢ A FOOT 6 FT. WIDE
4
GUARANTEED FIRST QUALITY WARD-O-LEUM WE SELL NO "SECONDS"
4½-INCH PATTERN
5
25¢ A FOOT 6 FT. WIDE
4½-INCH PATTERN
6
ANY ONE OF THESE FIVE 25¢ A FOOT 6 FT. WIDE
7
27¢ A FOOT 6 FT. WIDE
WARD-O-LEUM HALL RUNNER Extra Heavy
8
Descriptions and Prices on Opposite Page
EASY PAYMENTS READ PAGE 457
WARD-O-LEUM RUG BORDER
9
GENUINE INLAID LINOLEUMS
3-INCH PATTERN
10
89¢ A FOOT 6 FT. WIDE
11
ANY ONE OF THESE FIVE 82¢ A FOOT 6 FT. WIDE
12
$1.24 A FOOT 6 FT. WIDE
2-INCH PATTERN
WE SHOW SIZE OF PATTERNS ON SOME DESIGNS-ALL OTHER PATTERNS IN PROPORTION
13
$1.09 A FOOT 6 FT. WIDE
14
15
16
6-INCH PATTERN
17
OUR BEST

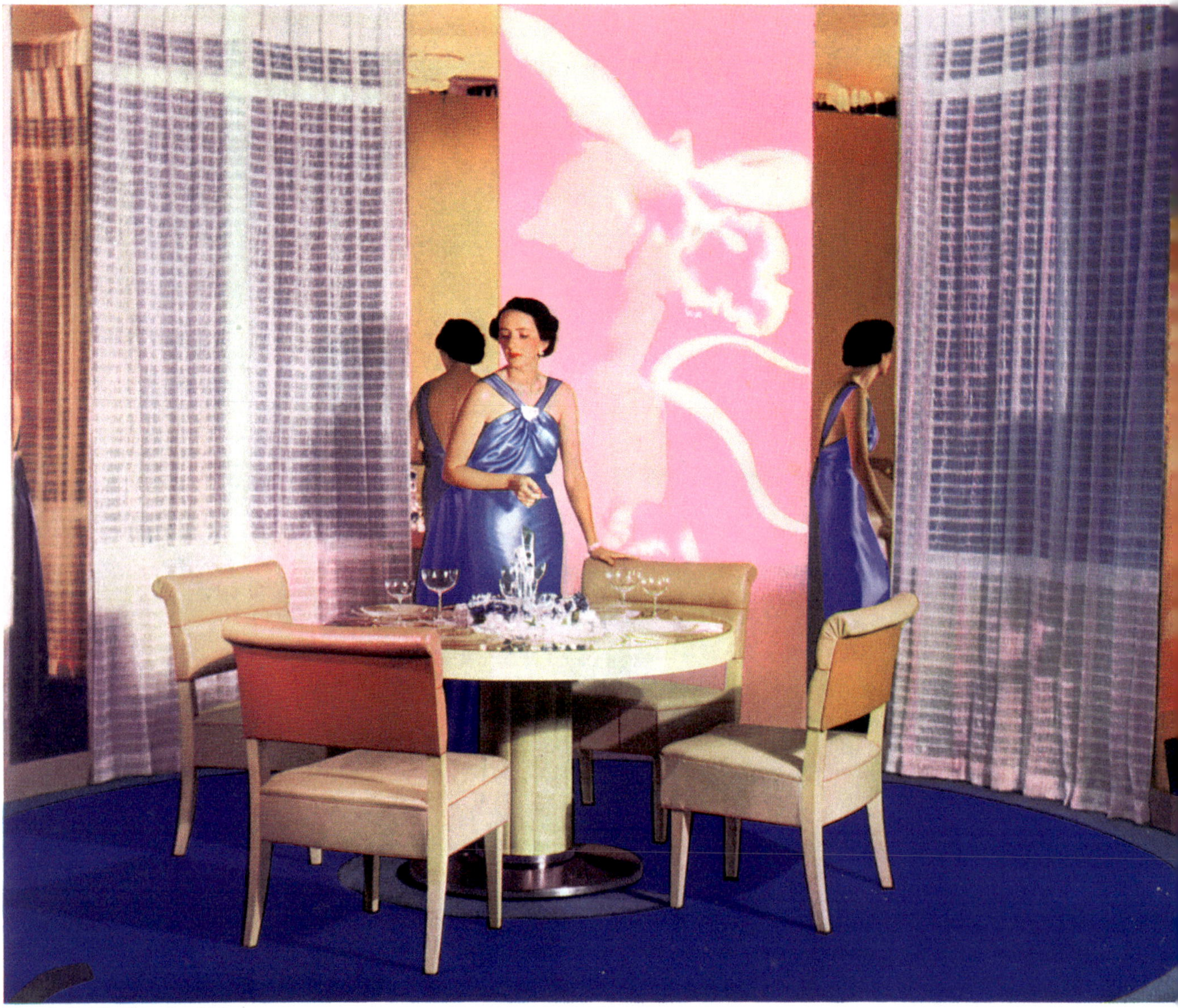

Interior by Paul MacAllister, Inc., A.I.D.

mirrors in *Color* suggest a wealth of new ideas

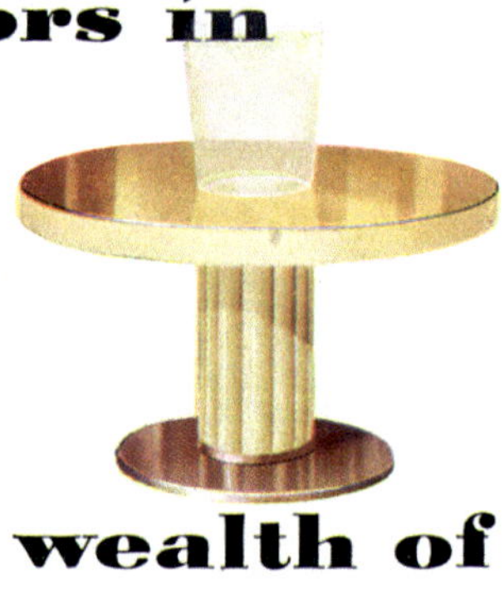

Colored plate glass mirrors in this intimately modern dining room give brilliant emphasis to the entire decorative scheme. This newest aid to the decorator's art is available in three shades of blue, a green and the rich peach used here. Its warmth and color immediately suggest a wealth of new ideas. The unique dining table presents a striking illustration. The top is of mirrored peach-color plate with the center unsilvered to permit illumination from a fixture concealed in the pedestal. Thus the softness of the candelabra of ancient d is reborn in the modern mann

On wall areas, the adroit use mirrored plate glass gives the lusion of greater space. The fa less beauty of colored plate gl will add richness and charm your home. Your interior de rator or the local L·O·F distri tor will offer you many help suggestions. Libbey·Owens·Fo Glass Company . . . Toledo, Oh

L O F

LIBBEY·OWENS·FOR

Quality Glas

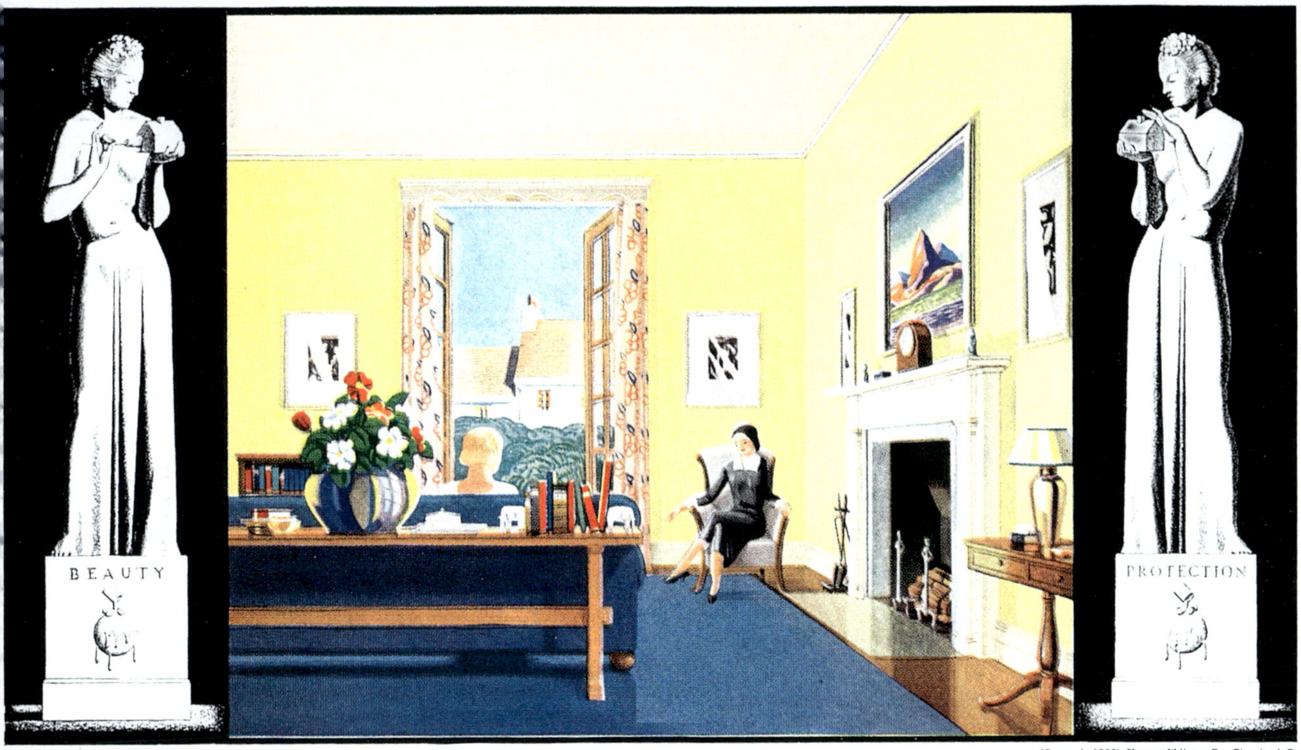

Painting by Rockwell Kent

BEAUTY AND PROTECTION

BY SHERWIN-WILLIAMS

From the use of paint—Sherwin-Williams paint—come pleasures few things can give. Every bit of your heart's desire for the color, freshness, and loveliness of a newly painted room is at your brush's bidding.

Your walls and woodwork become warm and friendly—almost animated—under the touch of colorful, easily applied S-W Flat-Tone. Should you wish a bright, quickly washable quality added to the color beauty, S-W Semi-Lustre awaits your commands. And chairs, tables, cabinets, kitchen, bathroom and breakfast room indispensables alluringly join the color magic parade when you repaint them with glistening S-W Enameloid.

Painting is fascinating . . . fascinating to watch and anticipate the final beauty on the big jobs where the painting is done by a master painter . . . fascinating to feel the flow from the brush as you recreate a table or chair yourself.

And a paint can . . . with a Sherwin-Williams label around it . . . is an indispensable part of your home's beauty and protection. Be it famous old SWP, America's best known and most widely used house paint; be it the interior paints mentioned; or be it any other of Sherwin-Williams well known products—furniture polish, floor waxes and finishes, etc.,—it is made to help you to beautifully identify your dearest possessions—to transform a house into a home.

"All you need to know about paint is Sherwin-Williams." Go to "paint headquarters" in your locality. There the Sherwin-Williams "cover the earth" emblem means help and service from a paint dealer able to aid and guide you.

COVER THE EARTH

You can have twelve to eighteen months to pay for your painting. Ask the Sherwin-Williams dealer in your locality about the S-W Budget Payment Plan. Write directly to Sherwin-Williams Co., Dept. F-2, Cleveland, O.

The new Sherwin-Williams Home Decorator, a source book of color and paint ideas can be had free of charge from the Sherwin-Williams dealer in your locality. Or write The Sherwin-Williams Co., Dept. F-2, Cleveland, O.

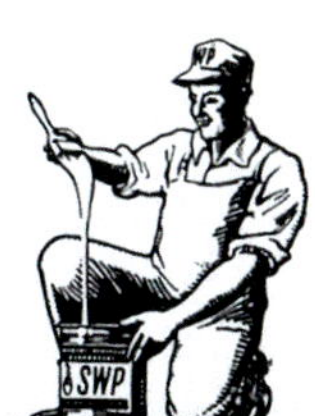

SHERWIN-WILLIAMS PAINTS

ALL YOU NEED TO KNOW ABOUT PAINT

Ward-O-Leum, 1931 ◄◄ *Libbey-Owens-Ford, 1937* ◄

Sherwin-Williams Paints, 1936

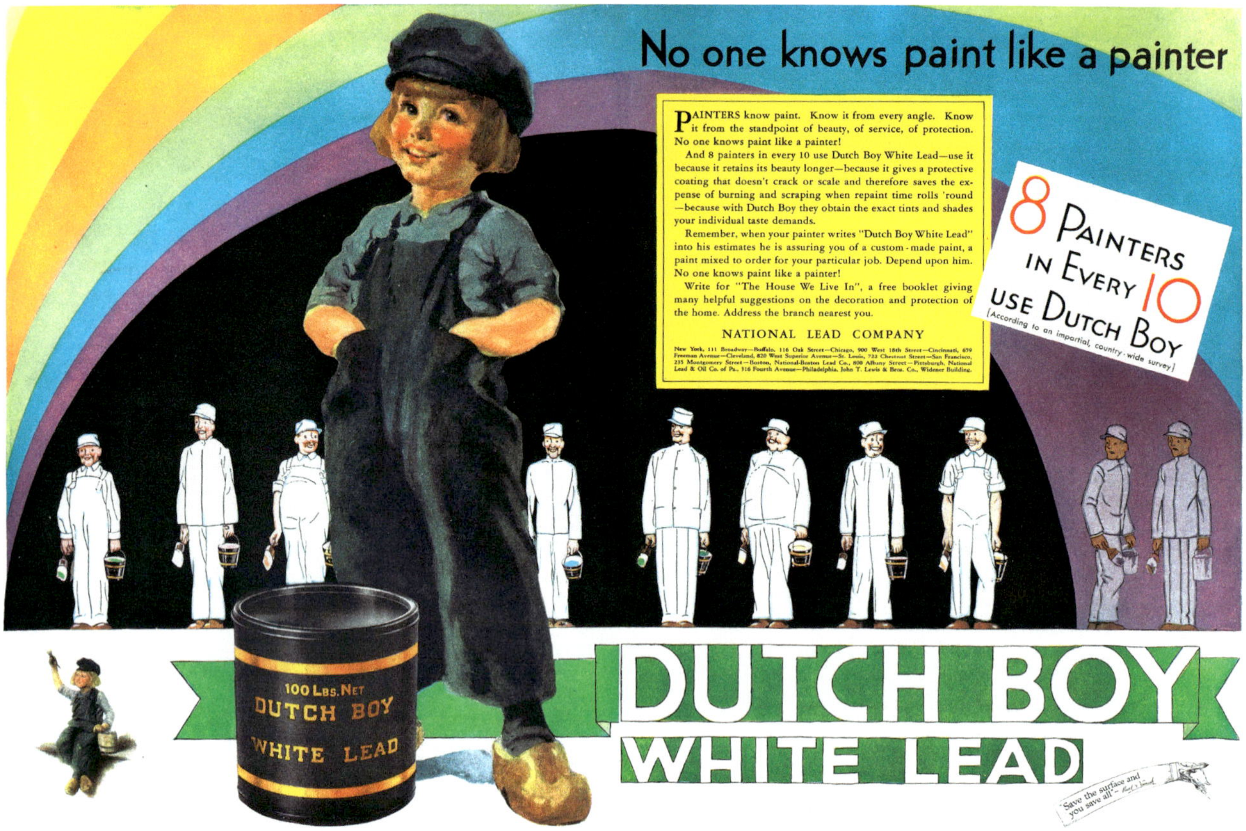

Dutch Boy Paint, 1930

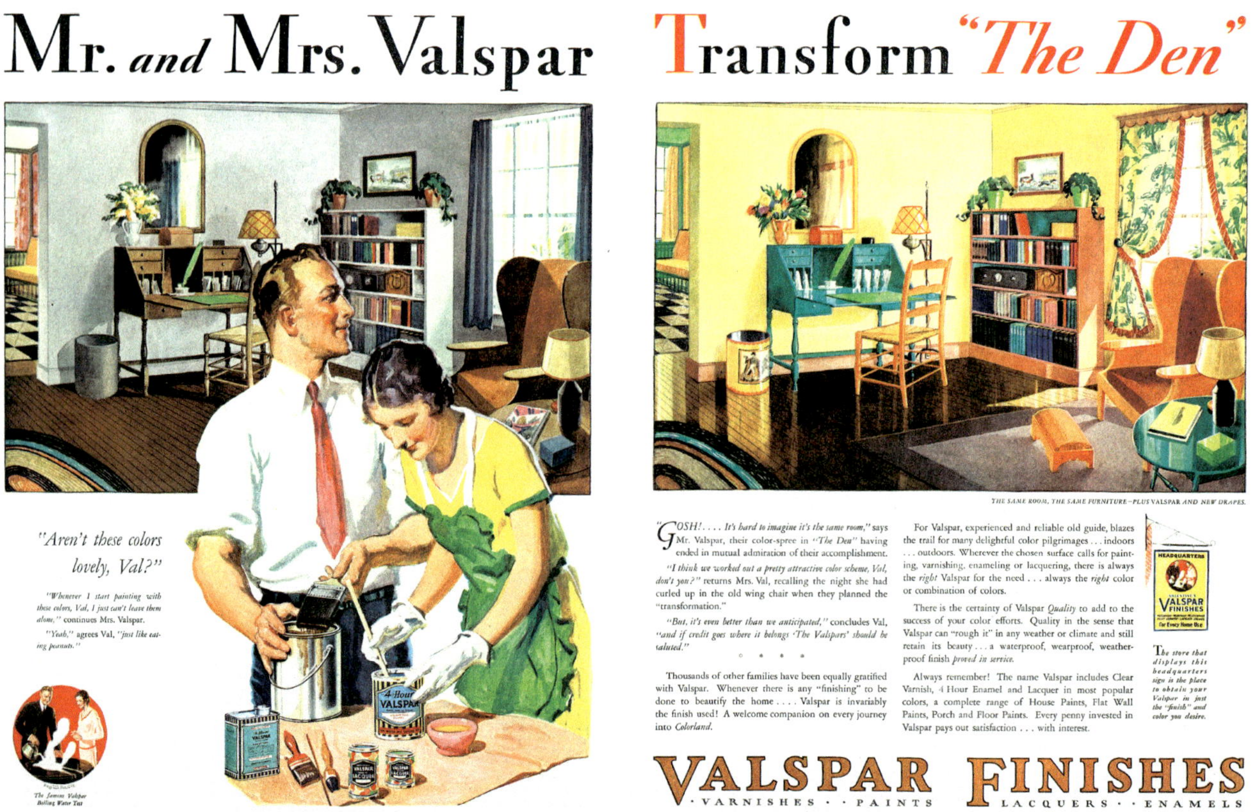

Valspar Finishes, 1930

▸ *Dutch Boy Paint, 1936*

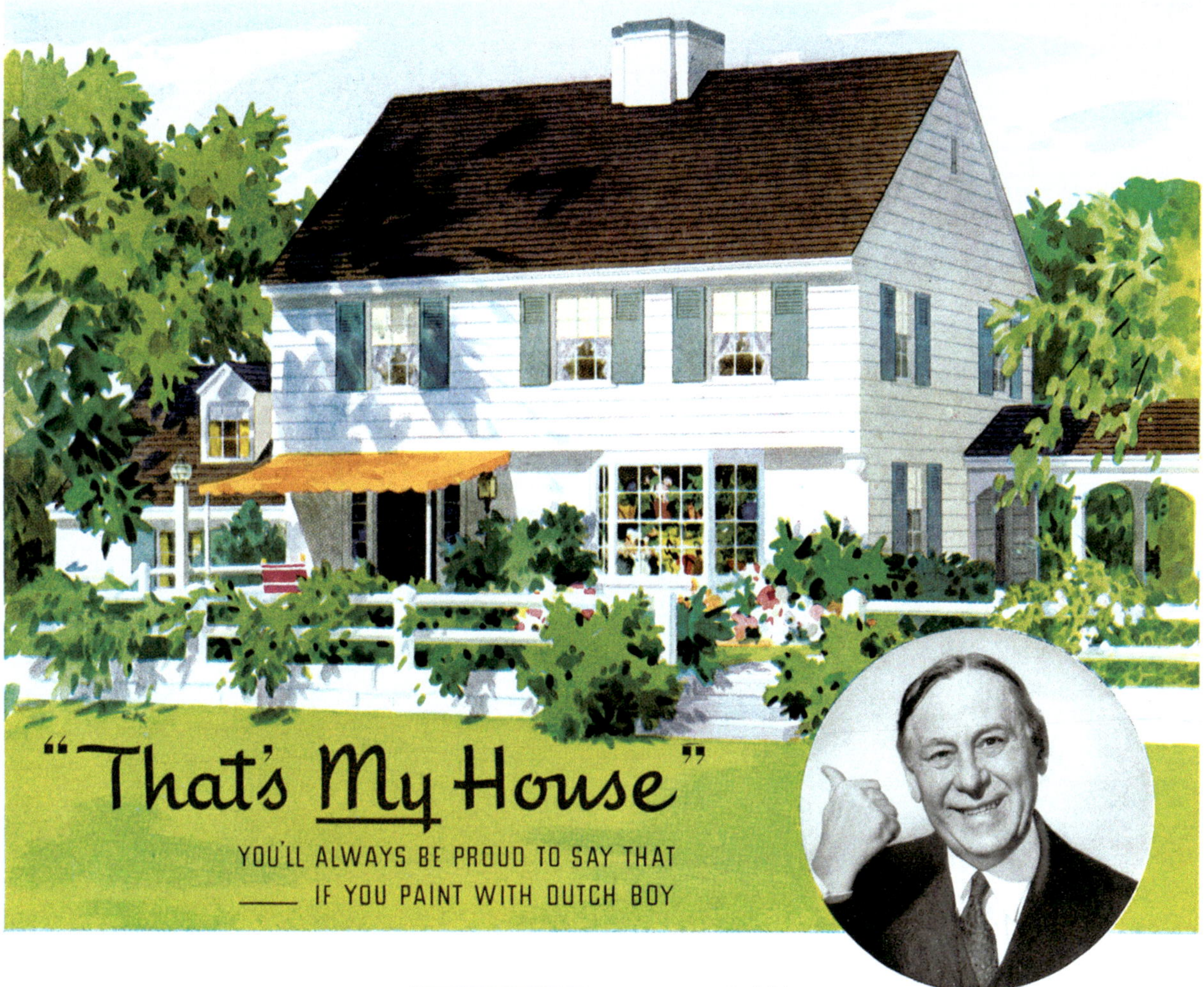

YOU'VE a right to be proud.

First of all, you *can't help* the feeling. For you know that you've given your home the best possible paint protection.

As time passes, you see that it is not only lasting protection, but lasting beauty. Dutch Boy wears well. So your house always *looks* well. Never does failure of the paint make you ashamed of your home's appearance.

And, then, when the time comes to repaint and you figure out what Dutch Boy costs per year, you've cause for pride again. You've spent less — much less — than the neighbor who used "cheap" paint, only to be humiliated by seeing it quickly disfigure his house and disgusted by having to do the job over so soon.

The unretouched photographs in the center are submitted as evidence. They tell a typical story of the difference between "cheap" paint and Dutch Boy.

Your painter knows this difference. By experience. The durability of Dutch Boy always backs up his reputation. Then, too, he can mix it to suit the requirements of your particular job and tint it to the exact color you specify. No one knows paint like a painter.

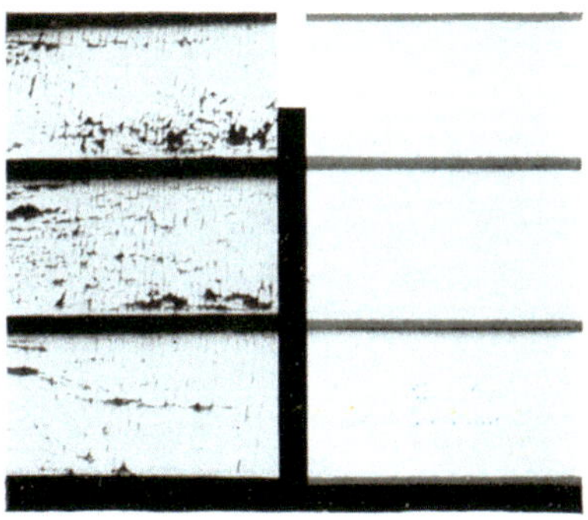

"CHEAP" PAINT	DUTCH BOY
After a few months. A short life and a sad one. Now the surface must be repainted. But first the old paint must be burned off and then an extra coat — a new priming coat — applied. And all this is expense the owner never figured on.	*After several years. Same location as "cheap" paint job. Look at the difference in condition. No cracking and scaling here. When repaint time does come, no burning and scraping and no new priming coat will be needed.*

Dutch Boy White Lead

GOOD PAINT'S OTHER NAME

How to Finance Painting

Don't say, "I'd like to paint, but haven't the cash just now." Under the new Dutch Boy Easy Payment Plan, the terms are — *nothing down and a little each month.*

If you want more details about this plan, check the coupon. But send in the coupon anyway and get our free 32-page booklet, illustrated in color, telling you how to improve your home with paint and how to buy the right kind of paint job. Address Dept. 218, nearest branch.

NATIONAL LEAD COMPANY—111 Broadway, New York; 116 Oak St., Buffalo; 900 W. 18th St., Chicago; 659 Freeman Ave., Cincinnati; 820 W. Superior Ave., Cleveland; 722 Chestnut St., St. Louis; 2240 24th St., San Francisco; National-Boston Lead Co., 800 Albany St., Boston; National Lead & Oil Co. of Penna., 316 Fourth Ave., Pittsburgh; John T. Lewis & Bros. Co., Widener Bldg., Philadelphia.

NATIONAL LEAD COMPANY
Department 218
(See list of branches above)

Please send me your free booklet "The House We Live In," containing color scheme suggestions and practical advice on interior and exterior painting.

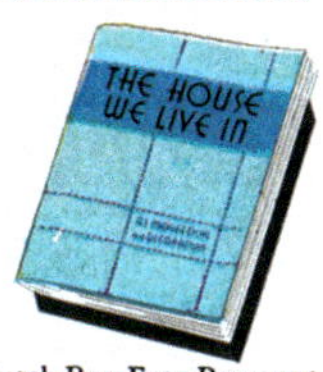

☐ Include folder describing Dutch Boy Easy Payment Plan.

Name ______________________

Street ______________________

City ______________ *State* ________

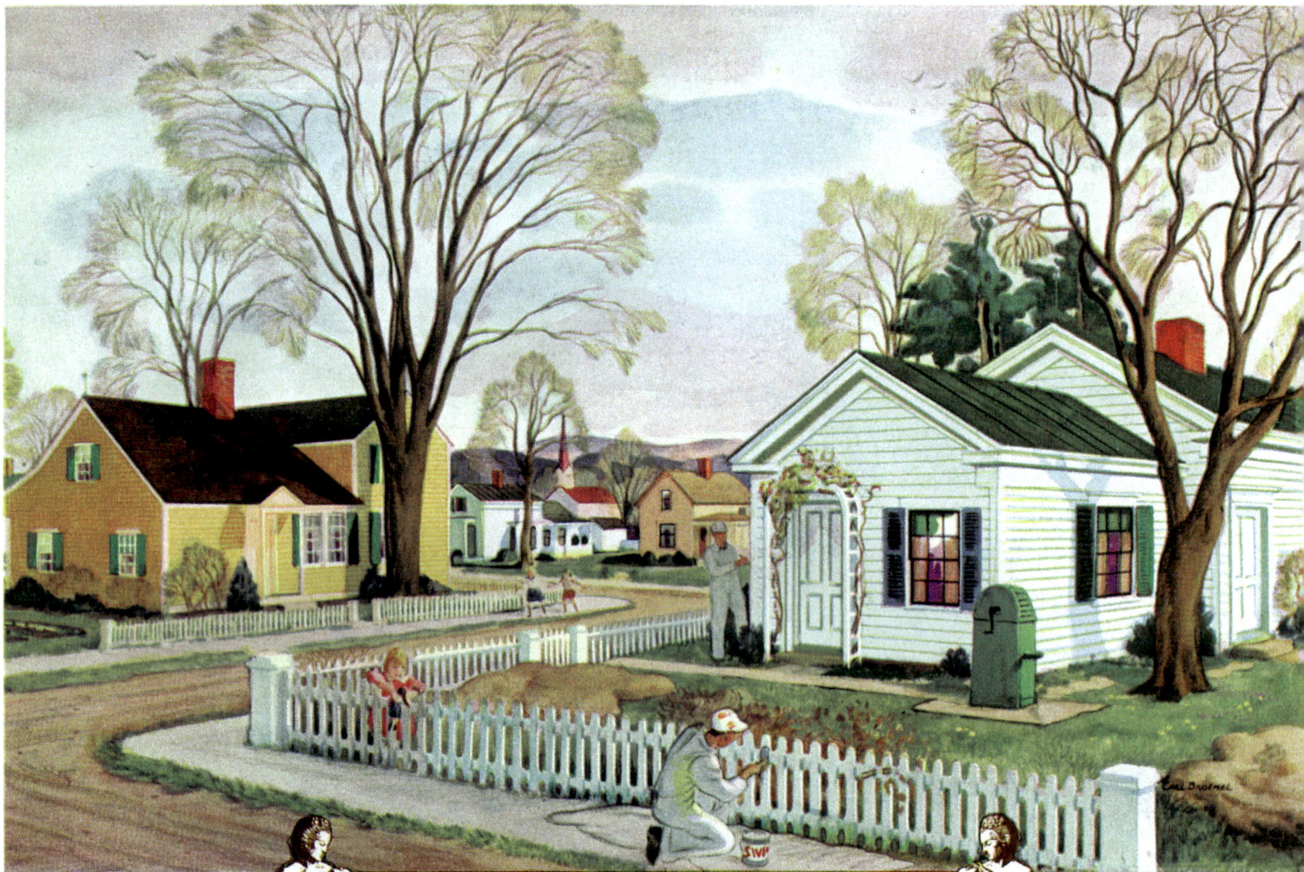

WHY are more homes painted with SWP than with any other brand of PAINT?

BEAUTY

PROTECTION

FIGURES BY ROCKWELL KENT—PAINTING BY CARL BROEMEL © 1937 THE SHERWIN-WILLIAMS CO.

A simple question, briefly answered—*SWP goes steps further to give homeowners each and every thing they want in a highest quality house paint!*

There's *beauty* . . . smoothness and richness of finish . . . SWP has it *plus*. Its white is whiter . . . its colors brighter, more permanent.

There's *protection*, complete . . . lasting. SWP has a tougher film of unequalled durability.

And there's *economy* . . . SWP covers more surface per gallon and covers it better. Further, it's quicker, easier to apply . . . cuts painting time and labor. And its *washability* can save you at least one repainting!

Chance had nothing to do with these superiorities of SWP. They were produced by the research, ingenuity and resources of the world's larges makers of paint anc varnish. Nothing has been overlooked tc make SWP look better, wear better and give greater economy than any other paint. Ask your neighborhood Sherwin-Williams dealer for "The Truth About House Paint" booklet for full details.

"All you need to know about paint is Sherwin-Williams." And city, town or hamlet, the famous Sherwin-Williams "Cover-the-Earth" symbol is "paint headquarters." There you will find a Sherwin-Williams dealer eager to help and serve you.

A new edition of the famous Home Decorator. Every page in color! Cover by the noted artist T. M. Cleland. Exteriors, room plans and color schemes of America's leading model homes. For your free copy see your neighborhood S-W dealer . . . or write The Sherwin-Williams Co., Dept. Z-21, Cleveland, Ohio.

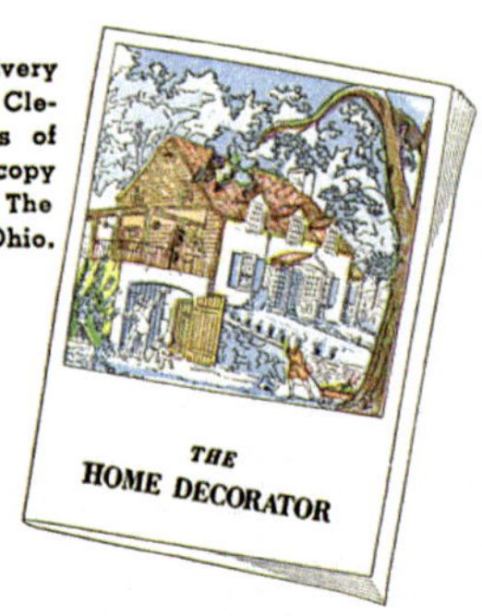

SHERWIN-WILLIAMS PAINTS

"ALL YOU NEED TO KNOW ABOUT PAINT"

COVER THE EARTH

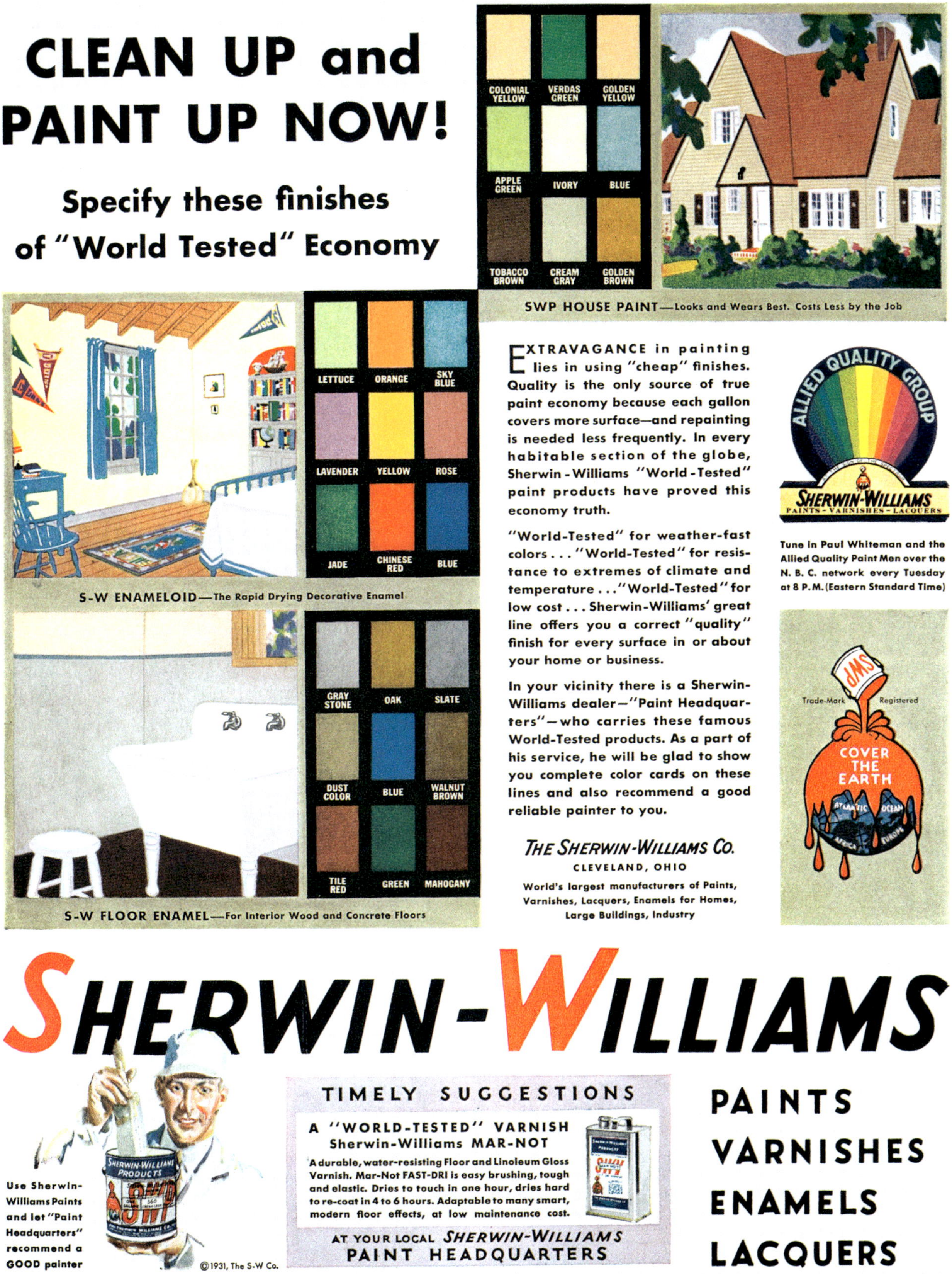

Sherwin-Williams Paints, 1937 ◄

Sherwin-Williams Paints, 1931

ABRAHAM & STRAUS
FULTON ST. AT HOYT . BROOKLYN

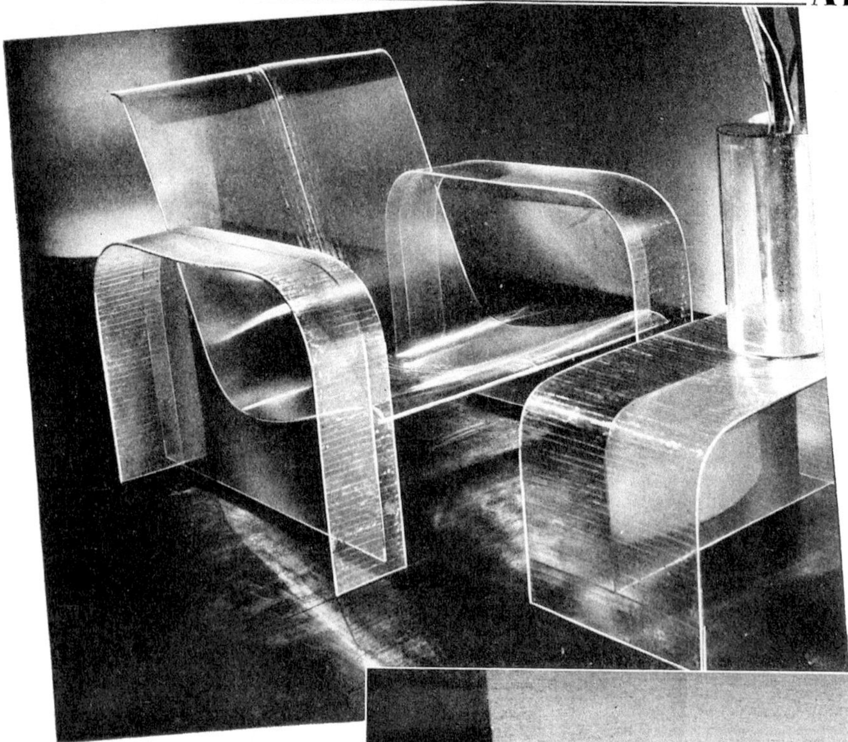

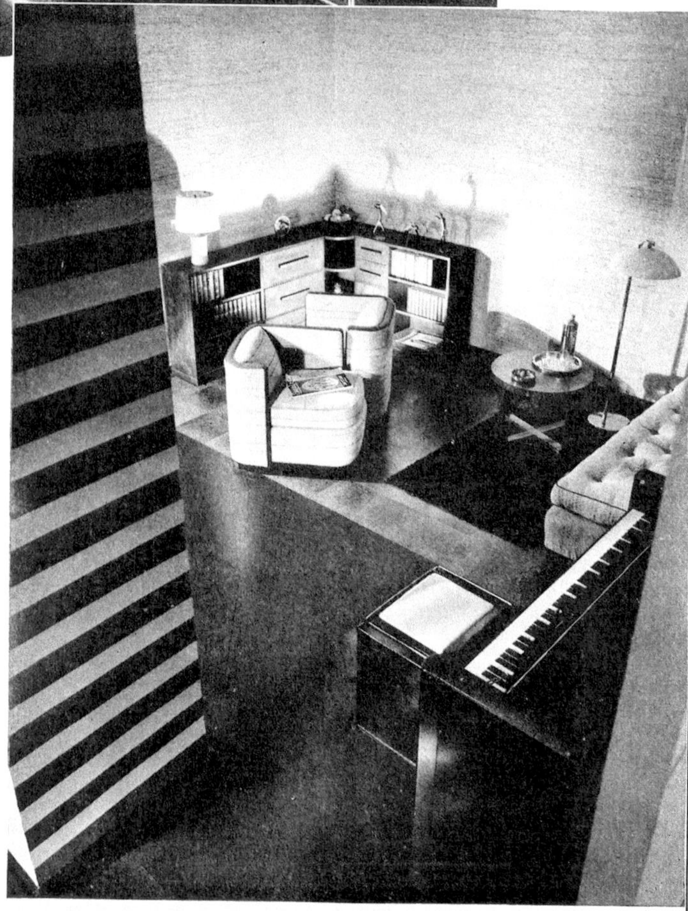

CHAIRS OF 'GLASS'

for Contemporary Cinderellas

Jewel setting for your lady. So magically inspired, it's like foretelling the future by gazing into a crystal. Knockout for a Manhattan terrace . . . for a country garden. Brilliance for an interior. Cora Scovil thought it up. Here is an original working model. Dupont's Plastex is the 'glass.' Chair to order, $175.

HIDE-OUT FOR A MAN

Leather on the walls in cheerful tangerine. Leather on deep twin barrel chairs in tobacco brown. A place for his books and drinks. A chance to try his hand at Rachmaninoff or Cole Porter on his own Minipiano. True Bachelor's quarters . . . even if you do have a daughter at Vassar. P. S. You can duplicate the works right to the wallpapers for $742.62.

HOW TO LIVE FOR TODAY AND TOMORROW AS SEEN IN A&S HOUSE OF PLANES FOR 1937 . . . INTERIOR DESIGNS BY ELEANOR LE MAIRE

Abraham & Straus, 1937

▸ *William F. Wholey Co., 1932*

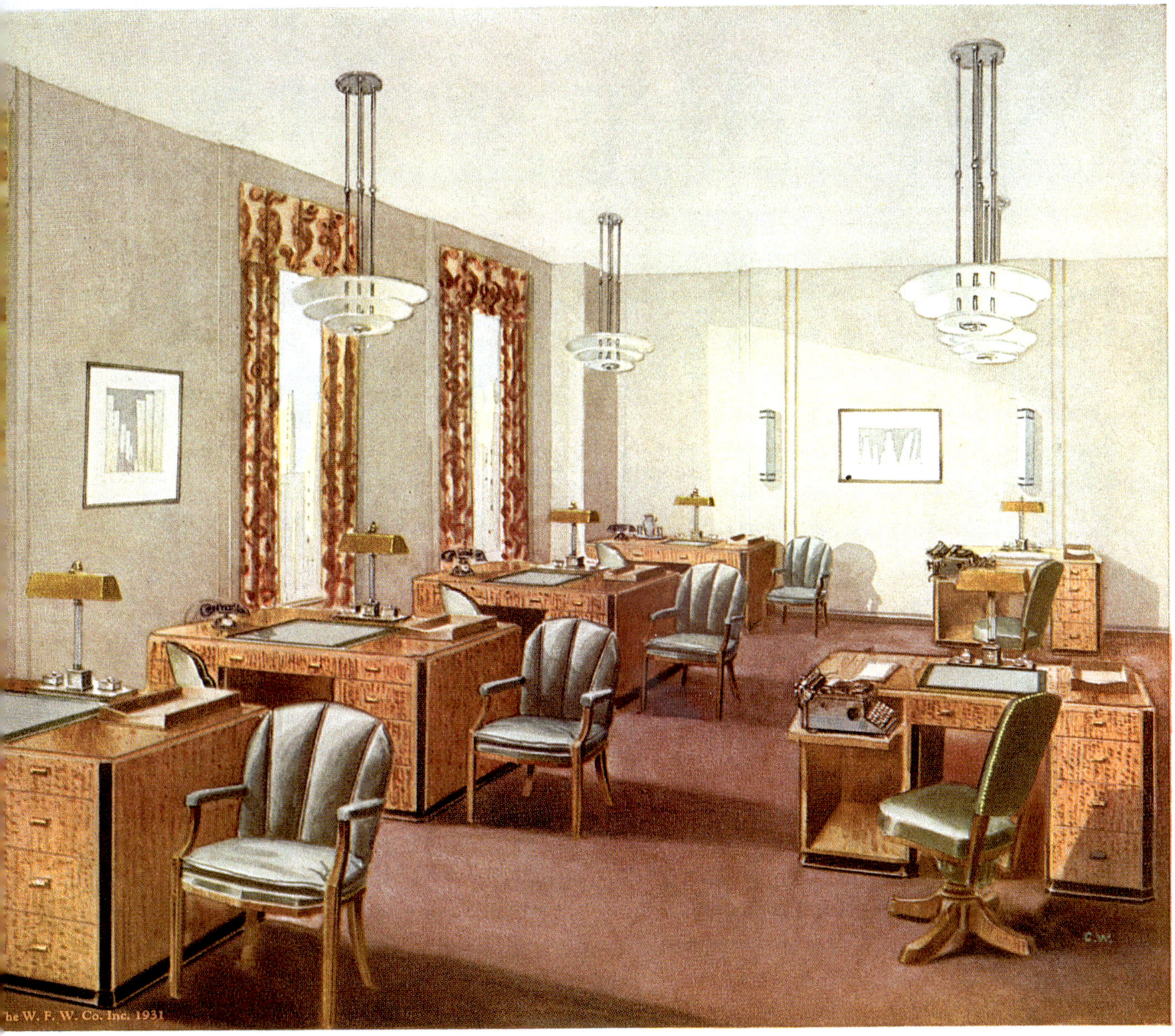

It Didn't Just Happen!

Being counsellors to many of the country's largest advertisers, The J. Walter Thompson Advertising Corporation recognizes the value of competent counsel in their own problems.

Months before their new Wall Street offices were to be occupied, the needs and inter-relations of their departments were being charted on the drawing boards of the Wholey designing staff.

Under the Wholey plan, no detail of office design is left to chance, nor need furnishings be selected from sketches alone. At the Wholey Showrooms, three floors are devoted to complete offices, reception rooms, board rooms . . . where decorative treatments and furnishings to suit all purposes and budgets may be compared, and preferences definitely established.

ICE PLANNING **WHOLEY** INTERIOR ARCHITECTURE · DECORATION · FURNITURE

E WILLIAM F. COMPANY INC. 11 EAST 36, NEW YORK

A Beautiful Chrometube Shop

complete ready for the most desirable patronage

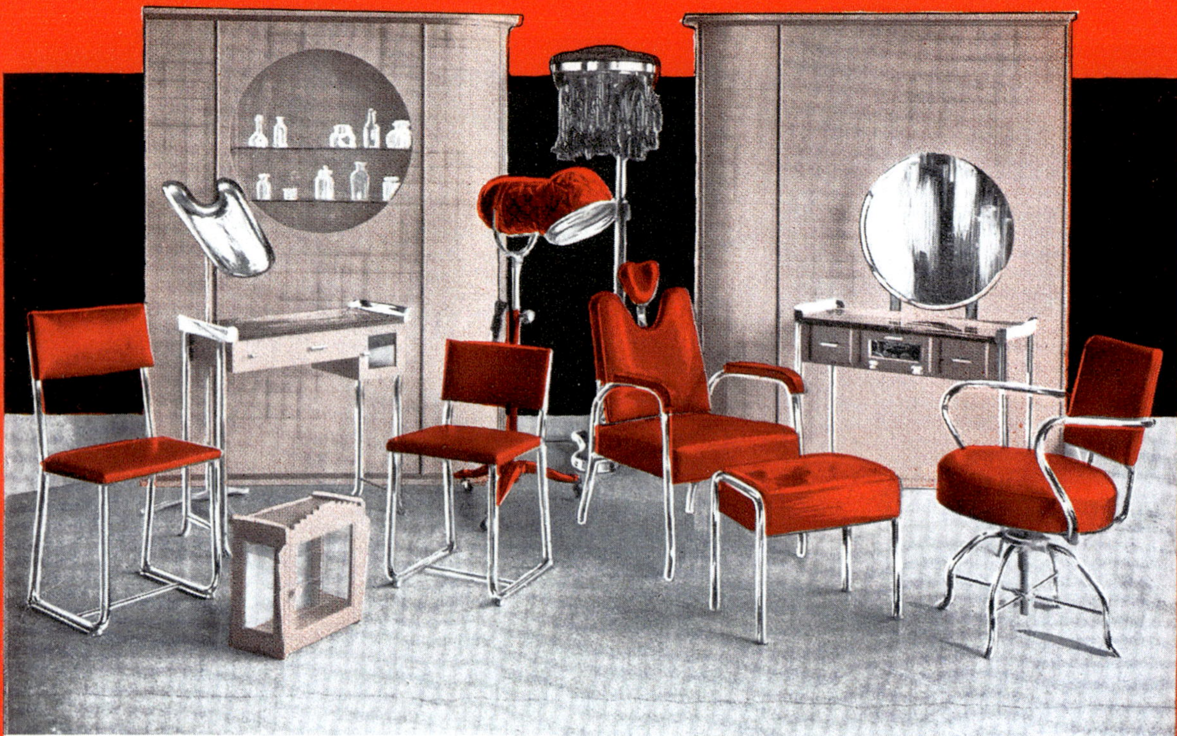

There is great satisfaction

in having a lovely Chrometube Shop . . .

It is business-like—the colors of upholstery may be just as lively or subdued as one wishes, and besides you know that your furniture is quality PAIDAR equipment. Shop owners like to buy the Paidar easy purchase way—small monthly payments—one contract for everything.

All Equipment

except permanent waving machine

$217.00

Waver extra according to make desired. Booth panels decorated in Plaid design in any standard color.

No. 1295 with show case—30″ x 6″ deep, $74.00.

No. 1296 with hat shelf and coat hangers in back, $60.00.

Buy the PAIDAR easy to pay way.

The Paidar catalog is very interesting and instructive. Ask for special literature on gas dryers.

EMIL J. Paidar COMPANY

32-34 West 20th St. New York City

1114 N. Wells St. Chicago

Manufacturers of

BEAUTY PARLOR CHAIRS
BOOTHS, DRESSERS
HAIR DRYERS

BARBER CHAIRS
MIRROR CASES
DISPLAY CASES

LAVATORIES, ETC.
BARBER POLES, ETC.
MANICURE TABLES, ETC.

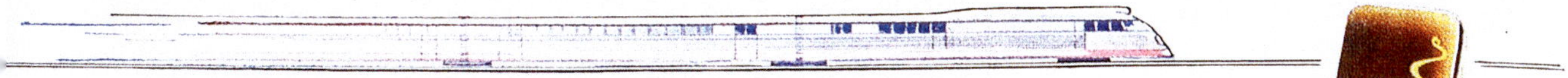

THE "CENTURY"

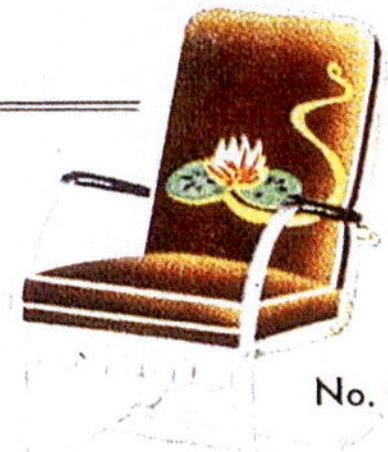

No. K-1577

Characteristic of Hettrick quality is this new modern styled glider. Tubular chrome front rail and white enameled back rail; torpedo type arms with chrome trim and fitted with ash receiver in each arm; sturdy embossed end panel; fluted metal front panel. Three individual sections of spring with nine coils in each. Ball bearing suspension; anti-sway lock; opens up to form a bed as shown on page 45. Six individual cushions covered with waterproofed Textileather, filled with cotton linters and double rope piped with stayform binding.

Spring Steel Chair—Constructed of heavy spring steel. Cushions are covered with waterproofed Textileather, filled with cotton linters and double rope piped; metal arm rests.

No. K-1376	Sh. Wt. 150 lbs.	$42.10
No. K-1371	Sh. Wt. 150 lbs.	42.10
No. K-1374	Sh. Wt. 150 lbs.	42.10
No. K-1577 Spring Steel Chair	Sh. Wt. 55 lbs.	14.88

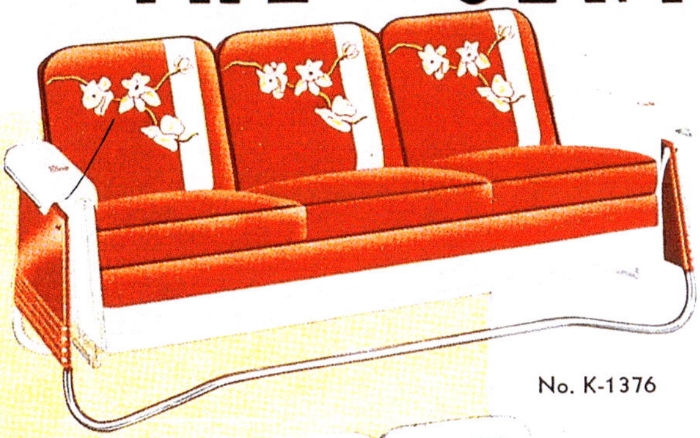

No. K-1376

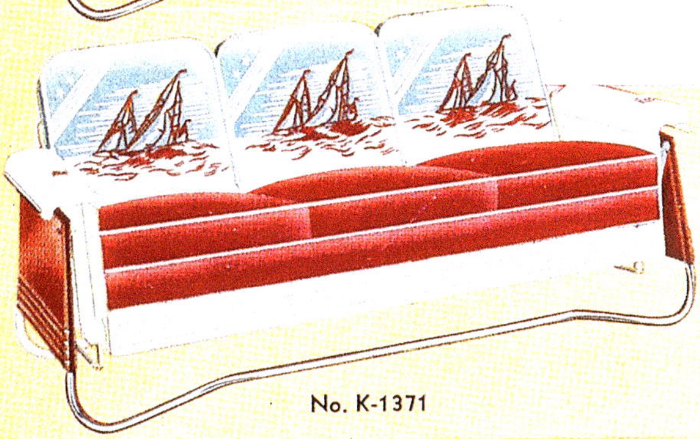

No. K-1371

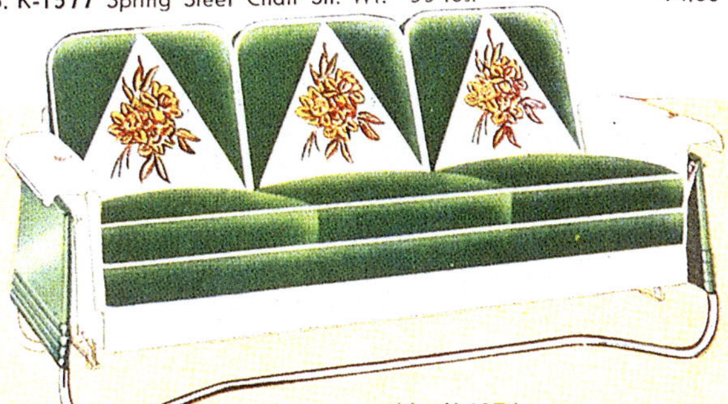

No. K-1374

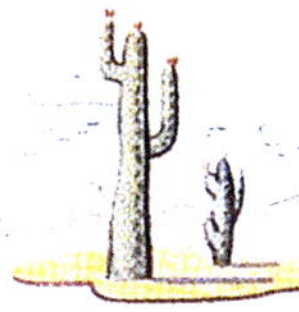

THE "CORANADO"

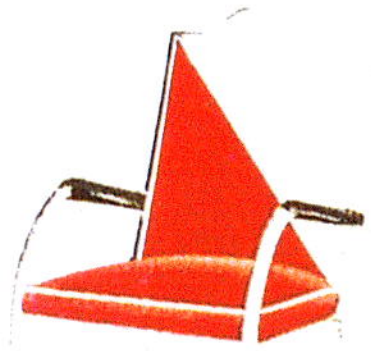

No. K-1586

Distinctive, appealing style, satisfactorily priced—one of the most modern glider creations on the market. White enameled tubular spreader rails; three individual springs with nine coils each; full depth pillow type arms; sturdy embossed end panel; fluted metal front panel; ball bearing suspension; anti-sway lock; opens up to form a bed as shown on page 45. Six individual cushions covered with waterproofed Textileather, filled with cotton linters and double rope piped with stayform binding; painted with the finest enamel pigments obtainable and baked in a modern infrared ray oven.

Spring Steel Chair—Constructed of heavy spring steel. Cushions are covered with waterproofed Textileather, filled with cotton linters and double rope piped; metal arm rests.

No. K-1368	Sh. Wt. 150 lbs.	$36.66
No. K-1360	Sh. Wt. 150 lbs.	36.66
No. K-1366	Sh. Wt. 150 lbs.	36.66
No. K-1586 Spring Steel Chair	Sh. Wt. 55 lbs.	14.88

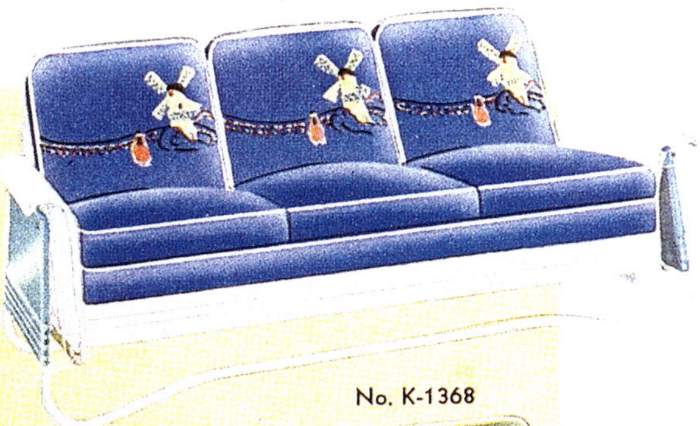

No. K-1368

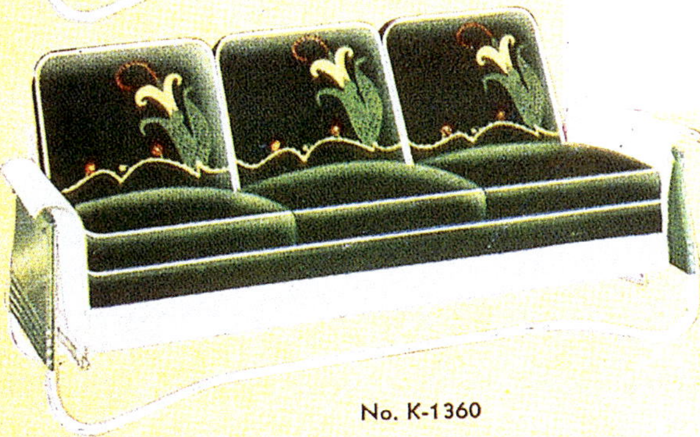

No. K-1360

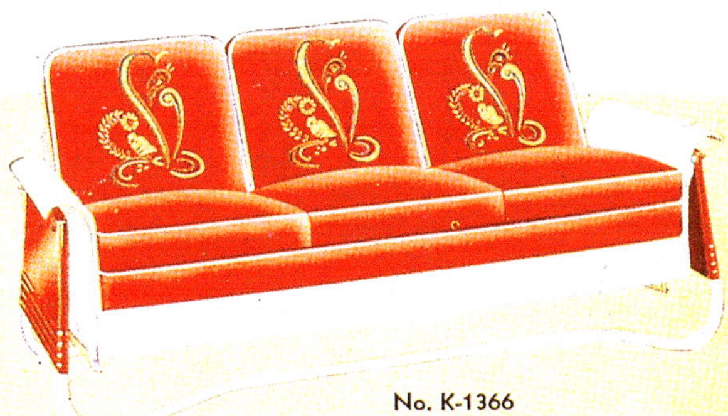

No. K-1366

Emil J. Paidar Co., 1936 ◂

Hettrick Gliders, 1935

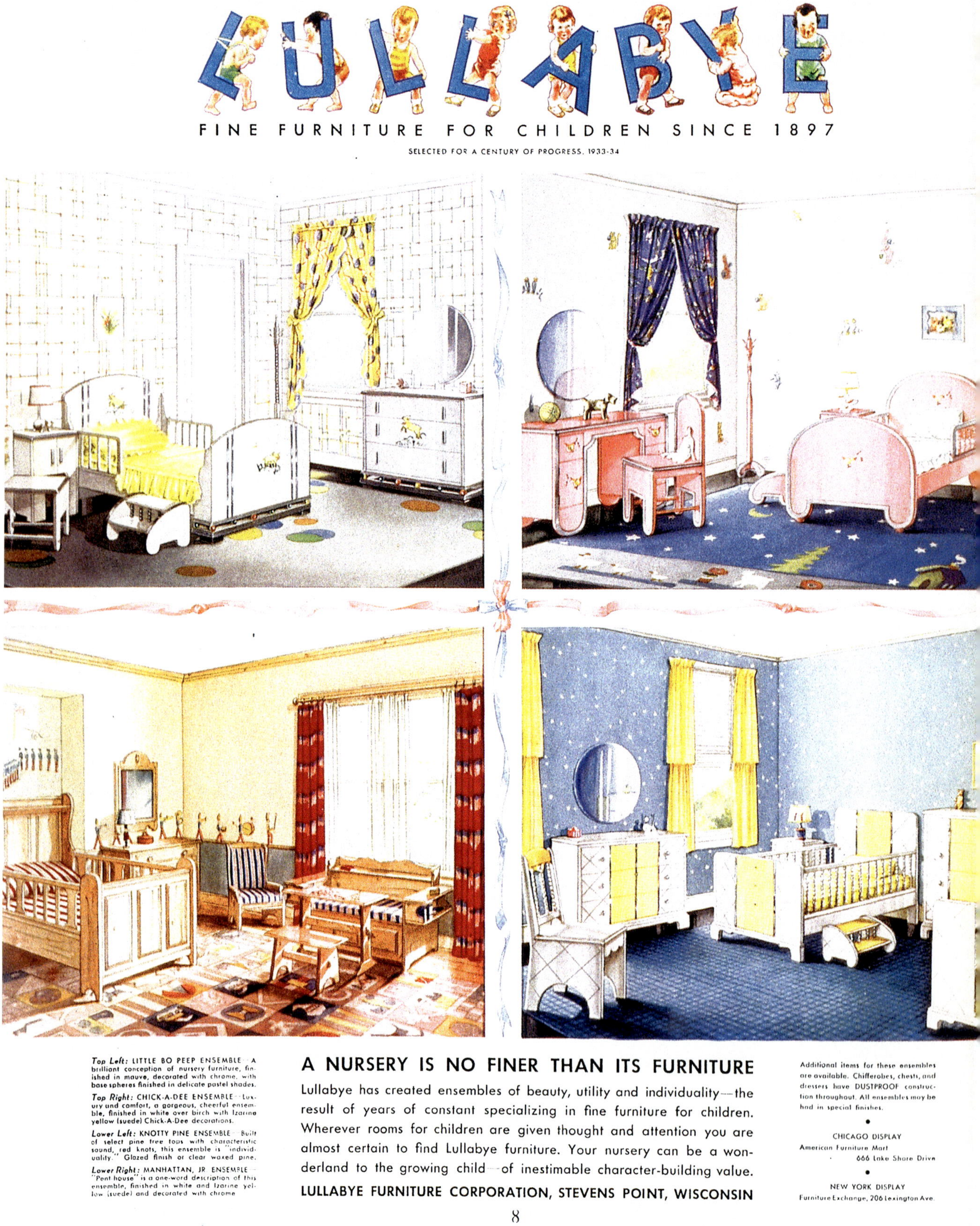

Lullabye Furniture Co., 1935

HETTRICK PLAY YARD EQUIPMENT...

HAVE FUN IN THE "OLE SWIMMIN' HOLE"

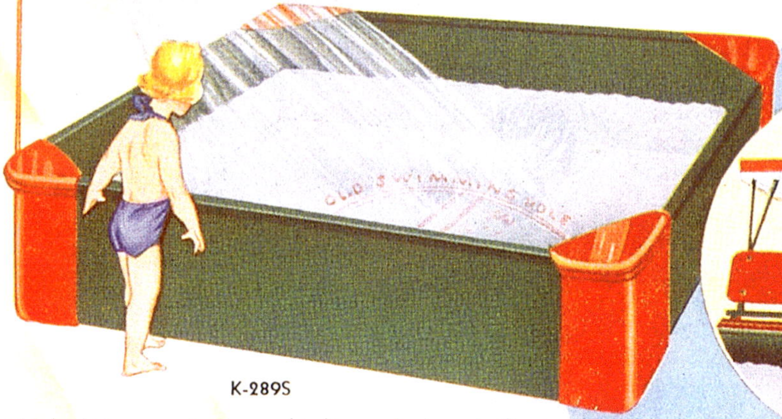

K-289S

Every child should have a swimming pool in his own back yard. Good, clean, healthful fun and an excellent means of keeping children off dangerous streets. Constructed of extra heavy waterproofed green oiled duck. Streamlined orange legs and seats, doing away with all sharp, injurious corners. Attractive orange design inside the bottom of pool. Green and orange bench fits on No. 290S and No. 294S pool, with orange canopy to fit on bench. Sturdy green angle iron frame. Drain plug in bottom for draining. Upright shower for No. 289S and No. 290S and double horizontal shower for No. 294S pool.

No.	Size	Sh. Wt.	Price
K-289S	3½′ x 3½′ x 12″ deep	23 lbs.	$10.34
K-290S	4½′ x 4½′ x 12″ deep	30 lbs.	11.88
K-294S	4½′ x 7′ x 12″ deep	35 lbs.	16.34

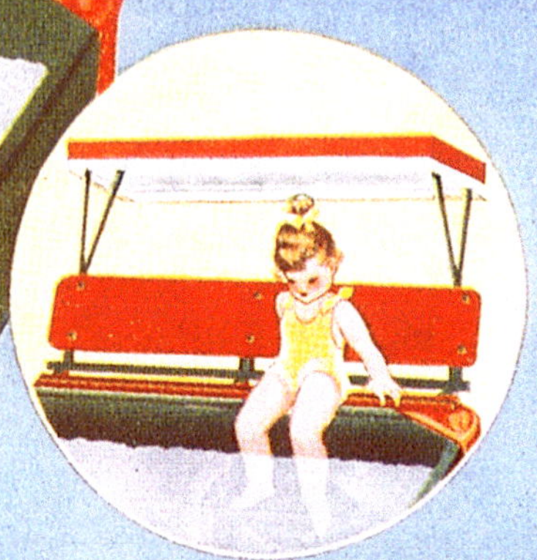

No.	Sh. Wt.	Price
K-272 Bench	10 lbs.	$4.34
K-273 Canopy	3 lbs.	2.22

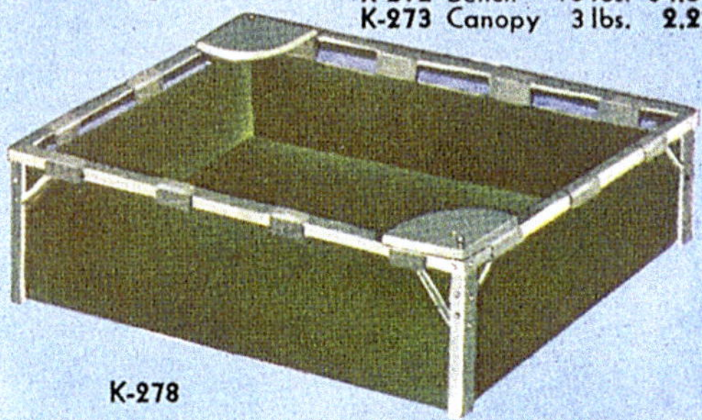

K-278

No.	Size	Sh. Wt.	Price
K-278 Without Shower	36″x46″x12″ deep	22 lbs.	$6.56
K-278S With Shower	36″x46″x12″ deep	25 lbs.	8.00

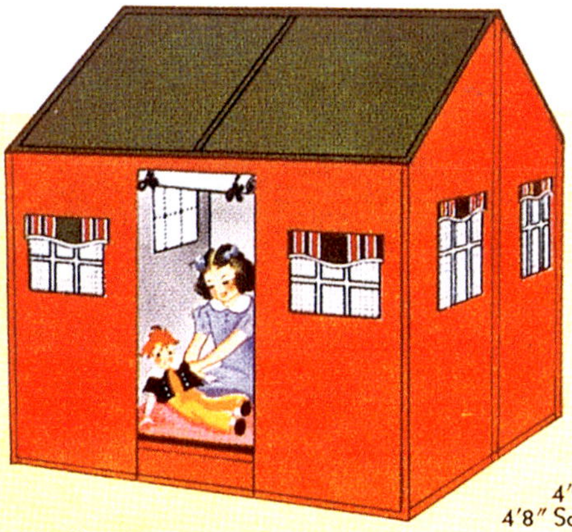

4′9″ High
4′8″ Square at Base

No. K-1852

"MARY ANN" PLAYHOUSE—One of the fastest selling tents on the market. No girl could resist it. A boon to every mother on a rainy day. Sturdy center poleless frame. No stakes necessary. High grade painted green and orange awning material. Double seamed throughout. Fine mesh bobbinet door, curtain and windows.

K-1852 Sh. Wt. 22 lbs. $12.12

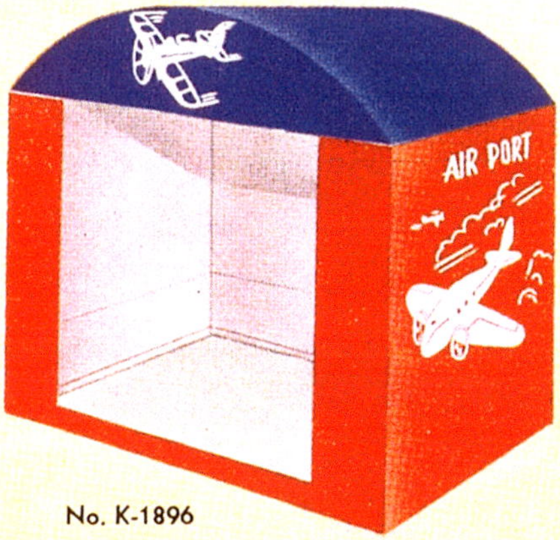

No. K-1896

AIRPORT—A real airport. One that will make the heart of every youngster jump with joy. Constructed of high count painted tent material, having wood frame and metal arches, blue top and red sides. Appropriate aeronautical designs in white on both sides and front. Size 3′2″ x 4′6″ at the base with 4′ center, 3′2″ wall. Airport has door opening 3′ wide and 2′10″ high.

K-1896 Sh. Wt. 18 lbs. $7.30

Hettrick Play Equipment, 1935

HERE'S HOW TO BEAUTIFY A ROOM WITH... PAINT *and* GLASS

by PITTSBURGH PLATE GLASS CO.

There are hundreds of ways in which paint and glass may be used to beautify and improve your home. (Our free booklet describes them in detail). The charm of paint on walls or woodwork . . . the enlivening brightness of glass in its many forms . . . these add to the gracious welcome of well planned rooms.

The "Pittsburgh" name on any paint or glass product is a positive assurance of high quality. The 73 branches of the Pittsburgh Plate Glass Co., its thousands of dealers, make these products conveniently available no matter where you live.

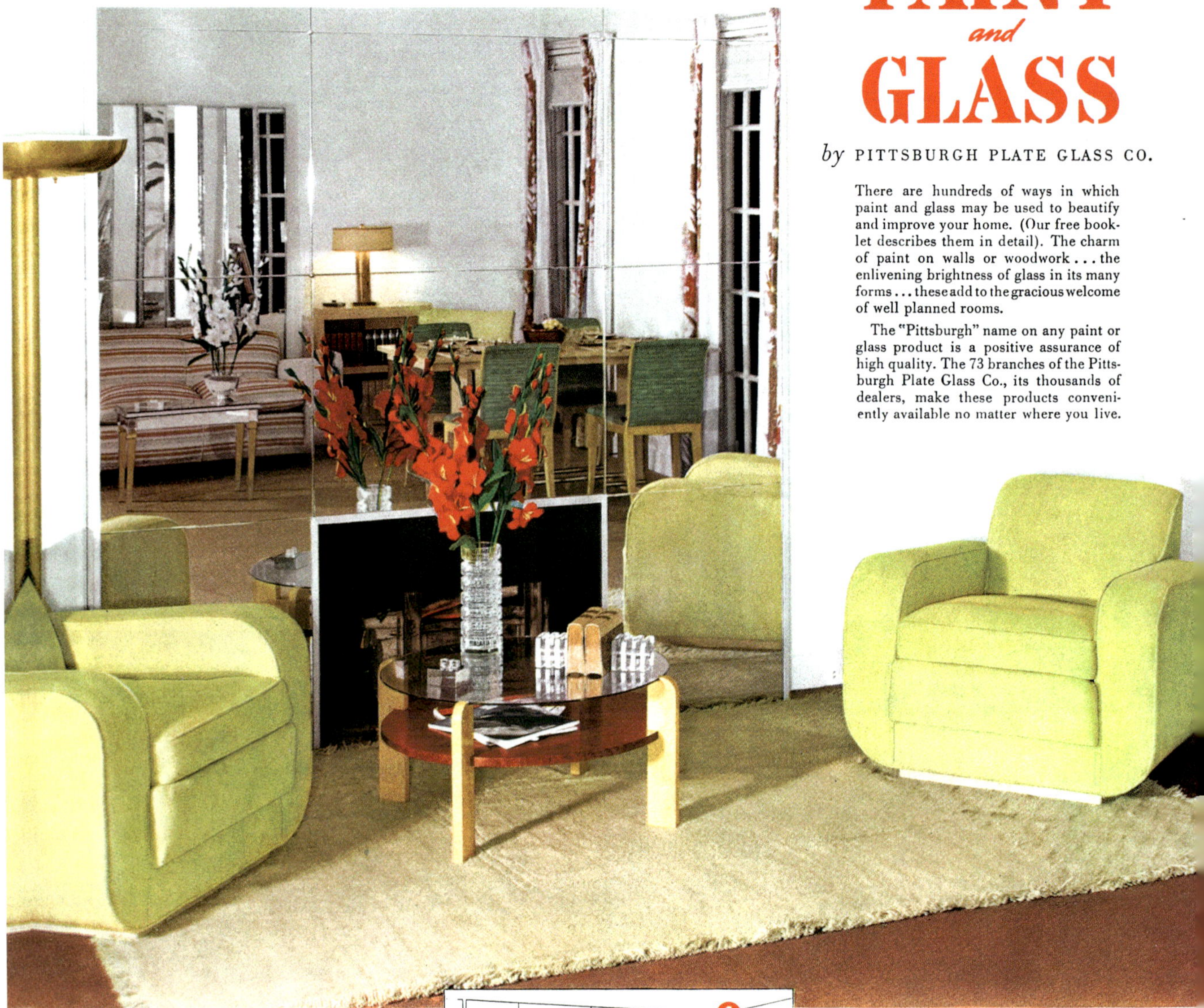

COLOR PHOTOGRAPH BY METTEE-FRITTITA TAKEN IN W. & J. SLOANE'S HOUSE OF YEARS, NEW YORK

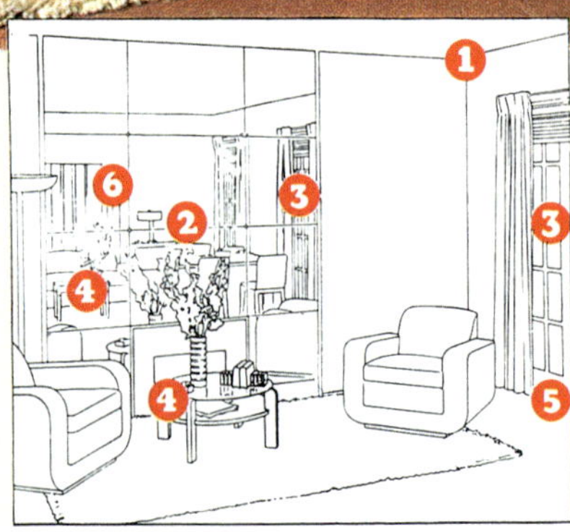

1 Notice how soft, evenly-tinted walls and ceiling, finished in quick-drying Pittsburgh Wallhide Paint, set the stage for the decoration of this room.

2 See how large mirror panels, reflecting warm color and creating an atmosphere of spaciousness and light, can add charm to the family fireside.

3 These French doors, glazed with clear, brilliant Pennvernon Window Glass, invite more daylight into the room, and bring Nature's beauty indoors.

4 Look at these two small tables . . . and see how polished plate glass and facings of mirror glass blend beauty with utility in incidental furniture.

5 Note how the woodwork, finished in smooth, rich Pittsburgh Waterspar Enamel, accentuates the clean sweep of Pittsburgh Wallhide walls and ceiling.

6 Always successful . . . an accordion screen completely faced with mirror glass and slightly folded to afford a host of warm, interesting reflections.

SEND FOR FREE BOOK
A new fascinating book on home improvement and decoration, fully illustrated and filled with practical suggestions to fit your budget. Whether you own, rent or plan to build, be sure to send the coupon for your free copy of "Practical Suggestions for the Interesting Use of Paint and Glass in Your Home." This book is absolutely free.

Paint · PITTSBURGH PLATE GLASS COMPANY · *Glass*

Makers of WALLHIDE PAINT · WATERSPAR ENAMEL *and* VARNISH · SUN-PROOF PAINT · FLORHIDE · GOLD STRIPE PAINT BRUSHES · POLISHED PLATE GLASS · MIRRORS · PENNVERNON WINDOW GLASS · CARRARA STRUCTURAL GLASS · DUPLATE SAFETY GLASS

PITTSBURGH PLATE GLASS COMPANY
2384-B Grant Building, Pittsburgh, Pa.

Please send me, without obligation, your new book "Practical Suggestions for the Interesting Use of Paint and Glass in Your Home."

Name____________________

Street____________________

City__________ State__________

MODERN FURNITURE UTILIZES

TUF-FLEX GLASS

FOR GREATER STRENGTH*

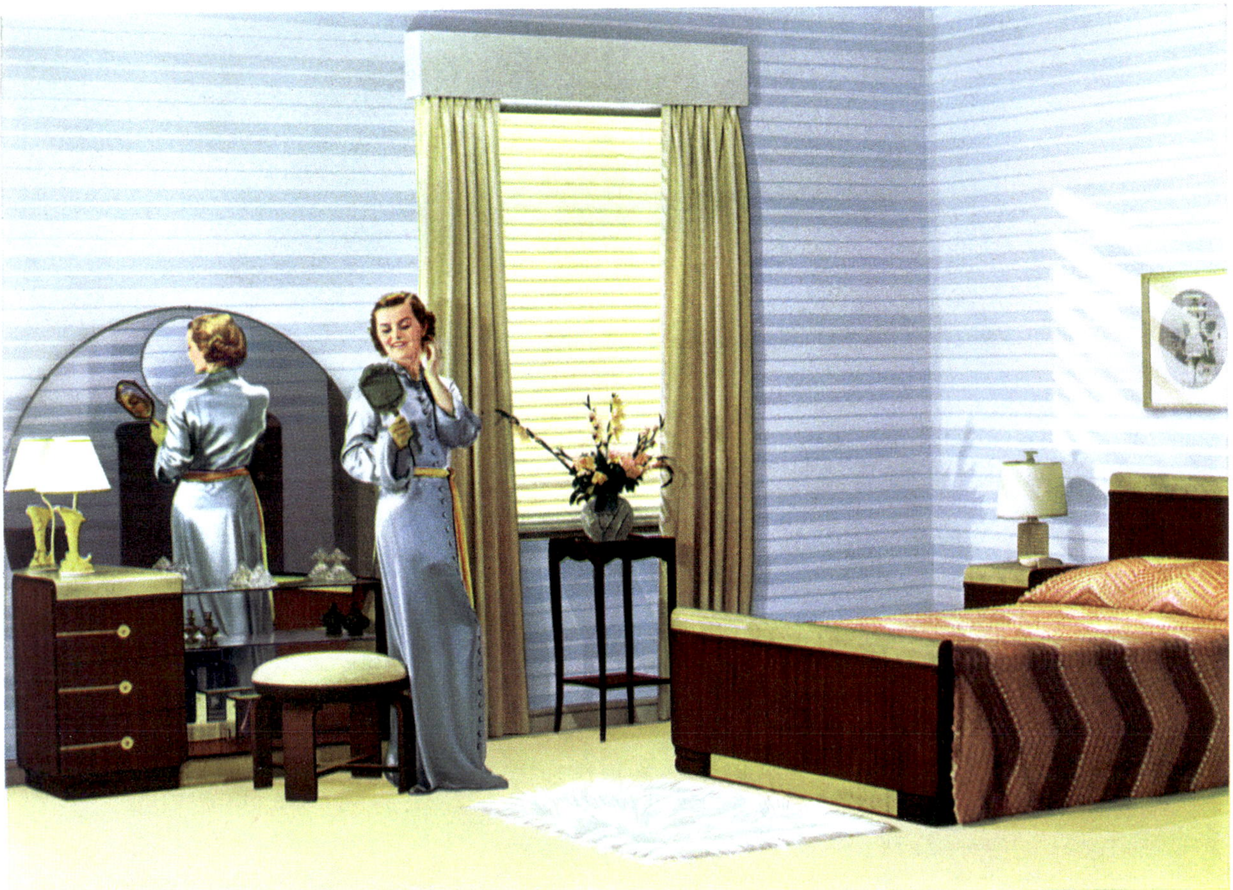

When the designers of Fashion Flow Furniture created their new bedroom pieces they took full advantage of the trend toward a more generous use of glass in the home. For instance, milady's vanity, illustrated here, offers an excellent example of how the sparkling beauty of glass is made to blend with modern furniture design. This vanity has a large mirror of polished plate and shelves of Tuf-Flex Glass—the new tempered plate glass which is from three to seven times as strong as ordinary plate glass. Women appreciate the fact that glass is stain-proof in ordinary use. Toilet accessories show to advantage on glass and here the use of Tuf-Flex tempered plate glass, for the first time, makes the long brilliant glass shelves more practical. The whole ensemble adds a noticeable touch of smartness to the room.

LIBBEY·OWENS·FORD GLASS COMPANY, TOLEDO, OHIO

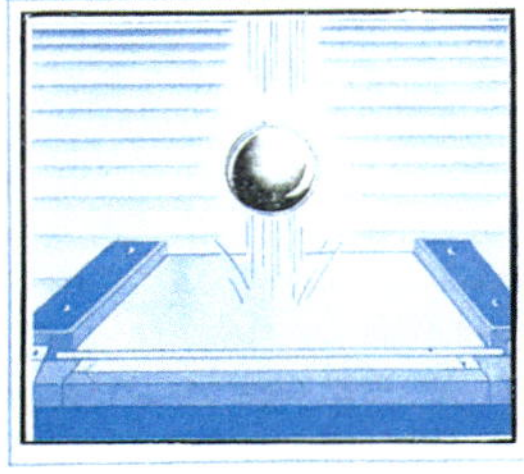

● *A 2-pound steel ball bounds back from a 12x12-in. light of ¼-in. Tuf-Flex, after a drop of 5 feet.*

** While Tuf-Flex is not unbreakable, its tempering process limits its susceptibility. Chipping or puncturing exposed edges or surfaces causes the glass to disintegrate into small crystals, and if not framed, the crystals have a tendency to fly apart.*

Pittsburgh Plate Glass Co., 1937 ◄

W & J Sloane, 1933

NEO-CLASSIC BATH
PEMBROKE MODEL IN A POMPEIAN SETTING.

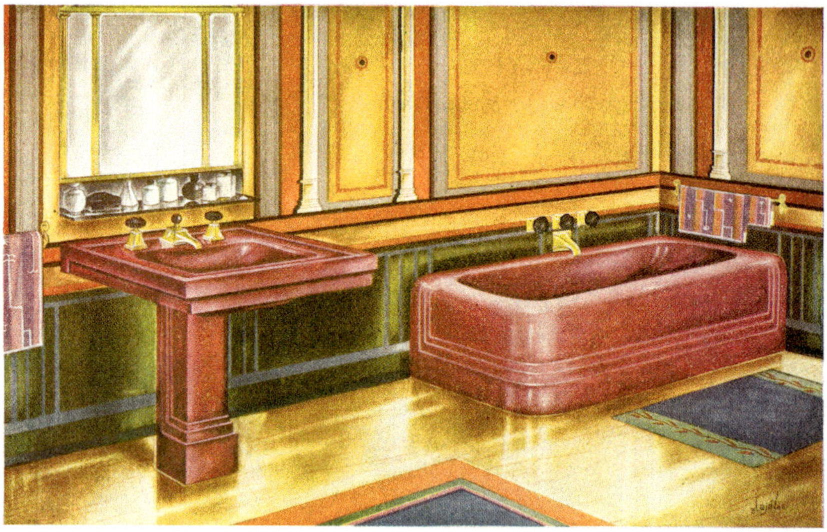

NEO-CLASSIC

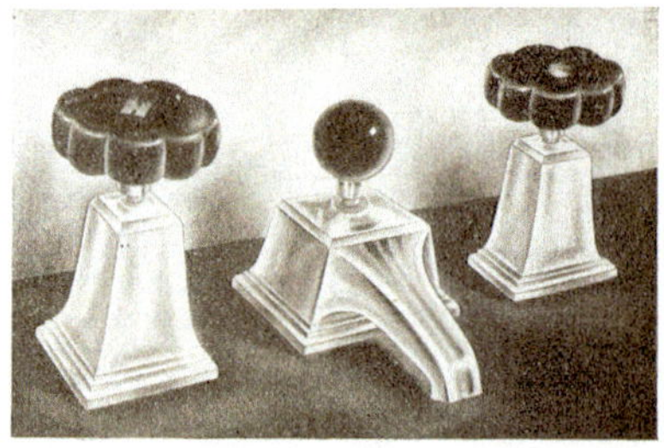

WITH FITTINGS OF HARMONIOUS DESIGN

A new form for plumbing fixtures modelled by a designer of recognized authority, and faithfully reproduced by "Standard" . . . Neo-Classic form is a distinct departure from the usual plumbing fixture design . . . Its individuality is grounded in that simplicity which is at once classic and modern. And it is this very simplicity which permits the Neo-Classic to be used with distinction in both period and contemporary settings.

The simplicity of the Neo-Classic motif has this further advantage—it is carried out equally well in the design of bath, lavatory and water closet; in fittings for these fixtures; in towel-bar and lighting fixtures . . . This makes possible, for the first time, an ensemble of perfect harmony in design as well as color.

You are invited to visit a "Standard" Showroom to see the Neo-Classic designs which, in the bath models, may be had in regular enamel or "Standard" Acid-Resisting enamel . . . The Neo-Classic lavatory and water closet models are available in vitreous china . . . All Neo-Classic fixtures, bath, lavatory and water closet, are available in white and each of the nine "Standard" colors. A Copy of the book "Standard" Plumbing Fixtures for the Home" will be mailed on request.

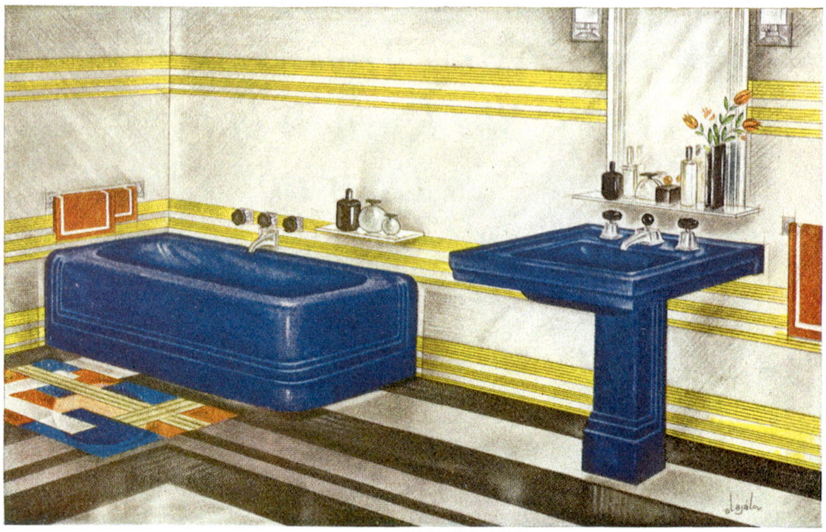

NEO-CLASSIC BATH
PEMBROKE MODEL IN A CONTEMPORARY SETTING.

"Standard"
PLUMBING FIXTURES

Standard Sanitary Mfg. Co. 106 SIXTH STREET, PITTSBURGH

DIVISION OF AMERICAN RADIATOR & STANDARD SANITARY CORPORATION

Standard Plumbling Fixtures, 1931

▸ *Pittsburgh Plate Glass Co., 1937*

IT'S THRILLING TO HAVE A BATHROOM

THAT *everyone* ADMIRES!

THAT'S one reason why so many people these days are building their bathrooms with walls of Carrara Structural Glass. These walls make any bathroom beautiful. Or any kitchen, for that matter. They're smooth, polished, highly reflective. They're mellow and rich in color, forming an ideal background for fixtures or furniture. They're permanent. And one of the nicest things about them is, they're so easy to keep clean. You just give them an occasional rubdown with a damp cloth.

Are you planning a new home? Let Carrara Walls make you proud of your bathroom. Are you going to remodel your present bathroom or kitchen? Let Carrara Walls bring back its youth and beauty in full measure. And meanwhile, send today for our brochure "Personality Bathrooms and Character Kitchens." It is illustrated in full color, and contains complete facts. Address Pittsburgh Plate Glass Company, 2178 Grant Bldg., Pittsburgh, Pa.

Paint · PITTSBURGH PLATE GLASS COMPANY · *Glass*

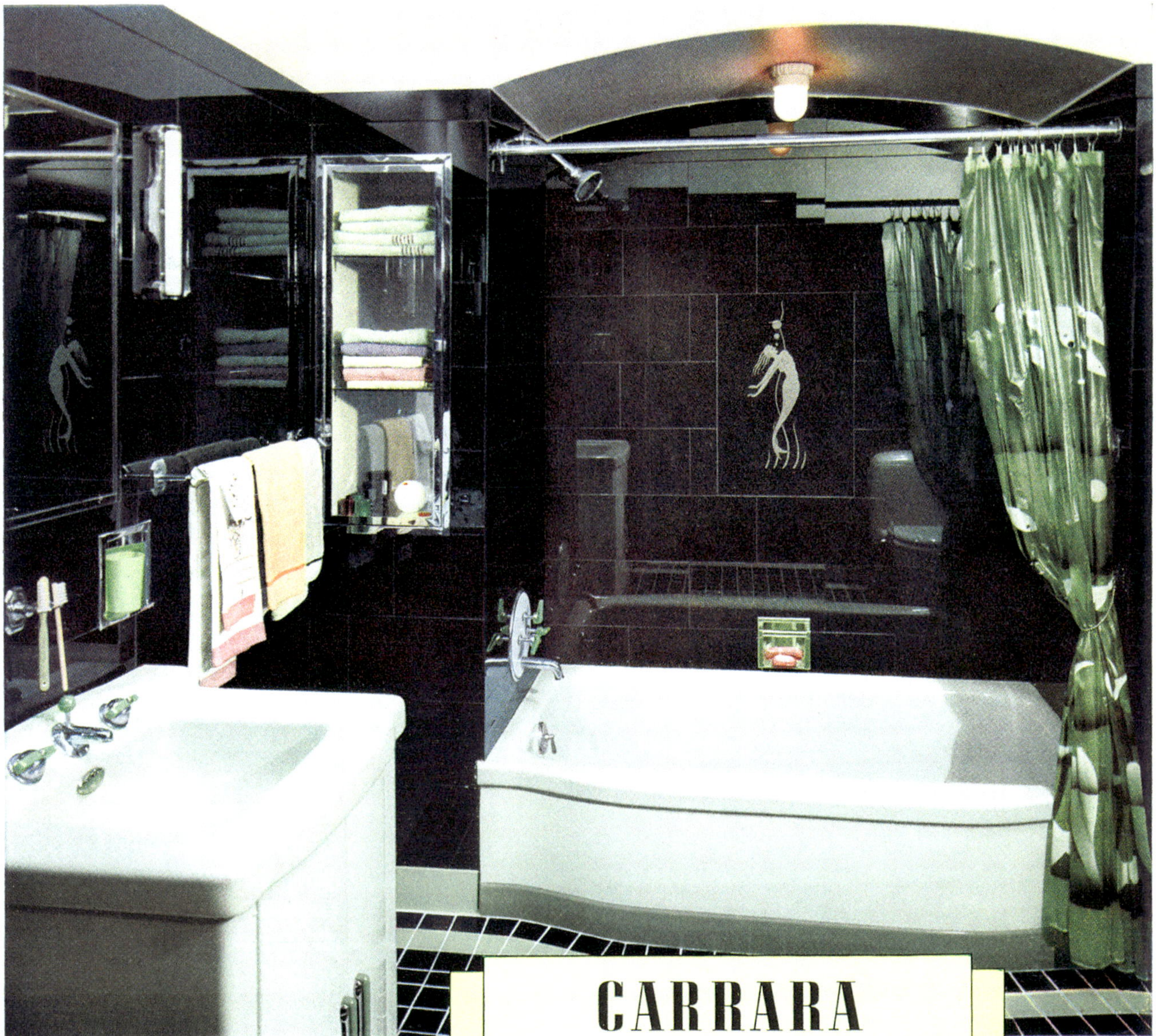

A charming Carrara bathroom in the home of Mr. and Mrs. H. D. Clark of Detroit. A Black Carrara wainscot, with Jade Carrara trim and fixtures of jade green, is the secret of the room's beauty and utility.

CARRARA

THE MODERN STRUCTURAL GLASS

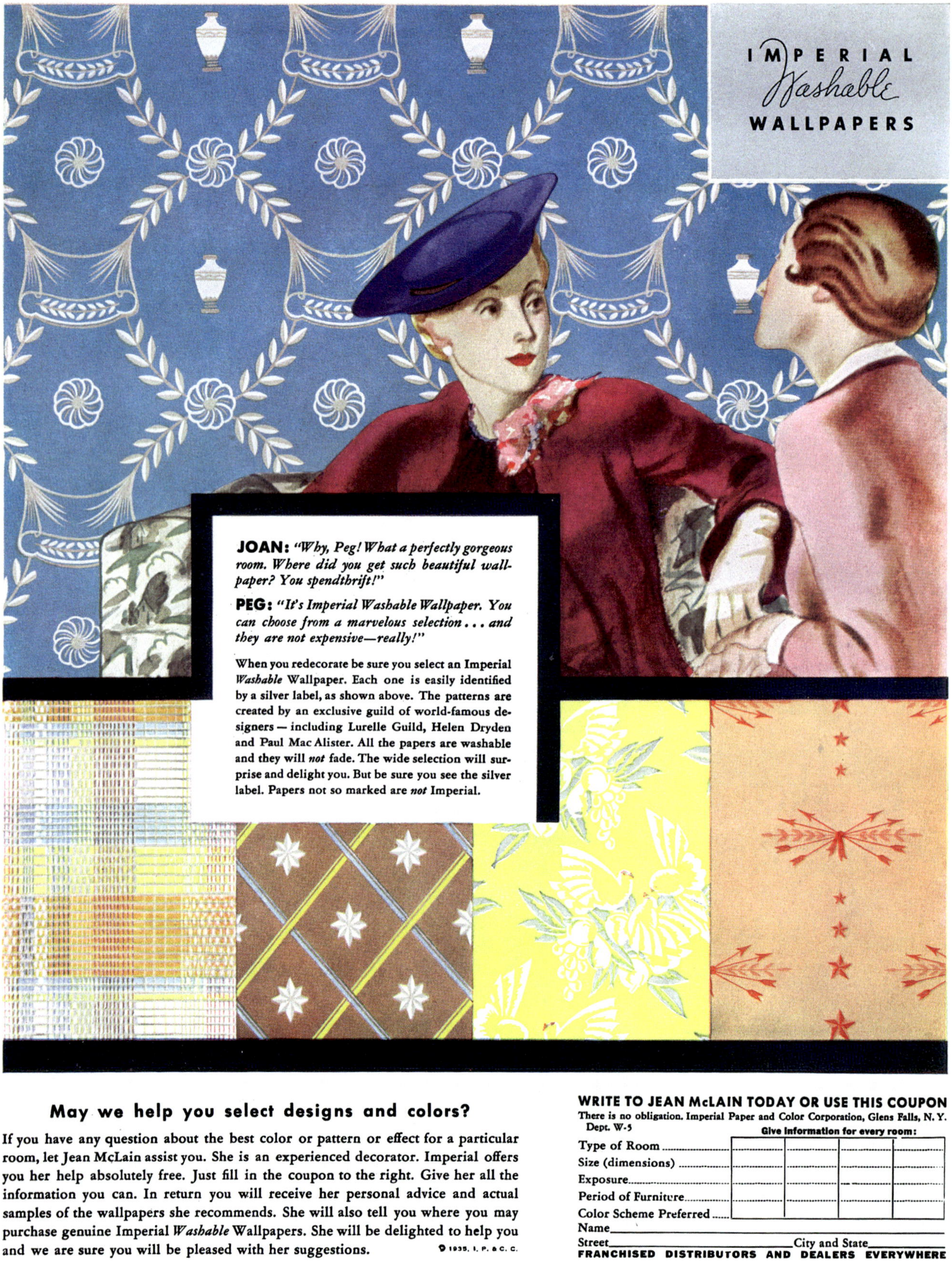

Imperial Wallpapers, 1935

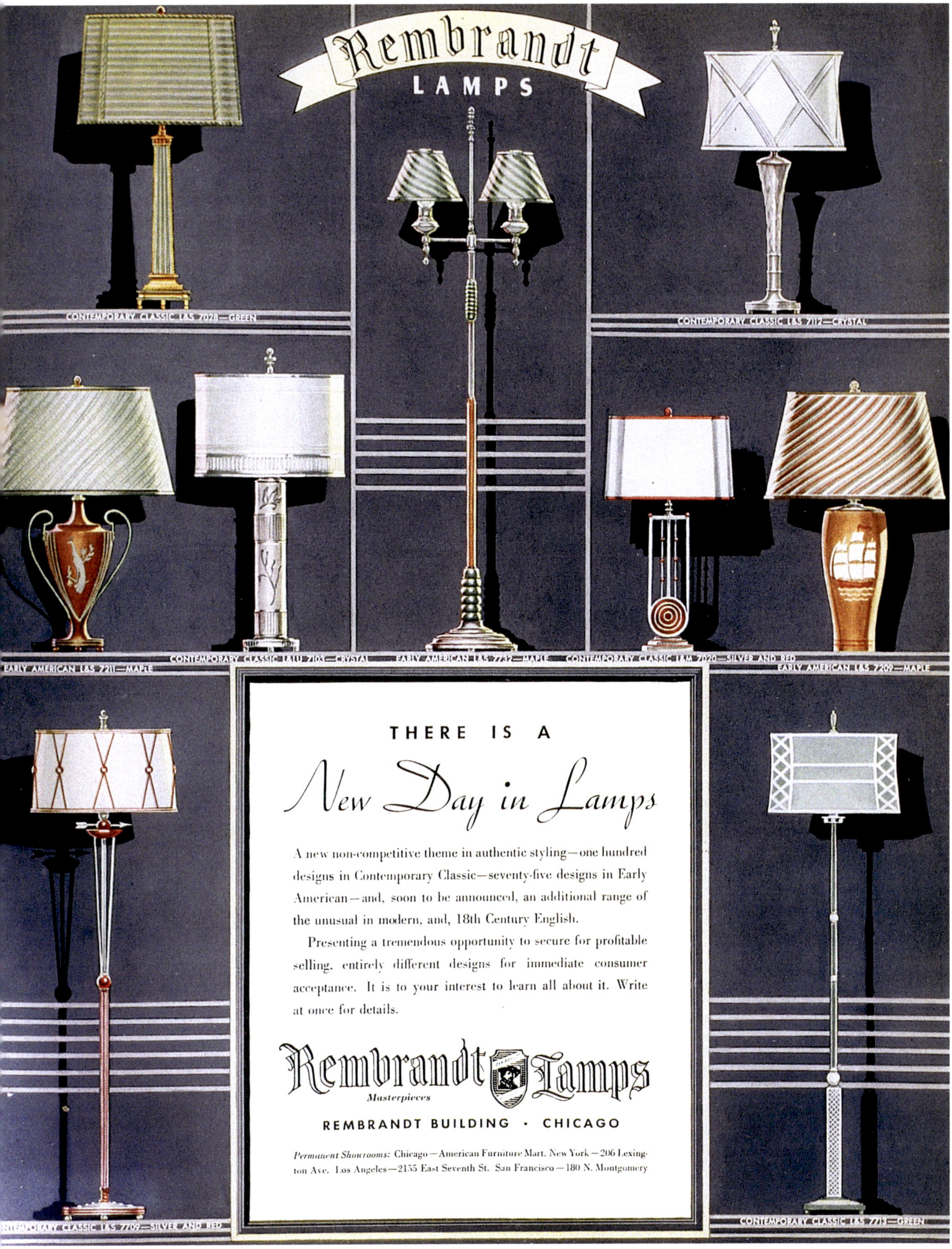

Rembrandt Lamps, 1935

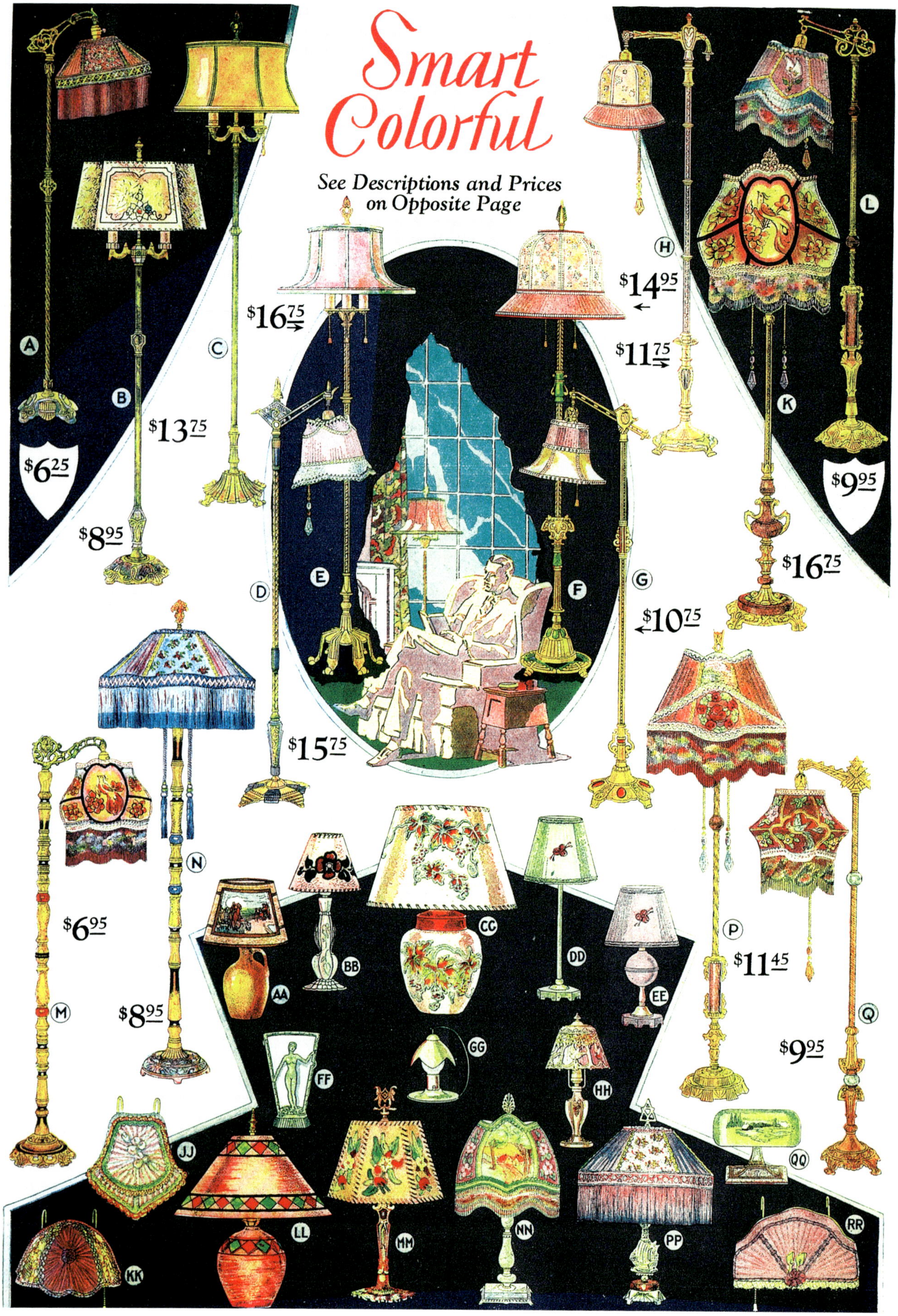
Smart
Colorful
See Descriptions and Prices
on Opposite Page
A
$6.25
B
$8.95
C
$13.75
$16.75
D
E
$15.75
F
G
H
$14.95
$11.75
$10.75
K
L
$9.95
$16.75
M
$6.95
N
$8.95
P
$11.45
Q
$9.95
AA
BB
CC
DD
EE
FF
GG
HH
JJ
KK
LL
MM
NN
PP
QQ
RR

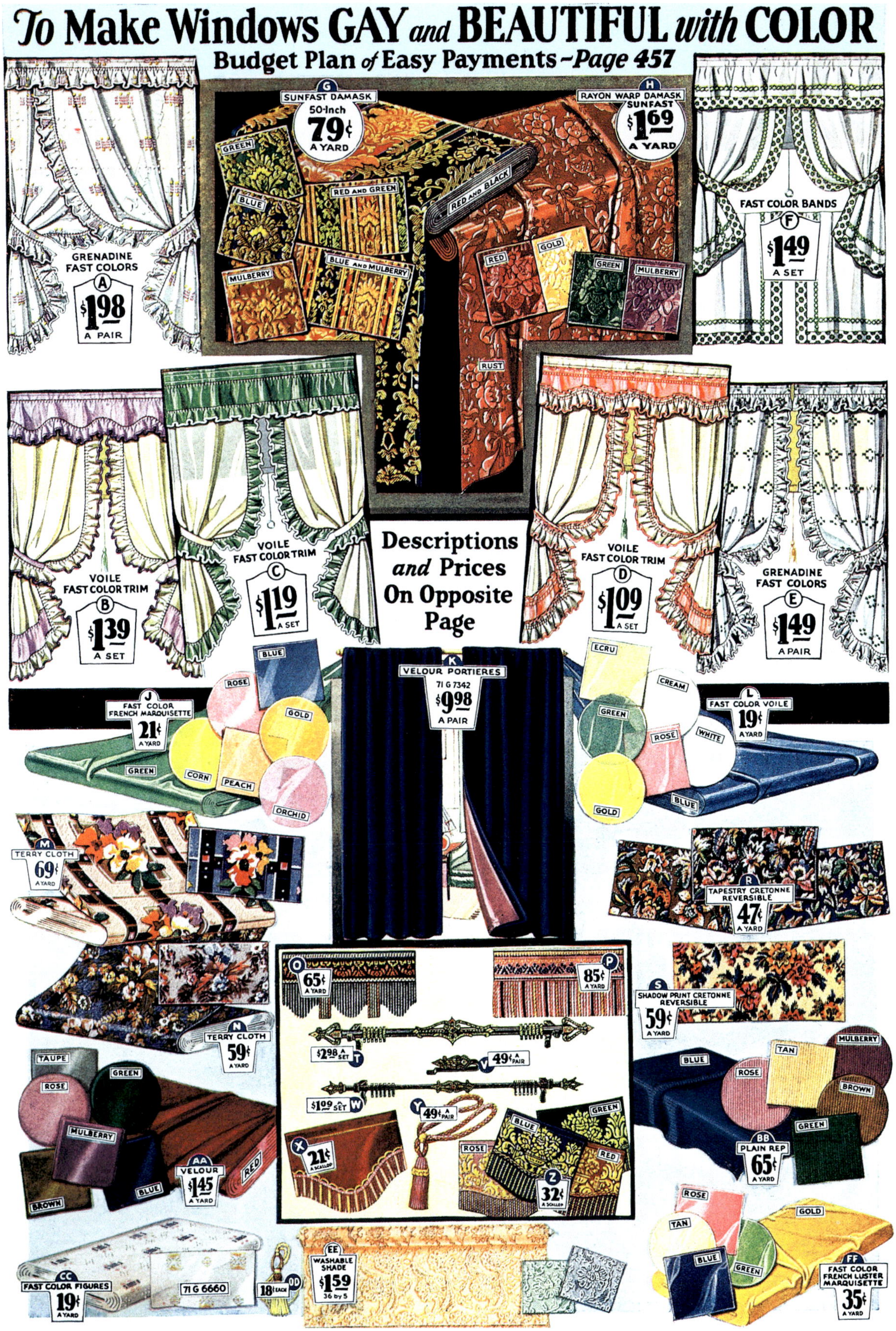
To Make Windows GAY and BEAUTIFUL with COLOR
Budget Plan of Easy Payments–Page 457
G SUNFAST DAMASK 50-Inch 79¢ A YARD
GREEN
BLUE
MULBERRY
RED AND GREEN
BLUE AND MULBERRY
RED AND BLACK
H RAYON WARP DAMASK SUNFAST $1.69 A YARD
RED
GOLD
GREEN
MULBERRY
RUST
GRENADINE FAST COLORS A $1.98 A PAIR
FAST COLOR BANDS F $1.49 A SET
VOILE FAST COLOR TRIM B $1.39 A SET
VOILE FAST COLOR TRIM C $1.19 A SET
Descriptions and Prices On Opposite Page
VOILE FAST COLOR TRIM D $1.09 A SET
GRENADINE FAST COLORS E $1.49 A PAIR
J FAST COLOR FRENCH MARQUISETTE 21¢ A YARD
ROSE
BLUE
GOLD
GREEN
CORN
PEACH
ORCHID
K VELOUR PORTIERES 71 G 7342 $9.98 A PAIR
ECRU
CREAM
GREEN
ROSE
WHITE
GOLD
BLUE
L FAST COLOR VOILE 19¢ A YARD
M TERRY CLOTH 69¢ A YARD
R TAPESTRY CRETONNE REVERSIBLE 47¢ A YARD
N TERRY CLOTH 59¢ A YARD
O 65¢ A YARD
P 85¢ A YARD
S SHADOW PRINT CRETONNE REVERSIBLE 59¢ A YARD
$2.98 A SET T
V 49¢ A PAIR
$1.09 A SET W
Y 49¢ A PAIR
X 21¢ A SCALLOP
Z 32¢ A SCALLOP
TAUPE
ROSE
GREEN
MULBERRY
BLUE
BROWN
AA VELOUR $1.45 A YARD
RED
BLUE
TAN
ROSE
MULBERRY
BROWN
GREEN
BB PLAIN REP 65¢ A YARD
CC FAST COLOR FIGURES 19¢ A YARD
71 G 6660
18¢ EACH DD
EE WASHABLE SHADE $1.59 36 by 5
ROSE
TAN
BLUE
GREEN
GOLD
FF FAST COLOR FRENCH LUSTER MARQUISETTE 35¢ A YARD

SEE HOW MUCH A FEW CENTS' WORTH OF ELECTRICITY NOW BUYS

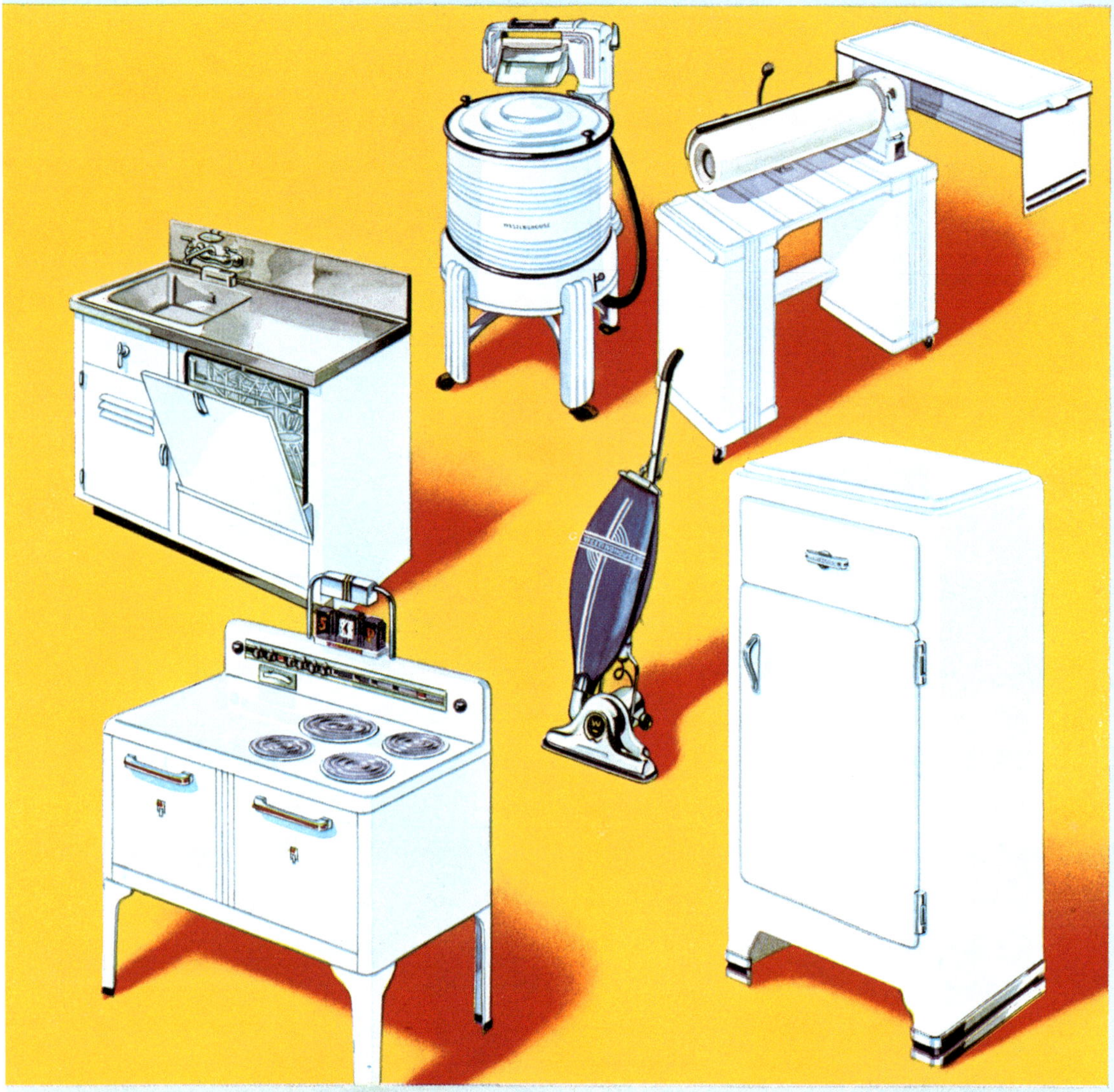

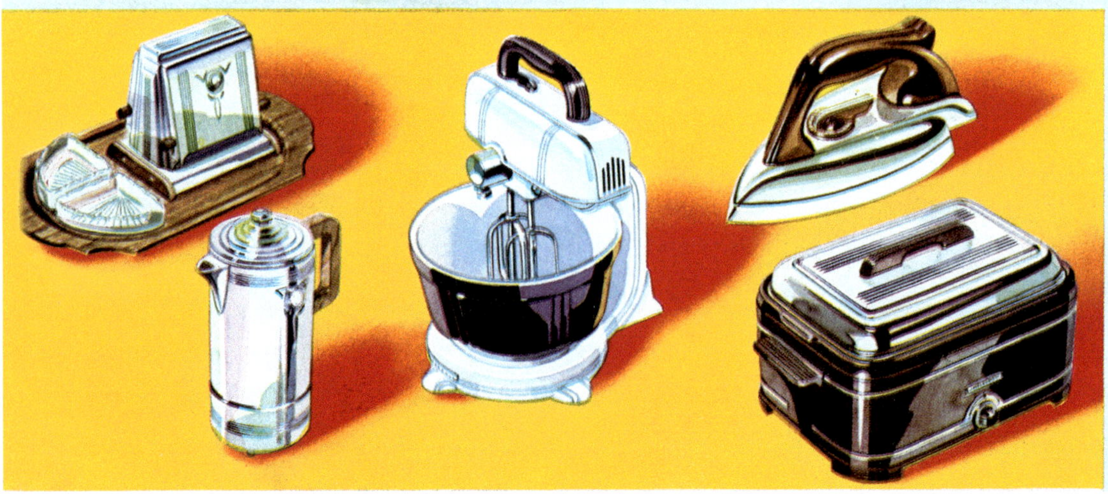

• The Westinghouse name assures world-famous quality, moderate prices, and *low operating cost*. Costs below are national averages. Select *Westinghouse* and *save*.

• ELECTRIC DISH-WASHER. 1c washes all day's dishes . . . cleaner, more safely than by hand. Sliding racks fill from the front; top usable for work space.

• DE LUXE WASHER. Washes 9 pounds of clothing, dry weight, for less than 2c. Natural washing action. Massive wringer with every safety feature.

• DE LUXE ADJUST-O-MATIC IRONER. 6c worth of electricity irons washer-load of clothing. You merely guide the pieces. Thermostatic control maintains any desired heat; two speeds.

• VACUUM CLEANER. Just 1c vacuums a 9′ x 12′ rug thoroughly. Westinghouse combines gentleness with super-cleaning.

• ELECTRIC RANGE. This dinner for six: Roast Canadian bacon, au gratin potatoes and California mince pie, cooks for *less* than 4½c.

• REFRIGERATOR. 4 to 6c a day keeps food in perfect condition and makes frozen desserts. Mechanism hermetically sealed; never needs oiling. Fast-freezing Eject-o-Cube Ice Tray; 5-year Protection Plan.

• TOASTER SET. Less than 1c makes delicious breakfast toast for family of 4.

• PERCOLATOR. 8 cups of flavorful, fragrant coffee, the same every time, for 1c.

• FOOD CRAFTER. Does all those arm-tiring food-preparing jobs; super-power without separate gear stand . . . averages less than 1c per day for electricity.

• DE LUXE ADJUST-O-MATIC ROASTER. Spend all afternoon out. It roasts meat, with potatoes and string beans for eight or ten . . . 3½c per hour.

• STREAMLINE IRON. 3½c an hour. Ultramodern, fast, light, fatigue-proof.

▲► *Westinghouse, 1936*

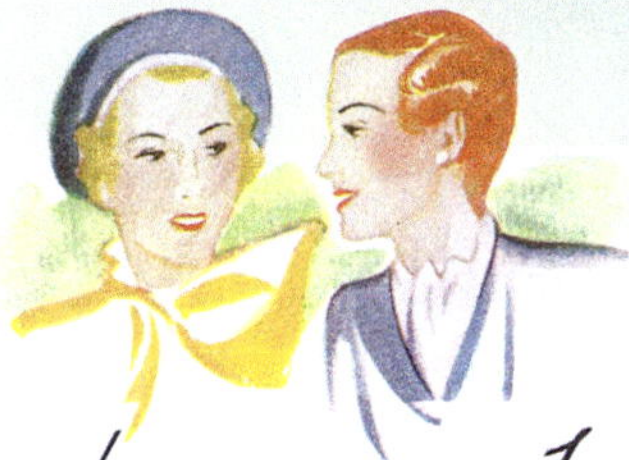

"It's a joy to work in a Kitchen like this"

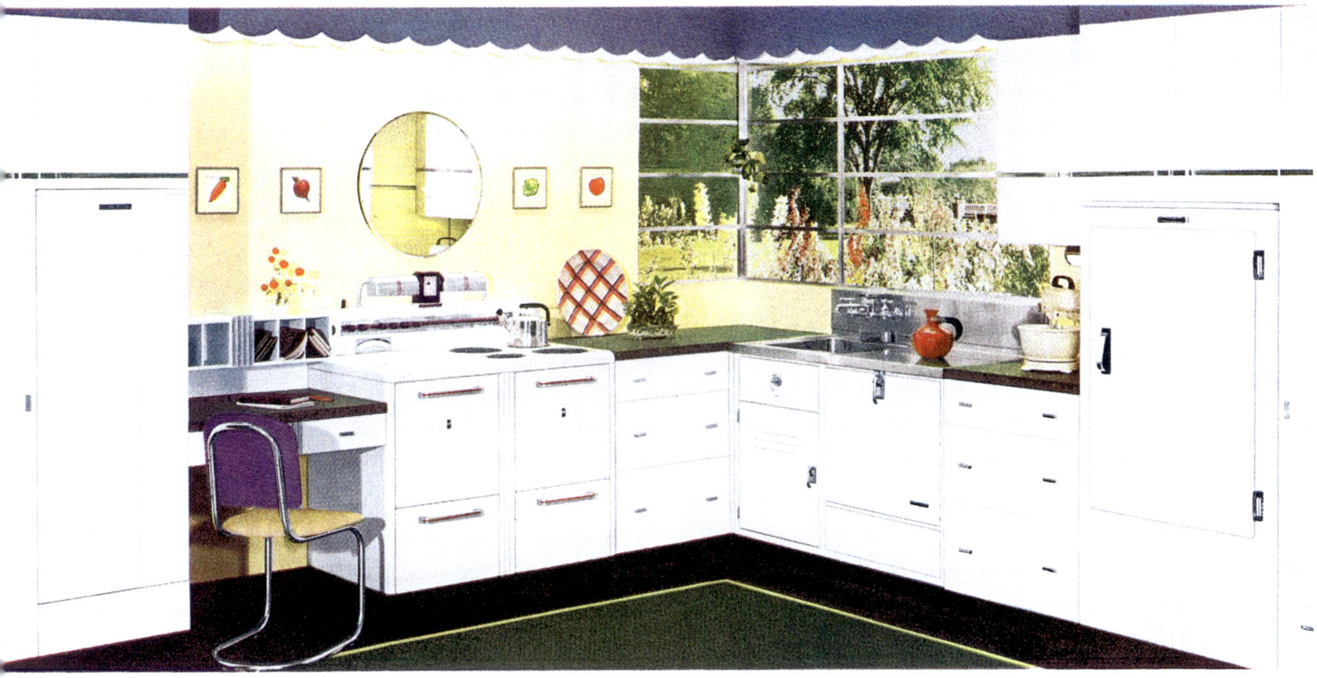

NOW YOU CAN HAVE ONE...EASILY

● Imagine the thrill of having a beautiful, modern kitchen where everything is convenient . . . where electricity cooks meals automatically . . . even prepares frozen salads and desserts . . . then does the dishes!

The Westinghouse Kitchen Planning Department will design such a kitchen for your home, arranging it scientifically to save all extra steps and motions. The layout will include the modern appliances you now have, plus the equipment you will want for a *completely* modernized kitchen. A friendly budgeting plan makes it surprisingly easy to obtain all this beauty and convenience on a simple step-by-step plan.

In celebration of its Golden Jubilee year, Westinghouse brings to America's kitchens the most modern, beautifully styled electric appliances you have ever seen. The line is headed by the Westinghouse Golden Jubilee Refrigerator that sets a new standard of refrigerator value . . . the sensational Golden Jubilee Ranges with their new "Economizer" speed units that cut electric cooking costs 18% . . . and a complete line of great Golden Jubilee appliances for every home need.

On the next page is shown a beautiful 7-color portfolio that tells the whole entrancing story. On its 24 big pages are "before" and "after" pictures of kitchens, showing what *you* can accomplish, economically. Mail coupon with 10c to cover partial cost. Portfolio will be sent you at once.

WESTINGHOUSE 1886 W 1936 GOLDEN JUBILEE

Every house needs

Westinghouse

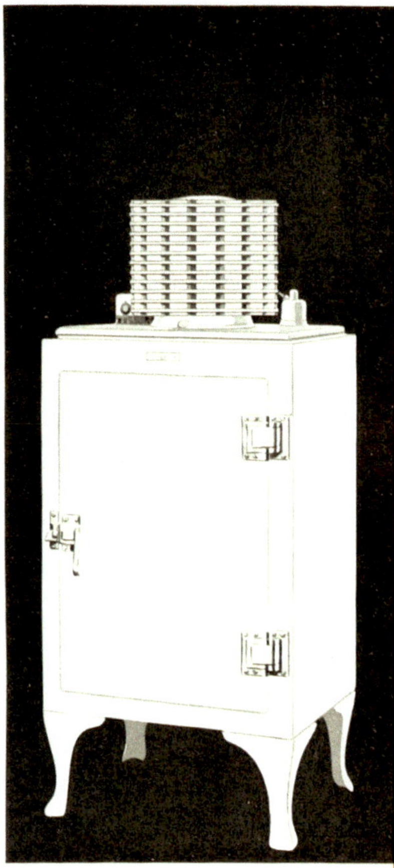

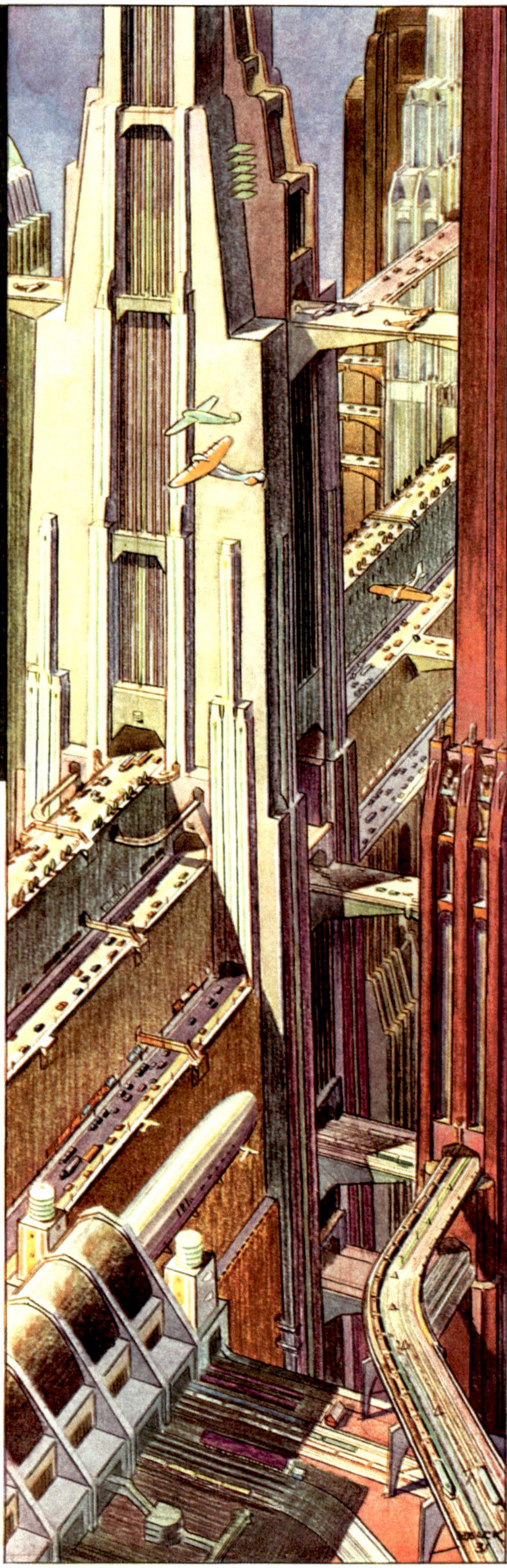

Daringly · distinctively · modern

TRUE to this dynamic age, when beauty is the unconscious outgrowth of the practical, the staunch lines of the General Electric reflect the spirit of modern art, thought, and architecture. Its distinctive design heralds a more advanced type of refrigeration service. In its Monitor Top is a simple modern mechanism, hushed in a blanket of oil—sealed, in a fortress of steel, against time and wear. Because this modern Refrigerator is so well-conceived and so ably constructed—and because it is so basically correct in contour—time blends it well into the setting of any kitchen. Its appearance literally grows on one. Like things we treasure most, it wears well, both mechanically and visually.

General Electric Company, Electric Refrigeration Department, Section B5, Hanna Building, 1400 Euclid Avenue, Cleveland, Ohio

GENERAL ELECTRIC

ALL-STEEL REFRIGERATOR

DOMESTIC, APARTMENT HOUSE, AND COMMERCIAL REFRIGERATORS, ELECTRIC WATER COOLERS

Join us in the General Electric Program, broadcast every Saturday evening, on a nation-wide N. B. C. network

INVEST IN AN ELECTRIC REFRIGERATOR

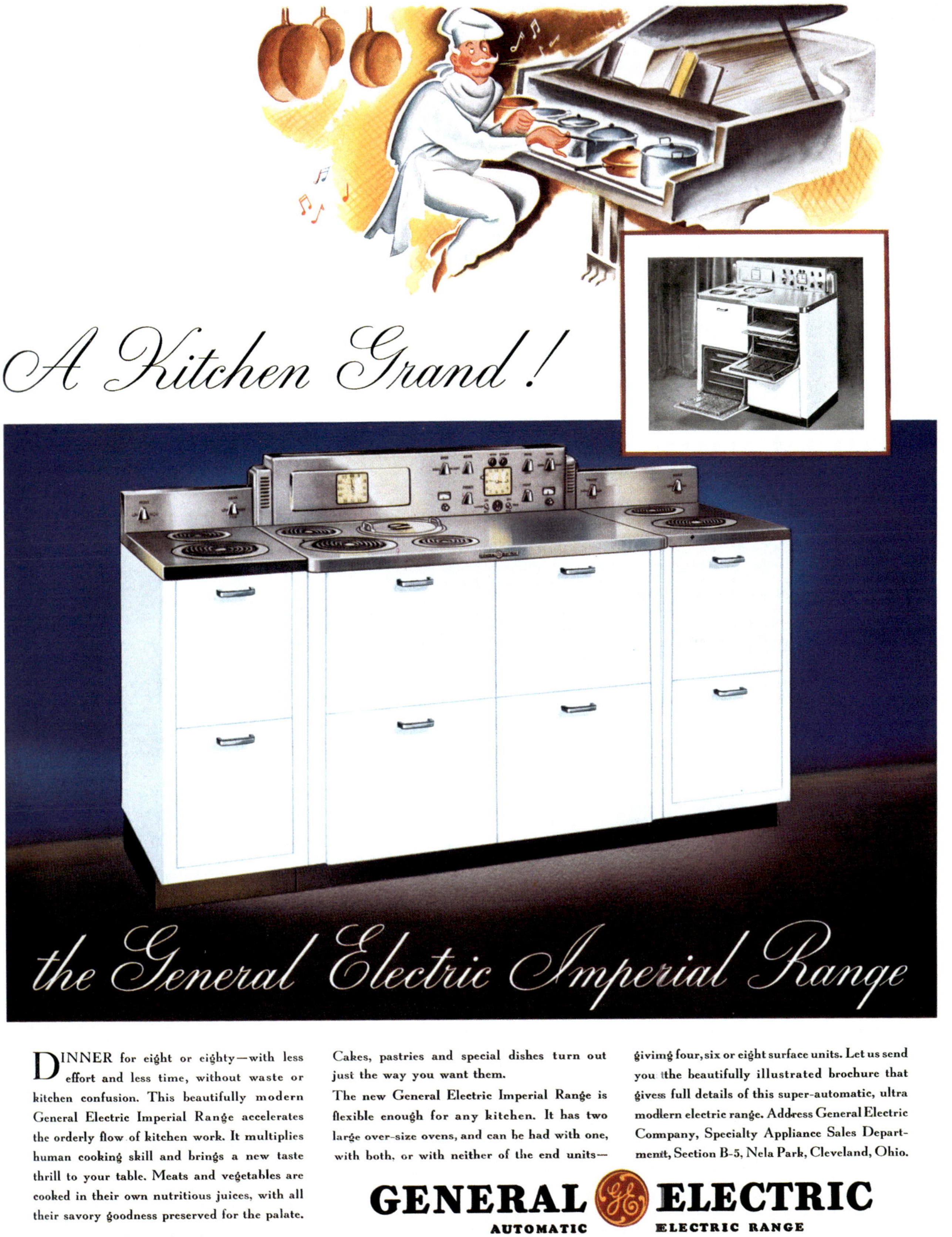

General Electric, 1931 ◄

General Electric, 1935

WASHERS MADE

Wardway Gyrator Quickest

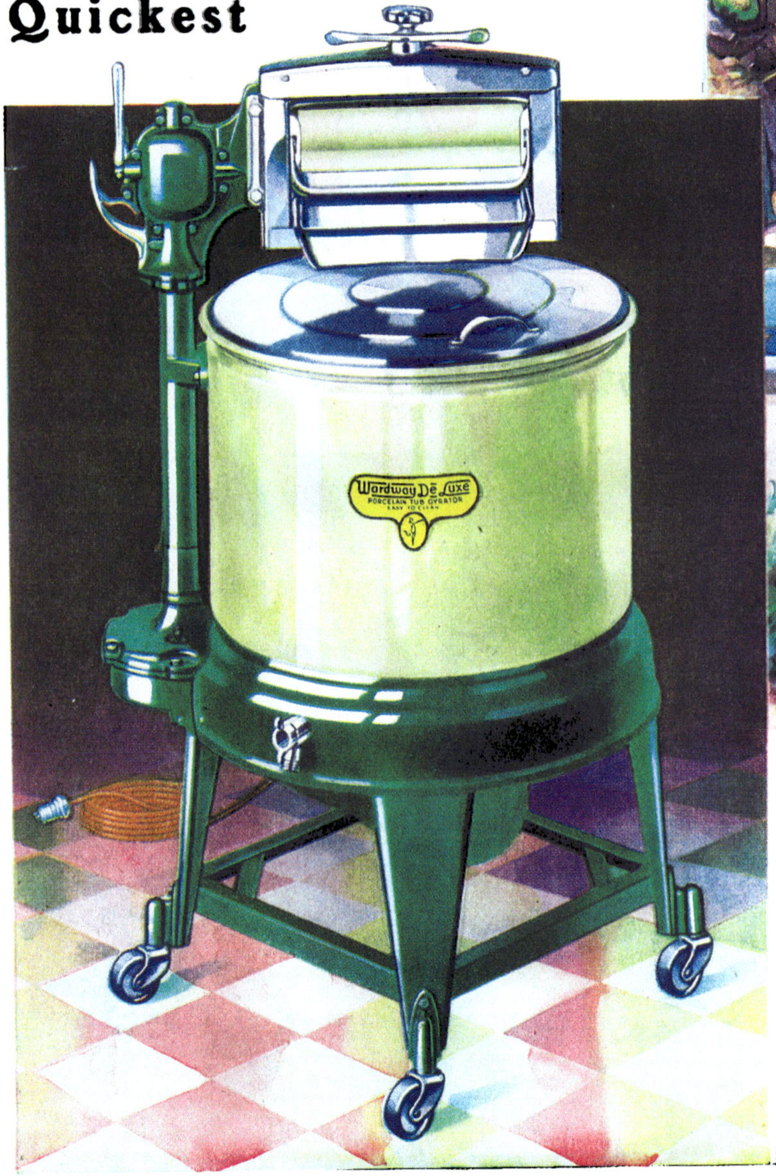

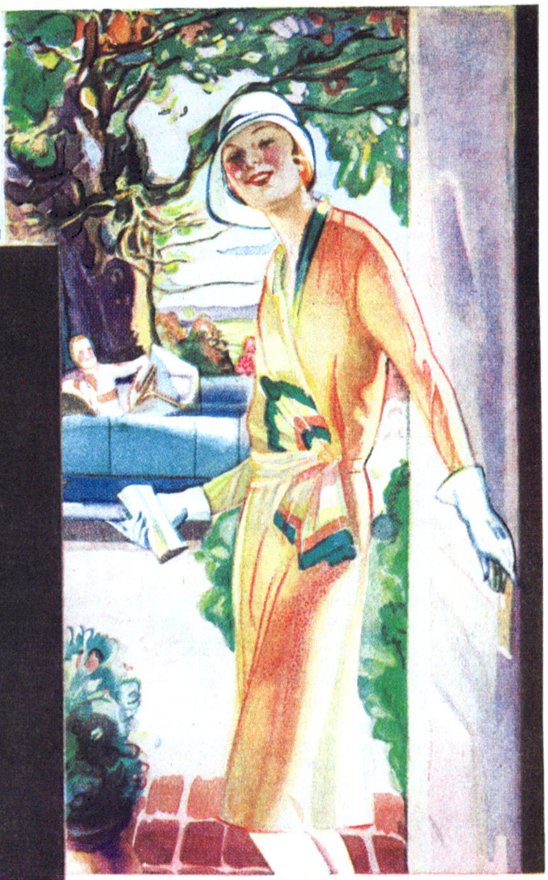

GLISTENING PORCELAIN

Our Beautiful Wardway De Luxe Model

FEATURES WITH $155 WASHERS

⑤ Newest V-Belt Drive

Conserves and puts to work every ounce of motor power. Quiet, vibration free. All working parts fully enclosed for safety and cleanliness.

⑥ Improved 3-Fin Agitator

At Last! A gyrator agitator that eliminates the awkward center post—no longer danger of catching or tearing clothes—no hard-to-clean places in your tub.

Our new 3-fin agitator is of smooth, strong, cast aluminum. Sixty swift reverse turns a minute produce the most thorough gyrator action known. Actual tests prove it washes CLEANER....QUICKER!

⑦ Porcelain—Enamel or Copper Tub

Extra capacity tub; holds 6 to 8 large sheets or their equivalent Your choice of our famous, highly polished Copper Tub or the glistening porcelain enamel tub of our De Luxe Model Gyrator.

⑧ Tub Drain Threaded For Hose

Big, oversize faucet drains tub quickly. Easy to reach—easy to turn on or off. Can be connected by pipe or hose to sink or drain. Splash-proof cover—machine is water-tight.

⑨ Strong Silent Motor

One of the finest washing machine motors obtainable—strong, silent—dependable for years of service. Full ¼ H.P.—can operate full washer and wringer at same time. Completely enclosed by splash-proof housing and easy to reach.

⑩ Adjustable Swivel Casters

Caster adjusts to floor unevenness—machine always stands level, assuring proper motor performance. Rolls lightly—stands securely.

Gyrator takes floor space 25 in. sq. Ideal working height, 34 inches to top of tub.

Improved 3-Fin Agitator

Read Feature ⑥

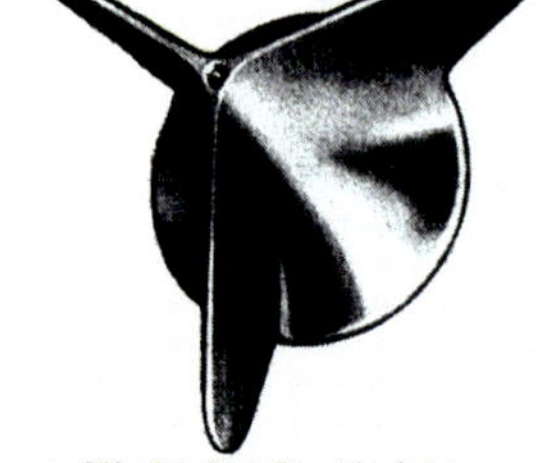

We Do Not Pay Freight

You, Too, Can Have Leisurely Mondays

"My large washing which formerly took up my entire morning is now done in TWO HOURS. It is a pleasure instead of a drudgery to do my own laundry work with a Wardway Gyrator," writes Mrs. V. A. Baty from Adrian, Texas.

$84.95 Cash Price

Luxury Washer at Ordinary Price

A gleaming porcelain enamel washer, so easy to clean, so lastingly beautiful ....the kind thousands have dreamed of as an unattainable luxury.... NOW at a price practical for EVERY home. The superb construction of our De Luxe model will be heartily approved by the "men folks"....for mechanically **it is similar to our famous Copper Tub Wardway.** Repeated scientific experiments, rigidly impartial, have PROVED its washing efficiency. Read about the conclusive State College Test (described on the opposite page) that establishes the superiority of the Wardway Gyrator over 9 nationally famous washers, $20 to $95 higher in price.

BEAUTIFUL! Sparkling Porcelain Easy to Clean as a China Dish

Inside and out, shining surfaces of cafe au lait enamel with jade green porcelain frame. Satin smooth.. .beautiful....practical, for porcelain enamel eliminates the last hateful drudgery of washday. A damp cloth....only a little effort NOW keep your washer immaculate, **spotless as a china dish.**

And now about DURABILITY! This heavy armor of porcelain enamel is fused right onto the tough, heavy Armco Ingot iron tub. Chip-proof with just ordinary carefulness, resistant to quick heat and cold....practical and lasting. Sturdy, braced steel frame including wringer shaft, motor and gear housings are lacquered a matching green with fittings of bright nickel.

Only $5 Down . . . $8 a Month

Keep It for 30 Days—Give It Every Test!

We want you to try this Washer yourself, for 30 days, in your own home. Let your neighbors try it, too ...give it every possible test.. .compare it point by point with other washers regardless of price. **Be your own demonstrator!**

One $5 payment brings it to your home. If at the end of a month you are not thoroughly satisfied....if you are not convinced that you actually save $25 to $80, write us for shipping instructions. We will gladly return all the money you have paid.

Ward's 10-Year Guarantee Protects You

"The Wardway Gyrator is so strongly built and mechanically correct that we can give you a SPECIAL GUARANTEE for ten years of ordinary family use against all defects in material or workmanship.

This guarantee is based on PERFORMANCE—running loaded for the equivalent of 20 years of weekly washings—torn down—inspected—it had barely begun to show wear.

Its Fine Mechanical Details Are Described at Left

All Wardway Gyrators have the quality features described at left. In addition to these our De Luxe Model has still further refinements:

The All Steel Lovell Wringer is **heavily nickel-plated**; drainboard is **cadmium plated**; RUST-PROOF throughout. Extra Capacity Tub of **heat staining seamless porcelain enamel**; 14¾ inches deep, 21¾ inches in diameter. Capacity 6 to 8 large sheets or their equivalent.

For easy payments use Order Blank in back of Catalogue. To include other articles in your Easy Payment Order, read Budget Plan of Easy Payments on Page 457. See Page 551 for ELECTRIC IRONER to attach to this De Luxe Gyrator.

Ship. wt. 230 lbs. **We Do Not Pay Freight. Shipped promptly from our stock in Oklahoma City, Okla.** Estimated Total Freight Charges: For 150 miles $1.82; 300 miles $2.88; 500 miles $3.75.

186 G 3086—Cash Price: Full amount with order..........**$84.95**
Easy Payment Price: Only $5 with order and $8 a month.......**$93.45**

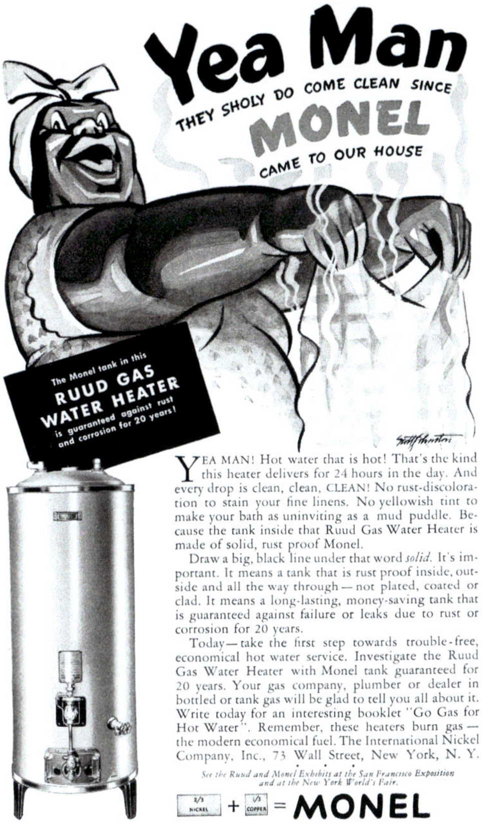

Monel, 1939

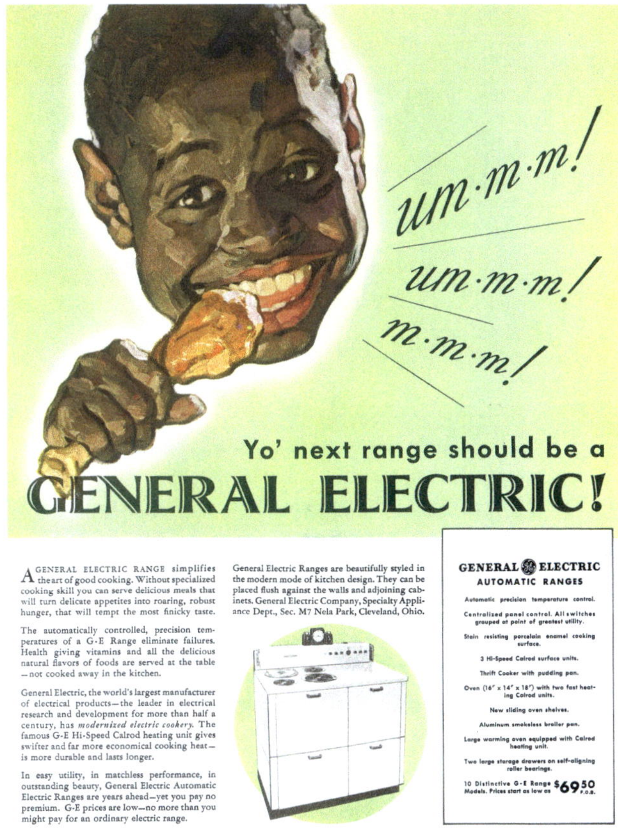

General Electric. 1935

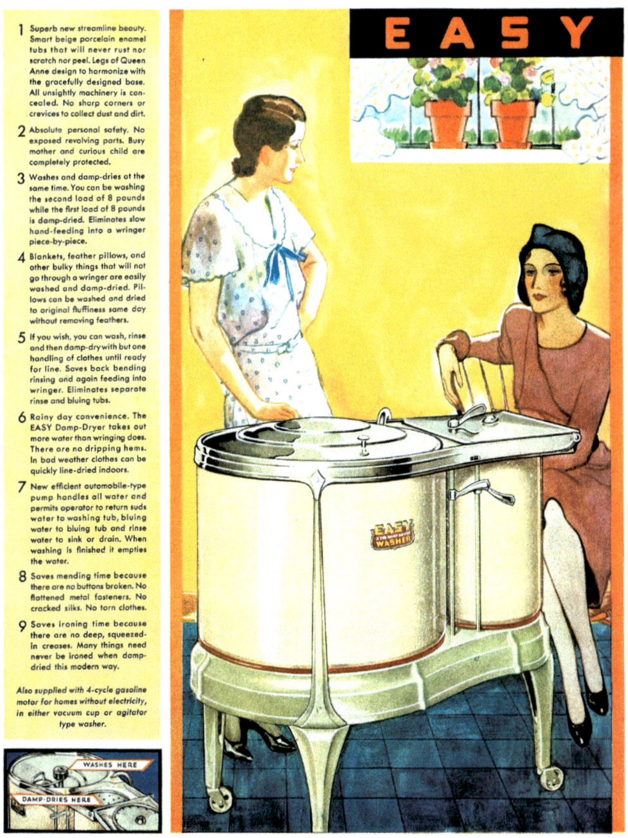

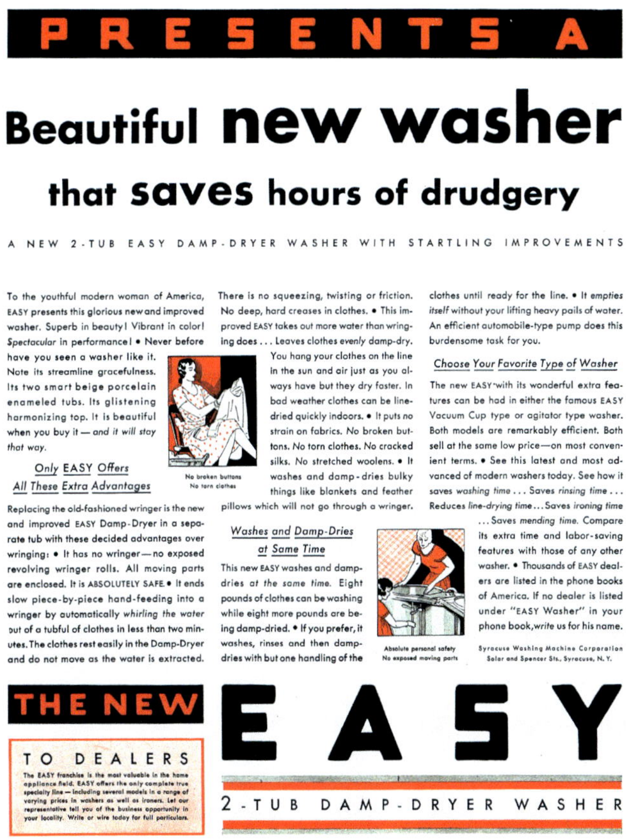

Wardway Gyrator Washer, 1931 ◄ Easy Washer, 1931

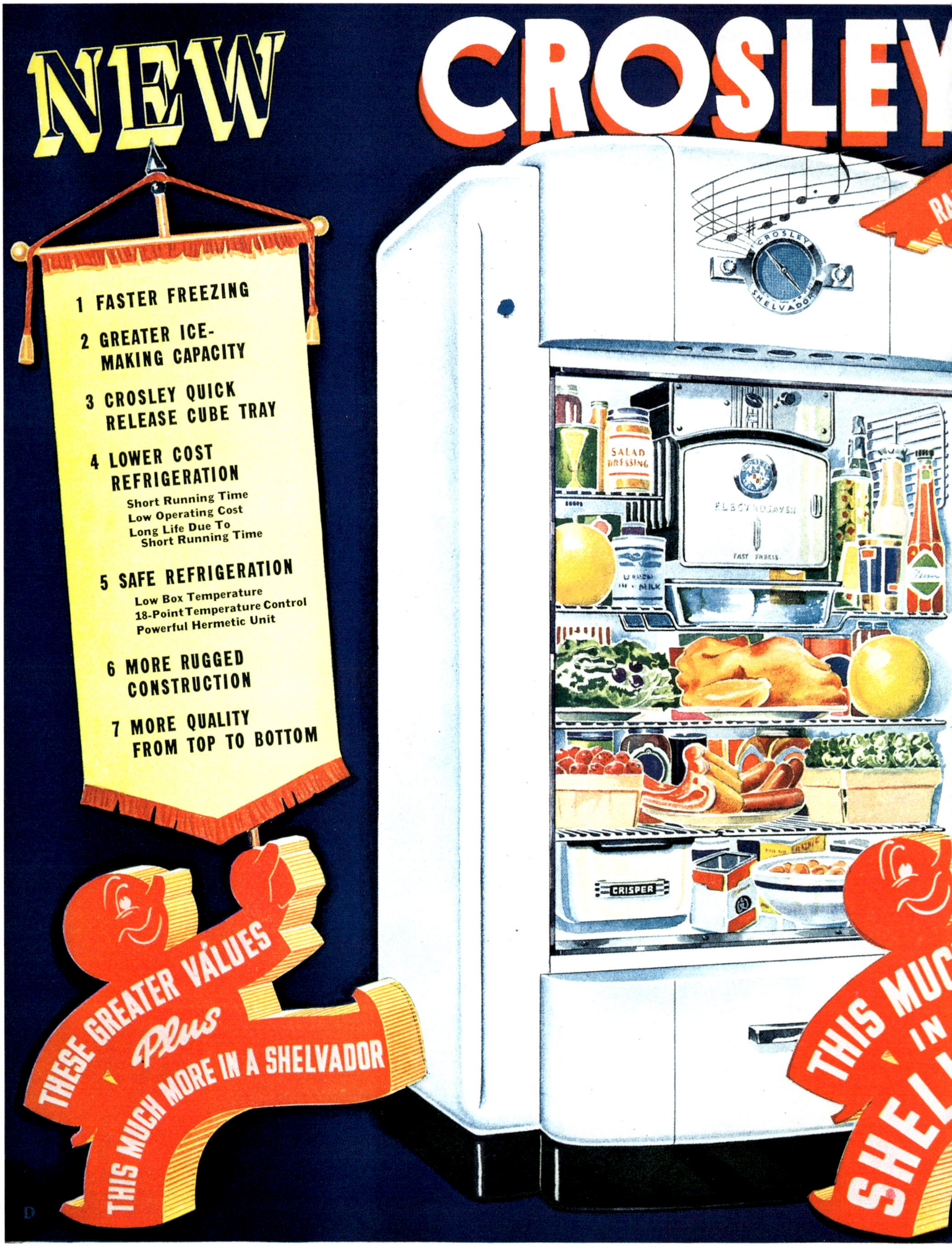

Crosley Shelvador, 1938

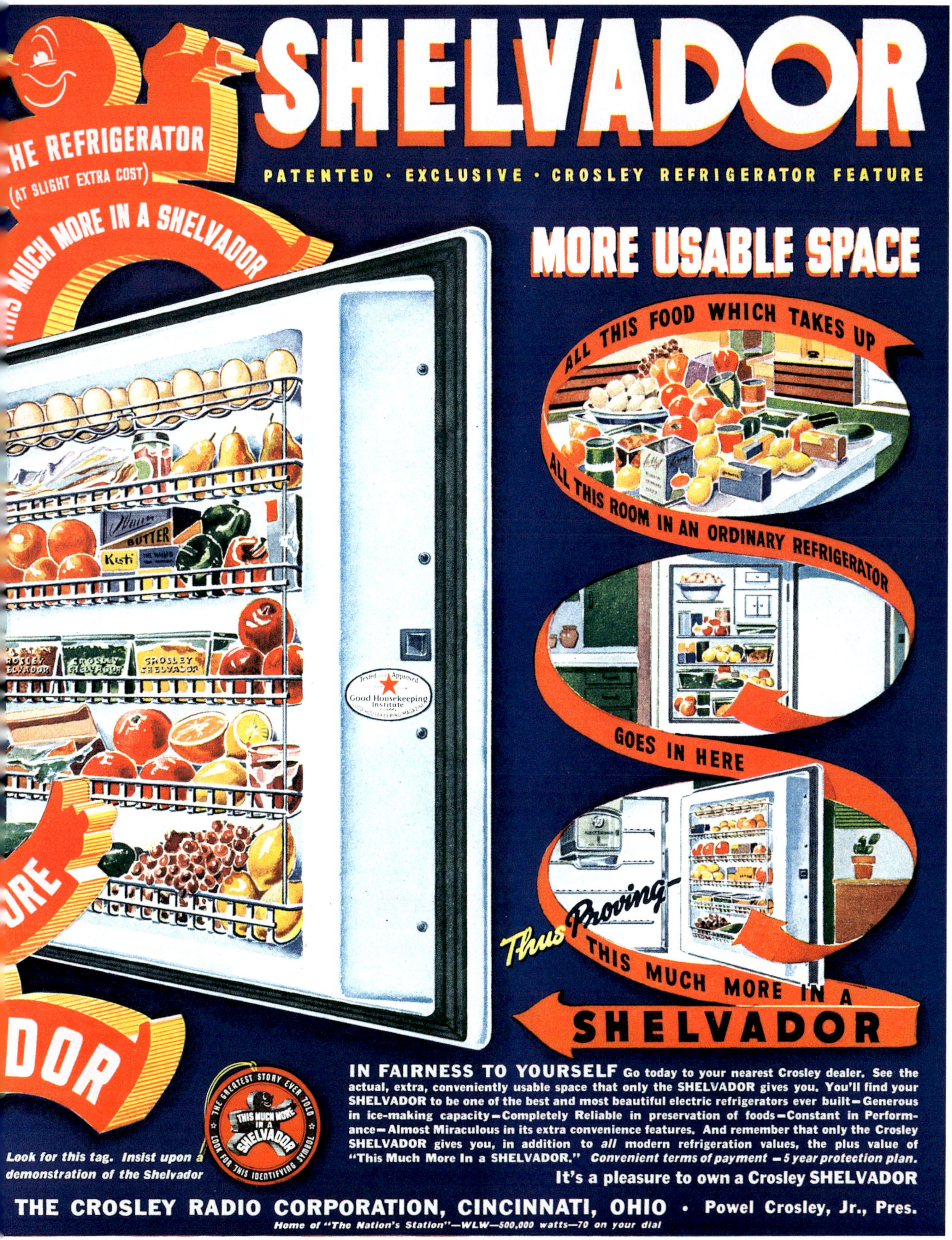
SHELVADOR
PATENTED · EXCLUSIVE · CROSLEY REFRIGERATOR FEATURE
HE REFRIGERATOR
(AT SLIGHT EXTRA COST)
MUCH MORE IN A SHELVADOR
MORE USABLE SPACE
ALL THIS FOOD WHICH TAKES UP
ALL THIS ROOM IN AN ORDINARY REFRIGERATOR
GOES IN HERE
Thus Proving—
THIS MUCH MORE IN A
SHELVADOR
Tested and Approved Good Housekeeping Institute
BUTTER
THE GREATEST STORY EVER TOLD
THIS MUCH MORE IN A SHELVADOR
LOOK FOR THIS IDENTIFYING SYMBOL
Look for this tag. Insist upon a demonstration of the Shelvador
IN FAIRNESS TO YOURSELF Go today to your nearest Crosley dealer. See the actual, extra, conveniently usable space that only the SHELVADOR gives you. You'll find your SHELVADOR to be one of the best and most beautiful electric refrigerators ever built—Generous in ice-making capacity—Completely Reliable in preservation of foods—Constant in Performance—Almost Miraculous in its extra convenience features. And remember that only the Crosley SHELVADOR gives you, in addition to all modern refrigeration values, the plus value of "This Much More In a SHELVADOR." Convenient terms of payment —5 year protection plan.
It's a pleasure to own a Crosley SHELVADOR
THE CROSLEY RADIO CORPORATION, CINCINNATI, OHIO · Powel Crosley, Jr., Pres.
Home of "The Nation's Station"—WLW—500,000 watts—70 on your dial

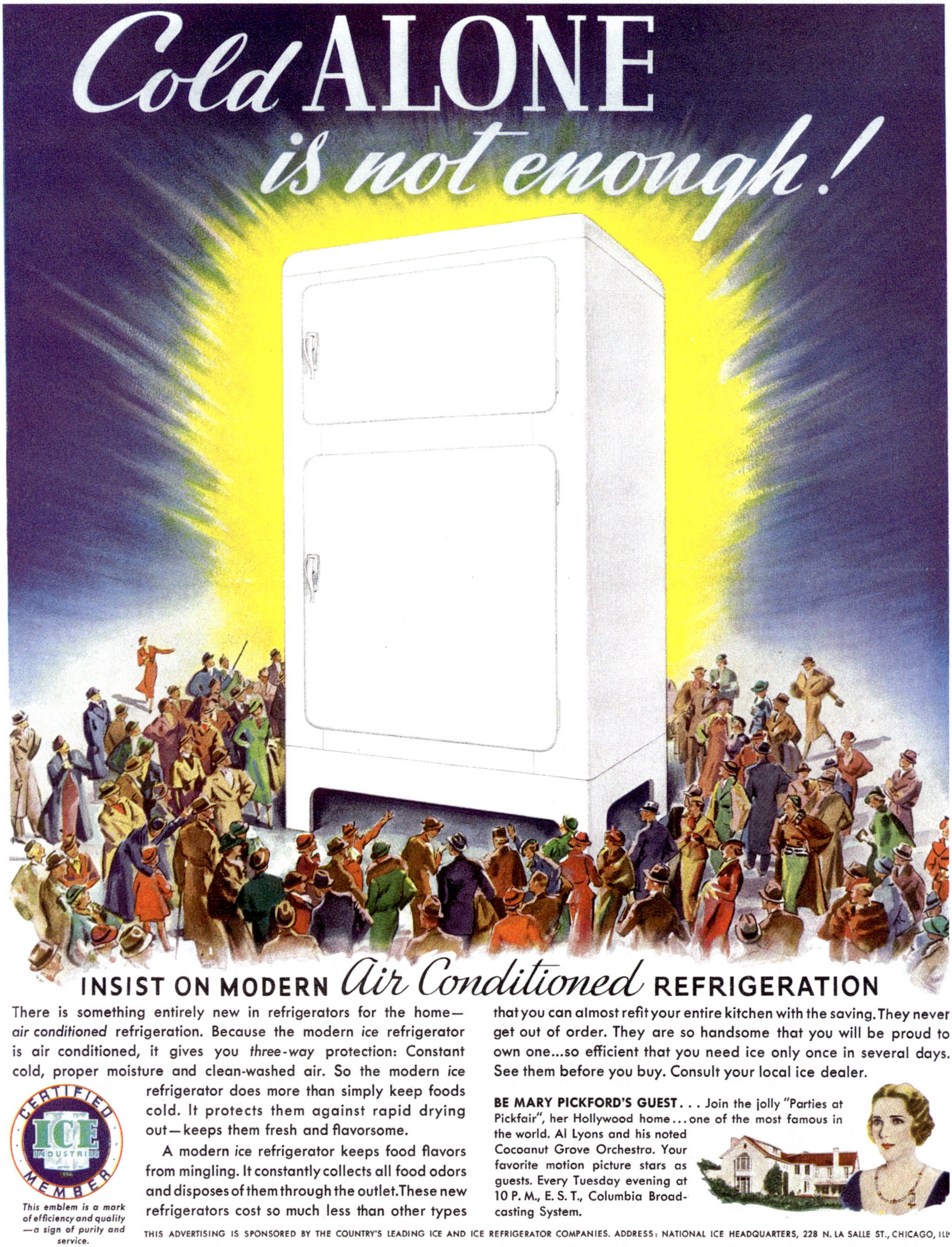

Certified ICE Member, 1936

► *Westinghouse, 1938*

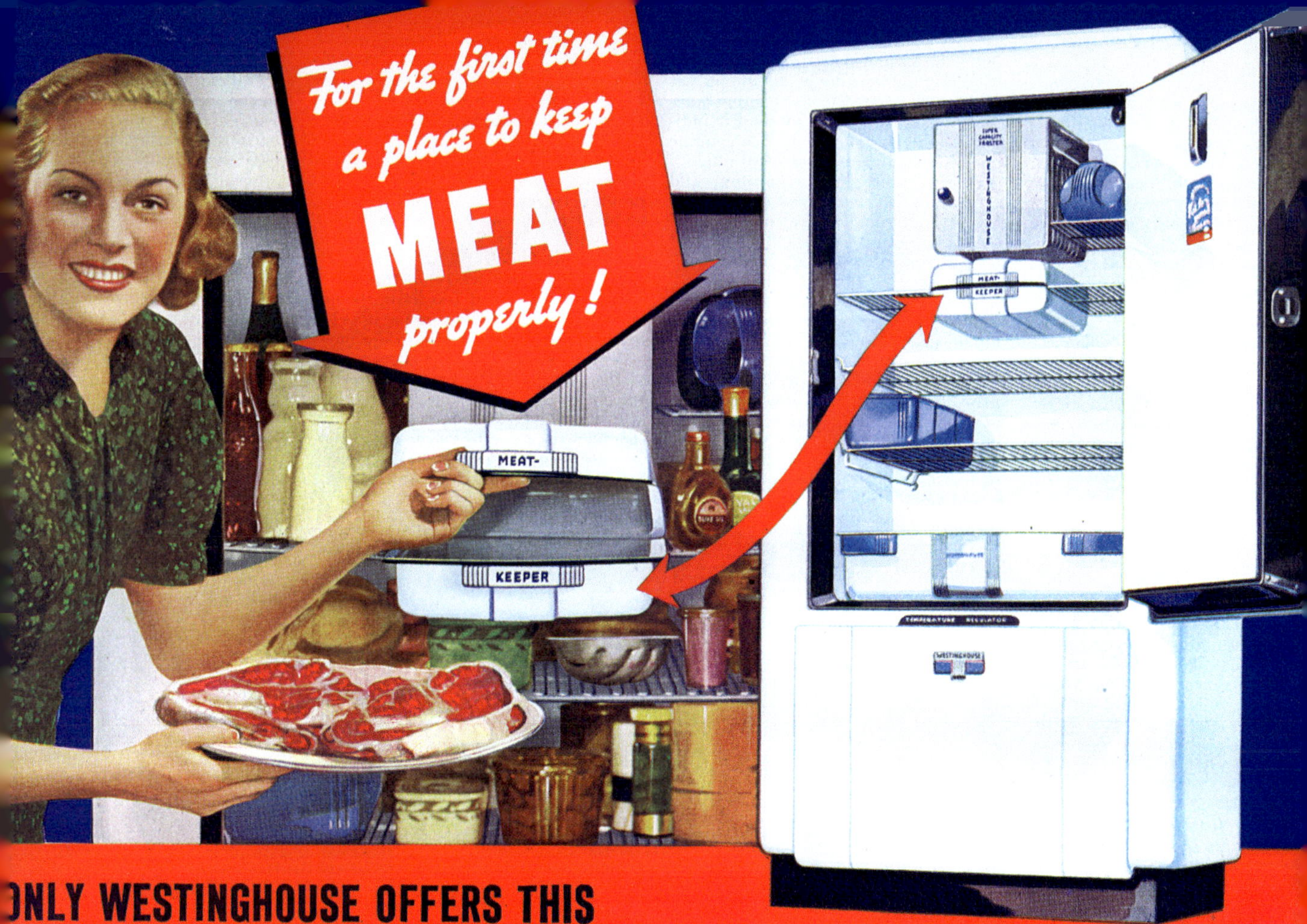

ONLY WESTINGHOUSE OFFERS THIS

Kitchen-proved MEAT-KEEPER

Greatest improvement in years! A big, covered, ventilated, all-porcelain meat compartment that keeps your steaks, chops, and roasts *fresher* for days *longer*. It conserves needed moisture at Safety Zone temperature. Gives the new 1938 Westinghouse Kitchen-proved Refrigerator the *most complete* food storage facilities ever developed. Together with the new glass-top Humidrawer for vegetables, the new Super-capacity Froster, Zoned Temperature Regulator, and improved Economizer Mechanism it makes possible Kitchen-proved Savings in *food, time,* and *money* like these:

1 *Saves* FOOD

Big food savings plus the low prices of the 1938 Westinghouse make it your budget's best friend. $1.07 on leftovers, $1.03 on quantity buying . . . these weekly average savings in 102 Proving Kitchens amount to

$9.10 a month

Kitchen-proved

2 *Saves* TIME

Ice cubes frozen in 56 minutes! That's average fastest time in 102 Westinghouse Proving Kitchens! Frozen desserts in 65 minutes! And a whole week's food shopping in one or two trips to the store.

SHOPPING TRIPS CUT IN HALF

Kitchen-proved

3 *Saves* MONEY

Operating cost amazingly low! Average, 62 cents a week less than previous methods of refrigeration in 102 Proving Kitchens! Only 4/5 of a kilowatt-hour daily average current consumption.

10 HOURS OUT OF 12 IT USES NO CURRENT AT ALL

Kitchen-proved

Get Personal Proof: Your nearest Westinghouse dealer can give you facts and figures on Kitchen-proved Savings in homes like yours. Find his name in your classified telephone directory under "Refrigerators, Electric." Westinghouse Electric & Manufacturing Co., Mansfield, Ohio

Westinghouse *Kitchen-proved* Refrigerator

EVERY HOUSE NEEDS WESTINGHOUSE

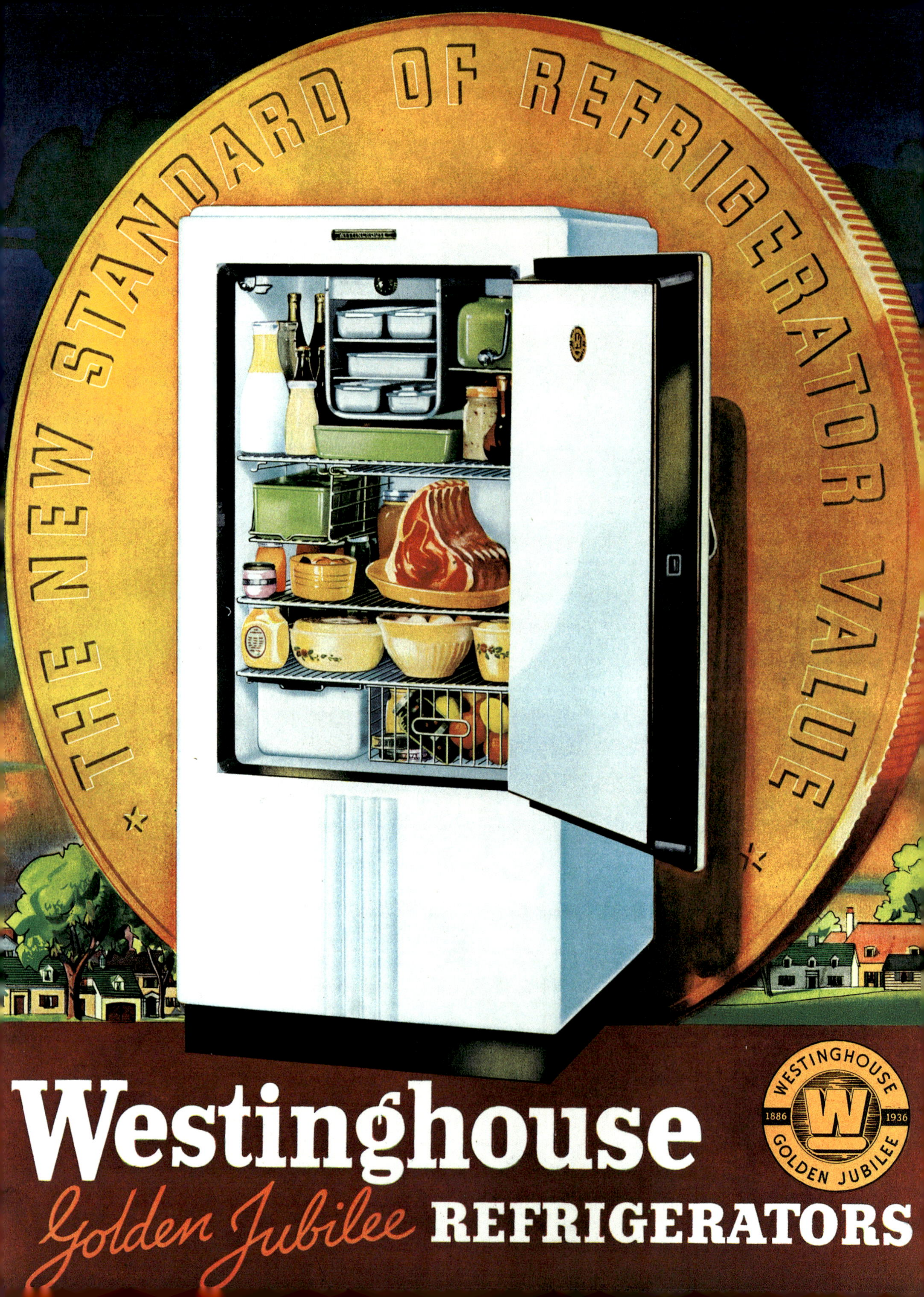
THE NEW STANDARD OF REFRIGERATOR VALUE
Westinghouse
Golden Jubilee REFRIGERATORS
WESTINGHOUSE
1886
W
1936
GOLDEN JUBILEE

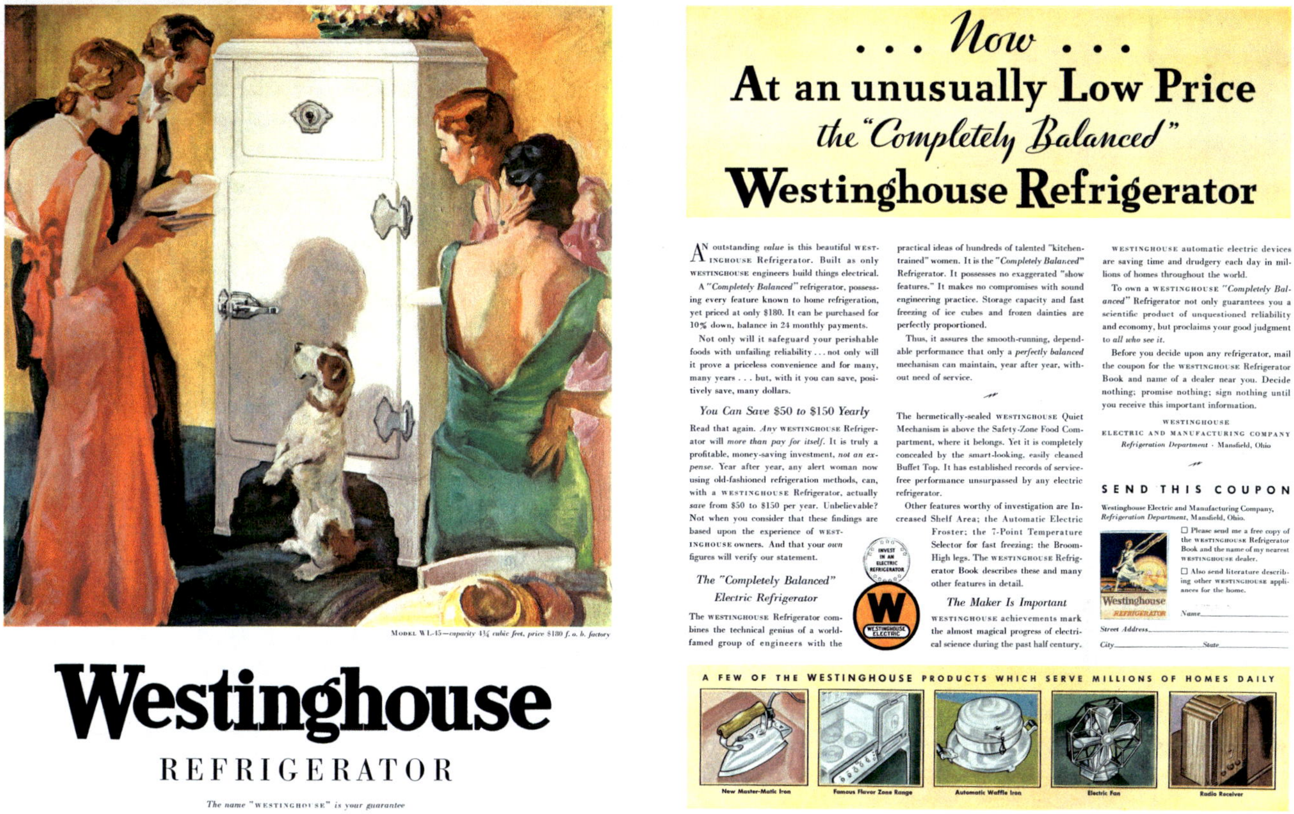

Westinghouse, 1931

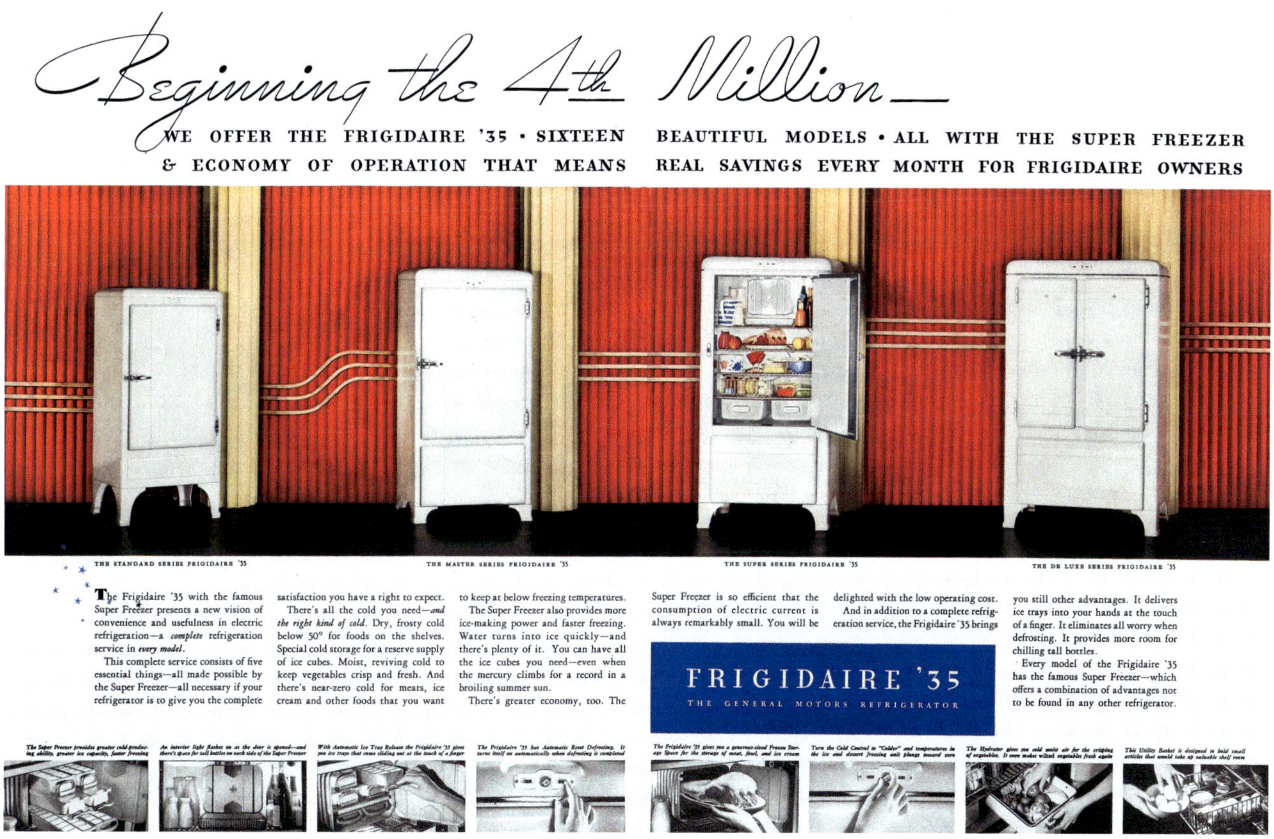

Westinghouse, 1936 ◄ *Frigidaire, 1935*

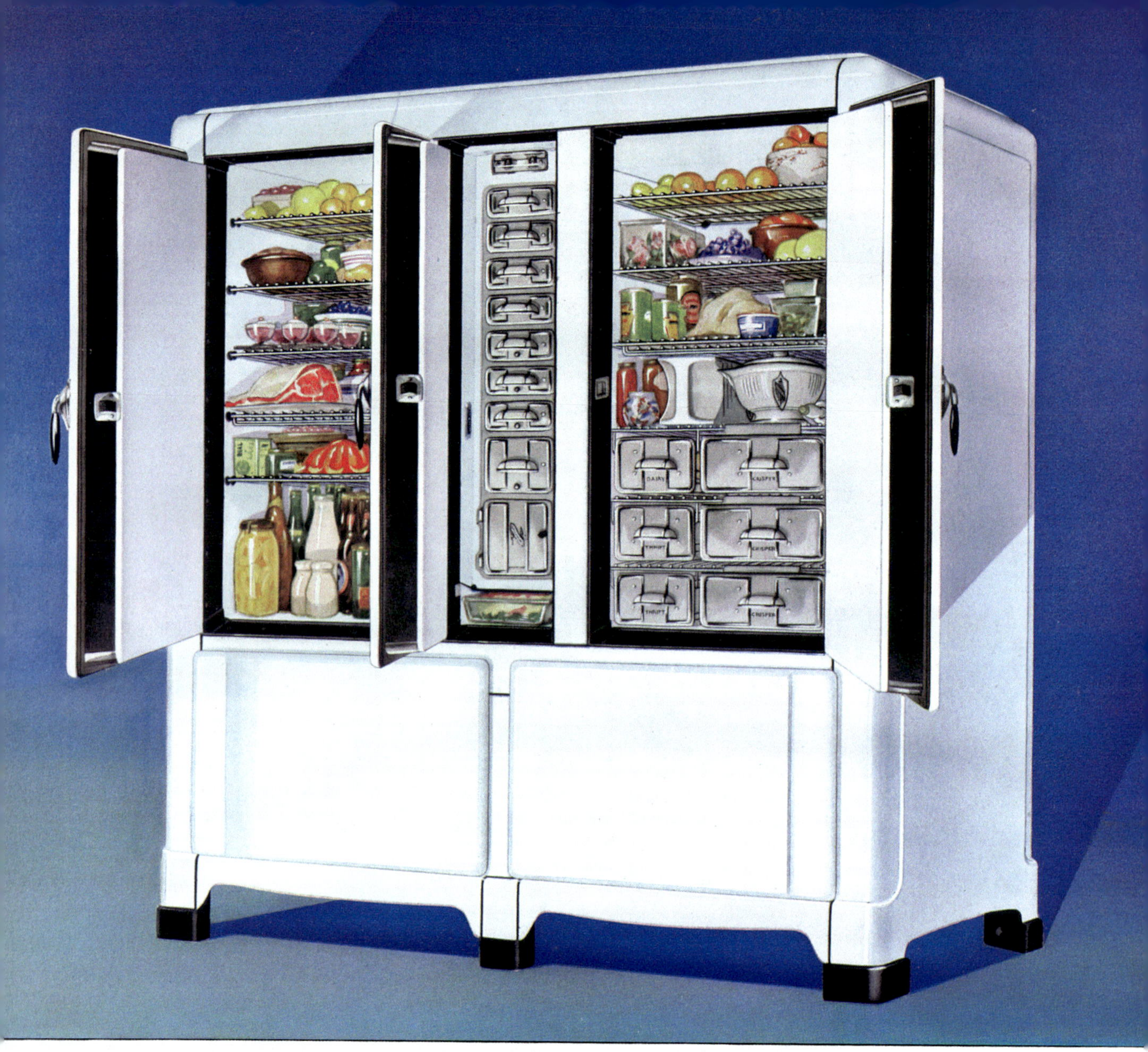

KELVINATOR

..the Finest in Electric Refrigeration

IF you knew as much as we do about the 20th Anniversary Kelvinator, we are sure you would agree with us, heartily. Without boasting—and with no intention of disparaging the other fine electric refrigerators being built to-day, we do believe the new 1934 De Luxe Kelvinator *is* the finest in electric refrigeration.

Of course, we are proud of it! Why shouldn't we be? We know how it is engineered—how it is built—of what fine materials it is made—and how it will perform. We know the tradition behind it. We know the brilliant record our engineers and designers have made as *pioneers* in the industry during the past twenty years—the longest experience in the industry. And finally, we know this is their greatest achievement.

The Kelvinator management extends a cordial invitation to the readers of Fortune in all the corners of the globe—an invitation to visit the nearest dealer and inspect the 20th Anniversary Kelvinators. Wherever Fortune goes, a Kelvinator dealer is very likely to be found. . . . KELVINATOR CORPORATION, *14287 Plymouth Road, Detroit, Michigan. Factories also in London, Ontario, and London, England.* 1914

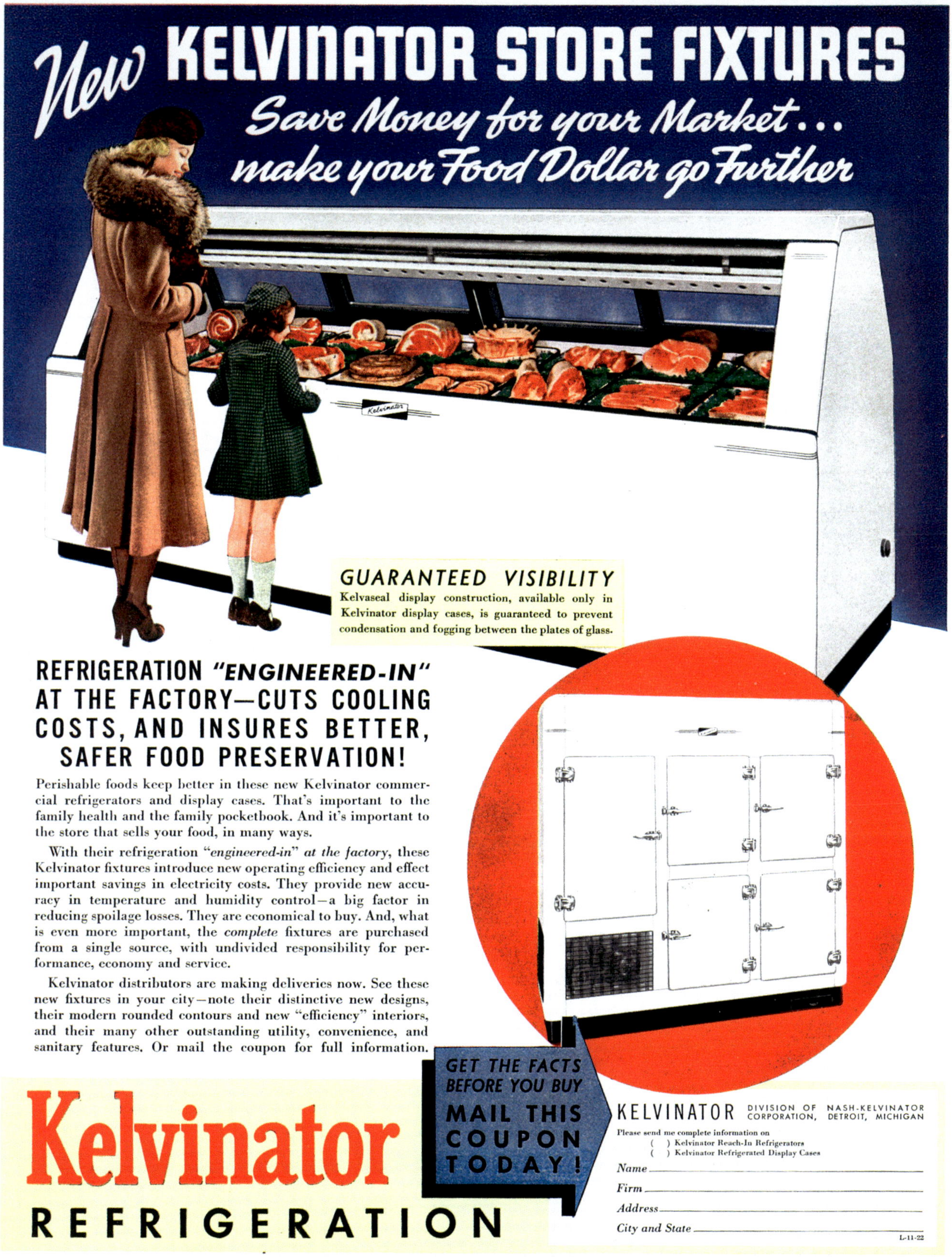

Kelvinator, 1934 ◄

Kelvinator, 1937

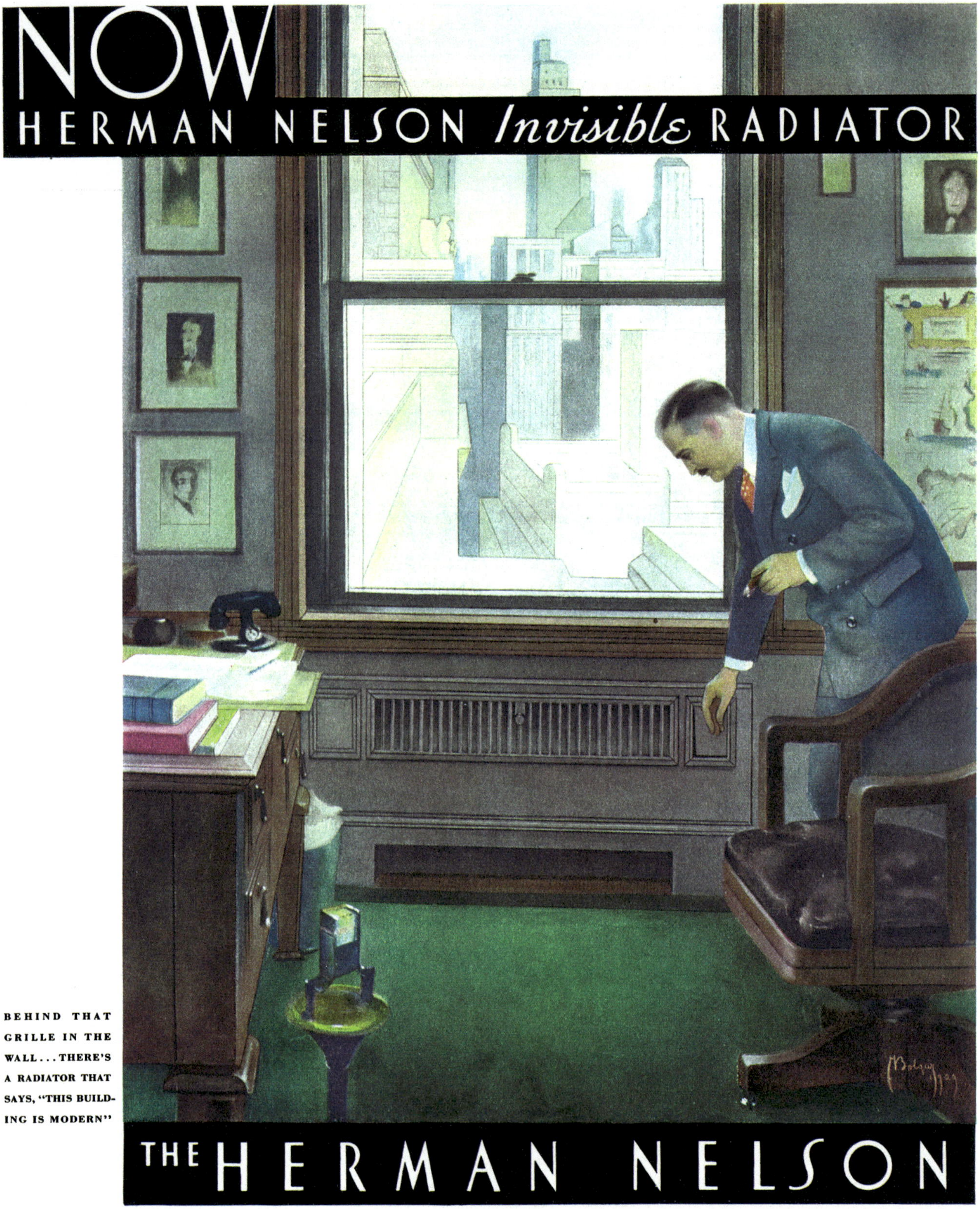

Makers of the *Herman Nelson Invisible Radiator*, for residences, apartments, hotels, offices and monumental structures—the *Univent*, for the ventilation of schools, offices, churches and all buildings having an acute ventilating problem—the *Herman Nelson hiJet Heater*, for economical distribution of heat in factories, mills, garages, warehouses, and smaller buildings.

Herman Nelson, 1930

HEAT WITH GAS!

INSTANT - CLEAN - NO ASHES - NO TROUBLE -

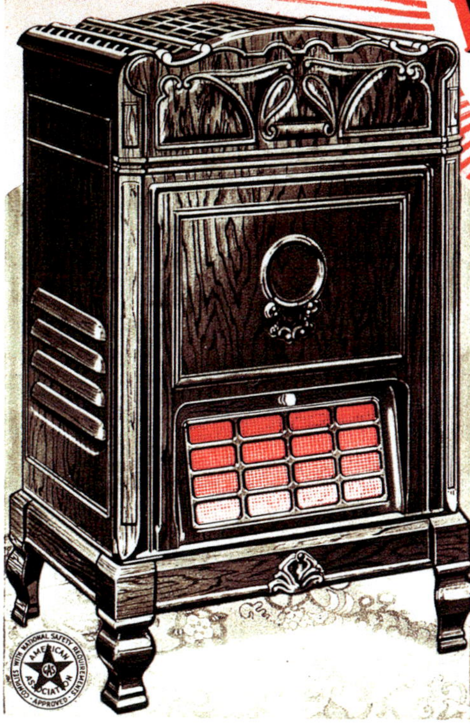

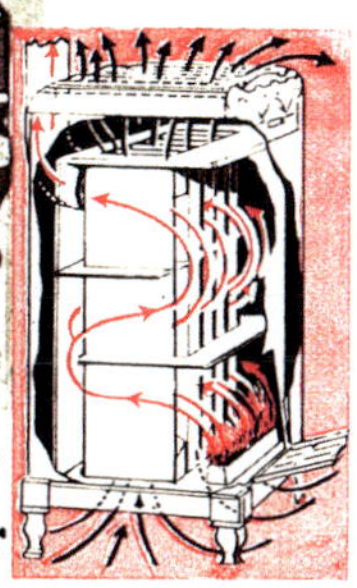

$59.85 CASH PRICE — HAWTHORNE Windsor

Reg. U.S. Pat. Off.

Improved Type Single Burner

Heats 2 or 3 Rooms

ALL the comforts of warm moist circulating air for your home with this beautiful Gas-Fired Circulating Heater. No trouble—no dirt—no ashes—no coal to carry. You simply turn on the gas and light the single extra powerful burner. Special low gas rates for heating purposes in most localities assures you a heat—costing less than 3 cents an hour to operate with natural gas at 50 cents per 1000 cubic feet, or only 8 cents an hour with manufactured gas at $1 per 1000 cubic feet. Tested and approved by American Gas Association Laboratory.

$5 DOWN
BALANCE IN TWELVE EQUAL MONTHLY PAYMENTS

Beautiful Style and Finish—Quality Clear Through

Cabinet charming furniture design, finished with Grained Walnut Porcelain Enamel that won't burn off. You can hardly detect the difference from actual walnut.

Heating Unit all cast iron of highly efficient design. Five cast iron heating chambers, each having eight vertical fins. Within the heating unit a single gas burner of exceptional efficiency sends heat from the gas flame into direct contact with ribbed cast iron surfaces. The heat strikes these surfaces three times on the way to the flue. Red arrows in cut-away picture above show course of heat through the unit.

Circulates Warm Moist Air

Air in your home passes through the heating unit in long straight passages as shown by the black arrows in cut-away picture above. This design reduces direct radiation from the sides of the heater to a minimum because rapid circulation is maintained. Adjoining rooms are heated as evenly and as quickly as the room in which the heater is installed. No burned gases ever come in contact with the circulating air—nothing but pure, healthful heat reaches the rooms. Water pan moistens heated air, assuring a healthful heat constantly.

MEASUREMENTS: Overall, 26¾ inches wide, by 22¾ inches deep including cast elbow, by 41 inches high; 4-inch flue, 36 inches from floor to top of collar.

For pipe see Page 669. If you desire to use a stoveboard with the Hawthorne, order the 30 by 38-inch on Page 673.

Specify whether for natural or manufactured gas.

Shipping weight 400 pounds. **Shipped Not Prepaid.**

For easy payments use Order Blank in back of catalogue and send only $5 with your order. To include additional items in your Easy Payment Order, see Budget Plan, Page 457.

168 G 5040—Walnut Porcelain Enameled.
Cash Price: Full amount with order.......... **$59.85**
Easy Payment Price: Only $5 with order and $5.25 a month.......... **$65.85**

Shipped promptly from stock at Kansas City or Oklahoma City. Send your order to house nearer you. Estimated Freight Charges per 100 lbs.: 150 miles 65¢; 300 miles $1.02; 500 miles $1.51.

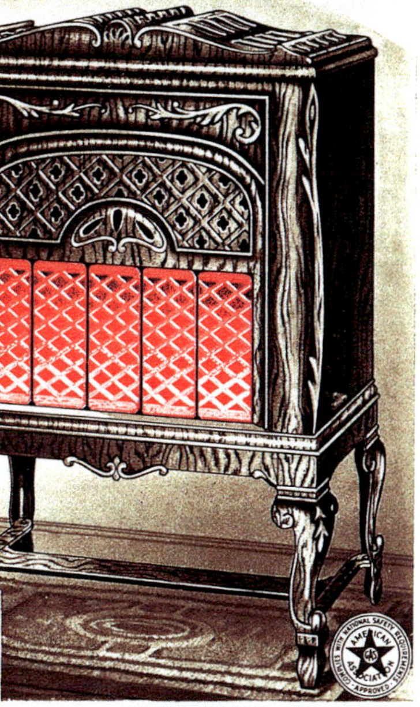

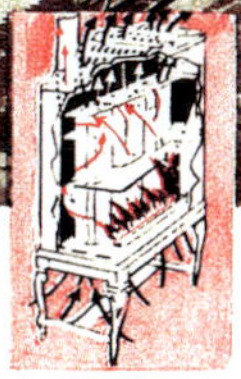

ARGYLE Windsor — $39.85 CASH PRICE

Reg. U.S. Pat. Off.

Heats 1 or 2 Rooms

Cabinet design to equal the finest product of the furniture maker's art—built to resemble a modern, attractive radio cabinet. An entirely new departure in Circulating Gas-Fired Heaters. Five double clay radiants permit you to enjoy the same cheerful glowing warmth of the ordinary Radiant Heater yet brings the advantages of moist air heat constantly circulated. Real, oldtime fireside cheer combined with this modern up-to-date heating method makes the Argyle a very distinctive heater.

$4 DOWN
FOUR DOLLARS A MONTH

Distinctive in Appearance—Quality-Built

Tested and approved by the American Gas Association Laboratory.

Cabinet is finished in walnut porcelain enamel and grained realistically.

Heating Unit is similar to Hawthorne except smaller. Three cast iron heating chambers. See cut-away view above. Red arrows show course of flame—strikes heating chambers three times on way to flue.

Warm Moist Air Circulates to all parts of the room. Passes through heating chambers in long straight passages, as shown by black arrows in cut-away view above. Single burner supplies clean instant heat—flame burns up through clay radiants giving the cheerful effect of an open fireplace. Heat is radiated as well as circulated.

MEASUREMENTS: Overall, 21 inches wide, by 16 inches deep including cast elbow, by 33 inches high; 4-inch flue. For pipe see Page 669. Specify whether for natural or manufactured gas.

Ship. wt. 200 lbs. **Shipped Not Prepaid.**

For easy payments use Order Blank in back of catalogue. To include additional items in your Easy Payment Order see Budget Plan, Page 457.

168 G 5042—Walnut Porcelain Enameled. Cash Price. **$39.85**
Easy Payment Price: $4 Down, $4 a month.......... **$43.85**

Shipped promptly from stock at Kansas City or Oklahoma City. Send your order to the house nearer you. Estimated Total Freight Charges: 150 miles $1.52; 300 miles $2.40; 500 miles $3.58.

Radiant Gas Heaters

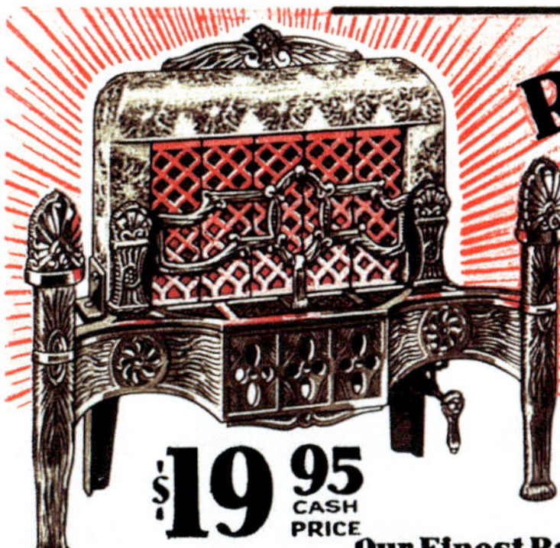

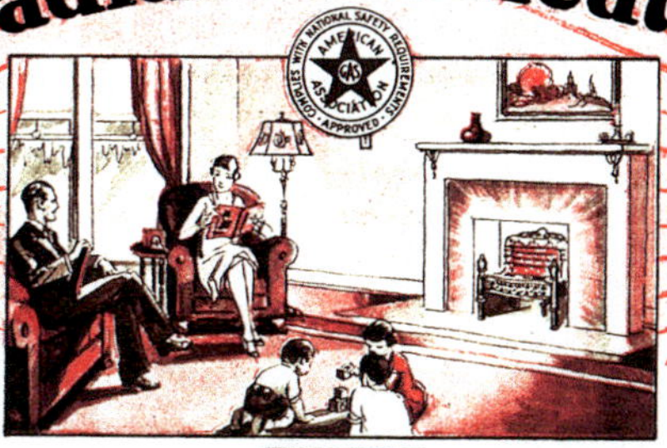

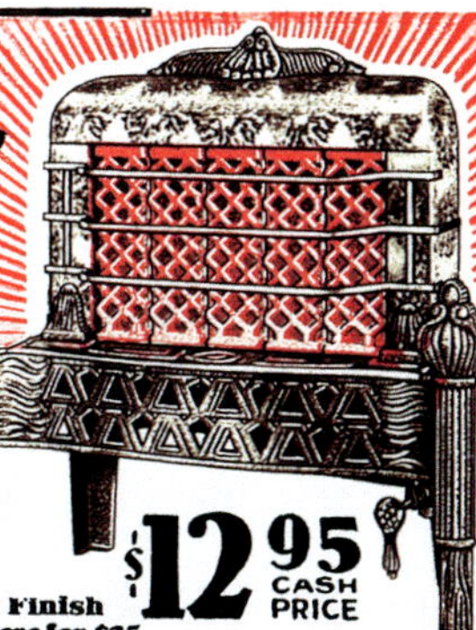

$19.95 CASH PRICE

Our Finest Radiant Heater

Most Stores Would Ask $30 to $35 For It

Our best Heater is a real beauty. Striking treatment of overhanging tile in perfect harmony with the handsome antique brass finish which will retain its luster even after years of service. New cast iron burner has patented features which give more heat from less gas. Approved by American Gas Association Laboratory. **Shipped from Kansas City or Oklahoma City. Send order to house nearer you. Shipped Not Prepaid.** To include other merchandise on your easy payment order, see Budget Plan, Page 457. Specify if for natural or manufactured gas.

168 G 5055—10-Radiant size. Width 27½ inches, depth 10½ inches, height 23½ inches. Ship. wt., 58 lbs. Cash Price: Full amount with order.......... **$19.95**
Easy Payment Price: **$3.00 Down, $4.00 a Month**.......... **22.95**

168 G 5056—12-Radiant size. Width 30½ inches, depth 10½ inches, height 12 inches. Ship. wt., 61 lbs. Cash Price: Full amount with order.......... **$22.95**
Easy Payment Price: **$3 Down, $4.00 a Month**.......... **25.95**

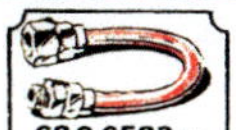

68 G 6583—Copper Connectors for Radiants. Connects ⅜-in. heater valve with ½-in. gas pipe. **Postpaid.**

12-inch..... **40¢**
18-inch..... **46¢**
24-inch..... **54¢**

$12.95 CASH PRICE

Autumn Brown Crackle Finish

Equal Quality Sells Elsewhere for $25

Low priced compact energetic heating unit, approved by the American Gas Association. The high temperature flame leaves no unburned gases. Tinted overhanging tile backwall and radiants tone harmoniously into the new Autumn brown crackle finish used so much by the manufacturers of steel radio cabinets—a lasting, attractive finish. **Shipped from Kansas City or Oklahoma City. Send orders to house nearer you. Shipped Not Prepaid.** To include this heater with other merchandise on easy payments, see Budget Plan, Page 457. Specify if for natural or manufactured gas. Ship. wts., 43, 47 and 50 lbs.

168 G 5052—6-Radiant size; 18½ in. wide by 9 in. deep by 22½ in. high.......... **$ 7.95**
168 G 5053—8-Radiant size; 18½ in. wide by 9 in. deep by 22½ in. high.......... **10.45**
168 G 5054—10-Radiant size; 22 in. wide by 9 in. deep by 22½ in. high.......... **12.95**

We carry a larger selection of Gas Radiant Heaters, Gas Bathroom Heaters and Gas Utility Heaters at Oklahoma City. Write to our Oklahoma City or Kansas City house for pictures, descriptions and prices.

Come and get it!

Sometimes we're so intent on relating all the features of the TOASTMASTER* automatic pop-up type toaster—that we neglect to sing the praises of the toast it pops out. Ah! here's toast that's fit company for fresh golden eggs and steaming, mellow coffee—crisp and golden and piping hot—toast that can't burn because it pops out the second it's ready—toast that comes out the exact shade *you* "order," once you've set the little knob to light, medium or dark. You have the Flexible Timer to thank for that. Just drop in two slices of bread—push down the handle, and—come and get it, perfect toast every tim The presence of the trademark "TOASTMASTER" upon this toaster is you guarantee of highest quality and perfection. Why don't you get one today

FREE! "The Party's On"—a new and interesting booklet on entertai ment ideas and games for young and old. Ask for your copy whereve TOASTMASTER Products are sold, or write direct to: McGraw Electri Company, Toastmaster Products Division, Dept. 157, Minneapolis, Min

*"TOASTMASTER" is a registered trad mark of McGraw Electric Compa

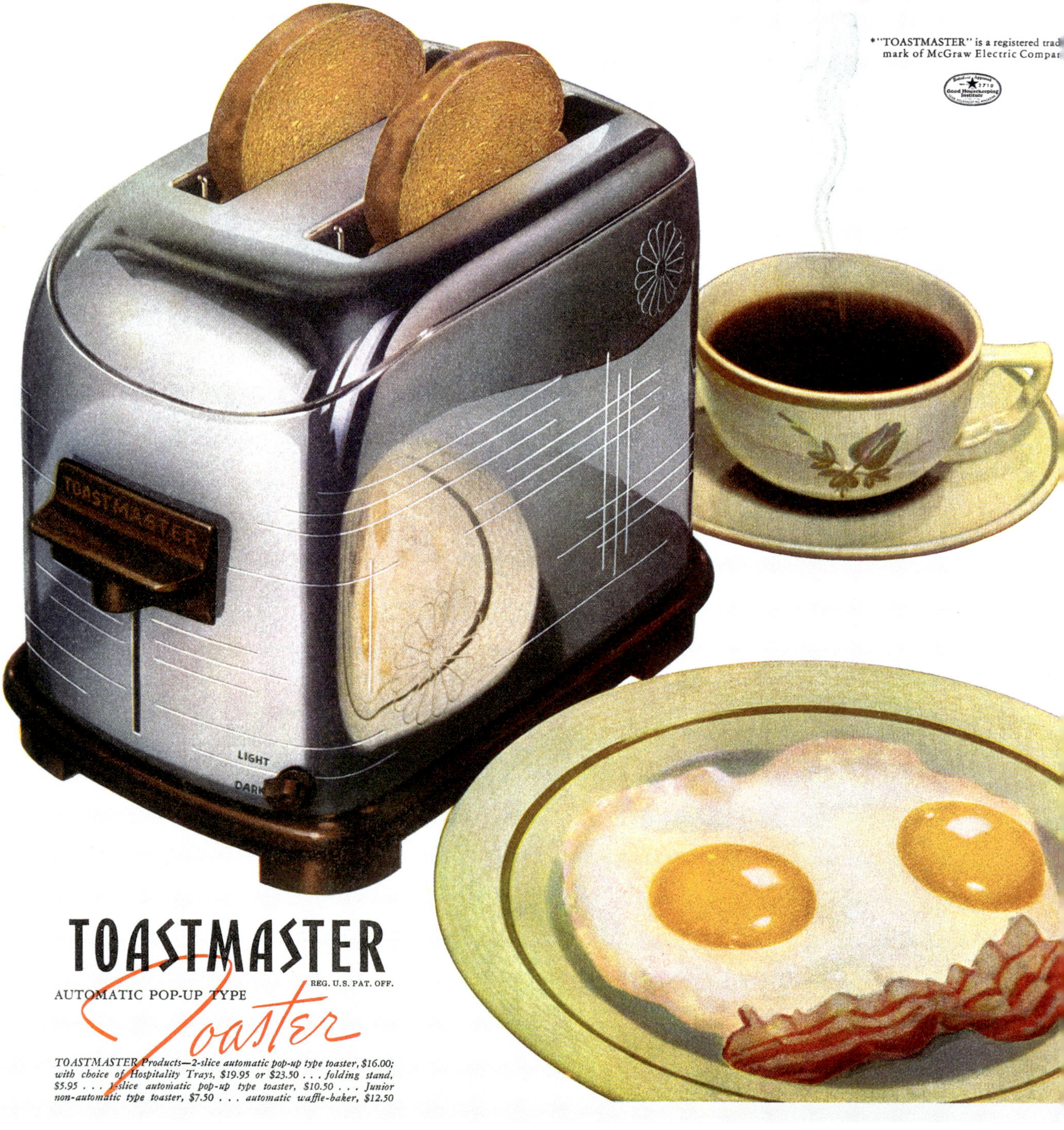

TOASTMASTER

REG. U.S. PAT. OFF.

AUTOMATIC POP-UP TYPE
Toaster

TOASTMASTER Products—2-slice automatic pop-up type toaster, $16.00; with choice of Hospitality Trays, $19.95 or $23.50 . . . folding stand, $5.95 . . . 1-slice automatic pop-up type toaster, $10.50 . . . Junior non-automatic type toaster, $7.50 . . . automatic waffle-baker, $12.50

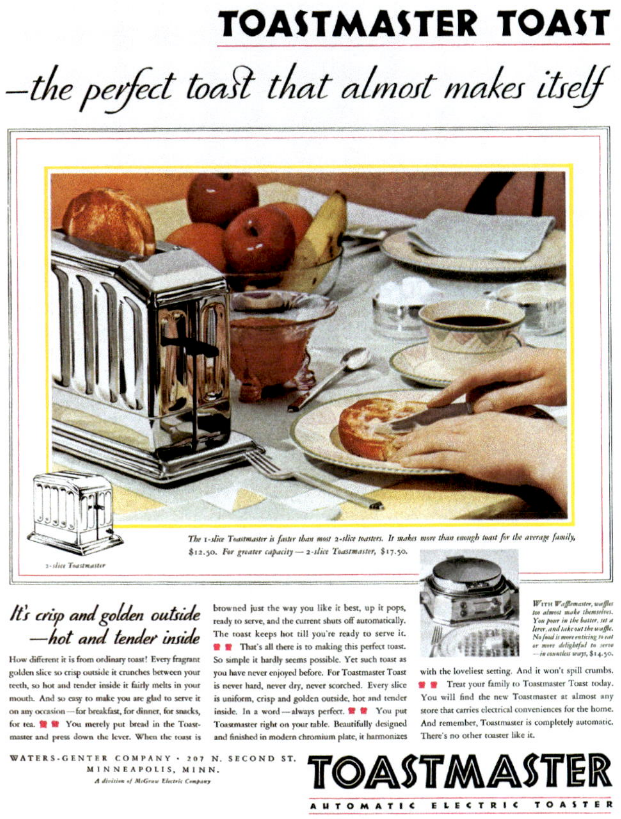

Toastmaster, 1931

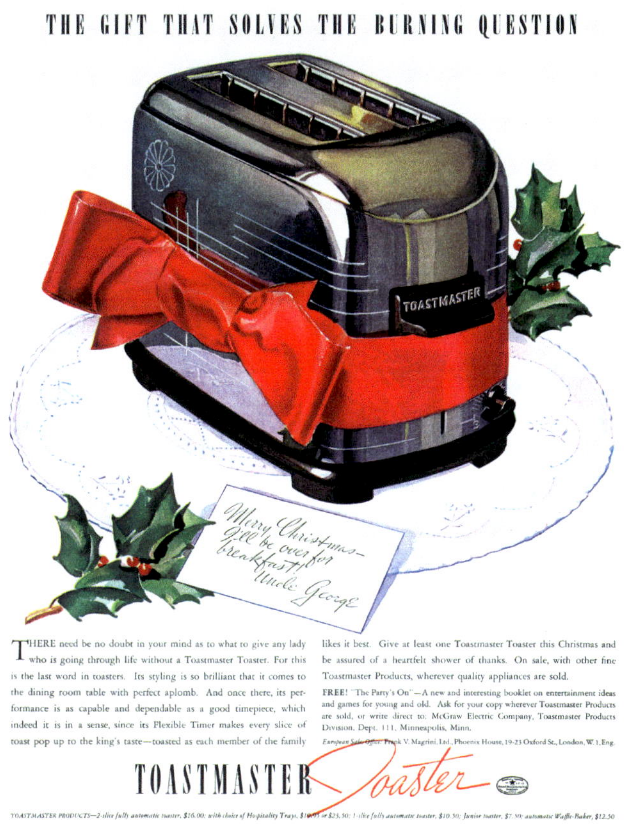

Toastmaster, 1937

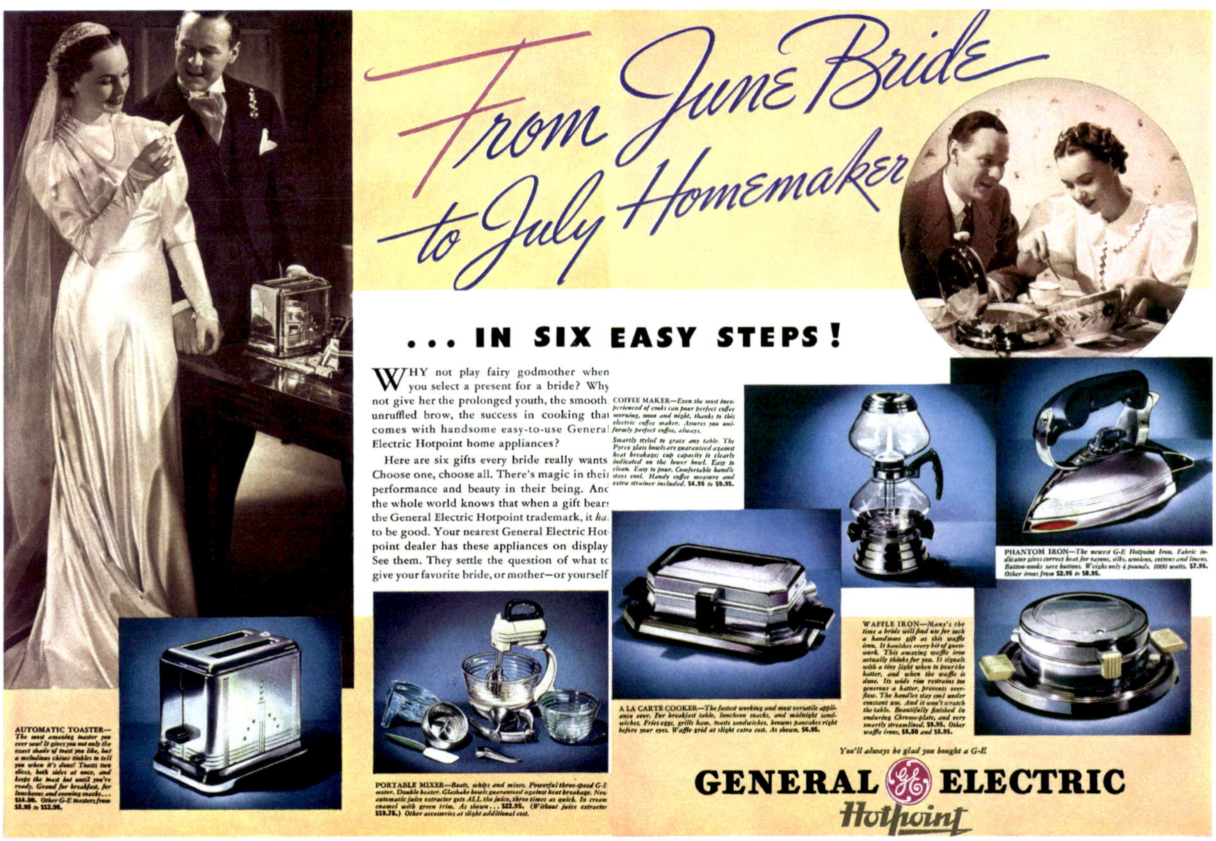

Toastmaster, 1938 ◄ General Electric, 1937

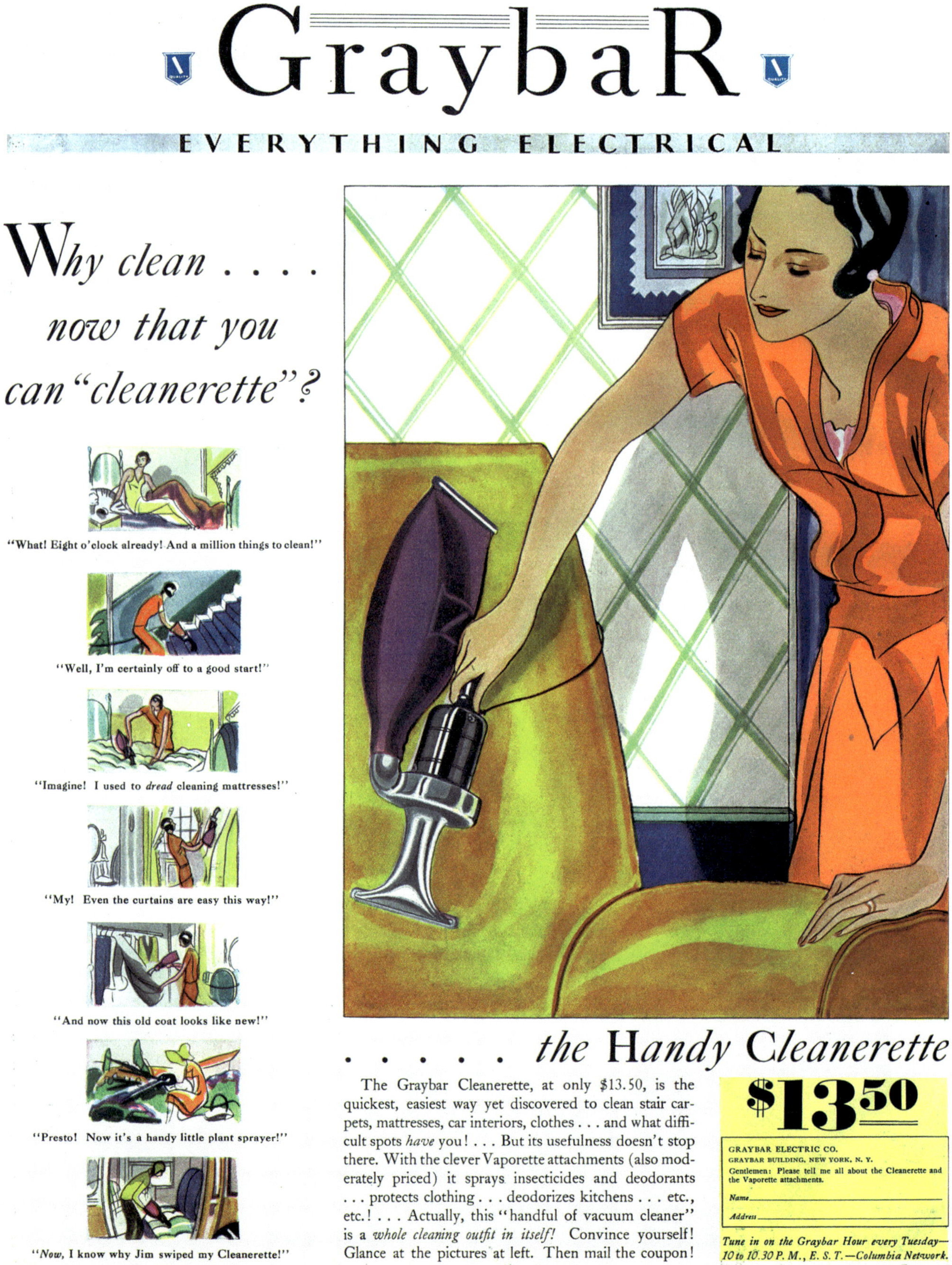

Graybar, 1930

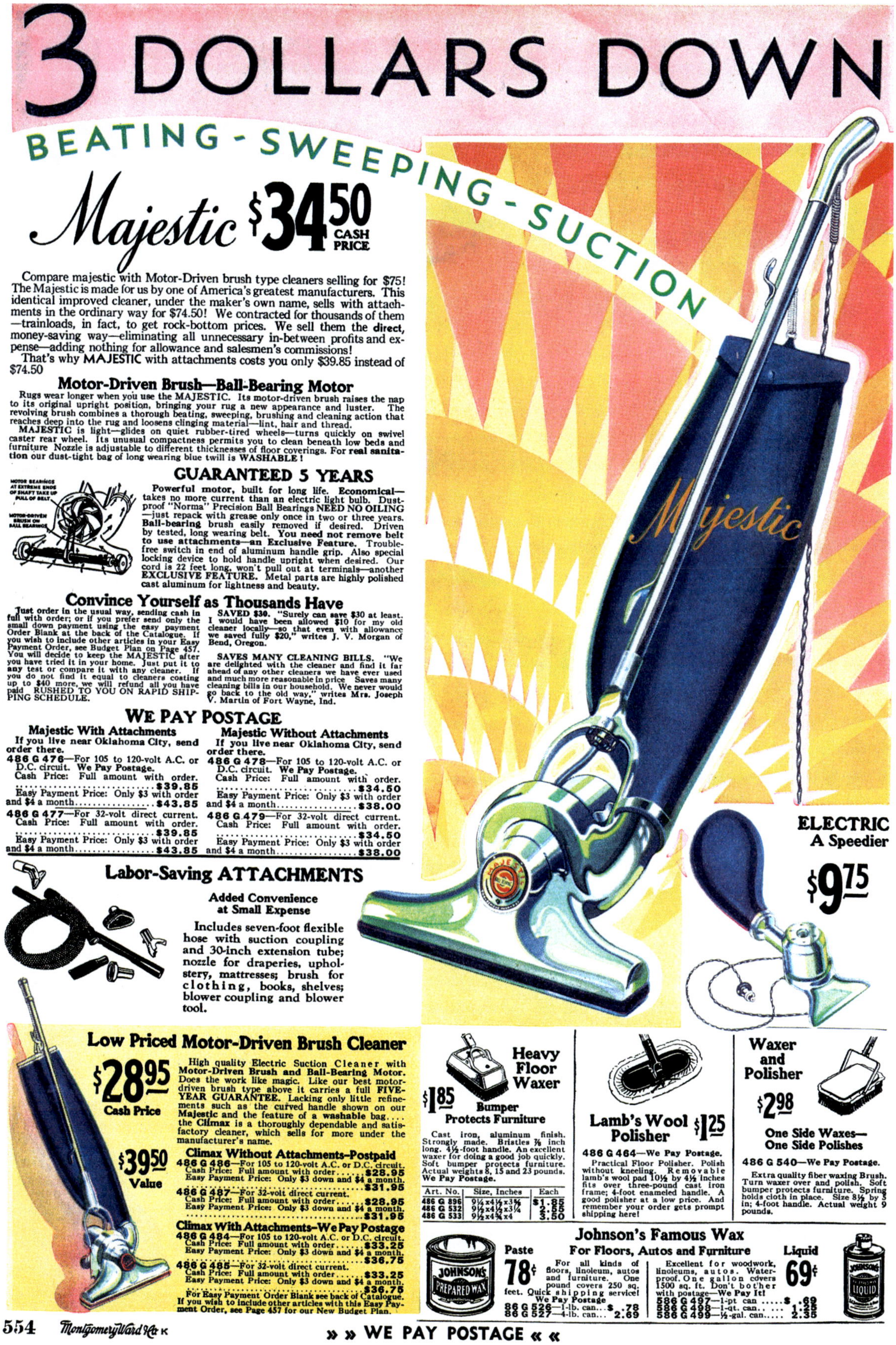

3 DOLLARS DOWN

BEATING - SWEEPING - SUCTION

Majestic $34.50 CASH PRICE

Compare majestic with Motor-Driven brush type cleaners selling for $75! The Majestic is made for us by one of America's greatest manufacturers. This identical improved cleaner, under the maker's own name, sells with attachments in the ordinary way for $74.50! We contracted for thousands of them—trainloads, in fact, to get rock-bottom prices. We sell them the **direct**, money-saving way—eliminating all unnecessary in-between profits and expense—adding nothing for allowance and salesmen's commissions!

That's why **MAJESTIC** with attachments costs you only $39.85 instead of $74.50

Motor-Driven Brush—Ball-Bearing Motor

Rugs wear longer when you use the MAJESTIC. Its motor-driven brush raises the nap to its original upright position, bringing your rug a new appearance and luster. The revolving brush combines a thorough beating, sweeping, brushing and cleaning action that reaches deep into the rug and loosens clinging material—lint, hair and thread.

MAJESTIC is light—glides on quiet rubber-tired wheels—turns quickly on swivel caster rear wheel. Its unusual compactness permits you to clean beneath low beds and furniture Nozzle is adjustable to different thicknesses of floor coverings. For **real sanitation** our dust-tight bag of long wearing blue twill is **WASHABLE!**

GUARANTEED 5 YEARS

MOTOR BEARINGS AT EXTREME ENDS OF SHAFT TAKE UP PULL OF BELT

MOTOR-DRIVEN BRUSH ON BALL BEARINGS

Powerful motor, built for long life. **Economical**—takes no more current than an electric light bulb. Dust-proof "Norma" Precision Ball Bearings NEED NO OILING—just repack with grease only once in two or three years. **Ball-bearing** brush easily removed if desired. Driven by tested, long wearing belt. **You need not remove belt to use attachments—an Exclusive Feature.** Trouble-free switch in end of aluminum handle grip. Also special locking device to hold handle upright when desired. Our cord is 22 feet long, won't pull out at terminals—another **EXCLUSIVE FEATURE.** Metal parts are highly polished cast aluminum for lightness and beauty.

Convince Yourself as Thousands Have

Just order in the usual way, sending cash in full with order; or if you prefer send only the small down payment using the easy payment Order Blank at the back of the Catalogue. If you wish to include other articles in your Easy Payment Order, see Budget Plan on Page 457. You will decide to keep the MAJESTIC after you have tried it in your home. Just put it to **any** test or compare it with any cleaner. If you do not find it equal to cleaners costing up to $40 more, we will refund all you have paid RUSHED TO YOU ON RAPID SHIPPING SCHEDULE.

SAVED $30. "Surely can save $30 at least. I would have been allowed $10 for my old cleaner locally—so that even with allowance we saved fully $20," writes J. V. Morgan of Bend, Oregon.

SAVES MANY CLEANING BILLS. "We are delighted with the cleaner and find it far ahead of any other cleaners we have ever used and much more reasonable in price Saves many cleaning bills in our household. We never would go back to the old way," writes Mrs. Joseph V. Martin of Fort Wayne, Ind.

WE PAY POSTAGE

Majestic With Attachments

If you live near Oklahoma City, send order there.

486 G 476—For 105 to 120-volt A.C. or D.C. circuit. **We Pay Postage.**
Cash Price: Full amount with order. **$39.85**
Easy Payment Price: Only $3 with order and $4 a month.......... **$43.85**

486 G 477—For 32-volt direct current.
Cash Price: Full amount with order. **$39.85**
Easy Payment Price: Only $3 with order and $4 a month.......... **$43.85**

Majestic Without Attachments

If you live near Oklahoma City, send order there.

486 G 478—For 105 to 120-volt A.C. or D.C. circuit. **We Pay Postage.**
Cash Price: Full amount with order. **$34.50**
Easy Payment Price: Only $3 with order and $4 a month.......... **$38.00**

486 G 479—For 32-volt direct current.
Cash Price: Full amount with order. **$34.50**
Easy Payment Price: Only $3 with order and $4 a month.......... **$38.00**

Labor-Saving ATTACHMENTS

Added Convenience at Small Expense

Includes seven-foot flexible hose with suction coupling and 30-inch extension tube; nozzle for draperies, upholstery, mattresses; brush for clothing, books, shelves; blower coupling and blower tool.

ELECTRIC A Speedier

$9.75

Low Priced Motor-Driven Brush Cleaner

$28.95 Cash Price

$39.50 Value

High quality Electric Suction Cleaner with **Motor-Driven Brush and Ball-Bearing Motor.** Does the work like magic. Like our best motor-driven brush type above it carries a full **FIVE-YEAR GUARANTEE.** Lacking only little refinements such as the curved handle shown on our **Majestic** and the feature of a **washable** bag.... the **Climax** is a thoroughly dependable and satisfactory cleaner, which sells for more under the manufacturer's name.

Climax Without Attachments–Postpaid

486 G 486—For 105 to 120-volt A.C. or D.C. circuit.
Cash Price: Full amount with order...... **$28.95**
Easy Payment Price: Only $3 down and $4 a month. **$31.95**

486 G 487—For 32-volt direct current.
Cash Price: Full amount with order...... **$28.95**
Easy Payment Price: Only $3 down and $4 a month. **$31.95**

Climax With Attachments–We Pay Postage

486 G 484—For 105 to 120-volt A.C. or D.C. circuit.
Cash Price: Full amount with order...... **$33.25**
Easy Payment Price: Only $3 down and $4 a month. **$36.75**

486 G 485—For 32-volt direct current.
Cash Price: Full amount with order...... **$33.25**
Easy Payment Price: Only $3 down and $4 a month. **$36.75**

For Easy Payment Order Blank see back of Catalogue. If you wish to include other articles with this Easy Payment Order, see Page 457 for our New Budget Plan.

Heavy Floor Waxer

$1.85

Bumper Protects Furniture

Cast iron, aluminum finish. Strongly made. Bristles ⅞ inch long. 4½-foot handle. An excellent waxer for doing a good job quickly. Soft bumper protects furniture. Actual weights 8, 15 and 23 pounds. **We Pay Postage.**

Art. No.	Size, Inches	Each
486 G 896	9¼x4½x3⅝	$1.85
486 G 532	9½x4½x3¼	2.55
486 G 533	9½x4¾x4	3.50

Lamb's Wool Polisher $1.25

486 G 464—We Pay Postage.

Practical Floor Polisher. Polish without kneeling. Removable lamb's wool pad 10½ by 4½ inches fits over three-pound cast iron frame; 4-foot enameled handle. A good polisher at a low price. And remember your order gets prompt shipping here!

Waxer and Polisher

$2.98

One Side Waxes—One Side Polishes

486 G 540—We Pay Postage.

Extra quality fiber waxing Brush. Turn waxer over and polish. Soft bumper protects furniture. Spring holds cloth in place. Size 8½ by 5 in; 4-foot handle. Actual weight 9 pounds.

Johnson's Famous Wax

For Floors, Autos and Furniture

JOHNSON'S PREPARED WAX

Paste 78¢

For all kinds of floors, linoleum, autos and furniture. One pound covers 250 sq. feet. Quick shipping service! **We Pay Postage**

86 G 526—1-lb. can... **$ .78**
86 G 527—4-lb. can... **2.69**

Liquid 69¢

Excellent for woodwork, linoleums, autos. Water-proof. One gallon covers 1500 sq. ft. Don't bother with postage—**We Pay It!**

586 G 497—1-pt can ..... **$ .69**
586 G 498—1-qt. can..... **1.25**
586 G 499—½-gal. can..... **2.35**

JOHNSON'S LIQUID

554 Montgomery Ward & Co K

» » WE PAY POSTAGE « «

Majestic Sweeper, 1931

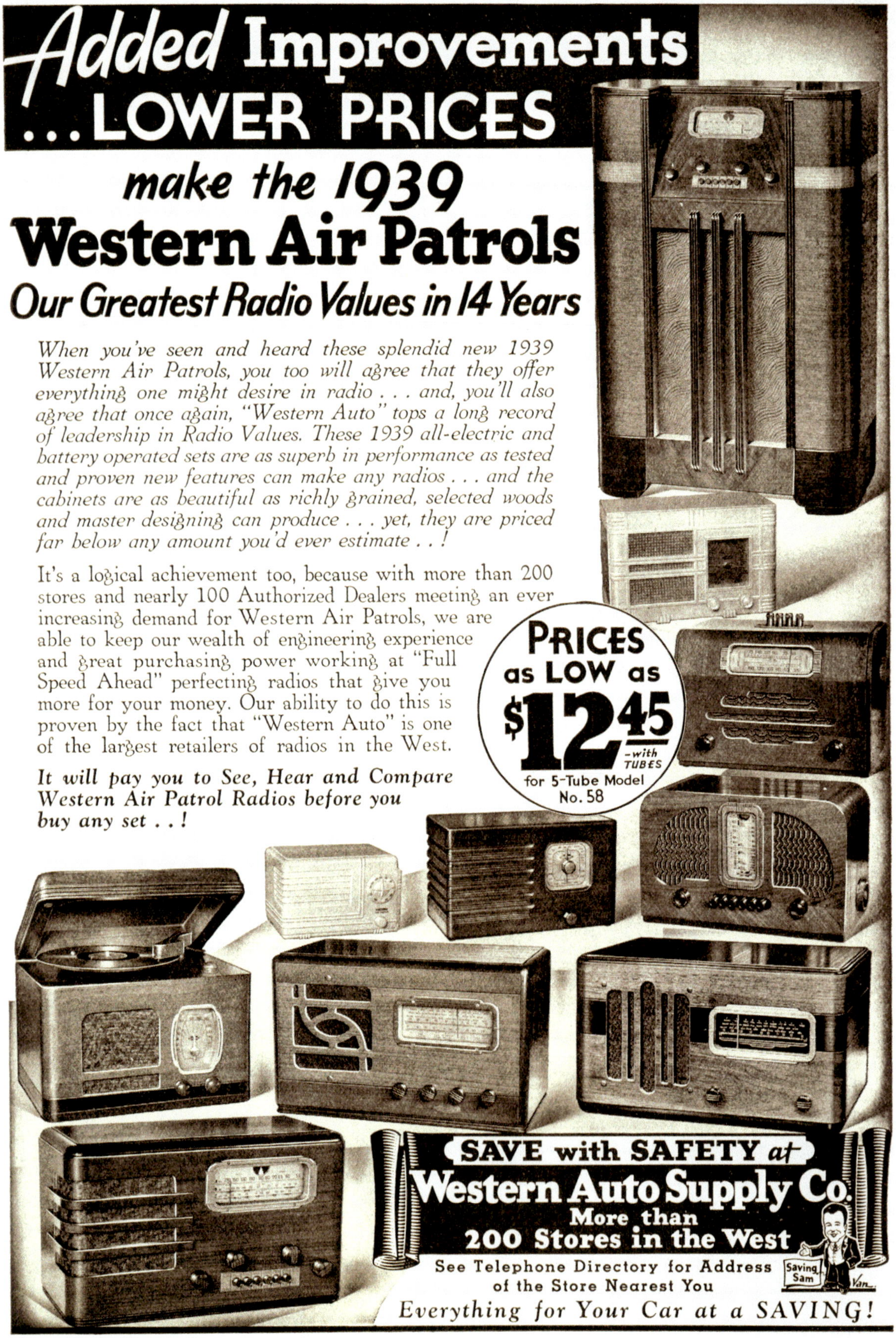

Western Air Patrol Radios, 1938

▸ *Majestic Radio, 1930*

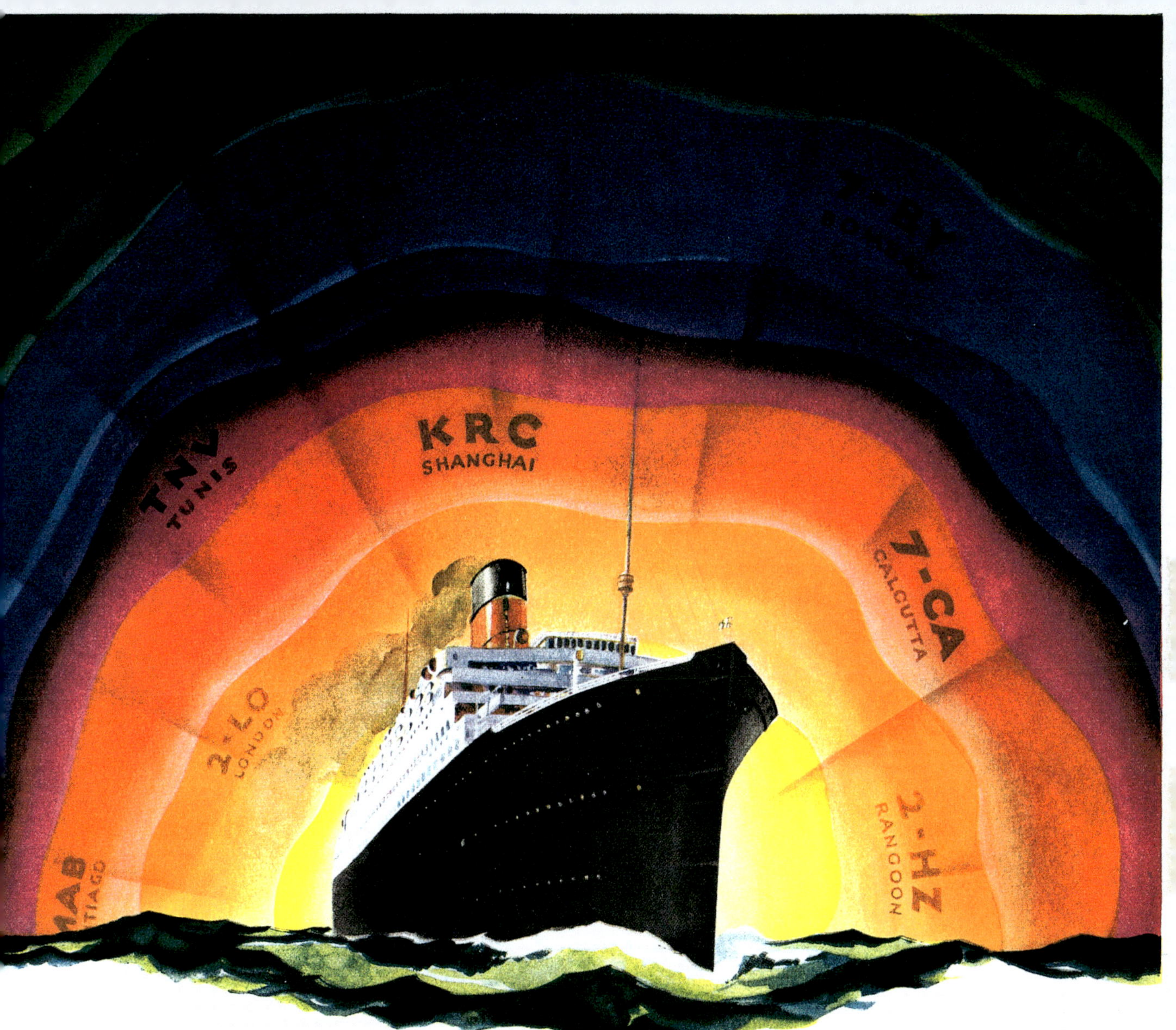

Chosen for another FAMOUS LINER because of its glorious COLORFUL TONE

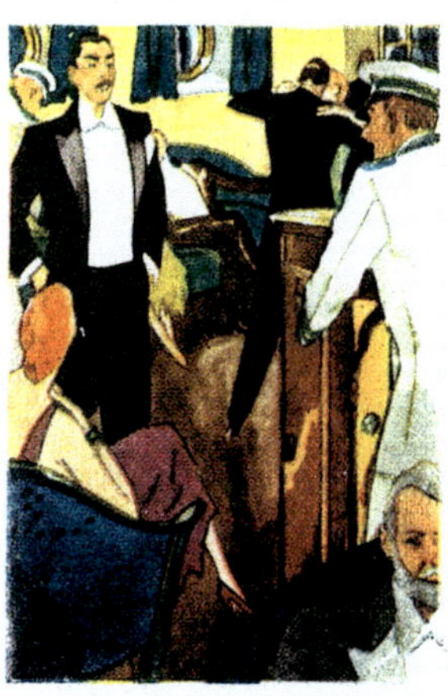

THE palatial Franconia, famous Cunard liner—most luxurious of World Cruise Steamships—chooses Majestic Radio for the 1930 cruise.

Again honored as the radio unaffected by changing latitude and various conditions—again recognized as the master of distance—the new Majestic is selected to entertain the Franconia's passengers on their six-months cruise round the world.

Picking up foreign stations from Algiers to Stamboul, from Bombay to Shanghai—reaching across dark jungles and tropic seas—Majestic brings in program after program in that unrivaled COLORFUL TONE that is exclusively Majestic's.

Chosen for the world flight of the Graf Zeppelin—chosen for the world cruise of the Franconia—chosen for 60 of America's finest trains—chosen by over two million owners—Majestic must unquestionably be your choice.

A trial in your home will convince you. No cost, no obligation. Call your dealer—and ask about Majestic's convenient payment plan.

GRIGSBY-GRUNOW COMPANY, CHICAGO, U. S. A. · WORLD'S LARGEST MANUFACTURERS OF COMPLETE RADIO RECEIVERS

Licensed under patents and applications of R. C. A. and R. F. L. also by Lektiphone, Lowell & Dunmore and Hogan License Associates.

TUNE IN Majestic Theatre of the Air over the Columbia Broadcasting System every Sunday evening from 9 to 10, Eastern Standard Time. Famous headliners of the stage and screen.

Majestic Radio

MIGHTY MONARCH OF THE AIR

SEE THIS SENSATIONAL NEW YEAR VALUE

Electric Tuning

RCA VICTOR RADIO

NOW ONLY $89.95

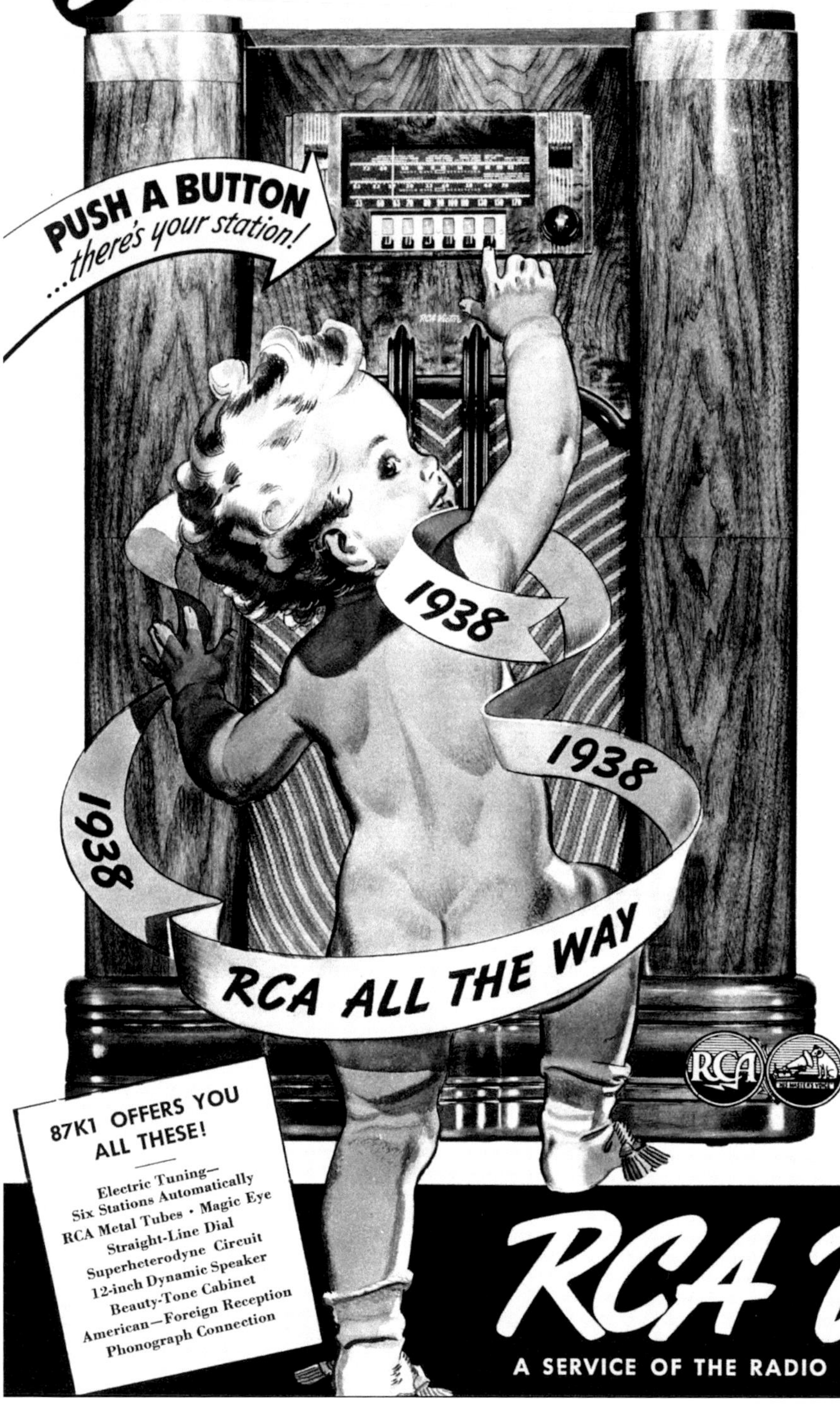

SO SIMPLE, A BABY CAN TUNE IT!

In this sensational RCA Victor value, and in every other RCA Victor radio, you get the benefit of RCA's unmatched experience in designing, building and operating the world's largest international communications system.

Quantity production, improved engineering, large-scale purchasing have all helped to make it possible for you to have the sensational model shown on this page at the amazingly low figure of $89.95*.

You can buy RCA Victor Radios on C. I. T. easy payment plan. Any radio instrument is better with an RCA Antenna System. *All prices f. o. b. Camden, N. J., subject to change without notice. When buying radio tubes, say "RCA"! First in Metal—Foremost in Glass—Finest in Tone!

Listen to the "Magic Key" every Sunday, 2 to 3 p.m., E. S. T., on NBC Blue Network.

This and Your Radio Play Victor Records

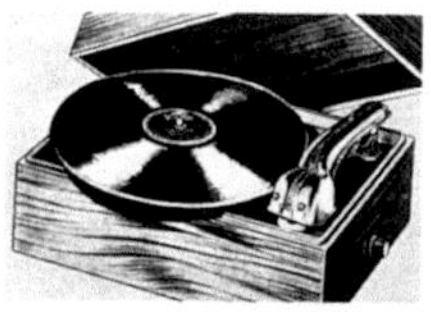

RCA Victor Record Player R-93A transforms any modern AC radio into an electric phonograph-radio. Can be attached easily and quickly. You can operate it from your armchair. . . $19.95*

RCA Victor

A SERVICE OF THE RADIO CORPORATION OF AMERICA

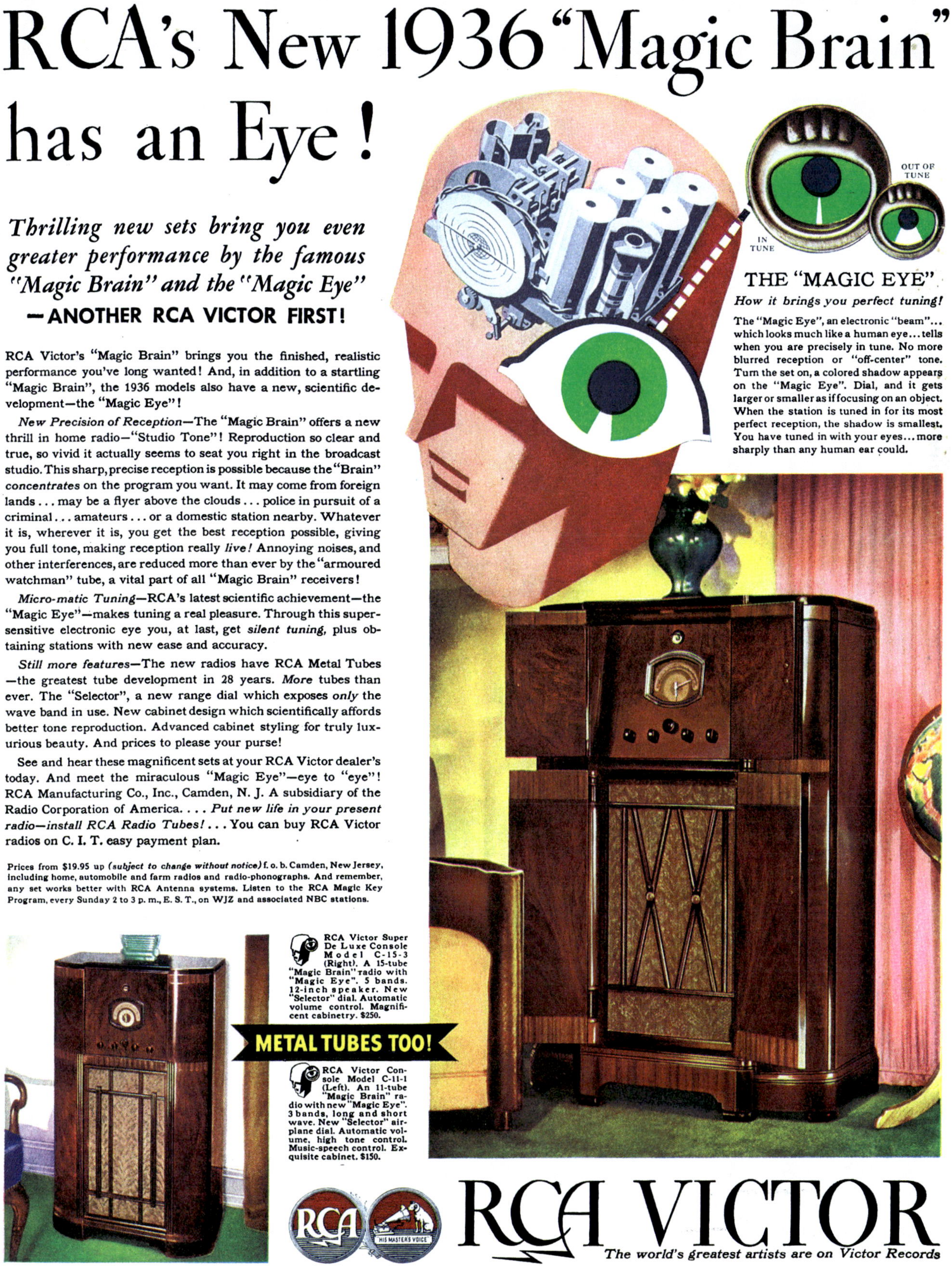

RCA Victor, 1938 ◂

RCA Victor, 1936

And the winner is...

Placating the Patron

"The customer is always right," coined by American department-store owner H. Gordon Selfridge for his new London store in the early 1900s, had been adopted as a hallmark of American business by the 1930s. Like much advertising, the claims of GF Allsteel® were well founded, but went to extremes by suggesting that an office would gain "greater character and dignity" through the use of its furniture. Nonetheless, the overriding idea that the customer is always right endures as a principle of business today.

Alles für König Kunde

Der von dem amerikanischen Warenhausbesitzer H. Gordon Selfridge Anfang des 20.Jahrhunderts für seine neue Londoner Filiale geprägte Slogan „Der Kunde hat immer Recht" war in den Dreißigern zum Leitspruch in der amerikanischen Geschäftswelt geworden. An der Werbebotschaft von GF Allsteel war sicherlich etwas Wahres dran, doch mit der Behauptung, man verleihe seinen Büroräumen mit ihrem Mobiliar „mehr Charakter und Würde", schoss man vielleicht etwas über das Ziel hinaus. Aber die Auffassung, der Kunde habe immer Recht, hat zumindest in der amerikanische Wirtschaft bis heute überlebt.

Comment caresser le consommateur dans le sens du poil

Dans les années 30, le monde des affaires américain avait fait sienne la devise « Le client a toujours raison », inventée au début du siècle par H. Gordon Selfridge pour son grand magasin londonien. Comme dans la plupart des publicités, les affirmations de GF Allsteel® étaient fondées, mais elles ne craignaient pas d'en rajouter en suggérant qu'avec ses meubles, un bureau « gagnerait en personnalité et en dignité ». Il n'en reste pas moins que l'idée selon laquelle le client est roi prévaut encore aujourd'hui.

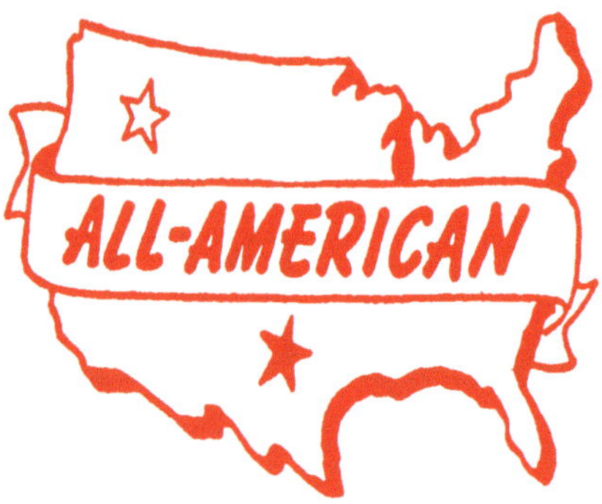

GF Allsteel, 1930

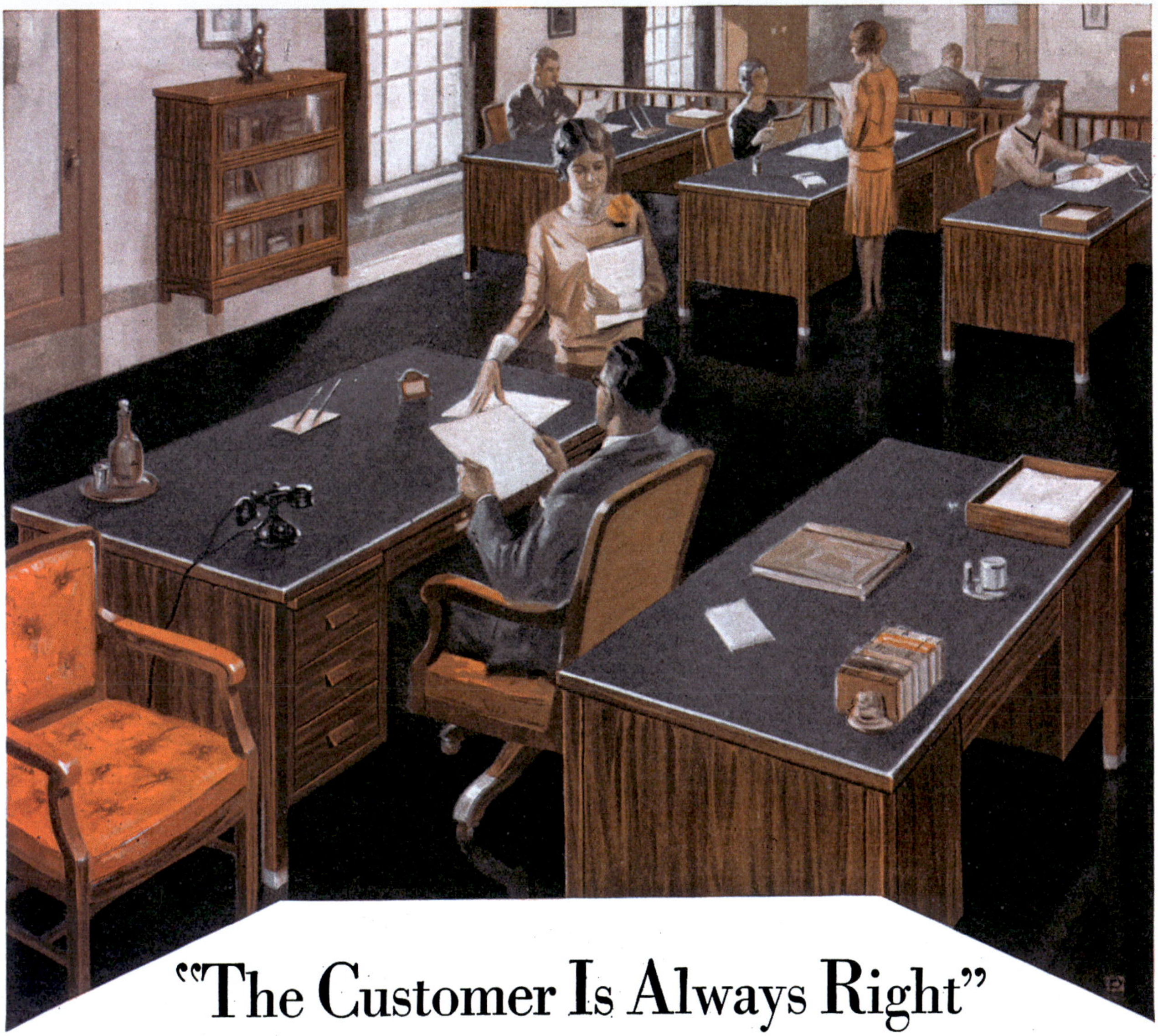

"The Customer Is Always Right"

AND his opinion of you and your business is just what you make it.

Let him find you and your co-workers in modern surroundings, equipped with the tools of modern business.

GF Allsteel Equipment supplies that up-to-the-minute touch in appearance. And because its utility is known and recognized, it never fails to create an impression of character and progress.

It brings you the strength and stamina of steel, for permanence; the resistance of steel to wear, to fire, to dampness, to every hazard of hard use; and the baked-on enamel finishes, possible only with steel, for enduring beauty.

With GF Allsteel Equipment, work is done with less effort and more speed.

Business leaders everywhere have proved that. And they have also found inspiration for workers in these finer offices, and a greater character and dignity that impresses every visitor.

THE GENERAL FIREPROOFING COMPANY
Youngstown, Ohio ·· *Canadian Plant, Toronto*
BRANCHES AND DEALERS IN ALL PRINCIPAL CITIES

GF Allsteel
"Serves and Survives"

COMPLETE OFFICE EQUIPMENT

Commercial Desks · from $45 *to* $80
Executive Desks · from $175 *to* $500
Slightly higher in the West and South

THE GENERAL FIREPROOFING CO. L.D. 868
Youngstown, Ohio

Please send me a copy of the GF Allsteel Office Equipment Catalog.

Name ____________________

Firm ____________________

Address ____________________

City ______________ *State* ________

DESKS ·· FILES ·· SAFES ·· SHELVING — FILING SUPPLIES

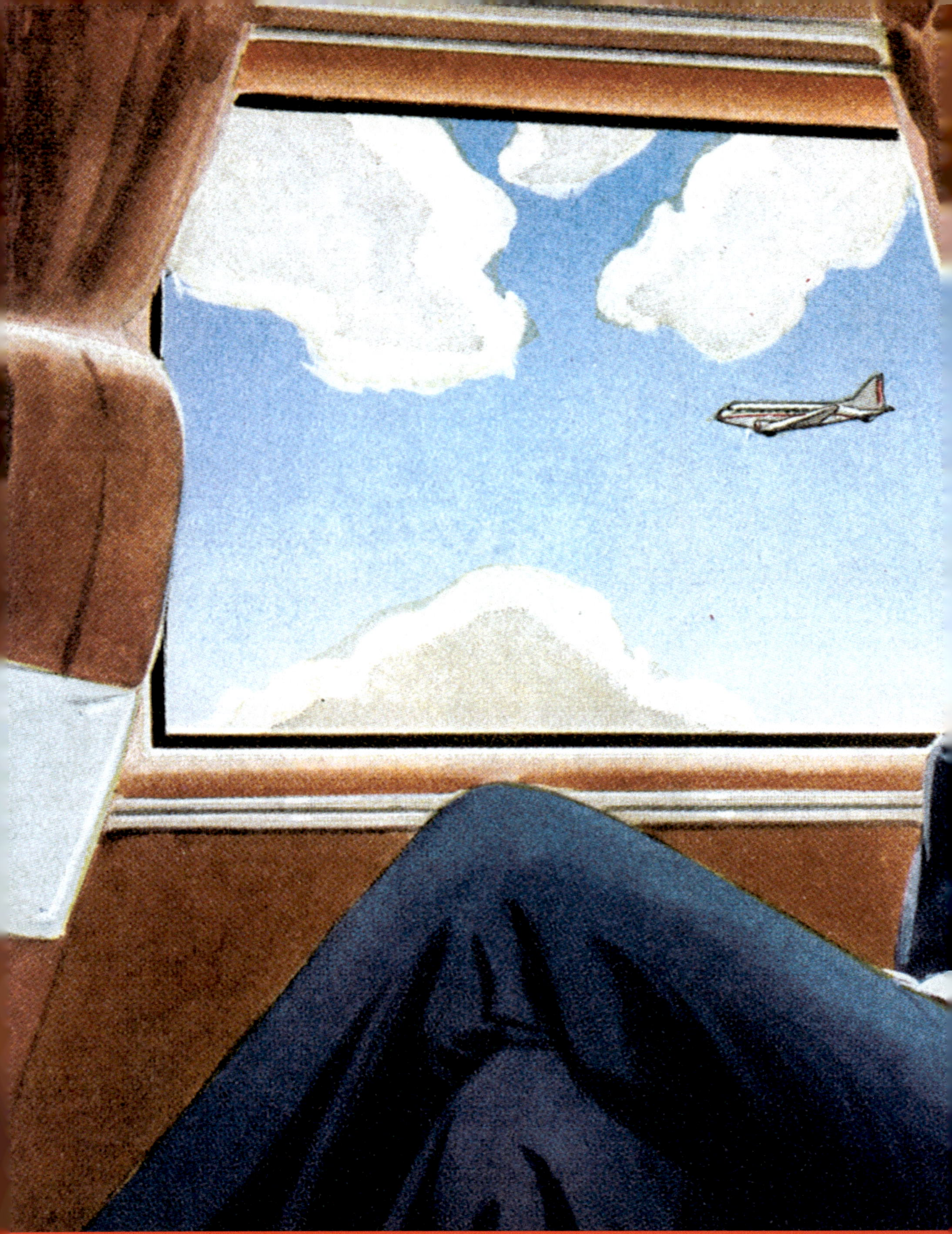

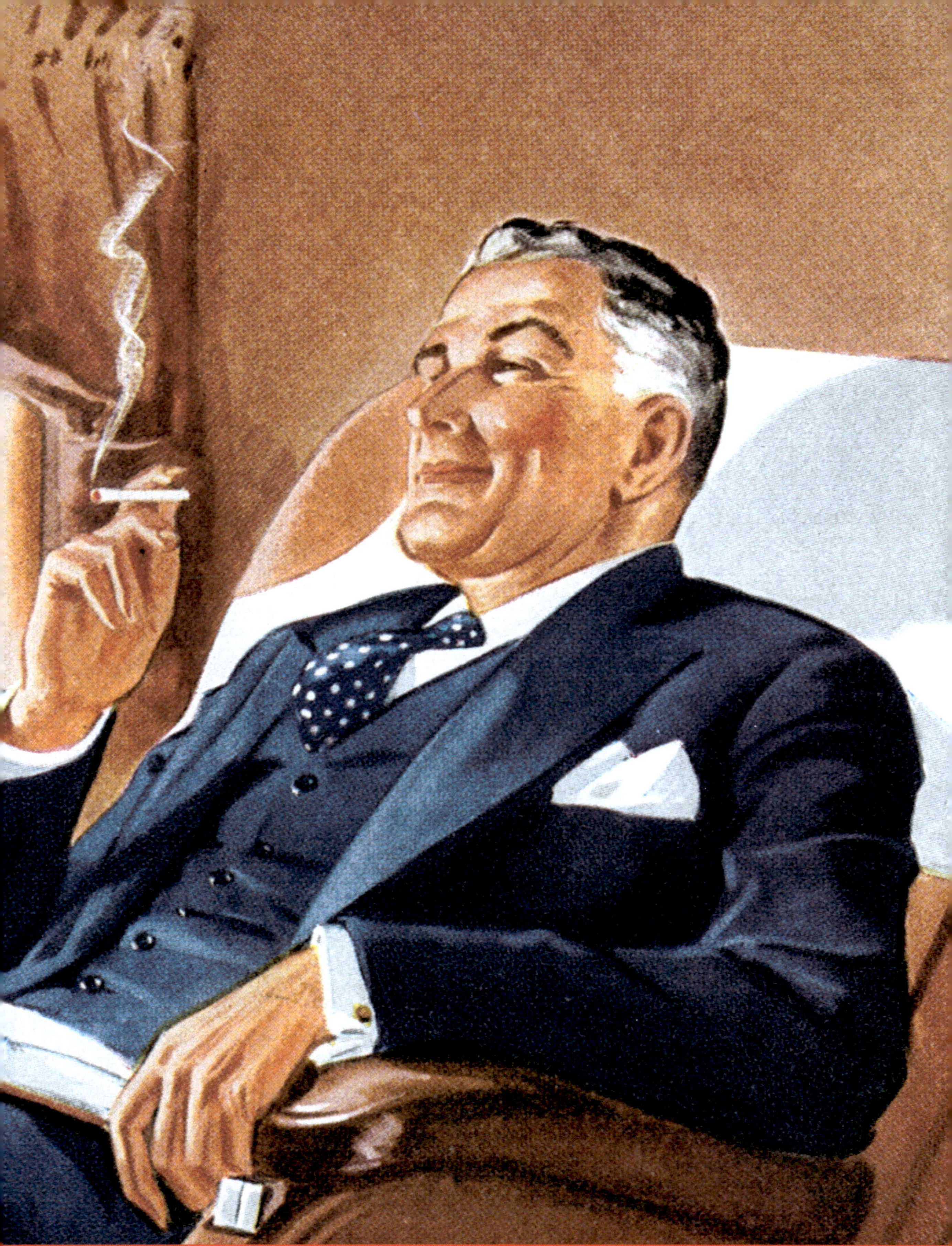

RIDE THE MOST BEAUTIFUL TRAIN IN AMERICA

See a hundred miles of Pacific Ocean on your Southern Pacific California trip!

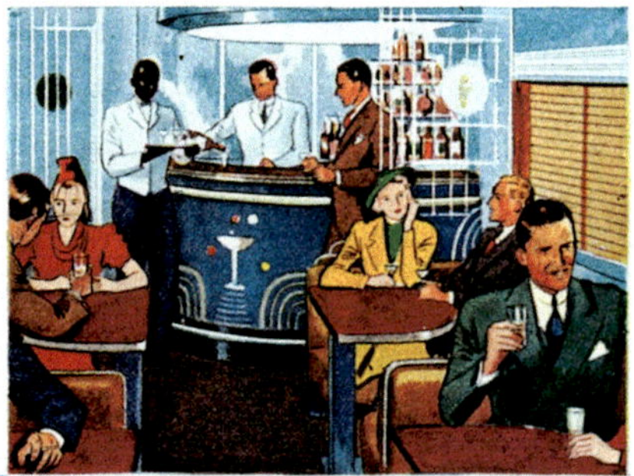

THE TAVERN on the *Daylight* is lined with cozy leather booths and illuminated with soft, colored lights. In this congenial atmosphere, you'll spend happy hours while California's beautiful coastal scenery glides by.

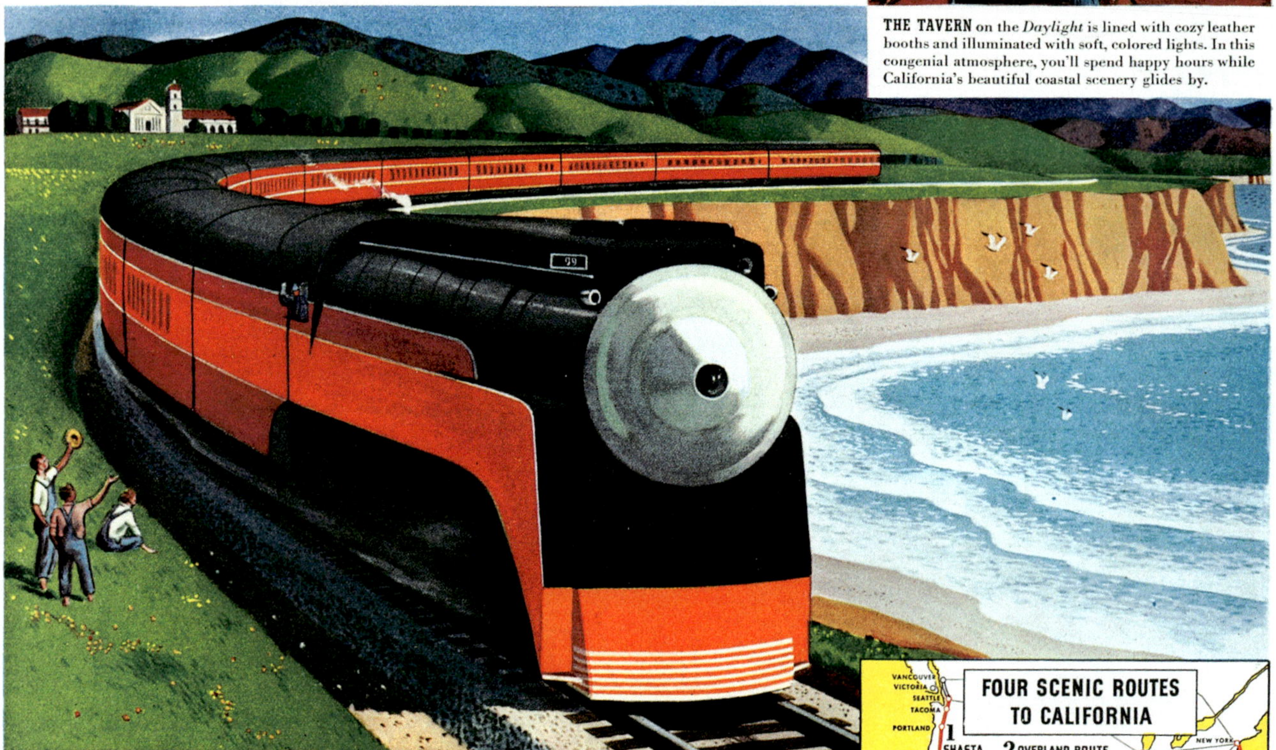

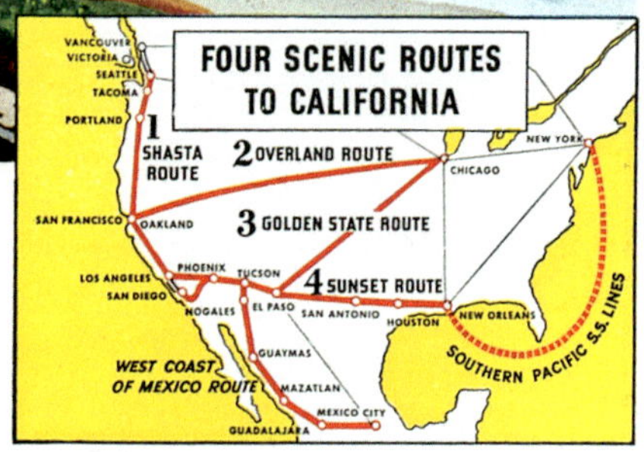

63,060 passengers in three months, 143,851 in six months, 198,540 in nine months! That's the impressive record of Southern Pacific's new *Daylight*, the most beautiful train in America. Every day this brilliant streamlined train speeds between Los Angeles and San Francisco over the route of the California Missions, through rolling mountains and rich valleys, following the very edge of the Pacific Ocean for more than a hundred miles.

Whether your Pacific Coast destination is Los Angeles, San Francisco, Portland or Seattle, you can include this *Daylight* trip in your ticket by going west on *one* of Southern Pacific's Four Scenic Routes and returning on *another* SP route (see explanation at right).

Costing more than $2,000,000, custom-built from stem to stern, the twin *Daylights* are the "flagships" of an impressive fleet of brand new trains recently placed in service by Southern Pacific. In the year just past, the thrifty *Californian* and *San Francisco Challenger*, the royal *Forty-Niner*, the new *Cascade*, the *Sunbeam* in Texas and the giant new streamliner *City of San Francisco* joined the *Golden State Limited*, the *Overland Limited*, the *Sunset Limited* and the other famous trains that serve the Southern Pacific West.

HOW TO SEE TWICE AS MUCH ON YOUR TRIP WEST

The *Daylight* is just one bonus you enjoy on a Southern Pacific ticket to the Coast. We have Four Scenic Routes to California (see map). By going on one of these routes and returning on another one, you see a different part of the United States each way. You see *twice as much* of California and the West as you would by going and returning on the same route. You enjoy the *Daylight* ride between Los Angeles and San Francisco. And from most eastern and mid-western places, such a "go one way, return another" SP ticket costs you not one cent more rail fare than the usual back-and-forth round trip.

FREE TRAVEL SERVICE! For Southern Pacific's liberally illustrated travel guide, *How to See the Whole Pacific Coast*, write O. P. Bartlett, Dept. SE-3, 310 So. Michigan Avenue, Chicago. He will also send you a post card for you to mail if you wish a detailed routing, with costs. No charge for this service. No obligation.

Southern Pacific's representatives in principal eastern cities are authorities on the West. They will be glad to personally assist you plan your trip. See your telephone directory.

SOUTHERN PACIFIC — THE WEST'S GREATEST TRANSPORTATION SYSTEM

American Airlines, 1939 ◂◂ Southern Pacific, 1938

▸ Southern Pacific, 1937 ▸▸ Pennsylvania Railroad, 1938

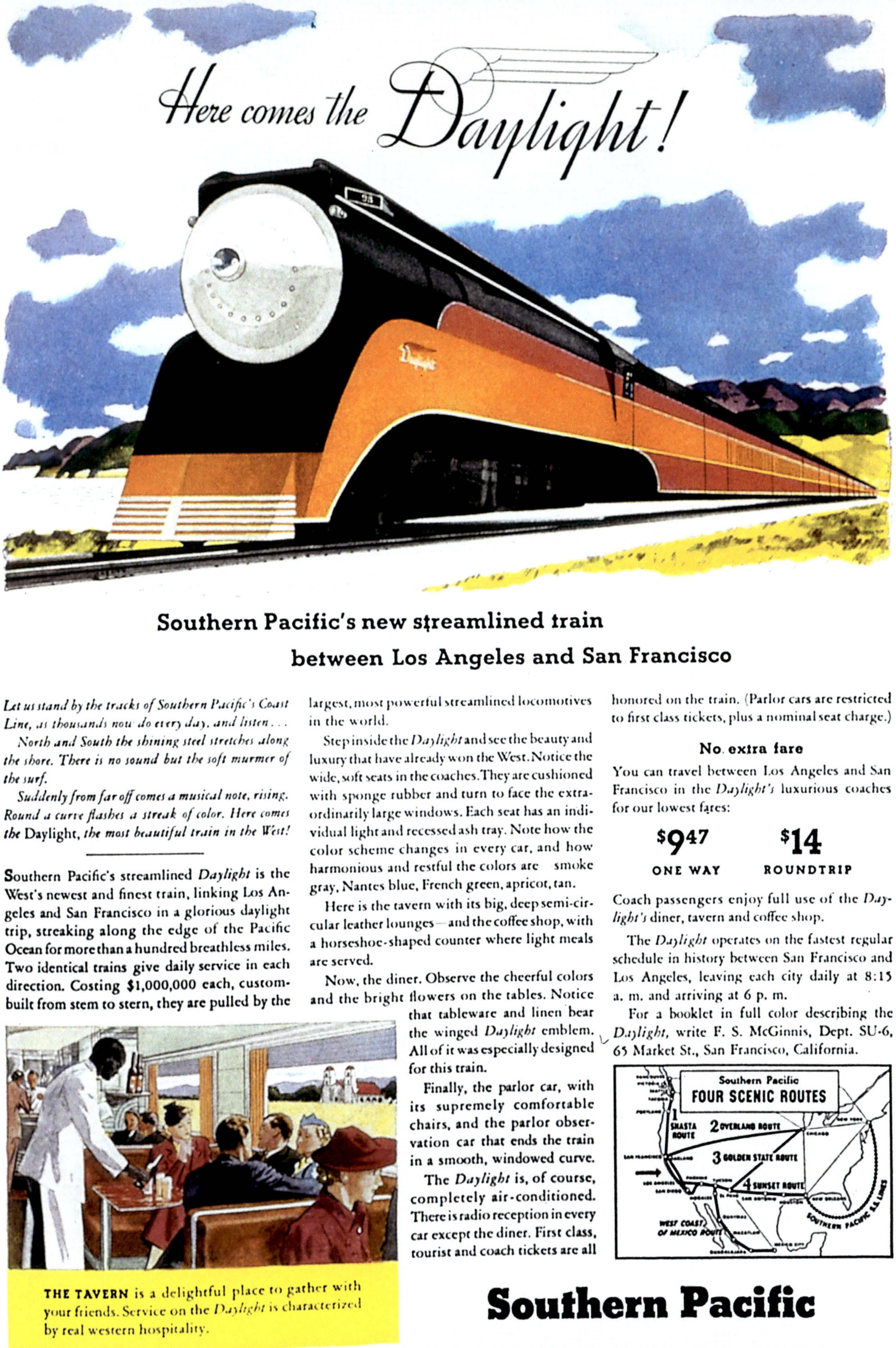
Here comes the Daylight!
Southern Pacific's new streamlined train
between Los Angeles and San Francisco
Let us stand by the tracks of Southern Pacific's Coast Line, as thousands now do every day, and listen . . .
North and South the shining steel stretches along the shore. There is no sound but the soft murmer of the surf.
Suddenly from far off comes a musical note, rising. Round a curve flashes a streak of color. Here comes the Daylight, *the most beautiful train in the West!*
Southern Pacific's streamlined *Daylight* is the West's newest and finest train, linking Los Angeles and San Francisco in a glorious daylight trip, streaking along the edge of the Pacific Ocean for more than a hundred breathless miles. Two identical trains give daily service in each direction. Costing $1,000,000 each, custom-built from stem to stern, they are pulled by the largest, most powerful streamlined locomotives in the world.
Step inside the *Daylight* and see the beauty and luxury that have already won the West. Notice the wide, soft seats in the coaches. They are cushioned with sponge rubber and turn to face the extraordinarily large windows. Each seat has an individual light and recessed ash tray. Note how the color scheme changes in every car, and how harmonious and restful the colors are — smoke gray, Nantes blue, French green, apricot, tan.
Here is the tavern with its big, deep semi-circular leather lounges — and the coffee shop, with a horseshoe-shaped counter where light meals are served.
Now, the diner. Observe the cheerful colors and the bright flowers on the tables. Notice that tableware and linen bear the winged *Daylight* emblem. All of it was especially designed for this train.
Finally, the parlor car, with its supremely comfortable chairs, and the parlor observation car that ends the train in a smooth, windowed curve.
The *Daylight* is, of course, completely air-conditioned. There is radio reception in every car except the diner. First class, tourist and coach tickets are all honored on the train. (Parlor cars are restricted to first class tickets, plus a nominal seat charge.)
No extra fare
You can travel between Los Angeles and San Francisco in the *Daylight's* luxurious coaches for our lowest fares:
$9.47 ONE WAY
$14 ROUNDTRIP
Coach passengers enjoy full use of the *Daylight's* diner, tavern and coffee shop.
The *Daylight* operates on the fastest regular schedule in history between San Francisco and Los Angeles, leaving each city daily at 8:15 a. m. and arriving at 6 p. m.
For a booklet in full color describing the *Daylight*, write F. S. McGinnis, Dept. SU-6, 65 Market St., San Francisco, California.
Southern Pacific
FOUR SCENIC ROUTES
1 SHASTA ROUTE
2 OVERLAND ROUTE
3 GOLDEN STATE ROUTE
4 SUNSET ROUTE
WEST COAST OF MEXICO ROUTE
SOUTHERN PACIFIC S.S. LINES
THE TAVERN is a delightful place to gather with your friends. Service on the *Daylight* is characterized by real western hospitality.
Southern Pacific

PENNSYLVANIA RAILROAD PRESENTS

A FLEET OF MODE

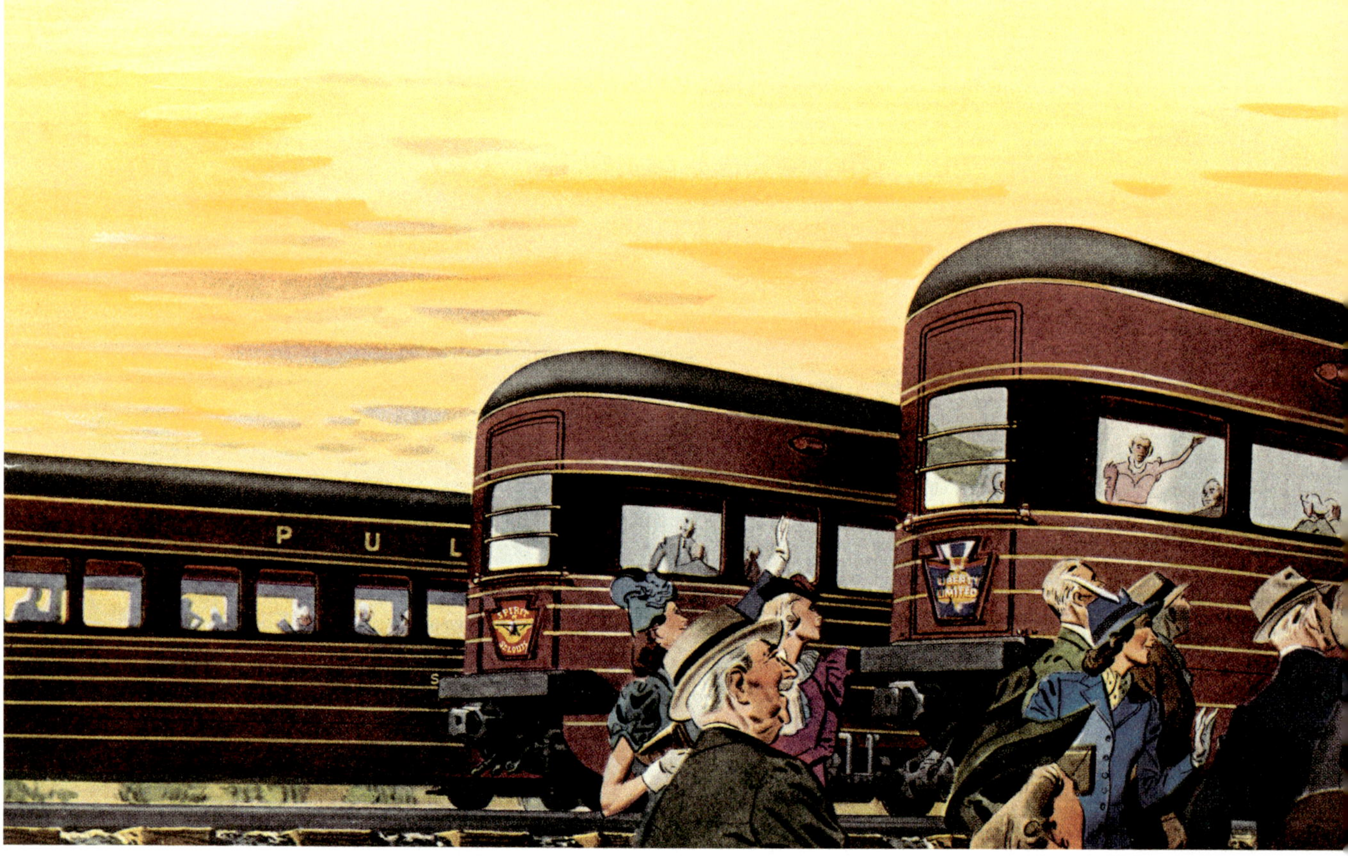

HERE'S THE FLEET OF MODERNISM!
(Standard Time)

BROADWAY LIMITED

Lv. New York..............5:00 P.M.
Lv. Philadelphia............6:20 P.M.
Ar. Chicago................8:00 A.M.

Lv. Chicago................3:30 P.M.
Ar. Philadelphia............7:09 A.M.
Ar. New York..............8:30 A.M.

THE GENERAL

Lv. New York..............3:40 P.M.
Lv. Philadelphia............5:09 P.M.
Ar. Chicago................7:50 A.M.

Lv. Chicago................3:15 P.M.
Ar. Philadelphia............8:01 A.M.
Ar. New York..............9:30 A.M.

LIBERTY LIMITED

Lv. Washington............5:10 P.M.
Lv. Baltimore..............5:55 P.M.
Ar. Chicago................8:35 A.M.

Lv. Chicago................3:10 P.M.
Ar. Baltimore..............8:02 A.M.
Ar. Washington............8:50 A.M.

"SPIRIT OF ST. LOUIS"

Lv. New York..............5:15 P.M.
Lv. Philadelphia............6:38 P.M.
Lv. Washington............5:30 P.M.
Ar. St. Louis..............12:42 P.M.

Lv. St. Louis..............12:15 P.M.
Ar. Washington............9:55 A.M.
Ar. Philadelphia............8:24 A.M.
Ar. New York..............9:50 A.M.

All trains air-conditioned. P.R.R. Luxury Coaches and Improved Section Sleepers on all trains except the all-room Pullman train — Broadway Limited.

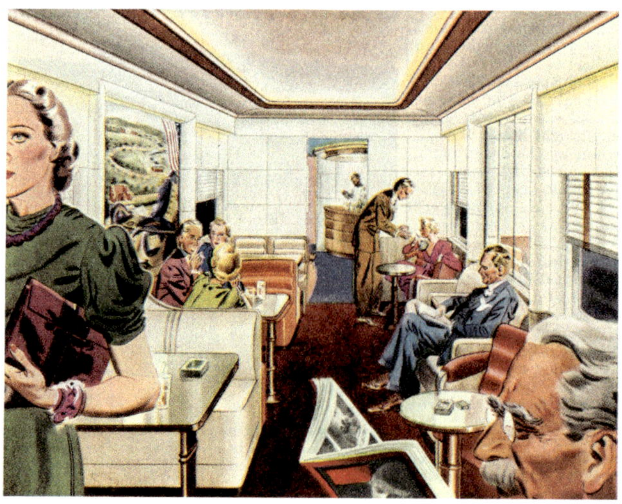

Bar Lounge: Designed in collaboration with the Pullman Company by Raymond Loewy, creator of smart modern interiors. Interestingly placed divans . . conversation corners in richly cushioned fabrics . . low broad upholstered settees . . venetian blinds . . a magnificent mural, facing long triple-panelled mirrors . . a fan-wise bar within easy hail. Soft shades predominate in the color scheme and lighting which are soothing, not flamboyant.

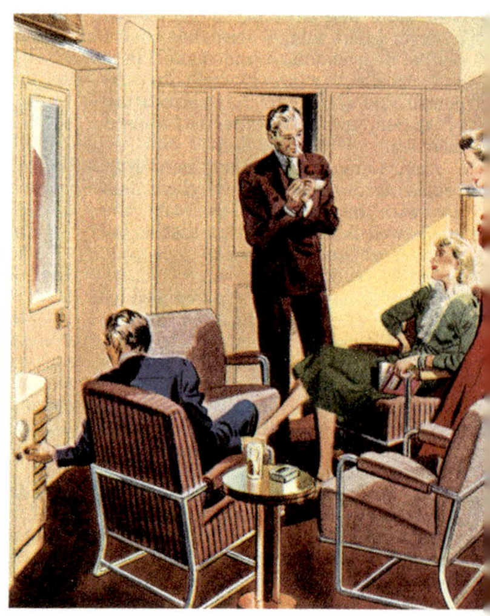

Master Suites (on Broadway and Liberty Limiteds) Something entirely new in private accommodations. Two rooms, not one. The first, a handsome lounge in soft colors, with radio and other modern furnishings (at night, twin beds); the second, a private bathroom with shower.

·ISM

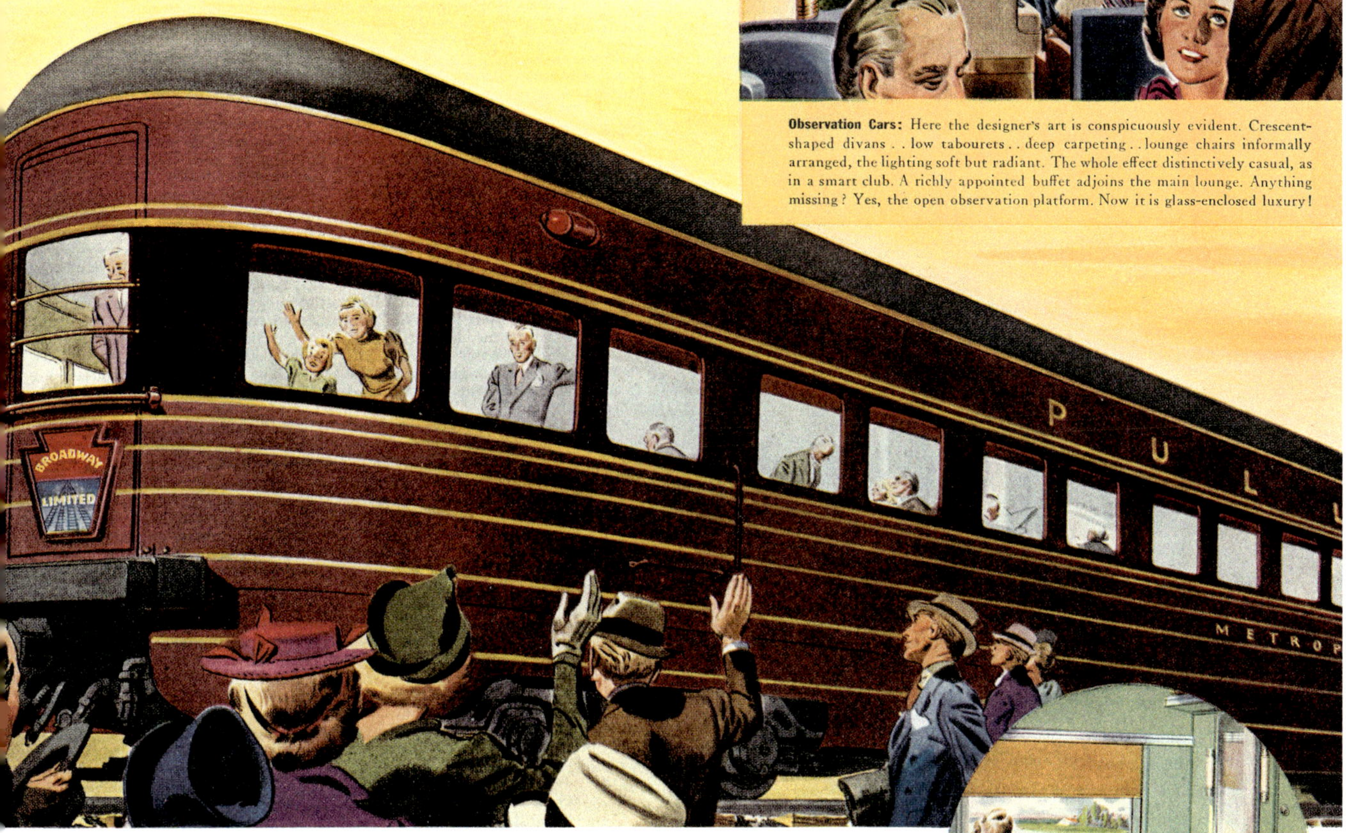

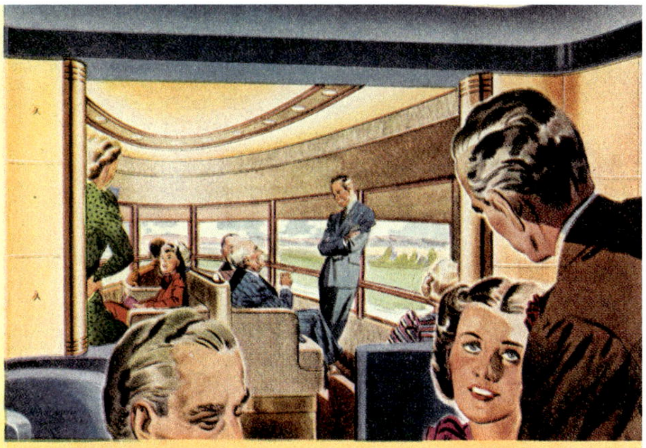

Observation Cars: Here the designer's art is conspicuously evident. Crescent-shaped divans . . low tabourets . . deep carpeting . . lounge chairs informally arranged, the lighting soft but radiant. The whole effect distinctively casual, as in a smart club. A richly appointed buffet adjoins the main lounge. Anything missing? Yes, the open observation platform. Now it is glass-enclosed luxury!

ES INTO SERVICE WEDNESDAY, JUNE 15, 1938, LED BY A NEW AND FINER

BROADWAY LIMITED

First All-Room Train in History. . Daily Between New York and Chicago. . 16 Hours!

RACK TRAINS are reborn—a whole fleet of them. liant innovations in comfort and style. Even car ghts and dimensions change. All this, achieved by aboration of Pennsylvania Railroad and Pullman npany engineers and Raymond Loewy, noted designer.

l it's all yours to enjoy in air-conditioned travel on nsylvania Railroad routes uniting New York, Phila- ohia, Baltimore, Washington and other leading cities n Chicago and St. Louis.

new types of private accommodations, a wider ge than ever before available on any train. In ad- on to new versions of drawing rooms, compart- nts, double bedrooms, you now have . . the Master Suite, the Roomette, the Duplex. Each has a definite individuality, and all have nice soft beds—6 feet, 5 inches long—and private toilet facilities.

Nor is that all. New personality is given the fleet leader . . *Broadway Limited*. Staffed with valet, barber, manicurist, maid and train secretary, this leader becomes an all-room Pullman train. Privacy for every passenger. New-style diners, too—excitingly different. Faster schedule also—New York to Chicago in 16 hours!

Coupled with the new electrified mileage east of Harrisburg, this *Fleet of Modernism* now makes travel on the Pennsylvania Railroad even more attractive than ever before. Enjoy it!

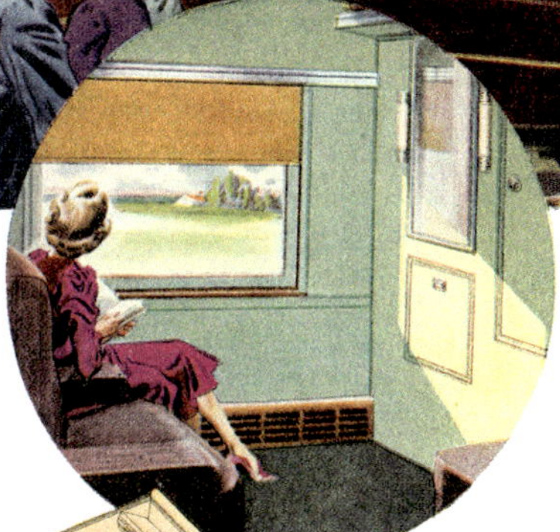

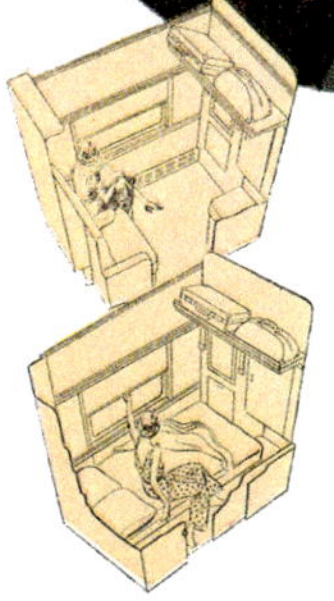

Roomettes give you a private little world of your own. Comfortably compact, this accommodation provides . . personal toilet and washing facilities, illuminated mirror, enclosed wardrobe and, at night, a full-length bed which dips down at your finger's touch.

BY DAY *a cheery sitting room*
BY NIGHT *a cozy bedroom*

Pennsylvania Railroad

SHORTEST ROUTE BETWEEN EAST AND WEST—HEAVIEST RAIL, FINEST ROADBED IN AMERICA. YOU CAN SLEEP *restfully*

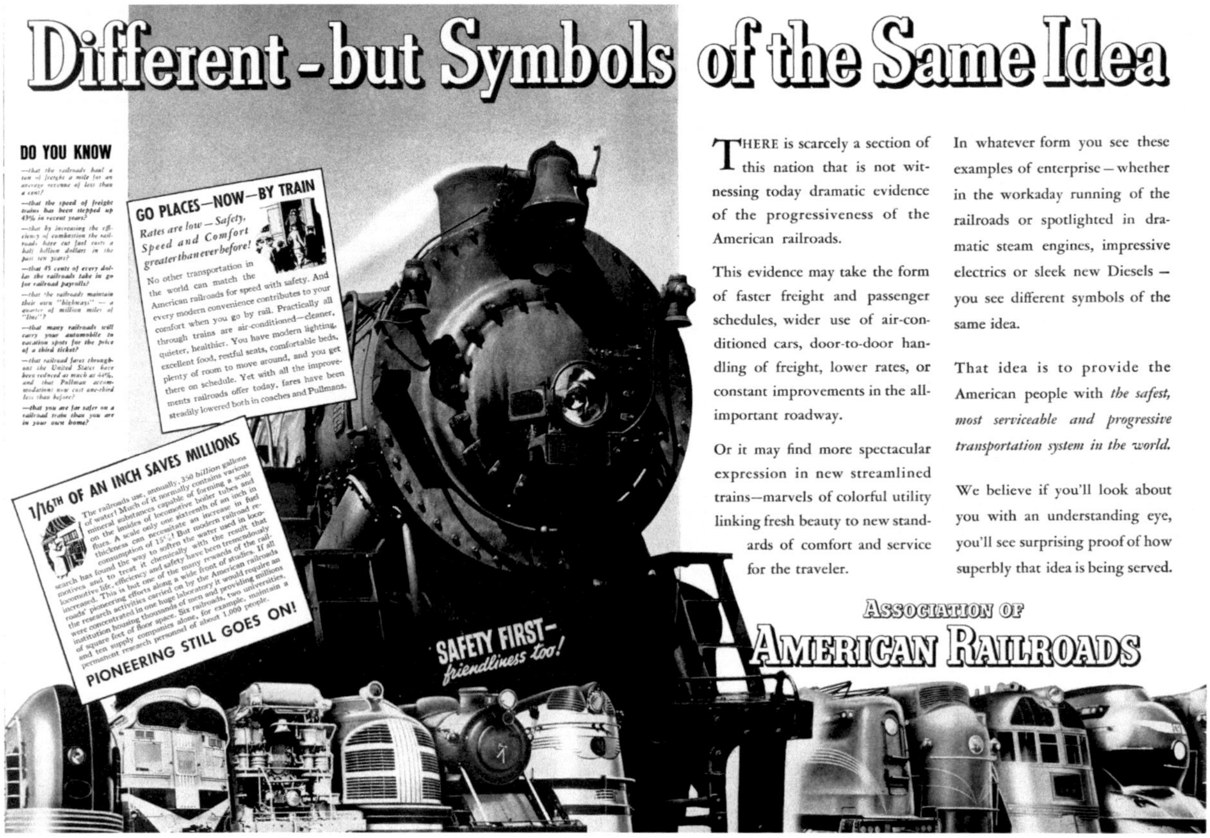

American Railroads, 1936

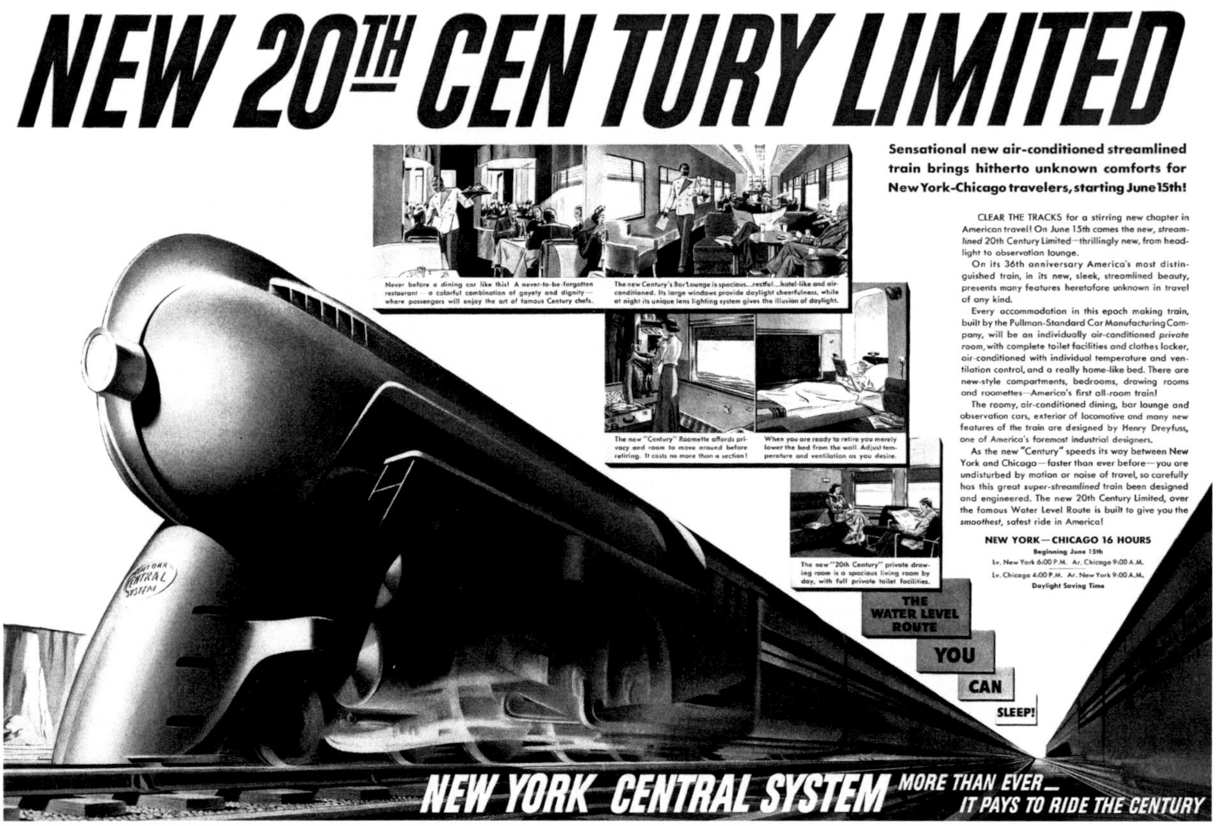

20th Century Limited, 1938

► *N.Y.K. Line, 1932*

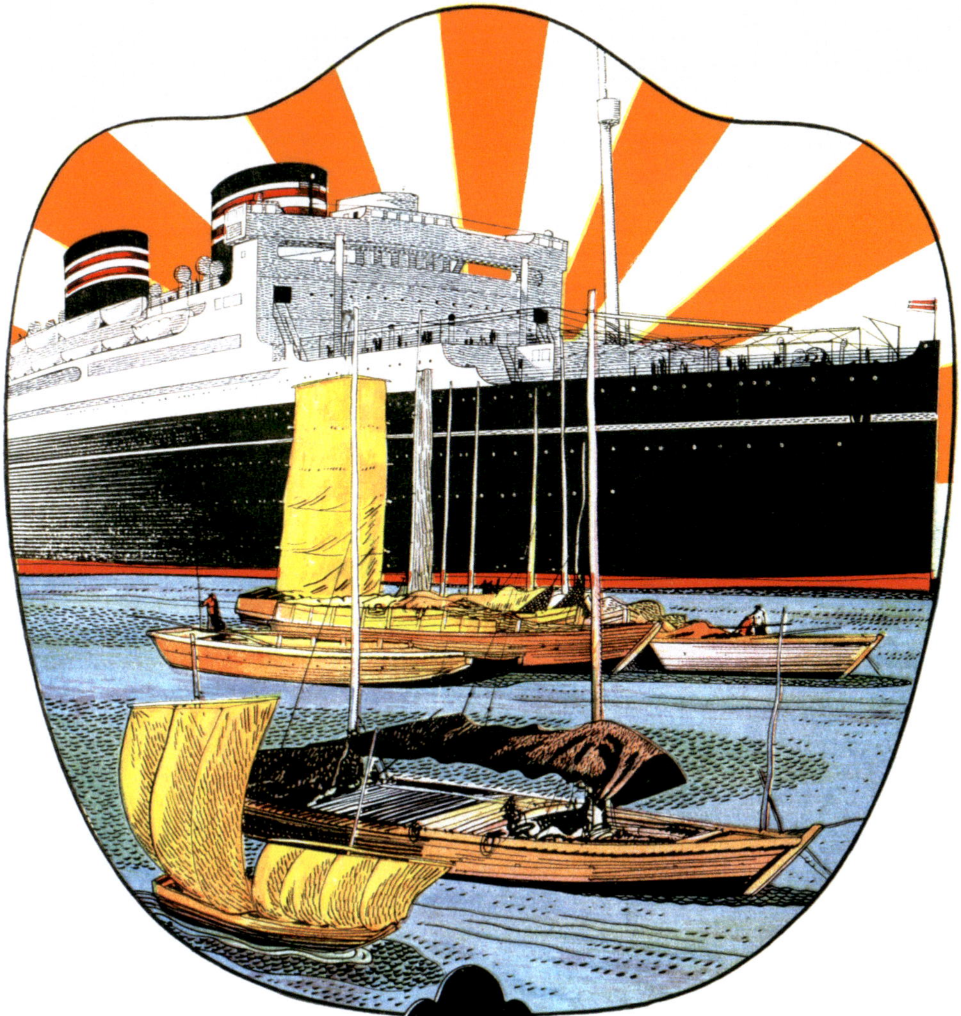

SPECIAL REDUCED FARES ....TO THE ORIENT

Low Summer Rates

● Never before have such attractive rates to the Orient been offered to the American public. Round trip summer rates to Yokohama are now equivalent to approximately one-and-one-half minimum rates first, cabin, second, and tourist classes. ● De luxe first, second, and cabin classes from San Francisco and Los Angeles via Honolulu. Every comfort of the twentieth century on great new express motor liners. Magnificent dancing salons ...tiled swimming pools...gymnasiums...public rooms, the work of European stylists...and menus that would make any languid appetite laugh in eager anticipation. ● Also splendid new cabin and tourist cabin motor liners almost as luxurious...from Seattle and Vancouver direct to Japan.

JAPAN, CHINA and the PHILIPPINES

From Pacific Coast to Japan and Return

FIRST CLASS	CABIN CLASS	TOURIST CABIN
• $465 •	$375 •	$195 UP •

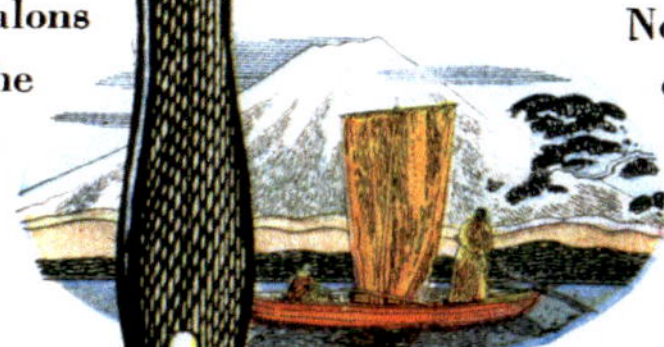

Now is the time to see the wonderful lands of the East. Full details as to rates and the exceptional service given on N.Y.K. ships are described in beautifully illustrated literature. Call or write to Department 19.

N·Y·K·LINE

(Japan Mail)

New York, 25 Broadway, 545 Fifth Avenue San Francisco, 551 Market Street · Seattle, 1404 Fourth Avenue · Chicago, 40 North Dearborn Street · Los Angeles, 605 South Grand Avenue · or any Cunard Line office. Consult your local tourist agent. He knows.

Christmas Present

A happy, carefree cruise Round the World... designed to your order... starting whenever you choose... taking 85 days to two years.

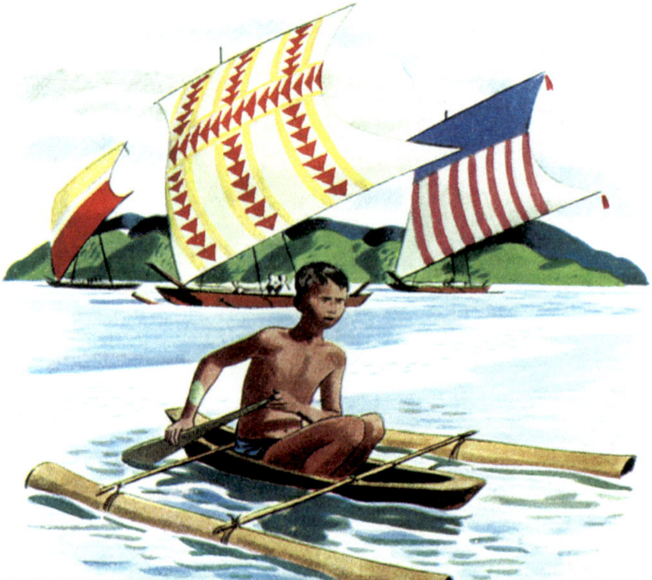

Visits to 21 Fascinating Ports — PHILIPPINE DUGOUT AND VINTAS

Exciting days and nights in the great cosmopolitan ports of Cuba and Panama, California, Hawaii, Japan, China, the Philippines, Malaya, India, Egypt, Italy, and France... 14 fascinating far-flung countries.

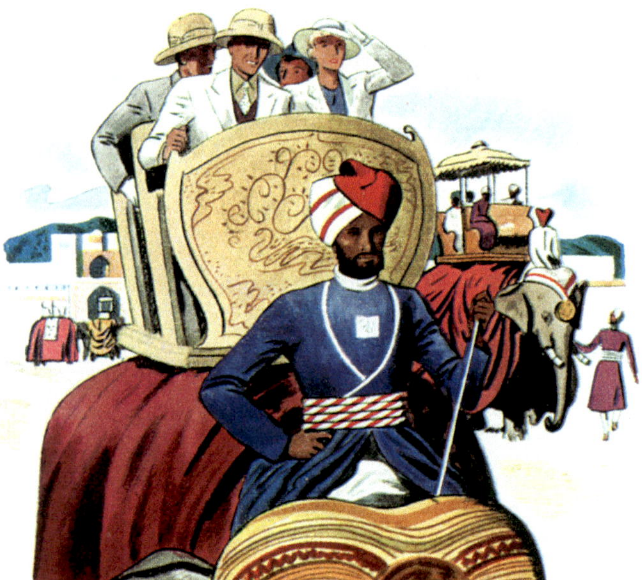

Low Shore Costs — INDIA HAS BRAND NEW THRILLS

Ask your own Travel Agent for all details. Or write Dollar Steamship Lines, 604 Fifth Avenue, New York; 110 South Dearborn Street, Chicago; 311 California Street, San Francisco. Offices in other principal cities.

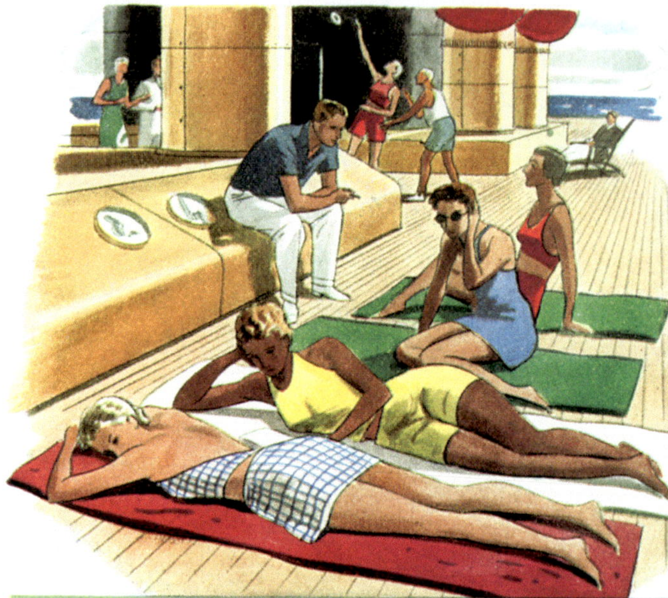

Luxurious Living — ALONG THE SUNSHINE ROUTE

World-famed President Liners have broad play-decks and an outdoor swimming pool... every stateroom outside (with real twin beds)... menus made up from the best the whole wide world affords.

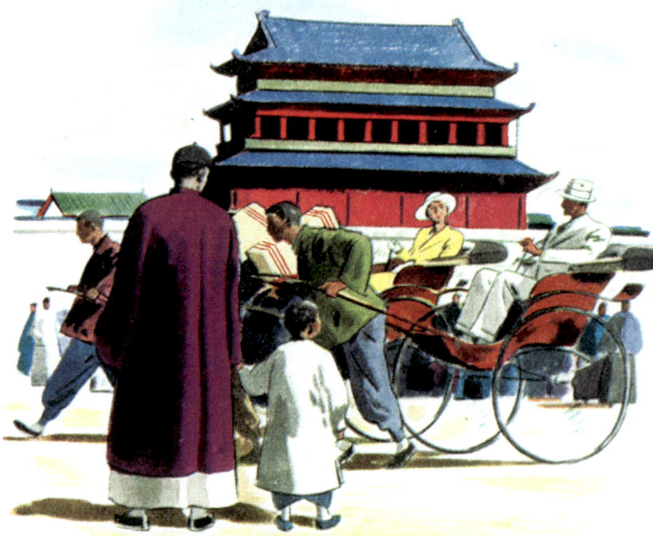

Stopovers and Sidetrips Anywhere — PEKING SIDETRIP

Weekly sailings from New York, Los Angeles and San Francisco allow stopovers and sidetrips anywhere en route... continuation on the next or another of these world's only regular-world-cruising ships.

Round the World

CRUISES TO ORDER

COST JUST $854 FIRST CLASS

•

DOLLAR
Steamship Lines

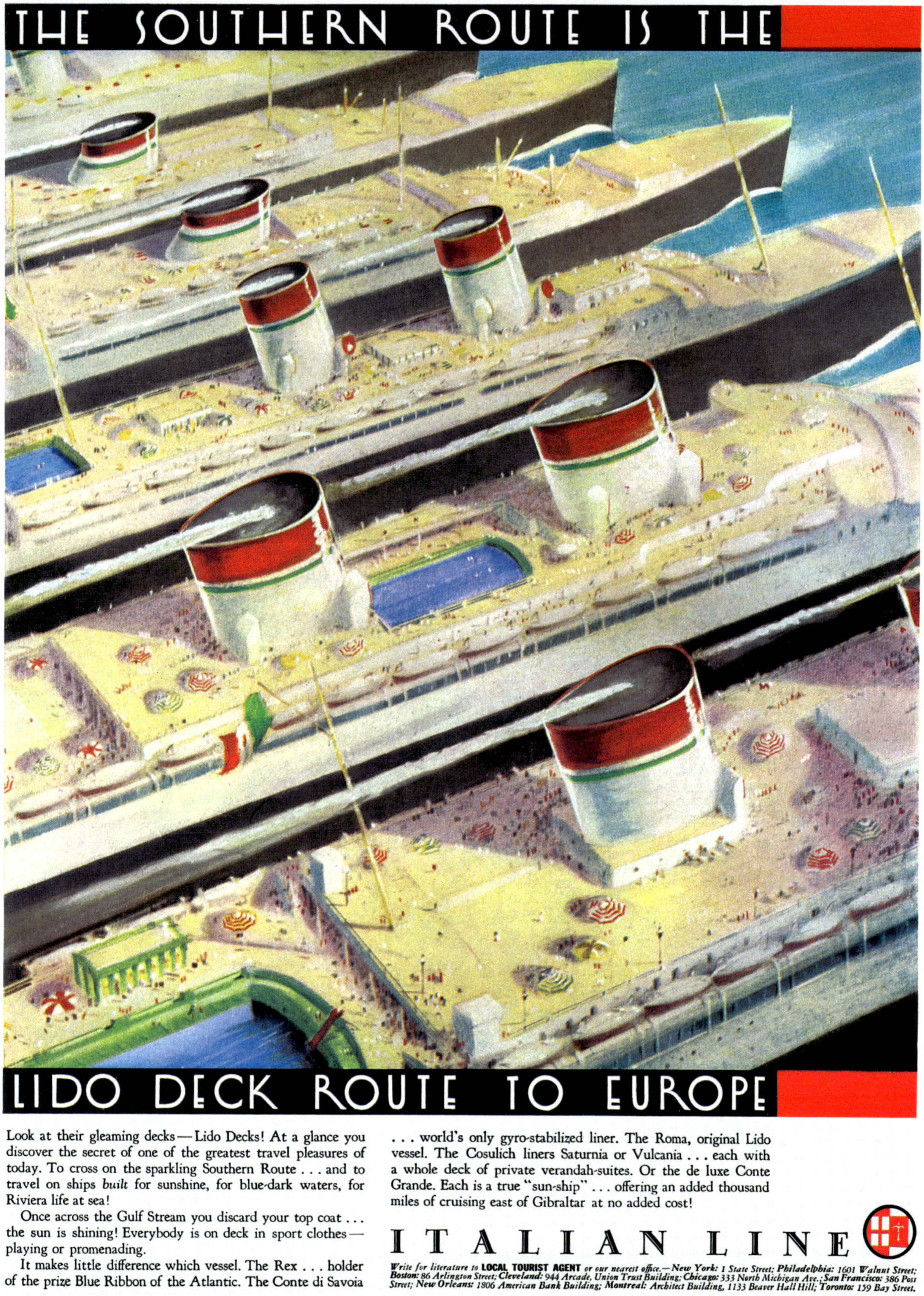

Dollar Steamship Lines, 1935 ◂

Italian Line, 1939

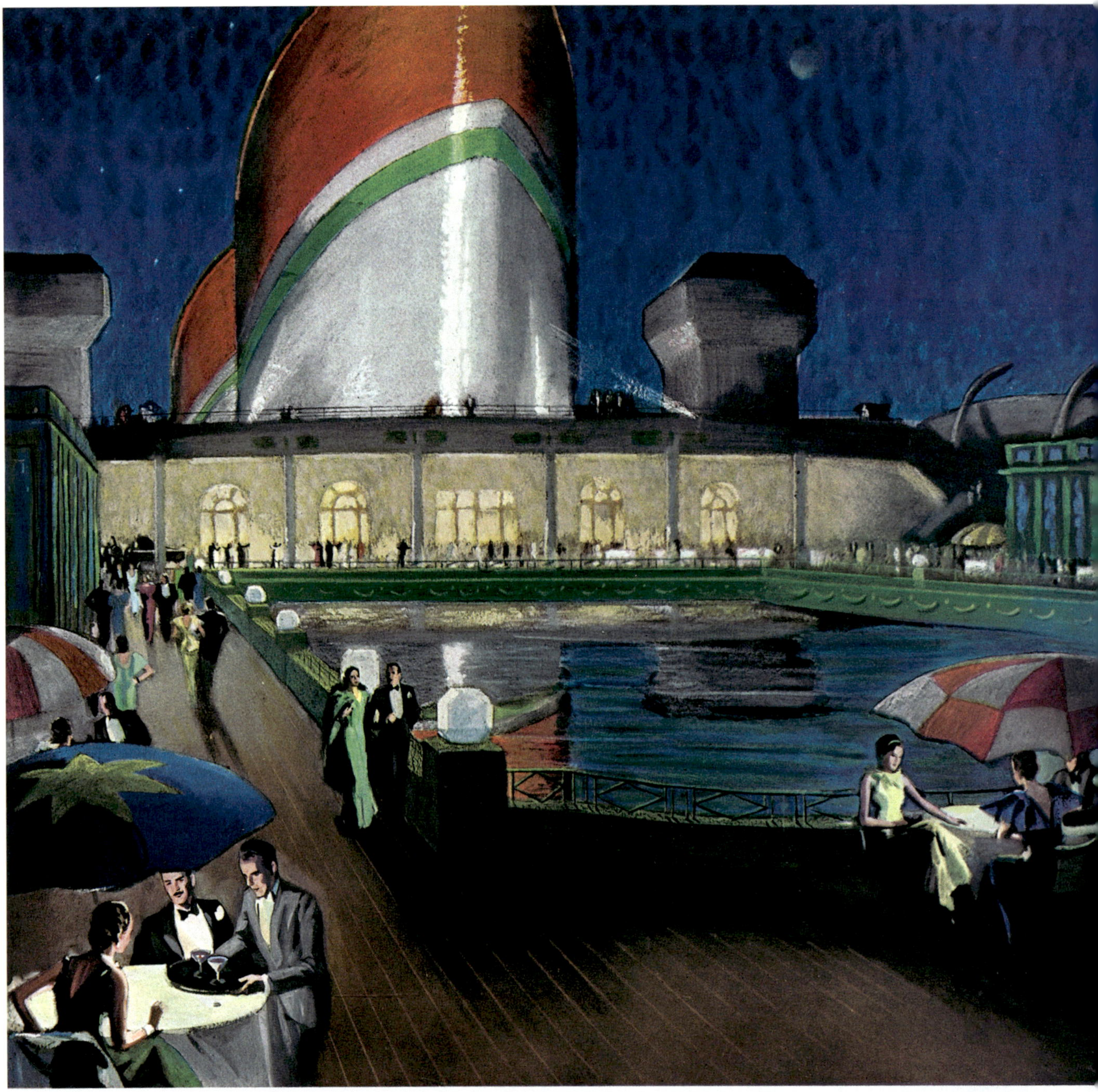

THE *Lido Life*

synonymous with the

SOUTHERN ROUTE

"Lido" is an Italian word . . the Lido Deck an Italian Line creation! In daytime, with the sun streaming down, here is the Lido of gay cabanas and beach costume. In the ghostly evening, stars and shaded lamps utterly transform the setting! Now you are formal—festive—as on the terrace of a Riviera casino, with the moon and the Mediterranean everywhere.

Only on the Southern Route can the "Lido life" be properly enjoyed. For a speedy crossing, choose the Rex, fastest liner afloat, or the Conte di Savoia, only gyro-stabilized liner. The Roma and Augustus offer the same Lido delights on a more leisurely itinerary—likewise the Cosulich liners Saturnia and Vulcania, which include as many as nine and ten ports en route. And remember that all six vessels offer 1000 miles or more of cruising "east of Gibraltar" at no extra cost!

*Write for illustrated literature to local agent or our nearest office. — **New York:** 1 State Street; **Philadelphia:** 1601 Walnut Street; **Boston:** 86 Arlington Street; **Cleveland:** 944 Arcade, Union Trust Building; **Chicago:** 333 North Michigan Avenue; **San Francisco:** 386 Post Street; **New Orleans:** 1806 American Bank Building; **Montreal:** Architect Building, 1133 Beaver Hall Hill; **Toronto:** 159 Bay Street.*

ITALIAN LINE

Italian Line, 1934

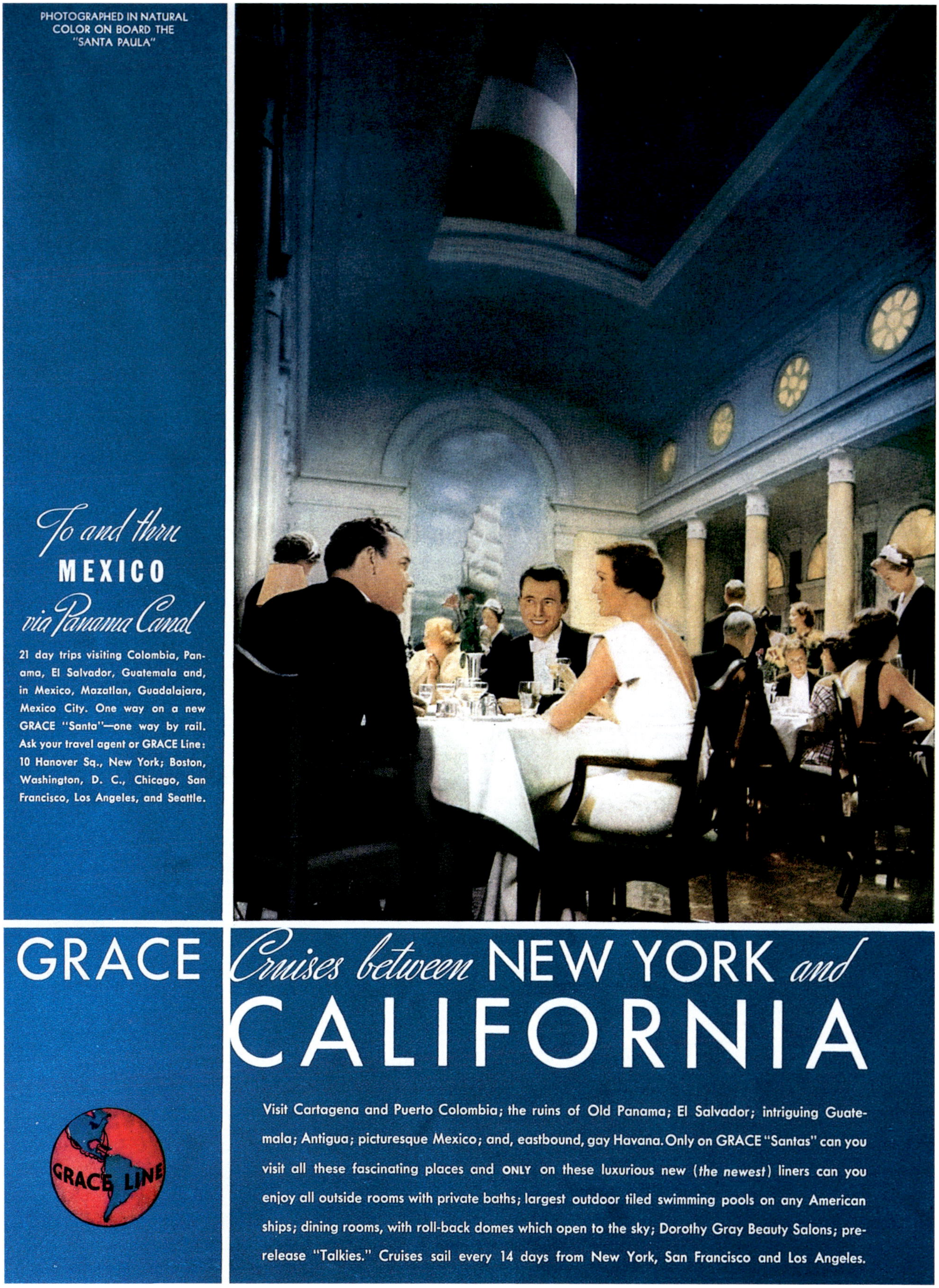

Grace Cruises, 1935

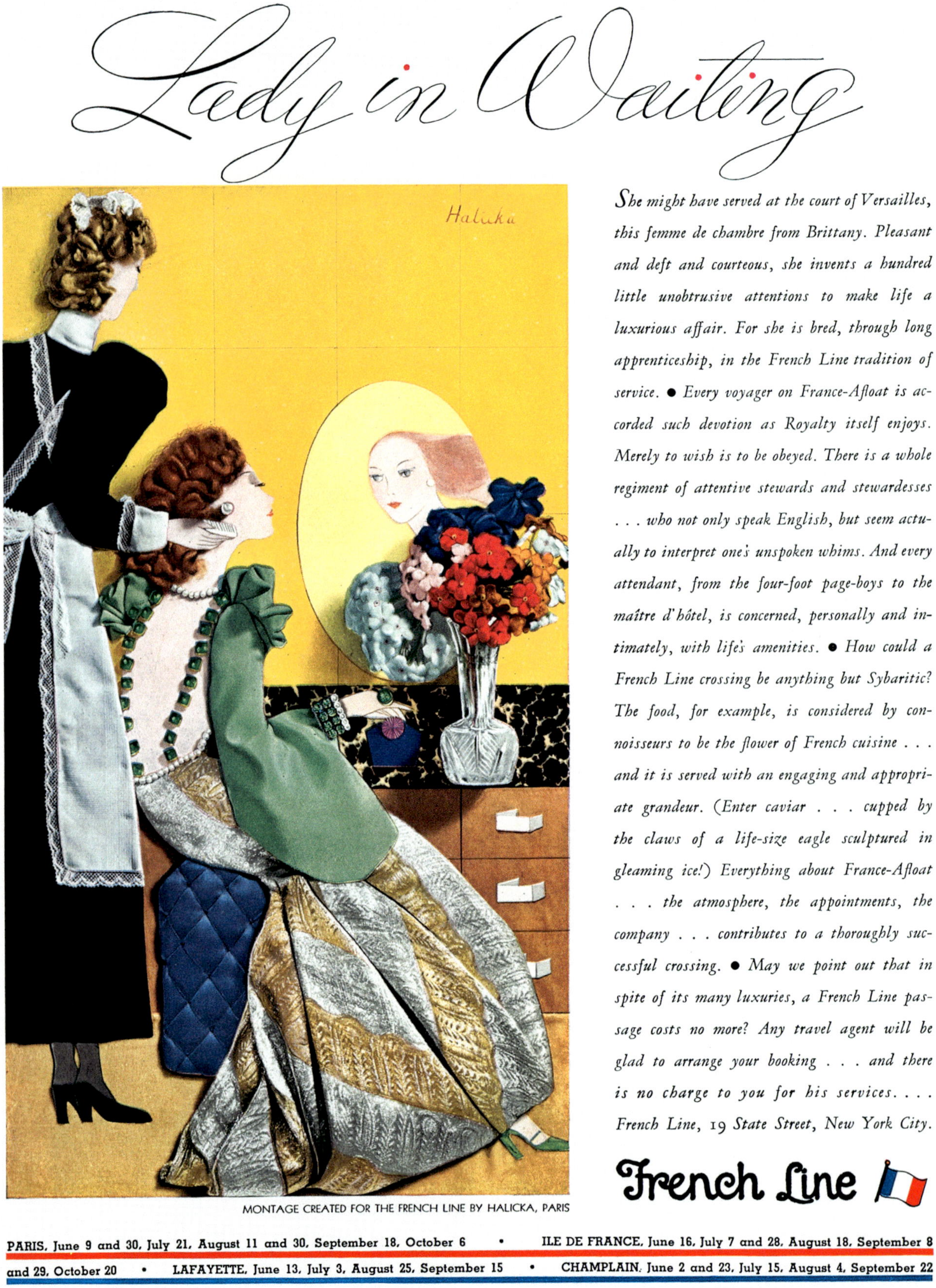

French Line, 1934

LAND OF CEREMONY

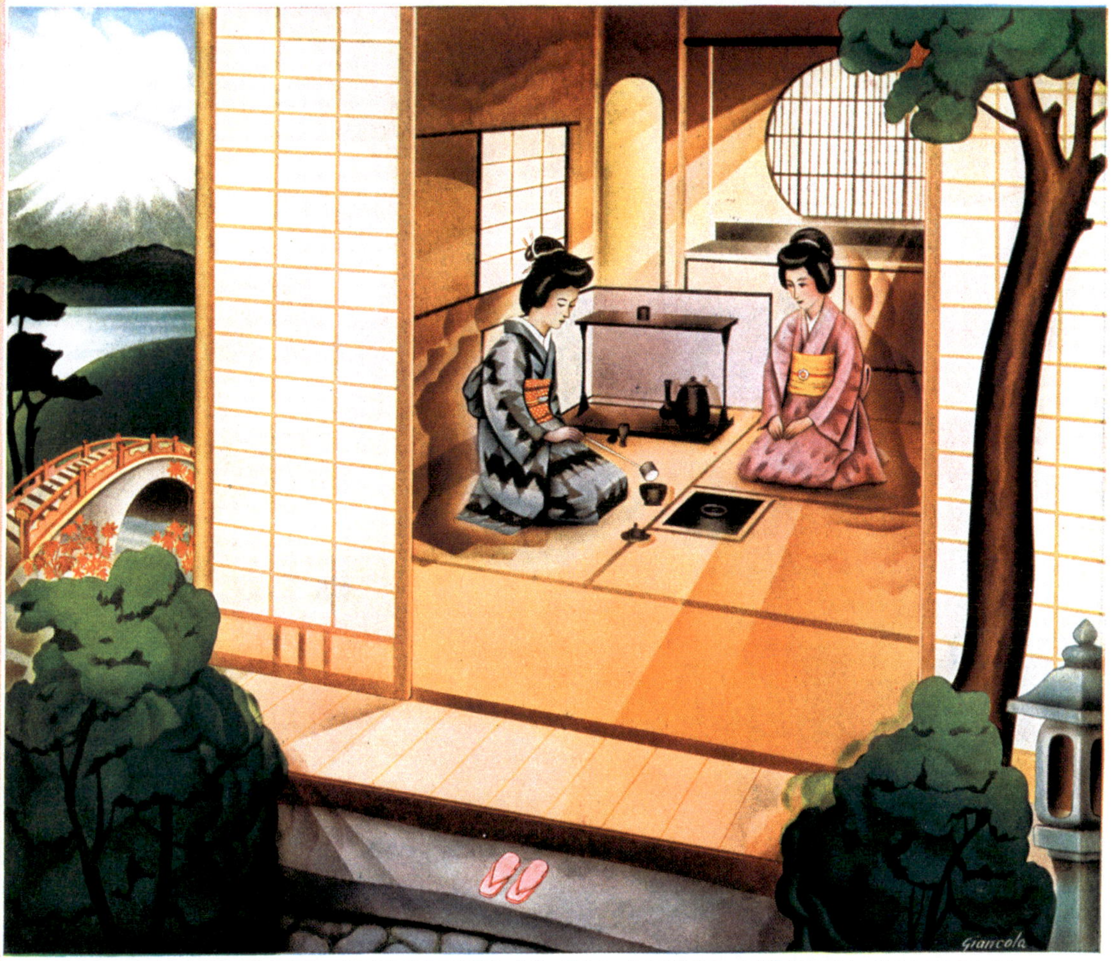

THE TEA CEREMONY—INTRODUCED BY THE SHOGUN ASHIKAGA YOSHIMASA

THE visitor to Old Japan is always delighted with the gracious ceremonies to which even the simplest acts are elevated. How perfectly this artistic reverence prepares one for the wonders of the Blossom Empire—its mirror lakes and painted valleys, the centuries-old craftsmanship, all the ancient loveliness of shrines and temples.

Most pleasantly surprising is the existence side by side with these ancient beauties of the modern miracles of traveling comfort and convenience. Swift, super-luxury express trains whisk the traveler from city to city. Large, modern hotels await him everywhere with all the familiar facilities and services. Automobiles spin into the remotest sections. Even the favorite sports are amply provided for—golf, tennis, baseball, riding or flying.

The Japan Tourist Bureau (a non-commercial organization) maintains an office in New York in addition to widespread facilities in Japan for the special service of visitors. It will be honored to help plan your itinerary, arrange all the details of accommodations, and serve you while in Japan, without additional cost. It will make your visit to "The All Year Paradise" an unforgettable experience.

The wonderlands of Japan, Korea, Manchuria and China are reached from the United States and Canada by frequent steamships sailing from San Francisco, Seattle and Vancouver. Full information will be furnished by any tourist agency or by the Japan Tourist Bureau. Write for Booklet.

JAPAN
TOURIST BUREAU

c/o Japanese Gov't Railways, One Madison Ave., N. Y. City
c/o Nippon Yusen Kaisha, 545 Fifth Ave., N. Y. City

Japan Tourist Bureau, 1930

Lido after dark

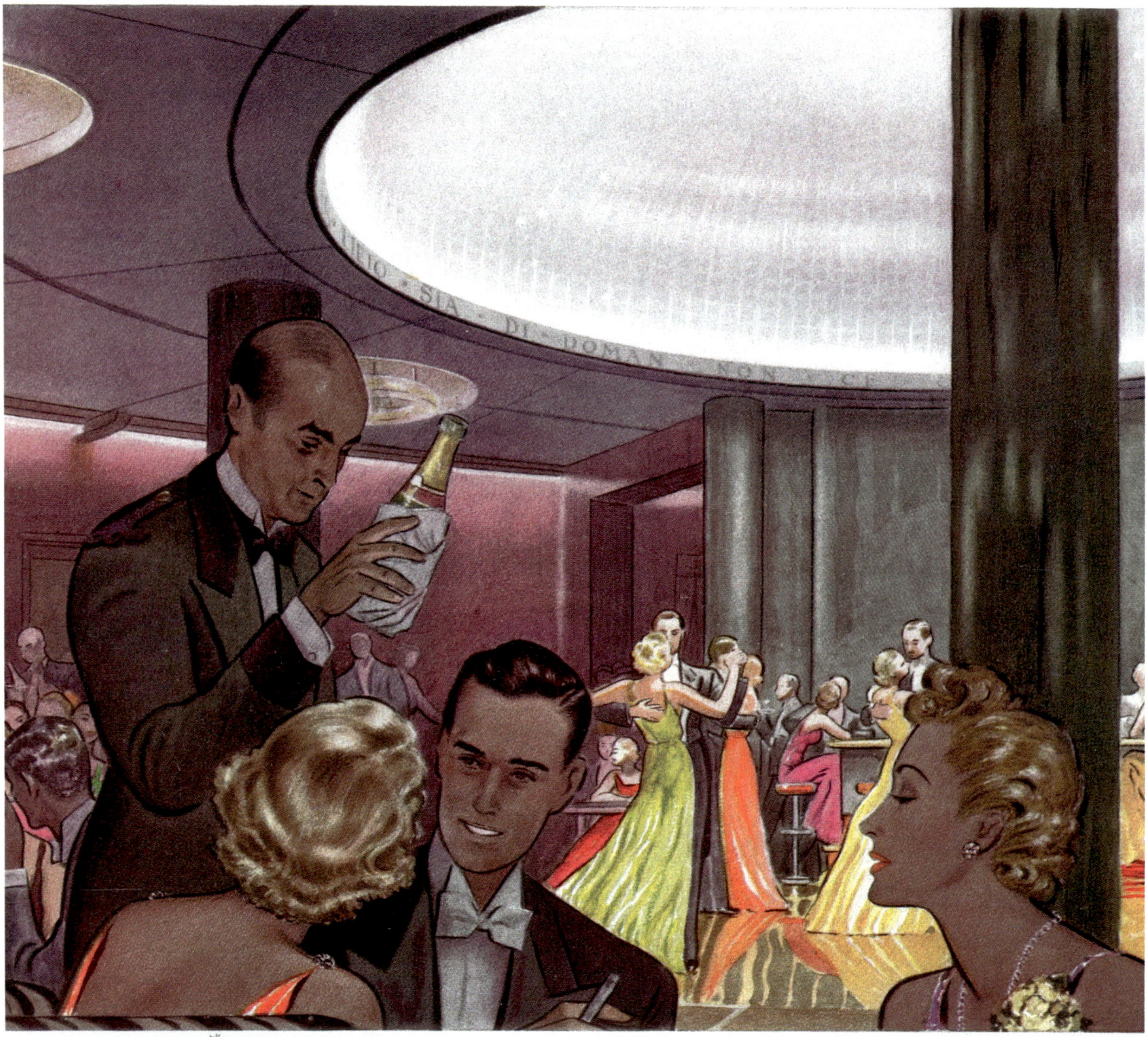

THE CONTE DI SAVOIA . . . MIDNIGHT!

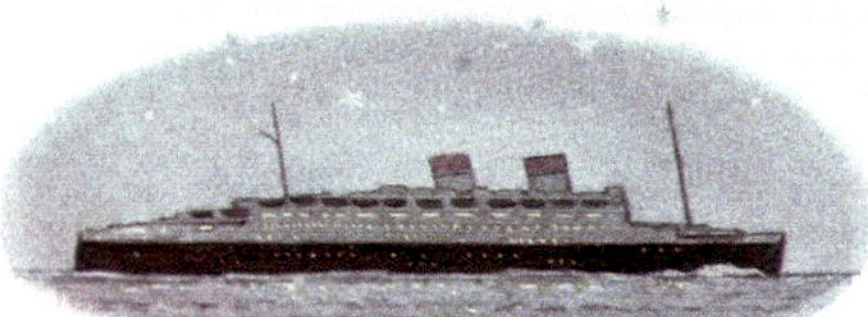

THE miraculous Southern Route sun has gone down . . . and the scene changes utterly. Instead of beach slacks . . . it's "white tie and tails". Instead of deck tennis, fencing, traps . . . it's music and champagne . . . or Asti Spumante, if you prefer to "do as the Romans do", as you probably will. For of course this is an Italian ship, offering all the warmth and subtlety of Italy's wines and table delicacies as well as those of other countries. Daytime Lido brought first fame to the Italian Line, with its sweeping play-decks and pools. Lido after dark brings the crowning mark of elegance to your Wintertime outdoor crossing.

Choose the great Rex, the gyro-stabilized Conte di Savoia, or the charming Roma, for an express voyage. Or enjoy the more leisurely route of the Vulcania or Saturnia, with their eight or nine extra ports to entertain you on the way. All are true Lido leaders . . . by day or night!

The leading **TRAVEL AGENTS** *in your city are our representatives. Consult them freely—their services are gratis. Or apply to our nearest office: New York, Philadelphia, Boston, Cleveland, Chicago, Los Angeles, San Francisco, New Orleans, Montreal, Toronto.*

ITALIAN LINE

Italian Line, 1937

► *Italian Line, 1938*

Winter takes a Lido holiday

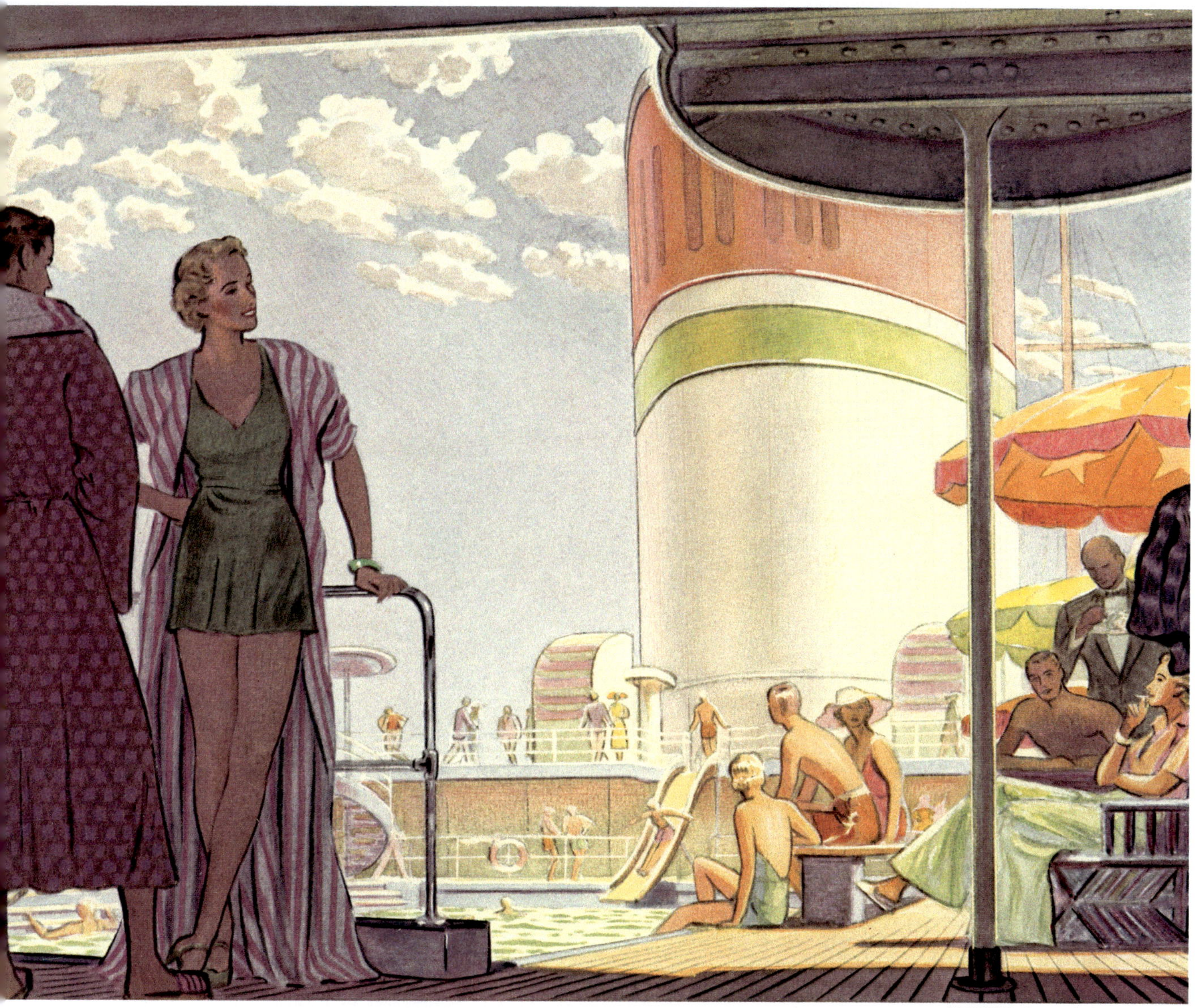

LIDO DECK—Conte di SAVOIA

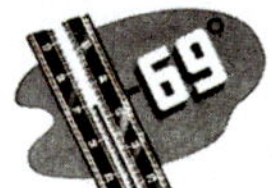

The Thermometer Tells the Story! . . . 69° is a fairly normal noon temperature on a typical Southern Route crossing . . . though it may be freezing at home. Ask your Travel Agent for our illustrated weather-map booklet giving comparative statistics: "Why It's Called the Mild Southern Route".

WINTER goes a-summering on the Southern Route! Though the calendar wears a frosty look, it knows no power to change the bright skies, the blue waters, the friendly temperatures . . . as your Italian liner approaches mid-ocean, skirts the Azores, pauses at Gibraltar and moves serenely on into the placid Mediterranean.

"Lido" takes command! Thanks to the beneficent weather . . . and thanks many times over to the design and construction of Lido ships . . . your Winter crossing is transformed into a beach-revel of warmth and sunshine. For this is the *open-air* way to all Europe, especially in the cold months. Board the great Rex, the gyro-stabilized Conte di Savoia or the charming Roma, for an express voyage. Or treat yourself to the leisurely nine or ten port itinerary of the popular Vulcania or Saturnia . . . if you can afford the time to *see more* on your way to Europe.

In either case, be sure to pack your favorite beach-robe and sandals!

The leading **TRAVEL AGENTS** *in your city are our representatives. Consult them freely—their services are gratis. Or apply to our nearest office: New York, Philadelphia, Boston, Cleveland, Chicago, Los Angeles, San Francisco, New Orleans, Montreal, Toronto.*

ITALIAN LINE

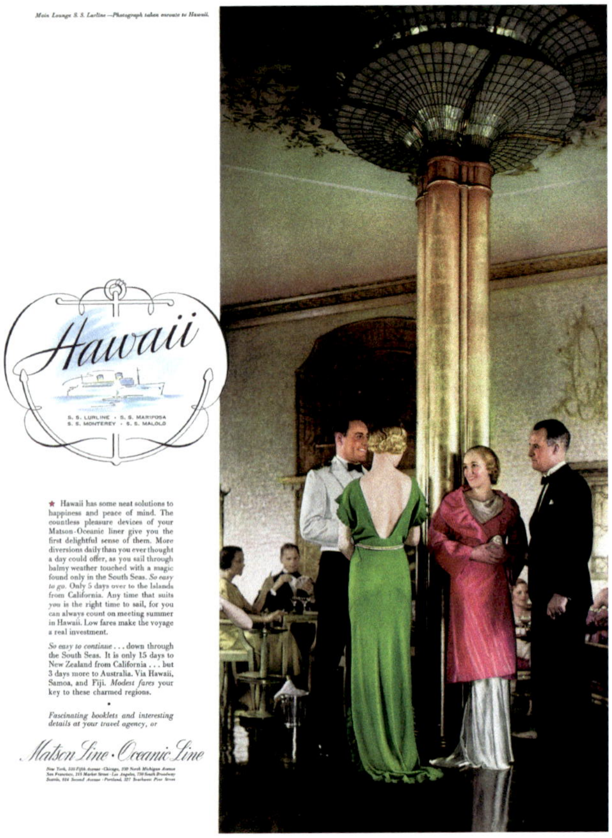

Matson Line, 1934

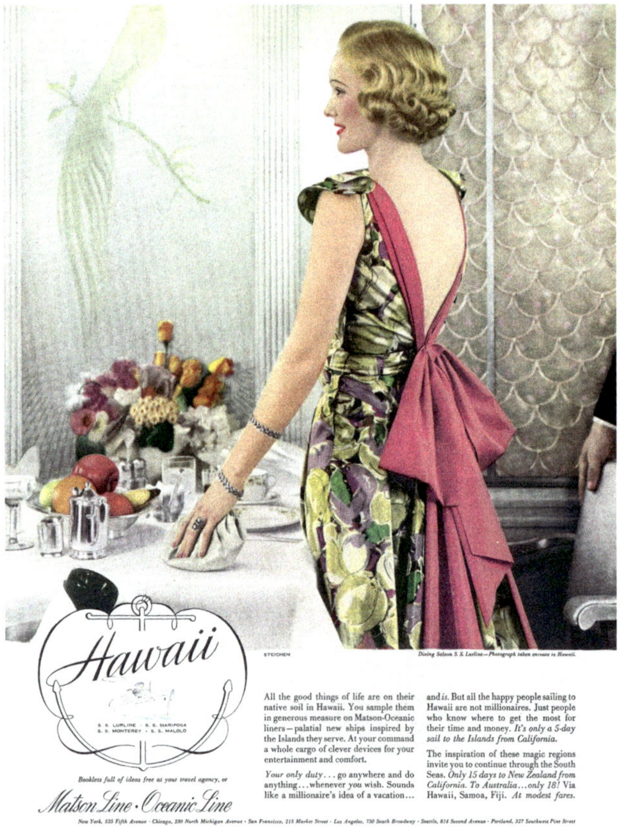

Matson Line, 1934

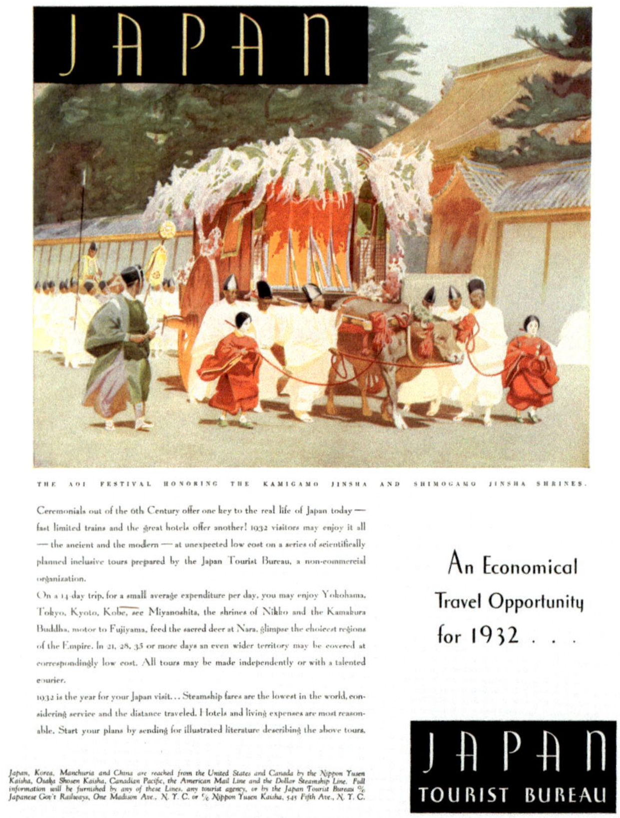

Japan Tourist Bureau, 1932

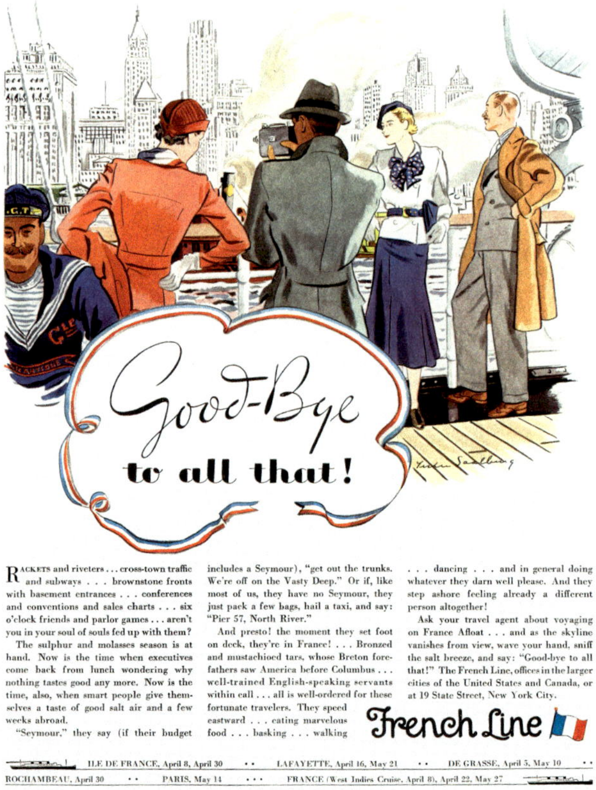

French Line, 1931

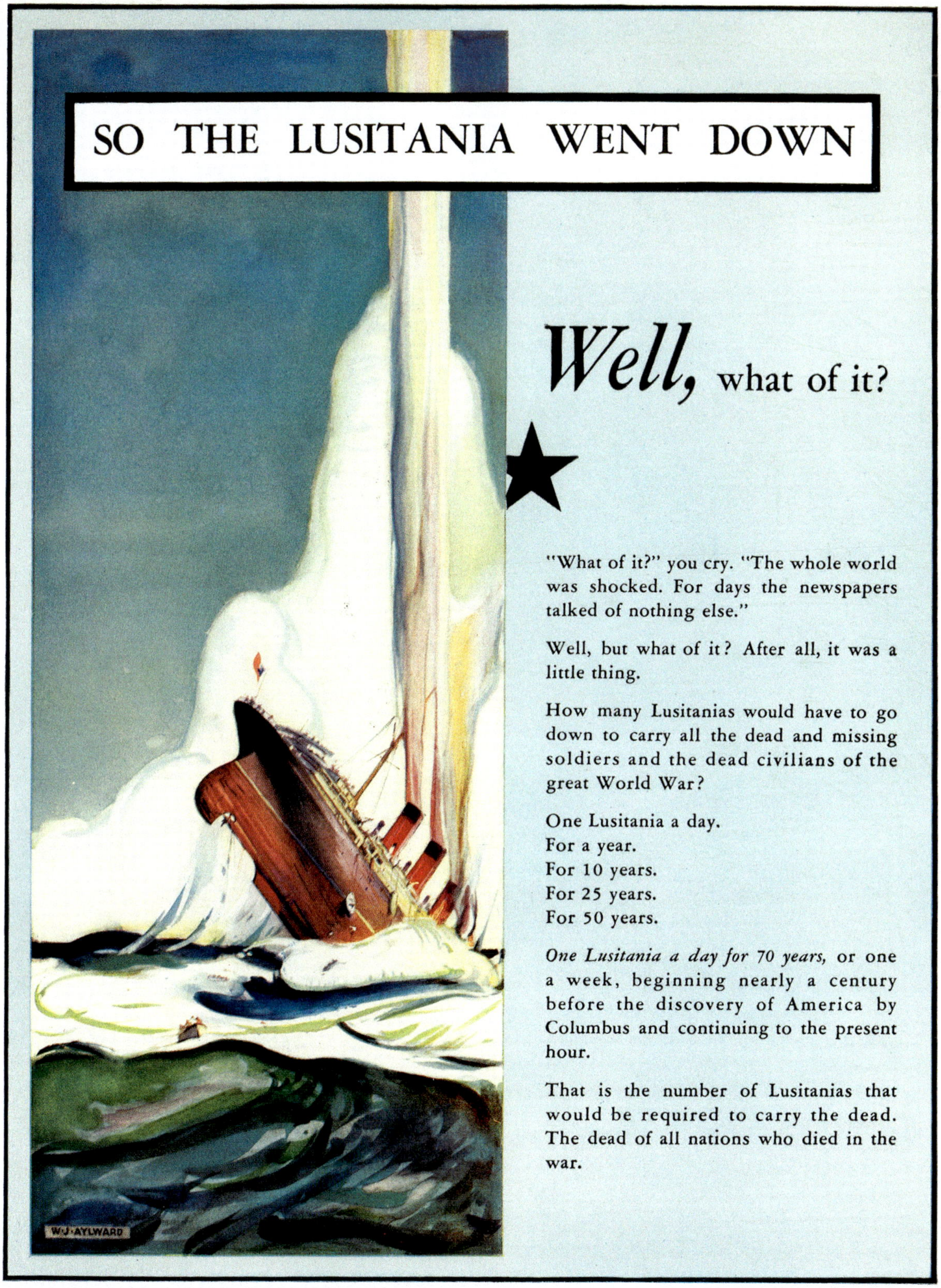

This advertisement, written by Bruce Barton, painted by W. J. Aylward and presented here through the co-operation of FORTUNE and the courtesy of the AMERICAN MAGAZINE, is the first exhibit of an educational campaign dramatizing the horrors of war; a campaign which Henry Ewald has called "a bold, practical plan which dwarfs all former use of advertising." Co-operation to develop this campaign into a persistent, extensive, efficient drive for Peace is invited by World Peaceways, Hotel Roosevelt, Madison Avenue at Forty-fifth Street, New York City.

World Peaceways, 1934

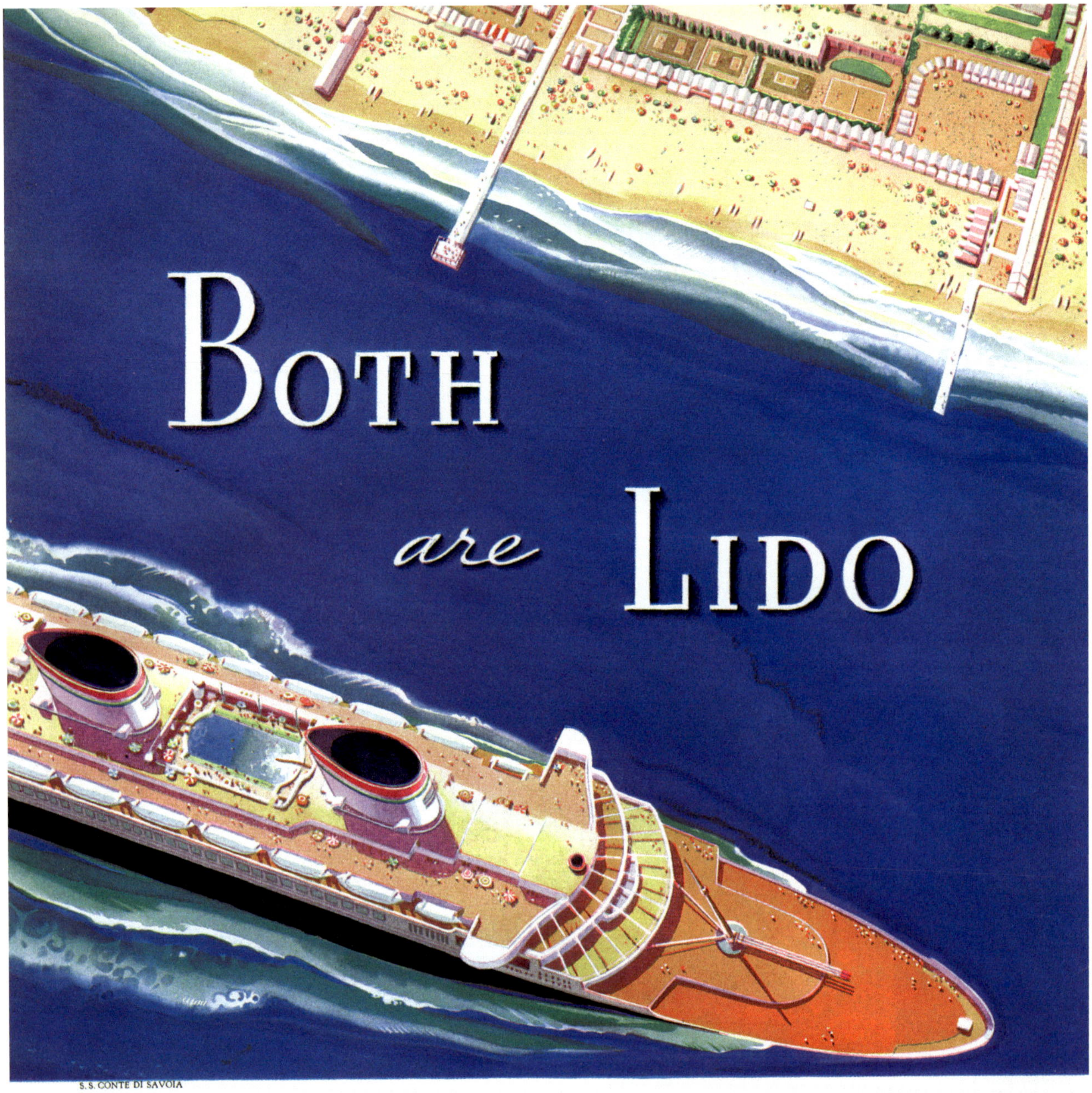

S.S. CONTE DI SAVOIA

The Lido of Venice . . . and the Lido of Italian liners . . . are sisters under the sun! The famed strip of golden, warm sands, splashed by the turquoise of the Adriatic and set off by the glories of Venice across the Lagoon . . . sees its splendor, its color, its charm, its *Lido life* mirrored on the sweeping decks of the super-liners Rex and Conte di Savoia . . . leaders of the equally famed Italian Line fleet!

Smart Europe flocks to Venice's Lido "in season". Smart America more and more is flocking to the Italian Line's Lido in *all* seasons—because of the outdoor delights, the mildness, the serene comforts of the Southern Route crossing, at any time of the year.

Soon you will be going abroad again. This time, give your trip the added glamour of a Lido crossing . . . and the added 1000 miles or more of Mediterranean cruising at no added cost. There are two ways to go—a direct, express crossing to Naples, Genoa or Nice on the Rex or Conte di Savoia . . . or a leisurely itinerary embracing as many as ten fascinating ports on the popular Roma, Saturnia or Vulcania. And at the end of your Lido voyage, fast trains will speed you to European capitals!

The leading **TRAVEL AGENTS** *in your city are our representatives. Consult them freely—their services are gratis. Or apply to our nearest office:* ***New York, Philadelphia, Boston, Cleveland, Chicago, San Francisco, New Orleans, Montreal, Toronto.***

ITALIAN LINE

Italian Line, 1937

► *Oceanic Steamship Co., 1934*

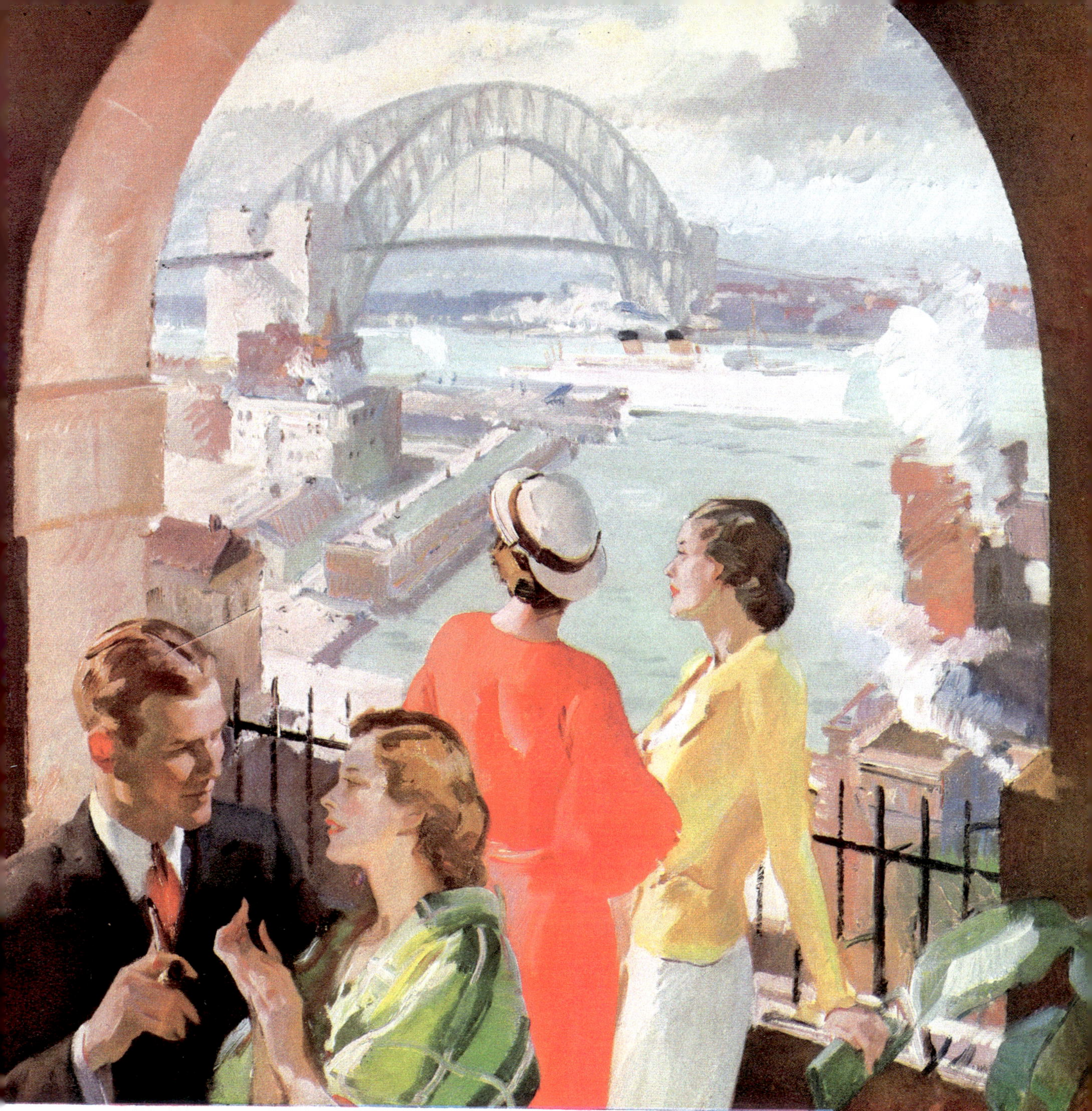

NEW ADVENTURE

A view of Sydney harbor . . . evoking admiration for Australia and the youthful vitality of its young civilization . . . playing . . . building . . . achieving a new order on the world's oldest continent. Strange contrasts—almost within sound of today's busy traffic—unique survivals of human and animal life found in no other part of the world. A voyage to this South Seas continent offers a *new adventure.*

Join a Matson *"South Pacific Cruise" personally escorted all-inclusive-cost—to Australia! via Hawaii! Samoa! Fiji! New Zealand!* Never before in travel! A 46-day cruise from California, *every month of the year.* No more than 5 days between ports. Smart elegance of magnificent liners..."Mariposa" or "Monterey"...emphasizing your enjoyment of the voyage. Similar attractive fares if you travel independently. ☆ *Your travel agent is an authority, see him for information, or any of our offices.*

The OCEANIC STEAMSHIP COMPANY
MATSON LINE

New York, 535 Fifth Ave. · Chicago, 230 No. Michigan Ave. · San Francisco, 215 Market St. · Los Angeles, 730 So. Broadway · Seattle, 814 Second Ave. · Portland, 327 Southwest Pine St.

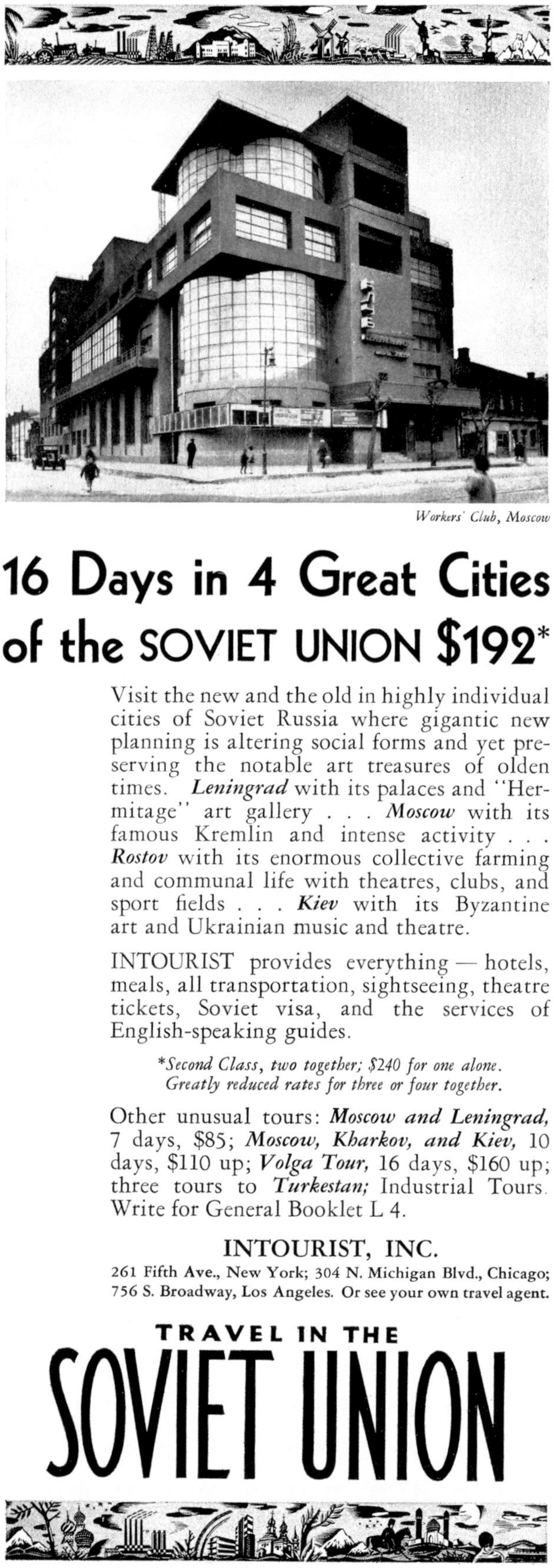

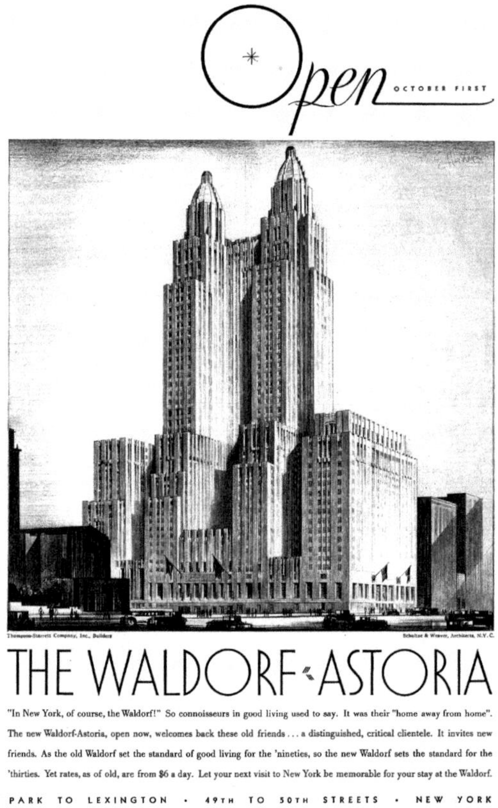

The Waldorf Astoria, 1931

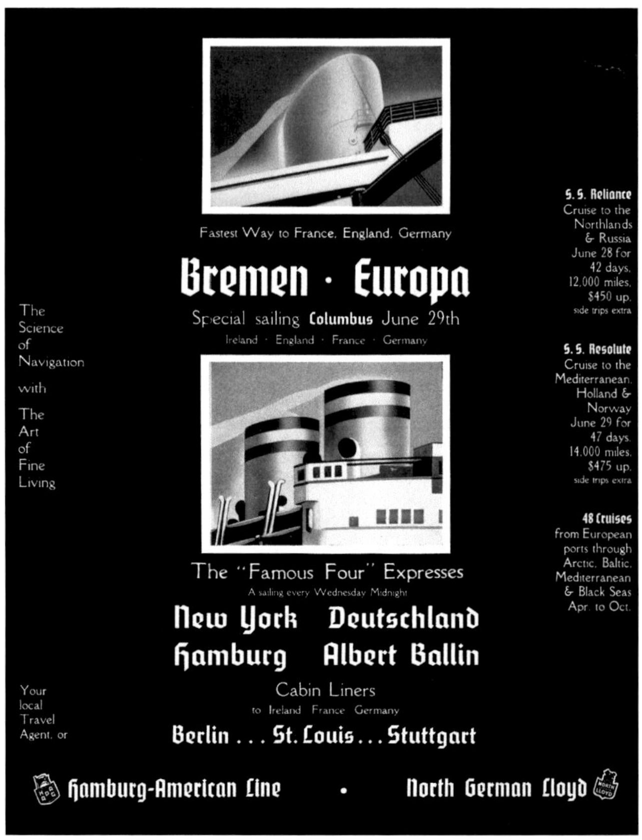

Intourist, Inc.,1931

Hamburg-American Line, 1935

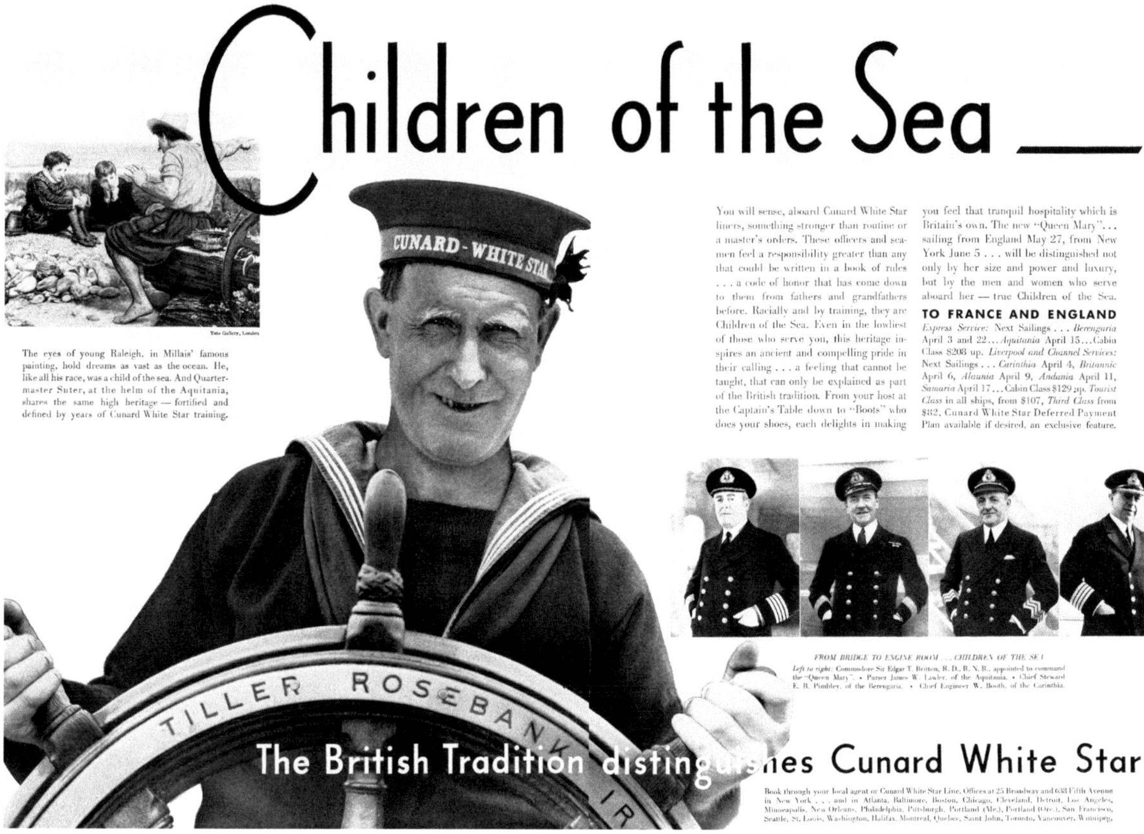

Cunard White Star, 1936

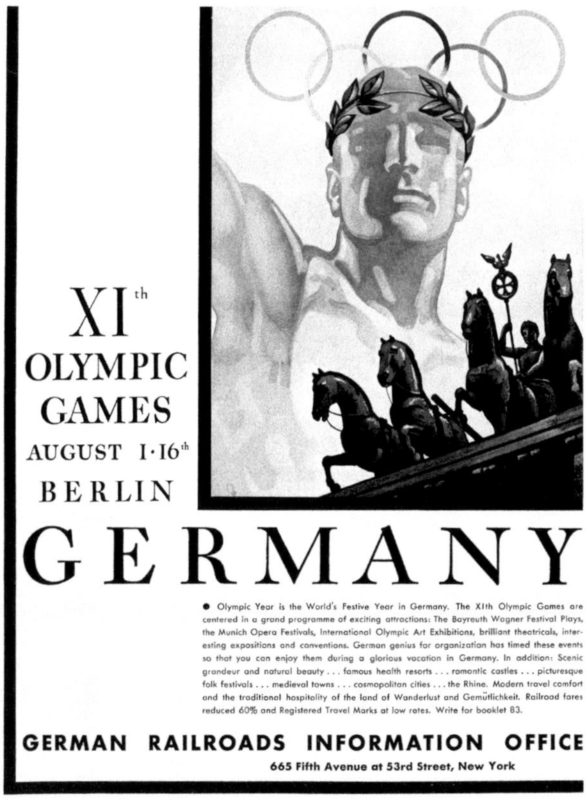

German Railroads Information Office, 1936

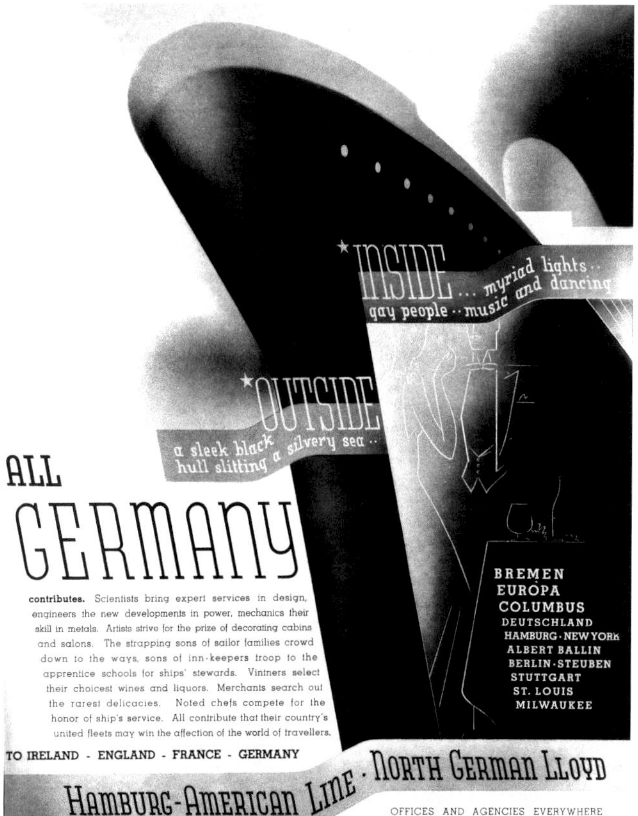

Hamburg-American Line, 1934

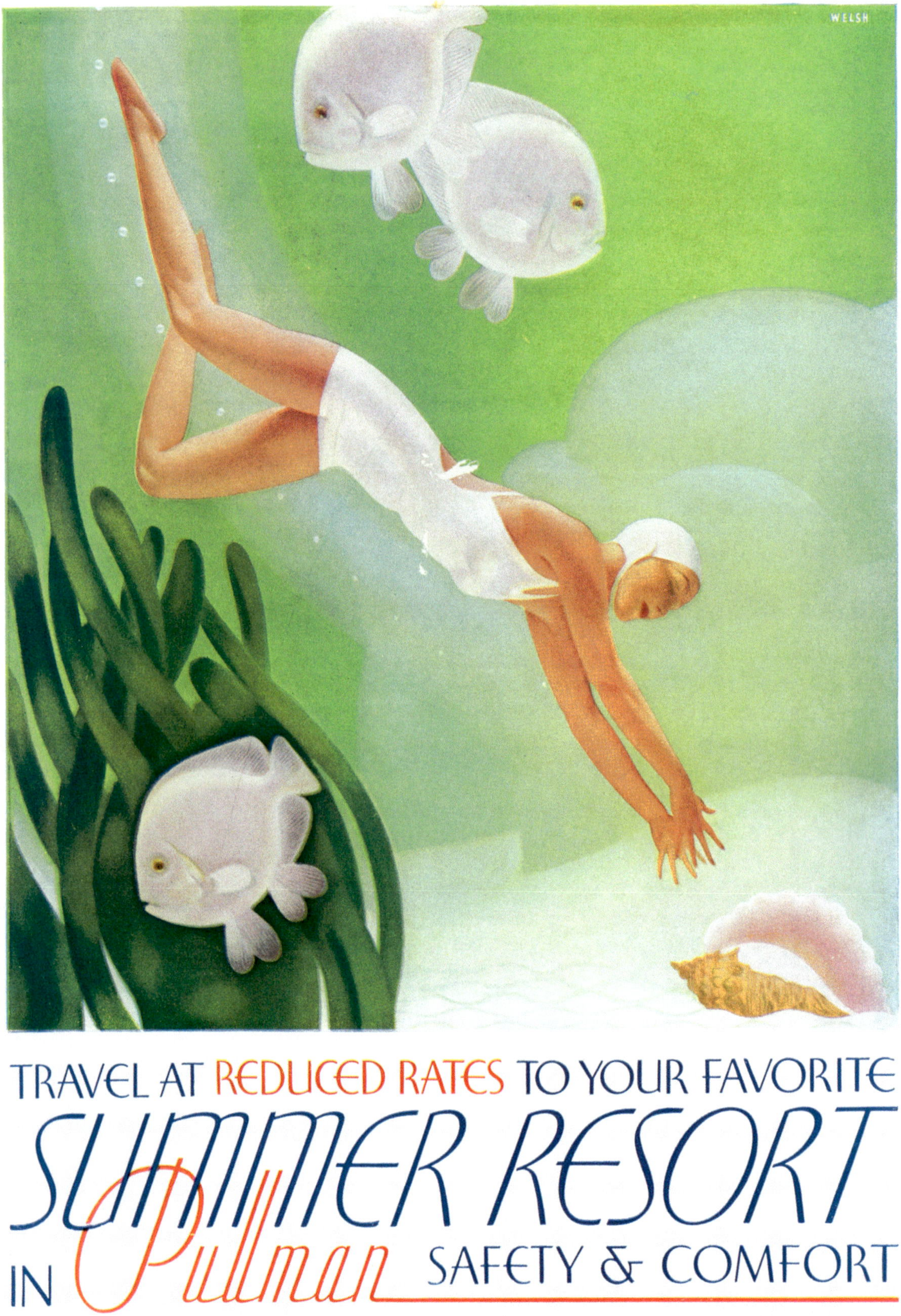

▲► *Pullman, 1937*

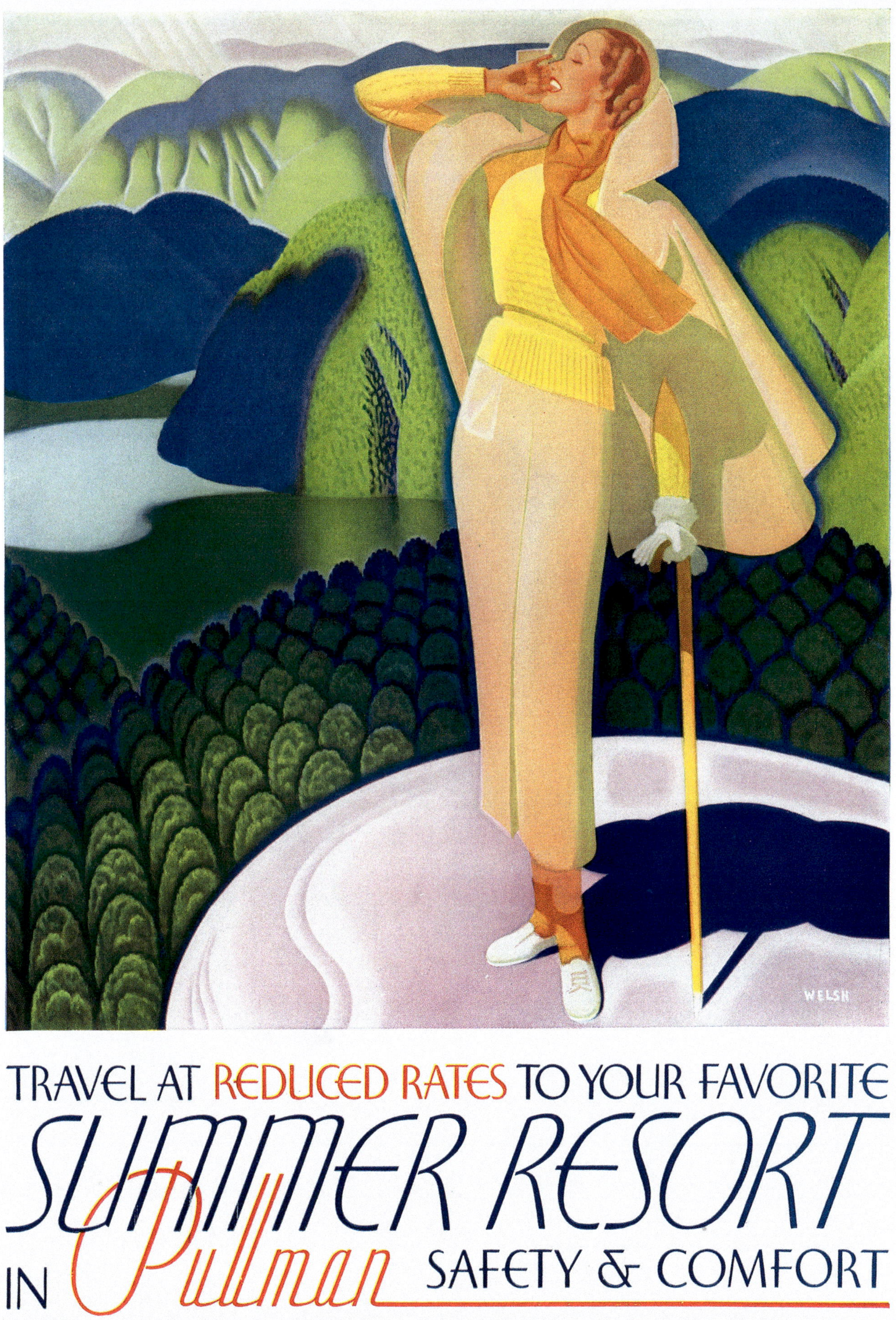
WELSH
TRAVEL AT REDUCED RATES TO YOUR FAVORITE
SUMMER RESORT
IN Pullman SAFETY & COMFORT

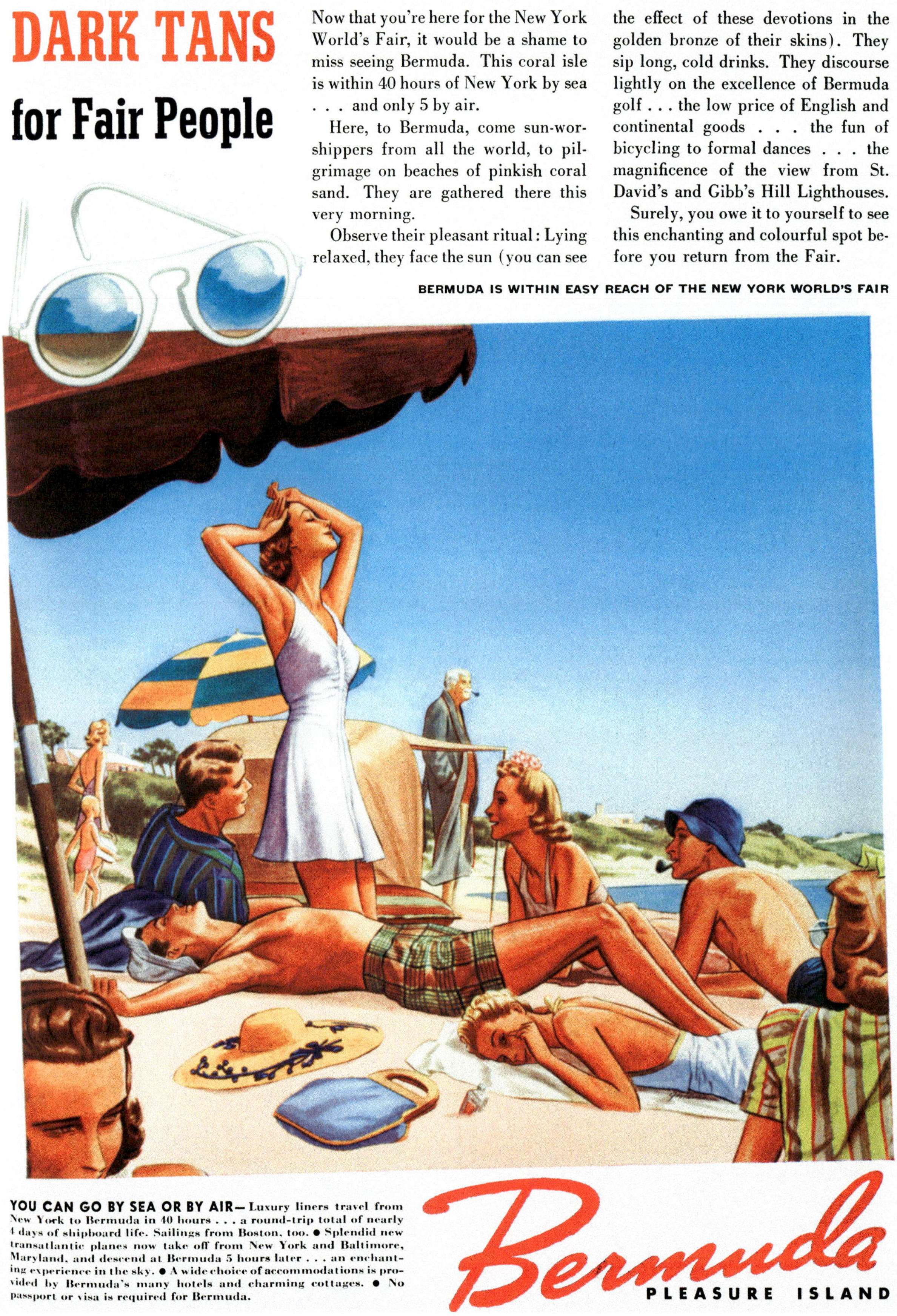

▲▶ *Bermuda, 1939*

Isles of Repose

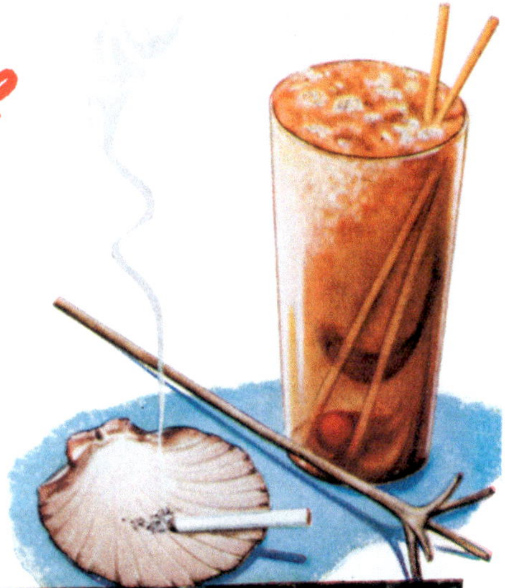

FOR VETERANS OF THE FAIR

When you've "done" the World's Fair, and you feel pretty well "done" yourself, come to this nearby tranquil retreat, Bermuda.

Nothing occurs with rush or clatter in this coral Arcady next door. Life is thrilling enough at bicycle pace. Motor traffic is banned by a humane Parliament, along with smoke-belching chimneys, fumes, and like disturbers of the peace.

Here, in this land of fun and flowers, is the balm for all your sorrows (including hay-fever). Even the climate beguiles you. Forever pleasant, it offers year-round indulgence in your favourite sports . . . golf . . . sailing . . . game fishing . . . tennis . . . bathing on rose-tinted beaches.

As a fillip to the Fair, nothing could be more fitting than a sojourn in this spot so beautifully strange.

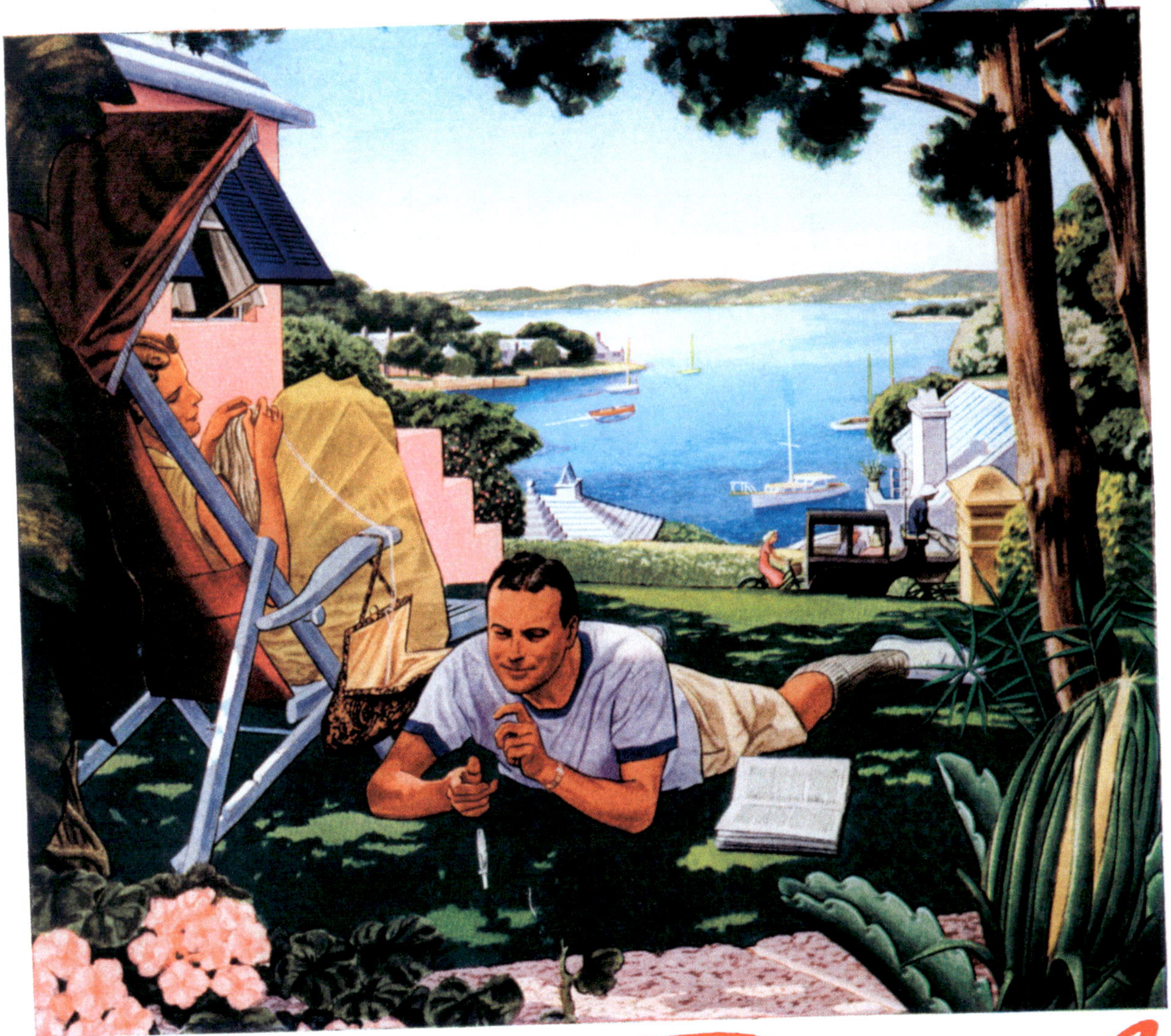

BERMUDA IS NEAR THE NEW YORK WORLD'S FAIR . . . BY SEA OR BY AIR — Luxury liners travel from New York to Bermuda in 40 hours . . . a round-trip total of nearly 4 days of shipboard life. Sailings from Boston, too. • Splendid new transatlantic planes now take off from New York and Baltimore, Maryland, and descend at Bermuda 5 hours later . . . an enchanting experience in the sky. • A wide choice of accommodations is provided by Bermuda's many hotels and charming cottages. • No passport or visa is required.

Bermuda

PLEASURE ISLAND

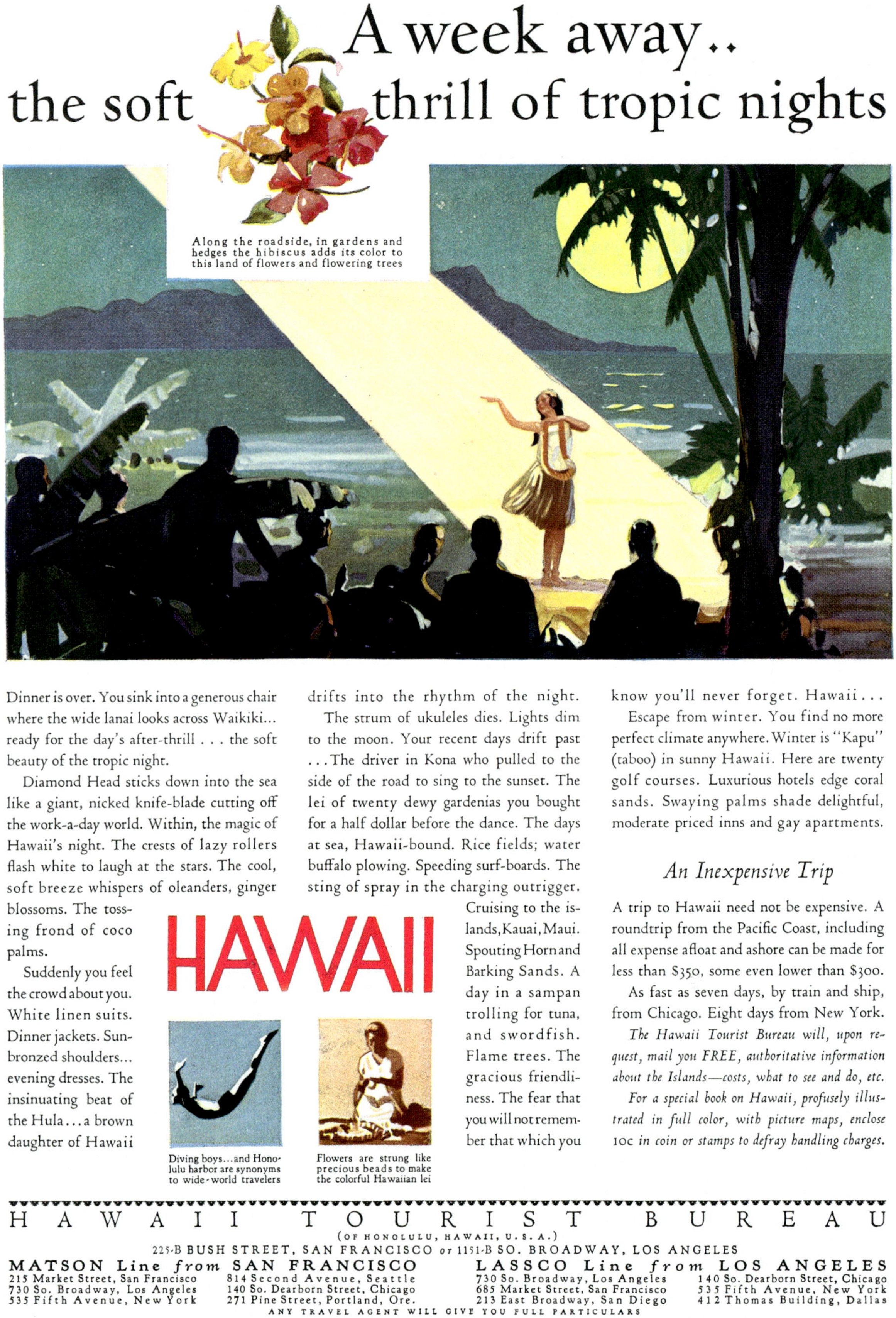

Hawaii, 1931

► *Matson Line, 1938*

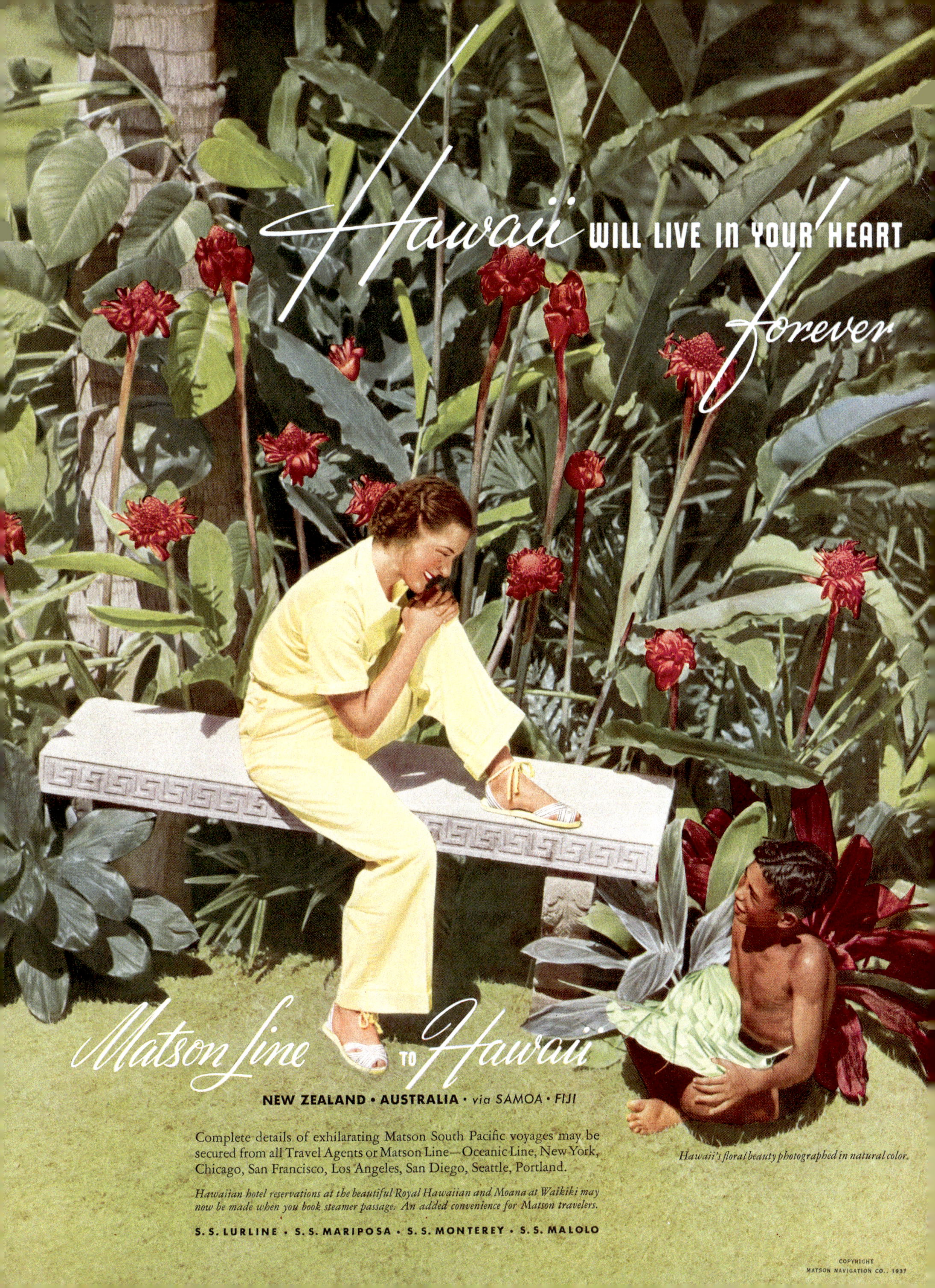

Hawaii WILL LIVE IN YOUR HEART forever
Matson Line TO Hawaii
NEW ZEALAND • AUSTRALIA • via SAMOA • FIJI
Complete details of exhilarating Matson South Pacific voyages may be secured from all Travel Agents or Matson Line—Oceanic Line, New York, Chicago, San Francisco, Los Angeles, San Diego, Seattle, Portland.
Hawaiian hotel reservations at the beautiful Royal Hawaiian and Moana at Waikiki may now be made when you book steamer passage. An added convenience for Matson travelers.
S. S. LURLINE • S. S. MARIPOSA • S. S. MONTEREY • S. S. MALOLO
Hawaii's floral beauty photographed in natural color.
COPYRIGHT MATSON NAVIGATION CO., 1937

HOLLYWOOD *alone is worth the trip*

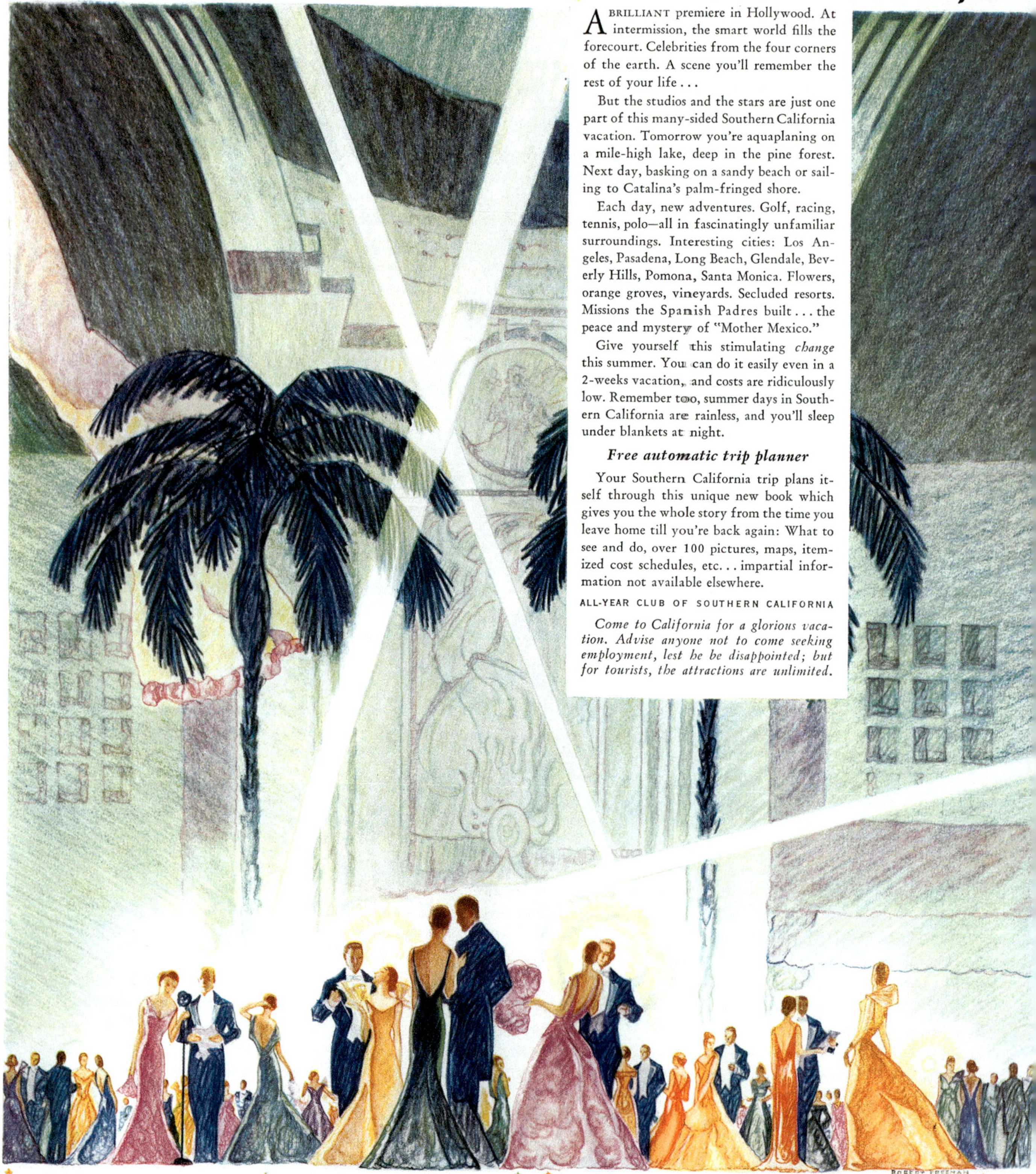

A BRILLIANT premiere in Hollywood. At intermission, the smart world fills the forecourt. Celebrities from the four corners of the earth. A scene you'll remember the rest of your life . . .

But the studios and the stars are just one part of this many-sided Southern California vacation. Tomorrow you're aquaplaning on a mile-high lake, deep in the pine forest. Next day, basking on a sandy beach or sailing to Catalina's palm-fringed shore.

Each day, new adventures. Golf, racing, tennis, polo—all in fascinatingly unfamiliar surroundings. Interesting cities: Los Angeles, Pasadena, Long Beach, Glendale, Beverly Hills, Pomona, Santa Monica. Flowers, orange groves, vineyards. Secluded resorts. Missions the Spanish Padres built . . . the peace and mystery of "Mother Mexico."

Give yourself this stimulating *change* this summer. You can do it easily even in a 2-weeks vacation, and costs are ridiculously low. Remember too, summer days in Southern California are rainless, and you'll sleep under blankets at night.

Free automatic trip planner

Your Southern California trip plans itself through this unique new book which gives you the whole story from the time you leave home till you're back again: What to see and do, over 100 pictures, maps, itemized cost schedules, etc. . . impartial information not available elsewhere.

ALL-YEAR CLUB OF SOUTHERN CALIFORNIA

Come to California for a glorious vacation. Advise anyone not to come seeking employment, lest he be disappointed; but for tourists, the attractions are unlimited.

SOUTHERN CALIFORNIA

All-Year Club of Southern California, Div. C-4, 1151 So. Broadway, Los Angeles, Calif.

Send me *free* book with complete details (including costs) of a Southern California vacation. Also send free routing by ☐ auto, ☐ rail, ☐ plane, ☐ bus, ☐ steamship. Also send free booklets about counties checked: ☐ Los Angeles, ☐ Santa Barbara, ☐ Orange, ☐ Inyo, ☐ Riverside, ☐ San Diego, ☐ Ventura, ☐ Imperial, ☐ Mission Trails, ☐ San Bernardino.

Name __________ *Street* __________

City __________ *State* __________

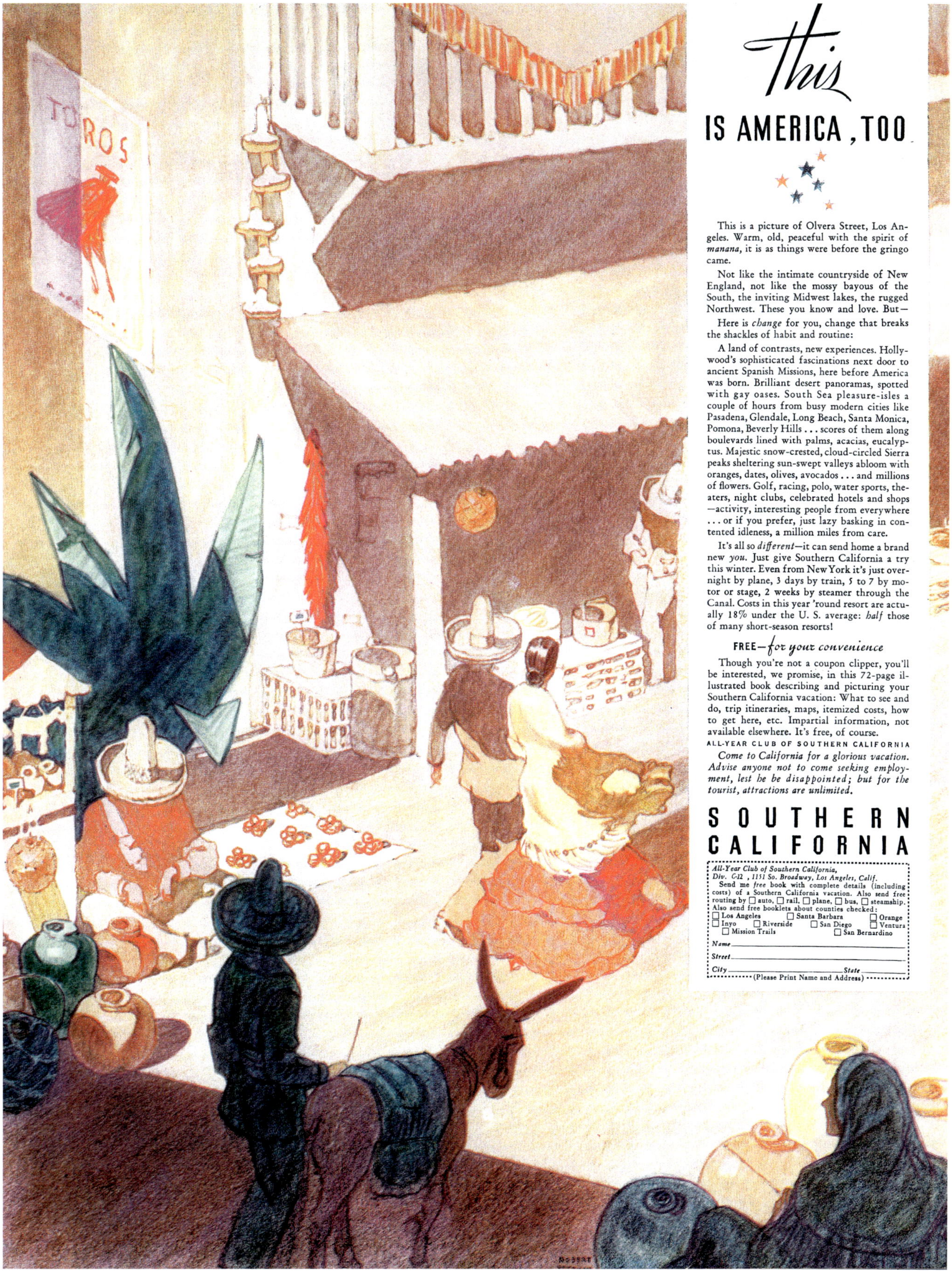

Southern California, 1935 ◄

Southern California, 1934

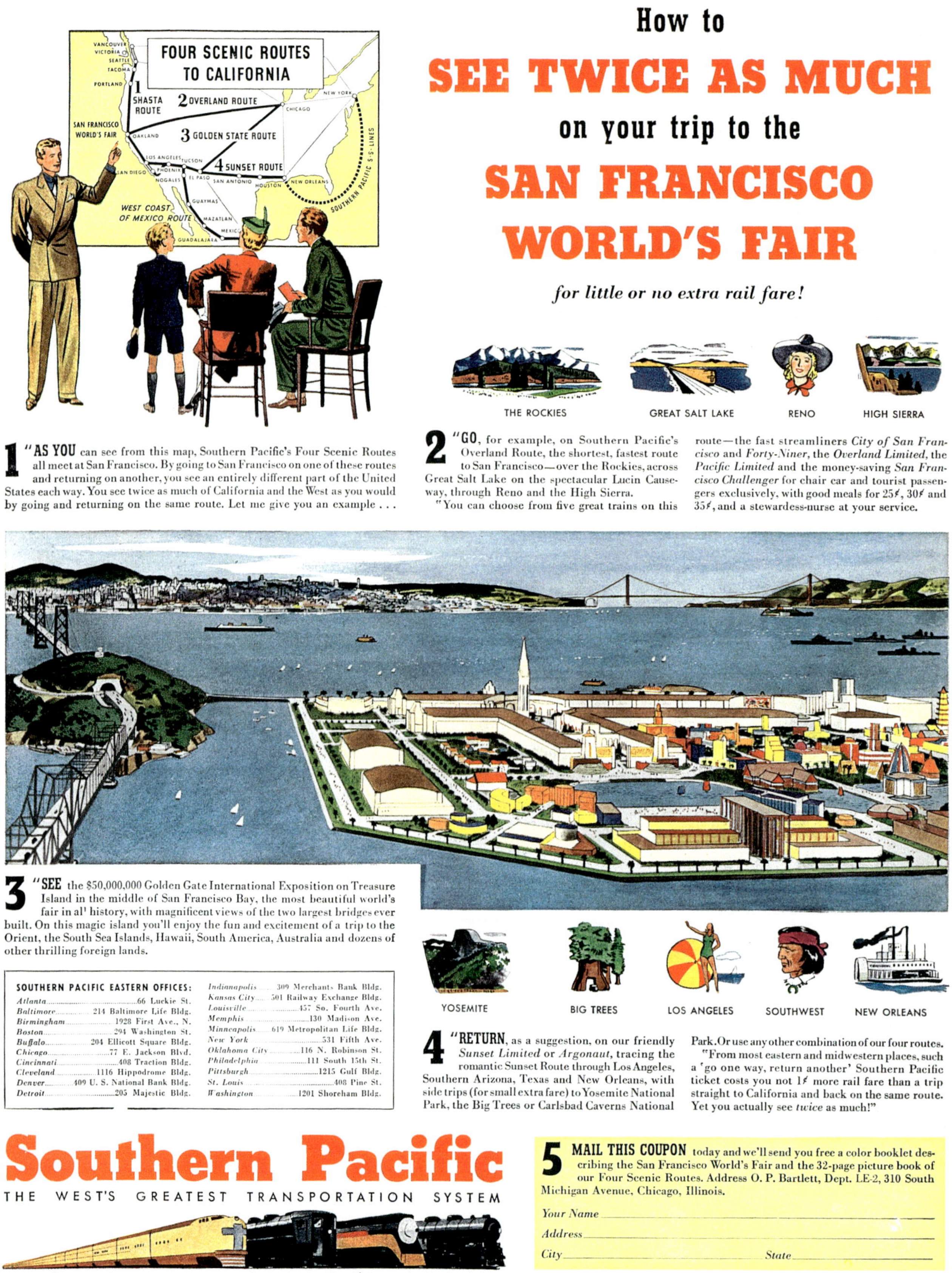

Southern Pacific, 1939

▸ *Californians, Inc., 1937*

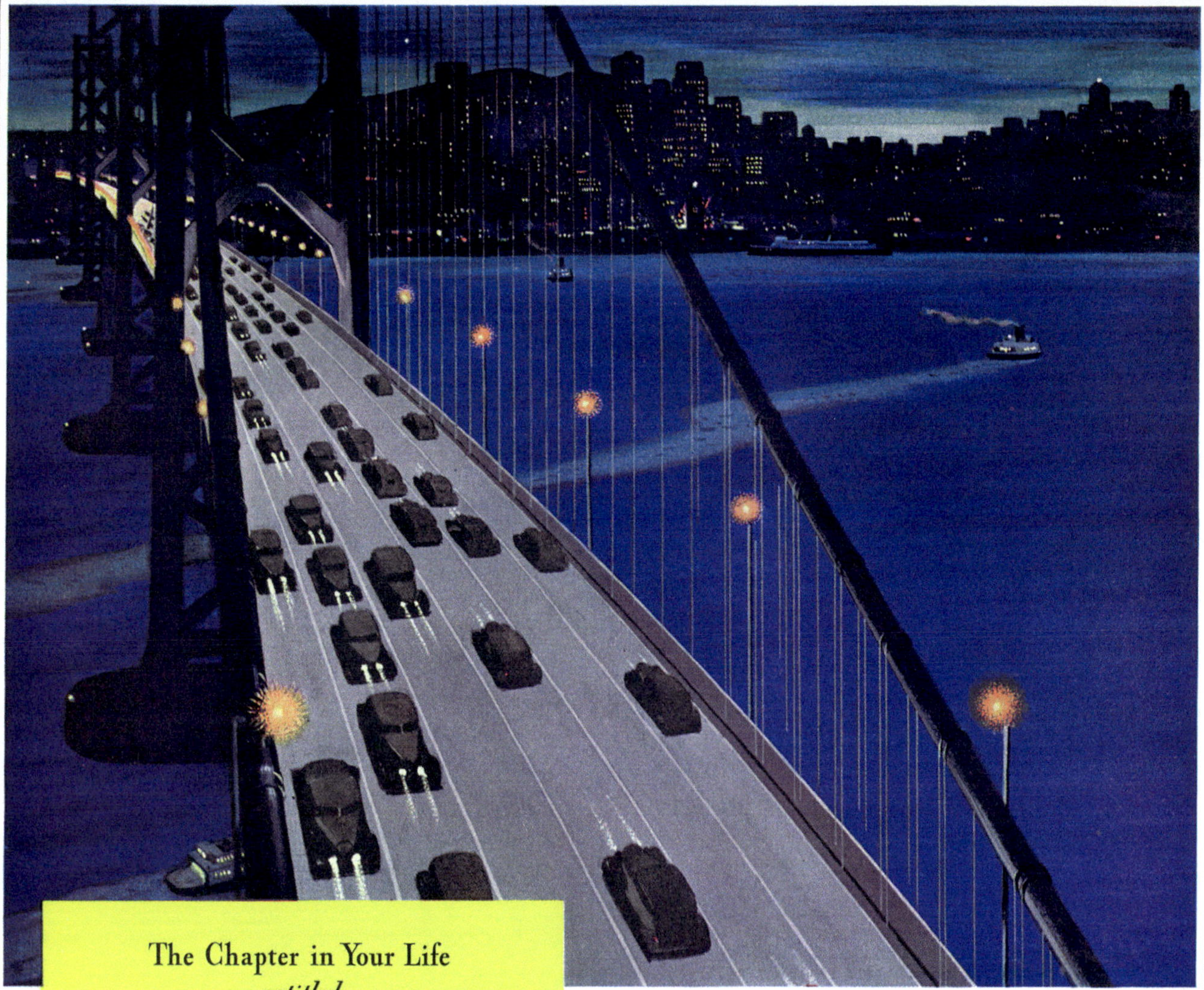

Approaching San Francisco on the 8¼ mile San Francisco-Oakland Bay Bridge

The Chapter in Your Life *entitled* SAN FRANCISCO

Its beginning takes your breath away!

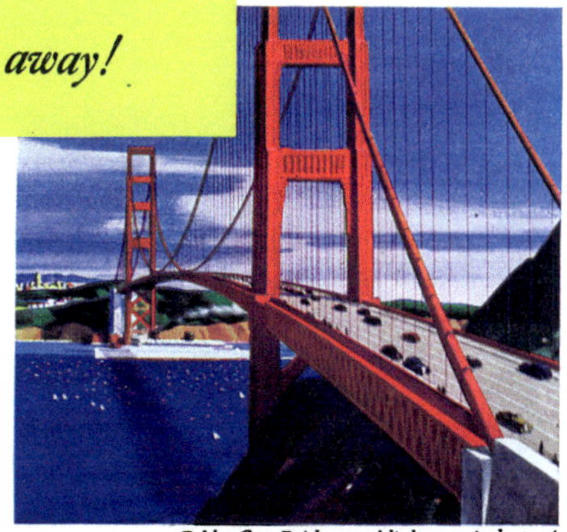

Golden Gate Bridge: world's longest single span!

SWIFTLY your car leaves the eastern shore and climbs above the Bay of San Francisco.

Three miles you hum along into the setting sun: when suddenly the great bridge turns. And now it is a white-tiled tunnel, pushed through an island's top!

Your breath comes short. *But it's coming shorter.*

For as you speed out through the tunnel's mouth, between the silver towers of this world's new longest bridge, San Francisco bursts upon you all at once. A high-piled blue and gold city, rising straight from a glistening sea.

A city like no other you have ever seen...yet, just as you knew it must be. There is Telegraph Hill, behind the ships. Nob Hill—above Chinatown. Russian Hill, with its cable cars. Tall serene Twin Peaks. And the sky-touching pillars of that other epic span—across the Golden Gate.

In an instant you know...the promise it has made you San Francisco is going to keep!

To be thrilling every minute you are here. On the hills and by the sea. In cosmopolitan hotels and world-famous restaurants. On green golf links and bridle paths and tennis courts...and on the Bay.

Any time you come you will find it the same. Sunny, hospitable, gay. Easy to get to by motor car or train or boat or plane. Your nearest railroad or travel agent, or your own auto club, will give you all travel details.

Write us for the new free book THE CHAPTER IN YOUR LIFE ENTITLED SAN FRANCISCO. Its subject, in pictures and prose, is the whole exciting outdoor-land this storied city centers:

The land of the Yosemite Valley and Lake Tahoe, high in the Sierra; the giant-Redwood Empire; beach-bordered Monterey, Carmel, Del Monte, Santa Cruz; flashing Feather River and Russian River; Mt. Shasta, volcanic Mt. Lassen . . . Gold Towns of the 'Forty-Niners.

Send the coupon now.

★ CALIFORNIANS INC.

Dept. 206, 703 Market St., San Francisco. Please send the new book and Official Tourist Map, free.

*Name*____________________

*Street*____________________

*City*__________ *State*__________

Tell anyone to come to California for a glorious vacation. But advise those seeking employment not to come here at this time, lest they be disappointed.

Follow the Vogue of Royalty

SEE THE HAUNTING BEAUTY OF CANADA ..LOVELIEST OF ALL AT

Banff AND Lake Louise

IN THE CANADIAN ROCKIES

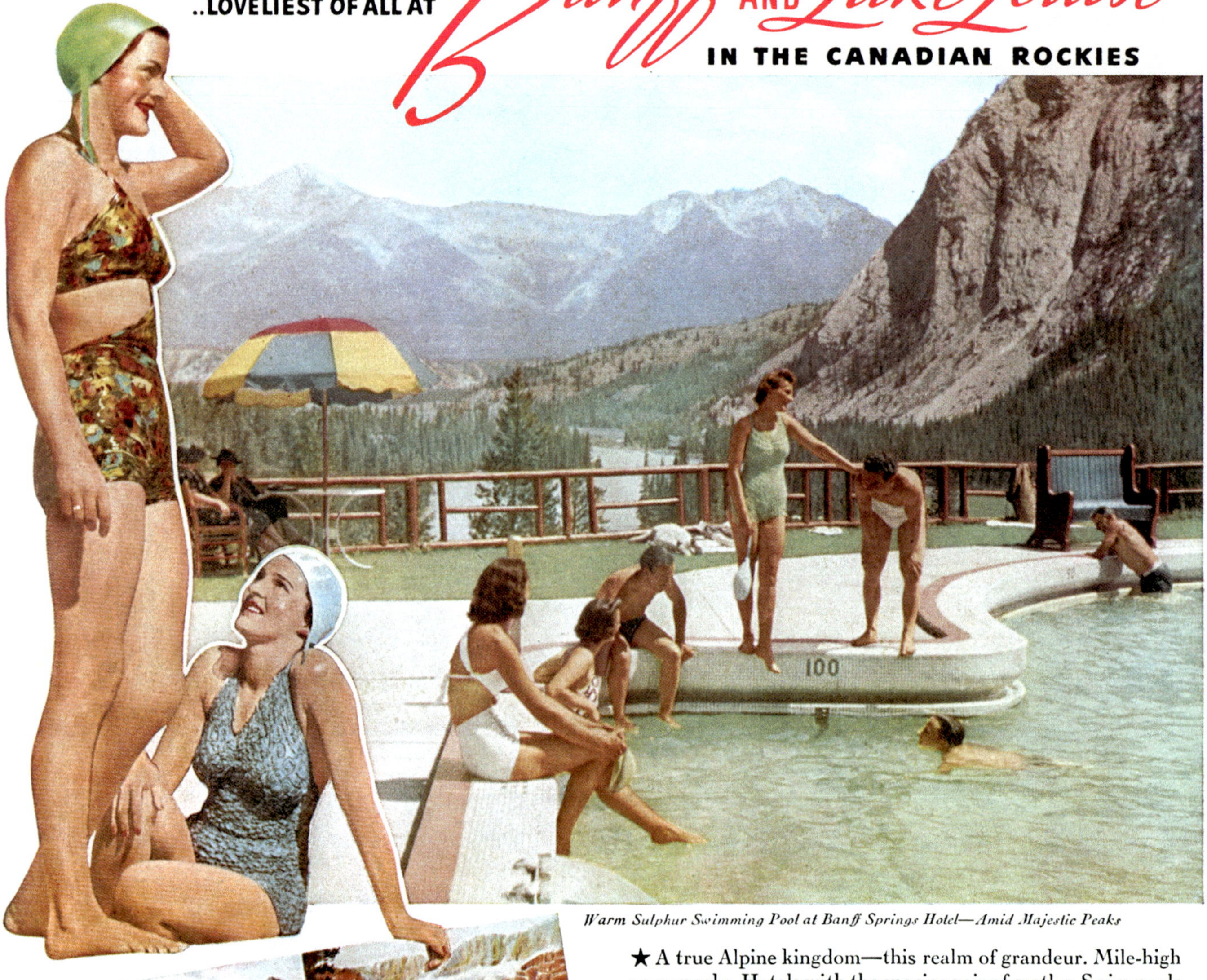

Warm Sulphur Swimming Pool at Banff Springs Hotel—Amid Majestic Peaks

★ A true Alpine kingdom—this realm of grandeur. Mile-high snow peaks. Hotels with the spacious air of castles. Swim pools of warm sulphur and fresh water. Trail rides and hikes on top of the world with cowboys and Swiss guides. And by night fun reigns in brilliant ballrooms. Come up this summer—see Canada's crowning glory. Travel the Columbia Icefield Highway ...America's newest, most spectacular drive...from Lake Louise.

Special rates for guests staying at Banff Springs Hotel or Chateau Lake Louise a week or longer.

Air-conditioned transcontinental trains. Low round-trip fares to Banff, North Pacific Coast, California, Alaska.

Ask Your Travel Agent or *Nearest Canadian Pacific Office*
NEW YORK • BOSTON • PHILADELPHIA • CHICAGO • SAN FRANCISCO • MONTREAL
and other large cities in U. S. and Canada

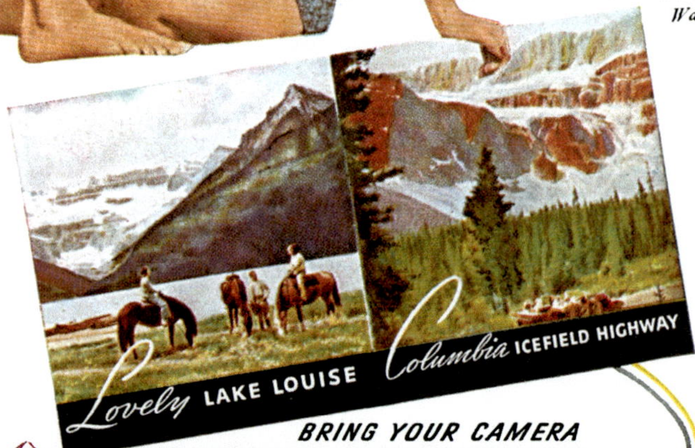

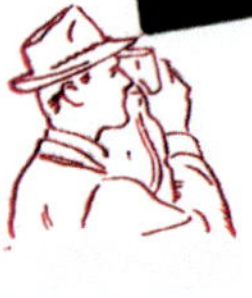

BRING YOUR CAMERA

$1,000 IN CASH PRIZES

Capture this brilliant paradise in color photos. Gleaming glaciers, purple peaks, mountain flowers, Alpine sunlight. Ask for contest details. 47 Cash Prizes.

Canadian Pacific

WORLD'S GREATEST TRAVEL SYSTEM

Banff Springs . . . *Cosmopolis of the Canadian Rockies*

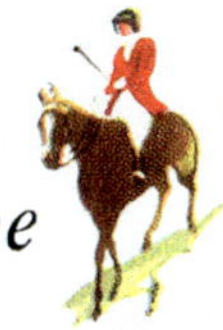

LIKE a continuous smart English houseparty . . . nonchalant, brilliant, informal. So go the stimulating days under the hospitable roof of Banff Springs Hotel, in the heart of the Canadian Rockies. Mornings . . . every one to his tastes . . . along with interesting companions. Pony rides up trails over 8,000 feet high. A climb up Sulphur Mountain. Golf on a $350,000 course with glacial river hazards. Luncheon, prepared by famous chefs. Archery with Indian bows . . . speedy tennis on red clay courts . . . canters on well-groomed saddle horses . . . motor trips to lovely Lake Louise, dips into a warm sulphur pool topped off with icy cold plunges. And then tea time in the lounge.

Now the scene takes on a more formal tone, tweeds and sports dresses give place to the graceful evening mode. And after a perfect dinner with exquisite music . . . and a light opera by the gay *Cruisaders*, a tete-a-tete under a silvery moon, with the stars looking down on Bow Valley's exquisite panorama.

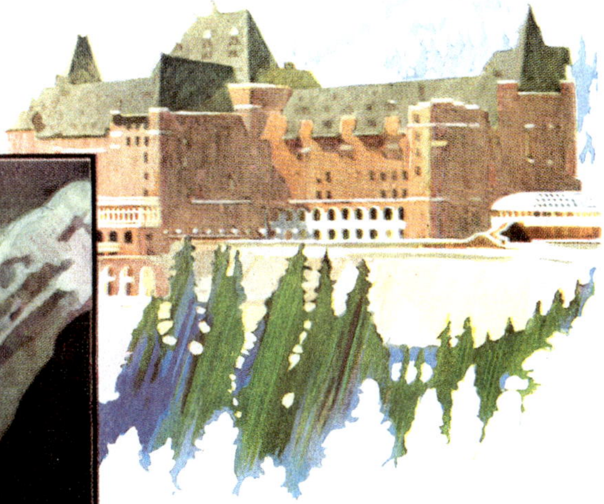

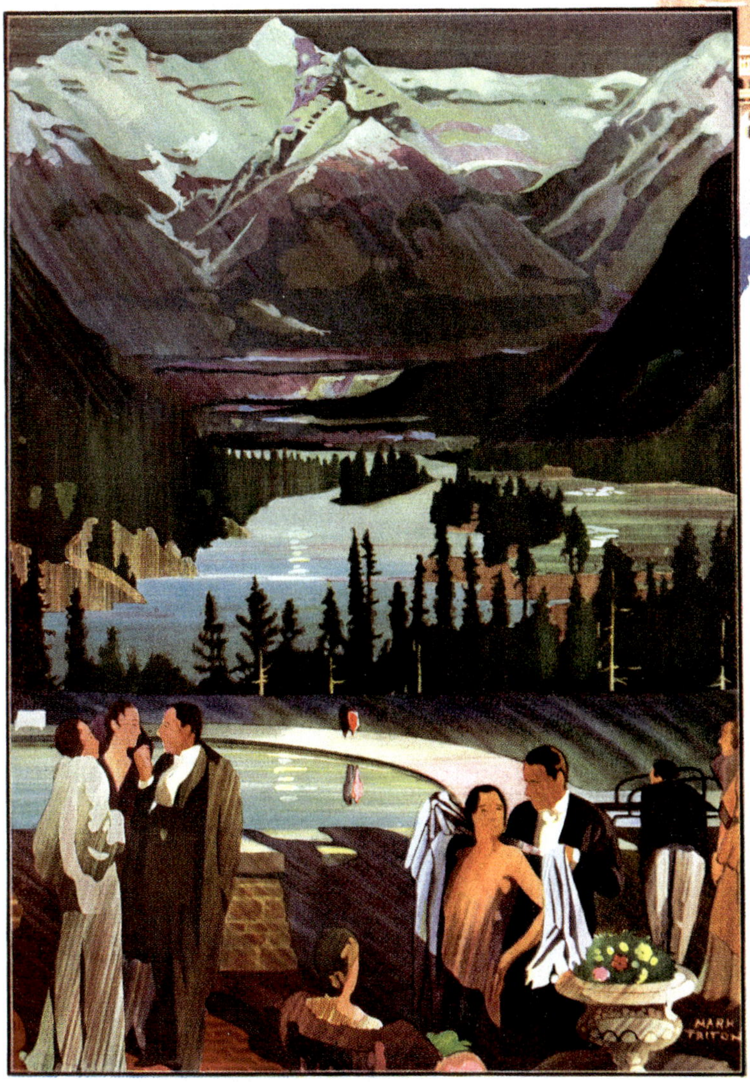

Come up this summer and stay! . . .

Special monthly rates, European Plan for typical room with bath, *single* — $8.00 up per day, *double* — $12.00 up. Period suites for two, $28.00 up. Special servants' quarters. Room rates about 20% lower during May, June, Sept. But arrange for all summer long. American Plan also, May 15th—June 15th and Sept. 7th to 30th, for stay one week or longer, room with bath and meals, *single*—$10.00 per person per day, *double* — $18.00 per day. ***Hotel opens May 15th.*** Reservations, rates, information, from any Canadian Pacific Office: New York, Boston, Philadelphia, Buffalo, Washington, D. C., Detroit, Chicago, San Francisco, and all important cities in the United States. *Canada:* Montreal, Winnipeg, Vancouver.

Banff

SPRINGS HOTEL

Canadian Pacific

Low fares—Pacific Coast Excursions—May 15—Sept. 30.

Ask for Pacific Coast Tours, Alaska, Conducted Tours Folders.

Canadian Pacific, 1939 ◂▴

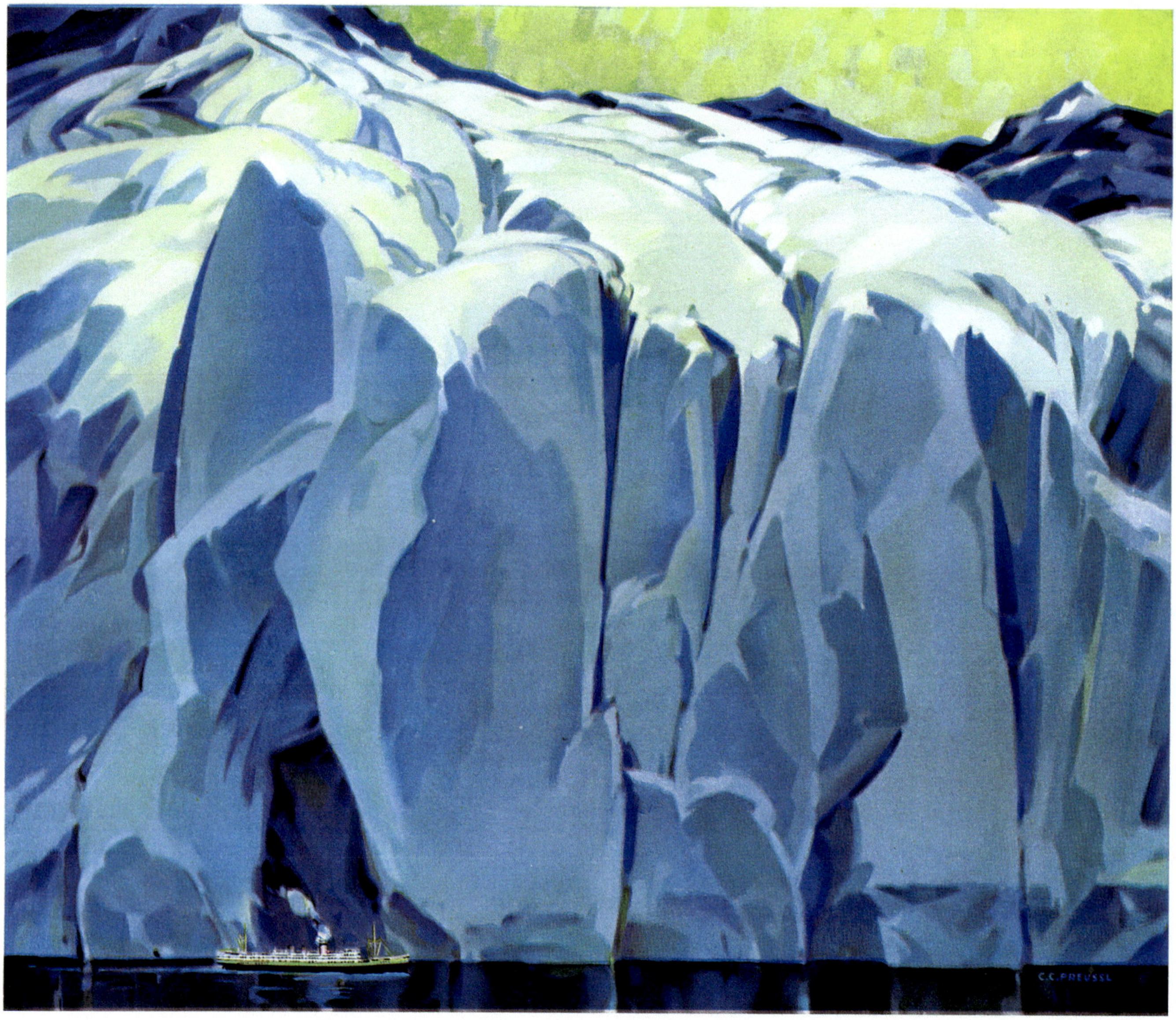

THE GLACIERS ARE BIGGER

1935 "See Alaska" YEAR

The largest glaciers in the world are along the coast of Alaska. You can snowball upon them in summer—yet in June and July, wild flowers in profusion fringe their edges!

A most unusual country is Alaska. Imagine, if you will, a land where a baseball game can be played at midnight without artificial light! Where totem poles stand next to telephone poles in modern towns. Where vines grow three inches over night, in gardens near glacial fields of ice.

Travel by train across America. We have *air-conditioned* trains which are cool, clean, quiet and safe. Relax as you ride. Arrive at Seattle, refreshed and ready to sail. How much vacation time have you? Two weeks, three, or four? We can give you an Alaskan trip to exactly fit your time and pocketbook. And nowhere in the world can you find a vacation paradise to equal this enchanted land. May we figure costs from your home town?

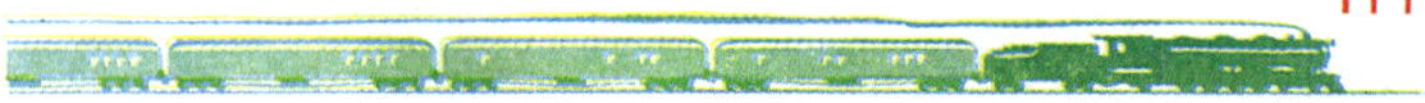

in ALASKA

For free Alaska literature, write any of The All-American Services to Alaska:

NORTH WESTERN LINE
Dept. N-8, Chicago, Illinois

ALASKA RAILROAD
Dept. R-8, 333 North Michigan Avenue, Chicago, Illinois

THE MILWAUKEE ROAD
Dept. M-8, Chicago, Illinois

BURLINGTON ROUTE
Dept. B-8, Chicago, Illinois

GREAT NORTHERN RAILWAY
Dept. G-8, St. Paul, Minnesota

NORTHERN PACIFIC RAILWAY
Dept. P-8, St. Paul, Minnesota

UNION PACIFIC RAILROAD
Dept. U-8, Omaha, Nebraska

ALASKA STEAMSHIP COMPANY
Dept. A-8, Seattle, Washington

NOVOLESCENCE

The Reason Why Our Hotels Are Always New

In Cincinnati NETHERLAND PLAZA
William O. Seelbach, Manager. 800 Rooms, starting as low as $3.00.

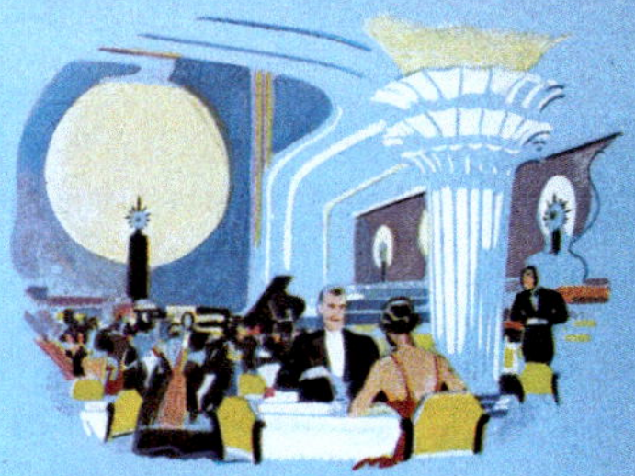

The new Pavillon Caprice, where smart Cincinnati sips, sups, steps, in a brilliant setting of crystal and chromium.

In New York HOTEL NEW YORKER
Frank L. Andrews, Manager. 2,500 Rooms, many as low as $3.00.

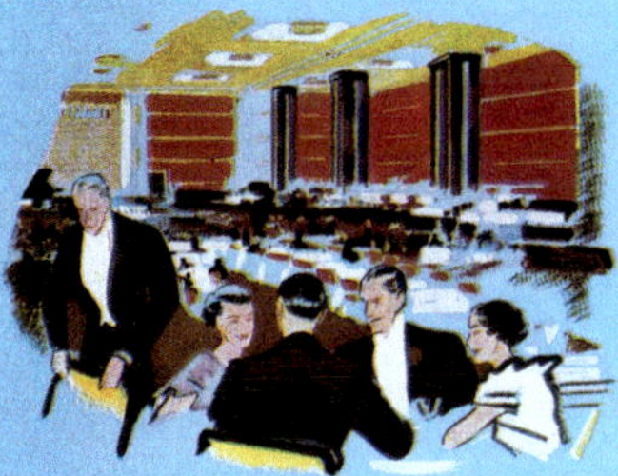

The new Terrace Restaurant, vivid, gay, where New York meets for dinner and supper dancing.

In Detroit THE BOOK-CADILLAC
J. E. Frawley, General Manager. 1,200 Rooms, $3.00 and up.

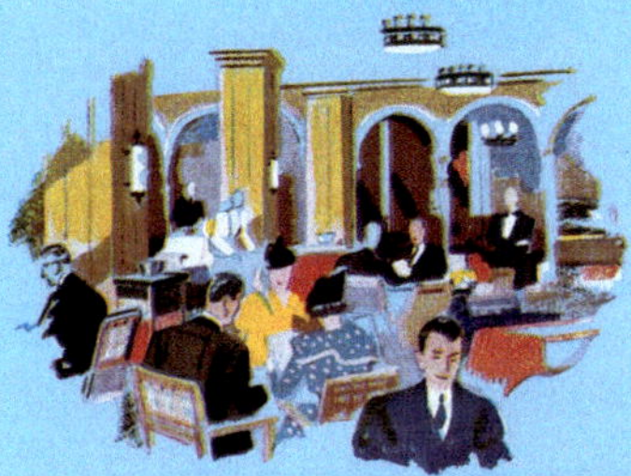

The new Cafe Cadillac, where perfect food and drink are served in a club-like atmosphere.

In New York HOTEL LEXINGTON
Charles E. Rochester, Manager. 801 Rooms, from $3.

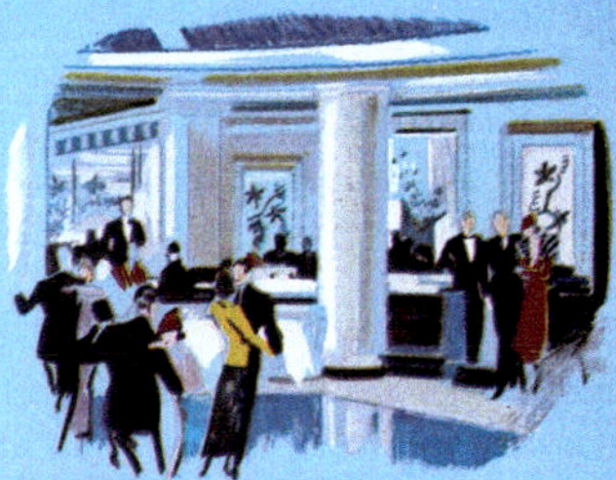

The new Silver Grill, charming, intimate, a favorite rendezvous on New York's smart East Side.

In Dayton HOTEL VAN CLEVE
H. F. Stevens, Manager. 300 Rooms, from $2.50.

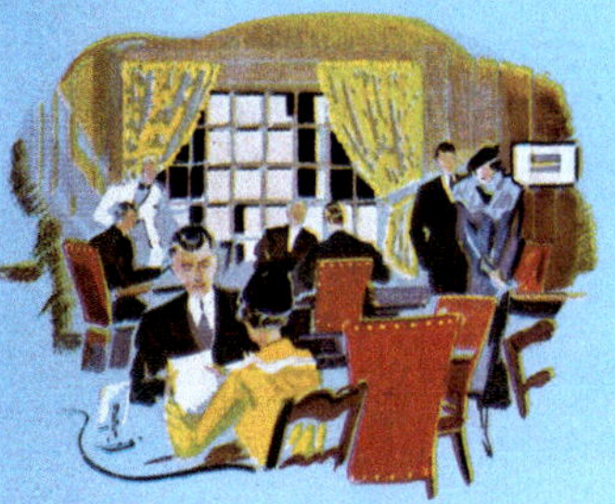

The new Pine Room, refreshingly simple and in good taste, a favorite spot for quiet luncheon or dinner.

In Dallas THE ADOLPHUS
Otis M. Harrison, Manager. 825 Rooms, starting at $2.

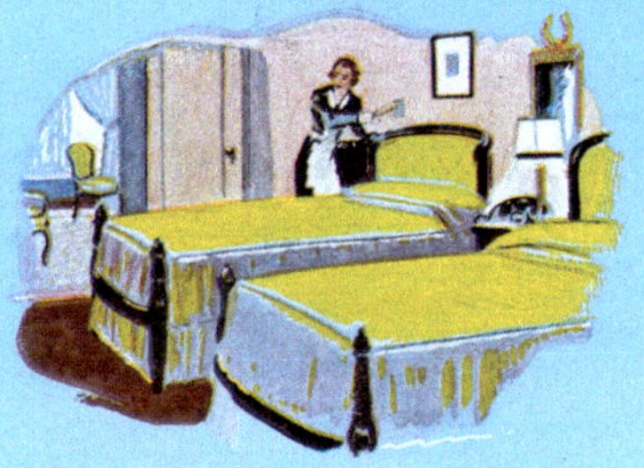

Newly decorated guest rooms combine the charm of a long-established hotel with modern comfort and convenience.

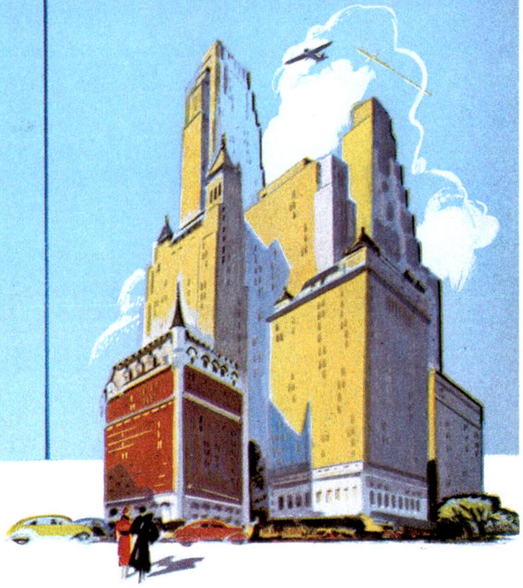

We've coined a new word for a new idea in hotel management—*"Novolescence"*—just the opposite of obsolescence. We don't allow our hotels to grow old—ever. Instead, we manage each year to make them better properties than they were the year before—*actually!*

We believe (in fact, we know from experience) that a better hotel results from spending $50,000 during each of five years for permanent improvements—than from waiting five years and spending a lump sum of $250,000. That is why guests, returning from time to time, always find something new to greet them. A new restaurant in this hotel. An old one rejuvenated in another. A public room completely refurnished. Guest rooms redecorated. And there is always that newness which the constant use of paint and soap and polish brings to light. Further, with six hotels, we're always in a position to use one as a "proving ground"—and, if an innovation is well received, we put it into effect with all. In fact, many pleasant hotel customs in general use today originated with us. We never rest. We never stop working. We never cease thinking of you.

That's why our hotels always look as though they'd just been opened this morning. That's why they become better year by year. That's why our personnel is always alert, our service always eager. With us *novolescence* is an obsession—and our guests sense it the minute they step through our doors. And until we modestly bill them goodbye!

Hotels directed by **NATIONAL HOTEL MANAGEMENT CO · INC** *Ralph Hitz, President*

Chicago Office: 77 West Washington Street   Washington Office: 830 National Press Building

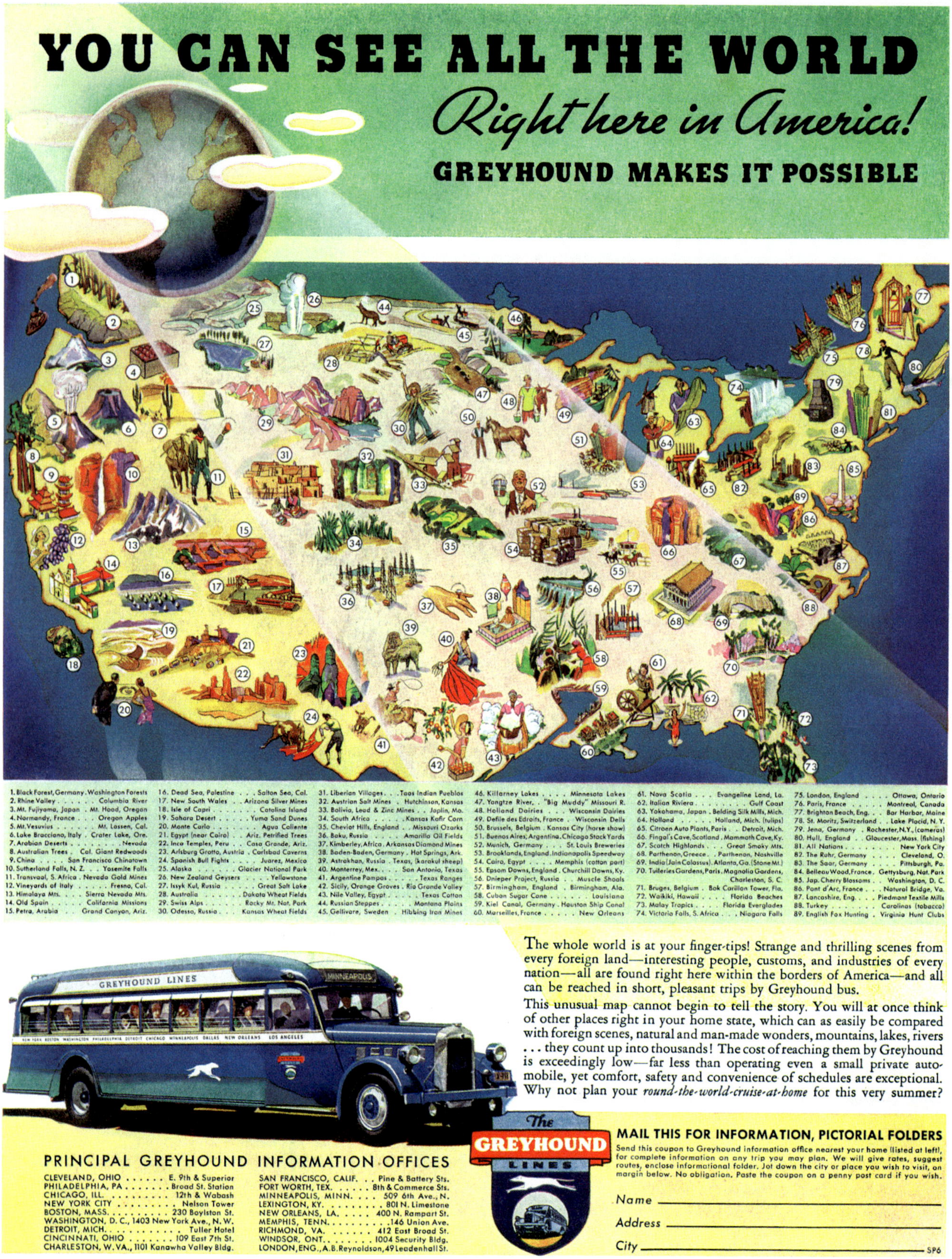

Greyhound, 1935

▸ Greyhound, 1938

"RIDE WITH US *in this* $20,000 AUTOMOBILE!"

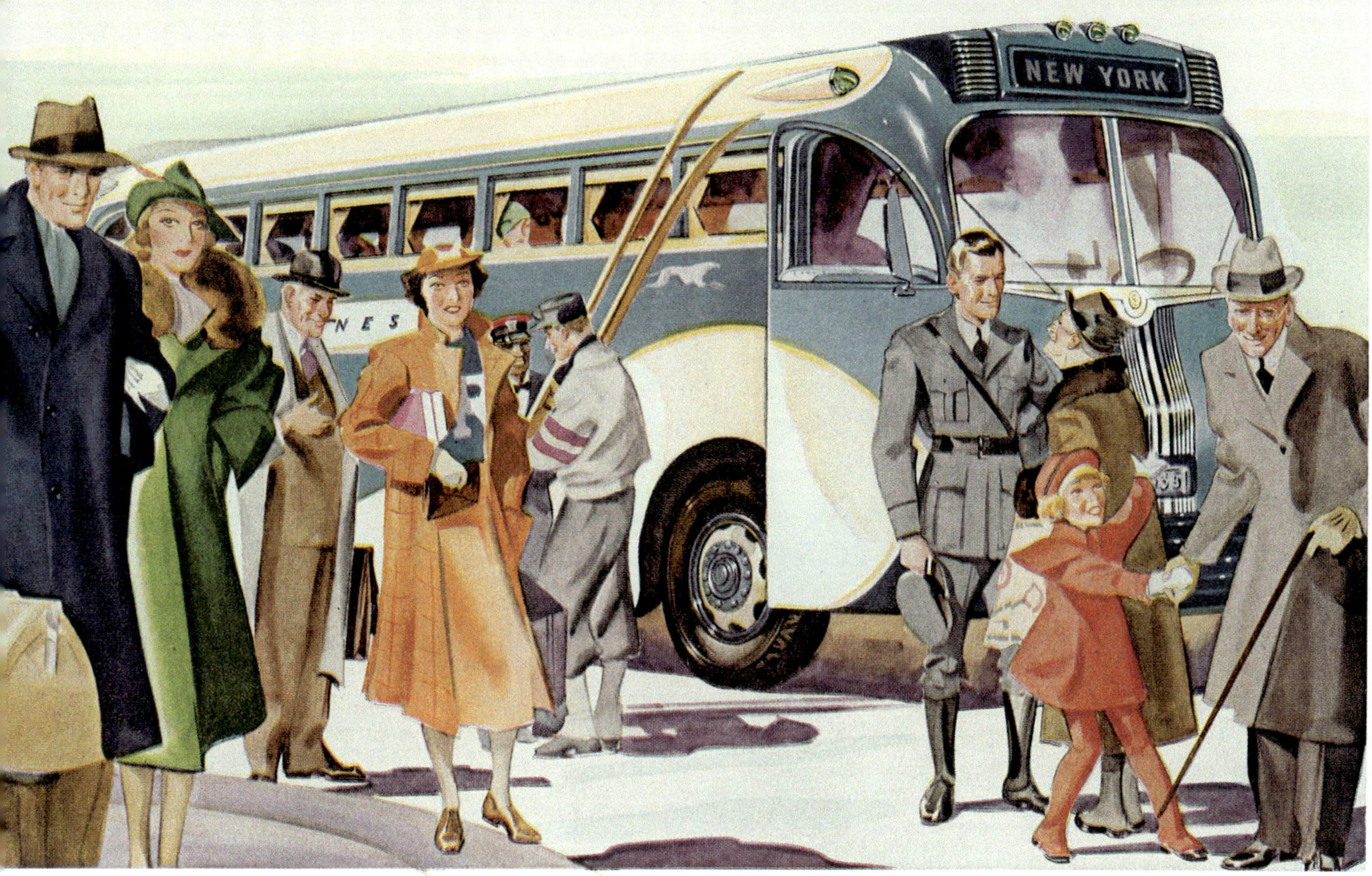

at far less cost than driving a small private car

NOT EVEN THE SWANKIEST FOREIGN-BUILT LIMOUSINE CAN MATCH THESE FEATURES!

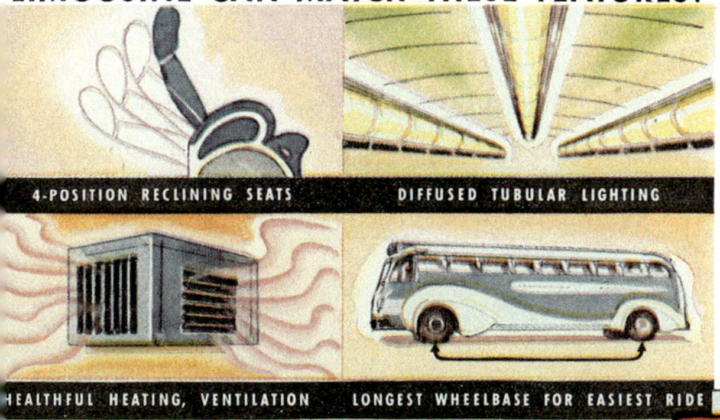

Hear this cordial invitation! It comes from the army of friendly and cosmopolitan people who have made more than *forty million* trips by Greyhound in the past year.

"A $20,000 automobile!" you say—"Why, even the snootiest foreign-built limousine doesn't cost that much money. How can *I* afford to travel in such a car?"

As a matter of fact, we doubt if you could purchase the new Greyhound Super-Coach for even that sum—as private automobiles are sold. It is actually worth a lot more, with its brilliantly designed aluminum alloy construction, deep-cushioned chairs adjustable to four positions, diffused tubular lighting, healthful heating and ventilation, advanced safety features found in no ordinary automobile. And remember, the service of America's most skilful drivers comes with the coach.

Would you believe that one can ride to nearly any part of America or Canada in this luxurious cruiser, at a third the cost of driving a small private car? More amazing, Greyhound fares have come steadily *down,* through the years, as comfort and convenience have gone *up*—despite the advance of nearly all living costs. In this new year, Greyhound offers America's biggest dollar's worth of travel—and that goes for trips to the next city or across the continent. *See for yourself.*

PRINCIPAL GREYHOUND INFORMATION OFFICES

Cleveland, O. . . . . E. 9th & Superior
Philadelphia, Pa. . . . Broad Street Station
New York City . . . . . 245 W. 50th Street
Chicago, Ill. . . . . 12th & Wabash
Charleston, W. Va. . . 155 Summers Street
Minneapolis, Minn. . 509 Sixth Avenue, N.
Boston, Mass. . . . . 60 Park Square
Washington, D.C., 1403 New York Ave., N.W.
Detroit, Mich., Washington Blvd. at Grand Riv.
St. Louis, Mo. . . Broadway & Delmar Blvd.
San Francisco, Cal. . Pine & Battery Streets
Ft. Worth, Tex. . . . 905 Commerce Street
Lexington, Ky. . . . . . . 801 N. Limestone
Memphis, Tenn. . . . . 527 N. Main Street
New Orleans, La. . 400 N. Rampart Street
Cincinnati, Ohio . . . . 630 Walnut Street
Richmond, Va. . . . . . 412 E. Broad Street
Toronto, Ont. . . . 1501 Royal Bank Bldg.
London, England . . . .
. . A. B. Reynoldson, 49 Leadenhall Street

The GREYHOUND LINES

For You—Bright Pictorial Booklets All About Winter Playgrounds

Break the spell of Winter with a trip to sunshine cities of the South or West! Mail this coupon to nearest information office, listed at left, for thrilling rotogravure section "FLORIDA AND GULF COAST" ☐, or colorful folders "CALIFORNIA, ALL THE WEST" ☐, "ACROSS AMERICA THROUGH SOUTHWEST" ☐. (Please check which one.) If fares and information on any special trip are desired, jot down place you wish to visit, on line below.

____

Name__________________________

Address________________________ SP-1

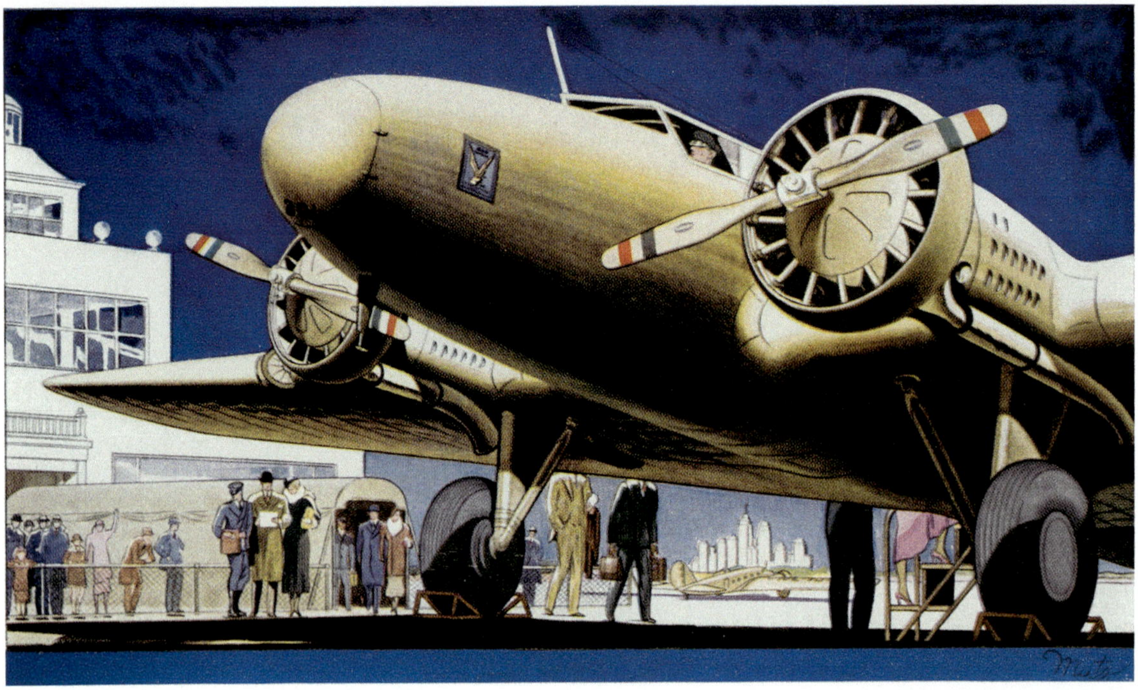

NEW WORLD'S RECORDS BY UNITED AIR LINES

☆ With a new fleet of 3-mile-a-minute, Wasp-powered Boeings, United Air Lines is giving the fastest service ever maintained with multi-motored planes. New York-Chicago is a morning, afternoon or evening flight. Chicago-Pacific Coast an overnight journey. And New York-California a trip of less than one day. These are world's records.
☆ The public's response to this service is to use it. During 1933 United Air Lines carried approximately 125,000 passengers. Another world's record.
☆ United's new Boeing planes make every provision for the passengers' comfort. Heated spacious cabins.

60,000,000 MILES FLYING EXPERIENCE

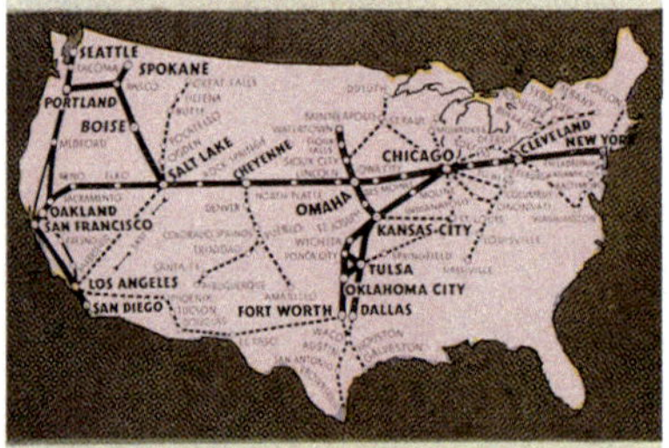

CALIFORNIA TO NEW YORK . . . 20 HRS.
3 flights daily each way

CHICAGO TO NEW YORK . . . 4¾ HRS.
10 flights daily each way

CALIFORNIA TO CHICAGO . . . 14¼ HRS.
3 flights daily each way

FT. WORTH-DALLAS TO CLEVELAND . . . 9 HRS.
2 flights daily each way

LOS ANGELES TO SEATTLE . . . 8 HRS.
2 flights daily each way

(West bound schedules slightly longer due to prevailing winds.)

Consult new United Air Lines' time table for schedule to intermediate and off-line points

UNITED AIR LINES

Subsidiary of United Aircraft & Transport Corporation

☆ Adjustable reclining chairs for relaxation or for sleeping during night flights.
☆ United Air Lines' year-round service utilizes every known aid to avigation. Multi-motored planes manned by two transport pilots. Two-way radio. Directive radio beam. Lighted airways. Frequent weather reports.
☆ Fly with United Air Lines — the fastest and most interesting way to travel. ☆ For schedules, tickets or reservations to 137 cities . . . call United Air Lines' ticket offices, Hotel Porters, Travel Bureaus, Postal or Western Union. ☆ Air Express — Phone Air Express Division, Railway Express Agency. Use Air Mail — it speeds business.

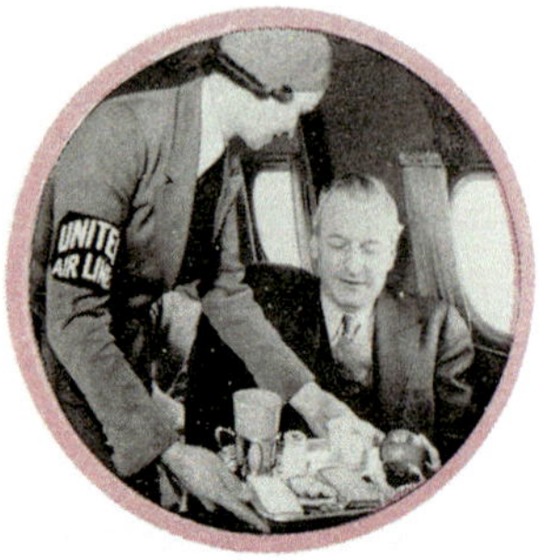

Stewardess service. Lunches served aloft included in economical fares.

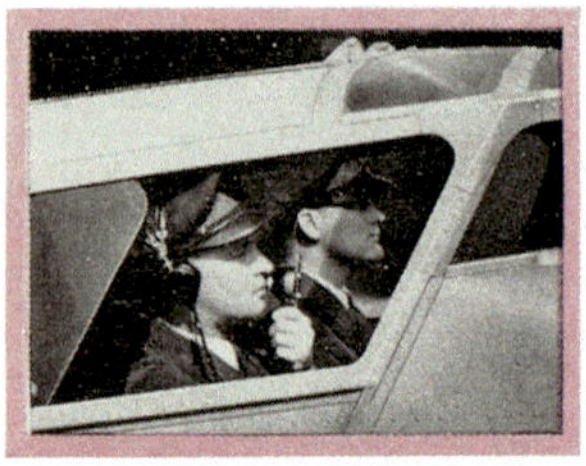

Two veteran pilots (averaging 4,000 hours of flying) on every multi-motored plane.

United Air Lines, 1934

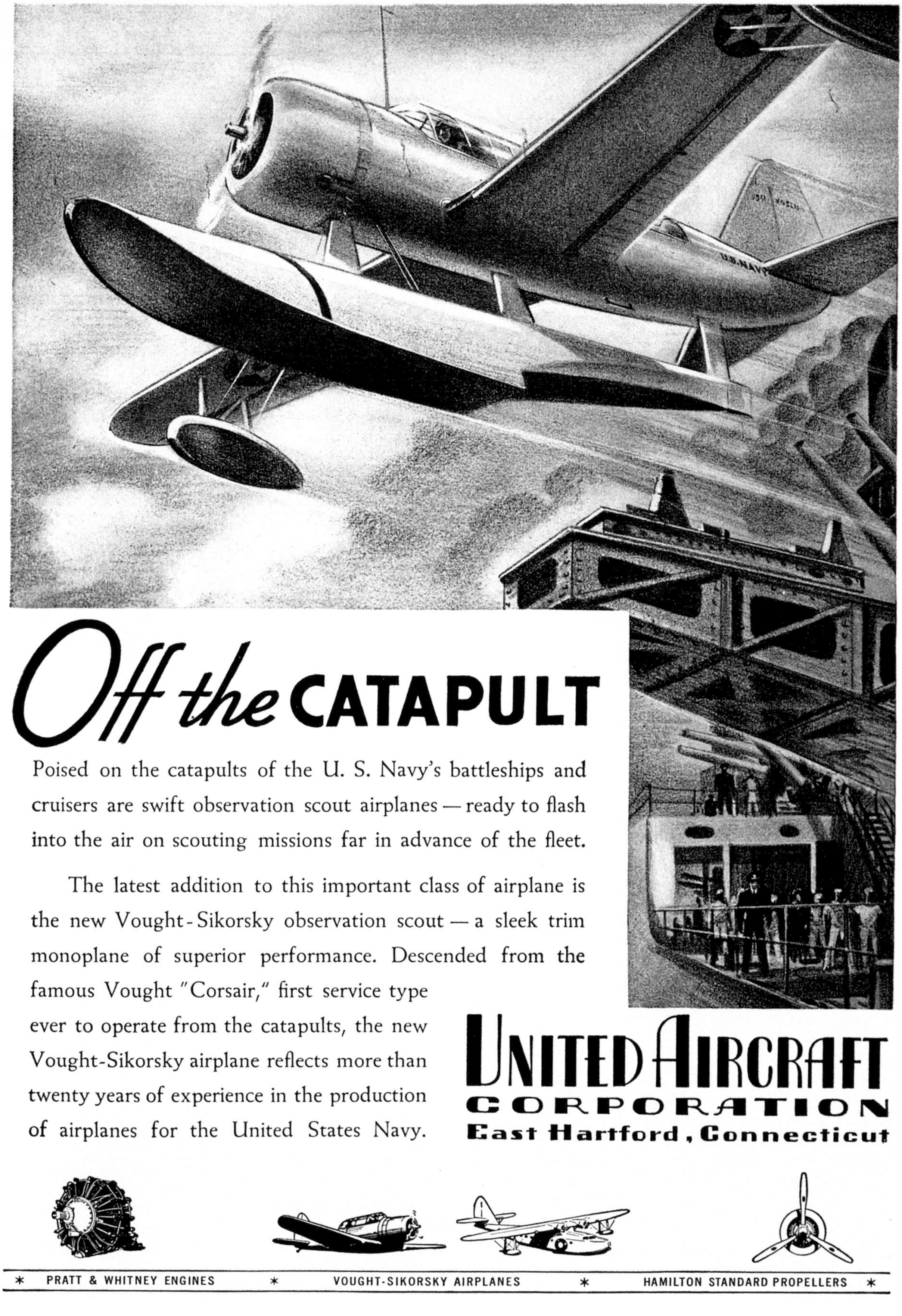

United Aircraft, 1939

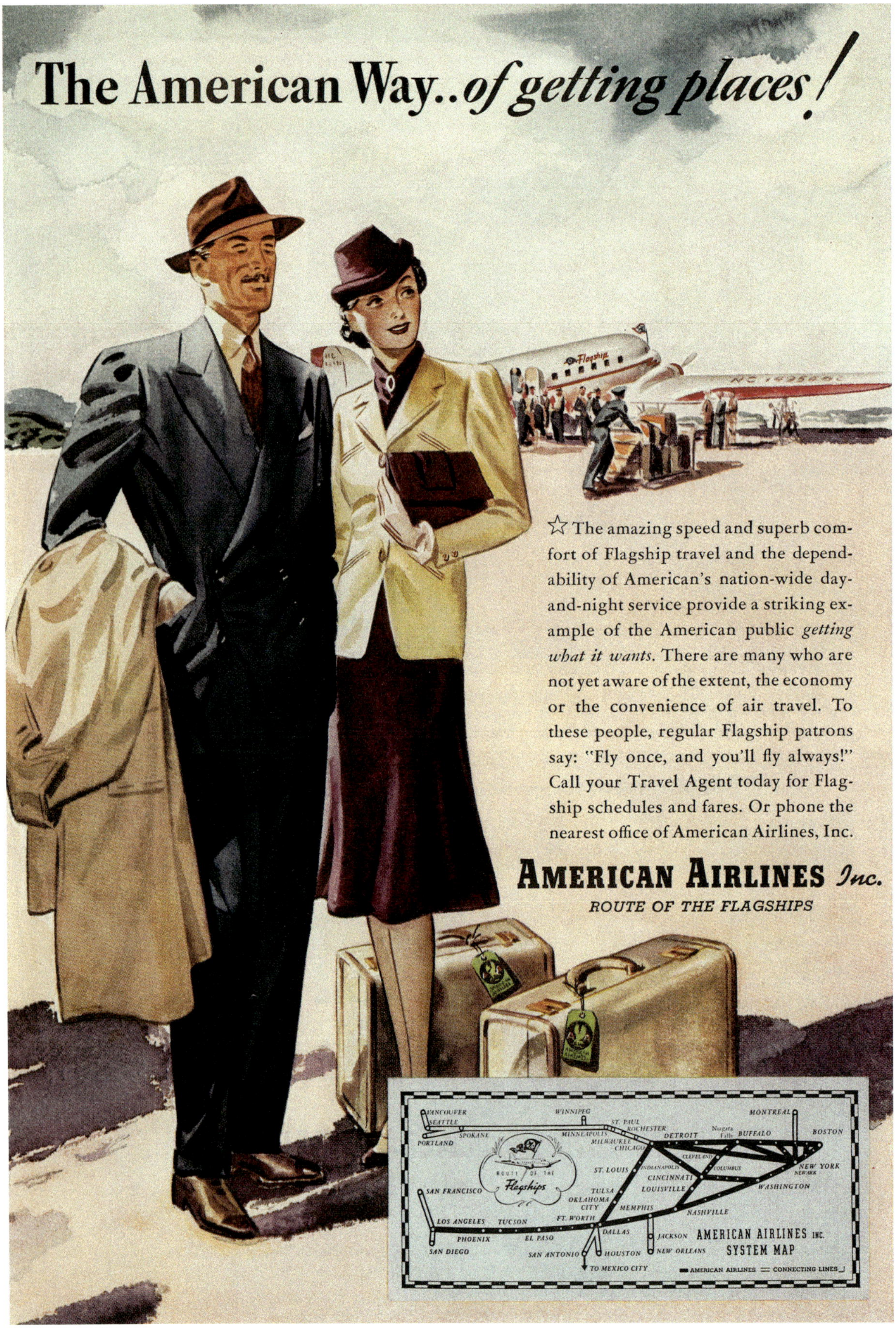

American Airlines, 1939

▸ *TWA, 1935*

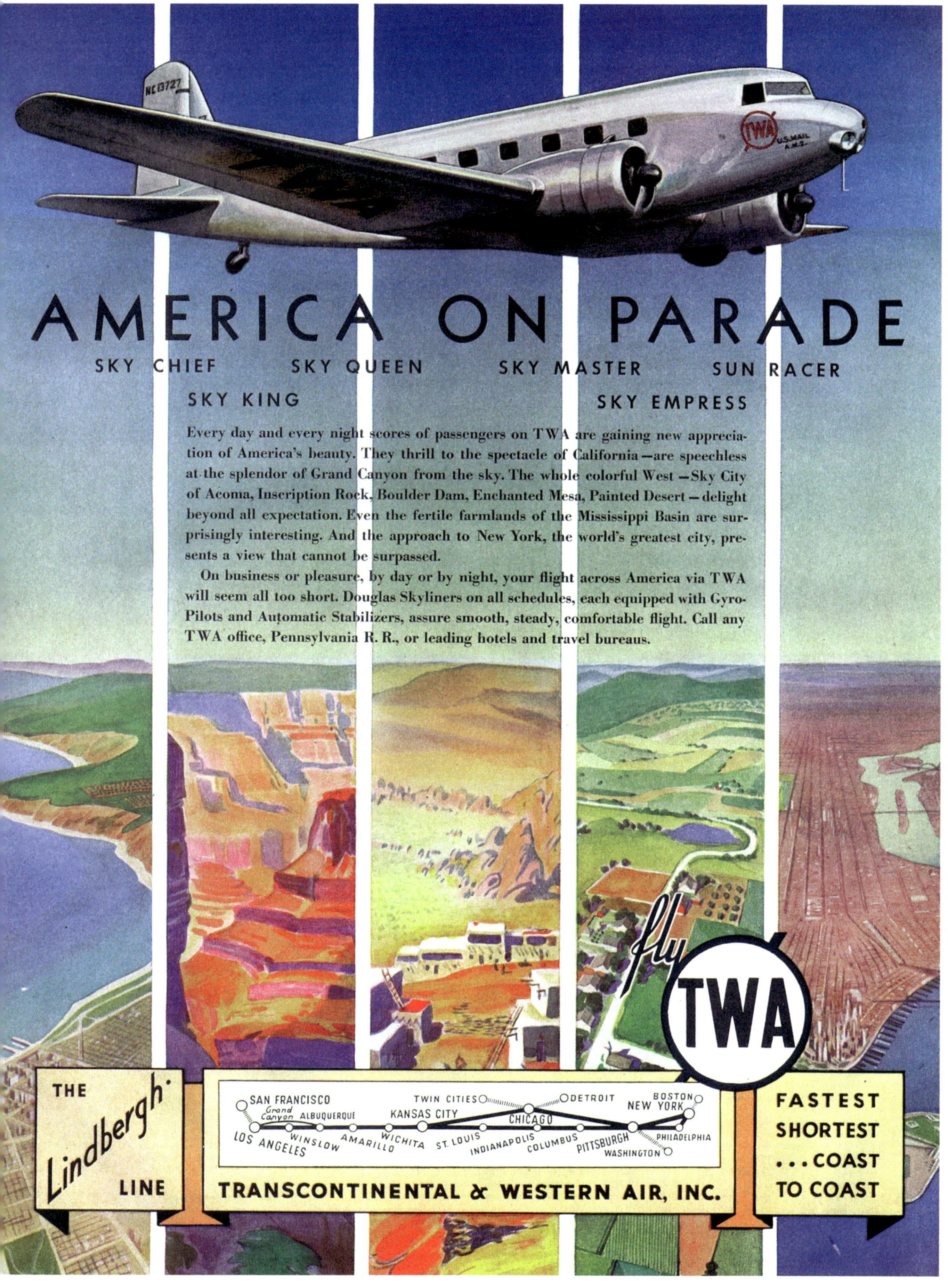
NC13727
TWA
U.S. MAIL A.M.2.
AMERICA ON PARADE
SKY CHIEF
SKY QUEEN
SKY MASTER
SUN RACER
SKY KING
SKY EMPRESS
Every day and every night scores of passengers on TWA are gaining new appreciation of America's beauty. They thrill to the spectacle of California—are speechless at the splendor of Grand Canyon from the sky. The whole colorful West—Sky City of Acoma, Inscription Rock, Boulder Dam, Enchanted Mesa, Painted Desert—delight beyond all expectation. Even the fertile farmlands of the Mississippi Basin are surprisingly interesting. And the approach to New York, the world's greatest city, presents a view that cannot be surpassed.
On business or pleasure, by day or by night, your flight across America via TWA will seem all too short. Douglas Skyliners on all schedules, each equipped with Gyro-Pilots and Automatic Stabilizers, assure smooth, steady, comfortable flight. Call any TWA office, Pennsylvania R. R., or leading hotels and travel bureaus.
fly TWA
THE Lindbergh LINE
SAN FRANCISCO
Grand Canyon
ALBUQUERQUE
LOS ANGELES
WINSLOW
AMARILLO
WICHITA
KANSAS CITY
TWIN CITIES
ST. LOUIS
INDIANAPOLIS
CHICAGO
COLUMBUS
DETROIT
PITTSBURGH
WASHINGTON
NEW YORK
BOSTON
PHILADELPHIA
TRANSCONTINENTAL & WESTERN AIR, INC.
FASTEST
SHORTEST
...COAST
TO COAST

And the winner is...

Basking in Post-Olympic Glory

Published in 1938, this ad from the German Tourist Board invites unsuspecting tourists to visit the land where "the world marches on". The copy offers the traveler the opportunity to experience Deutschland's glorious past, Berlin's gay nightlife, and romantic operas and festivals. Coyly bypassing any references to a Nazi presence—save for the party flag flying on the beach—and the firmly entrenched dictatorship of Adolf Hitler, invitations such as this would quickly evaporate as the country's aggressive pogrom began to breach German borders.

Deutschland sonnt sich im Glanze Olympias

1938 lud das deutsche Fremdenverkehrsamt ahnungslose Touristen ein, das Land zu besuchen, in dem die Zeit (im Stechschritt) „voranmarschierte". Der Text verhieß dem Reisenden eine Begegnung mit Deutschlands ruhmreicher Vergangenheit und dem schillerndem Nachtleben in Berlin, romantische Opern und Festspiele. Sieht man von der Hakenkreuzfahne am Strand ab, vermied man tunlichst jeden Hinweis auf das Nazi-Regime und Adolf Hitlers Terrorherrschaft. Als Deutschland jedoch begann, seine Grenzen neu zu ziehen, verschwanden diese Anzeigen rasch.

Les lauriers post-olympiques

Publiée en 1938, cette publicité de l'office du tourisme allemand invite les touristes à visiter le pays « qui va de l'avant ». Le texte propose au voyageur de découvrir le glorieux passé de l'Allemagne, la joyeuse vie nocturne de Berlin, avec ses opéras romantiques et ses festivals, mais reste très évasif quant à la présence nazie (exception faite du drapeau du parti flottant sur la plage) et à la dictature fermement établie d'Adolf Hitler. Ce genre d'invitation disparut rapidement à mesure que les rumeurs de pogroms se répandirent hors des frontières.

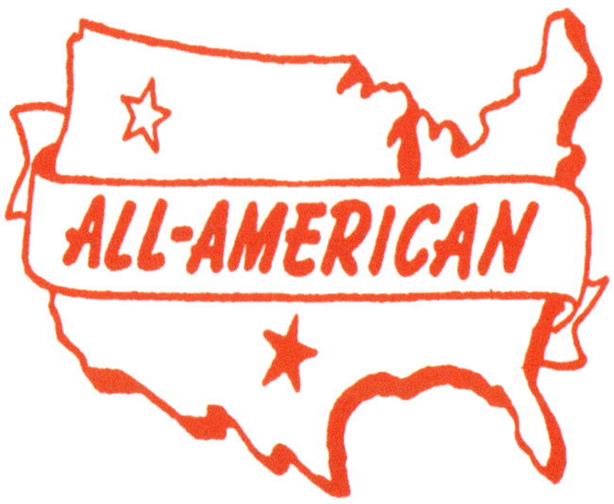

German Railroads Information Office, 1938

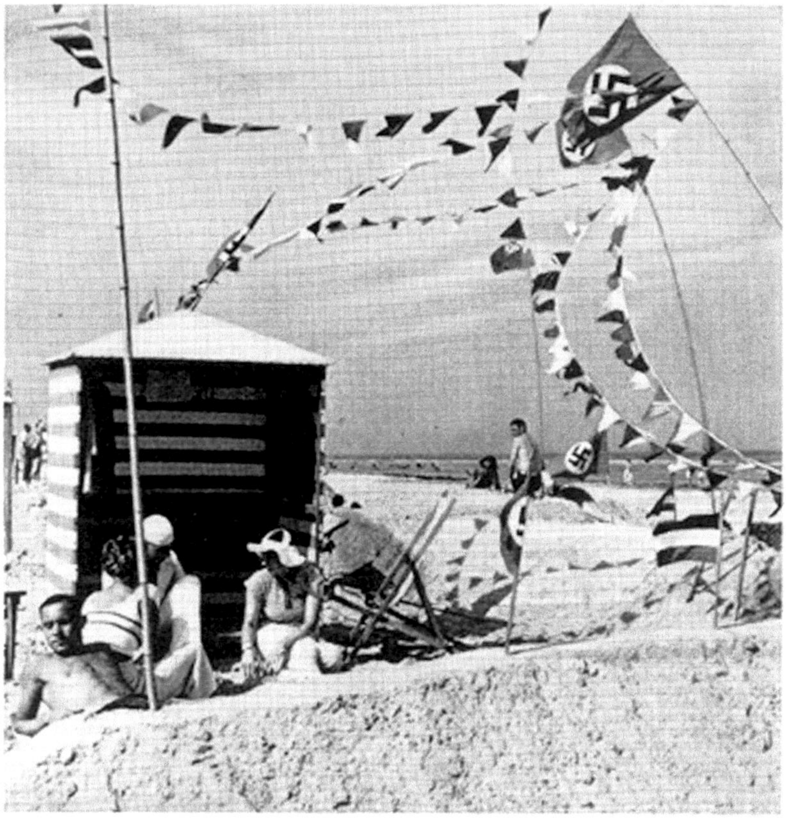

Plan Now

FOR A GLORIOUS TRIP TO

GERMANY

• Turn romantic pages of history in Germany. The time-mellowed ruins of ancient castles, the tomb of Charlemagne, the elaborate Guild Halls of medieval cities, the Romanesque and Gothic cathedrals of Cologne, Freiburg, Worms and Speyer, and Frederick the Great's palace of Sanssouci . . . these and many others . . . What glories of the past they echo! . . . What message of romance they bring you—as you tour through Germany . . . while operas and festivals, stage-craft and symphonies evidence in word and music the undying genius of Goethe, Wagner, Beethoven and Bach.

But the world marches on in Germany, also . . . Here you will find 20th Century progress. Or all modern sports and many that are uniquely German — piloting gliders on the Wasserkuppe or breasting the Rhine in a Faltboat. Then, too, there are great cities like Berlin, with their gay night life, splendid theatres, hotels and restaurants . . . And centers of culture, art and merrymaking like Munich, as famed for its museums as for its brew . . . Dresden, Nürnberg, Frankfurt, Stuttgart, Bayreuth, Weimar — all with a connotation of their own.

As for scenery: the Bavarian Alps, the Black Forest, Harz and Thuringia . . . the castles and vineyards of the Rhine and its gentle-flowing tributaries, the fruit trees and gardens of the Bergstrasse, the lovely sweep of sea and sky along the Baltic and North Sea. And the charm of Germany's famous health resorts.

All this you can enjoy, and more . . . in perfect comfort whether in hotel, train or steamer . . . good living at moderate prices, ***still further reduced by the use of registered Travel Marks.*** And the German Railroads grant you ***60% reduction of rail fares.*** Now is the time to see Germany. Begin planning your trip today.

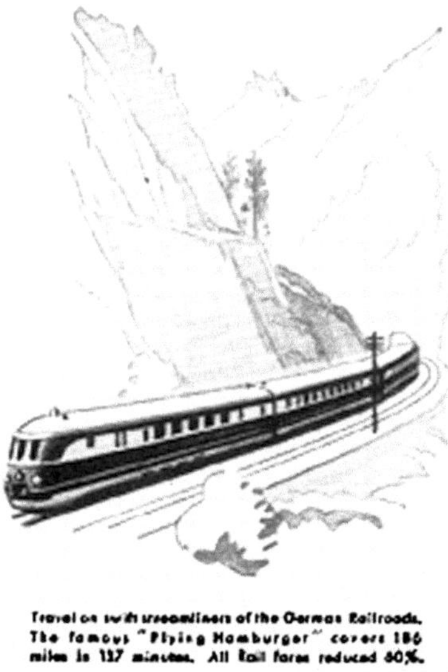

Travel on swift streamliners of the German Railroads. The famous "Flying Hamburger" covers 186 miles in 137 minutes. All Rail fares reduced 60%.

CONSULT YOUR TRAVEL AGENT AND WRITE FOR BOOKLET 48

GERMAN RAILROADS INFORMATION OFFICE

665 Fifth Avenue at 53rd Street, New York, N. Y.

Index

A Century of American Ads at Your Fingertips

The best of American consumer output is showcased in these comprehensive volumes presenting the buying habits, economic preferences, and cultural trends as viewed in advertisements from various decades from 1930 to 2010.

"Anyone who approaches with questions about how people lived, ate, felt and consumed in earlier decades will find the TASCHEN ad books an excellent investment."
The Toronto Star

All-American Ads of the 30s, 40s, 50s, 60s, 70s, 80s, 90s & 2000s
Jim Heimann
Multilingual edition in:
English / Deutsch / Français

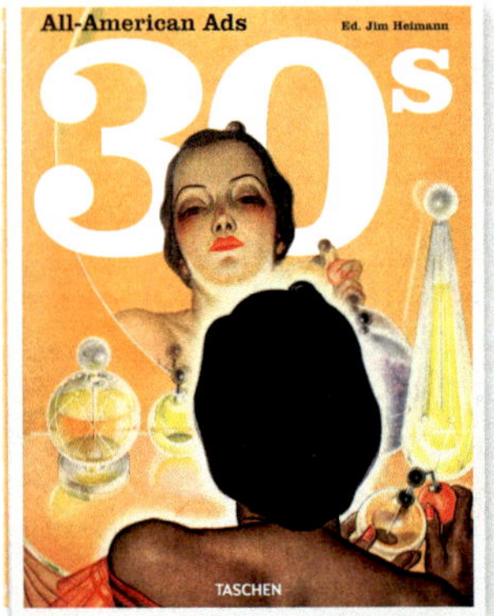

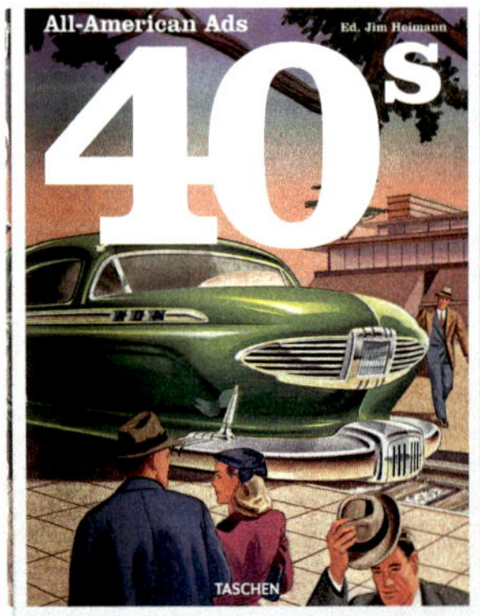

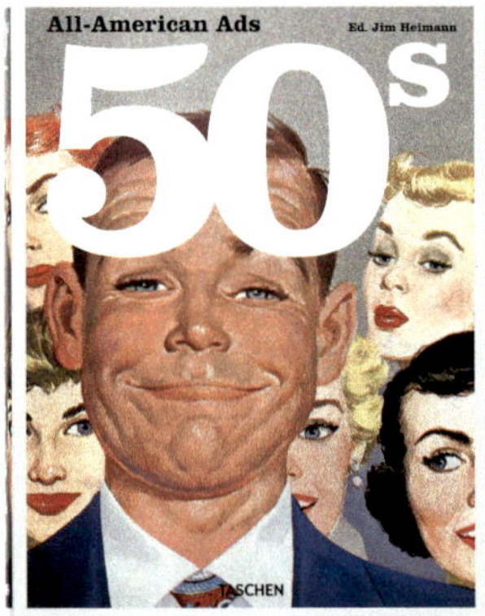

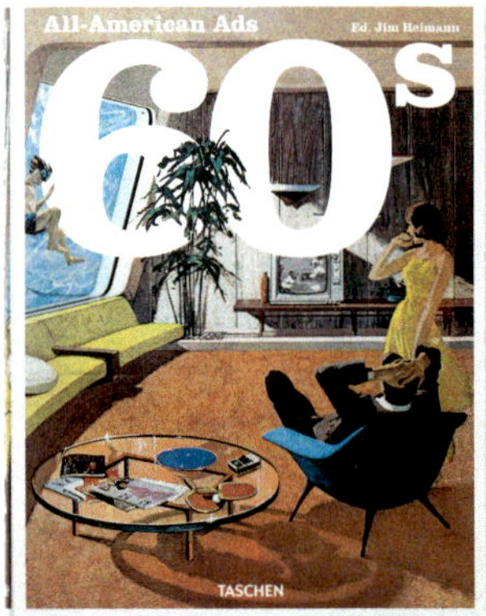

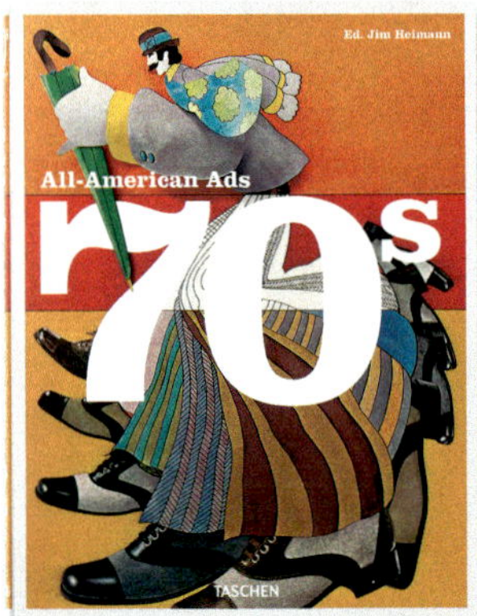

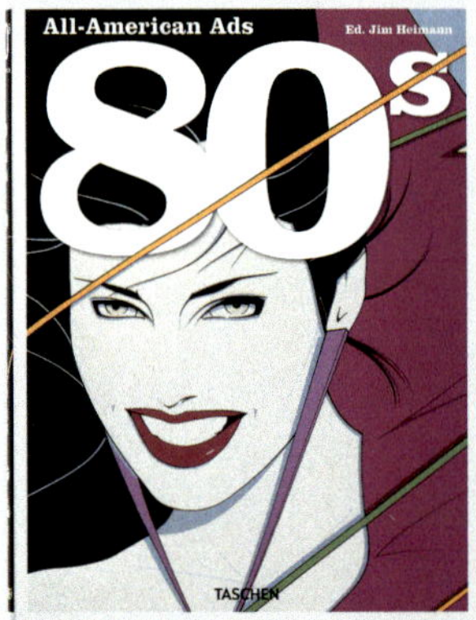

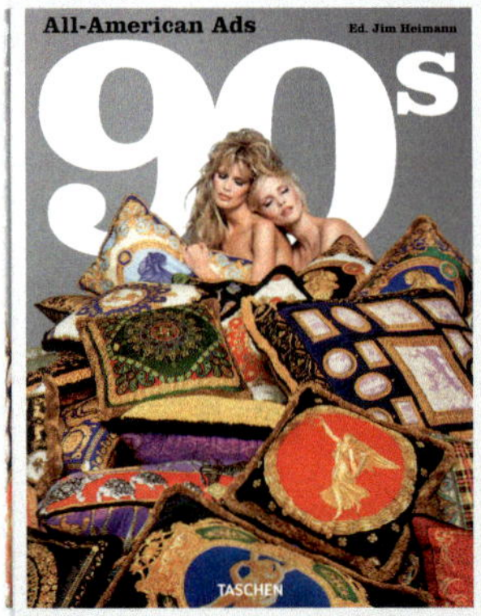

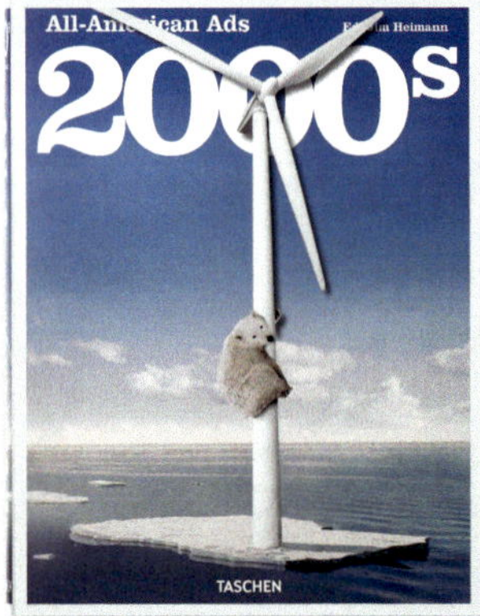